BASEBALL SABERMETRIC 1992

by
Brock J. Hanke
and the
Mad Aztec Press Crew

The Elysian Fields Press
Brown & Benchmark
A Division of Wm. C. Brown Communications, Inc.

Library of Congress Cataloging in Publication Data:

HANKE, BROCK J., 1947 -

BASEBALL SABERMETRIC 1992

Front Cover Photo Credit:

St. Louis Post-Dispatch

Thursday, May 13, 1969

L.T. "Jug" Spence

Umpires: John Kibler (out) and Ed Vargo (safe)

Bill Sudakis tagged by Mike Shannon

Library of Congress Catalog Card number: 92-70373

ISBN: 0-697-16612-0

Printed in the United States of America by The Elysian Fields Press, 2460 Kerper Boulevard, Dubuque, IA 52001.

10 9 8 7 6 5 4 3 2 1

Mission Statement of The Elysian Fields Press Imprint

The purpose and philosophy of The Elysian Fields Press is grounded in an appreciation of baseball as a central mythology of American culture. We wish to explore in print, via periodicals and books of essay, history, fiction, biography, poetry and anthology, the unifying romance of baseball as it connects us with our larger heritage and the natural cycles of generation.

Table of Contents

I

Introductions

Introduction for New Readers

You see, there used to be this book called THE BILL JAMES BASEBALL ABSTRACT. It was written by a man named, you guessed it, Bill James. The ABSTRACT was fun to read and full of controversial pronouncements to excite the blood of any baseball fan. But, more, it was full of statistical analysis, designed to back up the pronouncements, rather than just arguments in support of them. This was - and is - regarded as cheating by much of the sporting press, but many fans found the novel idea of honest and careful analysis most rewarding to read. And thus did the book sell and sell until 1988, when Bill James got tired of writing it, and turned his hand to the material which can now be found in the BILL JAMES BASEBALL BOOK, on sale at good bookstores everywhere.

When Bill gave up writing the ABSTRACT, he was aware that there would be writers who wanted to produce a continuation of the concept. When the inevitable proposals came to his attention, he chose to combine those of Brock J. Hanke and Rob Wood. This book was the 1989 BASEBALL ABSTRACT. Unfortunately, Rob and Brock ("I" am Brock) did not make a good collaborative pair, and thus it came to pass that neither one of them has the right to use the title BASEBALL ABSTRACT any more. This book, BASEBALL SABERMETRIC, is Brock's attempt to continue the concept of the ABSTRACT.

This is not to say that I write the book all by myself. No, what I have done is to put together a team of people who want to write material in the style of the ABSTRACT, and who I think are more than capable of doing so. The advantage of this is that you, the reader, get a much closer focus on each topic than I could possibly generate if I had to examine them all myself. You also get some variety in writing style, which may help in the reading; and some variety also in the ideas, which doubtless helps in the understanding.

My longtime friend Don Malcolm is the main collaborator. David Raglin has been with us for two years now, to my extreme delight. And Pete De Coursey is back, after a one-year hiatus, to write once again about the Phillies.

I should also mention STATS, Inc., which provides all the wonderful statistic lists you'll see here. STATS is the brainchild of John Dewan, who followed up on a Bill James suggestion to found an organization called PROJECT SCORESHEET. The Project was formed to score every game in the Major Leagues, so that statistics therefrom could be obtained by analysts for several thousand dollars less than the official statisticians, Elias, will sell them for. Project Scoresheet began as a volunteer organization and has remained so, while John formed STATS, Inc. to do the same thing on a more professional basis. Without STATS, I couldn't even attempt this book, as I couldn't afford the raw material. It is also true that John was the person who believed in my proposal to continue the ABSTRACT enough that he brought it to Bill James' attention....

STATS leads to a quick mention of Dick Cramer. Dick was one of the very first sabermetricians, and did the original computer programming for STATS. Fortunately for me, he lives in St. Louis, as do I, and does the programming for all those wonderful stats lists in the book here. Did I mention that Dick fits this in between his regular job and playing jazz and his wife and... I didn't? Well, he does, and I thank him as often as I can.

So enough of the publishing history. What kind of book do you have here? Well, Bill called what he was doing "sabermetrics," which is where the title comes from. My opinion is that sabermetrics amounts to "systems analysis of baseball." That is, sabermetricians take a look at the game of baseball as a system and attempt to figure out how it is working. That's why all the statistics; in order to analyze a system, you have to have enough mathematical information about it to make a mathematical model.

Needless to say, sabermetrics is not like sportswriting. That activity is inherently relies on "insider" information. Sportswriters, as you doubtless know, talk to players and managers and focus on their personal struggles, both with the game itself and with each other. I know very little about the insider aspect of baseball. I can't tell you how to adjust your swing to hit a curve, or how to correct a pitching motion or how to keep race problems from destroying a ballclub. But, in focusing on such things, insiders often lose the ability to see the proverbial forest through the trees. That is, they lose sight of the whole system in their need to focus on individual parts. Sabermetrics provides the most valuable service of retreating the focus and thereby widening the scope. Also, let's face it, most readers aren't baseball insiders, either. You who are reading this right now will probably get a better grasp of what I am doing than you will ever really have of what, say, Rickey Henderson does.

It may be no little help that the actual mathematics of sabermetrics is not very difficult. I have a degree in mathematics, but you won't be needing one. Even better, we have a nice big glossary of terms and methods in the back of this book, which I have tried to write in layman's language.

Feel free to dip into the SABERMETRIC wherever you want to start. The essays (we don't really have "chapters") are not organized in reading order, but by category. True, the introductory material, like this essay, comes first, but then we just collect the Team Comments together, then the Player Comments and, finally, the general essays, concluding with the Glossary. So use the Table of Contents to flip right to your favorite team or player, because it's finally come time for me to shut up.

Thanks for Reading,

Introduction for Old Readers

Well, hmm. We've got two sorts of old readers, here, you know. There's the old readers who were with us last year, and then the old readers who had no idea anyone was doing anything with the BASEBALL ABSTRACT concept. First, a few (well, four) paragraphs for the second category, those who only remember Bill James' book.

Bill, you will remember, gave up the ABSTRACT with the 1988 edition. Of the proposals he received, he decided to combine mine (I am Brock J. Hanke) with that of Rob Wood. We did produce a 1989 BASEBALL ABSTRACT, but then we found we were unable to continue as partners. So we both lost the right to use the ABSTRACT title. I, Brock, decided to continue doing an ABSTRACT-style book, with my own hand-picked team of collaborators, which was published last year as BASEBALL SABERMETRIC, 1990, and which is back again as what you have in your hands.

There are two big differences between this book and Bill's work. First, we are not so theoretically oriented as Bill. Bill did a lot of what can only be called groundbreaking analysis, devising new methods and approaches. We don't have nearly as much of that; instead, we rely heavily on Bill's methods, to which he relinquished copyright in the 1988 book. We do have some advancements upon that base, like my own Stolen Base Profit Method, but the basics in this book are going to seem awfully familiar to you old readers.

A lot of this is simply the result of Bill's getting a lot done during his decade of the ABSTRACT. I have always suspected that one of his primary motivations for quitting the book was that he was confronting the Law of Diminishing Returns in original analysis, doing more work for less result. The rest is probably my own personality. I have much more an engineer's background and mindset than Bill does; I like applying the same old methods, year after year, to different raw data, to see what small differences in results arise. My little essays on Innings Pitched are very much my interest showing. The original study of this sort of thing was done by Bill as a side issue in analyzing Billy Martin. I have followed the idea of "how many innings constitutes too many" for several years, and this year, I'm ready to say something. Yes, for those of you who remember this from last year, I have even more to say than I did then.

The second difference is that we have many more, and much more sophisticated, stat boxes than Bill ever had. This is the result of STATS, Inc. and their scoring database. Bill, you will recall, kept having to ask teams for whatever stats they'd send him, while I can just go to STATS, Inc. and ask for a report. I have to pay them, of course, but they're well within the reach of even this self-published enterprise. Trust me, STATS, Inc. bears no resemblance whatsoever to Elias.

Those of you who were with us last year will note that this is the same Introduction that you got then. That's because there has been very little change in the format of the book. I'm working with some new fonts to present stat lines, and would like some comment on that; otherwise, this is pretty much the same old format. Note that this means that, if you are unhappy, NOW is the time to gripe!

You'll also note that the pitcher study is still in the form of a report on work in progress. This is because I'm running into some brick walls. If you have pitcher studies, send them in. I need new ideas as to how to group pitchers together. The groupings I'm using now just don't hold together in any sort of detail analysis.

Also, and again like last year's book, you'll see very few general essays. This is partially because I got requests for the team profiles, and partially because general essays are hard to work with. You have to work the writer through the study to get the sort of quality I'd like to have. I promise to redouble my efforts on this, as I think the essays can be the most valuable part of the book. But again, you're the reader. Comments, please.

One thing I'm very pleased with is the Major League Equivalencies of minor league stats. They're in the back, and they're great. Brian Rodewald did them, and he did them right. I think this information can be mined for more than anything else here. Try to use them and let me know what happens. I've had at least one reader write me to ask what I think of Eric Karros. What I think is that his MLEs and Peak Projections speak for themsleves.

One last thing. You may have noticed that this book is actually published by Elysian Fields Press. These people are trying to break into the baseball field, and they're doing great, in my estimation. My own contact is Steve Lehman, who you may know from the MINNEAPOLIS REVIEW OF BASEBALL. It's a great little magazine, as is ELYSIAN FIELDS QUARTERLY. Get used to this imprint; it's going places.

As for this book, Steve has left me a lot of the control I used to have. Actually, I've produced camera-ready copy, and he's left me alone to do that. Just like the other years. This means that the typography is not Elysian Fields standard. It's doubtless worse. If typos bother you, blame me. They're not Steve's fault, and they're not Elysian Fields' fault, either.

Thanks Once Again for Reading,

Brock J. Hanke

Work in Progress

Innings Pitched and Arm Trouble

Brock J. Hanke

I wish I had more to report. But I don't. I just can't get the pitchers to group together so that I can find out things about a class of pitchers and have it consistently apply to the class. So, enough bitching; what have I found out?

First, the history. Pitcher workloads have always been going down. When professional baseball began, the pitcher was just one of the position players, like the center fielder. His responsibilities were to serve the ball up for the batter to hit and to field bunts. Soon, though, it was determined that the pitcher could control the batting result, if he threw with effort, rather than serving up tosses.

With the increased strain on the arm, came the sharing of the pitching responsibility. No longer could one man pitch all his team's game. The last man to really try was Old Hoss Radbourne, in 1884 for Providence. He didn't really want to, but his team's other pitcher had jumped to the Union Association, and the team could win the pennant if it had consistent pitching. Radbourne did win his team the pennant, but he also blew out his arm, and was through within just a couple of years.

As time progressed, the number of starting pitchers in teams' rotations kept increasing. First three, then four and now five. As a result, individual start totals went down, as did individual innings pitched totals and games won. The last 40-game winner pitched just after the turn of the century. Dizzy Dean had the last 30-win season in the National League, in 1930. Think about that. It means that it has been longer since anyone won 30 in the NL than it was from the beginning of the league to that season. It's 1875-1930 (56 years) as opposed to 1931-1991 (60 years).

And folks, the trend hasn't stopped. Pitchers of the fifties and sixties, like Don Drysdale and Bob Gibson, talk about modern starters as if they lacked guts, because they don't pitch 300 innings. Hoss Radbourne and Big Ed Walsh doubtless thought Don and Bob were wimps, too.

But it's not lack of character that's causing the problem, but lack of arm. Modern pitching requires the pitcher to throw pretty much as hard as he can for as long as he can. That strains the arm much more than older styles did. Also, pitching styles have changed to emphasize whole body use, rather than just arm use. Walter Johnson didn't have any kick at all, and even Drysdale's motion is nothing compared to Nolan Ryan's.

So what parameters have I found for the issue of innings pitched? Well, no one seems to pitch 275 innings any more. Most pitchers don't get 240. And some of them get hurt from it. Beyond that, I've got some notes to show, and some individuals to comment on. Let's look at some of the individuals first.

Dwight Gooden:

As you doubtless know, Doc is not the pitcher he was when he was 19. As you may not know, he pitched some awful loads when he was young. When he was 21, Gooden pitched 277 innings, going 24-4 and posting a 1.53 ERA. The next year, he pitched 250 innings, despite adding more than a run to the ERA. Then he pitched in the postseason. He has never matched that ERA again, much less the microscopic one. I think there is no doubt that the load was what did him in.

The Oakland A's:

One of the things that has happened to the A's is that they've been burning out pitchers at a ridiculous rate. Mike Moore went down after the 1990 season, in which he pitched 242 innings plus postseason. the next year, with Moore ineffective, Tony LaRussa gave 238 innings plus post to Bob Welch. The results of that experiment are now in. Please remember that both Moore and Welch were consistent pitchers before this happened.

Orel Hershiser:

Tummy Lasorda, ruiner of pitching arms, gave this man workloads of 265, 267 and 257 innings, with postseason work thrown in as well. You know what happened.

Bret Saberhagen:

Workloads of 257 and 261, followed by an attempt to pitch the Royals to the title by himself. 262 innings. 2.16 ERA. Blown out arm.

Now for the guys to whom this does not happen.

Dave Stewart:

This exception to the rule labored four years under ridiculous loads before he collapsed. But Dave didn't get his start as a pitcher. He was a catcher when he was young. He had no early stress to fight off.

Roger Clemens:

Roger has handled overloads for six years now. Roger Clemens is the best pitcher in baseball. Also, Roger is constantly complaining about arm trouble. And his postseason record is underwhelming, compared to the rest of his achievement.

Nolan Ryan:

Nolan was the last pitcher to get the fifties bonus baby treatment. It used to be that bonus babies had to stay on the Major League roster, whether they could pitch or not. Teams used to keep these kids around, with great arms but no idea of where the strike zone might be, because they had to. Then they started doing that just out of habit. Sandy Koufax put in some years as one of those, got very few innings. So did the aforementioned Bob Gibson.

Nolan Ryan was the last of those guys. He was 25 before he got over 152 innings. You know where he is now.

Charlie Hough:

Charlie is the last of the old knuckleball pitchers. It used to be rumored that knuckler guys could pitch hellacious loads. Then Wilber Wood's arm went. Well, Charlie has the knuckler, and he also didn't get overworked. So he's still around.

And then there's the source of the problem. It looks like I could get a study going, from what I've got here, doesn't it? I mean, all I have to do is get rid of the noise that the Dave Stewarts and Nolan Ryans create and I should be OK. Nope. There's always

Joe Magrane:

Joe Magrane pitched just over 200 innings in 1990, and his arm blew out. Why? Well, I've got an idea. You see, when Joe Magrane was drafted, the rap on his was that he'd been throwing exclusively curveballs in college, and had lost his fastball. The Cardinals responded by sending him to school to get those miles per hour back. That is, they sent him to fastball school. And it worked. He got his speed back, and became an ERA king. But the damage had already been done. It is known that curve balls are harder on the arm than fastballs. Joe's arm had been ruined in college.

That's the problem. I don't know everyone's history like I know Joe Magrane's. And they're not all so obvious anyway. I can't get the people who can handle 230 innings sorted out from the men who can't handle 200. Hell, I was confident that Ramon Martinez would hold everything he had shown because he had only thrown 230 frames.

Given that, what do I mean by "you can predict the next big arm collapse?" Well, I mean this. Virtually all the ace starters are in danger of overload. After all, their teams are counting on them to win. They, the Welches and Hershisers, get beat up so often that it's possible to set up some leading indicators just from their fiascos alone. Here they are:

If a starter gets more than 250 innings and his name is not Roger Clemens, he's going to have a big collapse the next year. Count on it, Greg Maddux. That idiot Don Zimmer gave you 263 innings last year, and the team wasn't even in contention. You're toast for 1992.

If a starter gets 240, unload him in your fantasy league; he's a bad gamble.

If a guy who had that sort of bad year gets under 220, he's going to improve the year after. That's what happened to Moore in 1991. He got little enough work in 1990 that his arm recovered some.

If a guy has trouble with a particular workload, that's probably his limit. If Joe Magrane gets more than 210 innings, he's in trouble.

I haven't talked about relievers yet. The story is much the same. About middle men there can be little said. They don't get comparable sorts of work. Some just mop up, some set up, some get one batter at a time. Some start part of the time. But about the ace closers, I have some ideas.

If a closer gets over 90 innings, he's toast. If not the next year, then certainly in two.

If a closer gets over 80 innings, he's a tremendous bet to have his ERA explode. Check out Bobby Thigpen.

If a closer gets between 60 and 75 innings a year, he should be good for five or six. This year, my confidence in the load limit was shaken by the collapses of Dennis Eckersley and Dave Smith. Those two men have always had reasonable workloads, and I got to thinking they were bulletproof. Mike Schooler got reasonable work, and couldn't handle it, either. For a couple of years, though, 60-75 is the good load.

Remember, these figures used to be higher, and they're still going down. I think there's going to be pressure soon for a six-man rotation. I think that's silly. At that point, you might as well go back to four starters, and have two "continuers," men who are expected to pitch the sixth and seventh, every other day.

You think I'm getting paranoid? Well, ask yourself this: when was the last time when none of the four postseason teams had an ace starter than they pitched in games 1, 4, and 7 of either the LCS or the World Series? Isn't that supposed to be standard procedure? Yet none of the 1991 participants did that. They had to go with their #4 man, even with everything on the line. There is going to be pressure for a six-man rotation, and it's going to be soon.

Well, that's about it for work in progress. As I said, I could use some help. If you've got some, send it in. In the meantime, check those workloads and UNLOAD GREG MADDUX.

Some Run Tracking Charts

Don Malcolm

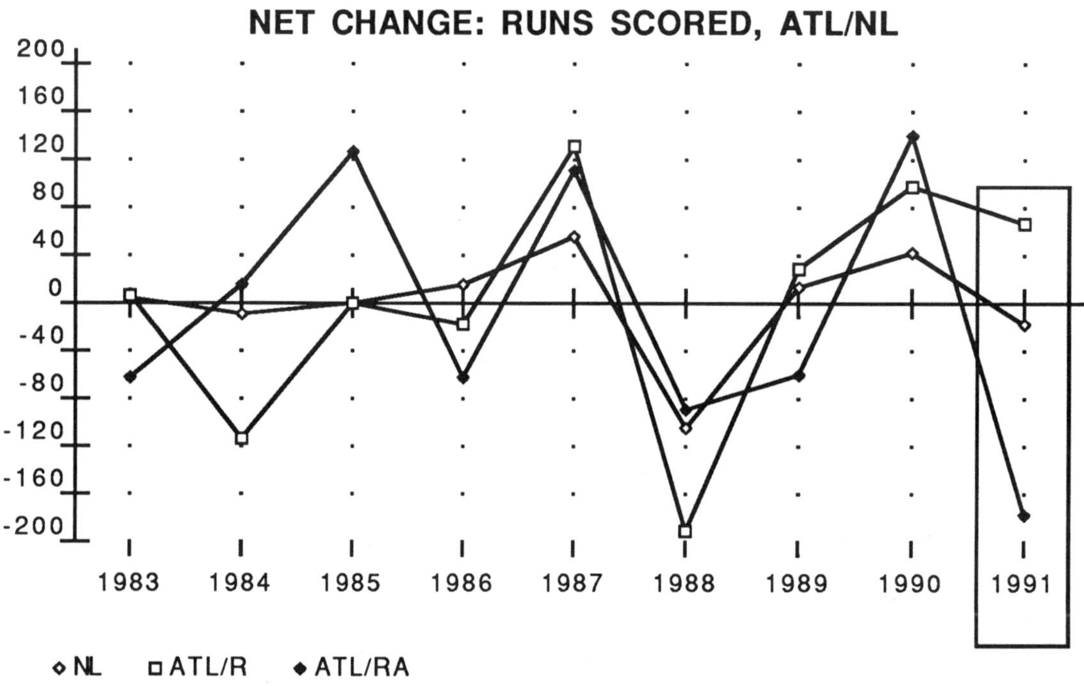

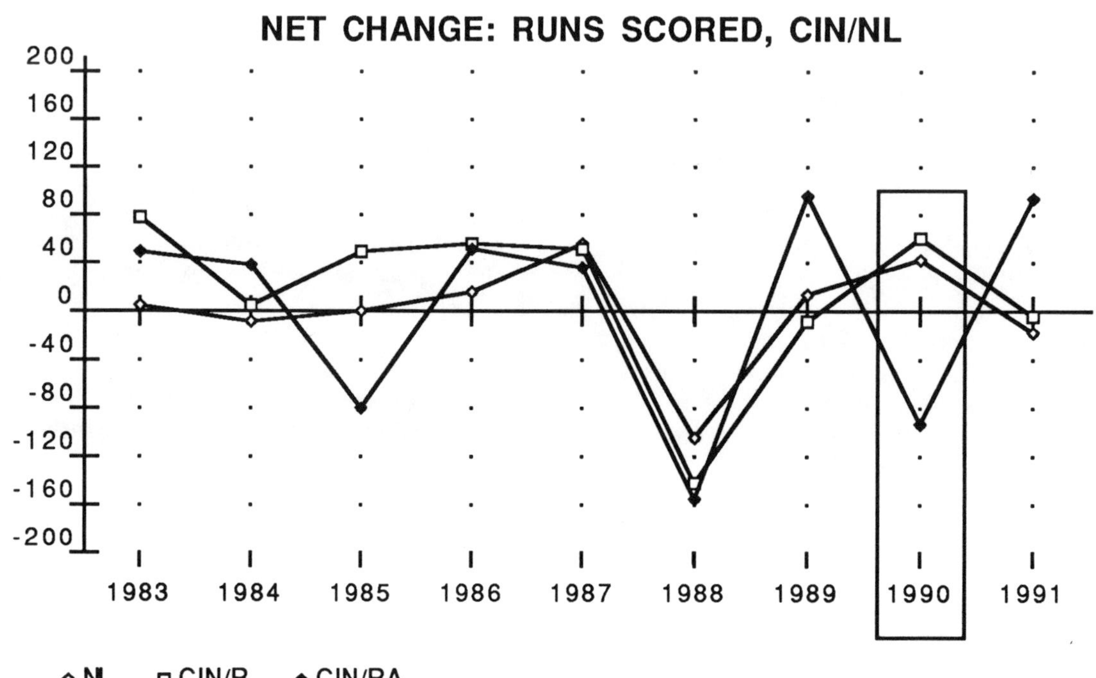

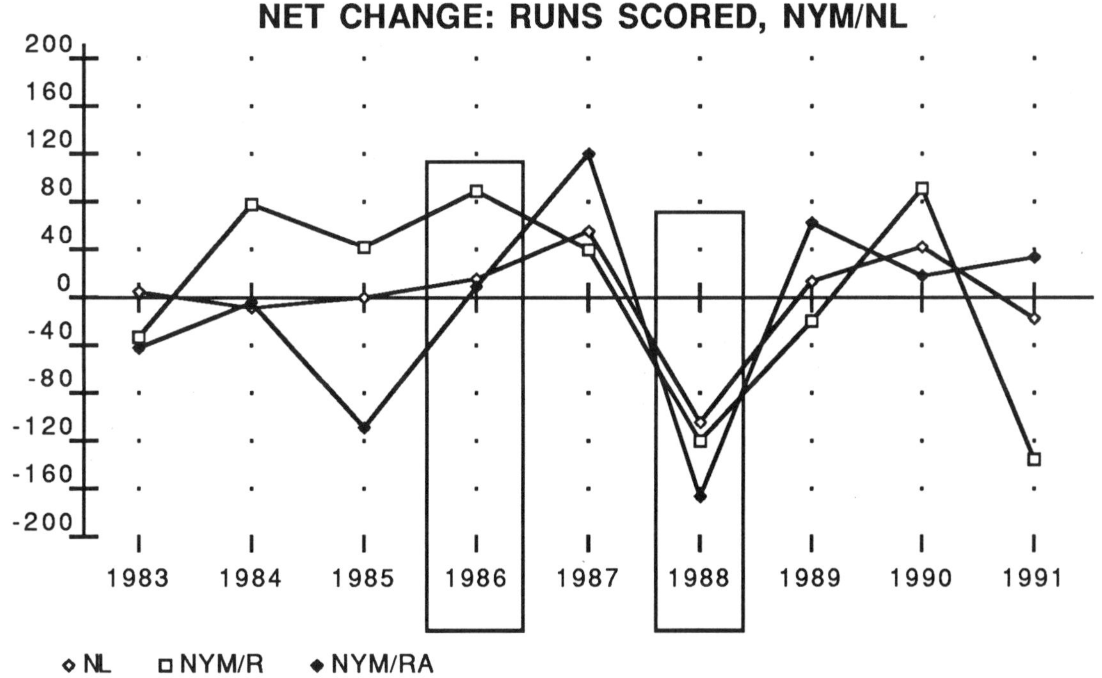

NET CHANGE: RUNS SCORED, NYM/NL
200
160
120
80
40
0
-40
-80
-120
-160
-200
1983
1984
1985
1986
1987
1988
1989
1990
1991
NL
NYM/R
NYM/RA

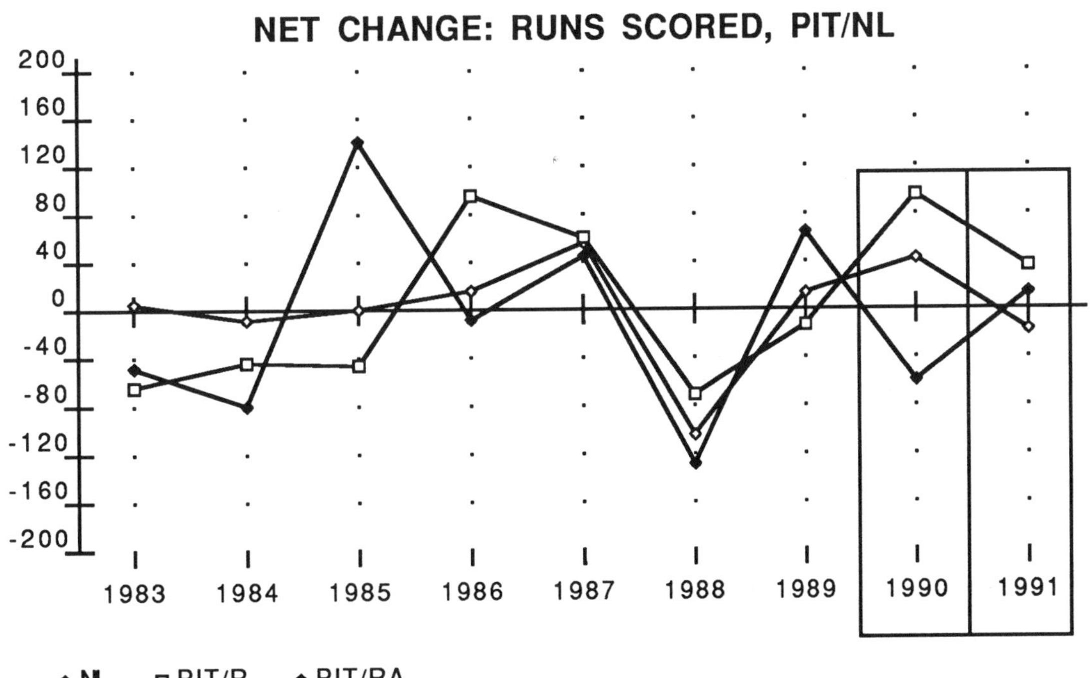

NET CHANGE: RUNS SCORED, PIT/NL
200
160
120
80
40
0
-40
-80
-120
-160
-200
1983
1984
1985
1986
1987
1988
1989
1990
1991
NL
PIT/R
PIT/RA

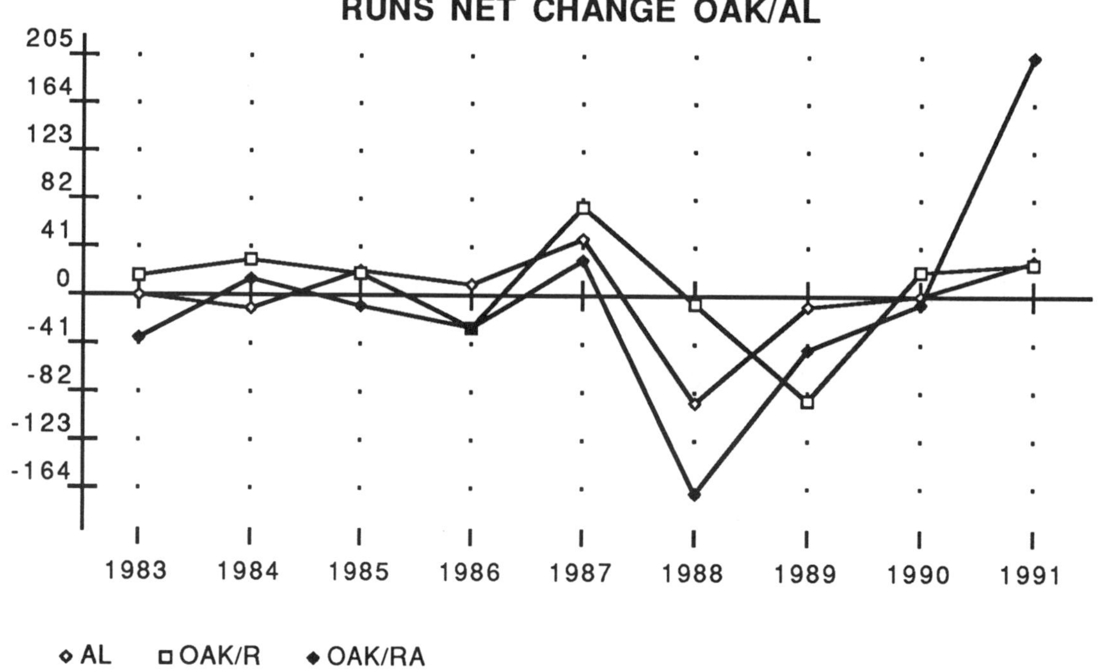
RUNS NET CHANGE OAK/AL
205
164
123
82
41
0
-41
-82
-123
-164
1983
1984
1985
1986
1987
1988
1989
1990
1991
AL
OAK/R
OAK/RA

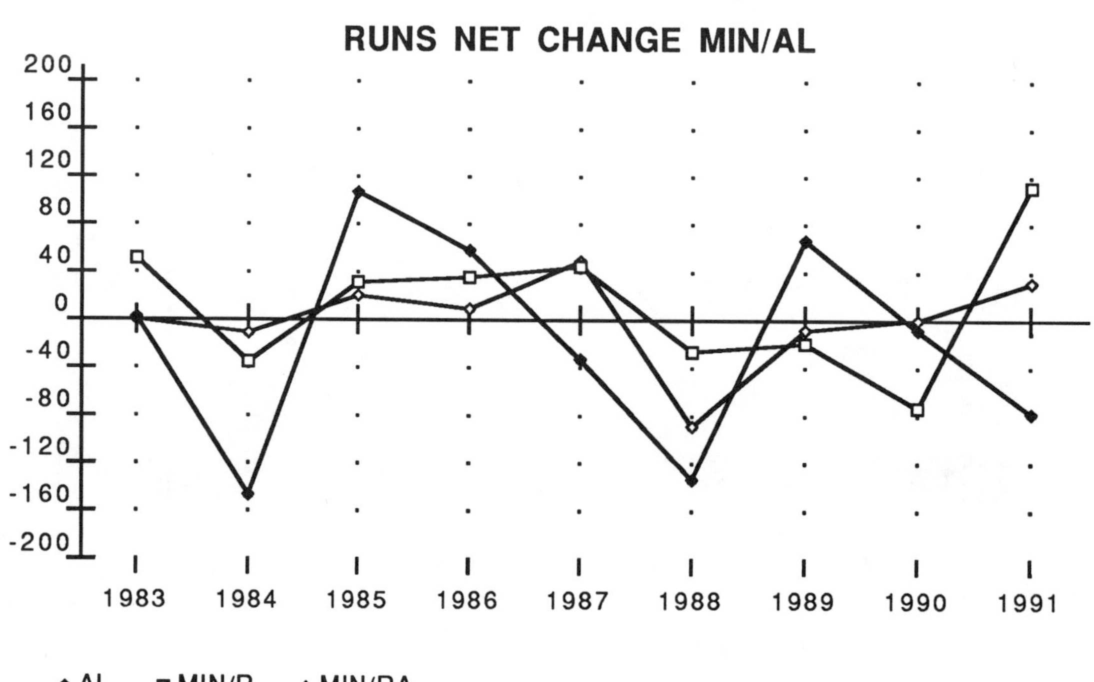
RUNS NET CHANGE MIN/AL
200
160
120
80
40
0
-40
-80
-120
-160
-200
1983
1984
1985
1986
1987
1988
1989
1990
1991
AL
MIN/R
MIN/RA

II

Team Essays

Three Quick Notes

Brock J. Hanke

I have three quick things to say before you get into the team essays. First, I don't get much feedback on the stat boxes, and I'd like some. I'm very proud of them, but I don't know if I should be. So look them over, and send me a comment, please.

Second, I have included team profiles for all teams this year. I don't know if they're really worth the 26 pages, but I did get some letters requesting them, so here they are. One reason I'm not sure that they're worth the space is that they're available on-line from STATS, Inc. Check out their ad in the back of the book.

Third, if you've been reading my advertising, you'll remember that I promised a lot of comments on team leaders, like Bobby Cox and Fred Claire. These are included in the team essays. If I didn't write the essay, I added the commment to what the other writer said. The writers were aware of the advertising, and tried to write to suit, but they had their own things to say. I feel very strongly that, if I advertise something, I should produce it, so my commments on the subjects at hand are mandatory. They should NOT be taken as criticism of the other writers' essays.

American League

Western Division

1. Minnesota Twins
2. Chicago White Sox
3. Texas Rangers
4. Oakland Athletics
5. Seattle Mariners
6. Kansas City Royals
7. California Angels

AL Western Division Team Batting

	G	AB	Run	Hit	2B	3B	HR	TB	RBI	W	K	IW	HB	SB	CS	GI DP	SH	SF	Avg	Slug	OBP	Runs Ctd
California	1628	5470	653	1396	245	29	115	2044	607	448	928	28	38	94	56	114	63	31	.255	.374	.314	642
Chicago	1875	5594	758	1464	226	39	139	2185	722	610	896	45	37	134	74	131	76	41	.262	.391	.336	745
Kansas City	1866	5584	727	1475	290	41	117	2198	689	523	969	47	35	119	68	127	53	47	.264	.394	.328	723
Minnesota	1866	5556	776	1557	270	42	140	2331	733	526	747	38	40	107	68	157	44	49	.280	.420	.344	789
Oakland	1806	5382	760	1340	245	19	159	2100	716	639	974	56	49	150	64	130	41	49	.249	.390	.331	716
Seattle	1855	5494	702	1400	268	29	126	2104	665	588	811	57	37	97	44	139	55	62	.255	.383	.328	702
Texas	1910	5678	827	1534	287	31	176	2411	772	590	1034	51	42	101	50	128	59	41	.270	.425	.341	831

AL Western Division Sabermetric Team Batting

	Ball Park Adjusted												Runs		Run/					
	AB	Run	Hit	2B	3B	HR	RBI	W	SO	Avg	Slug	OBP	Ctd	Outs	27o	OW%	OG	OWAR	DWAR	TWAR
California	5312	683	1417	264	40	108	641	438	901	.267	.393	.326	681	4143	4.44	.549	153	30.61	9.03	39.64
Chicago	5541	749	1435	223	39	132	713	616	907	.259	.385	.335	729	4419	4.45	.501	164	24.79	11.06	35.85
Kansas City	5778	768	1539	297	32	151	733	547	1048	.266	.407	.330	774	4553	4.59	.513	169	27.48	3.53	31.01
Minnesota	5597	748	1500	259	34	143	707	546	757	.268	.403	.335	738	4429	4.50	.510	164	26.29	8.83	35.29
Oakland	5411	813	1402	252	22	174	762	648	955	.259	.410	.342	776	4298	4.87	.512	159	25.76	6.08	31.86
Seattle	5400	697	1393	262	26	120	657	608	780	.258	.383	.334	702	4311	4.40	.517	160	26.72	9.67	36.39
Texas	5461	797	1481	279	24	175	750	578	959	.271	.427	.343	816	4238	5.20	.510	157	25.15	3.66	29.15

AL Western Division Team Pitching

	ERA	W	L	Pct	G	GS	CG	ShO	GF	Sv	IP	R	ER	H	2B	3B	HR	BB	IW	SO	HB	WP	BK
California	3.69	81	81	.500	472	162	18	3	144	50	1441.2	649	591	1351	250	21	141	543	29	990	38	49	11
Chicago	3.80	87	75	.537	500	162	28	5	134	40	1478.0	681	624	1302	215	30	154	601	25	923	31	44	6
Kansas City	3.92	82	80	.506	457	162	17	7	145	41	1466.0	722	639	1473	271	42	105	529	44	1004	43	47	5
Minnesota	3.69	95	67	.586	453	162	21	6	141	53	1449.1	652	595	1402	273	31	139	488	39	876	27	57	5
Oakland	4.58	84	77	.522	556	161	14	3	147	49	1435.1	773	731	1416	250	38	154	648	30	886	55	60	7
Seattle	3.79	83	79	.512	545	162	10	5	152	48	1464.1	674	617	1387	258	32	136	628	50	1003	47	82	7
Texas	4.50	84	77	.522	547	161	8	3	153	41	1470.0	814	735	1484	277	31	151	659	37	1015	44	77	12

AL Western Division Catchers

	G	PO	A	Er	TC	DP	PB	SB	CS	CS%	FPct	DI	DG	DW%	DWAR	ERA	ERA Wo-W
California	162	1018	111	6	1135	17	22	89	72	.447	.995	1433.2	10.0	.393	.43	3.69	
Chicago	162	970	91	9	1070	14	20	96	66	.407	.992	1478.0	10.0	.336	-.14	3.80	
Kansas City	162	1027	84	13	1124	10	11	94	56	.373	.988	1457.0	10.0	.287	-.63	3.92	
Minnesota	162	905	59	10	974	10	12	118	43	.267	.990	1449.1	10.0	.322	-.28	3.69	
Oakland	162	914	81	20	1015	10	8	116	60	.341	.980	1435.1	10.0	.169	-1.33	4.57	
Seattle	162	1027	83	9	1119	15	24	84	44	.344	.992	1464.1	10.0	.335	-.15	3.79	
Texas	162	1074	88	24	1186	10	15	107	58	.352	.980	1470.0	10.0	.178	-1.29	4.47	
LG.AVG	162	997	93	13	1103	10	12	137	67	.328	.988	1448.2					

AL Western Division First Base

	G	PO	A	Er	TC	DP	FPct	DI	DG	DW%	DWAR
California	162	1533	115	10	1658	139	.994	1433.2	3.0	.547	.59
Chicago	162	1438	100	13	1551	134	.992	1478.0	3.0	.495	.43
Kansas City	162	1435	100	9	1544	130	.994	1457.0	3.0	.530	.54
Minnesota	162	1537	125	11	1673	145	.993	1449.1	3.0	.572	.67
Oakland	162	1364	120	6	1490	134	.996	1435.1	3.0	.625	.82
Seattle	162	1468	118	6	1592	170	.996	1464.1	3.0	.556	.62
Texas	162	1418	105	12	1535	126	.992	1470.0	3.0	.498	.44
LG.AVG	162	1454	119	13	1586	112	.992	1448.2			

AL Western Division Second Base

	G	PO	A	Er	TC	DP	FPct	DI	DG	DW%	DWAR
California	162	366	494	21	881	116	.976	1433.2	8.0	.593	1.93
Chicago	162	342	470	13	825	102	.984	1478.0	8.0	.571	1.77
Kansas City	162	342	484	17	843	101	.980	1457.0	8.0	.474	.99
Minnesota	162	298	534	19	851	109	.978	1449.1	8.0	.555	1.64
Oakland	162	347	502	11	860	101	.987	1435.1	8.0	.543	1.53
Seattle	162	362	487	18	867	143	.979	1464.1	8.0	.636	2.29
Texas	162	333	444	14	791	91	.982	1470.0	8.0	.395	.36
LG.AVG	162	346	481	15	842	87	.982	1448.2			

AL Western Division Third Base

	G	PO	A	Er	TC	DP	FPct	DI	DG	DW%	DWAR
California	162	120	379	17	516	40	.967	1433.2	6.0	.659	1.85
Chicago	162	158	337	23	518	35	.956	1478.0	6.0	.621	1.63
Kansas City	162	127	331	17	475	27	.964	1457.0	6.0	.489	.83
Minnesota	162	105	366	19	490	39	.961	1449.1	6.0	.599	1.49
Oakland	162	141	266	17	424	33	.960	1435.1	6.0	.465	.69
Seattle	162	100	335	22	457	30	.952	1464.1	6.0	.452	.61
Texas	162	126	340	13	479	29	.973	1470.0	6.0	.533	1.09
LG.AVG	162	120	320	23	463	26	.950	1448.2			

AL Western Division Shortstop

	G	PO	A	Er	TC	DP	FPct	DI	DG	DW%	DWAR
California	162	239	512	21	772	96	.973	1433.2	11.0	.552	2.21
Chicago	162	275	490	26	791	102	.967	1478.0	11.0	.587	2.61
Kansas City	162	264	461	29	754	97	.962	1457.0	11.0	.445	1.03
Minnesota	162	261	496	11	768	99	.986	1449.1	11.0	.606	2.81
Oakland	162	268	425	22	715	92	.969	1435.1	11.0	.447	1.06
Seattle	162	291	510	20	821	129	.976	1464.1	11.0	.655	3.35
Texas	162	267	504	27	798	87	.966	1470.0	11.0	.459	1.19
LG.AVG	162	268	482	26	776	82	.966	1448.2			

AL Western Division Left Field

	G	PO	A	Er	TC	DP	FPct	DI	DG	DW%	DWAR
California	162	292	10	6	308	0	.981	1433.2	4.0	.468	.47
Chicago	162	337	13	5	355	3	.986	1478.0	4.0	.646	1.19
Kansas City	162	315	6	9	330	0	.973	1457.0	4.0	.371	.08
Minnesota	162	372	4	7	383	1	.982	1449.1	4.0	.489	.55
Oakland	162	400	11	10	421	1	.976	1435.1	4.0	.605	1.02
Seattle	162	330	4	8	342	1	.977	1464.1	4.0	.409	.24
Texas	162	344	3	10	357	1	.972	1470.0	4.0	.392	.17
LG.AVG	162	341	9	6	356	1	.983	1448.2			

AL Western Division Center Field

	G	PO	A	Er	TC	DP	FPct	DI	DG	DW%	DWAR
California	162	364	14	2	380	2	.995	1433.2	6.0	.564	1.28
Chicago	162	466	12	2	480	4	.996	1478.0	6.0	.725	2.25
Kansas City	162	461	3	5	469	0	.989	1457.0	6.0	.492	.85
Minnesota	162	416	15	6	437	6	.986	1449.1	6.0	.564	1.28
Oakland	162	443	10	2	455	2	.996	1435.1	6.0	.639	1.72
Seattle	162	416	17	6	439	5	.986	1464.1	6.0	.573	1.34
Texas	162	453	10	9	472	2	.981	1470.0	6.0	.508	.94
LG.AVG	162	407	8	6	421	2	.986	1448.2			

AL Western Division Right Field

	G	PO	A	Er	TC	DP	FPct	DI	DG	DW%	DWAR
California	162	283	8	6	297	0	.980	1433.2	5.0	.402	.26
Chicago	162	363	12	9	384	2	.977	1478.0	5.0	.614	1.32
Kansas City	162	291	4	10	305	0	.967	1457.0	5.0	.298	-.26
Minnesota	162	338	9	7	354	6	.980	1449.1	5.0	.491	.70
Oakland	162	318	9	9	336	1	.973	1435.1	5.0	.444	.47
Seattle	162	328	16	6	350	6	.983	1464.1	5.0	.624	1.37
Texas	162	304	14	9	327	3	.972	1470.0	5.0	.510	.79
LG.AVG	162	318	12	6	336	2	.982	1448.2			

Minnesota Twins

Don Malcolm and Brock J. Hanke

MINNESOTA											
YEAR	1982	1983	1984	1985	1986	1987	1988	1989	1990	1991	TOT
W	60	70	81	77	71	85	91	80	74	95	784
L	102	92	81	85	91	77	71	82	88	67	836
WPCT	0.370	0.432	0.500	0.475	0.438	0.525	0.562	0.494	0.457	0.586	0.484
R	657	709	673	705	741	786	759	740	666	776	7212
RA	819	822	675	782	839	806	672	738	729	652	7534
PWPT	0.392	0.427	0.499	0.448	0.438	0.487	0.561	0.501	0.455	0.586	0.478
PythW	63	69	81	73	71	79	91	81	74	95	77
PythL	99	93	81	89	91	83	71	81	88	67	85
LUCK	-3	1	0	4	0	6	0	-1	0	0	7

Defensive Efficiency Record: .7089

There are three basic classes of big reversal teams in baseball history. I call them the New Source of Talent teams, associated with the names Branch Rickey and Bill Veeck; the New Management teams, like the 1982 Milwaukee Brewers under Harvey Kuenn and the 1991 Atlanta Braves under Bobby Cox; and the Obvious Holes class, like the 1914 Miracle Braves. Before getting into where the Twins fit, though, here's Don Malcolm's contribution to the discussion. Remember what Don says here as you continue; it's more than a little important in analyzing the Twins.

The litany of questions concerning the Twins' success began to assault members of the Sabermetric staff sometime in July. They finally subsided around the middle of September, when it became clear to even the casual kibitzers that the Twins were going to win. With victory a certainty, the need for explanation ceased: this says something about human nature and the general nature of curiousity, but what it says is less than flattering.

For those people who do want to know how the Twins won the AL West, I offer the chart on the next page of their actual vs. projected individual offensive performances in 1991. The projections, by the way, have been reprinted from the STATS 1991 Handbook.

For purposes of comparison, I've lumped Chuck Knoblauch's actual data with the projection for Nelson Liriano, who was beat out for the second base job and wound up in the Kansas City farm system. And I've lumped the actuals for Scott Leius with the projections for John (Go Down) Moses, whose parachute didn't open. In all cases, the statistics with the higher RC27 listing appear in the top line of the comparison.

When we look at this offensive data, we are struck by several things. Ten of the fifteen players (or special combinations, as noted) exceeded their RC27 projections. And of the five who didn't exceed their projections, two (Kent Hrbek and Kirby Puckett) had seasons that were very close—about 95 to 98% of their projections. The biggest bust—Al Newman—never figured to be much of an offensive contributor. And, in context of the whole team, his dysfunctional offensive performance was just a minor blip on what is otherwise a superb example of a team that collectively exceeded what was projected for it.

And we can isolate the two main causes of this upsurge (truth told, they're not very hard to spot). Chili Davis had a monster year, providing nearly 25 more extra-base hits than what was projected. And, as good as Chili was, Shane Mack was even better. Although he didn't exceed his RC27 projection by as much as Chili, Mack's accumulated day-by-day performance had at least as much impact.

Also, the Twins were blessed with several fine seasons from players coming off the bench. Randy Bush, Gene Larkin, and Scott Leius were major contributors. Their combined totals for '91 amounted to another near All-Star caliber player:

AB	R	H	TB	D	T	HR	RBI	BB	SO	SB	CS	BA	SA	OBP	RC27
619	90	180	258	31	4	13	62	84	81	7	10	.291	.417	.376	5.96

The Twins had by far the best set of actuals based upon seasonal projections in baseball during 1991. The second best team in this category—interestingly enough—was Atlanta.

Hi. This is Brock again. There can be no doubt that big reversal years have a bit of player luck attached to them. Don has clearly identified that that was one of the things that happened with the 1991 Twins. But winning years of many types have to have a little luck to get over the top. What did the Twins do in addition to get them from last place to the unprecedented first?

T	Player	G	AB	R	H	TB	D	T	HR	RBI	BB	SO	SB	CS	BA	SA	OBP	RC27
A	Bush	93	165	21	50	80	10	1	6	23	24	25	0	2	.303	.485	.392	7.35
P	Bush	96	241	31	60	101	13	2	8	29	32	37	4	4	.249	.419	.337	5.08
A	Davis, C.	153	534	84	148	271	34	1	29	93	95	117	5	6	.277	.507	.386	7.32
P	Davis, C.	138	499	67	128	203	23	2	16	73	58	100	4	4	.257	.407	.334	4.93
A	Gagne	139	408	52	108	161	23	3	8	42	26	72	11	9	.265	.395	.309	4.47
P	Gagne	145	428	57	104	165	24	5	9	44	23	87	11	7	.243	.386	.282	3.87
P	Gladden	116	427	57	116	158	20	2	6	38	26	55	21	7	.272	.370	.313	4.30
A	Gladden	126	461	65	114	164	14	9	6	52	36	60	15	9	.247	.356	.302	3.85
A	Harper	123	441	54	137	195	26	1	10	69	14	22	1	2	.311	.442	.332	5.75
P	Harper	125	400	44	116	166	21	1	9	50	18	21	3	3	.290	.415	.321	5.06
P	Hrbek	136	487	67	141	238	26	1	23	82	68	47	3	2	.290	.489	.377	6.99
A	Hrbek	132	462	72	131	213	20	1	20	89	67	48	4	4	.284	.461	.374	6.50
A	Knoblauch	151	565	78	159	198	24	6	1	50	59	40	25	5	.281	.350	.349	4.60
P	Liriano	119	381	49	98	136	16	5	4	39	35	45	14	8	.257	.357	.320	4.15
A	Larkin, G.	98	255	34	73	95	14	1	2	19	30	21	2	3	.286	.373	.361	5.09
P	Larkin, G.	114	353	43	95	136	22	2	5	42	45	40	3	2	.269	.385	.352	5.01
A	Leius	109	199	35	57	83	7	2	5	20	30	35	5	5	.286	.417	.380	6.00
P	Moses	64	122	17	32	42	5	1	1	11	11	13	5	3	.262	.344	.323	4.07
A	Mack	143	442	79	137	234	27	8	18	74	34	79	13	9	.310	.529	.359	7.44
P	Mack	134	311	46	92	127	11	3	6	40	33	59	12	5	.296	.408	.363	5.69
A	Munoz	51	138	15	39	69	7	1	7	26	9	31	3	0	.283	.500	.327	6.14
P	Munoz	140	480	61	137	222	26	4	17	71	30	90	15	7	.285	.463	.327	5.72
P	Newman	118	299	37	69	82	11	1	0	23	34	31	13	6	.231	.274	.309	2.98
A	Newman	118	246	25	47	52	5	0	0	19	23	21	4	5	.191	.211	.260	1.84
P	Ortiz	91	212	17	58	69	8	0	1	23	17	17	2	3	.274	.325	.328	3.96
A	Ortiz	61	134	9	28	35	5	1	0	11	15	12	0	1	.209	.261	.289	2.57
A	Pagliarulo	121	365	38	102	140	20	0	6	36	21	55	1	2	.279	.384	.319	4.58
P	Pagliarulo	128	405	37	91	161	20	1	16	52	39	84	2	1	.225	.398	.293	4.05
P	Puckett	153	628	86	200	289	34	5	15	92	43	73	8	5	.318	.460	.362	6.60
A	Puckett	152	611	92	195	281	29	6	15	89	31	78	11	5	.319	.460	.352	6.42

A=ACTUAL P=PROJECTED

Well, first, the giant step wasn't completely unprecedented. After all, baseball is in divisions now. The Twins didn't have to overcome all the teams in the American League, just those in their own division. That's not the same task that faced teams before the divsion split. To be exact, the A's were the only real strong team in the Twins' division, and they had gotten complacent. The two good outfits who were still struggling to improve were the Red Sox and the Blue Jays, locked in mortal combat over in the East, safely away from the Twins' division race. Still, no one in division play has ever done this, either. So, what was special about the Twins?

My first class of reversal teams made their giant leaps by finding new sources of Major League talent lying around untapped. Branch Rickey, of course, developed the farm system for the Cardinals, finding a way to get talent into the St. Louis organization in large quantities. This was not all the farm system did, though. One of the main things it did was to organize the talent in areas of the country with no Major League baseball of their own. Before the farm, talent in the South and West of America was organized internally, into leagues like the Sally League (Ty Cobb and Eddie Cicotte) and the Pacific Coast League. What Rickey did was to get those leagues associated with the Majors by some method other than cutthroat commercial transaction. That is, instead of whichever owner had a quick influx of cash going out and buying Sally League prospects, Rickey tied them all up before they got expensive.

Later, with the Dodgers, Rickey was the first to bring African-American talent into the Majors. So, in the American League, was Bill Veeck. Even later, Rickey began to develop Latin talent for, off all teams, the Pittsburgh Pirates. I assume that, if he were still alive, The Mahatma would be working out trades with Japan and Taiwan (hint, O general managers, hint).

The second class of reversal teams is that class which already had winning talent on hand, but whose managements were in the way of winning. When the obstruction was removed, the winning began. Harvey Kuenn was brought in to replace a hard line manager. He just sat in the dugout and told all his players to have fun. They promptly did, until game 7 of the World Series. What Bobby Cox did, in moving down to the field job with the Braves, was the same thing. He decided that his predecessor was in the way of the talent, and replaced him with someone (himself) who would let them win. As early as 1925, Rogers Hornsby replaced a disliked Branch Rickey as the field manager of the Cardinals, who promptly played championship baseball despite the fact that their best player (Hornsby) had a horrible year (for him) in 1926. That Hornsby later became a jerk about it is no reason to ignore what happened then.

It is to the third class of reversals, though, that the Twins belong. That class is teams that have some championship talent, but some obvious holes as well. The team fills the holes with championship ballplayers and promptly wins. The Twins had no DH, no second baseman, a weak right field and left field corps, and only one serious starting pitcher. They didn't just fill the holes with journeymen. They brought in Chili Davis. They came up with Chuck Knoblauch, Rookie of the Year. They quit playing Dan Gladden all the time, and used Randy Bush and Shane Mack. They developed Scott Erickson and bought Jack Morris. That's half a team brought from weakness to strength. Since they already had strengths in the form of Kirby Puckett, Kent Hrbek, Brian Harper and Kevin Tapani, they were more than ready to contend, in one year's time.

Yes, some of it was luck. Knoblauch didn't have to be that good; neither did Erickson. Morris could have been really finished, as could Chili Davis. But you do have to give Andy MacPhail credit. He identified the holes and aggressively sought solutions. That's what I like in Fred Claire, and Andy did it too.

I rate as minor the contribution of Tom Kelly. He's a reasonable technical manager, but nothing more than that. He burned out Erickson in the first half with monstrous overwork. But he also put Chili at DH, and I think that helped. As long time readers may remember, I speculated on Chili and defense a couple of books ago. I noticed that, when Chili quit playing center field and moved to right for the Angels, his bat got big. I reasoned that maybe it helped his concentration at the plate to have a lesser defensive responsibility than he actually could have handled. Well, the ultimate in no defensive responsibility is DH, and Chili's bat responded again.

In this type of reversal, the Twins resemble the Miracle Braves. That team had been weak up the middle. Then Johnny Evers became available at second base, and kid Rabbit Maranville turned in the greatest defensive year any shortstop has ever had. They got a hot year out of some pitchers, and were on their way. That is, they went from very weak up the middle to very strong, and the team was solid enough elsewhere to make that a contender. That's the Twins' story, too. It's not just that they filled some holes. It's that they filled their weakest spots with championship quality players, and they already had some strong spots. In some ways, they are like the New Management teams. The weak spots were keeping Puckett and Hrbek and Tapani from winning. Once the impediments were removed, the championship trail began.

Minnesota Twins Home Park Performance Factors

	Outs	Runs	Hits	2b	3b	HR	W	K	SH	SF	HBP	IBB	SB	CS	GDP
Home LH Batters	1.010	.948	.947	.951	6.767	.920	.885	.954	.825	.677	6.767	.825	.825	1.692	.825
Home RH Batters	1.027	.948	.925	.981	.705	1.149	.995	1.052	.916	.968	1.052	.847	.973	1.278	.952
All Home Batters	1.027	.951	.934	.971	.743	1.078	.957	1.048	.951	.911	1.113	.860	.983	1.319	.938
Opp LH Batters	1.016	.944	.964	.895	.708	1.011	1.066	1.023	1.097	1.073	.545	.849	.763	1.011	.895
Opp RH Batters	1.031	.991	1.001	.982	.992	.979	1.147	.973	1.252	1.156	1.006	1.413	.968	1.480	1.045
All Opp Batters	1.022	.979	.994	.951	.877	.973	1.119	.981	1.171	1.073	.869	1.077	.878	1.277	.979
All LH Batters	1.013	.947	.957	.912	.848	.969	.984	.996	.994	.951	1.391	.840	.763	1.265	.864
All RH Batters	1.027	.968	.958	.981	.774	1.038	1.064	1.001	1.038	1.037	1.040	1.129	.974	1.349	.992
All Batters	1.024	.966	.963	.959	.795	1.019	1.033	1.007	1.050	.985	1.007	.970	.925	1.311	.959

Conventional Batting Records for Minnesota Twins

	G	AB	Run	Hit	2B	3B	HR	TB	RBI	W	K	IW	HB	SB	CS	BRng Eff	GI DP	SH	SF	Avg	Slug	OBP	Runs Ctd
Harper B	123	441	54	137	28	1	10	197	69	14	22	3	6	1	2	.347	14	2	6	.311	.447	.336	62
Hrbek	132	462	72	131	20	1	20	213	89	67	48	4	0	4	4	.298	15	3	2	.284	.461	.373	79
Knoblauch	151	565	78	159	24	6	1	198	50	59	40	0	4	25	5	.468	8	1	5	.281	.350	.351	76
Pagliarulo	121	365	38	102	20	0	6	140	36	21	55	3	3	1	2	.433	9	2	2	.279	.384	.322	44
Gagne	139	408	52	108	23	3	8	161	42	26	72	0	3	11	9	.467	15	5	5	.265	.395	.310	45
Gladden	126	461	65	114	14	9	6	164	52	36	60	1	5	15	9	.611	13	5	4	.247	.356	.306	49
Puckett	152	611	92	195	29	6	15	281	89	31	78	4	4	11	5	.520	27	8	7	.319	.460	.352	91
Mack	143	442	79	137	27	8	18	234	74	34	79	1	6	13	9	.500	11	2	5	.310	.529	.363	82
Davis C	153	534	84	148	34	1	29	271	93	95	117	13	1	5	6	.391	9	0	4	.277	.507	.385	109
Larkin G	98	255	34	73	14	1	2	95	19	30	21	3	1	2	3	.455	9	3	2	.286	.373	.361	34
Newman A	118	246	25	47	5	0	0	52	19	23	21	0	1	4	5	.475	5	5	3	.191	.211	.260	14
Leius	109	199	35	57	7	2	5	83	20	30	35	1	0	5	5	.500	4	5	1	.286	.417	.378	32
Bush	93	165	21	50	10	1	6	80	23	24	25	3	3	0	2	.276	5	0	0	.303	.485	.401	32
Munoz P	51	138	15	39	7	1	7	69	26	9	31	0	1	3	0	.526	2	1	2	.283	.500	.327	23
Ortiz	61	134	9	28	5	1	0	35	11	15	12	0	1	0	1	.280	6	1	0	.209	.261	.293	10
Sorrento	26	47	6	12	2	0	4	26	13	4	11	2	0	0	0	.333	3	0	0	.255	.553	.314	7
Brown J	38	37	10	8	0	0	0	8	0	2	8	0	0	7	1	.429	0	1	0	.216	.216	.256	3
Webster L	18	34	7	10	1	0	3	20	8	6	10	0	0	0	0	.444	2	0	1	.294	.588	.390	8
Castillo C	9	12	0	2	0	1	0	4	0	0	2	0	1	0	0	.000	0	0	0	.167	.333	.231	1
Guthrie	1	0	0	0	0	0	0	0	0	0	0	0	0	0	0	.000	0	0	0	.000	.000	.000	0
Aguilera	1	0	0	0	0	0	0	0	0	0	0	0	0	0	0	.000	0	0	0	.000	.000	.000	0
Abbott P	1	0	0	0	0	0	0	0	0	0	0	0	0	0	0	.000	0	0	0	.000	.000	.000	0
Wayne	1	0	0	0	0	0	0	0	0	0	0	0	0	0	0	.000	0	0	0	.000	.000	.000	0
Leach T	1	0	0	0	0	0	0	0	0	0	0	0	0	0	0	.000	0	0	0	.000	.000	.000	0
TOTALS	1866	5556	776	1557	270	42	140	2331	733	526	747	38	40	107	68	.452	157	44	49	.280	.420	.344	789

Sabermetric Batting Records for Minnesota Twins

	Ball Park Adjusted												Runs		Run/					
	AB	Run	Hit	2B	3B	HR	RBI	W	SO	Avg	Slug	OBP	Ctd	Outs	27o	OW%	OG	OWAR	DWAR	TWAR
Brown J	36	9	7	0	0	0	0	2	8	.194	.194	.237	2	31	1.74	.135	1	-0.25	-0.02	-0.26
Bush	163	19	47	9	3	5	20	23	24	.288	.472	.408	32	122	7.08	.721	5	1.68	0.19	1.87
Castillo C	11	0	1	0	0	0	0	0	2	.091	.091	.167	0	10	0.00	.000	0	-0.13	0.01	-0.12
Davis C	537	81	142	32	0	29	89	98	118	.264	.486	.376	102	413	6.67	.696	15	5.29	0.01	5.30
Gagne	411	50	103	22	2	8	41	27	72	.251	.372	.298	41	344	3.22	.348	13	-0.03	1.92	1.89
Gladden	465	63	109	13	7	6	51	38	60	.234	.331	.297	44	389	3.05	.324	14	-0.37	0.45	0.08
Harper B	443	52	131	27	0	10	68	14	22	.296	.424	.322	57	335	4.59	.521	12	2.12	0.12	2.24
Hrbek	460	68	125	18	3	19	78	65	47	.272	.448	.361	74	355	5.63	.620	13	3.55	0.52	4.06
Knoblauch	570	75	153	23	5	1	49	63	40	.268	.332	.343	71	436	4.40	.499	16	2.40	1.28	3.68
Larkin G	256	32	70	13	0	2	18	31	21	.273	.348	.351	31	201	4.16	.472	7	0.91	0.07	0.97
Leius	200	33	54	6	1	5	19	32	35	.270	.385	.369	29	161	4.86	.549	6	1.19	0.51	1.69
Mack	444	76	131	26	6	19	73	36	79	.295	.509	.352	76	342	6.00	.650	13	3.79	0.84	4.64
Munoz P	138	14	37	6	0	7	25	9	31	.268	.464	.313	21	105	5.40	.600	4	0.97	0.40	1.38
Newman A	248	24	45	4	0	0	18	23	21	.181	.198	.249	13	220	1.60	.116	8	-1.91	1.04	-0.86
Ortiz	135	8	26	4	0	0	10	16	12	.193	.222	.283	8	116	1.86	.151	4	-0.85	0.25	-0.60
Pagliarulo	363	35	97	18	0	5	31	20	54	.267	.358	.322	41	277	4.00	.451	10	1.04	1.09	2.13
Puckett	614	89	187	28	5	15	88	33	78	.305	.440	.340	84	474	4.78	.541	18	3.35	1.10	4.46
Sorrento	46	5	11	1	0	3	11	3	10	.239	.457	.286	5	37	3.65	.407	1	0.08	0.06	0.13
Webster L	33	6	9	0	0	3	7	6	10	.273	.545	.375	7	26	7.27	.731	1	0.37	0.08	0.44
TOTALS	5597	748	1500	259	34	143	707	546	757	.268	.403	.335	738	4429	4.50	.510	164	26.29	9.92	36.21

Pitching Records for Minnesota Twins

	ERA	W	L	Pct	G	GS	CG	ShO	GF	Sv	IP	R	ER	H	2B	3B	HR	BB	IW	SO	HB	WP	BK
Morris Jk	3.43	18	12	.600	35	35	10	2	0	0	246.2	107	94	226	28	6	18	92	5	163	5	15	1
Tapani	2.99	16	9	.640	34	34	4	1	0	0	244.0	84	81	225	48	4	23	40	0	135	2	3	3
Erickson S	3.18	20	8	.714	32	32	5	3	0	0	204.0	80	72	189	39	5	13	71	3	108	6	4	0
Anderson A	4.96	5	11	.313	29	22	2	0	4	0	134.1	82	74	148	26	2	24	42	4	51	5	3	0
West	4.54	4	4	.500	15	12	0	0	0	0	71.1	37	36	66	17	1	13	28	0	52	1	3	0
Edens	4.09	2	2	.500	8	6	0	0	0	0	33.0	15	15	34	8	2	2	10	1	19	0	1	0
Banks	5.71	1	1	.500	5	3	0	0	2	0	17.1	15	11	21	2	0	1	12	0	16	0	3	0
Guthrie	4.32	7	5	.583	41	12	0	0	13	2	98.0	52	47	116	19	5	11	41	2	72	1	7	0
Willis	2.63	8	3	.727	40	0	0	0	9	2	89.0	31	26	76	12	1	4	19	2	53	1	4	1
Bedrosian	4.42	5	3	.625	56	0	0	0	22	6	77.1	42	38	70	16	1	11	35	6	44	3	2	0
Aguilera	2.35	4	5	.444	63	0	0	0	60	42	69.0	20	18	44	9	2	3	30	6	61	1	3	0
Leach T	3.61	1	2	.333	50	0	0	0	22	0	67.1	28	27	82	19	0	3	14	5	32	0	1	0
Abbott P	4.75	3	1	.750	15	3	0	0	1	0	47.1	27	25	38	10	1	5	36	1	43	0	5	0
Neagle	4.05	0	1	.000	7	3	0	0	2	0	20.0	9	9	28	8	1	3	7	2	14	0	1	0
Casian	7.36	0	0	.000	15	0	0	0	4	0	18.1	16	15	28	9	0	4	7	2	6	1	2	0
Wayne	5.11	1	0	1.000	8	0	0	0	2	1	12.1	7	7	11	3	0	1	4	0	7	1	0	0
TOTALS	3.69	95	67	.586	453	162	21	6	141	53	1449.1	652	595	1402	273	31	139	488	39	876	27	57	5

Sabermetric Pitching Records for Minnesota Twins

	Adj	|-Expected-|			|——Opposing Batters——|												Supported				
	ERA	W	L	Pct	BFP	Avg	Slg	OBA	RC/G	GDP	SB	CS	PK	PKE	SH	SF	RSup	RSp/G	W	L	Pct
Abbott P	4.56	2	2	.445	210	.232	.396	.365	5.09	5	6	1	0	0	7	3	30	5.70	2	2	.610
Aguilera	2.22	7	2	.773	275	.183	.275	.274	2.61	6	7	0	0	0	1	3	23	3.00	6	3	.647
Anderson A	4.76	7	9	.425	584	.281	.474	.336	5.67	9	14	6	1	4	4	6	63	4.22	7	9	.441
Banks	5.19	1	1	.383	85	.288	.356	.388	5.72	2	2	0	0	0	0	0	10	5.19	1	1	.500
Bedrosian	4.19	4	4	.488	332	.243	.420	.327	4.82	6	4	1	0	0	2	4	37	4.31	4	4	.514
Casian	6.87	0	0	.261	87	.354	.620	.414	9.52	3	0	0	1	0	0	0	13	6.38	0	0	.463
Edens	3.82	2	2	.534	143	.256	.391	.308	4.46	1	2	1	0	0	0	0	15	4.09	2	2	.534
Erickson S	3.04	18	10	.643	851	.248	.364	.314	3.70	22	4	10	0	2	5	7	130	5.74	22	6	.780
Guthrie	4.13	6	6	.495	432	.303	.465	.369	5.75	16	9	5	1	3	4	3	51	4.68	7	5	.562
Leach T	3.48	2	1	.581	292	.299	.401	.332	4.98	4	10	2	0	0	3	1	29	3.88	2	1	.554
Morris Jk	3.28	18	12	.608	1032	.245	.347	.315	3.81	23	32	8	0	0	5	8	141	5.14	21	9	.711
Neagle	3.60	1	0	.563	92	.329	.553	.380	8.06	1	2	1	0	0	0	0	5	2.25	0	1	.281
Tapani	2.88	17	8	.669	974	.245	.382	.277	3.58	14	18	3	0	1	9	6	144	5.31	19	6	.773
Wayne	4.38	0	1	.466	52	.244	.378	.314	4.08	1	0	0	0	0	1	1	19	13.86	1	0	.909
West	4.29	4	4	.476	305	.244	.458	.314	5.05	3	3	2	0	0	2	3	26	3.28	3	5	.369
Willis	2.53	8	3	.723	355	.232	.311	.273	2.75	8	5	3	0	0	3	4	40	4.04	8	3	.719
TOTALS	3.56	92	70	.568	6101	.255	.392	.317	4.27	124	118	43	3	10	46	49	776	4.82	105	57	.646

Batting 'Splits' Records for Minnesota Twins

	G	AB	Run	Hit	2B	3B	HR	TB	RBI	W	K	IW	HB	SB	CS	GI DP	SH	SF	Avg	Slug	OBP	Runs Ctd
SPLITS for Davis C																						
vs LHP	98	174	24	47	9	0	11	89	32	25	36	4	0	1	1	4	0	2	.270	.511	.358	32
vs RHP	138	360	60	101	25	1	18	182	61	70	81	9	1	4	5	5	0	2	.281	.506	.397	76
Home	79	267	44	81	19	1	14	144	45	54	51	6	1	2	3	3	0	2	.303	.539	.420	64
Away	74	267	40	67	15	0	15	127	48	41	66	7	0	3	3	6	0	2	.251	.476	.348	45
Grass	57	203	32	55	14	0	12	105	42	33	49	6	0	2	2	6	0	1	.271	.517	.371	39
Turf	96	331	52	93	20	1	17	166	51	62	68	7	1	3	4	3	0	3	.281	.502	.393	70
April/June	73	270	43	76	16	0	19	149	51	40	60	7	1	1	3	2	0	2	.281	.552	.374	58
July/October	80	264	41	72	18	1	10	122	42	55	57	6	0	4	3	7	0	2	.273	.462	.396	51
SPLITS for Gagne																						
vs LHP	62	118	13	33	8	2	2	51	12	12	17	0	1	1	4	5	1	1	.280	.432	.348	16
vs RHP	110	290	39	75	15	1	6	110	30	14	55	0	2	10	5	10	4	4	.259	.379	.294	30
Home	68	194	28	51	7	3	3	73	18	15	28	0	2	4	4	7	3	1	.263	.376	.321	22
Away	71	214	24	57	16	0	5	88	24	11	44	0	1	7	5	8	2	4	.266	.411	.300	24
Grass	56	165	21	43	13	0	5	71	17	11	30	0	0	6	3	6	1	4	.261	.430	.300	20
Turf	83	243	31	65	10	3	3	90	25	15	42	0	3	5	6	9	4	1	.267	.370	.317	26
April/June	66	207	27	53	12	2	5	84	19	15	37	0	1	5	4	7	3	1	.256	.406	.308	24
July/October	73	201	25	55	11	1	3	77	23	11	35	0	2	6	5	8	2	4	.274	.383	.312	22
SPLITS for Gladden																						
vs LHP	57	118	10	30	5	4	1	46	19	16	10	0	1	3	3	3	1	3	.254	.390	.341	16
vs RHP	110	343	55	84	9	5	5	118	33	20	50	1	4	12	6	10	4	1	.245	.344	.293	33
Home	65	244	34	65	9	5	3	93	27	22	33	1	3	9	4	9	3	1	.266	.381	.333	30
Away	61	217	31	49	5	4	3	71	25	14	27	0	2	6	5	4	2	3	.226	.327	.275	19
Grass	49	180	28	43	4	2	3	60	19	9	20	0	1	5	5	3	2	2	.239	.333	.276	16
Turf	77	281	37	71	10	7	3	104	33	27	40	1	4	10	4	10	3	2	.253	.370	.325	33
April/June	66	239	39	62	8	4	4	90	23	22	26	1	3	7	5	7	4	1	.259	.377	.328	29
July/October	60	222	26	52	6	5	2	74	29	14	34	0	2	8	4	6	1	3	.234	.333	.282	20
SPLITS for Harper B																						
vs LHP	60	114	15	36	7	1	2	51	14	5	8	3	1	0	1	1	0	2	.316	.447	.344	18
vs RHP	108	327	39	101	21	0	8	146	55	9	14	0	5	1	1	13	2	4	.309	.446	.333	45
Home	60	217	27	74	14	1	4	102	35	7	12	2	3	1	1	7	2	4	.341	.470	.364	35
Away	63	224	27	63	14	0	6	95	34	7	10	1	3	0	1	7	0	2	.281	.424	.309	27
Grass	48	167	22	46	10	0	6	74	32	7	7	1	3	0	1	4	0	2	.275	.443	.313	22
Turf	75	274	32	91	18	1	4	123	37	7	15	2	3	1	1	10	2	4	.332	.449	.351	40
April/June	56	206	23	67	18	0	3	94	32	7	11	2	4	1	0	2	1	4	.325	.456	.353	34
July/October	67	235	31	70	10	1	7	103	37	7	11	1	2	0	2	12	1	2	.298	.438	.321	28
SPLITS for Knoblauch																						
vs LHP	67	148	25	38	8	1	0	48	6	14	10	0	1	2	1	0	0	0	.257	.324	.325	17
vs RHP	133	417	53	121	16	5	1	150	44	45	30	0	3	23	4	8	1	5	.290	.360	.360	59
Home	75	287	43	94	12	5	1	119	26	30	18	0	1	17	1	3	0	2	.328	.415	.391	52
Away	76	278	35	65	12	1	0	79	24	29	22	0	3	8	4	5	1	3	.234	.284	.310	26
Grass	59	212	27	51	9	0	0	60	17	24	14	0	2	7	2	5	1	2	.241	.283	.321	21
Turf	92	353	51	108	15	6	1	138	33	35	26	0	2	18	3	3	0	3	.306	.391	.369	56
April/June	69	255	33	72	10	3	0	88	22	28	17	0	1	8	1	5	0	2	.282	.345	.353	33
July/October	82	310	45	87	14	3	1	110	28	31	23	0	3	17	4	3	1	3	.281	.355	.349	43
SPLITS for Puckett																						
vs LHP	71	155	34	63	8	5	7	102	24	8	19	0	0	3	2	7	2	0	.406	.658	.436	40
vs RHP	139	456	58	132	21	1	8	179	65	23	59	4	4	8	3	20	6	7	.289	.393	.324	54
Home	80	328	54	107	16	4	7	152	45	16	45	2	2	6	2	12	4	5	.326	.463	.356	51
Away	72	283	38	88	13	2	8	129	44	15	33	2	2	5	3	15	4	2	.311	.456	.348	40
Grass	55	217	34	70	10	2	7	105	38	10	26	1	2	4	2	11	3	1	.323	.484	.357	33
Turf	97	394	58	125	19	4	8	176	51	21	52	3	2	7	3	16	5	6	.317	.447	.350	58
April/June	73	293	48	95	13	4	10	146	42	15	37	3	4	4	3	14	2	4	.324	.498	.361	48
July/October	79	318	44	100	16	2	5	135	47	16	41	1	0	7	2	13	6	3	.314	.425	.344	43
SPLITS for Minnesota Twins (all batters except pitchers)																						
vs LHP	821	1511	222	440	82	21	46	702	214	163	191	10	5	15	22	44	17	13	.291	.465	.359	244
vs RHP	1533	4045	554	1117	188	21	94	1629	519	363	556	28	35	92	46	113	27	36	.276	.403	.338	546
Home	941	2764	404	834	139	29	62	1217	383	276	354	23	20	53	25	81	22	28	.302	.440	.366	444
Away	925	2792	372	723	131	13	78	1114	350	250	393	15	20	54	43	76	22	21	.259	.399	.322	348
Grass	719	2159	308	572	106	8	67	895	289	198	293	12	14	40	34	60	18	15	.265	.415	.329	284
Turf	1147	3397	468	985	164	34	73	1436	444	328	454	26	26	67	34	97	26	34	.290	.423	.354	505
April/June	851	2583	340	707	121	19	68	1070	322	246	328	20	19	45	30	74	18	20	.274	.414	.339	356
July/October	1015	2973	436	850	149	23	72	1261	411	280	419	18	21	62	38	83	26	29	.286	.424	.348	433

1991 SPLITS FOR Minnesota Twins

BATTING SPLITS

	AVG	AB	R	H	2B	3B	HR	RBI	SB	CS	BB	K	OBA	SPCT
Total	.280	5556	776	1557	270	42	140	733	107	68	526	747	.344	.420

	#Pit	#P/PA	GB	FB	G/F	G	IBB	HB	SH	SF	GDP
Miscellaneous	21975	3.53	2230	1596	1.40	162	38	40	44	49	157

	AVG	AB	R	H	2B	3B	HR	RBI	SB	CS	BB	K	OBA	SPCT
vs. Left	.291	1511	...	440	82	21	46	214	15	22	163	191	.359	.465
vs. Right	.276	4045	...	1117	188	21	94	519	92	46	363	556	.338	.403
Home	.302	2764	404	834	139	29	62	383	53	25	276	354	.366	.440
Away	.259	2792	372	723	131	13	78	350	54	43	250	393	.322	.399
None on	.280	3066	...	858	155	24	68	68	0	0	260	400	.341	.413
Runners on	.281	2490	...	699	115	18	72	665	107	68	266	347	.348	.428
April	.262	656	82	172	25	7	16	77	6	8	71	93	.336	.395
May	.277	965	114	267	51	7	21	108	12	14	92	115	.340	.409
June	.279	962	144	268	45	5	31	137	27	8	83	120	.340	.432
July	.300	914	140	274	45	10	23	131	15	9	93	117	.363	.446
August	.289	1006	141	291	54	10	23	134	17	15	84	139	.347	.431
September	.277	839	132	232	40	3	18	124	23	12	80	131	.339	.396
October	.248	214	23	53	10	0	8	22	7	2	23	32	.328	.407
None on/out	.268	1356	...	364	59	8	30	30	0	0	113	161	.330	.390
Scoring Posn	.262	1433	...	376	66	10	37	556	17	13	191	230	.343	.400
Close & Late	.283	769	...	218	34	3	22	118	15	9	81	122	.355	.421
Bases Loaded	.254	118	...	30	6	3	4	99	0	0	9	24	.285	.458
Batting #1	.262	687	97	180	24	11	12	73	21	16	62	92	.325	.381
Batting #2	.278	659	92	183	29	5	5	66	26	5	71	52	.351	.360
Batting #3	.315	670	107	211	33	7	20	104	12	5	34	85	.349	.475
Batting #4	.284	606	97	172	30	1	29	116	5	8	94	73	.377	.480
Batting #5	.294	615	89	181	40	1	23	95	4	4	67	118	.364	.475
Batting #6	.293	608	78	178	34	9	16	84	9	7	53	73	.353	.457
Batting #7	.284	588	83	167	28	2	18	80	9	8	48	86	.342	.430
Batting #8	.258	566	74	146	28	4	9	58	6	7	56	84	.326	.369
Batting #9	.250	557	59	139	24	2	8	57	15	8	41	84	.301	.343
As c	.287	600	67	172	33	2	13	87	1	3	34	42	.329	.413
As 1b	.280	600	84	168	27	1	23	102	3	6	81	65	.364	.443
As 2b	.269	642	83	173	26	6	1	60	26	6	69	42	.341	.333
As 3b	.274	536	66	147	25	2	11	55	5	7	47	77	.334	.390
As ss	.242	538	59	130	26	3	8	47	12	11	37	89	.293	.346
As lf	.255	651	92	166	23	9	12	72	19	14	48	90	.311	.373
As cf	.297	664	95	197	29	7	17	92	14	5	37	93	.335	.438
As rf	.328	585	87	192	41	9	18	88	11	7	54	95	.386	.521
Outfield	.292	1900	274	555	93	25	47	252	44	26	139	278	.343	.442
0.0 count	.342	962	...	329	62	12	30	149	...	...	1	0	.347	.525
After (0.1)	.250	2314	...	579	79	12	46	264	...	...	133	471	.294	.354
After (1.0)	.285	2279	...	649	129	18	64	320	...	...	361	276	.382	.441
Two strikes	.203	2185	...	444	75	8	33	219	...	...	219	746	.278	.290
Grass	.265	2159	308	572	106	8	67	289	40	34	198	293	.329	.415
Turf	.290	3397	468	985	164	34	73	444	67	34	328	454	.354	.423
Day	.280	1641	235	460	84	13	45	216	30	22	168	203	.349	.430
Night	.280	3915	541	1097	186	29	95	517	77	46	358	544	.342	.415
Inning 1.6	.279	3742	515	1043	182	33	92	489	72	55	353	488	.342	.419
Inning 7+	.283	1814	261	514	88	9	48	244	35	13	173	259	.349	.421
vs.Bal	.305	426	69	130	25	3	13	63	13	4	35	57	.359	.469
vs.Bos	.286	419	69	120	23	5	11	65	8	6	41	60	.348	.444
vs.Cal	.224	419	51	94	22	5	9	48	9	3	40	66	.292	.365
vs.ChA	.257	444	58	114	18	0	18	56	9	5	46	51	.327	.419
vs.Cle	.293	413	66	121	20	2	10	61	4	6	34	40	.349	.424
vs.Det	.331	414	63	137	26	7	10	57	5	5	49	38	.401	.500
vs.KC	.265	441	55	117	23	3	8	53	13	5	32	65	.315	.385
vs.Mil	.290	424	57	123	23	3	10	57	5	4	36	52	.345	.429
vs.NYA	.289	418	64	121	16	2	16	64	9	5	31	61	.341	.452
vs.Oak	.302	447	66	135	21	3	11	65	8	10	43	61	.367	.436
vs.Sea	.306	445	66	136	19	7	9	60	3	4	50	53	.381	.440
vs.Tex	.271	465	64	126	19	2	9	58	11	5	51	73	.342	.378
vs.Tor	.218	381	28	83	15	0	6	26	10	6	38	70	.298	.304
vs.Atl	.000	0	0	0	0	0	0	0	0	0	0	0	.000	.000

PITCHING SPLITS

	ERA	W	L	SV	SVOP	GS	CG	SHO	IP	H	ER	HR	BB	IBB	K
Total	3.69	95	67	53	66	162	21	8	1449.1	1402	595	139	488	39	876

	#Pit	#P/IP	GB	FB	G/F	BRp9	RA	WP	BK	SH	SF	R	HB	Hld
Miscellaneous	21911	15.12	2052	1612	1.27	11.90	291	57	5	46	49	652	27	29

	ERA	W	L	SV	SVOP	GS	CG	SHO	IP	H	ER	HR	BB	IBB	K
ST	3.77	71	51	0	0	162	21	6	1000.2	982	419	102	324	14	582
REL	3.53	24	16	53	66	0	0	0	448.2	420	176	37	164	25	294
Home	3.90	51	30	26	31	81	9	4	743.0	725	322	75	224	18	469
Away	3.48	44	37	27	35	81	12	2	706.1	677	273	64	264	21	407
April	3.98	9	11	4	5	20	4	2	176.1	184	78	14	73	9	99
May	3.82	14	14	8	11	28	4	1	252.0	240	107	23	97	10	152
June	2.81	22	6	12	14	28	5	2	252.2	237	79	21	64	4	133
July	3.71	16	10	10	13	26	1	0	230.2	237	95	25	68	3	142
August	4.52	17	12	11	11	29	3	0	258.2	245	130	34	89	8	154
September	3.34	15	10	6	7	25	4	1	221.0	193	82	15	75	4	157
October	3.72	2	4	2	5	6	0	0	58.0	66	24	7	22	1	39
Grass	3.50	35	27	21	28	62	9	1	543.0	518	211	50	204	15	316
Turf	3.81	60	40	32	38	100	12	5	906.1	884	384	89	284	24	560
Day	3.74	26	21	11	16	47	6	2	423.0	428	176	43	140	10	247
Night	3.67	69	46	42	50	115	15	4	1026.1	974	419	96	348	29	629
vs.Bal	3.86	8	4	5	6	12	1	0	107.1	104	46	9	41	3	59
vs.Bos	2.72	9	3	4	5	12	2	1	109.0	95	33	8	28	2	51
vs.Cal	5.76	5	8	3	3	13	3	1	114.0	123	73	18	36	3	76
vs.ChA	4.01	5	8	2	5	13	3	1	119.0	116	53	15	47	2	68
vs.Cle	2.50	10	2	6	7	12	0	0	108.0	96	30	3	33	1	52
vs.Det	3.51	8	4	6	6	12	0	0	105.0	98	41	13	43	1	72
vs.KC	3.76	7	6	5	5	13	0	0	115.0	114	48	7	41	3	77
vs.Mil	4.56	6	6	3	6	12	1	0	106.2	117	54	11	32	3	66
vs.NYA	2.94	10	2	6	7	12	1	1	107.0	105	35	12	18	1	69
vs.Oak	3.77	8	5	6	6	13	2	0	117.0	106	49	13	47	5	80
vs.Sea	3.07	9	4	2	2	13	2	1	117.1	109	40	9	52	7	61
vs.Tex	4.31	6	7	2	3	13	3	0	119.0	119	57	11	40	6	86
vs.Tor	3.09	4	8	3	5	12	3	1	105.0	100	36	10	30	2	59
vs.Atl	0.00	0	0	0	0	0	0	0	0.0	0	0	0	0	0	0

OPPOSING BATTERS VS. PITCHERS.

	AVG	AB	R	H	2B	3B	HR	RBI	SB	CS	BB	K	OBA	SPCT
Total	.255	5491	652	1402	273	31	139	616	118	43	488	876	.317	.392
vs. Left	.267	2360	...	630	122	14	44	246	52	17	219	322	.327	.386
vs. Right	.247	3131	...	772	151	17	95	370	66	26	269	554	.308	.397
ST	.258	3813	459	982	186	25	102	411	86	32	324	582	.316	.400
REL	.250	1678	193	420	87	6	37	205	32	11	164	294	.317	.375
Home	.257	2821	342	725	149	18	75	322	72	18	224	469	.313	.402
Away	.254	2670	310	677	124	13	64	294	46	25	264	407	.320	.382
None on	.263	3184	...	837	169	17	81	81	0	0	256	527	.321	.403
Runners on	.245	2307	...	565	104	14	58	535	118	43	232	349	.310	.378
None on/out	.268	1402	...	376	75	8	46	46	0	0	101	205	.321	.432
Scoring Posn	.236	1314	...	310	55	8	30	450	25	7	173	229	.318	.358
vs 1st Batr	.200	265	...	53	10	0	5	29	3	2	19	41	.250	.294
1st IP	.256	1569	144	402	75	8	40	211	41	14	156	278	.321	.391
Inning 1.6	.260	3698	452	960	182	24	94	428	92	36	314	583	.317	.398
Inning 7+	.247	1793	200	442	91	7	45	188	26	7	174	293	.315	.380
Close & Late	.239	852	...	204	39	5	17	95	15	6	81	143	.307	.357
0.0 count	.295	864	...	255	57	3	25	118	...	...	21	0	.311	.455
After (0.1)	.232	2386	...	554	112	12	51	219	...	...	112	567	.270	.353
After (1.0)	.265	2241	...	593	104	16	63	279	...	...	355	309	.364	.410
Two strikes	.194	2360	...	458	100	9	37	191	...	...	184	876	.255	.291
Pitch 1.15	.262	1419	...	372	72	8	29	146	29	12	121	215	.320	.385
Pitch 16.30	.221	1061	...	234	41	4	29	124	21	9	100	198	.288	.349
Pitch 31.45	.291	804	...	234	46	2	25	97	23	7	76	111	.351	.447
Pitch 46.60	.256	699	...	179	39	3	15	82	16	6	55	103	.313	.385
Pitch 61.75	.244	577	...	141	27	6	17	67	14	5	47	87	.302	.400
Pitch 76.90	.274	456	...	125	21	4	12	53	8	3	47	70	.343	.417
Pitch 91.105	.253	328	...	83	16	4	8	34	6	1	21	61	.298	.399
Pitch 106.20	.221	131	...	29	9	0	3	10	1	0	17	27	.313	.359
Pitch 121.35	.316	19	...	6	2	0	1	4	0	0	5	4	.458	.579

Chicago White Sox

Don Malcolm

CHICAGO YEAR	1982	1983	1984	1985	1986	1987	1988	1989	1990	1991	TOT
W	87	99	74	85	72	77	71	69	94	87	815
L	75	63	88	77	90	85	90	92	68	75	803
WPCT	0.537	0.611	0.457	0.525	0.444	0.475	0.441	0.429	0.580	0.537	0.504
R	786	800	679	736	644	748	631	693	682	758	7157
RA	710	650	736	720	699	746	757	750	633	681	7082
PWPT	0.551	0.602	0.460	0.511	0.459	0.501	0.410	0.461	0.537	0.553	0.505
PythW	89	98	74	83	74	81	66	75	87	90	82
PythL	73	64	88	79	88	81	96	87	75	72	80
LUCK	-2	1	0	2	-2	-4	5	-6	7	-3	-2

Defensive Efficiency Record: .7257

CONFESSIONS, COMPLAINTS, AND KUDOS

As always, the Pythagorean figures do not lie. They inform us that the White Sox were a better team in 1991 than they were in 1990, despite having won seven fewer games. "Better despite": this could be a motto for hundreds of teams in the course of baseball history who have played better than their record indicated, who achieved less than what might have been expected or deserved.

And it would be nice to provide some definitive information on the fate of teams who have experienced what the White Sox did in '91: a Pythagorean improvement coupled with a real-life decline in wins. It would be very nice, but the data just doesn't exist at this point.

But the truth of the situation is that, even if we had a list of all the teams since 1901 who have experienced the same phenomenon that happened to the White Sox in 1990-91, we'd still have an amorphous pile of information with contradictory tendencies embedded in it. Sabermetrics is not a clean science: this is one of the reasons why its leading practitioner abandoned it. Without further refinement and application in a rigorous way, it will remain as a curio of a singular mind.

One of the great successes of sabermetrics, however, is the raw predictive power of major league equivalences (MLEs). While sabermetricians do not always agree, they do tend to throw a lot of weight behind the MLE. The reason: it works spectacularly well. The small areas of disagreement are dwarfed by the overall reliance on this tool. And so, while Brock Hanke and I might quibble over exactly how great Frank Thomas is going to be (Brock wasn't nearly so sure as I—or Bill James), the MLE framework creates a comfortable context for knowledge that is a hell of a lot more foolproof than the ouija board tactics seemingly employed by baseball managers and executives.

HERE HE IS, JUST IN TIME TO BUST UP YOUR BALLPARK

I'll let Paul White wax rhapsodic about Hector Villanueva. (Actually, I like Hector, but it's possible that with the advent of Jim Lefebvre to the manager's job on the north side, Villanueva's days as a cult player may be numbered.) It's really a lot more fun to be in on the rise of a truly dominant offensive performer.

Frank Thomas had a frighteningly great year in 1991. It was so great that it made me refer back to the 1986 Baseball Abstract to see whether Frank's 1991 season qualifies him as the All-Time All-Star at first base for the age of 23 (see 1986 Abstract, pp. 301-327).

It's close. Bill James picked Orlando Cepeda, whose 1961 season included 46 HR and 142 RBI. Cepeda's RC/G was a little less than eight and a half; Big Frank clocks in at just under ten. Still, you have to respect the extra homers and RBI, and the slugging average. Frank makes up his difference in the incredible walk total (138), which would rank him second among the group of 14 offensive players selected as All-Time All-Stars or Top Alternatives. (Ted Williams is first, with 145 walks in 1942.)

Also on the Alternatives list is Cleveland first baseman Hal Trosky, who in 1936 had a monster season (.343, 405 total bases, 42 HR, 162 RBI). His RC/G is about a tenth of a run higher than Frank's, due to the total bases and slugging average. Bill probably picked Cepeda over Trosky due to the offensive context: the 1936 American League is second only to the 1930 National League in terms of runs scored per team. This tends to dilute Trosky's achievement somewhat, and likely leaves the competition for best performance by a 23-year old first baseman between Thomas and Cepeda.

Frank's power totals were undoubtedly boosted by the White Sox' change in home ballparks: he hit 24 of his 32 homers in the new Comiskey, and was an absolute terror there (.371 BA, .708 SA). On the road, Frank wasn't quite so fearsome, but he did manage a .400 OBA. Frank's ability to generate numbers that represent "world domination" will hinge on whether he can bring his road stats up a notch or two.

The Brock2 career projections for Frank show him clocking in right around the Hall of Fame signature stats for great slugging hitters: right around 500 HRs and 3000 hits. Brock Hanke's speculation that Frank might not be able to sustain that length of a career due his size and relative lack of speed is not unwarranted, though. But at this moment it appears that Big Frank is on his way to the type of career that has been all too rare in the 70's and 80's: you know, the one where you mention the guy's name and millions instantly know who you're talking about. I think maybe there are three in the latest crop of star players, the ones who've come up in the past three years: Thomas, Griffey, and Justice.

HERE HE IS, JUST IN TIME TO COOL MY ENTHUSIASM

The White Sox really want to win a pennant in '92. Their recent acquisition of Steve Sax demonstrates just how deep this desire is, and might signal how misguided their attempts to win are becoming.

The best thing one can say about the acquisition of Sax is that new manager Gene Lamont may have enough sense not to lead him off. However, Tim Raines had an off-season in '91 and the thinking on the South Side might be to bat him behind Sax. Poor idea, guys: don't even consider it. Raines walks about twice as often as Sax, which makes him a far better leadoff man. Sax really isn't the best choice to bat #2 on this team either, but trading for him seems to destroy one of the more viable options: Craig Grebeck, who quietly had a fine little half-season for the Sox, with surprising power and excellent on-base. There is no regular position for Grebeck now that Sax is on the scene: it remains to be seen how well Craig does in a "supersub" role.

The other problem with the trade is what the Sox gave up. Melido Perez has the kind of stuff that makes for a big winner. Last season, he was used very effectively by Jeff Torborg as a true long man, one of the few instances where a pitcher has been utilized in this manner over the past few years. The White Sox are once again gambling on all of their kid pitchers (Alvarez, Garcia, Fernandez, Hernandez), hoping that three of them will pan out in support of McDowell, Hibbard, Hough, and the recently signed Kirk McCaskill. Once McCaskill (with his 78-74 lifetime mark) was signed, it was clear that Perez was history. I think it's a shame, because under the right circumstances, Melido could have won 18-20 games with this team.

The White Sox doubtless have rationalized this deal in several ways. First, Sax is a recognized name: he'll help attendance. Second, they think they'll be strong up the middle on a day-in, day-out basis. Third, Sax has been on winning teams before: they figure that he brings them some intangibles. All those things have a grain of truth in them, and it's likely that Sax will right around his lifetime average (.286). The problem is that he's a conservative ploy to win a pennant that, in reality, masks a bigger gamble on the pitching staff, and no amount of intangibles can bring back a pitcher with the stuff of Melido Perez. Stuff doesn't always translate into wins (ask Jose DeLeon) but it doesn't hurt, either.

The other thing this deals smacks of is economic collusion. Sax was given a big contract extension in 1990. The Yankees have just signed Danny Tartabull to a deal that would make a sheik blush with embarassment. After they pay off part of Steve's $3 million this year, the Yanks are free and clear, and the Sox get the declining years of Mr. Sax, who is 32 this year.

Ah, hell, I just don't like the whole idea of the deal. The Sox will win the pennant, probably, and they'll give Sax more of the credit than he'll deserve. He'll get credit for anchoring the infield, he'll get credit for being a sparkplug in the field and on the bases. He'll get credit for lot of things that he will have had absolutely no part in, he'll get credit for helping the White Sox achieve the highest number of doubleplays since the days of Nellie Fox. Every intangible item that can be credited to Sax will be credited to him, and the whole notion drives me buggy.

HERE THEY ARE, TRYING TO COVER THE GAP

Actually, if the pitching staff doesn't come together just right, all of this premonitory discomfort about Sax will be moot. We will find out a lot oabout Gene Lamont in the first couple of months of the season as he tries to make sense out of his pitching personnel.

As noted above, there's a lot to choose from, but very little decided in terms of roles to be played, except for McDowell as #1 starter and Thigpen as closer. The White Sox won a lot of games last year on offense: Hibbard, Fernandez, and Hough were not winning pitchers, and McCaskill brings an ERA of 3.75 over the past two seasons.

If I were Lamont, I think I'd give up on Hough as a starter and go with a rotation of McDowell, Hibbard, Fernandez, McCaskill, and Wilson (No-Hit) Alvarez. Hough can be the long man. The set-up men behind Thigpen (Radinsky, Pall, and Ken Patterson) are a pretty good unit, and may be the salvation of the team. It's an odd staff in that it represents the residue of Jeff Torborg's quirky style of handling pitchers, which evolved over his years with the Sox to a degree previously unmanifested. In order to win this year, the Sox will be placing an overly high degree of reliance on McDowell and Thigpen. The former really needs 20-23 wins, the latter 40-50 saves in order to put the Sox over the top.

McDowell has been built up carefully to be the big man, though, and he's never going to be much readier to don the mantle. He was used a bit heavily last season (253 IP, 15 complete games), but when you look at the makeup of the staff, this type of use is virtually unavoidable.

Thigpen was overused in '90 and paid for it last year, but the one thing that Torborg did last year that may serve Lamont in good stead is that he began to develop an alternate closer in Scott Radinsky. If anything should happen to Thigpen, or he's just not cutting it as the closer, Radinsky is available to step in.

But the feeling still persists that the Sox staff is a lot like chewing gum stretched on the back of a bedpost: the further you stretch it, the more little cracks and fissures become visible, and the ever-thinning coverage across the middle can only stretch so far before you wind up with shards. Shards where tendons used to be.

Chicago White Sox Home Park Performance Factors

	Outs	Runs	Hits	2b	3b	HR	W	K	SH	SF	HBP	IBB	SB	CS	GDP
Home LH Batters	.977	.949	.970	1.039	.917	.865	.995	.984	1.017	.711	.954	1.336	1.046	1.271	.986
Home RH Batters	1.001	.959	.958	.967	.967	.926	.907	1.004	1.030	.967	1.118	1.005	.967	1.118	.994
All Home Batters	.987	.960	.961	.998	.944	.906	.944	.998	1.011	.800	.956	1.060	1.004	1.105	.984
Opp LH Batters	1.089	1.055	1.074	1.034	1.177	1.055	1.234	1.112	1.648	1.131	1.420	1.756	1.138	.891	.945
Opp RH Batters	.958	.998	.983	.957	1.082	.958	1.017	.993	.910	1.193	1.098	3.178	.968	.949	.928
All Opp Batters	1.002	1.018	1.000	.980	1.074	.996	1.077	1.027	.980	1.125	1.228	1.928	1.040	.910	.934
All LH Batters	1.017	.991	1.012	1.023	1.003	.934	1.082	1.025	1.171	.871	1.108	1.497	1.086	1.095	.974
All RH Batters	.977	.980	.971	.961	1.038	.943	.963	.997	.957	1.100	1.107	1.280	.970	1.006	.957
All Batters	.994	.988	.981	.989	1.001	.949	1.007	1.012	.997	.955	1.071	1.299	1.023	.997	.959

Conventional Batting Records for Chicago White Sox

	G	AB	Run	Hit	2B	3B	HR	TB	RBI	W	K	IW	HB	SB	CS	BRng Eff	GI DP	SH	SF	Avg	Slug	OBP	Runs Ctd
Fisk	134	460	42	111	25	0	18	190	74	32	86	4	7	1	2	.422	19	0	2	.241	.413	.299	52
Pasqua	134	417	71	108	22	5	18	194	66	62	86	4	3	0	2	.370	9	1	1	.259	.465	.358	71
Fletcher S	90	248	14	51	10	1	1	66	28	17	26	0	3	0	2	.267	3	6	3	.206	.266	.262	18
Ventura	157	606	92	172	25	1	23	268	100	80	67	3	4	2	4	.402	22	8	7	.284	.442	.367	97
Guillen	154	524	52	143	20	3	3	178	49	11	38	1	0	21	15	.500	7	13	7	.273	.340	.284	48
Raines	155	609	102	163	20	6	5	210	50	83	68	9	5	51	15	.554	7	9	3	.268	.345	.359	86
Johnson L	160	588	72	161	14	13	0	201	49	26	58	2	1	26	11	.527	13	6	3	.274	.342	.304	59
Sosa	116	316	39	64	10	1	10	106	33	14	98	2	2	13	6	.488	5	5	1	.203	.335	.240	25
Thomas F	158	559	104	178	31	2	32	309	109	138	112	13	1	1	2	.386	20	0	2	.318	.553	.453	146
Cora	100	228	37	55	2	3	0	63	18	20	21	0	5	11	6	.470	1	8	3	.241	.276	.313	22
Grebeck	107	224	37	63	16	3	6	103	31	38	40	0	1	1	3	.345	3	4	1	.281	.460	.386	42
Karkovice	75	167	25	41	13	0	5	69	22	15	42	1	1	0	0	.417	2	9	1	.246	.413	.310	22
Merullo	80	140	8	32	1	0	5	48	21	9	18	1	0	0	0	.625	1	1	4	.229	.343	.268	14
Newson	71	132	20	39	5	0	4	56	25	28	34	1	0	2	2	.265	4	0	0	.295	.424	.419	25
Snyder C	50	117	10	22	4	0	3	35	11	6	41	1	0	0	0	.412	5	3	0	.188	.299	.228	7
Huff	51	97	14	26	4	1	1	35	15	12	18	2	2	3	2	.480	5	3	1	.268	.361	.357	12
Jackson B	23	71	8	16	4	0	3	29	14	12	25	1	0	0	1	.375	3	0	1	.225	.408	.333	9
Kittle	17	47	7	9	0	0	2	15	7	5	9	0	2	0	0	.500	2	0	1	.191	.319	.291	4
Wakamatsu	18	31	2	7	0	0	0	7	0	1	6	0	0	0	0	.250	0	0	0	.226	.226	.250	2
McCray	17	7	2	2	0	0	0	2	0	0	2	0	0	1	1	.600	0	0	0	.286	.286	.286	0
Beltre	8	6	0	1	0	0	0	1	0	1	1	0	0	1	0	.000	0	0	0	.167	.167	.286	1
TOTALS	1875	5594	758	1464	226	39	139	2185	722	610	896	45	37	134	74	.439	131	76	41	.262	.391	.336	745

Sabermetric Batting Records for Chicago White Sox

	Ball Park Adjusted									Runs		Run/								
	AB	Run	Hit	2B	3B	HR	RBI	W	SO	Avg	Slug	OBP	Ctd	Outs	27o	OW%	OG	OWAR	DWAR	TWAR
Beltre	4	0	0	0	0	0	0	0	0	.000	.000	.000	0	4	0.00	.000	0	-0.05	-0.00	-0.05
Cora	225	36	53	1	3	0	17	20	21	.236	.267	.310	21	187	3.03	.318	7	-0.22	0.18	-0.04
Fisk	448	41	107	24	0	16	72	30	85	.239	.400	.296	48	363	3.57	.393	13	0.57	0.29	0.87
Fletcher S	242	13	49	9	1	0	27	16	25	.202	.248	.258	16	205	2.11	.184	8	-1.26	1.11	-0.15
Grebeck	218	36	61	15	3	5	30	36	39	.280	.445	.383	39	166	6.34	.671	6	1.97	0.70	2.67
Guillen	539	52	146	20	3	2	50	12	39	.271	.330	.284	48	438	2.96	.307	16	-0.69	2.58	1.89
Huff	94	13	25	3	1	0	14	11	17	.266	.319	.352	10	78	3.46	.378	3	0.08	0.22	0.30
Jackson B	68	7	15	3	0	2	13	11	24	.221	.353	.325	8	57	3.79	.421	2	0.15	0.00	0.15
Johnson L	605	72	164	14	13	0	50	28	60	.271	.337	.303	61	473	3.48	.381	18	0.54	2.04	2.58
Karkovice	162	24	39	12	0	4	21	14	41	.241	.389	.303	20	133	4.06	.455	5	0.52	0.19	0.71
Kittle	45	6	8	0	0	1	6	4	8	.178	.244	.269	3	39	2.08	.179	1	-0.25	-0.00	-0.25
McCray	5	1	1	0	0	0	0	0	1	.200	.200	.200	0	5	0.00	.000	0	-0.06	0.04	-0.03
Merullo	143	8	32	1	0	4	21	10	18	.224	.315	.269	13	115	3.05	.321	4	-0.12	0.02	-0.11
Newson	135	20	39	5	0	3	25	31	35	.289	.393	.422	24	101	6.42	.676	4	1.22	0.13	1.35
Pasqua	429	71	110	22	5	17	68	69	90	.256	.450	.363	73	330	5.97	.644	12	3.59	0.46	4.06
Raines	602	100	159	19	6	4	49	83	68	.264	.336	.357	83	474	4.73	.531	18	3.18	1.17	4.35
Snyder C	114	9	21	3	0	2	10	5	40	.184	.263	.218	6	99	1.64	.120	4	-0.85	0.22	-0.63
Sosa	308	38	62	9	1	9	32	13	97	.201	.325	.238	23	261	2.38	.223	10	-1.23	0.76	-0.47
Thomas F	545	101	172	29	2	30	106	132	111	.316	.541	.449	138	396	9.41	.818	15	6.86	0.19	7.06
Ventura	623	92	175	25	1	22	103	89	70	.281	.430	.371	100	489	5.52	.607	18	4.66	1.44	6.09
Wakamatsu	29	1	6	0	0	0	0	0	5	.207	.207	.207	1	23	1.17	.065	1	-0.24	0.11	-0.13
TOTALS	5541	749	1435	223	39	132	713	616	907	.259	.385	.335	729	4419	4.45	.501	164	24.79	11.85	36.64

Pitching Records for Chicago White Sox

	ERA	W	L	Pct	G	GS	CG	ShO	GF	Sv	IP	R	ER	H	2B	3B	HR	BB	IW	SO	HB	WP	BK
McDowell J	3.41	17	10	.630	35	35	15	3	0	0	253.2	97	96	212	44	5	19	82	2	191	4	10	1
Hough	4.02	9	10	.474	31	29	4	1	1	0	199.1	98	89	167	28	10	21	94	0	107	11	5	1
Hibbard	4.31	11	11	.500	32	29	5	0	1	0	194.0	107	93	196	27	2	23	57	1	71	2	1	0
Fernandez A	4.51	9	13	.409	34	32	2	0	1	0	191.2	100	96	186	33	6	16	88	2	145	2	4	1
Garcia R	5.40	4	4	.500	16	15	0	0	0	0	78.1	50	47	79	14	0	13	31	2	40	2	0	2
Alvarez W	3.51	3	2	.600	10	9	2	1	0	0	56.1	26	22	47	7	1	9	29	0	32	0	2	0
Perez M	3.12	8	7	.533	49	8	0	0	16	1	135.2	49	47	111	16	1	15	52	0	128	1	11	1
Pall	2.41	7	2	.778	51	0	0	0	7	0	71.0	22	19	59	6	0	7	20	3	40	3	2	0
Radinsky	2.02	5	5	.500	67	0	0	0	19	8	71.1	18	16	53	9	0	4	23	2	49	1	0	0
Thigpen	3.49	7	5	.583	67	0	0	0	58	30	69.2	32	27	63	8	2	10	38	8	47	4	2	0
Patterson K	2.83	3	0	1.000	43	0	0	0	13	1	63.2	22	20	48	7	2	5	35	1	32	1	2	0
Drahman	3.23	3	2	.600	28	0	0	0	8	0	30.2	12	11	21	3	1	4	13	1	18	0	0	0
Edwards	3.86	0	2	.000	13	0	0	0	3	0	23.1	14	10	22	4	0	2	17	3	12	0	2	0
Hernandez R	7.80	1	0	1.000	9	3	0	0	1	0	15.0	15	13	18	4	0	1	7	0	6	0	1	0
Carter Jf	5.25	0	1	.000	5	2	0	0	1	0	12.0	8	7	8	3	0	1	5	0	2	0	0	0
Drees	12.27	0	0	.000	4	0	0	0	1	0	7.1	10	10	10	1	0	4	6	0	2	0	2	0
Wapnick	1.80	0	1	.000	6	0	0	0	4	0	5.0	1	1	2	1	0	0	4	0	1	0	0	0
TOTALS	3.80	87	75	.537	500	162	28	5	134	40	1478.0	681	624	1302	215	30	154	601	25	923	31	44	6

Sabermetric Pitching Records for Chicago White Sox

	Adj	Expected			Opposing Batters												Supported			
	ERA	W	L	Pct	BFP	Avg	Slg	OBA	RC/G	GDP	SB	CS	PK	PKE	SH	SF	RSup	RSp/G	W	L	Pct
Alvarez W	3.36	3	2	.598	237	.230	.407	.325	3.94	9	0	4	0	1	3	1	35	5.59	4	1	.735
Carter Jf	4.50	0	1	.452	49	.182	.318	.265	2.68	2	1	0	0	0	0	0	13	9.75	1	0	.824
Drahman	2.93	3	2	.660	125	.193	.349	.276	3.13	2	0	1	0	0	2	1	23	6.75	4	1	.841
Drees	11.05	0	0	.120	37	.345	.793	.444	13.02	1	1	0	0	0	1	1	0	0.00	0	0	.000
Edwards	3.47	1	1	.581	106	.259	.376	.375	4.90	5	2	0	0	0	2	2	2	0.77	0	2	.047
Fernandez A	4.41	10	12	.462	827	.259	.388	.337	4.57	13	15	11	1	1	7	11	72	3.38	8	14	.370
Garcia R	5.29	3	5	.374	332	.269	.449	.340	5.03	7	4	5	0	2	3	2	41	4.71	4	4	.443
Hernandez R	7.20	0	1	.244	69	.290	.403	.362	5.58	2	2	0	0	0	0	0	12	7.20	1	0	.500
Hibbard	4.22	11	11	.484	806	.266	.402	.320	4.05	27	6	8	0	2	8	2	105	4.87	13	9	.571
Hough	3.93	10	9	.520	858	.229	.381	.320	4.27	12	10	9	1	3	8	16	93	4.20	10	9	.533
McDowell J	3.34	16	11	.600	1028	.228	.347	.292	3.46	12	22	10	5	3	8	4	156	5.53	20	7	.734
Pall	2.28	7	2	.762	282	.231	.337	.295	2.98	8	4	5	0	2	4	0	54	6.85	8	1	.900
Patterson K	2.69	2	1	.699	265	.214	.330	.321	3.55	6	5	3	0	2	3	2	26	3.68	2	1	.652
Perez M	3.05	10	5	.642	553	.224	.352	.299	3.54	10	15	5	1	2	4	1	62	4.11	10	5	.645
Radinsky	1.89	8	2	.824	289	.206	.288	.270	2.71	4	1	0	0	0	4	4	44	5.55	9	1	.896
Thigpen	3.36	7	5	.597	309	.245	.409	.348	5.03	4	8	5	0	1	7	3	16	2.07	3	9	.275
Wapnick	0.00	0	0	.000	22	.111	.167	.273	2.02	0	0	0	0	0	0	0	4	7.20	0	0	.000
TOTALS	3.75	88	74	.543	6194	.239	.374	.315	3.96	124	96	66	8	19	64	50	758	4.62	98	64	.602

Batting 'Splits' Records for Chicago White Sox

	G	AB	Run	Hit	2B	3B	HR	TB	RBI	W	K	IW	HB	SB	CS	GI DP	SH	SF	Avg	Slug	OBP	Runs Ctd
SPLITS for Fisk																						
vs LHP	72	157	7	36	8	0	5	59	28	9	24	1	1	0	1	11	0	1	.229	.376	.274	13
vs RHP	117	303	35	75	17	0	13	131	46	23	62	3	6	1	1	8	0	1	.248	.432	.312	40
Home	71	233	21	55	13	0	9	95	39	18	41	3	2	0	1	9	0	1	.236	.408	.295	26
Away	63	227	21	56	12	0	9	95	35	14	45	1	5	1	1	10	0	1	.247	.419	.304	26
Grass	116	396	36	98	24	0	14	164	61	27	71	4	7	0	1	13	0	1	.247	.414	.306	47
Turf	18	64	6	13	1	0	4	26	13	5	15	0	0	1	1	6	0	1	.203	.406	.257	4
April/June	64	224	19	58	14	0	5	87	29	19	40	3	4	1	0	10	0	1	.259	.388	.327	27
July/October	70	236	23	53	11	0	13	103	45	13	46	1	3	0	2	9	0	1	.225	.436	.273	25
SPLITS for Guillen																						
vs LHP	88	161	9	34	3	0	1	40	9	1	15	0	0	2	6	2	5	2	.211	.248	.213	7
vs RHP	133	363	43	109	17	3	2	138	40	10	23	1	0	19	9	5	8	5	.300	.380	.315	43
Home	78	247	25	71	10	3	1	90	29	4	21	1	0	10	2	4	6	7	.287	.364	.291	27
Away	76	277	27	72	10	0	2	88	20	7	17	0	0	11	13	3	7	0	.260	.318	.278	21
Grass	133	449	48	123	18	3	3	156	44	11	34	1	0	17	13	6	12	7	.274	.347	.287	43
Turf	21	75	4	20	2	0	0	22	5	0	4	0	0	4	2	1	1	0	.267	.293	.267	6
April/June	72	253	28	69	9	2	0	82	18	6	18	1	0	13	4	3	4	4	.273	.324	.285	24
July/October	82	271	24	74	11	1	3	96	31	5	20	0	0	8	11	4	9	3	.273	.354	.283	24
SPLITS for Pasqua																						
vs LHP	43	49	9	13	2	1	3	26	8	9	12	0	0	0	1	1	0	0	.265	.531	.379	10
vs RHP	126	368	62	95	20	4	15	168	58	53	74	4	3	0	1	8	1	1	.258	.457	.355	61
Home	66	196	39	57	11	3	10	104	29	36	34	1	1	0	0	3	1	1	.291	.531	.402	44
Away	68	221	32	51	11	2	8	90	37	26	52	3	2	0	2	6	0	0	.231	.407	.317	28
Grass	114	349	59	87	18	4	14	155	52	55	69	1	3	0	1	9	1	1	.249	.444	.355	56
Turf	20	68	12	21	4	1	4	39	14	7	17	3	0	0	1	0	0	0	.309	.574	.373	15
April/June	54	164	24	41	7	2	7	73	23	22	30	2	0	0	0	2	1	1	.250	.445	.337	26
July/October	80	253	47	67	15	3	11	121	43	40	56	2	3	0	2	7	0	0	.265	.478	.372	45
SPLITS for Sosa																						
vs LHP	63	128	16	29	5	0	5	49	11	8	39	2	1	6	3	3	2	0	.227	.383	.277	13
vs RHP	78	188	23	35	5	1	5	57	22	6	59	0	1	7	3	2	3	1	.186	.303	.214	12
Home	61	145	15	27	5	1	3	43	10	7	44	1	0	5	3	5	2	1	.186	.297	.222	8
Away	55	171	24	37	5	0	7	63	23	7	54	1	2	8	3	0	3	0	.216	.368	.256	17
Grass	99	264	32	54	7	1	8	87	25	13	84	2	2	13	5	5	4	1	.205	.330	.246	21
Turf	17	52	7	10	3	0	2	19	8	1	14	0	0	0	1	0	1	0	.192	.365	.208	4
April/June	70	230	28	47	5	1	9	81	26	11	75	2	1	9	4	4	4	1	.204	.352	.243	19
July/October	46	86	11	17	5	0	1	25	7	3	23	0	1	4	2	1	1	0	.198	.291	.233	6
SPLITS for Thomas F																						
vs LHP	94	170	26	64	9	0	11	106	35	42	27	7	0	1	1	4	0	0	.376	.624	.500	56
vs RHP	141	389	78	114	22	2	21	203	74	96	85	6	1	0	1	16	0	2	.293	.522	.432	91
Home	81	267	65	99	16	1	24	189	61	76	60	7	0	1	1	8	0	1	.371	.708	.509	101
Away	77	292	39	79	15	1	8	120	48	62	52	6	1	0	1	12	0	1	.271	.411	.399	50
Grass	134	470	90	161	28	2	29	280	95	119	94	12	1	1	2	18	0	2	.343	.596	.475	138
Turf	24	89	14	17	3	0	3	29	14	19	18	1	0	0	0	2	0	0	.191	.326	.333	11
April/June	73	258	43	78	14	1	13	133	57	64	59	8	1	1	1	10	0	1	.302	.516	.441	61
July/October	85	301	61	100	17	1	19	176	52	74	53	5	0	0	1	10	0	1	.332	.585	.463	85
SPLITS for Ventura																						
vs LHP	102	192	23	50	6	0	5	71	20	31	29	0	2	0	2	9	5	3	.260	.370	.364	26
vs RHP	139	414	69	122	19	1	18	197	80	49	38	3	2	2	2	13	3	4	.295	.476	.369	72
Home	81	304	52	88	13	0	16	149	58	37	37	1	3	1	4	12	4	4	.289	.490	.368	52
Away	76	302	40	84	12	1	7	119	42	43	30	2	1	1	0	10	4	3	.278	.394	.367	45
Grass	134	518	80	147	22	1	23	240	93	66	57	2	4	2	4	20	8	5	.284	.463	.366	85
Turf	23	88	12	25	3	0	0	28	7	14	10	1	0	0	0	2	0	2	.284	.318	.375	12
April/June	71	269	30	74	9	0	4	95	28	32	26	2	1	2	2	9	7	1	.275	.353	.353	34
July/October	86	337	62	98	16	1	19	173	72	48	41	1	3	0	2	13	1	6	.291	.513	.378	64
SPLITS for Chicago White Sox (all batters except pitchers)																						
vs LHP	946	1782	205	459	63	6	47	675	194	186	305	18	11	38	31	45	26	9	.258	.379	.330	220
vs RHP	1494	3812	553	1005	163	33	92	1510	528	424	591	27	26	96	43	86	50	32	.264	.396	.339	525
Home	955	2713	378	735	108	20	74	1105	361	305	426	21	20	65	33	64	36	25	.271	.407	.346	390
Away	920	2881	380	729	118	19	65	1080	361	305	470	24	17	69	41	67	40	16	.253	.375	.326	356
Grass	1609	4765	655	1271	195	33	119	1889	622	526	756	38	35	115	66	111	70	36	.267	.396	.342	655
Turf	266	829	103	193	31	6	20	296	100	84	140	7	2	19	8	20	6	5	.233	.357	.303	91
April/June	822	2560	302	662	90	15	50	932	291	246	411	27	15	69	24	59	34	19	.259	.364	.325	311
July/October	1053	3034	456	802	136	24	89	1253	431	364	485	18	22	65	50	72	42	22	.264	.413	.345	435

1991 SPLITS FOR Chicago White Sox

BATTING SPLITS

	AVG	AB	R	H	2B	3B	HR	RBI	SB	CS	BB	K	OBA	SPCT
Total	.262	5594	758	1464	226	39	139	722	134	74	610	896	.336	.391

	#Pit	#P/PA	GB	FB	G/F	G	IBB	HB	SH	SF	GDP
Miscellaneous	23107	3.63	2119	1584	1.34	162	45	37	76	41	131

	AVG	AB	R	H	2B	3B	HR	RBI	SB	CS	BB	K	OBA	SPCT
vs. Left	.258	1782	...	459	63	6	47	194	38	31	186	305	.330	.379
vs. Right	.264	3812	...	1005	163	33	92	528	96	43	424	591	.339	.396
Home	.271	2713	378	735	108	20	74	361	65	33	305	426	.346	.407
Away	.253	2881	380	729	118	19	65	361	69	41	305	470	.326	.375
None on	.256	3207	...	821	129	18	68	68	0	0	298	526	.323	.371
Runners on	.269	2387	...	643	97	21	71	654	134	74	312	370	.352	.417
April	.271	601	77	163	26	3	13	75	13	6	57	83	.337	.389
May	.251	963	100	242	26	3	16	95	31	11	95	177	.319	.334
June	.258	996	125	257	38	9	21	121	25	7	94	151	.324	.378
July	.262	944	152	247	43	6	33	143	24	13	113	133	.345	.425
August	.275	1016	154	279	46	8	31	150	21	18	107	153	.344	.427
September	.247	857	125	212	37	9	19	115	16	15	117	168	.341	.378
October	.295	217	25	64	10	1	6	23	4	4	27	31	.368	.433
None on/out	.244	1388	...	338	61	7	27	27	0	0	116	232	.307	.356
Scoring Posn	.272	1406	...	382	64	12	35	557	23	9	224	237	.368	.409
Close & Late	.264	1109	...	293	45	7	27	144	32	15	124	172	.340	.390
Bases Loaded	.336	131	...	44	11	0	6	129	0	0	11	21	.361	.557
Batting #1	.265	667	107	177	22	6	6	55	53	15	91	76	.356	.343
Batting #2	.265	669	105	177	23	1	21	98	11	4	72	80	.338	.396
Batting #3	.294	605	103	178	28	1	29	95	4	3	129	113	.419	.488
Batting #4	.249	630	87	157	34	6	24	110	2	3	82	116	.340	.437
Batting #5	.254	618	78	157	27	4	22	104	4	8	82	128	.342	.417
Batting #6	.268	624	75	167	25	6	14	80	12	11	53	123	.326	.394
Batting #7	.235	618	76	145	21	9	11	57	19	8	39	131	.283	.351
Batting #8	.241	582	67	140	22	2	7	57	12	3	40	85	.289	.321
Batting #9	.286	581	60	166	24	4	5	66	17	19	22	44	.314	.367
As c	.264	607	63	160	36	0	22	92	1	2	42	118	.317	.432
As 1b	.259	606	95	157	28	2	25	90	0	2	93	119	.364	.436
As 2b	.229	547	53	125	17	5	1	49	7	8	51	60	.302	.283
As 3b	.281	636	92	179	27	2	24	104	2	5	84	72	.364	.443
As ss	.283	584	66	165	25	3	6	62	22	15	19	51	.302	.366
As lf	.253	636	107	161	19	4	7	57	44	15	93	82	.351	.329
As cf	.268	639	76	171	16	13	2	57	27	13	26	71	.297	.343
As rf	.235	579	71	136	22	5	18	84	13	7	55	156	.302	.383
Outfield	.252	1854	254	468	57	22	27	198	84	35	174	309	.318	.351
0.0 count	.301	853	...	257	45	7	21	111	...	...	1	0	.304	.444
After (0.1)	.245	2436	...	598	89	17	51	269	...	...	118	579	.285	.359
After (1.0)	.264	2305	...	609	92	15	67	342	...	...	458	317	.385	.404
Two strikes	.191	2352	...	449	71	11	41	203	...	...	258	896	.274	.283
Grass	.267	4765	655	1271	195	33	119	622	115	66	526	756	.342	.396
Turf	.233	829	103	193	31	6	20	100	19	8	84	140	.303	.357
Day	.266	1534	207	408	52	10	39	193	39	17	171	255	.340	.389
Night	.260	4060	551	1056	174	29	100	529	95	57	439	641	.335	.391
Inning 1.6	.258	3684	505	952	154	25	85	481	94	56	422	605	.337	.383
Inning 7+	.268	1910	253	512	72	14	54	241	40	18	188	291	.334	.405
vs.Bal	.268	411	58	110	20	1	12	58	7	4	38	63	.332	.409
vs.Bos	.239	427	45	102	13	1	7	41	11	4	35	77	.294	.323
vs.Cal	.246	448	50	110	12	0	12	47	8	12	40	78	.308	.353
vs.Cle	.261	399	45	104	17	2	8	44	14	6	35	63	.323	.373
vs.Det	.270	423	50	114	16	4	14	49	6	8	41	54	.333	.426
vs.KC	.272	441	68	120	15	5	7	68	11	2	44	71	.336	.376
vs.Mil	.276	449	68	124	21	1	13	66	10	6	57	56	.364	.414
vs.Min	.261	444	58	116	23	3	15	55	10	5	47	68	.330	.428
vs.NYA	.308	425	77	131	21	4	11	74	14	6	44	66	.378	.454
vs.Oak	.271	436	59	118	14	6	9	57	16	4	60	84	.363	.392
vs.Sea	.237	439	50	104	25	3	14	49	6	3	54	74	.322	.403
vs.Tex	.259	451	78	117	19	7	8	68	6	7	72	69	.364	.386
vs.Tor	.234	401	52	94	10	2	9	46	15	7	43	73	.313	.337

PITCHING SPLITS

	ERA	W	L	SV	SVOP	GS	CG	SHO	IP	H	ER	HR	BB	IBB	K
Total	3.79	87	75	40	64	162	28	12	1478.0	1302	622	154	601	25	923

	#Pit	#P/IP	GB	FB	G/F	BRp9	RA	WP	BK	SH	SF	R	HB	Hld
Miscellaneous	23017	15.57	1913	1721	1.11	11.78	338	44	6	64	50	681	31	41

	ERA	W	L	SV	SVOP	GS	CG	SHO	IP	H	ER	HR	BB	IBB	K
ST	4.23	54	55	0	0	162	28	5	1014.1	927	477	112	411	7	621
REL	2.85	33	20	40	64	0	0	0	463.2	375	147	42	190	18	302
Home	3.72	46	35	19	29	81	10	3	750.0	668	310	79	281	6	452
Away	3.88	41	40	21	35	81	18	2	728.0	634	314	75	320	19	471
April	4.30	11	6	6	8	17	2	0	157.0	139	75	17	84	3	125
May	4.11	10	17	3	9	27	4	0	252.0	236	115	28	126	11	161
June	3.34	17	12	9	11	29	6	1	264.0	214	98	28	84	3	153
July	3.48	19	8	10	15	27	5	0	251.0	220	97	30	80	6	124
August	4.23	12	18	5	9	30	7	2	261.2	245	123	22	101	0	175
September	3.20	15	11	6	9	26	4	2	236.1	192	84	19	98	2	155
October	5.14	3	3	1	3	6	0	0	56.0	56	32	10	28	0	30
Grass	3.74	74	64	35	55	138	22	5	1265.1	1104	526	129	521	22	807
Turf	4.15	13	11	5	9	24	6	0	212.2	198	98	25	80	3	116
Day	3.61	23	20	8	13	43	13	2	403.2	321	162	33	174	7	259
Night	3.87	64	55	32	51	119	15	3	1074.1	981	462	121	427	18	664
vs.Bal	3.21	8	4	4	5	12	3	2	109.1	83	39	9	44	0	84
vs.Bos	3.82	5	7	4	4	12	0	0	113.0	110	48	16	54	6	67
vs.Cal	3.49	5	8	1	3	13	1	1	116.0	120	45	10	42	0	67
vs.Cle	2.83	6	6	3	4	12	4	0	105.0	85	33	7	30	1	56
vs.Det	5.42	4	8	2	4	12	1	0	108.0	102	65	17	65	1	89
vs.KC	4.32	7	6	4	4	13	1	0	114.2	104	55	12	33	0	64
vs.Mil	4.02	7	5	2	4	12	2	0	118.2	111	53	10	48	7	60
vs.Min	4.20	8	5	3	7	13	1	0	120.0	114	56	18	46	1	51
vs.NYA	3.98	8	4	4	6	12	3	0	108.2	98	48	7	43	1	71
vs.Oak	3.23	7	6	3	5	13	3	1	117.0	79	42	11	55	3	85
vs.Sea	3.55	7	6	5	6	13	2	1	119.0	98	47	13	41	1	68
vs.Tex	3.73	8	5	2	5	13	2	0	120.2	97	50	14	63	3	88
vs.Tor	3.58	7	5	3	7	12	5	0	108.0	101	43	10	37	1	73

OPPOSING BATTERS VS. PITCHERS.

	AVG	AB	R	H	2B	3B	HR	RBI	SB	CS	BB	K	OBA	SPCT
Total	.239	5448	681	1302	215	30	154	648	96	66	601	923	.315	.374
vs. Left	.234	2163	...	507	89	16	51	252	47	28	236	365	.309	.361
vs. Right	.242	3285	...	795	126	14	103	396	49	38	365	558	.320	.383
ST	.245	3784	516	927	163	24	112	442	66	46	411	621	.320	.390
REL	.225	1664	165	375	52	6	42	206	30	20	190	302	.306	.340
Home	.241	2767	337	668	113	14	79	324	46	38	281	452	.312	.378
Away	.236	2681	344	634	102	16	75	324	50	28	320	471	.319	.370
None on	.229	3178	...	728	118	17	88	88	0	0	327	542	.305	.360
Runners on	.253	2270	...	574	97	13	66	560	96	66	274	381	.330	.394
None on/out	.238	1376	...	327	58	9	41	41	0	0	149	209	.317	.382
Scoring Posn	.257	1249	...	321	49	7	37	478	19	14	181	223	.342	.396
vs 1st Batr	.236	297	...	70	11	0	12	61	7	2	23	46	.293	.394
1st IP	.242	1612	231	390	60	9	53	245	39	22	163	296	.313	.389
Inning 1.6	.246	3622	508	891	155	25	106	482	66	41	398	617	.321	.390
Inning 7+	.225	1826	173	411	60	5	48	166	30	25	203	306	.305	.342
Close & Late	.231	985	...	228	33	2	26	109	22	17	121	174	.319	.348
0.0 count	.281	768	...	216	43	4	18	85	...	...	19	0	.300	.418
After (0.1)	.208	2397	...	498	78	12	54	250	...	...	129	597	.251	.318
After (1.0)	.258	2283	...	588	94	14	82	313	...	...	453	326	.380	.419
Two strikes	.166	2438	...	404	51	10	52	206	...	...	246	923	.244	.259
Pitch 1.15	.238	1463	...	348	52	8	45	173	29	20	135	232	.305	.377
Pitch 16.30	.234	997	...	233	38	6	25	126	17	11	134	193	.325	.359
Pitch 31.45	.232	704	...	163	34	1	13	75	18	9	89	116	.316	.338
Pitch 46.60	.270	589	...	159	34	4	22	100	13	8	70	104	.345	.453
Pitch 61.75	.221	575	...	127	20	5	16	62	5	4	46	100	.278	.357
Pitch 76.90	.249	494	...	123	14	2	11	43	7	8	47	73	.314	.352
Pitch 91.105	.262	374	...	98	17	2	13	41	5	3	43	60	.342	.422

Texas Rangers

Don Malcolm

TEXAS											
YEAR	1982	1983	1984	1985	1986	1987	1988	1989	1990	1991	TOT
W	64	77	69	62	87	75	70	83	83	85	755
L	98	85	92	99	75	87	91	79	79	77	862
WPCT	0.395	0.475	0.429	0.385	0.537	0.463	0.435	0.512	0.512	0.525	0.467
R	590	639	656	617	771	823	637	695	676	829	6933
RA	749	609	714	785	743	849	735	714	696	814	7408
PWPT	0.383	0.524	0.458	0.382	0.518	0.484	0.429	0.487	0.485	0.509	0.467
PythW	62	85	74	62	84	78	69	79	79	82	76
PythL	100	77	88	100	78	84	93	83	83	80	86
LUCK	2	-8	-5	0	3	-3	1	4	4	3	1

Defensive Efficiency Record: .6901

We called him Uncle Alan. He was a red-haired Marxist from Long Island with a wit so dry it crackled and a strangely endearing sneer. Somehow he lived for years (platonically) with a neurotic Jewish girl who had recently re-invented guilt on a scale slightly wider than Cinemascope. But mostly I remember him for two things: 1) his strategic absence one Saturday night, leaving me to wait on 350 surly customers in a four-hour shift at the Washington University campus greasy spoon all by myself (they carried me out after three-and-a-half hours because my eyes refused to focus), and 2) his oversized and undercoordinated weimaraner named Bakunin.

When I look at the Texas Rangers, I am instantly reminded of that ungainly dog, the quintessence of dishevelled, hapless aggression. Rarely has a team looked so imposing and inept in such a short span. This team has probably taken on more of its manager's professional personality traits than any other. Bobby Valentine, a classic extrovert if there ever was one, played baseball with his cerebellum. He is a prime example of the player gifted with abundant natural talent who could not or would not make the necessary mental adjustments to become a dominant player at the major league level. The Rangers, as a team, play the way Bobby Valentine played baseball: restless, often flashy, aggressively inept defense; impatient, edgy, high-octane offense that still somehow seems less than the sum of its parts.

Uncle Alan's weimaraner was still a growing puppy when he used to entertain us by charging around a corner and having all four legs go out from under him. The Rangers can be similarly entertaining. With Bakunin, though, you were pretty sure it was just a phase he was going through: the Rangers don't give you much of a signal that things will ever change.

A couple of years ago a very interesting sabermetric volume entitled The Diamond Appraised was published. It was written, mainly, by Craig Wright, who has been associated with the Rangers for more than ten years as a sabermetrician. The most interesting aspect of the volume, however, may not actually be found in the concise and well-argued concepts that Wright proposes, but in the nature of the dialogue between Wright and then-Rangers pitching coach Tom House. The inability of House (and, by extension, Bobby Valentine) to assimilate and implement any of Wright's suggestions concerning the use of starting pitchers is a glaring indictment of baseball's ongoing hostility to anything but the received wisdom that keeps the network of good-old-boy smoke-and-fog (the coined word is "gobsaf") spilling out unabated. It has also kept the Rangers from becoming what they most certainly should be, which is the dominant team in the AL West.

Maybe they'll make it anyway. Maybe, like Bakunin the klutzy pup, it's just a phase they're going through. They have an intriguing collection of hitters who could win a pennant with only minimal assistance from a pitching staff. We'll examine the hitting in a bit more detail below, using the Brock2 system to get a look at how the Rangers' Big Six shapes up over the next five years.

And if you see a copy of The Diamond Appraised (it's been showing up recently as a remainder), by all means snap it up. It's fascinating reading, both for the breadth and insight that Craig Wright brings to his work, but also for the thin veil of accommodation that the business of baseball has toward anyone would try to use scientific concepts to improve performance.

THE "BIG SIX": THE NEXT FIVE YEARS

No, we're not discussing Christy Mathewson, who had the nickname Big Six well before any of the Rangers' hitters were gleams in their great-grandfathers' eyes.

For our purposes here, the Rangers' Big Six hitters are: Julio Franco, Rafael Palmeiro, Ruben Sierra, Juan Gonzalez, Kevin Reimer, and Dean Palmer. The order of presentation is analogous to the sequence in which they bat, from second to seventh, in the Rangers' lineup. The Rangers are still missing a leadoff man (they're hoping that highly touted center field prospect Kevin Belcher will fill this void someday soon). Their #8 hitter is the young catcher Ivan Rodriguez, who's not likely to progress to a level where he'll provide anything but acceptable lower-in-the-order production. The #9 slot is currently occupied by shortstops Jeff Huson and Mario Diaz, quintessential exemplars of good field, no hit. They may be challenged by exciting but erratic Cristobal Colon, who'll probably play at Oklahoma City this year.

The Big Six was, as you can see, fairly potent in 1991:

PLAYER	AGE	G	AB	R	H	D	T	HR	RBI	BB
Franco, Julio	29	146	589	108	201	27	3	15	78	65
Gonzalez, Juan	21	142	545	78	144	34	1	27	102	42
Palmeiro, Rafael	26	159	630	115	203	49	3	26	88	68
Palmer, Dean	22	81	268	38	50	9	2	15	37	32
Reimer, Kevin	27	136	394	46	106	22	0	20	69	33
Sierra, Ruben	25	161	661	110	203	44	5	25	116	56
BIG 6 TOTALS			3087	495	907	185	14	128	490	296

Three players with more than 200 hits, something that hadn't happened since 1937, when the Detroit Tigers had four (Greenberg, Gehringer, Pete Fox, and Gee Walker). These six hitters (five full hitters, when you add up the at-bats) had more homers combined than 14 other major league teams in 1991.

So, given the quantity of hitting talent assembled in one place, and factoring in the inevitable perturbations that occur, this is one of the better hitting nuclei in recent memory. Palmer looks a lot like Rob Deer, but he can play third base. Let's see what the Brock2 system projects for them over the next five years:

PLAYER	AGE	G	AB	R	H	D	T	HR	RBI	BB
Franco, Julio	30	152	593	83	175	25	2	11	66	73
Gonzalez, Juan	22	154	581	92	162	38	2	31	101	43
Palmeiro, Rafael	27	156	604	97	188	40	4	22	93	58
Palmer, Dean	23	51	155	26	32	6	1	10	26	18
Reimer, Kevin	28	118	296	35	80	18	1	13	45	32
Sierra, Ruben	26	156	610	99	185	40	3	23	94	51
BIG 6 TOTALS (1992)			2839	432	823	168	12	110	425	277

Brock2, in the version we're using, is still a conservative, steady-state tool, so even though you might expect Sierra and Palmeiro to improve due to their age, the projections for '92 show them declining. Dean Palmer's .187 BA in '91 isn't treated kindly by Brock2, which limits his playing time severely. Kevin Reimer is similarly affected, though not nearly to the same degree.

So, just for the hell of it, let's prorate Palmer and Reimer out to 600 plate appearances and see how their numbers stack up:

YEAR	PLAYER	AGE	AB	R	H	D	T	HR	RBI	BB
1992	Palmer, Dean	23	538	90	111	21	3	35	90	62
1992	Reimer, Kevin	28	541	64	146	33	2	24	82	

Looks like Palmer would be a big homer threat, but the batting average (which has been left off to protect the guilty) is just barely over .200. It will take a lot of chutzpah on the part of Bobby Valentine to leave Palmer out there full-time. His slugging average against lefties in 1991, by the way, was .617.

It isn't until 1993 that the Brock2 system figures Palmer to be a full-time player, and as can be seen, the prorated home run totals above are right on track with the '93 projection:

PLAYER	AGE	G	AB	R	H	D	T	HR	RBI	BB
Franco, Julio	31	151	585	85	180	25	2	11	68	68
Gonzalez, Juan	23	155	583	95	163	38	2	32	103	47
Palmeiro, Rafael	28	156	603	106	197	44	3	23	97	67
Palmer, Dean	24	153	497	85	101	19	4	32	85	63
Reimer, Kevin	29	140	382	45	106	22	0	18	60	36
Sierra, Ruben	27	157	622	104	189	40	4	27	102	58
BIG 6 TOTALS (1993)			3272	520	936	189	14	143	515	340

All in all, 1993 shapes up as the Rangers' best bet: Franco has what Brock2 projects to be his last .300+ season, Palmeiro and Sierra have representative peak years, Gonzalez continues to improve, Reimer has his best season as projected, and Palmer cracks the 30 homer plateau (though still with a BA barely reaching .210). If the Rangers can get any kind of a leadoff hitter, they should score close to 900 runs. And if they can't win scoring 900 runs, then they'll probably never win.

It's interesting to see what the projections look like out to '96, although the likelihood that this aggregation of players will remain together in one lineup for that long is dubious indeed:

PLAYER	AGE	G	AB	R	H	D	T	HR	RBI	BB
Franco, Julio	32	152	583	77	173	25	2	9	63	69
Gonzalez, Juan	24	155	579	97	163	38	2	33	105	48
Palmeiro, Rafael	29	159	607	102	198	43	3	22	95	63
Palmer, Dean	25	148	475	88	100	18	4	33	86	64
Reimer, Kevin	30	137	377	38	98	21	0	14	52	38
Sierra, Ruben	28	155	603	102	189	40	3	24	96	58
BIG 6 TOTALS (1994)			3224	505	921	185	14	136	498	340

PLAYER	AGE	G	AB	R	H	D	T	HR	RBI	BB
Franco, Julio	33	151	573	75	171	24	2	9	61	71
Gonzalez, Juan	25	150	559	99	161	37	2	34	105	49
Palmeiro, Rafael	30	157	604	91	188	41	3	19	88	65
Palmer, Dean	26	154	495	101	108	20	4	40	100	63
Reimer, Kevin	31	144	385	38	101	21	0	14	53	38
Sierra, Ruben	29	159	616	103	193	41	3	25	99	58
BIG 6 TOTALS (1995)			3231	507	921	183	13	141	506	344

PLAYER	AGE	G	AB	R	H	D	T	HR	RBI	BB
Franco, Julio	34	151	566	67	163	23	1	7	57	63
Gonzalez, Juan	26	156	575	107	167	38	2	40	117	50
Palmeiro, Rafael	31	157	589	86	183	39	2	18	83	62
Palmer, Dean	27	152	488	106	108	20	4	43	106	67
Reimer, Kevin	32	145	387	35	99	21	0	12	49	39
Sierra, Ruben	30	156	609	89	181	38	2	21	89	58
BIG 6 TOTALS (1996)			3214	491	901	179	12	142	502	339

The system projects Palmer and Gonzalez to become slugging stars on the order of the Bash Brothers, along with a slow but still perceptible decline by present big guns Franco, Palmeiro, and Sierra. I think the general trend here is probably correct, although the actual numbers are not to be taken as gospel. This version of the Brock2 system has not been revised to reflect Bill James' calibrations to lower home runs, so the homer figures for Palmer and Gonzalez should be viewed as overly generous.

A quick theoretical digression: what is really needed with a systemic prediction tool like Brock2 is a way to create a little more "warble" in a player's year-to-year totals, but still retain an overall five-to-eight year curve. A fairly grandiose means of achieving this was discussed in the 1990 Sabermetric, but there are other, less data-intensive ways of producing such profiles: I'll try to address this issue in next year's book.

The Brock2 system as currently deployed kicks out some interesting lifetime figures for our "Big Six." Juan Gonzalez is targeted to hit 568 homers; Ruben Sierra is projected to crack 3000 hits; Palmeiro and Franco are geared to crack 2800 hits; and Dean Palmer is adjudged to be the 90's equivalent of Dave Kingman, hitting 413 lifetime homers with a batting average of .214. Stay tuned.

Texas Rangers Home Park Performance Factors

	Outs	Runs	Hits	2b	3b	HR	W	K	SH	SF	HBP	IBB	SB	CS	GDP
Home LH Batters	.932	.924	.950	.942	.999	.848	.863	.834	1.674	.930	.877	1.033	.781	.748	.748
Home RH Batters	.951	.928	.944	.882	.703	1.090	.925	.965	.903	.847	.728	.903	1.150	.812	1.112
All Home Batters	.943	.926	.941	.908	.720	.992	.915	.924	1.045	.978	.779	1.003	.952	.787	.924
Opp LH Batters	.983	1.014	1.042	1.042	1.030	1.030	1.213	.919	1.030	1.154	.918	7.210	.843	.753	1.057
Opp RH Batters	.973	.993	.961	1.053	.679	1.006	.955	.939	1.249	.772	1.112	.906	1.194	.679	.905
All Opp Batters	.973	.999	.985	1.033	.866	.989	1.034	.926	1.158	.903	1.075	1.248	1.037	.762	.918
All LH Batters	.957	.970	.997	.995	1.003	.934	1.027	.876	1.301	1.039	.918	1.622	.802	.741	.880
All RH Batters	.962	.960	.953	.965	.691	1.046	.939	.952	1.047	.788	.910	.907	1.172	.724	.999
All Batters	.958	.962	.963	.969	.789	.993	.974	.925	1.100	.925	.912	1.103	.994	.769	.923

Conventional Batting Records for Texas Rangers

	G	AB	Run	Hit	2B	3B	HR	TB	RBI	W	K	IW	HB	SB	CS	BRng Eff	GI DP	SH	SF	Avg	Slug	OBP	Runs Ctd
Rodriguez I	88	280	24	74	16	0	3	99	27	5	42	0	0	0	1	.381	10	2	1	.264	.354	.276	24
Palmeiro	159	631	115	203	49	3	26	336	88	68	72	10	6	4	3	.410	18	2	7	.322	.532	.389	130
Franco Ju	146	589	108	201	27	3	15	279	78	65	78	8	3	36	9	.458	13	0	2	.341	.474	.408	119
Buechele	121	416	58	111	17	2	18	186	66	39	69	4	5	0	4	.373	11	10	2	.267	.447	.335	60
Huson	119	268	36	57	8	3	2	77	26	39	32	0	0	8	3	.568	6	9	1	.213	.287	.312	26
Gonzalez Juan	142	545	78	144	34	1	27	261	102	42	118	7	5	4	4	.500	10	0	3	.264	.479	.321	82
Pettis	137	282	37	61	7	5	0	78	19	54	91	0	0	29	13	.484	4	6	1	.216	.277	.341	32
Sierra	161	661	110	203	44	5	25	332	116	56	91	7	0	16	4	.407	17	0	9	.307	.502	.357	118
Downing	123	407	76	113	17	2	17	185	49	58	70	7	8	1	1	.505	7	1	2	.278	.455	.377	73
Reimer	136	394	46	106	22	0	20	188	69	33	93	6	7	0	3	.298	10	0	6	.269	.477	.332	61
Palmer Dn	81	268	38	50	9	2	15	108	37	32	98	0	3	0	2	.469	4	1	0	.187	.403	.281	31
Petralli	87	199	21	54	8	1	2	70	20	21	25	1	0	2	1	.353	4	7	1	.271	.352	.339	25
Diaz Mar	96	182	24	48	7	0	1	58	22	15	18	0	0	0	1	.400	5	4	1	.264	.319	.318	18
Stanley M	95	181	25	45	13	1	3	69	25	34	44	0	2	0	0	.281	2	5	1	.249	.381	.372	29
Daugherty	58	144	8	28	3	2	1	38	11	16	23	1	0	1	0	.250	2	4	3	.194	.264	.270	12
Hernandez J	45	98	8	18	2	1	0	22	4	3	31	0	0	0	1	.556	2	6	0	.184	.224	.208	4
Walling	24	44	1	4	1	0	0	5	2	3	8	0	2	0	0	.286	3	0	0	.091	.114	.184	1
Fariss	19	31	6	8	1	0	1	12	6	7	11	0	0	0	0	.167	0	0	0	.258	.387	.395	5
Russell Jn	22	27	3	3	0	0	0	3	1	1	7	0	0	0	0	.600	0	0	1	.111	.111	.138	1
Green G	8	20	0	3	1	0	0	4	1	1	6	0	0	0	0	.000	0	2	0	.150	.200	.190	1
Maurer	13	16	0	1	1	0	0	2	2	2	6	0	1	0	0	.000	0	0	0	.063	.125	.211	1
Harris D	18	8	4	3	0	0	1	6	2	1	3	0	0	1	0	.500	0	0	0	.375	.750	.444	3
Scruggs	5	6	1	0	0	0	0	0	0	0	1	0	0	0	0	1.000	1	0	0	.000	.000	.000	0
Kreuter	3	4	0	0	0	0	0	0	0	0	1	0	0	0	0	.000	0	0	0	.000	.000	.000	0
Jeffcoat	2	1	1	1	1	0	0	2	1	0	0	0	0	0	0	.000	0	0	0	1.000	2.000	1.000	2
Parent	3	1	0	0	0	0	0	0	0	0	1	0	0	0	0	.000	0	0	0	.000	.000	.000	0
Capra	2	0	1	0	0	0	0	0	0	1	0	0	0	0	0	1.000	0	0	0	.000	.000	1.000	0
Russell Jf	1	0	0	0	0	0	0	0	0	0	0	0	0	0	0	.000	0	0	0	.000	.000	.000	0
Poole	1	0	0	0	0	0	0	0	0	0	0	0	0	0	0	.000	0	0	0	.000	.000	.000	0
Bohanon	1	0	0	0	0	0	0	0	0	0	0	0	0	0	0	.000	0	0	0	.000	.000	.000	0
Rogers	1	0	0	0	0	0	0	0	0	0	0	0	0	0	0	.000	0	0	0	.000	.000	.000	0
Rosenthal	1	0	0	0	0	0	0	0	0	0	0	0	0	0	0	.000	0	0	0	.000	.000	.000	0
TOTALS	1918	5703	829	1539	288	31	177	2420	774	596	1039	51	42	102	50	.426	129	59	41	.270	.424	.341	835

Sabermetric Batting Records for Texas Rangers

	Ball Park Adjusted												Runs		Run/					
	AB	Run	Hit	2B	3B	HR	RBI	W	SO	Avg	Slug	OBP	Ctd	Outs	27o	OW%	OG	OWAR	DWAR	TWAR
Buechele	398	55	105	16	1	18	64	36	65	.264	.445	.330	57	317	4.85	.478	12	1.51	1.21	2.71
Capra	0	0	0	0	0	0	0	0	0	.000	.000	.000	0	0	0.00	.000	0	0.00	0.00	0.00
Daugherty	137	7	26	2	1	0	10	15	21	.190	.219	.266	9	118	2.06	.142	4	-0.91	0.07	-0.84
Diaz Mar	173	23	45	6	0	1	21	14	17	.260	.312	.316	17	137	3.35	.304	5	-0.23	0.41	0.18
Downing	389	73	107	16	1	17	47	54	66	.275	.452	.373	69	291	6.40	.614	11	2.85	0.00	2.85
Fariss	29	5	7	0	0	1	5	6	10	.241	.345	.371	4	22	4.91	.484	1	0.11	0.11	0.22
Franco Ju	564	103	191	26	2	15	76	61	74	.339	.472	.404	114	393	7.83	.705	15	5.16	0.15	5.31
Gonzalez Juan	522	74	137	32	0	28	99	39	112	.262	.485	.317	79	399	5.35	.526	15	2.61	0.52	3.13
Green G	18	0	2	0	0	0	0	0	5	.111	.111	.111	0	18	0.00	.000	1	-0.23	0.11	-0.12
Harris D	6	3	2	0	0	1	1	0	2	.333	.833	.333	2	4	13.50	.876	0	0.08	0.02	0.10
Hernandez J	93	7	17	1	0	0	3	2	29	.183	.194	.200	4	84	1.29	.060	3	-0.90	0.32	-0.58
Huson	258	34	56	7	3	1	25	40	28	.217	.279	.321	26	222	3.16	.280	8	-0.58	0.51	-0.07
Kreuter	3	0	0	0	0	0	0	0	0	.000	.000	.000	0	3	0.00	.000	0	-0.04	-0.00	-0.04
Maurer	14	0	0	0	0	0	1	2	5	.000	.000	.125	0	14	0.00	.000	1	-0.18	0.02	-0.16
Palmeiro	611	111	202	48	3	24	84	70	63	.331	.537	.400	132	436	8.17	.722	16	6.01	0.35	6.36
Palmer Dn	256	36	47	8	1	15	36	30	93	.184	.398	.274	28	215	3.52	.325	8	-0.20	-0.13	-0.34
Parent	0	0	0	0	0	0	0	0	0	.000	.000	.000	0	0	0.00	.000	0	0.00	0.00	0.00
Petralli	191	20	53	7	1	1	19	21	21	.277	.340	.347	24	151	4.29	.417	6	0.38	-0.52	-0.14
Pettis	269	35	58	6	3	0	18	52	84	.216	.260	.343	30	230	3.52	.325	9	-0.21	0.33	0.12
Reimer	380	44	105	21	0	18	66	34	81	.276	.474	.340	61	292	5.64	.553	11	2.20	-0.01	2.18
Rodriguez I	268	23	70	15	0	3	26	4	39	.261	.351	.272	22	210	2.83	.237	8	-0.88	-0.34	-1.22
Russell Jn	25	2	2	0	0	0	0	0	6	.080	.080	.080	0	23	0.00	.000	1	-0.30	0.03	-0.27
Scruggs	5	0	0	0	0	0	0	0	0	.000	.000	.000	0	6	0.00	.000	0	-0.08	0.01	-0.06
Sierra	633	105	195	42	3	24	112	54	84	.308	.498	.358	113	464	6.58	.627	17	4.76	1.01	5.77
Stanley M	172	24	42	12	0	3	24	31	41	.244	.366	.363	25	137	4.93	.486	5	0.69	-0.40	0.28
Walling	41	0	3	0	0	0	1	3	7	.073	.073	.156	0	40	0.00	.000	1	-0.52	0.01	-0.51
TOTALS	5470	797	1482	279	24	175	750	580	960	.271	.427	.343	817	4246	5.20	.512	157	25.49	3.79	29.28

Pitching Records for Texas Rangers

	ERA	W	L	Pct	G	GS	CG	ShO	GF	Sv	IP	R	ER	H	2B	3B	HR	BB	IW	SO	HB	WP	BK
Brown Kev	4.40	9	12	.429	33	33	0	0	0	0	210.2	116	103	233	40	4	17	90	5	96	13	12	3
Ryan	2.91	12	6	.667	27	27	2	2	0	0	173.0	58	56	102	25	3	12	72	0	203	5	8	0
Guzman	3.08	13	7	.650	25	25	5	1	0	0	169.2	67	58	152	33	1	10	84	1	125	4	8	1
Witt B	6.09	3	7	.300	17	16	1	1	0	0	88.2	66	60	84	18	2	4	74	1	82	1	8	0
Boyd	6.68	2	7	.222	12	12	0	0	0	0	62.0	47	46	81	15	1	12	17	1	33	0	0	1
Bohanon	4.84	4	3	.571	11	11	1	0	0	0	61.1	35	33	66	13	0	4	23	0	34	2	3	1
Chiamparino	4.03	1	0	1.000	5	5	0	0	0	0	22.1	11	10	26	2	1	1	12	0	8	0	0	0
Fajardo	5.68	0	2	.000	4	3	0	0	1	0	19.0	13	12	25	6	1	2	4	0	15	1	0	0
Rogers	5.42	10	10	.500	63	9	0	0	20	5	109.2	80	66	121	22	3	14	61	7	73	6	3	1
Alexander G	5.24	5	3	.625	30	9	0	0	4	0	89.1	56	52	93	15	3	11	48	7	50	3	3	1
Barfield Jn	4.54	4	4	.500	28	9	0	0	4	1	83.1	51	42	96	19	3	11	22	3	27	0	0	2
Jeffcoat	4.63	5	3	.625	70	0	0	0	21	1	79.2	46	41	104	13	5	8	25	3	43	4	3	0
Russell Jf	3.29	6	4	.600	68	0	0	0	56	30	79.1	36	29	71	6	0	11	26	1	52	1	6	0
Rosenthal	5.25	1	4	.200	36	0	0	0	8	1	70.1	43	41	72	16	2	9	36	1	61	1	8	1
Mathews T	3.61	4	0	1.000	34	2	0	0	8	1	57.1	24	23	54	19	1	5	18	3	51	1	5	0
Gossage	3.57	4	2	.667	44	0	0	0	16	1	40.1	16	16	33	6	1	4	16	1	28	3	3	0
Manuel	1.13	1	0	1.000	8	0	0	0	5	0	16.0	2	2	7	1	0	0	6	0	5	0	2	0
Bitker	6.75	1	0	1.000	9	0	0	0	2	0	14.2	11	11	17	4	0	4	8	3	16	0	2	0
Arnsberg	8.38	0	1	.000	9	0	0	0	2	0	9.2	9	9	10	0	0	5	5	0	8	0	1	1
Petkovsek	14.46	0	1	.000	4	1	0	0	1	0	9.1	16	15	21	3	0	4	4	0	6	0	2	0
Poole	4.50	0	0	.000	5	0	0	0	2	1	6.0	4	3	10	2	0	0	3	0	4	0	0	0
Schiraldi	11.57	0	1	.000	3	0	0	0	1	0	4.2	6	6	5	0	0	3	5	0	1	0	0	0
Nolte	3.38	0	0	.000	3	0	0	0	2	0	2.2	1	1	3	0	0	0	3	0	1	0	0	0
TOTALS	4.47	85	77	.525	548	162	9	4	153	41	1479.0	814	735	1486	278	31	151	662	37	1022	45	77	12

Sabermetric Pitching Records for Texas Rangers

	Adj	|-Expected-|			|------Opposing Batters------|												Supported				
	ERA	W	L	Pct	BFP	Avg	Slg	OBA	RC/G	GDP	SB	CS	PK	PKE	SH	SF	RSup	RSp/G	W	L	Pct
Alexander G	5.04	3	5	.397	402	.272	.430	.364	5.71	6	7	3	0	0	6	3	67	6.75	5	3	.642
Arnsberg	7.45	0	1	.232	44	.256	.641	.341	7.81	1	0	0	0	0	0	0	2	1.86	0	1	.059
Barfield Jn	4.32	4	4	.472	361	.289	.464	.330	5.40	5	1	3	1	1	3	4	48	5.18	5	3	.590
Bitker	6.14	0	1	.307	70	.274	.532	.357	7.81	0	1	0	0	0	0	0	3	1.84	0	1	.083
Bohanon	4.55	3	4	.447	273	.274	.378	.336	4.91	3	5	0	0	0	2	5	42	6.16	5	2	.647
Boyd	6.39	3	6	.291	277	.314	.519	.356	6.80	3	3	3	0	0	2	0	28	4.06	3	6	.288
Brown Kev	4.23	10	11	.483	934	.284	.404	.362	4.95	30	5	11	3	2	6	4	107	4.57	11	10	.539
Chiamparino	3.63	1	0	.560	101	.295	.375	.380	5.12	4	2	0	0	0	1	0	16	6.45	1	0	.760
Fajardo	5.21	1	1	.381	84	.329	.513	.357	6.95	0	4	2	0	0	0	3	7	3.32	1	1	.288
Gossage	3.35	4	2	.599	167	.228	.366	.317	3.97	1	2	2	1	0	3	0	30	6.69	5	1	.800
Guzman	2.92	13	7	.663	730	.239	.341	.330	3.91	11	12	13	1	1	2	3	98	5.20	15	5	.760
Jeffcoat	4.41	4	4	.463	363	.321	.466	.373	6.32	9	5	2	0	0	5	4	48	5.42	5	3	.602
Manuel	0.56	1	0	.981	58	.143	.163	.224	1.30	1	0	0	1	0	0	3	7	3.94	1	0	.980
Mathews T	3.45	2	2	.584	236	.251	.419	.312	4.53	2	8	3	0	0	2	0	35	5.49	3	1	.717
Nolte	0.00	0	0	.000	14	.273	.273	.429	5.53	0	0	0	0	0	0	0	0	0.00	0	0	.000
Petkovsek	13.50	0	1	.084	53	.438	.750	.472	16.65	1	1	0	0	0	0	1	7	6.75	0	1	.200
Poole	3.00	0	0	.650	31	.370	.444	.419	8.39	0	0	0	0	0	0	1	3	4.50	0	0	.692
Rogers	5.17	8	12	.385	511	.281	.444	.375	6.04	11	1	3	2	1	9	5	76	6.24	12	8	.593
Rosenthal	4.99	2	3	.402	321	.257	.425	.341	5.71	1	6	1	0	0	1	3	31	3.97	2	3	.387
Russell Jf	3.06	6	4	.640	336	.236	.365	.295	3.61	10	1	0	0	0	3	4	30	3.40	6	4	.552
Ryan	2.76	12	6	.687	683	.172	.285	.263	2.61	6	24	8	1	1	3	9	95	4.94	14	4	.763
Schiraldi	9.64	0	1	.152	25	.263	.737	.417	12.64	0	1	0	0	0	1	0	0	0.00	0	1	.000
Witt B	5.79	3	7	.333	413	.254	.356	.388	5.55	5	18	4	0	1	3	4	49	4.97	4	6	.425
TOTALS	4.30	77	85	.475	6487	.262	.402	.341	4.89	110	107	58	10	7	52	56	829	5.04	94	68	.579

Batting 'Splits' Records for Texas Rangers

	G	AB	Run	Hit	2B	3B	HR	TB	RBI	W	K	IW	HB	SB	CS	GI DP	SH	SF	Avg	Slug	OBP	Runs Ctd
SPLITS for Buechele																						
vs LHP	55	97	15	28	5	1	6	53	17	15	15	3	2	0	0	1	3	1	.289	.546	.391	22
vs RHP	114	319	43	83	12	1	12	133	49	24	54	1	3	0	4	10	7	1	.260	.417	.317	39
Home	56	190	26	57	12	0	7	90	23	18	26	3	3	0	3	4	6	1	.300	.474	.368	32
Away	65	226	32	54	5	2	11	96	43	21	43	1	2	0	1	7	4	1	.239	.425	.308	28
Grass	104	358	50	95	17	1	14	156	53	32	56	3	4	0	3	10	7	2	.265	.436	.331	50
Turf	17	58	8	16	0	1	4	30	13	7	13	1	1	0	1	1	3	0	.276	.517	.364	11
April/June	66	228	33	61	10	1	11	106	33	26	41	2	1	0	3	5	9	1	.268	.465	.344	36
July/October	55	188	25	50	7	1	7	80	33	13	28	2	4	0	1	6	1	1	.266	.426	.325	25
SPLITS for Downing																						
vs LHP	67	139	32	39	5	0	9	71	17	25	24	6	3	1	0	1	0	0	.281	.511	.401	31
vs RHP	109	268	44	74	12	2	8	114	32	33	46	1	5	0	1	6	1	2	.276	.425	.364	43
Home	63	204	45	52	8	2	8	88	23	32	39	4	4	0	1	3	1	1	.255	.431	.365	34
Away	60	203	31	61	9	0	9	97	26	26	31	3	4	1	0	4	0	1	.300	.478	.389	39
Grass	105	348	63	93	15	2	13	151	41	50	64	5	7	1	1	7	1	2	.267	.434	.369	58
Turf	18	59	13	20	2	0	4	34	8	8	6	2	1	0	0	0	0	0	.339	.576	.426	15
April/June	54	189	31	51	7	1	7	81	23	29	34	6	5	1	0	4	1	1	.270	.429	.379	33
July/October	69	218	45	62	10	1	10	104	26	29	36	1	3	0	1	3	0	1	.284	.477	.375	40
SPLITS for Gonzalez Juan																						
vs LHP	73	147	24	44	7	0	9	78	27	16	28	4	0	1	2	3	0	1	.299	.531	.366	28
vs RHP	135	398	54	100	27	1	18	183	75	26	90	3	5	3	2	7	0	2	.251	.460	.304	55
Home	73	262	37	70	16	0	7	107	40	19	62	3	5	1	1	4	0	1	.267	.408	.328	35
Away	69	283	41	74	18	1	20	154	62	23	56	4	0	3	3	6	0	2	.261	.544	.315	46
Grass	119	444	66	125	28	0	22	219	83	34	94	6	5	3	4	8	0	3	.282	.493	.337	73
Turf	23	101	12	19	6	1	5	42	19	8	24	1	0	1	0	2	0	0	.188	.416	.248	10
April/June	56	220	37	66	16	0	10	112	50	27	44	6	1	4	4	5	0	2	.300	.509	.376	42
July/October	86	325	41	78	18	1	17	149	52	15	74	1	4	0	0	5	0	1	.240	.458	.281	41
SPLITS for Texas Rangers (all batters except pitchers)																						
vs LHP	849	1516	239	417	76	11	63	704	219	180	268	19	9	27	15	39	24	11	.275	.464	.353	249
vs RHP	1628	4187	590	1122	212	20	114	1716	555	416	771	32	33	75	35	90	35	30	.268	.410	.337	586
Home	940	2734	404	738	143	21	79	1160	368	292	508	21	25	51	29	64	26	17	.270	.424	.344	401
Away	978	2969	425	801	145	10	98	1260	406	304	531	30	17	51	21	65	33	24	.270	.424	.339	433
Grass	1615	4757	707	1299	239	27	153	2051	663	512	869	36	37	86	48	112	51	35	.273	.431	.346	715
Turf	303	946	122	240	49	4	24	369	111	84	170	15	5	16	2	17	8	6	.254	.390	.316	120
April/June	806	2511	365	692	126	14	67	1047	345	286	412	29	14	52	29	51	40	21	.276	.417	.350	376
July/October	1112	3192	464	847	162	17	110	1373	429	310	627	22	28	50	21	78	19	20	.265	.430	.334	459

1991 SPLITS FOR Texas Rangers

BATTING SPLITS

	AVG	AB	R	H	2B	3B	HR	RBI	SB	CS	BB	K	OBA	SPCT
Total	.270	5703	829	1539	288	31	177	774	102	50	596	1039	.341	.424

	#Pit	#P/PA	GB	FB	G/F	G	IBB	HB	SH	SF	GDP
Miscellaneous	24280	3.77	2023	1687	1.20	162	51	42	59	41	129

	AVG	AB	R	H	2B	3B	HR	RBI	SB	CS	BB	K	OBA	SPCT
vs. Left	.275	1516	...	417	76	11	63	219	27	15	180	268	.353	.464
vs. Right	.268	4187	...	1122	212	20	114	555	75	35	416	771	.337	.410
Home	.270	2734	404	738	143	21	79	368	51	29	292	508	.344	.424
Away	.270	2969	425	801	145	10	98	406	51	21	304	531	.339	.424
None on	.258	3144	...	810	158	15	86	86	0	0	309	595	.328	.399
Runners on	.285	2559	...	729	130	16	91	688	102	50	287	444	.357	.455
April	.254	532	65	135	25	2	13	63	10	6	51	81	.323	.382
May	.306	992	164	304	54	7	29	152	20	11	117	148	.379	.463
June	.256	987	136	253	47	5	25	130	22	12	118	183	.336	.390
July	.268	920	131	247	44	6	35	122	12	12	80	178	.332	.443
August	.285	1115	174	318	56	7	39	164	15	3	96	213	.344	.453
September	.255	998	142	254	56	4	33	129	19	6	117	202	.336	.418
October	.176	159	17	28	6	0	3	14	4	0	17	34	.260	.270
None on/out	.261	1394	...	364	71	4	46	46	0	0	142	251	.334	.417
Scoring Posn	.274	1454	...	398	66	12	48	573	27	19	202	273	.359	.435
Close & Late	.265	993	...	263	36	3	32	138	24	11	109	183	.340	.404
Bases Loaded	.280	125	...	35	7	2	2	89	0	0	5	23	.297	.416
Batting #1	.240	679	109	163	20	6	23	71	10	2	88	138	.334	.389
Batting #2	.314	671	113	211	40	4	17	85	19	6	79	90	.390	.462
Batting #3	.315	685	113	216	49	4	21	108	10	5	56	86	.364	.491
Batting #4	.299	656	119	196	37	4	28	111	22	5	71	114	.367	.495
Batting #5	.276	648	100	179	34	1	33	115	10	8	60	131	.342	.485
Batting #6	.235	617	79	145	30	5	22	88	5	5	68	134	.315	.407
Batting #7	.254	599	76	152	28	2	22	80	2	3	65	138	.330	.417
Batting #8	.252	602	58	152	31	2	8	68	1	5	39	104	.298	.350
Batting #9	.229	546	62	125	19	3	3	48	23	11	70	104	.317	.291
As p	1.000	1	1	1	1	0	0	1	0	0	0	0	1.000	2.000
As c	.265	578	63	153	31	2	8	62	1	2	39	87	.311	.367
As 1b	.312	658	118	205	50	4	26	91	4	3	74	80	.383	.518
As 2b	.330	658	119	217	29	3	16	87	35	9	74	91	.401	.456
As 3b	.225	582	79	131	23	4	25	83	0	6	66	134	.309	.407
As ss	.232	508	58	118	18	4	3	49	7	5	52	76	.303	.301
As lf	.246	627	79	154	27	1	25	102	3	4	59	135	.317	.411
As cf	.248	589	78	146	25	5	19	77	28	13	79	153	.337	.404
As rf	.304	678	110	206	43	5	25	115	16	4	55	97	.352	.493
Outfield	.267	1894	267	506	95	11	69	294	47	21	193	385	.336	.438
0.0 count	.338	650	...	220	33	6	21	96	...	...	1	0	.339	.505
After (0.1)	.242	2556	...	619	114	13	65	303	...	...	153	669	.290	.373
After (1.0)	.280	2497	...	700	141	12	91	375	...	...	405	370	.381	.456
Two strikes	.191	2647	...	505	95	12	53	242	...	...	232	1038	.261	.296
Grass	.273	4757	707	1299	239	27	153	663	86	48	512	869	.346	.431
Turf	.254	946	122	240	49	4	24	111	16	2	84	170	.316	.390
Day	.274	1098	171	301	63	4	32	161	23	6	122	173	.351	.426
Night	.269	4605	658	1238	225	27	145	613	79	44	474	866	.339	.424
Inning 1.6	.273	3782	562	1032	198	26	120	523	69	31	384	675	.342	.434
Inning 7+	.264	1921	267	507	90	5	57	251	33	19	212	364	.340	.405
vs.Bal	.238	404	47	96	16	1	12	44	7	3	39	82	.312	.371
vs.Bos	.313	415	75	130	28	2	16	72	4	6	46	71	.382	.506
vs.Cal	.276	463	71	128	27	2	16	67	8	7	60	107	.361	.447
vs.ChA	.224	433	63	97	16	2	14	57	10	7	63	88	.323	.367
vs.Cle	.280	414	65	116	25	1	10	62	6	3	35	63	.340	.418
vs.Det	.305	440	73	134	16	4	14	66	10	7	57	65	.384	.455
vs.KC	.258	493	56	127	30	5	8	48	7	1	48	98	.329	.387
vs.Mil	.289	440	72	127	20	3	17	71	4	2	42	75	.352	.464
vs.Min	.263	453	59	119	27	3	11	57	6	4	40	86	.318	.408
vs.NYA	.288	431	63	124	24	3	17	59	12	2	26	69	.330	.476
vs.Oak	.256	449	64	115	21	1	15	60	13	3	56	74	.343	.408
vs.Sea	.267	461	74	123	21	1	17	68	7	3	59	81	.354	.427
vs.Tor	.253	407	47	103	17	3	10	43	8	2	25	80	.300	.383

PITCHING SPLITS

	ERA	W	L	SV	SVOP	GS	CG	SHO	IP	H	ER	HR	BB	IBB	K
Total	4.47	85	77	41	63	162	9	9	1479.0	1486	734	151	662	37	1022

	#Pit	#P/IP	GB	FB	G/F	BRp9	RA	WP	BK	SH	SF	R	HB	Hld
Miscellaneous	24094	16.29	2071	1646	1.26	13.34	386	77	12	52	56	814	45	35

	ERA	W	L	SV	SVOP	GS	CG	SHO	IP	H	ER	HR	BB	IBB	K
ST	4.63	52	53	0	0	162	9	4	948.0	968	488	92	442	10	653
REL	4.19	33	24	41	63	0	0	0	531.0	518	247	59	220	27	369
Home	4.31	46	35	25	29	81	4	2	749.0	741	359	77	312	16	553
Away	4.64	39	42	16	34	81	5	2	730.0	745	376	74	350	21	469
April	4.00	8	8	5	5	16	1	1	144.0	117	64	15	60	0	106
May	4.26	18	9	9	14	27	1	1	249.1	257	118	19	138	7	156
June	4.26	13	14	4	9	27	3	1	261.2	265	124	32	117	13	153
July	4.38	13	14	9	14	27	0	0	238.1	224	116	40	110	4	196
August	4.91	15	16	8	11	31	1	0	276.2	305	151	22	111	7	187
September	4.57	16	13	6	10	29	2	1	264.0	272	134	19	107	3	187
October	5.60	2	3	0	0	5	1	0	45.0	46	28	4	19	3	37
Grass	4.58	71	66	35	51	137	8	4	1245.0	1252	634	136	542	28	877
Turf	3.88	14	11	6	12	25	1	0	234.0	234	101	15	120	9	145
Day	4.38	17	13	7	14	30	1	0	275.1	263	134	25	137	8	195
Night	4.49	68	64	34	49	132	8	4	1203.2	1223	601	126	525	29	827
vs.Bal	5.09	3	9	2	2	12	0	0	106.0	107	60	13	42	0	92
vs.Bos	4.33	7	5	5	6	12	0	0	104.0	117	50	4	56	2	59
vs.Cal	3.42	8	5	2	4	13	1	0	121.0	110	46	13	49	2	85
vs.ChA	5.07	5	8	2	6	13	1	1	120.2	117	68	8	72	6	69
vs.Cle	4.46	8	4	7	8	12	1	1	107.0	114	53	9	41	2	73
vs.Det	4.46	6	6	2	5	12	0	0	111.0	104	55	18	60	4	101
vs.KC	4.39	6	7	2	3	13	1	0	125.0	122	61	12	60	7	91
vs.Mil	5.01	5	7	1	3	12	0	0	109.2	117	61	12	41	3	57
vs.Min	4.50	7	6	5	8	13	0	0	120.0	126	60	9	51	2	73
vs.NYA	3.42	7	5	2	3	12	1	0	110.2	110	42	15	34	2	70
vs.Oak	5.23	9	4	3	4	13	2	1	117.0	112	68	16	56	3	89
vs.Sea	4.54	8	5	4	5	13	1	0	123.0	129	62	9	56	2	72
vs.Tor	4.24	6	6	4	6	12	1	1	104.0	101	49	13	44	2	91

OPPOSING BATTERS VS. PITCHERS.

	AVG	AB	R	H	2B	3B	HR	RBI	SB	CS	BB	K	OBA	SPCT
Total	.262	5669	814	1486	278	31	151	761	107	58	662	1022	.341	.402
vs. Left	.249	2313	...	576	100	18	47	296	50	24	283	403	.331	.369
vs. Right	.271	3356	...	910	178	13	104	465	57	34	379	619	.348	.425
ST	.265	3654	541	968	194	18	92	459	82	44	442	653	.346	.403
REL	.257	2015	273	518	84	13	59	302	25	14	220	369	.332	.400
Home	.259	2857	400	741	133	17	77	376	55	35	312	553	.333	.399
Away	.265	2812	414	745	145	14	74	385	52	23	350	469	.349	.405
None on	.256	3116	...	797	148	18	82	82	0	0	341	599	.333	.394
Runners on	.270	2553	...	689	130	13	69	679	107	58	321	423	.350	.412
None on/out	.261	1389	...	362	67	7	32	32	0	0	133	250	.328	.388
Scoring Posn	.254	1505	...	383	72	5	35	576	27	7	233	272	.350	.379
vs 1st Batr	.301	339	...	102	14	1	7	59	4	2	36	55	.370	.410
1st IP	.260	1802	251	468	79	9	47	308	35	20	229	340	.344	.392
Inning 1.6	.264	3734	555	985	194	21	96	519	88	48	450	667	.345	.404
Inning 7+	.259	1935	259	501	84	10	55	242	19	10	212	355	.334	.398
Close & Late	.235	1036	...	243	43	5	29	126	12	7	129	207	.322	.370
0.0 count	.337	769	...	259	50	4	24	134	...	...	34	0	.366	.506
After (0.1)	.225	2414	...	544	109	11	44	248	...	...	149	629	.274	.334
After (1.0)	.275	2486	...	683	119	16	83	379	...	...	479	393	.392	.436
Two strikes	.182	2533	...	462	96	11	29	214	...	...	267	1022	.264	.263
Pitch 1.15	.272	1567	...	426	68	8	41	232	27	16	182	273	.348	.404
Pitch 16.30	.228	1141	...	260	58	5	26	140	17	6	136	237	.313	.356
Pitch 31.45	.296	813	...	241	46	6	24	114	16	12	89	120	.367	.456
Pitch 46.60	.273	626	...	171	30	5	22	100	14	6	63	101	.340	.442
Pitch 61.75	.258	516	...	133	24	3	9	55	17	5	69	96	.345	.368
Pitch 76.90	.263	452	...	119	23	1	14	63	8	4	56	71	.353	.412
Pitch 91.105	.234	329	...	77	17	2	6	37	5	6	35	76	.311	.353
Pitch 106.20	.262	183	...	48	12	1	8	18	2	2	26	33	.351	.470
Pitch 121.35	.273	44	...	12	1	0	1	4	1	1	6	14	.360	.364
Pitch 136.50	.000	1	...	0	0	0	0	0	0	0	1	1	.500	.000

Oakland Athletics

Brock J. Hanke

OAKLAND YEAR	1982	1983	1984	1985	1986	1987	1988	1989	1990	1991	TOT
W	68	74	77	77	76	81	104	99	103	84	843
L	94	88	85	85	86	81	58	63	59	78	777
WPCT	0.420	0.457	0.475	0.475	0.469	0.500	0.642	0.611	0.636	0.519	0.520
R/OAK	691	708	738	757	731	806	800	712	733	760	7436
RA/OAK	819	782	796	787	760	789	620	576	570	776	7275
PWPT	0.416	0.450	0.462	0.481	0.481	0.511	0.625	0.604	0.623	0.490	0.511
PythW	67	73	75	78	78	83	101	98	101	79	83
PythL	95	89	87	84	84	79	61	64	61	83	79
LUCK	1	1	2	-1	-2	-2	3	1	2	5	10

Defensive Efficiency Record: .7038

First, let's not be confused. The A's collapse was worse than it looked. They were a full five games lucky. That takes them from an above-average team to below average; from a contender on a bad year to a team in trouble. And, if you look at what they have and don't have, you'll see that all the danger signs are there.

First, their offense is all coming from the hitting positions. The only people with over two Offensive Wins Above Replacement are the outfielders, first baseman and DH. What that means is that they have no easy way to improve. Everybody's looking for a middle infielder who can hit, and a catcher. Actually, the A's look to lose ground; the only infielder who gave them any offense at all, Mike Gallego, has moved to the Yankees. In addition, consider that Mark McGwire was just barely over the two-OWAR mark. That means that the A's have only a four-man offense. And it's an old offense, too.

The defense is undistinguished. The Hendersons can play, and so can (presumably) new second baseman Lance Blankenship, and Jose Canseco has range when he's healthy, but there are questions elsewhere. Brook Jacoby looks finished at third. There are better first basemen than Mark McGwire, although he doesn't hurt the team. Neither Walt Weiss nor any of his backups is especially great at shortstop. Terry Steinbach was absolutely awful. He had a Defensive Winning Percentage of .182 and a catcher's ERA of 4.69, which was .42 above his backup's. Normally, the starting catcher has a better ERA than the backup, because the pitchers are more familiar with his style. Steinbach's backup, by the way, was Jamie Quirk.

Oakland's pitching was even worse than I expected, and I expected even less than Don Malcolm did. Bob Welch did his overwork el foldo, just as I predicted he would, but Dave Stewart and Dennis Eckersley didn't help out. As you know if you've read my pitcher essay, I really don't know what to make of the bad years from those two, Dave Smith and Mike Schooler. It may be that there are only so many years a pitcher can put in of even reasonable workloads. In any case, the A's desperately need both Stewart and Eck if they're to return to contention.

The only bright spot was Mike Moore, who returned to form as a result of 1990's light workload. That workload, of course, was a result of 1989's overload, which caused Mike to pitch so badly in 1990 that no one would give him innings. Now, Mike has had 210 in 1991. That really shouldn't be enough to throw him off again, but you never know. What you do know is that the A's don't have any depth to cover for Moore or Welch or Stewart.

So much for the problems; let's focus on possible solutions. I submit that the following player acquisitions would be enough to return to A's to the top of the heap:

The A's need a middle infielder who can hit. He doesn't have to play shortstop, though. A second or third baseman would be fine. It would help if he could hold down Carney Lansford's old #2 sot in the batting order. Let's say Tony Phillips.

The A's need another starter who can pick up some real quality innings. They can probably get away with Ron Darling in the #4 slot, and they probably want to try Todd Van Poppel in #5. But all that assumes that Stewart, Welch and Moore are all going to be up to the challenge of #1, #2 and #3 again. That's unlikely. So, let's get them a reserve, say, Scott Sanderson.

Are you getting the message? Do I have to note that the infield would really fill out if they added Mike Gallego to the above? Or that, if they still had Willie McGee, they could work some arrangement to platoon Mark McGwire and skim what cream there is in his homers and walks? In short, do I need to say that the difference between the A's now and the dynasty they were is the free agents they've given away for draft pick futures?

Here it is:

R. Henderson lf
Tony Phillips 3b
D. Henderson cf
Canseco rf or DH
Baines 1b
McGee DH or rf
Gallego 2b
Steinbach c
Weiss ss

You want to compete with that? With Mark McGwire as a pinch hitter and Lance Blankenship as a late inning defensive replacement? If I add that the pitching rotation consists of the best five of Stewart, Welch, Moore, Sanderson, Darling and Van Poppel; and that the closers are Todd Burns and The Eck? I didn't think so.

Now, let's assume that Sandy Alderson isn't stupid. That seems fair. If you assume that, you have to assume that he could see what he was doing to the team by letting Phillips, Sanderson, McGee and Gallego go. Even if he, like Tony LaRussa, didn't see that the top starters were being overworked; and even if he was counting completely on the health of the Hendersons, Canseco, Baines and McGwire; he could see the holes he was leaving in the infield. So, why did he do what he did?

The plea, of course, was poverty. It always is. Never mind that no Major League baseball team ever goes bankrupt. Never mind that people like George Steinbrenner have used their teams to shore up their filing commercial enterprises. It was poverty, of course. The A's just don't compete in one of those big markets, you know. they can't afford a winning team.

Nonsense. I can't say what's really going on in Oakland, but team poverty isn't it. Maybe it's what happened in New York. Maybe Walter Haas is having financial trouble elsewhere. Maybe he has to bleed money from the team to keep other entities out of bankruptcy. Or maybe it's what's going on in St. Louis, where the ownership wants to be the star and is having trouble sharing the credit with ballplayers. Or maybe it's what has happened in so many franchises, where the owner just got reactionary and stubborn. I don't know. But it's not poverty. And, whatever it is, it seems likely to cost the A's the dynasty they were on the verge of maintaining.

I don't mean to claim that the A's are absolutely through. They still have that great core of stars. They still have the Hendersons, and Jose, and Harold Baines; and Stewart, Moore and Welch. They still have Eckersley. Van Poppel could be everything he's supposed to be. They can win an occasional division title with that. But they can't be a dynasty. To truly dominate, they have to fill in the gaps. They have to get infielders who can hit. They have to get some pitching depth. They have to get a real hitting bench. They have to do the little things that they used to do, but that they scrimp on now. They have to get the nails and the horseshoes and shoe the horse, if they want to ride him.

Oakland Athletics Home Park Performance Factors

	Outs	Runs	Hits	2b	3b	HR	W	K	SH	SF	HBP	IBB	SB	CS	GDP
Home LH Batters	.975	1.048	1.036	.882	1.682	.902	.884	.855	.596	.820	1.682	.961	.961	1.519	1.085
Home RH Batters	1.003	1.031	1.023	1.021	1.112	1.048	.955	1.045	1.006	.934	1.333	.676	.984	1.077	1.017
All Home Batters	.996	1.031	1.026	.992	1.234	1.018	.939	1.004	.899	.916	1.360	.794	.996	1.129	1.039
Opp LH Batters	.993	1.254	1.065	1.202	.769	1.446	1.196	1.014	.883	1.086	.937	7.359	.994	.761	1.125
Opp RH Batters	.968	1.016	1.060	.979	1.390	1.078	1.037	.904	1.031	1.295	.971	1.148	.916	1.028	1.032
All Opp Batters	.988	1.110	1.067	1.070	1.092	1.177	1.092	.957	.933	1.154	1.030	1.441	.970	.902	1.079
All LH Batters	.987	1.177	1.053	1.080	.944	1.193	1.071	.950	.778	.995	1.104	1.296	.966	.869	1.115
All RH Batters	.989	1.025	1.038	1.004	1.274	1.061	.985	.984	1.017	1.050	1.133	.809	.960	1.060	1.024
All Batters	.992	1.069	1.046	1.030	1.129	1.091	1.009	.982	.916	1.031	1.165	.952	.986	1.012	1.058

Conventional Batting Records for Oakland Athletics

																BRng	GI						Runs
	G	AB	Run	Hit	2B	3B	HR	TB	RBI	W	K	IW	HB	SB	CS	Eff	DP	SH	SF	Avg	Slug	OBP	Ctd
Steinbach	129	456	50	125	31	1	6	176	67	22	70	4	7	2	2	.398	15	0	9	.274	.386	.312	52
McGwire	154	483	62	97	22	0	22	185	75	93	116	3	3	2	1	.375	13	1	5	.201	.383	.330	66
Gallego	159	482	67	119	15	4	12	178	49	67	84	3	5	6	9	.444	8	10	3	.247	.369	.343	63
Riles	108	281	30	60	8	4	5	91	32	31	42	3	1	3	2	.500	8	4	4	.214	.324	.290	27
Bordick	90	235	21	56	5	1	0	63	21	14	37	0	3	3	4	.444	3	12	1	.238	.268	.289	19
Henderson R	134	470	105	126	17	1	18	199	57	98	73	7	7	58	18	.545	7	0	3	.268	.423	.400	92
Henderson D	150	572	86	158	33	0	25	266	85	58	113	3	4	6	6	.505	8	1	2	.276	.465	.346	93
Canseco	154	572	115	152	32	1	44	318	122	78	152	8	9	26	6	.500	16	0	6	.266	.556	.359	117
Baines	141	488	76	144	25	1	20	231	90	72	67	22	1	0	1	.385	12	0	5	.295	.473	.383	91
Wilson W	113	294	38	70	14	4	0	92	28	18	43	1	4	20	5	.480	11	1	1	.238	.313	.290	26
Quirk	76	203	16	53	4	0	1	60	17	16	28	1	2	0	3	.280	7	3	0	.261	.296	.321	18
Jacoby	56	188	14	40	12	0	0	52	20	11	22	1	1	2	0	.250	6	0	4	.213	.277	.255	13
Blankenship L	90	185	33	46	8	0	3	63	21	23	42	0	3	12	3	.490	2	2	3	.249	.341	.336	24
Law V	74	134	11	28	7	1	0	37	9	18	27	0	0	0	0	.500	4	5	0	.209	.276	.303	12
Weiss	40	133	15	30	6	1	0	38	13	12	14	0	0	6	0	.522	3	1	2	.226	.286	.286	12
Brosius	36	68	9	16	5	0	2	27	4	3	11	0	0	3	1	.267	2	1	0	.235	.397	.268	7
Howitt	21	42	5	7	1	0	1	11	3	1	12	0	0	0	0	.667	1	0	1	.167	.262	.182	2
Komminsk	24	25	1	3	1	0	0	4	2	2	9	0	0	1	0	.000	0	0	0	.120	.160	.185	1
Hemond	23	23	4	5	0	0	0	5	0	1	7	0	0	1	2	1.000	0	0	0	.217	.217	.250	1
Manrique	9	21	2	3	0	0	0	3	0	2	1	0	0	0	0	.000	1	0	0	.143	.143	.217	1
Witmeyer	11	19	0	1	0	0	0	1	0	0	5	0	0	0	0	.000	1	0	0	.053	.053	.053	0
Lansford	5	16	0	1	0	0	0	1	1	0	2	0	0	0	0	.000	0	0	0	.063	.063	.063	0
Afenir	5	11	0	1	0	0	0	1	0	0	2	0	0	0	0	.000	1	0	0	.091	.091	.091	0
Jennings	8	9	0	1	0	0	0	1	0	2	2	0	0	0	1	.000	1	0	0	.111	.111	.273	0
Allison	1	0	0	0	0	0	0	0	0	0	0	0	0	0	0	.000	0	0	0	.000	.000	.000	0
Welch	1	0	0	0	0	0	0	0	0	0	0	0	0	0	0	.000	0	0	0	.000	.000	.000	0
Show	1	0	0	0	0	0	0	0	0	0	0	0	0	0	0	.000	0	0	0	.000	.000	.000	0
Moore M	1	0	0	0	0	0	0	0	0	0	0	0	0	0	0	.000	0	0	0	.000	.000	.000	0
Honeycutt	1	0	0	0	0	0	0	0	0	0	0	0	0	0	0	.000	0	0	0	.000	.000	.000	0
Young C	1	0	0	0	0	0	0	0	0	0	0	0	0	0	0	.000	0	0	0	.000	.000	.000	0
Slusarski	1	0	0	0	0	0	0	0	0	0	0	0	0	0	0	.000	0	0	0	.000	.000	.000	0
Eckersley	3	0	0	0	0	0	0	0	0	0	0	0	0	0	0	.000	0	0	0	.000	.000	.000	0
TOTALS	1820	5410	760	1342	246	19	159	2103	716	642	981	56	50	151	64	.450	130	41	49	.248	.389	.331	716

Sabermetric Batting Records for Oakland Athletics

	Ball Park Adjusted												Runs		Run/					
	AB	Run	Hit	2B	3B	HR	RBI	W	SO	Avg	Slug	OBP	Ctd	Outs	27o	OW%	OG	OWAR	DWAR	TWAR
Afenir	10	0	1	0	0	0	0	0	1	.100	.100	.100	0	10	0.00	.000	0	-0.13	-0.02	-0.15
Baines	489	87	151	26	1	23	96	74	62	.309	.507	.398	101	356	7.66	.723	13	4.92	0.01	4.93
Blankenship L	183	33	47	7	0	3	22	22	40	.257	.344	.341	24	146	4.44	.467	5	0.63	0.69	1.32
Bordick	234	21	58	4	1	0	22	13	36	.248	.274	.295	19	196	2.62	.234	7	-0.84	0.74	-0.11
Brosius	67	9	16	4	0	2	4	2	10	.239	.388	.261	6	55	2.95	.279	2	-0.15	0.18	0.03
Canseco	571	117	158	31	1	46	128	77	148	.277	.576	.369	123	441	7.53	.716	16	5.98	0.16	6.14
Gallego	480	68	123	14	5	12	51	66	81	.256	.381	.350	66	387	4.60	.485	14	1.94	0.97	2.92
Hemond	22	4	5	0	0	0	0	0	6	.227	.227	.227	1	19	1.42	.082	1	-0.19	0.05	-0.13
Henderson D	572	88	164	32	0	26	89	57	110	.287	.479	.354	98	425	6.23	.633	16	4.45	1.58	6.04
Henderson R	470	107	131	16	1	19	59	97	71	.279	.438	.408	96	367	7.06	.689	14	4.61	0.78	5.39
Howitt	41	5	7	1	0	1	3	1	11	.171	.268	.190	2	35	1.54	.096	1	-0.33	0.09	-0.24
Jacoby	186	14	41	11	0	0	20	10	21	.220	.280	.259	13	155	2.26	.186	6	-0.94	0.45	-0.49
Jennings	8	0	1	0	0	0	0	2	1	.125	.125	.300	0	9	0.00	.000	0	-0.12	0.03	-0.09
Komminsk	24	1	3	0	0	0	2	1	8	.125	.125	.160	1	21	1.29	.069	1	-0.22	0.09	-0.13
Lansford	15	0	1	0	0	0	1	0	1	.067	.067	.067	0	14	0.00	.000	1	-0.18	0.00	-0.18
Law V	133	11	29	6	1	0	9	17	26	.218	.278	.307	12	113	2.87	.268	4	-0.34	0.04	-0.30
Manrique	20	2	3	0	0	0	0	1	0	.150	.150	.190	0	18	0.00	.000	1	-0.23	-0.01	-0.25
McGwire	481	63	101	21	0	23	78	92	113	.210	.397	.337	69	400	4.66	.491	15	2.09	0.72	2.81
Quirk	202	18	55	4	0	1	18	16	26	.272	.307	.332	19	159	3.23	.317	6	-0.20	-0.19	-0.39
Riles	280	34	63	8	4	5	34	32	39	.225	.336	.304	29	232	3.38	.336	9	-0.12	0.40	0.28
Steinbach	456	51	130	30	1	6	70	21	68	.285	.395	.321	55	353	4.21	.441	13	1.18	-1.09	0.09
Weiss	133	16	31	6	1	0	13	12	13	.233	.293	.293	12	107	3.03	.290	4	-0.24	0.31	0.08
Wilson W	295	40	73	14	4	0	29	18	42	.247	.322	.299	28	239	3.16	.308	9	-0.37	0.40	0.03
Witmeyer	18	0	1	0	0	0	0	0	4	.056	.056	.056	0	18	0.00	.000	1	-0.23	0.03	-0.21
TOTALS	5438	813	1404	253	22	174	762	651	962	.258	.409	.341	776	4323	4.85	.511	160	25.78	6.41	32.20

Pitching Records for Oakland Athletics

	ERA	W	L	Pct	G	GS	CG	ShO	GF	Sv	IP	R	ER	H	2B	3B	HR	BB	IW	SO	HB	WP	BK
Stewart D	5.18	11	11	.500	35	35	2	1	0	0	226.0	135	130	245	44	8	24	105	1	144	9	13	0
Welch	4.58	12	13	.480	35	35	7	1	0	0	220.0	124	112	220	34	4	25	91	3	101	11	3	2
Moore M	2.96	17	8	.680	33	33	3	1	0	0	210.0	75	69	176	35	0	11	105	1	153	5	14	0
Slusarski	5.27	5	7	.417	20	19	1	0	0	0	109.1	69	64	121	17	3	14	52	1	60	4	4	0
Hawkins	4.79	4	4	.500	15	14	1	0	1	0	77.0	41	41	68	14	4	5	36	0	40	5	0	1
Darling	4.08	3	7	.300	12	12	0	0	0	0	75.0	34	34	64	12	2	7	38	2	60	2	3	1
Dressendorfer	5.45	3	3	.500	7	7	0	0	0	0	34.2	28	21	33	7	0	5	21	0	17	0	3	0
Van Poppel	9.64	0	0	.000	1	1	0	0	0	0	4.2	5	5	7	0	1	1	2	0	6	0	0	0
Eckersley	2.96	5	4	.556	67	0	0	0	59	43	76.0	26	25	60	8	2	11	9	3	87	1	1	0
Young C	5.00	4	2	.667	41	1	0	0	6	0	68.1	38	38	74	11	2	8	34	2	27	2	2	1
Klink	4.35	10	3	.769	62	0	0	0	10	2	62.0	30	30	60	10	1	4	21	5	34	5	4	0
Chitren	4.33	1	4	.200	56	0	0	0	20	4	60.1	31	29	59	10	3	8	32	4	47	4	2	1
Show	5.92	1	2	.333	23	5	0	0	6	0	51.2	36	34	62	17	1	5	17	1	20	0	2	1
Nelson G	6.84	1	5	.167	44	0	0	0	11	0	48.2	38	37	60	9	4	12	23	1	23	3	0	0
Honeycutt	3.58	2	4	.333	43	0	0	0	7	0	37.2	16	15	37	6	2	3	20	3	26	2	0	0
Campbell K	2.74	1	0	1.000	14	0	0	0	2	0	23.0	7	7	13	3	0	4	14	0	16	1	0	0
Briscoe	7.07	0	0	.000	11	0	0	0	9	0	14.0	11	11	12	3	0	3	10	0	9	0	3	0
Burns	3.38	1	0	1.000	9	0	0	0	5	0	13.1	5	5	10	3	0	2	8	1	3	0	1	0
Walton B	6.23	1	0	1.000	12	0	0	0	5	0	13.0	9	9	11	2	0	3	6	0	10	1	3	0
Allison	7.36	1	1	.500	11	0	0	0	4	0	11.0	9	9	16	2	1	0	5	1	4	0	0	0
Guzman R	9.00	1	0	1.000	5	0	0	0	1	0	5.0	5	5	11	4	0	0	2	0	3	0	0	0
Harris R	12.00	0	0	.000	2	0	0	0	1	0	3.0	4	4	5	1	0	0	3	1	2	0	2	0
Law V	0.00	0	0	.000	1	0	0	0	1	0	0.2	0	0	1	1	0	0	1	0	0	0	0	0
TOTALS	4.57	84	78	.519	559	162	14	3	148	49	1444.1	776	734	1425	253	38	155	655	30	892	55	60	7

Sabermetric Pitching Records for Oakland Athletics

	Adj	|-Expected-|			|——Opposing Batters——|												Supported				
	ERA	W	L	Pct	BFP	Avg	Slg	OBA	RC/G	GDP	SB	CS	PK	PKE	SH	SF	RSup	RSp/G	W	L	Pct
Allison	7.36	0	2	.236	49	.381	.476	.438	6.73	3	0	0	0	0	1	1	8	6.55	1	1	.441
Briscoe	7.07	0	0	.251	62	.235	.471	.355	5.35	3	0	0	0	0	0	1	5	3.21	0	0	.171
Burns	3.38	1	0	.595	57	.217	.413	.321	4.40	2	1	0	0	0	1	2	6	4.05	1	0	.590
Campbell K	2.74	1	0	.690	94	.167	.359	.301	3.57	2	1	0	0	0	1	0	9	3.52	1	0	.623
Chitren	4.48	2	3	.455	271	.258	.432	.356	5.65	5	5	0	0	0	4	2	32	4.77	3	2	.532
Darling	4.32	5	5	.472	319	.237	.374	.331	4.42	5	7	1	1	0	5	4	23	2.76	3	7	.290
Dressendorfer	5.71	2	4	.339	159	.244	.407	.344	5.20	2	3	2	1	1	2	1	29	7.53	4	2	.635
Eckersley	3.08	6	3	.638	299	.208	.365	.235	3.07	0	8	1	1	0	1	0	19	2.25	3	6	.348
Guzman R	9.00	0	1	.171	24	.500	.682	.542	11.67	3	0	0	0	0	0	0	10	18.00	1	0	.800
Harris R	12.00	0	0	.104	15	.455	.545	.533	9.44	2	1	0	0	0	0	1	1	3.00	0	0	.059
Hawkins	5.03	3	5	.398	333	.237	.366	.329	4.37	2	7	5	0	0	2	3	47	5.49	4	4	.544
Honeycutt	3.82	3	3	.533	167	.261	.394	.358	5.19	3	5	1	0	0	2	1	11	2.63	2	4	.321
Klink	4.65	6	7	.436	266	.260	.364	.335	3.99	9	4	2	0	0	8	0	40	5.81	8	5	.610
Law V	0.00	0	0	.000	4	.333	.667	.500	15.51	0	0	0	0	0	0	0	0	0.00	0	0	.000
Moore M	3.13	16	9	.631	887	.229	.318	.324	3.54	19	19	12	0	0	5	4	102	4.37	17	8	.661
Nelson G	7.21	1	5	.243	229	.306	.577	.381	8.31	3	4	1	0	0	3	4	25	4.62	2	4	.291
Show	6.27	1	2	.298	231	.300	.464	.346	6.00	3	4	1	0	2	2	4	26	4.53	1	2	.343
Slusarski	5.60	4	8	.348	486	.283	.436	.364	5.58	11	5	5	1	0	0	3	63	5.19	6	6	.462
Stewart D	5.50	8	14	.356	1014	.278	.428	.356	5.58	19	23	9	0	0	5	15	154	6.13	12	10	.555
Van Poppel	9.64	0	0	.152	21	.368	.632	.429	9.62	0	1	1	0	1	0	0	2	3.86	0	0	.138
Walton B	6.23	0	1	.301	56	.229	.458	.321	5.35	1	2	0	0	0	0	1	4	2.77	0	1	.165
Welch	4.87	10	15	.414	950	.263	.404	.341	4.68	17	12	16	1	1	6	6	102	4.17	11	14	.424
Young C	5.27	2	4	.376	306	.278	.425	.363	5.39	8	4	3	0	1	3	1	42	5.53	3	3	.524
TOTALS	4.89	67	95	.412	6299	.260	.405	.342	4.87	122	116	60	5	6	51	54	760	4.74	78	84	.484

Batting 'Splits' Records for Oakland Athletics

	G	AB	Run	Hit	2B	3B	HR	TB	RBI	W	K	IW	HB	SB	CS	GI DP	SH	SF	Avg	Slug	OBP	Runs Ctd
SPLITS for Canseco																						
vs LHP	70	136	27	34	9	0	8	67	21	24	41	5	2	11	2	4	0	0	.250	.493	.370	26
vs RHP	143	436	88	118	23	1	36	251	101	54	111	3	7	15	4	12	0	6	.271	.576	.356	90
Home	76	267	56	72	15	0	16	135	46	39	80	4	5	18	2	9	0	2	.270	.506	.371	53
Away	78	305	59	80	17	1	28	183	76	39	72	4	4	8	4	7	0	4	.262	.600	.349	64
Grass	128	467	93	120	27	1	33	248	91	67	124	7	8	23	4	16	0	6	.257	.531	.356	90
Turf	26	105	22	32	5	0	11	70	31	11	28	1	1	3	2	0	0	0	.305	.667	.376	27
April/June	70	255	52	62	18	0	18	134	49	44	68	4	4	12	2	10	0	3	.243	.525	.359	49
July/October	84	317	63	90	14	1	26	184	73	34	84	4	5	14	4	6	0	3	.284	.580	.359	67
SPLITS for Henderson D																						
vs LHP	67	144	27	51	14	0	8	89	24	15	23	1	1	1	4	4	0	1	.354	.618	.416	35
vs RHP	133	428	59	107	19	0	17	177	61	43	90	2	3	5	2	4	1	1	.250	.414	.322	59
Home	76	282	40	73	9	0	15	127	39	29	57	3	1	1	3	2	1	1	.259	.450	.329	43
Away	74	290	46	85	24	0	10	139	46	29	56	0	3	5	3	6	0	1	.293	.479	.362	50
Grass	129	488	76	140	25	0	23	234	77	51	99	3	3	5	6	7	1	2	.287	.480	.357	84
Turf	21	84	10	18	8	0	2	32	8	7	14	0	1	1	0	1	0	0	.214	.381	.283	9
April/June	72	270	53	84	17	0	18	155	50	33	47	2	1	4	4	6	0	1	.311	.574	.387	59
July/October	78	302	33	74	16	0	7	111	35	25	66	1	3	2	2	2	1	1	.245	.368	.308	36
SPLITS for Henderson R																						
vs LHP	54	114	31	33	3	0	8	60	17	21	19	6	1	8	6	2	0	1	.289	.526	.401	24
vs RHP	118	356	74	93	14	1	10	139	40	77	54	1	6	50	12	5	0	2	.261	.390	.399	68
Home	71	248	54	69	10	0	8	103	28	48	36	6	4	27	10	4	0	2	.278	.415	.401	47
Away	63	222	51	57	7	1	10	96	29	50	37	1	3	31	8	3	0	1	.257	.432	.399	45
Grass	116	415	95	112	15	1	14	171	47	81	62	7	6	51	14	7	0	2	.270	.412	.395	78
Turf	18	55	10	14	2	0	4	28	10	17	11	0	1	7	4	0	0	1	.255	.509	.432	14
April/June	58	198	44	56	6	1	4	76	21	52	28	1	2	29	10	3	0	1	.283	.384	.435	41
July/October	76	272	61	70	11	0	14	123	36	46	45	6	5	29	8	4	0	2	.257	.452	.372	51
SPLITS for McGwire																						
vs LHP	70	130	16	26	5	0	5	46	19	23	28	2	0	0	0	5	0	2	.200	.354	.316	15
vs RHP	136	353	46	71	17	0	17	139	56	70	88	1	3	2	1	8	1	3	.201	.394	.336	51
Home	77	243	34	45	10	0	15	100	48	52	55	3	1	1	0	7	0	2	.185	.412	.329	35
Away	77	240	28	52	12	0	7	85	27	41	61	0	2	1	1	6	1	3	.217	.354	.332	30
Grass	129	400	55	82	18	0	21	163	69	80	96	3	3	1	0	9	0	4	.205	.407	.339	60
Turf	25	83	7	15	4	0	1	22	6	13	20	0	0	1	1	4	1	1	.181	.265	.289	6
April/June	75	231	32	47	10	0	13	96	40	57	64	2	1	1	1	5	1	2	.203	.416	.361	38
July/October	79	252	30	50	12	0	9	89	35	36	52	1	2	1	0	8	0	3	.198	.353	.300	28
SPLITS for Riles																						
vs LHP	15	21	0	3	0	0	0	3	1	0	2	0	0	0	0	1	1	0	.143	.143	.143	0
vs RHP	103	260	30	57	8	4	5	88	31	31	40	3	1	3	2	7	3	4	.219	.338	.301	27
Home	57	148	16	35	7	1	3	53	18	18	25	2	0	1	1	4	4	0	.236	.358	.319	17
Away	51	133	14	25	1	3	2	38	14	13	17	1	1	2	1	4	0	4	.188	.286	.258	10
Grass	93	247	24	55	8	3	5	84	29	25	35	3	1	3	1	8	4	3	.223	.340	.293	25
Turf	15	34	6	5	0	1	0	7	3	6	7	0	0	0	1	0	0	1	.147	.206	.268	2
April/June	60	171	22	45	5	3	3	65	22	23	23	1	1	2	2	6	3	3	.263	.380	.348	23
July/October	48	110	8	15	3	1	2	26	10	8	19	2	0	1	0	2	1	1	.136	.236	.193	5
SPLITS for Steinbach																						
vs LHP	64	139	11	37	11	0	3	57	15	7	17	2	1	0	0	5	0	2	.266	.410	.302	16
vs RHP	112	317	39	88	20	1	3	119	52	15	53	2	6	2	2	10	0	7	.278	.375	.316	36
Home	66	220	23	61	19	0	1	83	31	14	29	3	1	2	0	9	0	7	.277	.377	.314	25
Away	63	236	27	64	12	1	5	93	36	8	41	1	6	0	2	6	0	2	.271	.394	.310	27
Grass	106	371	39	104	26	1	4	144	58	19	52	4	4	2	2	13	0	9	.280	.388	.315	43
Turf	23	85	11	21	5	0	2	32	9	3	18	0	3	0	0	2	0	0	.247	.376	.297	9
April/June	57	205	25	60	15	0	5	90	31	8	30	0	5	2	1	7	0	2	.293	.439	.332	28
July/October	72	251	25	65	16	1	1	86	36	14	40	4	2	0	1	8	0	7	.259	.343	.296	25
SPLITS for Oakland Athletics (all batters except pitchers)																						
vs LHP	709	1336	177	349	71	1	42	548	167	154	218	19	7	28	20	38	14	10	.261	.410	.338	183
vs RHP	1508	4074	583	993	175	18	117	1555	549	488	763	37	43	123	44	92	27	39	.244	.382	.328	532
Home	908	2627	357	633	121	7	76	996	342	336	473	34	17	68	27	61	23	25	.241	.379	.328	340
Away	912	2783	403	709	125	12	83	1107	374	306	508	22	33	83	37	69	18	24	.255	.398	.333	375
Grass	1527	4531	634	1126	211	15	133	1766	599	538	810	50	38	118	49	114	36	43	.249	.390	.330	599
Turf	293	879	126	216	35	4	26	337	117	104	171	6	12	33	15	16	5	6	.246	.383	.332	117
April/June	813	2475	360	638	118	11	76	1006	340	345	433	22	19	74	34	68	21	20	.258	.406	.350	363
July/October	1007	2935	400	704	128	8	83	1097	376	297	548	34	31	77	30	62	20	29	.240	.374	.313	354

1991 SPLITS FOR Oakland Athletics

BATTING SPLITS

	AVG	AB	R	H	2B	3B	HR	RBI	SB	CS	BB	K	OBA	SPCT
Total	.248	5410	760	1342	246	19	159	716	151	64	642	981	.331	.389

	#Pit	#P/PA	GB	FB	G/F	G	IBB	HB	SH	SF	GDP
Miscellaneous	23346	3.77	1885	1594	1.18	162	56	50	41	49	130

	AVG	AB	R	H	2B	3B	HR	RBI	SB	CS	BB	K	OBA	SPCT
vs. Left	.261	1336	...	349	71	1	42	167	28	20	154	218	.338	.410
vs. Right	.244	4074	...	993	175	18	117	549	123	44	488	763	.328	.382
Home	.241	2627	357	633	121	7	76	342	68	27	336	473	.328	.379
Away	.255	2783	403	709	125	12	83	374	83	37	306	508	.333	.398
None on	.239	3047	...	728	142	6	84	84	0	0	338	545	.321	.372
Runners on	.260	2363	...	614	104	13	75	632	151	64	304	436	.343	.410
April	.254	646	91	164	34	5	13	84	17	10	89	125	.349	.382
May	.263	923	151	243	42	4	28	142	33	13	137	150	.358	.408
June	.255	906	118	231	42	2	35	114	24	11	119	158	.344	.422
July	.246	952	152	234	47	2	25	139	17	10	100	161	.323	.378
August	.236	950	110	224	40	3	33	105	29	11	86	167	.303	.388
September	.235	855	112	201	34	2	20	109	15	8	91	179	.311	.350
October	.253	178	26	45	7	1	5	23	16	1	20	41	.330	.388
None on/out	.248	1353	...	335	68	2	43	43	0	0	148	227	.327	.396
Scoring Posn	.261	1354	...	353	52	11	47	556	50	13	217	259	.357	.419
Close & Late	.241	843	...	203	33	5	26	122	22	8	107	176	.329	.384
Bases Loaded	.295	112	...	33	8	1	7	115	0	0	8	19	.316	.571
Batting #1	.262	629	127	165	25	3	18	66	68	23	117	96	.383	.397
Batting #2	.253	680	106	172	36	0	23	88	12	5	56	135	.316	.407
Batting #3	.262	638	125	167	32	1	46	129	27	7	85	167	.354	.531
Batting #4	.274	613	95	168	33	1	20	108	6	0	90	91	.364	.429
Batting #5	.261	606	66	158	32	2	15	80	4	4	70	106	.335	.394
Batting #6	.209	594	63	124	24	3	10	73	5	4	58	111	.283	.310
Batting #7	.235	567	58	133	32	2	10	72	8	4	62	91	.311	.351
Batting #8	.229	551	60	126	18	4	13	56	13	7	52	97	.297	.347
Batting #9	.242	532	60	129	14	3	4	44	8	10	52	87	.316	.303
As c	.265	614	60	163	34	1	7	75	2	4	35	93	.309	.358
As 1b	.199	552	63	110	23	0	21	82	3	2	97	123	.321	.355
As 2b	.250	517	76	129	21	3	13	54	10	10	65	97	.340	.377
As 3b	.219	567	57	124	27	3	4	58	10	2	53	86	.284	.298
As ss	.223	515	51	115	12	4	3	42	10	6	46	72	.289	.280
As lf	.255	619	116	158	29	3	16	74	65	22	104	93	.368	.389
As cf	.277	647	103	179	37	1	25	91	9	7	63	130	.346	.453
As rf	.252	630	110	159	29	2	40	110	27	7	78	156	.338	.495
Outfield	.262	1896	329	496	95	6	81	275	101	36	245	379	.351	.446
0.0 count	.326	737	...	240	45	2	30	127	...	...	6	0	.339	.514
After (0.1)	.202	2417	...	489	83	4	51	256	...	...	165	635	.258	.303
After (1.0)	.272	2256	...	613	118	13	78	333	...	...	435	346	.389	.439
Two strikes	.182	2525	...	460	80	7	39	235	...	...	267	980	.263	.266
Grass	.249	4531	634	1126	211	15	133	599	118	49	538	810	.330	.390
Turf	.246	879	126	216	35	4	26	117	33	15	104	171	.332	.383
Day	.258	1778	269	458	88	7	58	258	36	18	199	332	.335	.413
Night	.243	3632	491	884	158	12	101	458	115	46	443	649	.329	.377
Inning 1.6	.249	3632	523	904	176	11	105	495	109	50	437	627	.332	.390
Inning 7+	.246	1778	237	438	70	8	54	221	42	14	205	354	.328	.386
vs.Bal	.286	427	77	122	17	2	13	72	8	2	37	67	.345	.426
vs.Bos	.247	417	55	103	24	1	14	49	3	2	47	83	.328	.410
vs.Cal	.237	410	50	97	19	3	9	48	6	6	46	69	.321	.363
vs.ChA	.196	403	45	79	10	1	11	45	5	8	55	85	.296	.308
vs.Cle	.281	438	73	123	19	3	12	63	11	6	41	66	.343	.420
vs.Det	.255	396	54	101	17	1	16	54	10	5	49	58	.336	.424
vs.KC	.255	436	67	111	19	1	12	63	14	4	65	77	.354	.385
vs.Mil	.247	388	46	96	15	1	10	46	18	4	44	68	.323	.369
vs.Min	.244	435	55	106	18	3	13	50	19	7	47	80	.324	.389
vs.NYA	.251	399	59	100	24	1	9	55	16	6	56	66	.346	.383
vs.Sea	.251	419	51	105	22	1	15	48	12	7	42	88	.321	.415
vs.Tex	.249	450	72	112	29	1	16	71	16	1	56	89	.337	.424
vs.Tor	.222	392	56	87	13	0	9	52	13	6	57	85	.322	.324

PITCHING SPLITS

	ERA	W	L	SV	SVOP	GS	CG	SHO	IP	H	ER	HR	BB	IBB	K
Total	4.57	84	78	49	73	162	14	14	1444.1	1425	734	155	655	30	892

	#Pit	#P/IP	GB	FB	G/F	BRp9	RA	WP	BK	SH	SF	R	HB	Hld
Miscellaneous	23902	16.55	1861	1664	1.12	13.30	397	60	7	51	54	776	55	65

	ERA	W	L	SV	SVOP	GS	CG	SHO	IP	H	ER	HR	BB	IBB	K
ST	4.50	56	56	0	0	162	14	3	986.2	965	493	98	460	9	585
REL	4.74	28	22	49	73	0	0	0	457.2	460	241	57	195	21	307
Home	4.05	47	34	20	30	81	9	2	744.0	678	335	67	306	11	474
Away	5.13	37	44	29	43	81	5	1	700.1	747	399	88	349	19	418
April	3.73	13	7	8	9	20	1	0	176.1	165	73	14	80	4	88
May	5.41	15	12	7	9	27	1	0	239.2	260	144	30	115	3	143
June	4.91	13	15	11	17	28	4	1	244.0	226	133	21	118	5	147
July	4.30	15	12	7	13	27	4	1	251.1	239	120	34	93	2	150
August	4.44	15	14	9	15	29	2	0	259.1	262	128	25	107	7	146
September	4.29	11	15	6	9	26	1	1	230.2	230	110	28	122	9	182
October	5.44	2	3	1	1	5	1	0	43.0	43	26	3	20	0	36
Grass	4.21	76	60	41	61	136	14	3	1224.2	1149	573	124	552	22	758
Turf	6.60	8	18	8	12	26	0	0	219.2	276	161	31	103	8	134
Day	4.54	32	22	18	24	54	3	1	483.2	470	244	50	202	9	326
Night	4.59	52	56	31	49	108	11	2	960.2	955	490	105	453	21	566
vs.Bal	3.63	9	3	3	4	12	1	0	109.0	95	44	14	53	2	64
vs.Bos	4.68	4	8	2	5	12	3	1	109.2	110	57	10	48	2	61
vs.Cal	2.29	12	1	10	10	13	1	0	118.0	94	30	7	39	2	66
vs.ChA	4.51	6	7	3	5	13	0	0	115.2	118	58	9	60	5	84
vs.Cle	5.46	7	5	1	5	12	2	0	112.0	125	68	11	42	1	60
vs.Det	4.00	8	4	5	6	12	1	0	108.0	98	48	10	71	2	85
vs.KC	6.00	7	6	7	7	13	0	0	114.0	134	76	16	40	3	80
vs.Mil	6.08	4	8	4	7	12	0	0	103.2	103	70	14	52	2	56
vs.Min	4.99	5	8	3	6	13	2	0	115.1	135	64	11	43	0	61
vs.NYA	4.80	6	6	4	5	12	0	0	105.0	98	56	16	44	0	66
vs.Sea	4.24	6	7	3	5	13	0	0	110.1	99	52	11	59	5	49
vs.Tex	4.40	4	9	0	3	13	3	2	116.2	115	57	15	56	3	74
vs.Tor	4.54	6	6	4	5	12	1	0	107.0	101	54	11	48	3	86

OPPOSING BATTERS VS. PITCHERS.

	AVG	AB	R	H	2B	3B	HR	RBI	SB	CS	BB	K	OBA	SPCT
Total	.260	5481	776	1425	253	38	155	750	116	60	655	892	.342	.405
vs. Left	.264	2687	...	709	122	21	55	341	58	33	331	378	.344	.386
vs. Right	.256	2794	...	716	131	17	100	409	58	27	324	514	.340	.423
ST	.258	3737	530	965	169	22	98	473	78	52	460	585	.342	.394
REL	.264	1744	246	460	84	16	57	277	38	8	195	307	.341	.428
Home	.245	2772	351	678	119	18	67	342	60	35	306	474	.323	.373
Away	.276	2709	425	747	134	20	88	408	56	25	349	418	.361	.437
None on	.249	3043	...	758	138	17	87	87	0	0	339	493	.330	.391
Runners on	.274	2438	...	667	115	21	68	663	116	60	316	399	.356	.422
None on/out	.243	1350	...	328	64	7	39	39	0	0	145	211	.321	.387
Scoring Posn	.279	1409	...	393	70	18	38	580	24	8	219	255	.370	.435
vs 1st Batr	.223	363	...	81	12	1	8	53	6	1	27	73	.281	.328
1st IP	.266	1835	235	489	84	15	58	306	44	17	198	326	.341	.423
Inning 1.6	.261	3684	527	962	169	24	97	506	81	51	457	580	.345	.399
Inning 7+	.258	1797	249	463	84	14	58	244	35	9	198	312	.336	.417
Close & Late	.251	914	...	229	41	7	29	133	27	6	106	184	.335	.406
0.0 count	.323	703	...	227	42	7	30	120	...	...	24	0	.350	.531
After (0.1)	.230	2444	...	563	97	15	47	254	...	...	154	569	.281	.340
After (1.0)	.272	2334	...	635	114	16	78	376	...	...	477	323	.396	.435
Two strikes	.190	2392	...	454	83	8	37	203	...	...	281	892	.280	.278
Pitch 1.15	.274	1628	...	446	79	16	52	241	36	13	156	254	.342	.438
Pitch 16.30	.254	982	...	249	43	4	26	128	20	10	126	211	.341	.385
Pitch 31.45	.245	705	...	173	26	4	8	77	11	16	94	101	.337	.328
Pitch 46.60	.248	552	...	137	31	5	13	79	12	6	76	82	.342	.393
Pitch 61.75	.247	566	...	140	29	2	16	75	15	9	56	84	.318	.390
Pitch 76.90	.271	454	...	123	27	3	18	73	10	2	61	62	.359	.463
Pitch 91.105	.262	336	...	88	9	3	13	47	4	2	51	55	.356	.423
Pitch 106.20	.298	191	...	57	7	1	7	22	4	2	21	30	.376	.455
Pitch 121.35	.203	59	...	12	2	0	2	10	3	0	12	9	.347	.339
Pitch 136.50	.167	12	...	2	1	0	0	0	1	0	4	4	.375	.250
Pitch 151+	.000	1	...	0	0	0	0	0	0	0	0	0	.000	.000

Seattle Mariners

Brock J. Hanke

SEATTLE YEAR	1982	1983	1984	1985	1986	1987	1988	1989	1990	1991	TOT
W	76	60	74	74	67	78	68	73	77	83	730
L	86	102	88	88	95	84	93	89	85	79	889
WPCT	0.469	0.370	0.457	0.457	0.414	0.481	0.422	0.451	0.475	0.512	0.451
R	651	558	682	719	718	760	664	694	640	702	6788
RA	712	740	774	818	835	801	744	728	680	674	7506
PWPT	0.455	0.362	0.437	0.436	0.425	0.474	0.443	0.476	0.470	0.520	0.450
PythW	74	59	71	71	69	77	72	77	76	84	73
PythL	88	103	91	91	93	85	90	85	86	78	89
LUCK	2	1	3	3	-2	1	-4	-4	1	-1	0

Defensive Efficiency Record: .7011

Well, now. What's this? The Mariners in contention? Looks like it. You know, you guys in Seattle have never had us sabermetrics types look at what your team could do to put itself over the top. Well, that's over now. All the M's lack is the finishing touches. So what are those touches, and how can the Mariner brain trust put them on?

First, let's take a look at what the Mariners have. In the field, I rate them championship-quality at third base, left field (assuming that's where Kevin Mitchell will play), and center. They are certainly not hurting at second base, shortstop(!), and right field (Jay Buhner). That's right, shortstop. To my intense surprise, Omar Vizquel, who cannot hit Major League pitching at all, came in second in the shortstop rankings. What the stats say is that Omar is clearly the Gold Glove at the position, and that nobody else (except Cal Ripken, of course) hits very much anyway. There are a few shortstops who can hit a little, but their defense is much weaker than Omar's. Altogether, I don't figure Omar will keep that ranking up. Alan Trammell can probably still hit enough to outrank him, if he doesn't get hurt again. Bill Spiers and Dick Schofield probably can too, if they get a little team stability. But, still, Omar probably is legitimately within the top four, the position being what it is right now.

As for pitchers, the M's can likely count on Randy Johnson, Eric Hanson and Brian Holman to pitch at least well, if not better. I rate the three of them in that order, as Johnson seems to have gotten his control down at last. None of them were overworked last year, so none of them figure for arm trouble. They'll probably get a decent year out of either Rich Delucia or Bill Krueger as well. Delucia is younger, but I give a 70/30 bet on Krueger. Bill's 1991 season is not at all out of the context of the previous two. Rich's good 1990 stats were fueled by unrealistically low walk totals, indicating that the hitters didn't know what he could and couldn't throw for strikes. He's going to have to improve his real control to move up. If you look at other teams, those five starters look pretty good. It's a team strength. This, of course, presumes that they do sign Krueger. As of this writing, they were threatening to not offer him a contract. That would be a big mistake. The M's are not deep enough at pitcher to do that.

In relief, the M's have to hope for Mike Schooler to return to form. A couple of years ago, Schooler was a good bet for the Rolaids Award, as he was one of the few closers who hadn't been overworked. However, he proved unable to cope with even the 70-inning load he got in 1989. One of the Mariner needs is a second closer to keep Mike down to 60 innings or so. With Bill Swift and Mike Jackson gone, Bill Plummer needs to open competition in the spring.

Now, what to the M's lack? Well, the most obvious thing they don't have is a killer bat at either first base or DH. Almost all the division winners have at least one of those spots filled with a real big stick. They could also use a better bat behind the plate, especially since they've got to hit Vizquel somewhere. That may not seem like much to Seattle fans accustomed to large groupings of holes; but for a contender, it's a lot. The real hot bats don't come often, or cheap. And catchers are scarce, particularly now. But those are not the greatest of the Mariner needs.

What the Mariners need most is to get their lineup sorted out. The problem, as it so often is, is at the transition spot of #2. Right now, the Mariners would probably like to hit Ken Griffey Jr. in the #3 slot, with Kevin Mitchell cleanup and Jay Buhner #5. There are two problems with this. First, it requires you to bat Edgar Martinez leadoff, and Edgar runs poorly. This is a minor problem. Edgar, like Wade Boggs, gets on base so much that he's going to score runs in job lots whether he can run or not. He's also not going to make many outs, which is going to help the rest of the Mariner offense.

The second problem is that this plan sets up Harold Reynolds to bat second. The M's may not think this is a problem, but it is. Harold, you see, has stopped hitting .280, and has started hitting

.250. That's just age to Harold, but it's a 30 point drop in batting average to the Mariners. More important, it's a 30 point drop in on-base percentage. Last year, Harold only got on at a .332 clip. That's decent, but not at the top of an American League batting order. To give you an idea, Jay Buhner, whose forte is power and who hit .244, got on base .337. Harold also doesn't steal 70 bases any more, though his percentage stealing is still very good. In sum, Harold Reynolds has slowly slipped down out of contention for the #2 spot in the Mariner order.

What would be nice would be if someone could fill both the #2 lineup slot and also play first base or DH. That doesn't seem like much, but the Mariners roster doesn't have many such people. Henry Cotto can probably bat #2 against lefty pitching, but all the other guys are slow sluggers except for Greg Briley, who doesn't look like he can hit at all. I think Alonzo Powell can play, but he's a righty like Cotto. If I were Woody Woodword, I'd be working the trade phones even now. The chance of ending up with a lineup like:

Griffey
Martinez
Mitchell
Buhner
Pete O'Brien
Tino Martinez
Reynolds
Valle
Vizquel

is all too great. For those Seattle fans who thinks it looks fine compared to what they've seen before, the problems are complete lack of speed i the middle of the lineup and too many guys who make outs and hit homers and nothing else.

The odd things is that the best #2 hitter on last year's roster has retired. That's right, I'm taking about Griffey Senior. At last look, he could still hit .260 or more, and take walks in truckloads. He got on base .380 and, on this team, he could even run a little. He's also a lefty, and could platoon with Cotto.

The bench needs sorting out. It's old at the skill positions and overloaded with right handed hitters. There's enough talent there, but it needs to be converted into more useful forms. Tracy Jones has no value to the ballclub, and neither does Dave Cochrane, unless he can really catch, in which case Dave Valle has no value. What the M's bench needs is 1) a young middle infielder who can handle shortstop, so they can pinch hit for Vizquel in the late innings; 2) a lefty bat, unless they get a better lefty DH; and 3) a good defensive catcher, so they can pinch hit there, too. The pinch hitters, of course, will come from whoever loses the first base and DH contests.

The pitching staff is in much better shape. It really lacks only two things: a real staff ace and depth. The staff ace is a real problem, but the Mariners have the one best solution. That's young pitchers with good arms, one of whom will very likely develop into the ace they need. Randy Johnson, who has the best arm, is by far the best bet. Those of you who have been getting this book all along will remember that I said I'd rather have Johnson than Eric Hanson a couple of years ago, when Eric had his real good year and Randy was struggling with the strike zone. The reason for that, and the reason for this pick of him to become the ace, is the strikeout stats. Randy Johnson's problems with control can be solved with work. Other pitchers' problems with throwing speed can't. Randy has the arm, and that gives him the edge.

After Johnson, I rate Hanson, and then Holman. Actually, Holman's strikeout stats are awfully weak for staff ace caliber pitching. He, and Krueger too, would have to quit walking people altogether and also stop giving up hits to turn into the John Tudor sort of ace. After Hanson, the best bet might be Delucia. He doesn't give up many hits; he just throws the homer ball too much. If someone could find out what the batters are hitting the taters off, he might be able to just stop throwing it. I give Johnson a 70% chance of winning 20 games someday; Hanson 25%, Delucia 10%, and the others only a nominal chance.

Of the bench pitchers, the best one looks to be Calvin Jones. He seems to have an arm, and his control is not terrible. This, you understand, is only on the basis of 46 innings. That's what I mean by lack of depth. After their four starters and Schooler, the M's don't have a lot of pitching. If Delucia doesn't get those homers under control, there are precious few options. Still, I'd rather gamble on that than not have Kevin Mitchell.

What can the Mariners do to solve the problems? Well, the first thing they can do is to run every available catcher through spring training. I mean they need to work the waiver wire all March. It doesn't take much to measure up to current standards behind the plate. The good teams keep track of the available floating talent pool at each position and have an idea of who to call in when they need just a little improvement. The Mariners are not famous for doing this. They may lack the coaches needed to do the spring evaluations. If so, they need to hire coaches. No one should lose a division title because they can't improve on Dave Valle's 1991 season.

The same situation exists for the bench. The waiver wire bears watching. The Mariners have never worried about how good their second string was before, because it's never made any difference in the pennant race. Now it might. They need to find that real good fielding shortstop for late inning defense. They also could use a backup center fielder who can go get them. They absolutely must sort through their reserve outfielders and pick up a left handed pinch hitter. They may need a pinch runner, considering their team speed. Scouting those people, and organizing them, is Bill Plummer's main job.

His secondary job, but the first he'll have to do, is to get the first base and DH prospects sorted out for the two starting spots. Those prospects, of course, are the same people who will constitute the pinch hitting bench.

As for pitching, that's not Bill Plummer's problem. It's Woody Woodword's. Woody needs to get some bulk pitching in there, like the Bosox do every year. He needs to scour the waiver wires and set up a lefty-righty plan and get those arms in there and see who's got something left. Plummer's job is to see if Schooler has come back, or if he's got to go with Calvin Jones all year.

You will note that I think that the Mariners have many things to do with secondary players, and few to do with the top men. That's correct. The main characteristic of consistent winners is that they take care of the little things. They have good enough systems, or enough money, to get enough of the big guys without hard work. They work on things like the backup catcher and the lefty/righty balance of their pinch hitters. The Dodgers do that, and the Bosox. The Cubs and the Mets don't, which is why they don't win that often, despite all the superstars.

The Mariners now are at the crossroads. They have enough stars to contend. Now they need to grow up, and start acting like an adult organization. You readers from the northwest keep track of their bench, and then write me. Does it have somebody for every role? Does it have good late defense and good pinch offense? Does it have lefty/righty balance, both in hitting and pitching? Does the lineup concentrate the top bats at the top of the order? In short, did the Mariners do the little things? If so, they'll eventually win. If not, well, welcome to Cleveland.

Seattle Mariners Home Park Performance Factors

	Outs	Runs	Hits	2b	3b	HR	W	K	SH	SF	HBP	IBB	SB	CS	GDP
Home LH Batters	1.002	.917	.962	.937	1.122	.760	.992	.995	1.054	1.009	.766	1.164	1.054	1.026	1.456
Home RH Batters	.947	.988	1.056	1.098	.864	1.102	.881	.925	.708	.795	.932	.767	1.171	1.304	.909
All Home Batters	.980	.936	.981	.962	.831	.903	.926	.960	.861	.955	.931	.985	1.074	1.178	1.073
Opp LH Batters	.963	1.059	1.019	1.045	1.101	1.248	1.191	.949	1.081	1.242	.996	1.225	.924	.996	1.039
Opp RH Batters	.988	1.038	1.014	.971	.952	.970	1.102	.997	.871	.819	1.091	.798	1.084	1.136	1.057
All Opp Batters	.978	1.050	1.010	.997	.999	1.013	1.142	.966	1.021	.905	1.107	.965	1.037	1.070	1.043
All LH Batters	.986	.975	.984	.976	1.108	.894	1.067	.975	1.065	1.065	.918	1.186	1.024	1.022	1.217
All RH Batters	.972	1.020	1.029	1.011	.917	1.017	1.010	.968	.794	.808	1.020	.787	1.100	1.168	.993
All Batters	.979	.991	.995	.980	.916	.957	1.030	.961	.935	.933	1.022	.977	1.057	1.120	1.055

Conventional Batting Records for Seattle Mariners

																BRng	GI						Runs
	G	AB	Run	Hit	2B	3B	HR	TB	RBI	W	K	IW	HB	SB	CS	Eff	DP	SH	SF	Avg	Slug	OBP	Ctd
Valle	132	324	38	63	8	1	8	97	32	34	49	0	9	0	2	.358	19	6	3	.194	.299	.286	26
O'Brien P	152	560	58	139	29	3	17	225	88	44	61	7	1	0	1	.448	14	3	9	.248	.402	.300	67
Reynolds H	161	631	95	160	34	6	3	215	57	72	63	2	5	28	8	.559	11	14	6	.254	.341	.332	78
Martinez E	150	544	98	167	35	1	14	246	52	84	72	9	8	0	3	.464	19	2	4	.307	.452	.405	101
Vizquel	142	426	42	98	16	4	1	125	41	45	37	0	0	7	2	.370	8	8	3	.230	.293	.302	40
Briley	139	381	39	99	17	3	2	128	26	27	51	0	0	23	11	.387	7	1	3	.260	.336	.307	39
Griffey Jr	154	548	76	179	42	1	22	289	100	71	82	21	1	18	6	.584	10	4	9	.327	.527	.399	120
Buhner	137	406	64	99	14	4	27	202	77	53	117	5	6	0	1	.437	10	2	4	.244	.498	.337	69
Davis A	145	462	39	102	15	1	12	155	69	56	78	9	0	0	3	.211	8	0	10	.221	.335	.299	49
Cochrane	65	178	16	44	13	0	2	63	22	9	38	0	1	0	1	.259	3	1	1	.247	.354	.286	18
Cotto	66	177	35	54	6	2	6	82	23	10	27	0	2	16	3	.474	7	2	1	.305	.463	.347	28
Jones Tr	79	175	30	44	8	1	3	63	24	18	22	2	1	2	0	.452	8	1	2	.251	.360	.321	20
Bradley S	83	172	10	35	7	0	0	42	11	19	19	2	0	0	0	.345	2	5	2	.203	.244	.280	13
Schaefer	84	164	19	41	7	1	1	53	11	5	25	0	0	3	1	.308	7	6	0	.250	.323	.272	13
Martinez Tino	36	112	11	23	2	0	4	37	9	11	24	0	0	0	0	.333	2	0	2	.205	.330	.272	10
Powell A	57	111	16	24	6	1	3	41	12	11	24	0	1	0	2	.533	1	0	2	.216	.369	.288	12
Griffey	30	85	10	24	7	0	1	34	9	13	13	0	1	0	0	.611	2	0	1	.282	.400	.380	14
Amaral	14	16	2	1	0	0	0	1	0	1	5	0	1	0	0	.250	1	0	0	.063	.063	.167	0
Sinatro	5	8	1	2	0	0	0	2	1	1	1	0	0	0	0	1.000	0	0	0	.250	.250	.333	1
Lennon	9	8	2	1	1	0	0	2	1	3	1	0	0	0	0	.600	0	0	0	.125	.250	.364	1
Howard C	9	6	1	1	1	0	0	2	0	1	2	0	0	0	0	1.000	0	0	0	.167	.333	.286	1
Swift	3	0	0	0	0	0	0	0	0	0	0	0	0	0	0	.000	0	0	0	.000	.000	.000	0
Jackson M	1	0	0	0	0	0	0	0	0	0	0	0	0	0	0	.000	0	0	0	.000	.000	.000	0
Murphy R	1	0	0	0	0	0	0	0	0	0	0	0	0	0	0	.000	0	0	0	.000	.000	.000	0
Schooler	1	0	0	0	0	0	0	0	0	0	0	0	0	0	0	.000	0	0	0	.000	.000	.000	0
TOTALS	1855	5494	702	1400	268	29	126	2104	665	588	811	57	37	97	44	.442	139	55	62	.255	.383	.328	702

Sabermetric Batting Records for Seattle Mariners

	Ball Park Adjusted								Runs				Run/							
	AB	Run	Hit	2B	3B	HR	RBI	W	SO	Avg	Slug	OBP	Ctd	Outs	27o	OW%	OG	OWAR	DWAR	TWAR
Amaral	15	2	1	0	0	0	0	0	4	.067	.067	.125	0	14	0.00	.000	1	-0.18	0.06	-0.12
Bradley S	168	9	34	6	0	0	11	20	18	.202	.238	.284	13	143	2.45	.250	5	-0.53	-0.01	-0.54
Briley	375	38	98	16	3	2	27	29	49	.261	.336	.312	39	300	3.51	.406	11	0.62	0.19	0.81
Buhner	399	64	102	14	3	27	76	52	112	.256	.509	.348	72	311	6.25	.684	12	3.85	1.11	4.96
Cochrane	174	15	43	12	0	1	21	9	36	.247	.333	.288	16	135	3.20	.362	5	0.06	-0.13	-0.07
Cotto	174	35	55	6	1	6	22	9	25	.316	.466	.357	29	129	6.07	.671	5	1.54	0.27	1.81
Davis A	454	38	101	14	1	12	74	61	75	.222	.337	.308	50	376	3.59	.417	14	0.93	0.05	0.98
Griffey Jr	539	75	177	41	1	22	107	77	79	.328	.531	.406	121	394	8.29	.792	15	6.45	1.34	7.79
Griffey	82	9	23	6	0	1	9	14	12	.280	.390	.381	13	62	5.66	.640	2	0.67	0.05	0.71
Howard C	5	1	1	1	0	0	0	0	1	.200	.400	.200	0	4	0.00	.000	0	-0.05	0.04	-0.01
Jones Tr	171	30	45	8	0	3	23	17	21	.263	.363	.332	20	134	4.03	.474	5	0.61	0.14	0.76
Lennon	7	2	1	1	0	0	0	2	0	.143	.286	.333	1	6	4.50	.529	0	0.04	0.00	0.04
Martinez E	536	99	172	36	0	14	51	83	69	.321	.466	.417	106	389	7.36	.750	14	5.76	0.82	6.59
Martinez Tino	109	10	22	1	0	4	9	12	23	.202	.321	.276	10	91	2.97	.328	3	-0.07	0.09	0.01
O'Brien P	550	57	137	28	3	17	94	48	59	.249	.404	.304	66	444	4.01	.472	16	2.00	0.49	2.49
Powell A	108	16	24	6	0	3	11	10	23	.222	.361	.292	12	87	3.72	.435	3	0.27	-0.00	0.27
Reynolds H	619	94	159	33	5	2	56	74	60	.257	.336	.339	77	497	4.18	.492	18	2.62	2.06	4.68
Schaefer	161	19	42	7	0	1	10	4	24	.261	.323	.279	13	130	2.70	.288	5	-0.30	0.47	0.18
Sinatro	7	1	2	0	0	0	0	0	0	.286	.286	.286	1	5	5.40	.618	0	0.05	0.06	0.11
Valle	317	38	65	8	0	8	31	33	47	.205	.306	.296	26	278	2.53	.261	10	-0.91	0.49	-0.42
Vizquel	418	41	97	15	3	0	40	46	35	.232	.282	.307	39	340	3.10	.347	13	-0.04	3.00	2.96
TOTALS	5400	697	1393	262	26	120	657	608	780	.258	.383	.334	702	4311	4.40	.517	160	26.72	10.60	37.32

Pitching Records for Seattle Mariners

	ERA	W	L	Pct	G	GS	CG	ShO	GF	Sv	IP	R	ER	H	2B	3B	HR	BB	IW	SO	HB	WP	BK
Johnson R	3.98	13	10	.565	33	33	2	1	0	0	201.1	96	89	151	32	1	15	152	0	228	12	12	2
Holman B	3.69	13	14	.481	30	30	5	3	0	0	195.1	86	80	199	36	4	16	77	0	108	10	8	1
Delucia	5.09	12	13	.480	32	31	0	0	0	0	182.0	107	103	176	35	3	31	78	4	98	4	10	0
Krueger	3.60	11	8	.579	35	25	1	0	2	0	175.0	82	70	194	34	4	15	60	4	91	4	10	1
Hanson	3.81	8	8	.500	27	27	2	1	0	0	174.2	82	74	182	36	7	16	56	2	143	2	14	1
Bankhead	4.90	3	6	.333	17	9	0	0	2	0	60.2	35	33	73	16	1	8	21	2	28	2	0	0
Swift	1.99	1	2	.333	71	0	0	0	30	17	90.1	22	20	74	6	1	3	26	4	48	1	2	1
Jackson M	3.25	7	7	.500	72	0	0	0	35	14	88.2	35	32	64	10	3	5	34	11	74	6	3	0
Swan	3.43	6	2	.750	63	0	0	0	11	2	78.2	35	30	81	17	0	8	28	7	33	0	8	0
Murphy R	3.00	0	1	.000	57	0	0	0	26	4	48.0	17	16	47	12	3	4	19	4	34	1	4	0
Jones Cd	2.53	2	2	.500	27	0	0	0	6	2	46.1	14	13	33	4	1	0	29	5	42	1	6	0
Burba	3.68	2	2	.500	22	2	0	0	11	1	36.2	16	15	34	7	2	6	14	3	16	0	1	0
Schooler	3.67	3	3	.500	34	0	0	0	23	7	34.1	14	14	25	2	1	2	10	0	31	0	2	1
Rice P	3.00	1	1	.500	7	2	0	0	0	0	21.0	10	7	18	0	0	3	10	1	12	1	0	0
Fleming	6.62	1	0	1.000	9	3	0	0	3	0	17.2	13	13	19	6	1	3	3	0	11	3	1	0
Harris Ge	4.05	0	0	.000	8	0	0	0	3	1	13.1	8	6	15	4	0	1	10	3	6	0	1	0
Comstock	54.00	0	0	.000	1	0	0	0	0	0	0.1	2	2	2	1	0	0	1	0	0	0	0	0
TOTALS	3.79	83	79	.512	545	162	10	5	152	48	1464.1	674	617	1387	258	32	136	628	50	1003	47	82	7

Sabermetric Pitching Records for Seattle Mariners

	Adj	Expected			Opposing Batters												Supported				
	ERA	W	L	Pct	BFP	Avg	Slg	OBA	RC/G	GDP	SB	CS	PK	PKE	SH	SF	RSup	RSp/G	W	L	Pct
Bankhead	4.75	4	5	.426	271	.297	.467	.354	6.29	5	8	0	0	0	0	2	26	3.86	4	5	.398
Burba	3.44	2	2	.586	153	.245	.453	.314	4.53	5	1	1	0	0	0	0	24	5.89	3	1	.746
Comstock	27.00	0	0	.022	4	.667	1.000	.750	66.51	0	0	0	0	0	0	0	0	0.00	0	0	.000
Delucia	5.04	10	15	.396	779	.260	.457	.333	5.14	13	4	9	1	0	5	14	111	5.49	14	11	.542
Fleming	6.11	0	1	.309	73	.284	.537	.342	5.59	3	1	1	0	0	0	0	7	3.57	0	1	.254
Hanson	3.76	9	7	.542	744	.269	.414	.323	4.54	16	11	10	0	0	2	8	100	5.15	10	6	.652
Harris Ge	3.38	0	0	.595	66	.273	.400	.385	6.18	1	0	0	0	0	1	0	4	2.70	0	0	.390
Holman B	3.64	15	12	.558	839	.268	.392	.343	4.56	22	4	5	1	2	6	3	79	3.64	14	13	.500
Jackson M	3.15	9	5	.628	363	.201	.298	.290	3.05	5	5	0	0	0	4	0	32	3.25	7	7	.516
Johnson R	3.93	12	11	.519	889	.213	.325	.358	4.15	22	18	9	0	6	9	8	112	5.01	14	9	.618
Jones Cd	2.33	3	1	.755	194	.209	.247	.335	2.95	6	5	1	0	0	6	0	21	4.08	3	1	.754
Krueger	3.55	11	8	.570	751	.289	.418	.346	4.99	19	11	5	4	2	6	9	81	4.17	11	8	.579
Murphy R	2.81	1	0	.679	211	.250	.410	.322	4.99	2	5	0	0	0	3	0	10	1.88	0	1	.308
Rice P	2.57	1	1	.717	91	.234	.351	.319	3.86	2	0	1	0	0	0	3	12	5.14	2	0	.800
Schooler	3.41	4	2	.590	138	.198	.278	.255	2.52	2	3	0	0	0	1	1	4	1.05	1	5	.086
Swan	3.32	5	3	.603	336	.269	.405	.330	4.42	13	7	1	0	0	6	1	30	3.43	4	4	.517
Swift	1.89	2	1	.823	359	.224	.276	.283	2.24	19	1	1	0	1	2	0	49	4.88	3	0	.869
TOTALS	3.76	88	74	.542	6261	.253	.386	.332	4.37	155	84	44	6	11	51	49	702	4.31	92	70	.569

Batting 'Splits' Records for Seattle Mariners

	G	AB	Run	Hit	2B	3B	HR	TB	RBI	W	K	IW	HB	SB	CS	GI DP	SH	SF	Avg	Slug	OBP	Runs Ctd
SPLITS for Buhner																						
vs LHP	81	146	20	35	5	2	9	71	26	28	28	4	3	0	0	5	0	1	.240	.486	.371	27
vs RHP	102	260	44	64	9	2	18	131	51	25	89	1	3	0	1	5	2	3	.246	.504	.316	41
Home	72	212	33	45	9	2	14	100	41	31	71	4	4	0	0	7	2	2	.212	.472	.321	32
Away	65	194	31	54	5	2	13	102	36	22	46	1	2	0	1	3	0	2	.278	.526	.355	37
Grass	52	153	28	46	3	2	12	89	32	19	35	1	1	0	1	3	0	2	.301	.582	.377	34
Turf	85	253	36	53	11	2	15	113	45	34	82	4	5	0	0	7	2	2	.209	.447	.313	36
April/June	58	144	22	32	5	2	9	68	28	23	47	3	2	0	0	3	2	0	.222	.472	.337	24
July/October	79	262	42	67	9	2	18	134	49	30	70	2	4	0	1	7	0	4	.256	.511	.337	45
SPLITS for Griffey Jr																						
vs LHP	95	159	20	50	10	0	5	75	26	20	30	4	1	1	2	3	4	4	.314	.472	.386	30
vs RHP	132	389	56	129	32	1	17	214	74	51	52	17	0	17	4	7	0	5	.332	.550	.404	91
Home	79	282	44	103	23	0	16	174	59	36	47	10	1	9	1	1	3	5	.365	.617	.432	81
Away	75	266	32	76	19	1	6	115	41	35	35	11	0	9	5	9	1	4	.286	.432	.364	42
Grass	59	206	25	57	14	1	4	85	33	27	29	8	0	6	4	8	1	3	.277	.413	.356	30
Turf	95	342	51	122	28	0	18	204	67	44	53	13	1	12	2	2	3	6	.357	.596	.425	93
April/June	73	249	27	68	17	0	7	106	32	35	42	9	0	6	0	3	1	5	.273	.426	.356	42
July/October	81	299	49	111	25	1	15	183	68	36	40	12	1	12	6	7	3	4	.371	.612	.435	80
SPLITS for Martinez E																						
vs LHP	84	156	27	56	13	0	2	75	12	24	11	8	0	0	0	7	1	1	.359	.481	.442	33
vs RHP	130	388	71	111	22	1	12	171	40	60	61	1	8	0	3	12	1	3	.286	.441	.390	68
Home	72	250	47	80	14	1	8	120	28	45	33	5	4	0	2	11	0	3	.320	.480	.427	52
Away	78	294	51	87	21	0	6	126	24	39	39	4	4	0	1	8	2	1	.296	.429	.385	49
Grass	59	222	37	64	13	0	5	92	17	32	31	3	2	0	0	6	2	0	.288	.414	.383	36
Turf	91	322	61	103	22	1	9	154	35	52	41	6	6	0	3	13	0	4	.320	.478	.419	65
April/June	69	241	40	75	10	0	5	100	24	38	35	4	4	0	2	10	0	1	.311	.415	.412	41
July/October	81	303	58	92	25	1	9	146	28	46	37	5	4	0	1	9	2	3	.304	.482	.399	60
SPLITS for Reynolds H																						
vs LHP	91	174	21	46	7	0	1	56	16	17	14	1	0	5	1	5	4	2	.264	.322	.326	19
vs RHP	147	457	74	114	27	6	2	159	41	55	49	1	5	23	7	6	10	4	.249	.348	.334	59
Home	81	314	58	94	20	5	1	127	27	42	27	2	3	15	1	7	7	0	.299	.404	.387	54
Away	80	317	37	66	14	1	2	88	30	30	36	0	2	13	7	4	7	6	.208	.278	.276	26
Grass	61	238	30	47	10	0	1	60	24	26	29	0	2	10	6	4	7	5	.197	.252	.277	18
Turf	100	393	65	113	24	6	2	155	33	46	34	2	3	18	2	7	7	1	.288	.394	.366	62
April/June	74	293	46	81	18	1	1	104	27	35	20	1	2	12	5	4	4	3	.276	.355	.354	40
July/October	87	338	49	79	16	5	2	111	30	37	43	1	3	16	3	7	10	3	.234	.328	.312	38
SPLITS for Valle																						
vs LHP	65	112	17	26	1	0	6	45	17	10	14	0	5	0	0	4	1	1	.232	.402	.320	14
vs RHP	98	212	21	37	7	1	2	52	15	24	35	0	4	0	2	15	5	2	.175	.245	.269	12
Home	72	173	15	28	4	1	0	34	8	17	27	0	1	0	1	10	4	2	.162	.197	.238	7
Away	60	151	23	35	4	0	8	63	24	17	22	0	8	0	1	9	2	1	.232	.417	.339	20
Grass	45	112	16	31	4	0	7	56	21	11	16	0	4	0	1	6	1	1	.277	.500	.359	18
Turf	87	212	22	32	4	1	1	41	11	23	33	0	5	0	1	13	5	2	.151	.193	.248	10
April/June	64	155	13	20	0	0	3	29	7	20	25	0	5	0	0	7	1	0	.129	.187	.250	8
July/October	68	169	25	43	8	1	5	68	25	14	24	0	4	0	2	12	5	3	.254	.402	.321	19
SPLITS for Vizquel																						
vs LHP	62	87	12	20	4	0	0	24	11	7	5	0	0	1	0	3	2	1	.230	.276	.284	7
vs RHP	132	339	30	78	12	4	1	101	30	38	32	0	0	6	2	5	6	2	.230	.298	.306	33
Home	69	206	24	52	11	4	1	74	24	21	21	0	0	1	1	3	4	2	.252	.359	.319	25
Away	73	220	18	46	5	0	0	51	17	24	16	0	0	6	1	5	4	1	.209	.232	.286	16
Grass	56	167	15	36	3	0	0	39	13	17	10	0	0	5	0	5	4	1	.216	.234	.286	12
Turf	86	259	27	62	13	4	1	86	28	28	27	0	0	2	2	3	4	2	.239	.332	.311	28
April/June	64	200	18	43	7	3	0	56	17	21	13	0	0	2	2	5	5	2	.215	.280	.287	17
July/October	78	226	24	55	9	1	1	69	24	24	24	0	0	5	0	3	3	1	.243	.305	.315	24
SPLITS for Seattle Mariners (all batters except pitchers)																						
vs LHP	961	1651	228	432	80	4	41	643	211	176	233	19	12	15	7	51	24	17	.262	.389	.334	216
vs RHP	1500	3843	474	968	188	25	85	1461	454	412	578	38	25	82	37	88	31	45	.252	.380	.325	487
Home	930	2706	374	701	137	19	69	1083	353	314	411	28	19	44	16	63	30	31	.259	.400	.337	377
Away	925	2788	328	699	131	10	57	1021	312	274	400	29	18	53	28	76	25	31	.251	.366	.319	326
Grass	709	2127	260	544	93	7	47	792	248	211	308	22	11	37	20	64	21	25	.256	.372	.323	254
Turf	1146	3367	442	856	175	22	79	1312	417	377	503	35	26	60	24	75	34	37	.254	.390	.331	448
April/June	840	2515	306	618	107	10	52	901	288	282	360	26	17	46	23	57	19	20	.246	.358	.324	300
July/October	1015	2979	396	782	161	19	74	1203	377	306	451	31	20	51	21	82	36	42	.263	.404	.331	402

1991 SPLITS FOR Seattle Mariners

BATTING SPLITS

	AVG	AB	R	H	2B	3B	HR	RBI	SB	CS	BB	K	OBA	SPCT
Total	.255	5494	702	1400	268	29	126	665	97	44	588	811	.328	.383

	#Pit	#P/PA	GB	FB	G/F	G	IBB	HB	SH	SF	GDP
Miscellaneous	23074	3.70	2091	1661	1.26	162	57	37	55	62	139

	AVG	AB	R	H	2B	3B	HR	RBI	SB	CS	BB	K	OBA	SPCT
vs. Left	.262	1651	...	432	80	4	41	211	15	7	176	233	.334	.389
vs. Right	.252	3843	...	968	188	25	85	454	82	37	412	578	.325	.380
Home	.259	2706	374	701	137	19	69	353	44	16	314	411	.337	.400
Away	.251	2788	328	699	131	10	57	312	53	28	274	400	.319	.366
None on	.247	3126	...	773	145	17	63	63	0	0	305	486	.318	.365
Runners on	.265	2368	...	627	123	12	63	602	97	44	283	325	.340	.407
April	.257	708	84	182	28	2	17	81	16	9	85	96	.340	.374
May	.245	913	115	224	34	6	21	107	18	6	99	133	.318	.365
June	.237	894	107	212	45	2	14	100	12	8	98	131	.316	.339
July	.275	924	132	254	48	9	26	122	17	7	69	124	.326	.431
August	.257	927	112	238	54	3	25	107	18	5	108	139	.333	.402
September	.255	965	122	246	51	5	18	120	12	7	109	158	.330	.374
October	.270	163	30	44	8	2	5	28	4	2	20	30	.349	.436
None on/out	.247	1378	...	341	63	9	28	28	0	0	123	199	.313	.367
Scoring Posn	.265	1340	...	355	62	9	28	505	16	7	201	202	.352	.387
Close & Late	.246	928	...	228	51	6	20	117	15	10	100	154	.320	.378
Bases Loaded	.243	111	...	27	5	1	4	95	0	0	10	15	.277	.414
Batting #1	.257	668	106	172	39	3	14	58	20	6	79	74	.338	.388
Batting #2	.263	653	99	172	29	7	8	60	29	11	70	86	.337	.366
Batting #3	.334	632	88	211	45	1	24	115	20	7	79	90	.404	.522
Batting #4	.275	621	82	171	35	2	16	95	0	2	67	103	.346	.415
Batting #5	.220	623	73	137	18	2	18	78	1	5	56	101	.283	.342
Batting #6	.240	583	75	140	31	4	18	71	4	4	79	121	.334	.400
Batting #7	.237	590	65	140	27	5	18	80	12	3	55	94	.301	.392
Batting #8	.227	569	58	129	24	2	1	49	2	1	53	80	.294	.281
Batting #9	.231	555	56	128	20	3	9	59	9	5	50	62	.299	.326
As c	.206	509	52	105	17	1	8	46	0	2	52	70	.287	.291
As 1b	.233	617	60	144	27	2	18	80	0	3	47	73	.284	.371
As 2b	.256	648	97	166	35	6	3	57	28	8	72	67	.332	.343
As 3b	.299	615	103	184	40	2	14	64	1	3	89	87	.392	.439
As ss	.239	536	53	128	22	4	2	48	9	3	50	54	.303	.306
As lf	.265	597	77	158	29	3	14	60	20	7	51	83	.323	.394
As cf	.325	625	92	203	46	1	26	117	21	7	76	96	.393	.526
As rf	.237	595	81	141	22	7	27	86	13	5	62	151	.313	.434
Outfield	.276	1817	250	502	97	11	67	263	54	19	189	330	.344	.452
0.0 count	.300	659	...	198	41	4	9	87	...	...	3	0	.306	.416
After (0.1)	.225	2438	...	549	106	13	50	230	...	...	125	540	.268	.341
After (1.0)	.272	2397	...	653	121	12	67	348	...	...	423	271	.379	.417
Two strikes	.189	2305	...	436	79	12	33	204	...	...	235	809	.266	.277
Grass	.256	2127	260	544	93	7	47	248	37	20	211	308	.323	.372
Turf	.254	3367	442	856	175	22	79	417	60	24	377	503	.331	.390
Day	.257	1430	182	367	67	7	33	176	28	18	132	238	.319	.383
Night	.254	4064	520	1033	201	22	93	489	69	26	456	573	.331	.383
Inning 1.6	.252	3637	468	917	170	18	85	441	70	28	393	524	.325	.379
Inning 7+	.260	1857	234	483	98	11	41	224	27	16	195	287	.332	.391
vs.Bal	.268	407	63	109	22	2	14	58	3	3	39	44	.334	.435
vs.Bos	.257	404	47	104	23	2	5	45	3	7	38	64	.319	.361
vs.Cal	.257	439	50	113	26	1	10	49	9	3	43	74	.324	.390
vs.ChA	.228	429	50	98	15	2	13	49	8	1	41	68	.295	.364
vs.Cle	.310	413	68	128	25	3	10	64	13	3	38	63	.364	.458
vs.Det	.257	400	55	103	21	1	9	49	8	0	65	60	.362	.382
vs.KC	.242	442	63	107	18	5	8	59	6	7	49	76	.317	.360
vs.Mil	.246	411	57	101	15	3	10	56	8	6	41	51	.317	.370
vs.Min	.247	441	44	109	24	0	9	42	11	3	52	61	.329	.363
vs.NYA	.257	409	43	105	16	4	9	39	10	1	26	65	.303	.381
vs.Oak	.248	399	54	99	17	1	11	53	7	4	59	49	.345	.378
vs.Tex	.270	477	69	129	30	2	9	64	3	3	56	72	.349	.398
vs.Tor	.225	423	39	95	16	3	9	38	8	3	41	64	.296	.340

PITCHING SPLITS

	ERA	W	L	SV	SVOP	GS	CG	SHO	IP	H	ER	HR	BB	IBB	K
Total	3.79	83	79	48	64	162	10	10	1464.1	1387	616	136	628	50	1003

	#Pit	#P/IP	GB	FB	G/F	BRp9	RA	WP	BK	SH	SF	R	HB	Hld
Miscellaneous	23284	15.90	2024	1557	1.30	12.67	383	82	7	51	49	674	47	49

	ERA	W	L	SV	SVOP	GS	CG	SHO	IP	H	ER	HR	BB	IBB	K
ST	4.11	60	59	0	0	162	10	5	974.2	961	445	102	432	11	688
REL	3.16	23	20	48	64	0	0	0	489.2	426	172	34	196	39	315
Home	3.46	45	36	22	30	81	8	4	760.0	697	292	69	273	26	534
Away	4.15	38	43	26	34	81	2	1	704.1	690	325	67	355	24	469
April	3.94	10	11	4	5	21	3	1	185.0	185	81	16	90	8	116
May	3.50	15	12	8	9	27	1	1	247.0	235	96	23	108	10	176
June	4.04	14	13	11	11	27	1	0	234.0	198	105	30	114	5	166
July	2.80	15	12	6	12	27	3	2	244.0	224	76	17	87	8	166
August	3.84	13	15	8	12	28	1	1	253.1	255	108	27	95	7	175
September	4.96	12	15	7	10	27	1	0	256.0	263	141	19	114	12	178
October	2.00	4	1	4	5	5	0	0	45.0	27	10	4	20	0	26
Grass	3.92	32	30	22	26	62	2	1	537.2	510	234	55	273	17	370
Turf	3.72	51	49	26	38	100	8	4	926.2	877	383	81	355	33	633
Day	4.33	17	26	8	11	43	4	3	374.1	357	180	42	162	13	247
Night	3.61	66	53	40	53	119	6	2	1090.0	1030	437	94	466	37	756
vs.Bal	3.00	8	4	3	4	12	0	0	108.0	96	36	12	45	2	75
vs.Bos	6.32	3	9	3	5	12	0	0	105.1	132	74	13	60	8	72
vs.Cal	2.95	7	6	6	7	13	0	0	119.0	106	39	12	47	4	88
vs.ChA	3.58	6	7	5	8	13	0	0	118.0	104	47	14	54	2	74
vs.Cle	3.03	10	2	6	7	12	0	0	107.0	101	36	5	33	1	81
vs.Det	5.47	4	8	4	5	12	0	0	103.2	103	63	17	61	2	75
vs.KC	3.53	6	7	4	5	13	1	1	119.2	107	47	6	50	3	71
vs.Mil	2.78	9	3	4	5	12	2	1	110.0	84	34	2	51	4	71
vs.Min	4.70	4	9	0	2	13	2	1	115.0	136	60	9	50	2	53
vs.NYA	1.91	9	3	4	4	12	1	1	113.0	97	24	8	40	3	82
vs.Oak	3.79	7	6	3	3	13	2	1	111.2	105	47	15	42	4	88
vs.Tex	4.98	5	8	4	5	13	1	0	121.0	123	67	17	59	8	81
vs.Tor	3.42	5	7	2	4	12	1	0	113.0	93	43	6	36	7	92

OPPOSING BATTERS VS. PITCHERS.

	AVG	AB	R	H	2B	3B	HR	RBI	SB	CS	BB	K	OBA	SPCT
Total	.253	5486	674	1387	258	32	136	630	84	44	628	1003	.332	.386
vs. Left	.257	2089	...	536	100	15	42	239	27	11	230	320	.331	.379
vs. Right	.251	3397	...	851	158	17	94	391	57	33	398	683	.332	.390
ST	.262	3670	483	961	191	20	102	424	55	38	432	688	.342	.408
REL	.235	1816	191	426	67	12	34	206	29	6	196	315	.312	.341
Home	.246	2833	319	697	130	16	69	301	41	22	273	534	.314	.376
Away	.260	2653	355	690	128	16	67	329	43	22	355	469	.351	.396
None on	.249	3103	...	772	139	17	86	86	0	0	311	563	.322	.388
Runners on	.258	2383	...	615	119	15	50	544	84	44	317	440	.345	.384
None on/out	.247	1371	...	338	60	7	39	39	0	0	137	230	.320	.386
Scoring Posn	.246	1342	...	330	58	10	25	468	30	8	229	268	.351	.360
vs 1st Batr	.254	342	...	87	21	2	4	36	7	1	27	60	.311	.363
1st IP	.257	1802	196	464	78	10	44	243	36	9	206	327	.336	.385
Inning 1.6	.261	3633	486	947	181	21	98	452	58	37	449	661	.344	.403
Inning 7+	.237	1853	188	440	77	11	38	178	26	7	179	342	.308	.352
Close & Late	.246	956	...	235	40	6	17	96	13	3	99	187	.319	.354
0.0 count	.294	810	...	238	41	7	26	98	...	...	38	0	.329	.458
After (0.1)	.226	2301	...	519	86	9	55	234	...	...	161	622	.281	.342
After (1.0)	.265	2375	...	630	131	16	55	298	...	...	429	381	.378	.403
Two strikes	.172	2373	...	409	77	9	35	204	...	...	273	1003	.262	.257
Pitch 1.15	.264	1630	...	431	71	7	44	179	35	8	146	256	.329	.398
Pitch 16.30	.210	1034	...	217	44	8	19	110	4	4	136	204	.304	.323
Pitch 31.45	.279	706	...	197	36	5	21	83	18	10	86	120	.361	.433
Pitch 46.60	.265	592	...	157	33	5	20	96	6	3	79	109	.350	.439
Pitch 61.75	.251	550	...	138	22	2	10	55	6	5	55	113	.321	.353
Pitch 76.90	.237	443	...	105	22	4	13	47	5	6	61	88	.332	.393
Pitch 91.105	.268	328	...	88	18	1	8	42	5	5	39	65	.348	.402
Pitch 106.20	.264	148	...	39	7	0	1	11	3	2	17	29	.343	.331
Pitch 121.35	.283	53	...	15	5	0	0	7	2	1	10	16	.391	.377
Pitch 136.50	.000	4	...	0	0	0	0	0	0	0	0	3	.000	.000

Kansas City Royals

Don Malcolm

KANSAS CITY											
YEAR	1982	1983	1984	1985	1986	1987	1988	1989	1990	1991	TOT
W	90	79	84	91	76	83	84	92	75	82	836
L	72	83	78	71	86	79	77	70	86	80	782
WPCT	0.556	0.488	0.519	0.562	0.469	0.512	0.522	0.568	0.466	0.506	0.517
R	784	696	673	687	654	715	704	690	707	727	7037
RA	717	767	686	639	673	691	648	635	709	722	6887
PWPT	0.545	0.452	0.490	0.536	0.486	0.517	0.541	0.541	0.499	0.503	0.511
PythW	88	73	79	87	79	84	88	88	81	82	83
PythL	74	89	83	75	83	78	74	74	81	80	79
LUCK	2	6	5	4	-3	-1	-4	4	-6	0	7

Defensive Efficiency Record: .6857

TREADMILL

You've seen the symptoms. Even in your own life. The nasty indicators that no matter what you do, no matter how hard you work, things aren't going to change much one way or the other. The decisions you make, the things you do have little material effect on the quailty of your life or the achievements in it.

For awhile you wallow in it, then—because the animalistic streak is unavoidably close to the surface—you decide to take violent action against it just because you cañ, and not because you expect it to matter, but just because you can. You transform yourself, you look like a different person, but inside things really haven't changed. You look into the mirror and you see the relapse coming, you see that nothing has changed except a loss of energy. You resolve at this point that there will be no more glimpses into that mirror...

This is your life, Herk Robinson. This is the process that you and your organization has entered into, the process that must inevitably result in agonizingly slow dessication and decline. There is nothing worse in any system or organization than the unavoidable apprehension of stasis, stagnation, lack of progress. What tends to happen in situations of this type is that the organization makes an effort to restructure its operations, revamp its methods, and winds up with something worse than what was originally in place.

Yes, this is your life, Herk Robinson. You succeeded a successful and well-regarded executive in John Schuerholz. You have struggled through a difficult first year at the helm, a year in which your team spent much of its time in the cellar. You have watched Schuerholz' new team, the Atlanta Braves, rise like a meteor from the lower depths of the NL West to achievement and adulation. You want desperately to do something similar. After all, that was what you were hired to do.

But in reality, you were given the job as a reward for years of faithful service to an organization that needs to be gutted and completely rebuilt. You have been a consummate company man, and now you've been given a chance to handle the most delicate, most qualitative, least cut-and-dried, least predictable set of tasks that can be assigned to anyone in major baseball. Develop the personnel, deliver a winner: you've got to ensure that you're never more than a year away from winning. The proud tradition of the Kansas City Royals, still the most successful expansion team ever, is slowly decaying, showing the signs of inevitable cracks and fissures. You are a wild-eyed man with a trowel, slapping cement everywhere you think it will help, not realizing that you have already been painted into a corner by previous events.

So now you've made a blockbuster trade, one that you're getting incredible press for having engineered. People in Kansas City are doubtless thinking that you've got the touch, that it rubbed off from being in the same county with John Schuerholz. Three everyday players for one starting pitcher and a utility man. What brilliance! Surely the Royals have solved their problems: the man with the trowel has patched all the leaks.

But imagine how you will feel—and trust me, this is exactly how you will feel—when you wake up on October 5th, 1992 and find that all of your machinating has made virtually no difference in your team's fortunes. The forceful, bold, cunning, desperately orchestrated actions, the hand signals and jerkings of the knee, all will have amounted to the most minimal of blips on the screen. How will you feel? Like a man who has grown old overnight, one who wishes only to sleep, one who defines motion as the absence of rest and vice-versa, and has quit searching for meaning and purpose, or explanations as to why these things tend not to exist.

You've seen the symptoms. There is nothing more you can do. You've done all you can. The fates have dealt you a hand that is satisfactory neither for offense nor defense: you can only watch yourself slowly be consumed. And it is the pace, the leaden assurance at which it creeps along, that will first disarm you, then slowly shorten your breath, afflict your eyes, your appetite, the use of your limbs. Torture as torpor: the visible symptoms of demise are manifested in a sudden recognition of the loss of desire, and in the inability to long for its recovery. You will feel like a man walled up behind cement, and you will see that you are the man who put you behind the wall, and it will not matter.

THE TRADE, ITS SUBTEXT, AND WHY IT WON'T MATTER

Perhaps the main reason why the trade will not matter is that its seductive design (three starting position players for a starting pitcher and a utility man) so effectively masks the other off-season personnel action, the one that really does matter: the loss of Danny Tartabull to free agency.

One of the basic misconceptions in baseball is that you can replace someone truly great with two players who, added up, give approximately the same value. The lingering racist tinge in baseball is reinforced by the ceaseless application of this bogus maxim, for when a player is "trouble" it means that he is too demonstrative about his ethnicity. And whenever ethnicity is an issue it means that it issues from a series of objections raised, via prototypically circular racist methods, by whites against non-whites. The departure of two "ethnic" players (Bo Jackson and Danny Tartabull) from the Royals even as they hire Hal McRae, the company token black, as manager shows that the forces of racism remain deeply embedded in the fabric of the game. The Royals have encrypted their particular strain with a series of actions that would attempt to deny or at least mask what is at work.

The Royals will doubtless cry foul at these assertions and insinuations, but they are speaking from both sides of their mouths at once. They have let their two best offensive performers go. Both of these men were black. They have traded for or signed, with one exception, all white players over the past three seasons. The only black player they have promoted into the starting lineup happens to be the manager's son. There is something doubly awful happening here, and it is strangling what used to be one of the most progressive organizations in baseball. The new cleanup hitter for the Royals just might turn out to be David Duke.

Replacing Danny Tartabull and his nine runs created per game with Kevin McReynolds (4.88 RC/G) and Greg Jefferies (4.66 RC/G) is part of this ongoing obscenity. Baseball is saying to blacks and latins: you can be great, but we don't want to hear you saying it. Take the money and be quiet. Don't cause dissension, don't force us to examine our policies or our prejudices. Shut up and get in on the gravy train. We'll let you be economically equal if you just keep your mouth closed. If you make too much noise, we're going to find a way to move you elsewhere, even if it costs us on the field. Because we are not going to admit that we have a problem. There will be no meetings of Racists Anonymous here. We are not racist, we just want to be in control. We are giving you this opportunity, don't bite the hand that feeds you. Bite us and we'll turn the public against you. Bare your teeth and we'll paint you blacker than you already are. We'll replace you with white boys who can't carry your jock strap and insult you by saying that we're stronger without you.

There is no way to replace Danny Tartabull. Players do not exceed nine runs created per game often enough to make them interchangeable. Two players who create nine runs per game combined do not constitute a replacement, they are an indictment of a team's inability to assess talent objectively and build its team according to the imperatives of those objective evaluations.

Ah, but let's look at what else the Royals have done, you say. They have signed another star hitter. They have signed Wally Joyner. (For one year.) Surely this makes up for the loss of Tartabull. Joyner averages more than six runs created per game.

It's staggering, but true: baseball people just don't understand the calculus of process. Peak is not a function of linear progression, it's a function of unique forces that then add value to the lesser numbers in the surrounding series. One man in the middle of a bunch of players rated at 110 (league average being 100) who peaks at 200 affects the value of the surrounding players at 110. Their value is heightened by proximity to the peak. You can't simulate a 200 peak with two 105's and a 120, or three more 110's. It is not the same. It cannot be the same. You've got to keep the 200 and add value to what surrounds it. But baseball rarely does this—unless the player is white.

Here is the Royals' opening day lineup:

1. McRae, cf
2. Jefferies, lf
3. Brett, dh
4. Joyner, 1b
5. McReynolds, rf
6. Seitzer, 3b
7. McFarlane, c
8. Miller, 2b
9. Stillwell, ss

It's not going to cut it. The peak power men will barely crack 20 homers. Brett is 39. McRae, the lone black and the manager's son, is an absymal leadoff man, who made a mighty contribution to the Royals having the lowest OBP from the #1 slot in the AL (and fourth worst in all of baseball).

The only hope that the Royals have is that Jefferies blossoms and can become a legitimate #3 hitter, Joyner goes on a season-long salary drive and hits .320, Miller can actually hit .280 with some walks and bat first or second, and that McRae folds up enough so that his father has no choice but to platoon him with someone like Kirk Gibson (the kid hits lefties OK, but his ,270 OBA against righthanders is just lethal). If all that happens, the Royals might score as many runs in 1992 as they did in 1991.

And, of course, there is no longer a Bret Saberhagen on the Royals pitching staff. No longer a still young (28) ace to anchor a staff that has been erratic and streaky for the past several years. The Royals have traded peak performance, that rarest of commodities, for an abundance of semi-precious stones. They have exchanged two diamond necklaces for seven or eight cultured pearls. Yes, they're better than paste, better than colored glass, but they can't compare to what has been pawned away, bartered and abandoned, tossed aside as if the treasures of the gods rain down upon man in never-ceasing showers. The Royals have sucker-punched themselves, and they don't even know that they're lying face-down on the canvas. Would that happen to every team that decides to fight equipped only with white gloves.

Kansas City Royals Home Park Performance Factors

	Outs	Runs	Hits	2b	3b	HR	W	K	SH	SF	HBP	IBB	SB	CS	GDP
Home LH Batters	1.046	1.158	1.064	1.222	.745	1.486	1.055	1.135	.896	1.002	.970	.959	.970	1.088	1.018
Home RH Batters	.994	1.061	1.003	.998	.771	1.059	.977	1.066	.626	1.652	.823	.991	.871	.934	1.248
All Home Batters	1.019	1.086	1.024	1.054	.757	1.204	.995	1.097	.739	1.099	.856	.962	.917	1.030	1.143
Opp LH Batters	.991	.988	1.004	.922	.886	1.921	1.099	1.074	1.299	1.006	1.006	1.133	.845	1.354	.903
Opp RH Batters	1.077	1.020	1.067	1.037	.655	1.225	1.074	1.075	1.785	1.287	.907	1.129	.976	.878	1.018
All Opp Batters	1.045	1.027	1.063	.998	.811	1.381	1.097	1.067	1.468	1.135	.916	1.131	.945	1.005	.995
All LH Batters	1.017	1.069	1.034	1.050	.825	1.682	1.073	1.103	1.156	.998	.995	1.046	.910	1.232	.963
All RH Batters	1.038	1.038	1.039	1.024	.715	1.146	1.031	1.068	.927	1.452	.868	1.066	.929	.915	1.080
All Batters	1.032	1.055	1.044	1.025	.785	1.287	1.046	1.080	1.009	1.119	.887	1.040	.934	1.020	1.062

Conventional Batting Records for Kansas City Royals

	G	AB	Run	Hit	2B	3B	HR	TB	RBI	W	K	IW	HB	SB	CS	BRng Eff	GI DP	SH	SF	Avg	Slug	OBP	Runs Ctd
Macfarlane	84	267	34	74	18	2	13	135	41	17	52	0	6	1	0	.388	4	1	4	.277	.506	.330	45
Benzinger	78	293	29	86	15	3	2	113	40	17	46	2	3	2	6	.339	5	1	1	.294	.386	.338	36
Shumpert	144	369	45	80	16	4	5	119	34	30	75	0	5	17	11	.593	10	10	3	.217	.322	.283	32
Pecota	125	398	53	114	23	2	6	159	45	41	45	6	2	16	7	.471	12	7	0	.286	.399	.356	56
Stillwell	122	385	44	102	17	1	6	139	51	33	56	5	1	3	4	.455	8	5	4	.265	.361	.322	45
Gibson K	132	462	81	109	17	6	16	186	55	69	103	3	6	18	4	.474	9	1	2	.236	.403	.341	69
McRae B	152	629	86	164	28	9	8	234	64	24	99	1	2	20	11	.594	12	3	5	.261	.372	.288	64
Tartabull	132	484	78	153	35	3	31	287	100	65	121	6	3	6	3	.393	9	0	5	.316	.593	.397	116
Brett	131	505	77	129	40	2	10	203	61	58	75	10	0	2	0	.434	20	1	8	.255	.402	.327	65
Eisenreich	135	375	47	113	22	3	2	147	47	20	35	1	1	5	3	.488	11	3	6	.301	.392	.333	47
Howard D	94	236	20	51	7	0	1	61	17	16	45	0	1	3	2	.382	1	9	2	.216	.258	.267	18
Seitzer	85	234	28	62	11	3	1	82	25	29	21	3	2	4	1	.487	4	1	1	.265	.350	.350	31
Mayne	85	231	22	58	8	0	3	75	31	23	42	4	0	2	4	.361	6	2	3	.251	.325	.315	23
Thurman	80	184	24	51	9	0	2	66	13	11	42	0	1	15	5	.583	4	3	1	.277	.359	.320	21
Cromartie	69	131	13	41	7	2	1	55	20	15	18	0	0	1	3	.414	3	1	1	.313	.420	.381	20
Martinez Crm	44	121	17	25	6	0	4	43	17	27	25	3	0	0	1	.192	4	0	0	.207	.355	.351	16
Spehr	37	74	7	14	5	0	3	28	14	9	18	0	1	1	0	.308	2	3	1	.189	.378	.282	8
Berry	31	60	5	8	3	0	0	11	1	5	23	0	1	0	0	.444	1	0	0	.133	.183	.212	2
Pulliam	18	33	4	9	1	0	3	19	4	3	9	1	0	0	0	1.000	1	1	0	.273	.576	.333	6
Morman	12	23	1	6	0	0	0	6	1	1	5	1	0	0	0	.500	0	0	0	.261	.261	.292	2
Liriano	10	22	5	9	0	0	0	9	1	0	2	0	0	0	1	.625	0	1	0	.409	.409	.409	3
Pedre	10	19	2	5	1	1	0	8	3	3	5	0	0	0	0	.000	0	0	0	.263	.421	.364	3
Puhl	15	18	0	4	0	0	0	4	3	3	2	1	0	0	0	.000	1	0	0	.222	.222	.333	1
Moore R	18	14	3	5	1	0	0	6	0	1	2	0	0	3	2	.429	0	0	0	.357	.429	.400	2
Clark D	11	10	1	2	0	0	0	2	1	1	1	0	0	0	0	.000	0	0	0	.200	.200	.273	1
Cole S	9	7	1	1	0	0	0	1	0	2	2	0	0	0	0	.500	0	0	0	.143	.143	.333	1
Zuvella	2	0	0	0	0	0	0	0	0	0	0	0	0	0	0	.000	0	0	0	.000	.000	.000	0
Gordon	1	0	0	0	0	0	0	0	0	0	0	0	0	0	0	.000	0	0	0	.000	.000	.000	0
TOTALS	1866	5584	727	1475	290	41	117	2198	689	523	969	47	35	119	68	.452	127	53	47	.264	.394	.328	723

Sabermetric Batting Records for Kansas City Royals

	Ball Park Adjusted								Runs		Run/									
	AB	Run	Hit	2B	3B	HR	RBI	W	SO	Avg	Slug	OBP	Ctd	Outs	27o	OW%	OG	OWAR	DWAR	TWAR
Benzinger	302	30	89	15	2	2	42	17	49	.295	.377	.335	36	226	4.30	.480	8	1.09	0.24	1.33
Berry	61	5	8	3	0	0	1	5	24	.131	.180	.197	2	54	1.00	.048	2	-0.60	0.15	-0.45
Brett	515	82	133	42	1	17	66	62	82	.258	.443	.333	75	410	4.94	.549	15	3.03	0.01	3.04
Clark D	10	1	2	0	0	0	1	1	1	.200	.200	.273	1	8	3.38	.363	0	0.00	-0.00	0.00
Cole S	7	1	1	0	0	0	0	2	2	.143	.143	.333	1	6	4.50	.503	0	0.03	-0.00	0.03
Cromartie	133	13	42	7	1	1	21	16	19	.316	.406	.387	21	98	5.79	.626	4	1.00	0.07	1.07
Eisenreich	382	50	116	23	2	3	51	21	38	.304	.398	.335	49	288	4.59	.513	11	1.74	0.02	1.76
Gibson K	471	86	112	18	4	27	59	74	113	.238	.465	.346	81	374	5.85	.631	14	3.89	0.03	3.92
Howard D	243	21	53	7	0	1	18	16	48	.218	.259	.264	18	204	2.38	.221	8	-0.97	0.59	-0.38
Liriano	22	5	9	0	0	0	1	0	2	.409	.409	.409	3	15	5.40	.593	1	0.14	0.06	0.20
Macfarlane	275	35	76	18	1	14	43	17	55	.276	.502	.325	46	209	5.94	.638	8	2.23	0.07	2.30
Martinez Crm	124	17	25	6	0	4	17	27	26	.202	.347	.344	16	103	4.19	.468	4	0.45	0.15	0.60
Mayne	235	23	59	8	0	5	33	24	46	.251	.349	.317	26	190	3.69	.406	7	0.39	0.11	0.50
McRae B	650	90	171	28	7	10	68	25	107	.263	.374	.289	67	510	3.55	.386	19	0.68	0.86	1.54
Moore R	14	3	5	1	0	0	0	1	2	.357	.429	.400	2	10	5.40	.593	0	0.09	0.03	0.12
Morman	23	1	6	0	0	0	1	1	5	.261	.261	.292	2	17	3.18	.335	1	-0.01	0.03	0.03
Pecota	412	55	118	23	1	6	47	42	48	.286	.391	.354	56	321	4.71	.526	12	2.09	0.80	2.89
Pedre	19	2	5	1	0	0	3	3	5	.263	.316	.364	2	14	3.86	.427	1	0.04	-0.03	0.01
Puhl	18	0	4	0	0	0	3	3	2	.222	.222	.333	2	14	3.86	.427	1	0.04	-0.00	0.04
Pulliam	33	4	9	1	0	3	4	3	9	.273	.576	.333	6	26	6.23	.660	1	0.30	0.02	0.32
Seitzer	242	29	64	11	2	1	26	29	22	.264	.339	.344	30	184	4.40	.492	7	0.97	0.16	1.13
Shumpert	381	46	82	16	2	5	35	30	80	.215	.307	.277	32	335	2.58	.250	12	-1.25	0.73	-0.52
Spehr	76	7	14	5	0	3	14	9	19	.184	.368	.267	8	68	3.18	.335	3	-0.04	0.03	-0.01
Stillwell	398	46	106	17	0	7	54	34	60	.266	.362	.321	46	313	3.97	.440	12	1.05	0.33	1.38
Tartabull	500	81	158	35	2	35	105	66	129	.316	.604	.393	121	361	9.05	.804	13	6.07	-0.32	5.75
Thurman	189	24	52	9	0	2	13	11	44	.275	.354	.313	21	149	3.81	.420	6	0.39	0.24	0.63
Zuvella	0	0	0	0	0	0	0	0	0	.000	.000	.000	0	0	0.00	.000	0	0.00	0.00	0.00
TOTALS	5778	768	1539	297	32	151	733	547	1048	.266	.407	.330	774	4553	4.59	.513	169	27.48	4.40	31.88

Pitching Records for Kansas City Royals

	ERA	W	L	Pct	G	GS	CG	ShO	GF	Sv	IP	R	ER	H	2B	3B	HR	BB	IW	SO	HB	WP	BK
Appier	3.42	13	10	.565	34	31	6	3	1	0	207.2	97	79	205	41	1	13	61	3	158	2	7	1
Saberhagen	3.07	13	8	.619	28	28	7	2	0	0	196.1	76	67	165	28	4	12	45	5	136	9	8	1
Boddicker	4.08	12	12	.500	30	29	1	0	1	0	180.2	89	82	188	41	7	13	59	0	79	13	3	2
Gubicza	5.68	9	12	.429	26	26	0	0	0	0	133.0	90	84	168	27	3	10	42	1	89	6	5	0
Wagner H	7.20	1	1	.500	2	2	0	0	0	0	10.0	10	8	16	5	0	2	3	0	5	0	0	0
Gordon	3.87	9	14	.391	45	14	1	0	11	1	158.0	76	68	129	16	8	16	87	6	167	4	5	0
Aquino	3.44	8	4	.667	38	18	1	1	9	3	157.0	67	60	152	33	5	10	47	5	80	4	1	0
Davis Storm	4.96	3	9	.250	51	9	1	1	22	2	114.1	69	63	140	21	3	11	46	9	53	1	1	0
Montgomery	2.90	4	4	.500	67	0	0	0	55	33	90.0	32	29	83	15	2	6	28	2	77	2	6	0
Davis Mrk	4.45	6	3	.667	29	5	0	0	8	1	62.2	36	31	55	11	1	6	39	0	47	1	1	0
Magnante	2.45	0	1	.000	38	0	0	0	10	0	55.0	19	15	55	15	1	3	23	3	42	0	1	0
Crawford	5.98	3	2	.600	33	0	0	0	17	1	46.2	31	31	60	8	4	3	18	5	38	1	5	0
Johnston	0.40	1	0	1.000	13	0	0	0	1	0	22.1	1	1	9	1	0	0	9	3	21	0	0	0
McGaffigan	4.50	0	0	.000	4	0	0	0	1	0	8.0	5	4	14	2	1	0	2	0	3	0	0	0
Maldonado C	8.22	0	0	.000	5	0	0	0	2	0	7.2	9	7	11	3	0	0	9	1	1	0	4	0
Schatzeder	9.45	0	0	.000	8	0	0	0	2	0	6.2	9	7	11	3	0	0	7	1	4	0	0	0
Gardner W	1.59	0	0	.000	3	0	0	0	2	0	5.2	4	1	5	0	1	0	2	0	3	0	0	0
Pecota	4.50	0	0	.000	1	0	0	0	1	0	2.0	1	1	4	1	1	0	0	0	0	0	0	0
Corbin	3.86	0	0	.000	2	0	0	0	2	0	2.1	1	1	3	0	0	0	2	0	1	0	0	1
TOTALS	3.92	82	80	.506	457	162	17	7	145	41	1466.0	722	639	1473	271	42	105	529	44	1004	43	47	5

Sabermetric Pitching Records for Kansas City Royals

	Adj	|-Expected-|			|------	Opposing	Batters	------|									Supported				
	ERA	W	L	Pct	BFP	Avg	Slg	OBA	RC/G	GDP	SB	CS	PK	PKE	SH	SF	RSup	RSp/G	W	L	Pct
Appier	3.60	13	10	.564	881	.255	.357	.307	3.86	12	10	8	0	1	8	6	109	4.72	15	8	.633
Aquino	3.61	7	5	.562	661	.253	.374	.308	4.05	9	10	6	1	2	2	7	88	5.04	8	4	.661
Boddicker	4.28	11	13	.477	775	.272	.408	.340	4.70	18	17	10	2	3	10	1	90	4.48	13	11	.523
Corbin	3.86	0	0	.529	12	.300	.300	.417	5.73	0	0	0	0	0	0	0	4	15.43	0	0	.941
Crawford	6.17	2	3	.305	216	.311	.440	.367	6.57	1	9	2	0	0	1	3	23	4.44	2	3	.341
Davis Mrk	4.60	4	5	.442	276	.240	.376	.347	4.57	6	4	3	0	1	2	5	30	4.31	4	5	.468
Davis Storm	5.20	5	7	.382	515	.306	.437	.367	5.64	16	2	2	0	0	6	4	55	4.33	5	7	.410
Gardner W	1.59	0	0	.869	26	.217	.304	.280	3.37	0	0	0	0	0	0	0	0	0.00	0	0	.000
Gordon	4.04	12	11	.505	684	.221	.357	.324	4.12	8	9	7	0	0	5	3	70	3.99	11	12	.493
Gubicza	5.95	7	14	.320	601	.308	.424	.361	5.67	14	18	6	0	2	3	5	63	4.26	7	14	.339
Johnston	0.40	1	0	.990	85	.120	.133	.214	1.02	1	1	1	0	0	1	0	14	5.64	1	0	.995
Magnante	2.45	1	0	.735	236	.262	.386	.333	4.39	5	1	2	0	0	2	1	32	5.24	1	0	.820
Maldonado C	8.22	0	0	.198	43	.333	.424	.476	8.77	1	0	0	0	0	1	0	2	2.35	0	0	.075
McGaffigan	4.50	0	0	.452	39	.389	.500	.410	7.71	2	0	0	0	0	0	1	8	9.00	0	0	.800
Montgomery	3.00	5	3	.650	376	.246	.355	.305	3.78	7	4	0	0	0	6	2	30	3.00	4	4	.500
Pecota	4.50	0	0	.452	9	.444	.778	.444	10.58	1	0	0	0	0	0	0	2	9.00	0	0	.800
Saberhagen	3.21	13	8	.619	789	.228	.327	.280	2.98	14	9	9	4	3	8	3	94	4.31	14	7	.643
Schatzeder	9.45	0	0	.158	37	.367	.467	.486	9.26	2	0	0	0	0	0	0	2	2.70	0	0	.075
Wagner H	7.20	0	2	.244	49	.348	.587	.388	9.20	1	0	0	0	0	0	0	11	9.90	1	1	.654
TOTALS	4.14	80	82	.494	6310	.261	.380	.327	4.35	118	94	56	7	12	55	41	727	4.46	87	75	.538

Batting 'Splits' Records for Kansas City Royals

	G	AB	Run	Hit	2B	3B	HR	TB	RBI	W	K	IW	HB	SB	CS	GIDP	SH	SF	Avg	Slug	OBP	Runs Ctd
SPLITS for Brett																						
vs LHP	90	167	16	39	12	1	2	59	18	20	28	0	0	1	0	10	0	4	.234	.353	.309	17
vs RHP	117	338	61	90	28	1	8	144	43	38	47	10	0	1	0	10	1	4	.266	.426	.337	49
Home	62	243	32	60	19	2	3	92	27	30	33	4	0	2	0	9	0	3	.247	.379	.326	30
Away	69	262	45	69	21	0	7	111	34	28	42	6	0	0	0	11	1	5	.263	.424	.329	35
Grass	54	211	34	53	18	0	5	86	26	19	32	3	0	0	0	11	0	3	.251	.408	.309	24
Turf	77	294	43	76	22	2	5	117	35	39	43	7	0	2	0	9	1	5	.259	.398	.340	41
April/June	46	181	25	45	14	0	2	65	23	20	28	4	0	0	0	2	0	2	.249	.359	.320	22
July/October	85	324	52	84	26	2	8	138	38	38	47	6	0	2	0	18	1	6	.259	.426	.332	43
SPLITS for Eisenreich																						
vs LHP	58	87	13	28	2	1	1	35	16	4	12	0	1	1	1	1	1	2	.322	.402	.351	13
vs RHP	114	288	34	85	20	2	1	112	31	16	23	1	0	4	2	10	2	4	.295	.389	.328	35
Home	69	193	25	60	9	2	2	79	25	9	14	1	1	3	3	6	3	5	.311	.409	.337	25
Away	66	182	22	53	13	1	0	68	22	11	21	0	0	2	0	5	0	1	.291	.374	.330	22
Grass	51	145	19	44	12	0	0	56	16	7	18	0	0	2	0	3	0	1	.303	.386	.333	19
Turf	84	230	28	69	10	3	2	91	31	13	17	1	1	3	3	8	3	5	.300	.396	.333	29
April/June	63	211	20	64	14	1	1	83	20	10	22	0	1	2	2	4	1	1	.303	.393	.336	27
July/October	72	164	27	49	8	2	1	64	27	10	13	1	0	3	1	7	2	5	.299	.390	.330	20
SPLITS for McRae B																						
vs LHP	89	204	30	60	13	2	2	83	19	9	16	1	1	7	1	5	1	1	.294	.407	.326	27
vs RHP	136	425	56	104	15	7	6	151	45	15	83	0	1	13	10	7	2	4	.245	.355	.270	38
Home	78	318	46	85	16	6	3	122	29	17	52	1	2	10	5	5	2	4	.267	.384	.305	37
Away	74	311	40	79	12	3	5	112	35	7	47	0	0	10	6	7	1	1	.254	.360	.270	27
Grass	55	237	31	64	9	3	3	88	25	3	33	0	0	8	5	7	1	1	.270	.371	.278	21
Turf	97	392	55	100	19	6	5	146	39	21	66	1	2	12	6	5	2	4	.255	.372	.294	43
April/June	69	272	38	69	9	4	4	98	32	14	45	1	0	8	7	6	1	3	.254	.360	.287	26
July/October	83	357	48	95	19	5	4	136	32	10	54	0	2	12	4	6	2	2	.266	.381	.288	38
SPLITS for Kansas City Royals (all batters except pitchers)																						
vs LHP	954	1820	226	481	95	11	36	706	211	171	297	12	14	37	19	46	22	12	.264	.388	.330	233
vs RHP	1498	3764	501	994	195	30	81	1492	478	352	672	35	21	82	49	81	31	35	.264	.396	.328	490
Home	937	2767	344	732	143	29	47	1074	328	273	437	25	22	67	32	54	36	23	.265	.388	.333	367
Away	929	2817	383	743	147	12	70	1124	361	250	532	22	13	52	36	73	17	24	.264	.399	.324	357
Grass	705	2154	299	572	115	7	59	878	284	182	412	17	9	35	26	57	16	22	.266	.408	.322	276
Turf	1161	3430	428	903	175	34	58	1320	405	341	557	30	26	84	42	70	37	25	.263	.385	.332	448
April/June	799	2516	323	648	122	15	59	977	311	220	431	22	9	48	27	49	21	20	.258	.388	.317	311
July/October	1067	3068	404	827	168	26	58	1221	378	303	538	25	26	71	41	78	32	27	.270	.398	.338	412

1991 SPLITS FOR Kansas City Royals

BATTING SPLITS

	AVG	AB	R	H	2B	3B	HR	RBI	SB	CS	BB	K	OBA	SPCT
Total	.264	5584	727	1475	290	41	117	689	119	68	523	969	.328	.394

	#Pit	#P/PA	GB	FB	G/F	G	IBB	HB	SH	SF	GDP
Miscellaneous	22830	3.66	2052	1568	1.31	162	47	35	53	47	127

	AVG	AB	R	H	2B	3B	HR	RBI	SB	CS	BB	K	OBA	SPCT
vs. Left	.264	1820	...	481	95	11	36	211	37	19	171	297	.330	.388
vs. Right	.264	3764	...	994	195	30	81	478	82	49	352	672	.328	.396
Home	.265	2767	344	732	143	29	47	328	67	32	273	437	.333	.388
Away	.264	2817	383	743	147	12	70	361	52	36	250	532	.324	.399
None on	.258	3173	...	819	176	22	65	65	0	0	253	575	.317	.389
Runners on	.272	2411	...	656	114	19	52	624	119	68	270	394	.343	.400
April	.250	637	70	159	34	5	9	68	9	5	45	126	.299	.361
May	.247	897	103	222	37	5	20	98	24	11	82	148	.313	.367
June	.272	982	150	267	51	5	30	145	15	11	93	157	.333	.426
July	.303	945	157	286	55	7	24	148	26	15	93	143	.368	.452
August	.263	972	110	256	56	13	15	101	24	15	91	174	.328	.394
September	.244	979	117	239	48	5	15	110	19	9	106	178	.320	.349
October	.267	172	20	46	9	1	4	19	2	2	13	43	.324	.401
None on/out	.271	1410	...	382	88	15	38	38	0	0	97	259	.323	.435
Scoring Posn	.290	1412	...	409	73	12	30	554	23	14	209	257	.374	.422
Close & Late	.236	938	...	221	37	12	15	91	15	13	114	174	.319	.349
Bases Loaded	.282	124	...	35	6	1	7	109	0	0	5	21	.286	.516
Batting #1	.267	705	89	188	34	5	7	59	32	15	44	113	.311	.359
Batting #2	.273	670	108	183	37	8	12	81	16	10	58	113	.337	.406
Batting #3	.266	646	96	172	47	4	14	79	5	0	72	104	.336	.416
Batting #4	.304	624	101	190	39	3	33	114	11	4	80	132	.382	.535
Batting #5	.270	636	75	172	37	5	12	87	9	11	54	88	.328	.401
Batting #6	.278	608	72	169	21	7	10	79	16	5	61	91	.349	.385
Batting #7	.255	581	64	148	34	1	12	72	4	3	52	104	.317	.379
Batting #8	.232	569	62	132	20	2	9	62	8	10	55	117	.300	.322
Batting #9	.222	545	60	121	21	6	8	56	18	10	47	107	.287	.327
As p	.000	1	0	0	0	0	0	0	0	0	0	0	.000	.000
As c	.254	552	61	140	29	3	18	82	4	4	51	109	.319	.415
As 1b	.272	610	66	166	32	5	4	73	3	12	60	92	.339	.361
As 2b	.224	505	58	113	20	4	5	46	20	13	44	102	.292	.309
As 3b	.260	578	76	150	30	4	7	56	17	5	62	76	.335	.362
As ss	.258	565	59	146	24	1	6	67	6	6	43	82	.310	.336
As lf	.269	629	96	169	28	7	13	68	22	8	64	116	.342	.397
As cf	.272	703	95	191	39	9	8	73	23	13	26	107	.297	.387
As rf	.316	618	96	195	41	3	34	122	12	5	79	140	.391	.557
Outfield	.285	1950	287	555	108	19	55	263	57	26	169	363	.343	.444
0.0 count	.317	791	...	251	57	6	24	132	...	...	3	0	.324	.496
After (0.1)	.233	2519	...	586	113	14	42	248	...	...	117	619	.269	.339
After (1.0)	.281	2274	...	638	120	21	51	309	...	...	370	350	.381	.419
Two strikes	.200	2493	...	498	92	6	38	218	...	...	217	968	.266	.287
Grass	.266	2154	299	572	115	7	59	284	35	26	182	412	.322	.408
Turf	.263	3430	428	903	175	34	58	405	84	42	341	557	.332	.385
Day	.258	1626	204	419	84	11	34	192	30	14	148	293	.320	.386
Night	.267	3958	523	1056	206	30	83	497	89	54	375	676	.332	.397
Inning 1.6	.269	3714	508	1000	205	24	78	484	90	49	326	633	.330	.400
Inning 7+	.254	1870	219	475	85	17	39	205	29	19	197	336	.326	.380
vs.Bal	.284	464	71	132	30	5	11	67	10	5	43	76	.342	.442
vs.Bos	.235	379	34	89	25	5	3	31	10	5	36	78	.305	.351
vs.Cal	.260	438	51	114	25	1	8	47	11	5	47	88	.333	.377
vs.ChA	.245	424	55	104	21	3	12	54	5	6	33	64	.302	.394
vs.Cle	.247	401	36	99	16	4	4	35	7	5	17	73	.276	.337
vs.Det	.290	421	70	122	19	4	14	67	9	5	38	58	.346	.454
vs.Mil	.294	415	57	122	17	0	10	55	10	6	41	64	.363	.407
vs.Min	.257	444	53	114	21	4	7	50	16	3	41	77	.320	.369
vs.NYA	.277	422	59	117	31	5	10	56	7	2	31	78	.330	.445
vs.Oak	.293	457	79	134	21	3	16	76	4	8	40	80	.352	.457
vs.Sea	.245	436	49	107	21	3	6	46	9	3	50	71	.330	.349
vs.Tex	.261	467	71	122	23	1	12	67	9	7	60	91	.343	.392
vs.Tor	.238	416	42	99	20	3	4	38	12	8	46	71	.317	.329

PITCHING SPLITS

	ERA	W	L	SV	SVOP	GS	CG	SHO	IP	H	ER	HR	BB	IBB	K
Total	3.92	82	80	41	53	162	17	9	1466.0	1473	639	105	529	44	1004

	#Pit	#P/IP	GB	FB	G/F	BRp9	RA	WP	BK	SH	SF	R	HB	Hld
Miscellaneous	23564	16.07	2101	1586	1.32	12.55	295	47	5	55	41	722	43	23

	ERA	W	L	SV	SVOP	GS	CG	SHO	IP	H	ER	HR	BB	IBB	K
ST	3.98	63	59	0	0	162	17	7	1002.2	990	443	75	327	13	638
REL	3.81	19	21	41	53	0	0	0	463.1	483	196	30	202	31	366
Home	3.92	40	41	17	24	81	8	2	765.0	746	333	40	257	21	513
Away	3.93	42	39	24	29	81	9	5	701.0	727	306	65	272	23	491
April	3.66	8	11	5	5	19	2	1	167.0	166	68	15	53	2	104
May	3.74	13	14	5	7	27	6	0	238.0	228	99	12	79	5	145
June	4.47	12	15	8	13	27	2	1	255.2	282	127	20	95	4	164
July	4.40	16	10	9	9	26	0	0	241.1	263	118	20	92	14	180
August	2.64	18	11	7	10	29	5	4	266.0	234	78	13	83	11	192
September	4.54	14	15	7	9	29	2	1	256.0	263	129	20	107	5	187
October	4.29	1	4	0	0	5	0	0	42.0	37	20	5	20	3	32
Grass	3.96	31	31	19	23	62	6	5	534.2	557	235	55	211	15	371
Turf	3.90	51	49	22	30	100	11	2	931.1	916	404	50	318	29	633
Day	3.84	23	23	12	16	46	4	2	419.0	420	179	37	167	12	305
Night	3.95	59	57	29	37	116	13	5	1047.0	1053	460	68	362	32	699
vs.Bal	3.86	8	4	4	7	12	0	0	119.0	125	51	11	42	6	79
vs.Bos	2.71	5	7	2	3	12	1	1	103.0	89	31	9	42	4	62
vs.Cal	4.74	4	9	2	2	13	0	0	112.0	125	59	8	35	2	87
vs.ChA	4.94	6	7	2	2	13	3	2	113.0	120	62	7	44	1	71
vs.Cle	2.11	8	4	4	4	12	4	2	111.0	100	26	5	14	0	77
vs.Det	5.63	4	8	2	2	12	0	0	104.0	115	65	15	56	5	98
vs.Mil	3.76	9	3	8	9	12	1	0	110.0	114	46	5	27	1	66
vs.Min	4.15	6	7	2	2	13	2	0	115.0	117	53	8	32	2	65
vs.NYA	3.58	7	5	3	3	12	1	1	108.0	99	43	5	40	4	65
vs.Oak	4.30	6	7	2	4	13	1	1	113.0	111	54	12	65	4	77
vs.Sea	4.39	7	6	2	4	13	4	0	119.0	107	58	8	49	2	76
vs.Tex	3.48	7	6	5	8	13	0	0	126.2	127	49	8	48	4	98
vs.Tor	3.36	5	7	3	3	12	0	0	112.1	124	42	4	35	9	83

OPPOSING BATTERS VS. PITCHERS.

	AVG	AB	R	H	2B	3B	HR	RBI	SB	CS	BB	K	OBA	SPCT
Total	.261	5640	722	1473	271	42	105	672	94	56	529	1004	.327	.380
vs. Left	.279	2699	...	753	142	28	46	343	43	30	267	434	.344	.403
vs. Right	.245	2941	...	720	129	14	59	329	51	26	262	570	.311	.358
ST	.258	3838	496	990	188	28	75	428	64	47	327	638	.320	.380
REL	.268	1802	226	483	83	14	30	244	30	9	202	366	.342	.380
Home	.255	2927	378	746	150	29	40	345	54	31	257	513	.319	.367
Away	.268	2713	344	727	121	13	65	327	40	25	272	491	.336	.394
None on	.254	3143	...	798	159	25	54	54	0	0	272	563	.317	.372
Runners on	.270	2497	...	675	112	17	51	618	94	56	257	441	.339	.390
None on/out	.251	1378	...	346	73	10	21	21	0	0	113	223	.312	.364
Scoring Posn	.262	1473	...	386	67	13	27	541	17	10	178	283	.340	.380
vs 1st Batr	.268	257	...	69	17	2	4	44	6	3	31	48	.355	.397
1st IP	.264	1605	204	423	84	12	19	226	34	16	191	293	.342	.366
Inning 1.6	.259	3716	483	961	185	28	75	459	62	47	343	633	.324	.384
Inning 7+	.266	1924	239	512	86	14	30	213	32	9	186	371	.333	.372
Close & Late	.254	934	...	237	31	4	15	106	18	7	86	185	.321	.344
0.0 count	.348	788	...	274	47	8	23	127	...	...	42	0	.384	.515
After (0.1)	.230	2500	...	574	97	16	42	273	...	...	141	636	.275	.332
After (1.0)	.266	2352	...	625	127	18	40	272	...	...	346	368	.360	.386
Two strikes	.193	2594	...	501	96	12	28	217	...	...	215	1004	.258	.272
Pitch 1.15	.265	1366	...	362	74	11	17	143	24	15	149	225	.340	.373
Pitch 16.30	.248	1132	...	281	56	5	14	142	21	6	126	238	.325	.344
Pitch 31.45	.260	831	...	216	36	6	17	105	15	8	76	145	.323	.379
Pitch 46.60	.277	696	...	193	35	7	18	97	13	9	58	104	.335	.425
Pitch 61.75	.267	607	...	162	29	7	14	69	5	7	40	111	.317	.407
Pitch 76.90	.268	481	...	129	21	3	11	63	7	7	37	81	.323	.393
Pitch 91.105	.243	334	...	81	12	2	7	33	6	4	26	56	.304	.353
Pitch 106.20	.250	160	...	40	8	0	6	20	3	0	14	33	.313	.412
Pitch 121.35	.286	35	...	10	1	1	1	3	0	0	3	10	.359	.457
Pitch 136.50	.000	2	...	0	0	0	0	0	0	0	0	1	.000	.000

California Angels

Don Malcolm and Brock J. Hanke

CALIFORNIA YEAR	1982	1983	1984	1985	1986	1987	1988	1989	1990	1991	TOT
W	93	70	81	90	92	75	75	91	80	81	828
L	69	92	81	72	70	87	87	71	82	81	792
WPCT	0.574	0.432	0.500	0.556	0.568	0.463	0.463	0.562	0.494	0.500	0.511
R	814	722	696	732	786	770	714	669	690	653	7246
RA	670	779	697	703	684	803	771	578	706	649	7040
PWPT	0.596	0.462	0.499	0.520	0.569	0.479	0.462	0.573	0.489	0.503	0.514
PythW	97	75	81	84	92	78	75	93	79	81	83
PythL	65	87	81	78	70	84	87	69	83	81	79
LUCK	-4	-5	0	6	0	-3	0	-2	1	0	-7

Defensive Efficiency Record: .7053

WHAT'S IN STORE FROM WHITEY
or A WALK THROUGH A MASTER'S METHODS

Yes, this is Brock again, slipping in my comment beofre Don Malcolm gets his. Or, rather, before I get mine; just wait until you read Don's comment. At any rate, the reason for this is that Don writes these art comments. I ask him to. I like his work, and I think it's important that sabermetricians get used to something other than dry exposition. Besides, I'd never have thought of comparing Darryl Strawberry to a film noir heroine. "Leggy and fragile" indeed. I also like the metaphor of Whitey Herzog in Disneyland, having been dragged off the Matterhorn ride by someone he's "wedded" to in some metaphorical way....

Now, on the subject of Whitey. Those of you who got the 1989 BASEBALL ABSTRACT will recall a Whitey Herzog Manager's Box I wrote therein. A lot of this will be a repeat of a lot of that. Why should Whitey have changed, anyway? For those of you who haven't got that book, the thesis of the box was that Whitey Herzog did have a type of team and an approach to winning that he maneuvered to acquire and activate. You all in Anaheim are going to get to see that now, and so I thought I'd give you some advance notice. By the way, there's nothig here about stealing bases. That was a sideshow for Whitey, an adaptation to the St. Louis ballpark. Your stadium does not encourace it.

First, keep track of the walks column in your offense. For the entire reign of Herzog in St. Louis, the team that won the NL East always led the division in walks taken. Always. When the Phillies won, they brought in Joe Morgan and Pete Rose to add to Mike Scmidt and Von Hayes. When the Mets won, they developed Howard Johnson to go with Darryl Strawberry and Keith Hernandez. Essentially, Whitey forced you to beat him at his own game.

In that light, the trade for the aforementioned Hayes makes perfect sense. The Angels don't get on base. They will do more of that now. Hayes, if he has nothing else left, still takes walks. Look it up in the Phillie stats. It'll give you practice. You're going to have to keep close track of that column if you're going to make sense of any of Whitey's moves.

Aside from trying to lead the league in walks, Whitey tries to keep his offense balanced. I did a chart in the 1989 box, tracking all of Whitey's lineups by offensive emphasis. What I mean by emphasis is that many players have one thing they do very well, much better than they do anything else. For example, Lance Parrish has power and nothing else left. Von Hayes gets on base. Junior Felix hits for a high batting average. In the National League, Whitey always had:

2 on base men (Tommy Herr)
2 power men (Jack Clark)
2 batting average men (Willie McGee)
1 complete hitter (Keith Hernandez)
1 defensive specialist (Ozzie Smith)

I assume that the American League will induce Whitey to get one more complete hitter, not another power man who doesn't get on base. It's worth noting that, when Whitey won, it was often because the defensive specialist contributed something to the offense. It's also worth noting that some players can have two offensive emphases, because they do two things well. When Tommy Herr, for example, was hitting .280 or .300, he could be an on base man or a batting average man. In general, the on base men batted first and second, while the batting average men tended to bat fifth and sixth, where they could drive in runs from scoring position, rather than wasting the opportunity with a walk.

Right now, the Angels have the following men with emphases: Von Hayes and Donnie Hill get on base. Lance Parrish and Gary Gaetti have power. Luis Polonia and Junior Felix hit for high averages.

Note that I pencil in Donnie Hill ahead of Luis Sojo. That's because Dick Schofield is the defensive specialist and Whitey will have only one. Sojo does not have an offensive emphasis. He's a midding hitter with no power, and he doesn't take walks. I don't think he'll play, unless Buck Rodgers overrides Whitey. One thing Whitey will not abide is a guy who has no offensive specialty at all. You know the type, if you think about it. He hits .265 or .270. He takes some walks, but not much more than average. He hits 8-14 homers. In the entire time Whitey was with the Cardinals, he had only one hitter of that type. It was Mike Heath, who Whitey was trying to make into a power hitter. When that failed after one year, Heath was gone. That's one reason I don't think Hubie Brooks will start.

If you look, you'll see that this leaves two big fat screaming holes under complete hitter. What Whitey had in mind, of course, was Bobby Bonilla and Wally Joyner. Not having them means that the Angels don't have a real offense. I don't know what Whitey will do about that. He's got Lee Stevens, who might solve one problem for him. He's got Hubie Brooks, but I think Hubie was acquired as a backup and injury filler, not a projected starter. I know this: Whitey's not through trading.

But what will he trade? Well, get used to it, Angel fans, Whitey Herzog has no repsect for top starting pitching. The best starters he's ever had were Dennis Leonard and John Tudor. He's never been afraid to trade starters. You guys could lose that rotation to get the hitters. What I think is that Whitey does not like to put too many apples in one basket. He doesn't like to concentrate too much of his team's quality in one fragile arm. He gets top relief closers because he must, to compete. Especially, he must if he's not going to get top starters. Brian Harvey is not going anywhere, as you know from his new contract. Langston, Abbott, and Finley are different questions.

The key to a Whitey team, though, is the bench. It's going to be organized, and it's going to get on base. It will have a lefty and a righty primary pinch hitter (Hubie Brooks, if you're lucky). It's going to have a reserve second/third baseman who can get on. It's going to have a good glove spare shortstop. And it's going to have the dreaded third string catcher. This is one of Whitey's most humorous - and effective - ploys. What he does is find a good defensive infielder who can't hit enough to start. In St. Louis, the men were Tom Lawless and then Tim Jones. There are rumors here that he's going to try to trade for Jones. If he does, be aware that he sent Jones to instructional league to learn to catch. He's the spare part. The third string catcher. If Whitey doesn't get Jones, he'll get one of your infielders to learn to catch. Whitey is that organized.

The pitching bench will be like that, too. The staff will probably be 11 men, six righties and five lefties, or vice versa, depending on the starters. (Note: the starters will be either two left and three right or vice versa. Whitey will have blaance that way.) One lefty and one righty will be closers, including Harvey. One lefty and one righty will be there specifically for their curveballs. They will be specialists in getting one man of the same hand out. Ricky Horton did that for years in St. Louis. He had a wicked lefty sinker curve, and could retire Darryl Strawberry and Keith Hernandez any time he wanted. But Kevin McReynolds must have hit .600 against him.

The other thing you should be aware of is Whitey's plan for player development. When a player first comes to the Angels from the farm system, keep track of what his job is. If he's put on the bench, that's Whitey's way of saying that he's never going to be a starter in the Major Leagues, at least not in Whitey's assessment. If he starts immediately, Whitey thinks he can. This is very strong. If Whitey bring a man up for just an injury replacement, and then leaves him on the bench when the injured starter returns, then the replacement has been written off as a career starter.

Here's how strong this is: when Vince Coleman came up to the Cardinals, it was to hold the fort while Lonnie Smith was on the Injured Reserve for a few weeks. When Lonnie came back, Vince had shown enough that Whitey thought he could start in the Majors. So Whitey traded Lonnie Smith! That's how strong this is. Whitey will not keep a starter on the bench. He'll start, either on the Angels or in the minors.

So to review:

1. The Angels will have two of each batting specialty and one defensive man who does not need to hit to keep his job.

2. As an offensive team, the Angels will take walks and get on base. Thus the "walk" through Whitey's methods.

3. The pitching staff will have right/left balance.

4. There will be a top closer.

5. The bench will be organized, balanced and well defined, down to the last man on the roster, who will be able to catch.

6. There will be people for very specialized roles, down to retiring one hitter or backing up one starting spot.

7. If there is someone just up from the minors, he'll be doing on the Angels what Whitey thinks he'll be doing as a career in the Major Leagues. The only exception is if he's filling in for an injury. Then, you'll find out when the starter returns.

Oh, one more thing. You've seen it already. Whitey Herzog is not afraid to lose a trade to win the division title. There is no doubt that he lost the Kyle Abbott deal, in terms of player value. But Von Hayes gets on base, and Whitey needs that. Besides, Whitey has no respect for starters. The trade was typical, typical Whitey. There will be more. Judge the man by whether he wins, not by how he does it.

And now, speaking of judging men and their karma, here's Don Malcolm....

HANKE AND MALCOLM IN DISNEYLAND

Hanke: Well, Don, I told you so.

Malcolm: Now, wait a minute, Dev. I told you so. I told you that the Rooster would get axed.

Hanke: The Angels need the Mule.

Malcolm: Do you think our readers remember anything about the Mule?

Hanke: They better. Not too many four-legged Babe Ruths running around loose in real life.

Malcolm: If only teams could make up fictitious four-legged Babe Ruths, and play them....

Hanke: It would solve Whitey's biggest problem. No cleanup hitter.

Malcolm: Not to mention no number three hitter.

Hanke: They don't want to sign with the Angels.

Malcolm: Why not?

Hanke: Bad karma.

Malcolm: That's what I said about the Royals last year. Is there some superabundance of malevolent spiritual essence that has become circumambient in baseball?

Hanke: Jeez, can you crank out the six-bit words. That fifth straight trip on the Pirates of the Caribbean seems to gotten you out of kilter.

Malcolm: No, it was the three straight times on Mr. Toad's Wild Ride that put me over the edge. Besides, my mom says that my first words as an infant were polysyllabic. I've always talked funny.

Hanke: It's bad karma—Jackie Autry has created a malevolent spiritual essence that is circumnavigating the Big A. Two can play at that polysyllabic stuff, kemosabe.

Malcolm: So who the hell will Whitey bat third?

Hanke: Well, technically speaking, it ain't Whitey's decision, it's Buck Rodgers. I think that old Buck will probably swallow real hard, and then—very gingerly—write in the name of Von Hayes.

Malcolm: He had a very bad year.

Hanke: It wasn't too vintage. And Whitey got burned a bit on that trade, I think, because he expected to re-sign McCaskill. He let Kyle Abbott get away in that deal, and now the fourth starter has to be chosen from a bunch of real porkers.

Malcolm: Cliff Young.

Hanke: Mike Fetters.

Malcolm: Scott Lewis.

Hanke: Joe Grahe.

Malcolm: How low can you go, Dev, how low can you go?

Hanke: It's bad karma, Don. It's like being trapped in an elevator with someone who hasn't bathed in six months. Every second is an eternity, every minute a millennium!!

Malcolm: I think that the trip on the Matterhorn sort of crossed several of your wires, big guy.

Hanke: Don't stop me now, Don, I'm all cranked up!!

Malcolm: So what are we going to tell the authorities when they come fish us out of the Matterhorn pond that you jumped into—

Hanke: Excuse me. I didn't jump, I was pushed.

Malcolm: Pushed? Out of a seat belt?? This sounds like one of your infamous fabulations.

Hanke: It was bad karma, Don, bad karma. And that's fabrications, not fabulations. Those six bit words are going to be the death of you yet...

Malcolm: But why did you pull me out of the car too?

Hanke: Sabermetricians got to stick together. They're a vanishing breed.

Malcolm: So listen, Mr. Bad Karma, while we wait for the guys in white suits, who is Whitey going to play this season?

Hanke: You mean—

Malcolm: OK, OK: who is Buck going to play?

Hanke: Well, it'll be another dreary year of Lance Parrish behind the plate. It looks like Lee Stevens will get another chance at first, since Joyner flew the coop.

Malcolm: Think he'll make it this time?

Hanke: He's no Joyner, but he might hit 20 homers. It'll be the same crew in the rest of the infield: Sojo at second, Schofield at short, Gaetti at third.

Malcolm: How does that infield stack up defensively?

Hanke: It's very good. Sojo and Gaetti are near the top at their positions in range factor, and Schofield is quite competent. Finley and Abbott didn't win eighteen games apiece last year on their high heaters, you know.

Malcolm: So what about the outfield?

Hanke: Figure on an outfield of Polonia in left, Felix in center, and Hubie Brooks in right.

Malcolm: What is likely to DH? Hayes?

Hanke: Yeah. Here they come. They don't look too happy with us.

Malcolm: Who?

Hanke: The guys in the white suits. (loudly) Why'd you push me in, Don?

Malcolm: Wh—I didn't—why, you—

Attendants: OK, boys, let's get out of the water now. This isn't Wet and Wild.

Hanke: (wailing loudly) Why did you do it, Don? Why?

Malcolm: (glowering at Hanke as they are escorted out of the pond and down to the Disneyland police station) Bad karma, Dev. Bad karma.

Hi. Brock here again for a quick comment on Don's trip. First, for those of you who don't know, my nickname is Dev. It's a long story, but Don knows me by that name, not Brock. Second, there are a couple of things I don't agree with here that Don wrote in for me. First, I don't think the Kyle Abbott trade was a disaster. See my reasoning above. And second, I think Von Hayes is slated for the outfield, possibly center. Hayes can still field, and Luis Polonia is not very good at that, no matter how fast he can run. The Angels are strong in infield defense, but weak in the outfield. Polonia may well be the DH. Or maybe Hubie Brooks, who may have to be started. But I doubt Hayes. Anyway, all that's a quibble. I like Don's metaphor here, and I like the romp. I also like Pirates of the Carribean, but that's another story.

California Angels Home Park Performance Factors

	Outs	Runs	Hits	2b	3b	HR	W	K	SH	SF	HBP	IBB	SB	CS	GDP
Home LH Batters	.958	1.135	1.066	1.268	1.022	.985	.887	1.044	.880	1.201	1.523	.774	1.330	.993	1.036
Home RH Batters	.940	1.020	.955	1.046	1.177	.913	.908	.947	.793	1.194	1.262	1.177	.902	.902	1.000
All Home Batters	.943	1.048	.995	1.144	1.032	.927	.899	.980	.800	1.170	1.273	.875	1.128	.927	1.010
Opp LH Batters	.938	.967	.982	.947	.923	.948	1.017	1.031	.587	1.114	1.114	.822	.873	.923	1.052
Opp RH Batters	.986	1.083	1.065	1.055	1.998	.972	1.078	.956	.845	.983	1.086	.775	1.313	.903	1.008
All Opp Batters	.969	1.047	1.036	1.019	1.760	.957	1.058	.964	.799	.947	1.076	.766	1.106	.935	1.004
All LH Batters	.950	1.066	1.032	1.119	.998	.970	.935	1.039	.737	1.170	1.326	.787	1.192	.965	1.044
All RH Batters	.963	1.050	1.011	1.050	1.543	.940	.996	.950	.826	1.033	1.160	.862	1.116	.885	1.002
All Batters	.956	1.047	1.015	1.077	1.255	.940	.978	.970	.805	1.033	1.162	.812	1.120	.927	1.004

Conventional Batting Records for California Angels

	G	AB	Run	Hit	2B	3B	HR	TB	RBI	W	K	IW	HB	SB	CS	BRng Eff	GI DP	SH	SF	Avg	Slug	OBP	Runs Ctd
Parrish Ln	119	402	38	87	12	0	19	156	51	35	117	2	5	0	1	.215	7	0	3	.216	.388	.285	45
Joyner	143	551	79	166	34	3	21	269	96	52	66	4	1	2	0	.406	11	2	5	.301	.488	.360	98
Sojo	113	364	38	94	14	1	3	119	20	14	26	0	5	4	2	.355	12	19	0	.258	.327	.295	33
Gaetti	152	586	58	144	22	1	18	222	66	33	104	3	8	5	5	.429	13	2	5	.246	.379	.293	63
Schofield	134	427	44	96	9	3	0	111	31	50	69	2	3	8	4	.385	3	7	0	.225	.260	.310	39
Polonia	150	604	92	179	28	8	2	229	50	52	74	4	1	48	23	.597	11	2	3	.296	.379	.352	81
Felix	66	230	32	65	10	2	2	85	26	11	55	0	3	7	5	.373	5	0	2	.283	.370	.321	26
Winfield	150	568	75	149	27	4	28	268	86	56	109	4	1	7	2	.376	21	2	6	.262	.472	.326	84
Parker D	119	466	45	108	22	2	11	167	56	29	91	3	3	3	2	.286	9	0	3	.232	.358	.279	46
Gallagher	90	270	32	79	17	0	1	99	30	24	43	0	2	2	4	.393	6	10	0	.293	.367	.355	35
Hill D	77	209	36	50	8	1	1	63	20	30	21	1	0	1	0	.412	1	3	0	.239	.301	.335	24
Venable	82	187	24	46	8	2	3	67	21	11	30	2	2	2	1	.484	5	4	2	.246	.358	.292	19
Tingley	45	115	11	23	7	0	1	33	13	8	34	0	1	1	1	.389	1	4	0	.200	.287	.258	9
Abner	41	101	12	23	6	1	2	37	9	4	18	0	0	1	2	.545	3	0	0	.228	.366	.257	8
Howell Jk	32	81	11	17	2	0	2	25	7	11	11	0	0	1	1	.267	1	0	0	.210	.309	.304	8
Orton	29	69	7	14	4	0	0	18	3	10	17	0	1	0	1	.333	2	4	0	.203	.261	.313	6
Rose	22	65	5	18	5	1	1	28	8	3	13	0	0	0	0	.667	1	0	1	.277	.431	.304	8
Stevens	18	58	8	17	7	0	0	24	9	6	12	2	0	1	2	.308	0	1	1	.293	.414	.354	9
Disarcina	18	57	5	12	2	0	0	14	3	3	4	0	2	0	0	.455	0	2	0	.211	.246	.274	4
Amaro	10	23	0	5	1	0	0	6	2	3	3	1	0	0	0	.000	1	0	0	.217	.261	.308	2
Cron	6	15	0	2	0	0	0	2	0	2	5	0	0	0	0	.000	0	0	0	.133	.133	.235	1
Flora	3	8	1	1	0	0	0	1	0	1	5	0	0	1	0	.500	1	1	0	.125	.125	.222	0
Marshall	2	7	0	0	0	0	0	0	0	0	1	0	0	0	0	.000	0	0	0	.000	.000	.000	0
Lyons Bar	2	5	0	1	0	0	0	1	0	0	0	0	0	0	0	.000	0	0	0	.200	.200	.200	0
Davis M	3	2	0	0	0	0	0	0	0	0	0	0	0	0	0	.000	0	0	0	.000	.000	.000	0
Harvey	2	0	0	0	0	0	0	0	0	0	0	0	0	0	0	.000	0	0	0	.000	.000	.000	0
TOTALS	1628	5470	653	1396	245	29	115	2044	607	448	928	28	38	94	56	.401	114	63	31	.255	.374	.314	642

Sabermetric Batting Records for California Angels

	Ball Park Adjusted								Runs		Run/								
	AB	Run	Hit	2B	3B	HR	RBI	W	SO	Avg	Slug	OBP	Ctd	Outs	27o	OW%	OG	OWAR	DWAR	TWAR
Abner	98	12	23	6	1	1	9	3	17	.235	.347	.257	8	79	2.73	.315	3	-0.10	0.40	0.30
Amaro	22	0	5	1	0	0	2	2	2	.227	.273	.292	2	18	3.00	.357	1	0.00	0.01	0.01
Cron	14	0	2	0	0	0	0	1	4	.143	.143	.200	0	12	0.00	.000	0	-0.16	0.03	-0.13
Davis M	1	0	0	0	0	0	0	0	0	.000	.000	.000	0	1	0.00	.000	0	-0.01	-0.00	-0.02
Disarcina	55	5	12	2	0	0	3	2	3	.218	.255	.271	4	44	2.45	.271	2	-0.13	-0.00	-0.13
Felix	223	33	66	10	2	1	27	10	53	.296	.372	.332	27	168	4.34	.537	6	1.16	-0.08	1.08
Flora	7	1	1	0	0	0	0	0	4	.143	.143	.143	0	7	0.00	.000	0	-0.09	-0.02	-0.11
Gaetti	570	60	145	23	1	16	69	32	98	.254	.382	.302	64	448	3.86	.478	17	2.13	1.65	3.78
Gallagher	262	33	79	17	0	0	31	23	40	.302	.366	.362	35	200	4.72	.579	7	1.70	0.98	2.68
Hill D	202	37	50	8	1	0	21	29	20	.248	.297	.342	23	155	4.01	.497	6	0.85	0.76	1.61
Howell Jk	77	11	17	2	0	1	7	10	11	.221	.286	.310	8	61	3.54	.436	2	0.19	0.21	0.40
Joyner	533	83	169	37	2	20	103	49	68	.317	.507	.372	101	381	7.16	.759	14	5.78	0.52	6.30
Lyons Bar	4	0	1	0	0	0	0	0	0	.250	.250	.250	0	3	0.00	.000	0	-0.04	0.01	-0.03
Marshall	6	0	0	0	0	0	0	0	0	.000	.000	.000	0	6	0.00	.000	0	-0.08	-0.00	-0.08
Orton	66	7	14	4	0	0	3	9	16	.212	.273	.316	6	57	2.84	.332	2	-0.04	0.17	0.13
Parker D	449	47	110	24	1	10	60	27	94	.245	.370	.290	48	352	3.68	.455	13	1.37	0.00	1.37
Parrish Ln	390	39	87	12	0	17	53	34	111	.223	.385	.292	45	313	3.88	.482	12	1.52	0.91	2.44
Polonia	585	96	183	31	7	1	53	49	76	.313	.395	.365	85	439	5.23	.627	16	4.51	0.26	4.77
Rose	63	5	18	5	1	0	8	2	12	.286	.397	.303	7	47	4.02	.499	2	0.26	0.18	0.44
Schofield	414	46	96	9	4	0	32	49	65	.232	.273	.318	40	329	3.28	.399	12	0.60	1.84	2.44
Sojo	353	39	94	14	1	2	21	13	24	.266	.329	.302	33	287	3.10	.373	11	0.24	1.60	1.84
Stevens	55	8	17	7	0	0	9	5	12	.309	.436	.361	9	40	6.07	.695	1	0.51	0.05	0.56
Tingley	111	11	23	7	0	0	13	7	32	.207	.270	.261	8	92	2.35	.254	3	-0.33	-0.00	-0.33
Venable	180	25	47	8	1	2	22	10	31	.261	.350	.304	19	142	3.61	.446	5	0.50	0.13	0.64
Winfield	553	78	150	28	6	26	90	55	103	.271	.485	.335	87	432	5.44	.646	16	4.73	0.58	5.31
TOTALS	5312	683	1417	264	40	108	641	438	901	.267	.393	.326	681	4143	4.44	.548	153	30.43	10.19	40.62

Pitching Records for California Angels

	ERA	W	L	Pct	G	GS	CG	ShO	GF	Sv	IP	R	ER	H	2B	3B	HR	BB	IW	SO	HB	WP	BK
Langston	3.00	19	8	.704	34	34	7	0	0	0	246.1	89	82	190	34	2	30	96	3	183	2	6	0
Abbott	2.89	18	11	.621	34	34	5	1	0	0	243.0	85	78	222	35	3	14	73	6	158	5	1	4
Finley C	3.80	18	9	.667	34	34	4	2	0	0	227.1	102	96	205	43	3	23	101	1	171	8	6	3
McCaskill	4.26	10	19	.345	30	30	1	0	0	0	177.2	93	84	193	36	5	19	66	1	71	3	6	0
Grahe	4.81	3	7	.300	18	10	1	0	2	0	73.0	43	39	84	20	3	2	33	0	40	3	2	0
Lewis S	6.27	3	5	.375	16	11	0	0	0	0	60.1	43	42	81	16	0	9	21	0	37	2	3	0
Abbott K	4.58	1	2	.333	5	3	0	0	0	0	19.2	11	10	22	4	0	2	13	0	12	1	1	1
Valenzuela	12.15	0	2	.000	2	2	0	0	0	0	6.2	10	9	14	3	0	3	3	0	5	0	1	0
Eichhorn	1.98	3	3	.500	70	0	0	0	23	1	81.2	21	18	63	16	2	2	13	1	49	2	0	0
Harvey	1.60	2	4	.333	67	0	0	0	63	46	78.2	20	14	51	7	0	6	17	3	101	1	2	2
Robinson JD	5.37	0	3	.000	39	0	0	0	16	3	57.0	34	34	56	13	0	9	29	4	57	2	10	0
Bailes	4.18	1	2	.333	42	0	0	0	14	0	51.2	26	24	41	7	1	5	22	5	41	4	2	0
Fetters	4.84	2	5	.286	19	4	0	0	8	0	44.2	29	24	53	7	0	4	28	2	24	3	4	0
Beasley	3.38	0	1	.000	22	0	0	0	8	0	26.2	14	10	26	5	0	2	10	1	14	1	2	0
Bannister F	3.96	0	0	.000	16	0	0	0	2	0	25.0	12	11	25	3	2	5	10	1	16	0	1	0
Young Cli	4.26	1	0	1.000	11	0	0	0	6	0	12.2	6	6	12	1	0	3	3	1	6	0	0	0
McClure	9.31	0	0	.000	13	0	0	0	2	0	9.2	11	10	13	0	0	3	5	0	5	1	2	1
TOTALS	3.69	81	81	.500	472	162	18	3	144	50	1441.2	649	591	1351	250	21	141	543	29	990	38	49	11

Sabermetric Pitching Records for California Angels

	Adj	|-Expected-|			|——Opposing Batters——|												Supported				
	ERA	W	L	Pct	BFP	Avg	Slg	OBA	RC/G	GDP	SB	CS	PK	PKE	SH	SF	RSup	RSp/G	W	L	Pct
Abbott	3.00	19	10	.650	1002	.244	.336	.302	3.32	21	12	14	1	6	7	7	127	4.70	21	8	.711
Abbott K	4.58	1	2	.444	90	.301	.438	.414	5.95	3	1	2	0	0	3	0	7	3.20	1	2	.329
Bailes	4.35	1	2	.468	219	.218	.346	.310	3.72	2	2	3	0	0	3	2	12	2.09	1	2	.187
Bannister F	3.96	0	0	.516	104	.266	.500	.337	4.99	5	0	1	0	0	0	0	7	2.52	0	0	.288
Beasley	3.38	1	0	.595	113	.257	.366	.327	3.99	3	0	1	2	0	0	1	16	5.40	1	0	.719
Eichhorn	1.98	5	1	.809	311	.219	.309	.255	2.24	11	3	3	0	0	5	3	34	3.75	5	1	.781
Fetters	5.04	3	4	.397	206	.305	.414	.410	5.90	8	6	4	0	0	1	0	18	3.63	2	5	.341
Finley C	3.96	14	13	.516	955	.244	.385	.330	4.20	21	15	14	0	0	4	3	136	5.38	18	9	.649
Grahe	4.93	4	6	.407	330	.288	.397	.365	5.44	4	9	5	0	0	1	1	21	2.59	2	8	.216
Harvey	1.60	5	1	.867	309	.178	.266	.225	2.19	3	12	0	0	0	3	2	19	2.17	4	2	.648
Langston	3.11	17	10	.634	992	.215	.360	.291	3.35	16	10	15	4	8	4	6	125	4.57	18	9	.684
Lewis S	6.41	2	6	.289	281	.316	.484	.373	7.12	2	6	2	0	0	2	0	38	5.67	4	4	.439
McCaskill	4.41	13	16	.463	762	.283	.435	.347	5.05	22	8	6	1	0	6	6	62	3.14	10	19	.337
McClure	9.31	0	0	.162	48	.317	.537	.396	8.89	0	0	0	0	0	0	1	1	0.93	0	0	.010
Robinson JD	5.53	1	2	.354	252	.259	.444	.349	5.52	6	4	0	1	0	3	2	16	2.53	1	2	.173
Valenzuela	12.15	0	2	.102	36	.452	.839	.486	17.76	0	0	0	1	0	1	1	0	0.00	0	2	.000
Young Cli	4.26	0	1	.479	49	.261	.478	.306	3.73	2	1	2	0	1	0	0	14	9.95	1	0	.845
TOTALS	3.86	86	76	.529	6059	.250	.383	.321	4.11	129	89	72	10	15	43	35	653	4.08	85	77	.528

Batting 'Splits' Records for California Angels

	G	AB	Run	Hit	2B	3B	HR	TB	RBI	W	K	IW	HB	SB	CS	GIDP	SH	SF	Avg	Slug	OBP	Runs Ctd
SPLITS for Felix																						
vs LHP	27	55	9	16	3	1	0	21	9	0	17	0	0	1	0	1	0	1	.291	.382	.286	6
vs RHP	61	175	23	49	7	1	2	64	17	11	38	0	3	6	5	4	0	1	.280	.366	.332	20
Home	31	105	19	32	2	1	2	42	11	6	20	0	2	3	3	3	0	1	.305	.400	.351	14
Away	35	125	13	33	8	1	0	43	15	5	35	0	1	4	2	2	0	1	.264	.344	.295	13
Grass	52	182	28	54	7	2	2	71	19	9	42	0	2	5	4	5	0	1	.297	.390	.335	22
Turf	14	48	4	11	3	0	0	14	7	2	13	0	1	2	1	0	0	1	.229	.292	.269	4
April/June	43	147	19	38	6	2	1	51	13	7	42	0	3	4	3	2	0	2	.259	.347	.302	15
July/October	23	83	13	27	4	0	1	34	13	4	13	0	0	3	2	3	0	0	.325	.410	.356	11
SPLITS for Sojo																						
vs LHP	56	114	16	34	7	1	0	43	5	5	6	0	0	0	1	5	5	0	.298	.377	.328	12
vs RHP	92	250	22	60	7	0	3	76	15	9	20	0	5	4	1	7	14	0	.240	.304	.280	21
Home	56	176	16	42	5	0	1	50	6	11	11	0	1	2	0	6	8	0	.239	.284	.287	14
Away	57	188	22	52	9	1	2	69	14	3	15	0	4	2	2	6	11	0	.277	.367	.303	19
Grass	97	305	29	78	10	0	1	91	12	14	21	0	4	4	2	10	15	0	.256	.298	.297	26
Turf	16	59	9	16	4	1	2	28	8	0	5	0	1	0	0	2	4	0	.271	.475	.283	7
April/June	51	157	16	36	8	1	0	46	10	5	9	0	3	0	0	5	12	0	.229	.293	.267	12
July/October	62	207	22	58	6	0	3	73	10	9	17	0	2	4	2	7	7	0	.280	.353	.317	22
SPLITS for Winfield																						
vs LHP	82	160	24	48	9	1	11	92	27	20	24	3	1	1	0	4	0	0	.300	.575	.381	35
vs RHP	144	408	51	101	18	3	17	176	59	36	85	1	0	6	2	17	2	6	.248	.431	.304	50
Home	73	271	33	66	10	1	13	117	33	25	54	2	0	4	1	12	1	2	.244	.432	.305	33
Away	77	297	42	83	17	3	15	151	53	31	55	2	1	3	1	9	1	4	.279	.508	.345	51
Grass	126	475	58	119	21	3	18	200	53	48	89	4	1	7	2	20	1	5	.251	.421	.318	60
Turf	24	93	17	30	6	1	10	68	33	8	20	0	0	0	0	1	1	1	.323	.731	.373	26
April/June	67	265	41	76	16	4	16	148	53	20	45	2	0	1	0	9	1	4	.287	.558	.332	47
July/October	83	303	34	73	11	0	12	120	33	36	64	2	1	6	2	12	1	2	.241	.396	.322	38
SPLITS for California Angels (all batters except pitchers)																						
vs LHP	802	1561	193	397	77	8	32	586	182	120	254	7	7	20	12	35	19	6	.254	.375	.309	179
vs RHP	1436	3909	460	999	168	21	83	1458	425	328	674	21	31	74	44	79	44	25	.256	.373	.316	463
Home	814	2650	291	645	94	13	59	942	266	235	438	16	14	38	29	51	38	13	.243	.355	.307	291
Away	814	2820	362	751	151	16	56	1102	341	213	490	12	24	56	27	63	25	18	.266	.391	.321	352
Grass	1358	4514	515	1131	188	23	90	1635	475	371	749	23	31	74	49	91	53	24	.251	.362	.310	507
Turf	270	956	138	265	57	6	25	409	132	77	179	5	7	20	7	23	10	7	.277	.428	.333	136
April/June	731	2539	341	675	113	20	53	987	313	201	416	11	24	46	17	54	30	15	.266	.389	.324	323
July/October	897	2931	312	721	132	9	62	1057	294	247	512	17	14	48	39	60	33	16	.246	.361	.306	320

1991 SPLITS FOR California Angels

BATTING SPLITS

	AVG	AB	R	H	2B	3B	HR	RBI	SB	CS	BB	K	OBA	SPCT
Total	.255	5470	653	1396	245	29	115	607	94	56	448	928	.314	.374

	#Pit	#P/PA	GB	FB	G/F	G	IBB	HB	SH	SF	GDP
Miscellaneous	22157	3.66	2001	1619	1.24	162	28	38	63	31	114

	AVG	AB	R	H	2B	3B	HR	RBI	SB	CS	BB	K	OBA	SPCT
vs. Left	.254	1561	...	397	77	8	32	182	20	12	120	254	.309	.375
vs. Right	.256	3909	...	999	168	21	83	425	74	44	328	674	.316	.373
Home	.243	2650	291	645	94	13	59	266	38	29	235	438	.307	.355
Away	.266	2820	362	751	151	16	56	341	56	27	213	490	.321	.391
None on	.243	3124	...	760	140	18	73	73	0	0	244	555	.302	.370
Runners on	.271	2346	...	636	105	11	42	534	94	56	204	373	.330	.379
April	.270	679	84	183	27	6	12	78	15	7	62	112	.336	.380
May	.259	919	129	238	43	8	22	118	15	6	71	152	.316	.395
June	.270	941	128	254	43	6	19	117	16	4	68	152	.323	.389
July	.254	871	101	221	35	2	18	97	9	8	68	148	.308	.361
August	.232	960	100	223	41	3	32	93	14	11	79	173	.293	.381
September	.252	950	90	239	50	3	7	84	20	17	80	164	.311	.333
October	.253	150	21	38	6	1	5	20	5	3	20	27	.339	.407
None on/out	.243	1345	...	327	57	7	28	28	0	0	120	214	.311	.358
Scoring Posn	.275	1354	...	372	66	7	24	480	34	13	150	209	.344	.387
Close & Late	.231	746	...	172	23	1	13	57	12	7	67	138	.297	.316
Bases Loaded	.269	93	...	25	5	2	3	77	0	0	3	11	.284	.462
Batting #1	.294	671	100	197	29	8	4	58	48	23	61	79	.352	.379
Batting #2	.266	651	85	173	35	3	14	86	7	5	53	88	.322	.393
Batting #3	.298	635	91	189	35	6	23	103	6	1	60	85	.356	.480
Batting #4	.220	635	69	140	27	2	21	82	7	3	49	139	.276	.369
Batting #5	.252	619	69	156	28	1	20	80	2	4	46	112	.308	.397
Batting #6	.227	598	60	136	22	2	15	58	5	5	53	137	.297	.346
Batting #7	.266	595	56	158	27	2	11	53	4	5	28	111	.302	.373
Batting #8	.222	544	69	121	26	3	6	49	5	5	50	94	.295	.314
Batting #9	.241	522	54	126	16	2	1	38	10	5	48	83	.314	.285
As c	.215	553	53	119	23	0	19	65	1	3	50	156	.287	.360
As 1b	.293	631	87	185	40	4	21	105	3	0	58	87	.351	.469
As 2b	.246	558	63	137	22	2	3	31	6	3	45	50	.308	.308
As 3b	.240	629	64	151	22	1	19	69	6	5	35	110	.287	.369
As ss	.231	537	60	124	14	3	1	45	8	4	62	81	.316	.274
As lf	.291	660	96	192	31	8	4	57	45	22	60	84	.349	.380
As cf	.269	587	75	158	29	3	6	64	8	9	34	118	.313	.359
As rf	.270	610	78	165	34	6	23	88	8	4	53	103	.328	.459
Outfield	.277	1857	249	515	94	17	33	209	61	35	147	305	.331	.400
0.0 count	.322	749	...	241	42	3	23	112	...	...	2	0	.328	.478
After (0.1)	.230	2426	...	558	81	10	42	246	...	...	88	600	.262	.324
After (1.0)	.260	2295	...	597	122	16	50	249	...	...	339	328	.356	.393
Two strikes	.195	2488	...	485	94	14	35	212	...	...	186	926	.256	.286
Grass	.251	4514	515	1131	188	23	90	475	74	49	371	749	.310	.362
Turf	.277	956	138	265	57	6	25	132	20	7	77	179	.333	.428
Day	.268	1375	183	368	77	8	31	172	27	14	110	236	.325	.403
Night	.251	4095	470	1028	168	21	84	435	67	42	338	692	.311	.364
Inning 1.6	.262	3725	485	975	171	21	86	451	75	44	299	631	.319	.388
Inning 7+	.241	1745	168	421	74	8	29	156	19	12	149	297	.304	.343
vs.Bal	.263	399	41	105	13	2	9	40	7	6	18	60	.297	.373
vs.Bos	.226	380	40	86	19	3	7	37	2	1	29	73	.282	.347
vs.ChA	.270	444	55	120	19	2	10	49	9	8	42	67	.332	.390
vs.Cle	.258	434	55	112	14	5	3	50	3	1	29	78	.307	.334
vs.Det	.269	409	42	110	15	2	9	38	9	6	17	56	.299	.381
vs.KC	.281	445	67	125	22	2	8	63	5	7	35	87	.335	.393
vs.Mil	.242	385	32	93	14	1	2	30	7	3	31	64	.305	.299
vs.Min	.276	446	74	123	22	2	18	71	8	2	36	76	.330	.455
vs.NYA	.262	405	64	106	27	2	10	60	9	5	44	59	.340	.412
vs.Oak	.220	427	32	94	12	2	7	27	11	7	39	66	.296	.307
vs.Sea	.243	436	45	106	22	3	12	42	6	3	47	88	.319	.390
vs.Tex	.243	452	53	110	23	1	13	50	5	5	49	85	.318	.385
vs.Tor	.260	408	53	106	23	2	7	50	13	2	32	69	.318	.377

PITCHING SPLITS

	ERA	W	L	SV	SVOP	GS	CG	SHO	IP	H	ER	HR	BB	IBB	K
Total	3.69	81	81	50	63	162	18	15	1441.2	1351	591	141	543	29	990

	#Pit	#P/IP	GB	FB	G/F	BRp9	RA	WP	BK	SH	SF	R	HB	Hld
Miscellaneous	22608	15.68	2077	1506	1.38	12.06	310	49	11	43	35	649	38	42

	ERA	W	L	SV	SVOP	GS	CG	SHO	IP	H	ER	HR	BB	IBB	K
ST	3.81	70	67	0	0	162	18	3	1042.0	1009	441	102	404	11	660
REL	3.38	11	14	50	63	0	0	0	399.2	342	150	39	139	18	330
Home	3.30	40	41	24	30	81	10	2	748.0	649	274	74	251	20	520
Away	4.11	41	40	26	33	81	8	1	693.2	702	317	67	292	9	470
April	3.35	10	10	5	5	20	2	1	180.0	158	67	14	64	3	117
May	3.62	16	11	9	10	27	3	1	238.2	229	96	25	81	4	165
June	4.53	15	12	8	12	27	2	1	242.1	251	122	31	104	6	195
July	3.95	11	15	6	7	26	4	0	230.0	220	101	26	73	1	154
August	3.49	11	18	9	10	29	2	0	255.0	240	99	19	92	6	147
September	3.42	15	13	12	15	28	4	0	252.2	213	96	23	114	8	171
October	2.09	3	2	1	4	5	1	0	43.0	40	10	3	15	1	41
Grass	3.70	64	71	39	49	135	18	3	1208.2	1125	497	125	449	26	830
Turf	3.63	17	10	11	14	27	0	0	233.0	226	94	16	94	3	160
Day	3.81	22	18	13	14	40	4	0	354.0	347	150	33	133	5	266
Night	3.65	59	63	37	49	122	14	3	1087.2	1004	441	108	410	24	724
vs.Bal	3.69	6	6	4	5	12	2	0	105.0	99	43	14	36	1	69
vs.Bos	3.03	8	4	6	7	12	2	1	104.0	85	35	6	41	2	59
vs.ChA	3.54	8	5	6	9	13	1	0	119.1	110	47	12	40	3	78
vs.Cle	3.16	7	5	3	3	12	0	0	111.0	107	39	7	36	0	66
vs.Det	3.84	5	7	3	5	12	1	0	105.1	95	45	20	39	1	96
vs.KC	3.55	9	4	5	6	13	1	0	114.0	114	45	8	47	2	88
vs.Mil	4.24	6	6	5	5	12	2	0	104.0	115	49	7	48	4	60
vs.Min	3.52	8	5	3	4	13	1	1	115.0	94	45	9	40	1	66
vs.NYA	3.79	6	6	2	2	12	3	1	107.0	99	45	13	30	1	67
vs.Oak	3.50	1	12	0	0	13	3	0	113.0	97	44	9	46	4	69
vs.Sea	3.43	6	7	6	6	13	0	0	118.0	113	45	10	43	2	74
vs.Tex	4.88	5	8	4	6	13	0	0	120.0	128	65	16	60	4	107
vs.Tor	3.74	6	6	3	5	12	2	0	106.0	95	44	10	37	4	91

OPPOSING BATTERS VS. PITCHERS.

	AVG	AB	R	H	2B	3B	HR	RBI	SB	CS	BB	K	OBA	SPCT
Total	.250	5399	649	1351	250	21	141	609	89	72	543	990	.321	.383
vs. Left	.272	1669	...	454	90	5	42	216	29	21	140	275	.329	.407
vs. Right	.240	3730	...	897	160	16	99	393	60	51	403	715	.318	.372
ST	.257	3927	480	1009	190	15	102	426	63	60	404	660	.328	.391
REL	.232	1472	169	342	60	6	39	183	26	12	139	330	.302	.361
Home	.237	2744	303	649	122	5	74	281	41	38	251	520	.303	.366
Away	.264	2655	346	702	128	16	67	328	48	34	292	470	.340	.400
None on	.248	3105	...	771	143	10	75	75	0	0	307	535	.319	.373
Runners on	.253	2294	...	580	107	11	66	534	89	72	236	455	.324	.395
None on/out	.248	1344	...	333	61	2	32	32	0	0	133	220	.319	.368
Scoring Posn	.253	1267	...	321	67	6	38	459	28	16	167	272	.336	.406
vs 1st Batr	.219	283	...	62	16	0	7	36	4	3	24	56	.282	.350
1st IP	.238	1565	156	372	78	4	40	218	41	14	165	307	.314	.369
Inning 1.6	.256	3649	460	935	187	16	90	432	58	58	384	610	.330	.390
Inning 7+	.238	1750	189	416	63	5	51	177	31	14	159	380	.303	.367
Close & Late	.220	861	...	189	26	1	21	92	16	10	81	199	.287	.325
0.0 count	.302	768	...	232	47	2	21	90	...	...	21	0	.324	.451
After (0.1)	.224	2407	...	539	88	5	52	215	...	...	134	642	.270	.329
After (1.0)	.261	2224	...	580	115	14	68	304	...	...	387	348	.370	.417
Two strikes	.183	2454	...	450	66	7	46	210	...	...	240	990	.260	.272
Pitch 1.15	.245	1414	...	346	73	3	37	159	38	13	125	242	.310	.379
Pitch 16.30	.215	952	...	205	33	2	23	108	10	9	112	213	.301	.327
Pitch 31.45	.254	696	...	177	35	8	16	74	12	12	74	127	.327	.397
Pitch 46.60	.285	608	...	173	36	3	16	88	6	11	63	110	.353	.433
Pitch 61.75	.249	550	...	137	19	3	15	60	5	11	52	97	.314	.376
Pitch 76.90	.276	519	...	143	24	0	16	53	6	7	50	82	.343	.414
Pitch 91.105	.255	380	...	97	19	2	5	38	11	5	36	67	.321	.355
Pitch 106.20	.268	209	...	56	10	0	9	18	1	4	20	34	.330	.445
Pitch 121.35	.235	68	...	16	1	0	4	10	0	0	12	17	.350	.426
Pitch 136.50	.250	4	...	1	0	0	0	1	0	0	1	1	.400	.250

American League

Eastern Division

1. Toronto Blue Jays
2. Boston Red Sox
3. Detroit Tigers
4. Milwaukee Brewers
5. New York Yankees
6. Baltimore Orioles
7. Cleveland Indians

AL Eastern Division Team Batting

	G	AB	Run	Hit	2B	3B	HR	TB	RBI	W	K	IW	HB	SB	CS	GIDP	SH	SF	Avg	Slug	OBP	Runs Ctd
Baltimore	1821	5571	685	1414	253	29	170	2235	659	528	964	33	33	49	33	145	47	45	.254	.401	.320	709
Boston	1722	5508	730	1481	304	25	125	2210	690	592	817	49	32	59	39	143	50	51	.269	.401	.340	758
Cleveland	1720	5470	576	1390	236	26	79	1915	546	449	888	24	43	84	58	145	62	46	.254	.350	.313	593
Detroit	1732	5547	817	1372	259	26	209	2310	778	699	1185	40	31	109	47	90	38	44	.247	.416	.333	803
Milwaukee	1642	5611	799	1523	247	53	116	2224	750	556	802	48	23	106	68	136	52	66	.271	.396	.336	750
New York	1706	5541	674	1418	249	19	147	2146	630	473	861	38	39	109	36	126	37	50	.256	.387	.316	686
Toronto	1753	5489	684	1412	295	45	133	2196	649	499	1043	49	58	148	53	108	56	65	.257	.400	.322	727

AL Eastern Division Sabermetric Team Batting

	|-------- Ball Park Adjusted --------|												Runs		Run/					
	AB	Run	Hit	2B	3B	HR	RBI	W	SO	Avg	Slug	OBP	Ctd	Outs	27o	OW%	OG	OWAR	DWAR	TWAR
Baltimore	5402	675	1388	252	42	168	648	521	916	.257	.412	.324	718	4269	4.54	.494	158	22.82	9.31	32.22
Boston	5503	717	1440	278	29	120	684	566	837	.262	.388	.331	716	4337	4.46	.498	161	23.83	6.18	30.17
Cleveland	5637	614	1420	248	23	116	588	475	960	.252	.366	.312	631	4536	3.76	.454	168	17.44	4.83	22.27
Detroit	5796	826	1440	294	30	196	774	692	1207	.248	.411	.330	817	4592	4.80	.483	170	22.58	7.99	30.57
Milwaukee	5795	794	1573	244	67	117	740	544	795	.271	.397	.333	773	4547	4.59	.482	168	22.16	7.58	29.74
New York	5333	633	1368	241	27	127	597	451	850	.257	.383	.316	651	4208	4.18	.465	156	17.96	6.63	24.59
Toronto	5658	671	1404	293	47	121	632	525	1076	.248	.381	.314	696	4562	4.12	.511	169	27.18	6.84	34.02

AL Eastern Division Team Pitching

	ERA	W	L	Pct	G	GS	CG	ShO	GF	Sv	IP	R	ER	H	2B	3B	HR	BB	IW	SO	HB	WP	BK
Baltimore	4.60	67	94	.416	530	161	8	2	153	42	1448.2	794	741	1528	293	25	145	501	39	860	28	49	8
Boston	4.04	83	78	.516	489	161	14	4	147	45	1430.2	711	642	1398	283	34	147	530	59	989	31	42	4
Cleveland	4.24	57	105	.352	451	162	22	3	140	33	1441.1	759	679	1551	279	38	110	441	61	862	39	48	6
Detroit	4.54	84	78	.519	488	162	18	4	144	38	1450.1	794	731	1570	257	45	148	593	88	739	24	50	5
Milwaukee	4.18	83	79	.512	503	162	23	6	139	41	1463.2	744	679	1498	254	22	147	527	31	859	45	53	5
New York	4.43	71	91	.438	539	162	3	2	159	37	1444.0	777	711	1510	295	42	152	506	29	936	42	53	14
Toronto	3.50	91	71	.562	509	162	10	2	152	60	1462.2	622	569	1301	217	22	121	523	41	971	43	55	8

AL Eastern Division Catchers

	G	PO	A	Er	TC	DP	PB	SB	CS	CS%	FPct	DI	DG	DW%	DWAR	ERA	ERA Wo-W
Baltimore	162	890	79	2	971	11	8	111	51	.315	.998	1439.2	10.0	.282	-.67	4.57	
Boston	162	1019	77	8	1104	14	11	97	53	.353	.993	1422.0	10.0	.296	-.54	4.02	
Cleveland	162	916	64	11	991	10	19	102	47	.315	.989	1433.1	10.0	.235	-.56	4.24	
Detroit	162	786	79	11	876	3	12	88	58	.397	.987	1441.1	10.0	.213	-.99	4.54	
Milwaukee	162	901	90	6	997	16	16	115	47	.290	.994	1454.2	10.0	.292	-.58	4.18	
New York	162	988	65	9	1062	8	13	134	50	.272	.992	1436.0	10.0	.232	-.73	4.43	
Toronto	162	1001	85	17	1103	11	22	118	53	.310	.985	1462.2	10.0	.347	-.03	3.50	
LG.AVG	162	997	93	13	1103	10	12	137	67	.328	.988	1448.2					

AL Eastern Division First Base

	G	PO	A	Er	TC	DP	FPct	DI	DG	DW%	DWAR
Baltimore	162	1453	143	19	1615	150	.988	1439.2	3.0	.457	.32
Boston	162	1437	126	15	1578	147	.990	1422.0	3.0	.481	.39
Cleveland	162	1407	107	19	1533	135	.988	1433.1	3.0	.395	.14
Detroit	162	1446	113	9	1568	156	.994	1441.1	3.0	.509	.47
Milwaukee	162	1452	138	16	1606	158	.990	1454.2	3.0	.533	.55
New York	162	1462	100	12	1574	163	.992	1436.0	3.0	.529	.53
Toronto	162	1474	103	8	1585	104	.995	1462.2	3.0	.509	.48
LG.AVG	162	1454	119	13	1586	112	.992	1448.2			

AL Eastern Division Second Base

	G	PO	A	Er	TC	DP	FPct	DI	DG	DW%	DWAR
Baltimore	162	331	500	17	848	117	.980	1439.2	8.0	.540	1.50
Boston	162	339	488	15	842	123	.982	1422.0	8.0	.601	1.99
Cleveland	162	340	503	26	869	111	.970	1433.1	8.0	.464	.90
Detroit	162	379	505	7	891	132	.992	1441.1	8.0	.654	2.42
Milwaukee	162	347	567	27	941	127	.971	1454.2	8.0	.599	1.98
New York	162	309	487	9	805	122	.989	1436.0	8.0	.555	1.63
Toronto	162	338	459	15	812	82	.982	1462.2	8.0	.473	.98
LG.AVG	162	346	481	15	842	87	.982	1448.2			

AL Eastern Division Third Base

	G	PO	A	Er	TC	DP	FPct	DI	DG	DW%	DWAR
Baltimore	162	105	297	11	413	31	.973	1439.2	6.0	.480	.77
Boston	162	113	332	18	463	38	.961	1422.0	6.0	.543	1.14
Cleveland	162	103	354	36	493	40	.927	1433.1	6.0	.411	.37
Detroit	162	111	315	21	447	27	.953	1441.1	6.0	.405	.33
Milwaukee	162	108	285	17	410	31	.959	1454.2	6.0	.427	.46
New York	162	108	332	36	476	26	.924	1436.0	6.0	.319	-.19
Toronto	162	125	354	31	510	24	.939	1462.2	6.0	.480	.78
LG.AVG	162	120	320	23	463	26	.950	1448.2			

AL Eastern Division Shortstop

	G	PO	A	Er	TC	DP	FPct	DI	DG	DW%	DWAR
Baltimore	162	267	533	12	812	113	.985	1439.2	11.0	.627	3.01
Boston	162	216	513	32	761	104	.958	1422.0	11.0	.489	1.51
Cleveland	162	264	472	14	750	92	.981	1433.1	11.0	.496	1.59
Detroit	162	260	531	22	813	118	.973	1441.1	11.0	.568	2.38
Milwaukee	162	254	463	23	740	117	.969	1454.2	11.0	.522	1.88
New York	162	264	531	30	825	137	.964	1436.0	11.0	.596	2.69
Toronto	162	252	450	22	724	73	.970	1462.2	11.0	.461	1.22
LG.AVG	162	268	482	26	776	82	.966	1448.2			

AL Eastern Division Left Field

	G	PO	A	Er	TC	DP	FPct	DI	DG	DW%	DWAR
Baltimore	162	327	17	6	350	2	.983	1439.2	4.0	.625	1.09
Boston	162	306	9	5	320	3	.984	1422.0	4.0	.462	.44
Cleveland	162	356	11	11	378	1	.971	1433.1	4.0	.493	.57
Detroit	162	353	11	9	373	1	.976	1441.1	4.0	.529	.71
Milwaukee	162	383	6	4	393	1	.990	1454.2	4.0	.551	.80
New York	162	334	14	6	354	2	.983	1436.0	4.0	.573	.89
Toronto	162	312	6	11	329	0	.967	1462.2	4.0	.393	.17
LG.AVG	162	341	9	6	356	1	.983	1448.2			

AL Eastern Division Center Field

	G	PO	A	Er	TC	DP	FPct	DI	DG	DW%	DWAR
Baltimore	162	450	10	3	463	1	.994	1439.2	6.0	.612	1.55
Boston	162	382	2	3	387	1	.992	1422.0	6.0	.421	.42
Cleveland	162	441	9	11	461	2	.976	1433.1	6.0	.430	.48
Detroit	162	495	7	7	509	3	.986	1441.1	6.0	.542	1.14
Milwaukee	162	446	1	3	450	1	.993	1454.2	6.0	.516	.99
New York	162	412	5	8	425	0	.981	1436.0	6.0	.379	.17
Toronto	162	457	8	2	467	2	.996	1462.2	6.0	.639	1.73
LG.AVG	162	407	8	6	421	2	.986	1448.2			

AL Eastern Division Right Field

	G	PO	A	Er	TC	DP	FPct	DI	DG	DW%	DWAR
Baltimore	162	358	19	5	382	6	.987	1439.2	5.0	.699	1.72
Boston	162	346	8	6	360	2	.983	1422.0	5.0	.487	.68
Cleveland	162	386	15	10	411	1	.976	1433.1	5.0	.619	1.34
Detroit	162	408	13	9	430	4	.979	1441.1	5.0	.638	1.43
Milwaukee	162	357	16	7	380	7	.982	1454.2	5.0	.647	1.48
New York	162	347	17	3	367	6	.992	1436.0	5.0	.689	1.68
Toronto	162	321	16	6	343	2	.983	1462.2	5.0	.645	1.48
LG.AVG	162	318	12	6	336	2	.982	1448.2			

Toronto Blue Jays

Dave Raglin

TORONTO											
YEAR	1982	1983	1984	1985	1986	1987	1988	1989	1990	1991	TOT
W	78	89	89	99	86	96	87	89	86	91	890
L	84	73	73	62	76	66	75	73	76	71	729
WPCT	0.481	0.549	0.549	0.615	0.531	0.593	0.537	0.549	0.531	0.562	0.550
R	651	795	750	759	809	845	763	731	767	684	7554
RA	701	726	696	588	733	655	680	651	661	622	6713
PWPT	0.463	0.545	0.537	0.625	0.549	0.625	0.557	0.558	0.574	0.547	0.559
PythW	75	88	87	101	89	101	90	90	93	89	91
PythL	87	74	75	61	73	61	72	72	69	73	71
LUCK	3	1	2	-2	-3	-5	-3	-1	-7	2	-13

Defensive Efficiency Record: .7184

It was a fantasy owner's dream, a hot stove league special. It was the biggest trade in years. How often are four players who are considered stars traded for one another? It was so close to being a challenge trade--one middle infielder for another, one big slugger for another.

Who got the better of the trade? A question made for a sabermetrician. Actually, a better question is who benefitted from the trade. Just because San Diego may have benefitted doesn't mean that Toronto made a bad trade. Both teams can benefit, and both teams can lose in a trade. It's not a zero-sum game.

We'll start by comparing their 1990 and 1991 seasons--but not do it by player--Roberto Alomar 1990 vs. Roberto Alomar 1991-but by team. After all, the way to tell if the Blue Jays improved themselves in the middle infield part of the deal was to measure what Alomar did for them in 1991 compared to Tony Fernandez in 1990. Below are four comparisons, for each team and "position" (MIF is middle infielder, SLG is slugger). The first pair looks at the Jays, the second two, the Padres. Below that are the totals for Toronto and San Diego. The runs created and runs created numbers below were calculated using the advanced formula, including statistics not shown here.

The Toronto-San Diego Trade--Who Benefitted, 1990 vs 1991 by Team and "Position"

Tm	Pos	YrPlayer	G	AB	BB	R	H	2B	3B	HR	BI	BA	RC	RC/G
TOR	MIF	1990Fernandez	161	635	71	84	175	27	17	4	66	.276	87	4.8
TOR	MIF	1991Alomar	161	637	57	88	188	41	11	9	69	.295	104	5.9
TOR	SLG	1990McGriff	153	557	94	91	167	21	1	35	88	.300	118	7.8
TOR	SLG	1991Carter	162	638	49	89	174	42	3	33	108	.273	103	5.7
SDP	MIF	1990Alomar	147	586	48	80	168	27	5	6	60	.287	78	4.8
SDP	MIF	1991Fernandez	145	558	55	81	152	27	5	4	38	.272	69	4.3
SDP	SLG	1990Carter	162	634	48	79	147	27	1	24	115	.232	72	3.8
SDP	SLG	1991McGriff	153	528	105	84	147	19	1	31	106	.278	104	7.1

Tm	Pos	YrPlayer	G	AB	BB	R	H	2B	3B	HR	BI	BA	RC	RC/G
TOR	ALL	1990Fer/McG	314	1192	165	175	342	48	18	39	154	.287	203	6.1
TOR	ALL	1991Alo/Car	323	1275	106	177	362	83	14	42	177	.284	207	5.8
SDP	ALL	1990Alo/Car	309	1220	96	159	315	54	6	30	175	.258	150	4.3
SDP	ALL	1991Fer/McG	298	1086	160	165	299	46	6	35	144	.275	172	5.6

Alomar was a big improvement offensively for Toronto over Fernandez; Fernandez was a good hitter for a shortstop, Alomar was in the top fifteen American Leaguers in runs created. Joe Carter created almost as many runs as Fred McGriff (we'll talk about that later) but used many more outs to do so.

For the Padres, Fernandez in 1991 was not quite as good as Alomar in 1990, but McGriff was much better than Carter for San Diego. Defensively, Fernandez had more range compared to others at his position than Alomar did, but Carter played the outfield while McGriff played first, so defensively, they're a wash. Overall, the 1991 Padres in the deal performed better than the 1990 pair.

That brings up an interesting aspect to this trade. Everybody said it was the most even trade they'd seen in years, especially considering that each team traded one middle infielder and one slugger. Their performance in the season before the trade wasn't, though. The Blue Jays-to-San Diego had 203 runs created, 6.1 runs created per game, while the 1990 Padre pair had 150 and 4.3. Alomar and especially Carter had seasons in 1990 that were below expectations. In fact, Carter had about as bad of a season a player could have and still drive in 115 runs. Playing in every game and batting in the middle of the lineup, he scored only 79 runs.

So the Padres got more improvement but the Blue Jays got more total production and won the East with their best record since 1987. Part of the production for the Jays is the ballpark; San Diego is a good home run park and decent offensive park by National League standards, but the Skydome has been a hitter's paradise in the hitter's league the past two seasons, especially for home runs. For the last two seasons, there have been 9.5% more runs scored by both teams in Toronto games at home than on the road, and 33.1% more homers. For 1991, I think both sides are winners.

Let's divert for a minute here from the trade talk. It is my opinion McGriff is as good as his runs created formula says he is. In last year's Oriole article, I talked about the runs created formula. I said while it was overall a very good statistical model, there were times where it, like any model, was not accurate. The theory that the formula overestimates the value of walks for sluggers who walk a lot, and my example involved Mickey Tettleton. Sluggers like Tettleton and McGriff who walk a lot tend to walk A LOT with runners in scoring position. The pitcher was happy to let them walk because the next hitter was far less likely to be able to drive in the runs. That's the job of a cleanup hitter, after all, to drive in runs. Tettleton was the extreme case; in 1990, he hit .155 with runners in scoring position (16 for 110), but with 44 walks.

McGriff wasn't that extreme, but his walks were way up and his slugging down with runners in scoring position the last four seasons since he became a regular. From 1988 to 1991, McGriff hit .252 (135 for 535) with runners in scoring position with 149 walks to register a .407 on-base percentage and a .430 slugging percentage, compared to a .292 batting average (478 for 1637), .378 on-base percentage with 227 base on balls, and .563 slugging percentage when there were no runners in scoring position. That jump in walks is consistent with the overall jump with runners in scoring position, but McGriff was high to begin with.

The key stat is the difference in slugging percentage, .407 vs. .563. McGriff is the number four hitter, a better hitter than the number five hitters he's had behind him (the Padre number five hitters had a .262 average, but with a .317 on-base percentage and a low .395 slugging percentage) and he's there to drive in runs. The runs created formula assumes a value for walks which doesn't take into account runners stranded at third while the big RBI man is standing on first. McGriff's walks are worth less than Rickey Henderson's--he's batting leadoff with Canseco and Dave Henderson coming up behind him, while McGriff had Jerald Clark and Scott Coolbaugh. (On the other hand, Henderson's home runs with Mike Bordick and Mike Gallego to drive in are worth less than McGriff's with Tony Clark and Tony Fernandez hitting ahead of him.)

McGriff's walks have value, no doubt, I'm not denying that. Nor am I saying that McGriff's propensity to walk too much and not slug enough with runners in scoring position is worse than Joe Carter's .308 on-base percentage. It's just that his value to scoring runs for the Padres is less than the formula indicates.

Now back to our regularly scheduled trade discussion. Since we've looked at 1991, let's look into the future now. The chart below uses Bill James' Brock2 formulas (that predict the rest of a player's career based on the player's age, position, and continued ability) to project the next four seasons, 1992 to 1995, for the four players. Why four seasons? Because with the freedom of players, a team really controls a player for a short time, so it's unrealistic to use what Roberto Alomar hits in 2005 to evaluate the trade. Plus, the shorter the time period, the more accurate the formulas.

There was a small adjustment made to the Brock2 formulas, concerning Joe Carter. The formulas have a column which predict a player's playing time based on whether his previous performance was above a replacement-level ballplayer using runs created per game as the measure of performance. However, because of his poor on-base percentage, Carter earns low runs created per game figures. His 1990 runs created per game of 3.8 is below the replacement-level of a left fielder in the model, so it start to drastically cut his playing time immediately in 1992. Obviously, no matter what the formula says, the baseball world does not and has never considered Joe Carter below replacement-level, so I tinkered with the formulas to leave him as pretty much a regular for the four years of the projection. The first four lines show each individual player, and the last two show the totals by team.

The Future for the Players in the Big Trade

Tm	Pos	YrPlayer	G	AB	BB	R	H	2B	3B	HR	BI	BA	RC	RC/G
TOR	MIF	92-95Alomar	619	2403	233	350	739	145	33	38	288	.307	329	5.0
TOR	SLG	92-95Carter	626	2368	191	240	573	125	6	88	317	.242	253	3.6
SDP	MIF	92-95Fernandez	608	2317	244	299	599	100	27	12	197	.259	228	3.4
SDP	SLG	92-95McGriff	621	2153	412	303	587	76	3	110	345	.273	364	5.9
TOR	ALL	92-95Alo/Car	1245	4772	424	590	1312	269	40	126	605	.275	582	4.3
SDP	ALL	92-95Fer/McG	1229	4470	656	602	1186	177	30	121	542	.265	582	4.5

You can't get much closer than that--582 runs created for the two Jays, 582 runs created for the two Padres. The runs created per game for the Padres is slightly higher because they are projected to make 176 less outs (3284 vs. 3460) than the two Toronto hitters. Also notice that the formulas project Fernandez and Carter to be fading while Alomar and McGriff will be still starring (even considering the overestimating of McGriff's runs created).

So who will make out better in the long run? The numbers are almost a dead heat. I'd rather be on the Jays' end of this because Alomar is the best player in the trade. He's the most likely to exceed his projection for the next four seasons. He has been mentioned prominetely as a future MVP candidate; I don't see any others ever earning that award. This looks like one of those trades that at least both teams won't be hurt by, and in the long run, both might just benefit from. It's a photo finish for one of the biggest, and most daring trades in history.

Toronto Blue Jays Home Park Performance Factors

	Outs	Runs	Hits	2b	3b	HR	W	K	SH	SF	HBP	IBB	SB	CS	GDP
Home LH Batters	1.048	1.086	.990	.934	.725	1.069	.967	1.052	1.035	.884	.659	1.098	1.449	7.246	1.220
Home RH Batters	1.006	.932	.966	1.016	1.206	.870	1.071	.985	.999	1.172	.788	.970	.880	1.084	1.093
All Home Batters	1.023	.967	.976	.945	.895	.905	.993	1.019	1.072	1.045	.783	1.003	.946	1.170	1.068
Opp LH Batters	1.048	1.087	1.068	1.167	1.007	1.348	1.103	.978	1.196	1.023	1.404	1.023	1.076	.982	1.498
Opp RH Batters	1.070	.954	.989	1.014	1.215	.789	1.131	1.075	1.399	1.370	.895	3.297	1.119	1.031	.928
All Opp Batters	1.064	.997	1.014	1.043	1.203	.919	1.112	1.045	1.283	1.188	.972	1.289	1.076	.973	1.077
All LH Batters	1.047	1.085	1.034	1.028	.896	1.211	1.038	1.013	1.138	.948	.956	1.049	1.073	1.130	1.341
All RH Batters	1.043	.947	.980	1.016	1.222	.832	1.105	1.037	1.224	1.275	.846	1.222	1.007	1.056	.991
All Batters	1.044	.984	.997	.994	1.014	.914	1.055	1.033	1.181	1.113	.868	1.123	1.013	1.047	1.077

Conventional Batting Records for Toronto Blue Jays

	G	AB	Run	Hit	2B	3B	HR	TB	RBI	W	K	IW	HB	SB	CS	BRng Eff	GI DP	SH	SF	Avg	Slug	OBP	Runs Ctd
Myers G	107	309	25	81	22	0	8	127	36	21	45	4	0	0	0	.217	13	0	3	.262	.411	.306	36
Olerud	139	454	64	116	30	1	17	199	68	68	84	9	6	0	2	.333	12	3	10	.256	.438	.353	73
Alomar R	161	637	88	188	41	11	9	278	69	57	86	3	4	53	11	.468	5	16	5	.295	.436	.354	108
Gruber	113	429	58	108	18	2	20	190	65	31	70	5	6	12	7	.464	7	3	5	.252	.443	.308	58
Lee M	138	445	41	104	18	3	0	128	29	24	107	0	2	7	2	.420	10	10	4	.234	.288	.274	35
Carter J	162	638	89	174	42	3	33	321	108	49	112	12	10	20	9	.500	7	0	9	.273	.503	.330	108
White D	156	642	110	181	40	10	17	292	60	55	135	1	7	33	10	.537	7	5	6	.282	.455	.342	105
Whiten	46	149	12	33	4	3	2	49	19	11	35	1	1	0	1	.625	5	0	3	.221	.329	.274	13
Mulliniks	97	240	27	60	12	1	2	80	24	44	44	2	0	0	0	.321	9	0	2	.250	.333	.364	31
Borders	105	291	22	71	17	0	5	103	36	11	45	1	1	0	0	.294	8	6	3	.244	.354	.271	27
Wilson M	86	241	26	58	12	4	2	84	28	8	35	0	5	11	3	.451	4	2	2	.241	.349	.277	24
Tabler	82	185	20	40	5	1	1	50	21	29	21	5	1	0	0	.318	3	2	5	.216	.270	.318	19
Maldonado	52	177	26	49	9	0	7	79	28	23	53	4	6	3	0	.289	4	0	2	.277	.446	.375	32
Sprague	61	160	17	44	7	0	4	63	20	19	43	2	3	0	3	.438	2	0	1	.275	.394	.361	23
Gonzales R	71	118	16	23	3	0	1	29	6	12	22	0	4	0	0	.300	5	6	1	.195	.246	.289	9
Hill G	35	99	14	25	5	2	3	43	11	7	24	0	0	2	2	.429	2	0	2	.253	.434	.296	12
Ducey	39	68	8	16	2	2	1	25	4	6	26	0	0	2	0	.462	1	1	0	.235	.368	.297	8
Snyder C	21	49	4	7	0	1	0	9	6	3	19	0	0	0	0	.286	1	1	1	.143	.184	.189	2
Parker D	13	36	2	12	4	0	0	16	3	4	7	0	0	0	1	1.000	0	0	0	.333	.444	.400	6
Williams K	13	29	5	6	2	0	1	11	3	4	5	0	1	1	0	.600	1	0	1	.207	.379	.314	4
Bell D	18	28	5	4	0	0	0	4	1	6	5	0	1	3	2	.600	0	0	0	.143	.143	.314	2
Zosky	18	27	2	4	1	1	0	7	2	0	8	0	0	0	0	1.000	1	1	0	.148	.259	.148	1
Giannelli	9	24	2	4	1	0	0	5	0	5	9	0	0	1	0	.000	0	0	0	.167	.208	.310	2
Ward T	8	13	1	4	0	0	0	4	2	1	2	0	0	0	0	.000	1	0	0	.308	.308	.357	1
Knorr	3	1	0	0	0	0	0	0	0	1	1	0	0	0	0	.000	0	0	0	.000	.000	.500	0
TOTALS	1753	5489	684	1412	295	45	133	2196	649	499	1043	49	58	148	53	.422	108	56	65	.257	.400	.322	727

Sabermetric Batting Records for Toronto Blue Jays

	Ball Park Adjusted								Runs		Run/								
	AB	Run	Hit	2B	3B	HR	RBI	W	SO	Avg	Slug	OBP	Ctd	Outs	27o	OW%	OG	OWAR	DWAR	TWAR
Alomar R	655	86	187	40	11	8	67	59	88	.285	.417	.345	103	507	5.49	.649	19	5.62	1.02	6.64
Bell D	27	4	3	0	0	0	0	6	5	.111	.111	.273	1	26	1.04	.062	1	-0.28	-0.05	-0.32
Borders	297	20	69	17	0	4	33	12	46	.232	.330	.260	24	246	2.63	.299	9	-0.46	0.58	0.12
Carter J	651	83	170	42	3	27	101	53	115	.261	.459	.320	98	508	5.21	.625	19	5.18	0.95	6.13
Ducey	70	8	16	2	1	1	4	6	26	.229	.329	.289	7	56	3.38	.412	2	0.13	0.02	0.14
Giannelli	24	2	4	1	0	0	0	5	9	.167	.208	.310	2	20	2.70	.310	1	-0.03	-0.00	-0.03
Gonzales R	120	15	22	3	0	0	5	13	22	.183	.208	.277	8	111	1.95	.189	4	-0.66	0.45	-0.22
Gruber	438	54	105	18	2	16	60	34	72	.240	.400	.298	52	356	3.94	.489	13	1.83	0.91	2.75
Hill G	100	13	24	5	2	2	10	7	24	.240	.390	.284	10	82	3.29	.400	3	0.15	0.13	0.28
Knorr	1	0	0	0	0	0	0	1	1	.000	.000	.500	0	1	0.00	.000	0	-0.01	0.01	-0.00
Lee M	458	40	103	17	3	0	28	25	110	.225	.275	.264	34	382	2.40	.262	14	-1.24	0.77	-0.48
Maldonado	179	24	47	9	0	5	26	25	54	.263	.397	.365	28	138	5.48	.649	5	1.53	0.24	1.77
Mulliniks	249	29	61	12	0	2	25	45	44	.245	.317	.359	29	201	3.90	.483	7	0.99	0.01	1.00
Myers G	321	27	83	23	0	9	38	21	45	.259	.414	.302	35	257	3.68	.454	10	0.99	0.02	1.01
Olerud	473	69	119	31	0	20	73	70	85	.252	.444	.349	72	390	4.98	.605	14	3.68	0.38	4.06
Parker D	37	2	12	4	0	0	3	4	7	.324	.432	.390	5	29	4.66	.572	1	0.24	0.00	0.24
Snyder C	49	3	6	0	1	0	5	3	19	.122	.163	.170	1	46	0.59	.021	2	-0.56	0.32	-0.24
Sprague	162	16	42	7	0	3	18	20	44	.259	.358	.346	20	126	4.29	.531	5	0.84	-0.00	0.84
Tabler	189	18	39	5	1	0	19	31	21	.206	.243	.310	17	161	2.85	.333	6	-0.10	0.01	-0.09
Ward T	12	0	3	0	0	0	1	1	2	.250	.250	.308	1	10	2.70	.310	0	-0.01	0.22	0.20
White D	661	108	180	39	10	15	58	57	139	.272	.430	.333	99	509	5.25	.629	19	5.26	1.87	7.13
Whiten	153	11	32	3	3	1	18	11	36	.209	.288	.257	11	130	2.28	.243	5	-0.51	1.13	0.62
Williams K	28	4	5	2	0	0	2	4	5	.179	.250	.273	2	25	2.16	.223	1	-0.12	0.12	-0.00
Wilson M	247	25	57	11	4	1	27	8	36	.231	.320	.264	21	201	2.82	.329	7	-0.16	0.11	-0.05
Zosky	26	1	3	1	1	0	1	0	8	.115	.231	.115	0	25	0.00	.000	1	-0.32	0.14	-0.18
TOTALS	5658	671	1404	293	47	121	632	525	1076	.248	.381	.314	696	4562	4.12	.511	169	27.18	9.35	36.53

Pitching Records for Toronto Blue Jays

	ERA	W	L	Pct	G	GS	CG	ShO	GF	Sv	IP	R	ER	H	2B	3B	HR	BB	IW	SO	HB	WP	BK
Stottlemyre	3.78	15	8	.652	34	34	1	0	0	0	219.0	97	92	194	27	5	21	75	3	116	12	4	0
Key	3.05	16	12	.571	33	33	2	2	0	0	209.1	84	71	207	36	2	12	44	3	125	3	1	0
Wells	3.72	15	10	.600	40	28	2	0	3	1	198.1	88	82	188	37	2	24	49	1	106	2	10	3
Guzman J	2.99	10	3	.769	23	23	1	0	0	0	138.2	53	46	98	13	2	6	66	0	123	4	10	0
Candiotti	2.98	6	7	.462	19	19	3	0	0	0	129.2	47	43	114	27	6	6	45	1	81	4	5	0
Stieb	3.17	4	3	.571	9	9	1	0	0	0	59.2	22	21	52	8	1	4	23	0	29	2	0	0
Boucher	4.58	0	3	.000	7	7	0	0	0	0	35.1	20	18	39	12	0	6	16	1	16	2	0	4
Timlin	3.16	11	6	.647	63	3	0	0	17	3	108.1	43	38	94	6	1	6	50	11	85	1	5	0
Ward D	2.77	7	6	.538	81	0	0	0	46	23	107.1	36	33	80	10	1	3	33	3	132	2	6	0
Acker	5.20	3	5	.375	54	4	0	0	11	1	88.1	53	51	77	10	1	16	36	5	44	2	7	0
MacDonald	2.85	3	3	.500	45	0	0	0	10	0	53.2	19	17	51	7	0	5	25	4	24	0	1	1
Henke	2.32	0	2	.000	49	0	0	0	43	32	50.1	13	13	33	8	1	4	11	2	53	0	1	0
Fraser	6.15	0	2	.000	13	1	0	0	6	0	26.1	20	18	33	6	0	4	11	2	12	3	2	0
Weathers	4.91	1	0	1.000	15	0	0	0	4	0	14.2	9	8	15	4	0	1	17	3	13	2	0	0
Hentgen	2.45	0	0	.000	3	1	0	0	1	0	7.1	2	2	5	2	0	1	3	0	3	2	1	0
Wills	16.62	0	1	.000	4	0	0	0	3	0	4.1	8	8	8	1	0	2	5	0	2	1	0	0
Dayley	6.23	0	0	.000	8	0	0	0	3	0	4.1	3	3	7	0	0	0	5	0	3	1	2	0
Horsman	0.00	0	0	.000	4	0	0	0	2	0	4.0	0	0	2	0	0	0	3	1	2	0	0	0
Weston	0.00	0	0	.000	2	0	0	0	2	0	2.0	0	0	1	1	0	0	1	1	1	0	0	0
Leiter	27.00	0	0	.000	3	0	0	0	1	0	1.2	5	5	3	2	0	0	5	0	1	0	0	0
TOTALS	3.50	91	71	.562	509	162	10	2	152	60	1462.2	622	569	1301	217	22	121	523	41	971	43	55	8

Sabermetric Pitching Records for Toronto Blue Jays

	Adj	|-Expected-|			|------Opposing Batters------|												Supported				
	ERA	W	L	Pct	BFP	Avg	Slg	OBA	RC/G	GDP	SB	CS	PK	PKE	SH	SF	RSup	RSp/G	W	L	Pct
Acker	5.09	3	5	.392	374	.238	.424	.314	4.63	5	10	3	0	0	7	5	39	3.97	3	5	.378
Boucher	4.33	1	2	.471	162	.279	.493	.358	6.48	2	1	1	0	2	3	1	12	3.06	1	2	.333
Candiotti	2.92	9	4	.663	539	.236	.354	.304	3.83	6	16	5	2	1	3	4	45	3.12	7	6	.534
Dayley	4.15	0	0	.492	26	.368	.368	.500	10.55	0	2	0	0	0	0	1	4	8.31	0	0	.800
Fraser	5.81	1	1	.331	123	.303	.468	.382	7.00	2	5	1	0	0	0	0	11	3.76	1	1	.295
Guzman J	2.92	9	4	.662	574	.197	.268	.294	2.82	7	11	6	0	0	2	5	92	5.97	10	3	.807
Henke	2.15	2	0	.784	190	.184	.307	.232	2.22	4	2	0	1	0	0	0	9	1.61	1	1	.360
Hentgen	1.23	0	0	.917	30	.208	.417	.345	4.57	1	1	0	0	0	1	0	2	2.45	0	0	.800
Horsman	0.00	0	0	.000	16	.167	.167	.333	2.36	0	0	0	0	0	1	0	1	2.25	0	0	.000
Key	2.97	18	10	.655	877	.254	.347	.293	3.57	14	6	2	0	1	10	5	107	4.60	20	8	.706
Leiter	21.60	0	0	.035	13	.429	.714	.667	22.76	0	0	0	0	0	1	0	2	10.80	0	0	.200
MacDonald	2.68	4	2	.699	231	.252	.361	.332	4.22	3	5	4	0	2	2	2	29	4.86	5	1	.767
Stieb	3.02	5	2	.647	244	.243	.346	.321	3.45	7	5	5	2	1	4	1	26	3.92	4	3	.628
Stottlemyre	3.70	13	10	.550	921	.235	.356	.305	3.97	11	24	3	0	2	0	8	110	4.52	14	9	.599
Timlin	3.07	11	6	.639	463	.233	.297	.317	3.39	8	11	5	0	0	6	2	57	4.74	12	5	.704
Ward D	2.68	9	4	.699	428	.207	.262	.271	2.39	7	7	4	0	0	3	4	27	2.26	5	8	.416
Weathers	4.30	0	1	.475	79	.263	.386	.442	7.61	1	4	1	0	0	2	1	12	7.36	1	0	.746
Wells	3.63	14	11	.559	811	.252	.403	.297	3.91	11	8	13	3	9	6	6	99	4.49	15	10	.605
Weston	0.00	0	0	.000	8	.143	.286	.250	2.63	0	0	0	0	0	0	0	0	0.00	0	0	.000
Wills	14.54	0	1	.073	27	.421	.789	.560	18.99	0	0	0	0	0	2	0	0	0.00	0	1	.000
TOTALS	3.44	95	67	.586	6136	.238	.352	.307	3.78	89	118	53	8	18	53	45	684	4.21	97	65	.600

Batting 'Splits' Records for Toronto Blue Jays

	G	AB	Run	Hit	2B	3B	HR	TB	RBI	W	K	IW	HB	SB	CS	GIDP	SH	SF	Avg	Slug	OBP	Runs Ctd
SPLITS for Alomar R																						
vs LHP	92	191	28	47	12	3	5	80	27	11	35	0	3	11	3	1	7	2	.246	.419	.295	25
vs RHP	144	446	60	141	29	8	4	198	42	46	51	3	1	42	8	4	9	3	.316	.444	.379	83
Home	80	313	47	93	23	8	6	150	40	35	36	2	2	28	5	4	7	4	.297	.479	.367	60
Away	81	324	41	95	18	3	3	128	29	22	50	1	2	25	6	1	9	1	.293	.395	.341	48
Grass	63	255	34	68	14	1	1	87	22	15	41	0	1	18	4	1	7	1	.267	.341	.309	30
Turf	98	382	54	120	27	10	8	191	47	42	45	3	3	35	7	4	9	4	.314	.500	.383	80
April/June	75	295	39	81	24	5	5	130	34	31	41	2	1	25	4	2	10	1	.275	.441	.345	50
July/October	86	342	49	107	17	6	4	148	35	26	45	1	3	28	7	3	6	4	.313	.433	.363	58
SPLITS for Carter J																						
vs LHP	84	188	27	63	12	1	10	107	32	11	28	4	0	9	1	4	0	3	.335	.569	.366	40
vs RHP	146	450	62	111	30	2	23	214	76	38	84	8	10	11	8	3	0	6	.247	.476	.315	69
Home	81	321	49	93	23	1	23	187	64	23	65	9	8	9	4	4	0	4	.290	.583	.348	66
Away	81	317	40	81	19	2	10	134	44	26	47	3	2	11	5	3	0	5	.256	.423	.311	43
Grass	63	247	33	65	12	1	10	109	37	21	35	2	2	8	5	1	0	3	.263	.441	.322	36
Turf	99	391	56	109	30	2	23	212	71	28	77	10	8	12	4	6	0	6	.279	.542	.335	72
April/June	76	295	42	91	24	1	17	168	54	25	50	8	5	12	6	2	0	4	.308	.569	.368	63
July/October	86	343	47	83	18	2	16	153	54	24	62	4	5	8	3	5	0	5	.242	.446	.297	46
SPLITS for Whiten																						
vs LHP	28	41	2	6	1	0	1	10	3	4	12	1	0	0	0	1	0	1	.146	.244	.217	2
vs RHP	41	108	10	27	3	3	1	39	16	7	23	0	1	0	1	4	0	2	.250	.361	.297	11
Home	23	74	7	15	1	3	2	28	8	7	21	0	1	0	1	3	0	0	.203	.378	.280	7
Away	23	75	5	18	3	0	0	21	11	4	14	1	0	0	0	2	0	3	.240	.280	.268	6
Grass	19	59	2	14	1	0	0	15	9	3	13	0	0	0	0	2	0	3	.237	.254	.262	4
Turf	27	90	10	19	3	3	2	34	10	8	22	1	1	0	1	3	0	0	.211	.378	.283	9
April/June	46	149	12	33	4	3	2	49	19	11	35	1	1	0	1	5	0	3	.221	.329	.274	13
July/October	No plate appearances																					
SPLITS for Toronto Blue Jays (all batters except pitchers)																						
vs LHP	869	1666	207	428	90	10	47	679	196	142	288	17	12	36	15	30	19	23	.257	.408	.316	219
vs RHP	1449	3823	477	984	205	35	86	1517	453	357	755	32	46	112	38	78	37	42	.257	.397	.325	508
Home	868	2695	359	724	162	27	75	1165	340	255	504	25	37	77	22	52	25	31	.269	.432	.337	406
Away	885	2794	325	688	133	18	58	1031	309	244	539	24	21	71	31	56	31	34	.246	.369	.308	325
Grass	667	2137	258	526	103	9	48	791	248	193	419	17	14	52	23	44	24	29	.246	.370	.309	250
Turf	1086	3352	426	886	192	36	85	1405	401	306	624	32	44	96	30	64	32	36	.264	.419	.331	479
April/June	780	2544	316	666	145	26	53	1022	299	251	465	18	25	70	26	54	24	28	.262	.402	.331	347
July/October	973	2945	368	746	150	19	80	1174	350	248	578	31	33	78	27	54	32	37	.253	.399	.315	380

Boston Red Sox

Brock J. Hanke

BOSTON											
YEAR	1982	1983	1984	1985	1986	1987	1988	1989	1990	1991	TOT
W	89	78	86	81	95	78	89	83	88	84	851
L	73	84	76	81	66	84	73	79	74	78	768
WPCT	0.549	0.481	0.531	0.500	0.590	0.481	0.549	0.512	0.543	0.519	0.526
R	753	724	810	800	794	842	813	774	699	731	7740
RA	713	775	764	720	696	825	689	735	664	712	7293
PWPT	0.527	0.466	0.529	0.552	0.565	0.510	0.582	0.526	0.526	0.513	0.530
PythW	85	75	86	90	92	83	94	85	85	83	86
PythL	77	87	76	72	70	79	68	77	77	79	76
LUCK	4	3	0	-9	3	-5	-5	-2	3	1	-7

Defensive Efficiency Record: .6968

OK, so who would I keep if I were trying to sort out the Red Sox outfielder/first base/DH platoon, and why?

I would keep Jack Clark because he's still helping and he has no market value. I would keep Phil Plantier because he's the hottest prospect. I would keep Ellis Burks because he's the only center fielder. I would have kept Steve Lyons, because he's a versatile backup, but Bobby Cox snarfed him up. I'd have to keep Mike Greenwell because neither Mo Vaughn nor Jack Clark (any more) can play in the outfield, and Carlos Quintana is untested out there. That leaves a debate between Carlos and Mo for the last starting spot.

None of the usual indicators makes the decision for me. They're the same type of hitter, so batting order needs don't apply. Mo is young, at age 24, but Carlos is only 26. Mo has more rep, and Carlos didn't show much at age 25, but Carlos power stats have moved right up, and he now has to be taken seriously. Carlos fields better, but this is first base. Carlos is right handed, while Mo bats left, but the Bosox are balanced in that regard. Both men hit most of their home runs out of Fenway. That's normal for Carlos. He's right handed, and has to contend with the Monster. Mo, on the other hand, ought to be able to learn to exploit Fenway, and therefore should show more power in the future.

Carlos has played a little outfield, and isn't awful. If Mike Greenwell should collapse completely, Carlos could probably handle the job. Mo Vaughn has, as far as I know, never played outfield. He's also an inch shorter and 30 pounds heavier than Carlos. That should indicate that he can't play anywhere but first and DH, and would be a point fore keeping Carlos. But Vaughn seems to have some speed. His doubles stats are fine, and he attempts the occasional stolen base. Carlos doesn't.

All in all, I don't see a whole lot to choose from here. All in all, what I think I'd try to do is shop one of Scott Cooper/Wade Boggs and one of Mo/Carlos, and see what combination would get me the best collection of pitchers and a catcher. That probably means letting Mo go. I'll bet, though, that you can get as much for Mo and Wade as for Mo and Scott, so you can keep one of the kids. I'll also bet you can get our choice of Whitey Herzog's pitchers for that, and a catcher as well. Even if you don't want the Angels' catchers and have to make Whitey trade for one first.

What the Bosox seem to be trying to do is deal Greenwell and/or Burks. I really don't see why. If they deal Burks, they have to put a really untested kid in center. If they deal Greenwell, they have to play Carlos Quintana in the outfield. Unless the Boston management knows something I don't (injury or drugs or something like that), I'd keep Mike and especially Ellis. What I think is that the Sox are trying to get rid of the older men and keep all this kids. I would usually agree with this, but the Bosox aren't going to have Wade Boggs and Roger Clemens and Frank Viola forever. They have to compete with the Blue Jays now. They can get more now value for the kids than for the veterans. Besides, what do they think - their farm system is going to quit producing hitters or something?

As far as pitching goes, I guess you readers can figure out that I love the acquisition of Frank Viola. Starting pitching has been the Bosox weakness for some years now. What they've been doing, for you new readers, is this: every year they pick up a bunch of has beens and journeymen and let them fight it out for the rotation spots behind Roger. What they get, of course, is a bunch of .400 pitchers. Since they have a .600 offense, that produces a .500 record out of the team except for Roger. Then they figure that Roger will go 15 or 20 games over .500, which is what they need as a team in order to contend. Well, the Jays have recently upped the ante, and Roger can't really do it himself. Getting Frank gives them a real good chance to get 25 games over .500 before they get into the journeymen. That can win against anything.

Regarding Tony Pena: he may be through. You've got a 35-year-old catcher here, and he's put more than the usual stress on his legs, with the squats he uses. I know that the position is unusually weak right now, and there are a lot of teams with catchers who can't hit; but, if I were the Sox, I'd be looking for some help there. That comment I made above about using Cooper and Vaughn to trade for one wasn't just something off the top of my head.

When I first started doing these books, the first article I wrote on the Boston Red Sox was an answer to a particularly silly comment in the ELIAS BASEBALL ANALYST. That comment had to do with Walt Hriniak and his influence of Red Sox hitters, and so it's a bit irrelevant now. But one of the things that I wrote there is still working. I noted that, offense or no offense, the Red Sox won the division whenever their team ERA went below 4.00. They didn't win when they pitched worse. That's still true, and it's another reason why I like the pickup of Viola.

Well, that's bout all I've got to write about the Sox this year. You know, year in and year out, this is the shortest, and one of the easiest, articles I get to write. The reason is simple: this is an obvious ballclub. Their strengths are obvious, as are their weaknesses. Part of that is the ballpark; it forces extremes. Part of it is Roger. He's the best, pure and simple, and the rest of the Boston pitching staff is not. But part of it is the management. They are very straightforward and very organized. I don't always agree with their decisions. For example, I would not have buried Scott Cooper for nearly this many years. I'd have either found a place for him or traded him for something I needed. But, whether for good or bad, the Boston management is organized, and they know what they're trying to do. It leads to short articles for you Boston readers to look at in this book, but it also probably helps the team you look at all year.

Boston Red Sox Home Park Performance Factors

	Outs	Runs	Hits	2b	3b	HR	W	K	SH	SF	HBP	IBB	SB	CS	GDP
Home LH Batters	.988	.920	.897	.723	.737	.847	.856	1.126	.490	.909	2.122	.699	1.114	1.490	.909
Home RH Batters	.987	.939	.972	.870	1.443	.906	.939	.997	.891	1.287	1.035	.967	.937	.999	.921
All Home Batters	.985	.934	.947	.819	1.021	.887	.912	1.021	.833	1.117	1.129	.772	1.017	1.096	.915
Opp LH Batters	.987	1.009	.936	.891	2.454	1.074	.951	1.041	1.084	.951	1.211	.740	.893	1.084	.829
Opp RH Batters	1.048	1.026	1.005	1.042	1.159	1.025	1.008	1.037	1.416	1.021	1.008	1.382	1.083	.976	.917
All Opp Batters	1.031	1.028	.994	1.012	1.322	1.027	.999	1.028	1.124	1.023	1.066	.999	1.039	1.015	.918
All LH Batters	.986	.957	.915	.790	1.026	.941	.897	1.068	.753	.929	1.468	.717	.992	1.182	.873
All RH Batters	1.014	.977	.985	.942	1.231	.960	.970	1.012	1.023	1.154	1.028	1.187	1.007	.989	.919
All Batters	1.006	.978	.969	.902	1.165	.953	.952	1.018	.941	1.072	1.097	.874	1.020	1.041	.916

Conventional Batting Records for Boston Red Sox

	G	AB	Run	Hit	2B	3B	HR	TB	RBI	W	K	IW	HB	SB	CS	BRng Eff	GI DP	SH	SF	Avg	Slug	OBP	Runs Ctd
Pena T	141	464	45	107	23	2	5	149	48	37	53	1	4	8	3	.444	23	4	3	.231	.321	.291	40
Quintana	149	478	69	141	21	1	11	197	71	61	66	2	2	1	0	.339	17	6	3	.295	.412	.375	74
Reed Jd	153	618	87	175	42	2	5	236	60	60	53	2	4	6	5	.435	15	11	3	.283	.382	.349	83
Boggs W	144	546	93	181	42	2	8	251	51	89	32	25	0	1	2	.287	16	0	6	.332	.460	.421	109
Rivera L	129	414	64	107	22	3	8	159	40	35	86	0	3	4	4	.475	10	12	4	.258	.384	.318	50
Greenwell	147	544	76	163	26	6	9	228	83	43	35	6	3	15	5	.429	11	1	7	.300	.419	.350	81
Burks	130	474	56	119	33	3	14	200	56	39	81	2	6	6	11	.487	7	2	3	.251	.422	.314	61
Brunansky	142	459	54	105	24	1	16	179	70	49	72	2	3	1	2	.344	8	0	8	.229	.390	.303	56
Clark Jk	140	481	75	120	18	1	28	224	87	96	133	3	3	0	2	.313	17	0	5	.249	.466	.374	86
Vaughn M	74	219	21	57	12	0	4	81	32	26	43	2	2	2	1	.371	7	0	4	.260	.370	.339	28
Lyons S	87	212	15	51	10	1	4	75	17	11	35	2	0	10	3	.367	1	3	1	.241	.354	.277	22
Plantier	53	148	27	49	7	1	11	91	35	23	38	2	1	1	0	.484	3	0	2	.331	.615	.420	40
Brumley	63	118	16	25	5	0	0	30	5	10	22	0	0	2	0	.474	0	4	0	.212	.254	.273	9
Marzano	49	114	10	30	8	0	0	38	9	1	16	0	1	0	0	.429	5	1	2	.263	.333	.271	9
Marshall	22	62	4	18	4	0	1	25	7	0	19	0	0	0	0	.429	2	0	0	.290	.403	.290	6
Naehring	20	55	1	6	1	0	0	7	3	6	15	0	0	0	0	.500	0	4	0	.109	.127	.197	2
Romine	44	55	7	9	2	0	1	14	7	3	10	0	0	1	1	.357	1	0	0	.164	.255	.207	3
Cooper S	14	35	6	16	4	2	0	24	7	2	2	0	0	0	0	.438	0	0	0	.457	.686	.486	12
Zupcic	18	25	3	4	0	0	1	7	3	1	6	0	0	0	0	.000	0	1	0	.160	.280	.192	1
Housie	11	8	2	2	1	0	0	3	0	1	3	0	0	1	0	.000	1	1	0	.250	.375	.333	1
Wedge	1	1	0	1	0	0	0	1	0	0	0	0	0	0	0	.000	0	0	0	1.000	1.000	1.000	1
Reardon	1	0	0	0	0	0	0	0	0	0	0	0	0	0	0	.000	0	0	0	.000	.000	.000	0
TOTALS	1732	5530	731	1486	305	25	126	2219	691	593	820	49	32	59	39	.387	144	50	51	.269	.401	.340	760

Sabermetric Batting Records for Boston Red Sox

	Ball Park Adjusted								Runs		Run/									
	AB	Run	Hit	2B	3B	HR	RBI	W	SO	Avg	Slug	OBP	Ctd	Outs	27o	OW%	OG	OWAR	DWAR	TWAR
Boggs W	525	89	165	33	3	7	47	80	34	.314	.429	.402	94	380	6.68	.692	14	4.82	1.03	5.84
Brumley	117	15	24	4	0	0	4	9	22	.205	.239	.262	8	96	2.25	.203	4	-0.52	0.26	-0.26
Brunansky	463	53	103	22	1	15	71	47	73	.222	.371	.293	53	377	3.80	.421	14	0.99	0.65	1.64
Burks	478	55	117	31	3	13	57	37	82	.245	.404	.305	57	382	4.03	.450	14	1.42	0.33	1.75
Clark Jk	485	73	118	17	1	27	89	93	135	.243	.449	.365	83	388	5.78	.627	14	3.98	0.00	3.98
Cooper S	32	5	14	3	3	0	6	1	2	.438	.719	.455	11	18	16.50	.932	1	0.39	0.01	0.40
Greenwell	525	73	149	20	9	8	76	38	37	.284	.402	.333	72	397	4.90	.547	15	2.90	0.65	3.55
Housie	7	1	1	0	0	0	0	0	3	.143	.143	.143	0	6	0.00	.000	0	-0.08	0.00	-0.08
Lyons S	204	14	46	8	1	3	15	9	37	.225	.319	.258	18	163	2.98	.309	6	-0.24	0.45	0.21
Marshall	61	3	17	3	0	0	7	0	19	.279	.328	.279	5	45	3.00	.312	2	-0.06	-0.01	-0.07
Marzano	114	9	29	7	0	0	9	0	16	.254	.316	.256	8	92	2.35	.217	3	-0.45	-0.08	-0.53
Naehring	54	0	5	0	0	0	3	5	15	.093	.093	.169	1	53	0.51	.013	2	-0.66	0.04	-0.62
Pena T	468	44	105	21	2	4	49	36	53	.224	.303	.284	38	393	2.61	.256	15	-1.37	0.29	-1.08
Plantier	141	26	44	5	1	10	32	20	41	.312	.574	.399	34	100	9.18	.809	4	1.70	0.14	1.84
Quintana	481	67	139	20	1	10	72	59	67	.289	.397	.367	71	366	5.24	.580	14	3.12	0.47	3.59
Reed Jd	622	85	172	40	2	4	61	58	53	.277	.367	.341	79	482	4.43	.497	18	2.62	1.66	4.28
Rivera L	417	62	105	21	3	7	41	34	87	.252	.367	.310	48	341	3.80	.421	13	0.90	1.50	2.40
Romine	54	6	8	1	0	0	7	2	10	.148	.167	.179	2	46	1.17	.065	2	-0.49	0.05	-0.44
Vaughn M	211	20	52	9	0	3	29	23	46	.246	.332	.325	23	169	3.67	.405	6	0.34	0.02	0.36
Wedge	0	0	0	0	0	0	0	0	0	.000	.000	.000	0	0	0.00	.000	0	0.00	0.00	0.00
Zupcic	24	2	3	0	0	0	3	0	6	.125	.125	.125	0	22	0.00	.000	1	-0.29	-0.03	-0.32
TOTALS	5518	717	1442	279	29	120	684	566	839	.261	.388	.331	716	4350	4.44	.499	161	23.99	7.43	31.42

Pitching Records for Boston Red Sox

	ERA	W	L	Pct	G	GS	CG	ShO	GF	Sv	IP	R	ER	H	2B	3B	HR	BB	IW	SO	HB	WP	BK
Clemens	2.62	18	10	.643	35	35	13	4	0	0	271.1	93	79	219	46	8	15	65	12	241	5	6	0
Gardiner	4.85	9	10	.474	22	22	0	0	0	0	130.0	79	70	140	26	2	18	47	2	91	0	1	0
Bolton	5.24	8	9	.471	25	19	0	0	4	0	110.0	72	64	136	22	4	16	51	2	64	1	3	0
Young Mt	5.18	3	7	.300	19	16	0	0	1	0	88.2	55	51	92	12	0	4	53	2	69	2	5	0
Morton	4.59	6	5	.545	16	15	1	0	0	0	86.1	49	44	93	23	2	9	40	2	45	1	1	1
Darwin	5.16	3	6	.333	12	12	0	0	0	0	68.0	39	39	71	17	1	15	15	1	42	4	2	0
Harris GA	3.85	11	12	.478	53	21	1	0	15	2	173.0	79	74	157	30	4	13	69	5	127	5	6	1
Hesketh	3.29	12	4	.750	39	17	0	0	5	0	153.1	59	56	142	32	5	19	53	3	104	0	8	0
Lamp	4.70	6	3	.667	51	0	0	0	12	0	92.0	54	48	100	21	4	8	31	7	57	3	1	0
Gray	2.34	2	3	.400	50	0	0	0	20	1	61.2	17	16	39	11	1	7	10	4	41	1	2	0
Reardon	3.03	1	4	.200	57	0	0	0	51	40	59.1	21	20	54	11	2	9	16	3	44	1	0	0
Fossas	3.47	3	2	.600	64	0	0	0	18	1	57.0	27	22	49	10	0	3	28	9	29	3	2	0
Kiecker	7.36	2	3	.400	18	5	0	0	3	0	40.1	34	33	56	8	0	6	23	4	21	2	3	2
Petry	4.43	0	0	.000	13	0	0	0	7	1	22.1	17	11	21	5	0	3	12	2	12	1	0	0
Irvine	6.00	0	0	.000	9	0	0	0	5	0	18.0	13	12	25	8	1	2	9	1	8	2	1	0
Plympton	0.00	0	0	.000	4	0	0	0	3	0	5.1	0	0	5	1	0	0	4	0	2	0	1	0
Lyons S	0.00	0	0	.000	1	0	0	0	1	0	1.0	0	0	2	1	0	0	0	0	1	0	0	0
Dopson	18.00	0	0	.000	1	0	0	0	1	0	1.0	2	2	2	1	0	0	1	0	0	0	0	0
Manzanillo J	18.00	0	0	.000	1	0	0	0	1	0	1.0	2	2	2	1	0	0	3	0	1	0	0	0
TOTALS	4.02	84	78	.519	490	162	15	4	147	45	1439.2	712	643	1405	286	34	147	530	59	999	31	42	4

Sabermetric Pitching Records for Boston Red Sox

	Adj ERA	Expected W	Expected L	Expected Pct	Opposing Batters BFP	Avg	Slg	OBA	RC/G	GDP	SB	CS	PK	PKE	SH	SF	Supported RSup	RSp/G	W	L	Pct
Bolton	5.07	7	10	.394	499	.308	.485	.378	6.43	18	5	2	0	1	2	4	53	4.34	7	10	.422
Clemens	2.55	20	8	.719	1077	.221	.328	.270	2.85	18	23	16	1	3	6	8	134	4.44	21	7	.752
Darwin	5.03	4	5	.398	292	.263	.500	.309	5.75	1	5	1	0	0	1	2	27	3.57	3	6	.335
Dopson	9.00	0	0	.171	6	.500	.750	.500	17.18	0	0	0	0	0	0	1	0	0.00	0	0	.000
Fossas	3.32	3	2	.603	244	.236	.327	.335	3.63	9	5	2	0	1	5	0	21	3.32	3	2	.500
Gardiner	4.71	8	11	.430	562	.274	.438	.333	5.14	11	11	5	1	0	1	3	90	6.23	12	7	.637
Gray	2.19	4	1	.777	231	.181	.338	.219	2.24	3	5	3	0	0	3	1	24	3.50	4	1	.719
Harris GA	3.75	13	10	.544	731	.243	.363	.318	3.85	17	1	6	3	2	4	8	76	3.95	12	11	.527
Hesketh	3.17	10	6	.625	631	.250	.424	.313	4.12	19	7	8	1	5	7	3	87	5.11	12	4	.722
Irvine	5.50	0	0	.356	90	.321	.526	.404	8.74	1	1	0	0	0	1	0	10	5.00	0	0	.452
Kiecker	7.14	1	4	.247	194	.344	.503	.429	8.11	4	7	3	0	1	5	1	31	6.92	2	3	.484
Lamp	4.50	4	5	.452	403	.275	.420	.335	4.94	14	10	0	0	0	3	2	63	6.16	6	3	.652
Lyons S	0.00	0	0	.000	5	.400	.600	.400	10.97	0	0	0	0	0	0	0	0	0.00	0	0	.000
Manzanillo J	9.00	0	0	.171	8	.400	.600	.625	21.43	0	0	0	0	0	0	0	0	0.00	0	0	.000
Morton	4.48	5	6	.454	379	.284	.448	.356	5.58	9	4	2	1	1	3	7	59	6.15	7	4	.653
Petry	4.03	0	0	.507	98	.250	.417	.347	4.93	3	2	1	0	0	0	1	14	5.64	0	0	.662
Plympton	0.00	0	0	.000	24	.263	.316	.375	4.28	1	0	0	0	0	0	1	0	0.00	0	0	.000
Reardon	2.88	3	2	.668	248	.236	.419	.286	4.29	2	3	1	0	0	0	2	6	0.91	0	5	.091
Young Mt	4.97	4	6	.403	404	.266	.335	.365	4.55	11	8	3	0	0	1	2	36	3.65	4	6	.351
TOTALS	3.93	84	78	.520	6126	.257	.402	.323	4.42	141	97	53	7	14	42	46	731	4.57	93	69	.575

Batting 'Splits' Records for Boston Red Sox

	G	AB	Run	Hit	2B	3B	HR	TB	RBI	W	K	IW	HB	SB	CS	GIDP	SH	SF	Avg	Slug	OBP	Runs Ctd
SPLITS for Boggs W																						
vs LHP	81	166	27	44	6	2	2	60	13	17	10	1	0	0	0	9	0	0	.265	.361	.333	18
vs RHP	134	380	66	137	36	0	6	191	38	72	22	24	0	1	2	7	0	6	.361	.503	.456	93
Home	69	252	50	98	28	2	6	148	32	47	12	15	0	0	1	8	0	2	.389	.587	.482	73
Away	75	294	43	83	14	0	2	103	19	42	20	10	0	1	1	8	0	4	.282	.350	.368	40
Grass	119	445	75	147	34	2	8	209	47	72	24	22	0	1	2	12	0	5	.330	.470	.420	91
Turf	25	101	18	34	8	0	0	42	4	17	8	3	0	0	0	4	0	1	.337	.416	.429	19
April/June	70	264	38	82	21	0	5	118	31	47	17	11	0	1	1	10	0	2	.311	.447	.412	50
July/October	74	282	55	99	21	2	3	133	20	42	15	14	0	0	1	6	0	4	.351	.472	.430	60
SPLITS for Greenwell																						
vs LHP	88	168	26	55	9	2	4	80	34	8	12	0	2	4	1	5	1	4	.327	.476	.357	28
vs RHP	138	376	50	108	17	4	5	148	49	35	23	6	1	11	4	6	0	3	.287	.394	.347	53
Home	71	255	35	77	17	3	5	115	42	27	13	6	0	5	1	5	1	3	.302	.451	.365	43
Away	76	289	41	86	9	3	4	113	41	16	22	0	3	10	4	6	0	4	.298	.391	.337	38
Grass	123	442	62	132	23	3	8	185	68	41	22	6	3	12	4	9	1	6	.299	.419	.358	68
Turf	24	102	14	31	3	3	1	43	15	2	13	0	0	3	1	2	0	1	.304	.422	.314	13
April/June	71	272	41	86	11	3	5	118	41	23	18	2	0	10	0	6	0	3	.316	.434	.366	45
July/October	76	272	35	77	15	3	4	110	42	20	17	4	3	5	5	5	1	4	.283	.404	.334	36
SPLITS for Quintana																						
vs LHP	80	153	30	52	7	0	5	74	26	26	21	2	0	0	0	8	1	0	.340	.484	.436	32
vs RHP	124	325	39	89	14	1	6	123	45	35	45	0	2	1	0	9	5	3	.274	.378	.345	43
Home	74	236	31	69	10	0	2	85	30	34	31	1	1	1	0	7	4	1	.292	.360	.382	34
Away	75	242	38	72	11	1	9	112	41	27	35	1	1	0	0	10	2	2	.298	.463	.368	40
Grass	125	398	56	116	20	1	6	156	56	50	54	2	2	1	0	15	6	3	.291	.392	.371	58
Turf	24	80	13	25	1	0	5	41	15	11	12	0	0	0	0	2	0	0	.313	.512	.396	16
April/June	70	243	34	74	11	0	5	100	29	28	32	1	2	0	0	6	5	0	.305	.412	.381	39
July/October	79	235	35	67	10	1	6	97	42	33	34	1	0	1	0	11	1	3	.285	.413	.369	35
SPLITS for Boston Red Sox (all batters except pitchers)																						
vs LHP	826	1481	231	426	81	9	39	642	212	159	197	8	5	12	8	50	15	19	.288	.433	.355	225
vs RHP	1513	4049	500	1060	224	16	87	1577	479	434	623	41	27	47	31	94	35	32	.262	.389	.335	536
Home	882	2749	378	762	183	12	69	1176	359	316	389	31	13	28	17	76	29	21	.277	.428	.352	415
Away	850	2781	353	724	122	13	57	1043	332	277	431	18	19	31	22	68	21	30	.260	.375	.328	346
Grass	1477	4646	609	1242	261	18	105	1854	580	512	686	45	25	51	32	127	43	43	.267	.399	.340	635
Turf	255	884	122	244	44	7	21	365	111	81	134	4	7	8	7	17	7	8	.276	.413	.339	125
April/June	738	2454	309	638	129	9	57	956	297	270	360	19	12	28	13	64	22	17	.260	.390	.334	323
July/October	994	3076	422	848	176	16	69	1263	394	323	460	30	20	31	26	80	28	34	.276	.411	.345	437

1991 SPLITS FOR Boston Red Sox

BATTING SPLITS

	AVG	AB	R	H	2B	3B	HR	RBI	SB	CS	BB	K	OBA	SPCT
Total	.269	5530	731	1486	305	25	126	691	59	39	593	820	.340	.401

	#Pit	#P/PA	GB	FB	G/F	G	IBB	HB	SH	SF	GDP
Miscellaneous	23077	3.69	2096	1532	1.37	162	49	32	50	51	144

	AVG	AB	R	H	2B	3B	HR	RBI	SB	CS	BB	K	OBA	SPCT
vs. Left	.288	1481	...	426	81	9	39	212	12	8	159	197	.355	.433
vs. Right	.262	4049	...	1060	224	16	87	479	47	31	434	623	.335	.389
Home	.277	2749	378	762	183	12	69	359	28	17	316	389	.352	.428
Away	.260	2781	353	724	122	13	57	332	31	22	277	431	.328	.375
None on	.266	3001	...	799	155	14	70	70	0	0	287	445	.335	.397
Runners on	.272	2529	...	687	150	11	56	621	59	39	306	375	.346	.406
April	.239	607	62	145	28	2	16	58	3	3	62	93	.315	.371
May	.282	968	140	273	52	5	21	132	18	4	114	123	.357	.411
June	.250	879	107	220	49	2	20	107	7	6	94	144	.322	.379
July	.262	961	120	252	49	5	27	113	8	7	99	139	.330	.408
August	.282	996	136	281	57	8	18	123	7	9	97	138	.346	.410
September	.278	905	142	252	53	1	22	135	15	9	108	148	.358	.412
October	.294	214	24	63	17	2	2	23	1	1	19	35	.350	.421
None on/out	.276	1356	...	374	84	6	31	31	0	0	121	181	.338	.415
Scoring Posn	.264	1437	...	379	80	7	34	553	11	4	231	221	.356	.400
Close & Late	.225	805	...	181	33	3	9	76	3	5	87	165	.303	.307
Bases Loaded	.354	147	...	52	14	0	5	142	0	0	17	19	.400	.551
Batting #1	.322	670	112	216	49	5	12	52	3	8	92	53	.403	.464
Batting #2	.269	661	92	178	43	1	9	72	9	4	69	74	.339	.378
Batting #3	.285	629	93	179	30	4	20	95	9	1	87	89	.369	.440
Batting #4	.241	605	90	146	27	2	28	103	2	3	98	157	.348	.431
Batting #5	.306	624	86	191	36	3	13	94	13	8	53	62	.364	.436
Batting #6	.241	609	73	147	34	2	24	98	3	4	58	95	.305	.422
Batting #7	.276	591	61	163	35	4	7	71	7	4	55	103	.339	.384
Batting #8	.228	587	54	134	29	1	6	56	8	3	38	70	.278	.312
Batting #9	.238	554	70	132	22	3	7	50	5	4	43	117	.296	.327
As c	.236	576	55	136	31	2	5	56	8	3	38	68	.287	.323
As 1b	.291	592	83	172	24	1	12	77	2	1	79	92	.374	.395
As 2b	.286	660	88	189	43	2	6	65	8	5	63	61	.351	.385
As 3b	.324	638	103	207	48	4	8	58	2	3	93	44	.407	.450
As ss	.237	531	75	126	25	3	8	47	5	4	47	115	.301	.341
As lf	.301	632	91	190	32	6	15	104	16	5	52	57	.353	.441
As cf	.246	619	69	152	42	4	17	70	15	13	47	102	.303	.409
As rf	.235	595	74	140	29	2	24	94	1	2	63	103	.308	.412
Outfield	.261	1846	234	482	103	12	56	268	32	20	162	262	.322	.421
0.0 count	.317	804	...	255	62	3	23	134	...	...	1	0	.319	.488
After (0.1)	.235	2415	...	568	108	13	52	256	...	...	132	511	.277	.355
After (1.0)	.287	2311	...	663	135	9	51	301	...	...	421	309	.396	.419
Two strikes	.193	2392	...	461	82	7	33	217	...	...	233	818	.268	.274
Grass	.267	4646	609	1242	261	18	105	580	51	32	512	686	.340	.399
Turf	.276	884	122	244	44	7	21	111	8	7	81	134	.339	.413
Day	.269	1808	259	486	103	5	38	241	16	9	201	271	.342	.394
Night	.269	3722	472	1000	202	20	88	450	43	30	392	549	.339	.405
Inning 1.6	.281	3796	554	1067	219	20	97	525	50	28	424	519	.353	.426
Inning 7+	.242	1734	177	419	86	5	29	166	9	11	169	301	.311	.347
vs.Bal	.261	421	51	110	22	1	9	49	5	4	29	66	.308	.382
vs.Cal	.228	372	38	85	16	0	6	36	2	2	41	59	.305	.320
vs.ChA	.253	435	57	110	20	2	16	50	10	3	54	67	.336	.418
vs.Cle	.280	457	60	128	30	2	2	55	3	5	49	61	.353	.368
vs.Det	.299	452	64	135	25	2	8	63	0	0	44	47	.359	.416
vs.KC	.234	380	37	89	16	3	9	35	1	4	42	62	.313	.363
vs.Mil	.278	449	70	125	21	0	12	68	10	2	49	89	.352	.405
vs.Min	.236	403	37	95	19	3	8	36	3	3	28	51	.284	.357
vs.NYA	.258	442	53	114	23	1	13	50	7	6	44	60	.329	.403
vs.Oak	.263	418	58	110	35	4	10	58	2	2	48	61	.341	.438
vs.Sea	.308	428	79	132	29	2	13	75	8	3	60	72	.390	.477
vs.Tex	.283	414	56	117	26	2	4	52	5	3	56	59	.363	.384
vs.Tor	.296	459	71	136	23	3	16	64	3	2	49	66	.368	.464

PITCHING SPLITS

	ERA	W	L	SV	SVOP	GS	CG	SHO	IP	H	ER	HR	BB	IBB	K
Total	4.01	84	78	45	61	162	15	12	1439.2	1405	642	147	530	59	999

	#Pit	#P/IP	GB	FB	G/F	BRp9	RA	WP	BK	SH	SF	R	HB	Hld
Miscellaneous	22557	15.67	2053	1435	1.43	12.29	328	42	4	42	46	712	31	56

	ERA	W	L	SV	SVOP	GS	CG	SHO	IP	H	ER	HR	BB	IBB	K
ST	4.22	65	61	0	0	162	15	4	984.1	984	462	103	341	26	711
REL	3.58	19	17	45	61	0	0	0	455.1	421	181	44	189	33	288
Home	3.91	43	38	23	30	81	7	2	749.0	757	325	76	285	33	523
Away	4.14	41	40	22	31	81	8	2	690.2	648	318	71	245	26	476
April	2.76	11	7	9	11	18	1	1	163.0	125	50	8	70	4	115
May	4.94	15	13	7	9	28	1	0	244.0	249	134	31	99	11	180
June	3.66	11	16	5	7	27	2	0	236.0	229	96	26	80	9	157
July	4.39	11	16	5	8	27	2	0	250.0	266	122	31	83	11	166
August	3.72	18	11	9	12	29	5	1	254.0	239	105	25	87	12	190
September	3.73	17	10	9	13	27	3	2	238.2	234	99	20	83	5	150
October	6.17	1	5	1	1	6	1	0	54.0	63	37	6	28	7	41
Grass	4.05	70	67	36	49	137	12	4	1225.2	1200	551	128	454	48	863
Turf	3.87	14	11	9	12	25	3	0	214.0	205	92	19	76	11	136
Day	4.52	25	28	12	18	53	4	1	471.2	491	237	54	184	18	327
Night	3.77	59	50	33	43	109	11	3	968.0	914	406	93	346	41	672
vs.Bal	4.35	5	8	2	3	13	1	0	113.2	116	55	17	42	2	84
vs.Cal	3.00	4	8	2	2	12	1	0	102.0	86	34	7	29	2	73
vs.ChA	3.00	7	5	3	6	12	1	0	114.0	102	38	7	35	5	77
vs.Cle	3.20	9	4	4	6	13	1	1	121.0	106	43	9	48	3	87
vs.Det	4.94	5	8	3	3	13	2	1	113.0	118	62	24	48	7	105
vs.KC	2.68	7	5	6	8	12	1	0	104.0	89	31	3	36	8	78
vs.Mil	4.18	7	6	4	5	13	1	0	114.0	121	53	5	38	4	71
vs.Min	5.43	3	9	2	4	12	0	0	106.0	120	64	11	41	6	60
vs.NYA	3.99	6	7	2	4	13	2	1	115.0	107	51	17	37	2	63
vs.Oak	4.30	8	4	4	5	12	1	1	111.0	103	53	14	47	8	83
vs.Sea	3.42	9	3	4	5	12	1	0	108.0	104	41	5	38	6	64
vs.Tex	6.38	5	7	3	3	12	1	0	103.0	130	73	16	46	6	71
vs.Tor	3.52	9	4	6	7	13	2	0	115.0	103	45	12	45	0	83

OPPOSING BATTERS VS. PITCHERS.

	AVG	AB	R	H	2B	3B	HR	RBI	SB	CS	BB	K	OBA	SPCT
Total	.257	5477	712	1405	286	34	147	664	97	53	530	999	.323	.402
vs. Left	.247	2093	...	517	110	13	36	228	48	27	205	370	.315	.364
vs. Right	.262	3384	...	888	176	21	111	436	49	26	325	629	.328	.425
ST	.261	3768	509	984	201	24	103	413	64	39	341	711	.323	.409
REL	.246	1709	203	421	85	10	44	251	33	14	189	288	.324	.385
Home	.264	2865	374	757	149	14	76	343	50	29	285	523	.331	.406
Away	.248	2612	338	648	137	20	71	321	47	24	245	476	.314	.397
None on	.255	3131	...	799	162	20	81	81	0	0	256	593	.315	.397
Runners on	.258	2346	...	606	124	14	66	583	97	53	274	406	.334	.408
None on/out	.262	1368	...	358	75	10	40	40	0	0	119	244	.324	.419
Scoring Posn	.253	1359	...	344	74	10	33	497	27	17	206	236	.345	.395
vs 1st Batr	.235	289	...	68	15	4	9	55	5	2	25	49	.301	.408
1st IP	.251	1690	220	424	83	9	46	264	32	13	173	305	.323	.392
Inning 1.6	.262	3722	515	974	198	22	98	477	75	38	350	702	.325	.406
Inning 7+	.246	1755	197	431	88	12	49	187	22	15	180	297	.319	.393
Close & Late	.235	839	...	197	42	10	17	85	17	9	95	150	.317	.369
0.0 count	.321	758	...	243	48	4	27	120	...	...	48	0	.363	.501
After (0.1)	.226	2437	...	551	102	13	56	251	...	...	136	644	.270	.348
After (1.0)	.268	2282	...	611	136	17	64	293	...	...	346	355	.363	.426
Two strikes	.176	2474	...	436	91	9	37	194	...	...	214	998	.245	.265
Pitch 1.15	.254	1510	...	383	80	11	39	196	32	12	137	240	.318	.399
Pitch 16.30	.241	1071	...	258	43	5	32	140	19	5	106	241	.314	.380
Pitch 31.45	.246	748	...	184	41	6	15	72	13	11	71	127	.312	.377
Pitch 46.60	.252	646	...	163	37	2	17	78	14	4	46	132	.300	.395
Pitch 61.75	.299	572	...	171	36	2	17	83	5	7	60	91	.363	.458
Pitch 76.90	.260	438	...	114	24	3	15	53	8	9	54	73	.341	.432
Pitch 91.105	.283	321	...	91	18	3	7	27	4	1	40	57	.363	.424
Pitch 106.20	.244	131	...	32	8	1	3	10	1	2	9	27	.293	.389
Pitch 121.35	.286	42	...	12	2	1	2	8	1	2	5	10	.354	.524
Pitch 136.50	.000	4	...	0	0	0	0	0	0	0	2	1	.333	.000

Detroit Tigers

Dave Raglin and Brock J. Hanke

DETROIT											
YEAR	1982	1983	1984	1985	1986	1987	1988	1989	1990	1991	TOT
W	83	92	104	84	87	98	88	59	79	84	858
L	79	70	58	77	75	64	74	103	83	78	761
WPCT	0.512	0.568	0.642	0.522	0.537	0.605	0.543	0.364	0.488	0.519	0.530
R	729	789	829	729	798	896	703	617	750	817	7657
RA	685	679	643	688	714	735	658	816	754	794	7166
PWPT	0.531	0.575	0.624	0.529	0.555	0.598	0.533	0.364	0.497	0.514	0.533
PythW	86	93	101	86	90	97	86	59	81	83	86
PythL	76	69	61	76	72	65	76	103	81	79	76
LUCK	-3	-1	3	-2	-3	1	2	0	-2	1	-4

Defensive Efficiency Record: .6912

The 1991 Detroit Tigers were the ultimate sabermetric team. Let's list a couple of big ways:

(1) For years, we've heard the old line that pitching is 75% or 90% or some huge percentage of winning games. Proponents of that view always trot out some example of a team with a weak offense and great pitching that was very successful. What about the other side, though?

The 1991 Tigers turned that theory on its head. The Tigers allowed 794 runs, third worst in the league, yet still posted a winning record, 84-78. How? They were second in the league in runs scored, with 817. Using the Pythagoreom Theorem developed by Bill James, predicted winning percentage = $RF^2 / (RF^2 + RA^2)$, 819 runs for and 794 runs against should produce a winning percentage of .514. The Tigers' winning percentage was .519.

(2) The 1991 Tigers were second in the league in runs scored despite finishing **last** in the league in batting average.

It was fascinating to watch the transformation in the sports pages as the summer went on. First, the writers had to mention that the Tigers were in the pennant race despite being last in the AL, at the time, in the two "most important" (my quotes) statistics, ERA and batting average. Boy, were some of them puzzled over that! Then, they started to notice that Detroit was near the top of the league in runs scored, and that they had actually scored a few more runs than they had given up, still despite being last in the league in batting average, by seven to nine points on average! They started writing that the Tigers were scoring runs by hitting gobs of home runs and a few even mentioned the number of **walks** the Tigers had accumulated! I think this team helped raise the consciousness of quite a few fans and sportswriters. It wasn't like a religious conversion, but I think that because of this team, people will look at the other facets of offense beyond batting average a little more.

Those facets are captured in a statistic invented by James a few years ago called Secondary Average (SEC). Secondary average does just what it says--captures the other parts of offense that are not part of most people's primary offensive statistic, batting average. The formula is (extra bases on hits + BB + SB) / AB. Extra bases on hits is simply the bases on a hit after first (one for a double, two for a triple, and three for a home run). James set up secondary average so that the league average would be about the same as the league average for batting average, even though the spread is larger; the best players are usually near .500 while the worst are in the low .100s. As expected, Detroit laps the field:

Secondary Average, American League, 1991

	AB	H	R	D	T	HR	BB	SB	BA	SEC
DET	**5547**	**1372**	**817**	**259**	**26**	**209**	**699**	**109**	**.247**	**.315**
OAK	5410	1342	760	246	19	159	642	151	.248	.287
TEX	5703	1539	829	288	31	177	596	102	.270	.277
TOR	5489	1412	684	295	56	133	499	148	.257	.265
CHW	5594	1464	758	226	39	139	610	134	.262	.262
SEA	5494	1400	702	268	29	126	588	97	.255	.253
MIN	5556	1557	776	270	42	140	526	107	.280	.253
BAL	5604	1421	686	256	29	170	528	50	.254	.250

BOS	5530	1486	731	305	25	126	593	59	.269	.250
KCR	5584	1475	727	290	41	117	523	119	.264	.244
MIL	5611	1523	799	247	53	116	556	106	.271	.243
NYY	5541	1418	674	249	19	147	473	109	.256	.236
CAL	5470	1396	653	245	29	115	448	94	.255	.218
CLE	5470	1390	576	236	26	79	449	84	.254	.193
AL	77603	20195	10172	3680	464	1953	7730	1469	.260	.253

How did the Tigers compile such a high secondary average? Look at the table--they lead the league in home runs by 32 and the league in walks by 57! Of course, we're not saying that batting average is not an important statistic; it took an outstanding team in both home runs and bases on balls to finish second in runs scored despite finishing last in batting average.

The top Tiger in SEC was Mickey Tettleton, with his 31 homers and 101 free passes helping lead him to a .435 SEC, fourth in the league. The other top Tigers were Lou Whitaker (.411), Rob Deer (.408), and Cecil Fielder (.377).

My favorite Tiger has become Tony Phillips. After Cecil Fielder, he was the most valuable Tiger in 1991, even more valuable than Mickey Tettleton and Lou Whitaker. You just got to love him--he does so much for the team.

First of all, his defensive versatility. Phillips will play anywhere. In 1991, he played 46 games at third (the position the Tigers originally signed him to play), 36 at second, 25 in left, 23 in right, 13 at short, 9 in center (and 18 as the DH). Sparky has become the big maneuverer in his later years, and Phillips is perfect for it. Phillips' only regular position was leadoff, for which his .371 on-base percentage was ideal. Phillips played all of those positions well. He had a better range factor than the best regular at four positions; second, short, left, and right. At third and in center, his range factor was in the top third. (Part of that was the Tiger pitching staff which struck out the least men of any team in the league, but each team records about 4374 outs in a season (162*27) and the difference in the top and bottom strikeout teams was only 283, so most of Phillips' good range factors was Phillips.)

To get an idea of the day-to-day effect of having a Tony Phillips, let's look at where Phillips played in the field for the first 30 games (which he started as the Tigers' leadoff hitter):

Phillips in the Field, First 30 Games, 1991

1-DH	7-2B	13-SS	19-LF	25-DH
2-2B	8-2B	14-2B,RF	20-LF	26-CF,2B
3-2B	9-DH,LF	15-3B	21-LF,CF	27-2B,3B
4-2B	10-2B	16-LF	22-LF,3B	28-2B,LF
5-CF	11-SS	17-2B,CF	23-LF	29-SS
6-DH	12-SS,CF	18-LF	24-3B	30-RF

In these 30 games, Phillips played second 11 times because Lou Whitaker was off to a slow start. Phillips, although a switch-hitter, hits lefthanders much better, which usually give Whitaker fits. He played 11 games in left because of injuries to Lloyd Moseby. Milt Cuyler had a little trouble getting acclimated to the majors at first, so Phillips was in center five times during this stretch. Nine times Phillips played two positions in one game, and only five times did Phillips play the same positions in consecutive games.

Phillips' defensive versatility helped in other ways. In a desperate search for anyone who could pitch, Sparky had 12 pitchers for awhile last year, something he couldn't have done if he hadn't had Phillips. He could do that because if Sparky wanted to pinch hit for somebody, Phillips could move to that position, allowing the pinch hitter to stay in the game. In Games 21 and 22 above, that's what happened. Both times, Phillips started in leftfield, but moved when Dave Bergman came in to pinch hit, first for Milt Cuyler and then for Travis Fryman.

Beyond his have glove, will travel role, Phillips had an excellent year in 1991. He hit .284 and slugged .438 to go with the .371 on-base percentage. He had 79 walks, 17 home runs, and 28 doubles while playing in 146 games. Although this was his best season ever at age 32, I don't think it was a fluke. The on-base percentage was in line with several of his previous seasons, the big improvement has been in power, the skill that tends to go last. He probably won't do quite as well in 1992, but it won't be that much worse. Phillips has played better the more he's been given a chance to play. One big reason he left the World Champion A's for the worst team in baseball after the 1989 season was for the chance to play everyday. He certainly can't complain about boredom with the Tigers, and we're glad to have him.

In his 1991 Baseball Book, Bill James wrote an article discussing the fact that Lou Whitaker and Alan Trammell have almost identical career statistics, but people in Detroit consider Trammell to be a much better player, and that the reason is racism. James said, "...there is, believe it or not, a widespread belief among the Detroit media that Trammell is a tough, aggressive player who has built himself up to this level by working hard, while

Lou is just, well, a kind of shiftless black guy who has a lot ability but hasn't done much with it." He gives several compelling examples to back up his argument from what he has read in the Detroit media and heard from callers on radio talk shows. Even though I am a Tiger fan and write a sabermetric newsletter on the team, I have lived in the Washington DC area for about eight years, and I cannot dispute what James is saying.

I've done a lot of thinking about this article because I have to admit that I have thought of Trammell as being better than Whitaker. For example, the last few years, when people suggested to me that the Tigers should trade one of their veteran stars, I'd suggest Whitaker but never Trammell. I am not a racist, so why did I feel this way, I asked myself. After thinking about it, I came up with three reasons.

First, Alan Trammell's best seasons have been better than Lou Whitaker's. In 1987, when the Tigers had the best record in baseball and won one of the most thrilling pennant races of all time, Alan Trammell had an MVP season. He only finished second in the balloting, but just because the writers didn't award it to him doesn't mean that he didn't deserve it--he did. Trammell has had over 90 runs created five times, over 6.0 runs created per game five times, and hit .300 six times. Conversely, Whitaker has had only 90 runs created three times, 6.0 runs created per game two times, and hit .300 once. Trammell has gotten votes in the MVP balloting seven times, to two times for Whitaker. Their career numbers are almost the same because Trammell has also had some horrendous seasons due to injuries--he has been on the disabled list three of the last four seasons, and that's not counting the time his career was threatened in the mid-'80s due to arm trouble--but Whitaker has been more consistent.

Trammell has been a superstar at times, Whitaker has been a star. Not to put Whitaker down, but the feeling about Trammell is, if it hadn't been for the injuries...

Secondly is a point that James made and then dismissed--the fact that Trammell is more outgoing than Whitaker. As James said, "Trammell is a visible on-field 'leader', a holler guy; Whitaker is quiet, laid back." Whitaker belong to a religion that does not believe in honoring anybody but God, not the kind of person who goes looking for the headlines.

I don't think that the point can be dismissed so easily. To illustrate, let's look at another sport, for a situation where two players are linked together forever, even though in this case they've always been opponents. One is black, one is white. One is outgoing, the life of the party, one is more private. However, in this case, it's the black athlete who is the more outgoing. Now you tell me, who is more famous and admired, Magic Johnson or Larry Bird. The news of Magic's illness made the top of the front page in most papers around the country; I don't think that would have happened for Bird. That may be an extreme example, but look who the most famous athletes in this country are--Magic, Michael Jordan, and Bo Jackson. All outgoing, and all black.

The third reason is plain and simple luck. Alan Trammell happened to have his best season in 1987, a hitter's year when the Tigers won the Eastern pennant. He also had a great season in 1984, where he was the fastest starter on the 35-5 team that won the Series. On the other hand, the two season Lou Whitaker topped 100 runs created were 1983 and 1985. His career high in home runs came in 1989, the year the rest of team collapsed.

Whitaker and Trammell's similarities and propensity for luck don't end on the field. Both players have suffered embarrassing off-the-field injuries. Trammell's came early in his career when he injured himself in a Halloween costume, an injury that he recovered from before the next season. Whitaker's came dancing with a month to go in the hot 1988 pennant race; without him, the Tigers lost the East by one game.

I do not doubt that there are people who regard Trammell higher because of the color of his skin. We have not eradicated racism from our society. However, I disagree with James' argument that racism is the only reason, or even the primary reason. You can't judge society by nuts who call talk shows or senile old writers like News sportswriter Joe Falls. As I've pointed out, there are several good reasons why Trammell could be more highly regarded that Whitaker.

Again, I must point out that none of this is meant to be an insult to Lou Whitaker. Lou has been a great player, and if he plays well for a few more years, may deserve consideration for a place in Cooperstown. Whitaker right now is a more valuable property that Trammell, and I hope to be calling out "Lou" for years to come. We never appreciate the great ones as much as we should when we have them, but I'm trying my best to appreciate them. Both of them.

NOTE FROM BROCK: You may remember something in my ads about a "fifties" offense. What Dave has written here is, basically, what I was talking about. The baseball of the 1950's was, compared to our current game, riddled with power and lacking in speed on offense. There were many home runs, compared to batting average. There were many, many walks. There were very few stolen bases. That's what last year's Tigers were like.

I have a problem calling this a "sabermetric" offense. That would imply that sabermetricians think it's a better offense than any other. I don't agree with that, and neither does any sabermetrician I know, including Dave. What I will acknowledge, though, is that it is a hidden offense. Most baseball people focus so heavily on batting average that they completely forget that walks exist. They do remember home runs, but the people who score in front of them get forgotten. To that extent, the Tiger offense was "sabermetric." It exploitedskills that traditional baseball forget, and that's what sabermetrics tries to bring to light.

This sort of offense, by the way, is a reasonable response to the Detroit ballpark, itself a leftover from the fifties. Or, rather, from the 1920's. The defining feature of fifties baseball was that the parks hadn't changed in years. They were, relative to the newer, bigger ballplayers of the time, too small. They were easy to hit home runs out of.

The players themselves had not responded any too well to the home run, either. We know now that the way to counter a power offense is with ground-ball pitching. You keep the ball down, it doesn't go out. The pitchers of the 1930's and 1940's, though, tried to counter the longball offense by making the hitters pay for their homers in the form of strikeouts. Unfortunately, that works very poorly. Even the monstrous strikeout pitchers of the fifties couldn't keep the home run offense under control. Strikeouts just aren't that big a negative. What's more, the focus on throwing overly hard led to bad control, and therefore to walks. That relieved the homer hitter from having to get on base with hits. He could concentrate on homers and let the walks provide men for him to drive in.

All things concerned, I'm glad that developmental logjam of the fifties was broken. I like to see our current game, with its mix of speed, averages and power. But I'll miss the last few of these old dinosaur ballparks as they disappear. They're part of the current diversity, too. Without them, the option of playing this sort of game will collapse in futility. I don't know that we exactly run a risk of returning to a one-style game, but I will miss ballparks like Tiger Stadium, and the teams like this that suit them.

Detroit Tigers Home Park Performance Factors

	Outs	Runs	Hits	2b	3b	HR	W	K	SH	SF	HBP	IBB	SB	CS	GDP
Home LH Batters	1.104	.977	1.028	1.130	1.095	.942	.890	1.072	.766	.935	1.248	1.095	1.248	.723	.888
Home RH Batters	1.011	.968	1.019	1.173	.613	.963	.953	1.023	1.215	.829	.757	1.147	1.087	1.101	1.081
All Home Batters	1.042	.958	1.023	1.157	.876	.970	.911	1.056	1.121	.872	.872	1.020	.980	1.034	1.052
Opp LH Batters	1.086	.990	1.021	1.100	1.202	.928	1.085	1.062	1.217	1.025	2.311	1.355	1.009	1.449	1.420
Opp RH Batters	1.035	1.115	1.110	1.142	1.597	.894	1.054	.958	1.243	1.043	1.640	.984	1.099	.962	1.033
All Opp Batters	1.046	1.066	1.077	1.116	1.448	.911	1.070	.982	1.204	1.052	1.603	1.123	1.082	1.191	1.140
All LH Batters	1.093	.984	1.023	1.111	1.170	.935	.986	1.069	1.051	.983	1.555	1.282	1.086	1.196	1.266
All RH Batters	1.024	1.043	1.066	1.157	1.119	.940	1.005	1.004	1.215	.953	1.055	.996	1.090	1.015	1.041
All Batters	1.044	1.012	1.050	1.134	1.185	.947	.986	1.030	1.165	.969	1.109	1.080	1.031	1.118	1.099

Conventional Batting Records for Detroit Tigers

	G	AB	Run	Hit	2B	3B	HR	TB	RBI	W	K	IW	HB	SB	CS	BRng Eff	GI DP	SH	SF	Avg	Slug	OBP	Runs Ctd
Tettleton	154	501	85	132	17	2	31	246	89	101	131	9	2	3	3	.400	12	0	4	.263	.491	.387	100
Fielder	162	624	102	163	25	0	44	320	133	78	151	12	6	0	0	.405	17	0	4	.261	.513	.347	111
Whitaker	138	470	94	131	26	2	23	230	78	90	45	6	2	4	2	.446	3	2	8	.279	.489	.391	100
Fryman T	149	557	65	144	36	3	21	249	91	40	149	0	3	12	5	.465	13	6	6	.259	.447	.309	75
Trammell	101	375	57	93	20	0	9	140	55	37	39	1	3	11	2	.439	7	5	1	.248	.373	.320	47
Moseby	74	260	37	68	15	1	6	103	35	21	43	2	3	8	1	.487	3	1	3	.262	.396	.321	35
Cuyler	154	475	77	122	15	7	3	160	33	52	92	0	5	41	10	.590	4	12	2	.257	.337	.335	61
Deer	134	448	64	80	14	2	25	173	64	89	175	1	0	1	3	.339	3	0	2	.179	.386	.314	60
Incaviglia	97	337	38	72	12	1	11	119	38	36	92	0	1	1	3	.286	6	1	2	.214	.353	.290	35
Phillips	146	564	87	160	28	4	17	247	72	79	95	5	3	10	5	.427	8	3	6	.284	.438	.371	97
Bergman	86	194	23	46	10	1	7	79	29	35	40	2	0	1	1	.308	2	0	2	.237	.407	.351	30
Barnes	75	159	28	46	13	2	5	78	17	9	24	1	0	10	7	.500	1	2	1	.289	.491	.325	24
Allanson	60	151	10	35	10	0	1	48	16	7	31	0	0	0	1	.286	3	2	0	.232	.318	.266	12
Shelby	53	143	19	22	8	1	3	41	8	8	23	1	1	0	2	.450	3	1	0	.154	.287	.204	7
Livingstone	44	127	19	37	5	0	2	48	11	10	25	0	0	2	1	.364	0	1	1	.291	.378	.341	17
Salas	33	57	2	5	1	0	1	9	7	0	10	0	2	0	0	.667	0	0	1	.088	.158	.117	1
Delossantos	16	30	1	5	2	0	0	7	0	2	4	0	0	0	0	.333	2	0	0	.167	.233	.219	1
Moses	13	21	5	1	1	0	0	2	1	2	7	0	0	4	0	.400	0	1	0	.048	.095	.130	1
Hare	9	19	0	1	1	0	0	2	0	2	1	0	0	0	0	.000	3	0	0	.053	.105	.143	0
Paredes	16	18	4	6	0	0	0	6	0	0	1	0	0	1	1	.250	0	0	0	.333	.333	.333	2
Bernazard	6	12	0	2	0	0	0	2	0	0	4	0	0	0	0	.000	0	0	0	.167	.167	.167	0
Rowland	4	4	0	1	0	0	0	1	1	1	2	0	0	0	0	.000	0	0	1	.250	.250	.333	1
Tanana	1	1	0	0	0	0	0	0	0	0	1	0	0	0	0	.000	0	0	0	.000	.000	.000	0
Henneman	4	0	0	0	0	0	0	0	0	0	0	0	0	0	0	.000	0	0	0	.000	.000	.000	0
Dalton	1	0	0	0	0	0	0	0	0	0	0	0	0	0	0	.000	0	0	0	.000	.000	.000	0
Gullickson	1	0	0	0	0	0	0	0	0	0	0	0	0	0	0	.000	0	1	0	.000	.000	.000	0
Gibson P	1	0	0	0	0	0	0	0	0	0	0	0	0	0	0	.000	0	0	0	.000	.000	.000	0
TOTALS	1732	5547	817	1372	259	26	209	2310	778	699	1185	40	31	109	47	.427	90	38	44	.247	.416	.333	803

Sabermetric Batting Records for Detroit Tigers

	Ball Park Adjusted												Runs		Run/					
	AB	Run	Hit	2B	3B	HR	RBI	W	SO	Avg	Slug	OBP	Ctd	Outs	27o	OW%	OG	OWAR	DWAR	TWAR
Allanson	155	10	37	11	0	0	15	7	30	.239	.310	.272	12	124	2.61	.217	5	-0.61	-0.40	-1.01
Barnes	163	29	48	15	2	4	16	9	23	.294	.485	.331	25	125	5.40	.542	5	0.89	0.38	1.27
Bergman	209	22	47	11	1	6	28	34	42	.225	.373	.332	28	166	4.55	.457	6	0.65	0.16	0.82
Bernazard	12	0	2	0	0	0	0	0	4	.167	.167	.167	0	10	0.00	.000	0	-0.13	0.04	-0.09
Cuyler	496	77	128	17	8	2	32	51	93	.258	.337	.334	63	397	4.28	.426	15	1.12	0.90	2.02
Delossantos	30	1	5	2	0	0	0	2	3	.167	.233	.219	1	27	1.00	.039	1	-0.31	0.01	-0.30
Deer	461	66	85	16	2	23	63	89	173	.184	.377	.316	60	383	4.23	.420	14	1.00	0.78	1.78
Fielder	644	106	173	28	0	40	132	78	149	.269	.498	.352	113	491	6.21	.610	18	4.73	0.27	5.00
Fryman T	575	67	153	41	3	19	90	40	147	.266	.447	.315	79	452	4.72	.474	17	2.08	0.60	2.68
Hare	20	0	1	1	0	0	0	1	1	.050	.100	.095	0	22	0.00	.000	1	-0.29	0.07	-0.22
Incaviglia	346	39	76	13	1	10	37	36	91	.220	.350	.294	36	281	3.46	.326	10	-0.25	0.26	0.01
Livingstone	135	18	37	5	0	1	10	9	26	.274	.333	.319	15	99	4.09	.404	4	0.20	0.22	0.42
Moseby	279	36	69	16	1	5	34	20	45	.247	.366	.307	34	216	4.25	.422	8	0.58	-0.03	0.55
Moses	21	5	1	1	0	0	0	1	7	.048	.095	.091	0	21	0.00	.000	1	-0.27	0.03	-0.24
Paredes	18	4	6	0	0	0	0	0	0	.333	.333	.333	2	13	4.15	.411	0	0.03	0.04	0.07
Phillips	588	88	167	31	4	15	71	78	96	.284	.427	.368	98	442	5.99	.592	16	3.96	1.82	5.78
Rowland	4	0	1	0	0	0	0	1	1	.250	.250	.400	1	3	9.00	.766	0	0.05	0.01	0.06
Salas	61	1	5	1	0	0	6	0	10	.082	.098	.125	1	56	0.48	.009	2	-0.71	-0.00	-0.71
Shelby	149	19	23	9	1	2	7	7	23	.154	.268	.197	7	132	1.43	.077	5	-1.34	0.35	-0.99
Tettleton	523	85	138	19	2	29	88	100	133	.264	.474	.382	99	404	6.62	.639	15	4.33	-0.59	3.74
Trammell	387	59	99	23	0	8	54	37	38	.256	.377	.326	50	303	4.46	.446	11	1.07	1.33	2.41
Whitaker	505	92	134	28	2	21	75	88	48	.265	.453	.373	94	384	6.61	.639	14	4.11	1.41	5.51
TOTALS	5796	826	1440	294	30	196	774	692	1207	.248	.411	.330	817	4592	4.80	.483	170	22.64	7.65	30.29

Pitching Records for Detroit Tigers

	ERA	W	L	Pct	G	GS	CG	ShO	GF	Sv	IP	R	ER	H	2B	3B	HR	BB	IW	SO	HB	WP	BK
Gullickson	3.90	20	9	.690	35	35	4	0	0	0	226.1	109	98	256	51	7	22	44	13	91	4	4	0
Terrell	4.24	12	14	.462	35	33	8	2	1	0	218.2	115	103	257	48	8	16	79	10	80	2	8	0
Tanana	3.77	13	12	.520	33	33	3	2	0	0	217.1	98	91	217	34	4	26	78	9	107	2	3	1
Aldred	5.18	2	4	.333	11	11	1	0	0	0	57.1	37	33	58	6	1	9	30	2	35	0	3	1
Leiter M	4.21	9	7	.563	38	15	1	0	7	1	134.2	66	63	125	20	5	16	50	4	103	6	2	0
Gibson P	4.59	5	7	.417	68	0	0	0	28	8	96.0	51	49	112	10	4	10	48	8	52	3	4	0
Cerutti	4.57	3	6	.333	38	8	1	0	10	2	88.2	49	45	94	11	4	9	37	9	29	2	4	1
Henneman	2.88	10	2	.833	60	0	0	0	50	21	84.1	29	27	81	17	2	2	34	8	61	0	5	0
Gleaton	4.06	3	2	.600	47	0	0	0	16	2	75.1	37	34	74	11	4	7	39	8	47	0	1	1
Gakeler	5.74	1	4	.200	31	7	0	0	11	2	73.2	52	47	73	12	1	5	39	6	43	1	7	0
Petry	4.94	2	3	.400	17	6	0	0	1	0	54.2	35	30	66	10	3	9	19	3	18	0	0	0
Searcy	8.41	1	2	.333	16	5	0	0	4	0	40.2	40	38	52	7	1	8	30	0	32	0	4	0
Meacham R	5.20	2	1	.667	10	4	0	0	1	0	27.2	17	16	35	8	0	4	11	0	14	0	0	1
Ritz	11.74	0	3	.000	11	5	0	0	3	0	15.1	22	20	17	3	0	1	22	1	9	2	0	0
Haas D	6.75	1	0	1.000	11	0	0	0	0	0	10.2	8	8	8	1	0	1	12	3	6	1	1	0
Munoz	9.64	0	0	.000	6	0	0	0	4	0	9.1	10	10	14	2	0	0	5	0	3	0	1	0
Dalton	3.38	0	0	.000	4	0	0	0	1	0	8.0	3	3	12	1	1	2	2	0	4	0	2	0
Kiely	14.85	0	1	.000	7	0	0	0	3	0	6.2	11	11	13	4	0	0	9	2	1	1	1	0
Kaiser	9.00	0	1	.000	10	0	0	0	4	2	5.0	5	5	6	1	0	1	5	2	4	0	0	0
TOTALS	4.54	84	78	.519	488	162	18	4	144	38	1450.1	794	731	1570	257	45	148	593	88	739	24	50	5

Sabermetric Pitching Records for Detroit Tigers

	Adj	|-Expected-|			|——Opposing Batters——|												Supported				
	ERA	W	L	Pct	BFP	Avg	Slg	OBA	RC/G	GDP	SB	CS	PK	PKE	SH	SF	RSup	RSp/G	W	L	Pct
Aldred	5.18	2	4	.384	253	.266	.427	.352	5.33	5	5	2	1	1	3	2	24	3.77	2	4	.346
Cerutti	4.57	4	5	.445	389	.276	.412	.348	5.11	7	5	2	0	2	7	3	42	4.26	4	5	.466
Dalton	3.38	0	0	.595	38	.333	.583	.368	8.30	1	0	0	0	0	0	0	8	9.00	0	0	.877
Gakeler	5.74	2	3	.336	331	.256	.358	.345	4.80	3	7	1	0	0	3	3	39	4.76	2	3	.408
Gibson P	4.59	5	7	.442	432	.297	.424	.379	5.60	13	5	5	1	2	2	2	50	4.69	6	6	.510
Gleaton	4.06	3	2	.503	319	.269	.415	.355	4.81	7	8	8	2	5	1	4	43	5.14	3	2	.615
Gullickson	3.94	15	14	.519	954	.288	.435	.321	4.75	22	15	8	1	0	8	8	146	5.81	20	9	.685
Haas D	6.75	0	1	.268	50	.242	.364	.438	5.02	3	0	1	0	0	2	2	11	9.28	1	0	.654
Henneman	2.88	8	4	.668	358	.258	.344	.326	3.80	10	3	2	0	0	5	5	37	3.95	8	4	.653
Kaiser	9.00	0	1	.171	26	.286	.476	.423	8.64	0	0	0	0	0	0	0	2	3.60	0	1	.138
Kiely	14.85	0	1	.070	42	.448	.586	.575	15.67	0	0	0	0	0	2	1	4	5.40	0	1	.117
Leiter M	4.21	8	8	.485	578	.245	.397	.316	4.37	8	6	6	0	2	5	6	90	6.01	11	5	.671
Meacham R	5.20	1	2	.382	126	.315	.495	.368	6.87	2	1	0	0	0	1	3	26	8.46	2	1	.725
Munoz	9.64	0	0	.152	46	.350	.400	.413	6.37	1	0	1	0	1	0	1	2	1.93	0	0	.038
Petry	4.94	2	3	.407	240	.300	.495	.356	6.11	7	5	2	0	0	1	0	34	5.60	3	2	.562
Ritz	11.74	0	3	.108	86	.288	.390	.482	8.62	2	3	0	0	0	1	2	7	4.11	0	3	.109
Searcy	8.41	1	2	.191	201	.313	.512	.412	8.07	5	2	1	0	0	2	3	17	3.76	1	2	.167
Tanana	3.81	13	12	.535	920	.265	.412	.327	4.53	17	17	14	0	7	12	9	125	5.18	16	9	.649
Terrell	4.28	12	14	.477	954	.301	.433	.358	5.19	35	6	5	0	0	10	9	110	4.53	14	12	.528
TOTALS	4.59	72	90	.443	6343	.281	.422	.348	5.11	148	88	58	5	20	65	63	817	5.07	89	73	.550

Batting 'Splits' Records for Detroit Tigers

	G	AB	Run	Hit	2B	3B	HR	TB	RBI	W	K	IW	HB	SB	CS	GIDP	SH	SF	Avg	Slug	OBP	Runs Ctd
ctober	49	170	22	37	4	1	6	61	18	22	43	0	0	0	2	4	1	0	.218	.359	.307	18
SPLITS for Tettleton																						
vs LHP	68	109	16	27	4	0	9	58	25	17	32	3	1	0	1	5	0	2	.248	.532	.349	19
vs RHP	145	392	69	105	13	2	22	188	64	84	99	6	1	3	2	7	0	2	.268	.480	.397	80
Home	77	239	42	63	7	2	15	119	44	56	63	6	2	2	2	6	0	4	.264	.498	.402	52
Away	77	262	43	69	10	0	16	127	45	45	68	3	0	1	1	6	0	0	.263	.485	.371	49
Grass	130	425	72	115	14	2	26	211	81	87	113	8	2	2	3	12	0	4	.271	.496	.394	87
Turf	24	76	13	17	3	0	5	35	8	14	18	1	0	1	0	0	0	0	.224	.461	.344	13
April/June	69	217	46	59	5	2	14	110	41	45	54	3	2	2	2	4	0	3	.272	.507	.397	47
July/October	85	284	39	73	12	0	17	136	48	56	77	6	0	1	1	8	0	1	.257	.479	.378	53
SPLITS for Trammell																						
vs LHP	52	113	17	24	6	0	4	42	17	8	10	0	1	0	0	3	2	1	.212	.372	.268	11
vs RHP	94	262	40	69	14	0	5	98	38	29	29	1	2	11	2	4	3	0	.263	.374	.341	36
Home	59	218	33	53	11	0	6	82	39	22	17	0	2	6	0	4	3	0	.243	.376	.318	28
Away	42	157	24	40	9	0	3	58	16	15	22	1	1	5	2	3	2	1	.255	.369	.322	19
Grass	88	324	46	79	17	0	8	120	49	33	34	1	2	10	2	6	5	1	.244	.370	.317	40
Turf	13	51	11	14	3	0	1	20	6	4	5	0	1	1	0	1	0	0	.275	.392	.339	7
April/June	66	247	37	58	15	0	6	91	30	25	24	1	3	8	2	7	5	0	.235	.368	.313	29
July/October	35	128	20	35	5	0	3	49	25	12	15	0	0	3	0	0	0	1	.273	.383	.333	18
SPLITS for Whitaker																						
vs LHP	70	97	16	24	3	0	2	33	14	15	15	0	1	0	0	0	2	0	.247	.340	.354	13
vs RHP	130	373	78	107	23	2	21	197	64	75	30	6	1	4	2	3	0	8	.287	.528	.400	87
Home	72	237	56	72	13	1	15	132	51	61	23	1	0	2	1	2	2	3	.304	.557	.442	65
Away	66	233	38	59	13	1	8	98	27	29	22	5	2	2	1	1	0	5	.253	.421	.335	36
Grass	116	400	83	118	23	2	20	205	70	80	36	5	1	4	2	2	2	6	.295	.512	.409	93
Turf	22	70	11	13	3	0	3	25	8	10	9	1	1	0	0	1	0	2	.186	.357	.289	8
April/June	64	206	44	50	7	2	10	91	34	47	21	2	2	1	2	2	2	4	.243	.442	.382	39
July/October	74	264	50	81	19	0	13	139	44	43	24	4	0	3	0	1	0	4	.307	.527	.399	61
SPLITS for Detroit Tigers (all batters except pitchers)																						
vs LHP	838	1529	219	390	79	7	60	663	206	181	307	13	12	22	21	26	16	12	.255	.434	.336	226
vs RHP	1514	4018	598	982	180	19	149	1647	572	518	878	27	19	87	26	64	22	32	.244	.410	.331	577
Home	856	2680	437	673	110	14	109	1138	416	399	554	21	19	61	22	43	16	26	.251	.425	.349	425
Away	876	2867	380	699	149	12	100	1172	362	300	631	19	12	48	25	47	22	18	.244	.409	.316	379
Grass	1461	4683	694	1168	218	22	174	1952	666	615	995	37	24	94	43	77	30	36	.249	.417	.337	689
Turf	271	864	123	204	41	4	35	358	112	84	190	3	7	15	4	13	8	8	.236	.414	.306	114
April/June	774	2483	368	589	100	14	93	996	351	330	512	18	16	48	23	45	21	23	.237	.401	.328	342
July/October	958	3064	449	783	159	12	116	1314	427	369	673	22	15	61	24	45	17	21	.256	.429	.336	462

1991 SPLITS FOR Detroit Tigers

BATTING SPLITS

	AVG	AB	R	H	2B	3B	HR	RBI	SB	CS	BB	K	OBA	SPCT
Total	.247	5547	817	1372	259	26	209	778	109	47	699	1185	.333	.416

	#Pit	#P/PA	GB	FB	G/F	G	IBB	HB	SH	SF	GDP
Miscellaneous	24381	3.83	1725	1627	1.06	162	40	31	38	44	90

	AVG	AB	R	H	2B	3B	HR	RBI	SB	CS	BB	K	OBA	SPCT
vs. Left	.255	1529	...	390	79	7	60	206	22	21	181	307	.336	.434
vs. Right	.244	4018	...	982	180	19	149	572	87	26	518	878	.331	.410
Home	.251	2680	437	673	110	14	109	416	61	22	399	554	.349	.425
Away	.244	2867	380	699	149	12	100	362	48	25	300	631	.316	.409
None on	.241	3154	...	760	147	14	106	106	0	0	364	680	.322	.397
Runners on	.256	2393	...	612	112	12	103	672	109	47	335	505	.345	.442
April	.229	637	97	146	32	4	22	90	13	6	80	132	.318	.396
May	.246	920	146	226	41	4	33	142	26	8	139	186	.344	.407
June	.234	926	125	217	27	6	38	119	9	9	111	194	.318	.400
July	.270	915	142	247	56	3	41	131	13	6	85	199	.333	.472
August	.235	1033	160	243	52	4	42	153	26	9	160	263	.339	.415
September	.265	887	112	235	38	5	25	109	20	6	97	157	.338	.404
October	.253	229	35	58	13	0	8	34	2	3	27	54	.331	.415
None on/out	.223	1365	...	305	54	8	43	43	0	0	158	284	.306	.369
Scoring Posn	.257	1345	...	345	65	7	48	538	36	10	217	305	.352	.422
Close & Late	.218	911	...	199	38	1	28	114	19	7	115	221	.308	.355
Bases Loaded	.277	141	...	39	5	1	5	120	0	0	13	31	.315	.433
Batting #1	.270	675	106	182	31	6	13	69	21	8	87	121	.354	.391
Batting #2	.286	653	125	187	41	4	26	101	10	3	92	70	.374	.481
Batting #3	.237	654	99	155	39	1	25	97	9	2	74	119	.317	.414
Batting #4	.259	634	104	164	26	0	44	134	0	1	79	153	.344	.508
Batting #5	.260	593	94	154	18	2	36	94	5	4	106	153	.371	.479
Batting #6	.219	606	89	133	25	3	27	90	8	5	77	165	.307	.404
Batting #7	.239	594	68	142	30	3	18	76	11	10	63	162	.314	.391
Batting #8	.191	576	59	110	29	2	13	71	8	4	68	134	.276	.316
Batting #9	.258	562	73	145	20	5	7	46	37	10	53	108	.324	.349
As p	.000	1	0	0	0	0	0	0	0	0	0	1	.000	.000
As c	.248	565	80	140	23	2	24	83	3	3	90	131	.351	.423
As 1b	.262	602	100	158	24	1	38	121	1	1	85	139	.358	.495
As 2b	.283	621	111	176	34	2	28	89	8	5	110	68	.388	.480
As 3b	.265	616	76	163	30	1	14	77	11	10	45	130	.315	.385
As ss	.267	649	96	173	41	3	22	102	16	3	58	118	.330	.441
As lf	.217	627	76	136	30	3	18	79	12	7	52	130	.277	.360
As cf	.256	570	89	146	22	8	4	37	40	11	58	107	.330	.344
As rf	.190	574	74	109	23	2	26	72	5	3	100	190	.309	.373
Outfield	.221	1771	239	391	75	13	48	188	57	21	210	427	.305	.359
0.0 count	.276	733	...	202	36	7	32	109	...	...	0	0	.276	.475
After (0.1)	.225	2441	...	549	88	7	82	300	...	...	179	755	.281	.367
After (1.0)	.262	2372	...	621	135	12	95	369	...	...	490	430	.387	.449
Two strikes	.177	2615	...	463	73	6	64	244	...	...	315	1184	.269	.283
Grass	.249	4683	694	1168	218	22	174	666	94	43	615	995	.337	.417
Turf	.236	864	123	204	41	4	35	112	15	4	84	190	.306	.414
Day	.251	1764	265	443	89	10	65	255	31	19	223	374	.336	.423
Night	.246	3783	552	929	170	16	144	523	78	28	476	811	.331	.413
Inning 1.6	.254	3748	588	951	174	22	149	561	77	36	492	759	.341	.431
Inning 7+	.234	1799	229	421	85	4	60	217	32	11	207	426	.315	.386
vs.Bal	.271	468	76	127	26	0	13	74	10	3	54	84	.345	.410
vs.Bos	.266	444	73	118	27	0	24	69	8	6	48	105	.339	.489
vs.Cal	.241	395	48	95	16	2	20	46	2	8	39	96	.313	.443
vs.ChA	.243	419	73	102	25	4	17	69	9	5	65	89	.344	.444
vs.Cle	.270	437	54	118	20	5	9	53	13	2	34	86	.324	.400
vs.KC	.277	415	82	115	21	3	15	71	6	2	56	98	.365	.451
vs.Mil	.226	465	57	105	18	2	18	56	7	5	51	80	.302	.389
vs.Min	.242	405	47	98	22	2	13	45	13	1	43	72	.316	.402
vs.NYA	.243	436	77	106	24	1	21	76	15	3	63	100	.343	.447
vs.Oak	.243	404	51	98	22	2	10	50	7	4	71	85	.357	.381
vs.Sea	.256	403	68	103	9	3	17	63	5	2	61	75	.353	.419
vs.Tex	.246	422	62	104	13	1	18	61	9	5	60	101	.341	.410
vs.Tor	.191	434	49	83	16	1	14	45	5	1	54	114	.283	.329

PITCHING SPLITS

	ERA	W	L	SV	SVOP	GS	CG	SHO	IP	H	ER	HR	BB	IBB	K
Total	4.51	84	78	38	55	162	18	7	1450.1	1570	726	148	593	88	739

	#Pit	#P/IP	GB	FB	G/F	BRp9	RA	WP	BK	SH	SF	R	HB	Hld
Miscellaneous	22844	15.75	2040	1658	1.23	13.57	326	50	5	65	63	794	24	25

	ERA	W	L	SV	SVOP	GS	CG	SHO	IP	H	ER	HR	BB	IBB	K
ST	4.48	60	60	0	0	162	18	4	961.1	1074	478	99	333	42	436
REL	4.66	24	18	38	55	0	0	0	489.0	496	253	49	260	46	303
Home	4.60	49	32	22	27	81	5	0	740.0	784	378	89	295	42	405
Away	4.47	35	46	16	28	81	13	4	710.1	786	353	59	298	46	334
April	3.43	10	9	6	9	19	1	1	170.2	174	65	10	67	15	85
May	5.27	13	14	6	10	27	1	0	244.1	303	143	32	110	18	111
June	4.45	14	14	7	10	28	4	1	249.0	253	123	24	108	12	125
July	5.87	14	12	5	7	26	1	0	227.0	284	148	28	100	11	110
August	4.23	18	12	8	12	30	5	2	272.1	288	128	33	106	17	148
September	4.03	11	15	5	5	26	5	0	230.0	213	103	18	80	13	124
October	3.32	4	2	1	2	6	1	0	57.0	55	21	3	22	2	36
Grass	4.55	74	63	32	46	137	16	4	1235.1	1321	624	134	503	77	642
Turf	4.48	10	15	6	9	25	2	0	215.0	249	107	14	90	11	97
Day	4.82	26	25	10	16	51	6	1	456.0	523	244	46	187	31	236
Night	4.41	58	53	28	39	111	12	3	994.1	1047	487	102	406	57	503
vs.Bal	4.24	8	5	2	4	13	2	0	121.0	121	57	14	44	4	78
vs.Bos	4.58	8	5	4	6	13	1	0	114.0	135	58	8	44	6	47
vs.Cal	3.14	7	5	3	4	12	4	1	106.0	110	37	9	17	1	56
vs.ChA	3.82	8	4	4	5	12	2	2	110.2	114	47	14	41	6	54
vs.Cle	3.41	6	7	4	4	13	4	0	111.0	116	42	4	34	7	56
vs.KC	5.35	8	4	5	6	12	0	0	106.0	122	63	14	38	4	58
vs.Mil	6.86	4	9	1	3	13	1	0	122.0	138	93	17	63	10	53
vs.Min	5.07	4	8	3	3	12	0	0	103.0	137	58	10	49	5	38
vs.NYA	4.64	8	5	2	3	13	1	1	116.1	127	60	9	56	11	59
vs.Oak	4.29	4	8	3	6	12	0	0	107.0	101	51	16	49	7	58
vs.Sea	4.46	8	4	4	5	12	2	0	105.0	103	52	9	65	11	60
vs.Tex	5.47	6	6	0	2	12	0	0	110.1	134	67	14	57	10	65
vs.Tor	3.51	5	8	3	4	13	1	0	118.0	112	46	10	36	6	57

OPPOSING BATTERS VS. PITCHERS.

	AVG	AB	R	H	2B	3B	HR	RBI	SB	CS	BB	K	OBA	SPCT
Total	.281	5596	794	1570	257	45	148	752	88	58	593	739	.348	.422
vs. Left	.281	2126	...	597	104	19	61	289	34	27	229	220	.349	.434
vs. Right	.280	3470	...	973	153	26	87	463	54	31	364	519	.348	.415
ST	.286	3751	521	1074	184	29	99	442	59	38	333	436	.343	.430
REL	.269	1845	273	496	73	16	49	310	29	20	260	303	.358	.405
Home	.274	2860	402	784	124	14	89	388	44	25	295	405	.340	.421
Away	.287	2736	392	786	133	31	59	364	44	33	298	334	.357	.423
None on	.273	3129	...	854	156	21	86	86	0	0	271	429	.333	.419
Runners on	.290	2467	...	716	101	24	62	666	88	58	322	310	.367	.426
None on/out	.278	1394	...	387	70	8	40	40	0	0	109	167	.332	.425
Scoring Posn	.288	1413	...	407	64	13	31	581	26	7	239	190	.380	.418
vs 1st Batr	.268	276	...	74	10	4	3	56	3	3	41	44	.364	.366
1st IP	.270	1627	299	439	66	17	37	267	34	22	220	245	.356	.400
Inning 1.6	.282	3768	535	1063	180	31	106	505	70	40	378	473	.347	.431
Inning 7+	.277	1828	259	507	77	14	42	247	18	18	215	266	.352	.404
Close & Late	.272	882	...	240	36	6	19	128	12	9	105	142	.346	.391
0.0 count	.318	781	...	248	29	9	27	135	...	...	61	0	.365	.481
After (0.1)	.252	2433	...	613	90	18	49	274	...	...	111	485	.284	.364
After (1.0)	.298	2382	...	709	138	18	72	343	...	...	421	254	.402	.461
Two strikes	.216	2343	...	505	84	15	42	249	...	...	212	737	.280	.318
Pitch 1.15	.277	1451	...	402	62	14	35	211	29	17	177	196	.353	.411
Pitch 16.30	.267	1145	...	306	54	6	31	135	14	14	126	194	.343	.406
Pitch 31.45	.274	849	...	233	37	8	23	121	16	7	79	101	.334	.418
Pitch 46.60	.287	656	...	188	24	5	19	85	8	4	76	75	.357	.425
Pitch 61.75	.272	552	...	150	30	4	11	63	8	7	46	69	.326	.400
Pitch 76.90	.282	486	...	137	25	5	13	67	7	5	46	55	.344	.434
Pitch 91.105	.360	311	...	112	16	2	13	47	3	2	29	34	.410	.550
Pitch 106.20	.271	107	...	29	5	0	3	18	3	1	10	8	.336	.402
Pitch 121.35	.323	31	...	10	4	1	0	4	0	1	5	4	.405	.516
Pitch 136.50	.375	8	...	3	0	0	0	1	0	0	1	3	.444	.375

Milwaukee Brewers

Dave Raglin

MILWAUKEE											
YEAR	1982	1983	1984	1985	1986	1987	1988	1989	1990	1991	TOT
W	95	87	67	71	77	91	87	81	74	83	813
L	67	75	94	90	84	71	75	81	88	79	804
WPCT	0.586	0.537	0.416	0.441	0.478	0.562	0.537	0.500	0.457	0.512	0.503
R	891	764	641	690	667	862	682	707	732	799	7435
RA	717	708	734	802	734	817	616	679	760	744	7311
PWPT	0.607	0.538	0.433	0.425	0.452	0.527	0.551	0.520	0.481	0.536	0.508
PythW	98	87	70	69	73	85	89	84	78	87	82
PythL	64	75	92	93	89	77	73	78	84	75	80
LUCK	-3	0	-3	2	4	6	-2	-3	-4	-4	-7

Defensive Efficiency Record: .6961

It was looking like another long summer in a part of the country where summers are short. As they woke up on the morning on Sunday August 4th, the Milwaukee Brewers were a disappointing 43-60, a 67-win pace for the season. But just as the thoughts of Wisconsin boys were starting to turn towards the Pack, something happened.

For the rest of the season, the Brewers were hotter than a vacant Detroit house on Devil's Night. They were on fire--of their last 59 games, Milwaukee won 40 of them, a 110-win pace.

What happened? Was this streak a preview of thing to come, or just some good play that was too little too late? Well, this is the sort of thing us sabermetricians are supposed to be able to answer, so let's go...

The first step is to find out whether it was the offense or the defense (pitching/fielding) which led the way. In those 59 games, Milwaukee scored 324 runs (5.49 per game) and allowed 223 (3.78 per game). To compare, the top offensive team in the league for 1991, Texas, averaged 5.11 runs per game, and the best at keeping runs off the scoreboard, Toronto, allowed 3.84. The league average was 4.49. It seems that it the Brewers' streak was a team effort-not one dominated by either the offense or the defense.

Let's start with the bats. Below are the hitters' stats for the 59 games:

Milwaukee Brewer Hitters, Last 59 Games, August 4-October 6, 1991, Ranked by Runs Created

	AB	BB	R	H	2B	3B	HR	BI	BA	RC	RC/G
Molitor	247	35	57	82	11	4	7	34	.332	51	7.8
Surhoff	204	10	30	71	9	3	5	32	.348	38	7.3
Randolph	225	41	37	73	9	2	0	28	.324	37	6.2
Vaughn	217	22	35	57	10	2	9	37	.263	32	5.2
Spiers	161	14	32	57	6	4	3	26	.354	32	7.7
Hamilton	207	17	34	65	7	3	1	35	.314	31	5.5
Gantner	222	12	30	63	10	2	2	21	.284	26	4.2
Yount	190	24	20	47	7	1	1	33	.247	20	3.5
Bichette	133	4	14	29	6	2	3	15	.218	11	2.7
Sveum	67	8	8	21	7	0	0	13	.313	10	5.8
Stubbs	85	10	12	17	4	0	2	8	.200	8	3.1
Dempsey	51	10	5	13	1	0	1	7	.255	6	4.1
Canale	34	8	6	6	2	0	3	10	.176	6	5.3
McIntosh	11	0	2	4	1	0	1	1	.364	3	10.8
Maldonado	9	0	0	1	0	0	0	0	.111	0	0.4

Molitor was the man--on base 117 times (a 321 pace), 57 runs (a 158 pace), and 82 hits (a 225 pace). Surhoff and Spiers were in another universe. Randolph had a .429 on-base percentage. Vaughn continued his power burst while improving his average. Hamilton was a Enos Cabell-great-average-not-much-else clone.

Noticeable for his absence from the top of the list is Robin Yount. The future first ballot Hall-of-Famer drove in 33 runs (a 91 pace) but with Molitor and Randolph batting in front of him, that's not that great. Otherwise, Yount might be showing signs of age. He has now had two disappointing seasons in a row. Two more Brewers who didn't hit well during the streak were Dante Bichette and Franklin Stubbs.

What are the chances of the big six doing it in 1992? Molitor, Vaughn, and Hamilton didn't really do that much better during the streak, so while they probably won't do quite as well, they probably will be in the neighborhood (DHing seems to helped Molitor stay healthy). Surhoff and Spiers seemed to be in another universe. Since they were 26 and 25, respectively, and each been in the majors for several years, chalk up those streaks as getting hot at the right time and nothing else.

Let's look at the pitchers. Here, there is more hope for the future:

Milwaukee Brewer Pitchers, Last 59 Games, August 4-October 6, 1991, Starters First, Then Relievers

	G	IP	H	ER	BB	SO	HR	W	L	S	ERA	WHIP
Wegman	12	97.0	81	24	18	48	9	9	1	0	2.23	1.02
Bosio	12	77.0	71	28	16	42	4	7	2	0	3.27	1.13
Navarro	12	85.0	75	33	26	35	8	7	3	0	3.49	1.19
Plesac	10	48.0	52	25	21	33	5	2	3	0	4.69	1.52
August	9	37.7	59	30	17	22	6	1	3	0	7.17	2.02
Eldred	3	16.0	20	8	6	10	2	2	0	0	4.50	1.63
Henry	24	27.0	11	2	9	20	0	1	1	15	0.67	0.74
Machado	22	37.7	23	12	18	43	6	3	1	1	2.87	1.09
Crim	20	31.3	39	11	9	16	2	3	0	0	3.16	1.53
Lee	22	21.0	20	8	11	11	1	2	2	0	3.43	1.48
Ignasiak	4	12.7	7	8	8	10	2	2	1	0	5.68	1.18
Nunez	12	12.3	14	8	2	7	4	1	0	5	5.84	1.30
George	2	6.0	8	2	0	2	0	0	0	0	3.00	1.33
Hunter	1	3.3	7	5	2	1	0	0	1	0	13.50	2.70

Five pitchers pitched especially well during this stretch, starters Bill Wegman, Chris Bosio, and Jamie Navarro, and relievers Doug Henry and Julio Machado. Wegman had been getting better, but had still been mediocre when he came up with arm injuries in 1989. Last year, he put it all together for the first time; the question is, will it continue. The Brewers' front office obviously thinks so; they gave Wegman a big long-term contract after the season.

Chris Bosio continued his pattern of pitching well when healthy--unfortunetly, that has not been too often the last couple of seasons. Jamie Navarro had good numbers, but any pitcher with a 35-26 SO/BB ratio in 85 innings while pitching well has to be considered suspect.

In the pen, Doug Henry was amazing--11 hits in 27 innings for starters. He became the ace after Dan Plesac couldn't hold the job. (Fill in more on Henry.) Julio Machado had been considered a good prospect with a blazing fastball for the Phillies' and Mets' organizations, but he finally put it together; 43 Ks and only 23 hits allowed in 37.2 innings. This kid is for real!! If Henry turns out to be a fluke, Machado could handle the save man job. (Hint--a good fantasy team pickup if you have a spot on your staff to gamble a bit with.)

Notice that the mainstays of the Brewer staffs the last few years aren't on this list. Teddy Higuera was hurt most of the year and didn't pitch during this stretch, Dan Plesac lost his bullpen job and did not pitch that well in the rotation, and Chuck Crim became the third man in the pen behind Henry and Machado.

How will those five pitchers do in 1992? I don't know, it could go both ways. On the plus side, they are all young, and we really don't know their upside potential yet. On the downside, only Machado has a great fastball, and Wegman and Bosio have a history of arm trouble.

Maybe this is what they mean by the saying that pitching is 60% or 75% or whatever percentage of the game. We've got a reasonable good idea of what the Brewer hitters will do in 1992. Hitters are a lot more predictable than pitchers. However, the pitchers who carried the team down the stretch could continue to pitch well in 1992, or they could bomb. In that sense, pitching is more "important" than hitting, because we can't tell as well what pitchers will do. In that narrow sense, pitching is the key to the 1992 Brewers.

Milwaukee Brewers Home Park Performance Factors

	Outs	Runs	Hits	2b	3b	HR	W	K	SH	SF	HBP	IBB	SB	CS	GDP
Home LH Batters	.995	.948	.968	.870	.999	1.045	.824	.920	.937	1.342	.854	.563	1.129	.959	.818
Home RH Batters	1.005	.970	1.017	.900	.872	.904	.954	1.023	.914	.909	.778	1.085	1.078	1.161	.835
All Home Batters	1.004	.964	1.002	.893	.934	.933	.908	.984	.964	1.078	.818	.886	1.103	1.060	.837
Opp LH Batters	1.060	.984	1.082	1.008	.962	1.109	1.110	1.009	1.716	1.578	1.029	1.716	1.052	1.471	.885
Opp RH Batters	1.075	1.062	1.071	1.158	1.845	1.076	1.042	1.010	1.307	.876	1.380	.986	1.180	.962	1.140
All Opp Batters	1.061	1.025	1.064	1.089	1.623	1.093	1.052	.999	1.298	1.078	1.270	1.208	1.162	1.018	1.031
All LH Batters	1.022	.963	1.017	.928	1.030	1.052	.943	.955	1.089	1.441	.930	.855	1.119	1.095	.846
All RH Batters	1.037	1.012	1.042	1.014	1.058	.982	.996	1.011	1.157	.903	1.080	1.079	1.122	1.076	.971
All Batters	1.031	.993	1.031	.982	1.093	1.010	.974	.987	1.114	1.086	1.053	1.003	1.130	1.055	.925

Conventional Batting Records for Milwaukee Brewers

	G	AB	Run	Hit	2B	3B	HR	TB	RBI	W	K	IW	HB	SB	CS	BRng Eff	GI DP	SH	SF	Avg	Slug	OBP	Runs Ctd
Surhoff BJ	142	503	56	146	19	4	5	188	67	25	33	2	0	5	8	.473	21	13	8	.290	.374	.319	54
Stubbs	103	362	48	77	16	2	11	130	38	35	71	3	2	13	4	.423	4	0	5	.213	.359	.282	39
Randolph	123	427	59	140	14	2	0	158	53	75	38	3	0	4	2	.435	14	3	3	.328	.370	.426	72
Gantner	139	522	63	148	27	4	2	189	47	27	34	5	3	4	6	.437	12	7	4	.284	.362	.320	58
Spiers	132	411	70	115	12	6	8	163	54	34	55	0	2	13	8	.483	9	10	4	.280	.397	.335	54
Vaughn G	145	542	81	132	24	5	27	247	98	62	125	2	1	2	2	.513	5	2	7	.244	.456	.319	82
Yount	129	499	66	129	20	4	10	187	77	54	79	8	4	6	4	.524	13	1	9	.259	.375	.330	63
Bichette	133	441	52	105	18	3	15	174	59	22	105	4	1	14	8	.396	9	1	6	.238	.395	.272	45
Molitor	157	661	132	215	32	12	17	322	74	77	62	16	6	19	8	.497	11	0	1	.325	.487	.400	133
Hamilton	121	402	63	125	15	6	1	155	56	32	37	2	0	16	6	.534	9	7	3	.311	.386	.359	57
Sveum	90	266	33	64	19	1	4	97	43	32	78	0	1	2	4	.320	8	5	4	.241	.365	.320	31
Sheffield	50	175	25	34	12	2	2	56	22	19	15	1	3	5	5	.478	3	1	5	.194	.320	.277	16
Dempsey	60	147	15	34	5	0	4	51	21	23	20	1	0	0	2	.053	7	1	3	.231	.347	.329	16
Maldonado	34	111	11	23	6	0	5	44	20	13	23	0	0	1	0	.308	4	0	1	.207	.396	.288	12
Brock	31	60	9	17	4	0	1	24	6	14	9	1	0	1	1	.308	1	1	0	.283	.400	.419	11
Canale	20	30	6	5	1	0	3	15	8	8	6	0	0	0	0	.667	4	0	2	.167	.500	.325	4
McIntosh	7	11	2	4	1	0	1	8	1	0	4	0	0	0	0	.500	0	0	0	.364	.727	.364	3
Olander	12	9	2	0	0	0	0	0	0	2	5	0	0	0	0	1.000	0	0	0	.000	.000	.182	0
Carrillo	3	0	0	0	0	0	0	0	0	0	0	0	0	0	0	.000	0	0	0	.000	.000	.000	0
Henry D	1	0	0	0	0	0	0	0	0	0	0	0	0	0	0	.000	0	0	0	.000	.000	.000	0
George	1	0	0	0	0	0	0	0	0	0	0	0	0	0	0	.000	0	0	0	.000	.000	.000	0
TOTALS	1633	5579	793	1513	245	51	116	2208	744	554	799	48	23	105	68	.459	134	52	65	.271	.396	.336	744

Sabermetric Batting Records for Milwaukee Brewers

	Ball Park Adjusted												Runs		Run/					
	AB	Run	Hit	2B	3B	HR	RBI	W	SO	Avg	Slug	OBP	Ctd	Outs	27o	OW%	OG	OWAR	DWAR	TWAR
Bichette	458	52	109	18	4	14	56	21	106	.238	.386	.270	46	371	3.35	.330	14	-0.27	1.12	0.85
Brock	61	8	17	3	0	1	6	13	8	.279	.377	.405	11	46	6.46	.647	2	0.51	0.09	0.60
Canale	30	5	5	0	0	3	8	7	5	.167	.467	.308	4	30	3.60	.363	1	0.01	0.05	0.06
Carrillo	0	0	0	0	0	0	0	0	0	.000	.000	.000	0	0	0.00	.000	0	0.00	0.00	0.00
Dempsey	152	15	35	5	0	3	20	22	20	.230	.322	.324	16	128	3.38	.334	5	-0.08	0.02	-0.06
Gantner	535	60	151	25	3	2	47	26	32	.282	.351	.315	57	415	3.71	.377	15	0.42	0.90	1.32
Hamilton	412	60	128	14	5	1	56	30	35	.311	.376	.354	56	311	4.86	.510	12	1.84	0.65	2.49
Maldonado	115	11	24	6	0	4	19	12	23	.209	.365	.283	12	94	3.45	.343	3	-0.02	0.03	0.01
McIntosh	11	2	4	1	0	0	0	0	4	.364	.455	.364	2	7	7.71	.724	0	0.10	-0.00	0.09
Molitor	687	134	224	32	16	16	71	76	63	.326	.489	.398	138	481	7.75	.725	18	6.69	0.08	6.76
Olander	9	2	0	0	0	0	0	1	5	.000	.000	.100	0	9	0.00	.000	0	-0.12	0.02	-0.10
Randolph	444	59	146	14	2	0	51	74	38	.329	.369	.423	74	318	6.28	.635	12	3.35	1.43	4.78
Sheffield	181	25	35	12	2	1	21	18	15	.193	.298	.272	15	158	2.56	.224	6	-0.74	-0.13	-0.87
Spiers	421	67	117	11	5	8	54	32	53	.278	.385	.327	53	338	4.23	.441	13	1.14	1.52	2.66
Stubbs	370	46	78	15	1	11	38	33	68	.211	.346	.273	38	306	3.35	.331	11	-0.22	0.35	0.13
Surhoff BJ	515	54	149	17	3	5	68	24	31	.289	.363	.315	55	420	3.54	.355	16	0.08	0.02	0.10
Sveum	274	32	66	18	1	4	42	31	77	.241	.358	.316	31	228	3.67	.372	8	0.19	0.54	0.73
Vaughn G	563	82	137	24	6	26	94	61	127	.243	.446	.315	83	440	5.09	.533	16	2.98	0.76	3.74
Yount	518	67	134	20	5	9	74	53	80	.259	.369	.328	64	409	4.22	.440	15	1.36	0.71	2.07
TOTALS	5761	788	1562	242	65	117	734	542	792	.271	.397	.333	767	4522	4.58	.480	167	21.76	8.16	29.92

Pitching Records for Milwaukee Brewers

	ERA	W	L	Pct	G	GS	CG	ShO	GF	Sv	IP	R	ER	H	2B	3B	HR	BB	IW	SO	HB	WP	BK
Navarro	3.92	15	12	.556	34	34	10	2	0	0	234.0	117	102	237	39	3	18	73	3	114	6	10	0
Bosio	3.25	14	10	.583	32	32	5	1	0	0	204.2	80	74	187	28	4	15	58	0	117	8	5	0
Wegman	2.88	14	7	.667	27	27	6	2	0	0	184.1	74	59	170	29	3	15	39	0	84	6	5	0
August	5.47	9	8	.529	28	23	1	1	3	0	138.1	87	84	166	22	3	18	47	2	62	3	5	0
Brown K	5.51	2	4	.333	15	10	0	0	0	0	63.2	39	39	66	16	1	6	34	2	30	1	6	0
Higuera	4.46	3	2	.600	7	6	0	0	1	0	36.1	18	18	37	8	0	2	10	0	33	1	0	0
Knudson	7.97	1	3	.250	12	7	0	0	3	0	35.0	33	31	54	12	1	8	15	0	23	1	1	0
Hunter	7.26	0	5	.000	8	6	0	0	0	0	31.0	26	25	45	8	0	3	17	0	14	4	3	0
Eldred	4.50	2	0	1.000	3	3	0	0	0	0	16.0	9	8	20	1	0	2	6	0	10	0	0	0
George	3.00	0	0	.000	2	1	0	0	1	0	6.0	2	2	8	3	0	0	0	0	2	0	0	0
Robinson R	6.23	0	1	.000	1	1	0	0	0	0	4.1	3	3	6	2	1	0	3	1	0	1	0	0
Plesac	4.29	2	7	.222	45	10	0	0	25	8	92.1	49	44	92	20	2	12	39	1	61	3	2	1
Crim	4.63	8	5	.615	66	0	0	0	29	3	91.1	52	47	115	15	0	9	25	9	39	2	3	3
Machado	3.45	3	3	.500	54	0	0	0	13	3	88.2	36	34	65	11	0	12	55	1	98	3	5	0
Holmes	4.72	1	4	.200	40	0	0	0	9	3	76.1	43	40	90	15	1	6	27	1	59	1	6	0
Lee	3.86	2	5	.286	62	0	0	0	9	1	67.2	33	29	72	11	1	10	31	7	43	1	0	0
Henry D	1.00	2	1	.667	32	0	0	0	25	15	36.0	4	4	16	6	0	1	14	1	28	0	0	0
Nunez E	6.04	2	1	.667	23	0	0	0	18	8	25.1	20	17	28	5	1	6	13	2	24	0	0	1
Ignasiak	5.68	2	1	.667	4	1	0	0	0	0	12.2	8	8	7	0	1	2	8	0	10	0	0	0
Austin	8.31	0	0	.000	5	0	0	0	1	0	8.2	8	8	8	2	0	1	11	1	3	3	1	0
Dempsey	4.50	0	0	.000	2	0	0	0	2	0	2.0	1	1	3	1	0	0	1	0	0	0	0	0
TOTALS	4.19	82	79	.509	502	161	22	6	139	41	1454.2	742	677	1492	254	22	146	526	31	854	44	52	5

Sabermetric Pitching Records for Milwaukee Brewers

	Adj	|-Expected-|			|------Opposing Batters------|												Supported			
	ERA	W	L	Pct	BFP	Avg	Slg	OBA	RC/G	GDP	SB	CS	PK	PKE	SH	SF	RSup	RSp/G	W	L	Pct
August	5.40	6	11	.364	613	.301	.450	.358	5.76	16	18	4	1	0	9	3	102	6.64	10	7	.602
Austin	7.27	0	0	.240	46	.276	.448	.500	8.24	2	0	0	0	0	2	1	1	1.04	0	0	.020
Bosio	3.21	15	9	.619	840	.244	.350	.302	3.49	22	9	4	2	0	2	6	105	4.62	16	8	.674
Brown K	5.37	2	4	.367	285	.270	.418	.361	5.28	6	5	4	0	1	5	1	23	3.25	2	4	.268
Crim	4.53	6	7	.449	408	.305	.416	.351	5.58	7	12	1	0	1	3	1	69	6.80	9	4	.692
Dempsey	0.00	0	0	.000	10	.333	.444	.400	7.75	0	0	0	0	0	0	0	0	0.00	0	0	.000
Eldred	3.94	1	1	.519	73	.299	.403	.356	5.58	1	3	1	0	0	0	0	7	3.94	1	1	.500
George	1.50	0	0	.881	25	.333	.458	.320	5.08	1	1	0	0	0	0	1	2	3.00	0	0	.800
Henry D	0.75	3	0	.967	137	.133	.208	.221	1.55	1	0	1	0	0	1	2	13	3.25	3	0	.949
Higuera	4.21	2	3	.485	153	.262	.362	.314	4.06	4	5	0	0	1	0	1	33	8.17	4	1	.790
Holmes	4.60	2	3	.441	344	.295	.410	.351	5.22	5	1	3	0	2	8	3	24	2.83	1	4	.275
Hunter	6.97	1	4	.256	152	.349	.481	.437	7.82	8	4	0	1	0	1	1	16	4.65	2	3	.308
Ignasiak	4.97	1	2	.403	51	.163	.349	.294	3.55	1	2	0	0	0	0	0	15	10.66	2	1	.821
Knudson	7.71	1	3	.219	174	.355	.605	.409	10.34	0	4	1	0	0	3	3	16	4.11	1	3	.221
Lee	3.72	4	3	.546	291	.283	.453	.362	5.13	13	6	4	0	2	4	1	29	3.86	4	3	.518
Machado	3.35	4	2	.598	371	.211	.364	.334	3.91	10	5	5	1	1	3	2	58	5.89	5	1	.755
Navarro	3.88	14	13	.526	1002	.261	.370	.318	4.18	20	23	7	0	0	7	8	127	4.88	17	10	.613
Nunez E	5.68	1	2	.341	119	.277	.525	.353	7.17	1	2	0	0	0	3	2	13	4.62	1	2	.398
Plesac	4.19	4	5	.488	402	.263	.434	.336	5.04	7	4	5	0	0	3	7	34	3.31	3	6	.385
Robinson R	4.15	0	1	.492	21	.353	.588	.476	10.33	1	1	0	0	0	0	0	0	0.00	0	1	.000
Wegman	2.83	14	7	.676	751	.244	.359	.289	3.38	16	9	7	1	3	6	3	106	5.18	16	5	.770
TOTALS	4.16	79	82	.492	6268	.267	.398	.332	4.60	142	114	47	6	11	60	46	793	4.91	94	67	.582

Batting 'Splits' Records for Milwaukee Brewers

	G	AB	Run	Hit	2B	3B	HR	TB	RBI	W	K	IW	HB	SB	CS	GI DP	SH	SF	Avg	Slug	OBP	Runs Ctd
SPLITS for Milwaukee Brewers (all batters except pitchers)																						
vs LHP	851	1606	202	419	59	10	29	585	194	189	238	21	7	23	19	36	15	18	.261	.364	.338	203
vs RHP	1409	3973	591	1094	186	41	87	1623	550	365	561	27	16	82	49	98	37	47	.275	.409	.335	541
Home	801	2666	392	719	134	25	62	1089	370	297	391	25	14	44	31	78	26	28	.270	.408	.343	371
Away	832	2913	401	794	111	26	54	1119	374	257	408	23	9	61	37	56	26	37	.273	.384	.330	374
Grass	1380	4697	694	1293	206	44	102	1893	648	494	657	45	20	88	60	120	45	54	.275	.403	.343	651
Turf	253	882	99	220	39	7	14	315	96	60	142	3	3	17	8	14	7	11	.249	.357	.296	95
April/June	752	2518	349	650	114	19	61	985	331	248	393	26	14	50	32	67	28	25	.258	.391	.325	318
July/October	881	3061	444	863	131	32	55	1223	413	306	406	22	9	55	36	67	24	40	.282	.400	.345	427

1991 SPLITS FOR Milwaukee Brewers

BATTING SPLITS

	AVG	AB	R	H	2B	3B	HR	RBI	SB	CS	BB	K	OBA	SPCT
Total	.271	5611	799	1523	247	53	116	750	106	68	556	802	.336	.396

	#Pit	#P/PA	GB	FB	G/F	G	IBB	HB	SH	SF	GDP
Miscellaneous	22635	3.59	2102	1629	1.29	162	48	23	52	66	136

	AVG	AB	R	H	2B	3B	HR	RBI	SB	CS	BB	K	OBA	SPCT
vs. Left	.260	1614	...	420	59	11	29	196	23	19	189	240	.337	.364
vs. Right	.276	3997	...	1103	188	42	87	554	83	49	367	562	.336	.409
Home	.270	2698	398	729	136	27	62	376	45	31	299	394	.343	.410
Away	.273	2913	401	794	111	26	54	374	61	37	257	408	.330	.384
None on	.257	3121	...	802	140	25	64	64	0	0	269	441	.319	.379
Runners on	.290	2490	...	721	107	28	52	686	106	68	287	361	.357	.418
April	.252	650	91	164	36	2	19	86	13	8	60	93	.316	.402
May	.267	971	119	259	44	10	22	116	23	7	94	141	.330	.401
June	.253	897	139	227	34	7	20	129	14	17	94	159	.326	.373
July	.261	907	115	237	40	10	15	109	18	10	80	134	.320	.377
August	.305	1045	164	319	51	10	20	152	23	18	104	125	.364	.431
September	.258	865	116	223	29	10	18	109	10	7	104	116	.336	.377
October	.341	276	55	94	13	4	2	49	5	1	20	34	.383	.438
None on/out	.263	1400	...	368	60	11	38	38	0	0	104	178	.317	.403
Scoring Posn	.283	1449	...	410	64	23	38	636	28	11	209	230	.362	.438
Close & Late	.270	960	...	259	37	8	21	139	19	12	103	151	.342	.391
Bases Loaded	.352	122	...	43	9	2	4	123	0	0	7	15	.345	.557
Batting #1	.319	683	136	218	32	13	18	78	21	8	79	63	.394	.483
Batting #2	.317	662	86	210	31	7	4	91	7	9	78	49	.387	.403
Batting #3	.247	663	80	164	24	7	6	99	14	9	50	83	.295	.332
Batting #4	.240	633	80	152	29	2	17	94	8	5	69	124	.312	.373
Batting #5	.253	620	86	157	28	2	23	101	13	5	62	108	.320	.416
Batting #6	.266	616	86	164	24	9	13	68	9	9	56	106	.327	.398
Batting #7	.265	608	84	161	26	4	17	84	13	5	47	92	.317	.405
Batting #8	.261	574	72	150	27	3	10	55	7	8	59	81	.329	.371
Batting #9	.266	552	89	147	26	6	8	80	14	10	56	96	.333	.379
As c	.273	604	69	165	22	4	8	85	5	9	45	47	.318	.363
As 1b	.257	607	104	156	30	5	20	78	22	10	81	89	.343	.422
As 2b	.312	603	87	188	25	4	0	63	7	5	90	49	.401	.367
As 3b	.257	626	70	161	34	4	7	66	7	10	39	70	.301	.358
As ss	.269	540	87	145	25	7	8	79	14	10	53	93	.333	.385
As lf	.243	630	88	153	26	5	28	109	6	2	64	135	.311	.433
As cf	.284	641	92	182	28	4	12	97	10	7	65	93	.349	.396
As rf	.248	636	77	158	24	7	14	81	20	11	30	130	.280	.374
Outfield	.259	1907	257	493	78	16	54	287	36	20	159	358	.314	.401
0.0 count	.317	867	...	275	30	11	25	135	...	...	2	0	.313	.464
After (0.1)	.238	2373	...	565	85	21	34	265	...	...	118	511	.276	.335
After (1.0)	.288	2371	...	683	132	21	57	350	...	...	403	291	.390	.434
Two strikes	.200	2304	...	461	81	12	30	237	...	...	209	802	.268	.285
Grass	.276	4729	700	1303	208	46	102	654	89	60	496	660	.343	.404
Turf	.249	882	99	220	39	7	14	96	17	8	60	142	.296	.357
Day	.281	1585	239	445	77	13	37	229	33	20	177	221	.351	.416
Night	.268	4026	560	1078	170	40	79	521	73	48	379	581	.330	.389
Inning 1.6	.271	3713	528	1008	177	37	77	492	76	49	365	518	.335	.401
Inning 7+	.271	1898	271	515	70	16	39	258	30	19	191	284	.337	.387
vs.Bal	.287	450	65	129	30	4	8	61	12	4	43	52	.350	.424
vs.Bos	.274	442	59	121	17	4	5	55	13	3	38	71	.328	.364
vs.Cal	.288	399	53	115	15	4	7	47	3	10	48	60	.366	.398
vs.ChA	.252	441	55	111	12	4	10	53	7	7	48	60	.325	.365
vs.Cle	.299	469	68	140	24	5	7	62	5	3	34	63	.346	.416
vs.Det	.292	472	97	138	25	4	17	95	4	4	63	53	.369	.470
vs.KC	.268	425	51	114	20	4	5	48	7	6	27	66	.312	.369
vs.Min	.285	410	57	117	25	5	11	55	8	2	32	66	.336	.451
vs.NYA	.282	450	64	127	15	10	6	57	10	5	44	73	.345	.400
vs.Oak	.260	396	75	103	17	5	14	72	11	6	52	56	.349	.434
vs.Sea	.215	390	34	84	13	2	2	33	8	6	51	71	.304	.274
vs.Tex	.273	429	69	117	18	1	12	61	8	6	41	57	.335	.403
vs.Tor	.244	438	52	107	16	1	12	51	10	6	35	54	.295	.368

PITCHING SPLITS

	ERA	W	L	SV	SVOP	GS	CG	SHO	IP	H	ER	HR	BB	IBB	K
Total	4.14	83	79	41	62	162	23	11	1463.2	1498	674	147	527	31	859

	#Pit	#P/IP	GB	FB	G/F	BRp9	RA	WP	BK	SH	SF	R	HB	Hld
Miscellaneous	22965	15.69	2138	1653	1.29	12.73	341	53	5	60	47	744	45	46

	ERA	W	L	SV	SVOP	GS	CG	SHO	IP	H	ER	HR	BB	IBB	K
ST	4.17	62	52	0	0	162	23	6	974.2	1012	452	88	314	6	502
REL	4.18	21	27	41	62	0	0	0	489.0	486	227	59	213	25	357
Home	4.26	43	37	19	30	80	9	3	746.0	762	353	73	275	14	468
Away	4.09	40	42	22	32	82	14	3	717.2	736	326	74	252	17	391
April	4.34	10	9	5	7	19	1	0	174.0	179	84	19	61	2	118
May	3.74	12	15	7	13	27	4	1	257.1	243	107	27	86	10	150
June	4.30	12	15	4	8	27	2	2	238.2	237	114	23	88	7	142
July	5.38	9	18	3	7	27	7	0	234.1	286	140	22	102	4	115
August	4.30	19	10	10	13	29	3	1	264.0	281	126	34	97	2	145
September	3.43	15	11	9	10	26	5	1	233.1	201	89	21	77	4	150
October	2.76	6	1	3	4	7	1	1	62.0	71	19	1	16	2	39
Grass	4.06	75	62	34	51	137	20	6	1246.2	1257	563	122	450	28	742
Turf	4.81	8	17	7	11	25	3	0	217.0	241	116	25	77	3	117
Day	4.40	26	19	10	17	45	6	1	421.0	445	206	39	173	13	255
Night	4.08	57	60	31	45	117	17	5	1042.2	1053	473	108	354	18	604
vs.Bal	4.23	10	3	6	8	13	1	0	117.0	128	55	15	34	0	68
vs.Bos	5.05	6	7	5	6	13	1	0	114.0	125	64	12	49	3	89
vs.Cal	2.50	6	6	1	2	12	2	0	104.1	93	29	2	31	1	64
vs.ChA	4.36	5	7	1	4	12	4	0	117.2	124	57	13	57	4	56
vs.Cle	3.13	8	5	4	6	13	3	2	115.0	112	40	7	28	3	52
vs.Det	4.01	9	4	3	3	13	1	0	125.2	105	56	18	51	4	80
vs.KC	4.46	3	9	3	5	12	0	0	107.0	122	53	10	41	3	64
vs.Min	4.15	6	6	4	7	12	2	0	106.1	123	49	10	36	3	52
vs.NYA	4.59	6	7	3	7	13	3	1	117.2	125	60	10	30	4	63
vs.Oak	3.77	8	4	2	3	12	2	2	105.0	96	44	10	44	2	68
vs.Sea	4.35	3	9	1	2	12	2	1	107.2	101	52	10	41	1	51
vs.Tex	5.06	7	5	4	4	12	1	0	110.1	127	62	17	42	0	75
vs.Tor	4.50	6	7	4	5	13	1	0	116.0	117	58	13	43	3	77

OPPOSING BATTERS VS. PITCHERS.

	AVG	AB	R	H	2B	3B	HR	RBI	SB	CS	BB	K	OBA	SPCT
Total	.266	5623	744	1498	254	22	147	725	115	47	527	859	.332	.398
vs. Left	.266	2674	...	712	111	11	69	363	54	23	257	346	.332	.393
vs. Right	.267	2949	...	786	143	11	78	362	61	24	270	513	.332	.402
ST	.268	3774	497	1012	173	18	88	438	83	29	314	502	.327	.393
REL	.263	1849	247	486	81	4	59	287	32	18	213	357	.341	.407
Home	.266	2866	398	762	126	6	73	389	52	26	275	468	.332	.390
Away	.267	2757	346	736	128	16	74	336	63	21	252	391	.332	.406
None on	.265	3129	...	829	142	13	84	84	0	0	278	481	.330	.399
Runners on	.268	2494	...	669	112	9	63	641	115	47	249	378	.334	.396
None on/out	.265	1383	...	367	61	6	42	42	0	0	130	226	.333	.409
Scoring Posn	.280	1409	...	394	65	7	40	574	33	11	169	228	.352	.421
vs 1st Batr	.268	298	...	80	14	2	12	51	4	2	36	59	.353	.450
1st IP	.263	1721	247	453	78	7	42	264	44	18	195	305	.340	.390
Inning 1.6	.266	3732	491	993	178	17	88	475	83	32	330	559	.329	.394
Inning 7+	.267	1891	253	505	76	5	59	250	32	15	197	300	.337	.406
Close & Late	.257	930	...	239	33	0	36	135	15	9	101	148	.330	.409
0.0 count	.318	867	...	276	53	5	23	125	...	...	22	0	.338	.471
After (0.1)	.232	2397	...	556	85	7	55	274	...	...	128	567	.275	.342
After (1.0)	.282	2359	...	666	116	10	69	326	...	...	377	292	.382	.428
Two strikes	.204	2373	...	483	77	7	53	256	...	...	214	857	.273	.309
Pitch 1.15	.269	1505	...	405	71	5	40	188	39	15	149	249	.338	.403
Pitch 16.30	.225	1122	...	253	42	3	27	148	15	9	120	207	.300	.340
Pitch 31.45	.282	865	...	244	31	2	25	108	20	10	73	139	.343	.409
Pitch 46.60	.299	679	...	203	41	2	19	99	11	5	67	88	.364	.449
Pitch 61.75	.259	552	...	143	23	6	12	70	12	4	33	69	.300	.388
Pitch 76.90	.268	441	...	118	31	2	13	53	7	1	43	54	.336	.435
Pitch 91.105	.278	291	...	81	13	2	2	26	8	1	21	32	.333	.357
Pitch 106.20	.293	140	...	41	1	0	6	22	3	2	20	16	.374	.429
Pitch 121.35	.345	29	...	10	1	0	3	11	0	0	2	5	.406	.690
Pitch 136.50	.000	1	...	0	0	0	0	0	0	0	0	0	.000	.000
Pitch 151+	.000	0	...	0	0	0	0	0	0	0	0	0	.000	.000

New York Yankees

Dave Raglin

NEW YORK											
YEAR	1982	1983	1984	1985	1986	1987	1988	1989	1990	1991	TOT
W	79	91	87	97	90	89	85	74	67	71	830
L	83	71	75	64	72	73	76	87	95	91	787
WPCT	0.488	0.562	0.537	0.602	0.556	0.549	0.528	0.460	0.414	0.438	0.513
R	709	770	758	839	790	788	772	698	603	674	7401
RA	716	703	679	660	738	758	748	792	749	777	7320
PWPT	0.495	0.545	0.555	0.618	0.534	0.519	0.516	0.437	0.393	0.429	0.506
PythW	80	88	90	100	87	84	84	71	64	70	82
PythL	82	74	72	62	75	78	78	91	98	92	80
LUCK	-1	3	-3	-3	3	5	1	3	3	1	12

Defensive Efficiency Record: .6826

The New York Yankees have been rightly criticized the last few years for some of their crazy decisions (Andy Hawkins, the Rickey Henderson trade, etc.), so it was interesting to see them come under intense criticism for what I see as one of their best decisions in years, the hiring of Buck Showalter as their manager for 1992.

I'm not really sure why everybody was so against Showalter. I guess it was mostly because he hasn't been a successful manager with another team or wasn't a good player. In other words, he was (gasp) unknown. (These are some of the same people who have rightly criticized the Yankees for signing known retread free agents instead of building up the farm system.)

If these people had been paying attention to the farm system, though, they would have noticed that Buck Showalter has been doing a great job there. His overall minor league managing record is 360-207. He became a manager in 1985 after a seven-year playing career in the New York system and one year as a coach for the Yanks' farm club in Fort Lauderdale. In his first year at the helm, he led Oneonta of the New York-Penn League to a league-record 55-23 mark.

That record lasted only a year, because his 1986 team went 59-18. His next stop was Fort Lauderdale, where he finished first for the third straight season, going 85-53. In 1988, for the first and only time so far, his team didn't finish first; Fort Lauderdale was third with a 69-65 record. However, he made up for that faux pas in Albany-Colonie in 1989.

This was the first time I heard of Buck Showalter, because I was following the Tigers' team in London. That A/C team finished 92-46, but was even doing much better than that until most of the key players were called up to Columbus. On a visit to Albany for the 1989 SABR Convention, I read several stories in the paper about Showalter. The players respected him and couldn't say enough good things about him, and he was mentioned in both the Albany media and Baseball America as a top managerial prospect. By the way, the Albany-Colonie team finished first and won the playoffs, the third playoff championship in five seasons for a Showalter team. After the 1989 season, he was named the Yankees "eye-in-the-sky" coach, and was promoted to the third base coaching job in June when Stump Merrill became manager.

One of the things that Bill James mentioned in one of his Abstracts that has stuck with me is that most successful major league managers were successful managers in the minors. Take a look around the majors at the successful managers and you'll see what I mean. Sparky Anderson managed in the minors five seasons, finishing first in three half-seasons, before becoming a major league coach. Tommy Lasorda managed in the Dodger system eight seasons and finished first five times, before becoming a Dodger coach. Tony LaRussa's 1978 Knoxville team, his first, finished 49-21 in the first half and started 4-4 in the second when LaRussa was called up to the White Sox' coaching ranks. He went back to the minors in 1979, compiling an ok 54-52 record, when in early August he was named the manager in Chicago. He struggled for a few years as a major league manager, then became one of the best.

Jimmy Leyland managed in the Tigers' system for 12 years, winning three full pennants and one half-season one in his last five years before becoming a White Sox coach and later skipper of the Pirates. From the 1991 World Series, Tom Kelly ran teams in the Twins' system for five years, winning three Manager-of-the-Year titles, before being promoted to the Minnesota coaching staff, and ultimately, manager of the Twins. Bobby Cox ran teams in the Yankees' system for six summers, never compiling a losing record. One of the media's top choices for every managerial opening lately, Davey Johnson, got his training as a very successful manager in the Mets' organization.

I don't want to beat a dead horse into the ground, but I think I've made my point. In my opinion, Buck Showalter was the obvious, logical, and perfect choice to manage the New York Yankees in 1992. He knows the players, he knows the organization, and he's been very successful. What more do you want, other than having a "big" name. When Sparky Anderson was hired by the Reds, the headline read "Sparky Who?", similarly for Walter Alston in Brooklyn. It may be funny to look back at the criticisms of Buck Showalter in twenty years after he's won, let's say, six divisional pennants, four league championships, and two World Series rings.

This move also shows that the Yankees' front office has a grip on reality. They seem to realize that they are not one or two big names away from winning it all (although Michael's want of Steve Buechele would be an argument against that), and that they have to rebuild from the ground up. It won't happen overnight; Showalter is likely to suffer his first losing season; but if they give him a chance and hold on to their young players, they will eventually turn it around. If they lose patience with Showalter and don't give him enough time, he'll just become another one of the Yankee prospects, like Doug Drabek and Fred McGriff, that made it big elsewhere.

And now, for you David Letterman fans, straight from the home office in Rochester Hills, Michigan, are the Top Ten McDonalds Menu Items and 1991 New York Yankee Statistics. Drum roll, please (tap hands on table)...

10. Only two AL teams walked less often (473 times)
9. Chicken McNuggets
8. Breakfast Burritos
7. The Bronx Bombers had the best stolen base percentage in the league, 75% (109-36)
6. The starters had the second worst ERA in the league (5.07) and threw the fewest innings (5.5 per game)
5. The Big Mac
4. The bullpen had the fourth best ERA in the league (3.41)
3. The Yanks were 11th in the league in runs scored with 674 and 12th in runs allowed with 777
2. Large Fries

And, the Number One McDonalds Menu Item and 1991 New York Yankee Statistic...

1. This was the first time in four years that their manager made it through an entire season (of course, they fired him as soon as the season was over)

New York Yankees Home Park Performance Factors

	Outs	Runs	Hits	2b	3b	HR	W	K	SH	SF	HBP	IBB	SB	CS	GDP
Home LH Batters	.915	.849	.944	.860	1.193	.824	.852	.950	5.965	.799	.954	.882	.924	1.193	.990
Home RH Batters	.969	.900	.967	.950	1.321	.832	.929	1.005	1.035	1.218	1.118	1.023	.849	.977	1.028
All Home Batters	.944	.877	.949	.907	1.202	.835	.895	.980	1.020	.961	1.051	.955	.818	.987	1.011
Opp LH Batters	.953	.980	.954	1.148	2.397	.835	1.032	.929	.680	.929	.929	.680	1.027	.614	.915
Opp RH Batters	1.003	.993	.989	.965	1.601	.959	.978	1.029	1.130	.809	.876	.991	1.020	1.096	1.138
All Opp Batters	.980	1.001	.981	1.035	1.658	.903	1.016	.996	.949	.897	.928	.913	1.023	.878	1.033
All LH Batters	.931	.905	.947	.981	1.820	.829	.924	.938	.728	.844	.947	.839	.973	.688	.933
All RH Batters	.986	.947	.978	.956	1.472	.896	.954	1.017	1.081	.967	.967	.995	.918	1.036	1.082
All Batters	.961	.937	.964	.970	1.457	.867	.953	.986	.972	.938	.981	.939	.916	.913	1.018

Conventional Batting Records for New York Yankees

	G	AB	Run	Hit	2B	3B	HR	TB	RBI	W	K	IW	HB	SB	CS	BRng Eff	GI DP	SH	SF	Avg	Slug	OBP	Runs Ctd
Nokes	135	456	52	122	20	0	24	214	77	25	49	5	5	3	2	.308	6	0	7	.268	.469	.308	66
Mattingly	152	587	64	169	35	0	9	231	68	46	42	11	4	2	0	.359	21	0	9	.288	.394	.339	77
Sax S	158	652	85	198	38	2	10	270	56	41	38	2	3	31	11	.489	16	5	6	.304	.414	.345	92
Kelly P	96	298	35	72	12	4	3	101	23	15	52	0	5	12	1	.471	5	2	2	.242	.339	.287	31
Espinoza	148	480	51	123	23	2	5	165	33	16	57	0	2	4	1	.429	10	9	2	.256	.344	.282	45
Hall M	141	492	67	140	23	2	19	224	80	26	40	6	3	0	1	.416	6	0	6	.285	.455	.321	72
Williams B	85	320	43	76	19	4	3	112	34	48	57	0	1	10	5	.364	4	2	3	.237	.350	.336	41
Barfield Je	84	284	37	64	12	0	17	127	48	36	80	6	0	1	0	.559	11	0	1	.225	.447	.312	38
Maas	148	500	69	110	14	1	23	195	63	83	128	3	4	5	1	.439	4	0	5	.220	.390	.333	72
Kelly	126	486	68	130	22	2	20	216	69	45	77	2	5	32	9	.527	14	2	5	.267	.444	.333	72
Meulens	96	288	37	64	8	1	6	92	29	18	97	1	4	3	0	.439	7	1	2	.222	.319	.276	25
Velarde	80	184	19	45	11	1	1	61	15	18	43	0	3	3	1	.464	6	5	0	.245	.332	.322	20
Geren	64	128	7	28	3	0	2	37	12	9	31	0	0	0	1	.067	5	3	0	.219	.289	.270	9
Sheridan	62	113	13	23	3	0	4	38	7	13	30	1	0	1	1	.333	6	1	0	.204	.336	.286	10
Leyritz	32	77	8	14	3	0	0	17	4	13	15	0	0	0	1	.150	0	1	0	.182	.221	.300	6
Lovullo	22	51	0	9	2	0	0	11	2	5	7	1	0	0	0	1.000	0	3	0	.176	.216	.250	3
Humphreys	25	40	9	8	0	0	0	8	3	9	7	0	0	2	0	.600	0	1	0	.200	.200	.347	4
Rodriguez C	15	37	1	7	0	0	0	7	2	1	2	0	0	0	0	.400	3	1	0	.189	.189	.211	1
Blowers	15	35	3	7	0	0	1	10	1	4	3	0	0	0	0	.250	1	1	0	.200	.286	.282	3
Ramos J	10	26	4	8	1	0	0	9	3	1	3	0	0	0	0	.417	1	0	2	.308	.346	.310	3
Lusader	11	7	2	1	0	0	0	1	1	1	3	0	0	0	1	1.000	0	0	0	.143	.143	.250	0
Guetterman	1	0	0	0	0	0	0	0	0	0	0	0	0	0	0	.000	0	0	0	.000	.000	.000	0
TOTALS	1706	5541	674	1418	249	19	147	2146	630	473	861	38	39	109	36	.424	126	37	50	.256	.387	.316	686

Sabermetric Batting Records for New York Yankees

	Ball Park Adjusted								Runs		Run/									
	AB	Run	Hit	2B	3B	HR	RBI	W	SO	Avg	Slug	OBP	Ctd	Outs	27o	OW%	OG	OWAR	DWAR	TWAR
Barfield Je	278	35	62	11	0	15	48	34	81	.223	.424	.307	35	228	4.14	.461	8	0.94	1.15	2.09
Blowers	33	2	6	0	0	0	1	3	3	.182	.182	.250	2	29	1.86	.147	1	-0.22	-0.09	-0.31
Espinoza	471	48	120	22	2	4	33	15	57	.255	.335	.278	43	373	3.11	.326	14	-0.34	2.34	2.01
Geren	125	6	27	2	0	1	12	8	31	.216	.256	.263	8	107	2.02	.169	4	-0.72	-0.11	-0.83
Hall M	460	61	132	23	3	15	71	24	37	.287	.448	.322	67	338	5.35	.588	13	2.98	0.66	3.64
Humphreys	38	8	7	0	0	0	3	8	7	.184	.184	.326	3	32	2.53	.242	1	-0.13	-0.01	-0.14
Kelly P	292	33	70	11	5	2	23	14	52	.240	.332	.282	29	232	3.38	.362	9	0.11	0.15	0.26
Kelly	478	64	127	21	2	17	69	42	78	.266	.425	.327	66	382	4.66	.520	14	2.41	0.31	2.72
Leyritz	75	7	13	2	0	0	4	12	15	.173	.200	.287	5	64	2.11	.182	2	-0.40	-0.15	-0.55
Lovullo	48	0	8	1	0	0	1	4	6	.167	.188	.231	2	42	1.29	.076	2	-0.43	0.07	-0.36
Lusader	5	1	0	0	0	0	0	0	2	.000	.000	.000	0	5	0.00	.000	0	-0.06	0.01	-0.06
Maas	468	63	104	14	1	19	56	78	120	.222	.378	.335	67	371	4.88	.542	14	2.64	0.04	2.69
Mattingly	550	58	160	35	0	7	61	43	39	.291	.393	.342	72	417	4.66	.520	15	2.63	0.57	3.20
Meulens	282	35	62	7	1	5	29	17	98	.220	.305	.270	23	230	2.70	.267	9	-0.71	0.24	-0.47
Nokes	426	47	115	20	0	19	69	23	46	.270	.451	.309	60	323	5.02	.556	12	2.47	-0.55	1.92
Ramos J	24	3	7	0	0	0	3	0	3	.292	.292	.269	2	20	2.70	.267	1	-0.06	-0.00	-0.07
Rodriguez C	34	0	6	0	0	0	1	0	1	.176	.176	.176	1	31	0.87	.036	1	-0.36	0.13	-0.23
Sax S	640	80	193	36	2	8	56	39	38	.302	.402	.341	86	486	4.78	.532	18	3.28	1.39	4.67
Sheridan	105	11	21	3	0	3	6	12	28	.200	.314	.282	9	92	2.64	.258	3	-0.31	0.28	-0.03
Velarde	181	17	44	10	1	0	15	17	43	.243	.309	.315	18	149	3.26	.347	6	-0.02	0.49	0.47
Williams B	307	40	73	18	5	2	32	45	56	.238	.349	.333	39	245	4.30	.479	9	1.17	0.18	1.35
TOTALS	5333	633	1368	241	27	127	597	451	850	.257	.383	.316	651	4208	4.18	.465	156	17.96	7.10	25.06

Pitching Records for New York Yankees

	ERA	W	L	Pct	G	GS	CG	ShO	GF	Sv	IP	R	ER	H	2B	3B	HR	BB	IW	SO	HB	WP	BK
Sanderson	3.81	16	10	.615	34	34	2	2	0	0	208.0	95	88	200	46	5	22	29	0	130	3	4	1
Johnson J	5.95	6	11	.353	23	23	0	0	0	0	127.0	89	84	156	21	5	15	33	1	62	6	5	1
Leary	6.49	4	10	.286	28	18	1	0	4	0	120.2	89	87	150	32	2	20	57	1	83	4	10	0
Taylor W	6.27	7	12	.368	23	22	0	0	0	0	116.1	85	81	144	28	4	13	53	0	72	7	3	3
Perez P	3.18	2	4	.333	14	14	0	0	0	0	73.2	26	26	68	6	3	7	24	1	41	0	3	2
Eiland	5.33	2	5	.286	18	13	0	0	4	0	72.2	51	43	87	20	5	10	23	1	18	3	0	0
Kamieniecki	3.90	4	4	.500	9	9	0	0	0	0	55.1	24	24	54	12	3	8	22	1	34	3	1	0
Cary	5.91	1	6	.143	10	9	0	0	0	0	53.1	35	35	61	13	1	6	32	2	34	0	2	1
Hawkins	9.95	0	2	.000	4	3	0	0	1	0	12.2	15	14	23	2	0	5	6	0	5	0	1	0
Witt M	10.13	0	1	.000	2	2	0	0	0	0	5.1	7	6	8	2	0	1	1	0	0	0	1	0
Cadaret	3.62	8	6	.571	68	5	0	0	17	3	121.2	52	49	110	21	4	8	59	6	105	2	3	1
Plunk	4.76	2	5	.286	43	8	0	0	6	0	111.2	69	59	128	22	5	18	62	1	103	1	6	2
Habyan	2.30	4	2	.667	66	0	0	0	16	2	90.0	28	23	73	17	3	2	20	2	70	2	1	2
Guetterman	3.68	3	4	.429	64	0	0	0	37	6	88.0	42	36	91	19	2	6	25	5	35	3	4	0
Farr	2.19	5	5	.500	60	0	0	0	48	23	70.0	19	17	57	12	0	4	20	3	60	5	2	0
Howe S	1.68	3	1	.750	37	0	0	0	10	3	48.1	12	9	39	8	0	1	7	2	34	3	2	0
Monteleone	3.64	3	1	.750	26	0	0	0	10	0	47.0	27	19	42	10	0	5	19	3	34	0	1	1
Mills A	4.41	1	1	.500	6	2	0	0	3	0	16.1	9	8	16	2	0	1	8	0	11	0	2	0
Chapin	5.06	0	1	.000	3	0	0	0	2	0	5.1	3	3	3	2	0	0	6	0	5	0	2	0
Espinoza	0.00	0	0	.000	1	0	0	0	1	0	0.2	0	0	0	0	0	0	0	0	0	0	0	0
TOTALS	4.43	71	91	.438	539	162	3	2	159	37	1444.0	777	711	1510	295	42	152	506	29	936	42	53	14

Sabermetric Pitching Records for New York Yankees

	Adj	|-Expected-|			|——Opposing Batters——|													Supported			
	ERA	W	L	Pct	BFP	Avg	Slg	OBA	RC/G	GDP	SB	CS	PK	PKE	SH	SF	RSup	RSp/G	W	L	Pct
Cadaret	3.33	8	6	.601	517	.246	.365	.335	4.04	14	11	8	0	1	6	3	71	5.25	10	4	.713
Cary	5.40	3	4	.364	247	.285	.439	.378	6.19	7	7	1	0	1	1	0	20	3.38	2	5	.281
Chapin	3.38	1	0	.595	25	.158	.263	.360	4.33	0	1	0	0	0	0	0	2	3.37	1	0	.500
Eiland	4.95	3	4	.405	317	.302	.510	.356	6.13	13	6	1	0	0	0	3	24	2.97	2	5	.265
Espinoza	0.00	0	0	.000	2	.000	.000	.000	0.25	0	0	0	0	0	0	0	0	0.00	0	0	.000
Farr	1.93	8	2	.818	285	.219	.312	.288	2.88	8	2	2	0	0	0	0	12	1.54	4	6	.390
Guetterman	3.38	4	3	.595	376	.268	.388	.320	4.16	11	4	3	0	1	4	4	36	3.68	4	3	.543
Habyan	2.10	5	1	.791	349	.225	.315	.274	2.68	10	4	1	4	0	2	1	38	3.80	5	1	.766
Hawkins	9.24	0	2	.164	66	.383	.667	.439	12.54	0	0	1	0	1	0	0	6	4.26	0	2	.176
Howe S	1.49	4	0	.883	189	.222	.284	.262	2.27	7	1	0	0	0	2	1	26	4.84	4	0	.914
Johnson J	5.53	6	11	.354	562	.305	.453	.351	5.77	13	18	4	1	4	7	4	59	4.18	6	11	.364
Kamieniecki	3.58	5	3	.566	239	.256	.455	.333	5.20	5	4	2	2	0	2	1	27	4.39	5	3	.601
Leary	6.04	4	10	.314	551	.312	.511	.388	7.10	13	10	5	0	0	7	2	64	4.77	5	9	.384
Mills A	3.86	1	1	.529	72	.254	.333	.333	4.44	1	3	0	1	0	0	1	6	3.31	1	1	.424
Monteleone	3.26	2	2	.612	201	.236	.376	.307	4.01	3	2	2	0	0	2	2	28	5.36	3	1	.731
Perez P	2.93	4	2	.660	299	.250	.371	.311	3.49	11	4	4	0	0	3	0	24	2.93	3	3	.500
Plunk	4.43	3	4	.460	521	.286	.478	.371	7.01	7	28	3	1	1	6	4	44	3.55	3	4	.390
Sanderson	3.55	15	11	.570	837	.252	.405	.279	3.66	19	16	7	0	0	5	5	115	4.98	17	9	.663
Taylor W	5.80	6	13	.332	528	.314	.477	.388	6.51	17	12	6	2	2	2	7	68	5.26	9	10	.451
Witt M	8.44	0	1	.190	26	.320	.520	.346	8.08	0	1	0	0	0	0	0	4	6.75	0	1	.390
TOTALS	4.15	80	82	.492	6209	.271	.421	.334	4.83	159	134	50	11	11	49	38	674	4.20	82	80	.506

Batting 'Splits' Records for New York Yankees

	G	AB	Run	Hit	2B	3B	HR	TB	RBI	W	K	IW	HB	SB	CS	GI DP	SH	SF	Avg	Slug	OBP	Runs Ctd
SPLITS for Barfield Je																						
vs LHP	56	108	20	34	4	0	9	65	24	17	22	6	0	1	0	3	0	0	.315	.602	.408	27
vs RHP	72	176	17	30	8	0	8	62	24	19	58	0	0	0	0	8	0	1	.170	.352	.250	14
Home	42	130	21	30	7	0	11	70	30	20	31	2	0	1	0	6	0	1	.231	.538	.331	22
Away	42	154	16	34	5	0	6	57	18	16	49	4	0	0	0	5	0	0	.221	.370	.294	16
Grass	71	236	33	51	10	0	14	103	39	30	63	4	0	1	0	10	0	1	.216	.436	.303	30
Turf	13	48	4	13	2	0	3	24	9	6	17	2	0	0	0	1	0	0	.271	.500	.352	9
April/June	70	243	29	55	11	0	15	111	44	30	70	6	0	1	0	10	0	1	.226	.457	.310	33
July/October	14	41	8	9	1	0	2	16	4	6	10	0	0	0	0	1	0	0	.220	.390	.319	5
SPLITS for Maas																						
vs LHP	103	181	24	40	7	0	9	74	31	30	51	0	3	1	1	3	0	2	.221	.409	.338	27
vs RHP	131	319	45	70	7	1	14	121	32	53	77	3	1	4	0	1	0	3	.219	.379	.330	45
Home	73	236	28	42	8	0	8	74	25	40	55	1	3	3	0	3	0	3	.178	.314	.301	26
Away	75	264	41	68	6	1	15	121	38	43	73	2	1	2	1	1	0	2	.258	.458	.361	48
Grass	124	415	55	87	13	0	18	154	51	71	109	3	4	4	1	3	0	4	.210	.371	.328	57
Turf	24	85	14	23	1	1	5	41	12	12	19	0	0	1	0	1	0	1	.271	.482	.357	16
April/June	70	252	44	63	9	1	13	113	33	52	59	1	2	2	1	2	0	2	.250	.448	.380	48
July/October	78	248	25	47	5	0	10	82	30	31	69	2	2	3	0	2	0	3	.190	.331	.282	26
SPLITS for Williams B																						
vs LHP	52	104	16	21	6	0	2	33	13	17	11	0	0	3	2	1	0	2	.202	.317	.309	11
vs RHP	76	216	27	55	13	4	1	79	21	31	46	0	1	7	3	3	2	1	.255	.366	.349	30
Home	42	159	20	42	10	2	1	59	19	23	22	0	0	7	2	2	2	1	.264	.371	.355	23
Away	43	161	23	34	9	2	2	53	15	25	35	0	1	3	3	2	0	2	.211	.329	.317	18
Grass	74	276	37	68	17	4	2	99	31	42	43	0	1	9	3	2	2	3	.246	.359	.345	38
Turf	11	44	6	8	2	0	1	13	3	6	14	0	0	1	2	2	0	0	.182	.295	.280	3
April/June	No plate appearances																					
July/October	85	320	43	76	19	4	3	112	34	48	57	0	1	10	5	4	2	3	.237	.350	.336	41
SPLITS for New York Yankees (all batters except pitchers)																						
vs LHP	1016	2002	280	542	89	3	61	820	257	189	289	12	18	44	17	52	10	19	.271	.410	.336	277
vs RHP	1359	3539	394	876	160	16	86	1326	373	284	572	26	21	65	19	74	27	31	.248	.375	.305	410
Home	858	2685	356	692	129	7	82	1081	333	242	394	18	16	63	16	56	17	24	.258	.403	.320	354
Away	848	2856	318	726	120	12	65	1065	297	231	467	20	23	46	20	70	20	26	.254	.373	.313	332
Grass	1464	4687	583	1193	211	13	128	1814	548	414	715	31	32	95	32	101	32	44	.255	.387	.317	584
Turf	242	854	91	225	38	6	19	332	82	59	146	7	7	14	4	25	5	6	.263	.389	.314	102
April/June	752	2468	313	632	105	6	78	983	296	214	410	16	15	39	13	56	9	16	.256	.398	.317	313
July/October	954	3073	361	786	144	13	69	1163	334	259	451	22	24	70	23	70	28	34	.256	.378	.315	373

1991 SPLITS FOR New York Yankees

BATTING SPLITS

	AVG	AB	R	H	2B	3B	HR	RBI	SB	CS	BB	K	OBA	SPCT
Total	.256	5541	674	1418	249	19	147	630	109	36	473	861	.316	.387
	#Pit	#P/PA	GB	FB	G/F	G	IBB	HB	SH	SF	GDP			
Miscellaneous	21803	3.55	2070	1710	1.21	162	38	39	37	50	126			
	AVG	AB	R	H	2B	3B	HR	RBI	SB	CS	BB	K	OBA	SPCT
vs. Left	.271	2002	...	542	89	3	61	257	44	17	189	289	.336	.410
vs. Right	.248	3539	...	876	160	16	86	373	65	19	284	572	.305	.375
Home	.258	2685	356	692	129	7	82	333	63	16	242	394	.320	.403
Away	.254	2856	318	726	120	12	65	297	46	20	231	467	.313	.373
None on	.254	3215	...	818	134	14	87	87	0	0	243	499	.310	.386
Runners on	.258	2326	...	600	115	5	60	543	109	36	230	362	.324	.389
April	.254	574	79	146	21	3	13	75	11	7	79	96	.342	.369
May	.239	927	111	222	46	1	35	102	7	3	80	169	.304	.405
June	.273	967	123	264	38	2	30	119	21	3	55	145	.314	.410
July	.255	868	109	221	44	2	26	101	18	6	79	138	.320	.400
August	.263	1044	137	275	44	7	20	126	25	10	88	154	.323	.376
September	.241	943	85	227	43	4	15	79	21	7	74	135	.297	.343
October	.289	218	30	63	13	0	8	28	6	0	18	24	.342	.459
None on/out	.267	1407	...	376	58	5	38	38	0	0	95	194	.315	.397
Scoring Posn	.257	1296	...	333	66	3	33	470	38	8	160	212	.334	.389
Close & Late	.244	881	...	215	35	1	28	112	14	4	89	162	.318	.381
Bases Loaded	.257	105	...	27	7	0	1	74	0	0	3	17	.248	.352
Batting #1	.260	677	94	176	37	3	11	58	31	10	63	97	.325	.372
Batting #2	.285	671	80	191	32	3	12	64	17	11	48	62	.331	.395
Batting #3	.284	641	75	182	38	0	12	86	17	2	60	61	.347	.399
Batting #4	.272	617	91	168	25	3	26	87	5	1	74	93	.349	.449
Batting #5	.246	622	85	153	25	2	33	100	7	4	53	118	.304	.452
Batting #6	.239	611	72	146	24	0	20	76	8	1	41	109	.294	.376
Batting #7	.220	574	65	126	18	0	20	69	3	2	57	124	.290	.355
Batting #8	.229	572	51	131	22	2	8	43	4	3	41	107	.285	.316
Batting #9	.261	556	61	145	28	6	5	47	17	2	36	90	.311	.360
As p	.000	1	0	0	0	0	0	0	0	0	0	0	.000	.000
As c	.264	580	63	153	24	0	26	90	2	3	33	80	.306	.440
As 1b	.287	644	76	185	34	0	14	84	4	0	55	63	.344	.405
As 2b	.299	665	86	199	39	2	10	59	33	11	42	46	.344	.409
As 3b	.223	539	49	120	20	4	6	39	12	3	47	89	.290	.308
As ss	.248	569	58	141	26	3	4	36	5	1	20	76	.275	.325
As lf	.270	604	85	163	24	2	28	98	17	3	45	110	.324	.455
As cf	.246	637	88	157	32	5	14	71	26	12	71	117	.323	.378
As rf	.231	610	69	141	24	2	22	73	3	1	55	120	.294	.385
Outfield	.249	1851	242	461	80	9	64	242	46	16	171	347	.314	.406
0.0 count	.301	830	...	250	48	2	26	130	...	...	2	0	.311	.458
After (0.1)	.223	2412	...	539	91	7	45	210	...	...	106	567	.259	.323
After (1.0)	.274	2299	...	629	110	10	76	290	...	...	337	294	.365	.429
Two strikes	.188	2287	...	430	75	8	44	195	...	...	196	858	.254	.286
Grass	.255	4687	583	1193	211	13	128	548	95	32	414	715	.317	.387
Turf	.263	854	91	225	38	6	19	82	14	4	59	146	.314	.389
Day	.261	1746	243	456	83	10	44	228	41	17	195	254	.336	.396
Night	.253	3795	431	962	166	9	103	402	68	19	278	607	.307	.383
Inning 1.6	.262	3727	473	977	181	14	92	440	85	28	305	535	.319	.392
Inning 7+	.243	1814	201	441	68	5	55	190	24	8	168	326	.310	.377
vs.Bal	.260	442	59	115	20	1	13	55	5	4	43	65	.323	.398
vs.Bos	.250	428	55	107	21	2	17	53	13	1	37	63	.314	.428
vs.Cal	.244	405	48	99	23	0	13	44	8	1	30	67	.303	.398
vs.ChA	.245	400	52	98	14	1	7	49	7	5	43	71	.320	.338
vs.Cle	.269	453	54	122	25	2	12	50	9	1	33	55	.315	.413
vs.Det	.283	449	69	127	20	3	9	65	10	7	56	59	.357	.401
vs.KC	.245	404	46	99	19	3	5	40	8	2	40	65	.317	.344
vs.Mil	.268	466	61	125	22	1	10	60	12	1	30	63	.313	.384
vs.Min	.259	406	46	105	15	2	12	41	7	1	18	69	.291	.394
vs.Oak	.249	394	56	98	15	1	16	53	10	4	44	66	.330	.414
vs.Sea	.230	421	32	97	23	0	8	27	4	2	40	82	.302	.342
vs.Tex	.255	431	46	110	15	1	15	44	7	3	34	70	.316	.399
vs.Tor	.262	442	50	116	17	2	10	49	9	4	25	66	.304	.378

PITCHING SPLITS

	ERA	W	L	SV	SVOP	GS	CG	SHO	IP	H	ER	HR	BB	IBB	K
Total	4.42	71	91	37	52	162	3	10	1444.0	1510	709	152	506	29	936
	#Pit	#P/IP	GB	FB	G/F	BRp9	RA	WP	BK	SH	SF	R	HB	Hld	
Miscellaneous	23118	16.01	2050	1627	1.26	12.83	377	53	14	49	38	777	42	51	
	ERA	W	L	SV	SVOP	GS	CG	SHO	IP	H	ER	HR	BB	IBB	K
ST	5.07	45	68	0	0	162	3	2	892.0	984	502	108	304	7	528
REL	3.41	26	23	37	52	0	0	0	552.0	526	209	44	202	22	408
Home	4.31	39	42	18	24	81	1	0	739.0	761	354	84	243	15	466
Away	4.56	32	49	19	28	81	2	2	705.0	749	357	68	263	14	470
April	5.19	6	11	1	1	17	1	0	149.0	162	86	16	62	5	102
May	3.49	14	13	6	8	27	1	1	245.1	227	95	20	102	8	139
June	4.25	13	14	10	11	27	0	0	241.1	255	114	22	65	1	153
July	4.36	13	13	9	9	26	1	1	231.0	250	112	24	63	2	142
August	5.54	12	19	3	7	31	0	0	274.2	300	169	42	102	8	215
September	4.10	9	19	5	9	28	0	0	243.2	255	111	24	94	5	151
October	3.66	4	2	3	7	6	0	0	59.0	61	24	4	18	0	34
Grass	4.36	64	74	33	44	138	2	1	1235.2	1271	599	133	442	24	797
Turf	4.84	7	17	4	8	24	1	1	208.1	239	112	19	64	5	139
Day	4.98	23	29	11	16	52	0	0	459.1	498	254	51	195	15	307
Night	4.18	48	62	26	36	110	3	2	984.2	1012	457	101	311	14	629
vs.Bal	3.74	8	5	5	8	13	0	0	118.0	125	49	15	32	4	73
vs.Bos	3.88	7	6	3	5	13	0	0	116.0	114	50	13	44	1	60
vs.Cal	5.21	6	6	4	4	12	1	1	107.0	106	62	10	44	0	59
vs.ChA	6.28	4	8	1	1	12	0	0	106.0	131	74	11	44	1	66
vs.Cle	2.87	7	6	6	9	13	0	0	116.0	115	37	5	36	1	77
vs.Det	5.59	5	8	1	3	13	0	0	114.1	106	71	21	63	6	100
vs.KC	4.63	5	7	1	1	12	1	0	107.0	117	55	10	31	4	78
vs.Mil	4.54	7	6	4	5	13	0	0	117.0	127	59	6	44	1	73
vs.Min	5.12	2	10	0	1	12	0	0	103.2	121	59	16	31	2	61
vs.Oak	4.11	6	6	4	4	12	0	0	105.0	100	48	9	56	2	66
vs.Sea	3.43	3	9	1	2	12	1	1	110.1	105	42	9	26	4	65
vs.Tex	4.61	5	7	3	3	12	0	0	109.1	124	56	17	26	0	69
vs.Tor	3.86	6	7	4	6	13	0	0	114.1	119	49	10	29	3	89

OPPOSING BATTERS VS. PITCHERS.

	AVG	AB	R	H	2B	3B	HR	RBI	SB	CS	BB	K	OBA	SPCT
Total	.271	5574	777	1510	295	42	152	736	134	50	506	936	.334	.421
vs. Left	.272	2300	...	625	123	19	65	283	61	21	220	363	.337	.427
vs. Right	.270	3274	...	885	172	23	87	453	73	29	286	573	.332	.417
ST	.283	3483	532	984	188	34	108	470	86	35	304	528	.342	.449
REL	.252	2091	245	526	107	8	44	266	48	15	202	408	.320	.374
Home	.269	2831	380	761	137	12	84	363	65	28	243	466	.329	.415
Away	.273	2743	397	749	158	30	68	373	69	22	263	470	.339	.427
None on	.268	3141	...	841	169	23	76	76	0	0	248	520	.326	.409
Runners on	.275	2433	...	669	126	19	76	660	134	50	258	416	.344	.436
None on/out	.271	1381	...	374	88	9	37	37	0	0	114	222	.331	.428
Scoring Posn	.280	1416	...	396	76	15	41	561	47	8	180	263	.357	.441
vs 1st Batr	.240	341	...	82	16	1	5	44	5	2	32	61	.307	.337
1st IP	.252	1846	227	466	89	13	38	245	55	23	169	351	.318	.376
Inning 1.6	.279	3784	567	1057	205	32	110	536	104	39	352	595	.343	.438
Inning 7+	.253	1790	210	453	90	10	42	200	30	11	154	341	.316	.385
Close & Late	.252	819	...	206	34	4	17	91	13	7	80	152	.323	.365
0.0 count	.335	776	...	260	47	8	24	125	...	...	21	0	.357	.509
After (0.1)	.242	2547	...	617	116	18	57	277	...	...	102	616	.277	.369
After (1.0)	.281	2251	...	633	132	16	71	334	...	...	383	320	.385	.449
Two strikes	.206	2533	...	522	100	12	47	256	...	...	227	933	.275	.311
Pitch 1.15	.258	1647	...	425	83	13	31	164	45	16	133	280	.317	.381
Pitch 16.30	.269	1160	...	312	68	5	33	167	29	11	110	217	.332	.422
Pitch 31.45	.269	832	...	224	40	6	17	110	16	4	81	141	.339	.393
Pitch 46.60	.280	661	...	185	27	6	25	101	12	5	55	117	.337	.452
Pitch 61.75	.299	555	...	166	31	5	16	88	15	10	64	81	.373	.459
Pitch 76.90	.275	418	...	115	25	3	20	71	11	2	42	46	.343	.493
Pitch 91.105	.288	233	...	67	15	3	9	29	4	1	17	38	.337	.494
Pitch 106.20	.227	66	...	15	6	1	0	4	2	1	4	15	.292	.348
Pitch 121.35	.250	4	...	1	0	0	1	2	0	0	0	1	.250	1.000

Baltimore Orioles

Dave Raglin

BALTIMORE											
YEAR	1982	1983	1984	1985	1986	1987	1988	1989	1990	1991	TOT
W	94	98	85	83	73	67	54	87	76	67	784
L	68	64	77	78	89	95	107	75	85	95	833
WPCT	0.580	0.605	0.525	0.516	0.451	0.414	0.335	0.537	0.472	0.414	0.485
R	774	799	681	818	708	729	550	708	669	686	7122
RA	687	652	667	764	760	880	789	686	698	796	7379
PWPT	0.559	0.600	0.510	0.534	0.465	0.407	0.327	0.516	0.479	0.426	0.482
PythW	91	97	83	87	75	66	53	84	78	69	78
PythL	71	65	79	75	87	96	109	78	84	93	84
LUCK	3	1	2	-4	-2	1	1	3	-2	-2	1

Defensive Efficiency Record: .6907

I'm not sure if my worst prediction of 1991 was for the Baltimore Orioles to win the AL Eastern Division pennant. After all, I also predicted both the Twins and Braves to repeat as cellar dwellers, too. My fantasy teams even had bad seasons. If someone had told me in March that Cal Ripken was going to win the American League's Most Valuable Player award, I'd have considered flying to Vegas and putting a lot on money on the Birds.

Let's start by looking at the good news of 1991 as far as the O's were concerned. Cal Ripken. Actually, that's not quite true, as we'll see later, but there wasn't much else to cheer about during the last season on 33rd Street (except for the demise of the park itself--I did not like Memorial Stadium at all).

When it was announced in November that Cal had won the MVP, a loud stink was heard from about 550 miles to the northwest. Cecil Fielder thought he, not Ripken, deserved the award. As Joe Friday would say (if he hadn't died already), just the facts...

Below is a list of the top ten offensive players in the American League for 1991, ranked by Runs Created. Notice that it's good for Cecil that we listed ten players, because he's number 10.

American League 1991, Top Ten Players in Runs Created

	G	AB	BB	R	H	2B	3B	HR	BI	BA	OBP	SLG	RC	RC/G
Thomas	158	559	138	104	178	31	2	32	109	.318	.453	.553	145	9.7
Ripken	162	650	53	99	210	46	5	34	114	.323	.374	.566	134	7.9
Molitor	158	665	77	133	216	32	13	17	75	.325	.399	.489	132	7.6
Palmeiro	159	631	68	115	203	49	3	26	88	.322	.389	.532	129	7.7
Griffey	154	548	71	76	179	42	1	22	100	.327	.399	.527	118	8.3
Franco	146	589	65	108	201	27	3	15	78	.341	.408	.474	118	7.8
Sierra	161	661	56	110	203	44	5	25	116	.307	.357	.502	117	6.6
Canseco	154	572	78	115	152	32	1	44	122	.266	.359	.556	116	7.1
Tartabull	132	484	65	78	153	35	3	31	100	.316	.397	.593	116	9.1
Fielder	162	624	78	102	163	25	0	44	133	.261	.347	.513	110	6.2

Cal finished second in runs created behind Frank Thomas of the White Sox. Only Thomas and Danny Tartabull, the often-injured ex-Royal who had his best season ever in his free-agency year, had more runs created per game among the top ten. But Thomas led the league in both runs created and runs created per game by a wide margin. Shouldn't he have leapfrogged both Ripken and Fielder and everybody else to win the award?

Yes, if the award was for the top offensive player. However, defense has to count. How do we take it into account that Ripken played shortstop, and played it very well (finishing with the second best range in the league), while Thomas and Paul Molitor were essentially designated hitters?

If you look in the back of this book, you'll see a list of names and numbers titled "Defensive Wins Above Replacement". Using formulas developed by Bill James, this statistic estimates the number of wins the given player won for his team defensively compared to a replacement-level player. Cal Ripken lead the majors with 3.09 defensive wins above replacement, meaning that it is estimated that the Orioles won about three more games just because of Ripken's defense compared to a replacement-level ballplayer, say Manny Lee or Mike Bordick.

Bill James has estimated that each 10 runs is worth about a win, so 3.09 wins above replacement equals about 31 runs above replacement. The chart below shows the runs created for each of the top ten above, their defensive runs above replacement, and the total:

Total Runs =
Runs Created + Defensive Runs Above Replacement,

Top Ten American Leaguers in Runs Created, 1991

	RC	DRAR	Total
Ripken	134	31	165
Thomas	145	0	145
Molitor	132	1	133
Palmeiro	129	4	133
Griffey	118	13	131
Sierra	117	10	127
Franco	118	2	120
Canseco	116	2	118
Tartabull	116	-3	113
Fielder	110	3	113

Notice the huge difference between Ripken and the other players. Franco, the only other middle infielder on the list, was not a good defensive player in 1991. The second-best defensive player here was Ken Griffey, who also plays an important defensive position, centerfield. Tartabull, is actually below replacement-level in rightfield, costing his team runs. After looking at defense, it's clear that Ripken was the best position player in the league.

Next are the pitchers. I have no problem awarding the MVP to a pitcher if he deserves it, but I don't see anybody out there who was better than Ripken, so I'm going to plead laziness and not analyze the best pitcher, Roger Clemens, compared to Cal. If you want to, the methodology is in the 1987 Abstract.

Now comes the argument that got Cecil steamed, the contender-noncontender thing. First of all, it isn't like the Tigers were in the race all year. They were on the fringes of it all year, thanks to the weak East, but were in thick of it for only about a month, from early August to early September. But it's true that the Orioles finished sixth with Cal and, given the Indians, would have finished sixth without him.

But that ignores the context of a season over time. Seasons are not isolated events, but part of a chain of seasons, each independent in a way but also dependent in a way. The 1987 Red Sox had what may have first appeared to be an unsuccessful season--a losing record after coming within one strike of winning it all in 1986--but they spent the summer redoing their lineup, bringing in people like Ellis Burks and Mike Greenwell, and won two of the next three Eastern pennants.

Another example which is closer to Cecil's heart is the 1990 Tigers. True, they had a losing record, 79-83, but after 1989's 59-103, it looked like it would be years until the Tigers would be a force again. The 1990 season proved to be a springboard into 1991, when the Tigers returned to the winning side of the ledger and, as mentioned before, were in the race for a little while. Cecil might have had been on a losing team in 1990, but the value of his season to the franchise was great. Henderson still deserved the MVP because he had a better season than Cecil, but Cecil did deserve serious consideration.

If the Orioles hadn't had Cal this season, let's say he had gotten hurt on Opening Day but would be healthy in 1992, they would now be looking back at another season similar to 1988. The hope for 1992 would be extremely dim. (After all, how many seasons like the 1989 Orioles are there?) If Glenn Davis had been there all year as expected, they would have been a better team in 1991 with a better outlook for 1992.

The point is that there is value in a player on a bad team having a great year. All things being equal, I'd choose a team on a top contender, but that wasn't the choice here. The choice between Cecil and Cal was a choice between a player who had a much better season vs one on a marginal contender. The choice was clear. Cal deserved the award, and I'm glad the writers saw it that way. It shows how much the writers many have learned in a short time due to sabermetrics--in 1987, they gave Alan Trammell's MVP to George Bell. I just wish they had known as much then as they seem to now.

So looking back, why did I say that Baltimore would win the East in 1991? Looking at Ben McDonald's numbers for 1990, a 2.43 ERA and a 8-5 record, a 65-35 SO/BB ratio, and allowing only 88 hits in 118.2 innings, I thought for sure that he was all set to become the next Roger Clemens. A couple of other starters come through with decent seasons, and with Olson and Williamson in the pen, the pitching would be fine. A lineup with Ripken, Milligan, Davis, and something from Dwight Evans would score some runs.

Things started falling apart in Florida. After a couple of scoreless performances, McDonald came up with arm trouble. The mood in the Baltimore media started to approach panic.

You see, Ben McDonald, even before the Orioles went through the formality of drafting him, has been considered the savior in Baltimore. He became the focus of the team. That is not good, unless the player is as good as a Wayne Gretzky or a Babe Ruth and can play at that level.

A good example of this is Bo Jackson with Kansas City in 1987. He became the focus of the Royals, which turned into a problem after he announced his intention to play for the Raiders. "It was a major distraction; it just ruined our season," said Danny Tartabull. Jackson had not been playing that well anyway after a good start (which built everything up), but from then on, he was awful, and so were the Royals. After the announcement, Kansas City went 3-12 and fell out of the race for good.

The point is that both became the focus of their teams when they weren't that good, and their falling severely hurt their teams psychologically. After the O's lost on Opening Day with Ben on the DL, the mood among fans and the local media was, so much for 1991.

That was just the knockdown. The knockout came when Glenn

Davis went down with back problems in April. At that point, the few remaining optimists gave up, Frank was fired, and everybody spent the summer watching the new ballpark go up.

The Orioles early problems weren't limited to the early part of the season. They had problems with the early parts of games, too. According to Dave Smith of SportsSource, the O's scored 67 runs in the first inning and allowed 134. After one inning, they were ahead 30 times, behind 50, and tied in 82 games. Here's how that compared throughout the majors:

The Worst Five Teams in the First Inning in Various Categories, 1991

Least Scored		Most Allowed		Least Leads		Most Behind		Most Under .500	
Team	Runs	Team	Runs	Team	Leads	Team	Behind	Team	Under
BAL	**67**	**BAL**	**134**	CLE	28	**BAL**	**50**	**BAL**	**-20**
STL	69	CIN	112	**BAL**	**30**	HOU	49	HOU	-14
CLE	70	HOU	109	STL	30	CIN	48	CLE	-12
SDP	72	SDP	103	PIT	31	SEA	44	PIT	-10
KCR	74	KCR	103	CHW	32	CHC	44	CHW	-10
Avg	91	Avg	91	Avg	39	Avg	39	Avg	0

The Orioles scored the least runs of any major league team in the first, allowed the most by far, were ahead fewer times than any other team except for the Indians, were behind more than any other team, and were more games under .500 than any other team.

It certainly was not news in Baltimore that the Orioles allowed a lot of runs in the first inning--talk about trying to hide an elephant. The Oriole starting pitchers had a 5.29 ERA, going 42-69 (the bullpen went 25-26) while allowing 1025 hits in exactly 900 innings with a 479-318 SO/BB ratio. That's a 1.49 WHIP (Walks + Hits / Innings Pitched, basically men on base per inning) if you're scoring at home.

However, it wasn't widely publicized that the Orioles had trouble scoring in the first. This is especially amazing because Baltimore had the league MVP coming up third in the order every game. I'm sure your first reaction was that it's hard coming up in the bottom of the first down by several runs, but that wasn't the reason.

The Oriole leadoff and number two hitters were awful in 1991. The top of the order, mostly Mike Devereaux with a little bit of Brady Anderson and Luis Mercedes thrown in for seasoning, hit only .256 with an on-base percentage of .318 and a slugging percentage of .404. The number two hitters, Joe Orsulak about half of the time, Brady Anderson some, and a potpourri for the rest, hit .244 with a .309 on-base percentage and an appalling .342 slugging percentage. (To compare, the league as a whole hit .260 with a .329 on-base percentage and a .395 slugging percentage.) The number two hitter is at least supposed to have bat control. The Baltimore number two hitters struck out 102 times. No wonder Fielder had 19 more RBIs than Ripken.

So can the Orioles win the East in 1992? Actually, they aren't as far away as you might think for a 67-95 team. They are certainly closer than the Twins or the Braves were at this time last year.

What has to happen? First, Mike Mussina, who looked like what McDonald was supposed to be, has to continue. If they make a trade for a starter (possibly including Milligan), and either McDonald or top prospect Arthur Rhodes comes through, they'll have the basis of a decent rotation. If both McDonald and Rhodes com through, they'll have a very good rotation. Gregg Olson should improve with Dick Bosman as pitching coach instead of Al Jackson, and one of the most unheralded middle relievers in the game, Mark Williamson, is supposedly healthy.

The middle of the order looks strong. Baltimore was third in the league in home runs in 1991 with 170 and tied for fourth in slugging percentage at .401, and having a healthy Davis in the lineup instead of Milligan should make up for a drop in Ripken's numbers. Then the biggest need is for hitters at the top of the order, as was pointed out earlier. Outfielder Luis Mercedes (.334 average, .435 on-base at Rochester) may be the answer at the top of the order.

The odds of this all happening are small, of course, but not outrageous. This is the AL East, after all. With the excitement of moving into Oriole Park at Camden Yards providing a little extra shove, it could happen. If you're in Vegas this spring and want to take a chance on a longshot, put down $20 on the O's. If you win, though, I want a cut.

Maryland Governor William Donald Schaefer and Orioles' owner Eli Jacobs spent the summer in a childish battle of will over the name of the new stadium. The lease between the state and the team states that both had to agree on the name. The Governor wanted to call it Camden Yards, because of its being built on the site of the old Camden Yards railway station (which I agreed with). Jacobs wanted the taxpayer-fianaced stadium named after his team, Oriole Park. Months after the supposed final deadline for naming the park, they announced the unwieldy compromise "Oriole Park at Camden Yards". The next day, I was talking to the witty Oriole announcer Jon Miller when somebody asked him what he would call the new stadium on the air. Miller replied matter-of-factly, "Oriole Park at Camden Yards Near the Inner Harbor Just a Few Blocks From Babe Ruth's Birthplace."

Baltimore Orioles Home Park Performance Factors

	Outs	Runs	Hits	2b	3b	HR	W	K	SH	SF	HBP	IBB	SB	CS	GDP
Home LH Batters	.944	.854	.914	.956	6.154	.813	.892	1.022	.816	.783	.816	1.810	1.017	.879	.821
Home RH Batters	.923	.982	.972	.934	1.249	.990	.945	.938	.815	1.118	1.121	.892	1.047	.961	.885
All Home Batters	.932	.943	.965	.950	1.349	.948	.936	.961	.861	1.008	1.004	.991	1.022	.934	.875
Opp LH Batters	1.019	.995	.960	1.024	1.584	.950	1.037	.940	.930	1.002	.540	.883	.766	.716	1.113
Opp RH Batters	.996	1.048	1.015	1.041	1.592	1.086	1.018	.934	1.363	1.007	1.410	1.216	.879	.940	.986
All Opp Batters	1.000	1.030	.999	1.048	1.600	1.033	1.038	.940	1.131	.983	.944	1.027	.879	.862	1.010
All LH Batters	.986	.932	.938	.995	2.084	.887	.971	.983	.879	.918	.674	.947	.848	.751	.985
All RH Batters	.953	1.007	.987	.978	1.385	1.030	.977	.937	1.009	1.089	1.240	1.003	.902	.940	.927
All Batters	.964	.984	.979	.996	1.466	.989	.985	.953	.979	.994	.976	1.004	.901	.879	.938

Conventional Batting Records for Baltimore Orioles

	G	AB	Run	Hit	2B	3B	HR	TB	RBI	W	K	IW	HB	SB	CS	BRng Eff	GI DP	SH	SF	Avg	Slug	OBP	Runs Ctd
Hoiles	107	341	36	83	15	0	11	131	31	29	61	1	1	0	2	.353	11	0	1	.243	.384	.304	37
Milligan	141	483	57	127	17	2	16	196	70	84	108	4	2	0	5	.298	23	0	2	.263	.406	.373	71
Ripken B	104	287	24	62	11	1	0	75	14	15	31	0	0	0	1	.375	14	11	2	.216	.261	.253	17
Gomez L	118	391	40	91	17	2	16	160	45	40	82	0	2	1	1	.327	11	5	7	.233	.409	.302	48
Ripken C	162	650	99	210	46	5	34	368	114	53	46	15	5	6	1	.390	19	0	9	.323	.566	.374	135
Orsulak	143	486	57	135	22	1	5	174	43	28	45	1	4	6	2	.443	9	0	3	.278	.358	.321	56
Devereaux	149	608	82	158	27	10	19	262	59	47	115	2	2	16	9	.485	13	7	4	.260	.431	.313	80
Evans Dw	101	270	35	73	9	1	6	102	38	54	54	2	2	2	3	.500	7	1	2	.270	.378	.393	43
Horn	121	317	45	74	16	0	23	159	61	41	99	4	3	0	0	.342	10	0	1	.233	.502	.326	51
Anderson B	113	256	40	59	12	3	2	83	27	38	44	0	5	12	5	.500	1	11	3	.230	.324	.338	33
Melvin	79	228	11	57	10	0	1	70	23	11	46	2	0	0	0	.222	5	1	5	.250	.307	.279	20
Martinez C	67	216	32	58	12	1	13	111	33	11	51	0	0	1	1	.536	1	0	1	.269	.514	.303	34
Segui	86	212	15	59	7	0	2	72	22	12	19	2	0	1	1	.267	7	3	1	.278	.340	.316	21
Bell Ju	100	209	26	36	9	2	1	52	15	8	51	0	0	0	0	.514	1	4	2	.172	.249	.201	11
Hulett	79	206	29	42	9	0	7	72	18	13	49	0	1	0	1	.325	3	1	0	.204	.350	.255	18
Davis G	49	176	29	40	9	1	10	81	28	16	29	0	5	4	0	.375	2	0	2	.227	.460	.307	27
Worthington	31	102	11	23	3	0	4	38	12	12	14	0	1	0	1	.200	3	1	0	.225	.373	.313	12
Whitt	35	62	5	15	2	0	0	17	3	8	12	0	0	0	0	.500	3	0	0	.242	.274	.329	5
Mercedes	19	54	10	11	2	0	0	13	2	4	9	0	0	0	0	.545	1	1	0	.204	.241	.259	3
McKnight	16	41	2	7	1	0	0	8	2	2	7	0	0	1	0	.167	2	0	0	.171	.195	.209	1
Tackett	6	8	1	1	0	0	0	1	0	2	2	0	0	0	0	.500	0	1	0	.125	.125	.300	1
Turner	4	1	0	0	0	0	0	0	0	0	0	0	0	0	0	1.000	0	0	0	.000	.000	.000	0
Flanagan	1	0	0	0	0	0	0	0	0	0	0	0	0	0	0	.000	0	0	0	.000	.000	.000	0
Mesa	1	0	0	0	0	0	0	0	0	0	0	0	0	0	0	.000	0	0	0	.000	.000	.000	0
Olson Gregg	1	0	0	0	0	0	0	0	0	0	0	0	0	0	0	.000	0	0	0	.000	.000	.000	0
TOTALS	1833	5604	686	1421	256	29	170	2245	660	528	974	33	33	50	33	.398	146	47	45	.254	.401	.319	710

Sabermetric Batting Records for Baltimore Orioles

	Ball Park Adjusted												Runs		Run/					
	AB	Run	Hit	2B	3B	HR	RBI	W	SO	Avg	Slug	OBP	Ctd	Outs	27o	OW%	OG	OWAR	DWAR	TWAR
Anderson B	248	36	55	11	11	1	26	36	43	.222	.367	.325	34	207	4.43	.485	8	1.03	0.24	1.27
Bell Ju	202	25	35	8	2	0	14	7	48	.173	.233	.200	10	171	1.58	.106	6	-1.54	0.31	-1.23
Davis G	169	29	39	8	1	10	27	15	27	.231	.467	.313	27	133	5.48	.589	5	1.18	0.06	1.24
Devereaux	587	83	156	26	14	19	57	46	107	.266	.455	.319	83	462	4.85	.529	17	3.07	1.38	4.45
Evans Dw	260	35	72	8	1	6	37	53	50	.277	.385	.401	44	199	5.97	.630	7	2.06	0.47	2.53
Gomez L	377	40	90	16	2	16	44	39	76	.239	.419	.308	49	309	4.28	.467	11	1.34	0.43	1.77
Hoiles	329	36	82	14	0	11	30	28	57	.249	.392	.309	38	259	3.96	.429	10	0.75	0.17	0.92
Horn	307	41	69	15	0	20	60	39	97	.225	.469	.316	45	247	4.92	.536	9	1.70	0.00	1.70
Hulett	198	29	41	8	0	7	17	12	45	.207	.354	.256	18	160	3.04	.306	6	-0.26	0.17	-0.09
Martinez C	209	29	54	11	3	11	32	10	50	.258	.498	.292	31	155	5.40	.582	6	1.33	0.37	1.70
McKnight	38	1	6	0	0	0	1	1	6	.158	.158	.179	1	33	0.82	.031	1	-0.39	0.05	-0.34
Melvin	220	11	56	9	0	1	22	10	43	.255	.309	.281	19	174	2.95	.294	6	-0.36	-0.26	-0.63
Mercedes	51	10	10	1	0	0	1	3	8	.196	.216	.241	3	42	1.93	.151	2	-0.31	0.03	-0.28
Milligan	467	57	126	16	2	16	68	82	101	.270	.415	.380	73	368	5.36	.578	14	3.11	0.21	3.32
Orsulak	470	52	126	21	3	4	42	26	44	.268	.351	.308	51	355	3.88	.418	13	0.90	1.72	2.62
Ripken B	276	24	61	10	1	0	13	14	29	.221	.264	.257	17	241	1.90	.148	9	-1.81	1.25	-0.56
Ripken C	630	100	208	45	7	35	111	52	43	.330	.590	.382	141	448	8.50	.775	17	7.06	3.09	10.14
Segui	204	14	57	6	0	1	21	11	18	.279	.324	.316	20	155	3.48	.367	6	0.10	0.16	0.26
Tackett	6	1	0	0	0	0	0	1	1	.000	.000	.143	0	7	0.00	.000	0	-0.09	0.05	-0.04
Turner	0	0	0	0	0	0	0	0	0	.000	.000	.000	0	0	0.00	.000	0	0.00	0.00	0.00
Whitt	60	4	14	1	0	0	2	7	11	.233	.250	.313	5	48	2.81	.274	2	-0.13	-0.05	-0.19
Worthington	97	11	22	2	0	4	11	11	13	.227	.371	.312	12	78	4.15	.452	3	0.29	0.11	0.40
TOTALS	5434	676	1395	255	42	168	649	521	925	.257	.412	.323	719	4295	4.52	.494	159	22.91	9.95	32.86

Pitching Records for Baltimore Orioles

	ERA	W	L	Pct	G	GS	CG	ShO	GF	Sv	IP	R	ER	H	2B	3B	HR	BB	IW	SO	HB	WP	BK
Milacki	4.01	10	9	.526	31	26	3	1	1	0	184.0	86	82	175	39	0	17	53	3	108	1	1	2
McDonald	4.84	6	8	.429	21	21	1	0	0	0	126.1	71	68	126	22	3	16	43	2	85	1	3	0
Ballard	5.60	6	12	.333	26	22	0	0	1	0	123.2	91	77	153	33	4	16	28	2	37	2	3	1
Mesa	5.97	6	11	.353	23	23	2	1	0	0	123.2	86	82	151	33	2	11	62	2	64	3	3	0
Robinson JM	5.18	4	9	.308	21	19	0	0	0	0	104.1	62	60	119	22	1	12	51	2	65	6	8	0
Mussina	2.87	4	5	.444	12	12	2	0	0	0	87.2	31	28	77	14	1	7	21	0	52	1	3	1
Johnson D	7.07	4	8	.333	22	14	0	0	4	0	84.0	68	66	127	20	2	18	24	3	38	4	0	0
Smith Roy	5.60	5	4	.556	17	14	0	0	0	0	80.1	52	50	99	18	2	9	24	0	25	1	3	1
Rhodes A	8.00	0	3	.000	8	8	0	0	0	0	36.0	35	32	47	8	1	4	23	0	23	0	2	0
Flanagan	2.38	2	7	.222	64	1	0	0	24	3	98.1	27	26	84	13	0	6	25	6	55	3	2	2
Frohwirth	1.87	7	3	.700	51	0	0	0	10	3	96.1	24	20	64	14	3	2	29	3	77	1	0	0
Williamson	4.48	5	5	.500	65	0	0	0	21	4	80.1	42	40	87	16	2	9	35	7	53	0	7	0
Olson Gregg	3.18	4	6	.400	72	0	0	0	62	31	73.2	28	26	74	5	2	1	29	5	72	1	8	1
Kilgus	5.08	0	2	.000	38	0	0	0	14	1	62.0	38	35	60	13	0	8	24	2	32	3	2	0
Poole	2.00	3	2	.600	24	0	0	0	3	0	36.0	10	8	19	2	0	3	9	2	34	0	2	0
Telford	4.05	0	0	.000	9	1	0	0	4	0	26.2	12	12	27	5	0	3	6	1	24	0	1	0
Hickey	9.00	1	0	1.000	19	0	0	0	6	0	14.0	14	14	15	4	2	3	6	0	10	0	0	0
Jones S	4.09	0	0	.000	4	1	0	0	0	0	11.0	6	5	11	6	0	1	5	0	10	0	0	0
Bautista	16.88	0	1	.000	5	0	0	0	3	0	5.1	10	10	13	5	0	1	5	0	3	1	1	0
De La Rosa	4.50	0	0	.000	2	0	0	0	1	0	4.0	3	2	6	2	0	0	2	0	1	0	0	0
TOTALS	4.59	67	95	.414	534	162	8	2	154	42	1457.2	796	743	1534	294	25	147	504	40	868	28	49	8

Sabermetric Pitching Records for Baltimore Orioles

	Adj	|-Expected-|			|———Opposing Batters———|												Supported				
	ERA	W	L	Pct	BFP	Avg	Slg	OBA	RC/G	GDP	SB	CS	PK	PKE	SH	SF	RSup	RSp/G	W	L	Pct
Ballard	5.46	6	12	.359	540	.302	.478	.340	5.72	11	1	4	0	0	1	3	59	4.29	7	11	.382
Bautista	15.19	0	1	.068	34	.464	.750	.559	21.31	0	0	0	0	0	0	0	2	3.37	0	1	.047
De La Rosa	2.25	0	0	.768	20	.353	.471	.400	8.18	0	0	0	0	0	0	1	3	6.75	0	0	.900
Flanagan	2.29	7	2	.761	391	.236	.323	.289	2.93	12	6	3	0	0	4	3	37	3.39	6	3	.687
Frohwirth	1.78	8	2	.841	372	.190	.267	.255	2.15	9	10	4	1	0	4	1	38	3.55	8	2	.800
Hickey	8.36	0	1	.193	62	.278	.593	.339	7.19	1	0	0	0	0	0	2	15	9.64	1	0	.571
Johnson D	6.86	3	9	.262	393	.349	.563	.394	8.53	6	3	3	0	0	0	1	48	5.14	4	8	.360
Jones S	3.27	0	0	.609	49	.256	.465	.327	5.48	1	0	0	0	0	0	1	15	12.27	0	0	.934
Kilgus	4.94	1	1	.407	267	.256	.415	.328	4.65	6	2	2	0	1	2	4	22	3.19	1	1	.295
McDonald	4.70	6	8	.431	532	.261	.418	.321	4.67	11	14	3	0	1	2	3	71	5.06	8	6	.536
Mesa	5.82	6	11	.330	566	.307	.449	.385	6.46	9	12	5	0	0	5	4	75	5.46	8	9	.468
Milacki	3.91	10	9	.522	758	.253	.383	.305	3.86	18	12	6	0	1	7	5	84	4.11	10	9	.524
Mussina	2.77	6	3	.685	349	.239	.354	.286	3.15	9	4	4	0	0	3	2	38	3.90	6	3	.665
Olson Gregg	3.05	6	4	.642	319	.262	.305	.332	3.91	5	13	1	0	0	5	1	6	0.73	1	9	.054
Poole	1.75	4	1	.845	135	.157	.248	.212	1.62	2	0	1	0	1	3	2	17	4.25	4	1	.855
Rhodes A	7.75	1	2	.218	174	.320	.469	.405	7.66	2	7	2	0	0	1	3	22	5.50	1	2	.335
Robinson JM	5.09	5	8	.392	472	.289	.434	.375	5.83	12	10	5	0	1	3	0	44	3.80	5	8	.357
Smith Roy	5.49	3	6	.357	348	.311	.465	.358	5.68	9	6	5	0	0	2	3	36	4.03	3	6	.351
Telford	3.71	0	0	.548	109	.265	.402	.303	4.06	3	1	0	0	0	0	1	14	4.73	0	0	.618
Williamson	4.37	5	5	.467	357	.275	.424	.343	5.28	8	10	3	0	0	1	5	40	4.48	5	5	.513
TOTALS	4.51	73	89	.451	6247	.273	.412	.333	4.76	134	111	51	1	5	43	45	686	4.24	76	86	.469

Batting 'Splits' Records for Baltimore Orioles

																GI						Runs
	G	AB	Run	Hit	2B	3B	HR	TB	RBI	W	K	IW	HB	SB	CS	DP	SH	SF	Avg	Slug	OBP	Ctd
SPLITS for Baltimore Orioles (all batters except pitchers)																						
vs LHP	782	1487	161	381	62	10	47	604	157	167	254	13	5	7	13	47	16	14	.256	.406	.331	195
vs RHP	1518	4117	525	1040	194	19	123	1641	503	361	720	20	28	43	20	99	31	31	.253	.399	.315	515
Home	926	2701	329	659	121	12	80	1044	318	258	463	15	15	22	16	77	25	21	.244	.387	.311	320
Away	907	2903	357	762	135	17	90	1201	342	270	511	18	18	28	17	69	22	24	.262	.414	.327	391
Grass	1571	4704	569	1178	207	24	147	1874	549	440	817	25	26	41	28	118	42	36	.250	.398	.316	587
Turf	262	900	117	243	49	5	23	371	111	88	157	8	7	9	5	28	5	9	.270	.412	.337	123
April/June	818	2507	307	634	110	9	75	987	295	271	446	17	18	27	21	68	22	17	.253	.394	.328	323
July/October	1015	3097	379	787	146	20	95	1258	365	257	528	16	15	23	12	78	25	28	.254	.406	.312	387

1991 SPLITS FOR Baltimore Orioles

BATTING SPLITS

	AVG	AB	R	H	2B	3B	HR	RBI	SB	CS	BB	K	OBA	SPCT
Total	.254	5604	686	1421	256	29	170	660	50	33	528	974	.319	.401

	#Pit	#P/PA	GB	FB	G/F	G	IBB	HB	SH	SF	GDP
Miscellaneous	23450	3.75	1976	1671	1.18	162	33	33	47	45	146

	AVG	AB	R	H	2B	3B	HR	RBI	SB	CS	BB	K	OBA	SPCT
vs. Left	.256	1487	...	381	62	10	47	157	7	13	167	254	.331	.406
vs. Right	.253	4117	...	1040	194	19	123	503	43	20	361	720	.315	.399
Home	.244	2701	329	659	121	12	80	318	22	16	258	463	.311	.387
Away	.262	2903	357	762	135	17	90	342	28	17	270	511	.327	.414
None on	.256	3226	...	826	147	16	102	102	0	0	283	558	.319	.406
Runners on	.250	2378	...	595	109	13	68	558	50	33	245	416	.319	.393
April	.231	589	67	136	21	2	18	66	9	7	67	128	.315	.365
May	.252	917	105	231	39	1	28	100	11	7	104	164	.327	.388
June	.267	1001	135	267	50	6	29	129	7	7	100	154	.337	.416
July	.253	942	106	238	43	3	28	105	6	5	84	152	.314	.394
August	.257	1007	132	259	57	8	25	127	4	2	80	171	.311	.404
September	.255	923	120	235	41	4	37	112	12	4	76	164	.314	.428
October	.244	225	21	55	5	5	5	21	1	1	17	41	.298	.378
None on/out	.243	1409	...	342	60	6	45	45	0	0	121	234	.306	.390
Scoring Posn	.252	1265	...	319	62	9	32	462	11	4	175	249	.338	.391
Close & Late	.237	970	...	230	30	3	29	109	6	4	93	171	.305	.364
Bases Loaded	.324	105	...	34	4	1	5	91	0	0	6	22	.333	.524
Batting #1	.256	688	100	176	32	11	16	58	20	12	63	130	.318	.404
Batting #2	.244	667	84	163	29	3	10	61	8	2	59	102	.309	.342
Batting #3	.321	660	101	212	46	5	34	114	6	1	54	50	.372	.561
Batting #4	.261	624	89	163	30	1	28	108	4	2	74	122	.345	.447
Batting #5	.249	582	79	145	24	3	17	74	6	4	96	110	.358	.388
Batting #6	.272	615	66	167	23	1	28	88	3	6	58	123	.336	.449
Batting #7	.222	598	57	133	26	2	19	61	1	2	50	120	.282	.368
Batting #8	.242	596	56	144	24	0	11	52	2	3	40	114	.288	.337
Batting #9	.206	574	54	118	22	3	7	44	0	1	34	103	.250	.291
As c	.246	566	48	139	26	0	10	50	0	2	40	109	.294	.345
As 1b	.268	604	70	162	24	3	20	85	3	3	79	99	.357	.417
As 2b	.203	522	48	106	22	3	4	34	0	1	27	90	.241	.280
As 3b	.230	582	66	134	24	2	24	66	1	2	55	114	.297	.402
As ss	.319	661	100	211	46	5	34	114	6	1	54	50	.370	.558
As lf	.240	628	73	151	29	2	6	55	7	4	55	80	.306	.322
As cf	.266	687	100	183	31	12	19	67	22	12	62	128	.327	.429
As rf	.259	614	71	159	24	2	15	71	4	4	59	108	.325	.378
Outfield	.256	1929	244	493	84	16	40	193	33	20	176	316	.320	.378
0.0 count	.292	743	...	217	42	2	33	103	...	...	1	0	.297	.487
After (0.1)	.232	2449	...	567	100	14	68	261	...	...	123	601	.271	.367
After (1.0)	.264	2412	...	637	114	13	69	296	...	...	377	373	.363	.408
Two strikes	.196	2605	...	510	91	16	45	218	...	...	207	973	.257	.295
Grass	.250	4704	569	1178	207	24	147	549	41	28	440	817	.316	.398
Turf	.270	900	117	243	49	5	23	111	9	5	88	157	.337	.412
Day	.236	1427	162	337	62	6	36	151	14	9	140	271	.308	.364
Night	.260	4177	524	1084	194	23	134	509	36	24	388	703	.323	.413
Inning 1.6	.264	3745	498	987	190	24	119	475	38	27	339	627	.326	.422
Inning 7+	.233	1859	188	434	66	5	51	185	12	6	189	347	.306	.357
vs.Bos	.258	449	63	116	26	1	17	55	4	0	42	84	.324	.434
vs.Cal	.248	400	45	99	14	1	14	44	8	4	36	69	.309	.393
vs.ChA	.210	395	39	83	18	4	9	39	2	2	44	84	.291	.344
vs.Cle	.262	451	48	118	12	1	14	47	3	2	29	73	.311	.386
vs.Det	.261	464	63	121	19	7	14	60	1	1	44	78	.325	.422
vs.KC	.268	466	56	125	27	3	11	54	2	2	42	79	.335	.410
vs.Mil	.278	460	60	128	27	2	15	59	5	2	34	68	.330	.443
vs.Min	.256	407	50	104	22	1	9	48	3	3	41	59	.321	.381
vs.NYA	.271	462	55	125	25	2	15	54	5	4	32	73	.320	.431
vs.Oak	.235	405	44	95	19	0	14	44	5	1	53	64	.320	.385
vs.Sea	.241	399	41	96	14	1	12	39	1	3	45	75	.320	.371
vs.Tex	.263	407	66	107	17	4	13	63	6	4	42	92	.333	.420
vs.Tor	.237	439	56	104	16	2	13	54	5	5	44	76	.306	.371

PITCHING SPLITS

	ERA	W	L	SV	SVOP	GS	CG	SHO	IP	H	ER	HR	BB	IBB	K
Total	4.59	67	95	42	58	162	8	6	1457.2	1534	743	147	504	40	868

	#Pit	#P/IP	GB	FB	G/F	BRp9	RA	WP	BK	SH	SF	R	HB	Hld
Miscellaneous	22604	15.51	2073	1627	1.27	12.76	372	49	8	43	45	796	28	47

	ERA	W	L	SV	SVOP	GS	CG	SHO	IP	H	ER	HR	BB	IBB	K
ST	5.29	42	69	0	0	162	8	2	900.0	1025	529	104	318	13	479
REL	3.45	25	26	42	58	0	0	0	557.2	509	214	43	186	27	389
Home	4.33	33	48	15	22	81	3	1	744.0	775	358	72	245	19	478
Away	4.86	34	47	27	36	81	5	1	713.2	759	385	75	259	21	390
April	4.85	6	12	3	4	18	0	0	159.2	170	86	17	61	5	76
May	4.69	10	17	6	9	27	2	1	236.0	250	123	23	92	6	131
June	5.01	14	14	11	15	28	0	0	257.0	284	143	26	96	9	148
July	4.77	10	17	8	11	27	1	0	245.1	252	130	28	66	6	135
August	4.29	13	16	6	9	29	1	0	260.0	269	124	25	86	6	165
September	4.11	13	14	7	9	27	4	1	241.0	253	110	21	83	7	171
October	4.14	1	5	1	1	6	0	0	58.2	56	27	7	20	1	42
Grass	4.45	58	80	36	47	138	6	2	1238.0	1284	612	120	428	33	732
Turf	5.37	9	15	6	11	24	2	0	219.2	250	131	27	76	7	136
Day	4.69	16	26	13	21	42	1	0	376.1	382	196	40	126	7	222
Night	4.55	51	69	29	37	120	7	2	1081.1	1152	547	107	378	33	646
vs.Bos	3.87	8	5	5	6	13	1	0	114.0	110	49	9	29	6	66
vs.Cal	2.74	6	6	3	4	12	2	1	105.0	105	32	9	18	2	60
vs.ChA	4.54	4	8	2	3	12	0	0	107.0	110	54	12	38	2	63
vs.Cle	4.00	7	6	6	6	13	1	0	119.1	125	53	5	40	4	68
vs.Det	5.26	5	8	4	5	13	0	0	119.2	127	70	13	54	2	84
vs.KC	4.88	4	8	3	6	12	1	0	118.0	132	64	11	43	2	76
vs.Mil	4.87	3	10	2	3	13	0	0	114.2	129	62	8	43	6	52
vs.Min	5.68	4	8	1	3	12	0	0	104.2	130	66	13	35	5	57
vs.NYA	4.17	5	8	3	5	13	1	1	116.2	115	54	13	43	2	65
vs.Oak	5.99	3	9	2	3	12	0	0	106.2	122	71	13	37	3	67
vs.Sea	5.01	4	8	3	4	12	0	0	106.0	109	59	14	39	3	44
vs.Tex	3.80	9	3	4	5	12	1	0	109.0	96	46	12	39	0	82
vs.Tor	4.85	5	8	4	5	13	1	0	117.0	124	63	15	46	3	84

OPPOSING BATTERS VS. PITCHERS.

	AVG	AB	R	H	2B	3B	HR	RBI	SB	CS	BB	K	OBA	SPCT
Total	.273	5626	796	1534	294	25	147	757	111	51	504	868	.333	.412
vs. Left	.264	2511	...	664	117	11	58	328	49	26	240	400	.328	.389
vs. Right	.279	3115	...	870	177	14	89	429	62	25	264	468	.337	.431
ST	.288	3555	566	1025	206	16	104	480	67	36	318	479	.348	.443
REL	.246	2071	230	509	88	9	43	277	44	15	186	389	.308	.359
Home	.270	2871	387	775	138	7	72	371	63	30	245	478	.328	.398
Away	.275	2755	409	759	156	18	75	386	48	21	259	390	.338	.427
None on	.256	3201	...	818	144	12	84	84	0	0	263	513	.316	.387
Runners on	.295	2425	...	716	150	13	63	673	111	51	241	355	.355	.446
None on/out	.257	1406	...	362	63	6	47	47	0	0	104	199	.313	.411
Scoring Posn	.303	1340	...	406	79	10	37	593	29	8	186	222	.379	.460
vs 1st Batr	.222	334	...	74	8	2	8	57	5	2	25	59	.272	.329
1st IP	.268	1797	251	482	91	11	43	331	50	15	200	322	.341	.403
Inning 1.6	.284	3804	594	1081	207	17	115	564	74	34	340	547	.343	.438
Inning 7+	.249	1822	202	453	87	8	32	193	37	17	164	321	.312	.358
Close & Late	.241	912	...	220	44	6	16	99	22	12	96	157	.315	.355
0.0 count	.338	834	...	282	60	2	25	141	...	...	30	0	.361	.505
After (0.1)	.235	2433	...	571	103	9	50	247	...	...	127	569	.276	.346
After (1.0)	.289	2359	...	681	131	14	72	369	...	...	347	299	.378	.448
Two strikes	.201	2374	...	478	80	10	41	222	...	...	199	867	.265	.295
Pitch 1.15	.259	1632	...	422	83	8	33	224	44	15	153	275	.323	.380
Pitch 16.30	.287	1133	...	325	58	6	41	182	19	9	116	178	.352	.457
Pitch 31.45	.263	848	...	223	38	5	18	107	16	13	70	139	.319	.383
Pitch 46.60	.278	654	...	182	39	3	18	85	14	3	55	96	.338	.430
Pitch 61.75	.278	568	...	158	22	1	19	74	5	1	38	80	.325	.421
Pitch 76.90	.311	411	...	128	30	0	10	44	7	4	32	45	.361	.457
Pitch 91.105	.249	241	...	60	16	2	4	25	2	2	29	34	.332	.382
Pitch 106.20	.279	111	...	31	6	0	4	15	3	3	7	14	.322	.441

Cleveland Indians

Dave Raglin

CLEVELAND											
YEAR	1982	1983	1984	1985	1986	1987	1988	1989	1990	1991	TOT
W	78	70	75	60	84	61	78	73	77	57	713
L	84	92	87	102	78	101	84	89	85	105	907
WPCT	0.481	0.432	0.463	0.370	0.519	0.377	0.481	0.451	0.475	0.352	0.440
R	683	704	761	729	831	742	666	604	732	576	7028
RA	748	785	766	861	841	957	731	654	737	759	7839
PWPT	0.455	0.446	0.497	0.418	0.494	0.375	0.454	0.460	0.497	0.365	0.446
PythW	74	72	80	68	80	61	73	75	80	59	72
PythL	88	90	82	94	82	101	89	87	82	103	90
LUCK	4	-2	-5	-8	4	0	5	-2	-3	-2	-9

Defensive Efficiency Record: .6763

What can you say about this franchise? In 1992, they will tie the record for the most seasons in a row without a contender by a franchise in one city, currently held at 33 seasons by the 1917-1949 Philadelphia Phillies. None of the current Indians were even alive when the Indians last contended in 1959.

However, before the 1991 season, the Indians had a brilliant idea (and if someone understands the logic behind it, please write me c/o Baseball Sabermetric and let me in on it). One of the very few bright spots for the 1990 Indians had been the play of Alex Cole. Acquired from the Padres' system during the season, his third organization in less than a year, he was called up at the end of July. I happened to be at his first game in the majors, a doubleheader against the Yankees during the 1990 SABR Convention. He was exciting; bunting for his first major league hit, running with abandon, tracking down everything in center. Considering that the Indians lost four of the five games to the then-last place Yankees, Cole was the only bright spot in an embarrassing weekend for Cleveland.

That was a prologue to an exciting two months. By the time the 1990 season was over, Cole had stolen 40 bases while hitting .300. An intelligent organization would have patted themselves on the back for such a steal, penciled in Cole as the leadoff hitter/centerfielder, and worked to get some more bats to go along with Sandy Alomar (the Rookie of the Year) and Carlos Baerga. That could be the making of a good offense.

Instead, they decided to press their luck. They decided to remake their whole team, their whole ballpark, around a twice-traded, previously marginal prospect who had had two good months. They announced to the world that the Indians were going to become a "speed-and-defense" team, and to help facilitate that, they moved the fences back into Lake Erie.

Every now and then, we see a team announce that they are going to become a "speed-and-defense" team. Generally, announcements like that are made by general managers who don't know what they're talking about, like Hank Peters of the Indians and Ken Harrelson when they let him play with the White Sox a few years ago. The only guy who has been able to win with a "speed-and-defense" strategy consistently was Whitey Herzog with the Cardinals. I think that the "speed-and-defense" strategy is attractive to people like Peters and Harrelson because it's easier to get "speed-and-defense" people than good power hitters who will win you more games.

As we all know, the Indians pressed their luck to the breaking point. The 1991 Cleveland Indians went 57-105, a pathetic season even by their own lowly standards. They finished 34 1/2 games out of first, ten games out of sixth. In how many ways was this move the fences back maneuver a stupid idea? Got some time...

(1) Out of all of the key Indians at the end of the 1990 season, the move the fences back idea really benefitted only Cole. Who were the other top Indian hitters? Baerga, Alomar, and Jacoby, all more power hitters than speedsters. In 1991, Jacoby was traded, but another power hitter emerged, Albert Belle.

On the pitching staff, the top three pitchers were Candiotti, Swindell, and Doug Jones. Both Candiotti and Swindell gave up a lot of home runs in 1990 (1.13 and 1.02 per nine innings pitched, compared to the league average of 0.80), but in 1989 and 1988, neither gave up that many home runs (Swindell, .79 in 1989, .69 in 1988; Candiotti, .44 and .62). Doug Jones had always been stingy with the homers (.53 in 1990, .45 in 1989, and .11, one home run, in 1988). Who else but Cole on the team benefitted from the moving out of the fences? Maybe Mitch Webster, but you don't move your fences for Mitch Webster.

It's the same as the Harrelson situation--the management declared they wanted a "speed-and-defense" team, but the personnel did not fit the plan.

(2) For a team that was so committed to a player that they would change the configuration of the ballpark, the Indians gave

up on Cole awfully quick. True, Cole didn't help because of injuries, and poor basestealing, but if you build your team around one ballplayer, you at least show the courage of your convictions and give him every chance.

Cole dislocated his shoulder in spring training (as it turned out, this is something that happens quite frequently), but made it back for the start of the season. However, injuries forced him to the bench in early May with a .309 average but only two stolen bases in five attempts. When he came back, he played only four to five days a week; the immortal Mike Huff had played well while Cole was hurt. He wasn't doing good--at the All-Star Break, he had only nine steals in 21 attempts. It took until August for his RBI total to pass his stolen base total, but it was nip and tuck all the way. (What else did the Cleveland fans have to watch, anyway, Albert Belle throwing baseballs in the stands?) By then, he wasn't playing much, and one of the Indians' main acquisitions in the offseason was a speedy centerfielder. Rumor has it they're going to move the fences back in, too.

(3) Another problem the Indians have had is lack of attendance. I'm not criticizing the people of Northern Ohio--you have to really love baseball to pay good, hard-earned money to watch in Indians. But if you're having a hard time drawing people, it seems silly to change your ballpark in a way that makes the games less exciting. As the chart below shows, the Indians hit only 22 home runs at home. You either had to be lucky or go to a lot of games to see even two home runs by the home team.

(4) Let's now look at the stats--for Cleveland and the opposition both in Cleveland and in the opposition's parks:

Team	Where	AB	*R*	H	HR	SB	CS	BA	OBP	SLG
CLE	CLE	2693	271	705	22	33	28	.262	.321	.343
OPP	CLE	2900	377	788	41	51	29	.272	.321	.373
CLE	OPP	2777	305	685	57	51	30	.247	.306	.357
OPP	OPP	2723	382	763	69	51	18	.280	.337	.423
TOT	CLE	5593	648	1493	63	84	57	.267	.321	.359
TOT	OPP	5500	687	1448	126	102	48	.263	.320	.390

The opposition benefitted more by the changes to Municipal Stadium than did the Indians! Cleveland was outhomered almost two-to-one at home, 41 to 22, but only 69 to 57 on the road. The Indians' speed game also failed them at home, 33 steals and 28 caught stealings! That's the kind of stolen base record teams in the '60s used to have. The average game in Cleveland had exactly eight runs scored by both teams. That'll bring in the crowd, especially with less than one home run a game.

How can people so stupid be entrusted to run a multi-million dollar business? I've seen Rotisserie owners who think like these people, but it's usually because they have three kids running around the house and they don't have to time to spend with it.

Do they even care if they win? The silliest statement of the 1991 season must have been Hank Peters defending the charge that the Indians won't spend to keep their ballplayers. Peters was indignant, responding that there was no evidence to support that charge, none at all.

No evidence?! What more evidence do we need, the murdered witnessed and photographed with the murder weapon in front of 60,000 people? (As the murderer in the musical Chicago said, "He ran into my knife. Fifteen times.") Who have they spent to keep. Nobody. Who have they lost because of money? Joe Carter, Brett Butler, Tom Candiotti, and now Greg Swindell. True, they made out like bandits for Carter, but Butler left as a free agent, and they got a bunch of perineal prospects for Candiotti or Swindell. Glenallen Hill, who'se had an up-and-down career, is probably the best of the bunch, but with all of the outfielders the Indians have, will they play him everyday in 1992? They sure didn't in 1991. For Swindell, the Reds dumped Jack Armstrong (5.48 ERA and Scott Scudder (51 Ks and 56 walks in 101 innings).

If the owners of the Indians are going to blackmail the taxpayers of Cleveland to give them a new ballpark, the least the team can do is try and win, and they aren't doing that now. The first major move the team made after being given the ballpark was to give their best pitcher away, Swindell, for a couple of nothings. The people of Cleveland deserve better than the idiots they have now running their team, especially if they are supposed to give those millionaires tax dollars that could be spent helping people hurt by the recession or lowering high tax rates that stifle business growth. I'm sorry if you think I have been cruel to the Indians' management in this article, but they deserve it. Cleveland is a great baseball town, but we won't see it until the club is sold to people who care about it, and that's sad.

Here are the batting averages, on-base percentages, and slugging percentages for the Indians in 1991 by batting order position. No comments are necessary.

	BA	OBP	SLG
First	.275	.368	.355
Second	.232	.285	.282
Third	.289	.340	.370
Fourth	.265	.313	.454
Fifth	.238	.288	.361
Sixth	.261	.319	.392
Seventh	.246	.311	.337
Eighth	.215	.278	.278
Ninth	.261	.309	.311

Cleveland Indians Home Park Performance Factors

	Outs	Runs	Hits	2b	3b	HR	W	K	SH	SF	HBP	IBB	SB	CS	GDP
Home LH Batters	1.063	1.173	1.174	1.133	1.292	7.934	.996	1.115	1.443	1.010	.882	.829	1.368	1.229	.858
Home RH Batters	1.019	1.007	.946	.923	.716	1.507	.987	1.116	.753	.934	.874	.807	1.089	1.072	1.013
All Home Batters	1.019	1.040	.984	.961	.875	1.617	.980	1.104	.889	.957	.901	.812	1.181	1.065	1.001
Opp LH Batters	1.059	1.096	1.083	1.217	.901	1.208	1.115	1.051	.872	1.122	.936	.936	.905	.872	1.322
Opp RH Batters	1.054	1.103	1.051	1.111	.904	1.340	1.156	1.081	1.230	.866	.837	1.369	.985	.937	1.161
All Opp Batters	1.048	1.093	1.061	1.148	.932	1.328	1.136	1.059	1.087	.967	.907	1.131	1.011	.910	1.178
All LH Batters	1.060	1.120	1.111	1.191	1.003	1.379	1.055	1.078	1.037	1.099	.927	.913	1.109	1.072	1.126
All RH Batters	1.036	1.052	.996	1.012	.812	1.384	1.068	1.096	.943	.887	.863	1.122	1.044	.992	1.080
All Batters	1.034	1.065	1.023	1.056	.903	1.413	1.057	1.081	.983	.954	.905	1.010	1.085	.991	1.085

Conventional Batting Records for Cleveland Indians

	G	AB	Run	Hit	2B	3B	HR	TB	RBI	W	K	IW	HB	SB	CS	BRng Eff	GI DP	SH	SF	Avg	Slug	OBP	Runs Ctd
Skinner J	99	284	23	69	14	0	1	86	24	14	67	1	1	0	2	.295	8	4	2	.243	.303	.279	23
Jacoby	66	231	14	54	9	1	4	77	24	16	32	2	2	0	1	.333	7	0	0	.234	.333	.289	21
Baerga	157	590	79	168	27	2	11	232	68	48	74	5	5	3	2	.403	12	4	3	.285	.393	.342	80
Thome	27	98	7	25	4	2	1	36	9	5	16	1	1	1	1	.214	4	0	0	.255	.367	.298	10
Fermin	129	424	30	111	13	2	0	128	31	26	27	0	3	5	4	.324	16	13	3	.262	.302	.307	37
Belle	122	458	60	129	31	1	28	246	94	24	99	1	5	3	1	.406	24	0	5	.282	.537	.321	70
Cole	121	383	58	114	17	3	0	137	20	58	46	2	1	27	17	.536	8	3	2	.298	.358	.390	56
Whiten	70	258	34	66	14	4	7	109	26	19	50	1	2	4	2	.600	7	0	2	.256	.422	.310	33
James C	115	437	31	104	16	2	5	139	41	18	61	2	4	3	4	.434	9	2	2	.238	.318	.273	36
Lewis M	83	310	29	82	15	1	0	99	30	15	44	0	0	2	1	.467	12	2	5	.265	.319	.294	27
Browne J	106	286	27	66	5	2	1	78	29	26	28	0	1	2	4	.381	5	12	4	.231	.273	.293	24
Martinez Crl	71	253	21	72	14	0	4	98	28	10	42	2	2	3	2	.294	10	1	5	.285	.387	.311	28
Alomar S	51	184	10	40	9	0	0	49	7	8	24	1	4	0	4	.308	4	2	1	.217	.266	.264	12
Aldrete	84	182	22	48	6	1	1	59	19	36	37	1	0	1	2	.357	0	1	2	.264	.324	.382	26
Huff	51	146	28	35	6	1	2	49	10	25	30	0	4	11	2	.595	2	3	1	.240	.336	.364	22
Manto	47	128	15	27	7	0	2	40	13	14	22	0	4	2	0	.480	3	1	1	.211	.313	.306	13
Allred	48	125	17	29	3	0	3	41	12	25	35	2	1	2	2	.250	2	3	2	.232	.328	.359	17
Hill G	37	122	15	32	3	0	5	50	14	16	30	0	0	4	2	.417	5	1	1	.262	.410	.345	17
Jefferson R	26	101	10	20	3	0	2	29	12	3	22	0	0	0	0	.429	1	0	1	.198	.287	.219	6
Ward T	40	100	11	23	7	0	0	30	5	10	16	0	0	0	0	.421	1	4	0	.230	.300	.300	10
Lopez L	34	79	6	17	4	1	0	23	7	4	7	1	1	0	0	.429	0	1	1	.215	.291	.259	6
Gonzalez Jo	32	67	9	11	2	1	1	18	4	10	26	0	1	6	0	.643	2	0	0	.164	.269	.282	6
Taubensee	25	62	5	14	2	1	0	18	8	5	15	1	0	0	0	.600	1	0	2	.226	.290	.275	5
Kirby	20	42	4	9	2	0	0	11	5	2	6	0	0	1	2	.500	2	1	1	.214	.262	.244	2
Webster M	13	32	2	4	0	0	0	4	0	3	9	0	0	2	2	.250	0	1	0	.125	.125	.200	1
Perezchica	17	22	4	8	2	0	0	10	0	3	5	0	0	0	0	.455	0	0	0	.364	.455	.440	5
Medina	5	16	0	1	0	0	0	1	0	1	7	0	0	0	0	.000	0	1	0	.063	.063	.118	0
Escobar J	10	15	0	3	0	0	0	3	1	1	4	0	0	0	0	.000	0	1	0	.200	.200	.250	1
Magallanes	3	2	0	0	0	0	0	0	0	1	1	0	0	0	0	.000	0	0	0	.000	.000	.333	0
TOTALS	1711	5445	572	1381	235	25	78	1900	542	447	884	23	42	82	57	.415	145	62	46	.254	.349	.313	587

Sabermetric Batting Records for Cleveland Indians

	Ball Park Adjusted								Runs			Run/								
	AB	Run	Hit	2B	3B	HR	RBI	W	SO	Avg	Slug	OBP	Ctd	Outs	27o	OW%	OG	OWAR	DWAR	TWAR
Aldrete	196	24	54	7	1	4	21	37	40	.276	.383	.387	33	147	6.06	.684	5	1.82	0.17	1.99
Allred	133	19	32	3	0	13	13	26	37	.241	.556	.360	28	110	6.87	.736	4	1.57	0.20	1.78
Alomar S	188	10	39	9	0	0	7	8	26	.207	.255	.251	11	158	1.88	.172	6	-1.04	-0.01	-1.05
Baerga	607	84	171	28	1	16	73	50	80	.282	.410	.339	85	455	5.04	.600	17	4.21	1.16	5.37
Belle	469	63	128	31	0	39	99	25	108	.273	.588	.313	74	372	5.37	.630	14	3.85	0.28	4.13
Browne J	298	29	67	5	1	1	31	28	31	.225	.258	.289	24	253	2.56	.279	9	-0.67	-0.04	-0.71
Cole	417	65	128	19	3	0	23	61	50	.307	.367	.394	64	320	5.40	.632	12	3.34	0.30	3.64
Escobar J	14	0	2	0	0	0	1	1	4	.143	.143	.200	0	12	0.00	.000	0	-0.16	0.06	-0.09
Fermin	434	31	110	13	1	0	32	27	29	.253	.288	.299	35	359	2.63	.290	13	-0.80	1.51	0.71
Gonzalez Jo	68	9	10	2	0	1	4	10	28	.147	.221	.256	5	60	2.25	.230	2	-0.27	0.15	-0.12
Hill G	124	15	31	3	0	7	14	17	32	.250	.444	.340	18	100	4.86	.582	4	0.86	0.07	0.93
Huff	149	29	34	6	0	2	10	26	32	.228	.309	.354	20	121	4.46	.540	4	0.85	0.44	1.30
Jacoby	236	14	53	9	0	5	25	17	35	.225	.326	.280	20	191	2.83	.320	7	-0.21	0.19	-0.02
James C	448	32	103	16	1	7	43	19	67	.230	.317	.265	36	360	2.70	.300	13	-0.66	0.34	-0.32
Jefferson R	103	10	20	3	0	2	12	3	23	.194	.282	.217	6	84	1.93	.180	3	-0.53	0.10	-0.43
Kirby	45	4	10	2	0	0	5	2	6	.222	.267	.250	2	41	1.32	.093	2	-0.39	0.19	-0.20
Lewis M	317	30	81	15	0	0	31	16	48	.256	.303	.288	25	255	2.65	.292	9	-0.55	0.20	-0.35
Lopez L	80	6	16	4	0	0	7	4	7	.200	.250	.238	5	64	2.11	.208	2	-0.34	-0.01	-0.35
Magallanes	2	0	0	0	0	0	0	1	1	.000	.000	.333	0	2	0.00	.000	0	-0.03	-0.00	-0.03
Manto	130	15	26	7	0	2	13	15	24	.200	.300	.297	12	107	3.03	.351	4	0.00	0.00	0.01
Martinez Crl	258	22	71	14	0	5	29	10	46	.275	.388	.300	27	203	3.59	.432	8	0.61	-0.04	0.58
Medina	15	0	0	0	0	0	0	1	7	.000	.000	.063	0	15	0.00	.000	1	-0.19	0.00	-0.19
Perezchica	21	4	7	2	0	0	0	3	5	.333	.429	.417	4	14	7.71	.778	1	0.22	-0.01	0.21
Skinner J	290	24	68	14	0	1	25	15	73	.234	.293	.271	21	236	2.40	.254	9	-0.84	-0.21	-1.05
Taubensee	65	5	15	2	1	0	9	5	16	.231	.292	.278	6	53	3.06	.355	2	0.01	-0.25	-0.24
Thome	105	7	28	4	2	4	10	5	17	.267	.457	.300	13	82	4.28	.519	3	0.51	-0.04	0.47
Ward T	102	11	23	7	0	0	5	10	17	.225	.294	.295	10	83	3.25	.384	3	0.10	0.21	0.31
Webster M	32	2	4	0	0	0	0	3	9	.125	.125	.200	1	29	0.93	.049	1	-0.32	0.07	-0.25
Whiten	265	36	67	14	3	10	28	20	54	.253	.442	.307	35	207	4.57	.551	8	1.54	0.72	2.26
TOTALS	5620	612	1416	248	23	114	586	473	957	.252	.365	.312	628	4522	3.75	.453	167	17.25	5.76	23.01

Pitching Records for Cleveland Indians

	ERA	W	L	Pct	G	GS	CG	ShO	GF	Sv	IP	R	ER	H	2B	3B	HR	BB	IW	SO	HB	WP	BK
Swindell	3.48	9	16	.360	33	33	7	0	0	0	238.0	112	92	241	48	4	21	31	1	169	3	3	1
Nagy	4.13	10	15	.400	33	33	6	1	0	0	211.1	103	97	228	45	8	15	66	7	109	6	6	2
King E	4.60	6	11	.353	25	24	2	1	0	0	150.2	83	77	166	33	4	7	44	4	59	3	2	2
Nichols Rod	3.57	2	11	.154	30	16	3	1	4	1	136.0	63	54	144	18	1	6	30	3	75	6	3	0
Candiotti	2.24	7	6	.538	15	15	3	0	0	0	108.1	35	27	88	14	4	6	28	0	86	2	6	0
Otto	4.13	2	7	.222	17	13	1	0	0	0	93.2	46	43	100	14	3	6	25	6	44	3	3	0
Boucher	8.34	1	4	.200	5	5	0	0	0	0	22.2	21	21	35	9	1	6	8	0	13	0	1	0
Mutis	11.68	0	3	.000	3	3	0	0	0	0	12.1	16	16	23	5	2	1	7	1	6	0	1	0
Gozzo	19.29	0	0	.000	2	2	0	0	0	0	4.2	10	10	9	5	0	0	7	0	3	0	2	0
Hillegas	4.34	3	4	.429	51	3	0	0	31	7	83.0	42	40	67	12	1	7	46	7	66	2	5	0
Shaw	3.36	0	5	.000	29	1	0	0	9	1	72.1	34	27	72	10	1	6	27	5	31	4	6	0
Jones D	5.54	4	8	.333	36	4	0	0	29	7	63.1	42	39	87	23	2	7	17	5	48	0	1	0
Olin	3.36	3	6	.333	48	0	0	0	32	17	56.1	26	21	61	10	1	2	23	7	38	1	0	0
Orosco	3.74	2	0	1.000	47	0	0	0	20	0	45.2	20	19	52	8	0	4	15	8	36	1	1	1
Blair	6.75	2	3	.400	11	5	0	0	1	0	36.0	27	27	58	8	0	7	10	0	13	1	1	0
York	6.75	1	4	.200	14	4	0	0	3	0	34.2	29	26	45	7	4	2	19	3	19	2	2	0
Bell E	0.51	4	0	1.000	9	0	0	0	2	0	17.2	2	1	5	0	0	0	5	0	7	1	0	0
Valdez	5.51	1	0	1.000	6	0	0	0	1	0	16.1	11	10	15	1	0	3	5	1	11	0	1	0
Valdez E	1.50	0	0	.000	7	0	0	0	0	0	6.0	1	1	5	0	0	0	3	1	1	1	0	0
Egloff	4.76	0	0	.000	6	0	0	0	2	0	5.2	3	3	8	2	0	0	4	1	8	0	2	0
Seanez	16.20	0	0	.000	5	0	0	0	0	0	5.0	12	9	10	2	0	2	7	0	7	0	2	0
Walker MC	2.08	0	1	.000	5	0	0	0	3	0	4.1	1	1	6	2	0	0	2	1	2	1	0	0
Kiser	9.64	0	0	.000	7	0	0	0	1	0	4.2	5	5	7	0	0	0	4	0	3	1	0	0
Kramer T	17.36	0	0	.000	4	0	0	0	1	0	4.2	9	9	10	3	1	1	6	0	4	0	0	0
TOTALS	4.24	57	104	.354	448	161	22	3	139	33	1433.1	753	675	1542	279	37	109	439	61	858	38	48	6

Sabermetric Pitching Records for Cleveland Indians

	Adj	|-Expected-|			|——Opposing Batters——|												Supported				
	ERA	W	L	Pct	BFP	Avg	Slg	OBA	RC/G	GDP	SB	CS	PK	PKE	SH	SF	RSup	RSp/G	W	L	Pct
Bell E	0.51	4	0	.985	60	.093	.093	.183	0.53	3	2	0	0	0	0	0	14	7.13	4	0	.995
Blair	7.00	1	4	.254	168	.377	.565	.413	8.35	7	1	1	0	0	1	2	12	3.00	1	4	.155
Boucher	8.74	1	4	.180	108	.350	.640	.398	10.12	2	2	0	0	1	0	0	5	1.99	0	5	.049
Candiotti	2.33	10	3	.755	442	.218	.317	.268	3.06	3	10	3	1	0	1	7	48	3.99	10	3	.746
Egloff	4.76	0	0	.424	28	.333	.417	.429	6.92	1	0	0	0	0	0	0	1	1.59	0	0	.100
Gozzo	19.29	0	0	.043	28	.450	.700	.571	16.29	2	1	0	0	0	0	1	8	15.43	0	0	.390
Hillegas	4.55	3	4	.446	359	.223	.340	.324	3.95	6	6	3	0	1	4	7	28	3.04	2	5	.308
Jones D	5.83	4	8	.330	293	.320	.496	.357	6.90	5	4	0	0	0	2	2	27	3.84	4	8	.302
King E	4.90	7	10	.411	656	.279	.384	.328	4.62	9	8	3	0	0	7	8	68	4.06	7	10	.407
Kiser	9.64	0	0	.152	25	.368	.368	.500	7.96	1	1	0	0	0	1	0	3	5.78	0	0	.265
Kramer T	17.36	0	0	.053	30	.476	.857	.533	21.76	0	0	0	0	0	0	3	1	1.93	0	0	.012
Mutis	12.41	0	3	.098	68	.397	.603	.455	12.37	0	0	0	0	0	2	1	6	4.38	0	3	.111
Nagy	4.39	12	13	.465	914	.275	.403	.330	4.70	22	23	7	0	1	5	9	80	3.41	9	16	.376
Nichols Rod	3.77	7	6	.540	573	.273	.345	.317	3.83	10	16	8	0	0	6	4	40	2.65	4	9	.330
Olin	3.51	5	4	.575	249	.274	.354	.344	4.17	9	3	2	0	0	2	0	17	2.72	3	6	.374
Orosco	3.94	1	1	.518	202	.286	.396	.338	5.21	2	5	0	0	0	1	3	16	3.15	1	1	.390
Otto	4.32	4	5	.472	396	.280	.387	.329	4.24	11	4	3	1	0	7	4	39	3.75	4	5	.429
Seanez	16.20	0	0	.060	33	.385	.692	.515	18.41	0	0	0	0	0	0	0	5	9.00	0	0	.236
Shaw	3.48	3	2	.579	311	.262	.371	.332	3.94	13	1	3	0	0	1	4	31	3.86	3	2	.551
Swindell	3.71	14	11	.549	971	.263	.393	.287	3.73	15	9	11	2	8	13	8	96	3.63	12	13	.490
Valdez E	1.50	0	0	.881	27	.238	.238	.346	3.57	0	0	0	0	0	1	1	2	3.00	0	0	.800
Valdez	5.51	0	1	.355	70	.238	.397	.290	4.25	1	2	0	0	0	1	1	5	2.76	0	1	.200
Walker MC	2.08	1	0	.795	22	.316	.421	.409	7.50	0	0	0	0	0	0	0	1	2.07	1	0	.500
York	7.01	1	4	.254	163	.333	.489	.412	7.38	4	4	2	0	0	3	4	18	4.67	2	3	.308
TOTALS	4.51	73	88	.451	6196	.276	.397	.329	4.61	126	102	46	4	11	58	69	571	3.59	62	99	.387

Batting 'Splits' Records for Cleveland Indians

	G	AB	Run	Hit	2B	3B	HR	TB	RBI	W	K	IW	HB	SB	CS	GI DP	SH	SF	Avg	Slug	OBP	Runs Ctd
SPLITS for Baerga																						
vs LHP	74	161	27	53	8	0	2	67	20	8	14	2	4	0	0	6	1	0	.329	.416	.376	24
vs RHP	146	432	53	118	20	2	9	169	49	40	60	3	2	3	2	6	3	3	.273	.391	.335	58
Home	81	299	33	87	13	2	2	110	32	20	31	3	2	1	1	5	2	2	.291	.368	.337	37
Away	77	294	47	84	15	0	9	126	37	28	43	2	4	2	1	7	2	1	.286	.429	.355	45
Grass	135	508	73	150	23	2	11	210	65	40	53	5	4	3	1	10	4	2	.295	.413	.350	74
Turf	23	85	7	21	5	0	0	26	4	8	21	0	2	0	1	2	0	1	.247	.306	.323	8
April/June	69	246	36	68	8	1	8	102	30	27	23	1	2	2	2	5	2	0	.276	.415	.353	36
July/October	89	347	44	103	20	1	3	134	39	21	51	4	4	1	0	7	2	3	.297	.386	.341	46
SPLITS for Belle																						
vs LHP	57	132	17	38	11	1	8	75	34	5	27	1	0	2	0	9	0	1	.288	.568	.312	19
vs RHP	114	329	43	92	20	1	20	174	61	20	72	1	5	1	1	15	0	4	.280	.529	.327	52
Home	63	236	23	60	15	0	8	99	35	11	49	0	3	2	0	13	0	2	.254	.419	.294	25
Away	60	225	37	70	16	2	20	150	60	14	50	2	2	1	1	11	0	3	.311	.667	.352	47
Grass	110	413	55	115	26	2	26	223	85	24	88	2	4	3	1	21	0	4	.278	.540	.321	64
Turf	13	48	5	15	5	0	2	26	10	1	11	0	1	0	0	3	0	1	.313	.542	.333	7
April/June	49	186	25	48	12	1	10	92	32	11	42	0	3	3	0	13	0	0	.258	.495	.310	24
July/October	74	275	35	82	19	1	18	157	63	14	57	2	2	0	1	11	0	5	.298	.571	.331	48
SPLITS for Cole																						
vs LHP	40	62	13	24	5	1	0	31	8	14	7	0	1	6	5	3	2	1	.387	.500	.500	15
vs RHP	106	325	45	90	12	2	0	106	13	44	40	2	0	21	12	5	2	1	.277	.326	.362	41
Home	56	182	28	53	9	0	0	62	14	33	27	1	1	11	9	3	0	2	.291	.341	.399	27
Away	66	205	30	61	8	3	0	75	7	25	20	1	0	16	8	5	4	0	.298	.366	.374	29
Grass	101	330	53	93	13	2	0	110	19	48	43	2	1	24	15	7	2	2	.282	.333	.373	43
Turf	21	57	5	21	4	1	0	27	2	10	4	0	0	3	2	1	2	0	.368	.474	.463	13
April/June	45	145	15	43	5	1	0	50	6	19	16	0	1	8	9	3	2	1	.297	.345	.380	18
July/October	77	242	43	71	12	2	0	87	15	39	31	2	0	19	8	5	2	1	.293	.360	.390	37
SPLITS for Cleveland Indians (all batters except pitchers)																						
vs LHP	742	1504	167	394	66	9	22	544	160	127	233	10	13	25	22	44	15	18	.262	.362	.321	170
vs RHP	1444	3965	409	996	170	17	57	1371	386	322	655	14	30	59	36	101	47	28	.251	.346	.310	422
Home	864	2693	271	705	122	15	22	923	253	221	393	15	24	33	28	72	33	23	.262	.343	.321	293
Away	855	2776	305	685	114	11	57	992	293	228	495	9	19	51	30	73	29	23	.247	.357	.306	299
Grass	1471	4669	517	1209	201	25	72	1676	490	395	729	23	37	74	51	122	52	39	.259	.359	.319	530
Turf	248	800	59	181	35	1	7	239	56	54	159	1	6	10	7	23	10	7	.226	.299	.278	65
April/June	749	2428	239	599	93	11	34	816	227	213	370	10	19	37	25	62	36	15	.247	.336	.311	253
July/October	970	3041	337	791	143	15	45	1099	319	236	518	14	24	47	33	83	26	31	.260	.361	.315	340

1991 SPLITS FOR Cleveland Indians

BATTING SPLITS

	AVG	AB	R	H	2B	3B	HR	RBI	SB	CS	BB	K	OBA	SPCT
Total	.254	5470	576	1390	236	26	79	546	84	58	449	888	.313	.350

	#Pit	#P/PA	GB	FB	G/F	G	IBB	HB	SH	SF	GDP
Miscellaneous	21774	3.59	2172	1436	1.51	162	24	43	62	46	145

	AVG	AB	R	H	2B	3B	HR	RBI	SB	CS	BB	K	OBA	SPCT
vs. Left	.262	1504	...	394	66	9	22	160	25	22	127	233	.321	.362
vs. Right	.251	3966	...	996	170	17	57	386	59	36	322	655	.310	.346
Home	.262	2693	271	705	122	15	22	253	33	28	221	393	.321	.343
Away	.247	2777	305	685	114	11	57	293	51	30	228	495	.306	.357
None on	.249	3127	...	780	130	13	47	47	0	0	259	529	.312	.344
Runners on	.260	2343	...	610	106	13	32	499	84	58	190	359	.315	.358
April	.235	583	46	137	21	3	9	44	9	7	48	99	.300	.328
May	.271	912	124	247	40	6	17	118	19	10	83	146	.335	.384
June	.230	933	69	215	32	2	8	65	9	8	82	125	.294	.295
July	.259	911	96	236	36	4	18	91	12	9	71	150	.315	.367
August	.260	1028	121	267	49	4	18	114	14	12	78	185	.316	.368
September	.257	853	93	219	45	5	8	90	15	10	67	150	.312	.349
October	.276	250	27	69	13	2	1	24	6	2	20	33	.322	.356
None on/out	.255	1349	...	344	58	8	21	21	0	0	134	211	.327	.357
Scoring Posn	.254	1278	...	325	54	8	16	443	21	12	135	224	.322	.347
Close & Late	.218	1043	...	227	28	5	11	91	16	7	84	209	.279	.286
Bases Loaded	.266	79	...	21	5	0	1	57	0	1	4	17	.292	.367
Batting #1	.275	637	94	175	28	4	5	36	39	19	93	95	.368	.355
Batting #2	.232	656	62	152	26	2	1	54	3	6	47	88	.285	.282
Batting #3	.289	640	74	185	25	3	7	70	4	2	48	94	.340	.370
Batting #4	.265	637	75	169	32	2	28	103	6	0	39	134	.313	.454
Batting #5	.238	621	70	148	28	3	14	69	5	8	43	102	.288	.361
Batting #6	.261	597	61	156	29	5	13	67	5	6	49	92	.319	.392
Batting #7	.246	581	54	143	30	1	7	58	4	6	50	103	.311	.337
Batting #8	.215	554	44	119	20	3	3	44	8	2	41	104	.278	.278
Batting #9	.261	547	42	143	18	3	1	45	10	9	39	76	.309	.311
As c	.235	548	40	129	28	2	1	44	0	6	28	108	.278	.299
As 1b	.236	598	54	141	20	3	10	74	1	3	45	107	.287	.329
As 2b	.240	629	60	151	23	4	3	64	3	3	38	85	.285	.304
As 3b	.269	592	72	159	27	3	11	62	6	4	60	71	.340	.380
As ss	.280	572	48	160	23	2	0	48	6	5	38	54	.325	.327
As lf	.276	594	75	164	28	2	27	93	6	6	57	126	.343	.466
As cf	.267	617	88	165	23	3	7	40	37	19	87	93	.361	.348
As rf	.237	560	66	133	31	5	8	49	12	5	54	109	.308	.354
Outfield	.261	1771	229	462	82	10	42	182	55	30	198	328	.339	.390
0.0 count	.335	817	...	274	54	3	15	101	...	...	0	0	.337	.464
After (0.1)	.227	2374	...	538	81	7	26	197	...	...	118	580	.267	.299
After (1.0)	.254	2279	...	578	101	16	38	248	...	...	312	308	.345	.362
Two strikes	.190	2364	...	449	79	9	23	184	...	...	194	886	.255	.260
Grass	.259	4670	517	1209	201	25	72	490	74	51	395	729	.319	.359
Turf	.226	800	59	181	35	1	7	56	10	7	54	159	.278	.299
Day	.255	1626	188	415	71	8	28	183	24	18	153	280	.321	.360
Night	.254	3844	388	975	165	18	51	363	60	40	296	608	.310	.346
Inning 1.6	.258	3634	402	938	157	17	51	383	63	47	303	562	.317	.353
Inning 7+	.246	1836	174	452	79	9	28	163	21	11	146	326	.305	.345
vs.Bal	.276	453	53	125	25	1	5	53	13	4	40	68	.335	.369
vs.Bos	.233	454	48	106	17	4	9	45	5	7	48	87	.313	.348
vs.Cal	.262	408	43	107	15	2	7	38	6	7	36	66	.324	.360
vs.ChA	.224	380	33	85	16	0	7	33	7	5	30	56	.282	.321
vs.Det	.276	420	45	116	21	4	4	42	6	8	34	56	.334	.374
vs.KC	.242	413	28	100	15	1	5	27	2	7	14	77	.271	.320
vs.Mil	.260	431	45	112	16	3	7	42	4	3	28	52	.307	.360
vs.Min	.239	401	35	96	15	0	3	31	2	4	33	52	.303	.299
vs.NYA	.264	435	42	115	20	2	5	40	7	5	36	77	.317	.354
vs.Oak	.286	437	81	125	18	5	11	78	10	3	42	60	.351	.426
vs.Sea	.256	395	38	101	20	0	5	37	6	2	33	81	.315	.344
vs.Tex	.276	413	58	114	23	4	9	54	9	2	41	73	.344	.416
vs.Tor	.205	430	27	88	15	0	2	26	7	1	34	83	.265	.253

PITCHING SPLITS

	ERA	W	L	SV	SVOP	GS	CG	SHO	IP	H	ER	HR	BB	IBB	K
Total	4.23	57	105	33	51	162	22	18	1441.1	1551	678	110	441	61	862

	#Pit	#P/IP	GB	FB	G/F	BRp9	RA	WP	BK	SH	SF	R	HB	Hld
Miscellaneous	22272	15.45	2102	1549	1.36	12.68	289	48	6	59	69	759	39	10

	ERA	W	L	SV	SVOP	GS	CG	SHO	IP	H	ER	HR	BB	IBB	K
ST	4.21	42	79	0	0	162	22	3	1032.1	1124	483	77	261	19	596
REL	4.31	15	26	33	51	0	0	0	409.0	427	196	33	180	42	266
Home	4.10	30	52	14	19	82	15	2	747.0	788	340	41	207	28	447
Away	4.39	27	53	19	32	80	7	1	694.1	763	339	69	234	33	415
April	2.61	7	10	5	7	17	1	0	155.1	136	45	6	37	3	104
May	4.64	10	17	3	7	27	5	0	238.2	256	123	22	72	9	162
June	3.99	7	21	4	4	28	3	0	248.0	260	110	19	83	14	155
July	4.21	9	18	5	9	27	5	1	239.2	266	112	20	80	15	142
August	4.71	10	20	6	11	30	3	2	265.1	299	139	21	81	10	151
September	4.20	11	15	8	10	26	5	0	229.1	238	107	17	71	9	119
October	5.95	3	4	2	3	7	0	0	65.0	96	43	5	17	1	29
Grass	4.15	53	85	30	46	138	19	3	1241.0	1323	572	92	369	49	746
Turf	4.81	4	20	3	5	24	3	0	200.1	228	107	18	72	12	116
Day	3.97	19	29	9	15	48	7	0	424.1	441	187	33	133	16	256
Night	4.35	38	76	24	36	114	15	3	1017.0	1110	492	77	308	45	606
vs.Bal	3.42	6	7	4	5	13	1	0	118.1	118	45	14	29	7	73
vs.Bos	4.18	4	9	3	6	13	0	0	118.1	128	55	2	49	4	61
vs.Cal	3.32	5	7	3	5	12	3	0	111.0	112	41	3	29	6	78
vs.ChA	3.26	6	6	4	4	12	1	1	105.0	104	38	8	35	2	63
vs.Det	3.89	7	6	5	6	13	2	0	111.0	118	48	9	34	3	86
vs.KC	2.64	4	8	2	4	12	2	0	109.0	99	32	4	17	4	73
vs.Mil	4.62	5	8	2	4	13	2	1	115.0	140	59	7	34	2	63
vs.Min	5.37	2	10	2	2	12	0	0	104.0	121	62	10	34	5	40
vs.NYA	3.88	6	7	5	6	13	3	0	116.0	122	50	12	33	4	55
vs.Oak	5.09	5	7	1	5	12	1	0	111.1	123	63	12	41	5	66
vs.Sea	5.40	2	10	0	1	12	2	0	103.1	128	62	10	38	7	63
vs.Tex	5.31	4	8	2	3	12	1	1	105.0	116	62	10	35	6	63
vs.Tor	4.89	1	12	0	0	13	4	0	114.0	122	62	9	33	6	78

OPPOSING BATTERS VS. PITCHERS.

	AVG	AB	R	H	2B	3B	HR	RBI	SB	CS	BB	K	OBA	SPCT
Total	.276	5623	759	1551	279	38	110	708	102	47	441	862	.329	.398
vs. Left	.290	2306	...	669	112	21	32	284	57	16	201	311	.346	.399
vs. Right	.266	3317	...	882	167	17	78	424	45	31	240	551	.317	.397
ST	.278	4043	539	1124	210	33	77	452	73	39	261	596	.322	.403
REL	.270	1580	220	427	69	5	33	256	29	8	180	266	.346	.383
Home	.272	2900	377	788	128	22	41	346	51	29	207	447	.321	.373
Away	.280	2723	382	763	151	16	69	362	51	18	234	415	.337	.423
None on	.271	3118	...	844	154	22	50	50	0	0	205	492	.320	.382
Runners on	.282	2505	...	707	125	16	60	658	102	47	236	370	.340	.417
None on/out	.267	1396	...	373	72	12	28	28	0	0	83	226	.314	.396
Scoring Posn	.273	1423	...	389	70	11	31	574	30	6	177	222	.344	.403
vs 1st Batr	.283	247	...	70	12	0	3	61	3	0	29	43	.363	.368
1st IP	.278	1581	214	440	69	7	35	288	36	6	157	275	.343	.397
Inning 1.6	.277	3787	508	1048	192	32	77	478	77	35	260	564	.324	.405
Inning 7+	.274	1836	251	503	87	6	33	230	25	12	181	298	.340	.382
Close & Late	.266	927	...	247	45	4	15	117	17	8	105	156	.340	.372
0.0 count	.310	804	...	249	46	5	18	126	...	...	47	0	.347	.447
After (0.1)	.254	2508	...	637	102	14	44	280	...	...	97	557	.286	.358
After (1.0)	.288	2311	...	665	131	19	48	302	...	...	297	305	.366	.423
Two strikes	.202	2379	...	481	90	12	27	194	...	...	163	861	.258	.284
Pitch 1.15	.278	1365	...	380	64	4	30	211	34	5	122	213	.338	.397
Pitch 16.30	.276	1043	...	288	53	7	20	146	12	9	104	198	.342	.398
Pitch 31.45	.289	841	...	243	44	10	18	98	16	10	59	117	.336	.429
Pitch 46.60	.261	712	...	186	33	8	9	77	9	9	48	99	.308	.368
Pitch 61.75	.255	588	...	150	26	2	12	51	14	7	34	77	.297	.367
Pitch 76.90	.286	510	...	146	29	4	12	64	7	2	35	77	.338	.429
Pitch 91.105	.284	348	...	99	21	1	4	32	7	4	28	49	.337	.385
Pitch 106.20	.292	161	...	47	8	1	4	24	3	1	9	22	.324	.429
Pitch 121.35	.184	49	...	9	1	1	1	4	0	0	2	10	.212	.306
Pitch 136.50	.500	8	...	4	0	0	0	1	0	0	0	0	.500	.500

National League

Western Division

1. Atlanta Braves
2. Los Angeles Dodgers
3. San Diego Padres
4. San Francisco Giants
5. Cincinnati Reds
6. Houston Astros

NL Western Division Team Batting

	G	AB	Run	Hit	2B	3B	HR	TB	RBI	W	K	IW	HB	SB	CS	GIDP	SH	SF	Avg	Slug	OBP	Runs Ctd
Atlanta	2349	5456	749	1407	255	30	141	2145	704	563	906	55	32	165	76	104	86	45	.258	.393	.328	723
Cincinnati	2216	5496	688	1417	250	27	164	2213	654	488	1004	54	32	124	56	85	72	41	.258	.403	.320	724
Houston	2302	5504	605	1345	240	43	79	1908	570	502	1027	45	35	125	68	87	63	43	.244	.347	.309	609
Los Angeles	2375	5408	665	1366	191	29	108	1939	605	583	957	50	28	126	68	110	94	46	.253	.359	.326	653
San Diego	2173	5408	636	1321	204	36	121	1960	591	501	1069	60	32	101	64	121	78	38	.244	.362	.310	609
San Francisco	2296	5463	649	1345	215	48	141	2079	605	471	973	59	40	95	57	92	90	33	.246	.381	.309	651

NL Western Division Sabermetric Team Batting

	|-------- Ball Park Adjusted --------|												Runs		Run/					
	AB	Run	Hit	2B	3B	HR	RBI	W	SO	Avg	Slug	OBP	Ctd	Outs	27o	OW%	OG	OWAR	DWAR	TWAR
Atlanta	5399	670	1327	247	32	120	636	580	946	.246	.370	.320	666	4369	4.12	.475	162	20.24	6.39	26.64
Cincinnati	5703	664	1432	240	28	141	622	470	1074	.251	.377	.311	685	4534	4.08	.478	168	21.56	5.55	27.11
Houston	5586	642	1381	230	35	111	604	515	1011	.247	.361	.313	642	4485	3.86	.473	166	20.42	3.66	24.07
Los Angeles	5551	690	1404	218	45	110	621	584	950	.253	.368	.326	678	4478	4.09	.537	166	31.01	7.64	38.65
San Diego	5285	625	1313	207	42	113	588	478	1033	.248	.368	.311	600	4282	3.78	.478	159	20.24	8.23	28.47
San Francisco	5307	669	1345	212	45	144	626	467	952	.253	.392	.317	675	4220	4.32	.519	156	26.48	7.89	34.36

NL Western Division Team Pitching

	ERA	W	L	Pct	G	GS	CG	ShO	GF	Sv	IP	R	ER	H	2B	3B	HR	BB	IW	SO	HB	WP	BK
Atlanta	3.49	94	68	.580	507	162	18	3	144	48	1452.2	644	564	1304	235	41	118	481	39	969	28	66	13
Cincinnati	3.83	74	88	.457	516	162	7	1	155	43	1440.0	691	613	1372	231	35	127	560	41	997	28	60	9
Houston	4.00	65	97	.401	527	162	7	3	155	36	1453.0	717	646	1347	248	30	129	651	62	1033	29	46	17
Los Angeles	3.07	93	69	.574	529	162	15	7	147	40	1458.0	565	497	1312	202	28	96	500	77	1028	28	48	12
San Diego	3.58	84	78	.519	496	162	14	4	148	47	1452.2	646	578	1385	196	32	139	457	56	921	13	49	13
San Francisco	4.03	75	87	.463	496	162	10	6	152	45	1442.0	697	646	1397	233	30	143	544	60	905	36	44	14

NL Western Division Catchers

	G	PO	A	Er	TC	DP	PB	SB	CS	CS%	FPct	DI	DG	DW%	DWAR	ERA	ERA Wo-W
Atlanta	162	981	86	6	1073	11	14	149	59	.284	.994	1434.2	10.0	.409	.59	3.49	
Cincinnati	162	1051	74	19	1144	13	19	139	59	.298	.983	1423.0	10.0	.274	-.75	3.79	
Houston	162	1085	82	15	1182	12	16	143	60	.296	.987	1436.0	10.0	.265	-.84	4.00	
Los Angeles	162	1063	97	13	1173	10	8	145	60	.293	.989	1450.0	10.0	.439	.89	3.07	
San Diego	162	934	110	14	1058	15	9	108	65	.376	.987	1443.2	10.0	.365	.15	3.57	
San Francisco	162	924	101	16	1041	14	9	129	83	.392	.985	1424.0	10.0	.259	-.90	4.03	
LG.AVG	162	997	93	13	1103	10	12	137	67	.328	.988	1442.0					

NL Western Division First Base

	G	PO	A	Er	TC	DP	FPct	DI	DG	DW%	DWAR
Atlanta	162	1511	117	15	1643	111	.991	1434.2	3.0	.451	.30
Cincinnati	162	1306	127	14	1447	112	.990	1423.0	3.0	.493	.42
Houston	162	1372	114	13	1499	104	.991	1436.0	3.0	.505	.46
Los Angeles	162	1468	153	10	1631	111	.994	1450.0	3.0	.600	.74
San Diego	162	1455	90	15	1560	115	.990	1443.2	3.0	.405	.16
San Francisco	162	1449	128	5	1582	133	.997	1424.0	3.0	.594	.72
LG.AVG	162	1454	119	13	1586	112	.992	1442.0			

NL Western Division Second Base

	G	PO	A	Er	TC	DP	FPct	DI	DG	DW%	DWAR
Atlanta	162	357	472	24	853	88	.972	1434.2	8.0	.487	1.08
Cincinnati	162	318	427	17	762	90	.978	1423.0	8.0	.401	.40
Houston	162	298	487	17	802	82	.979	1436.0	8.0	.402	.41
Los Angeles	162	335	497	18	850	87	.979	1450.0	8.0	.497	1.17
San Diego	162	343	465	15	823	91	.982	1443.2	8.0	.506	1.24
San Francisco	162	370	460	10	840	111	.988	1424.0	8.0	.605	2.02
LG.AVG	162	346	481	15	842	87	.982	1442.0			

NL Western Division Third Base

	G	PO	A	Er	TC	DP	FPct	DI	DG	DW%	DWAR
Atlanta	162	124	379	29	532	33	.945	1434.2	6.0	.589	1.41
Cincinnati	162	99	264	15	378	24	.960	1423.0	6.0	.378	.16
Houston	162	141	319	26	486	30	.947	1436.0	6.0	.473	.73
Los Angeles	162	132	282	21	435	24	.952	1450.0	6.0	.426	.45
San Diego	162	113	332	19	464	21	.959	1443.2	6.0	.470	.71
San Francisco	162	144	321	21	486	31	.957	1424.0	6.0	.535	1.09
LG.AVG	162	120	320	23	463	26	.950	1442.0			

NL Western Division Shortstop

	G	PO	A	Er	TC	DP	FPct	DI	DG	DW%	DWAR
Atlanta	162	242	484	29	755	74	.962	1434.2	11.0	.468	1.28
Cincinnati	162	306	492	20	818	86	.976	1423.0	11.0	.556	2.24
Houston	162	255	392	39	686	79	.943	1436.0	11.0	.296	-.58
Los Angeles	162	258	531	38	827	72	.954	1450.0	11.0	.468	1.29
San Diego	162	276	482	27	785	86	.966	1443.2	11.0	.520	1.87
San Francisco	162	269	487	27	783	94	.966	1424.0	11.0	.522	1.86
LG.AVG	162	268	482	26	776	82	.966	1442.0			

NL Western Division Left Field

	G	PO	A	Er	TC	DP	FPct	DI	DG	DW%	DWAR
Atlanta	162	297	12	8	317	3	.975	1434.2	4.0	.510	.63
Cincinnati	162	344	6	6	356	1	.983	1423.0	4.0	.466	.46
Houston	162	385	6	5	396	1	.987	1436.0	4.0	.543	.76
Los Angeles	162	315	9	5	329	0	.985	1450.0	4.0	.493	.57
San Diego	162	332	5	7	344	1	.980	1443.2	4.0	.441	.36
San Francisco	162	317	13	9	339	2	.973	1424.0	4.0	.541	.75
LG.AVG	162	341	9	6	356	1	.983	1442.0			

NL Western Division Center Field

	G	PO	A	Er	TC	DP	FPct	DI	DG	DW%	DWAR
Atlanta	162	382	8	6	396	1	.985	1434.2	6.0	.430	.48
Cincinnati	162	413	7	11	431	4	.974	1423.0	6.0	.388	.23
Houston	162	399	17	5	421	3	.988	1436.0	6.0	.572	1.32
Los Angeles	162	389	8	1	398	3	.997	1450.0	6.0	.548	1.18
San Diego	162	466	4	2	472	2	.996	1443.2	6.0	.604	1.53
San Francisco	162	413	9	4	426	5	.991	1424.0	6.0	.532	1.08
LG.AVG	162	407	8	6	421	2	.986	1442.0			

NL Western Division Right Field

	G	PO	A	Er	TC	DP	FPct	DI	DG	DW%	DWAR
Atlanta	162	311	10	11	332	0	.967	1434.2	5.0	.465	.57
Cincinnati	162	335	15	3	353	2	.992	1415.0	5.0	.685	1.66
Houston	162	296	19	14	329	3	.957	1436.0	5.0	.523	.86
Los Angeles	162	260	14	5	279	2	.982	1450.0	5.0	.494	.72
San Diego	162	346	12	5	363	4	.986	1434.2	5.0	.616	1.32
San Francisco	162	308	4	8	320	1	.975	1424.0	5.0	.384	.17
LG.AVG	162	318	12	6	336	2	.982	1442.0			

Atlanta Braves

Don Malcolm

ATLANTA											
YEAR	1982	1983	1984	1985	1986	1987	1988	1989	1990	1991	TOT
W	89	88	80	66	72	69	54	63	65	94	740
L	73	74	82	96	89	92	106	97	97	68	874
WPCT	0.549	0.543	0.494	0.407	0.447	0.429	0.338	0.394	0.401	0.580	0.458
R	739	746	632	632	615	747	555	584	682	749	6681
RA	702	640	655	781	719	829	741	680	821	644	7212
PWPT	0.526	0.576	0.482	0.396	0.423	0.448	0.359	0.424	0.408	0.575	0.462
PythW	85	93	78	64	68	73	58	69	66	93	75
PythL	77	69	84	98	94	89	104	93	96	69	87
LUCK	4	-5	2	2	4	-4	-4	-6	-1	1	-7

Defensive Efficiency Record: .7118

FACT ONE

Braves' leadoff hitters scored 13 more runs than the Dodgers in 1991 (127 to 114). This was due, in part, to the fact that the Braves leadoff hitters slugged 10 more homers than the Dodgers' leadoff hitters (12 to 2). As I keep saying, put a little power in the #1 slot: it can't hurt...

HOW, LONNIE, HOW?

Rags to riches stories aren't quite what they used to be. But how could Bobby Cox know that he was supposed to pinch-run for Lonnie Smith? Well, they do call him Skates, and he's not considered by anyone in the less-than-Foucaultian world o' baseball to be a raving mental giant. But, sheesh, Lonnie, of all the times to revert to form....

ARE THE KID PITCHERS FOR REAL?

Y-e-s. Look at their overall opponents' batting averages. Glavine, .222. Avery .240. Smoltz, .243. Remember that they pitch half their games in the Pad, where the league scored 788 runs in 81 games, the highest total of any National League ballpark. As a team, the Braves' road ERA was 3.17, which was a close second to the Dodgers (3.10).

It's an impressive threesome, and if Cox is on the ball, they might be joined by someone like Kent Mercker, who has the stuff to be a starter. The only difficulty is that moving Mercker out of the bullpen brings the Braves down to one lefty in the pen, but it's likely to be a pretty deep pen now that Al Pena has been retained. Lefty Mike Stanton was supposed to be the Braves' closer in 1990, but hurt himself trying to impress everyone. He's back and ready to be the lefty counterpart to Pena. Don't be too surprised if Mercker is in the Braves' rotation this year.

FACT TWO

The Braves cleanup slot was tied with the Giants' #3 slot for the most RBI by an indivdual batting orderf position (133). The difference between the Braves and Pirates and the rest of the league is that they had longer sequence offenses: they had more RBI later in the batting order than any of the other teams.

WHY DIDN'T WE GET IT RIGHT?

In other words, why didn't we predict in the '91 book that the Braves would do what they did? Readers of the earlier editions of the book may recall that in 1990 we expected big things from the Braves, and kind of envisioned them as a new version of the late 60s Mets. 1990 was supposed to have been a building year, where the Braves would add 10 to 12 wins to their total, and then have a breakthrough year in 1991.

Because the Braves' pitching backslid in 1990, we backed off from this scenario, which turned out to be the correct one after all. It just shows you that there are many variations within the classic patterns of improvement, and that the signals are still valid even when the classic pattern isn't followed. The Braves were clearly ready to be a contending team in 1991, but they got all the little things (a career year from Terry Pendleton, breakthroughs from Glavine and Avery, an abundance of strong and effective relievers, the development of Brian Hunter just in time to fill in for the injured Bream, the timely return of David Justice, etc., etc.). Hell, they should have been World Champs. One of these years now, they probably will be.

WHY, LONNIE, WHY?

Let's remember how much Lonnie contributed to the Braves offense during the Series. He hit a couple of big homers, and was instrumental in the Braves taking a 3-2 lead back to the Metrodome. It's his added power in the leadoff slot that gave the Braves an extra dimension in the offense, and helped them have the best overall production at that slot in the NL last year.

But I can help wishing (for once) that baseball had adopted Finley's orange ball. Lonnie would have been able to pick up an orange ball in the Metrodome (I think).

FACT THREE

The #7 slot in the Braves batting order, despite hitting just .237, had the highest number of RBI (77) in the NL. Another benefit of the long sequence offense...

IS SID THROUGH?

Y-e-s, I'm afraid so. His knee is so bad that it is beginning to seriously affect all areas of his game. The Braves would be better off handing the first base job to Brian Hunter and seeing if he can learn to handle righties. Sid was used so much as an escape valve by the Twins that you just hated to see him even come to the plate in the Series. At best, Sid should be in a platoon with Hunter this year, but in an arrangement that features more exposure to righties for Brian, so as to prepare him for full-time play. Hunter projects to be a 30-homer man in this park, which would give the Braves a pretty good Murderer's Row.

LET JUSTICE PREVAIL

He drove in 87 runs in 109 games last season, which translates to a 130 RBI pace for a full year. But his biggest hit must have been the homer off Rob Dibble to cap the Braves' rally from a 6-0 Reds lead on September 30. It was at that point that it became clear to me that the Braves would indeed win their division.

Justice is projected to crack the 30 homer threshhold this season, and I can't see much of a reason to doubt that he will. He might end up being a bigger money player for them than Dale Murphy was. His concentration at the plate is impressive, and he has done an excellent job of minimizing the pitchers' ability to take advantage of his somewhat long swing. I think we're in for a long ride with Dave in the driver's seat,

FACT FOUR

We should have expected the Braves to beat the Pirates in the playoffs. During the regular season the Braves won nine of twelve, outscoring the Bucs 71-51. That translates to a .660 Pythagorean winning percentage, or 107-55 if the Braves were to play the Pirates a full season.

CAN THEY DO IT AGAIN?

Y-e-s. But they'll likely have to overcome a return to earth from Pendleton. But there is enough depth and versatility here to overcome an off-season or two. Still, what made the Braves so formidable was that steady punch from 1-5 in the batting order: any serious disruption of that might drag them down to third place.

The pitching, though, looks strong and deep and, most of all, young. It remains to be seen if Al Pena can keep up the killer save pace that he achieved in the stretch drive last year: after all, his total of 15 saves (11 with the Braves) represents a career high. But Cox is pretty savvy, and he's done a wonderful job in getting the pieces to fit together. There are alternatives for all of the potential problem areas on the team (closer, number four starter, first base, third base, left field). I don't see any reason to doubt that the Braves will be in the thick of it again, and probably for the next three to five years.

NOTE FROM BROCK: This is the third team in a row that has done this under Bobby Cox. The 1982 Braves, the ones that won for Joe Torre, were created by Cox before he left for Toronto. That team featured the following position players:

	POS	AGE
Chris Chambliss	1b	33
Glenn Hubbard	2b	24
Rafael Ramirez	ss	24
Bob Horner	3b	24
Claudell Washington	lf	27
Dale Murphy	cf	26
Rufino Linares	rf	27
Bruce Benedict	c	26

Many of the bellwether pitchers were old, but the young pitchers included Bob Walk, Steve Bedrosian, Ken Dayley and Pascual Perez. That's a tremendous team, and it was Cox's team as built. It even had Brett Butler on the way. You may remember that the Braves management post Cox traded a lot of the team away for little return, and that its pitching didn't develop under Torre and Bob Gibson. But the team that won, the team that could have been, was a Bobby Cox team.

If you think about it, it's obvious that the Blue Jays of the late 1980's were Cox's creation as well. After all, he went there from the Braves. To a large extent, the Jays still are a Cox team, though current management is having to handle a transition. And it, too, was a young team when it first got good.

As are the current Braves. It's not as if the BASEBALL SABERMETRIC crew didn't see it coming. As Don mentions, he had them down for a team on the make two years ago, but lost a little faith when they took steps backward in 1990. I didn't lose faith. What I saw was that the team was not very well managed on the field. There was a lot of confusion about roles, and the pitching staff was erratically handled, with a lot of riding of hot hands. I also saw that the manager had been fired, and Bobby Cox was about to take the field reins. I predicted them to contend.

What Bobby Cox did was what he has always done. First, he got the roles defined. That always helps, especially for a player like Ron Gant. Gant had been a coming superstar for years, but he was always being retrained for new field positions. Bobby just put him out in center and told him that was his job. It worked for Lou Brock in 1964, and it worked for Gant in 1991.

Cox also got the pitching staff under control. Yes, he had some help from the very fast development of Steve Avery, but it wasn't all Steve. Bobby got all the other guys to contribute. Glavine and Leibrandt and Berenguer and even Alejandro Pena all were helped by defined roles and regular work assignments.

The final thing that Cox did was to identify the needs of the club that he could not fill from within and arrange to fill them from without. I know that installing Sid Bream at first base was not a good move in terms of player value, but it did solidify the team. Terry Pendleton, please remember, was obtained to settle the infield defense. His bat was a surprise plus. The settled third base spot allowed Cox to make a real bat/glove platoon out of Jeff Blauser and Rafael Belliard at short, and another out of Treadway and Lemke at second.

In all of this, Bobby Cox has maintained a low profile. He took no credit for whatever it was that happened to Pendleton's bat. People hardly remember that he was ever associated with the Jays, much less the early Braves. But he was, and he built those teams. And make no mistake, he's in charge of this one. John Schuerholz, who gets a lot of press, is just an organization man who is executing Cox's ideas. It's Bobby Cox's team, with Bobby Cox's role definition and Bobby Cox's regular work assignments. And it's about time it was Bobby Cox's credit that was given, as well.

Atlanta Braves Home Park Performance Factors

	Outs	Runs	Hits	2b	3b	HR	W	K	SH	SF	HBP	IBB	SB	CS	GDP
Home LH Batters	.947	.888	.973	1.004	.819	.976	.976	.984	1.490	.647	.718	.799	.862	1.323	.769
Home RH Batters	.996	.860	.911	1.018	1.115	.783	.971	1.020	1.025	1.271	1.172	1.066	1.242	1.266	.926
All Home Batters	.984	.873	.926	.982	1.075	.839	.977	1.015	1.152	.926	1.017	.939	1.020	1.214	.872
Opp LH Batters	1.033	.967	.969	1.005	1.770	.822	1.101	1.103	.824	.749	.563	.923	1.239	1.138	.855
Opp RH Batters	1.034	.885	.962	.919	.832	.891	1.067	1.064	.806	.752	.958	1.427	1.191	.937	.928
All Opp Batters	1.028	.917	.961	.961	1.108	.866	1.085	1.075	.825	.776	.873	1.135	1.187	.976	.879
All LH Batters	.988	.926	.970	1.005	1.245	.915	1.036	1.041	1.062	.695	.664	.857	1.052	1.219	.810
All RH Batters	1.015	.873	.936	.968	.935	.834	1.016	1.041	.898	.928	1.053	1.193	1.205	1.092	.924
All Batters	1.005	.895	.944	.972	1.087	.854	1.028	1.044	.965	.844	.943	1.021	1.100	1.093	.874

Conventional Batting Records for Atlanta Braves

	G	AB	Run	Hit	2B	3B	HR	TB	RBI	W	K	IW	HB	SB	CS	BRng Eff	GI DP	SH	SF	Avg	Slug	OBP	Runs Ctd
Olson Greg	133	411	46	99	25	0	6	142	44	44	48	3	3	1	1	.342	13	2	4	.241	.345	.316	45
Bream	91	265	32	67	12	0	11	112	45	25	31	5	0	0	3	.313	8	4	4	.253	.423	.313	33
Treadway	106	306	41	98	17	2	3	128	32	23	19	1	2	2	2	.564	8	2	3	.320	.418	.368	46
Pendleton	153	586	94	187	34	8	22	303	86	43	70	8	1	10	2	.396	16	7	7	.319	.517	.363	108
Belliard	149	353	36	88	9	2	0	101	27	22	63	2	2	3	1	.443	4	7	1	.249	.286	.296	31
Smith Lo	122	353	58	97	19	1	7	139	44	50	64	3	9	9	5	.468	4	2	2	.275	.394	.377	57
Gant	154	561	101	141	35	3	32	278	105	71	104	8	5	34	15	.614	6	0	5	.251	.496	.338	97
Justice	109	396	67	109	25	1	21	199	87	65	81	9	3	8	8	.446	4	0	5	.275	.503	.377	79
Nixon O	124	401	81	119	10	1	0	131	26	47	40	3	2	72	21	.520	5	7	3	.297	.327	.371	58
Blauser	129	352	49	91	14	3	11	144	54	54	59	4	2	5	6	.439	4	4	3	.259	.409	.358	54
Hunter B	97	271	32	68	16	1	12	122	50	17	48	0	1	0	2	.548	6	0	2	.251	.450	.296	34
Lemke	136	269	36	63	11	2	2	84	23	29	27	2	0	1	2	.426	9	6	4	.234	.312	.305	26
Heath	49	139	4	29	3	1	1	37	12	7	26	5	1	0	0	.357	4	2	1	.209	.266	.250	9
Sanders	54	110	16	21	1	2	4	38	13	12	23	0	0	11	3	.500	1	0	0	.191	.345	.270	11
Gregg	72	107	13	20	8	1	1	33	4	12	24	2	1	2	2	.529	1	0	0	.187	.308	.275	9
Cabrera	44	95	7	23	6	0	4	41	23	6	20	0	0	1	1	.375	5	0	1	.242	.432	.284	10
Avery	37	79	4	17	1	1	0	20	2	4	31	0	0	1	0	.300	1	5	0	.215	.253	.253	5
Glavine	36	74	1	17	1	0	0	18	6	6	19	0	0	1	0	.333	1	15	0	.230	.243	.287	6
Leibrandt	36	70	1	3	2	1	0	7	2	3	18	0	0	0	0	.500	1	12	0	.043	.100	.082	1
Mitchell Kth	48	66	11	21	0	0	2	27	5	8	12	0	0	3	1	.200	1	0	0	.318	.409	.392	11
Smoltz	38	65	7	7	3	0	0	10	3	5	28	0	0	0	0	.250	0	8	0	.108	.154	.171	2
Bell M	17	30	4	4	0	0	1	7	1	2	7	0	0	1	0	.429	2	0	0	.133	.233	.188	1
Willard	17	14	1	3	0	0	1	6	4	2	5	0	0	0	0	.000	0	0	0	.214	.429	.313	2
Heep	14	12	4	5	1	0	0	6	3	1	4	0	0	0	1	.500	0	0	0	.417	.500	.462	2
Smith P	14	12	1	2	0	0	0	2	0	1	5	0	0	0	0	.000	0	1	0	.167	.167	.231	1
Mercker	50	10	0	1	0	0	0	1	2	1	7	0	0	0	0	.000	0	0	0	.100	.100	.182	0
Freeman M	34	7	0	0	0	0	0	0	0	0	5	0	0	0	0	.000	0	0	0	.000	.000	.000	0
Reynoso	6	7	0	0	0	0	0	0	0	1	5	0	0	0	0	.000	0	0	0	.000	.000	.125	0
Stanton M	74	6	0	3	1	0	0	4	1	1	1	0	0	0	0	1.000	0	0	0	.500	.667	.571	2
Berenguer	49	5	0	0	0	0	0	0	0	0	3	0	0	0	0	.000	0	0	0	.000	.000	.000	0
Mahler R	13	5	0	1	1	0	0	2	0	0	2	0	0	0	0	.000	0	1	0	.200	.400	.200	0
Petry	10	5	1	1	0	0	0	1	0	0	0	0	0	0	0	1.000	0	0	0	.200	.200	.200	0
Castilla	12	5	1	1	0	0	0	1	0	0	2	0	0	0	0	.333	0	1	0	.200	.200	.200	0
Clancy	24	3	0	0	0	0	0	0	0	0	1	0	0	0	0	.000	0	0	0	.000	.000	.000	0
St.Claire	19	2	0	1	0	0	0	1	0	0	0	0	0	0	0	.000	0	0	0	.500	.500	.500	1
Wohlers	17	1	0	0	0	0	0	0	0	0	1	0	0	0	0	.000	0	0	0	.000	.000	.000	0
Pena A	15	1	0	0	0	0	0	0	0	0	1	0	0	0	0	.000	0	0	0	.000	.000	.000	0
Rossy	5	1	0	0	0	0	0	0	0	0	1	0	0	0	0	.000	0	0	0	.000	.000	.000	0
Berryhill	1	1	0	0	0	0	0	0	0	0	1	0	0	0	0	.000	0	0	0	.000	.000	.000	0
Sisk	14	0	0	0	0	0	0	0	0	0	0	0	0	0	0	.000	0	0	0	.000	.000	.000	0
Parrett	18	0	0	0	0	0	0	0	0	1	0	0	0	0	0	.000	0	0	0	.000	.000	1.000	0
Castillo T	7	0	0	0	0	0	0	0	0	0	0	0	0	0	0	.000	0	0	0	.000	.000	.000	0
Bielecki	2	0	0	0	0	0	0	0	0	0	0	0	0	0	0	.000	0	0	0	.000	.000	.000	0
TOTALS	2349	5456	749	1407	255	30	141	2145	704	563	906	55	32	165	76	.448	104	86	45	.258	.393	.328	723

Sabermetric Batting Records for Atlanta Braves

	|—— Ball Park Adjusted							——|		Runs	Run/									
	AB	Run	Hit	2B	3B	HR	RBI	W	SO	Avg	Slug	OBP	Ctd	Outs	27o	OW%	OG	OWAR	DWAR	TWAR
Bell M	28	3	3	0	0	0	0	2	7	.107	.107	.167	1	26	1.04	.054	1	-0.28	-0.00	-0.29
Belliard	351	31	82	8	1	0	24	22	65	.234	.262	.282	28	280	2.70	.280	10	-0.72	1.18	0.46
Berryhill	1	0	0	0	0	0	0	0	1	.000	.000	.000	0	1	0.00	.000	0	-0.01	0.01	-0.01
Blauser	349	42	85	13	2	9	48	55	61	.244	.370	.347	48	279	4.65	.536	10	1.92	0.23	2.15
Bream	261	29	65	12	0	9	41	25	32	.249	.398	.313	32	211	4.09	.473	8	0.96	0.26	1.22
Cabrera	94	6	21	5	0	3	20	6	20	.223	.372	.267	8	79	2.73	.285	3	-0.19	-0.10	-0.28
Castilla	4	0	0	0	0	0	0	0	2	.000	.000	.000	0	4	0.00	.000	0	-0.05	0.02	-0.03
Gant	558	88	132	33	2	26	94	72	108	.237	.443	.327	85	452	5.08	.579	17	3.84	0.31	4.15
Gregg	105	12	19	8	1	0	3	12	25	.181	.276	.265	8	88	2.45	.244	3	-0.35	0.10	-0.25
Heath	138	3	27	2	0	0	10	7	27	.196	.210	.238	7	116	1.63	.124	4	-0.97	0.09	-0.88
Heep	10	3	4	1	0	0	2	1	4	.400	.500	.455	2	7	7.71	.761	0	0.11	-0.00	0.11
Hunter B	269	27	63	15	0	10	44	17	50	.234	.401	.280	29	215	3.64	.415	8	0.52	0.06	0.58
Justice	389	62	105	25	1	18	79	67	84	.270	.478	.376	73	299	6.59	.699	11	3.86	0.62	4.48
Lemke	266	32	59	10	2	1	20	29	28	.222	.286	.295	23	224	2.77	.291	8	-0.49	0.67	0.18
Mitchell Kth	64	9	19	0	0	1	4	8	12	.297	.344	.375	9	46	5.28	.599	2	0.42	0.05	0.47
Nixon O	395	72	112	9	1	0	23	48	41	.284	.311	.361	54	317	4.60	.531	12	2.12	0.68	2.80
Olson Greg	408	40	92	24	0	5	39	44	50	.225	.321	.303	40	334	3.23	.358	12	0.10	0.58	0.69
Pendleton	577	84	176	33	8	18	77	44	73	.305	.484	.351	97	428	6.12	.667	16	5.02	1.44	6.46
Rossy	1	0	0	0	0	0	0	0	1	.000	.000	.000	0	1	0.00	.000	0	-0.01	-0.00	-0.01
Sanders	108	14	20	1	2	3	11	12	24	.185	.315	.267	10	91	2.97	.320	3	-0.10	0.13	0.03
Smith Lo	349	50	90	18	0	5	39	50	66	.258	.352	.363	50	270	5.00	.572	10	2.22	0.06	2.28
Treadway	300	38	95	17	2	2	29	23	19	.317	.407	.365	44	217	5.47	.616	8	2.13	0.24	2.38
Willard	12	0	2	0	0	0	3	2	5	.167	.167	.286	1	10	2.70	.280	0	-0.03	-0.00	-0.03
TOTALS	5399	670	1327	247	32	120	636	580	946	.246	.370	.320	666	4369	4.12	.475	162	20.24	6.63	26.87

Pitching Records for Atlanta Braves

	ERA	W	L	Pct	G	GS	CG	ShO	GF	Sv	IP	R	ER	H	2B	3B	HR	BB	IW	SO	HB	WP	BK
Glavine	2.55	20	11	.645	34	34	9	1	0	0	246.2	83	70	201	35	6	17	69	6	192	2	10	2
Smoltz	3.80	14	13	.519	36	36	5	0	0	0	229.2	101	97	206	38	7	16	77	1	148	3	20	2
Leibrandt	3.49	15	13	.536	36	36	1	1	0	0	229.2	105	89	212	38	5	18	56	3	128	4	5	3
Avery	3.38	18	8	.692	35	35	3	1	0	0	210.1	89	79	189	33	4	21	65	0	137	3	4	1
Smith P	5.06	1	3	.250	14	10	0	0	2	0	48.0	33	27	48	13	2	5	22	3	29	0	1	4
Reynoso	6.17	2	1	.667	6	5	0	0	1	0	23.1	18	16	26	4	3	4	10	1	10	3	2	0
Stanton M	2.88	5	5	.500	74	0	0	0	20	7	78.0	27	25	62	9	2	6	21	6	54	1	0	0
Mercker	2.58	5	3	.625	50	4	0	0	28	6	73.1	23	21	56	9	2	5	35	3	62	1	4	1
Berenguer	2.24	0	3	.000	49	0	0	0	35	17	64.1	18	16	43	7	2	5	20	2	53	3	0	0
Freeman M	3.00	1	0	1.000	34	0	0	0	6	1	48.0	19	16	37	6	0	2	13	1	34	2	4	0
Clancy	5.71	3	2	.600	24	0	0	0	9	3	34.2	23	22	36	8	4	3	14	1	17	1	5	0
St.Claire	4.08	0	0	.000	19	0	0	0	5	0	28.2	17	13	31	6	0	4	9	3	30	0	4	0
Mahler R	5.65	1	1	.500	13	2	0	0	1	0	28.2	20	18	33	9	0	2	13	1	10	2	1	0
Petry	5.55	0	0	.000	10	0	0	0	4	0	24.1	17	15	29	7	0	2	14	1	9	1	2	0
Parrett	6.33	1	2	.333	18	0	0	0	9	1	21.1	18	15	31	4	1	2	12	2	14	0	4	0
Wohlers	3.20	3	1	.750	17	0	0	0	4	2	19.2	7	7	17	5	1	1	13	3	13	2	0	0
Pena A	1.40	2	0	1.000	15	0	0	0	12	11	19.1	3	3	11	0	0	1	3	0	13	0	0	0
Sisk	5.02	2	1	.667	14	0	0	0	2	0	14.1	14	8	21	2	2	1	8	2	5	0	0	0
Castillo T	7.27	1	1	.500	7	0	0	0	5	0	8.2	9	7	13	1	0	3	5	0	8	0	0	0
Bielecki	0.00	0	0	.000	2	0	0	0	1	0	1.2	0	0	2	1	0	0	2	0	3	0	0	0
TOTALS	3.49	94	68	.580	507	162	18	3	144	48	1452.2	644	564	1304	235	41	118	481	39	969	28	66	13

Sabermetric Pitching Records for Atlanta Braves

	Adj	Expected			Opposing Batters												Supported				
	ERA	W	L	Pct	BFP	Avg	Slg	OBA	RC/G	GDP	SB	CS	PK	PKE	SH	SF	RSup	RSp/G	W	L	Pct
Avery	3.00	16	10	.601	868	.240	.372	.299	3.72	16	21	11	0	2	8	4	126	5.39	20	6	.764
Berenguer	1.96	2	1	.779	255	.189	.303	.261	2.68	3	3	1	0	0	2	2	23	3.22	2	1	.730
Bielecki	0.00	0	0	.000	9	.286	.429	.444	8.55	0	0	0	0	0	0	0	0	0.00	0	0	.000
Castillo T	6.23	1	1	.258	44	.342	.605	.419	10.56	0	0	0	0	0	1	0	9	9.35	1	1	.692
Clancy	4.93	2	3	.357	153	.267	.452	.336	5.62	2	2	0	1	0	1	2	17	4.41	2	3	.445
Freeman M	2.63	1	0	.662	190	.214	.283	.275	2.39	6	2	2	0	0	1	1	38	7.13	1	0	.880
Glavine	2.26	22	9	.725	989	.222	.330	.277	2.99	19	18	10	0	8	7	6	129	4.71	25	6	.812
Leibrandt	3.10	16	12	.585	949	.245	.363	.292	3.80	6	35	11	4	10	19	6	103	4.04	18	10	.630
Mahler R	5.02	1	1	.348	133	.282	.410	.364	5.77	1	6	3	0	0	1	0	14	4.40	1	1	.434
Mercker	2.21	6	2	.734	306	.211	.316	.303	3.51	5	10	0	0	0	2	2	29	3.56	6	2	.722
Parrett	5.48	1	2	.310	109	.326	.453	.402	7.76	1	1	0	0	0	2	0	13	5.48	2	1	.500
Pena A	0.93	2	0	.940	70	.167	.212	.203	1.23	2	0	0	0	0	1	0	2	0.93	1	1	.500
Petry	4.81	0	0	.368	116	.296	.429	.389	6.46	2	6	2	0	0	3	0	6	2.22	0	0	.176
Reynoso	5.40	1	2	.316	103	.299	.552	.390	7.21	2	1	1	5	0	3	0	12	4.63	1	2	.424
Sisk	4.40	1	2	.411	73	.333	.476	.403	7.94	2	2	0	0	0	1	1	16	10.04	3	0	.839
Smith P	4.50	2	2	.400	211	.262	.437	.335	5.53	4	13	1	0	0	2	4	25	4.69	2	2	.520
Smoltz	3.37	15	12	.543	947	.243	.360	.305	3.62	18	14	13	2	2	9	9	114	4.47	17	10	.637
St.Claire	3.45	0	0	.531	123	.282	.445	.333	4.96	1	1	3	0	0	3	1	12	3.77	0	0	.543
Stanton M	2.54	7	3	.677	314	.217	.325	.273	2.98	7	9	1	0	1	6	0	46	5.31	8	2	.814
Wohlers	2.75	3	1	.641	89	.239	.380	.368	5.24	3	5	0	0	0	2	1	15	6.86	3	1	.862
TOTALS	3.12	94	68	.580	6051	.240	.364	.303	3.80	100	149	59	12	23	74	39	749	4.64	112	50	.688

Batting 'Splits' Records for Atlanta Braves

	G	AB	Run	Hit	2B	3B	HR	TB	RBI	W	K	IW	HB	SB	CS	GI DP	SH	SF	Avg	Slug	OBP	Runs Ctd
SPLITS for Olson Greg																						
vs LHP	64	100	15	29	8	0	2	43	17	10	12	1	0	1	1	2	0	2	.290	.430	.348	15
vs RHP	118	311	31	70	17	0	4	99	27	34	36	2	3	0	0	11	2	2	.225	.318	.306	30
Home	64	202	25	58	11	0	6	87	31	15	18	2	0	0	0	8	1	4	.287	.431	.330	27
Away	69	209	21	41	14	0	0	55	13	29	30	1	3	1	1	5	1	0	.196	.263	.303	18
Grass	98	306	38	76	18	0	6	112	34	29	34	3	1	1	1	10	2	4	.248	.366	.312	34
Turf	35	105	8	23	7	0	0	30	10	15	14	0	2	0	0	3	0	0	.219	.286	.328	10
April/June	51	149	15	39	7	0	3	55	15	12	14	0	2	0	0	7	1	1	.262	.369	.323	17
July/October	82	262	31	60	18	0	3	87	29	32	34	3	1	1	1	6	1	3	.229	.332	.312	28
SPLITS for Pendleton																						
vs LHP	93	177	31	53	10	3	4	81	23	15	9	3	0	5	1	7	2	2	.299	.458	.351	27
vs RHP	139	409	63	134	24	5	18	222	63	28	61	5	1	5	1	9	5	5	.328	.543	.368	81
Home	75	285	51	97	18	3	13	160	48	18	30	4	1	6	1	7	1	4	.340	.561	.377	60
Away	78	301	43	90	16	5	9	143	38	25	40	4	0	4	1	9	6	3	.299	.475	.350	49
Grass	112	426	70	139	27	4	18	228	69	30	47	7	1	7	1	13	5	6	.326	.535	.367	82
Turf	41	160	24	48	7	4	4	75	17	13	23	1	0	3	1	3	2	1	.300	.469	.351	26
April/June	65	226	41	74	16	3	7	117	32	22	24	5	0	7	2	5	6	3	.327	.518	.382	45
July/October	88	360	53	113	18	5	15	186	54	21	46	3	1	3	0	11	1	4	.314	.517	.350	63
SPLITS for Smith Lo																						
vs LHP	63	115	25	39	9	1	0	50	11	18	22	1	3	1	0	2	0	2	.339	.435	.435	24
vs RHP	97	238	33	58	10	0	7	89	33	32	42	2	6	8	5	2	2	0	.244	.374	.348	33
Home	63	193	33	56	10	0	6	84	31	23	35	0	4	2	2	1	2	2	.290	.435	.374	34
Away	59	160	25	41	9	1	1	55	13	27	29	3	5	7	3	3	0	0	.256	.344	.380	23
Grass	92	280	42	78	14	0	7	113	37	39	48	2	6	4	4	3	2	2	.279	.404	.376	45
Turf	30	73	16	19	5	1	0	26	7	11	16	1	3	5	1	1	0	0	.260	.356	.379	11
April/June	49	140	21	36	6	1	3	53	20	20	26	1	4	4	2	2	1	1	.257	.379	.364	21
July/October	73	213	37	61	13	0	4	86	24	30	38	2	5	5	3	2	1	1	.286	.404	.386	36
SPLITS for Atlanta Braves (all batters except pitchers)																						
vs LHP	939	1591	240	425	81	11	36	636	225	157	241	18	6	50	20	33	29	16	.267	.400	.332	216
vs RHP	1643	3865	509	982	174	19	105	1509	479	406	665	37	26	115	56	71	57	29	.254	.390	.327	507
Home	1200	2709	418	739	127	12	83	1139	388	275	427	28	15	79	30	58	35	24	.273	.420	.340	396
Away	1149	2747	331	668	128	18	58	1006	316	288	479	27	17	86	46	46	51	21	.243	.366	.317	329
Grass	1710	4008	568	1058	189	19	114	1627	529	403	641	46	22	110	54	83	60	35	.264	.406	.332	548
Turf	639	1448	181	349	66	11	27	518	175	160	265	9	10	55	22	21	26	10	.241	.358	.319	175
April/June	1064	2472	336	647	115	18	60	978	320	242	392	28	18	88	42	50	42	20	.262	.396	.330	328
July/October	1285	2984	413	760	140	12	81	1167	384	321	514	27	14	77	34	54	44	25	.255	.391	.327	395

1991 SPLITS FOR Atlanta Braves

BATTING SPLITS

	AVG	AB	R	H	2B	3B	HR	RBI	SB	CS	BB	K	OBA	SPCT
Total	.258	5456	749	1407	255	30	141	704	165	76	563	906	.328	.393

	#Pit	#P/PA	GB	FB	G/F	G	IBB	HB	SH	SF	GDP
Miscellaneous	21913	3.54	1921	1648	1.17	161	55	32	86	45	104

	AVG	AB	R	H	2B	3B	HR	RBI	SB	CS	BB	K	OBA	SPCT
vs. Left	.267	1591	...	425	81	11	36	225	50	20	157	241	.332	.400
vs. Right	.254	3865	...	982	174	19	105	479	115	56	406	665	.327	.390
Home	.273	2709	418	739	127	12	83	388	79	30	275	427	.340	.420
Away	.243	2747	331	668	128	18	58	316	86	46	288	479	.317	.366
None on	.249	3098	...	772	137	16	81	81	0	0	283	527	.315	.382
Runners on	.269	2358	...	635	118	14	60	623	165	76	280	379	.345	.408
April	.237	603	75	143	28	5	12	71	22	9	61	95	.305	.360
May	.287	882	145	253	41	6	27	139	32	17	98	132	.360	.439
June	.254	987	116	251	46	7	21	110	34	16	83	165	.316	.379
July	.281	866	145	243	43	4	28	130	29	15	86	136	.345	.436
August	.255	1009	127	257	42	2	28	121	22	12	97	177	.320	.384
September	.234	943	115	221	50	5	20	108	22	6	121	165	.323	.362
October	.235	166	26	39	5	1	5	25	4	1	17	36	.310	.367
None on/out	.268	1377	...	369	58	9	45	45	0	0	118	214	.329	.421
Scoring Posn	.285	1445	...	412	79	9	36	550	27	9	205	235	.367	.427
Close & Late	.242	823	...	199	34	6	13	106	25	12	100	145	.327	.345
Bases Loaded	.316	117	...	37	7	1	3	97	0	0	8	13	.328	.470
Batting #1	.298	667	127	199	20	4	12	61	84	25	74	88	.371	.394
Batting #2	.276	663	113	183	30	5	12	73	17	8	57	76	.333	.391
Batting #3	.288	643	101	185	37	6	20	90	14	3	61	94	.353	.457
Batting #4	.270	608	111	164	36	3	37	133	23	15	84	120	.361	.521
Batting #5	.285	599	89	171	40	1	24	111	12	13	77	100	.366	.476
Batting #6	.229	584	64	134	21	5	20	84	6	5	81	73	.321	.385
Batting #7	.237	590	53	140	34	2	11	77	2	3	50	90	.299	.358
Batting #8	.245	575	59	141	21	2	4	48	4	2	39	96	.294	.310
Batting #9	.171	527	32	90	16	2	1	27	3	2	40	169	.231	.214
As p	.151	352	13	53	9	2	0	16	2	0	21	127	.198	.188
As c	.239	590	55	141	32	1	12	74	1	1	54	81	.304	.358
As 1b	.234	593	66	139	30	1	21	93	3	6	48	86	.292	.395
As 2b	.284	609	76	173	32	7	10	77	4	6	67	50	.354	.409
As 3b	.311	644	104	200	38	8	23	89	11	2	50	74	.357	.502
As ss	.248	544	64	135	14	2	5	48	6	4	49	104	.313	.309
As lf	.263	624	104	164	23	4	11	73	34	12	85	106	.359	.365
As cf	.261	628	115	164	37	3	33	110	47	20	77	110	.344	.487
As rf	.290	618	105	179	29	2	23	98	47	19	87	106	.377	.455
Outfield	.271	1870	324	507	89	9	67	281	128	51	249	322	.360	.436
0.0 count	.337	879	...	296	54	6	25	140	...	...	3	0	.341	.497
After (0.1)	.231	2325	...	537	98	13	43	248	...	...	124	592	.270	.340
After (1.0)	.255	2251	...	574	103	11	73	316	...	...	388	314	.366	.408
Two strikes	.171	2324	...	397	73	9	30	210	...	...	177	901	.231	.249
Grass	.264	4008	568	1058	189	19	114	529	110	54	403	641	.332	.406
Turf	.241	1448	181	349	66	11	27	175	55	22	160	265	.319	.358
Day	.257	1396	182	359	60	6	37	172	49	21	129	240	.322	.388
Night	.258	4060	567	1048	195	24	104	532	116	55	434	666	.331	.395
Inning 1.6	.259	3691	500	957	167	19	104	472	114	60	365	613	.327	.399
Inning 7+	.255	1765	249	450	88	11	37	232	51	16	198	293	.332	.380
vs.Min	.000	0	0	0	0	0	0	0	0	0	0	0	.000	.000
vs.ChN	.296	406	62	120	21	3	5	54	13	6	35	58	.348	.399
vs.Cin	.254	626	89	159	28	6	17	85	17	5	57	126	.315	.399
vs.Hou	.243	606	71	147	27	4	14	66	19	5	67	110	.316	.370
vs.LA	.217	604	62	131	23	2	9	55	24	8	70	112	.302	.306
vs.Mon	.266	403	53	107	14	4	9	49	14	4	41	63	.336	.387
vs.NYN	.254	386	49	98	21	3	13	48	6	5	29	51	.310	.425
vs.Phi	.279	437	69	122	28	1	12	67	12	6	53	76	.361	.430
vs.Pit	.270	389	71	105	19	2	16	66	21	7	49	66	.354	.452
vs.StL	.286	399	73	114	24	1	13	73	11	10	50	63	.363	.449
vs.SD	.248	604	71	150	22	1	16	67	9	13	56	91	.310	.368
vs.SF	.258	596	79	154	28	3	17	74	19	7	56	90	.329	.401

PITCHING SPLITS

	ERA	W	L	SV	SVOP	GS	CG	SHO	IP	H	ER	HR	BB	IBB	K
Total	3.49	94	67	48	59	162	18	8	1452.2	1304	563	118	481	39	969

	#Pit	#P/IP	GB	FB	G/F	BRp9	RA	WP	BK	SH	SF	R	HB	Hld
Miscellaneous	22352	15.39	2043	1553	1.32	11.23	345	66	13	74	39	644	28	37

	ERA	W	L	SV	SVOP	GS	CG	SHO	IP	H	ER	HR	BB	IBB	K
ST	3.46	72	49	0	0	162	18	3	1009.0	897	388	80	310	13	661
REL	3.57	22	19	48	59	0	0	0	443.2	407	176	38	171	26	308
Home	3.81	48	33	25	29	81	6	0	740.0	711	313	73	227	17	461
Away	3.17	46	35	23	30	81	12	3	712.2	593	251	45	254	22	508
April	2.95	8	10	3	4	18	2	1	164.2	141	54	8	63	8	114
May	3.18	17	9	8	11	26	4	0	235.0	222	83	26	60	2	153
June	4.12	12	17	6	8	29	2	1	258.0	250	118	21	93	8	164
July	4.31	16	10	8	8	26	2	0	225.2	205	108	23	80	5	138
August	3.31	19	11	10	11	30	4	0	269.0	242	99	23	86	8	196
September	2.93	18	10	10	14	28	3	1	255.1	207	83	13	80	8	179
October	3.80	4	1	3	3	5	1	0	45.0	37	19	4	19	0	25
Grass	3.55	70	50	36	42	120	14	2	1075.1	969	424	96	331	24	683
Turf	3.34	24	18	12	17	42	4	1	377.1	335	140	22	150	15	286
Day	3.49	22	19	10	13	41	6	0	364.0	328	141	31	114	9	256
Night	3.50	72	49	38	46	121	12	3	1088.2	976	423	87	367	30	713
vs.Min	0.00	0	0	0	0	0	0	0	0.0	0	0	0	0	0	0
vs.ChN	4.50	6	6	3	4	12	1	0	104.0	93	52	18	30	1	59
vs.Cin	4.09	11	7	6	7	18	1	0	165.0	159	75	14	68	5	112
vs.Hou	2.25	13	5	6	7	18	3	1	168.0	127	42	7	62	3	127
vs.LA	3.16	7	11	0	0	18	4	2	162.1	146	57	9	41	6	103
vs.Mon	5.33	5	7	5	7	12	1	0	103.0	123	61	10	41	1	91
vs.NYN	2.69	9	3	6	6	12	2	0	107.0	78	32	8	27	3	46
vs.Phi	4.08	5	7	1	4	12	0	0	108.0	112	49	12	40	6	89
vs.Pit	3.86	9	3	7	7	12	0	0	105.0	99	45	11	38	1	54
vs.StL	2.30	9	3	2	3	12	1	0	109.1	79	28	4	35	5	67
vs.SD	3.18	11	7	8	10	18	2	0	164.0	143	58	14	47	1	118
vs.SF	3.73	9	9	4	4	18	3	0	157.0	145	65	11	52	7	103

OPPOSING BATTERS VS. PITCHERS.

	AVG	AB	R	H	2B	3B	HR	RBI	SB	CS	BB	K	OBA	SPCT
Total	.240	5429	644	1304	235	41	118	597	149	59	481	969	.303	.364
vs. Left	.263	1870	...	492	91	21	35	212	55	24	206	317	.335	.390
vs. Right	.228	3559	...	812	144	20	83	385	94	35	275	652	.286	.350
ST	.239	3753	438	897	165	28	80	381	105	47	310	661	.298	.362
REL	.243	1676	206	407	70	13	38	216	44	12	171	308	.316	.368
Home	.254	2801	368	711	127	19	73	340	64	32	227	461	.311	.391
Away	.226	2628	276	593	108	22	45	257	85	27	254	508	.295	.335
None on	.233	3198	...	744	135	18	66	66	0	0	262	572	.294	.348
Runners on	.251	2231	...	560	100	23	52	531	149	59	219	397	.317	.386
None on/out	.246	1392	...	342	67	7	36	36	0	0	104	234	.301	.381
Scoring Posn	.259	1295	...	336	60	13	34	464	36	15	169	241	.341	.405
vs 1st Batr	.241	316	...	76	11	2	5	35	1	3	24	55	.302	.335
1st IP	.247	1750	176	433	68	21	41	247	50	25	183	337	.321	.381
Inning 1.6	.240	3611	439	866	159	31	75	411	114	47	328	650	.304	.363
Inning 7+	.241	1818	205	438	76	10	43	186	35	12	153	319	.302	.365
Close & Late	.217	903	...	196	31	5	13	83	15	9	89	167	.290	.306
0.0 count	.312	791	...	247	53	4	17	111	...	...	26	0	.334	.454
After (0.1)	.202	2455	...	496	90	16	33	209	...	...	117	628	.241	.292
After (1.0)	.257	2183	...	561	92	21	68	277	...	...	338	341	.357	.412
Two strikes	.171	2484	...	424	71	16	30	184	...	...	204	968	.236	.248
Pitch 1.15	.251	1529	...	384	63	16	41	176	40	19	148	275	.321	.394
Pitch 16.30	.230	1082	...	249	44	9	17	120	33	9	101	213	.295	.335
Pitch 31.45	.237	734	...	174	29	5	14	74	15	8	65	146	.299	.347
Pitch 46.60	.234	611	...	143	35	4	12	68	19	9	54	98	.299	.363
Pitch 61.75	.202	540	...	109	25	3	13	55	20	4	41	105	.258	.331
Pitch 76.90	.281	455	...	128	23	2	10	48	12	8	39	55	.339	.407
Pitch 91.105	.252	322	...	81	9	2	3	36	8	1	20	59	.295	.320
Pitch 106.20	.256	133	...	34	7	0	6	17	1	1	11	10	.317	.444
Pitch 121.35	.125	24	...	3	0	0	2	4	1	0	3	8	.214	.375
Pitch 136.50	.000	1	...	0	0	0	0	0	0	0	0	0	.000	.000

Los Angeles Dodgers

Don Malcolm

LOS ANGELES											
YEAR	1982	1983	1984	1985	1986	1987	1988	1989	1990	1991	TOT
W	88	91	79	95	73	73	94	77	86	93	849
L	74	71	83	67	89	89	67	83	76	69	768
WPCT	0.543	0.562	0.488	0.586	0.451	0.451	0.584	0.481	0.531	0.574	0.525
R	691	654	580	682	638	635	628	554	728	665	6455
RA	612	609	600	579	679	675	544	536	685	565	6084
PWPT	0.560	0.536	0.483	0.581	0.469	0.469	0.571	0.517	0.530	0.581	0.530
PythW	91	87	78	94	76	76	93	84	86	94	86
PythL	71	75	84	68	86	86	69	78	76	68	76
LUCK	-3	4	1	1	-3	-3	1	-7	0	-1	-10

Defensive Efficiency Record: .7061

WHO'S RUNNING THE STORE?

Bill James was right: to hell with sabermetrics. The world doesn't deserve it. Like most so-called "breakthroughs," it has been misapplied, distorted, or just plain ignored. A sabermetrician is nothing more than an iconoclast with an incurable addiction to baseball statistics, and wonders why the numbers say one thing and everyone inside the business of baseball says something else. (Answer: it's just about like any other business.)

That broadside out of the way, let's talk about business. Funny business, Dodger style. Baseball as practiced by the Dodgers has a lot more smoke and fog than film noir and a lot less narrative coherence. (Which is saying a mouthful, since even the best film noir was always kinda shaky in terms of cause and effect.)

The Dodgers are going through top-name players like film noir goes through plot twists. More and more, Fred Claire is beginning to resemble the prototypical noir hero: the seemingly moral man fatally tempted by lust, money, or both. Just like the characters portrayed by Edward G. Robinson in two seminal Fritz Lang noirs of the 40s (The Woman in the Window and Scarlet Street), Claire is being tempted by visions of virtually limitless resources. His own imagination is feeding his actions, fueling his desires, pushing him into a fatal assignation. But who would have thought that the femme fatale, played so well in the two Lang films by Joan Bennett, would turn out to be—Darryl Strawberry??

(You know, this isn't as far-fetched a metaphor as one might think. In Scarlet Street, Dan Duryea—that quintessential cad—has a nickname for Joan Bennett. It's a pet name symbolizing the wanton nature of their bond, one that reveals the manipulative aspect of sexuality at its most primal. The nickname? "Lazy Legs." And what has been the rap on Darryl Strawberry since about day seventy-three of his major league career? That he's lazy. "Selfish.")

How much of a baseball executive's acquisitive zeal is based on some lustful desire to possess the ballplayer's basic set of statistics, an erotic attachment to a set of idealized numbers? It's just what Brock Hanke was pointing out when he did his hilarious routine about Roy Hofheinz and Jimmy Wynn. "We got the Toy Cannon." (Remember that they actually called Wynn this? Need we go into the imagery associated with a cannon, or the symbology of its uses??) "He's gonna hit .330"—pronounced "three thuhty"—"hit 30 homers" (pronounced "homuhs"), "an' drive in 130 runs." Idealized numbers, to be sure. Not as ideal, perhaps, as 38-23-36, or so some would declaim, but baseball's curves are meant to be hit, not pawed. So the baseball executive, being in the main a prototypical male—plus or minus a few foot fetishes—must create this sublimated erotic aura around a set of numbers that represent baseball's version of consummation. Hence Darryl Strawberry is to Fred Claire what Joan Bennett is to Edward G. Robinson—a spoiled-but-still-enticing tendril of doom, oozing with the rotten perfume of corruption (to paraphrase General Sternwood in The Big Sleep).

And it is the aura of lust surrounding what Darryl's numbers might be, what orgasmic statistical heights might be reached, etc., etc., if only he were motivated, that has set Fred Claire on a course of action right out of Scarlet Street. But in the case of Darryl Strawberry, we aren't talking about a languid, leggy strumpet: what we have here is a high-strung, high-cost, $20 million outfielder. All right, a languid, leggy $20 million outfielder. In order to get the production his eroticizied calculations have projected for Darryl, Fred must keep Straw happy. He must give him what he wants. And ultimately, inevitably, he must allow Darryl Strawberry to run the Dodgers, to set the team's priorities, to dictate who must stay and who must go, to pontificate and insinuate over matters usually reserved for the secrecy of the general manager's office, such as who should be acquired to make the Dodger clubhouse a place of worship for the swollen and easily bruised ego of the Straw.

And now, for the lawyers out there in the audience, let me present my evidence. My simple, single, yet unassailable piece of evidence.

Eric Davis.

Ever since Darryl Strawberry was outfitted in Dodger Blue, there have been rumblings and whisperings—in the fringes of the mainstream media, which means that it's the truth but no one is supposed to print it—that Eric Davis, a tight buddy of the Straw's, would wind up in Los Angeles. As a matter of fact, Strawberry himself began campaigning for such a scenario during his last season with the Mets—before he even signed with the Dodgers.

So what do we see after a season where the Dodgers showed that their pitching was still potent but fragile? We see them trade away two pitchers, one of whom the only pitcher to throw more than 200 innings for LA in the past three seasons, for the most brittle of superstars.

But look at those stats. 80 stolen bases. (He hasn't come close to that in five years.) 37 home runs. (He's only been over 30 one other time.) Don't be surprised if Fred Claire takes to calling him "Eric the Cannon."

For Fred Claire, this extremely risky trade is based upon a bizarre combination of lust, avarice, naivete, and arrogance, a good bit of which has been fueled (perhaps brought to a broil is more appropriate) by the signing of Strawberry. How many of you lawyers out there are aware that the Dodgers, with their vaunted offense last year, actually scored fewer runs than they did in 1990, when Lenny Harris and Stan Javier led off, and there was no Straw? (Or Brett Butler, for that matter.)

Don't get me wrong. Eric Davis is, or was, a great player. Even in a lost season, he gives you a great deal of bang for the buck. He was not close to being a great player last year, for many reasons. The question remains whether he will be a great player again. Riverfront Stadium is a much better park to hit in than Dodger Stadium. Davis' power totals could be impacted significantly by the move.

But Fred Claire decided that if he could make the Straw happy, he'd magically add those 12 missing homers (the 12 that, added to the 28 Darryl hit in '91, give Fred that tingly fortysomething thrill) back into the kitty. And he'd have a happy Davis, too, which would make for God knows what type of synergy. Why, the two of 'em might hit 100 homers next season if they were happy.

Right. And Edward G. Robinson might get to take a tumble with Joan Bennett, too. Fred's delusions of grandeur aren't quite as pathetic as what Fritz Lang does to Edward G. in Scarlet Street, but they're clearly in the same continuum. What's far more serious about the situation Fred finds himself in is that it signals a distinct de facto power shift in the Dodger organization.

It used to be that the Dodger organization was something akin to a vast edifice, an imperial force unto itself. The myth of the Dodger farm system is still with us, long after its heyday, as some kind of supernatural structure that turns out Hall of Fame players like a heavenly assembly line (is it possible to forget—no matter how much one tries—the Big Dodger in the Sky?). But what Fred Claire is doing is to create a huge rift in the middle of a myth the Dodgers are still trying to sell. By catering to the Straw, he is creating a tidal wave of opposing tensions in the organization that can only be destructive. The ultimate victim of these destructive tensions will almost certainly be Fred Claire himself, and probably before the end of the Straw's five-year contract.

Darryl Strawberry is a great ballplayer. He is probably, however, neither a great general manager nor an acute judge of baseball talent and how it should be blended together to make a winning team. He's been on one World Series team in nine years, so he is no expert by example on winning. Therefore he probably should not be making pronouncements about who should stay or go in order to put the Dodgers over the top. But if Fred Claire continues his policy of rapprochement and accommodation, Darryl will only get bolder. The question "Who is running the Dodgers?" has come out into the open with an almost hysterical insistence. Fred Claire needs to make a stand soon, if he wants to be the person in charge in 1994.

WHY DO YOU THINK THEY CALL IT A ROTATION?

That great strong suit of the Dodgers is a lot more interchangeable than the Boys in blue would like you to believe. Consider the following chart of the Dodgers starting pitchers—actuals in 1988-91, projected for 1992:

YEAR	1988	1989	1990	1991	1992
PITCHERS IN DODGERS STARTING ROTATION	Hershiser Leary Tudor** Belcher (Valenzuela) Sutton	Hershiser Leary** Belcher Morgan (Tudor) Valenzuela Martinez Wetteland	(Hershiser) Martinez Belcher Morgan Neidlinger Hartley Valenzuela Cook	Hershiser Martinez Belcher Morgan Ojeda Gross	Hershiser Martinez Candiotti Ojeda Gross
SYMBOLS:	(pitcher injured) **pitcher acquired or traded during season				

The Dodgers would like you to believe that they are a pitching-rich organization that develops an incredible abundance of Hall of Fame-caliber hurlers. Don't you believe it. Consulting the chart shows that, going into 1992, the Dodgers have two starters who are products of their own farm system, Orel Hershiser and Ramon Martinez. The other home-grown pitcher (Valenzuela) bit the dust after ten seasons. Tim Belcher, although he was brought up from the minors by the dodgers, was in reality acquired from the A's. Several other pitchers brought up from the minors in 1990 during the Dodgers pitching crunch (Neidlinger, Hartley) were originally from other farm systems. John Wetteland, the only other Dodger farmhand on the list, began as a starter and didn't cut it, was given a bizarre trial as a reliever and, in part due to the self-fulfilling prophecy of failure imposed upon him, got demoted and finally traded to Montreal, where he may actually blossom.

So there is very little stability in the Dodger starting rotation, partially due to the vagaries of the latter-day phase of the free agency situation, but also due to the burnout factor that issues forth from Tommy Lasorda's fifties-based managerial methodologies.

It is important to remember that both Tommy Lasorda and that other destroyer of pitchers' arms, Roger Craig, spent many years in the Dodger organiation during the fifties. Tommy's practices took at least five years off Valenzuela's career, and may still have a significant effect on Hershiser's longevity. Such a trend may very well be continuing with Ramon Martinez, who is being pitched too much at an early age and may very well go the route of Fernando. In Ramon's case, it could happen sooner, since he is a more fragile body type. It certainly affected the Dodgers' pennant hopes in 1991, when the starting rotation required juggling due to Ramon's tender and tired arm.

The Dodgers had incredible good fortune to bring the number of runs allowed back into contending range last season. The bullpen problem was attacked by throwing as many available bodies at the problem as could found. And, miraculously, it worked. But to count on such success again is to go beyond wishful thinking all the way to psychotic delusion. The Dodgers have, as usual, too many right-handed relievers. Jay Howell is injury-prone and aging; Roger McDowell appears to be on the wane; Jim Gott doesn't seem to be viewed as the closer even though he may be the best bet. It figures to be another year of pseudo-committee and riding the hot hand for the Dodgers.

The main piece of luck the Dodgers have going for them is their ballpark. It makes all of their pitchers about three-quarters of a run better. This is one reason why, despite all of the inchoate machination that they employ with respect to the structure of the team in general and the makeup of the pitching staff in particular, they will likely continue to contend—but fall short—for another couple of years or so. But this Dodger rotation is the oldest and most brittle one yet. There are a few pitching prospects in the wings to maybe take up the slack for Ojeda and Gross (who failed abysmally as a starter last season and has a great deal to prove this season): Pedro Martinez, Ramon's younger brother, is perhaps the best of the bunch. But by 1994 the Dodgers will need to add three new starters to their rotation, and unless they continue to go shopping, I don't think they'll be able to sustain even the level of quality that they have.

GET A REAL JOB, JUAN...

Almost as irritating as the Darryl Strawberry-runs-the-Dodgers situation is the ongoing silliness with Juan Samuel. He is, as you may know, a far-less-than-wonderful second baseman, and his hitting rates as marginal when you consider where the Dodgers tried to bat him last season. Why not just give Harris and Sharperson the job at second and let Dave Hansen have a crack at third base?

Perhaps the real reason has to do with the Dodgers' not-so-subterranean fear that Jose Offerman is not going to make it. The disaster scenario calls for Lenny Harris to move to shortstop, and it's clear that the Dodgers don't want to play Sharperson full-time. Not having another second baseman means that if Offerman turns into a disaster, the Dodgers are forced to play Harris and Sharperson full time at short and second.

What this does, though, is mortgage the future of the one rookie the Dodgers should be trying to develop as a bonafide member of the offense. Dave Hansen is ready. If the Dodgers don't want to risk a rookie left side of the infield, then they should trade for Ozzie Smith and try to develop another shortstop via the draft. Juan Samuel is not a band-aid for the Dodgers' skittishness, he is a tourniquet being applied around Dave Hansen's neck.

THE FEARLESS PICK

Oh, yes. When all is said and done, where will the Dodgers finish this year? Why, in second place, of course. The Giants and Astros can't win, but one of the remaining three teams (Reds, Braves, Padres—in that order of likelihood) will make the Dodgers into bridesmaids for the third year in a row.

Los Angeles Dodgers Home Park Performance Factors

	Outs	Runs	Hits	2b	3b	HR	W	K	SH	SF	HBP	IBB	SB	CS	GDP
Home LH Batters	1.023	.973	.979	1.030	1.327	.940	.962	1.045	.926	1.094	1.327	.973	.988	.908	1.142
Home RH Batters	.989	1.051	1.049	1.265	2.670	1.137	.964	.962	.870	1.265	1.001	.858	.916	1.070	.945
All Home Batters	1.008	.979	1.003	1.112	1.604	.964	.942	1.006	.909	1.036	1.142	.885	.983	.933	1.033
Opp LH Batters	1.015	1.098	1.021	1.092	1.279	1.033	1.028	.936	.855	1.200	1.138	1.110	1.070	.842	1.564
Opp RH Batters	1.058	1.126	1.073	1.222	1.793	1.114	1.105	1.002	1.028	.940	2.021	1.317	.960	1.072	1.356
All Opp Batters	1.044	1.097	1.054	1.176	1.503	1.090	1.063	.981	.946	1.047	1.603	1.154	1.039	.974	1.391
All LH Batters	1.020	1.012	.994	1.054	1.300	.971	.984	.997	.895	1.130	1.245	1.039	1.019	.885	1.262
All RH Batters	1.033	1.100	1.064	1.242	2.074	1.112	1.053	.987	.959	1.008	1.400	1.198	.944	1.073	1.191
All Batters	1.025	1.035	1.028	1.143	1.548	1.024	.999	.990	.930	1.042	1.334	1.030	1.010	.955	1.189

Conventional Batting Records for Los Angeles Dodgers

	G	AB	Run	Hit	2B	3B	HR	TB	RBI	W	K	IW	HB	SB	CS	BRng Eff	GI DP	SH	SF	Avg	Slug	OBP	Runs Ctd
Scioscia	119	345	39	91	16	2	8	135	40	47	32	3	3	4	3	.273	5	5	4	.264	.391	.353	51
Murray E	153	576	69	150	23	1	19	232	96	55	74	17	0	10	3	.239	17	0	8	.260	.403	.321	74
Samuel	153	594	74	161	22	6	12	231	58	49	133	4	3	23	8	.400	8	10	3	.271	.389	.328	79
Harris L	145	429	59	123	16	1	3	150	38	37	32	5	5	12	3	.564	17	12	2	.287	.350	.349	52
Griffin Alf	109	350	27	85	6	2	0	95	27	22	49	5	1	5	4	.447	5	7	5	.243	.271	.286	28
Daniels	137	461	54	115	15	1	17	183	73	63	116	4	1	6	1	.370	9	0	6	.249	.397	.337	66
Butler	161	615	112	182	13	5	2	211	38	108	79	4	1	38	28	.539	3	4	2	.296	.343	.401	93
Strawberry	139	505	86	134	22	4	28	248	99	75	125	4	3	10	8	.559	8	0	5	.265	.491	.361	92
Carter G	101	248	22	61	14	0	6	93	26	22	26	1	7	2	2	.341	11	1	2	.246	.375	.323	28
Sharperson	105	216	24	60	11	2	2	81	20	25	24	0	1	1	3	.366	2	10	0	.278	.375	.355	30
Javier	121	176	21	36	5	3	1	50	11	16	36	0	0	7	1	.520	4	3	2	.205	.284	.268	14
Gwynn C	94	139	18	35	5	1	5	57	22	10	23	1	1	1	0	.550	5	1	3	.252	.410	.301	17
Offerman	52	113	10	22	2	0	0	24	3	25	32	2	1	3	2	.320	5	1	0	.195	.212	.345	10
Hamilton J	41	94	4	21	4	0	1	28	14	4	21	0	0	0	0	.286	2	1	0	.223	.298	.255	7
Martinez R	33	77	6	9	1	0	1	13	9	1	25	0	0	0	0	.300	1	8	0	.117	.169	.128	2
Morgan M	34	76	2	7	0	0	0	7	3	1	11	0	0	0	0	.167	1	8	2	.092	.092	.101	1
Webster M	58	74	12	21	5	1	1	31	10	9	21	0	0	0	1	.600	0	1	0	.284	.419	.361	12
Belcher	33	67	3	8	2	0	0	10	3	0	26	0	0	0	0	.167	1	7	0	.119	.149	.119	1
Ojeda	31	56	2	9	0	0	1	12	3	3	10	0	0	0	0	.000	1	6	1	.161	.214	.200	3
Hansen	53	56	3	15	4	0	1	22	5	2	12	0	0	1	0	.429	2	0	0	.268	.393	.293	6
Hershiser	21	31	6	8	2	0	0	10	2	3	8	0	0	1	0	.167	0	4	0	.258	.323	.324	4
Gonzalez Jo	42	28	3	0	0	0	0	0	0	2	9	0	0	0	0	.429	0	0	0	.000	.000	.067	0
Gross K	48	25	4	7	1	0	0	8	3	2	14	0	0	0	0	.333	0	2	0	.280	.320	.333	3
Hernandez C	15	14	1	3	1	0	0	4	1	0	5	0	1	1	0	.667	2	0	1	.214	.286	.250	1
Karros	14	14	0	1	1	0	0	2	1	1	6	0	0	0	0	.000	0	0	0	.071	.143	.133	0
Lyons Bar	9	9	0	0	0	0	0	0	0	0	2	0	0	0	0	.500	0	0	0	.000	.000	.000	0
Goodwin	16	7	3	1	0	0	0	1	0	0	0	0	0	1	1	.750	0	0	0	.143	.143	.143	0
Hartley	40	4	0	0	0	0	0	0	0	0	1	0	0	0	0	.000	1	0	0	.000	.000	.000	0
Smith G	5	3	1	0	0	0	0	0	0	0	2	0	0	0	0	.000	0	1	0	.000	.000	.000	0
Gott	55	2	0	1	0	0	0	1	0	0	1	0	0	0	0	.000	0	1	0	.500	.500	.500	1
Crews	60	1	0	0	0	0	0	0	0	1	1	0	0	0	0	.000	0	0	0	.000	.000	.500	0
Davis Butch	1	1	0	0	0	0	0	0	0	0	0	0	0	0	0	.000	0	0	0	.000	.000	.000	0
Cook D	20	1	0	0	0	0	0	0	0	0	1	0	0	0	0	.000	0	1	0	.000	.000	.000	0
Wilson S	11	1	0	0	0	0	0	0	0	0	0	0	0	0	0	.000	0	0	0	.000	.000	.000	0
Candelaria	59	0	0	0	0	0	0	0	0	0	0	0	0	0	0	.000	0	0	0	.000	.000	.000	0
Howell Jay	44	0	0	0	0	0	0	0	0	0	0	0	0	0	0	.000	0	0	0	.000	.000	.000	0
McDowell R	34	0	0	0	0	0	0	0	0	0	0	0	0	0	0	.000	0	0	0	.000	.000	.000	0
Wetteland	6	0	0	0	0	0	0	0	0	0	0	0	0	0	0	.000	0	0	0	.000	.000	.000	0
Christopher	3	0	0	0	0	0	0	0	0	0	0	0	0	0	0	.000	0	0	0	.000	.000	.000	0
TOTALS	2375	5408	665	1366	191	29	108	1939	605	583	957	50	28	126	68	.424	110	94	46	.253	.359	.326	653

Sabermetric Batting Records for Los Angeles Dodgers

	Ball Park Adjusted								Runs		Run/									
	AB	Run	Hit	2B	3B	HR	RBI	W	SO	Avg	Slug	OBP	Ctd	Outs	27o	OW%	OG	OWAR	DWAR	TWAR
Butler	622	115	181	13	6	1	38	107	78	.291	.336	.395	92	474	5.24	.656	18	5.37	1.31	6.68
Carter G	255	23	64	17	0	6	28	22	25	.251	.388	.332	31	207	4.04	.531	8	1.39	0.45	1.85
Daniels	466	55	114	15	1	16	74	62	114	.245	.384	.331	62	370	4.52	.587	14	3.25	0.52	3.76
Davis Butch	1	0	0	0	0	0	0	0	0	.000	.000	.000	0	1	0.00	.000	0	-0.01	0.00	-0.01
Gonzalez Jo	28	3	0	0	0	0	0	2	8	.000	.000	.067	0	28	0.00	.000	1	-0.36	0.08	-0.29
Goodwin	6	3	0	0	0	0	0	0	0	.000	.000	.000	0	6	0.00	.000	0	-0.08	0.03	-0.05
Griffin Alf	358	28	87	6	3	0	27	22	48	.243	.277	.285	29	291	2.69	.334	11	-0.17	1.18	1.01
Gwynn C	139	18	34	5	1	4	22	9	22	.245	.381	.289	14	114	3.32	.433	4	0.35	0.17	0.52
Hamilton J	96	4	22	4	0	1	15	4	20	.229	.302	.260	7	76	2.49	.300	3	-0.14	-0.00	-0.14
Hansen	55	3	14	4	0	0	5	1	11	.255	.327	.268	4	43	2.51	.304	2	-0.07	0.11	0.04
Harris L	433	61	122	16	1	2	38	36	31	.282	.337	.344	49	347	3.81	.502	13	1.96	0.72	2.68
Hernandez C	14	1	3	1	0	0	1	0	4	.214	.286	.250	1	14	1.93	.205	1	-0.08	0.01	-0.07
Javier	180	21	37	5	4	1	11	16	35	.206	.294	.268	15	151	2.68	.333	6	-0.10	0.24	0.14
Karros	14	0	1	1	0	0	1	1	5	.071	.143	.133	0	13	0.00	.000	0	-0.17	0.02	-0.15
Lyons Bar	9	0	0	0	0	0	0	0	1	.000	.000	.000	0	9	0.00	.000	0	-0.12	-0.00	-0.12
Murray E	591	71	154	26	1	19	98	55	73	.261	.404	.320	75	467	4.34	.566	17	3.74	0.69	4.43
Offerman	115	10	22	2	0	0	3	25	31	.191	.209	.340	9	100	2.43	.291	4	-0.22	0.06	-0.16
Samuel	613	80	170	27	13	13	62	50	130	.277	.427	.334	89	472	5.09	.643	17	5.12	0.73	5.85
Scioscia	348	40	90	16	2	7	40	46	31	.259	.376	.347	49	274	4.83	.618	10	2.72	0.42	3.14
Sharperson	222	26	63	13	4	2	21	25	23	.284	.405	.359	33	173	5.15	.648	6	1.91	0.20	2.11
Smith G	3	1	0	0	0	0	0	0	1	.000	.000	.000	0	3	0.00	.000	0	-0.04	-0.00	-0.04
Strawberry	511	89	133	23	5	27	101	74	123	.260	.483	.354	90	399	6.09	.720	15	5.47	0.45	5.92
Webster M	75	12	21	5	1	1	10	9	20	.280	.413	.357	12	54	6.00	.714	2	0.73	0.12	0.85
TOTALS	5551	690	1404	218	45	110	621	584	950	.253	.368	.326	678	4478	4.09	.537	166	31.01	7.49	38.50

Pitching Records for Los Angeles Dodgers

	ERA	W	L	Pct	G	GS	CG	ShO	GF	Sv	IP	R	ER	H	2B	3B	HR	BB	IW	SO	HB	WP	BK
Morgan M	2.78	14	10	.583	34	33	5	1	1	1	236.1	85	73	197	22	6	12	61	10	140	3	6	0
Martinez R	3.27	17	13	.567	33	33	6	4	0	0	220.1	89	80	190	33	1	18	69	4	150	7	6	0
Belcher	2.62	10	9	.526	33	33	2	1	0	0	209.1	76	61	189	26	3	10	75	3	156	2	7	0
Ojeda	3.18	12	9	.571	31	31	2	1	0	0	189.1	78	67	181	31	4	15	70	9	120	3	4	2
Hershiser	3.46	7	2	.778	21	21	0	0	0	0	112.0	43	43	112	18	2	3	32	6	73	5	2	4
Gross K	3.58	10	11	.476	46	10	0	0	16	3	115.2	55	46	123	13	2	10	50	6	95	2	3	0
Gott	2.96	4	3	.571	55	0	0	0	26	2	76.0	28	25	63	6	2	5	32	7	73	1	6	3
Crews	3.43	2	3	.400	60	0	0	0	17	6	76.0	30	29	75	17	1	7	19	11	53	0	3	1
Hartley	4.42	2	0	1.000	40	0	0	0	11	1	57.0	29	28	53	8	2	7	37	7	44	3	8	1
Howell Jay	3.18	6	5	.545	44	0	0	0	35	16	51.0	19	18	39	8	2	3	11	3	40	1	0	0
McDowell R	2.55	6	3	.667	33	0	0	0	18	7	42.1	12	12	39	6	2	3	16	8	22	0	1	0
Candelaria	3.74	1	1	.500	59	0	0	0	10	2	33.2	16	14	31	9	1	3	11	2	38	0	1	1
Cook D	0.51	1	0	1.000	20	1	0	0	5	0	17.2	3	1	12	3	0	0	7	1	8	0	0	0
Wetteland	0.00	1	0	1.000	6	0	0	0	3	0	9.0	2	0	5	1	0	0	3	0	9	1	1	0
Wilson S	0.00	0	0	.000	11	0	0	0	3	2	8.1	0	0	1	0	0	0	4	0	5	0	0	0
Christopher	0.00	0	0	.000	3	0	0	0	2	0	4.0	0	0	2	1	0	0	3	0	2	0	0	0
TOTALS	3.07	93	69	.574	529	162	15	7	147	40	1458.0	565	497	1312	202	28	96	500	77	1028	28	48	12

Sabermetric Pitching Records for Los Angeles Dodgers

	Adj	|-Expected-|			|——Opposing Batters——|														Supported		
	ERA	W	L	Pct	BFP	Avg	Slg	OBA	RC/G	GDP	SB	CS	PK	PKE	SH	SF	RSup	RSp/G	W	L	Pct
Belcher	2.71	12	7	.648	880	.240	.318	.306	3.38	15	17	10	0	1	11	3	80	3.44	12	7	.617
Candelaria	3.74	1	1	.491	138	.252	.415	.307	3.61	6	1	3	0	0	1	3	11	2.94	1	1	.382
Christopher	0.00	0	0	.000	15	.167	.250	.333	1.74	2	0	0	0	0	0	0	1	2.25	0	0	.000
Cook D	0.51	1	0	.981	69	.203	.254	.279	2.24	2	1	1	2	1	1	2	9	4.59	1	0	.988
Crews	3.55	3	2	.517	318	.256	.392	.299	4.30	2	10	2	2	0	4	2	28	3.32	2	3	.466
Gott	2.96	4	3	.606	322	.223	.312	.304	3.46	6	8	0	0	0	6	1	45	5.33	5	2	.764
Gross K	3.66	11	10	.502	509	.275	.380	.348	4.90	6	15	6	0	1	6	4	59	4.59	13	8	.612
Hartley	4.42	1	1	.408	258	.245	.398	.362	5.59	3	10	1	0	0	1	1	26	4.11	1	1	.463
Hershiser	3.54	5	4	.519	473	.259	.330	.316	3.78	8	11	2	2	1	2	1	77	6.19	7	2	.754
Howell Jay	3.18	6	5	.572	202	.213	.328	.259	2.93	1	3	1	0	0	5	2	11	1.94	3	8	.272
Martinez R	3.35	16	14	.546	916	.229	.337	.293	3.51	6	16	9	1	2	8	4	121	4.94	21	9	.685
McDowell R	2.55	6	3	.675	174	.257	.382	.324	3.93	5	6	3	0	0	4	2	22	4.68	7	2	.771
Morgan M	2.86	15	9	.623	949	.226	.307	.278	2.81	23	24	7	2	2	10	4	96	3.66	15	9	.621
Ojeda	3.28	12	9	.556	802	.257	.376	.323	4.15	12	23	15	0	5	15	9	72	3.42	11	10	.521
Wetteland	0.00	0	0	.000	36	.161	.194	.250	1.70	1	0	0	0	1	0	1	4	4.00	0	0	.000
Wilson S	0.00	0	0	.000	28	.042	.042	.179	0.26	2	0	0	0	0	0	0	3	3.24	0	0	.000
TOTALS	3.17	93	69	.573	6089	.241	.341	.306	3.63	100	145	60	9	14	74	39	665	4.10	101	61	.626

Batting 'Splits' Records for Los Angeles Dodgers

	G	AB	Run	Hit	2B	3B	HR	TB	RBI	W	K	IW	HB	SB	CS	GI DP	SH	SF	Avg	Slug	OBP	Runs Ctd
SPLITS for Butler																						
vs LHP	116	256	48	72	2	3	0	80	14	49	41	0	0	13	13	2	1	0	.281	.313	.397	35
vs RHP	129	359	64	110	11	2	2	131	24	59	38	4	1	25	15	1	3	2	.306	.365	.404	59
Home	80	295	59	92	7	2	2	109	22	59	29	2	0	17	16	1	2	1	.312	.369	.425	51
Away	81	320	53	90	6	3	0	102	16	49	50	2	1	21	12	2	2	1	.281	.319	.377	43
Grass	119	451	85	137	10	2	2	157	34	79	50	3	0	26	22	2	3	2	.304	.348	.406	70
Turf	42	164	27	45	3	3	0	54	4	29	29	1	1	12	6	1	1	0	.274	.329	.387	24
April/June	73	288	52	83	5	2	1	95	15	47	40	1	1	17	13	1	1	1	.288	.330	.389	41
July/October	88	327	60	99	8	3	1	116	23	61	39	3	0	21	15	2	3	1	.303	.355	.411	53
SPLITS for Daniels																						
vs LHP	101	206	21	52	8	0	6	78	36	19	52	0	0	0	0	2	0	5	.252	.379	.309	26
vs RHP	102	255	33	63	7	1	11	105	37	44	64	4	1	6	1	7	0	1	.247	.412	.359	40
Home	73	242	35	60	7	0	12	103	48	31	63	3	1	4	1	5	0	3	.248	.426	.332	36
Away	64	219	19	55	8	1	5	80	25	32	53	1	0	2	0	4	0	3	.251	.365	.343	30
Grass	105	357	45	89	12	1	15	148	61	49	94	4	1	5	1	7	0	4	.249	.415	.338	53
Turf	32	104	9	26	3	0	2	35	12	14	22	0	0	1	0	2	0	2	.250	.337	.333	13
April/June	65	226	30	59	6	0	10	95	41	21	54	1	1	3	0	6	0	4	.261	.420	.321	31
July/October	72	235	24	56	9	1	7	88	32	42	62	3	0	3	1	3	0	2	.238	.374	.351	34
SPLITS for Harris L																						
vs LHP	65	87	15	21	0	0	1	24	9	6	8	0	3	0	1	6	8	1	.241	.276	.309	7
vs RHP	130	342	44	102	16	1	2	126	29	31	24	5	2	12	2	11	4	1	.298	.368	.359	46
Home	70	211	30	58	6	0	1	67	17	18	18	3	3	5	2	6	8	0	.275	.318	.341	23
Away	75	218	29	65	10	1	2	83	21	19	14	2	2	7	1	11	4	2	.298	.381	.357	29
Grass	104	313	43	83	11	1	2	102	28	24	24	3	3	6	2	14	9	1	.265	.326	.323	32
Turf	41	116	16	40	5	0	1	48	10	13	8	2	2	6	1	3	3	1	.345	.414	.417	22
April/June	64	192	25	58	4	1	1	67	17	19	16	3	1	6	2	7	4	0	.302	.349	.368	25
July/October	81	237	34	65	12	0	2	83	21	18	16	2	4	6	1	10	8	2	.274	.350	.333	27
SPLITS for Samuel																						
vs LHP	107	250	38	63	11	2	7	99	27	14	59	3	1	7	3	3	5	0	.252	.396	.294	29
vs RHP	122	344	36	98	11	4	5	132	31	35	74	1	2	16	5	5	5	3	.285	.384	.352	50
Home	77	295	37	75	12	1	4	101	26	25	67	2	2	11	4	5	4	2	.254	.342	.315	33
Away	76	299	37	86	10	5	8	130	32	24	66	2	1	12	4	3	6	1	.288	.435	.342	46
Grass	115	450	55	121	16	4	9	172	46	34	103	4	2	16	7	7	8	2	.269	.382	.322	56
Turf	38	144	19	40	6	2	3	59	12	15	30	0	1	7	1	1	2	1	.278	.410	.348	23
April/June	72	287	46	92	12	1	8	130	39	24	60	1	0	10	5	4	5	3	.321	.453	.369	49
July/October	81	307	28	69	10	5	4	101	19	25	73	3	3	13	3	4	5	0	.225	.329	.290	31
SPLITS for Scioscia																						
vs LHP	68	106	14	20	2	0	3	31	13	11	12	0	3	3	1	1	3	3	.189	.292	.276	10
vs RHP	97	239	25	71	14	2	5	104	27	36	20	3	0	1	2	4	2	1	.297	.435	.388	42
Home	62	163	15	47	9	0	3	65	22	26	15	2	0	1	2	2	4	3	.288	.399	.380	27
Away	57	182	24	44	7	2	5	70	18	21	17	1	3	3	1	3	1	1	.242	.385	.329	24
Grass	89	250	29	73	14	2	5	106	33	34	21	2	0	2	2	4	5	4	.292	.424	.372	42
Turf	30	95	10	18	2	0	3	29	7	13	11	1	3	2	1	1	0	0	.189	.305	.306	10
April/June	61	178	21	49	12	1	3	72	22	28	17	2	2	2	1	2	0	2	.275	.404	.376	30
July/October	58	167	18	42	4	1	5	63	18	19	15	1	1	2	2	3	5	2	.251	.377	.328	21
SPLITS for Strawberry																						
vs LHP	110	228	34	63	9	2	11	109	43	34	59	0	1	5	5	2	0	2	.276	.478	.370	42
vs RHP	107	277	52	71	13	2	17	139	56	41	66	4	2	5	3	6	0	3	.256	.502	.353	50
Home	71	257	44	73	12	2	14	131	54	38	55	1	0	9	4	4	0	2	.284	.510	.374	51
Away	68	248	42	61	10	2	14	117	45	37	70	3	3	1	4	4	0	3	.246	.472	.347	41
Grass	101	367	64	99	18	3	20	183	71	55	85	2	2	10	7	5	0	4	.270	.499	.364	69
Turf	38	138	22	35	4	1	8	65	28	20	40	2	1	0	1	3	0	1	.254	.471	.350	23
April/June	53	183	39	41	9	1	7	73	26	33	50	0	2	7	4	1	0	2	.224	.399	.345	28
July/October	86	322	47	93	13	3	21	175	73	42	75	4	1	3	4	7	0	3	.289	.543	.370	64
SPLITS for Los Angeles Dodgers (all batters except pitchers)																						
vs LHP	1193	2322	281	565	75	13	41	789	256	230	444	12	15	44	32	49	51	21	.243	.340	.313	252
vs RHP	1388	3086	384	801	116	16	67	1150	349	353	513	38	13	82	36	61	43	25	.260	.373	.336	402
Home	1185	2625	342	667	82	8	57	936	309	315	464	30	12	62	37	54	51	23	.254	.357	.334	326
Away	1190	2783	323	699	109	21	51	1003	296	268	493	20	16	64	31	56	43	23	.251	.360	.318	327
Grass	1751	3985	510	1018	138	18	86	1450	461	432	691	39	19	88	54	81	76	36	.255	.364	.328	490
Turf	624	1423	155	348	53	11	22	489	144	151	266	11	9	38	14	29	18	10	.245	.344	.319	163
April/June	1041	2474	319	631	86	11	46	877	287	261	428	26	10	58	31	50	37	24	.255	.354	.326	295
July/October	1334	2934	346	735	105	18	62	1062	318	322	529	24	18	68	37	60	57	22	.251	.362	.326	358

1991 SPLITS FOR Los Angeles Dodgers

BATTING SPLITS

	AVG	AB	R	H	2B	3B	HR	RBI	SB	CS	BB	K	OBA	SPCT
Total	.253	5408	665	1366	191	29	108	605	126	68	583	957	.326	.359

	#Pit	#P/PA	GB	FB	G/F	G	IBB	HB	SH	SF	GDP
Miscellaneous	22695	3.68	2125	1324	1.60	162	50	28	94	46	110

	AVG	AB	R	H	2B	3B	HR	RBI	SB	CS	BB	K	OBA	SPCT
vs. Left	.243	2322	...	565	75	13	41	256	44	32	230	444	.313	.340
vs. Right	.260	3086	...	801	116	16	67	349	82	36	353	513	.336	.373
Home	.254	2625	342	667	82	8	57	309	62	37	315	464	.334	.357
Away	.251	2783	323	699	109	21	51	296	64	31	268	493	.318	.360
None on	.241	3114	...	750	108	12	57	57	0	0	300	550	.310	.338
Runners on	.269	2294	...	616	83	17	51	548	126	68	283	407	.347	.386
April	.250	661	85	165	24	3	11	78	11	6	54	108	.306	.345
May	.242	881	118	213	29	3	19	105	30	8	118	176	.332	.346
June	.271	932	116	253	33	5	16	104	17	17	89	144	.334	.369
July	.251	857	109	215	32	6	18	100	24	12	89	158	.323	.365
August	.251	963	101	242	29	5	18	95	25	15	124	184	.338	.348
September	.253	947	126	240	40	7	23	115	17	10	101	153	.327	.383
October	.228	167	10	38	4	0	3	8	2	0	8	34	.266	.305
None on/out	.250	1364	...	341	41	6	25	25	0	0	122	223	.313	.344
Scoring Posn	.259	1323	...	342	42	11	33	485	30	10	212	245	.354	.382
Close & Late	.268	961	...	258	36	7	15	128	29	9	128	185	.355	.367
Bases Loaded	.213	141	...	30	5	2	3	91	0	0	12	23	.255	.340
Batting #1	.297	640	114	190	14	5	2	39	39	28	110	83	.400	.344
Batting #2	.292	655	93	191	30	6	10	68	21	9	59	113	.351	.402
Batting #3	.246	634	94	156	22	4	23	97	17	6	74	138	.320	.402
Batting #4	.251	622	76	156	29	1	25	110	12	5	70	110	.325	.421
Batting #5	.270	599	84	162	17	3	23	86	4	3	77	115	.352	.424
Batting #6	.265	599	61	159	27	4	7	59	13	6	47	67	.323	.359
Batting #7	.242	561	60	136	24	1	11	54	7	4	61	90	.324	.348
Batting #8	.233	554	40	129	16	2	1	47	8	6	60	92	.308	.274
Batting #9	.160	544	43	87	12	3	6	45	5	1	25	149	.199	.226
As p	.142	339	22	48	6	0	2	23	1	0	11	97	.167	.177
As c	.260	558	55	145	29	2	14	62	7	4	60	56	.338	.394
As 1b	.252	627	77	158	25	1	18	94	10	4	60	83	.315	.381
As 2b	.278	643	83	179	26	6	13	63	24	8	56	136	.339	.398
As 3b	.278	569	62	158	23	3	5	55	12	5	44	69	.331	.355
As ss	.239	527	40	126	12	2	0	36	8	6	55	82	.312	.269
As lf	.254	602	71	153	16	4	21	86	10	2	79	144	.338	.399
As cf	.295	633	113	187	14	5	2	39	39	28	108	82	.398	.343
As rf	.260	605	100	157	30	4	29	105	12	9	84	140	.349	.466
Outfield	.270	1840	284	497	60	13	52	230	61	39	271	366	.362	.402
0.0 count	.309	805	...	249	35	4	13	114	...	...	0	0	.309	.411
After (0.1)	.223	2392	...	534	78	9	38	220	...	...	147	608	.270	.311
After (1.0)	.264	2211	...	583	78	16	57	271	...	...	393	349	.374	.391
Two strikes	.189	2543	...	481	61	10	34	199	...	...	230	956	.258	.261
Grass	.255	3985	510	1018	138	18	86	461	88	54	432	691	.328	.364
Turf	.245	1423	155	348	53	11	22	144	38	14	151	266	.319	.344
Day	.255	1496	177	381	56	9	21	158	31	20	136	270	.317	.346
Night	.252	3912	488	985	135	20	87	447	95	48	447	687	.329	.363
Inning 1.6	.251	3624	430	908	124	17	68	397	90	48	376	623	.322	.350
Inning 7+	.257	1784	235	458	67	12	40	208	36	20	207	334	.335	.375
vs.Atl	.245	597	68	146	21	4	9	60	7	8	41	103	.293	.338
vs.ChN	.283	413	68	117	21	3	10	65	10	6	50	60	.361	.421
vs.Cin	.255	599	87	153	27	4	7	78	13	8	88	106	.352	.349
vs.Hou	.238	602	77	143	24	1	19	75	19	7	88	129	.337	.375
vs.Mon	.232	375	42	87	14	1	6	35	9	5	36	73	.299	.323
vs.NYN	.245	396	58	97	9	3	13	52	14	8	32	79	.303	.381
vs.Phi	.264	405	46	107	13	3	6	41	14	3	53	69	.349	.356
vs.Pit	.242	392	34	95	10	2	5	32	7	7	30	67	.303	.316
vs.StL	.265	408	41	108	12	3	5	36	8	7	36	66	.324	.346
vs.SD	.266	617	79	164	20	4	19	74	15	1	58	104	.327	.404
vs.SF	.247	604	65	149	20	1	9	57	10	8	71	101	.325	.328

PITCHING SPLITS

	ERA	W	L	SV	SVOP	GS	CG	SHO	IP	H	ER	HR	BB	IBB	K
Total	3.06	93	69	40	56	162	15	8	1458.0	1312	496	96	500	77	1028

	#Pit	#P/IP	GB	FB	G/F	BRp9	RA	WP	BK	SH	SF	R	HB	Hld
Miscellaneous	22189	15.22	2084	1400	1.49	11.36	367	48	12	74	39	565	28	54

	ERA	W	L	SV	SVOP	GS	CG	SHO	IP	H	ER	HR	BB	IBB	K
ST	3.06	65	48	0	0	162	15	7	1023.0	926	348	62	332	33	679
REL	3.08	28	21	40	56	0	0	0	435.0	386	149	34	168	44	349
Home	3.04	54	27	21	28	81	9	4	750.0	671	253	46	256	36	566
Away	3.10	39	42	19	28	81	6	3	708.0	641	244	50	244	41	462
April	2.97	10	10	2	2	20	5	3	176.0	157	58	16	47	10	128
May	3.11	17	10	11	11	27	1	0	237.0	230	82	15	97	10	166
June	2.75	18	9	9	17	27	4	1	252.1	213	77	8	90	15	177
July	3.45	13	13	3	4	26	4	2	229.2	220	88	14	84	15	139
August	3.37	13	16	6	10	29	1	1	264.1	234	99	21	81	14	186
September	2.82	20	8	7	10	28	0	0	255.2	219	80	18	93	10	195
October	2.72	2	3	2	2	5	0	0	43.0	39	13	4	8	3	37
Grass	3.04	75	45	33	45	120	12	6	1097.0	985	371	74	366	58	788
Turf	3.14	18	24	7	11	42	3	1	361.0	327	126	22	134	19	240
Day	3.06	24	21	11	13	45	4	1	394.0	362	134	24	137	19	277
Night	3.07	69	48	29	43	117	11	6	1064.0	950	363	72	363	58	751
vs.Atl	2.78	11	7	7	9	18	1	0	165.1	131	51	9	70	9	112
vs.ChN	3.27	10	2	5	7	12	1	1	110.0	104	40	6	22	3	83
vs.Cin	3.46	12	6	5	8	18	0	0	164.0	157	63	17	47	7	111
vs.Hou	3.14	10	8	4	5	18	0	0	166.0	153	58	11	58	7	128
vs.Mon	2.70	5	7	3	3	12	3	1	103.1	76	31	5	41	3	69
vs.NYN	4.11	7	5	3	4	12	1	0	105.0	106	48	8	50	6	51
vs.Phi	3.26	7	5	3	3	12	2	1	105.0	104	38	5	39	7	72
vs.Pit	2.12	7	5	3	4	12	1	0	106.0	88	25	4	41	7	75
vs.StL	2.98	6	6	1	5	12	2	1	108.2	94	36	3	38	7	67
vs.SD	3.16	10	8	4	5	18	2	2	162.1	157	57	12	43	8	129
vs.SF	2.77	8	10	2	3	18	2	1	162.1	142	50	16	51	13	131

OPPOSING BATTERS VS. PITCHERS.

	AVG	AB	R	H	2B	3B	HR	RBI	SB	CS	BB	K	OBA	SPCT
Total	.241	5448	565	1312	202	28	96	529	145	60	500	1028	.306	.341
vs. Left	.247	2639	...	652	99	17	41	243	83	33	274	476	.319	.344
vs. Right	.235	2809	...	660	103	11	55	286	62	27	226	552	.294	.338
ST	.241	3837	396	926	138	17	62	349	96	48	332	679	.303	.335
REL	.240	1611	169	386	64	11	34	180	49	12	168	349	.312	.356
Home	.240	2799	280	671	90	9	46	265	74	33	256	566	.303	.328
Away	.242	2649	285	641	112	19	50	264	71	27	244	462	.309	.355
None on	.242	3191	...	771	124	14	63	63	0	0	236	608	.297	.348
Runners on	.240	2257	...	541	78	14	33	466	145	60	264	420	.318	.331
None on/out	.244	1399	...	341	52	6	28	28	0	0	92	260	.295	.350
Scoring Posn	.232	1323	...	307	42	12	17	421	32	15	194	273	.325	.320
vs 1st Batr	.266	323	...	86	19	1	6	54	5	1	35	90	.332	.387
1st IP	.245	1707	140	419	75	14	27	202	55	20	159	349	.310	.353
Inning 1.6	.239	3631	376	868	134	14	61	352	96	48	313	662	.301	.334
Inning 7+	.244	1817	189	444	68	14	35	177	49	12	187	366	.316	.355
Close & Late	.232	969	...	225	39	8	12	102	30	9	110	196	.311	.326
0.0 count	.312	785	...	245	39	3	15	85	...	...	65	0	.371	.427
After (0.1)	.206	2467	...	509	81	9	32	201	...	...	114	697	.242	.285
After (1.0)	.254	2196	...	558	82	16	49	243	...	...	321	331	.349	.373
Two strikes	.150	2428	...	364	56	11	25	148	...	...	209	1027	.219	.213
Pitch 1.15	.250	1537	...	385	72	14	23	155	52	15	131	299	.308	.360
Pitch 16.30	.225	1016	...	229	29	2	21	88	18	12	92	230	.293	.320
Pitch 31.45	.261	706	...	184	24	6	15	81	25	12	64	142	.325	.375
Pitch 46.60	.225	626	...	141	23	1	10	58	14	6	59	110	.290	.313
Pitch 61.75	.236	580	...	137	16	0	6	52	12	6	50	83	.297	.295
Pitch 76.90	.228	479	...	109	22	3	7	46	11	7	47	84	.302	.330
Pitch 91.105	.251	303	...	76	9	1	6	28	8	1	30	51	.319	.347
Pitch 106.20	.247	158	...	39	3	1	5	15	5	0	20	23	.333	.373
Pitch 121.35	.289	45	...	13	4	0	3	8	0	1	7	6	.385	.578
Pitch 136.50	.000	0	...	0	0	0	0	0	0	0	0	0	.000	.000

San Diego Padres

Don Malcolm

SAN DIEGO											
YEAR	1982	1983	1984	1985	1986	1987	1988	1989	1990	1991	TOT
W	81	81	92	83	74	65	83	89	75	84	807
L	81	81	70	79	88	97	78	73	87	78	812
WPCT	0.500	0.500	0.568	0.512	0.457	0.401	0.516	0.549	0.463	0.519	0.498
R	675	653	686	650	656	668	594	642	673	636	6533
RA	658	653	634	622	722	763	583	626	673	646	6580
PWPT	0.513	0.500	0.539	0.522	0.452	0.434	0.509	0.513	0.500	0.492	0.496
PythW	83	81	87	85	73	70	83	83	81	80	80
PythL	79	81	75	77	89	92	79	79	81	82	82
LUCK	-2	0	5	-2	1	-5	0	6	-6	4	1

Defensive Efficiency Record: .7088

First: let's give Greg Riddoch some credit. He survived. In the context of the Padres' recent history of instability and melodrama, survival is a significant achievement.

But the question must be asked: for what purpose? Is survival really so desirable? What does Greg have to look forward to now that he has dodged what appeared to be an unerring bullet?

Answer: more bullets. It's a cruel world out there, due in no small measure to the Republicans, with TV money and the basic agreement due to go bellyup in tandem two years hence. The fur is already beginning to fly, and the Padres are looking to retrench. Fiscal conservatism is going to reign in Mission Valley.

This megatrend will put premature furrows into Riddoch's brow as he tries to devise a way to take a team that is stagnating (see the Pythagorean numbers above) and move it in a constructive direction. As of this writing, the Padres had pulled out of the Danny Tartabull sweepstakes (looking more like a pale sequel to the Bonilla giveaway, and a shame too, since Tartabull's potential peak season makes Bobby look a bit pale himself), vowing to stay the course and win with what they've got.

Question: How?? Answer: Beats the hell outta me, boys and girls. There wasn't nearly enough offense here last year, even with the Big Four of Roberts, Fernandez, Gwynn, and McGriff. All that combo managed to do, really, was inflate Benito Santiago's RBI totals and make some people believe that Benny really contributed something valuable to the offense with his .288 on-base percentage. Now Bip is gone, sent to Cincinnati where he will probably hit .300+ again.

So: no real leadoff man. Oh, the Padres still have "the incomparable" Tony Gwynn (I think George Will thought up that sobriquet), but they have never seen Tony as a leadoff hitter and, unless there is a tsunami with sufficient height to ravage Mount Everest, it is doubtful that such a concept will hit the Padres' mental beach. Given the nature of what they have done to themselves, Gwynn is their best bet, although I must admit that the idea of leading Darrin Jackson off is intriguing. Riddoch actually did this: he had his second leading homer man in the leadoff spot about twelve times last season. It's too bad Darrin can't draw walks, or it just might be a good plan. Desperation—as some wise man (or was it a wiseass?) said—is inherently intriguing, but only intermittently illuminating.

Actually, a reasonable method of determining a lineup could be constructed from a simple application of the players' offensive winning percentages. The rule of thumb would be something like this:

—Highest win percentage bats third.
—Second highest bats fourth, unless the player has less than 30% extrabase hits or less than 10% homers-to-hits.
—Third highest bats leadoff, unless the player has less than 10 stolen bases.
—Fourth highest bats second no matter what.
—Fifth through eighth bat in the 5-through-8 spots.

The batting order for the 1991 Padres, based on the above rules:

1) Gwynn
2) Fernandez
3) McGriff
4) Jackson
5) Roberts
6) Teufel
7) Santiago
8) pick a third baseman

The batting order for the 1992 Padres, based on last year's stats and on trades and signings thus far:

1) Gwynn
2) Fernandez
3) McGriff
4) Jackson
5) Teufel
6) Howard
7) Santiago
8) pick a third baseman

The classical lineup puts Roberts in the leadoff spot, moves Gwynn to third, McGriff to fourth, and Jackson to fifth. Why? On-base percentage. Speed. These are, superficially at least, sound reasons. But look what happens in the Padres' case. They put three singles hitters up in a row, three guys all with a long hit percentage ("long hits" are triples and homers) of less than 9%. That means that in the first inning, when run scoring is at its most crucial, the Padres have three guys who need to manufacture at least two hits in a row to manufacture a "sure rally" (man on third, no one out).

PLAYER	H	D	T	HR	XB%	LH%	HR%
ROBERTS	119	13	3	3	16.0	5.0	2.5
FERNANDEZ	152	27	5	4	23.7	5.9	2.6
GWYNN	168	27	11	4	25.0	8.9	2.4
MCGRIFF	147	19	1	31	34.7	21.8	21.1
JACKSON	94	12	1	21	36.2	23.4	22.3

By contrast, getting McGriff and/or Jackson up in the first inning enhances the chances of scoring due to the potential for long hits with men on base.

PLAYER	H	D	T	HR	XB%	LH%	HR%
GWYNN	168	27	11	4	25.0	8.9	2.4
FERNANDEZ	152	27	5	4	23.7	5.9	2.6
MCGRIFF	147	19	1	31	34.7	21.8	21.1
JACKSON	94	12	1	21	36.2	23.4	22.3
ROBERTS	119	13	3	3	16.0	5.0	2.5

It's possible to think of the batting order (in the NL at least) as a symmetrical construction of functions based around four hitters in a sequence and a null spot. Maybe one's fifth batter shouldn't necessarily be one who is a lesser version of the cleanup hitter, but instead a second leadoff hitter. Of course, the optimum situation is when your hitter is both: witness the rise of the Pirates when they took Barry Bonds out of the leadoff spot and batted him fifth, where his ancillary leadoff skills also provide a way of generating runs from the hits of the 6-7-8 hitters as well as driving in the 1-2-3-4 hitters.

But Barry Bonds is something of an anomaly, and one that is in danger of extinction due to the departure of Bonilla to (literally) greener pastures. The Padres have managed to return to the dilemma of the 1-4 offense despite all efforts to develop a more balanced lineup. Now they're down to a three-man offense (if you consider an offense to be comprised of those players with offensive winning percentages above .500).

Just three? What about Santiago? OWP of .447. "But he had 87 RBI." Offensive winning percentage of .447. Look up Benny's situational stats in Elias (do it in the bookstore, and save your money for a book with personality, like this one). You'll see that he had more opportunities that just about anyone to drive in runs. Santiago should bat eighth on a team with a good offense, but on the Padres he bats fifth.

The real question revolves around Darrin Jackson. Is he for real? How do you tell a fluke season, anyhow? Didn't John Shelby hit 20 homers once for the Dodgers? Everybody knows that he's a bum.

Actually, Shelby hit 22 homers for the Dodgers in 1987 (seems a lot longer ago than that, though, due to this lingering recession...). His OWP was .622. What you had with Shelby, as Bill James pointed out in the 1988 Abstract, was a fluke season. In 1988, Shelby lost a lot of his power, adjusted a bit by hitting for average, and wound up with an OWP of .565. In 1989, the roof fell in on him: his OWP was .181.

Every year there are about 50-75 major league regulars who post OWP's of .600 or higher. On this list there are usually four or five flukes, players who never achieve such a high figure again. For example, in 1988 there were 52 players with a .600 or higher OWP, including Marvell Wynne (.603), Dave Bergman (.604), and Johnny Ray (.600). None of these guys could be expected to reach this level without mitigating factors (Wynne played less than a full season and got hot, Bergman was platooned, Ray had his best season ever and just made it). In 1989, 62 players cracked .600, including such erstwhile heroes as Carney Lansford (.664), Jerry Browne (.618), Jose Gonzalez (.621) and Oddibe McDowell (.680). Lansford had to hit .336 to get there; Browne is a player who has been mishandled since, but right now looks like a fluke; and Gonzalez and McDowell have gone south in an uninterrupted trajectory.

So the odds are good that Jackson is for real, but you never really know. His overall career data (shown below, in context with his 1991 season) is not particularly encouraging: it doesn't show a steady pattern of power to mitigate the lack of strike-zone judgement. Bill James' 1992 projection for Jackson doesn't look too pretty: it rings him up at about 3.95 RC/G, a .244 BA, .402 SA, .291 on-base—an OWP something less than .500.

PLAYER	H	D	T	HR	XB%	LH%	HR%	YEAR
JACKSON	94	12	1	21	36.2	23.4	22.3	1991
JACKSON	215	34	4	34	33.5	17.7	15.8	CAREER
JACKSON	121	22	3	13	31.4	13.2	10.7	w/o 1991
JACKSON	76	13	1	12	34.2	17.1	15.8	1992 PROJ

In short, this is not the guy you want to be batting cleanup—unless those 1991 numbers aren't flukes. Assuming you take the data above as cautionary, it's unlikely that a conservative manager (here come those Republicans again...) would use Darrin in the #5 slot either. The Padres' problem is that they have no one else.

I think that I'd try a lineup like the one above: Gwynn, Fernandez, McGriff, and Jackson. Just for the hell of it. If you're going to be stuck with a 1-4 offense, as the Padres seem invariably to be, then you might as well organize it to get the maximum on-base in front of the guys with power. But the big problem is that no one knows which version of Jackson is going to show up in '92: the one we saw last year, the one that looks like a projection of his overall career to date, or—worst of all—someone like the totals on the third line, the career data prior to 1991. That guy is a number seven hitter all the way.

So the conservative approach—use what you've got on hand—turns out to be a real crapshoot. Just like supply-side economics. The Padres have a trickle-down offense which has always looked better than it really is. They've thrown away some valuable offensive talent (John Kruk, Randy Ready, Jack Clark, Carlos Baerga, and two Alomar brothers) over the past three seasons. What remains are McGriff and Fernandez, along with an aging, hobbled Tony Gwynn. In an age of offensive scarcity, the Padres will be turning to their pitching staff for salvation.

But these guys are still the high priests of home runs. The nature of Jack Murphy Stadium ensures this feature, of course, but the Padres seem determined to encourage home runs from a team that really can't hit them, thus penalizing a pretty good pitching staff. A rotation of Benes, Hurst, Harris, Melendez, and Whitson isn't too shabby. Imagine how good these guys' numbers might look if the interior fence was gone. The team might actually be able to generate a home-field advantage, something that has been totally elusive to the Padres since the change in the fence prior to the '82 season.

The big question is what to do with Randy Myers. I think trying to make Myers into a starter was a crackpot concept, something Lou Piniella did because Myers probably bitched about being replaced as the lead closer. I think I'd just put him back into the closer role and cross my fingers that last year was a fluke. A committee of set-up men supporting Myers, pitchers like Lefferts, Larry Andersen, Mike Maddux, and Rich Rodriguez, could make for a fine bullpen. There are also prospects such as Jeremy Hernandez, who looked very impressive in his September stint with the big club.

So it's the pitching that needs to rise up and give the Padres an advantage. Getting rid of the interior fence would go a long way toward providing that advantage. Benes and Harris could become lethal pitchers at home via such a scenario. Ditto Jose Melendez.

What does such a move do to the Padres' hitting? Fifty-two of the team's 121 homers last year were hit by two men—McGriff and Jackson. The home/road splits on those 52 homers are as follows: 30/22, or 1.36 to 1. Removing the fence will make the ratio closer to even, maybe tilted a bit toward the road, say .92 to 1. McGriff and Jackson will hit less homers, but so will the opposition. The Padres will be playing something more like Astro and Cardinal offense, with more emphasis on speed and on-base and long sequences. More importantly, they will be forcing the opposition to do the same, while trotting out pitchers with low opposition batting averages (Benes, .232; Harris, .233; Melendez, .221, Hurst .241).

In this context it makes even more sense to bunch those top 4 hitters and hope to get an early lead, and rely on the pitching. It's the only strategy that seems viable given the Padres' Republican cloth coat mindset. Signing Danny Tartabull could make the Padres a contender, but signing Tartabull and removing the interior wall could make them lethal. I doubt either will happen, but then again, from the Padres' perspective at least, I'm registered with the wrong party.

San Diego Padres Home Park Performance Factors

	Outs	Runs	Hits	2b	3b	HR	W	K	SH	SF	HBP	IBB	SB	CS	GDP
Home LH Batters	.946	.891	.972	.982	1.174	.843	.838	.900	1.116	1.039	.488	.675	.606	2.683	.844
Home RH Batters	.940	.955	.948	.910	.993	.901	.965	.997	.960	.993	.783	.901	.901	1.287	.869
All Home Batters	.949	.939	.958	.969	1.141	.876	.925	.969	.982	1.075	.748	.750	.879	1.224	.891
Opp LH Batters	.971	.980	1.019	1.308	1.023	.939	.902	.907	1.074	1.045	.522	.867	1.023	1.014	1.166
Opp RH Batters	1.009	1.064	1.053	.988	1.554	1.048	1.016	1.021	.811	1.495	.844	1.107	1.336	1.063	1.234
All Opp Batters	.995	1.028	1.031	1.065	1.205	.998	.986	.964	.886	1.195	.773	.988	1.149	1.005	1.174
All LH Batters	.957	.934	.996	1.127	1.095	.890	.870	.903	1.091	1.033	.505	.737	.823	1.323	.984
All RH Batters	.976	1.010	1.000	.949	1.242	.976	.992	1.017	.884	1.217	.824	1.006	1.146	1.133	1.020
All Batters	.972	.983	.994	1.017	1.174	.937	.956	.970	.932	1.135	.770	.852	1.016	1.087	1.011

Conventional Batting Records for San Diego Padres

	G	AB	Run	Hit	2B	3B	HR	TB	RBI	W	K	IW	HB	SB	CS	BRng Eff	GI DP	SH	SF	Avg	Slug	OBP	Runs Ctd
Santiago	152	580	60	155	22	3	17	234	87	23	114	5	4	8	10	.457	21	0	7	.267	.403	.296	61
McGriff F	153	528	84	147	19	1	31	261	106	105	135	26	2	4	1	.275	14	0	7	.278	.494	.396	110
Roberts Bip	117	424	66	119	13	3	3	147	32	37	71	0	4	26	11	.350	6	4	3	.281	.347	.342	53
Coolbaugh	60	180	12	39	8	1	2	55	15	19	45	2	1	0	3	.296	8	4	1	.217	.306	.294	15
Fernandez T	145	558	81	152	27	5	4	201	38	55	74	0	0	23	9	.619	11	7	1	.272	.360	.337	70
Clark Je	118	369	26	84	16	0	10	130	47	31	90	2	6	2	1	.317	10	1	4	.228	.352	.295	38
Jackson Dar	122	359	51	94	12	1	21	171	49	27	66	2	2	5	3	.467	5	3	3	.262	.476	.315	54
Gwynn T	134	530	69	168	27	11	4	229	62	34	19	8	0	8	8	.424	11	0	5	.317	.432	.355	79
Teufel	97	307	39	70	16	0	11	119	42	49	69	4	1	8	2	.310	8	4	2	.228	.388	.334	42
Howard T	106	281	30	70	12	3	4	100	22	24	57	4	1	10	7	.476	4	2	1	.249	.356	.309	31
Howell Jk	58	160	24	33	3	1	6	56	16	18	33	1	0	0	0	.393	1	1	0	.206	.350	.287	17
Faries	57	130	13	23	3	1	0	28	7	14	21	0	1	3	1	.316	5	4	0	.177	.215	.262	8
Abner	53	115	15	19	4	1	1	28	5	7	25	4	1	0	0	.526	3	1	1	.165	.243	.218	6
Ward K	44	107	13	26	7	2	2	43	8	9	27	0	1	1	4	.368	3	1	0	.243	.402	.308	11
Shipley	37	91	6	25	3	0	1	31	6	2	14	0	1	0	1	.357	1	1	0	.275	.341	.298	9
Hurst	31	67	3	9	1	0	0	10	6	4	23	0	0	0	0	.125	0	12	0	.134	.149	.183	3
Benes	33	62	4	2	0	0	1	5	1	6	29	0	2	0	0	.400	2	7	0	.032	.081	.143	1
Presley	20	59	3	8	0	0	1	11	5	4	16	1	1	0	1	.250	2	1	1	.136	.186	.200	2
Lampkin	38	58	4	11	3	1	0	16	3	3	9	0	0	0	0	.333	0	0	0	.190	.276	.230	4
Templeton	32	57	5	11	1	1	1	17	6	1	9	0	0	0	1	.600	3	0	1	.193	.298	.203	2
Azocar	38	57	5	14	2	0	0	16	9	1	9	1	1	2	0	.333	1	0	1	.246	.281	.267	5
Rasmussen D	25	44	3	6	1	0	0	7	0	5	12	0	0	0	0	.286	0	3	0	.136	.159	.224	2
Harris GW	20	36	0	3	0	0	0	3	2	1	13	0	1	0	0	.000	1	7	0	.083	.083	.132	1
Mota	17	36	4	8	0	0	0	8	2	2	7	0	1	0	0	.400	0	2	0	.222	.222	.282	3
Bilardello	15	26	4	7	2	1	0	11	5	3	4	0	0	0	0	.500	0	0	0	.269	.423	.345	4
Whitson	13	24	1	3	0	0	0	3	1	1	6	0	0	0	0	.000	0	2	0	.125	.125	.160	1
Melendez J	31	20	1	2	1	0	0	3	0	1	14	0	0	0	0	.333	0	0	0	.100	.150	.143	0
Vatcher	17	20	3	4	0	0	0	4	2	4	6	0	0	1	0	.333	0	0	0	.200	.200	.333	2
Barrett M	12	16	1	3	1	0	1	7	3	0	3	0	1	0	0	.000	0	0	0	.188	.438	.235	2
Aldrete	12	15	2	0	0	0	0	0	1	3	4	0	0	0	1	1.000	1	0	0	.000	.000	.167	0
Maddux M	64	13	1	1	0	0	0	1	0	2	4	0	0	0	0	.000	0	3	0	.077	.077	.200	1
Peterson	13	13	0	0	0	0	0	0	0	2	9	0	0	0	0	.000	0	1	0	.000	.000	.133	0
Bones	11	13	1	1	0	0	0	1	1	2	5	0	0	0	0	1.000	0	4	0	.077	.077	.200	1
Dorsett	11	12	0	1	0	0	0	1	1	0	3	0	0	0	0	.000	0	0	0	.083	.083	.083	0
Nolte	6	9	2	1	0	0	0	1	0	0	6	0	0	0	0	.000	0	2	0	.111	.111	.111	0
Stephenson	11	7	0	2	0	0	0	2	0	2	3	0	0	0	0	.000	0	0	0	.286	.286	.444	1
Lefferts	54	6	0	0	0	0	0	0	0	0	4	0	0	0	0	.000	0	0	0	.000	.000	.000	0
Rodriguez Rich	65	5	0	0	0	0	0	0	0	0	2	0	0	0	0	.000	0	0	0	.000	.000	.000	0
Andersen L	38	2	0	0	0	0	0	0	0	0	1	0	0	0	0	.000	0	0	0	.000	.000	.000	0
Gardner W	14	2	0	0	0	0	0	0	0	0	2	0	0	0	0	.000	0	0	0	.000	.000	.000	0
Lilliquist	6	2	0	0	0	0	0	0	1	0	0	0	0	0	0	.000	0	0	0	.000	.000	.000	0
Lewis Js	12	2	0	0	0	0	0	0	0	0	1	0	0	0	0	.000	0	0	0	.000	.000	.000	0
Hernandez Jer	9	2	0	0	0	0	0	0	0	0	1	0	0	0	0	.000	0	0	0	.000	.000	.000	0
Clements P	12	1	0	0	0	0	0	0	0	0	1	0	0	0	0	.000	0	0	0	.000	.000	.000	0
Rosenberg	10	1	0	0	0	0	0	0	0	0	1	0	0	0	0	.000	0	0	0	.000	.000	.000	0
Costello	27	1	0	0	0	0	0	0	0	0	1	0	0	0	0	.000	0	1	0	.000	.000	.000	0
Hammaker	1	1	0	0	0	0	0	0	0	0	1	0	0	0	0	.000	0	0	0	.000	.000	.000	0
Scott Tim	2	0	0	0	0	0	0	0	0	0	0	0	0	0	0	.000	0	0	0	.000	.000	.000	0
TOTALS	2173	5408	636	1321	204	36	121	1960	591	501	1069	60	32	101	64	.397	121	78	38	.244	.362	.310	609

Sabermetric Batting Records for San Diego Padres

	Ball Park Adjusted												Runs	Run/					
	AB	Run	Hit	2B	3B	HR	RBI	W	SO	Avg	Slug	OBP	Ctd	Outs	27o	OW%	OG	OWAR	DWAR	TWAR
Abner	112	15	19	3	1	0	4	6	25	.170	.214	.210	5	97	1.39	.110	4	-0.86	0.36	-0.50
Aldrete	14	1	0	0	0	0	1	2	3	.000	.000	.125	0	16	0.00	.000	1	-0.21	0.05	-0.16
Azocar	54	4	13	2	0	0	9	0	8	.241	.278	.236	3	43	1.88	.185	2	-0.26	-0.02	-0.29
Barrett M	15	1	3	0	0	0	2	0	3	.200	.200	.200	1	12	2.25	.244	0	-0.05	0.06	0.01
Bilardello	25	4	7	1	1	0	4	2	4	.280	.400	.333	4	18	6.00	.697	1	0.23	0.10	0.34
Clark Je	361	26	84	15	0	9	45	30	90	.233	.349	.296	37	292	3.42	.428	11	0.84	0.41	1.25
Coolbaugh	176	12	39	7	1	1	14	18	45	.222	.290	.292	13	152	2.31	.254	6	-0.54	0.23	-0.31
Dorsett	11	0	1	0	0	0	0	0	3	.091	.091	.091	0	10	0.00	.000	0	-0.13	0.01	-0.12
Faries	127	13	23	2	1	0	6	13	21	.181	.213	.257	7	113	1.67	.152	4	-0.83	0.61	-0.22
Fernandez T	545	79	151	27	5	3	37	52	71	.277	.361	.339	68	422	4.35	.547	16	3.08	2.13	5.21
Gwynn T	513	64	167	30	12	3	63	29	17	.326	.448	.358	76	376	5.46	.655	14	4.25	0.88	5.14
Howard T	274	29	69	12	3	3	21	22	55	.252	.350	.306	29	218	3.59	.452	8	0.82	0.74	1.56
Howell Jk	153	22	32	3	1	5	16	15	29	.209	.340	.280	15	123	3.29	.409	5	0.27	0.48	0.75
Jackson Dar	352	51	94	11	1	20	47	26	66	.267	.474	.317	53	271	5.28	.640	10	2.91	0.68	3.59
Lampkin	55	3	10	3	1	0	3	2	8	.182	.273	.211	3	45	1.80	.171	2	-0.30	-0.02	-0.32
McGriff F	511	78	146	21	1	27	109	91	121	.286	.489	.390	102	387	7.12	.764	14	5.93	0.16	6.09
Mota	34	3	7	0	0	0	1	1	6	.206	.206	.229	2	28	1.93	.192	1	-0.16	0.01	-0.16
Presley	57	3	8	0	0	0	4	3	16	.140	.140	.180	1	53	0.51	.016	2	-0.66	-0.06	-0.72
Roberts Bip	414	64	118	13	3	2	31	35	68	.285	.345	.343	51	320	4.30	.542	12	2.27	0.61	2.88
Santiago	569	60	155	20	3	16	85	22	115	.272	.402	.299	60	455	3.56	.447	17	1.64	0.02	1.67
Shipley	89	6	25	2	0	0	5	1	14	.281	.303	.289	7	66	2.86	.344	2	-0.02	-0.02	-0.04
Stephenson	5	0	1	0	0	0	0	1	2	.200	.200	.333	0	4	0.00	.000	0	-0.05	0.00	-0.05
Templeton	54	4	10	1	1	0	5	0	8	.185	.241	.182	1	49	0.55	.019	2	-0.60	0.54	-0.06
Teufel	300	39	70	15	0	10	41	48	69	.233	.383	.337	41	245	4.52	.566	9	1.96	0.20	2.16
Vatcher	19	3	4	0	0	0	1	3	6	.211	.211	.318	2	15	3.60	.453	1	0.06	0.01	0.07
Ward K	104	13	26	6	2	1	7	8	27	.250	.375	.304	10	85	3.18	.392	3	0.13	0.07	0.20
TOTALS	5285	625	1313	207	42	113	588	478	1033	.248	.368	.311	600	4282	3.78	.478	159	20.24	8.23	28.47

Pitching Records for San Diego Padres

	ERA	W	L	Pct	G	GS	CG	ShO	GF	Sv	IP	R	ER	H	2B	3B	HR	BB	IW	SO	HB	WP	BK
Benes	3.03	15	11	.577	33	33	4	1	0	0	223.0	76	75	194	24	6	23	59	7	167	4	3	4
Hurst	3.29	15	8	.652	31	31	4	0	0	0	221.2	89	81	201	30	1	17	59	3	141	3	5	1
Rasmussen D	3.74	6	13	.316	24	24	1	1	0	0	146.2	74	61	155	17	6	12	49	3	75	2	1	1
Harris GW	2.23	9	5	.643	20	20	3	2	0	0	133.0	42	33	116	17	0	16	27	6	95	1	2	0
Whitson	5.03	4	6	.400	13	12	2	0	0	0	78.2	47	44	93	11	3	13	17	3	40	0	1	1
Peterson	4.45	3	4	.429	13	11	0	0	0	0	54.2	33	27	50	7	3	10	28	2	37	0	7	1
Bones	4.83	4	6	.400	11	11	0	0	0	0	54.0	33	29	57	7	1	3	18	0	31	0	4	0
Nolte	11.05	3	2	.600	6	6	0	0	0	0	22.0	27	27	37	5	1	6	10	0	15	0	1	1
Hammaker	5.79	0	1	.000	1	1	0	0	0	0	4.2	7	3	8	1	0	0	3	0	1	0	1	0
Maddux M	2.46	7	2	.778	64	1	0	0	27	5	98.2	30	27	78	10	3	4	27	3	57	1	5	0
Melendez J	3.27	8	5	.615	31	9	0	0	10	3	93.2	35	34	77	16	1	11	24	3	60	1	3	2
Rodriguez Ric	3.26	3	1	.750	64	1	0	0	19	0	80.0	31	29	66	11	1	8	44	8	40	0	4	1
Lefferts	3.91	1	6	.143	54	0	0	0	40	23	69.0	35	30	74	11	3	5	14	3	48	1	3	1
Andersen L	2.30	3	4	.429	38	0	0	0	24	13	47.0	13	12	39	5	0	0	13	3	40	0	1	0
Costello	3.09	1	0	1.000	27	0	0	0	6	0	35.0	15	12	37	4	1	2	17	3	24	0	2	0
Gardner W	7.08	0	1	.000	14	0	0	0	2	1	20.1	16	16	27	2	1	1	12	1	9	0	1	0
Clements P	3.77	1	0	1.000	12	0	0	0	4	0	14.1	8	6	13	3	0	0	9	4	8	0	0	0
Lilliquist	8.79	0	2	.000	6	2	0	0	1	0	14.1	14	14	25	6	0	3	4	1	7	0	0	0
Hernandez Jer	0.00	0	0	.000	9	0	0	0	7	2	14.1	1	0	8	2	0	0	5	0	9	0	2	0
Lewis Js	4.15	0	0	.000	12	0	0	0	2	0	13.0	7	6	14	3	1	2	11	2	10	0	1	0
Rosenberg	6.94	1	1	.500	10	0	0	0	5	0	11.2	9	9	11	1	0	3	5	1	6	0	2	0
Jackson Dar	9.00	0	0	.000	1	0	0	0	1	0	2.0	2	2	3	2	0	0	2	0	0	0	0	0
Scott Tim	9.00	0	0	.000	2	0	0	0	0	0	1.0	2	1	2	1	0	0	0	0	1	0	0	0
TOTALS	3.58	84	78	.519	496	162	14	4	148	47	1452.2	646	578	1385	196	32	139	457	56	921	13	49	13

Sabermetric Pitching Records for San Diego Padres

	Adj	|-Expected-|			|——Opposing Batters——|												Supported				
	ERA	W	L	Pct	BFP	Avg	Slg	OBA	RC/G	GDP	SB	CS	PK	PKE	SH	SF	RSup	RSp/G	W	L	Pct
Andersen L	2.11	5	2	.753	188	.232	.262	.284	2.64	2	6	2	0	0	4	2	17	3.26	5	2	.705
Benes	2.95	16	10	.608	908	.232	.358	.285	3.40	11	10	11	0	0	5	4	82	3.31	15	11	.558
Bones	4.67	4	6	.383	234	.269	.354	.321	4.16	4	3	1	0	0	0	4	43	7.17	7	3	.702
Clements P	3.14	1	0	.578	63	.255	.314	.349	3.78	3	0	0	0	0	0	3	7	4.40	1	0	.662
Costello	2.83	1	0	.628	157	.276	.366	.353	4.71	5	4	0	0	0	4	2	14	3.60	1	0	.618
Gardner W	6.64	0	1	.234	99	.310	.391	.394	6.49	1	2	0	0	0	0	0	3	1.33	0	1	.038
Hammaker	3.86	0	1	.476	27	.364	.409	.440	8.14	1	1	0	0	0	2	0	1	1.93	0	1	.200
Harris GW	2.17	10	4	.742	537	.233	.363	.273	3.37	3	13	8	0	0	9	2	49	3.32	10	4	.701
Hernandez Jer	0.00	0	0	.000	56	.157	.196	.232	1.53	1	0	0	0	0	0	0	1	0.63	0	0	.000
Hurst	3.21	13	10	.567	909	.241	.340	.292	3.39	14	11	6	4	3	8	4	116	4.71	16	7	.683
Jackson Dar	4.50	0	0	.400	10	.375	.625	.500	12.50	0	0	0	0	0	0	0	1	4.50	0	0	.500
Lefferts	3.78	3	4	.485	290	.285	.408	.318	4.40	4	6	4	0	1	10	5	17	2.22	2	5	.256
Lewis Js	3.46	0	0	.530	64	.275	.490	.403	7.33	2	1	0	0	0	2	0	10	6.92	0	0	.800
Lilliquist	8.16	0	2	.168	70	.379	.606	.414	10.32	0	0	1	0	1	0	0	7	4.40	0	2	.225
Maddux M	2.37	6	3	.706	388	.221	.300	.277	2.59	7	5	7	0	1	5	2	59	5.38	8	1	.837
Melendez J	3.17	7	6	.573	381	.221	.368	.269	3,30	2	1	6	0	0	2	6	38	3.65	7	6	.570
Nolte	10.64	1	4	.107	111	.378	.633	.423	11.76	1	9	1	0	1	0	3	24	9.82	2	3	.460
Peterson	4.28	3	4	.424	241	.242	.449	.329	5.00	4	2	4	0	0	4	2	17	2.80	2	5	.299
Rasmussen D	3.62	10	9	.507	633	.271	.385	.328	4.52	13	21	6	0	4	4	6	58	3.56	9	10	.491
Rodriguez Rich	3.15	2	2	.576	335	.234	.365	.335	3.86	12	6	4	0	2	7	2	36	4.05	2	2	.623
Rosenberg	6.17	1	1	.262	49	.250	.477	.327	4.93	1	0	1	0	0	0	0	4	3.09	0	2	.200
Scott Tim	0.00	0	0	.000	5	.400	.600	.400	5.57	0	0	1	0	0	0	0	0	0.00	0	0	.000
Whitson	4.92	4	6	.358	337	.299	.479	.332	5.40	10	8	2	0	0	6	3	32	3.66	4	6	.356
TOTALS	3.52	84	78	.521	6092	.252	.375	.308	3.96	101	109	65	4	13	72	50	636	3.94	90	72	.556

Batting 'Splits' Records for San Diego Padres

	G	AB	Run	Hit	2B	3B	HR	TB	RBI	W	K	IW	HB	SB	CS	GI DP	SH	SF	Avg	Slug	OBP	Runs Ctd
SPLITS for Coolbaugh																						
vs LHP	28	52	5	12	4	0	1	19	7	7	11	0	0	0	0	3	1	1	.231	.365	.317	6
vs RHP	47	128	7	27	4	1	1	36	8	12	34	2	1	0	3	5	3	0	.211	.281	.284	9
Home	31	89	6	21	8	0	1	32	10	10	24	1	1	0	2	5	3	1	.236	.360	.317	9
Away	29	91	6	18	0	1	1	23	5	9	21	1	0	0	1	3	1	0	.198	.253	.270	6
Grass	43	129	9	23	8	1	1	36	12	15	38	1	1	0	2	6	3	1	.178	.279	.267	9
Turf	17	51	3	16	0	0	1	19	3	4	7	1	0	0	1	2	1	0	.314	.373	.364	6
April/June	45	149	11	36	6	1	2	50	13	14	34	1	0	0	3	8	4	1	.242	.336	.305	13
July/October	15	31	1	3	2	0	0	5	2	5	11	1	1	0	0	0	0	0	.097	.161	.243	2
SPLITS for Gwynn T																						
vs LHP	98	211	29	62	7	4	2	83	19	13	7	0	0	2	0	4	0	2	.294	.393	.332	28
vs RHP	110	319	40	106	20	7	2	146	43	21	12	8	0	6	8	7	0	3	.332	.458	.370	51
Home	63	244	32	75	13	4	1	99	21	17	12	6	0	5	1	7	0	3	.307	.406	.348	34
Away	71	286	37	93	14	7	3	130	41	17	7	2	0	3	7	4	0	2	.325	.455	.361	44
Grass	95	371	51	119	20	7	3	162	37	29	16	6	0	5	3	9	0	3	.321	.437	.367	59
Turf	39	159	18	49	7	4	1	67	25	5	3	2	0	3	5	2	0	2	.308	.421	.325	20
April/June	77	308	45	110	19	8	2	151	46	17	10	4	0	4	6	6	0	4	.357	.490	.386	56
July/October	57	222	24	58	8	3	2	78	16	17	9	4	0	4	2	5	0	1	.261	.351	.313	24
SPLITS for McGriff F																						
vs LHP	111	213	34	58	7	1	14	109	48	39	56	1	1	2	1	6	0	5	.272	.512	.380	43
vs RHP	126	315	50	89	12	0	17	152	58	66	79	25	1	2	0	8	0	2	.283	.483	.406	66
Home	74	239	46	67	7	0	18	128	53	60	68	17	2	4	0	6	0	2	.280	.536	.426	60
Away	79	289	38	80	12	1	13	133	53	45	67	9	0	0	1	8	0	5	.277	.460	.369	50
Grass	113	387	71	111	14	0	25	200	79	78	101	20	2	4	0	10	0	5	.287	.517	.405	86
Turf	40	141	13	36	5	1	6	61	27	27	34	6	0	0	1	4	0	2	.255	.433	.371	24
April/June	74	254	41	69	8	1	15	124	50	55	65	14	1	1	1	9	0	2	.272	.488	.401	52
July/October	79	274	43	78	11	0	16	137	56	50	70	12	1	3	0	5	0	5	.285	.500	.391	58
SPLITS for San Diego Padres (all batters except pitchers)																						
vs LHP	927	1799	238	452	71	13	57	720	224	167	316	8	7	24	17	44	30	16	.251	.400	.315	224
vs RHP	1490	3609	398	869	133	23	64	1240	367	334	753	52	25	77	47	77	48	22	.241	.344	.308	385
Home	1103	2640	315	646	97	14	65	966	293	247	512	38	20	52	26	62	37	16	.245	.366	.312	304
Away	1070	2768	321	675	107	22	56	994	298	254	557	22	12	49	38	59	41	22	.244	.359	.308	306
Grass	1604	3983	493	979	145	25	99	1471	459	360	796	46	24	74	41	84	58	25	.246	.369	.310	460
Turf	569	1425	143	342	59	11	22	489	132	141	273	14	8	27	23	37	20	13	.240	.343	.309	150
April/June	1019	2598	304	654	98	23	49	945	283	253	490	33	16	45	35	57	39	19	.252	.364	.320	304
July/October	1154	2810	332	667	106	13	72	1015	308	248	579	27	16	56	29	64	39	19	.237	.361	.301	306

1991 SPLITS FOR San Diego Padres

BATTING SPLITS

	AVG	AB	R	H	2B	3B	HR	RBI	SB	CS	BB	K	OBA	SPCT
Total	.244	5408	636	1321	204	36	121	591	101	64	501	1069	.310	.362

	#Pit	#P/PA	GB	FB	G/F	G	IBB	HB	SH	SF	GDP
Miscellaneous	21978	3.63	2040	1238	1.65	162	60	32	78	38	121

	AVG	AB	R	H	2B	3B	HR	RBI	SB	CS	BB	K	OBA	SPCT
vs. Left	.251	1799	...	452	71	13	57	224	24	17	167	316	.315	.400
vs. Right	.241	3609	...	869	133	23	64	367	77	47	334	753	.308	.344
Home	.245	2640	315	646	97	14	65	293	52	26	247	512	.312	.366
Away	.244	2768	321	675	107	22	56	298	49	38	254	557	.308	.359
None on	.229	3177	...	728	114	16	68	68	0	0	272	622	.293	.339
Runners on	.266	2231	...	593	90	20	53	523	101	64	229	447	.333	.395
April	.253	704	83	178	21	7	10	78	10	6	63	140	.315	.345
May	.236	952	112	225	35	12	21	100	16	14	90	193	.305	.364
June	.266	942	109	251	42	4	18	105	19	15	100	157	.338	.377
July	.217	787	64	171	30	1	15	55	10	7	68	157	.281	.315
August	.242	983	123	238	34	6	31	117	19	12	79	212	.300	.384
September	.240	870	119	209	34	5	24	111	21	8	93	172	.317	.374
October	.288	170	26	49	8	1	2	25	6	2	8	38	.317	.382
None on/out	.237	1373	...	325	45	6	33	33	0	0	120	259	.302	.350
Scoring Posn	.267	1302	...	348	54	13	36	470	29	13	169	282	.347	.412
Close & Late	.252	932	...	235	31	6	22	112	14	7	89	181	.319	.369
Bases Loaded	.316	114	...	36	4	0	4	98	0	1	5	25	.318	.456
Batting #1	.262	673	102	176	23	6	9	52	34	19	52	110	.317	.354
Batting #2	.260	647	100	168	30	7	8	44	18	7	64	95	.326	.365
Batting #3	.312	648	89	202	32	12	7	78	13	9	47	37	.355	.431
Batting #4	.274	577	94	158	21	1	33	113	7	2	105	142	.385	.485
Batting #5	.262	623	61	163	22	2	19	100	10	10	50	130	.317	.395
Batting #6	.226	611	57	138	25	3	19	64	7	7	38	140	.276	.370
Batting #7	.206	567	45	117	23	2	13	63	5	9	53	132	.276	.323
Batting #8	.243	543	56	132	18	2	8	41	7	0	54	100	.319	.328
Batting #9	.129	519	32	67	10	1	5	36	0	1	38	183	.193	.181
As p	.086	325	16	28	3	0	1	12	0	0	24	135	.156	.105
As c	.261	635	66	166	26	4	17	92	8	10	27	122	.293	.395
As 1b	.274	569	88	156	20	1	32	112	5	1	109	149	.389	.482
As 2b	.266	586	78	156	22	4	10	57	26	9	66	109	.345	.369
As 3b	.194	571	54	111	15	3	14	52	2	7	65	128	.278	.305
As ss	.275	633	87	174	31	5	4	46	23	9	55	84	.334	.359
As lf	.229	594	58	136	23	2	15	64	10	8	50	126	.292	.350
As cf	.254	619	85	157	24	3	18	52	15	9	43	107	.304	.389
As rf	.305	636	82	194	32	12	6	75	12	9	43	49	.347	.421
Outfield	.263	1849	225	487	79	17	39	191	37	26	136	282	.315	.388
0.0 count	.335	789	...	264	39	0	27	119	...	...	1	0	.335	.487
After (0.1)	.203	2481	...	504	81	19	33	214	...	...	127	735	.245	.291
After (1.0)	.259	2138	...	553	84	17	61	258	...	...	326	334	.358	.399
Two strikes	.162	2468	...	399	71	13	32	169	...	...	226	1068	.235	.240
Grass	.246	3983	493	979	145	25	99	459	74	41	360	796	.310	.369
Turf	.240	1425	143	342	59	11	22	132	27	23	141	273	.309	.343
Day	.241	1528	184	368	68	15	39	173	32	19	137	312	.306	.382
Night	.246	3880	452	953	136	21	82	418	69	45	364	757	.312	.355
Inning 1.6	.243	3610	432	879	137	27	80	402	78	48	333	699	.309	.363
Inning 7+	.246	1798	204	442	67	9	41	189	23	16	168	370	.312	.362
vs.Atl	.234	610	70	143	24	10	14	65	10	6	47	118	.289	.375
vs.ChN	.249	389	62	97	14	2	12	58	11	6	55	87	.346	.388
vs.Cin	.255	601	63	153	24	3	9	61	18	8	66	137	.329	.349
vs.Hou	.239	590	75	141	26	4	15	68	12	11	67	123	.321	.373
vs.LA	.253	620	72	157	22	2	12	69	11	4	43	129	.301	.353
vs.Mon	.221	412	45	91	13	4	8	36	8	6	40	70	.298	.330
vs.NYN	.207	376	37	78	10	0	8	31	4	5	28	87	.260	.298
vs.Phi	.210	391	33	82	19	2	6	32	4	1	35	67	.274	.315
vs.Pit	.274	423	47	116	13	2	11	46	6	7	27	78	.318	.392
vs.StL	.242	384	39	93	16	0	8	39	6	5	31	58	.301	.346
vs.SF	.278	612	93	170	23	7	18	86	11	5	62	115	.348	.426

PITCHING SPLITS

	ERA	W	L	SV	SVOP	GS	CG	SHO	IP	H	ER	HR	BB	IBB	K
Total	3.57	84	78	47	64	162	14	12	1452.2	1385	577	139	457	56	921

	#Pit	#P/IP	GB	FB	G/F	BRp9	RA	WP	BK	SH	SF	R	HB	Hld
Miscellaneous	21653	14.91	2005	1433	1.40	11.49	334	49	13	72	50	646	13	41

	ERA	W	L	SV	SVOP	GS	CG	SHO	IP	H	ER	HR	BB	IBB	K
ST	3.68	65	61	0	0	162	14	4	1011.1	978	413	112	285	27	636
REL	3.36	19	17	47	64	0	0	0	441.1	407	165	27	172	29	285
Home	3.48	42	39	22	32	81	5	2	744.0	691	288	72	232	29	501
Away	3.68	42	39	25	32	81	9	2	708.2	694	290	67	225	27	420
April	4.25	11	10	8	11	21	0	0	188.1	197	89	23	63	7	126
May	4.20	13	15	6	11	28	4	0	257.0	263	120	30	103	12	152
June	3.47	14	14	5	8	28	3	1	246.2	231	95	26	71	9	131
July	3.45	10	14	5	6	24	2	0	213.2	190	82	18	78	13	125
August	3.35	15	14	9	13	29	3	3	263.0	235	98	19	64	8	186
September	2.92	17	10	11	12	27	2	0	240.0	219	78	17	71	7	165
October	3.27	4	1	3	3	5	0	0	44.0	50	16	6	7	0	36
Grass	3.67	62	58	34	48	120	10	3	1080.1	1027	440	107	336	40	676
Turf	3.34	22	20	13	16	42	4	1	372.1	358	138	32	121	16	245
Day	3.95	26	20	15	18	46	6	2	407.2	417	179	44	127	12	246
Night	3.44	58	58	32	46	116	8	2	1045.0	968	399	95	330	44	675
vs.Atl	3.44	7	11	2	6	18	4	1	162.1	150	62	16	56	10	91
vs.ChN	3.46	8	4	3	4	12	2	1	106.2	112	41	11	21	1	62
vs.Cin	3.06	10	8	6	6	18	1	1	159.0	155	54	21	42	4	122
vs.Hou	3.36	12	6	10	12	18	2	0	163.1	139	61	7	50	3	115
vs.LA	4.18	8	10	4	6	18	0	0	161.2	164	75	19	58	2	104
vs.Mon	3.82	6	6	2	4	12	1	0	113.0	116	48	9	45	10	79
vs.NYN	4.12	5	7	4	4	12	0	0	102.2	103	47	9	35	4	56
vs.Phi	4.49	3	9	1	3	12	1	0	106.1	114	53	11	37	5	57
vs.Pit	2.72	5	7	2	3	12	0	0	109.0	99	33	10	33	6	70
vs.StL	2.40	9	3	3	4	12	2	1	108.2	82	29	4	23	4	66
vs.SF	4.22	11	7	10	12	18	1	0	160.0	151	75	22	57	7	99

OPPOSING BATTERS VS. PITCHERS.

	AVG	AB	R	H	2B	3B	HR	RBI	SB	CS	BB	K	OBA	SPCT
Total	.252	5499	646	1385	196	32	139	607	109	65	457	921	.308	.375
vs. Left	.245	2249	...	551	73	18	59	248	42	25	203	390	.305	.372
vs. Right	.257	3250	...	834	123	14	80	359	67	40	254	531	.310	.377
ST	.253	3867	462	978	129	21	112	412	79	42	285	636	.304	.384
REL	.249	1632	184	407	67	11	27	195	30	23	172	285	.318	.354
Home	.246	2808	320	691	94	13	72	297	49	34	232	501	.304	.366
Away	.258	2691	326	694	102	19	67	310	60	31	225	420	.313	.385
None on	.249	3268	...	814	117	20	87	87	0	0	242	559	.302	.377
Runners on	.256	2231	...	571	79	12	52	520	109	65	215	362	.317	.372
None on/out	.243	1413	...	343	51	13	44	44	0	0	100	216	.294	.391
Scoring Posn	.251	1205	...	302	44	7	25	446	26	15	153	210	.327	.361
vs 1st Batr	.286	301	...	86	10	3	8	43	3	1	22	45	.328	.419
1st IP	.260	1679	140	436	66	11	31	236	44	22	162	313	.322	.367
Inning 1.6	.251	3693	434	927	128	23	105	408	76	43	281	608	.303	.383
Inning 7+	.254	1806	212	458	68	9	34	199	33	22	176	313	.318	.358
Close & Late	.237	972	...	230	33	3	15	114	22	17	93	185	.302	.323
0.0 count	.312	876	...	273	34	5	30	120	...	...	45	0	.344	.465
After (0.1)	.219	2548	...	557	79	10	50	251	...	...	101	621	.247	.316
After (1.0)	.267	2075	...	555	83	17	59	236	...	...	311	300	.362	.409
Two strikes	.187	2448	...	458	65	10	41	203	...	...	167	920	.240	.272
Pitch 1.15	.261	1545	...	403	57	9	32	162	29	20	127	270	.315	.372
Pitch 16.30	.252	1058	...	267	48	6	25	150	23	20	118	197	.327	.380
Pitch 31.45	.247	744	...	184	24	3	25	84	15	4	42	111	.287	.388
Pitch 46.60	.237	619	...	147	25	4	15	56	14	8	49	95	.295	.363
Pitch 61.75	.254	574	...	146	18	6	19	59	9	6	38	96	.300	.406
Pitch 76.90	.256	484	...	124	9	3	14	52	10	4	46	65	.320	.374
Pitch 91.105	.230	322	...	74	12	1	5	27	5	3	25	58	.281	.320
Pitch 106.20	.260	131	...	34	3	0	3	15	3	0	7	24	.302	.351
Pitch 121.35	.300	20	...	6	0	0	1	3	1	0	2	4	.364	.450
Pitch 136.50	.333	3	...	1	0	0	0	0	0	0	2	1	.600	.333
Pitch 151+	.000	0	...	0	0	0	0	0	0	0	1	0	1.000	.000

San Francisco Giants

Don Malcolm

SAN FRANCISCO											
YEAR	1982	1983	1984	1985	1986	1987	1988	1989	1990	1991	TOT
W	87	79	66	62	83	90	83	92	85	75	802
L	75	83	96	100	79	72	79	70	77	87	818
WPCT	0.537	0.488	0.407	0.383	0.512	0.556	0.512	0.568	0.525	0.463	0.495
R	673	687	682	556	698	783	670	699	719	649	6816
RA	687	697	807	674	618	669	626	600	710	697	6785
PWPT	0.490	0.493	0.417	0.405	0.561	0.578	0.534	0.576	0.506	0.464	0.502
PythW	79	80	67	66	91	94	86	93	82	75	81
PythL	83	82	95	96	71	68	76	69	80	87	81
LUCK	8	-1	-1	-4	-8	-4	-3	-1	3	0	-11

Defensive Efficiency Record: .7039

THE TRADE OF DOOM

Mark down December 9, 1991 in your baseball history books, gang. It's going to be remembered as one of the blackest days in the annals of the Giants. For it is entirely possible that Al Rosen has made the worst trade in the history of baseball.

Consider Kevin Mitchell. He's rough—a history of running with a bad crowd. Naturally, he's ornery, hard to deal with, someone who has no patience with the standard type of rules set up for baseball (which ought to be a lot like boot camp as far as the executives in charge are concerned, most of whom grew up and/or played ball in the pre-free agent period).

Of course, no one wants a troublemaker on their team. Even people with a reasonable tolerance of differences in lifestyle, outlook, ethnic background, etc. wishes to avoid strife. It's human nature. No matter how valuable an individual might be, there is always a point of no return at which an organization has to jettison the individual in order to retain its sovereignty.

So at such a point, when there is obvious conflict, a very dispassionate examination of the problem is needed, an exacting process of evaluation that allows for a set of scenarios to be created that can make the relationship workable, or that provides a clear set of indicators with respect to the sources of conflict, their potential remedies, and the actions that will be taken should none of the attempts at reconciliation work.

Nowhere in any of the materials surrounding the Kevin Mitchell trade is there any evidence that Al Rosen—or any member of the San Francisco Giants management—made any effort along the lines described above. When a player like Kevin Mitchell, who has hit 108 home runs in the past three seasons, begins demonstrating symptoms of malaise, it is the duty of the organization to work with that individual in an intensive manner to resolve differences. It is somewhat akin to marriage counseling: if you have a loved one with whom things are going haywire, you don't just give your husband or wife their unconditional release.

Like it not, Al Rosen, the world has changed. A $3 million ballplayer brings a certain set of additional problems along with him, even if he is realtively well-adjusted. Kevin Mitchell has been a member of the San Francisco Giants since July 4, 1987: there is no possible way for you to plead ignorance concerning his troubled background. There is no evidence that what you have done (trading Mitchell for Bill Swift and Mike Jackson, two middling relievers from the Mariners, and Dave Burba, a marginal prospect) is based on a series of steps that left you no alternative. Instead, this trade smells like a panic-stricken manuever based on an unfounded rape charge, engineered to relieve pressure from the media and other, more obscure sources of tension within the Giants organization itself.

The world has changed. The world of baseball continues to oscillate between the 1950's mentality of labor relations and the 1980's cynosure of greed, a pas-de-deux of incompatible partners that keeps lurching the game closer and closer to doom like a runaway train. The world of baseball has changed, but many of the game's prime movers have shown no inkling of the implications lurking within the changes. Consequently, they try to operate like robber barons in an age where the individual player has become a mini-generalissimo in his own right, complete with stock options, entourage, and a rapidly thickening mythology.

Something's got to give, guys. You've got to start looking at the human factors involved in the mess you're creating, and you've got to quit passing the buck like Al Rosen did. He will doubtless be rewarded by his management for getting rid of a terrible problem in the clubhouse and lowering the Giants' payroll. But he has utterly failed—totally, unredeemably abrogated—the moral obligations and requirements of management.

Doubtless the fifties generation harbors an incredible resentment of the 80's ballplayer, due to the total upside-down realignment of the game's economic basis. But they need to look at who is really responsible for the situation that they find themselves in. The players did not create the conditions of the game that ultimately required what amounted to an historic labor movement. The players did not pen language into any basic agreement that forced salaries to escalate at a precipitously irresponsible rate. The players did not create the strange new world of societal pressures that make the job of manager and general manager into schizoid tasks.

The problem for Al Rosen is that he cannot trade Bob Lurie. The GM's of baseball, like any group of people in what really is middle management (they are kowtowing to what is generally an absentee caste of corporate ownership), have no choice but to deal with all of the problems of the game that move from both directions—down from the owners, up from the players—right at them. The joke in government contracting circles about having to train your supervisor is a poignant reality in baseball. The "owner virus" of the game has spread to the available population faster than AIDS, and appears to be intensifying its effects. At best, GM's are forced to be carriers: at worst, they succumb to the rhetoric of the disease, and become more virulent exponents of a fatal position.

So the Mitchell trade is emblematic of baseball's escalating malaise, and, to make matters worse, it's a real turkey of a deal for the Giants personnel-wise. All right, Mitchell is gone. The middle of your order still has Will Clark and Matt Williams, but Matt's a poor choice for a cleanup hitter because he has little plate discipline. And with no one behind him for protection, he's probably going to further expand his strike zone to try to handle the psychological demands of batting fourth. OK, maybe you don't buy any of that reasoning. Let's wait and see about Matt. But let's look at what we're going to trot out there in the outfield now that Mitchell is gone.

GLOOM: IT RHYMES WITH DOOM AND IT'S PLENTIFUL AT CANDLESTICK

Roger Craig has already stated that he will be platooning-and-shifting in the outfield in '92. Against righties, he claims that it will be Mark Leonard in left, Willie McGee in center, and Kevin Bass in right. Against lefties, it's going to be Bass in left, Darren Lewis in center, and McGee in right. This is the type of platooning that flies in the face of several profound implications in Jamesian theory, but that is all-too-common in baseball. In virtually all cases, managers will opt for even a mediocre veteran over a relatively untested younger player when such an option exists. Hence the reasoning for continuing to play an over-the-hill stiff like Kevin Bass over two younger players (Leonard and Lewis).

It's poor reasoning. Bass is 33 and his best role on any team at this point in his career is as a backup player, a fourth outfielder. If Craig really wants to take some steps that can help his team, he should play an outfield of Leonard in left, Lewis in center, and McGee in right. This gives him a good centerfielder and a decent leadoff hitter with good strike zone judgement on a fulltime basis. It allows McGee to bat second, where he's probably best used, on a fulltime basis. It allows the best remaining hitting prospect the Giants have—Mark Leonard—to get a full shot at being the number five hitter to protect Matt Williams.

What, you may ask, is the "profound implication in Jamesian theory" being ignored by Craig? It is simply this: younger players should be given a shot as soon as humanly possible, just as soon as you think they might be ready based upon major-league equivalences (MLE's). A young player is a great deal more likely to exceed expectations than an old one. Hence, younger players should be given more playing time when the choice is between a rookie and a journeyman.

It's a precept that is almost never followed, except when circumstances make it unavoidable, or when a rookie is considered to be so "hot" that the organization decides to make an exception. Much of the evaluation process of a rookie is based upon factors that do not contribute to a profile of his likely performance, however. Hence a player at a non-critical defensive position (left field, right field, first base) who is a 27th round pick (e.g. Mark Leonard) has a tough time getting a long look if there is anything in his way—a player drafted earlier or a journeyman player of any kind (and Kevin Bass and Mike Felder bookend the range within the class of journeymen). The Giants doubtless kept Mark Leonard in Class A ball at least a season more than necessary, but that's what happens when you're a 27th round draft pick. What they ought to see is that here's a 27 year old player with a .317 lifetime minor league average who is never going to be more ready to hold a major-league job than he is now. The cumulative MLE data for Mark Leonard as he goes into 1992 looks like this:

AB	R	H	TB	D	T	HR	RBI	BB	SO	SB	CS
480	70	131	213	30	3	16	84	71	96	6	5

This translates to a .274 BA, with a .448 SA and .368 OBP. The RC27 for this projected season: 6.08. This is better than anything that any of the remaining Giant outfielders can produce.

But Roger Craig is more likely to look at the numbers he's handed by the drones who use the abacus in Wind Tunnel 112 at the Stick, discern brightly that Leonard hit .100 against lefties last year, and start patting Kevin Bass on his rapidly aging fanny. And, of course, it's true: Mark Leonard did hit .100 against lefties in '91. He was 1-for-10 against them—the type of sample size that put the Elias Sports Bureau where they are today.

So it will likely be the platoon of doom at the Stick this year, which rhymes with gloom, and we all know that it must be the prevailing foggy conditions in San Francisco that make even the sharpest minds list in whatever direction appears to have the greatest amount of soft-focus. But I'm not convinced that Roger Craig's mind has ever been of sufficient caliber to make the type of decisions that permit a team to have long-term, ongoing success. The gloom boom continues unabated when we visit the scene of the biggest crime at Candlestick: the pitching staff.

THREE MORE FOR THE MEAT MACHINE

I feel for Messrs. Swift, Jackson, and Burba. They are joining a group of athletes who need protection above and beyond what any mere players' union can provide. They are going to become members of a Roger Craig pitching staff, a.k.a the Meat Machine.

But before we smack Roger around some more, let's return to the Mitchell trade and ask one of my favorite questions (Brock Hanke knows what's coming...):

Why??

Well, you can never have enough pitching, right?

But the truth is that you never have enough of the right pitching, so you've got to improvise: you either have to make some of the wrong ingredients work in a makeshift recipe, or you have to (and read my lips very carefully) trade for exactly what function you don't have covered.

Did the Giants do this when they traded Kevin Mitchell?

Of course not.

The Giants need three more righty relievers like most of us need a second head. Last year they used Brantley as the right-handed stopper, and had Kelly Downs, Francisco Oliveras, Don Robinson, and Rod Beck behind him. Subtract Robinson, and add Swift, Jackson, and Burba, all of whom relieved last season in Seattle, and you have seven righties whose primary role last year was relief.

What the Giants needed was a lefty reliever. Presently they have one: Dave Righetti. The staff is, in a phrase, woefully unbalanced. Trading a franchise player away is rash enough, but to have completely failed to address a critical team need in such a key transaction borders on criminal activity.

So what are you going to do with all those relievers, Rog? Well, let's see: Oliveras, Swift, Burba, and Beck have all started a lot in the minors. But Oliveras and Swift were ineffective as starters in the majors. So, if you're conservative, you give Burba and Beck a shot as starters and see if one of them pans out. Knowing Craig—and knowing the way baseball people tend to think—it will probably be Burba, even though Beck looks like the better prospect.

Here's my favorite question again...

Why?

Because Burba is older. (Never mind that Beck, who's two years younger, has actually been in the minors a year longer.) And—even more importantly—because the Giants are gonna try as hard as they can to make the Mitchell trade look good. They're going to probably make Swift into the righty closer and hope he'll rack up a bunch of saves early so that they can point to the trade and say, "See? It's working." They're going to talk a lot about Michael Jackson (yes, it will be Michael: they want you to think of that angry young androgynous semi-black billionaire whose next costume change will make him look like an anorexic Napoleon) has such a great arm. I can hear it now: "Michael is such a take-charge kind of guy. He's the type of take-charge guy we've been needing down in the pen."

You won't hear about it (his arm, that is) when it falls off in July, however, after Rog has burned him out. And Burba will get about 9 starts before his ERA settles in at about 5.27, whereupon he will be quietly sent to the bullpen to look forlorn and hold a mop for approximately five weeks, after which he will even more quietly be shipped to Phoenix in a plain brown wrapper.

It's all so predictable, it makes me sick. And it ought to make you sick, too. Humm baby, my ass.

Oh, yeah: did I mention that the Giants also unloaded a lefty pitcher named Mike Remlinger in the Mitchell deal? You'd probably do well to remember that name. Remlinger was the Giants' #1 pick in 1987. He was injured in 1988, and hasn't come back to where he was at the point. The Giants are virtually hopeless at rehabilitation (truth be told, they're downright poor at development, too), so one gets the feeling that the change of scenery could do wonders for Remlinger. Don't be surprised if he gets a long look in Seattle, what with the rotator cuff injury to Brian Holman. Fifty homers from Mitchell and 15 wins from Remlinger still might not be enough to put Al Rosen on the bread line, however.

But we can hope...

San Francisco Giants Home Park Performance Factors

	Outs	Runs	Hits	2b	3b	HR	W	K	SH	SF	HBP	IBB	SB	CS	GDP
Home LH Batters	.942	.967	.998	.788	.930	.847	.974	.934	.870	2.093	.797	.747	1.860	1.288	.930
Home RH Batters	.978	.945	.943	.929	.775	1.002	.922	1.057	.929	1.178	1.041	.844	.925	.810	.761
All Home Batters	.957	.961	.957	.904	.869	.945	.933	1.000	.894	1.219	1.036	.837	.968	.901	.835
Opp LH Batters	.973	1.122	1.020	.946	1.374	1.179	1.095	.985	.992	.992	1.190	1.113	.974	.913	.971
Opp RH Batters	.975	1.118	1.063	1.150	.876	1.093	1.018	.956	1.125	1.169	1.029	.997	1.336	.913	.888
All Opp Batters	.967	1.102	1.044	1.069	1.038	1.098	1.052	.958	1.068	1.142	1.066	1.052	1.178	.950	.912
All LH Batters	.961	1.059	1.010	.874	1.113	1.011	1.046	.964	.929	1.186	.966	.928	1.000	.918	.952
All RH Batters	.976	1.026	1.001	1.037	.817	1.045	.969	1.007	1.016	1.177	1.034	.921	1.112	.861	.827
All Batters	.962	1.032	1.000	.986	.939	1.018	.994	.980	.971	1.170	1.052	.942	1.082	.925	.875

Conventional Batting Records for San Francisco Giants

	G	AB	Run	Hit	2B	3B	HR	TB	RBI	W	K	IW	HB	SB	CS	BRng Eff	GI DP	SH	SF	Avg	Slug	OBP	Runs Ctd
Decker S	79	233	11	48	7	1	5	72	24	16	44	1	3	0	1	.320	7	2	4	.206	.309	.262	18
Clark W	148	565	84	170	32	7	29	303	116	51	91	12	2	4	2	.375	5	0	4	.301	.536	.359	111
Thompson Ro	144	492	74	129	24	5	19	220	48	63	95	2	6	14	7	.517	5	11	1	.262	.447	.352	82
Williams MD	157	589	72	158	24	5	34	294	98	33	128	6	6	5	5	.385	11	0	7	.268	.499	.310	88
Uribe	90	231	23	51	8	4	1	70	12	20	33	6	0	3	4	.417	2	1	0	.221	.303	.283	20
Mitchell K	113	371	52	95	13	1	27	191	69	43	57	8	5	2	3	.286	6	0	4	.256	.515	.338	65
McGee	131	497	67	155	30	3	4	203	43	34	74	3	2	17	9	.474	11	8	2	.312	.408	.357	71
Bass K	124	361	43	84	10	4	10	132	40	36	56	8	4	7	4	.348	12	2	3	.233	.366	.307	40
Felder	132	348	51	92	10	6	0	114	18	30	31	2	1	21	6	.557	2	4	0	.264	.328	.325	41
Anderson D	100	226	24	56	5	2	2	71	13	12	35	2	0	2	4	.432	8	2	0	.248	.314	.286	18
Lewis D	72	222	41	55	5	3	1	69	15	36	30	0	2	13	7	.426	1	7	0	.248	.311	.358	28
Manwaring	67	178	16	40	9	0	0	49	19	9	22	0	3	1	1	.375	2	7	2	.225	.275	.271	14
Kennedy	69	171	12	40	7	1	3	58	13	11	31	4	1	0	0	.375	4	0	1	.234	.339	.283	16
Leonard M	64	129	14	31	7	1	2	46	14	12	25	1	1	0	1	.400	3	1	2	.240	.357	.306	14
Litton	59	127	13	23	7	1	1	35	15	11	25	0	1	0	2	.563	2	3	1	.181	.276	.250	9
Kingery	91	110	13	20	2	2	0	26	8	15	21	1	0	1	0	.368	3	0	0	.182	.236	.280	8
Benjamin	54	106	12	13	3	0	2	22	8	7	26	2	2	3	0	.500	1	3	2	.123	.208	.188	5
Black	35	71	3	13	3	0	0	16	6	0	20	0	0	0	0	.000	0	9	0	.183	.225	.183	3
Herr	32	60	6	15	1	1	0	18	7	13	7	1	0	2	0	.200	3	0	0	.250	.300	.384	8
Burkett	36	55	0	5	1	0	0	6	1	3	26	0	0	0	0	.000	0	9	0	.091	.109	.138	1
Wilson Tr	48	51	7	12	1	0	1	16	5	4	16	0	1	0	0	.167	2	8	0	.235	.314	.304	5
Perezchica	23	48	2	11	4	1	0	17	3	2	12	0	0	0	1	.429	0	0	0	.229	.354	.260	4
Robinson D	35	40	1	6	1	0	0	7	4	1	13	0	0	0	0	.000	0	0	0	.150	.175	.171	1
Clayton	9	26	0	3	1	0	0	4	2	1	6	0	0	0	0	.000	1	0	0	.115	.154	.148	0
Wood	10	25	0	3	0	0	0	3	1	2	11	0	0	0	0	.000	0	1	0	.120	.120	.185	1
Downs	45	23	3	2	0	0	0	2	1	1	5	0	0	0	0	.250	0	2	0	.087	.087	.125	0
McClellan	13	21	0	3	0	0	0	3	1	1	3	0	0	0	0	.000	0	2	0	.143	.143	.182	1
Coles	11	14	1	3	0	0	0	3	0	0	2	0	0	0	0	.333	1	0	0	.214	.214	.214	0
Parker R	13	14	0	1	0	0	0	1	1	1	5	0	0	0	0	.000	0	0	0	.071	.071	.133	0
Hickerson	17	12	0	0	0	0	0	0	0	0	6	0	0	0	0	.000	0	1	0	.000	.000	.000	0
Oliveras	55	10	0	2	0	0	0	2	0	0	4	0	0	0	0	.000	0	0	0	.200	.200	.200	0
LaCoss	18	9	2	2	0	0	0	2	0	1	6	0	0	0	0	.000	0	0	0	.222	.222	.300	1
Remlinger	8	7	1	0	0	0	0	0	0	1	2	0	0	0	0	.000	0	4	0	.000	.000	.125	0
Heredia G	7	7	0	3	0	0	0	3	0	1	1	0	0	0	0	.000	0	0	0	.429	.429	.500	2
Garrelts	11	4	1	0	0	0	0	0	0	0	1	0	0	0	0	.500	0	1	0	.000	.000	.000	0
Brantley J	67	3	0	0	0	0	0	0	0	0	1	0	0	0	0	.000	0	1	0	.000	.000	.000	0
Righetti	61	3	0	0	0	0	0	0	0	0	2	0	0	0	0	.000	0	1	0	.000	.000	.000	0
Reuschel	4	2	0	0	0	0	0	0	0	0	0	0	0	0	0	.000	0	0	0	.000	.000	.000	0
Beck	31	2	0	1	0	0	0	1	0	0	0	0	0	0	0	.000	0	0	0	.500	.500	.500	1
Gunderson	2	0	0	0	0	0	0	0	0	0	0	0	0	0	0	.000	0	0	0	.000	.000	.000	0
Segura	11	0	0	0	0	0	0	0	0	0	0	0	0	0	0	.000	0	0	0	.000	.000	.000	0
TOTALS	2296	5463	649	1345	215	48	141	2079	605	471	973	59	40	95	57	.409	92	90	33	.246	.381	.309	651

Sabermetric Batting Records for San Francisco Giants

	Ball Park Adjusted												Runs		Run/					
	AB	Run	Hit	2B	3B	HR	RBI	W	SO	Avg	Slug	OBP	Ctd	Outs	27o	OW%	OG	OWAR	DWAR	TWAR
Anderson D	221	24	56	5	1	2	13	11	35	.253	.312	.289	18	176	2.76	.306	7	-0.28	0.56	0.27
Bass K	350	44	84	9	3	10	41	35	54	.240	.369	.314	41	283	3.91	.470	10	1.26	0.33	1.59
Benjamin	103	12	13	3	0	2	8	6	26	.126	.214	.186	5	95	1.42	.105	4	-0.86	0.88	0.01
Clark W	549	87	171	27	8	29	121	52	87	.311	.548	.368	115	390	7.96	.786	14	6.30	0.61	6.90
Clayton	25	0	3	1	0	0	2	0	6	.120	.160	.120	0	22	0.00	.000	1	-0.29	-0.07	-0.36
Coles	13	1	3	0	0	0	0	0	2	.231	.231	.231	1	10	2.70	.297	0	-0.02	-0.01	-0.03
Decker S	228	11	48	7	0	5	25	15	44	.211	.307	.264	19	191	2.69	.295	7	-0.39	-0.16	-0.55
Felder	338	52	92	9	5	0	18	29	30	.272	.328	.332	41	255	4.34	.522	9	1.62	0.43	2.05
Herr	58	6	15	0	0	0	7	12	6	.259	.259	.386	7	45	4.20	.505	2	0.26	0.67	0.92
Kennedy	165	12	40	6	1	3	13	11	29	.242	.345	.288	16	129	3.35	.394	5	0.21	-0.42	-0.21
Kingery	106	13	20	1	2	0	8	15	20	.189	.236	.289	8	88	2.45	.259	3	-0.30	0.13	-0.17
Leonard M	124	14	31	6	1	2	14	12	23	.250	.363	.309	14	99	3.82	.458	4	0.40	0.06	0.46
Lewis D	218	42	55	5	2	1	15	34	30	.252	.307	.358	28	176	4.30	.517	7	1.09	0.68	1.76
Litton	124	13	23	7	0	1	15	10	25	.185	.266	.250	9	107	2.27	.230	4	-0.48	0.30	-0.18
Manwaring	174	16	40	9	0	0	19	8	22	.230	.282	.273	15	144	2.81	.314	5	-0.19	-0.24	-0.43
McGee	484	69	155	29	2	4	44	33	72	.320	.413	.365	73	355	5.55	.641	13	3.83	0.20	4.03
Mitchell K	364	53	95	13	0	28	72	41	57	.261	.527	.341	68	279	6.58	.715	10	3.77	0.32	4.09
Parker R	13	0	1	0	0	0	1	0	5	.077	.077	.077	0	12	0.00	.000	0	-0.16	0.01	-0.14
Perezchica	47	2	11	4	0	0	3	1	12	.234	.319	.250	4	36	3.00	.343	1	-0.01	0.05	0.04
Thompson Ro	483	76	129	24	4	19	50	61	95	.267	.451	.356	83	376	5.96	.673	14	4.50	1.88	6.38
Uribe	224	23	51	7	3	1	12	19	32	.228	.299	.288	20	177	3.05	.350	7	0.00	0.63	0.63
Williams MD	578	74	158	24	4	35	102	32	128	.273	.510	.314	91	441	5.57	.643	16	4.78	1.09	5.87
Wood	24	0	3	0	0	0	1	2	10	.125	.125	.192	1	21	1.29	.087	1	-0.20	-0.02	-0.22
TOTALS	5307	669	1345	212	45	144	626	467	952	.253	.392	.317	675	4220	4.32	.519	156	26.48	7.89	34.36

Pitching Records for San Francisco Giants

	ERA	W	L	Pct	G	GS	CG	ShO	GF	Sv	IP	R	ER	H	2B	3B	HR	BB	IW	SO	HB	WP	BK
Black	3.99	12	16	.429	34	34	3	3	0	0	214.1	104	95	201	31	5	25	71	8	104	4	6	6
Burkett	4.18	12	11	.522	36	34	3	1	0	0	206.2	103	96	223	31	2	19	60	2	131	10	5	0
Wilson Tr	3.56	13	11	.542	44	29	2	1	6	0	202.0	87	80	173	32	5	13	77	4	139	5	5	3
McClellan	4.56	3	6	.333	13	12	1	0	1	0	71.0	41	36	68	12	1	12	25	1	44	1	5	0
Remlinger	4.37	2	1	.667	8	6	1	1	1	0	35.0	17	17	36	9	0	5	20	1	19	0	2	1
Heredia G	3.82	0	2	.000	7	4	0	0	1	0	33.0	14	14	27	3	1	4	7	2	13	0	1	0
Robinson D	4.38	5	9	.357	34	16	0	0	7	1	121.1	64	59	123	25	5	12	50	7	78	1	1	0
Downs	4.19	10	4	.714	45	11	0	0	4	0	111.2	59	52	99	16	2	12	53	9	62	3	4	1
Brantley J	2.45	5	2	.714	67	0	0	0	39	15	95.1	27	26	78	13	1	8	52	10	81	5	6	0
Oliveras	3.86	6	6	.500	55	1	0	0	17	3	79.1	36	34	69	7	1	12	22	4	48	1	2	2
Righetti	3.39	2	7	.222	61	0	0	0	49	24	71.2	29	27	64	12	0	4	28	6	51	3	1	1
Beck	3.78	1	1	.500	31	0	0	0	10	1	52.1	22	22	53	11	2	4	13	2	38	1	0	0
Hickerson	3.60	2	2	.500	17	6	0	0	4	0	50.0	20	20	53	11	0	3	17	3	43	0	2	0
LaCoss	7.23	1	5	.167	18	5	0	0	6	0	47.1	39	38	61	10	2	4	24	0	30	2	2	0
Garrelts	6.41	1	1	.500	8	3	0	0	2	0	19.2	14	14	25	3	1	5	9	0	8	0	0	0
Segura	4.41	0	1	.000	11	0	0	0	2	0	16.1	11	8	20	0	1	1	5	0	10	0	2	0
Reuschel	4.22	0	2	.000	4	1	0	0	1	0	10.2	5	5	17	5	0	0	7	1	4	0	0	0
Gunderson	5.40	0	0	.000	2	0	0	0	1	1	3.1	4	2	6	2	0	0	1	0	2	0	0	0
Litton	9.00	0	0	.000	1	0	0	0	1	0	1.0	1	1	1	0	1	0	3	0	0	0	0	0
TOTALS	4.03	75	87	.463	496	162	10	6	152	45	1442.0	697	646	1397	233	30	143	544	60	905	36	44	14

Sabermetric Pitching Records for San Francisco Giants

	Adj	|-Expected-|			|——Opposing Batters——|												Supported				
	ERA	W	L	Pct	BFP	Avg	Slg	OBA	RC/G	GDP	SB	CS	PK	PKE	SH	SF	RSup	RSp/G	W	L	Pct
Beck	3.78	1	1	.485	214	.273	.412	.319	4.24	4	2	3	0	0	4	2	24	4.13	1	1	.543
Black	4.07	13	15	.448	893	.251	.396	.313	4.07	20	14	11	1	5	11	7	96	4.03	14	14	.495
Brantley J	2.45	5	2	.691	411	.225	.338	.332	4.23	6	17	2	0	0	4	4	25	2.36	3	4	.480
Burkett	4.31	10	13	.421	890	.277	.392	.332	4.51	14	17	16	3	0	8	8	97	4.22	11	12	.490
Downs	4.27	6	8	.425	479	.239	.373	.326	4.31	10	15	4	0	1	4	4	64	5.16	8	6	.593
Garrelts	6.41	0	2	.247	90	.313	.563	.378	7.88	2	4	1	0	0	0	1	24	10.98	1	1	.746
Gunderson	5.40	0	0	.316	18	.353	.471	.389	8.72	0	0	0	0	0	0	0	0	0.00	0	0	.000
Heredia G	3.82	1	1	.481	126	.233	.379	.274	2.94	4	2	2	0	0	2	1	7	1.91	0	2	.200
Hickerson	3.60	2	2	.510	212	.275	.378	.333	4.16	6	6	4	0	1	2	0	21	3.78	2	2	.524
LaCoss	7.42	1	5	.197	225	.314	.448	.392	6.69	5	5	2	0	0	3	2	24	4.56	2	4	.275
Litton	9.00	0	0	.143	7	.250	.750	.571	19.61	0	0	0	0	0	0	0	3	27.00	0	0	.900
McClellan	4.69	3	6	.380	300	.252	.437	.316	4.67	6	12	5	0	0	3	1	33	4.18	4	5	.443
Oliveras	3.97	6	6	.461	316	.242	.400	.296	3.51	6	5	9	0	0	5	3	38	4.31	6	6	.541
Remlinger	4.37	1	2	.414	155	.271	.451	.364	5.43	6	1	1	0	1	1	1	21	5.40	2	1	.604
Reuschel	4.22	1	1	.431	54	.370	.478	.453	8.76	1	0	0	0	0	1	0	1	0.84	0	2	.038
Righetti	3.39	5	4	.540	304	.240	.330	.317	3.67	5	8	4	0	4	4	2	13	1.63	2	7	.188
Robinson D	4.45	6	8	.405	525	.265	.417	.334	4.94	8	10	5	0	1	4	5	48	3.56	5	9	.390
Segura	4.41	0	1	.410	72	.303	.379	.352	4.35	3	3	2	0	0	1	0	11	6.06	1	0	.654
Wilson Tr	3.65	12	12	.503	841	.234	.343	.308	3.45	18	8	12	0	7	14	5	99	4.41	14	10	.593
TOTALS	4.16	71	91	.438	6132	.257	.390	.326	4.32	124	129	83	4	20	71	46	649	4.05	79	83	.487

Batting 'Splits' Records for San Francisco Giants

	G	AB	Run	Hit	2B	3B	HR	TB	RBI	W	K	IW	HB	SB	CS	GIDP	SH	SF	Avg	Slug	OBP	Runs Ctd
SPLITS for Bass K																						
vs LHP	59	113	19	27	5	0	6	50	15	5	15	1	2	2	1	4	0	3	.239	.442	.276	13
vs RHP	102	248	24	57	5	4	4	82	25	31	41	7	2	5	3	8	2	0	.230	.331	.320	26
Home	63	167	21	35	2	2	5	56	17	21	35	4	1	4	1	5	2	2	.210	.335	.298	17
Away	61	194	22	49	8	2	5	76	23	15	21	4	3	3	3	7	0	1	.253	.392	.315	22
Grass	91	249	30	57	4	4	8	93	25	26	47	6	3	5	2	7	2	2	.229	.373	.307	29
Turf	33	112	13	27	6	0	2	39	15	10	9	2	1	2	2	5	0	1	.241	.348	.306	11
April/June	60	204	18	47	7	1	4	68	16	18	29	6	2	4	3	9	0	0	.230	.333	.299	18
July/October	64	157	25	37	3	3	6	64	24	18	27	2	2	3	1	3	2	3	.236	.408	.317	21
SPLITS for Felder																						
vs LHP	57	107	19	29	5	1	0	36	4	7	8	1	0	5	1	2	3	0	.271	.336	.316	12
vs RHP	101	241	32	63	5	5	0	78	14	23	23	1	1	16	5	0	1	0	.261	.324	.328	29
Home	68	168	22	48	5	3	0	59	10	13	13	2	0	10	1	1	1	0	.286	.351	.337	22
Away	64	180	29	44	5	3	0	55	8	17	18	0	1	11	5	1	3	0	.244	.306	.313	19
Grass	103	270	42	78	7	5	0	95	17	21	26	2	1	17	5	2	4	0	.289	.352	.342	35
Turf	29	78	9	14	3	1	0	19	1	9	5	0	0	4	1	0	0	0	.179	.244	.264	6
April/June	70	219	37	64	5	6	0	81	10	17	20	1	1	17	4	1	2	0	.292	.370	.346	31
July/October	62	129	14	28	5	0	0	33	8	13	11	1	0	4	2	1	2	0	.217	.256	.289	10
SPLITS for Williams MD																						
vs LHP	75	165	21	46	8	0	7	75	25	9	34	4	1	2	4	3	0	3	.279	.455	.315	22
vs RHP	144	424	51	112	16	5	27	219	73	24	94	2	5	3	1	8	0	4	.264	.517	.309	66
Home	78	289	35	83	12	3	17	152	46	16	60	5	2	3	3	5	0	2	.287	.526	.327	48
Away	79	300	37	75	12	2	17	142	52	17	68	1	4	2	2	6	0	5	.250	.473	.294	41
Grass	117	444	51	126	19	3	24	223	71	20	92	6	4	5	5	8	0	5	.284	.502	.317	68
Turf	40	145	21	32	5	2	10	71	27	13	36	0	2	0	0	3	0	2	.221	.490	.290	21
April/June	73	280	25	64	13	2	10	111	41	13	52	4	2	2	3	4	0	2	.229	.396	.266	28
July/October	84	309	47	94	11	3	24	183	57	20	76	2	4	3	2	7	0	5	.304	.592	.349	62
SPLITS for San Francisco Giants (all batters except pitchers)																						
vs LHP	828	1597	204	399	73	11	45	629	194	126	253	18	9	28	22	24	24	15	.250	.394	.306	193
vs RHP	1615	3866	445	946	142	37	96	1450	411	345	720	41	31	67	35	68	66	18	.245	.375	.310	458
Home	1115	2642	306	645	108	25	69	1010	283	234	454	33	17	46	28	50	48	12	.244	.382	.308	313
Away	1181	2821	343	700	107	23	72	1069	322	237	519	26	23	49	29	42	42	21	.248	.379	.309	338
Grass	1676	4005	457	984	150	35	105	1519	424	336	716	50	27	72	44	70	68	21	.246	.379	.307	469
Turf	620	1458	192	361	65	13	36	560	181	135	257	9	13	23	13	22	22	12	.248	.384	.315	182
April/June	1041	2546	292	621	100	25	64	963	274	213	449	37	16	52	28	48	42	17	.244	.378	.304	295
July/October	1255	2917	357	724	115	23	77	1116	331	258	524	22	24	43	29	44	48	16	.248	.383	.313	356

1991 SPLITS FOR San Francisco Giants

BATTING SPLITS

	AVG	AB	R	H	2B	3B	HR	RBI	SB	CS	BB	K	OBA	SPCT
Total	.246	5463	649	1345	215	48	141	605	95	57	471	973	.309	.381

	#Pit	#P/PA	GB	FB	G/F	G	IBB	HB	SH	SF	GDP
Miscellaneous	21895	3.59	2056	1499	1.37	162	59	40	90	33	92

	AVG	AB	R	H	2B	3B	HR	RBI	SB	CS	BB	K	OBA	SPCT
vs. Left	.250	1597	...	399	73	11	45	194	28	22	126	253	.306	.394
vs. Right	.245	3866	...	946	142	37	96	411	67	35	345	720	.310	.375
Home	.244	2642	306	645	108	25	69	283	46	28	234	454	.308	.382
Away	.248	2821	343	700	107	23	72	322	49	29	237	519	.309	.379
None on	.240	3212	...	770	132	27	81	81	0	0	242	602	.297	.373
Runners on	.255	2251	...	575	83	21	60	524	95	57	229	371	.325	.391
April	.257	682	93	175	23	8	25	88	7	6	63	122	.320	.424
May	.237	970	89	230	37	9	21	82	21	12	72	174	.291	.359
June	.242	894	110	216	40	8	18	104	24	10	78	153	.307	.365
July	.266	808	110	215	30	5	33	106	11	9	64	147	.324	.438
August	.263	1041	134	274	58	10	24	122	11	12	85	174	.322	.407
September	.218	911	94	199	23	7	15	86	18	5	89	166	.292	.308
October	.229	157	19	36	4	1	5	17	3	3	20	37	.318	.363
None on/out	.242	1374	...	333	57	13	33	33	0	0	106	236	.304	.375
Scoring Posn	.243	1297	...	315	42	14	27	434	24	5	168	234	.326	.359
Close & Late	.242	918	...	222	35	9	16	115	13	11	115	176	.327	.352
Bases Loaded	.265	132	...	35	4	4	2	94	0	0	8	26	.304	.402
Batting #1	.250	661	107	165	23	12	5	36	32	10	64	93	.321	.343
Batting #2	.274	668	89	183	38	5	10	64	17	12	46	115	.322	.391
Batting #3	.310	659	96	204	35	7	31	133	7	4	49	105	.357	.525
Batting #4	.259	615	89	159	23	3	38	105	7	5	65	107	.335	.491
Batting #5	.251	610	66	153	20	6	28	89	8	8	56	123	.316	.441
Batting #6	.235	599	65	141	21	5	16	45	12	7	57	107	.305	.367
Batting #7	.230	570	47	131	25	2	9	62	3	3	44	87	.291	.328
Batting #8	.194	567	45	110	15	8	3	39	7	6	46	98	.254	.265
Batting #9	.193	514	45	99	15	0	1	32	2	2	44	138	.260	.228
As p	.155	317	15	49	6	0	1	18	0	0	13	106	.190	.183
As c	.216	564	37	122	22	2	8	54	1	2	35	93	.268	.305
As 1b	.289	647	95	187	33	7	31	124	6	4	53	106	.343	.505
As 2b	.261	595	84	155	30	6	19	61	15	8	74	113	.348	.427
As 3b	.264	628	73	166	25	6	34	100	5	5	40	135	.311	.486
As ss	.204	544	48	111	19	7	4	32	6	8	39	97	.258	.287
As lf	.257	614	86	158	22	6	30	93	11	5	67	96	.336	.459
As cf	.283	653	94	185	29	6	5	38	29	14	64	87	.350	.369
As rf	.243	642	75	156	22	5	9	58	18	11	55	99	.304	.335
Outfield	.261	1909	255	499	73	17	44	189	58	30	186	282	.330	.387
0.0 count	.316	790	...	250	50	8	24	109	...	...	1	0	.323	.491
After (0.1)	.217	2420	...	525	66	16	42	211	...	...	110	623	.255	.310
After (1.0)	.253	2253	...	570	99	24	75	285	...	...	314	350	.346	.418
Two strikes	.172	2413	...	415	60	19	31	158	...	...	168	970	.229	.251
Grass	.246	4005	457	984	150	35	105	424	72	44	336	716	.307	.379
Turf	.248	1458	192	361	65	13	36	181	23	13	135	257	.315	.384
Day	.259	2077	261	537	87	22	53	239	43	25	174	364	.320	.398
Night	.239	3386	388	808	128	26	88	366	52	32	297	609	.302	.370
Inning 1.6	.246	3672	429	903	149	32	103	403	71	43	296	643	.306	.388
Inning 7+	.247	1791	220	442	66	16	38	202	24	14	175	330	.315	.365
vs.Atl	.245	592	76	145	26	8	11	70	20	8	52	103	.307	.372
vs.ChN	.238	390	45	93	18	6	5	41	7	3	36	69	.313	.354
vs.Cin	.247	607	71	150	22	4	15	64	8	3	50	93	.307	.371
vs.Hou	.249	614	86	153	19	5	16	78	9	3	74	119	.333	.375
vs.LA	.233	609	56	142	19	2	16	51	13	6	51	131	.296	.350
vs.Mon	.225	418	44	94	20	5	11	41	8	4	43	84	.300	.376
vs.NYN	.255	419	50	107	15	3	14	49	6	7	26	79	.302	.406
vs.Phi	.258	411	50	106	21	2	14	49	7	5	37	75	.325	.421
vs.Pit	.273	407	46	111	20	1	8	44	8	6	21	66	.309	.386
vs.StL	.239	389	44	93	16	6	9	42	4	7	24	55	.284	.380
vs.SD	.249	607	81	151	19	6	22	76	5	5	57	99	.313	.409

PITCHING SPLITS

	ERA	W	L	SV	SVOP	GS	CG	SHO	IP	H	ER	HR	BB	IBB	K
Total	4.03	75	87	45	61	162	10	13	1442.0	1397	646	143	544	60	905

	#Pit	#P/IP	GB	FB	G/F	BRp9	RA	WP	BK	SH	SF	R	HB	Hld
Miscellaneous	22183	15.38	1971	1596	1.23	12.34	334	44	14	71	46	697	36	35

	ERA	W	L	SV	SVOP	GS	CG	SHO	IP	H	ER	HR	BB	IBB	K
ST	4.18	54	63	0	0	162	10	6	945.0	933	439	94	340	26	562
REL	3.75	21	24	45	61	0	0	0	497.0	464	207	49	204	34	343
Home	3.41	43	38	25	30	81	8	5	744.0	653	282	62	250	27	479
Away	4.69	32	49	20	31	81	2	1	698.0	744	364	81	294	33	426
April	4.63	8	12	4	8	20	2	1	173.0	181	89	12	75	10	106
May	4.14	8	20	3	6	28	2	2	260.2	254	120	30	102	11	156
June	3.12	17	10	12	15	27	1	1	242.0	219	84	17	101	8	128
July	3.53	15	9	10	11	24	2	1	211.1	183	83	21	76	5	129
August	4.51	14	16	7	9	30	1	0	267.2	266	134	31	95	17	193
September	4.64	10	18	7	10	28	1	0	242.1	254	125	30	84	9	159
October	2.20	3	2	2	2	5	1	1	45.0	40	11	2	11	0	34
Grass	3.75	58	62	33	45	120	9	6	1081.0	1013	451	100	398	43	677
Turf	4.86	17	25	12	16	42	1	0	361.0	384	195	43	146	17	228
Day	3.47	34	27	16	25	61	6	5	552.0	495	213	58	209	19	362
Night	4.38	41	60	29	36	101	4	1	890.0	902	433	85	335	41	543
vs.Atl	4.17	9	9	6	6	18	0	0	157.2	154	73	17	56	8	90
vs.ChN	3.69	6	6	5	6	12	0	0	105.0	110	43	14	40	6	51
vs.Cin	3.86	8	10	3	4	18	2	0	158.2	137	68	23	50	9	100
vs.Hou	5.07	9	9	6	6	18	1	1	158.0	177	89	11	62	7	109
vs.LA	3.14	10	8	6	9	18	1	1	163.1	149	57	9	71	7	101
vs.Mon	3.86	5	7	4	5	12	0	0	114.1	108	49	14	40	5	75
vs.NYN	3.11	6	6	2	5	12	3	2	110.0	100	38	8	42	6	61
vs.Phi	3.82	6	6	5	6	12	0	0	106.0	85	45	11	37	2	69
vs.Pit	4.42	5	7	3	4	12	1	1	106.0	105	52	10	42	3	73
vs.StL	4.11	4	8	3	5	12	0	0	105.0	102	48	8	42	1	61
vs.SD	4.78	7	11	2	5	18	2	1	158.0	170	84	18	62	6	115

OPPOSING BATTERS VS. PITCHERS.

	AVG	AB	R	H	2B	3B	HR	RBI	SB	CS	BB	K	OBA	SPCT
Total	.257	5435	697	1397	233	30	143	665	129	83	544	905	.326	.390
vs. Left	.267	2259	...	604	92	14	60	297	71	42	256	354	.341	.400
vs. Right	.250	3176	...	793	141	16	83	368	58	41	288	551	.316	.383
ST	.260	3587	474	933	161	21	94	419	79	57	340	562	.326	.395
REL	.251	1848	223	464	72	9	49	246	50	26	204	343	.327	.379
Home	.237	2750	305	653	105	14	62	291	50	41	250	479	.303	.353
Away	.277	2685	392	744	128	16	81	374	79	42	294	426	.350	.427
None on	.251	3124	...	784	133	11	89	89	0	0	271	534	.315	.386
Runners on	.265	2311	...	613	100	19	54	576	129	83	273	371	.341	.395
None on/out	.260	1367	...	355	58	2	37	37	0	0	124	206	.324	.386
Scoring Posn	.273	1375	...	376	60	15	29	509	26	12	195	234	.358	.402
vs 1st Batr	.201	299	...	60	13	2	5	31	0	1	27	62	.267	.308
1st IP	.254	1753	130	445	80	12	40	255	53	23	205	313	.335	.382
Inning 1.6	.262	3690	491	968	163	24	97	469	85	58	354	591	.328	.398
Inning 7+	.246	1745	206	429	70	6	46	196	44	25	190	314	.322	.372
Close & Late	.246	894	...	220	28	2	24	104	30	16	118	154	.335	.362
0.0 count	.336	833	...	280	45	7	36	149	...	...	49	0	.372	.537
After (0.1)	.214	2361	...	505	92	12	37	194	...	...	133	604	.261	.310
After (1.0)	.273	2241	...	612	96	11	70	322	...	...	362	301	.373	.419
Two strikes	.170	2358	...	402	69	12	27	167	...	...	204	904	.241	.244
Pitch 1.15	.260	1547	...	402	68	11	36	173	43	19	159	263	.332	.388
Pitch 16.30	.253	1156	...	293	54	2	29	155	29	22	132	203	.332	.379
Pitch 31.45	.271	797	...	216	36	4	18	94	19	9	82	120	.340	.394
Pitch 46.60	.277	620	...	172	30	3	26	109	13	8	57	106	.333	.461
Pitch 61.75	.246	586	...	144	19	7	21	74	14	9	41	92	.297	.410
Pitch 76.90	.249	409	...	102	12	3	10	36	7	12	42	69	.323	.367
Pitch 91.105	.204	226	...	46	9	0	2	13	2	2	20	38	.267	.270
Pitch 106.20	.243	74	...	18	4	0	1	9	1	1	14	12	.371	.338
Pitch 121.35	.222	18	...	4	1	0	0	2	1	1	0	2	.222	.278
Pitch 136.50	.000	2	...	0	0	0	0	0	0	0	1	0	.333	.000

Cincinnati Reds

Don Malcolm

CINCINNATI YEAR	1982	1983	1984	1985	1986	1987	1988	1989	1990	1991	TOT
W	61	74	70	89	86	84	87	75	91	74	791
L	101	88	92	72	76	78	74	87	71	88	827
WPCT	0.377	0.457	0.432	0.553	0.531	0.519	0.540	0.463	0.562	0.457	0.489
R	545	623	627	677	732	783	641	632	693	689	6642
RA	661	710	747	666	717	752	596	691	597	691	6828
PWPT	0.405	0.435	0.413	0.508	0.510	0.520	0.536	0.455	0.574	0.499	0.486
PythW	66	70	67	82	83	84	87	74	93	81	79
PythL	96	92	95	80	79	78	75	88	69	81	83
LUCK	-5	4	3	7	3	0	0	1	-2	-7	4

Defensive Efficiency Record: .6988

RECANTATION 1

Did I say 87-91 wins?? Must have been my evil twin. Seriously, I can't remember ever having said...

SURREALISTIC FANTASY 1

I am the ghost of Marge Schott. Oh, you say she hasn't died yet? Are you sure that isn't Mickey Rooney cross-dressing for kicks? No? Then why do I have this urge to go on TV and sell used cars? This never happened to me before...well, there was that time in Veracruz—but we won't go into that....

YOUR STARTING LINEUP, LOU (PART ONE)...

A certain someone who writes for this book didn't think much of your offensive players, Lou. As a matter of fact, he thought the Dodgers had a far superior offense than you going into 1991. It's interesting to note, then, that your poor offense, which struggled along without the mighty Eric Davis (now a D-D-Dodger), scored only four fewer runs than the 1990 World Champeen team, and 24 more runs than the D's.

Also interesting is the fact that your guys played seven games under your Pythagorean projection last year. That's usually a good sign for a resurgence in the following year.

But about that lineup. May I be the first to suggest to you that Bip Roberts, newly acquired for the mercurial Randall K. Myers, should not bat leadoff?? Here, primarily for the sake of controversy, is a revisionist sabermetric notion of what the Reds 1992 batting order should look like:

1. Larkin, ss
2. Doran, 2b
3. Morris, 1b
4. O'Neill, rf
5. Sabo, 3b
6. Roberts, cf
7. Braggs, lf
8. Oliver/Reed, c

I'll give you (and all the other mortified readers) a chance to let this sink in while we return to TV land...

RECANTATION 2

Did I give Lou credit for how to handle a pitching staff? Must have been slipped in by the copy editor. Either that or I had some bad linguini the night I wrote the article and, in a hallucinatory state, confused Lou with his evil twin, Pat Corrales...

GIMME MO

The great thing about the off-season moves made by the Reds? There's still room for Mo Sanford in their starting rotation.

Who the hell is Mo Sanford, you ask? Meredith (Mo) Sanford is a 6'6", 220 pound right-handed torcher who was a 32nd round draft choice by the Reds in 1988. No, that's not a misprint: 32nd round. All Mo did in four years in the Reds farm system is the following:

IP	H	ER	BB	SO	W	L	ERA	K/9	H/9
493	346	150	221	566	38	18	2.74	10.33	6.31

Mo is a little wild, but he has struck out better than a man an inning at every stop along the way. He is one of the big reasons why the Reds didn't think twice about trading Jack Armstrong and Scott Scudder to the Indians in the Greg Swindell deal.

Mo got five starts with the Reds late last season. He was a little wilder in the majors than he was in the minors, of course, and he got stung for a couple of big innings, but overall he did nothing to dispel the notion that he has a chance to be a dominating pitcher. The league hit .186 against him, slugged .294, got on-base .291. These figures would rank him at or near the top in the National League for 1991. His hits per nine innings (6.11) was almost a full hit better than the NL leader in '91 (Pete Harnisch, 7.02).

If Mo can tighten his control a bit, he could be a very big winner in the NL. His stats have potential ace written all over him. The Reds have thinned out their pool of starting pitchers down to a Big Four (Rijo, Swindell, Browning, and Belcher), which leaves Chris Hammond as Mo's adversary for the number five job. Hammond had two absolutely dominating years in the high minors, including a 15-1 season at Nashville in 1990, but he has struggled with pitch selection and had some arm trouble last year. His strikeout totals were way off his minor league rates, unlike Sanford.

It strikes me that Hammond is likelier to be the better pitcher to put into relief than Mo, although both pitchers have seen very little work in the bullpen in their minor league careers. I think I'd see what Mo brings to the party in spring training; if he's smokin', I'd give him the ball.

SURREALISTIC FANTASY 2

Pete Rose is elected mayor of Cincinnati...

YOUR STARTING LINEUP, LOU (PART TWO)...

The batting order I modestly proposed (somewhat in the manner of Jonathan Swift, who stewed when he should have waffled) was as follows:

1. Larkin, ss
2. Doran, 2b
3. Morris, 1b
4. O'Neill, rf
5. Sabo, 3b
6. Roberts, cf
7. Braggs, lf
8. Oliver/Reed, c

1. You may think that Barry Larkin, who batted third for much of last year, should remain in that spot in the order. I disagree. Even if Larkin's 20 homers last year were not a fluke (his previous high was 12), I'd still use him in the #1 slot due to his speed and on-base percentage—over the past three seasons, it's the highest of all the available players the Reds have, including Bip.

2. So here is likely where the biggest objection occurs: OK, bat Larkin leadoff, fine, but why not bat Bip second? The reasons: power, on-base, and bat-handling experience. Doran is more likely to do the things that will let Larkin steal, he's better on the hit-and-run than Bip, and he has more power. It strengthens the first inning scoring scenarios to put Doran in the #2 slot.

3. It seems likely that Hal Morris will be the Reds' best overall hitter for the next few years, and one of the best in the NL. He's a legitimate threat to win several batting titles, and his power numbers are increasing without a significant drop in batting average. The only time you might want to modify the batting order is when a lefty is pitching: Morris hit just .252 against them in '91.

4. Paul O'Neill made the power jump last season (36 doubles, 28 homers) that makes him an acceptable cleanup hitter. Not awesome or anything, but solid. His walks also rose to a career high last season, which offsets the marginal drop in BA he experienced. I expect that O'Neill can hold right about at the level he performed at in '91 for several seasons (he's 29).

5. Sabo had a helluva year in '91, and has the perfect mix of skills to bat fifth: he combines attributes of the #1, #3, and #4 hitters into a whole that makes him a multi-dimensional threat. Power, batting average, and speed are seamlessly blended in ol' Spuds: the Reds have the best left side of the infield in baseball right now.

6. Here is where I'd put Bip. Research indicates that the #6 hitter leads off innings more frequently than any other slot (except, of course, for #1), so Bip can still function as a delayed leadoff hitter, which adds further dimension to the Reds lineup. His BA is likely to go back over .300 playing more on turf, so he's valuable in the #6 slot also due to his ability to drive in more runs with just singles (he's easily the least powerful hitter in the Reds' lineup, including the catching platoon). Batting Bip sixth maximizes the scoring strategies for both the first and second innings, the innings in which you want to manufacture as many runs as you can.

7. Forget Hatcher. And don't rush Reggie Sanders. Give Braggs a legitimate shot at playing full-time in left field this year. He just might hit .270 with 20 homers and help put the Reds back on top. Even if he hits .250, he's going to generate more runs than Hatcher. Use Dave Martinez, acquired from Montreal, as the fourth outfielder, and give Sanders a full year at Nashville so that he'll be ready to take a starting job in '93.

8. This looks like a classic platoon situation to me: Oliver has good power against lefties, Reed hits righties pretty well. Individually and collectively they don't make you forget Johnny Bench, but they get the job done.

The team does not have the same punch as it did in the heyday seasons of Davis ('86 and '87). But the Reds haven't been over 700 runs in the last four seasons with Davis, so waxing nostalgic for Eric isn't particularly realistic. This Reds squad has a good chance to break the 700 run barrier—if everyone stays healthy. But the brilliant thing about the Dave Martinez acquisition is that if something happens to Doran, who's 34 and has had a bad back for some time, the Reds can just shift Bip to second and play Dave in center with little or no impact on the offense.

THE NAME OF THE GAME

I know where Robert Stack is, but what the hell happened to Tony

Franciosa, anyway? Was that him in the short-lived Bay City Blues TV show, playing the oversexed groundskeeper? (Hell, they were all oversexed on that show....)

Actually, the "name of the game," as Tommy Boswell would say in his overly-oiled haute jouranalaise (rhymes with bernaise, in case you were wondering), is pitching. And the Reds probably have enough to make a run at it this year, despite sending Armstrong, Myers, and Scudder packing.

You know about the Big Four (Rijo, Swindell, Browning and Belcher). And I've just finished prosletyzing for Mo Sanford. And of course there's Chris Hammond. But what about the bullpen? Myers is gone, so that leaves Dibble to close, and Norm Charlton to be the key left-handed setup man and alternate closer. The rest of the bullpen cast will come from the likes of veteran Ted Power, rookies Milt Hill and Steve Foster, and other marginalia like Tim Layana and Gino Minutelli. Of these guys, Minutelli is the only lefty, so the Reds would probably like him to make it, but he really got hammered last year.

So it's probable that the Reds will start the year with a rotation of Rijo, Swindell, Browning, Belcher, and Hammond, with Sanford tucked away in Nashville to start every five days, and a pen of Dibble, Charlton, Power, Hill, and Foster (sorry, Gino: maybe Tony Franciosa can get you a gig as an extra in Hollywood). If Hammond isn't cutting it as the #5 starter, he could be shifted, say around June, to the pen as a middle reliever and Sanford brought up to take the rotation slot. That's about as good as the crystal ball can get: after all, I bought it used...

RECANTATION 3

Did I ever define what "recantation" meant? It means: anything I say can be taken back, denied, retracted, etc., and is void where prohibited.

SURREALISTIC FANTASY 3

May the ghost of Bart Giamatti visit each and every owner on Opening Day, and slap them upside the head...

Cincinnati Reds Home Park Performance Factors

	Outs	Runs	Hits	2b	3b	HR	W	K	SH	SF	HBP	IBB	SB	CS	GDP
Home LH Batters	.999	.924	.943	.829	.687	.754	.994	1.036	1.009	1.039	.761	1.081	1.116	1.229	1.061
Home RH Batters	1.043	.946	.967	.867	1.154	.851	.960	1.022	1.054	1.034	1.431	.998	.834	1.008	.855
All Home Batters	1.027	.936	.961	.853	.961	.816	.968	1.032	1.037	1.059	1.247	1.047	.893	1.046	.895
Opp LH Batters	1.142	.941	1.045	1.115	.988	.857	1.005	1.177	1.177	1.027	1.524	1.314	1.085	1.122	1.107
Opp RH Batters	1.024	1.031	1.061	1.042	1.678	.893	.934	1.072	1.110	.962	1.290	1.042	1.197	1.158	1.131
All Opp Batters	1.069	.997	1.062	1.083	1.131	.912	.966	1.112	1.171	.944	1.360	1.224	1.102	1.072	1.083
All LH Batters	1.069	.927	.995	.956	.861	.811	.983	1.105	1.094	1.016	1.217	1.194	1.061	1.160	1.072
All RH Batters	1.034	.981	1.006	.937	1.323	.867	.947	1.044	1.080	.998	1.383	1.016	.932	1.068	.971
All Batters	1.047	.966	1.009	.951	1.045	.860	.963	1.070	1.101	.988	1.301	1.123	.988	1.058	.986

Conventional Batting Records for Cincinnati Reds

	G	AB	Run	Hit	2B	3B	HR	TB	RBI	W	K	IW	HB	SB	CS	BRng Eff	GI DP	SH	SF	Avg	Slug	OBP	Runs Ctd
Reed Jf	91	270	20	72	15	2	3	100	31	23	38	3	1	0	1	.302	6	1	5	.267	.370	.321	32
Morris H	136	478	72	152	33	1	14	229	59	46	61	7	1	10	4	.426	4	5	7	.318	.479	.374	90
Doran	111	361	51	101	12	2	6	135	35	46	39	1	0	5	4	.308	4	0	3	.280	.374	.359	51
Sabo	153	582	91	175	35	3	26	294	88	44	79	3	6	19	6	.516	13	5	3	.301	.505	.354	103
Larkin B	123	464	88	140	27	4	20	235	69	55	64	1	3	24	6	.500	7	3	2	.302	.506	.378	93
Hatcher B	138	442	45	116	25	3	4	159	41	26	55	4	7	11	9	.423	9	4	3	.262	.360	.312	48
Davis E	89	285	39	67	10	0	11	110	33	48	92	5	5	14	2	.383	4	0	2	.235	.386	.353	44
O'Neill	152	532	71	136	36	0	28	256	91	73	107	14	1	12	7	.446	8	0	1	.256	.481	.346	91
Duncan	100	333	46	86	7	4	12	137	40	12	57	0	3	5	4	.455	0	5	3	.258	.411	.288	40
Oliver	94	269	21	58	11	0	11	102	41	18	53	5	0	0	0	.105	14	4	0	.216	.379	.265	23
Braggs	85	250	36	65	10	0	11	108	39	23	46	3	2	11	3	.452	4	0	4	.260	.432	.323	36
Quinones L	97	212	15	47	4	3	4	69	20	21	31	3	2	1	2	.353	2	1	1	.222	.325	.297	21
Winningham	98	169	17	38	6	1	1	49	4	11	40	1	0	4	4	.419	2	2	0	.225	.290	.272	13
Martinez Crm	53	138	12	32	5	0	6	55	19	15	37	1	0	0	0	.222	1	0	3	.232	.399	.301	18
Benzinger	51	123	7	23	3	2	1	33	11	10	20	2	0	2	0	.238	2	1	2	.187	.268	.244	9
Jones Chris	52	89	14	26	1	2	2	37	6	2	31	0	0	2	1	.667	2	0	1	.292	.416	.304	11
Browning	36	70	3	12	3	0	1	18	5	3	19	0	0	0	1	.000	0	10	0	.171	.257	.205	4
Rijo	31	67	7	14	0	0	0	14	5	2	13	0	0	0	1	.429	0	9	0	.209	.209	.232	4
Benavides	24	63	11	18	1	0	0	19	3	1	15	1	1	1	0	.368	1	1	1	.286	.302	.303	6
Armstrong	27	43	3	4	1	0	0	5	2	1	18	0	0	0	0	.000	1	5	0	.093	.116	.114	1
Sanders R	9	40	6	8	0	0	1	11	3	0	9	0	0	1	1	.833	1	0	0	.200	.275	.200	2
Hammond	20	34	4	12	3	0	0	15	1	2	10	0	0	0	0	.250	0	1	0	.353	.441	.389	6
Myers R	58	29	3	5	1	0	0	6	2	1	16	0	0	0	0	.333	0	3	0	.172	.207	.200	1
Scudder	27	29	2	3	0	0	1	6	1	0	11	0	0	0	0	.333	0	2	0	.103	.207	.103	1
Charlton	41	23	1	1	1	0	0	2	0	0	10	0	0	0	0	.500	0	4	0	.043	.087	.043	0
Gross Kip	29	22	1	2	0	0	0	2	1	0	6	0	0	0	0	.000	0	3	0	.091	.091	.091	0
Jefferson	13	19	2	1	0	0	0	1	0	1	3	0	0	2	0	.250	0	0	0	.053	.053	.100	0
Scott D	10	19	0	3	0	0	0	3	0	0	2	0	0	0	0	.000	0	0	0	.158	.158	.158	0
Sutko	10	10	0	1	0	0	0	1	1	2	6	0	0	0	0	.000	0	0	0	.100	.100	.250	0
Sanford	5	8	0	0	0	0	0	0	0	0	5	0	0	0	0	.000	0	2	0	.000	.000	.000	0
Jefferson R	5	7	1	1	0	0	1	4	1	1	2	0	0	0	0	1.000	0	0	0	.143	.571	.250	1
Lee T	3	6	0	0	0	0	0	0	0	0	2	0	0	0	0	.000	0	0	0	.000	.000	.000	0
Carman	28	5	0	0	0	0	0	0	1	0	3	0	0	0	0	.000	0	0	0	.000	.000	.000	0
Power	68	3	0	0	0	0	0	0	1	1	3	0	0	0	0	.000	0	0	0	.000	.000	.250	0
Minutelli	16	3	0	0	0	0	0	0	0	0	1	0	0	0	0	.000	0	0	0	.000	.000	.000	0
Dibble	67	2	0	0	0	0	0	0	0	0	0	0	0	0	0	.000	0	1	0	.000	.000	.000	0
Layana	23	1	0	0	0	0	0	0	0	0	1	0	0	0	0	.000	0	0	0	.000	.000	.000	0
Hillmi	22	1	0	0	0	0	0	0	0	0	1	0	0	0	0	.000	0	0	0	.000	.000	.000	0
Brown Kth	11	0	0	0	0	0	0	0	0	0	0	0	0	0	0	.000	0	0	0	.000	.000	.000	0
Foster S	11	0	0	0	0	0	0	0	0	0	0	0	0	0	0	.000	0	0	0	.000	.000	.000	0
TOTALS	2217	5501	689	1419	250	27	164	2215	654	488	1006	54	32	124	56	.405	85	72	41	.258	.403	.320	725

Sabermetric Batting Records for Cincinnati Reds

	Ball Park Adjusted								Runs		Run/									
	AB	Run	Hit	2B	3B	HR	RBI	W	SO	Avg	Slug	OBP	Ctd	Outs	27o	OW%	OG	OWAR	DWAR	TWAR
Benavides	64	10	18	0	0	0	2	0	15	.281	.281	.292	6	47	3.45	.396	2	0.08	0.12	0.20
Benzinger	127	6	23	2	2	0	10	9	21	.181	.228	.232	7	108	1.75	.144	4	-0.82	0.09	-0.74
Braggs	256	35	65	9	0	9	38	21	48	.254	.395	.312	33	200	4.45	.522	7	1.28	0.13	1.41
Davis E	292	38	67	9	0	9	32	45	96	.229	.353	.343	41	231	4.79	.559	9	1.79	0.39	2.18
Doran	374	49	102	11	2	5	33	44	41	.273	.353	.347	49	282	4.69	.548	10	2.07	0.33	2.40
Duncan	342	45	87	6	5	10	39	11	59	.254	.389	.284	39	266	3.96	.463	10	1.12	0.41	1.53
Hatcher B	453	44	117	23	4	3	40	24	57	.258	.347	.307	47	359	3.53	.408	13	0.77	0.36	1.13
Jefferson R	7	0	1	0	0	0	0	0	2	.143	.143	.143	0	6	0.00	.000	0	-0.08	0.01	-0.07
Jefferson	19	1	1	0	0	0	0	0	3	.053	.053	.053	0	18	0.00	.000	1	-0.23	0.00	-0.23
Jones Chris	91	13	26	0	2	1	5	1	32	.286	.363	.293	9	67	3.63	.420	2	0.17	0.10	0.27
Larkin B	475	87	141	25	5	17	67	52	67	.297	.478	.370	89	350	6.87	.722	13	4.82	1.82	6.65
Lee T	6	0	0	0	0	0	0	0	2	.000	.000	.000	0	6	0.00	.000	0	-0.08	0.02	-0.06
Martinez Crm	141	11	32	4	0	5	18	14	38	.227	.362	.293	16	111	3.89	.455	4	0.43	0.14	0.57
Morris H	499	67	151	32	0	11	53	45	67	.303	.433	.357	81	368	5.94	.661	14	4.23	0.39	4.63
O'Neill	558	66	135	34	0	22	83	72	118	.242	.421	.329	79	440	4.85	.564	16	3.49	1.49	4.98
Oliver	276	20	58	10	0	9	40	17	55	.210	.344	.256	21	235	2.41	.243	9	-0.93	-0.55	-1.49
Quinones L	219	14	47	3	3	3	19	20	33	.215	.297	.285	19	177	2.90	.316	7	-0.22	0.00	-0.22
Reed Jf	282	18	71	14	1	2	28	22	42	.252	.330	.303	29	224	3.50	.402	8	0.44	0.00	0.44
Sabo	597	89	177	33	4	22	86	41	82	.296	.476	.349	99	445	6.01	.665	16	5.20	0.27	5.47
Sanders R	41	5	8	0	0	0	2	0	9	.195	.195	.195	1	34	0.79	.034	1	-0.40	0.06	-0.34
Scott D	19	0	3	0	0	0	0	0	2	.158	.158	.158	0	16	0.00	.000	1	-0.21	-0.02	-0.23
Sutko	10	0	1	0	0	0	0	1	6	.100	.100	.182	0	9	0.00	.000	0	-0.12	-0.02	-0.14
Winningham	177	15	37	5	0	0	3	10	44	.209	.237	.251	10	148	1.82	.155	5	-1.07	0.02	-1.05
TOTALS	5714	666	1435	241	28	141	625	471	1078	.251	.377	.311	686	4542	4.08	.478	168	21.58	5.56	27.13

Pitching Records for Cincinnati Reds

	ERA	W	L	Pct	G	GS	CG	ShO	GF	Sv	IP	R	ER	H	2B	3B	HR	BB	IW	SO	HB	WP	BK
Browning	4.18	14	14	.500	36	36	1	0	0	0	230.1	124	107	241	40	5	32	56	4	115	4	3	1
Rijo	2.51	15	6	.714	30	30	3	1	0	0	204.1	69	57	165	33	4	8	55	4	172	3	2	4
Armstrong	5.48	7	13	.350	27	24	1	0	1	0	139.2	90	85	158	24	4	25	54	2	93	2	2	1
Scudder	4.35	6	9	.400	27	14	0	0	4	1	101.1	52	49	91	19	3	6	56	4	51	6	7	0
Hammond	4.06	7	7	.500	20	18	0	0	0	0	99.2	51	45	92	17	2	4	48	3	50	2	3	0
Sanford	3.86	1	2	.333	5	5	0	0	0	0	28.0	14	12	19	2	0	3	15	1	31	1	4	0
Myers R	3.55	6	13	.316	58	12	1	0	18	6	132.0	61	52	116	18	3	8	80	5	108	1	2	1
Charlton	2.91	3	5	.375	39	11	0	0	10	1	108.1	37	35	92	13	4	6	34	4	77	6	11	0
Power	3.62	5	3	.625	68	0	0	0	22	3	87.0	37	35	87	18	2	6	31	5	51	2	6	1
Gross Kip	3.47	6	4	.600	29	9	1	0	6	0	85.2	43	33	93	12	1	8	40	2	40	0	5	1
Dibble	3.17	3	5	.375	67	0	0	0	57	31	82.1	32	29	67	9	3	5	25	2	124	0	5	0
Carman	5.25	0	2	.000	28	0	0	0	10	1	36.0	23	21	40	8	0	8	19	1	15	1	2	0
Hillmi	3.78	1	1	.500	22	0	0	0	8	0	33.1	14	14	36	8	1	1	8	2	20	0	1	0
Minutelli	6.04	0	2	.000	16	3	0	0	2	0	25.1	17	17	30	5	2	5	18	1	21	0	3	0
Layana	6.97	0	2	.000	22	0	0	0	9	0	20.2	18	16	23	1	0	1	11	0	14	0	3	0
Foster S	1.93	0	0	.000	11	0	0	0	5	0	14.0	5	3	7	1	0	1	4	0	11	0	0	0
Brown Kth	2.25	0	0	.000	11	0	0	0	3	0	12.0	4	3	15	3	1	0	6	1	4	0	1	0
TOTALS	3.83	74	88	.457	516	162	7	1	155	43	1440.0	691	613	1372	231	35	127	560	41	997	28	60	9

Sabermetric Pitching Records for Cincinnati Reds

	Adj	|-Expected-|			|------	Opposing Batters	------|											Supported			
	ERA	W	L	Pct	BFP	Avg	Slg	OBA	RC/G	GDP	SB	CS	PK	PKE	SH	SF	RSup	RSp/G	W	L	Pct
Armstrong	5.28	7	13	.326	611	.293	.491	.354	6.16	7	12	8	6	3	6	9	75	4.83	9	11	.456
Brown Kth	1.50	0	0	.857	56	.306	.408	.382	6.03	0	3	2	0	1	1	0	3	2.25	0	0	.692
Browning	4.02	13	15	.454	983	.266	.427	.309	4.74	13	21	6	1	2	8	9	122	4.77	16	12	.584
Carman	5.00	1	1	.350	164	.286	.514	.373	7.15	1	3	1	0	1	3	1	12	3.00	1	1	.265
Charlton	2.74	5	3	.642	438	.236	.336	.306	3.29	10	10	7	0	5	7	1	36	2.99	4	4	.543
Dibble	3.06	5	3	.590	334	.223	.322	.280	3.27	1	16	5	0	0	5	3	19	2.08	3	5	.315
Foster S	1.29	0	0	.891	53	.143	.224	.208	1.47	1	0	0	0	0	0	0	10	6.43	0	0	.962
Gross Kip	3.26	6	4	.560	381	.279	.393	.355	4.91	11	8	3	0	2	6	2	56	5.88	8	2	.765
Hammond	3.88	7	7	.472	425	.250	.340	.339	3.90	13	8	3	1	4	6	1	39	3.52	6	8	.451
Hillmi	3.51	1	1	.523	137	.295	.402	.331	4.03	4	4	4	0	1	4	3	17	4.59	1	1	.631
Layana	6.53	0	2	.240	95	.277	.325	.362	4.69	2	5	1	0	1	1	0	12	5.23	1	1	.390
Minutelli	5.68	1	1	.295	124	.288	.519	.387	8.36	0	2	0	0	0	0	2	4	1.42	0	2	.059
Myers R	3.41	10	9	.537	575	.242	.342	.347	4.06	14	4	7	0	1	8	6	58	3.95	11	8	.574
Power	3.41	4	4	.537	371	.265	.387	.329	4.55	5	12	4	0	0	6	4	31	3.21	4	4	.469
Rijo	2.42	15	6	.697	825	.219	.305	.272	2.84	15	16	3	4	3	4	8	128	5.64	18	3	.844
Sanford	3.54	2	1	.519	118	.186	.294	.297	3.36	1	4	0	0	0	0	0	16	5.14	2	1	.679
Scudder	4.17	7	8	.436	443	.246	.362	.352	4.58	6	12	6	0	0	8	3	51	4.53	8	7	.541
TOTALS	3.69	81	81	.497	6133	.253	.379	.323	4.29	104	140	60	12	24	73	52	689	4.31	93	69	.576

Batting 'Splits' Records for Cincinnati Reds

	G	AB	Run	Hit	2B	3B	HR	TB	RBI	W	K	IW	HB	SB	CS	GI DP	SH	SF	Avg	Slug	OBP	Runs Ctd
SPLITS for Sabo																						
vs LHP	84	193	37	69	17	1	9	115	29	16	23	1	2	7	2	6	2	0	.358	.596	.412	46
vs RHP	137	389	54	106	18	2	17	179	59	28	56	2	4	12	4	7	3	3	.272	.460	.325	58
Home	79	298	48	101	24	2	15	174	45	25	37	2	2	9	3	8	3	1	.339	.584	.393	67
Away	74	284	43	74	11	1	11	120	43	19	42	1	4	10	3	5	2	2	.261	.423	.314	38
Grass	44	176	27	50	6	1	7	79	28	12	25	1	2	9	3	4	1	2	.284	.449	.333	26
Turf	109	406	64	125	29	2	19	215	60	32	54	2	4	10	3	9	4	1	.308	.530	.363	77
April/June	69	260	40	70	12	2	11	119	34	30	45	0	3	9	1	8	3	2	.269	.458	.349	43
July/October	84	322	51	105	23	1	15	175	54	14	34	3	3	10	5	5	2	1	.326	.543	.359	61
SPLITS for Cincinnati Reds (all batters except pitchers)																						
vs LHP	917	1749	223	446	86	9	49	697	212	167	359	12	10	34	18	29	27	16	.255	.399	.321	229
vs RHP	1539	3752	466	973	164	18	115	1518	442	321	647	42	22	90	38	56	45	25	.259	.405	.319	496
Home	1128	2704	373	737	151	15	104	1230	361	257	476	26	13	70	27	48	35	19	.273	.455	.336	420
Away	1089	2797	316	682	99	12	60	985	293	231	530	28	19	54	29	37	37	22	.244	.352	.304	309
Grass	644	1699	211	440	56	9	47	655	197	132	326	19	10	35	19	19	26	14	.259	.386	.314	211
Turf	1573	3802	478	979	194	18	117	1560	457	356	680	35	22	89	37	66	46	27	.257	.410	.323	514
April/June	1008	2473	309	639	114	16	75	1010	295	253	444	29	22	70	25	37	39	21	.258	.408	.330	349
July/October	1209	3028	380	780	136	11	89	1205	359	235	562	25	10	54	31	48	33	20	.258	.398	.311	377

1991 SPLITS FOR Cincinnati Reds

BATTING SPLITS

	AVG	AB	R	H	2B	3B	HR	RBI	SB	CS	BB	K	OBA	SPCT
Total	.258	5501	689	1419	250	27	164	654	124	56	488	1006	.320	.403

	#Pit	#P/PA	GB	FB	G/F	G	IBB	HB	SH	SF	GDP
Miscellaneous	22277	3.63	1996	1610	1.24	162	54	32	72	41	85

	AVG	AB	R	H	2B	3B	HR	RBI	SB	CS	BB	K	OBA	SPCT
vs. Left	.255	1749	...	446	86	9	49	212	34	18	167	359	.321	.399
vs. Right	.259	3752	...	973	164	18	115	442	90	38	321	647	.319	.405
Home	.273	2704	373	737	151	15	104	361	70	27	257	476	.336	.455
Away	.244	2797	316	682	99	12	60	293	54	29	231	530	.304	.352
None on	.256	3219	...	823	145	11	99	99	0	0	241	608	.311	.400
Runners on	.261	2282	...	596	105	16	65	555	124	56	247	398	.331	.407
April	.230	634	64	146	30	2	14	59	13	5	60	115	.300	.350
May	.242	884	98	214	31	8	28	95	22	12	75	146	.306	.390
June	.292	955	147	279	53	6	33	141	35	8	118	183	.372	.464
July	.274	849	109	233	41	1	23	101	12	10	64	153	.324	.406
August	.250	1055	127	264	47	5	30	121	21	12	93	203	.312	.390
September	.252	953	125	240	40	5	32	119	17	8	65	170	.300	.405
October	.251	171	19	43	8	0	4	18	4	1	13	36	.304	.368
None on/out	.254	1389	...	353	66	3	48	48	0	0	111	258	.313	.410
Scoring Posn	.255	1312	...	334	56	15	32	471	40	11	177	246	.337	.393
Close & Late	.236	890	...	210	25	7	14	84	24	7	90	188	.308	.327
Bases Loaded	.238	101	...	24	7	1	2	77	0	0	8	16	.286	.386
Batting #1	.265	680	92	180	28	1	14	59	21	10	57	103	.323	.371
Batting #2	.287	641	105	184	28	5	24	76	20	10	70	92	.358	.459
Batting #3	.282	634	97	179	34	4	18	84	22	6	69	94	.355	.434
Batting #4	.286	605	94	173	41	1	28	98	25	6	81	123	.373	.496
Batting #5	.265	616	76	163	32	3	25	100	14	6	51	103	.320	.448
Batting #6	.267	614	64	164	26	5	16	77	11	9	41	108	.316	.404
Batting #7	.241	590	58	142	26	5	16	71	8	7	52	115	.302	.383
Batting #8	.240	575	60	138	21	3	14	58	2	0	43	97	.293	.360
Batting #9	.176	546	43	96	14	0	9	31	1	2	24	171	.211	.251
As p	.157	338	24	53	9	0	2	19	0	2	10	115	.181	.201
As c	.240	554	40	133	25	2	14	73	0	1	43	93	.294	.368
As 1b	.298	615	82	183	37	2	17	77	9	4	64	89	.360	.447
As 2b	.261	635	76	166	18	7	15	63	8	6	56	87	.321	.383
As 3b	.293	635	94	186	36	3	27	93	20	7	50	87	.349	.487
As ss	.298	634	116	189	30	5	22	84	26	7	58	95	.360	.465
As lf	.257	642	74	165	26	3	17	79	21	10	39	120	.303	.386
As cf	.230	617	73	142	23	2	13	46	20	10	67	140	.312	.337
As rf	.251	597	82	150	42	1	31	98	14	7	82	119	.342	.481
Outfield	.246	1856	229	457	91	6	61	223	55	27	188	379	.319	.400
0.0 count	.307	784	...	241	42	4	29	107	...	...	2	0	.311	.482
After (0.1)	.215	2441	...	526	90	12	47	212	...	...	92	674	.248	.320
After (1.0)	.286	2276	...	652	118	11	88	335	...	...	347	332	.380	.464
Two strikes	.167	2439	...	408	64	12	29	174	...	...	181	1004	.227	.239
Grass	.259	1699	211	440	56	9	47	197	35	19	132	326	.314	.386
Turf	.257	3802	478	979	194	18	117	457	89	37	356	680	.323	.410
Day	.269	1433	183	385	66	8	49	175	22	10	127	244	.330	.428
Night	.254	4068	506	1034	184	19	115	479	102	46	361	762	.316	.394
Inning 1.6	.263	3725	505	979	182	17	123	482	91	41	334	660	.325	.420
Inning 7+	.248	1776	184	440	68	10	41	172	33	15	154	346	.310	.367
vs.Atl	.256	621	88	159	33	4	14	81	14	8	68	112	.336	.390
vs.ChN	.291	436	70	127	24	1	15	64	10	4	31	76	.338	.454
vs.Hou	.234	598	69	140	22	2	19	65	11	4	58	102	.302	.373
vs.LA	.255	616	66	157	23	0	17	64	12	6	47	111	.306	.375
vs.Mon	.263	399	61	105	20	3	16	58	18	2	43	74	.342	.449
vs.NYN	.314	437	63	137	26	3	9	61	15	4	37	94	.363	.449
vs.Phi	.278	396	62	110	24	2	9	58	9	2	52	78	.360	.417
vs.Pit	.206	389	34	80	16	2	13	33	9	4	28	79	.259	.357
vs.StL	.272	412	44	112	22	2	8	44	9	8	32	58	.330	.393
vs.SD	.255	609	64	155	17	5	21	59	9	8	42	122	.302	.402
vs.SF	.233	588	68	137	23	3	23	67	8	6	50	100	.297	.400

PITCHING SPLITS

	ERA	W	L	SV	SVOP	GS	CG	SHO	IP	H	ER	HR	BB	IBB	K
Total	3.83	74	88	43	58	162	7	9	1440.0	1372	613	127	560	41	997

	#Pit	#P/IP	GB	FB	G/F	BRp9	RA	WP	BK	SH	SF	R	HB	Hld
Miscellaneous	22579	15.68	1877	1608	1.17	12.25	354	60	9	73	52	691	28	23

	ERA	W	L	SV	SVOP	GS	CG	SHO	IP	H	ER	HR	BB	IBB	K
ST	3.98	59	65	0	0	162	7	1	966.0	930	427	94	359	21	614
REL	3.53	15	23	43	58	0	0	0	474.0	442	186	33	201	20	383
Home	4.24	39	42	26	35	81	2	0	737.0	696	347	77	321	17	482
Away	3.41	35	46	17	23	81	5	1	703.0	676	266	50	239	24	515
April	2.95	11	8	9	10	19	0	0	174.0	144	57	12	46	4	119
May	4.08	12	15	8	10	27	1	0	234.0	227	106	19	94	5	159
June	3.69	18	10	13	14	28	1	0	251.0	233	103	26	113	7	171
July	4.57	8	16	3	7	24	2	0	210.2	226	107	23	82	8	125
August	3.55	15	16	5	8	31	1	1	281.2	250	111	30	112	5	213
September	3.65	10	18	5	8	28	1	0	246.2	245	100	14	98	11	174
October	6.21	0	5	0	1	5	1	0	42.0	47	29	3	15	1	36
Grass	3.33	22	26	7	11	48	4	1	421.1	403	156	33	141	13	312
Turf	4.04	52	62	36	47	114	3	0	1018.2	969	457	94	419	28	685
Day	3.82	20	22	11	15	42	5	1	372.0	361	158	27	138	11	250
Night	3.83	54	66	32	43	120	2	0	1068.0	1011	455	100	422	30	747
vs.Atl	4.41	7	11	1	3	18	0	0	163.1	159	80	17	57	5	126
vs.ChN	3.50	8	4	5	6	12	1	0	110.2	106	43	12	25	2	67
vs.Hou	2.97	9	9	7	9	18	0	0	160.2	136	53	9	53	8	128
vs.LA	4.39	6	12	4	7	18	0	0	162.0	153	79	7	88	5	106
vs.Mon	3.74	6	6	2	3	12	0	0	106.0	101	44	10	41	2	76
vs.NYN	4.50	5	7	3	4	12	1	1	106.0	103	53	14	60	3	69
vs.Phi	3.28	9	3	7	7	12	1	0	107.0	96	39	11	28	1	79
vs.Pit	5.85	2	10	2	4	12	0	0	103.0	111	67	16	48	4	58
vs.StL	3.38	4	8	3	6	12	1	0	104.0	104	39	7	44	4	58
vs.SD	3.35	8	10	5	5	18	1	0	158.1	153	59	9	66	4	137
vs.SF	3.23	10	8	4	4	18	2	0	159.0	150	57	15	50	3	93

OPPOSING BATTERS VS. PITCHERS.

	AVG	AB	R	H	2B	3B	HR	RBI	SB	CS	BB	K	OBA	SPCT
Total	.253	5420	691	1372	231	35	127	647	140	60	560	997	.323	.379
vs. Left	.254	2278	...	579	106	18	46	281	80	29	284	437	.338	.377
vs. Right	.252	3142	...	793	125	17	81	366	60	31	276	560	.313	.380
ST	.254	3657	484	930	155	25	94	422	80	33	359	614	.322	.387
REL	.251	1763	207	442	76	10	33	225	60	27	201	383	.327	.361
Home	.252	2758	376	696	113	17	77	358	68	32	321	482	.329	.389
Away	.254	2662	315	676	118	18	50	289	72	28	239	515	.317	.368
None on	.240	3152	...	757	128	18	77	77	0	0	284	591	.307	.365
Runners on	.271	2268	...	615	103	17	50	570	140	60	276	406	.345	.398
None on/out	.249	1367	...	340	48	7	41	41	0	0	126	246	.316	.384
Scoring Posn	.270	1334	...	360	65	9	21	492	45	10	192	273	.351	.379
vs 1st Batr	.287	314	...	90	19	2	4	41	2	0	34	66	.351	.398
1st IP	.273	1796	125	490	88	17	34	292	72	32	218	360	.351	.398
Inning 1.6	.252	3673	482	927	163	21	92	455	93	36	372	623	.322	.383
Inning 7+	.255	1747	209	445	68	14	35	192	47	24	188	374	.327	.370
Close & Late	.269	825	...	222	33	6	13	99	30	13	97	199	.345	.371
0.0 count	.318	795	...	253	46	7	29	126	...	...	35	0	.345	.503
After (0.1)	.221	2459	...	543	91	10	46	238	...	...	130	661	.262	.322
After (1.0)	.266	2166	...	576	94	18	52	283	...	...	395	336	.379	.398
Two strikes	.182	2509	...	456	78	9	37	192	...	...	242	994	.256	.264
Pitch 1.15	.277	1537	...	425	76	15	31	211	59	26	167	286	.348	.406
Pitch 16.30	.237	1110	...	263	42	5	20	125	30	16	119	235	.310	.338
Pitch 31.45	.233	756	...	176	27	6	20	88	13	7	72	147	.298	.364
Pitch 46.60	.248	634	...	157	20	3	18	68	17	3	59	101	.312	.374
Pitch 61.75	.260	570	...	148	25	1	16	65	10	3	50	93	.323	.391
Pitch 76.90	.271	450	...	122	24	1	15	56	7	1	46	71	.341	.429
Pitch 91.105	.200	245	...	49	11	2	7	24	3	3	28	38	.282	.347
Pitch 106.20	.294	102	...	30	4	2	0	9	1	1	15	22	.378	.373
Pitch 121.35	.167	18	...	3	2	0	0	4	0	0	5	4	.333	.278
Pitch 136.50	.000	1	...	0	0	0	0	0	0	0	1	0	.500	.000

Houston Astros

Don Malcolm

HOUSTON YEAR	1982	1983	1984	1985	1986	1987	1988	1989	1990	1991	TOT
W	77	85	80	83	96	76	82	86	75	65	805
L	85	77	82	79	66	86	80	76	87	97	815
WPCT	0.475	0.525	0.494	0.512	0.593	0.469	0.506	0.531	0.463	0.401	0.497
R	569	643	693	706	654	648	617	647	573	605	6355
RA	620	646	630	691	569	678	631	669	656	717	6507
PWPT	0.457	0.498	0.548	0.511	0.569	0.477	0.489	0.483	0.433	0.416	0.488
PythW	74	81	89	83	92	77	79	78	70	67	79
PythL	88	81	73	79	70	85	83	84	92	95	83
LUCK	3	4	-9	0	4	-1	3	8	5	-2	15

Defensive Efficiency Record: .6985

FIVE REASONS TO WATCH THE ASTROS THIS SEASON

Watch the Astros do what? Why, lose about 91 games, of course. It's an improvement over last year, to be sure, but it still feels like a slap in the face. But then again if you get slapped enough, it actually feels good when it stops.

1. Jeff Bagwell.
2. Pete Harnisch.
3. Steve Finley.
4. Luis Gonzalez.
5. Al Osuna.

These five players are the main hopes for the future, the players who can be the nucleus for success down the road. Let's examine them in more detail:

BAGWELL—Very likely will become the first Astro player to win a batting title. Had a tremendously consistent rookie season. Showed no weaknesses whatsoever, and got stronger as the season wore on (higher BA, better power and OBP). Has enough size to be a 20+ HR man even with half his games in the Dome. At his peak, Bagwell will be a significantly superior player than Glenn Davis.

HARNISCH—Moving to the Dome really helped, but it appeared that Harnisch got over the hump in terms of his mechanics and pitch selection last year. A classic power pitcher, Harnisch was among the leaders in hits per nine innings, and opponent batting average, slugging average and OBP. He's for real, and with a better offense, he should be a big winner for many years to come.

FINLEY—He's a key to any kind of quick improvement that the Astros might make. Can he progress to hitting .300 and getting his walks high enough to crack the .360 OBP barrier? This is what the Astros need out of him to create a viable offense. All eight of his home runs came on the road in '91: he needs to get tha total into the low teens (13-14) to be the multi-dimensional hitter than the Astros need, especially on the road.

GONZALEZ—Rushed up from AA ball, Gonzalez more than held his own against righties (.282, .490 SA). A better, but noticeably less powerful, hitter in the second half of the season. Has the potential to team with Bagwell to provide a consistent 20+ HR tandem, something that the Astros haven't had very often. Excellent range in the outfield, although his arm is a little suspect. The Astros need for him to be their cleanup hitter for the nineties, especially since Eric Anthony doesn't look as though he's going to pull it off.

OSUNA—Should be the Astros' closer. Excellent hit-to-IP ratio in '91. Had some problems with his control, but overall looked very impressive. Has a good chance to double last year's save total (12) if given the opportunity.

Which way the Astros go, both in '92 and in the next few years, will hinge most on these five players. These are the key positions and functions that the Astros need to develop anchors for: ace starter, closer, leadoff hitter, #3 hitter, #4 hitter. Everything else can be improvised or jcrry-rigged. It's rare when teams don't have at least four of these five functions well in control and somehow go on to win.

WHO IS EDDIE TAUBENSEE AND WHY DID THE ASTROS TRADE FOR HIM??

He's a 6'4", 210 lb. catching prospect, signed originally by the Reds in the 6th round of the 1986 draft. After scuffling around in the lower depths of the Reds' farm system for five seasons, Taubensse got picked up by the Cleveland Indians, who promoted him to their AAA farm club at Colorado Springs, where Taubensee proceeded to hit .310 and slug .547. The Astros acquired him in the deal that sent Kenny Lofton to the Indians last December.

The Astros are hoping that Taubensee can become their #1 catcher, because they'd like to be able to move Craig Biggio to the outfield, where it's likely that he'll be able to retain his speed (71 SB in 3+ seasons in the majors). Biggio's percentage of runners thrown out attempting to steal (CS%) is 26%, or about a 75 on a league average scale of 100.

Unfortunately, Taubensee's defensive statistics during last year's cup of coffee with the Indians (14% CS) don't seem to warrant the hope that he can free up Biggio for outfield duty. Journeyman Carl Nichols (lifetime .204 hitter) isn't perceived as someone to try, despite an impressive 40% CS rate lifetime.

But if Taubensee hits in the spring, don't be surprised if the Astros take a shot at moving Biggio. There's an outfield slot open: only Gonzalez and Finley are assured of starting jobs, so the scenario is definitely one that Houston is seriously considering. I'd say the odds are long that Taubensee can pull it off this season: despite his six years in the minors, he's only 23 and has only the one (possibly aberrant) year at AAA to go on. But stranger things have happened...

FIVE PLAYERS TO AVOID WATCHING ON THE ASTROS THIS SEASON

They'll take your breath away with their ineffectual mediocrity; their raw, unschooled approach to the game; their variable ability to throw strikes; their maddeningly predictable inconsistency. If you're watching a game with the Astros playing in it, or listening on the radio and these players appear or are introduced, look away from the screen or turn the volume down.

1. Mark Davidson
2. Rafael Ramirez
3. Mark Portugal
4. Dwayne Henry
5. Andujar Cedeno

DAVIDSON—A career built on quicksand. Lifetime .225 hitter, no power, little speed, 31 years old. They didn't want to put Karl Rhodes on the bench when he slumped last May, so they kept Davidson all year. You've got your pension in, Mark, why don't you do us a favor and sell insurance full-time?

RAMIREZ—The classic hands-of-stone utility player. He's lost it at short, has always had a suspect bat, and wouldn't even be here if it were not for the terrible feeling in the pit of the Astro stomach about their other options (Cedeno and Yelding).

PORTUGAL—The Astros need to realize now that the league is catching up with Portugal, and unload him to some unsuspecting team (say the Cubs: they'll always invest in a suspect pitcher). The most comical episode of the entire 1991 season came when the Astros tried out Portugal as a closer during the last week of the season. The results were spectacular. The Braves lit up Portugal three times en route to victories. They should've voted him a World Series share for his yeoman efforts in helping them get past the Dodgers.

HENRY—Some people are of the opinion that Dwayne "turned the corner" last year. After all, his ERA was 3.19. Don't you believe it. This guy is an arson specialist, wilder in the strike zone than out of it (which he is a predominant amount of the time), and is just one more example of how a guy with a great fastball and absolutely nothing else can get chance after chance.

CEDENO—This guy has it all at short: bad range and bad hands. "Raw" is somehow just not strong enough a term to describe the rough edges attached to this player, another Astro whom the Braves should have voted a World Series share. You'll probably have to turn your head most of the season, because the Astros seem determined to give him a full shot. He does have a little pop in his bat, but that OBP is turn-out-the-lights material. A poor intersection of names: Andujar ("one tough Dominican") and Cedeno ("one armed and dangerous Dominican").

Don't fret none, Art Howe: this time next year you and Tom Trebelhorn will be deliriously happy running that organic fruit and vegetable stand, just outside the shadow of the Astrodome...

Houston Astros Home Park Performance Factors

	Outs	Runs	Hits	2b	3b	HR	W	K	SH	SF	HBP	IBB	SB	CS	GDP
Home LH Batters	.981	1.053	.966	.915	.718	1.863	.924	1.036	1.045	.958	1.542	.769	.974	.958	.871
Home RH Batters	1.023	.978	.969	.838	.830	1.381	1.033	.982	1.223	1.066	.901	1.157	.768	1.169	1.444
All Home Batters	1.017	1.006	.978	.886	.773	1.424	.992	.996	1.132	.989	1.080	.893	.871	1.101	1.171
Opp LH Batters	1.031	1.130	1.100	1.127	.825	1.222	1.082	1.003	1.178	1.139	.997	1.236	1.186	.962	1.210
Opp RH Batters	.961	1.121	1.050	.967	.906	1.516	1.036	.921	.752	.975	1.025	.787	1.035	1.042	1.199
All Opp Batters	1.005	1.119	1.077	1.037	.882	1.397	1.062	.974	.902	1.036	1.095	1.062	1.076	1.029	1.162
All LH Batters	1.008	1.090	1.037	1.021	.773	1.348	1.009	1.014	1.116	1.054	1.232	1.008	1.081	.975	1.027
All RH Batters	.993	1.043	1.004	.898	.866	1.474	1.035	.953	.950	1.018	.953	.941	.875	1.104	1.297
All Batters	1.011	1.064	1.026	.958	.819	1.400	1.029	.985	1.000	1.013	1.089	.983	.968	1.067	1.165

Conventional Batting Records for Houston Astros

	G	AB	Run	Hit	2B	3B	HR	TB	RBI	W	K	IW	HB	SB	CS	BRng Eff	GI DP	SH	SF	Avg	Slug	OBP	Runs Ctd
Biggio	149	546	79	161	23	4	4	204	46	53	71	3	2	19	6	.487	2	5	3	.295	.374	.358	79
Bagwell	156	554	79	163	26	4	15	242	82	75	116	5	13	7	4	.457	12	1	7	.294	.437	.387	99
Candaele	151	461	44	121	20	7	4	167	50	40	49	7	0	9	3	.329	5	1	3	.262	.362	.319	56
Caminiti	152	574	65	145	30	3	13	220	80	46	85	7	5	4	5	.388	18	3	4	.253	.383	.312	65
Yelding	78	276	19	67	11	1	1	83	20	13	46	3	0	11	9	.500	4	3	1	.243	.301	.276	22
Gonzalez L	137	473	51	120	28	9	13	205	69	40	101	4	8	10	7	.368	9	1	4	.254	.433	.320	65
Finley S	159	596	84	170	28	10	8	242	54	42	65	5	2	34	18	.445	8	10	6	.285	.406	.331	80
Rhodes	44	136	7	29	3	1	1	37	12	14	26	3	1	2	2	.389	3	0	1	.213	.272	.289	11
Cedeno A	67	251	27	61	13	2	9	105	36	9	74	1	1	4	3	.545	3	1	2	.243	.418	.270	27
Ramirez R	101	233	17	55	10	0	1	68	20	13	40	1	0	3	3	.303	3	1	2	.236	.292	.274	19
Davidson M	85	142	10	27	6	0	2	39	15	12	28	0	2	0	0	.357	2	0	0	.190	.275	.263	11
Young G	108	142	26	31	3	1	1	39	11	24	17	0	0	16	5	.583	3	1	2	.218	.275	.327	15
Sims	49	123	18	25	5	0	3	39	16	18	38	0	0	1	0	.455	2	0	2	.203	.317	.301	13
Anthony	39	118	11	18	6	0	1	27	7	12	41	1	0	1	0	.286	2	0	2	.153	.229	.227	7
Mota A	27	90	4	17	2	0	1	22	6	1	17	0	0	2	0	.500	0	0	0	.189	.244	.198	5
Ortiz Ja	47	83	7	23	4	1	1	32	5	14	14	0	0	0	0	.091	3	0	0	.277	.386	.381	12
Lofton	20	74	9	15	1	0	0	16	0	5	19	0	0	2	1	.429	0	0	0	.203	.216	.253	4
Oberkfell	53	70	7	16	4	0	0	20	14	14	8	4	0	0	0	.333	0	0	0	.229	.286	.357	8
Harnisch	33	62	4	6	1	0	0	7	4	4	21	0	0	0	1	.167	1	7	1	.097	.113	.149	1
McLemore	21	61	6	9	1	0	0	10	2	6	13	0	0	0	1	.750	1	0	1	.148	.164	.221	2
Tolentino	44	54	6	14	4	0	1	21	6	4	9	0	0	0	0	.125	2	0	1	.259	.389	.305	6
Nichols C	20	51	3	10	3	0	0	13	1	5	17	1	0	0	0	.182	0	0	0	.196	.255	.268	4
Portugal	33	46	4	9	1	0	0	10	3	4	4	0	1	0	0	.200	0	6	1	.196	.217	.269	4
Rohde	29	41	3	5	0	0	0	5	0	5	8	0	0	0	0	.400	1	2	0	.122	.122	.217	1
Deshaies	28	41	1	4	0	0	0	4	0	4	16	0	0	0	0	.000	1	8	0	.098	.098	.178	1
Kile	37	38	2	0	0	0	0	0	1	3	23	0	0	0	0	.250	1	4	0	.000	.000	.073	0
Jones Jim	26	38	4	7	1	0	0	8	0	3	11	0	0	0	0	.333	0	2	0	.184	.211	.244	2
Servais	16	37	0	6	3	0	0	9	6	4	8	0	0	0	0	.000	0	1	0	.162	.243	.244	3
Bowen R	17	22	2	4	1	0	0	5	0	3	11	0	0	0	0	.667	0	1	0	.182	.227	.280	2
Eusebio	10	19	4	2	1	0	0	3	0	6	8	0	0	0	0	.400	1	0	0	.105	.158	.320	1
Cooper G	9	16	1	4	1	0	0	5	2	3	6	0	0	0	0	.000	0	0	0	.250	.313	.368	2
Hernandez X	32	10	0	0	0	0	0	0	0	2	7	0	0	0	0	.000	0	1	0	.000	.000	.167	0
Gardner C	5	5	0	0	0	0	0	0	0	1	1	0	0	0	0	.000	0	0	0	.000	.000	.167	0
Juden	4	5	0	0	0	0	0	0	0	0	4	0	0	0	0	.000	0	0	0	.000	.000	.000	0
Clancy	30	3	0	0	0	0	0	0	0	0	1	0	0	0	0	.000	0	1	0	.000	.000	.000	0
Schilling	56	3	0	1	0	0	0	1	1	0	0	0	0	0	0	.000	0	0	0	.333	.333	.333	0
Br.williams	2	3	0	0	0	0	0	0	0	0	0	0	0	0	0	.000	0	2	0	.000	.000	.000	0
Osuna	71	2	1	0	0	0	0	0	1	0	1	0	0	0	0	.000	0	1	0	.000	.000	.000	0
Scott M	2	1	0	0	0	0	0	0	0	0	0	0	0	0	0	.000	0	0	0	.000	.000	.000	0
Henry	52	1	0	0	0	0	0	0	0	0	1	0	0	0	0	.000	0	0	0	.000	.000	.000	0
Corsi	47	1	0	0	0	0	0	0	0	0	1	0	0	0	0	.000	0	0	0	.000	.000	.000	0
Wilkens	7	1	0	0	0	0	0	0	0	0	1	0	0	0	0	.000	0	0	0	.000	.000	.000	0
Mallicoat	24	1	0	0	0	0	0	0	0	0	0	0	0	0	0	.000	0	0	0	.000	.000	.000	0
Capel	25	0	0	0	0	0	0	0	0	0	0	0	0	0	0	.000	0	0	0	.000	.000	.000	0
TOTALS	2302	5504	605	1345	240	43	79	1908	570	502	1027	45	35	125	68	.413	87	63	43	.244	.347	.309	609

Sabermetric Batting Records for Houston Astros

	Ball Park Adjusted												Runs		Run/					
	AB	Run	Hit	2B	3B	HR	RBI	W	SO	Avg	Slug	OBP	Ctd	Outs	27o	OW%	OG	OWAR	DWAR	TWAR
Anthony	118	12	18	6	0	1	7	12	41	.153	.229	.227	7	104	1.82	.166	4	-0.71	0.39	-0.32
Bagwell	551	82	164	23	3	21	83	77	110	.298	.465	.391	103	413	6.73	.731	15	5.83	0.40	6.24
Biggio	543	82	162	20	3	5	46	54	67	.298	.374	.361	79	396	5.39	.635	15	4.19	-0.52	3.66
Caminiti	581	69	148	28	2	18	84	47	83	.255	.403	.314	69	465	4.01	.491	17	2.43	0.76	3.19
Candaele	467	46	124	19	5	5	53	41	48	.266	.360	.323	57	355	4.34	.530	13	2.37	0.72	3.09
Cedeno A	249	28	61	11	1	13	36	9	70	.245	.454	.269	29	196	3.99	.489	7	1.01	-0.44	0.57
Cooper G	15	1	4	0	0	0	2	3	5	.267	.267	.389	2	11	4.91	.591	0	0.10	0.00	0.10
Davidson M	141	10	27	5	0	2	15	12	26	.191	.270	.260	10	116	2.33	.246	4	-0.45	0.26	-0.19
Eusebio	18	4	2	0	0	0	0	6	7	.111	.111	.333	1	17	1.59	.132	1	-0.14	-0.07	-0.21
Finley S	603	91	175	28	7	12	60	42	66	.290	.420	.335	85	470	4.88	.589	17	4.16	0.90	5.05
Gonzalez L	478	55	123	28	6	20	77	40	102	.257	.467	.325	72	375	5.18	.617	14	3.71	0.56	4.27
Lofton	74	9	15	1	0	0	0	5	19	.203	.216	.253	5	59	2.29	.239	2	-0.24	0.04	-0.20
McLemore	61	6	9	0	0	0	2	6	12	.148	.148	.221	2	55	0.98	.055	2	-0.60	0.02	-0.58
Mota A	89	4	17	1	0	1	6	1	16	.191	.236	.200	4	72	1.50	.119	3	-0.62	-0.14	-0.76
Nichols C	50	3	10	2	0	0	1	5	16	.200	.240	.273	4	40	2.70	.305	1	-0.07	-0.12	-0.19
Oberkfell	70	7	16	4	0	0	15	14	8	.229	.286	.357	8	54	4.00	.490	2	0.28	0.03	0.31
Ortiz Ja	82	7	23	3	0	1	5	14	13	.280	.354	.385	12	62	5.23	.621	2	0.62	0.13	0.75
Ramirez R	231	17	55	9	0	1	20	13	38	.238	.290	.276	18	184	2.64	.295	7	-0.37	-0.04	-0.42
Rhodes	136	7	29	3	0	1	13	14	26	.213	.257	.289	11	112	2.65	.297	4	-0.22	0.28	0.06
Rohde	41	3	5	0	0	0	0	5	7	.122	.122	.217	1	39	0.69	.028	1	-0.47	0.08	-0.39
Servais	36	0	6	2	0	0	6	4	7	.167	.222	.250	2	30	1.80	.163	1	-0.21	-0.01	-0.22
Sims	122	18	25	4	0	4	16	18	36	.205	.336	.303	13	101	3.48	.420	4	0.26	0.03	0.30
Tolentino	54	6	14	4	0	1	6	4	9	.259	.389	.305	6	43	3.77	.460	2	0.18	0.02	0.20
Yelding	274	19	67	9	0	1	20	13	43	.245	.288	.278	20	224	2.41	.259	8	-0.76	-0.12	-0.88
Young G	143	27	31	2	0	1	11	24	16	.217	.252	.325	14	123	3.07	.362	5	0.05	0.50	0.56
TOTALS	5586	642	1381	230	35	111	604	515	1011	.247	.361	.313	642	4485	3.86	.473	166	20.42	3.66	24.07

Pitching Records for Houston Astros

	ERA	W	L	Pct	G	GS	CG	ShO	GF	Sv	IP	R	ER	H	2B	3B	HR	BB	IW	SO	HB	WP	BK
Harnisch	2.70	12	9	.571	33	33	4	2	0	0	216.2	71	65	169	28	5	14	83	3	172	5	5	2
Portugal	4.49	10	12	.455	32	27	1	0	3	1	168.1	91	84	163	29	3	19	59	5	120	2	4	1
Deshaies	4.98	5	12	.294	28	28	1	0	0	0	161.0	90	89	156	36	5	19	72	5	98	1	0	5
Kile	3.69	7	11	.389	37	22	0	0	5	0	153.2	81	63	144	28	5	16	84	4	100	6	5	4
Jones Jim	4.39	6	8	.429	26	22	1	1	0	0	135.1	73	66	143	18	5	9	51	3	88	3	4	0
Bowen R	5.15	6	4	.600	14	13	0	0	0	0	71.2	43	41	73	13	0	4	36	1	49	3	8	1
Gardner C	4.01	1	2	.333	5	4	0	0	0	0	24.2	12	11	19	2	0	5	14	1	12	0	0	0
Juden	6.00	0	2	.000	4	3	0	0	0	0	18.0	14	12	19	3	0	3	7	1	11	0	0	1
Br.williams	3.75	0	1	.000	2	2	0	0	0	0	12.0	5	5	11	0	0	2	4	0	4	1	0	0
Scott M	12.86	0	2	.000	2	2	0	0	0	0	7.0	10	10	11	3	0	2	4	1	3	1	0	0
Osuna	3.42	7	6	.538	71	0	0	0	32	12	81.2	39	31	59	13	1	5	46	5	68	3	3	1
Corsi	3.71	0	5	.000	47	0	0	0	15	0	77.2	37	32	76	9	1	6	23	5	53	0	1	1
Schilling	3.81	3	5	.375	56	0	0	0	34	8	75.2	35	32	79	15	3	2	39	7	71	0	4	1
Henry	3.19	3	2	.600	52	0	0	0	25	2	67.2	25	24	51	10	1	7	39	7	51	2	5	0
Hernandez X	4.71	2	7	.222	32	6	0	0	8	3	63.0	34	33	66	12	0	6	32	7	55	0	0	0
Clancy	2.78	0	3	.000	30	0	0	0	13	5	55.0	19	17	37	9	0	5	20	3	33	0	5	0
Capel	3.03	1	3	.250	25	0	0	0	13	3	32.2	14	11	33	10	0	3	15	1	23	0	0	0
Mallicoat	3.86	0	2	.000	24	0	0	0	4	1	23.1	10	10	22	5	0	2	13	1	18	2	1	0
Wilkens	11.25	2	1	.667	7	0	0	0	3	1	8.0	14	10	16	5	1	0	10	2	4	0	1	0
TOTALS	4.00	65	97	.401	527	162	7	3	155	36	1453.0	717	646	1347	248	30	129	651	62	1033	29	46	17

Sabermetric Pitching Records for Houston Astros

	Adj	-Expected-			Opposing Batters												Supported				
	ERA	W	L	Pct	BFP	Avg	Slg	OBA	RC/G	GDP	SB	CS	PK	PKE	SH	SF	RSup	RSp/G	W	L	Pct
Bowen R	5.40	3	7	.316	319	.268	.360	.353	4.95	5	12	1	0	2	2	6	51	6.40	6	4	.584
Capel	3.03	2	2	.595	143	.266	.419	.343	4.94	2	3	3	0	0	3	1	10	2.76	2	2	.452
Clancy	2.95	2	1	.609	215	.193	.318	.266	2.75	4	3	1	1	0	1	2	14	2.29	1	2	.377
Corsi	3.94	2	3	.465	322	.259	.357	.310	3.69	9	8	3	0	1	3	2	27	3.13	2	3	.387
Deshaies	5.25	6	11	.328	686	.259	.430	.336	4.87	12	21	14	1	9	4	7	60	3.35	5	12	.289
Gardner C	4.01	1	2	.456	103	.218	.414	.327	4.47	2	0	0	1	1	2	0	7	2.55	1	2	.288
Harnisch	2.87	13	8	.622	900	.212	.313	.288	3.33	6	27	6	0	1	9	7	84	3.49	13	8	.597
Henry	3.33	3	2	.550	282	.219	.361	.333	4.16	3	7	3	1	0	6	2	22	2.93	2	3	.436
Hernandez X	5.00	3	6	.350	285	.263	.382	.345	5.03	4	7	2	0	0	1	1	20	2.86	2	7	.246
Jones Jim	4.66	5	9	.384	593	.270	.374	.336	4.62	9	18	6	0	0	7	2	58	3.86	6	8	.407
Juden	6.00	1	1	.273	81	.275	.449	.329	5.26	2	3	1	0	1	2	3	3	1.50	0	2	.059
Kile	3.92	8	10	.467	689	.246	.393	.344	5.08	7	12	3	0	2	9	5	76	4.45	10	8	.563
Mallicoat	3.86	1	1	.476	103	.259	.388	.363	4.82	3	1	1	0	0	1	2	14	5.40	1	1	.662
Osuna	3.53	7	6	.520	353	.201	.304	.311	3.49	5	2	0	0	1	6	5	37	4.08	7	6	.572
Portugal	4.76	8	14	.373	710	.256	.400	.318	4.31	15	12	7	0	2	6	6	85	4.54	10	12	.477
Schilling	4.04	4	4	.452	336	.271	.364	.356	4.71	4	3	4	0	0	5	1	28	3.33	3	5	.404
Scott M	12.86	0	2	.075	35	.367	.667	.457	12.33	0	2	1	0	0	0	0	1	1.28	0	2	.010
Wilkens	11.25	0	3	.096	51	.410	.590	.531	14.40	0	1	2	0	0	2	0	6	6.75	1	2	.265
Br.williams	3.75	0	1	.490	49	.250	.386	.327	3.47	2	1	2	0	0	0	0	2	1.50	0	1	.138
TOTALS	4.26	69	93	.427	6255	.247	.374	.328	4.37	94	143	60	4	20	69	52	605	3.75	71	91	.437

Batting 'Splits' Records for Houston Astros

	G	AB	Run	Hit	2B	3B	HR	TB	RBI	W	K	IW	HB	SB	CS	GIDP	SH	SF	Avg	Slug	OBP	Runs Ctd
SPLITS for Bagwell																						
vs LHP	96	206	31	66	10	0	7	97	37	33	37	3	2	6	1	4	0	1	.320	.471	.417	44
vs RHP	138	348	48	97	16	4	8	145	45	42	79	2	11	1	3	8	1	6	.279	.417	.369	56
Home	77	274	44	81	15	2	6	118	35	36	52	3	8	4	1	4	0	1	.296	.431	.392	50
Away	79	280	35	82	11	2	9	124	47	39	64	2	5	3	3	8	1	6	.293	.443	.382	49
Grass	46	158	22	44	2	2	6	68	30	28	40	1	3	2	2	5	1	4	.278	.430	.389	28
Turf	110	396	57	119	24	2	9	174	52	47	76	4	10	5	2	7	0	3	.301	.439	.386	71
April/June	72	252	29	72	12	2	7	109	30	33	66	2	1	3	1	5	1	1	.286	.433	.369	42
July/October	84	302	50	91	14	2	8	133	52	42	50	3	12	4	3	7	0	6	.301	.440	.401	57
SPLITS for Biggio																						
vs LHP	90	186	31	51	10	2	1	68	11	21	19	3	0	12	1	0	2	1	.274	.366	.346	27
vs RHP	126	360	48	110	13	2	3	136	35	32	52	0	2	7	5	2	3	2	.306	.378	.364	52
Home	73	277	39	95	20	3	0	121	24	27	39	0	1	14	5	1	1	2	.343	.437	.401	52
Away	76	269	40	66	3	1	4	83	22	26	32	3	1	5	1	1	4	1	.245	.309	.313	29
Grass	46	173	21	42	2	0	2	50	15	13	21	3	0	1	0	0	2	0	.243	.289	.296	16
Turf	103	373	58	119	21	4	2	154	31	40	50	0	2	18	6	2	3	3	.319	.413	.385	64
April/June	70	251	33	81	11	0	3	101	16	25	30	2	1	11	5	1	2	2	.323	.402	.384	42
July/October	79	295	46	80	12	4	1	103	30	28	41	1	1	8	1	1	3	1	.271	.349	.335	38
SPLITS for Yelding																						
vs LHP	48	97	7	29	3	1	0	34	5	6	15	1	0	4	5	0	1	1	.299	.351	.337	11
vs RHP	63	179	12	38	8	0	1	49	15	7	31	2	0	7	4	4	2	0	.212	.274	.242	11
Home	36	137	7	31	3	0	0	34	10	5	28	1	0	8	3	1	3	1	.226	.248	.252	9
Away	42	139	12	36	8	1	1	49	10	8	18	2	0	3	6	3	0	0	.259	.353	.299	13
Grass	20	72	3	17	3	0	0	20	3	5	9	2	0	2	3	2	0	0	.236	.278	.286	5
Turf	58	204	16	50	8	1	1	63	17	8	37	1	0	9	6	2	3	1	.245	.309	.272	17
April/June	63	237	17	58	10	1	1	73	19	12	41	3	0	10	6	3	3	1	.245	.308	.280	20
July/October	15	39	2	9	1	0	0	10	1	1	5	0	0	1	3	1	0	0	.231	.256	.250	2
SPLITS for Houston Astros (all batters except pitchers)																						
vs LHP	999	1964	210	480	86	9	25	659	199	192	372	14	10	54	24	41	17	13	.244	.336	.313	212
vs RHP	1511	3540	395	865	154	34	54	1249	371	310	655	31	25	71	44	46	46	30	.244	.353	.307	397
Home	1156	2725	302	690	136	29	27	965	285	255	524	27	16	74	30	36	28	23	.253	.354	.318	323
Away	1146	2779	303	655	104	14	52	943	285	247	503	18	19	51	38	51	35	20	.236	.339	.300	286
Grass	671	1655	187	396	53	7	34	565	175	141	301	12	10	25	21	26	25	12	.239	.341	.301	173
Turf	1631	3849	418	949	187	36	45	1343	395	361	726	33	25	100	47	61	38	31	.247	.349	.313	437
April/June	1052	2535	239	606	107	18	34	851	224	243	448	22	11	57	36	35	28	22	.239	.336	.306	270
July/October	1250	2969	366	739	133	25	45	1057	346	259	579	23	24	68	32	52	35	21	.249	.356	.312	339

1991 SPLITS FOR Houston Astros

BATTING SPLITS

	AVG	AB	R	H	2B	3B	HR	RBI	SB	CS	BB	K	OBA	SPCT
Total	.244	5504	605	1345	240	43	79	570	125	68	502	1027	.309	.347

	#Pit	#P/PA	GB	FB	G/F	G	IBB	HB	SH	SF	GDP
Miscellaneous	22055	3.59	1962	1528	1.28	162	45	35	63	43	87

	AVG	AB	R	H	2B	3B	HR	RBI	SB	CS	BB	K	OBA	SPCT
vs. Left	.244	1964	...	480	86	9	25	199	54	24	192	372	.313	.336
vs. Right	.244	3540	...	865	154	34	54	371	71	44	310	655	.307	.353
Home	.253	2725	302	690	136	29	27	285	74	30	255	524	.318	.354
Away	.236	2779	303	655	104	14	52	285	51	38	247	503	.300	.339
None on	.237	3163	...	749	134	24	42	42	0	0	253	594	.298	.334
Runners on	.255	2341	...	596	106	19	37	528	125	68	249	433	.324	.364
April	.221	637	48	141	24	6	6	46	15	9	62	129	.291	.306
May	.260	945	110	246	44	10	15	102	21	12	87	150	.322	.376
June	.230	953	81	219	39	2	13	76	21	15	94	169	.299	.316
July	.267	834	118	223	41	11	16	111	15	12	76	139	.332	.400
August	.245	1013	137	248	50	8	14	130	19	8	104	208	.318	.351
September	.234	947	88	222	34	5	10	82	28	8	63	207	.285	.313
October	.263	175	23	46	8	1	5	23	6	4	16	25	.328	.406
None on/out	.245	1381	...	338	64	12	16	16	0	0	105	245	.303	.343
Scoring Posn	.255	1350	...	344	66	11	21	473	21	16	189	288	.341	.367
Close & Late	.253	988	...	250	40	3	10	113	18	15	96	198	.322	.330
Bases Loaded	.291	103	...	30	6	0	1	76	0	0	6	21	.295	.379
Batting #1	.256	684	93	175	30	9	8	51	29	17	54	98	.309	.361
Batting #2	.260	658	77	171	18	7	4	55	29	12	55	82	.318	.327
Batting #3	.281	631	89	177	30	6	13	77	16	7	66	98	.354	.409
Batting #4	.244	627	65	153	28	5	13	80	6	6	58	124	.316	.367
Batting #5	.266	610	78	162	41	4	11	91	10	4	66	124	.338	.400
Batting #6	.238	610	58	145	24	3	11	68	10	7	53	134	.300	.341
Batting #7	.253	596	53	151	28	5	11	68	12	10	50	125	.311	.372
Batting #8	.229	572	48	131	26	4	5	51	9	3	49	97	.288	.315
Batting #9	.155	516	44	80	15	0	3	29	4	2	51	145	.234	.202
As p	.110	283	17	31	4	0	0	10	0	1	24	103	.181	.124
As c	.274	623	85	171	28	4	4	49	19	6	66	94	.344	.352
As 1b	.290	594	86	172	30	4	14	85	7	4	84	119	.385	.424
As 2b	.231	601	54	139	22	4	5	56	9	4	46	89	.285	.306
As 3b	.254	629	67	160	31	3	13	87	4	5	50	92	.312	.375
As ss	.244	643	54	157	30	3	11	63	16	13	27	139	.274	.351
As lf	.259	621	61	161	32	12	15	77	13	8	47	121	.318	.422
As cf	.265	650	89	172	29	10	8	51	35	18	54	81	.320	.377
As rf	.225	586	60	132	22	3	6	57	16	7	60	133	.298	.304
Outfield	.250	1857	210	465	83	25	29	185	64	33	161	335	.312	.369
0.0 count	.317	819	...	260	55	2	20	115	...	...	1	0	.321	.463
After (0.1)	.215	2536	...	545	99	18	25	228	...	...	114	686	.252	.298
After (1.0)	.251	2149	...	540	86	23	34	227	...	...	351	341	.356	.360
Two strikes	.170	2474	...	420	75	16	18	167	...	...	213	1025	.239	.235
Grass	.239	1655	187	396	53	7	34	175	25	21	141	301	.301	.341
Turf	.247	3849	418	949	187	36	45	395	100	47	361	726	.313	.349
Day	.245	1280	143	313	68	7	21	134	32	18	126	243	.314	.358
Night	.244	4224	462	1032	172	36	58	436	93	50	376	784	.308	.343
Inning 1.6	.241	3624	391	875	151	29	51	364	90	49	320	672	.305	.341
Inning 7+	.250	1880	214	470	89	14	28	206	35	19	182	355	.318	.357
vs.Atl	.206	618	45	127	24	5	7	45	21	3	62	127	.281	.294
vs.ChN	.244	402	42	98	17	4	6	40	4	2	28	60	.293	.351
vs.Cin	.230	592	57	136	24	1	9	51	14	8	53	128	.296	.319
vs.LA	.243	629	66	153	23	7	11	61	10	8	58	128	.310	.355
vs.Mon	.215	414	33	89	17	2	2	30	8	8	40	83	.286	.280
vs.NYN	.261	410	46	107	19	1	8	42	11	7	29	78	.310	.371
vs.Phi	.248	411	45	102	18	3	5	43	8	2	51	74	.332	.343
vs.Pit	.293	417	57	122	30	5	4	53	13	6	35	63	.346	.417
vs.StL	.248	383	50	95	15	7	9	48	10	6	34	62	.314	.394
vs.SD	.229	606	66	139	27	3	7	60	13	7	50	115	.289	.318
vs.SF	.285	622	98	177	26	5	11	97	13	11	62	109	.352	.395

PITCHING SPLITS

	ERA	W	L	SV	SVOP	GS	CG	SHO	IP	H	ER	HR	BB	IBB	K
Total	4.00	65	97	36	59	162	7	16	1453.0	1347	646	129	651	62	1033

	#Pit	#P/IP	GB	FB	G/F	BRp9	RA	WP	BK	SH	SF	R	HB	Hld
Miscellaneous	23240	15.99	1970	1518	1.30	12.56	365	46	17	69	52	717	29	43

	ERA	W	L	SV	SVOP	GS	CG	SHO	IP	H	ER	HR	BB	IBB	K
ST	4.07	45	63	0	0	162	7	3	956.1	884	433	89	402	28	666
REL	3.86	20	34	36	59	0	0	0	496.2	463	213	40	249	34	367
Home	3.55	37	44	15	29	81	5	3	754.0	648	297	44	318	30	551
Away	4.49	28	53	21	30	81	2	0	699.0	699	349	85	333	32	482
April	3.96	8	11	5	8	19	0	0	172.2	156	76	12	73	11	104
May	4.28	10	18	7	9	28	1	0	246.0	235	117	23	122	17	169
June	3.28	11	17	6	10	28	2	2	258.0	214	94	19	109	10	168
July	3.94	12	13	5	7	25	3	1	219.1	220	96	20	96	5	152
August	4.38	12	17	4	12	29	1	0	265.0	256	129	24	122	8	221
September	4.07	10	18	8	12	28	0	0	250.0	228	113	26	107	11	181
October	4.50	2	3	1	1	5	0	0	42.0	38	21	5	22	0	38
Grass	4.26	18	30	12	16	48	0	0	410.0	399	194	50	205	19	283
Turf	3.90	47	67	24	43	114	7	3	1043.0	948	452	79	446	43	750
Day	3.91	15	23	9	11	38	1	1	331.2	305	144	32	156	9	243
Night	4.03	50	74	27	48	124	6	2	1121.1	1042	502	97	495	53	790
vs.Atl	3.62	5	13	3	7	18	1	1	164.0	147	66	14	67	3	110
vs.ChN	4.29	3	9	3	4	12	0	0	105.0	105	50	11	43	2	74
vs.Cin	3.66	9	9	5	7	18	2	1	160.0	140	65	19	58	8	102
vs.LA	4.05	8	10	4	8	18	0	0	164.1	143	74	19	88	8	129
vs.Mon	3.71	2	10	0	2	12	0	0	114.0	100	47	5	50	6	91
vs.NYN	3.22	7	5	5	7	12	1	1	109.0	96	39	5	53	4	60
vs.Phi	2.95	7	5	3	7	12	1	0	109.2	87	36	6	37	4	93
vs.Pit	5.31	4	8	4	5	12	1	0	105.0	116	62	12	56	6	72
vs.StL	5.00	5	7	2	3	12	1	0	104.1	119	58	7	58	6	60
vs.SD	3.85	6	12	3	4	18	0	0	159.0	141	68	15	67	8	123
vs.SF	4.59	9	9	4	5	18	0	0	158.2	153	81	16	74	7	119

OPPOSING BATTERS VS. PITCHERS.

	AVG	AB	R	H	2B	3B	HR	RBI	SB	CS	BB	K	OBA	SPCT
Total	.247	5454	717	1347	248	30	129	665	143	60	651	1033	.328	.374
vs. Left	.255	2793	...	712	123	19	62	346	89	29	379	540	.343	.379
vs. Right	.239	2661	...	635	125	11	67	319	54	31	272	493	.311	.369
ST	.245	3602	473	884	167	20	89	403	106	41	402	666	.322	.377
REL	.250	1852	244	463	81	10	40	262	37	19	249	367	.339	.369
Home	.234	2775	330	648	126	18	44	306	71	30	318	551	.313	.339
Away	.261	2679	387	699	122	12	85	359	72	30	333	482	.343	.411
None on	.235	3063	...	721	129	12	72	72	0	0	340	606	.314	.356
Runners on	.262	2391	...	626	119	18	57	593	143	60	311	427	.344	.398
None on/out	.245	1341	...	329	63	7	36	36	0	0	165	233	.330	.383
Scoring Posn	.259	1439	...	373	76	10	35	521	35	7	246	278	.359	.399
vs 1st Batr	.270	311	...	84	17	1	7	43	3	0	49	51	.367	.399
1st IP	.263	1773	194	467	95	7	37	284	59	26	267	330	.357	.387
Inning 1.6	.248	3681	481	912	166	18	97	441	111	43	407	683	.323	.382
Inning 7+	.245	1773	236	435	82	12	32	224	32	17	244	350	.337	.359
Close & Late	.249	951	...	237	45	7	18	141	22	8	140	188	.345	.368
0.0 count	.315	812	...	256	44	5	20	106	...	...	54	0	.362	.456
After (0.1)	.224	2353	...	528	95	9	47	251	...	...	149	650	.271	.332
After (1.0)	.246	2289	...	563	109	16	62	308	...	...	448	383	.369	.389
Two strikes	.170	2456	...	418	78	12	34	206	...	...	222	1032	.239	.253
Pitch 1.15	.274	1538	...	421	88	8	34	210	41	21	200	265	.356	.408
Pitch 16.30	.229	1164	...	267	33	3	29	132	32	10	139	245	.310	.338
Pitch 31.45	.245	762	...	187	41	5	16	96	18	11	83	162	.322	.375
Pitch 46.60	.254	611	...	155	32	2	21	87	19	7	75	93	.339	.416
Pitch 61.75	.219	521	...	114	16	5	11	54	9	3	61	114	.301	.332
Pitch 76.90	.270	437	...	118	24	5	12	58	14	5	45	72	.338	.430
Pitch 91.105	.212	278	...	59	12	1	6	20	8	1	28	59	.287	.327
Pitch 106.20	.217	115	...	25	2	1	1	7	0	1	22	19	.345	.278
Pitch 121.35	.074	27	...	2	0	0	0	3	2	1	2	4	.129	.074
Pitch 136.50	.000	2	...	0	0	0	0	0	0	0	0	0	.000	.000

National League

Eastern Division

1. Pittsburgh Pirates
2. St. Louis Cardinals
3. Philadelphia Phillies
4. Chicago Cubs
5. New York Mets
6. Montreal Expos

NL Eastern Division Team Batting

	G	AB	Run	Hit	2B	3B	HR	TB	RBI	W	K	IW	HB	SB	CS	GI DP	SH	SF	Avg	Slug	OBP	Runs Ctd
Chicago	2297	5522	695	1395	232	26	159	2156	654	442	879	41	36	123	64	86	75	55	.253	.390	.309	678
Montreal	2209	5412	579	1329	236	42	95	1934	536	484	1056	51	28	221	100	97	64	47	.246	.357	.308	610
New York	2197	5327	640	1297	249	24	117	1945	605	578	785	53	27	153	70	99	59	52	.243	.365	.318	642
Philadelphia	2209	5504	628	1331	248	33	111	1978	590	489	1024	48	21	92	30	112	52	49	.242	.359	.304	614
Pittsburgh	2224	5449	768	1433	259	50	126	2170	725	620	901	62	35	124	46	110	99	66	.263	.398	.338	768
St. Louis	2244	5362	651	1366	239	53	68	1915	599	532	857	48	21	202	110	94	58	47	.255	.357	.322	632

NL Eastern Division Sabermetric Team Batting

	|-------- Ball Park Adjusted --------|												Runs		Run/					
	AB	Run	Hit	2B	3B	HR	RBI	W	SO	Avg	Slug	OBP	Ctd	Outs	27o	OW%	OG	OWAR	DWAR	TWAR
Chicago	5592	673	1388	239	30	138	633	483	908	.248	.376	.309	665	4507	3.98	.440	167	15.03	4.77	19.81
Montreal	4650	558	1176	209	36	100	524	411	875	.253	.378	.315	564	3722	4.09	.533	138	25.18	7.11	32.29
New York	5675	668	1362	270	22	128	637	611	830	.240	.363	.315	666	4618	3.89	.487	171	23.49	4.50	27.99
Philadelphia	5641	638	1337	246	41	114	590	493	1047	.237	.356	.298	613	4551	3.64	.448	169	16.45	5.01	21.46
Pittsburgh	5416	781	1455	262	43	132	732	641	870	.269	.406	.346	801	4276	5.06	.578	158	36.12	9.70	45.82
St. Louis	5733	728	1502	253	48	84	671	556	954	.262	.367	.327	701	4562	4.15	.517	169	28.23	8.18	36.41

NL Eastern Division Team Pitching

	ERA	W	L	Pct	G	GS	CG	ShO	GF	Sv	IP	R	ER	H	2B	3B	HR	BB	IW	SO	HB	WP	BK
Chicago	4.05	77	83	.481	520	160	12	2	148	40	1456.2	734	655	1415	246	50	117	542	64	927	28	48	12
Montreal	3.64	71	90	.441	528	161	12	6	149	39	1440.1	655	583	1304	254	39	111	584	42	909	32	51	9
New York	3.57	77	83	.481	474	160	12	4	149	39	1431.1	645	568	1399	225	46	108	409	41	1027	25	59	14
Philadelphia	3.89	77	84	.478	482	161	15	5	146	35	1454.0	680	628	1338	260	36	111	670	58	984	43	81	6
Pittsburgh	3.44	98	64	.605	515	162	18	9	144	51	1456.2	632	557	1411	236	32	117	401	34	919	30	40	12
St. Louis	3.69	84	78	.519	531	162	9	0	153	51	1435.1	648	588	1367	251	42	114	454	52	822	47	33	7

NL Eastern Division Catchers

	G	PO	A	Er	TC	DP	PB	SB	CS	CS%	FPct	DI	DG	DW%	DWAR	ERA	ERA Wo-W
Chicago	162	967	104	20	1091	11	19	139	64	.315	.982	1447.2	10.0	.242	-.23	4.05	
Montreal	162	949	106	18	1073	11	22	149	81	.352	.983	1423.1	10.0	.325	-.25	3.64	
New York	162	1060	95	11	1166	8	12	134	74	.356	.991	1417.0	10.0	.375	.25	3.58	
Philadelphia	162	1007	76	12	1095	7	9	151	48	.241	.989	1444.0	10.0	.289	-.60	3.89	
Pittsburgh	162	943	85	7	1035	8	9	142	74	.343	.993	1436.2	10.0	.411	.61	3.44	
St. Louis	162	875	96	12	983	11	8	121	81	.401	.988	1426.1	10.0	.337	-.13	3.69	
LG.AVG	162	997	93	13	1103	10	12	137	67	.328	.988	1435.1					

NL Eastern Division First Base

	G	PO	A	Er	TC	DP	FPct	DI	DG	DW%	DWAR
Chicago	162	1558	166	9	1733	113	.995	1447.2	3.0	.696	1.03
Montreal	162	1421	127	15	1563	113	.990	1423.1	3.0	.489	.41
New York	162	1421	123	6	1550	95	.996	1417.0	3.0	.586	.70
Philadelphia	162	1402	89	12	1503	95	.992	1444.0	3.0	.394	.13
Pittsburgh	162	1489	97	21	1607	118	.987	1436.2	3.0	.394	.13
St. Louis	162	1432	97	21	1550	112	.986	1426.1	3.0	.368	.05
LG.AVG	162	1454	119	13	1586	112	.992	1435.1			

NL Eastern Division Second Base

	G	PO	A	Er	TC	DP	FPct	DI	DG	DW%	DWAR
Chicago	162	287	555	6	848	73	.993	1447.2	8.0	.499	1.19
Montreal	162	321	450	28	799	85	.965	1423.1	8.0	.377	.22
New York	162	368	447	14	829	67	.983	1409.0	8.0	.414	.51
Philadelphia	162	350	438	11	799	79	.986	1435.0	8.0	.450	.79
Pittsburgh	162	397	506	10	913	93	.989	1436.2	8.0	.624	2.16
St. Louis	162	358	514	13	885	92	.985	1426.1	8.0	.583	1.86
LG.AVG	162	346	481	15	842	87	.982	1435.1			

NL Eastern Division Third Base

	G	PO	A	Er	TC	DP	FPct	DI	DG	DW%	DWAR
Chicago	162	92	297	21	410	21	.949	1447.2	6.0	.349	-.01
Montreal	162	120	326	15	461	30	.967	1423.1	6.0	.553	1.20
New York	162	88	297	31	416	20	.925	1409.0	6.0	.253	-.58
Philadelphia	162	111	323	24	458	26	.948	1435.0	6.0	.437	.51
Pittsburgh	162	125	357	26	508	35	.949	1436.2	6.0	.559	1.23
St. Louis	162	137	305	26	468	21	.944	1426.1	6.0	.420	.42
LG.AVG	162	120	320	23	463	26	.950	1435.1			

NL Eastern Division Shortstop

	G	PO	A	Er	TC	DP	FPct	DI	DG	DW%	DWAR
Chicago	162	301	472	24	797	86	.970	1447.2	11.0	.515	1.81
Montreal	162	248	495	17	760	83	.978	1423.1	11.0	.540	2.06
New York	162	256	508	37	801	73	.954	1409.0	11.0	.425	.82
Philadelphia	162	263	459	23	745	71	.969	1435.0	11.0	.444	1.02
Pittsburgh	162	247	514	24	785	85	.969	1436.2	11.0	.528	1.93
St. Louis	162	277	422	10	709	87	.986	1426.1	11.0	.541	2.08
LG.AVG	162	268	482	26	776	82	.966	1435.1			

NL Eastern Division Left Field

	G	PO	A	Er	TC	DP	FPct	DI	DG	DW%	DWAR
Chicago	162	310	7	12	329	0	.964	1447.2	4.0	.369	.07
Montreal	162	338	6	9	353	2	.975	1423.1	4.0	.445	.37
New York	162	334	11	2	347	1	.994	1409.0	4.0	.607	1.01
Philadelphia	162	341	10	4	355	1	.989	1435.0	4.0	.594	.96
Pittsburgh	162	342	16	3	361	2	.992	1436.2	4.0	.711	1.42
St. Louis	162	384	15	3	402	1	.993	1426.1	4.0	.759	1.63
LG.AVG	162	341	9	6	356	1	.983	1435.1			

NL Eastern Division Center Field

	G	PO	A	Er	TC	DP	FPct	DI	DG	DW%	DWAR
Chicago	162	399	5	8	412	2	.981	1447.2	6.0	.383	.20
Montreal	162	416	12	7	435	2	.984	1423.1	6.0	.536	1.10
New York	162	330	9	8	347	2	.977	1409.0	6.0	.303	-.27
Philadelphia	162	430	8	9	447	4	.980	1435.0	6.0	.474	.73
Pittsburgh	162	368	9	5	382	1	.987	1436.2	6.0	.425	.44
St. Louis	162	433	10	8	451	3	.982	1426.1	6.0	.518	1.00
LG.AVG	162	407	8	6	421	2	.986	1435.1			

NL Eastern Division Right Field

	G	PO	A	Er	TC	DP	FPct	DI	DG	DW%	DWAR
Chicago	162	296	10	4	310	4	.987	1447.2	5.0	.499	.74
Montreal	162	370	19	6	395	3	.985	1423.1	5.0	.733	1.89
New York	162	286	14	9	309	4	.971	1409.0	5.0	.479	.63
Philadelphia	162	348	7	5	360	0	.986	1435.0	5.0	.524	.85
Pittsburgh	162	314	14	5	333	3	.985	1436.2	5.0	.595	1.21
St. Louis	162	298	15	3	316	2	.991	1426.1	5.0	.642	1.45
LG.AVG	162	318	12	6	336	2	.982	1435.1			

Pittsburgh Pirates

Dave Raglin

PITTSBURGH											
YEAR	1982	1983	1984	1985	1986	1987	1988	1989	1990	1991	TOT
W	84	84	75	57	64	80	85	74	95	98	796
L	78	78	87	104	98	82	75	88	67	64	821
WPCT	0.519	0.519	0.463	0.354	0.395	0.494	0.531	0.457	0.586	0.605	0.492
R	724	659	615	568	663	723	651	637	733	768	6741
RA	696	648	567	708	700	744	616	680	619	632	6610
PWPT	0.520	0.508	0.541	0.392	0.473	0.486	0.528	0.467	0.584	0.596	0.510
PythW	84	82	88	63	77	79	85	76	95	97	83
PythL	78	80	74	99	85	83	77	86	67	65	79
LUCK	0	2	-13	-6	-13	1	0	-2	0	1	-30

Defensive Efficiency Record: .6988

It's great to see all of the statistics that are available these days. A few years ago, we were happy to get left/right information after the season; today, we can dial up the STATS computer and pull down what each player or team did, let's say, with runners in scoring position through the night before.

However, one disturbing trend has developed, the misuse of this information. It's great that ESPN gives us on-base percentage with batting average for the hitters, but they also love to tell us things like how the player has done the last ten games or how he's hit with runners in scoring position since June. The problem with statistics like that is that they are given a significance they don't deserve. Elias started this trend, breathlessly touting their LIPS (late inning pressure situation) statistics. However, if you look at the top players in LIPS' batting average for a season, they're just as likely to hit .150 as .350 the next year. That's what you get for making judgements on 75 at-bats.

Statistics based on such a small sample do not mean anything. If you get anything out of this article, get this. There are times that it's useful to know what a player has done in the last ten games; like if he's coming off an injury, you want to see if he's been hitting .128; but for the most part, it's garbage.

The public isn't fooled. They know that the only thing many of these of these statistics prove is how much research the people in the media can do. The problem is that those people give us serious researchers a bad name. We have enough sense to know what numbers to use and how to use them, but the average fan lumps our numbers in with the batting-average-with-a-lefthander-on-cloudy-days-in-domed-stadiums people. That bothers me--I have a degree in statistics and am a professional mathematical statistician, and I am very careful to not misuse my data.

Sometimes a whole season is not enough. My favorite story on the subject goes back several years. While doing some research for my Tiger newsletter, I noticed that the California Angels had compiled a worse record at home than on the road for his one season. The answer was obvious--a lot of players are from Southern California and they are especially pumped up to play well in front of their families and friends. However, before I published this breathtaking information, I figured I should check with past season. As it turned out, it was a one season aberration--Other than that year, the Angels had a normal home-road differential.

What does that have to do with the Pittsburgh Pirates? I want to walk you through a study I did on the Pirates, show you what I found, and discuss what I felt was significance.

It started on a cold night in November. My friend Dave Smith of Newark, DE, sent me some numbers he had compiled from the SportsSource scoresheet database. Remember the charts Bill James compiled a few years ago showing the number of games each team was above/below .500 after each inning (i.e., a team ahead 44 times after one inning, behind 40, and tied the rest would be four games over .500)? Dave provided me that for 1991, as well as the number of runs scored and allowed by each team in each inning, and a couple of other things.

Since I was doing the Pirate article for Brock, I looked at their numbers, and boy, did I find an eyeful. After one inning, the Pirates, were ahead 31 times, behind 41 times, and tied in the remaining 90 games! As you might have seen in the Oriole article, only three teams were ahead less often after one, and only three teams were more games under .500 after the first. Considering that the Pirates had the best record in baseball, 98-64, 34 games over .500, that was interesting.

The next step was to find out if the problem was offensive (well, I'm sure most Pirate fans were offended) or defensive. In the first inning, the Pirates scored 75 runs and allowed 85. Since the major league average was 91, the problem was with the offense.

The Pirates had two unique strategies that I decided I should check on. First, their leadoff hitters were their first base platoon, Orlando Merced and Gary Redus (I don't think I've ever seen that before), and their number two hitter Jay Bell, is the king of the sacrifice bunt. Bell's 39 sacrifices in 1990 and 30 in 1991 both led the majors, and Jim Leyland is one of the few managers, him and Tommy Lasorda, who will bunt in the first inning.

That brings up a long-debated topic in sabermetrics--does the sacrifice bunt hurt more than help? The consensus at this time in the field is that the sacrifice bunt is a bad play. However, the two managers who use it the most year after year (and were one-two in 1991) are Leyland and Lasorda, two of the most-respected managers in the game today.

Let's start with the leadoff hitters first (no pun intended), because that one is easy. The Pirate leadoff hitters in 1991 were actually very good:

Pirate Leadoff	AB	BB	R	H	HR	SB	CS	BA	OBP
1991 Season	663	86	125	174	16	25	7	.262	.351

The look at the effect of Bell's sacrifices is a little more difficult. The raw data needed for that is not readily available. However, I called my friend Dave Smith back, and thanks to his programming and the generosity of SportsSource in allowing us to use their data, we were able to design a couple of studies.

We started by looking at all of the situations where the Pirates got the leadoff batter in the first on first, the usual situation which Bell, batting second, would sacrifice. In 1991, the Pirates' first hitter was on first 33 times. Keeping in mind that 33 is not a large sample size, we note that Bell sacrificed the runner to second 11 of those times. In those 11 innings, Pittsburgh scored 0, 1, 0, 1, 0, 0, 1, 0, 2, 1, and 0 runs (a total of 6), while in the other 22 cases (including three games where Bell did not play), they scored 1, 1, 3, 4, 0, 1, 1, 1, 0, 0, 0, 1, 0, 1, 0, 0, 1, 0, 2, 1, 0, and 0 runs (a total of 18). It wasn't anything like Bell sacrificing with only a lefthander on the mound or anything, either, we checked for things that.

At first glance, it appears that we have found something big. The sabermetrician's argument against the sacrifice bunt has always been that it hurts the chances for a big inning, although it helps the possibility of scoring one run. There are times where scoring one run is enough, but of course the first inning is not one of those times. In the eleven first innings where Bell sacrificed, the Pirates scored zero runs six times, one run four times, and two runs once. No big innings there.

However, look at when they had a runner on first and didn't sacrifice. Out of the 22 times, they scored no runs ten times and one run nine times, nabbing two, three, and four runs only once each. It doesn't look like they got too many big innings when they didn't bunt Bell.

That was the problem. While the average National League team scored two or more runs in 24 first innings, the Pirates, the highest scoring team in the league, did it only 16 times. As you can tell by the Pirate first inning statistics below, few Pirates hit well in the first inning, nobody with power.

The two main Pirate leadoff hitters, Merced and Redus, had a combined .284 on-base percentage with one home run in the first inning, and number two man Bell also did not hit in the first either (.267 on-base percentage, one home run).

Why didn't Pittsburgh hit in the first? Aren't they inspired by Smokestack Sam? (For those of you who don't get to Three Rivers, right before the Pirates come up in the bottom of the first, they have a cartoon of train revving up speed on the DiamondVision, with a guy sticking his head out of the engine, Smokestack Sam, going woo, woo, like a train whistle. The fans join in, and I love it. That's just one of the many nice touches the Pirates have put in at Three Rivers.) It looks like the bunting may hurt them a bit, but mostly it's random chance, coincidence, the luck of the draw, etc.

It's amazing how much random chance there is out there, how many things we look at as significant are just Lady Luck getting into the fray. I looked at the games above/behind .500 for each team, and very rarely (Toronto, for one) is it a smooth line. Usually, the path is so jagged it makes the Rockies look like Nebraska.

Pirate Hitters in the First Inning, 1991, Ranked by On-Base Percentage

	AB	BB	H	HR	RBI	BA	OBP	SLG
Bonilla	75	18	24	1	21	.320	.452	.467
VanSlyke	109	18	27	3	14	.248	.354	.413
Bonds	50	8	12	2	18	.240	.345	.400
Merced	80	12	16	0	0	.200	.304	.250
Bell	130	5	31	1	3	.238	.267	.346
Redus	52	4	10	1	1	.192	.250	.327
Others	102	8	24	2	16	.235	.291	.353
Totals	598	73	144	10	73	.241	.323	.365

Does that mean we ignore the peaks and valleys. Of course not, but we do have to put them into perspective. There is a big, huge difference between saying that the Pirates did not hit well in the first inning and the Pirates are a bad hitting team in the first. The first statement states the facts. The second statement predicts--the Pirates are (not were) a bad first inning hitting team, meaning that they should be in 1992. In all likelihood, they will score more runs in the first in 1992 than in 1991, even without Bonilla (especially after looking at the 1990 numbers below).

Compare this to the Orioles. The O's did not score in the first inning, but there was good reasons for that. Their number one and two hitters were awful all of the time, not just in the first. Merced, Redus, and Bell had good seasons hitting first and second, just not in the first inning. See the difference?

Here are the 1990 numbers I got from Dave Smith (I owe you, Dave). Looking at 1990 is ideal because Jimmy Leyland used the same bunting strategy that year, too. In 1990, the Pirates scored 94 runs in the first, 26 times two or more, just above the league average in both categories. Bell did not hit well (.200 average), but Bonds went nuts (19-for-49, .388, four homers, 20 ribbies). Forty times, Pittsburgh had the leadoff runner on first. Seventeen times, Bell bunted (on three occasions, the runner was forced at second), with the Pirates scoring 17 runs. In the 23 times Bell didn't bunt, the Pirates scored 34 runs.

Therefore, for each of the two years, they scored about 50% more runs when they started with a runner on first and didn't bunt Bell than when they did bunt Bell. This is not enough evidence to throw away the strategy by itself, but it does lay claim to the theory that it doesn't help you score more runs. Given this on top of the past evidence on the situation, I wouldn't bunt Bell in the first.

But that's not the main reason they didn't score runs in the first. The main reason was Lady Luck, that's all. Maybe she doesn't like Smokestack Sam.

Pittsburgh Pirates Home Park Performance Factors

	Outs	Runs	Hits	2b	3b	HR	W	K	SH	SF	HBP	IBB	SB	CS	GDP
Home LH Batters	.984	1.087	1.039	1.303	1.124	1.061	1.048	1.010	1.117	1.066	.884	1.124	1.299	1.110	1.039
Home RH Batters	.936	.906	.937	.840	.681	1.001	1.055	.908	.908	1.065	1.203	.866	1.079	.752	.908
All Home Batters	.957	.968	.979	.968	.869	.990	1.003	.961	.988	1.092	1.059	.998	1.142	.871	.962
Opp LH Batters	1.024	1.077	1.032	1.243	.647	.992	1.110	.956	.901	.923	.901	1.137	.944	1.051	1.529
Opp RH Batters	1.009	1.088	1.091	1.060	.990	1.168	1.031	.975	1.125	.857	.876	1.282	1.151	.921	.933
All Opp Batters	1.016	1.068	1.052	1.057	.853	1.118	1.066	.970	1.068	.895	.845	1.261	1.036	.943	1.010
All LH Batters	1.001	1.084	1.036	1.278	.901	1.037	1.073	.981	1.044	1.026	.891	1.136	1.140	1.073	1.187
All RH Batters	.973	.998	1.017	.950	.807	1.089	1.046	.941	1.006	.936	1.037	1.055	1.119	.845	.921
All Batters	.985	1.016	1.014	1.011	.871	1.052	1.037	.963	1.030	1.017	.945	1.098	1.084	.904	.986

Conventional Batting Records for Pittsburgh Pirates

	G	AB	Run	Hit	2B	3B	HR	TB	RBI	W	K	IW	HB	SB	CS	BRng Eff	GI DP	SH	SF	Avg	Slug	OBP	Runs Ctd
LaValliere	108	336	25	97	11	2	3	121	41	33	27	4	2	2	1	.194	10	1	5	.289	.360	.351	43
Merced	120	411	83	113	17	2	10	164	50	64	81	4	1	8	4	.538	6	1	1	.275	.399	.373	65
Lind	149	499	53	132	16	6	3	169	53	30	54	10	2	7	4	.417	19	4	6	.265	.339	.305	49
Bonilla B	156	574	102	172	44	6	18	282	100	89	67	8	2	2	4	.458	14	0	11	.300	.491	.389	113
Bell Jay	156	604	96	163	32	8	16	259	67	52	98	1	4	10	6	.588	15	30	3	.270	.429	.330	85
Bonds	152	506	94	147	28	5	25	260	116	107	73	25	4	42	13	.455	8	0	13	.291	.514	.410	119
Van Slyke	137	487	87	129	23	7	17	217	83	71	84	1	4	10	2	.546	5	0	11	.265	.446	.356	85
Varsho	98	187	23	51	11	2	4	78	23	19	34	2	2	9	2	.487	2	1	1	.273	.417	.344	29
Redus	97	248	45	62	12	2	7	99	24	28	39	2	3	17	3	.473	0	1	4	.250	.399	.329	38
Slaught	76	216	19	64	17	1	1	86	29	21	32	1	3	1	0	.308	5	5	1	.296	.398	.365	32
Wilkerson	84	190	20	36	9	1	2	53	18	15	39	0	0	2	1	.542	2	0	4	.189	.279	.244	14
McClendon	84	163	24	47	7	0	7	75	24	18	23	0	2	2	1	.391	2	0	0	.288	.460	.366	28
Buechele	30	112	16	28	5	1	4	47	19	8	27	0	2	0	1	.412	3	1	1	.250	.420	.309	14
King J	33	109	16	26	1	1	4	41	18	14	15	3	1	3	1	.286	3	0	1	.239	.376	.328	14
Wehner	37	106	15	36	7	0	0	43	7	7	17	0	0	3	0	.500	0	0	0	.340	.406	.381	18
Webster M	36	97	9	17	3	4	1	31	9	9	31	1	0	0	0	.333	3	0	0	.175	.320	.245	7
Drabek	35	83	6	15	1	0	0	16	2	1	28	0	0	0	0	.167	0	4	0	.181	.193	.190	3
Espy	42	81	7	20	4	0	1	27	11	5	16	0	0	4	0	.625	0	3	2	.247	.333	.284	9
Smith Z	36	71	3	13	3	0	0	16	10	3	8	0	1	0	0	.455	0	13	1	.183	.225	.224	5
Smiley	33	70	3	7	0	0	0	7	3	3	24	0	0	0	0	.429	1	6	0	.100	.100	.137	1
Tomlin R	32	52	5	10	1	0	0	11	2	2	18	0	0	0	0	.167	2	13	0	.192	.212	.222	3
Walk	25	39	2	8	1	0	1	12	5	1	11	0	0	0	0	1.000	1	2	0	.205	.308	.225	3
Prince	25	33	4	9	3	0	1	15	2	7	3	0	1	0	0	.429	3	0	0	.273	.455	.415	6
Garcia C	12	24	2	6	0	2	0	10	1	1	8	0	0	0	0	.500	1	0	0	.250	.417	.280	2
Gonzalez Jo	16	20	2	2	0	0	1	5	3	0	6	0	0	0	0	.000	0	2	1	.100	.250	.095	1
Redfield	11	18	1	2	0	0	0	2	0	4	1	0	0	0	1	1.000	0	1	0	.111	.111	.273	1
Martinez Crm	11	16	1	4	0	0	0	4	0	1	2	0	0	0	0	1.000	2	0	0	.250	.250	.294	1
Heaton	43	14	0	4	1	0	0	5	1	1	2	0	0	0	0	.500	0	0	0	.286	.357	.333	2
Palacios	36	14	0	1	0	0	0	1	0	0	7	0	0	0	0	.000	0	5	0	.071	.071	.071	0
Belinda	60	7	0	0	0	0	0	0	1	2	5	0	0	0	0	.000	1	2	0	.000	.000	.222	0
Landrum B	60	4	0	0	0	0	0	0	0	0	3	0	0	0	0	.000	0	1	0	.000	.000	.000	0
Patterson B	54	4	1	1	0	0	0	1	0	0	2	0	0	0	0	1.000	0	0	0	.250	.250	.250	0
Richardson	6	4	0	1	0	0	0	1	0	0	3	0	0	0	0	.000	0	0	0	.250	.250	.250	0
Bullett	11	4	2	0	0	0	0	0	0	0	3	0	1	1	1	.500	0	0	0	.000	.000	.200	0
Schulz	3	3	0	0	0	0	0	0	0	0	2	0	0	0	0	.000	0	0	0	.000	.000	.000	0
Miller P	1	3	0	0	0	0	0	0	0	0	0	0	0	0	0	.000	0	0	0	.000	.000	.000	0
Fajardo	2	3	0	0	0	0	0	0	0	0	1	0	0	0	0	.000	1	0	0	.000	.000	.000	0
Reed Rk	1	2	0	1	1	0	0	2	2	0	0	0	0	0	0	.000	0	0	0	.500	1.000	.500	1
Kipper	52	1	0	0	0	0	0	0	0	0	0	0	0	0	0	.000	0	1	0	.000	.000	.000	0
Banister	1	1	0	1	0	0	0	1	0	0	0	0	0	0	0	.000	0	0	0	1.000	1.000	1.000	1
Rodriguez Ro	17	1	0	0	0	0	0	0	0	0	0	0	0	0	0	.000	0	0	0	.000	.000	.000	0
Huismann	5	0	0	0	0	0	0	0	0	0	0	0	0	0	0	.000	0	0	0	.000	.000	.000	0
Mason R	23	0	1	0	0	0	0	0	0	1	0	0	0	0	0	.000	0	1	0	.000	.000	1.000	0
TOTALS	2206	5417	767	1425	258	50	126	2161	724	617	894	62	35	123	45	.457	109	98	66	.263	.399	.339	765

Sabermetric Batting Records for Pittsburgh Pirates

	Ball Park Adjusted												Runs		Run/					
	AB	Run	Hit	2B	3B	HR	RBI	W	SO	Avg	Slug	OBP	Ctd	Outs	27o	OW%	OG	OWAR	DWAR	TWAR
Banister	1	0	1	0	0	0	0	0	0	1.000	1.000	1.000	1	0	?????	.000	0	???????	0.00	???????
Bell Jay	593	95	165	30	6	17	68	54	92	.278	.435	.342	89	478	5.03	.575	18	3.99	1.90	5.88
Bonds	512	101	152	35	4	25	115	115	71	.297	.527	.421	127	396	8.66	.801	15	6.61	1.14	7.75
Bonilla B	570	103	174	44	5	18	101	92	64	.305	.495	.397	117	422	7.49	.750	16	6.25	1.14	7.39
Buechele	109	15	28	4	0	4	19	8	25	.257	.404	.319	14	84	4.50	.520	3	0.53	0.21	0.74
Bullett	3	2	0	0	0	0	0	0	2	.000	.000	.000	0	3	0.00	.000	0	-0.04	0.00	-0.04
Espy	80	7	20	4	0	1	11	5	15	.250	.338	.291	9	64	3.80	.436	2	0.20	0.08	0.29
Garcia C	23	1	6	0	1	0	1	1	7	.261	.348	.292	2	17	3.18	.351	1	0.00	0.08	0.08
Gonzalez Jo	19	1	2	0	0	1	3	0	5	.105	.263	.105	1	19	1.42	.098	1	-0.18	0.15	-0.03
King J	106	15	26	0	0	4	18	14	14	.245	.358	.339	14	82	4.61	.532	3	0.55	0.08	0.63
LaValliere	339	27	100	14	1	3	40	35	26	.295	.369	.359	45	257	4.73	.545	10	1.85	0.45	2.30
Lind	489	52	133	15	5	3	53	31	50	.272	.342	.315	51	385	3.58	.407	14	0.81	1.86	2.66
Martinez Crm	15	0	4	0	0	0	0	1	1	.267	.267	.313	1	12	2.25	.213	0	-0.06	0.13	0.07
McClendon	159	23	47	6	0	7	24	18	21	.296	.465	.374	30	113	7.17	.733	4	1.60	0.05	1.66
Merced	407	84	114	17	1	10	50	66	78	.280	.400	.381	67	302	5.99	.658	11	3.44	0.12	3.57
Prince	32	3	9	2	0	1	2	7	2	.281	.438	.425	6	25	6.48	.692	1	0.32	-0.07	0.24
Redfield	17	0	2	0	0	0	0	4	0	.118	.118	.286	1	16	1.69	.132	1	-0.13	-0.01	-0.14
Redus	242	44	62	11	1	7	24	29	36	.256	.397	.339	38	186	5.52	.620	7	1.86	0.11	1.97
Richardson	3	0	1	0	0	0	0	0	2	.333	.333	.333	0	2	0.00	.000	0	-0.03	-0.01	-0.03
Schulz	3	0	0	0	0	0	0	0	1	.000	.000	.000	0	3	0.00	.000	0	-0.04	0.00	-0.04
Slaught	211	18	64	16	0	1	29	21	30	.303	.393	.374	32	156	5.54	.622	6	1.57	0.24	1.81
Van Slyke	492	94	133	29	6	17	82	76	82	.270	.457	.365	90	377	6.45	.690	14	4.75	0.75	5.50
Varsho	188	24	52	14	1	4	22	20	33	.277	.426	.349	30	141	5.74	.639	5	1.51	0.29	1.80
Webster M	95	9	17	3	3	1	9	9	29	.179	.305	.250	7	80	2.36	.230	3	-0.36	0.19	-0.16
Wehner	104	14	36	6	0	0	7	7	16	.346	.404	.387	18	68	7.15	.732	3	0.96	0.24	1.20
Wilkerson	187	20	36	9	0	2	18	15	37	.193	.273	.249	14	155	2.44	.242	6	-0.62	0.59	-0.04
TOTALS	5384	780	1447	261	43	132	731	638	863	.269	.407	.346	798	4249	5.07	.579	157	36.09	9.70	45.79

Pitching Records for Pittsburgh Pirates

	ERA	W	L	Pct	G	GS	CG	ShO	GF	Sv	IP	R	ER	H	2B	3B	HR	BB	IW	SO	HB	WP	BK
Drabek	3.13	15	14	.517	34	34	5	2	0	0	229.2	92	80	238	40	5	16	61	6	140	3	5	0
Smith Z	3.20	16	10	.615	35	35	6	3	0	0	228.0	95	81	234	36	4	15	29	3	120	2	1	0
Smiley	3.08	20	8	.714	33	32	2	1	0	0	207.2	78	71	194	38	6	17	44	0	129	3	3	1
Tomlin R	2.98	8	7	.533	31	27	4	2	0	0	175.0	75	58	170	28	6	9	54	4	104	6	2	3
Walk	3.60	9	2	.818	25	20	0	0	0	0	115.0	53	46	104	21	1	10	35	2	67	5	11	2
Fajardo	9.95	0	0	.000	2	2	0	0	0	0	6.1	7	7	10	0	0	0	7	0	8	0	3	0
Miller P	5.40	0	0	.000	1	1	0	0	0	0	5.0	3	3	4	2	0	0	3	0	2	0	0	0
Reed Rk	10.38	0	0	.000	1	1	0	0	0	0	4.1	6	5	8	3	0	1	1	0	2	0	0	0
Palacios	3.75	6	3	.667	36	7	1	1	8	3	81.2	34	34	69	10	1	12	38	2	64	1	6	2
Belinda	3.45	7	5	.583	60	0	0	0	37	16	78.1	30	30	50	5	2	10	35	4	71	4	2	0
Landrum B	3.23	4	4	.500	60	0	0	0	43	17	75.1	32	27	75	7	2	4	18	5	45	0	3	2
Heaton	4.26	3	3	.500	41	1	0	0	5	0	67.2	36	32	70	14	0	6	21	2	33	4	0	1
Patterson B	4.11	4	3	.571	54	1	0	0	19	2	65.2	32	30	67	12	1	7	15	1	57	0	0	0
Kipper	4.65	2	2	.500	52	0	0	0	18	4	60.0	34	31	66	12	2	7	22	3	38	0	0	1
Mason R	2.51	3	1	.750	23	0	0	0	5	3	28.2	9	8	18	3	0	1	6	1	18	1	2	0
Rodriguez Ro	4.40	1	1	.500	17	0	0	0	8	6	14.1	7	7	14	2	0	1	8	0	9	1	2	0
Huismann	7.20	0	0	.000	5	0	0	0	0	0	5.0	6	4	7	1	1	0	2	1	5	0	0	0
TOTALS	3.44	98	63	.609	510	161	18	9	143	51	1447.2	629	554	1398	234	31	116	399	34	912	30	40	12

Sabermetric Pitching Records for Pittsburgh Pirates

	Adj ERA	Expected W	Expected L	Expected Pct	Opposing Batters BFP	Avg	Slg	OBA	RC/G	GDP	SB	CS	PK	PKE	SH	SF	RSup	Supported RSp/G	W	L	Pct
Belinda	3.45	6	6	.532	318	.184	.327	.283	3.33	2	13	3	0	0	4	3	35	4.02	7	5	.576
Drabek	3.17	17	12	.572	956	.272	.384	.320	4.23	13	28	15	3	6	12	6	125	4.90	20	9	.704
Fajardo	9.95	0	0	.120	35	.357	.357	.486	9.26	0	3	0	0	0	0	0	8	11.37	0	0	.566
Heaton	4.26	3	3	.427	288	.272	.397	.333	4.68	6	9	2	0	1	3	3	45	5.99	4	2	.664
Huismann	7.20	0	0	.206	25	.304	.435	.360	6.85	0	0	0	0	0	0	0	7	12.60	0	0	.754
Kipper	4.65	2	2	.384	264	.276	.431	.335	5.18	4	7	4	0	2	1	2	23	3.45	1	3	.355
Landrum B	3.23	5	3	.565	317	.253	.330	.294	3.62	3	8	1	1	0	1	1	20	2.39	3	5	.354
Mason R	2.51	3	1	.681	108	.182	.242	.234	1.72	1	0	2	0	0	1	1	14	4.40	3	1	.754
Miller P	5.40	0	0	.316	21	.222	.333	.333	3.52	1	0	0	0	0	0	0	3	5.40	0	0	.500
Palacios	3.75	4	5	.490	347	.228	.386	.315	4.26	2	3	4	0	0	4	1	51	5.62	6	3	.692
Patterson B	4.11	3	4	.444	270	.267	.406	.306	3.97	5	1	5	0	1	2	2	28	3.84	3	4	.466
Reed Rk	10.38	0	0	.111	21	.400	.700	.429	11.32	1	0	0	0	0	0	0	6	12.46	0	0	.590
Rodriguez Ro	4.40	1	1	.411	64	.259	.352	.365	4.52	1	0	1	0	0	1	0	4	2.51	0	2	.246
Smiley	3.12	16	12	.581	836	.251	.381	.292	3.65	11	18	13	0	6	11	4	110	4.77	20	8	.700
Smith Z	3.24	15	11	.563	916	.268	.370	.292	3.48	27	26	8	0	0	7	5	130	5.13	19	7	.715
Tomlin R	2.98	9	6	.603	736	.254	.354	.315	3.76	15	17	12	1	7	5	2	85	4.37	10	5	.682
Walk	3.60	6	5	.510	484	.240	.363	.302	3.80	7	7	4	1	1	7	4	73	5.71	8	3	.716
TOTALS	3.49	85	76	.525	6006	.255	.372	.307	3.89	99	140	74	6	24	59	34	767	4.77	105	56	.651

Batting 'Splits' Records for Pittsburgh Pirates

	G	AB	Run	Hit	2B	3B	HR	TB	RBI	W	K	IW	HB	SB	CS	GIDP	SH	SF	Avg	Slug	OBP	Runs Ctd
SPLITS for Bell Jay																						
vs LHP	99	191	39	55	13	5	6	96	28	26	18	1	0	1	4	5	3	1	.288	.503	.372	34
vs RHP	141	413	57	108	19	3	10	163	39	26	80	0	4	9	2	10	27	2	.262	.395	.310	51
Home	80	299	51	84	19	5	7	134	33	23	48	0	1	4	6	9	15	1	.281	.448	.333	41
Away	76	305	45	79	13	3	9	125	34	29	50	1	3	6	0	6	15	2	.259	.410	.327	43
Grass	40	160	18	38	8	3	2	58	13	13	21	0	2	0	0	4	9	1	.237	.363	.301	18
Turf	116	444	78	125	24	5	14	201	54	39	77	1	2	10	6	11	21	2	.282	.453	.341	67
April/June	70	264	38	71	13	4	8	116	34	20	41	0	2	6	4	3	19	2	.269	.439	.323	38
July/October	86	340	58	92	19	4	8	143	33	32	57	1	2	4	2	12	11	1	.271	.421	.336	46
SPLITS for Bonds																						
vs LHP	119	197	29	55	13	2	7	93	39	32	30	3	3	13	6	1	0	3	.279	.472	.383	39
vs RHP	136	309	65	92	15	3	18	167	77	75	43	22	1	29	7	7	0	10	.298	.540	.425	81
Home	78	257	46	69	8	1	12	115	51	49	42	10	3	15	6	3	0	7	.268	.447	.383	50
Away	74	249	48	78	20	4	13	145	65	58	31	15	1	27	7	5	0	6	.313	.582	.436	71
Grass	39	132	22	37	10	2	5	66	27	23	18	5	0	15	5	3	0	5	.280	.500	.375	27
Turf	113	374	72	110	18	3	20	194	89	84	55	20	4	27	8	5	0	8	.294	.519	.421	93
April/June	67	224	34	60	10	2	10	104	45	42	33	7	3	16	6	3	0	3	.268	.464	.386	44
July/October	85	282	60	87	18	3	15	156	71	65	40	18	1	26	7	5	0	10	.309	.553	.427	76
SPLITS for Varsho																						
vs LHP	11	5	2	1	0	0	0	1	0	0	1	0	1	0	0	0	1	0	.200	.200	.333	1
vs RHP	94	182	21	50	11	2	4	77	23	19	33	2	1	9	2	2	0	1	.275	.423	.345	28
Home	52	95	9	23	5	1	1	33	8	8	13	1	2	3	1	1	0	0	.242	.347	.314	11
Away	46	92	14	28	6	1	3	45	15	11	21	1	0	6	1	1	1	1	.304	.489	.375	18
Grass	23	43	9	16	3	1	2	27	8	8	7	1	0	5	0	1	1	1	.372	.628	.462	14
Turf	75	144	14	35	8	1	2	51	15	11	27	1	2	4	2	1	0	0	.243	.354	.306	16
April/June	42	79	8	19	6	0	0	25	5	10	16	1	1	3	0	0	0	0	.241	.316	.333	10
July/October	56	108	15	32	5	2	4	53	18	9	18	1	1	6	2	2	1	1	.296	.491	.353	19
SPLITS for Pittsburgh Pirates (all batters except pitchers)																						
vs LHP	1077	1870	264	482	88	19	51	761	254	208	295	20	13	39	21	34	33	21	.258	.407	.333	262
vs RHP	1534	3547	503	943	170	31	75	1400	470	409	599	42	22	84	24	75	65	45	.266	.395	.342	503
Home	1116	2670	381	689	130	27	61	1056	358	301	438	29	16	51	26	54	46	27	.258	.396	.334	364
Away	1090	2747	386	736	128	23	65	1105	366	316	456	33	19	72	19	55	52	39	.268	.402	.343	401
Grass	596	1501	189	393	60	13	36	587	183	140	232	13	9	37	10	30	32	20	.262	.391	.325	198
Turf	1610	3916	578	1032	198	37	90	1574	541	477	662	49	26	86	35	79	66	46	.264	.402	.344	567
April/June	951	2342	299	576	101	19	51	868	282	259	373	23	16	51	22	47	45	22	.246	.371	.322	292
July/October	1255	3075	468	849	157	31	75	1293	442	358	521	39	19	72	23	62	53	44	.276	.420	.351	475

1991 SPLITS FOR Pittsburgh Pirates

BATTING SPLITS

	AVG	AB	R	H	2B	3B	HR	RBI	SB	CS	BB	K	OBA	SPCT
Total	.263	5449	768	1433	259	50	126	725	124	46	620	901	.338	.398

	#Pit	#P/PA	GB	FB	G/F	G	IBB	HB	SH	SF	GDP
Miscellaneous	22694	3.62	1994	1689	1.18	162	62	35	99	66	110

	AVG	AB	R	H	2B	3B	HR	RBI	SB	CS	BB	K	OBA	SPCT
vs. Left	.258	1894	...	489	89	19	51	255	40	22	211	297	.333	.406
vs. Right	.266	3555	...	944	170	31	75	470	84	24	409	604	.341	.394
Home	.258	2702	382	697	131	27	61	359	52	27	304	445	.334	.394
Away	.268	2747	386	736	128	23	65	366	72	19	316	456	.343	.402
None on	.255	2988	...	761	142	23	59	59	0	0	318	486	.330	.377
Runners on	.273	2461	...	672	117	27	67	666	124	46	302	415	.349	.424
April	.252	651	97	164	28	4	14	90	10	6	64	88	.321	.372
May	.261	821	119	214	35	8	22	112	20	7	93	132	.336	.403
June	.228	870	83	198	38	7	15	80	21	9	102	153	.310	.339
July	.301	968	175	291	44	13	33	168	26	5	110	143	.371	.475
August	.260	982	133	255	58	5	21	123	19	7	105	189	.328	.393
September	.272	995	141	271	49	9	21	132	23	10	127	166	.355	.403
October	.247	162	20	40	7	4	0	20	5	2	19	30	.333	.340
None on/out	.259	1335	...	346	75	13	22	22	0	0	135	182	.331	.384
Scoring Posn	.270	1449	...	391	72	14	36	569	27	8	217	259	.355	.413
Close & Late	.248	855	...	212	41	5	19	117	18	9	117	158	.338	.374
Bases Loaded	.254	134	...	34	5	2	5	106	0	0	8	33	.277	.433
Batting #1	.262	663	125	174	31	4	16	71	25	7	86	121	.351	.394
Batting #2	.275	655	105	180	38	8	17	72	11	7	56	108	.334	.435
Batting #3	.263	624	105	164	29	8	18	94	16	3	86	111	.349	.421
Batting #4	.298	604	104	180	45	6	19	104	2	4	95	69	.390	.487
Batting #5	.300	577	107	173	30	5	29	129	43	14	106	80	.404	.520
Batting #6	.241	614	68	148	24	7	14	78	9	3	57	110	.308	.371
Batting #7	.281	587	58	165	26	3	6	69	8	3	63	71	.351	.366
Batting #8	.259	588	59	152	23	6	3	64	6	4	40	77	.305	.333
Batting #9	.181	537	37	97	13	3	4	44	4	1	31	154	.227	.238
As p	.163	368	21	60	8	0	1	26	0	0	13	108	.193	.193
As c	.301	572	48	172	30	2	5	70	3	2	57	58	.367	.386
As 1b	.272	646	129	176	31	4	15	69	17	6	90	103	.363	.402
As 2b	.248	596	60	148	22	6	3	63	8	4	37	83	.291	.320
As 3b	.286	623	88	178	31	4	16	85	6	4	62	99	.351	.425
As ss	.269	648	100	174	35	9	16	68	10	7	56	109	.329	.424
As lf	.279	570	102	159	30	5	31	132	43	13	109	87	.390	.512
As cf	.248	625	104	155	30	8	19	95	18	4	82	120	.334	.413
As rf	.277	584	86	162	34	10	14	88	14	5	84	84	.365	.442
Outfield	.268	1779	292	476	94	23	64	315	75	22	275	291	.363	.454
0.0 count	.323	848	...	274	47	9	18	140	...	...	1	0	.327	.463
After (0.1)	.223	2307	...	514	91	14	40	245	...	...	128	584	.265	.326
After (1.0)	.281	2293	...	644	121	27	68	339	...	...	442	317	.396	.446
Two strikes	.186	2365	...	441	84	19	37	208	...	...	234	899	.261	.285
Grass	.262	1501	189	393	60	13	36	183	37	10	140	232	.325	.391
Turf	.263	3948	579	1040	199	37	90	542	87	36	480	669	.344	.401
Day	.276	1469	233	406	79	13	37	223	27	9	178	259	.354	.423
Night	.258	3980	535	1027	180	37	89	502	97	37	442	642	.333	.389
Inning 1.6	.269	3717	547	1001	183	41	86	512	96	30	405	604	.341	.410
Inning 7+	.249	1732	221	432	76	9	40	213	28	16	215	297	.332	.373
vs.Atl	.243	408	51	99	15	2	11	46	16	3	38	54	.309	.370
vs.ChN	.286	646	116	185	29	12	22	110	13	2	74	96	.356	.471
vs.Cin	.282	394	73	111	20	3	16	70	10	2	48	58	.358	.470
vs.Hou	.283	410	70	116	18	3	12	65	8	1	56	72	.368	.429
vs.LA	.230	383	30	88	15	3	4	29	11	7	41	75	.303	.316
vs.Mon	.250	583	75	146	36	3	9	74	14	9	80	97	.344	.369
vs.NYN	.274	616	85	169	29	5	10	78	16	7	58	94	.337	.386
vs.Phi	.258	598	87	154	31	6	10	80	14	3	92	121	.359	.380
vs.StL	.268	600	82	161	28	8	12	77	11	7	58	91	.335	.402
vs.SD	.244	405	41	99	15	3	10	39	4	2	33	70	.299	.370
vs.SF	.259	406	58	105	23	2	10	57	7	3	42	73	.330	.399

PITCHING SPLITS

	ERA	W	L	SV	SVOP	GS	CG	SHO	IP	H	ER	HR	BB	IBB	K
Total	3.44	98	64	51	67	162	18	6	1456.2	1411	557	117	401	34	919

	#Pit	#P/IP	GB	FB	G/F	BRp9	RA	WP	BK	SH	SF	R	HB	Hld
Miscellaneous	21650	14.86	2096	1582	1.32	11.38	353	40	12	59	34	632	30	45

	ERA	W	L	SV	SVOP	GS	CG	SHO	IP	H	ER	HR	BB	IBB	K
ST	3.27	67	44	0	0	162	18	9	1005.0	991	365	72	244	16	594
REL	3.83	31	20	51	67	0	0	0	451.2	420	192	45	157	18	325
Home	3.14	52	32	26	29	84	10	6	765.0	721	267	55	196	13	508
Away	3.77	46	32	25	38	78	8	3	691.2	690	290	62	205	21	411
April	3.29	13	7	5	6	20	2	2	178.0	156	65	14	53	5	93
May	3.28	17	8	9	9	25	4	3	225.0	207	82	12	61	3	146
June	3.15	15	12	11	13	27	2	0	237.0	243	83	16	60	7	152
July	3.86	15	12	5	7	27	3	2	242.2	232	104	29	91	10	161
August	3.14	17	12	10	13	29	3	1	264.0	251	92	19	59	5	161
September	4.00	18	11	9	16	29	4	1	263.0	271	117	23	67	4	176
October	2.68	3	2	2	3	5	0	0	47.0	51	14	4	10	0	30
Grass	4.27	20	22	12	21	42	3	0	372.2	379	177	43	121	13	218
Turf	3.15	78	42	39	46	120	15	9	1084.0	1032	380	74	280	21	701
Day	3.79	25	18	14	19	43	5	1	382.1	386	161	37	91	11	225
Night	3.32	73	46	37	48	119	13	8	1074.1	1025	396	80	310	23	694
vs.Atl	5.56	3	9	2	3	12	1	0	102.0	105	63	16	49	5	66
vs.ChN	4.78	11	7	4	8	18	1	0	165.2	165	88	25	53	10	94
vs.Cin	2.78	10	2	5	5	12	1	1	107.0	80	33	13	28	2	79
vs.Hou	3.87	8	4	3	3	12	2	2	107.0	122	46	4	35	1	63
vs.LA	2.91	5	7	4	4	12	2	0	105.0	95	34	5	30	1	67
vs.Mon	2.39	12	6	8	9	18	1	1	162.0	154	43	7	38	2	116
vs.NYN	3.20	12	6	5	7	18	2	1	166.0	152	59	14	44	1	93
vs.Phi	2.91	12	6	7	9	18	2	1	163.2	161	53	8	35	5	114
vs.StL	2.96	11	7	3	5	18	4	2	161.1	150	53	6	41	2	83
vs.SD	3.68	7	5	6	8	12	0	0	110.0	116	45	11	27	4	78
vs.SF	3.36	7	5	4	6	12	2	1	107.0	111	40	8	21	1	66

OPPOSING BATTERS VS. PITCHERS.

	AVG	AB	R	H	2B	3B	HR	RBI	SB	CS	BB	K	OBA	SPCT
Total	.256	5522	632	1411	236	32	117	592	142	74	401	919	.308	.373
vs. Left	.258	1968	...	507	76	10	35	198	61	27	155	328	.314	.360
vs. Right	.254	3554	...	904	160	22	82	394	81	47	246	591	.304	.381
ST	.260	3814	425	991	174	22	72	370	99	56	244	594	.306	.374
REL	.246	1708	207	420	62	10	45	222	43	18	157	325	.311	.373
Home	.251	2870	314	721	122	21	55	295	73	43	196	508	.302	.366
Away	.260	2652	318	690	114	11	62	297	69	31	205	411	.314	.382
None on	.243	3240	...	788	133	17	63	63	0	0	226	533	.296	.353
Runners on	.273	2282	...	623	103	15	54	529	142	74	175	386	.324	.402
None on/out	.259	1403	...	363	66	6	30	30	0	0	93	219	.308	.378
Scoring Posn	.268	1314	...	352	60	9	27	456	41	8	137	221	.334	.389
vs 1st Batr	.221	326	...	72	8	2	9	32	5	2	24	52	.276	.340
1st IP	.261	1794	107	468	82	12	40	248	67	33	157	318	.320	.387
Inning 1.6	.256	3673	416	940	167	24	68	386	100	55	251	607	.305	.370
Inning 7+	.255	1849	216	471	69	8	49	206	42	19	150	312	.313	.380
Close & Late	.252	979	...	247	34	3	24	116	33	15	91	168	.321	.367
0.0 count	.318	801	...	255	48	4	15	105	...	...	29	0	.345	.444
After (0.1)	.228	2613	...	595	87	20	47	254	...	...	98	638	.258	.330
After (1.0)	.266	2108	...	561	101	8	55	233	...	...	274	281	.351	.400
Two strikes	.184	2467	...	453	79	10	36	183	...	...	151	918	.233	.268
Pitch 1.15	.268	1566	...	420	71	9	34	171	56	27	132	251	.326	.390
Pitch 16.30	.242	1128	...	273	45	8	31	147	20	18	89	218	.299	.379
Pitch 31.45	.233	742	...	173	31	2	11	65	18	8	45	142	.280	.325
Pitch 46.60	.256	665	...	170	34	3	15	66	14	11	43	90	.304	.383
Pitch 61.75	.233	580	...	135	21	6	7	47	16	3	27	95	.269	.326
Pitch 76.90	.292	463	...	135	15	3	11	63	11	3	40	66	.348	.408
Pitch 91.105	.264	277	...	73	10	1	6	22	4	2	17	44	.311	.372
Pitch 106.20	.323	96	...	31	9	0	3	13	3	2	9	9	.387	.510
Pitch 121.35	.250	8	...	2	0	0	0	0	0	0	0	4	.250	.250

St. Louis Cardinals

Brock J. Hanke

ST. LOUIS											
YEAR	1982	1983	1984	1985	1986	1987	1988	1989	1990	1991	TOT
W	92	79	84	101	79	95	76	86	70	84	846
L	70	83	78	61	82	67	86	76	92	78	773
WPCT	0.568	0.488	0.519	0.623	0.491	0.586	0.469	0.531	0.432	0.519	0.523
R	685	679	652	747	601	798	578	632	599	651	6622
RA	609	710	645	572	611	693	633	608	698	648	6427
PWPT	0.559	0.478	0.505	0.630	0.492	0.570	0.455	0.519	0.424	0.502	0.515
PythW	90	77	82	102	80	92	74	84	69	81	83
PythL	72	85	80	60	82	70	88	78	93	81	79
LUCK	2	2	2	-1	-1	3	2	2	1	3	15

Defensive Efficiency Record: .7085

As long-time readers know, I have lived in St. Louis all my life, and so I follow the Cardinals in more detail than any other team. Last year, I abandoned sabermetrics altogether for a tirade on the subject of corporate management and what it does to baseball team organizations. This year, I am prepared to return to sabermetrics, but not to abandon the theme. What is it, just two years now since Whitey Herzog was in control of this ballclub? And what is Whitey but the most thorough of team organizers? Two lousy years, and the Cardinals have been reduced to a state of chaos hard to believe. No order, no transition, just a collection of people thrown together to fight it out with politics as to who shall play and where. I'm going to take a look at this sorry outfit position group by position group, and expose it for the sham of a team that it is.

Catcher:

The Cardinals have the best catcher in the National League, possibly in all of baseball. His name is Todd Zeile. Unfortunately for their fans, they're playing him at third base. Tom Pagnozzi, who the Cardinals insist on catching, came in 6th at the position, behind Rick Cerone, who played 58 fewer games than Pags did. Pags played 138 games; the only man who played over 100 who came in under him was #7 Greg Olsen. Sixth is OK, I guess, but there are a lot of third basemen out there who are better players than Pagnozzi is. Yes, the Cardinals do too have some of them. The mechanism of how Todd Zeile came to be an infielder is ornately baroque and overtly political and I will discuss it under the infield, where it belongs.

The Infield (Second, Short and Third only):

Here's what happened. When Whitey was removed, Fred Kuhlmann, the brewery politician who won the internal political struggle for dominance, decided to rid himself of every possible "Whitey's player." That meant Willie McGee, Vince Coleman and Terry Pendelton; and yes, he's still trying to rid himself of Ozzie Smith. Unfortunately, the system had no obvious replacement for third baseman Pendelton, and the Cards were roundly pilloried in the St. Louis press for disposing of a man who had no backup.

The management team could have tried several things in response to this.

They could have traded for a third baseman, but that might have cost money. What's more, if they tried to get one and failed, they would have had to admit that the Pendelton move was a bad one. Instead, they picked up a grade B third base prospect named Stan Royer in the Willie McGee disposal. He wasn't at all ready, so they couldn't put him out there in 1991. He was, however, the best prospect they had of justifying their dispersals, so they do want him to succeed someday.

The Cardinals did have a third baseman down at AAA Louisville, name of Luis Alicea. Alicea had been drafted #1 as a second baseman, and had been rushed to the big club years ago when Whitey found himself having to trade Tommy Herr away. Luis wasn't ready, and then he got hurt, but he hit .348 for half the 1990 season at Louisville, and played a decent third base in the bargain. But Luis had been injury-prone, and the Cards wanted someone who could play all year and make the fans forget Terry Pendelton, and they also had a vested interest in leaving room for Stan Royer if he did in fact develop. They didn't want a kid third baseman coming up and performing well and clogging up the position.

The Cardinals also had a truly hot second base prospect coming up, name of Geronimo Pena. Pena is probably the best prospect the Cards have had since Andy Van Slyke. Whitey had tried to get Geronimo to learn third base down at Louisville, but it was no use. Now, Pena was out of options, and had to be carried on the 1991 Cardinal roster. Given the desperate need to play Pena, they could have moved incumbent second baseman Jose Oquendo to third base, a spot he has filled before. But, again, that would leave no room for Royer. Also, Oquendo had just had a big bust year, and they were afraid of his having another at the position they wanted to look good.

What they did do is move their catcher, Todd Zeile. Manager Joe Torre had himself switched from catcher to third, albeit with a season at first base in the middle, and his first year at third had been his career year with the bat. Never mind that Joe wasn't much of a defensive catcher, nor that the men he made room for were Dick Allen at first and Ted Simmons behind the plate. Never mind that he was much older than Todd Zeile when he made the move. It was a quick fix, and Todd could always be moved to first base later to make room for Royer; he had that sort of bat. Better yet, they could buy the unending loyalty of Tom Pagnozzi with the move. Pags had been cast by Whitey as a backup. Whitey had said that there were teams Tom could start for, but not good ones, not winners. Yes, Fred Kuhlmann could have a truly loyal player in the Cardinal clubhouse. And yes, it has worked out that way. When the front office made their announcement that they were not going to sign any top free agents, Tom Pagnozzi was the only player who defended the move.

There are only a few problems that this has caused; minor ones, really, nothing of any importance. They don't have a spot for Luis Alicea, of course. But, what of that? He only hit .330 down at Louisville in 1991. He also didn't hit at all well in his at-bat of the week, once he was promoted to the Cards to make room for Stan Royer. Now the Cards face the prospect of giving him up as a trade throw-in before they can find out whether he's for real.

They also have to find playing time for Ozzie Smith, Jose Oquendo and Geronimo Pena, with only two positions to allocate. Of course, what they want to do is dispose of Ozzie, the last of Whitey's men. That's the right move, given Jose and Geronimo and Luis Alicea, but they aren't exactly doing a wonderful job of performing the feat. You see, no one is offering them a prime-of-career All-Star for the 36-year-old shortstop. If they trade him for what they can get, they get pilloried. If they just refuse to exercise his option, they not only get pilloried, but they also lose a cheap year out of Ozzie. If they sign him to a long-term contract, they have to move Oquendo or Pena, and expose their mishandling of third base.

What they've done, as you could predict if you were as cynical as I am, is pick up Ozzie's one cheap year. That leaves them with Jose Oquendo at second base, Geronimo Pena spending two full development years sitting on the bench (he's out of options, remember), and finding out nothing at all about Luis Alicea, because all the backup playing time will go to Geronimo. They can't, of course, trade anyone but Ozzie, because they might get burned. The obvious fact, that both Geronimo Pena and Luis Alicea are better players than Tom Pagnozzi, doesn't cross their minds. It's not politically expedient to act on that, you see.

The Outfield and First Base (this is one position group, don't you agree?):

Believe it or not, this is worse. It didn't start out that way. The very best move the Cardinal front office has made since Whitey left threatened to save them. They were able to get the Oakland A's to pony up both Felix Jose and the aforementioned Stan Royer for one month's rental of Willie McGee (and, of course, the two free agent compensation picks when they lost Willie). Felix Jose proved to be ready for the big time. He showed every sign of solving the Cardinal right field problems for the next six to ten years. What's more, hot rookie Ray Lankford panned out too, and was at least decent in center field. That effectively replaced everything they had lost in Vince Coleman and Willie McGee.

They did have one small problem. Since both Lankford and Jose had worked, there was only left field remaining, and the team had both rookie Bernard Gilkey to develop and veteran Milt Thompson to play. Gilkey solved the problem for one year by getting hurt, but Milt insisted on making the future difficult by having a wonderful return year. There is no longer any doubt that Whitey Herzog was right when he traded for Milt. So, alright, you've got to find some way to decide between the untested rookie and the hot veteran, or you've got to move somebody. What's the problem? After all, aren't you about to lose your first baseman, Pedro Guerrero, to free agency?

Well, yes, and the Cardinals could replace him with either Thompson or Gilkey and gain defense in the bargain, except for one thing. Pedro was the team's cleanup man, there are no other real candidates to hold down the job. None of the four outfielders has any home run power, though Felix Jose is a true RBI man.

The Cardinal solution was typical. They refused to address the Thompson/Gilkey problem at all. They did trade a kid pitcher for Andres Galarraga, a first baseman coming off a dismal year. You may think that gambling with your cleanup spot looks like suicide, and I may agree with you, but the Cardinals had to get somebody, and they had already committed themselves to not spending any money on a high-priced ballplayer. After all, if they wanted to do that, they could have kept Whitey's guys. Or they could have gone after a free agent, like Bobby Bonilla or Danny Tartabull or Wally Joyner. If they're not going to do that, they've got to find a cheap cleanup man, and good, stable cleanup men just don't come cheap.

Then the roof fell in. Ol' Pedro Guerrero, with his bad knees, was having a bit of trouble getting himself signed as a free agent. The date for offering arbitration came up; if the Cards didn't offer Pedro arbitration, they wouldn't get the draft pick compensation when he did sign. So they offered. And he accepted. No one had made him any signing offers. The Cardinals were stuck with two right-handed gambles at first base and cleanup. They couldn't even see far enough ahead to acquire a left-handed gamble so they could platoon.

Now, O Sabermetrician, take a moment to think what you might do here. To review: you've got two center fielders, sophomore Ray Lankford and veteran Milt Thompson (Milt can play anywhere). You've got a good right fielder, Felix Jose. You've got a rookie left fielder, Bernard Gilkey, who you'd like to develop.

You've got, of all things, the market corner on right handed first basemen, with two. They are also the only cleanup men on your team. What do you do in '92?

Got your plan ready, oh Fred Kuhlmann wannabe? Well, here's the Cardinal press announcement: they're going to play Pedro Guerrero in left field. They're going to bench and waste both Milt Thompson and Bernard Gilkey, play a man with no speed in Busch Stadium's left field and clog up their batting order with two men who can't run, plus a converted catcher at third base.

The Bench:

Technically, the Cardinals only have three or four bench players. They have four if Tim Jones is up on the roster at the given time. Jones is a Whitey Herzog Special. He's a real good defensive shortstop, who can play anywhere in the infield, and who can catch in an emergency. He's not good enough to start in the big time. Whitey got him to learn to catch by promising him a steady Major League job, albeit as the emergency and injury last gasp. Joe Torre shuttles him between St. Louis and Louisville. Whitey, according to rumor, wants to trade for him and move him to the Angels.

The three real benchwarmers are Rex Hudler, Gerald Perry and Rich Gedman. Of the three, Gedman has a real job as the backup catcher. I do wonder about that, as Gedman was considered "good hit, no field" in his heyday with the Bosox, and he can't hit any more. On the other hand, his competition was Alex Trevino. Hudler is, supposedly, the backup outfielder/infielder. But his days of playing infield defense are long gone, so he's never used there. That makes him a backup outfielder on a team with two guys on the bench who could compete for starting jobs. He can play center field, but both Lankford and Thompson are much better. Perry can't play anywhere except first base. The Cards got him because Joe Torre remembered his two good years in Atlanta. He hasn't hit a lick since 1988, including last year with the Birds. That makes him the #3 first baseman, behind Andres and Pedro, and a lefty pinch hitter on a team with Milt Thompson on its bench. For this, they pay him $1 million per year.

The rest of the bench is Thompson, Gilkey, Alicea and Pena. These are not bench players. They are competitors for starting jobs. They're not happy. They're also not trained to fill specific bench roles. As last seen, Joe Torre was using Geronimo Pena, his best bench bat, to pinch-run for Jose Oquendo in the late innings when Jose took the inevitable walk with the pitcher coming up next. No, it didn't occur to Joe that batting an on-base specialist 8th is dumb.

Starting Pitching:

This is in pretty good shape, largely because Whitey was always trying to develop young pitchers. The Cards have just sort of stood by while Omar Olivares and Rheal Cormier came through. Last year, they had no lefties in the rotation, because John Tudor retired, Joe Magrane was hurt and Ricky Horton was the first Whitey's man they discarded. Now they have Cormier, and the promise of Magrane's recovery, so they look OK. With those two and Omar Olivares to add to Bryn Smith and Jose de Leon, they even had Ken Hill to trade for Galarraga.

Still, they really don't have a staff ace, unless Magrane comes back completely. they really should take a look at trading numbers for top level quality. They could pile up numbers with good quality if they could sort out their infield and outfield....

Relief Closer:

Whitey Herzog, you may know, absolutely requires a top closer to feel secure. When Todd Worrell got hurt, he traded for Lee Smith. Now the Cards face the pleasant prospect of Worrell's recovery. This is the only spot on the roster where the Cards are truly dominant.

Relief bench:

A disaster, devoid of left hands. Whitey had five when he left: Tudor, Magrane, Horton, Frank Di Pino and Ken Dayley. The new team let Dayley go free agent and did nothing to replace him until Di Pino got hurt along with Magrane. Then they acquired Juan Agosto, who had seen his ERA increase two full runs during the last half of his last season in Houston. His arm was dead, and they worked him anyway. Now, there's little reason to expect much recovery. Di Pino is through. That's all the lefty pitching bench the Cards have. Yes, they have troubles in the middle innings with Pittsburgh and Los Angeles, who have all those lefty bats.

Basically, rooting for this team gives me an idea of what it must be like to be a baseball fan in Cleveland. Of course, you guys up there have had to put up with this for a lot longer. Your upper managements are always squabbling over politics, too. Your teams have too many of this and too little of that, and you never get together and trade the surpluses for the shortages. You play people out of position. You have no long term plans. You won't spend for the top free agent who could put you over the top. Well, if it makes you feel any better, Whitey Herzog put his team together just as fast as Kuhlmann, Dal Maxvill and Joe Torre have dismantled it.

One last note: those of you who really follow the game may be aware that Fred Kuhlmann has "resigned" from his job atop the Cardinal heap. I put resigned in quotes because he really didn't do that. He, as of this writing, still has the perks. He sits on the ownership committees and does the voting and exercises all the privileges of ownership. Someone named Stuart Meyer gets to do the work. One presumes that, when Kuhlmann either dies or tires of this (he's 75), Meyer will "resign," take the perks and get another apprentice who'll do all the work and wait Meyer out. That's long term planning in St. Louis.

St. Louis Cardinals Home Park Performance Factors

	Outs	Runs	Hits	2b	3b	HR	W	K	SH	SF	HBP	IBB	SB	CS	GDP
Home LH Batters	1.022	1.012	1.143	1.379	.762	1.253	.981	1.150	.676	1.189	6.474	1.619	.908	1.031	.947
Home RH Batters	1.060	1.022	1.066	.947	1.166	.885	.972	1.123	1.091	1.132	.791	.804	1.060	1.398	1.045
All Home Batters	1.047	1.013	1.073	1.063	.870	1.072	.979	1.135	1.038	1.129	.880	.988	.975	1.173	1.037
Opp LH Batters	1.064	1.326	1.149	1.087	.884	1.547	1.252	1.057	1.168	1.168	1.001	1.248	1.318	.989	.890
Opp RH Batters	1.064	1.137	1.105	1.020	1.054	1.269	.997	1.087	1.039	.967	.871	.899	.929	1.066	1.052
All Opp Batters	1.071	1.224	1.128	1.061	.965	1.414	1.115	1.092	1.135	1.128	.931	1.108	1.057	1.044	.977
All LH Batters	1.047	1.171	1.145	1.159	.817	1.415	1.134	1.103	1.016	1.166	1.024	1.313	1.050	1.029	.893
All RH Batters	1.062	1.082	1.086	.985	1.102	1.124	.984	1.102	1.067	1.044	.843	.849	1.000	1.208	1.050
All Batters	1.059	1.115	1.100	1.059	.914	1.263	1.044	1.112	1.088	1.126	.904	1.050	1.013	1.115	1.003

Conventional Batting Records for St. Louis Cardinals

	G	AB	Run	Hit	2B	3B	HR	TB	RBI	W	K	IW	HB	SB	CS	BRng Eff	GI DP	SH	SF	Avg	Slug	OBP	Runs Ctd
Pagnozzi	140	459	38	121	24	5	2	161	57	36	63	6	4	9	13	.286	10	6	5	.264	.351	.319	49
Guerrero	115	427	41	116	12	1	8	154	70	37	46	2	1	4	2	.216	12	0	7	.272	.361	.326	50
Oquendo	127	366	37	88	11	4	1	110	26	67	48	13	1	1	2	.329	5	4	3	.240	.301	.357	45
Zeile	155	565	76	158	36	3	11	233	81	62	94	3	5	17	11	.410	15	0	6	.280	.412	.353	82
Smith O	150	550	96	157	30	3	3	202	50	83	36	2	1	35	9	.482	8	6	1	.285	.367	.380	86
Gilkey	81	268	28	58	7	2	5	84	20	39	33	0	1	14	8	.422	14	1	2	.216	.313	.316	25
Lankford	151	566	83	142	23	15	9	222	69	41	114	1	1	44	20	.485	4	4	3	.251	.392	.301	67
Jose	154	568	69	173	40	6	8	249	77	50	113	8	2	20	12	.371	12	0	5	.305	.438	.360	89
Thompson M	115	326	55	100	16	5	6	144	34	32	53	7	0	16	9	.443	4	2	1	.307	.442	.368	53
Perry G	109	242	29	58	8	4	6	92	36	22	34	1	0	15	8	.528	2	0	3	.240	.380	.300	28
Hudler	101	207	21	47	10	2	1	64	15	10	29	1	0	12	8	.440	1	2	2	.227	.309	.260	16
Pena G	104	185	38	45	8	3	5	74	17	18	45	1	5	15	5	.500	0	1	3	.243	.400	.322	27
Gedman	46	94	7	10	1	0	3	20	8	4	15	0	0	0	1	.333	2	0	2	.106	.213	.140	2
Wilson C	60	82	5	14	2	0	0	16	13	6	10	2	0	0	0	.750	2	0	2	.171	.195	.222	4
Alicea	56	68	5	13	3	0	0	16	0	8	19	0	0	0	1	.444	0	0	0	.191	.235	.276	5
Smith B	31	65	6	16	1	0	0	17	8	1	11	0	0	0	0	.000	0	7	1	.246	.262	.254	5
Tewksbury	30	58	5	9	1	0	0	10	2	4	16	0	0	0	0	.200	1	7	0	.155	.172	.210	3
Olivares	28	53	4	12	3	0	0	15	6	2	16	0	0	0	0	.714	0	4	0	.226	.283	.255	4
Hill K	30	50	2	5	0	0	0	5	3	4	12	0	0	0	0	1.000	0	7	0	.100	.100	.167	1
DeLeon J	28	46	0	2	0	0	0	2	0	0	17	0	0	0	0	.200	0	5	0	.043	.043	.043	0
Jones Tim	16	24	1	4	2	0	0	6	2	2	6	1	0	0	1	.333	0	0	1	.167	.250	.222	1
Cormier	11	21	2	5	0	0	0	5	1	0	5	0	0	0	0	.500	0	1	0	.238	.238	.238	1
Royer	9	21	1	6	1	0	0	7	1	1	2	0	0	0	0	.333	0	0	0	.286	.333	.318	2
Brewer R	19	13	0	1	0	0	0	1	1	0	5	0	0	0	0	.000	0	0	0	.077	.077	.077	0
Moyer	8	8	0	0	0	0	0	0	0	1	4	0	0	0	0	.000	0	0	0	.000	.000	.111	0
Terry	65	7	1	1	0	0	0	1	1	0	2	0	0	0	0	.000	0	0	0	.143	.143	.143	0
Clark M	7	7	0	0	0	0	0	0	0	0	2	0	0	0	0	.000	1	1	0	.000	.000	.000	0
Stephens	6	7	0	2	0	0	0	2	0	1	3	0	0	0	0	.000	0	0	0	.286	.286	.375	1
Carpenter	59	3	0	1	0	0	0	1	1	0	0	0	0	0	0	.000	1	0	0	.333	.333	.333	0
Agosto	72	3	0	1	0	0	0	1	0	1	2	0	0	0	0	.000	0	0	0	.333	.333	.500	1
Fraser	35	2	0	0	0	0	0	0	0	0	2	0	0	0	0	.000	0	0	0	.000	.000	.000	0
McClure	32	1	1	1	0	0	0	1	0	0	0	0	0	0	0	.000	0	0	0	1.000	1.000	1.000	1
Perez Mk	14	0	0	0	0	0	0	0	0	0	0	0	0	0	0	.000	0	0	0	.000	.000	.000	0
Smith Le	67	0	0	0	0	0	0	0	0	0	0	0	0	0	0	.000	0	0	0	.000	.000	.000	0
Sherill	10	0	0	0	0	0	0	0	0	0	0	0	0	0	0	.000	0	0	0	.000	.000	.000	0
Grater	3	0	0	0	0	0	0	0	0	0	0	0	0	0	0	.000	0	0	0	.000	.000	.000	0
TOTALS	2244	5362	651	1366	239	53	68	1915	599	532	857	48	21	202	110	.404	94	58	47	.255	.357	.322	632

Sabermetric Batting Records for St. Louis Cardinals

	Ball Park Adjusted												Runs		Run/					
	AB	Run	Hit	2B	3B	HR	RBI	W	SO	Avg	Slug	OBP	Ctd	Outs	27o	OW%	OG	OWAR	DWAR	TWAR
Alicea	72	5	14	3	0	0	0	8	21	.194	.236	.275	5	59	2.29	.246	2	-0.23	0.12	-0.11
Brewer R	13	0	1	0	0	0	1	0	5	.077	.077	.077	0	12	0.00	.000	0	-0.16	0.03	-0.12
Gedman	98	8	11	1	0	4	9	4	16	.112	.245	.144	3	91	0.89	.047	3	-1.02	-0.06	-1.08
Gilkey	285	30	62	6	2	5	21	38	36	.218	.305	.308	25	249	2.71	.314	9	-0.33	0.68	0.34
Guerrero	455	44	125	11	1	8	76	36	50	.275	.356	.323	52	351	4.00	.499	13	1.93	0.02	1.95
Hudler	220	22	51	9	2	1	16	9	32	.232	.305	.260	17	183	2.51	.281	7	-0.47	0.33	-0.13
Jones Tim	24	1	4	2	0	0	2	2	6	.167	.250	.222	1	22	1.23	.086	1	-0.22	0.01	-0.20
Jose	608	77	190	42	5	9	86	52	125	.313	.442	.365	97	448	5.85	.680	17	5.48	1.26	6.74
Lankford	604	97	162	28	12	12	78	45	125	.268	.414	.321	83	471	4.76	.585	17	4.10	0.73	4.82
Oquendo	390	41	96	11	3	1	29	70	53	.246	.297	.359	47	308	4.12	.514	11	1.87	1.40	3.27
Pagnozzi	490	41	131	23	5	2	62	35	69	.267	.347	.317	50	396	3.41	.420	15	1.02	-0.03	0.99
Pena G	197	42	49	8	2	6	19	18	50	.249	.401	.320	28	157	4.82	.591	6	1.40	0.23	1.63
Perry G	257	33	66	9	3	8	40	24	37	.257	.409	.317	35	203	4.66	.574	8	1.69	0.07	1.75
Royer	21	1	6	0	0	0	1	0	2	.286	.286	.286	2	15	3.60	.446	1	0.05	0.02	0.07
Smith O	588	107	172	31	2	3	56	86	40	.293	.367	.382	92	440	5.65	.665	16	5.13	2.11	7.24
Stephens	7	0	2	0	0	0	0	0	3	.286	.286	.286	1	5	5.40	.645	0	0.05	-0.00	0.05
Thompson M	349	64	114	19	4	8	38	35	58	.327	.473	.387	65	249	7.05	.756	9	3.74	0.82	4.56
Wilson C	87	5	15	1	0	0	14	5	11	.172	.184	.213	4	76	1.42	.112	3	-0.67	0.05	-0.62
Zeile	603	82	171	35	3	11	88	61	103	.284	.406	.350	84	466	4.87	.596	17	4.24	0.39	4.63
TOTALS	5733	728	1502	253	48	84	671	556	954	.262	.367	.327	701	4562	4.15	.517	169	28.23	8.18	36.41

Pitching Records for St. Louis Cardinals

	ERA	W	L	Pct	G	GS	CG	ShO	GF	Sv	IP	R	ER	H	2B	3B	HR	BB	IW	SO	HB	WP	BK
Smith B	3.85	12	9	.571	31	31	3	0	0	0	198.2	95	85	188	39	5	16	45	3	94	7	3	1
Tewksbury	3.25	11	12	.478	30	30	3	0	0	0	191.0	86	69	206	42	8	13	38	2	75	5	0	0
Hill K	3.57	11	10	.524	30	30	0	0	0	0	181.1	76	72	147	23	6	15	67	4	121	6	7	1
Olivares	3.71	11	7	.611	28	24	0	0	2	1	167.1	72	69	148	22	4	13	61	1	91	5	3	1
DeLeon J	2.71	5	9	.357	28	28	1	0	0	0	162.2	57	49	144	29	5	15	61	1	118	6	1	1
Cormier	4.12	4	5	.444	11	10	2	0	1	0	67.2	35	31	74	16	1	5	8	1	38	2	2	1
Moyer	5.74	0	5	.000	8	7	0	0	1	0	31.1	21	20	38	8	1	5	16	0	20	1	2	1
Agosto	4.81	5	3	.625	72	0	0	0	22	2	86.0	52	46	92	17	4	4	39	4	34	8	6	0
Terry	2.80	4	4	.500	65	0	0	0	13	1	80.1	31	25	76	11	2	1	32	14	52	0	0	0
Smith Le	2.34	6	3	.667	67	0	0	0	61	47	73.0	19	19	70	8	3	5	13	5	67	0	1	0
Carpenter	4.23	10	4	.714	59	0	0	0	19	0	66.0	31	31	53	17	0	6	20	9	47	0	1	0
Fraser	4.93	3	3	.500	35	0	0	0	16	0	49.1	28	27	44	6	1	9	21	3	25	3	4	0
McClure	3.13	1	1	.500	32	0	0	0	9	0	23.0	8	8	24	3	1	1	8	2	15	1	0	0
Clark M	4.03	1	1	.500	7	2	0	0	1	0	22.1	10	10	17	2	0	3	11	0	13	0	2	0
Perez Mk	5.82	0	2	.000	14	0	0	0	2	0	17.0	11	11	19	6	1	1	7	2	7	1	0	1
Sherill	8.16	0	0	.000	10	0	0	0	3	0	14.1	13	13	20	1	0	2	3	1	4	2	1	0
Grater	0.00	0	0	.000	3	0	0	0	2	0	3.0	0	0	5	0	0	0	2	0	0	0	0	0
Oquendo	27.00	0	0	.000	1	0	0	0	1	0	1.0	3	3	2	1	0	0	2	0	1	0	0	0
TOTALS	3.69	84	78	.519	531	162	9	0	153	51	1435.1	648	588	1367	251	42	114	454	52	822	47	33	7

Sabermetric Pitching Records for St. Louis Cardinals

	Adj	|-Expected-|			|——Opposing Batters——|													Supported			
	ERA	W	L	Pct	BFP	Avg	Slg	OBA	RC/G	GDP	SB	CS	PK	PKE	SH	SF	RSup	RSp/G	W	L	Pct
Agosto	5.34	3	5	.321	377	.291	.408	.380	5.07	14	7	5	0	1	11	3	34	3.56	2	6	.308
Carpenter	4.64	5	9	.386	266	.220	.365	.278	3.35	2	3	4	0	0	3	2	44	6.00	9	5	.626
Clark M	4.43	1	1	.407	93	.215	.354	.301	4.10	0	5	1	0	0	0	3	17	6.85	1	1	.705
Cormier	4.52	4	5	.397	281	.277	.401	.300	3.99	6	1	3	0	0	1	3	23	3.06	3	6	.314
DeLeon J	2.99	8	6	.602	679	.239	.378	.313	3.99	8	12	12	0	0	5	4	57	3.15	7	7	.527
Fraser	5.47	2	4	.311	210	.242	.434	.325	4.72	4	6	4	0	0	1	3	26	4.74	3	3	.429
Grater	0.00	0	0	.000	15	.385	.385	.467	6.68	0	0	1	0	0	0	0	5	15.00	0	0	.000
Hill K	3.97	10	11	.461	743	.224	.346	.299	3.48	11	19	11	0	0	7	7	70	3.47	9	12	.434
McClure	3.13	1	1	.579	98	.282	.376	.340	4.22	2	0	2	0	1	1	3	13	5.09	1	1	.725
Moyer	6.32	1	4	.253	142	.319	.529	.399	7.56	2	8	3	0	0	4	2	2	0.57	0	5	.008
Olivares	4.09	8	10	.447	688	.243	.356	.316	3.68	12	10	11	1	2	11	2	78	4.20	9	9	.513
Oquendo	27.00	0	0	.018	7	.400	.600	.571	18.27	0	0	0	0	0	0	0	0	0.00	0	0	.000
Perez Mk	6.35	1	1	.251	75	.288	.455	.365	5.95	1	2	1	0	0	1	0	5	2.65	0	2	.148
Sherill	8.79	0	0	.149	67	.339	.458	.379	6.96	1	2	0	0	0	1	2	3	1.88	0	0	.044
Smith B	4.26	9	12	.427	818	.251	.381	.297	3.88	11	19	8	0	0	10	7	121	5.48	13	8	.624
Smith Le	2.59	6	3	.668	300	.249	.352	.281	3.55	3	10	2	0	0	5	1	13	1.60	2	7	.277
Terry	3.02	5	3	.596	339	.249	.308	.320	3.50	6	7	3	0	0	2	0	47	5.27	6	2	.752
Tewksbury	3.58	12	11	.513	798	.281	.413	.317	4.30	19	10	10	0	0	12	10	93	4.38	14	9	.600
TOTALS	4.11	72	90	.444	5996	.255	.381	.315	4.06	102	121	81	1	4	75	52	651	4.08	81	81	.497

Batting 'Splits' Records for St. Louis Cardinals

	G	AB	Run	Hit	2B	3B	HR	TB	RBI	W	K	IW	HB	SB	CS	GI DP	SH	SF	Avg	Slug	OBP	Runs Ctd
SPLITS for Jose																						
vs LHP	104	262	35	78	18	2	2	106	30	23	51	7	0	10	7	7	0	0	.298	.405	.354	36
vs RHP	122	306	34	95	22	4	6	143	47	27	62	1	2	10	5	5	0	5	.310	.467	.365	53
Home	78	280	34	83	16	5	3	118	39	25	48	5	1	9	5	5	0	3	.296	.421	.353	42
Away	76	288	35	90	24	1	5	131	38	25	65	3	1	11	7	7	0	2	.313	.455	.367	47
Grass	41	163	17	44	12	1	3	67	22	6	41	2	0	4	3	6	0	1	.270	.411	.294	17
Turf	113	405	52	129	28	5	5	182	55	44	72	6	2	16	9	6	0	4	.319	.449	.385	72
April/June	70	262	37	87	23	3	2	122	39	28	46	4	2	9	8	3	0	1	.332	.466	.399	49
July/October	84	306	32	86	17	3	6	127	38	22	67	4	0	11	4	9	0	4	.281	.415	.325	40
SPLITS for Oquendo																						
vs LHP	76	150	14	36	8	1	1	49	15	29	21	6	1	0	2	0	2	1	.240	.327	.365	20
vs RHP	95	216	23	52	3	3	0	61	11	38	27	7	0	1	0	5	2	2	.241	.282	.352	24
Home	67	184	21	48	3	2	0	55	14	32	19	6	1	1	0	2	1	1	.261	.299	.372	23
Away	60	182	16	40	8	2	1	55	12	35	29	7	0	0	2	3	3	2	.220	.302	.342	21
Grass	33	96	8	16	2	0	0	18	8	24	15	6	0	0	1	2	1	1	.167	.188	.331	8
Turf	94	270	29	72	9	4	1	92	18	43	33	7	1	1	1	3	3	2	.267	.341	.367	37
April/June	65	181	15	39	3	3	1	51	10	39	22	11	0	1	2	3	3	1	.215	.282	.353	21
July/October	62	185	22	49	8	1	0	59	16	28	26	2	1	0	0	2	1	2	.265	.319	.361	24
SPLITS for Zeile																						
vs LHP	101	237	38	72	15	1	5	104	33	26	44	2	2	8	4	4	0	2	.304	.439	.375	40
vs RHP	132	328	38	86	21	2	6	129	48	36	50	1	3	9	7	11	0	4	.262	.393	.337	42
Home	80	279	40	83	20	2	7	128	50	33	40	2	3	8	2	11	0	3	.297	.459	.374	48
Away	75	286	36	75	16	1	4	105	31	29	54	1	2	9	9	4	0	3	.262	.367	.331	35
Grass	39	149	21	40	12	0	0	52	12	11	30	0	2	3	7	1	0	1	.268	.349	.325	16
Turf	116	416	55	118	24	3	11	181	69	51	64	3	3	14	4	14	0	5	.284	.435	.362	66
April/June	71	258	36	74	17	2	3	104	32	25	43	2	3	7	6	9	0	2	.287	.403	.354	35
July/October	84	307	40	84	19	1	8	129	49	37	51	1	2	10	5	6	0	4	.274	.420	.351	47
SPLITS for St. Louis Cardinals (all batters except pitchers)																						
vs LHP	1079	2275	270	573	118	21	23	802	244	219	382	26	11	86	49	37	29	19	.252	.353	.318	262
vs RHP	1355	3087	381	793	121	32	45	1113	355	313	475	22	10	116	61	57	29	28	.257	.361	.325	370
Home	1182	2707	345	682	116	34	32	962	313	290	394	27	13	113	47	48	29	21	.252	.355	.325	327
Away	1062	2655	306	684	123	19	36	953	286	242	463	21	8	89	63	46	29	26	.258	.359	.319	305
Grass	576	1438	166	360	72	10	14	494	154	119	263	16	4	39	33	22	14	12	.250	.344	.307	151
Turf	1668	3924	485	1006	167	43	54	1421	445	413	594	32	17	163	77	72	44	35	.256	.362	.327	482
April/June	1047	2492	328	660	113	30	23	902	301	270	348	32	11	95	51	50	25	24	.265	.362	.336	313
July/October	1197	2870	323	706	126	23	45	1013	298	262	509	16	10	107	59	44	33	23	.246	.353	.309	320

1991 SPLITS FOR St. Louis Cardinals

BATTING SPLITS

	AVG	AB	R	H	2B	3B	HR	RBI	SB	CS	BB	K	OBA	SPCT
Total	.255	5362	651	1366	239	53	68	599	202	110	532	857	.322	.357

	#Pit	#P/PA	GB	FB	G/F	G	IBB	HB	SH	SF	GDP
Miscellaneous	21780	3.62	2207	1365	1.62	162	48	21	58	47	94

	AVG	AB	R	H	2B	3B	HR	RBI	SB	CS	BB	K	OBA	SPCT
vs. Left	.252	2275	...	573	118	21	23	244	86	49	219	382	.318	.353
vs. Right	.257	3087	...	793	121	32	45	355	116	61	313	475	.325	.361
Home	.252	2707	345	682	116	34	32	313	113	47	290	394	.325	.355
Away	.258	2655	306	684	123	19	36	286	89	63	242	463	.319	.359
None on	.242	3052	...	739	128	19	47	47	0	0	269	496	.305	.343
Runners on	.271	2310	...	627	111	34	21	552	202	110	263	361	.343	.376
April	.260	691	87	180	26	9	8	75	23	14	88	84	.345	.359
May	.273	873	116	238	44	7	7	109	39	15	88	136	.339	.363
June	.261	928	125	242	43	14	8	117	33	22	94	128	.327	.363
July	.248	856	96	212	31	7	16	89	36	10	84	142	.315	.356
August	.255	924	103	236	39	10	9	96	33	23	76	162	.311	.348
September	.235	937	105	220	42	6	16	95	32	14	78	181	.295	.344
October	.248	153	19	38	14	0	4	18	6	12	24	24	.344	.418
None on/out	.260	1338	...	348	60	7	23	23	0	0	127	201	.325	.367
Scoring Posn	.272	1424	...	387	67	26	10	506	53	20	214	240	.360	.376
Close & Late	.251	926	...	232	34	7	13	110	40	22	110	159	.332	.344
Bases Loaded	.264	129	...	34	6	2	0	105	0	0	12	16	.310	.341
Batting #1	.247	676	89	167	31	11	10	67	45	28	56	119	.305	.370
Batting #2	.288	615	107	177	35	3	4	59	39	10	92	49	.382	.374
Batting #3	.256	636	88	163	28	11	11	80	35	12	63	111	.324	.387
Batting #4	.268	622	68	167	23	1	12	98	13	7	62	71	.331	.367
Batting #5	.298	617	73	184	42	7	9	81	23	14	46	112	.344	.433
Batting #6	.244	589	68	144	25	5	11	59	20	16	54	106	.309	.360
Batting #7	.243	571	56	139	26	9	5	65	14	12	39	85	.296	.347
Batting #8	.243	515	59	125	15	4	4	46	6	7	83	72	.346	.311
Batting #9	.192	521	43	100	14	2	2	44	7	4	37	132	.244	.238
As p	.163	325	21	53	5	0	0	22	0	0	13	89	.195	.178
As c	.239	552	45	132	25	5	5	64	9	13	41	81	.294	.330
As 1b	.256	637	65	163	20	4	13	92	16	8	52	73	.309	.361
As 2b	.231	527	63	122	19	7	6	38	10	3	79	92	.336	.328
As 3b	.269	609	76	164	37	3	11	84	17	11	64	99	.341	.394
As ss	.283	611	100	173	32	3	3	55	35	10	93	45	.377	.360
As lf	.248	613	77	152	24	5	10	44	29	20	66	95	.320	.352
As cf	.255	662	92	169	28	16	9	75	50	22	44	119	.301	.387
As rf	.300	616	73	185	40	8	9	87	21	12	53	121	.355	.435
Outfield	.268	1891	242	506	92	29	28	206	100	54	163	335	.325	.391
0.0 count	.309	838	...	259	43	11	9	110	...	...	2	0	.312	.419
After (0.1)	.222	2382	...	529	100	20	26	227	...	...	115	578	.258	.314
After (1.0)	.270	2141	...	578	96	22	33	262	...	...	379	279	.379	.382
Two strikes	.192	2351	...	451	78	13	18	178	...	...	200	856	.257	.259
Grass	.250	1438	166	360	72	10	14	154	39	33	119	263	.307	.344
Turf	.256	3924	485	1006	167	43	54	445	163	77	413	594	.327	.362
Day	.263	1536	212	404	82	18	30	199	43	30	149	215	.326	.398
Night	.251	3826	439	962	157	35	38	400	159	80	383	642	.320	.341
Inning 1.6	.256	3633	434	929	173	35	44	396	145	75	346	573	.320	.359
Inning 7+	.253	1729	217	437	66	18	24	203	57	35	186	284	.326	.353
vs.Atl	.202	391	31	79	16	1	4	29	15	5	35	67	.268	.279
vs.ChN	.255	599	70	153	31	5	6	68	15	15	68	91	.330	.354
vs.Cin	.269	387	45	104	16	2	7	43	15	9	44	58	.341	.375
vs.Hou	.289	412	70	119	19	5	7	63	24	4	58	60	.374	.410
vs.LA	.242	389	39	94	19	3	3	37	19	9	38	67	.307	.329
vs.Mon	.258	585	70	151	28	9	9	61	22	21	56	95	.325	.383
vs.NYN	.269	620	76	167	29	13	4	70	21	7	52	119	.326	.377
vs.Phi	.277	596	95	165	28	7	10	86	23	7	75	90	.355	.398
vs.Pit	.249	603	66	150	26	3	6	62	21	14	41	83	.300	.332
vs.SD	.210	391	38	82	11	3	4	33	11	6	23	66	.255	.284
vs.SF	.262	389	51	102	16	2	8	47	16	13	42	61	.334	.375

PITCHING SPLITS

	ERA	W	L	SV	SVOP	GS	CG	SHO	IP	H	ER	HR	BB	IBB	K
Total	3.69	84	78	51	68	162	9	14	1435.1	1367	588	114	454	52	822

	#Pit	#P/IP	GB	FB	G/F	BRp9	RA	WP	BK	SH	SF	R	HB	Hld
Miscellaneous	20811	14.50	1975	1605	1.23	11.71	369	33	7	75	52	648	47	49

	ERA	W	L	SV	SVOP	GS	CG	SHO	IP	H	ER	HR	BB	IBB	K
ST	3.54	54	57	0	0	162	9	0	1001.1	942	394	82	300	12	557
REL	4.02	30	21	51	68	0	0	0	434.0	425	194	32	154	40	265
Home	3.15	52	32	29	36	84	7	0	771.0	693	270	41	229	27	426
Away	4.31	32	46	22	32	78	2	0	664.1	674	318	73	225	25	396
April	3.02	13	8	10	11	21	0	0	188.0	163	63	12	65	4	117
May	4.99	11	14	5	9	25	2	0	220.0	231	122	21	73	7	124
June	3.19	16	12	8	12	28	0	0	251.1	233	89	13	74	15	136
July	4.40	13	13	7	8	26	3	0	229.0	239	112	24	83	6	129
August	3.37	16	12	10	12	28	0	0	248.1	236	93	21	62	9	137
September	3.09	13	16	9	13	29	4	0	256.2	227	88	17	79	11	150
October	4.50	2	3	2	3	5	0	0	42.0	38	21	6	18	0	29
Grass	4.62	15	27	7	12	42	2	0	354.2	372	182	40	113	15	210
Turf	3.38	69	51	44	56	120	7	0	1080.2	995	406	74	341	37	612
Day	3.33	24	22	14	18	46	3	0	403.0	381	149	32	122	12	236
Night	3.83	60	56	37	50	116	6	0	1032.1	986	439	82	332	40	586
vs.Atl	5.74	3	9	1	2	12	0	0	105.0	114	67	13	50	5	63
vs.ChN	4.19	8	10	5	6	18	0	0	159.0	150	74	16	54	4	95
vs.Cin	3.48	8	4	6	7	12	2	0	106.0	112	41	8	32	2	58
vs.Hou	4.03	7	5	1	3	12	3	0	105.0	95	47	9	34	2	62
vs.LA	3.15	6	6	3	6	12	0	0	108.2	108	38	5	36	8	66
vs.Mon	2.87	11	7	9	10	18	1	0	160.0	146	51	7	45	4	95
vs.NYN	3.68	11	7	6	7	18	2	0	159.0	154	65	17	38	4	75
vs.Phi	3.26	12	6	10	11	18	0	0	160.0	141	58	10	52	3	104
vs.Pit	4.03	7	11	4	6	18	0	0	160.2	161	72	12	58	8	91
vs.SD	3.00	3	9	0	2	12	0	0	105.0	93	35	8	31	11	58
vs.SF	3.36	8	4	6	8	12	1	0	107.0	93	40	9	24	1	55

OPPOSING BATTERS VS. PITCHERS.

	AVG	AB	R	H	2B	3B	HR	RBI	SB	CS	BB	K	OBA	SPCT
Total	.255	5368	648	1367	251	42	114	615	121	81	454	822	.315	.381
vs. Left	.254	2743	...	697	128	24	47	288	74	42	273	380	.323	.370
vs. Right	.255	2625	...	670	123	18	67	327	47	39	181	442	.307	.392
ST	.252	3737	441	942	177	30	82	387	83	58	300	557	.310	.381
REL	.261	1631	207	425	74	12	32	228	38	23	154	265	.327	.380
Home	.244	2840	293	693	134	26	41	275	66	45	229	426	.305	.353
Away	.267	2528	355	674	117	16	73	340	55	36	225	396	.327	.412
None on	.245	3172	...	778	137	24	64	64	0	0	235	497	.302	.364
Runners on	.268	2196	...	589	114	18	50	551	121	81	219	325	.333	.405
None on/out	.243	1369	...	333	60	10	31	31	0	0	101	206	.300	.370
Scoring Posn	.266	1280	...	341	71	11	29	477	28	7	166	208	.343	.407
vs 1st Batr	.291	326	...	95	13	3	6	46	5	1	31	45	.358	.405
1st IP	.269	1765	164	474	86	15	39	264	54	32	164	298	.333	.401
Inning 1.6	.250	3602	434	900	162	27	78	410	92	62	298	546	.310	.375
Inning 7+	.264	1766	214	467	89	15	36	205	29	19	156	276	.327	.393
Close & Late	.259	930	...	241	34	10	20	108	19	11	93	160	.328	.382
0.0 count	.317	878	...	278	56	8	20	131	...	...	43	0	.349	.467
After (0.1)	.230	2363	...	543	89	22	38	234	...	...	99	550	.268	.334
After (1.0)	.257	2127	...	546	106	12	56	250	...	...	312	272	.351	.397
Two strikes	.176	2232	...	393	59	18	27	168	...	...	162	821	.238	.255
Pitch 1.15	.275	1649	...	454	82	15	34	196	49	23	141	245	.336	.405
Pitch 16.30	.237	1038	...	246	48	5	21	131	18	19	81	181	.293	.354
Pitch 31.45	.237	729	...	173	29	5	17	69	16	13	59	115	.296	.361
Pitch 46.60	.245	620	...	152	24	4	14	75	17	12	49	98	.309	.365
Pitch 61.75	.239	586	...	140	29	3	13	61	7	6	50	79	.300	.365
Pitch 76.90	.259	440	...	114	20	5	8	52	12	1	41	67	.321	.382
Pitch 91.105	.276	232	...	64	13	4	5	24	2	6	22	25	.341	.431
Pitch 106.20	.295	61	...	18	5	1	1	6	0	1	9	11	.386	.459
Pitch 121.35	.417	12	...	5	1	0	0	0	0	0	2	1	.500	.500
Pitch 136.50	1.000	1	...	1	0	0	1	2	0	0	0	0	1.000	4.000

Philadelphia Phillies

Pete De Coursey

PHILADELPHIA											
YEAR	1982	1983	1984	1985	1986	1987	1988	1989	1990	1991	TOT
W	89	90	81	75	86	80	65	67	77	77	787
L	73	72	81	87	75	82	96	95	85	83	829
WPCT	0.549	0.556	0.500	0.463	0.534	0.494	0.404	0.414	0.475	0.481	0.487
R	664	696	720	667	739	702	597	629	646	629	6689
RA	654	635	690	673	713	749	734	735	729	680	6992
PWPT	0.508	0.546	0.521	0.496	0.518	0.468	0.398	0.423	0.440	0.461	0.478
PythW	82	88	84	80	84	76	65	68	71	75	77
PythL	80	74	78	82	78	86	97	94	91	87	85
LUCK	7	2	-3	-5	2	4	0	-1	6	2	14

Defensive Efficiency Record: .7085

Atlanta's Fulton County Stadium gave Dale Murphy an MVP award he may not have deserved. Before we let his longtime home ballpark unfairly and prematurely clinch his election to the Baseball Hall of Fame at Cooperstown, it's time to take a clear look at his record. The argument that Murphy's achievements entering this season already have punched his ticket to Cooperstown has been made by writers, radio hosts and even experts like Bill James and the numbers-crunchers at STATS Inc. of Lincolnwood Ill. The argument in favor of the right-handed slugger boils down to three facts: He has hit 396 career home runs. He has been awarded five gold gloves. He was twice selected the Most Valuable Player in the National League.

The third credential is the most important. To get into the Hall of Fame, you usually have to be one of the best players of your era. Winning two MVPs seems to clearly give Murphy, now with the Phillies, that honor. But his 1982 award was due to statistical Illiteracy by the voters, one of the few times they allowed a player's home park to fool them.

Year	Lg	MVP	Home	Road
1980	NL	Mike Schmidt	25	23
1981	NL	Mike Schmidt	17	14
1982	AL	Robin Yount	9	20
1982	NL	Dale Murphy	24	12
1983	AL	Cal Ripken Jr.	12	15
1983	NL	Dale Murphy	17	19
1985	AL	Don Mattingly	22	13
1986	NL	Mike Schmidt	20	17
1987	AL	George Bell	19	28
1987	NL	Andre Dawson	27	22
1988	AL	Jose Canseco	16	26
1989	NL	Kirk Gibson	14	11
1989	AL	Kevin Mitchell	22	25
1990	AL	Rickey Henderson	8	20
1990	NL	Barry Bonds	14	19
1991	AL	Cal Ripken Jr.	16	18

When you examine the 16 MVP winners since 1980 who hit more than 25 HRs you discover two things: Home run hitters usually win the MVP - 15 of those 22 hit more than 25 home runs. And those hitters tend to be as powerful at home as they were on the road: Eight of the 15 hit more homers on the road; four hit within three HRs of their home totals while batting in foreign climes.

The easy test of whether a home park is the driving force behind a player's numbers is to double his home and road stats. If we do that, we see that Rickey Henderson in 1990 was on a 40-home run pace on the road, but was held to 28 by a tough home park, one which also held back Jose Canseco when he was on a 52-HR road pace in 1988. It also works the other way. In 1982, Dale Murphy was having a 24-HR season in neutral ballparks, which looked better because 24 Fulton County Stadium homers pumped some helium into his home run numbers.

Incidentally, the Cubs' Andre Dawson, whose 1987 award usually is cited as an example of Wrigley Field advantage, hit 22 road homers that year to lead the league in road blasts as well as overall HRs. That's not park advantage, that's power. Murphy's 12 1982 homers away from home, on the other hand, did not place him in the top ten for road homers. That's park advantage.

When you look at the 1982 MVP election, Murphy edged out Lonnie Smith 283-218 in the MVP voting, while Pedro Guerrero hit .304 with 32 HRs (17 on the road) and 100 RBIs. I don't know whether Guerrero or Smith would have won that year, but if his HR column had listed a 24, it would not have been Murphy. To be fair, Murphy fully earned the MVP in 1983, when he hit home runs everywhere, but Joe Torre, Jeff Burroughs, Zoilo Versalles, Willie McGee, Don Baylor, Kirk Gibson, Elston Howard and Hank Sauer all won one MVP. None of them is an automatic Cooperstown inductee. It is thesecond MVP which combines with Murphy's career HR total to make him a lock. If it wasn't deserved, his induction shouldn't be a foregone conclusion.

Let's take a look at his career home run total, which also obviously benefited from playing in Fulton County Stadium. Murphy has 396 HRs, and with the exception of Dave Kingman, who had no value outside the HR column, every eligible hitter with more than 390 HRs is in Cooperstown. Darrell Evans (414) and Graig Nettles (390) are waiting to become eligible. It appears that Murphy needs only one more good season to lock up his election, but once again, we need to take a closer look. There are eight active players with more than 150 road HRs. The chart shows where they rank in percentage of home runs hit in neutral parks.

(Players active in 1991 with more than 150 road home runs)

Player	Home	Road	Total	%
George Brett	128	163	291	56
Dave Winfield	187	219	406	54
Jack Clark	155	180	335	54
Eddie Murray	187	211	398	53
Andre Dawson	176	201	377	53
Lance Parrish	145	159	304	51
Carlton Fisk	186	186	372	50
Dave Parker	170	169	339	50
Gary Carter	160	159	319	50
Dwight Evans	203	182	385	47
Dale Murphy	215	181	396	46

Compared to his peers, Murphy has benefited tremendously from his home park. He has hit only 46 percent of his homers on the road. Now you may say that it's only an 8 to 9 percent difference between him and Winfield, Murray, Dawson and Clark. But when you're talking about men who have hit more than 370 HRs, an 8 percent difference is 30 HRs. That's enough HRs to send Frank Howard (382), Rocky Colavito (374) or Norm Cash (377) over the 400 barrier and into the Hall of Fame. That's a lot of home runs, and that's the benefit Murphy has received from playing in Atlanta.

Contrast him with Jack Clark, whose parks have held him back and you see that benefit even more clearly. Let's put this into perspective. Dale Murphy has been an outstanding star for a decade, and thoroughly deserved to win the MVP in 1983. But compared to his peers, he has not been as great a player as Winfield and Dawson, who have hit more home runs in neutral parks, stolen more bases, driven in more runs and won more Gold Gloves. He should follow, not lead them into the Hall of Fame.

Murphy is not far from getting bronzed: Three more seasons should easily bring 28 more road home runs, and 60 or more total. No one has ever hit 438 homers, 200 road homers, won an MVP and five Gold Gloves and not been inducted, and no one who does that should be slighted. But those accomplishments are not yet agate lines in his record. Until they are, we are doing a disservice to Cooperstown and to Murphy when we allow his old stadium to lower our standards for baseball's greatest honor. Past blaster cheated by Parks.

When you look back into recent history, there is another player who hit more road home runs than Murphy without having a home park to inflate his career totals, Braves alumnus Joe Adcock, who hit 199 of his 336 HRs on the road. The big right-handed slugger played with the Milwaukee (later Atlanta) Braves from 1953 to 1962, and lost three to six HRs every year to a home park which didn't like to let baseballs escape the field. When you realized that Adcock hit 26 more road homers than Dale Murphy, despite having 42 fewer total home runs, it's hard not to think that if they switched eras, Murphy would be an obscure but fondly remembered slugger, and Adcock a lock for the Hall of Fame. Timing is everything, they say, but if the explosion of statistical information in baseball is to ultimately mean anything, it hopefully will mean that we can see hitters for what they did, not for where they played.

Jim Fregosi brought a 905-game record as a major league manager and a 1979 AL West division championship with him as he takes over the helm of the Phillies, and it gave and continues to give valuable information about how and where the former all star shortstop will lead the team. That record shows two things very clearly: 1) Fregosi has wrung a lot of fine years from a lot of journeymen pitchers; 2) After seven seasons, he has no track record as a developer of young position players.

Fregosi took over a veteran Angels (average age of 29) contending team in 1978, and coaxed big years from MVP Don Baylor, Bob Grich, Rod Carew, Joe Rudi, Brian Downing and Dan Ford in '79 to win the AL West. In 1980, the injured Angels (Rudi, Baylor and Downing all missed considerable time) fell to sixth, and by 1981, the aging Angels (same team, average of 31) were 22-25 in June and Fregosi was fired.

In Chicago from mid-1986-88, he had goofy bosses who made dumb moves, and he struggled valiantly to keep a decent team on the field. Fregosi's similarities to Nick Leyva run much deeper than their hard-nosed, aggressive personal styles. Leyva was continually indicted for playing Wally Backman and Randy Ready (both 31) instead of 25-year-old prospect Mickey Morandini. But back in 1979-80, when he managed the California Angels, Fregosi gave 37-year-old Bert Campaneris 145 games at shortstop, and brought in 35-year-old Fred Patek for 81, which meant 21-year-old prospect Dickie Thon played only 30 major league games at short over two seasons (he hit .339 in 56 ABs in '79).

In 1979, when the Angels won the AL West by three games, you can defend Fregosi's decision to play veterans, but in 1980, the Angels fell from 88-74 to 65-95, and you have to wonder why Fregosi chose to play Patek and Campaneris for 140 games instead of Thon, who went on to lead the NL in triples in 1982 and was named to several All-Star teams in 1983.

Leyva and Fregosi share another attribute: Neither developed a first-rate starting player during their tenures. While Leyva's tribulations and impatience with the development of Ricky Jordan, Charlie Hayes and Morandini are well-known, Fregosi's record is not demonstrably better. Only two major league regulars have Fregosi to thank for their regular gig in the bigs: Bobby Bonilla and Ken Landreaux. Both men received a half-season tryout from Fregosi, and were then immediately traded away, so it is still unknown how well he can develop young players. And this troubling pattern continued in 1991 as Morandini and Chamberlain made lackluster debuts, in part because Fregosi seemed unwilling to give Chamberlain the support and batting helps he needed and frightened of giving Morandini the kind of playing time which would determine whether he could play every day. Using Wally Backman and Randy Ready in the drive to win third place in September rather than Morandini does seem akin to draining the last few dregs of Patek and Campaneris while eschewing Thon.

Along the same line, Fregosi also brought up Kim Batiste, let him spend September watching Dickie Thon. The Phils skipper apparently thought the team could not win the coveted third slot without using Thon, even though the Phils made no real attempt to sign Thon, and thus enter this year without having a chance to watch Batiste play. Also true to form, the Phils went out and got veterans Mariano Duncan and Dale Sveum, who, along with Backman, will give Fregosi more at-bats and innings to take away from his young infield triumvirate of Morandini, Batiste and Hollins. His lack of success in developing young players, unlike Leyva's, is not due to an unwillingness to try, as this chart demonstrates

He gave them a chance (Players who first played more than 65 games in a season under Jim Fregosi)

	1st year					ever since			
Player	Yr	AB	HR	RBI	BA	AB	HR	BI	BA
Ken Landreaux	78	260	5	23	.223	3841	86	456	.271
Jim Anderson	79	234	3	23	.248	736	10	63	.208
Tom Donohoe	80	218	2	14	.188	never played again			
Bob Clark	80	261	5	23	.230	706	14	77	.242
John Cangelosi	86	438	2	32	.235	538	4	34	.242
Fred Manrique	87	298	4	29	.258	1039	16	121	.253
Bobby Bonilla	87	234	2	26	.269	3060	114	500	.284
Kenny Williams	87	391	11	50	.281	763	16	69	.186
Dave Gallagher	88	347	5	31	.303	1033	2	75	.266
Mickey Morandini	91	325	1	20	.249	???			
Wes Chamberlain	91	363	13	50	.240	???			

In seven seasons, those are the men Jim Fregosi made into even semi-regulars. The only ones who developed were the ones who left his tutelage early, and he seemed unable to pull the plug before nonentities liek Dave Gallagher consumed seasons worths of at-bats.

By contrast, in only 208 games ramrodding the Padres, Larry Bowa christened the careers of Roberto Alomar, Benito Santiago, Shane Mack, Stan Jefferson and Joey Cora. In only three seasons, Hal Lanier brought baseball Craig Biggio, Ken Caminiti and Gerald Young. If the Phillies' main agenda item is to find a developer of young players, clearly Fregosi's record does not merit his selection as manager. If they are looking for a man to reshape the pitching staff, however, they've come to the right dugout.

(Pitchers whose seasons for Fregosi are compared to the rest of their careers)

	for Fregosi			otherwise	
Pitcher	yrs	W-L	ERA	W-L	ERA
Dave LaPoint	87-8	17-14	3.25	63-72	4.12
Mel. Perez	88	12-10	3.79	32-37	4.43
Mark Clear	79-80	22-16	2.47	49-33	3.99
F.Bannister	86-7	26-25	3.56	107-117	4.09
Dave Frost	78-81	25-23	3.81	8-13	4.96
Andy Hassler	80-1	9-4	2.84	35-67	3.99
Tommy Greene	91	13-7	3.38	4-5	4.75

Everywhere hehas gone, Fregosi has come up with a star reliever. When Dave LaRoche began to fade on the Angels, Fregosi turned to Mark Clear. When Bob James ran out of gas, he began with a committee of Bobby Thigpen, Dave Schmidt, Gene Nelson, Barry Jones, and several others until Thigpen (22 in 1986 when he saved seven games with 1.77 ERA) was ready for the load.

Clear, Thigpen, Nelson and Jones all came out of the minors under Fregosi. Their continuing success attests to Fregosi's judgment of pitchers. But Fregosi's wonders were not limited to the talented. His pitching staffs have featured a fluke success or two every year he has managed. The chart at left illustrates this. Two of Fregosi's best moves didn't make it onto the list. In 1988, Jerry Reuss was 13-9 with a 3.44 ERA for Fregosi; from 1986-90, pitching for five other teams, Reuss won 15 and lost 25 with a 5.79 ERA. Chris Knapp won 36 games in six years with an ERA of 5.00, but won 14 for Fregosi in 1978 with a 4.21 ERA.

It's true that some of these improvements only lasted a season, but let's put it this way: if you can come up with an ace reliever and a good starter, and turn a Hassler, Frost or LaPoint into a success each year, you are doing exactly what Jim Fregosi has done throughout his career - an outstanding job with your pitchers. And you might notice that like Frost and Hassler, another tall, strong overachiever named Tommy Greene joined the list of Fregosi projects, as had Jose DeJesus a year before, when the current Phils manager was guru to several minor league pitchers. The Phillies are a veteran team on the field but are running a fire drill of veterans, castoffs, and precocious youths onto the mound.

It's easy to see why GM Lee Thomas desires Fregosi's ability to work with veteran hitters and young and castoff pitchers: That's what the Phils are now. Fregosi's success in boosting veteran hitters to career years while nurturing pitchers and finding one-year wonder hurlers could make the team respectable again soon. But if his substandard track record in developing field players means that young players like Wes Chamberlain, Dave Hollins, Ron Jones, Kim Batiste and Tony Longmire will be undeveloped and left to rot on the vine, that could become a very costly and short-lived respectability.

WILD THING, you make my pulse race, on each toss to the plate, cause you're a WILD THING WILD THING . . Bill Giles loves you. . . . but I don't know for sure. With cash he'll shower you, but you might be Dutch II

Mitch ""Wild Thing'' Williams is probably the last person on earth to qualify as a ""relief pitcher.'' I would like to meet someone, anyone, who is relieved when Mitch takes over the rubber in a tight game. His normal inning-opener is to walk the first guy, retire the second, and let the third man single to center. Then he'll run three-ball counts on everybody else. But despite making fans and managers cover their eyes while he pitches, Williams has just finished an eight-win, five-save month. It was the kind of month which made Phillies managing partner Bill Giles announce that signing Williams, a free agent at season's end, was a top priority; it also made Williams feel entitled to future compensation along the lines of several years at $2.5 to $3 million each.

But a closer look at the month reveals a different conclusion: In the best month of his career, Williams showed why he never will be a top closer, and why the Phillies should not give him big money over several years. The first requirement of a team's top reliever is that he hold leads. Williams came in nine times last month with a lead, and lost four of them. All four were one-run leads.

It's true that the Phillies came back all four times to win the game, but that's no credit to Williams, and those three wins (one was won eventually by Mike Hartley) were due to his teammates. A team's closer has to be able to bail his team out with men on base. Williams entered five games with men on base in August. Four of those times he had a lead, and he gave up that lead in two of the four appearances. In the fifth game, he entered a tie game, and gave up the winning run, taking the loss. In those five appearances, he pitched 6 2/3 innings, allowing five hits and five walks. So when opponents were already on the bags, Williams averaged a hit, a walk, or both every time he came in.

Some of you are no doubt saying that this was just one month, and anybody might slump for a mere 30 days. But you're missing the point. August wasn't a slump for Williams: He was NL Pitcher of the Month. He was a pitcher of the month who held only five of nine leads. He was a pitcher of the month who failed three of the five times he was brought in to strand runners. He was a pitcher of the month who walked 16 batters in 22 2/3 innings. If that's pitcher of the month, I'd hate to see what ineffective looks like. But if Giles wheels out the cash, that's what we'll be looking at next year, just as the Chicago Cubs, his former employers, watched his 4-4, 2.64 ERA, 36-save 1989 turn into a 1-8, 3.93 ERA, 16-save 1990.

And if you look at Williams in light of the other top relievers, (see box) you'll see he puts more runners on base and thus faces more batters per game than most pitchers. He's near the bottom of the class of top relievers, and paying him as if he were likely to do the same or better for the next several years is insane. So what should the Phils have done if someone else offered Williams more? Let him go. Since they didn't, it could be Dutch Daulton and Roger McDowell all over again: Superstar salaries for average production.

With his propensity for putting men on base, the Phillies can't stop their prize lefty from dancing on the rim of a volcano every time he takes the mound, but they could have made certain they weren't holding hands on a long-term contract when he falls into the flames. Or as Houdini's agent informed a younger peer when retiring, ""Son, narrow brushes with death are marvelous theater, but poor prospects for long term contracts WILD THING, you put men on base, I know our lead ain't safe, 'cause you're a WILD THING.

When Mitch was Pitcher of the Month (This chart shows the nine games in August when Phillies reliever Mitch Williams entered with a lead.)

Date	IP	H	BB	Inn-Held		Result	
Aug. 9	1.2	1	2	4-3	8th	no	W (7)
Aug.10	1	1	0	4-2	9th	yes	Sv (20)
Aug.11	1	0	1	5-4	9th	yes	Sv (21)
Aug.15	2	0	0	6-4	8th	yes	Sv (22)
Aug.17	1	0	1	5-2	9th	yes	Sv (23)
Aug.21	1.1	1	1	5-4	8th	no	W (8)
Aug.24	2	1	3	5-4	8th	no	W (9)
Aug.25	1.1	0	1	6-5	8th	yes	Sv (24)
Aug.28	2	3	1	8-7	8th	no	ND

(Pitchers with more than 30 saves in 1991 ranked by batters faced and walks per inning pitched. BF/IP is batters faced per inning pitched)

Pitcher	Sv	BB/IP	H/IP	HR/IP	BF/IP
Tom Henke	32	0.22	0.66	0.08	3.78
Lee Smith	47	0.18	0.96	0.07	4.11
Brian Harvey	46	0.22	0.65	0.08	3.93
Dennis Eckersley	43	0.12	0.79	0.15	3.93
Rick Aguilera	42	0.43	0.64	0.04	3.99
Jeff Reardon	40	0.26	0.91	0.15	4.18
Jeff Montgomery	33	0.31	0.92	0.07	4.18
Rob Dibble	31	0.30	0.81	0.06	4.06
Gregg Olson	31	0.39	1.00	0.01	4.33
John Franco	30	0.33	1.10	0.04	4.46
Jeff Russell	30	0.33	0.89	0.14	4.24
Mitch Williams	30	0.70	0.64	0.05	4.37
Bobby Thigpen	30	0.55	0.90	0.14	4.44

Philadelphia Phillies Home Park Performance Factors

	Outs	Runs	Hits	2b	3b	HR	W	K	SH	SF	HBP	IBB	SB	CS	GDP
Home LH Batters	.973	.889	.984	.979	1.106	.852	.900	.959	1.095	1.020	.768	.791	.957	.863	.896
Home RH Batters	1.058	.999	.975	.995	.950	.988	1.015	1.083	1.093	1.376	.784	.797	1.172	.832	1.051
All Home Batters	1.017	.944	.972	.968	1.044	.924	.958	1.025	1.040	1.125	.759	.796	1.042	.864	.987
Opp LH Batters	1.061	1.073	1.021	1.009	1.899	1.135	1.126	1.082	1.212	1.813	.903	1.583	.950	1.258	.835
Opp RH Batters	1.070	1.091	1.058	1.094	1.400	1.173	1.048	1.014	1.108	.950	.917	1.108	.920	.909	1.030
All Opp Batters	1.048	1.090	1.045	1.036	1.480	1.143	1.060	1.020	1.121	1.065	.908	1.338	.986	1.082	.967
All LH Batters	1.009	.962	.998	.988	1.361	.966	.992	1.009	1.123	1.266	.822	1.061	.948	1.069	.865
All RH Batters	1.064	1.043	1.013	1.041	1.148	1.070	1.030	1.049	1.098	1.084	.873	.907	.974	.869	1.047
All Batters	1.032	1.012	1.006	1.000	1.229	1.022	1.008	1.023	1.078	1.086	.842	1.009	.998	.978	.983

Conventional Batting Records for Philadelphia Phillies

	G	AB	Run	Hit	2B	3B	HR	TB	RBI	W	K	IW	HB	SB	CS	BRng Eff	GI DP	SH	SF	Avg	Slug	OBP	Runs Ctd
Daulton	89	285	36	56	12	0	12	104	42	41	66	4	2	5	0	.429	4	2	5	.196	.365	.297	34
Kruk	152	538	84	158	27	6	21	260	92	67	100	16	1	7	0	.379	10	0	9	.294	.483	.367	100
Morandini	98	325	38	81	11	4	1	103	20	29	45	0	2	13	2	.431	7	6	2	.249	.317	.313	35
Hayes C	142	460	34	106	23	1	12	167	53	16	75	3	1	3	3	.365	13	2	1	.230	.363	.257	39
Thon	146	539	44	136	18	4	9	189	44	25	84	6	0	11	5	.355	9	2	4	.252	.351	.283	53
Chamberlain	101	383	51	92	16	3	13	153	50	31	73	0	2	9	4	.419	8	1	0	.240	.399	.300	45
Dykstra	63	246	48	73	13	5	3	105	12	37	20	1	1	24	4	.470	1	0	0	.297	.427	.391	48
Murphy Dl	153	544	66	137	33	1	18	226	81	48	93	3	0	1	0	.402	20	0	7	.252	.415	.309	67
Jordan	101	301	38	82	21	3	9	136	49	14	49	2	2	0	2	.537	11	0	5	.272	.452	.304	38
Hayes V	77	284	43	64	15	1	0	81	21	31	42	1	3	9	2	.516	6	0	5	.225	.285	.303	27
Ready	76	205	32	51	10	1	1	66	20	47	25	3	1	2	1	.302	5	1	4	.249	.322	.385	30
Backman	94	185	20	45	12	0	0	57	15	30	30	0	0	3	2	.367	2	2	3	.243	.308	.344	22
Lake	58	158	12	36	4	1	1	45	11	2	26	1	0	0	0	.304	5	4	0	.228	.285	.237	10
Hollins	56	151	18	45	10	2	6	77	21	17	26	1	3	1	1	.478	2	0	1	.298	.510	.378	30
Fletcher D	46	136	5	31	8	0	1	42	12	5	15	0	0	0	1	.278	2	1	0	.228	.309	.255	10
Morris Jn	85	127	15	28	2	1	1	35	6	12	25	4	1	2	0	.269	1	0	0	.220	.276	.293	11
Lindeman	65	95	13	32	5	0	0	37	12	13	14	1	0	0	1	.391	1	2	1	.337	.389	.413	16
Mulholland	35	80	3	7	0	0	0	7	0	1	32	0	1	1	0	.200	2	5	0	.087	.087	.110	1
Greene	38	71	4	19	2	0	2	27	7	4	15	0	0	0	0	.000	1	3	0	.268	.380	.307	8
DeJesus J	31	62	3	8	0	0	0	8	4	2	39	0	0	0	0	.000	0	4	0	.129	.129	.156	2
Booker R	28	53	3	12	1	0	0	13	7	1	7	1	0	0	0	.333	1	1	1	.226	.245	.236	3
Castillo Br	28	52	3	9	3	0	0	12	2	1	15	0	0	1	1	.333	1	0	0	.173	.231	.189	2
Campusano	15	35	2	4	0	0	1	7	2	1	10	0	0	0	0	.000	0	1	0	.114	.200	.139	1
Cox	23	29	4	3	0	0	0	3	1	2	16	0	0	0	0	.286	0	4	0	.103	.103	.161	1
Batiste K	10	27	2	6	0	0	0	6	1	1	8	1	0	0	1	.000	0	0	0	.222	.222	.250	1
Jones Ron	28	26	0	4	2	0	0	6	3	2	9	0	0	0	0	.000	1	0	0	.154	.231	.214	1
Ruffin	31	24	0	0	0	0	0	0	0	4	18	0	0	0	0	.000	0	6	0	.000	.000	.143	0
Schu	17	22	1	2	0	0	0	2	2	1	7	0	0	0	0	.333	1	0	1	.091	.091	.125	0
Grimsley	12	17	2	1	0	0	0	1	0	2	6	0	0	0	0	.500	0	0	0	.059	.059	.158	0
Combs	14	15	5	2	0	0	0	2	0	2	7	0	1	0	0	.500	0	2	0	.133	.133	.278	1
Ashby A	8	12	0	1	0	0	0	1	0	0	9	0	0	0	0	.000	0	1	0	.083	.083	.083	0
Brantley C	6	8	0	0	0	0	0	0	0	0	4	0	0	0	0	.000	0	2	0	.000	.000	.000	0
Searcy	18	4	0	0	0	0	0	0	0	0	3	0	0	0	0	.000	0	0	0	.000	.000	.000	0
Boever	68	3	0	1	0	0	0	1	0	0	0	0	0	0	0	.000	0	0	0	.333	.333	.333	0
Akerfelds	30	3	0	0	0	0	0	0	0	0	3	0	0	0	0	.000	0	0	0	.000	.000	.000	0
Ritchie	39	3	0	0	0	0	0	0	0	0	2	0	0	0	0	.000	0	0	0	.000	.000	.000	0
Mauser	3	3	0	0	0	0	0	0	0	0	2	0	0	0	0	.000	0	0	0	.000	.000	.000	0
Lindsey D	1	3	0	0	0	0	0	0	0	0	3	0	0	0	0	.000	0	0	0	.000	.000	.000	0
McDowell R	38	2	0	0	0	0	0	0	0	0	0	0	0	0	0	.000	0	0	0	.000	.000	.000	0
LaPoint	2	2	0	0	0	0	0	0	0	0	1	0	0	0	0	.000	0	0	0	.000	.000	.000	0
Williams Mitch	69	1	0	0	0	0	0	0	0	1	1	0	0	0	0	.000	0	0	0	.000	.000	.500	0
Carreno	3	1	0	0	0	0	0	0	0	0	1	0	0	0	0	.000	0	0	0	.000	.000	.000	0
Hartley	18	1	0	0	0	0	0	0	0	0	0	0	0	0	0	.000	0	0	0	.000	.000	.000	0
TOTALS	2215	5521	629	1332	248	33	111	1979	590	490	1026	48	21	92	30	.397	114	52	49	.241	.358	.303	613

Sabermetric Batting Records for Philadelphia Phillies

	Ball Park Adjusted								Runs		Run/									
	AB	Run	Hit	2B	3B	HR	RBI	W	SO	Avg	Slug	OBP	Ctd	Outs	27o	OW%	OG	OWAR	DWAR	TWAR
Backman	189	20	45	12	0	0	15	30	30	.238	.302	.338	22	151	3.93	.487	6	0.76	-0.06	0.71
Batiste K	28	2	6	0	0	0	1	1	8	.214	.214	.241	2	22	2.45	.270	1	-0.07	0.09	0.03
Booker R	53	2	12	0	0	0	7	1	7	.226	.226	.236	3	43	1.88	.179	2	-0.27	0.04	-0.23
Campusano	36	2	4	0	0	1	2	1	10	.111	.194	.135	1	33	0.82	.039	1	-0.38	0.15	-0.23
Castillo Br	54	3	9	3	0	0	2	1	15	.167	.222	.182	2	46	1.17	.078	2	-0.46	0.11	-0.35
Chamberlain	402	53	93	16	3	14	50	31	76	.231	.391	.288	45	321	3.79	.467	12	1.40	0.33	1.73
Daulton	288	35	56	11	0	11	43	41	67	.194	.347	.291	33	244	3.65	.450	9	0.90	-0.57	0.33
Dykstra	248	47	73	12	7	2	12	37	20	.294	.423	.386	47	179	7.09	.755	7	2.68	0.27	2.96
Fletcher D	137	4	31	7	0	0	12	5	15	.226	.277	.254	9	109	2.23	.233	4	-0.47	0.25	-0.22
Hayes C	483	35	107	24	1	12	53	16	78	.222	.350	.246	38	394	2.60	.294	15	-0.82	0.74	-0.08
Hayes V	287	42	64	14	1	0	21	31	42	.223	.279	.297	27	237	3.08	.367	9	0.15	0.53	0.68
Hollins	154	18	45	10	2	6	21	17	26	.292	.500	.368	30	111	7.30	.765	4	1.71	-0.08	1.63
Jones Ron	26	0	4	1	0	0	3	2	9	.154	.192	.214	1	22	1.23	.084	1	-0.22	0.00	-0.22
Jordan	316	39	83	21	3	9	49	14	51	.263	.434	.292	37	250	4.00	.495	9	1.34	-0.04	1.30
Kruk	544	82	158	26	9	20	94	67	102	.290	.482	.361	101	406	6.72	.734	15	5.78	0.65	6.43
Lake	165	12	36	4	1	1	11	2	27	.218	.273	.228	9	138	1.76	.160	5	-0.97	-0.19	-1.16
Lindeman	99	13	32	5	0	0	12	13	14	.323	.374	.398	16	71	6.08	.694	3	0.90	0.12	1.02
Lindsey D	3	0	0	0	0	0	0	0	3	.000	.000	.000	0	3	0.00	.000	0	-0.04	-0.01	-0.05
Morandini	329	37	81	10	6	0	20	29	45	.246	.313	.307	34	264	3.48	.426	10	0.74	0.56	1.30
Morris Jn	128	14	28	1	1	0	6	12	25	.219	.242	.286	10	100	2.70	.309	4	-0.15	0.14	-0.01
Murphy Dl	572	68	139	34	1	19	81	49	97	.243	.406	.299	67	461	3.92	.485	17	2.31	0.58	2.89
Ready	214	33	51	10	1	1	20	48	26	.238	.308	.372	29	173	4.53	.557	6	1.32	0.32	1.64
Schu	23	1	2	0	0	0	2	1	7	.087	.087	.120	0	23	0.00	.000	1	-0.30	-0.01	-0.31
Thon	566	45	138	18	4	9	44	25	88	.244	.337	.274	52	447	3.14	.377	17	0.44	1.07	1.51
TOTALS	5667	639	1342	248	41	114	591	494	1049	.237	.355	.297	614	4574	3.62	.446	169	16.25	5.01	21.26

Pitching Records for Philadelphia Phillies

	ERA	W	L	Pct	G	GS	CG	ShO	GF	Sv	IP	R	ER	H	2B	3B	HR	BB	IW	SO	HB	WP	BK
Mulholland	3.61	16	13	.552	34	34	8	3	0	0	232.0	100	93	231	42	7	15	49	2	142	3	3	0
Greene	3.38	13	7	.650	36	27	3	2	3	0	207.2	85	78	177	35	4	19	66	4	154	3	9	1
DeJesus J	3.42	10	9	.526	31	29	3	0	1	1	181.2	74	69	147	32	4	7	128	4	118	4	10	0
Cox	4.57	4	6	.400	23	17	0	0	2	0	102.1	57	52	98	16	3	14	39	2	46	1	7	1
Combs	4.90	2	6	.250	14	13	1	0	0	0	64.1	41	35	64	13	0	7	43	1	41	2	7	0
Grimsley	4.87	1	7	.125	12	12	0	0	0	0	61.0	34	33	54	12	2	4	41	3	42	3	14	0
Ashby A	6.00	1	5	.167	8	8	0	0	0	0	42.0	28	28	41	9	2	5	19	0	26	3	6	0
Brantley C	3.41	2	2	.500	6	5	0	0	0	0	31.2	12	12	26	4	1	0	19	0	25	2	2	0
LaPoint	16.20	0	1	.000	2	2	0	0	0	0	5.0	10	9	10	3	0	0	6	0	3	1	0	0
Ruffin	3.78	4	7	.364	31	15	1	1	2	0	119.0	52	50	125	28	3	6	38	3	85	1	4	0
Boever	3.84	3	5	.375	68	0	0	0	27	0	98.1	45	42	90	15	3	10	54	11	89	0	6	1
Williams Mitc	2.34	12	5	.706	69	0	0	0	60	30	88.1	24	23	56	12	1	4	62	5	84	8	4	1
McDowell R	3.20	3	6	.333	38	0	0	0	16	3	59.0	28	21	61	14	0	1	32	12	28	2	1	0
Ritchie	2.50	1	2	.333	39	0	0	0	13	0	50.1	17	14	44	7	1	4	17	5	26	2	1	0
Akerfelds	5.26	2	1	.667	30	0	0	0	11	0	49.2	30	29	49	5	2	5	27	4	31	3	4	0
Searcy	4.15	2	1	.667	18	0	0	0	4	0	30.1	16	14	29	7	2	2	14	1	21	0	1	1
Hartley	3.76	2	1	.667	18	0	0	0	5	1	26.1	11	11	21	2	0	4	10	1	19	3	2	1
Mauser	7.59	0	0	.000	3	0	0	0	1	0	10.2	10	9	18	4	0	3	3	0	6	0	0	0
Carreno	16.20	0	0	.000	3	0	0	0	1	0	3.1	6	6	5	1	1	1	3	0	2	2	0	0
TOTALS	3.86	78	84	.481	483	162	16	6	146	35	1463.0	680	628	1346	261	36	111	670	58	988	43	81	6

Sabermetric Pitching Records for Philadelphia Phillies

	Adj	|-Expected-|			|——Opposing Batters——|													Supported			
	ERA	W	L	Pct	BFP	Avg	Slg	OBA	RC/G	GDP	SB	CS	PK	PKE	SH	SF	RSup	RSp/G	W	L	Pct
Akerfelds	5.26	1	2	.328	229	.257	.382	.354	5.23	1	6	3	0	0	6	2	20	3.62	1	2	.322
Ashby A	6.00	2	4	.273	186	.256	.431	.341	5.31	2	0	1	0	0	1	3	12	2.57	1	5	.155
Boever	3.84	4	4	.477	431	.245	.383	.336	4.94	2	12	2	1	0	3	6	44	4.03	4	4	.523
Brantley C	3.41	2	2	.537	140	.228	.281	.341	3.86	1	6	2	0	0	2	3	16	4.55	3	1	.640
Carreno	16.20	0	0	.049	20	.333	.733	.500	17.36	0	1	0	0	0	0	0	0	0.00	0	0	.000
Combs	4.90	3	5	.360	300	.254	.389	.365	5.54	6	12	2	0	1	1	2	30	4.20	3	5	.424
Cox	4.57	4	6	.392	433	.258	.426	.323	4.70	6	11	7	0	0	6	7	60	5.28	6	4	.571
DeJesus J	3.42	10	9	.536	801	.224	.318	.353	4.05	16	19	11	0	1	11	3	81	4.01	11	8	.579
Greene	3.38	11	9	.541	857	.230	.361	.290	3.66	9	18	7	1	1	9	11	102	4.42	13	7	.631
Grimsley	4.87	3	5	.363	272	.242	.368	.364	5.16	5	14	1	1	1	3	2	22	3.25	2	6	.308
Hartley	3.76	1	2	.488	110	.219	.365	.312	4.03	2	3	0	0	0	1	0	14	4.79	2	1	.618
LaPoint	16.20	0	1	.049	32	.435	.565	.548	16.69	0	3	0	0	0	1	1	7	12.60	0	1	.377
Mauser	7.59	0	0	.190	53	.367	.633	.404	10.81	0	0	0	0	0	1	0	6	5.06	0	0	.308
McDowell R	3.20	5	4	.568	271	.266	.341	.360	4.72	5	6	1	0	2	7	1	13	1.98	2	7	.277
Mulholland	3.65	15	14	.504	956	.260	.374	.299	3.80	16	6	5	4	4	11	6	110	4.27	17	12	.578
Ritchie	2.50	2	1	.683	213	.234	.346	.299	4.08	1	10	0	0	0	2	4	12	2.15	1	2	.424
Ruffin	3.78	5	6	.485	508	.272	.386	.327	4.32	12	7	4	0	1	6	4	38	2.87	4	7	.366
Searcy	4.15	1	2	.439	134	.252	.400	.328	5.11	1	5	0	0	0	3	2	14	4.15	2	1	.500
Williams Mitch	2.34	12	5	.711	386	.182	.266	.330	3.53	3	12	2	1	2	4	4	28	2.85	10	7	.597
TOTALS	3.91	76	86	.469	6332	.246	.367	.329	4.39	88	151	48	8	13	78	61	629	3.87	80	82	.495

Batting 'Splits' Records for Philadelphia Phillies

	G	AB	Run	Hit	2B	3B	HR	TB	RBI	W	K	IW	HB	SB	CS	GIDP	SH	SF	Avg	Slug	OBP	Runs Ctd
SPLITS for Chamberlain																						
vs LHP	61	140	24	38	8	1	7	69	26	16	18	0	1	4	0	5	1	0	.271	.493	.350	24
vs RHP	90	243	27	54	8	2	6	84	24	15	55	0	1	5	4	3	0	0	.222	.346	.270	22
Home	54	211	27	56	9	1	9	94	32	15	37	0	1	2	2	6	0	0	.265	.445	.317	28
Away	47	172	24	36	7	2	4	59	18	16	36	0	1	7	2	2	1	0	.209	.343	.280	17
Grass	25	94	15	20	4	0	3	33	12	6	19	0	0	3	0	2	0	0	.213	.351	.260	9
Turf	76	289	36	72	12	3	10	120	38	25	54	0	2	6	4	6	1	0	.249	.415	.313	37
April/June	18	63	6	20	4	0	1	27	6	2	8	0	1	3	1	1	0	0	.317	.429	.348	9
July/October	83	320	45	72	12	3	12	126	44	29	65	0	1	6	3	7	1	0	.225	.394	.291	36
SPLITS for Kruk																						
vs LHP	98	202	26	60	12	2	4	88	35	18	38	1	1	2	0	3	0	5	.297	.436	.350	32
vs RHP	127	336	58	98	15	4	17	172	57	49	62	15	0	5	0	7	0	4	.292	.512	.378	68
Home	78	276	41	79	17	1	8	122	48	35	50	11	1	4	0	7	0	5	.286	.442	.363	46
Away	74	262	43	79	10	5	13	138	44	32	50	5	0	3	0	3	0	4	.302	.527	.372	54
Grass	39	138	24	36	2	2	9	69	23	14	26	3	0	2	0	1	0	3	.261	.500	.323	24
Turf	113	400	60	122	25	4	12	191	69	53	74	13	1	5	0	9	0	6	.305	.477	.383	77
April/June	71	260	39	75	9	5	10	124	54	28	40	5	0	1	0	8	0	6	.288	.477	.350	44
July/October	81	278	45	83	18	1	11	136	38	39	60	11	1	6	0	2	0	3	.299	.489	.383	57
SPLITS for Murphy Dl																						
vs LHP	85	192	28	57	13	0	5	85	25	17	33	2	0	1	0	10	0	2	.297	.443	.351	28
vs RHP	135	352	38	80	20	1	13	141	56	31	60	1	0	0	0	10	0	5	.227	.401	.286	39
Home	82	279	38	78	21	0	9	126	54	29	48	2	0	1	0	7	0	4	.280	.452	.343	44
Away	71	265	28	59	12	1	9	100	27	19	45	1	0	0	0	13	0	3	.223	.377	.272	24
Grass	41	157	16	32	4	1	6	56	13	12	25	0	0	0	0	8	0	2	.204	.357	.257	13
Turf	112	387	50	105	29	0	12	170	68	36	68	3	0	1	0	12	0	5	.271	.439	.329	55
April/June	69	248	31	65	11	1	11	111	37	20	45	3	0	1	0	11	0	4	.262	.448	.313	32
July/October	84	296	35	72	22	0	7	115	44	28	48	0	0	0	0	9	0	3	.243	.389	.306	34
SPLITS for Philadelphia Phillies (all batters except pitchers)																						
vs LHP	997	2025	243	529	103	13	36	766	225	185	366	13	12	25	10	54	22	17	.261	.378	.324	249
vs RHP	1472	3496	386	803	145	20	75	1213	365	305	660	35	9	67	20	60	30	32	.230	.347	.291	365
Home	1161	2782	341	697	133	16	61	1045	325	261	509	32	15	45	17	60	26	23	.251	.376	.316	336
Away	1054	2739	288	635	115	17	50	934	265	229	517	16	6	47	13	54	26	26	.232	.341	.290	278
Grass	571	1473	165	350	56	7	35	525	154	126	276	10	3	27	7	33	15	15	.238	.356	.296	158
Turf	1644	4048	464	982	192	26	76	1454	436	364	750	38	18	65	23	81	37	34	.243	.359	.306	455
April/June	1039	2597	300	633	110	16	46	913	284	227	466	20	10	36	13	59	22	30	.244	.352	.304	282
July/October	1176	2924	329	699	138	17	65	1066	306	263	560	28	11	56	17	55	30	19	.239	.365	.302	331

1991 SPLITS FOR Philadelphia Phillies

BATTING SPLITS

	AVG	AB	R	H	2B	3B	HR	RBI	SB	CS	BB	K	OBA	SPCT
Total	.241	5521	629	1332	248	33	111	590	92	30	490	1026	.303	.358

	#Pit	#P/PA	GB	FB	G/F	G	IBB	HB	SH	SF	GDP
Miscellaneous	21990	3.59	2018	1476	1.37	162	48	21	52	49	114

	AVG	AB	R	H	2B	3B	HR	RBI	SB	CS	BB	K	OBA	SPCT
vs. Left	.261	2025	...	529	103	13	36	225	25	10	185	366	.324	.378
vs. Right	.230	3496	...	803	145	20	75	365	67	20	305	660	.291	.347
Home	.251	2782	341	697	133	16	61	325	45	17	261	509	.316	.376
Away	.232	2739	288	635	115	17	50	265	47	13	229	517	.290	.341
None on	.242	3163	...	764	133	18	63	63	0	0	266	593	.302	.355
Runners on	.241	2358	...	568	115	15	48	527	92	30	224	433	.304	.363
April	.248	735	94	182	34	3	15	90	15	5	77	134	.317	.363
May	.233	891	89	208	37	4	12	84	10	2	71	149	.290	.324
June	.250	971	117	243	39	9	19	110	11	6	79	183	.306	.368
July	.214	799	75	171	30	5	18	74	15	5	75	147	.285	.332
August	.243	986	136	240	49	7	29	125	24	7	111	191	.319	.396
September	.262	967	106	253	51	4	18	96	14	5	66	186	.309	.378
October	.203	172	12	35	8	1	0	11	3	0	11	36	.254	.262
None on/out	.253	1395	...	353	58	7	34	34	0	0	116	242	.313	.378
Scoring Posn	.239	1316	...	315	66	6	28	457	22	2	160	252	.314	.362
Close & Late	.235	1099	...	258	44	6	21	108	13	4	110	219	.305	.343
Bases Loaded	.330	97	...	32	9	0	6	103	0	0	7	19	.351	.608
Batting #1	.266	665	104	177	32	9	4	28	32	10	78	78	.345	.359
Batting #2	.247	643	81	159	27	3	5	62	19	5	67	107	.318	.322
Batting #3	.262	646	92	169	28	8	19	83	13	5	62	114	.325	.418
Batting #4	.274	634	93	174	33	3	24	96	7	1	63	126	.338	.450
Batting #5	.246	621	76	153	42	3	16	95	4	2	58	103	.311	.401
Batting #6	.249	599	55	149	36	3	22	101	5	2	54	103	.311	.429
Batting #7	.221	598	46	132	23	2	10	54	3	4	35	111	.264	.316
Batting #8	.242	583	42	141	17	2	8	46	7	1	36	88	.284	.319
Batting #9	.147	532	40	78	10	0	3	25	2	0	37	196	.204	.182
As p	.124	339	20	42	2	0	2	12	1	0	18	159	.173	.147
As c	.211	577	53	122	24	1	14	63	5	1	48	108	.273	.329
As 1b	.285	631	91	180	36	6	25	105	3	3	57	114	.343	.480
As 2b	.245	608	76	149	24	5	2	43	17	4	80	80	.332	.311
As 3b	.250	633	57	158	37	3	17	74	4	4	38	107	.295	.398
As ss	.250	613	48	153	20	4	9	53	11	6	28	95	.280	.339
As lf	.244	630	87	154	27	6	18	88	12	5	62	112	.311	.392
As cf	.250	616	91	154	28	6	4	33	33	6	71	90	.330	.334
As rf	.256	628	79	161	37	2	18	86	3	1	58	108	.316	.408
Outfield	.250	1874	257	469	92	14	40	207	48	12	191	310	.319	.378
0.0 count	.299	876	...	262	49	6	24	116	...	...	3	0	.305	.451
After (0.1)	.218	2475	...	540	112	11	38	230	...	...	99	686	.249	.318
After (1.0)	.244	2169	...	530	87	16	49	244	...	...	350	340	.347	.367
Two strikes	.175	2412	...	421	83	11	27	191	...	...	205	1025	.239	.252
Grass	.238	1473	165	350	56	7	35	154	27	7	126	276	.296	.356
Turf	.243	4048	464	982	192	26	76	436	65	23	364	750	.306	.359
Day	.238	1583	183	377	71	7	35	170	36	7	138	297	.298	.358
Night	.243	3938	446	955	177	26	76	420	56	23	352	729	.305	.359
Inning 1.6	.246	3680	447	904	170	21	79	425	68	25	316	661	.305	.368
Inning 7+	.232	1841	182	428	78	12	32	165	24	5	174	365	.299	.340
vs.Atl	.267	419	60	112	18	2	12	56	5	3	40	89	.327	.406
vs.ChN	.226	667	73	151	21	3	17	70	13	3	65	118	.296	.343
vs.Cin	.241	398	44	96	14	5	11	43	6	2	28	79	.293	.384
vs.Hou	.214	407	42	87	19	1	6	40	4	3	37	93	.277	.310
vs.LA	.259	402	39	104	15	4	5	36	8	1	39	72	.329	.353
vs.Mon	.239	590	74	141	34	3	10	64	10	2	68	99	.315	.358
vs.NYN	.233	601	58	140	26	3	10	54	10	5	52	132	.295	.336
vs.Pit	.256	629	66	161	28	5	8	59	10	1	35	114	.296	.355
vs.StL	.233	606	70	141	35	2	10	66	13	7	52	104	.295	.347
vs.SD	.273	417	57	114	18	3	11	56	7	1	37	57	.329	.410
vs.SF	.221	385	46	85	20	2	11	46	6	2	37	69	.289	.369

PITCHING SPLITS

	ERA	W	L	SV	SVOP	GS	CG	SHO	IP	H	ER	HR	BB	IBB	K
Total	3.86	78	84	35	54	162	16	12	1463.0	1346	628	111	670	58	988

	#Pit	#P/IP	GB	FB	G/F	BRp9	RA	WP	BK	SH	SF	R	HB	Hld
Miscellaneous	23535	16.09	1942	1589	1.22	12.67	321	81	6	78	61	680	43	29

	ERA	W	L	SV	SVOP	GS	CG	SHO	IP	H	ER	HR	BB	IBB	K
ST	3.98	51	63	0	0	162	16	6	964.0	900	426	74	419	15	631
REL	3.64	27	21	35	54	0	0	0	499.0	446	202	37	251	43	357
Home	3.64	47	36	18	28	83	7	3	773.0	702	313	53	347	23	536
Away	4.11	31	48	17	26	79	9	3	690.0	644	315	58	323	35	452
April	4.31	9	12	5	7	21	0	0	194.0	161	93	12	118	13	113
May	2.83	13	13	6	8	26	3	2	238.1	199	75	15	95	9	164
June	5.02	10	18	6	8	28	1	0	249.0	264	139	22	135	16	161
July	3.44	10	15	6	8	25	3	1	220.0	212	84	20	82	6	144
August	3.69	20	9	6	14	29	2	0	265.2	254	109	21	122	10	190
September	4.06	13	15	6	8	28	5	2	246.0	213	111	17	98	3	181
October	3.06	3	2	0	1	5	2	1	50.0	43	17	4	20	1	35
Grass	4.05	17	25	10	15	42	3	1	369.0	342	166	39	174	17	243
Turf	3.80	61	59	25	39	120	13	5	1094.0	1004	462	72	496	41	745
Day	4.30	20	26	10	16	46	4	3	410.2	387	196	41	198	18	279
Night	3.69	58	58	25	38	116	12	3	1052.1	959	432	70	472	40	709
vs.Atl	5.04	7	5	2	3	12	0	0	109.0	122	61	12	53	2	76
vs.ChN	3.33	10	8	4	6	18	1	0	178.1	147	66	16	75	6	109
vs.Cin	4.93	3	9	3	4	12	0	0	104.0	110	57	9	52	5	78
vs.Hou	3.47	5	7	2	3	12	2	1	109.0	102	42	5	51	7	74
vs.LA	3.43	5	7	3	4	12	1	0	105.0	107	40	6	53	4	69
vs.Mon	2.29	14	4	4	7	18	6	3	165.0	120	42	12	59	5	113
vs.NYN	3.98	7	11	3	5	18	3	1	160.2	131	71	11	88	9	116
vs.Pit	4.86	6	12	2	6	18	1	0	159.1	154	86	10	92	9	121
vs.StL	4.97	6	12	4	6	18	1	0	157.2	165	87	10	75	6	90
vs.SD	2.64	9	3	4	4	12	1	1	109.0	82	32	6	35	2	67
vs.SF	3.74	6	6	4	6	12	0	0	106.0	106	44	14	37	3	75

OPPOSING BATTERS VS. PITCHERS.

	AVG	AB	R	H	2B	3B	HR	RBI	SB	CS	BB	K	OBA	SPCT
Total	.246	5480	680	1346	261	36	111	634	151	48	670	988	.329	.367
vs. Left	.248	2246	...	557	102	18	44	276	78	29	331	382	.345	.368
vs. Right	.244	3234	...	789	159	18	67	358	73	19	339	606	.318	.366
ST	.249	3620	458	900	176	23	74	395	92	37	419	631	.327	.371
REL	.240	1860	222	446	85	13	37	239	59	11	251	357	.333	.359
Home	.244	2877	334	702	140	14	53	319	79	23	347	536	.328	.358
Away	.247	2603	346	644	121	22	58	315	72	25	323	452	.331	.378
None on	.242	3029	...	732	137	19	64	64	0	0	342	537	.324	.363
Runners on	.251	2451	...	614	124	17	47	570	151	48	328	451	.336	.373
None on/out	.232	1336	...	310	69	10	22	22	0	0	149	221	.315	.348
Scoring Posn	.240	1458	...	350	76	10	29	508	44	8	233	285	.337	.366
vs 1st Batr	.223	274	...	61	14	3	4	24	2	2	34	52	.314	.339
1st IP	.243	1651	173	401	88	13	26	231	63	18	243	327	.342	.359
Inning 1.6	.252	3656	480	922	178	26	76	445	102	39	445	647	.334	.377
Inning 7+	.232	1824	200	424	83	10	35	189	49	9	225	341	.319	.346
Close & Late	.237	1028	...	244	48	3	19	106	33	6	156	199	.341	.345
0.0 count	.287	759	...	218	49	8	15	106	...	...	45	0	.333	.432
After (0.1)	.213	2368	...	504	91	12	38	226	...	...	147	636	.259	.310
After (1.0)	.265	2353	...	624	121	16	58	302	...	...	478	352	.390	.404
Two strikes	.180	2499	...	449	81	11	26	176	...	...	262	987	.259	.252
Pitch 1.15	.255	1406	...	359	73	13	24	152	48	16	185	248	.345	.377
Pitch 16.30	.237	1132	...	268	54	3	23	145	32	6	155	214	.332	.351
Pitch 31.45	.227	758	...	172	32	7	14	75	20	6	99	151	.317	.343
Pitch 46.60	.286	625	...	179	28	5	23	106	17	9	67	101	.357	.458
Pitch 61.75	.228	539	...	123	27	2	8	50	12	4	58	97	.303	.330
Pitch 76.90	.240	437	...	105	23	2	6	44	12	4	55	76	.326	.343
Pitch 91.105	.238	341	...	81	12	3	8	32	7	2	32	60	.301	.361
Pitch 106.20	.250	180	...	45	6	1	5	20	3	1	15	26	.303	.378
Pitch 121.35	.268	56	...	15	6	0	0	11	0	0	3	12	.300	.375
Pitch 136.50	.000	7	...	0	0	0	0	0	0	0	1	3	.125	.000

Chicago Cubs

Brock J. Hanke

CHICAGO											
YEAR	1982	1983	1984	1985	1986	1987	1988	1989	1990	1991	TOT
W	73	71	96	77	70	76	77	93	77	77	787
L	89	91	65	84	90	85	85	69	85	83	826
WPCT	0.451	0.438	0.596	0.478	0.438	0.472	0.475	0.574	0.475	0.481	0.488
R	676	701	762	686	680	720	660	702	690	695	6972
RA	709	719	658	729	781	801	694	623	774	734	7222
PWPT	0.476	0.487	0.573	0.470	0.431	0.447	0.475	0.559	0.443	0.473	0.482
PythW	77	79	93	76	70	72	77	91	72	77	78
PythL	85	83	69	86	92	90	85	71	90	85	84
LUCK	-4	-8	3	1	0	4	0	2	5	0	3

Defensive Efficiency Record: .7011

Analyzing the 1991 Cubs is ridiculously easy. Of their batters who had more than ten at-bats, including the bench, exactly five (5) had Offensive Winning Percentages over .500. What's more, you know who they were: Sandberg, Grace, Dawson, Bell and Hector Villanueva. No one else contributed any offense, no one else had over 3 Total Wins Above Replacement, and there's nowhere to play Hector, unless you want to sacrifice defense at catcher.

The Cubs, needless to say, don't have the kind of pitching staff that can afford to sacrifice defense at catcher. They also don't have the kind of pitching that can cover for a team Offensive Winning Percentage of .443. They wouldn't have had that kind of pitching if Dave Smith had been healthy all year. Hell, they wouldn't have had that kind of pitching if Danny Jackson, Rick Sutcliffe and the rest of them had been healthy all year.

OK, so the best-case scenario for the Cubs would still look like the Mets without Howard Johnson and Doc Gooden. So what they really need to do is to redo their farm system, possibly by hiring someone like, say, Dallas Green. So they're not going to do that; they're going to buy some more free agents and reshuffle their administrative team. So let's not look at that depressing reality. Let's look at what a winning Cubbie outfit might look like if the team was rebuilt from the bottom up. That is, what have winning Cub teams looked like in the (long) past, and what could the Cubs do to make a team that looks like those winners?

First, a quick look at pre-Wrigley Chicago winners, to determine if there's something about Chicago - the elevation, or the air, or the water - that shapes the teams that win there. The first Chicago dynasty was a shamelessly bought and paid for import, from the Boston National Association team to be exact. William Hulbert founded the National League to replace the Association, owned the Chicago NL franchise, and was careful to make sure that it started out a winner. For the league's first decade, Chicago regularly led in Runs Scored, often by a ridiculous 20% or more over the next best team. Never mind the rest of the league. When Cap Anson's team - and it was Anson's team on the field - didn't score like that, they didn't win, because they never did develop dominant pitching. By the second half of the 1880's, the offense, including Anson, had aged. They couldn't dominate any more, and stopped winning altogether until after the start of the American League as a major in 1901.

In terms of a model for the Cubbies, this looks promising, but is actually useless. Yes, the White Stockings (as they were called) did probably play in a hitters' park, like Wrigley Field. But let's face it. Baseball has far too much parity now for any team to realistically try to lead the league in Runs Scored by 20%. This is because modern baseball ownerships are far too stable for the Cubbies to be buying up the Seattle Mariners, much less the Red Sox. So, no, the Cubs aren't going to win the pennant by combining two teams' talent into one like Hulbert did.

The Chicago White Sox won the first American League pennant. This was a dominant team, leading the league in ERA and in Runs Scored. Mostly, though, they did it with pitching, winning the ERA and shutout crowns behind Clark Griffith, and posting the only team ERA under 3.00 in the league. Their Runs Scored margin was not nearly so impressive as the ERA. On offense, what they had was walks and speed, leading the league in both free passes and stolen bases. They won again in 1906, but it was a fluke. Cleveland led the league in both ERA and Runs Scored, but finished third. The Sox led the league in only two team categories, shutouts (Ed Walsh ran amok) and walks.

The great team that became the Black Sox won their first pennant in 1917, with a truly dominant outfit that led the league by sincere margins in both ERA and Runs Scored. The only way the current Cubbies are going to get like that is to sign about $150 million of free agents, all at the skill positions. The 1919 team was not so strong, largely because 1917 relief ace Dave Danforth was ineffective. They won because they scored runs, and they scored runs because they had the highest batting average and the most stolen bases, not because, as myth would have it, they had the most power.

The Black Sox cursed Comiskey Park pretty seriously. The only pennant winner left to the field was the 1959 "go-go" White Sox, who won with pitching and defense, leading the league in almost nothing but ERA and Stolen Bases. Expansion didn't help. The only division title won in Comiskey came in 1983, when the Sox had a monster power outfield, like the Cubs have now, only better. The '83 team led the league in Runs Scored; and their division in Slugging Percentage and Walks, overcoming the efforts of a mediocre pitching staff.

Before we look at actual Cubbie teams in Wrigley Field, I want to dwell on the sort of teams that won in Comiskey. Of the four winners, three were offense driven. Those three teams led their league in Runs Scored, in spite of the fact that Comiskey was a notorious pitchers' park. That is, their offense was even more dominant than it seemed, and they won by defying the ballpark, rather than conforming to it. Remember that when we look at Wrigley winners.

Perhaps the greatest of all Chicago teams was the fabled "Tinker to Evers to Chance" NL pennant winners of 1906-1908 and 1910. This really should have been called the "Brown to Reulbach to Overall" team, in honor of the anchors of its brilliant pitching staff. Mordecai "Three Finger" Brown was the staff ace. Missing a finger due to a mining accident, Brown was perforce the inventor of the split-finger fastball. Obtained in 1905 from the Cardinals in a trade even more one-sided than Carlton for Rick Wise, Brown joined a team that already contained the double play combination and ace catcher Johnny Kling. Strong up the middle though that team was, it had been unable to overtake the Phillippe / Wagner Pirates or the Mathewson / McGinnity Giants.

In 1906, the dam broke. Frank Chance had his career year, scoring 103 runs, and the team scored 704, to lead the league by 79. Brown got his splitter completely under control and went 26-6 with a joke of a 1.06 ERA. Jack Pfiester arrived, at his peak at age 28. 23-year-old Ed Reulbach matured early, and posted a 1.05 ERA himself to complement Brown with a 19-4 record. Carl Lundgren pitched in with 17-6. And then, the midseason acquisitions came: 32-year-old Jack Taylor went 12-3, and Orval Overall matched that record at age 25. The result was a ludicrous six-man staff (in the days of three-man rotations) whose worst ERA was Lundgren's 2.21 (team ERA: 1.75) and whose worst winning percentage was Pfiester's .714 (20-8). They led the league in ERA by a brutal .57 runs per game, and won 116 games, still the record.

As it turned out, Chance and the offense were not for real, but the pitchers were. In 1907, the offense trailed the Pirates by 63, but the 1.73 team ERA led by .57 again. The Cubs won 107 games. In 1908, the Cubs won the closest of all NL races, by one game over both the Giants and the Pirates. The three team ERAs were 2.14, 2.14 and 2.12, respectively (Lundgren had collapsed), and the Giants actually outscored the Cubs by 27 runs. In 1909, the Cubs stripped Lundgren of his workload and won the ERA title by 32 points, but the Pirates outscored them by 69 runs and won 110 games. 1910 saw the arrival of King Cole, another ERA title, some offense from the outfield for a change, and therefore another pennant, but it was Overall's last good year, and Brown was aging at 34. The Cubs won the Runs Scored crown in 1911, but lost the ERA and the pennant to the Giants. That was Brown's, and the team's last top year.

The first good Wrigley Field team was the first team to use the park, the 1914-1915 Federal League Whales. 1914's edition led the league in ERA and finished second, one game behind Indianapolis. The 1915 team won the pennant, finishing second in ERA by .04 and second in Runs Scored by six.

Three years later, the 1918 Cubs slipped in a war-shortened pennant, tying the Reds in Runs Scored and leading the ERA race by .30 behind Hippo Vaughn. The team was not in general that good, though, and the next Cubbie contender was the 1929-1932 team that won both ends of that period. In general, this was an offense-driven team, winning the Runs Scored titles in 1929 and 1931, and finishing only 6 behind the 1930 Cards. The center of the offense was the outfield of Kiki Cuyler, Hack Wilson and Riggs Stephenson, along with catcher Gabby Hartnett and/or second sacker Rogers Hornsby. The 1932 pennant, though, was not won with offense (Wilson and Hornsby were through), but by leading the league in ERA, courtesy of hot rookie Lon Warneke.

Some say that the problem with the 1930-1931 losers was being managed by Rogers Hornsby, and it is true that he led those two teams and only those. If the problem was Hornsby, it was because he couldn't handle the pitching. The 1929 outfit came in second in ERA to complement the 1932 team, while the 1930-1931 staffs were mediocre. By 1933, no manager could help the Cubs, who had lost Hornsby and Wilson, while Stephenson, Cuyler and Hartnett were all well over 30.

By 1935, the Cubs had retooled, adding Stan Hack, Augie Galan and Phil Cavaretta on offense, and (original) Bill Lee and Larry French to the pitching staff. They led the league in both ERA and Runs Scored and won 100 games. After a couple of years chasing the Giants, they won again in 1938, leading the league in ERA once more. War-torn 1945 saw the last of the Cubbie pennants, featuring an ERA-leading staff headed by the immortal Hank Wyse (22-10) with a mighty assist from Hank Borowy's career half-year.

Since 1945, the Cubs have won a grand total of two division titles and no pennants. Both the 1984 and 1989 NL East winners led the division in Runs Scored, but not in ERA. And I think it's fair to say that winning the Runs Scored title has been the Cubbie strategy for the last couple of decades. And I also think it's fair to say that that's been a bad strategy.

It's not just that, of the six Wrigley Field pennant winners (including the Whales) four have won the league ERA title and two (including the Whales) have come in second. It's that those four winners are the only Wrigley Field teams to lead in ERA. In addition, the early Cubs played in a hitters' park too, and their great teams were ERA driven. In fact, from 1901-1910, only one team other than the Cubs managed to win the pennant without leading the league in Runs Scored, and that was the fluke 1901 season where the only offense besides Pittsburgh's was attached to a bad Cardinal pitching staff. In the Dead Ball Era, offense was rare enough that it generally won.

If you look at the White Sox teams, though, you see a different tale. Pale Hose winners have led in Runs Scored four times, and in ERA only three (counting double winners). The only dominant team Comiskey Park has ever seen was the offense-driven Black Sox, and the only recent winner was the offense-driven 1983 team. Comiskey, of course, has always been a pitchers' park.

In general, what the analysis seems to be saying is that Chicago teams win by attempting to dominate in the areas that their ballparks do not favor. Given that both Wrigley and Comiskey were pretty extreme examples of their biases, this makes sense, at least psychologically. I mean, to win in Wrigley by dominating offensively, you have to convince a team of hitters whose stats look just fine, and who are leading the league in Runs Scored, that this isn't enough. They've got to do more. That's not easy. On the other hand, you get some help in convincing your pitchers. They're stats won't look so hot, even if they're pitching well. They'll be easy to convince that there's another level yet to attain. The opposite, of course, is true in Comiskey.

Also, there's the effect, explored by Bill James in the ABSTRACTs, of having a bench with decent looking stats. It takes a rare breed of administrator to decide that a bench player with a reasonable batting average and some power is contributing nothing to the offense and needs to be replaced. The 1991 Cubs show obvious signs of this. Take the gas out of their bench stats, as Offensive Winning Percentage does, and you end up with no over-.500 players. Yet, the raw stats don't look that bad.

In the light of all this, I think the Cubbie pitching acquisitions were fine. That's not a popular opinion, but consider what you need in Wrigley. Yes, Danny Jackson's a gamble, but if he should stay healthy, he can dominate, not just be a #3 guy. Dave Smith is the same, and may yet pay off big. After all, 1991's problems could easily have been the results of the injury plus the problem of adjusting from the best pitchers' park in the league to the best hitters'. You need some luck to get both of them, plus the other Cubbie injury cases, to come through, but you always need a little luck to come up with a truly dominant pitching staff.

I have more questions about the batting order the Cubs have developed. As I mentioned last year, the Cubbie lineup is woefully weak in getting on base. Wrigley, as a hitters' park, is going to favor long-sequence offense, and the Cubs can't mount that long sequence. Note that those Comiskey teams that led their leagues in Runs Scored did have those walks. It's walks, not homers that generate the real run totals. The Cubs, though, have overloaded on right handed hitters with power but no walks. I can easily imagine good offenses (the Dodgers' for example) that would bat Ryne Sandberg fifth, much less Andre Dawson or George Bell. In the current Cubbie lineup, though, Sandberg has to be a table setter, and Mark Grace, the only Cub who does get on base a lot but also the only lefty, has to bat cleanup, where he lacks RBI power. I think there is little doubt that the Cubbie offense would improve if they traded George Bell for, say, Kal Daniels even up, and batted Grace or even Daniels leadoff, but who's going to do that?

Actually, I have doubts whether the Cubs have enough offense to really be trying to win right now. They're getting nothing out of short, third, center field and catcher, not to mention the bench. To win with that, they really are going to have to lead the league in ERA. Is it in fact yet time to cash in Sandberg for a horde of young pitching arms and a patient hitter who runs well? Well, I don't know about that, but Dawson or Bell? Yes.

Chicago Cubs Home Park Performance Factors

	Outs	Runs	Hits	2b	3b	HR	W	K	SH	SF	HBP	IBB	SB	CS	GDP
Home LH Batters	1.031	.928	1.011	.861	1.817	1.010	1.085	1.050	.848	1.649	1.272	1.147	.909	1.122	.681
Home RH Batters	.984	.913	.939	.982	1.124	.851	1.043	1.040	1.305	1.051	.781	1.065	1.088	1.543	1.196
All Home Batters	1.003	.929	.971	.956	1.267	.892	1.053	1.051	1.069	1.111	.889	1.132	.994	1.353	1.083
Opp LH Batters	1.070	1.008	.995	.997	1.038	.872	1.053	1.158	1.030	.968	.992	1.388	.918	.848	.977
Opp RH Batters	1.001	.984	1.037	1.251	1.104	.778	1.198	.927	1.280	1.086	1.891	1.205	1.262	.837	.932
All Opp Batters	1.035	1.009	1.021	1.109	1.049	.854	1.135	1.017	1.178	1.043	1.284	1.298	1.109	.880	.987
All LH Batters	1.055	.977	1.001	.945	1.184	.901	1.063	1.116	.952	1.074	1.124	1.289	.915	.967	.851
All RH Batters	.990	.942	.978	1.081	1.108	.840	1.107	.982	1.275	1.068	1.017	1.127	1.160	1.191	1.056
All Batters	1.019	.968	.995	1.029	1.108	.880	1.093	1.031	1.124	1.074	1.033	1.219	1.051	1.087	1.028

Conventional Batting Records for Chicago Cubs

	G	AB	Run	Hit	2B	3B	HR	TB	RBI	W	K	IW	HB	SB	CS	BRng Eff	GI DP	SH	SF	Avg	Slug	OBP	Runs Ctd
Wilkins R	86	203	21	45	9	0	6	72	22	19	56	2	6	3	3	.361	2	7	0	.222	.355	.307	23
Grace	160	619	87	169	28	5	8	231	58	70	53	7	3	3	4	.478	6	4	7	.273	.373	.346	85
Sandberg	158	585	104	170	32	2	26	284	100	87	89	4	2	22	8	.432	9	1	9	.291	.485	.379	115
Salazar L	103	333	34	86	14	1	14	144	38	15	45	1	1	0	3	.297	8	2	0	.258	.432	.292	39
Dunston	142	492	59	128	22	7	12	200	50	23	64	5	4	21	6	.563	9	4	11	.260	.407	.292	59
Bell Geo	149	558	63	159	27	0	25	261	86	32	62	6	4	2	6	.452	10	0	9	.285	.468	.323	82
Walton	123	270	42	59	13	1	5	89	17	19	55	0	3	7	3	.434	7	3	3	.219	.330	.275	24
Dawson	149	563	69	153	21	4	31	275	104	22	80	3	5	4	5	.358	10	0	6	.272	.488	.302	80
Walker C	124	374	51	96	10	1	6	126	34	33	57	2	0	13	5	.429	3	1	3	.257	.337	.315	42
Dascenzo	118	239	40	61	11	0	1	75	18	24	26	2	2	14	7	.547	3	6	1	.255	.314	.327	26
Villanueva	71	192	23	53	10	1	13	104	32	21	30	1	0	0	0	.118	3	0	1	.276	.542	.346	36
Smith Dw	90	167	16	38	7	2	3	58	21	11	32	2	1	2	3	.286	2	1	0	.228	.347	.279	16
Berryhill	62	159	13	30	7	0	5	52	14	11	41	1	1	1	2	.389	2	0	1	.189	.327	.244	12
Vizcaino	93	145	7	38	5	0	0	43	10	5	18	0	0	2	1	.333	1	2	2	.262	.297	.283	13
Maddux G	39	88	8	18	2	0	1	23	7	2	24	0	0	1	0	.429	1	11	0	.205	.261	.222	6
Landrum C	56	86	28	20	2	1	0	24	6	10	18	0	0	27	5	.607	2	3	0	.233	.279	.313	10
Scott G	31	79	8	13	3	0	1	19	5	13	14	4	3	0	1	.300	2	1	0	.165	.241	.305	6
Girardi	21	47	3	9	2	0	0	11	6	6	6	1	0	0	0	.333	0	1	0	.191	.234	.283	4
Bielecki	39	46	1	3	0	0	0	3	7	3	21	0	0	0	0	1.000	1	4	0	.065	.065	.122	1
Boskie	30	41	3	7	0	1	1	12	2	3	15	0	0	0	0	.500	0	3	0	.171	.293	.227	3
Castillo F	18	35	0	5	0	0	0	5	1	2	13	0	0	0	1	.000	0	6	0	.143	.143	.189	1
Sutcliffe	20	32	2	3	1	0	0	4	2	1	9	0	0	0	0	.667	1	5	0	.094	.125	.121	1
Lancaster	64	28	2	5	2	0	0	7	2	0	13	0	0	0	0	.667	0	6	0	.179	.250	.179	1
Scanlan	40	24	0	1	0	0	0	1	1	1	10	0	0	0	0	.000	3	2	0	.042	.042	.080	0
Jackson Dan	17	23	1	2	0	0	0	2	1	0	13	0	0	0	0	1.000	0	2	0	.087	.087	.087	0
Sanchez R	13	23	1	6	0	0	0	6	2	4	3	0	0	0	0	.429	0	0	0	.261	.261	.370	3
May D	15	22	4	5	2	0	1	10	3	2	1	0	0	0	0	.667	1	0	1	.227	.455	.280	3
Pappas	7	17	1	3	0	0	0	3	2	1	5	0	0	0	0	.667	0	0	0	.176	.176	.222	1
McElroy	71	10	1	3	1	0	0	4	2	0	3	0	0	0	1	1.000	0	0	0	.300	.400	.300	1
Strange	3	9	0	4	1	0	0	5	1	0	1	0	1	1	0	.000	0	0	1	.444	.556	.455	3
Harkey	4	5	2	2	0	0	0	2	0	1	0	0	0	0	0	.000	0	0	0	.400	.400	.500	1
Assenmacher	75	4	1	1	0	0	0	1	0	1	1	0	0	0	0	.000	0	0	0	.250	.250	.400	1
Smith Dv	35	1	0	0	0	0	0	0	0	0	0	0	0	0	0	.000	0	0	0	.000	.000	.000	0
Slocumb	52	1	0	0	0	0	0	0	0	0	0	0	0	0	0	.000	0	0	0	.000	.000	.000	0
Wilson S	9	1	0	0	0	0	0	0	0	0	1	0	0	0	0	.000	0	0	0	.000	.000	.000	0
Renfroe	4	1	0	0	0	0	0	0	0	0	0	0	0	0	0	.000	0	0	0	.000	.000	.000	0
Pavlas	1	0	0	0	0	0	0	0	0	0	0	0	0	0	0	.000	0	0	0	.000	.000	.000	0
May	2	0	0	0	0	0	0	0	0	0	0	0	0	0	0	.000	0	0	0	.000	.000	.000	0
Perez Y	3	0	0	0	0	0	0	0	0	0	0	0	0	0	0	.000	0	0	0	.000	.000	.000	0
TOTALS	2297	5522	695	1395	232	26	159	2156	654	442	879	41	36	123	64	.437	86	75	55	.253	.390	.309	678

Sabermetric Batting Records for Chicago Cubs

	Ball Park Adjusted												Runs		Run/					
	AB	Run	Hit	2B	3B	HR	RBI	W	SO	Avg	Slug	OBP	Ctd	Outs	27o	OW%	OG	OWAR	DWAR	TWAR
Bell Geo	552	59	157	30	0	20	84	35	60	.284	.447	.328	79	421	5.07	.560	16	3.27	0.02	3.29
Berryhill	160	12	29	7	0	4	13	12	42	.181	.300	.241	11	136	2.18	.191	5	-0.80	-0.22	-1.03
Dascenzo	241	38	60	11	0	0	17	26	26	.249	.295	.326	25	198	3.41	.365	7	0.11	0.05	0.16
Dawson	557	65	151	23	4	25	102	24	78	.271	.461	.305	76	427	4.81	.534	16	2.90	0.45	3.35
Dunston	487	55	126	24	7	9	49	25	62	.259	.392	.295	58	393	3.98	.440	15	1.31	1.51	2.83
Girardi	45	2	8	2	0	0	5	6	5	.178	.222	.275	3	38	2.13	.184	1	-0.23	-0.06	-0.30
Grace	641	84	169	26	7	7	54	74	58	.264	.359	.338	84	491	4.62	.514	18	2.98	1.03	4.01
Landrum C	89	27	20	1	1	0	5	10	19	.225	.258	.303	10	76	3.55	.385	3	0.10	0.02	0.12
May D	22	3	5	1	0	0	2	2	1	.227	.273	.280	2	18	3.00	.308	1	-0.03	0.07	0.04
Pappas	15	0	2	0	0	0	1	1	4	.133	.133	.188	0	13	0.00	.000	0	-0.17	-0.03	-0.19
Salazar L	329	32	84	15	1	11	37	16	44	.255	.407	.292	36	258	3.77	.413	10	0.60	0.09	0.69
Sanchez R	21	0	5	0	0	0	1	4	2	.238	.238	.360	2	16	3.38	.361	1	0.01	0.05	0.06
Sandberg	578	98	167	35	2	21	98	97	87	.289	.465	.388	113	439	6.95	.705	16	5.77	1.09	6.86
Scott G	77	7	12	3	0	0	4	14	13	.156	.195	.316	6	69	2.35	.214	3	-0.35	0.18	-0.17
Smith Dw	173	15	38	6	2	2	19	11	35	.220	.312	.270	15	138	2.93	.299	5	-0.26	0.18	-0.08
Strange	8	0	3	1	0	0	0	0	1	.375	.500	.400	2	6	9.00	.800	0	0.10	-0.03	0.07
Villanueva	189	21	52	11	1	10	31	23	29	.275	.503	.352	34	141	6.51	.677	5	1.71	-0.03	1.68
Vizcaino	146	6	37	5	0	0	9	5	18	.253	.288	.275	12	115	2.82	.282	4	-0.29	0.34	0.05
Walker C	378	49	95	10	1	5	32	36	58	.251	.323	.314	41	295	3.75	.411	11	0.66	0.27	0.93
Walton	267	39	58	14	1	4	16	21	54	.217	.322	.281	24	225	2.88	.291	8	-0.49	0.16	-0.33
Wilkins R	211	20	45	8	0	5	20	20	61	.213	.322	.300	22	175	3.39	.363	6	0.09	-0.36	-0.28
TOTALS	5592	673	1388	239	30	138	633	483	908	.248	.376	.309	665	4507	3.98	.440	167	15.03	4.77	19.81

Pitching Records for Chicago Cubs

	ERA	W	L	Pct	G	GS	CG	ShO	GF	Sv	IP	R	ER	H	2B	3B	HR	BB	IW	SO	HB	WP	BK
Maddux G	3.35	15	11	.577	37	37	7	2	0	0	263.0	113	98	232	34	9	18	66	9	198	6	6	3
Bielecki	4.50	13	11	.542	39	25	0	0	8	0	172.0	91	86	169	30	9	18	54	6	72	2	6	0
Boskie	5.23	4	9	.308	28	20	0	0	2	0	129.0	78	75	150	29	6	14	52	4	62	5	1	1
Castillo F	4.35	6	7	.462	18	18	4	0	0	0	111.2	56	54	107	23	2	5	33	2	73	0	5	1
Sutcliffe	4.10	6	5	.545	19	18	0	0	0	0	96.2	52	44	96	20	5	4	45	2	52	0	2	2
Jackson Dan	6.75	1	5	.167	17	14	0	0	0	0	70.2	59	53	89	15	1	8	48	4	31	1	1	1
Harkey	5.30	0	2	.000	4	4	0	0	0	0	18.2	11	11	21	4	0	3	6	1	15	0	1	0
Lancaster	3.52	9	7	.563	64	11	1	0	21	3	156.0	68	61	150	26	3	13	49	7	102	4	2	2
Scanlan	3.89	7	8	.467	40	13	0	0	16	1	111.0	60	48	114	19	5	5	40	3	44	3	5	1
Assenmacher	3.24	7	8	.467	75	0	0	0	31	15	102.2	41	37	85	13	4	10	31	6	117	3	4	0
McElroy	1.95	6	2	.750	71	0	0	0	12	3	101.1	33	22	73	10	1	7	57	7	92	0	1	0
Slocumb	3.45	2	1	.667	52	0	0	0	21	1	62.2	29	24	53	10	1	3	30	6	34	3	9	0
Smith Dv	6.00	0	6	.000	35	0	0	0	28	17	33.0	22	22	39	4	4	6	19	5	16	1	1	1
Wilson S	4.38	0	0	.000	8	0	0	0	2	0	12.1	7	6	13	3	0	1	5	1	9	0	0	0
Dascenzo	0.00	0	0	.000	3	0	0	0	3	0	4.0	0	0	2	0	0	0	2	0	2	0	0	0
Renfroe	13.50	0	1	.000	4	0	0	0	2	0	4.2	7	7	11	2	0	1	2	1	4	0	1	0
Perez Y	2.08	1	0	1.000	3	0	0	0	0	0	4.1	1	1	2	2	0	0	2	0	3	0	2	0
May	18.00	0	0	.000	2	0	0	0	1	0	2.0	4	4	6	2	0	0	1	0	1	0	1	0
Pavlas	18.00	0	0	.000	1	0	0	0	1	0	1.0	2	2	3	0	0	1	0	0	0	0	0	0
TOTALS	4.05	77	83	.481	520	160	12	2	148	40	1456.2	734	655	1415	246	50	117	542	64	927	28	48	12

Sabermetric Pitching Records for Chicago Cubs

	Adj	|-Expected-|			|——Opposing Batters——|												Supported				
	ERA	W	L	Pct	BFP	Avg	Slg	OBA	RC/G	GDP	SB	CS	PK	PKE	SH	SF	RSup	RSp/G	W	L	Pct
Assenmacher	3.07	9	6	.589	427	.223	.357	.284	3.54	3	8	5	0	1	8	4	50	4.38	10	5	.671
Bielecki	4.34	10	14	.417	718	.262	.420	.318	4.44	15	17	9	2	2	10	6	97	5.08	14	10	.577
Boskie	5.02	5	8	.348	582	.294	.456	.361	6.04	9	4	2	1	1	8	6	57	3.98	5	8	.385
Castillo F	4.19	6	7	.434	467	.252	.351	.304	3.75	5	7	4	0	1	6	3	50	4.03	6	7	.480
Dascenzo	0.00	0	0	.000	15	.154	.154	.267	1.18	1	0	0	0	0	0	0	4	9.00	0	0	.000
Harkey	4.82	1	1	.367	84	.273	.442	.321	5.55	1	2	0	0	0	0	1	7	3.38	1	1	.329
Jackson Dan	6.50	1	5	.242	347	.309	.451	.407	7.20	7	8	2	0	2	8	2	42	5.35	2	4	.404
Lancaster	3.40	9	7	.538	653	.256	.376	.315	4.02	6	14	14	1	0	9	4	76	4.38	10	6	.624
Maddux G	3.22	15	11	.566	1070	.237	.345	.288	3.44	14	25	7	5	0	16	3	130	4.45	17	9	.657
May	13.50	0	0	.069	12	.545	.727	.583	21.77	0	0	0	0	0	0	0	0	0.00	0	0	.000
McElroy	1.87	6	2	.795	419	.210	.305	.317	3.26	6	12	10	0	3	9	6	41	3.64	6	2	.792
Pavlas	9.00	0	0	.143	5	.750	1.500	.750	23.64	1	0	0	0	0	1	0	2	18.00	0	0	.800
Perez Y	0.00	0	0	.000	16	.167	.333	.250	2.20	0	0	1	0	1	0	2	5	10.38	0	0	.000
Renfroe	11.57	0	1	.092	27	.440	.640	.481	15.38	0	0	0	0	0	0	0	4	7.71	0	1	.308
Scanlan	3.73	7	8	.492	482	.269	.373	.332	4.20	11	5	7	0	0	8	6	39	3.16	6	9	.418
Slocumb	3.30	2	1	.553	274	.231	.323	.321	4.19	1	12	1	0	0	6	6	33	4.74	2	1	.673
Smith Dv	5.73	2	4	.291	151	.302	.535	.396	7.50	5	3	0	0	0	2	0	6	1.64	0	6	.075
Sutcliffe	3.91	5	6	.469	422	.264	.379	.338	4.69	12	21	2	0	0	5	8	49	4.56	6	5	.576
Wilson S	3.65	0	0	.503	53	.277	.404	.340	5.01	1	1	0	0	0	0	1	3	2.19	0	0	.265
TOTALS	3.91	75	85	.469	6224	.257	.384	.324	4.37	98	139	64	9	11	96	58	695	4.29	87	73	.547

Batting 'Splits' Records for Chicago Cubs

	G	AB	Run	Hit	2B	3B	HR	TB	RBI	W	K	IW	HB	SB	CS	GI DP	SH	SF	Avg	Slug	OBP	Runs Ctd
SPLITS for Chicago Cubs (all batters except pitchers)																						
vs LHP	961	2022	258	523	82	10	67	826	246	175	284	14	12	34	23	35	33	21	.259	.409	.318	265
vs RHP	1508	3500	437	872	150	16	92	1330	408	267	595	27	24	89	41	51	42	34	.249	.380	.304	413
Home	1200	2829	386	731	126	10	93	1156	362	217	425	17	21	66	23	40	37	26	.258	.409	.313	372
Away	1097	2693	309	664	106	16	66	1000	292	225	454	24	15	57	41	46	38	29	.247	.371	.305	307
Grass	1653	3945	526	1031	165	16	126	1606	497	301	605	28	24	87	44	60	53	38	.261	.407	.315	512
Turf	644	1577	169	364	67	10	33	550	157	141	274	13	12	36	20	26	22	17	.231	.349	.296	167
April/June	1068	2574	313	663	108	11	79	1030	298	196	406	25	22	50	31	44	32	24	.258	.400	.313	323
July/October	1229	2948	382	732	124	15	80	1126	356	246	473	16	14	73	33	42	43	31	.248	.382	.306	355

1991 SPLITS FOR Chicago Cubs

BATTING SPLITS

	AVG	AB	R	H	2B	3B	HR	RBI	SB	CS	BB	K	OBA	SPCT
Total	.253	5522	695	1395	232	26	159	654	123	64	442	879	.309	.390

	#Pit	#P/PA	GB	FB	G/F	G	IBB	HB	SH	SF	GDP
Miscellaneous	21798	3.56	1988	1577	1.26	159	41	36	75	55	86

	AVG	AB	R	H	2B	3B	HR	RBI	SB	CS	BB	K	OBA	SPCT
vs. Left	.259	2022	...	523	82	10	67	246	34	23	175	284	.318	.409
vs. Right	.249	3500	...	872	150	16	92	408	89	41	267	595	.304	.380
Home	.258	2829	386	731	126	10	93	362	66	23	217	425	.313	.409
Away	.247	2693	309	664	106	16	66	292	57	41	225	454	.305	.371
None on	.244	3268	...	799	133	12	91	91	0	0	243	527	.302	.376
Runners on	.264	2254	...	596	99	14	68	563	123	64	199	352	.320	.411
April	.231	698	87	161	31	3	19	81	17	5	63	99	.298	.365
May	.265	909	113	241	42	4	35	107	15	11	57	147	.311	.436
June	.270	967	113	261	35	4	25	110	18	15	76	160	.325	.392
July	.247	885	129	219	45	3	25	116	27	14	80	145	.311	.390
August	.257	1023	126	263	38	7	20	117	20	8	69	167	.304	.367
September	.246	881	104	217	32	5	29	102	18	10	74	130	.305	.393
October	.208	159	23	33	9	0	6	21	8	1	23	31	.304	.377
None on/out	.244	1412	...	344	69	6	45	45	0	0	102	219	.300	.397
Scoring Posn	.249	1286	...	320	51	9	41	482	28	12	146	215	.318	.398
Close & Late	.257	1134	...	292	49	7	26	138	35	12	101	206	.321	.382
Bases Loaded	.282	85	...	24	1	0	4	72	0	0	6	10	.291	.435
Batting #1	.243	672	105	163	22	2	8	41	30	10	55	100	.303	.317
Batting #2	.283	650	111	184	30	6	12	58	19	10	69	68	.349	.403
Batting #3	.280	604	89	169	31	1	21	105	17	6	89	76	.370	.439
Batting #4	.270	649	77	175	22	1	33	109	5	6	34	94	.304	.459
Batting #5	.278	643	82	179	33	4	25	100	10	10	35	79	.320	.459
Batting #6	.243	625	63	152	33	2	24	78	13	7	40	120	.290	.418
Batting #7	.249	594	63	148	25	4	15	58	14	8	36	103	.290	.380
Batting #8	.229	558	55	128	24	3	12	55	10	4	51	81	.305	.348
Batting #9	.184	527	50	97	12	3	9	50	5	3	33	158	.233	.269
As p	.144	340	20	49	6	1	2	25	1	1	13	122	.176	.185
As c	.230	570	55	131	27	0	23	69	3	5	54	127	.303	.398
As 1b	.265	637	89	169	28	5	8	59	3	4	72	52	.339	.363
As 2b	.288	617	107	178	33	1	26	101	23	8	89	90	.375	.472
As 3b	.255	619	68	158	20	1	16	55	7	6	38	93	.302	.368
As ss	.260	592	61	154	27	7	12	60	22	6	28	79	.292	.390
As lf	.282	639	75	180	30	1	24	92	6	8	41	71	.324	.444
As cf	.237	634	99	150	28	2	10	47	38	13	61	107	.306	.334
As rf	.268	650	74	174	25	5	31	111	5	6	29	93	.302	.465
Outfield	.262	1923	248	504	83	8	65	250	49	27	131	271	.311	.415
0.0 count	.311	749	...	233	46	7	28	110	...	...	2	0	.314	.503
After (0.1)	.227	2515	...	572	79	10	55	244	...	...	102	579	.260	.332
After (1.0)	.261	2258	...	590	107	9	76	300	...	...	309	300	.351	.418
Two strikes	.183	2428	...	445	65	10	46	192	...	...	167	876	.239	.275
Grass	.261	3945	526	1031	165	16	126	497	87	44	301	605	.315	.407
Turf	.231	1577	169	364	67	10	33	157	36	20	141	274	.296	.349
Day	.254	2761	363	701	112	12	84	335	69	28	213	431	.309	.394
Night	.251	2761	332	694	120	14	75	319	54	36	229	448	.310	.386
Inning 1.6	.249	3627	460	902	153	16	111	431	75	46	282	555	.304	.392
Inning 7+	.260	1895	235	493	79	10	48	223	48	18	160	324	.320	.388
vs.Atl	.242	385	55	93	11	1	18	53	10	6	30	59	.299	.416
vs.Cin	.251	422	49	106	22	0	12	46	10	6	25	67	.290	.389
vs.Hou	.259	406	60	105	26	1	11	55	6	6	43	74	.325	.409
vs.LA	.248	419	41	104	13	1	6	41	9	1	22	83	.288	.327
vs.Mon	.244	581	71	142	25	3	15	69	13	9	44	98	.296	.375
vs.NYN	.265	607	78	161	22	5	15	72	14	6	35	87	.308	.392
vs.Phi	.226	650	69	147	20	3	16	64	14	4	75	109	.311	.340
vs.Pit	.256	644	98	165	26	4	25	90	12	6	53	94	.316	.425
vs.StL	.250	599	83	150	34	4	16	75	21	5	54	95	.317	.401
vs.SD	.271	414	45	112	16	2	11	44	5	6	21	62	.305	.399
vs.SF	.278	395	46	110	17	2	14	45	9	9	40	51	.345	.438

PITCHING SPLITS

	ERA	W	L	SV	SVOP	GS	CG	SHO	IP	H	ER	HR	BB	IBB	K
Total	4.03	76	83	39	67	160	12	3	1456.2	1415	653	117	542	64	927

	#Pit	#P/IP	GB	FB	G/F	BRp9	RA	WP	BK	SH	SF	R	HB	Hld
Miscellaneous	22508	15.45	2156	1344	1.60	12.26	360	48	12	96	58	734	28	38

	ERA	W	L	SV	SVOP	GS	CG	SHO	IP	H	ER	HR	BB	IBB	K
ST	4.35	48	54	0	0	160	12	2	957.0	972	463	76	331	27	542
REL	3.46	29	29	40	67	0	0	0	499.2	443	192	41	211	37	385
Home	4.02	46	37	24	34	83	4	0	773.0	763	345	75	257	25	501
Away	4.08	31	46	16	33	77	8	2	683.2	652	310	42	285	39	426
April	3.68	10	11	7	12	21	0	0	188.1	158	77	15	68	10	107
May	3.95	14	12	11	13	26	1	0	236.2	220	104	18	83	11	141
June	4.08	10	18	7	13	28	0	0	249.1	254	113	16	117	17	164
July	4.86	14	11	6	8	25	4	1	235.1	274	127	22	61	7	159
August	3.50	17	12	4	10	29	4	0	269.2	249	105	22	98	10	179
September	4.60	8	18	4	7	26	1	0	228.2	220	117	22	98	9	150
October	2.22	4	1	1	4	5	2	1	48.2	40	12	2	17	0	27
Grass	4.16	59	56	29	43	115	8	0	1048.2	1039	485	93	377	44	679
Turf	3.75	18	27	11	24	45	4	2	408.0	376	170	24	165	20	248
Day	4.31	43	39	23	35	82	6	0	744.2	741	357	71	264	33	487
Night	3.77	34	44	17	32	78	6	2	712.0	674	298	46	278	31	440
vs.Atl	4.76	6	6	5	6	12	0	0	104.0	120	55	5	35	4	58
vs.Cin	5.15	4	8	3	4	12	0	0	108.1	127	62	15	31	7	76
vs.Hou	3.00	9	3	4	4	12	3	1	108.0	98	36	6	28	2	60
vs.LA	4.86	2	10	1	4	12	1	0	107.1	117	58	10	50	3	60
vs.Mon	3.27	10	7	8	11	17	0	0	157.0	143	57	12	52	9	123
vs.NYN	3.17	11	6	2	2	17	4	0	159.0	131	56	7	48	6	89
vs.Phi	3.38	8	10	3	8	18	1	1	178.2	151	67	17	65	7	118
vs.Pit	6.01	7	11	3	9	18	0	0	164.2	185	110	22	74	7	96
vs.StL	3.65	10	8	5	9	18	2	0	160.1	153	65	6	68	5	91
vs.SD	4.41	4	8	1	3	12	0	0	104.0	97	51	12	55	5	87
vs.SF	3.25	6	6	5	7	12	1	0	105.1	93	38	5	36	9	69

OPPOSING BATTERS VS. PITCHERS.

	AVG	AB	R	H	2B	3B	HR	RBI	SB	CS	BB	K	OBA	SPCT
Total	.257	5499	734	1415	246	50	117	686	139	64	542	927	.324	.384
vs. Left	.268	2827	...	757	128	32	64	365	85	35	299	447	.338	.404
vs. Right	.246	2672	...	658	118	18	53	321	54	29	243	480	.309	.363
ST	.266	3658	511	972	175	37	76	422	86	39	331	542	.327	.396
REL	.241	1841	223	443	71	13	41	264	53	25	211	385	.318	.360
Home	.260	2931	396	763	124	26	75	373	64	42	257	501	.319	.397
Away	.254	2568	338	652	122	24	42	313	75	22	285	426	.329	.369
None on	.244	3111	...	760	142	23	63	63	0	0	273	536	.308	.365
Runners on	.274	2388	...	655	104	27	54	623	139	64	269	391	.343	.408
None on/out	.260	1348	...	350	64	12	30	30	0	0	146	205	.337	.392
Scoring Posn	.276	1448	...	399	62	19	31	550	42	9	199	242	.353	.409
vs 1st Batr	.279	305	...	85	12	4	10	60	4	2	43	63	.369	.443
1st IP	.265	1748	238	463	85	14	44	289	58	27	221	325	.344	.405
Inning 1.6	.261	3627	491	947	177	36	72	464	92	41	354	554	.326	.389
Inning 7+	.250	1872	243	468	69	14	45	222	47	23	188	373	.320	.374
Close & Late	.269	1083	...	291	44	11	26	149	27	17	126	229	.346	.402
0.0 count	.321	800	...	257	36	8	18	123	...	...	60	0	.369	.454
After (0.1)	.219	2411	...	527	104	23	35	253	...	...	128	616	.259	.324
After (1.0)	.276	2288	...	631	106	19	64	310	...	...	354	311	.371	.423
Two strikes	.190	2374	...	450	79	21	27	211	...	...	206	927	.254	.275
Pitch 1.15	.265	1522	...	403	66	13	43	211	38	23	178	257	.340	.410
Pitch 16.30	.232	1141	...	265	52	9	18	130	36	10	109	239	.298	.341
Pitch 31.45	.266	772	...	205	37	6	15	95	14	9	78	141	.336	.387
Pitch 46.60	.250	660	...	165	27	10	8	80	11	5	54	84	.305	.358
Pitch 61.75	.265	592	...	157	28	5	15	70	16	9	47	71	.324	.405
Pitch 76.90	.233	430	...	100	16	2	8	46	16	3	41	75	.302	.335
Pitch 91.105	.320	281	...	90	17	3	6	40	5	3	20	41	.365	.466
Pitch 106.20	.286	91	...	26	3	1	4	11	3	2	14	17	.377	.473
Pitch 121.35	.308	13	...	4	0	1	0	3	0	0	1	2	.357	.462

New York Mets

Brock J. Hanke

NEW YORK											
YEAR	1982	1983	1984	1985	1986	1987	1988	1989	1990	1991	TOT
W	65	68	90	98	108	92	100	87	91	77	876
L	97	94	72	64	54	70	60	75	71	84	741
WPCT	0.401	0.420	0.556	0.605	0.667	0.568	0.625	0.537	0.562	0.478	0.542
R	609	575	652	695	783	823	703	683	775	640	6938
RA	723	680	676	568	578	698	532	595	613	646	6309
PWPT	0.415	0.417	0.482	0.600	0.647	0.582	0.636	0.569	0.615	0.495	0.547
PythW	67	68	78	97	105	94	103	92	100	80	89
PythL	95	94	84	65	57	68	59	70	62	82	73
LUCK	-2	0	12	1	3	-2	-3	-5	-9	-3	-8

Defensive Efficiency Record: .6868

Alright, let's get right down to the screaming and shouting. Do you think the Mets have become the front-runners in this division? Well, then consider the following trades:

Gregg Jeffries for Bobby Bonilla
Kevin McReynolds for Eddie Murray
Hubie Brooks for Dave Gallagher
Keith Miller for Willie Randolph and Bill Pecota
Frank Viola for Bret Saberhagen

I rate this set of player moves about even, for reasons laid out in the Bobby Bonilla player comment. Some of the moves gain quality, but lose age. Some gain age but lose quality. Overall, the quality gain is not better concentrated than it was before. Nor is it more in the skill positions. You might think that the Mets have picked up a couple of years of leadoff hitting in Willie Randolph, but they're going to hit Vince Coleman there. Coleman and Randolph is no better than Coleman and Jeffries. The Mets only win this collection if Jeffries never develops and/or Viola never comes back and Bret Saberhagen never collapses again. That's hardly enough to make up the godawful deficit the Mets have to gain on the Pirates.

What's more, the moves and their advertised consequences do not address the needs of the Mets. The Mets had plenty of pitching, even with an off year from Frank Viola. Bret Saberhagen will be better than Frank was in 1991, but so will Frank, in all likelihood. He doesn't really figure to help.

What the Mets needed was two things: strength up the middle, and to sort out their outfielders. As for the former, they gained not one whit. In fact, they lost ground. The current Met plan is to play an infield of Murray, Randolph, Elster and Magadan. That's Randolph and Elster up the middle. They have not changed their catching corps at all, so they gain nothing. Their center fielder is still Vince Coleman. The net change is Willie Randolph for Gregg Jeffries. That may look like a big gain on defense,until you realize how old Willie is. What's more, in the process, the Mets gave away Keith Miller, who is just as good a second baseman as Willie, and several years younger. They could always have replaced Jeffries with Miller, if they had wanted to.

That leads to the second need. The reason that the Mets wouldn't replace Gregg Jeffries with Keith Miller is that Gregg would have had to play the outfield, and the Mets were already full up with flycatchers. Although they had no real center fielders (no, Vince Coleman is not, either), they had a grand total of five candidates for the two other spots. There were the incumbents, Kevin McReynolds and Hubie Brooks. There was Darryl Boston. There was the aforementioned Jeffries. And there was also Mackey Sasser, who was being tortured with a plan to put him behind the plate, where he was losing ground to a phobia.

As of now, the Mets have ** candidates for the two spots. Acquiring Eddie Murray has induced the Mets to move first baseman Dave Magadan to third base, on the grounds that he'll be better on defense there than Howard Johnson, who plays badly at shortstop. That moves Hojo to the outfield. He joins the above Boston and Sasser. But they won't play; Hojo's partner will be Bobby Bo. Dave Gallagher is now Boston's caddy who is Coleman's caddy.

You might argue that Hojo and Bobby Bo are a whole lot better outfield pair than McReynolds and Hubie. I would agree with you, if that were the actual tradeoff. But it's not; there are four positions to be considered, because of the move of Hojo from third. The question is whether Hojo, Bobby, Dave Magadan and Eddie Murray are better than Hojo, Kevin McReynolds, Magadan and a platoon of Hubie and Gregg Jeffries, which is what the Mets would have had if they'd just put Miller at the keystone and let the dominos fall.

Ah, but Bobby Bonilla and Eddie Murray both switch hit! Well, so does Gregg Jeffries. So, for that matter, does a platoon of Mackey Sasser and Kevin McReynolds, if you must have switchers. What's more, the platoon might have done something to actually develop Sasser, who sure looks like he could hit if he only could get a settled job. All in all, the best things you can say about the moves are 1) Dave Gallagher is a better late-inning center field replacement than Darryl Boston, if you pinch hit for your leadoff man, and 2) Bill Pecota is a better backup second baseman and third baseman if you're going to pinch hit for your #2 batter or Dave Magadan, who is only in the lineup for his bat. There's still nobody to play shortstop if you pinch hit for Kevin Elster, as you should.

In the lineup, the Mets will realize a short-term gain over the 1991 season. the reason for this is that Gregg Jeffries, responding to being played out of position, hit very badly last year. If you look at the batting stats, you will see that Keith Miller actually outhit Gregg. And thus, the Met starting batting order of:

Coleman
Magadan
Jeffries
Hojo
McReynolds
Brooks
catcher
Elster

will improve at the #3 spot to something like:

Coleman
Randolph
Bonilla
Hojo
Murray
Magadan
catcher
Elster

The real problem with the first lineup, though, wasn't the #3 spot. That could have been fixed at any time by just moving Jeffries to the outfield. The real problem was that there was no way to pinch hit for the #8 man. Oh, the Mets tried. They would hit for Kevin Elster and then play Hojo at short. That's not exactly what is meant by "late inning defense." The fact remains that the Met lineup had a three-slot hole at #7, #8 and the pitcher, and only two of them could be covered in an emergency. Please remember that the Pirates will bat a lineup like:

Merced/Redus	1b
Bell	ss
Van Slyke	cf
Bonds	lf
Varsho/McClendon	rf
Lavalliere/Slaught	c
Buechele/King	3b
Lind	2b

That's not as strong in right field as you'd like but it's OK. It also has only one hole, at second base. Needless to say, it's easier to find a good-field-no-hit second baseman than a shortstop. Curtis Wilkerson is already on the roster. The Pirates can pinch hit at any time.

In all this light, I just don't see that the Mets have come close to catching the Pirates. I'm not even sure they've caught the Cardinals, and I think the Cardinal management is a disaster right now. I wouldn't be totally surprised to find out that the Cubs have passed the Mets, pitchers or no pitchers.

I'm also not completely sure that the Mets even have enough talent on hand to trade for the mighty team they'd like to build. They need to improve at three lineup spots: shortstop, catcher and center field. They also need some bench help. They have a couple of left/right fielders to trade. That and a pitcher, if they want to have a weak #5 spot. I don't think they can make that conversion. I sure wouldn't give them what they need for what they have, unless Saberhagen were the pitcher they had in mind.

What has happened to the Mets, for those of you who are snowblind from the media blizzard, is that the fabled Met farm system has failed to come through. The last top prospect they got was Jeffries, and that's been years. After him, they've got Sasser, who couldn't play a skill spot, either. Then, I guess it's David Innis, who isn't exactly Doc Gooden.

Books ago, I wrote about this. The Mets' success in the 1980's was largely fueled by Gooden and Darryl Strawberry, and the trade for Keith Hernandez. They got all three players because they were bad. Straw came as a #1 in the whole draft. That's just luck. Sometimes you get Darryl, sometimes it's Jeff King. Doc was, if I remember right, a #5 or something; again, high in the first round. Hernandez had to be unloaded on someone; Whitey decided to give him to the Mets because they were so bad at the time, it looked like Keith would never come back to haunt the Cardinals.

But, then, the Mets got good. They quit getting the ripoff trade offers. They quit getting top choices in the draft. And then, their farm system let them down. It didn't develop a top middle infielder. It didn't develop anybody who could hit and go get fly balls, either. It couldn't come up with a catcher. Instead, it came up with a string of left fielders who could hit. That's fine, but you can only play one at a time. And the Mets never did convert them into what they really needed. They kept trading for people whose skills duplicated the ones they already had. That was the weakness of the Dave Johnson organization; now Jeff Torborg has to pay for it.

New York Mets Home Park Performance Factors

	Outs	Runs	Hits	2b	3b	HR	W	K	SH	SF	HBP	IBB	SB	CS	GDP
Home LH Batters	1.016	.951	1.033	1.051	.691	.910	1.019	.900	1.102	.926	2.072	.811	.832	.731	1.712
Home RH Batters	1.066	1.063	1.046	1.022	1.099	1.221	1.058	1.192	1.577	.791	.927	1.064	.860	1.015	1.031
All Home Batters	1.041	1.010	1.029	1.039	.934	1.080	1.017	1.049	1.262	.871	1.025	.990	.911	.937	1.121
Opp LH Batters	1.113	1.107	1.061	1.145	1.111	1.120	1.203	1.060	1.074	.851	2.363	1.120	1.328	1.144	1.576
Opp RH Batters	1.086	1.053	1.074	1.105	.971	1.072	1.024	1.063	.971	.887	1.133	.827	.961	.923	1.384
All Opp Batters	1.099	1.079	1.071	1.131	.971	1.119	1.099	1.067	1.008	.891	1.244	.934	1.103	1.039	1.419
All LH Batters	1.070	1.038	1.044	1.104	.943	1.035	1.118	.991	1.100	.888	2.235	.999	1.145	.965	1.645
All RH Batters	1.076	1.056	1.060	1.062	.981	1.134	1.043	1.106	1.092	.844	1.022	.951	.918	.952	1.178
All Batters	1.071	1.045	1.049	1.086	.943	1.099	1.060	1.052	1.085	.882	1.128	.965	1.007	.989	1.255

Conventional Batting Records for New York Mets

	G	AB	Run	Hit	2B	3B	HR	TB	RBI	W	K	IW	HB	SB	CS	BRng Eff	GI DP	SH	SF	Avg	Slug	OBP	Runs Ctd
Cerone	90	227	18	62	13	0	2	81	16	30	24	2	1	1	1	.237	9	0	0	.273	.357	.360	29
Magadan	124	418	58	108	23	0	4	143	51	83	50	3	2	1	1	.477	5	7	7	.258	.342	.378	63
Jefferies	136	486	59	132	19	2	9	182	62	47	38	2	2	26	5	.391	12	1	3	.272	.374	.336	64
Johnson H	156	564	108	146	34	4	38	302	117	78	120	12	1	30	16	.444	4	0	15	.259	.535	.342	108
Elster	115	348	33	84	16	2	6	122	36	40	53	6	1	2	3	.333	4	1	4	.241	.351	.318	41
McReynolds	143	522	65	135	32	1	16	217	74	49	46	7	2	6	6	.447	8	1	4	.259	.416	.322	70
Coleman	72	278	45	71	7	5	1	91	17	39	47	0	0	37	14	.591	3	1	0	.255	.327	.347	35
Brooks	103	357	48	85	11	1	16	146	50	44	62	8	3	3	1	.453	7	0	3	.238	.409	.324	49
Miller K	98	275	41	77	22	1	4	113	23	23	44	0	5	14	4	.509	2	0	1	.280	.411	.345	42
Boston	137	255	40	70	16	4	4	106	21	30	42	0	0	15	8	.391	2	0	1	.275	.416	.350	38
Carreon	106	254	18	66	6	0	4	84	21	12	26	2	2	2	1	.286	14	1	1	.260	.331	.297	22
Sasser	96	228	18	62	14	2	5	95	35	9	19	2	1	0	2	.500	6	1	4	.272	.417	.298	26
Templeton	80	219	20	50	9	1	2	67	20	9	29	3	0	3	1	.344	7	4	2	.228	.306	.257	16
O'Brien C	69	168	16	31	6	0	2	43	14	17	25	1	4	0	2	.400	5	0	2	.185	.256	.272	12
Herr	70	155	17	30	7	0	1	40	14	32	21	4	0	7	2	.286	1	2	2	.194	.258	.328	17
Donnels	37	89	7	20	2	0	0	22	5	14	19	1	0	1	1	.364	0	1	0	.225	.247	.330	8
Cone	34	72	3	9	0	0	0	9	5	3	14	0	2	0	0	.250	4	6	1	.125	.125	.179	2
Viola	35	71	2	9	2	0	0	11	1	2	13	0	0	0	0	.000	1	10	0	.127	.155	.151	2
Gooden	27	63	7	15	3	0	1	21	6	0	9	0	0	1	1	.429	1	8	0	.238	.333	.238	5
Hundley	21	60	5	8	0	1	1	13	7	6	14	0	1	0	0	.500	3	1	1	.133	.217	.221	3
Gardner J	13	37	3	6	0	0	0	6	1	4	6	0	0	0	0	.000	0	0	1	.162	.162	.238	2
Teufel	20	34	2	4	0	0	1	7	2	2	8	0	0	1	1	.000	0	0	0	.118	.206	.167	1
Darling	17	34	0	4	3	0	0	7	1	0	14	0	0	0	0	1.000	0	5	0	.118	.206	.118	1
Whitehurst	36	33	2	6	1	0	0	7	0	2	6	0	0	0	0	.333	0	5	0	.182	.212	.229	2
Mcdaniel	23	29	3	6	1	0	0	7	2	1	11	0	0	2	0	.600	0	0	0	.207	.241	.233	2
Schourek	35	22	0	3	1	0	0	4	3	2	9	0	0	0	0	.000	0	0	0	.136	.182	.208	1
Young A	10	14	0	2	1	0	0	3	0	0	4	0	0	0	0	.500	0	1	0	.143	.214	.143	0
Fernandez S	8	13	1	2	1	0	0	3	0	0	7	0	0	0	0	.250	0	1	0	.154	.231	.154	1
Carr	12	11	1	2	0	0	0	2	1	0	2	0	0	1	0	.333	0	0	0	.182	.182	.182	0
Torve	10	8	0	0	0	0	0	0	0	0	1	0	0	0	0	.000	1	0	0	.000	.000	.000	0
Burke	35	5	0	0	0	0	0	0	0	0	4	0	0	0	0	.000	0	0	0	.000	.000	.000	0
Castillo T	10	4	0	0	0	0	0	0	0	0	0	0	0	0	0	.000	0	2	0	.000	.000	.000	0
Simons	42	3	0	0	0	0	0	0	0	0	0	0	0	0	0	.000	0	1	0	.000	.000	.000	0
Innis	69	2	0	0	0	0	0	0	0	0	1	0	0	0	0	.000	0	0	0	.000	.000	.000	0
Franco Jn	52	1	0	0	0	0	0	0	0	0	1	0	0	0	0	.000	0	0	0	.000	.000	.000	0
Pena A	44	0	0	0	0	0	0	0	0	0	0	0	0	0	0	.000	0	0	0	.000	.000	.000	0
Sauveur	6	0	0	0	0	0	0	0	0	0	0	0	0	0	0	.000	0	0	0	.000	.000	.000	0
Valera	2	0	0	0	0	0	0	0	0	0	0	0	0	0	0	.000	0	0	0	.000	.000	.000	0
Bross	8	0	0	0	0	0	0	0	0	0	0	0	0	0	0	.000	0	0	0	.000	.000	.000	0
Beatty	5	0	0	0	0	0	0	0	0	0	0	0	0	0	0	.000	0	0	0	.000	.000	.000	0
TOTALS	2206	5359	640	1305	250	24	117	1954	605	578	789	53	27	153	70	.416	99	60	52	.244	.365	.317	644

Sabermetric Batting Records for New York Mets

	Ball Park Adjusted								Runs		Run/									
	AB	Run	Hit	2B	3B	HR	RBI	W	SO	Avg	Slug	OBP	Ctd	Outs	27o	OW%	OG	OWAR	DWAR	TWAR
Boston	269	41	73	17	3	4	21	33	41	.271	.401	.351	40	206	5.24	.633	8	2.16	0.08	2.24
Brooks	382	50	90	11	1	18	54	45	69	.236	.411	.319	52	302	4.65	.575	11	2.52	0.24	2.76
Carr	11	1	2	0	0	0	1	0	2	.182	.182	.182	0	9	0.00	.000	0	-0.12	0.03	-0.08
Carreon	271	19	69	6	0	4	22	12	29	.255	.321	.291	21	219	2.59	.296	8	-0.44	0.21	-0.23
Cerone	242	19	65	13	0	2	17	31	27	.269	.347	.354	29	187	4.19	.524	7	1.20	0.14	1.34
Coleman	295	46	74	7	4	1	17	41	49	.251	.312	.342	36	238	4.08	.511	9	1.42	-0.07	1.35
Donnels	93	7	20	2	0	0	5	15	18	.215	.237	.324	9	74	3.28	.403	3	0.15	0.12	0.26
Elster	373	34	89	17	2	6	38	41	59	.239	.343	.313	42	294	3.86	.483	11	1.44	0.61	2.05
Gardner J	39	3	6	0	0	0	1	4	5	.154	.154	.233	2	33	1.64	.144	1	-0.25	-0.05	-0.30
Herr	164	17	31	7	0	1	14	33	22	.189	.250	.323	17	138	3.33	.410	5	0.30	0.65	0.96
Hundley	63	5	8	0	0	1	7	6	14	.127	.175	.214	2	59	0.92	.050	2	-0.66	0.17	-0.49
Jefferies	516	61	138	20	1	9	65	49	40	.267	.362	.332	64	400	4.32	.539	15	2.80	-0.33	2.47
Johnson H	600	112	153	36	3	41	123	82	126	.255	.530	.339	112	480	6.30	.713	18	6.46	0.03	6.49
Magadan	443	59	113	25	0	4	52	92	49	.255	.339	.383	66	351	5.08	.618	13	3.48	0.51	4.00
Mcdaniel	30	3	6	1	0	0	2	1	11	.200	.233	.226	2	24	2.25	.241	1	-0.10	0.04	-0.06
McReynolds	559	68	143	34	1	18	80	51	51	.256	.417	.319	74	434	4.60	.571	16	3.55	0.75	4.30
Miller K	294	43	81	23	1	4	24	23	49	.276	.401	.339	42	218	5.20	.629	8	2.25	0.52	2.78
O'Brien C	179	16	32	6	0	2	15	17	28	.179	.246	.264	11	155	1.92	.187	6	-0.94	0.14	-0.80
Sasser	240	18	64	15	1	5	35	9	18	.267	.400	.295	26	190	3.69	.461	7	0.78	-0.06	0.72
Templeton	232	20	52	9	0	2	21	9	30	.224	.289	.252	16	193	2.24	.239	7	-0.79	0.54	-0.26
Teufel	36	2	4	0	0	1	2	2	9	.111	.194	.158	1	32	0.84	.043	1	-0.36	0.04	-0.33
Torve	8	0	0	0	0	0	0	0	0	.000	.000	.000	0	9	0.00	.000	0	-0.12	0.01	-0.11
TOTALS	5708	668	1370	271	22	128	637	611	834	.240	.362	.315	668	4645	3.88	.486	172	23.38	4.32	27.71

Pitching Records for New York Mets

	ERA	W	L	Pct	G	GS	CG	ShO	GF	Sv	IP	R	ER	H	2B	3B	HR	BB	IW	SO	HB	WP	BK
Cone	3.29	14	14	.500	34	34	5	2	0	0	232.2	95	85	204	29	7	13	73	2	241	5	17	1
Viola	3.97	13	15	.464	35	35	3	0	0	0	231.1	112	102	259	41	4	25	54	4	132	1	6	1
Gooden	3.60	13	7	.650	27	27	3	1	0	0	190.0	80	76	185	33	6	12	56	2	150	3	5	2
Whitehurst	4.18	7	12	.368	36	20	0	0	6	1	133.1	67	62	142	24	5	12	25	3	87	4	3	4
Darling	3.87	5	6	.455	17	17	0	0	0	0	102.1	50	44	96	16	6	9	28	1	58	6	9	4
Young A	3.10	2	5	.286	10	8	0	0	2	0	49.1	20	17	48	8	1	4	12	1	20	1	1	0
Fernandez S	2.86	1	3	.250	8	8	0	0	0	0	44.0	18	14	36	3	1	4	9	0	31	0	0	0
Schourek	4.27	5	4	.556	35	8	1	1	7	2	86.1	49	41	82	14	6	7	43	4	67	2	1	0
Innis	2.66	0	2	.000	69	0	0	0	29	0	84.2	30	25	66	10	3	2	23	6	47	0	4	0
Pena A	2.71	6	1	.857	44	0	0	0	24	4	63.0	20	19	63	9	1	5	19	4	49	0	1	2
Simons	5.19	2	3	.400	42	1	0	0	11	1	60.2	40	35	55	13	1	5	19	5	38	2	3	0
Franco Jn	2.93	5	9	.357	52	0	0	0	48	30	55.1	27	18	61	8	3	2	18	4	45	1	6	0
Burke	2.75	3	3	.500	35	0	0	0	15	1	55.2	22	17	55	9	1	5	12	2	34	0	2	0
Castillo T	1.90	1	0	1.000	10	3	0	0	1	0	23.2	7	5	27	4	0	1	6	1	10	0	0	0
Bross	1.80	0	0	.000	8	0	0	0	4	0	10.0	2	2	7	1	0	1	3	0	5	0	0	0
Beatty	2.79	0	0	.000	5	0	0	0	1	0	9.2	3	3	9	3	0	0	4	1	7	0	1	0
Sauveur	10.80	0	0	.000	6	0	0	0	0	0	3.1	4	4	7	1	1	1	2	0	4	0	0	0
Valera	0.00	0	0	.000	2	0	0	0	1	0	2.0	0	0	1	0	0	0	4	1	3	0	0	0
TOTALS	3.56	77	84	.478	475	161	12	4	149	39	1437.1	646	569	1403	226	46	108	410	41	1028	25	59	14

Sabermetric Pitching Records for New York Mets

	Adj ERA	Expected W	Expected L	Expected Pct	Opposing Batters BFP	Avg	Slg	OBA	RC/G	GDP	SB	CS	PK	PKE	SH	SF	Supported RSup	RSp/G	W	L	Pct
Beatty	2.79	0	0	.634	42	.250	.333	.317	3.90	0	1	1	0	0	1	1	2	1.86	0	0	.308
Bross	1.80	0	0	.806	39	.200	.314	.263	2.57	1	0	0	0	0	1	0	6	5.40	0	0	.900
Burke	2.75	4	2	.641	231	.255	.375	.291	3.68	6	1	0	0	1	1	2	20	3.23	3	3	.581
Castillo T	1.90	1	0	.789	104	.281	.354	.320	4.33	1	3	1	1	0	1	1	10	3.80	1	0	.800
Cone	3.40	15	13	.538	966	.235	.329	.296	3.46	8	27	13	1	4	13	7	108	4.18	17	11	.601
Darling	3.96	5	6	.463	427	.251	.395	.310	4.39	4	12	2	3	4	7	4	44	3.87	5	6	.489
Fernandez S	2.86	2	2	.622	177	.222	.327	.262	2.99	1	3	1	0	0	5	1	21	4.30	3	1	.692
Franco Jn	2.93	9	5	.611	247	.271	.360	.328	4.25	6	4	2	0	2	3	0	12	1.95	4	10	.308
Gooden	3.74	10	10	.491	789	.257	.369	.311	3.88	15	33	16	0	2	5	4	108	5.12	13	7	.651
Innis	2.76	1	1	.638	336	.219	.291	.270	2.54	6	6	5	0	0	6	5	24	2.55	1	1	.460
Pena A	2.71	5	2	.647	261	.267	.377	.317	4.10	4	8	4	0	0	2	4	23	3.29	4	3	.594
Sauveur	10.80	0	0	.104	19	.467	.867	.529	18.67	0	0	0	0	0	2	0	0	0.00	0	0	.000
Schourek	4.38	4	5	.413	385	.248	.390	.334	5.17	1	12	0	0	0	5	4	39	4.07	4	5	.463
Simons	5.34	2	3	.321	258	.246	.379	.305	3.96	3	5	4	0	2	9	4	31	4.60	2	3	.426
Valera	0.00	0	0	.000	11	.143	.143	.455	5.32	0	1	0	0	0	0	0	0	0.00	0	0	.000
Viola	4.12	12	16	.442	980	.286	.423	.325	4.60	16	6	16	0	7	15	5	90	3.50	12	16	.419
Whitehurst	4.32	8	11	.420	556	.274	.409	.311	4.20	12	9	8	0	1	6	3	80	5.40	12	7	.610
Young A	3.10	4	3	.584	202	.257	.374	.303	3.85	4	3	1	0	0	1	1	22	4.01	4	3	.626
TOTALS	3.72	79	82	.494	6030	.257	.374	.309	3.99	88	134	74	5	23	83	46	640	4.01	86	75	.537

Batting 'Splits' Records for New York Mets

	G	AB	Run	Hit	2B	3B	HR	TB	RBI	W	K	IW	HB	SB	CS	GIDP	SH	SF	Avg	Slug	OBP	Runs Ctd
SPLITS for Brooks																						
vs LHP	57	121	16	30	5	0	5	50	17	18	13	1	0	2	1	2	0	1	.248	.413	.343	18
vs RHP	88	236	32	55	6	1	11	96	33	26	49	7	3	1	0	5	0	2	.233	.407	.315	31
Home	49	172	25	41	6	1	4	61	22	27	28	3	1	2	1	4	0	3	.238	.355	.340	22
Away	54	185	23	44	5	0	12	85	28	17	34	5	2	1	0	3	0	0	.238	.459	.309	27
Grass	77	270	39	68	9	1	10	109	37	32	47	4	1	3	1	7	0	3	.252	.404	.330	37
Turf	26	87	9	17	2	0	6	37	13	12	15	4	2	0	0	0	0	0	.195	.425	.307	12
April/June	62	220	35	60	8	1	13	109	40	31	37	5	2	2	0	4	0	3	.273	.495	.363	42
July/October	41	137	13	25	3	0	3	37	10	13	25	3	1	1	1	3	0	0	.182	.270	.258	10
SPLITS for Elster																						
vs LHP	74	159	12	47	9	0	1	59	14	17	16	3	0	1	2	1	0	1	.296	.371	.362	22
vs RHP	81	189	21	37	7	2	5	63	22	23	37	3	1	1	1	3	1	3	.196	.333	.282	19
Home	61	181	12	48	11	0	3	68	14	19	24	4	1	2	2	1	0	2	.265	.376	.335	24
Away	54	167	21	36	5	2	3	54	22	21	29	2	0	0	1	3	1	2	.216	.323	.300	17
Grass	77	232	18	62	14	1	3	87	21	24	29	6	1	2	2	3	1	3	.267	.375	.335	30
Turf	38	116	15	22	2	1	3	35	15	16	24	0	0	0	1	1	0	1	.190	.302	.286	11
April/June	49	148	12	35	8	1	3	54	22	17	21	4	0	1	1	1	0	2	.236	.365	.311	18
July/October	66	200	21	49	8	1	3	68	14	23	32	2	1	1	2	3	1	2	.245	.340	.323	23
SPLITS for Jefferies																						
vs LHP	79	174	25	51	10	1	1	66	18	15	9	0	1	9	2	4	0	0	.293	.379	.353	24
vs RHP	114	312	34	81	9	1	8	116	44	32	29	2	1	17	3	8	1	3	.260	.372	.328	40
Home	69	244	35	72	10	1	5	99	28	30	21	1	0	14	1	5	0	1	.295	.406	.371	40
Away	67	242	24	60	9	1	4	83	34	17	17	1	2	12	4	7	1	2	.248	.343	.300	25
Grass	99	364	45	101	14	1	7	138	44	33	30	1	0	17	4	10	0	3	.277	.379	.335	47
Turf	37	122	14	31	5	1	2	44	18	14	8	1	2	9	1	2	1	0	.254	.361	.341	17
April/June	56	206	28	56	11	0	5	82	32	21	19	0	1	15	3	4	1	1	.272	.398	.341	30
July/October	80	280	31	76	8	2	4	100	30	26	19	2	1	11	2	8	0	2	.271	.357	.333	34
SPLITS for New York Mets (all batters except pitchers)																						
vs LHP	1036	2051	209	510	94	4	34	714	196	191	291	18	8	53	25	46	21	16	.249	.348	.313	227
vs RHP	1407	3308	431	795	156	20	83	1240	409	387	498	35	19	100	45	53	39	36	.240	.375	.320	418
Home	1136	2670	332	657	123	12	57	975	307	300	390	28	14	88	39	46	24	32	.246	.365	.322	330
Away	1070	2689	308	648	127	12	60	979	298	278	399	25	13	65	31	53	36	20	.241	.364	.313	315
Grass	1576	3787	453	925	176	15	78	1365	425	398	558	40	16	110	53	72	43	42	.244	.360	.316	446
Turf	630	1572	187	380	74	9	39	589	180	180	231	13	11	43	17	27	17	10	.242	.375	.322	199
April/June	985	2413	327	594	124	12	60	922	307	302	344	31	9	87	37	39	29	25	.246	.382	.329	321
July/October	1221	2946	313	711	126	12	57	1032	298	276	445	22	18	66	33	60	31	27	.241	.350	.308	324

1991 SPLITS FOR New York Mets

BATTING SPLITS

	AVG	AB	R	H	2B	3B	HR	RBI	SB	CS	BB	K	OBA	SPCT
Total	.244	5359	640	1305	250	24	117	605	153	70	578	789	.317	.365

	#Pit	#P/PA	GB	FB	G/F	G	IBB	HB	SH	SF	GDP
Miscellaneous	22255	3.66	1868	1828	1.02	161	53	27	60	52	99

	AVG	AB	R	H	2B	3B	HR	RBI	SB	CS	BB	K	OBA	SPCT
vs. Left	.249	2051	...	510	94	4	34	196	53	25	191	291	.313	.348
vs. Right	.240	3308	...	795	156	20	83	409	100	45	387	498	.320	.375
Home	.246	2670	332	657	123	12	57	307	88	39	300	390	.322	.365
Away	.241	2689	308	648	127	12	60	298	65	31	278	399	.313	.364
None on	.240	3097	...	743	142	15	75	75	0	0	293	434	.308	.368
Runners on	.248	2262	...	562	108	9	42	530	153	70	285	355	.330	.360
April	.223	646	80	144	34	4	13	74	29	8	100	95	.327	.348
May	.263	859	115	226	41	4	22	110	36	14	85	138	.328	.397
June	.247	908	132	224	49	4	25	123	22	15	117	111	.332	.392
July	.244	893	106	218	41	1	17	103	17	9	95	115	.317	.349
August	.231	966	86	223	31	5	18	82	9	10	68	155	.283	.329
September	.241	893	100	215	45	4	18	92	35	14	96	142	.316	.361
October	.284	194	21	55	9	2	4	21	5	0	17	33	.344	.412
None on/out	.252	1357	...	342	71	4	37	37	0	0	129	178	.319	.392
Scoring Posn	.256	1357	...	347	68	5	22	472	41	5	202	224	.345	.362
Close & Late	.234	913	...	214	44	3	24	109	30	15	128	158	.328	.368
Bases Loaded	.252	127	...	32	3	1	4	99	0	0	10	29	.281	.386
Batting #1	.256	668	92	171	36	7	6	43	53	22	71	107	.330	.358
Batting #2	.272	615	92	167	34	3	10	70	15	6	92	80	.366	.385
Batting #3	.260	627	86	163	27	4	19	90	23	8	71	79	.332	.407
Batting #4	.265	615	90	163	40	1	25	94	11	8	67	90	.338	.455
Batting #5	.240	599	85	144	27	3	27	95	19	8	68	83	.314	.431
Batting #6	.249	595	60	148	16	2	12	67	12	9	55	74	.314	.343
Batting #7	.249	554	51	138	26	2	3	55	13	5	72	74	.334	.319
Batting #8	.213	555	44	118	26	2	8	55	2	2	54	81	.288	.310
Batting #9	.175	531	40	93	18	0	7	36	5	2	28	121	.218	.249
As p	.148	337	15	50	12	0	1	16	1	1	9	82	.175	.193
As c	.226	531	45	120	27	2	5	48	1	3	54	63	.304	.313
As 1b	.250	585	72	146	28	1	5	62	5	5	95	75	.352	.326
As 2b	.256	629	84	161	36	2	13	71	26	5	69	66	.331	.382
As 3b	.268	594	88	159	25	4	22	94	31	15	77	85	.350	.434
As ss	.230	578	61	133	30	3	15	67	5	4	58	92	.298	.370
As lf	.267	625	65	167	31	2	14	83	9	4	47	56	.320	.390
As cf	.267	637	95	170	29	8	8	48	50	23	75	95	.344	.375
As rf	.245	611	83	150	29	2	26	88	14	7	65	123	.317	.427
Outfield	.260	1873	243	487	89	12	48	219	73	34	187	274	.327	.397
0.0 count	.296	754	...	223	46	5	20	109	...	...	2	0	.301	.450
After (0.1)	.211	2400	...	507	84	8	51	231	...	...	126	510	.252	.317
After (1.0)	.261	2204	...	575	120	11	46	265	...	...	414	279	.376	.388
Two strikes	.189	2347	...	443	74	7	38	193	...	...	193	788	.252	.275
Grass	.244	3787	453	925	176	15	78	425	110	53	398	558	.316	.360
Turf	.242	1572	187	380	74	9	39	180	43	17	180	231	.322	.375
Day	.236	1743	200	412	94	7	38	191	49	23	190	257	.313	.364
Night	.247	3616	440	893	156	17	79	414	104	47	388	532	.320	.365
Inning 1.6	.241	3590	426	865	164	17	66	400	99	50	385	505	.315	.351
Inning 7+	.249	1769	214	440	86	7	51	205	54	20	193	284	.323	.392
vs.Atl	.204	382	35	78	26	1	8	34	7	2	27	46	.255	.340
vs.ChN	.231	568	63	131	25	5	7	60	18	10	48	89	.288	.329
vs.Cin	.256	402	63	103	13	2	14	58	11	3	60	69	.354	.403
vs.Hou	.243	395	43	96	28	2	5	40	11	8	53	60	.336	.362
vs.LA	.260	408	55	106	21	1	8	52	13	3	50	51	.342	.375
vs.Mon	.258	585	87	151	33	2	16	83	25	11	93	73	.360	.403
vs.Phi	.221	593	75	131	31	4	11	68	19	5	88	116	.320	.342
vs.Pit	.244	623	62	152	17	2	14	59	16	7	44	93	.297	.345
vs.StL	.256	601	68	154	20	5	17	65	13	5	38	75	.303	.391
vs.SD	.262	393	48	103	13	0	9	47	11	7	35	56	.321	.364
vs.SF	.244	409	41	100	23	0	8	39	9	9	42	61	.312	.359

PITCHING SPLITS

	ERA	W	L	SV	SVOP	GS	CG	SHO	IP	H	ER	HR	BB	IBB	K
Total	3.56	77	84	39	58	161	12	9	1437.1	1403	568	108	410	41	1028

	#Pit	#P/IP	GB	FB	G/F	BRp9	RA	WP	BK	SH	SF	R	HB	Hld
Miscellaneous	21868	15.21	2085	1443	1.44	11.51	314	59	14	83	46	646	25	21

	ERA	W	L	SV	SVOP	GS	CG	SHO	IP	H	ER	HR	BB	IBB	K
ST	3.71	57	65	0	0	161	12	4	1017.2	1007	419	81	277	14	748
REL	3.22	20	19	39	58	0	0	0	419.2	396	150	27	133	27	280
Home	3.74	40	42	21	28	82	6	3	750.0	760	312	55	215	26	554
Away	3.37	37	42	18	30	79	6	1	687.1	643	257	53	195	15	474
April	3.03	12	8	7	8	20	2	0	178.0	164	60	6	52	3	120
May	3.58	14	11	7	9	25	4	0	226.0	227	90	20	64	10	160
June	4.22	13	15	6	12	28	2	1	247.2	263	116	20	72	11	174
July	2.86	16	11	7	9	27	1	0	236.0	200	75	24	62	6	189
August	4.27	8	21	4	8	29	0	0	257.1	284	122	17	83	7	189
September	3.43	12	15	8	10	27	2	2	247.0	229	94	21	68	3	161
October	2.38	2	3	0	2	5	1	1	45.1	36	12	0	9	1	35
Grass	3.58	54	61	28	39	115	10	3	1036.1	1013	412	85	292	36	735
Turf	3.52	23	23	11	19	46	2	1	401.0	390	157	23	118	5	293
Day	3.67	24	29	12	17	53	6	2	471.1	466	192	36	132	16	340
Night	3.51	53	55	27	41	108	6	2	966.0	937	377	72	278	25	688
vs.Atl	4.15	3	9	2	4	12	0	0	104.0	98	48	13	29	4	51
vs.ChN	4.26	6	11	5	7	17	1	0	156.1	161	74	15	35	3	87
vs.Cin	4.96	7	5	4	7	12	1	0	107.0	137	59	9	37	3	94
vs.Hou	3.50	5	7	1	4	12	1	1	108.0	107	42	8	29	3	78
vs.LA	3.72	5	7	1	2	12	2	0	104.0	97	43	13	32	3	79
vs.Mon	2.26	14	4	8	8	18	3	1	163.0	142	41	4	32	4	128
vs.Phi	2.88	11	7	6	8	18	1	1	162.1	140	52	10	52	4	132
vs.Pit	4.09	6	12	3	5	18	0	0	163.0	169	74	10	58	3	94
vs.StL	3.94	7	11	2	4	18	2	1	157.2	167	69	4	52	5	119
vs.SD	2.27	7	5	4	5	12	1	0	103.0	78	26	8	28	6	87
vs.SF	3.39	6	6	3	4	12	0	0	109.0	107	41	14	26	3	79

OPPOSING BATTERS VS. PITCHERS.

	AVG	AB	R	H	2B	3B	HR	RBI	SB	CS	BB	K	OBA	SPCT
Total	.257	5466	646	1403	226	46	108	601	134	74	410	1028	.309	.374
vs. Left	.257	2443	...	628	108	22	36	239	74	36	199	461	.312	.363
vs. Right	.256	3023	...	775	118	24	72	362	60	38	211	567	.307	.383
ST	.259	3883	467	1007	160	33	81	407	104	58	277	748	.310	.380
REL	.250	1583	179	396	66	13	27	194	30	16	133	280	.307	.359
Home	.263	2886	348	760	113	29	55	327	71	41	215	554	.314	.380
Away	.249	2580	298	643	113	17	53	274	63	33	195	474	.303	.368
None on	.252	3152	...	793	139	25	56	56	0	0	214	581	.302	.365
Runners on	.264	2314	...	610	87	21	52	545	134	74	196	447	.319	.387
None on/out	.272	1395	...	380	65	12	29	29	0	0	80	247	.314	.399
Scoring Posn	.255	1367	...	348	42	13	31	471	28	14	159	288	.327	.372
vs 1st Batr	.250	284	...	71	13	4	6	40	2	1	21	52	.299	.387
1st IP	.242	1626	123	394	60	12	28	206	45	30	155	324	.309	.346
Inning 1.6	.258	3658	443	942	152	32	74	416	107	59	274	706	.310	.377
Inning 7+	.255	1808	203	461	74	14	34	185	27	15	136	322	.307	.368
Close & Late	.258	921	...	238	36	7	15	99	16	7	67	167	.308	.362
0.0 count	.325	830	...	270	51	8	28	126	...	...	31	0	.351	.507
After (0.1)	.217	2419	...	525	77	11	38	208	...	...	85	674	.246	.305
After (1.0)	.274	2217	...	608	98	27	42	267	...	...	294	354	.358	.400
Two strikes	.181	2488	...	451	62	9	31	190	...	...	171	1025	.235	.251
Pitch 1.15	.257	1484	...	381	61	12	29	157	35	22	122	261	.314	.373
Pitch 16.30	.230	1074	...	247	38	9	18	106	29	11	82	218	.286	.332
Pitch 31.45	.244	693	...	169	23	3	11	77	21	9	57	152	.302	.333
Pitch 46.60	.275	615	...	169	31	11	12	79	19	8	48	105	.327	.420
Pitch 61.75	.274	576	...	158	30	3	14	62	11	11	32	109	.313	.410
Pitch 76.90	.305	486	...	148	29	4	13	76	12	8	39	74	.358	.461
Pitch 91.105	.240	313	...	75	7	2	6	23	6	3	16	63	.272	.332
Pitch 106.20	.236	157	...	37	5	0	3	12	0	2	9	24	.277	.325
Pitch 121.35	.283	53	...	15	2	2	1	8	0	0	3	17	.316	.453
Pitch 136.50	.313	16	...	5	1	0	1	2	1	0	2	5	.389	.563

Montreal Expos

Brock J. Hanke

MONTREAL											
YEAR	1982	1983	1984	1985	1986	1987	1988	1989	1990	1991	TOT
W	86	82	78	84	78	91	81	81	85	71	817
L	76	80	83	77	83	71	81	81	77	90	799
WPCT	0.531	0.506	0.484	0.522	0.484	0.562	0.500	0.500	0.525	0.441	0.506
R	697	677	593	633	637	741	628	632	662	579	6479
RA	616	646	585	636	688	720	592	630	598	655	6366
PWPT	0.561	0.523	0.507	0.498	0.462	0.514	0.529	0.502	0.551	0.439	0.509
PythW	91	85	82	81	75	83	86	81	89	71	82
PythL	71	77	80	81	87	79	76	81	73	91	80
LUCK	-5	-3	-4	3	3	8	-5	0	-4	0	-7

Defensive Efficiency Record: .7099

Every year I swear I'm going to write a nice, long Expos article full of complex sabermetrics. And every year, it's one of the shortest in the book. Why? Well, for one thing, the Expos are very easy to analyze, very straightforward. For another, they have no great teams of the past to compare the current outfit to. They have not yet had much place in baseball history. I suppose I could write about the sabermetric effects of cracked domes, but that's mean. Besides, there hasn't been nearly enough evidence to justify such a thing. The main dome effect on my life is that I got to see three extra home games last year, here in St. Louis.

I do want to write a victory statement of sorts about Buck Rodgers. As far as I can tell, I was the person in the baseball world who thought the least of Buck's managerial skills. I thought his handling of the lineup, especially of Tim Raines, was horrid. I thought his development of his pitching staff left much to be desired. And, sure enough, the Expos now have a reasonable lineup, without Raines, and their pitching is in a state of collapse. I don't want to harp on this too much; there's only so much you can do when your pitching staff is traded out from under you. But a lot of people seemed to think he was some sort of miracle worker, who would soon bring the Expos to the promised land of division titledom. I never saw any reason to think that, and it did not in fact ever happen.

Right now, I think a lot of the Expo management team. They seem to have a real plan, and a real chance in a couple of years. They have addressed three of the Expo weaknesses. To wit:

1) They have rid themselves of the problem of having a right handed lineup anchor who played first base. That's always a short road to imbalance in the lineup. If you're going to do that sort of thing, and I am aware that Whitey Herzog did it for years, you'd better see to it that your outfielders are left handed. Otherwise, you end up where Buck's Expos were, with your first baseman, a right handed outfielder, and an infielder (always right handed) as the center of your lineup. Then you have to bat Tim Raines third just in order to break up the string. The Cubs, I'd like to note, are currently in the same pickle, but at least their first baseman is a lefty. They have three outfield spots with which to acquire a lefty hitter. The Expos only had two, and one of them was center.

2) They are starting to acquire some pitching. Trading for Ken Hill is a good move for the Expos, and that's not the end of it. Eventually, they'll develop some pitching. Whether they'll do so before they have to replace the right half of their infield remains to be seen.

3) They traded for age in the closer spot. Tim Burke might have still been able to pitch, but Barry Jones is four years younger. He's not the best closer, but he's alright, and he's going to be around.

The main problem they have yet to address is sorting out the catching corps. That, of course, was delayed by the injury to Mike Fitzgerald. If Fitz does come back, I expect to see either Nelson Santovenia or Gilberto Reyes departing soon. If he's not OK, Fitz will doubtless go. That would be a shame. He finally seemed to have won himself a job, as he deserved for years under Rodgers. For him to go down now would not be my idea of justice.

It is certainly true that the Expos are getting some help from their farm system, just as I and everyone else has seen coming for some time. They've already got Delino DeShields, Larry Walker and Marquis Grissom, and Bret Barberie looks just great. If he can truly play shortstop, the Expo age problem is solved. If not, Grissom is on the trade block, just like Dave Martinez and Otis Nixon. That's another thing I like about the current Expos. They're not afraid to let someone go, if he's clogging up a playing spot. They're not afraid to lose Otis, and have him star with the Braves, and then let Dave Martinez go as well. I've always approved of teams who were not afraid to lose a player transaction if it would help them win the title.

I give this team about two years to prove it can contend. If they can get their pitching straightened out before Tim Wallach gives into Father Time, I think it's a lock. I'd really like to see something like:

Barberie ss
DeShields 2b
Calderon rf
Walker lf
Wallach 3b
Grissom cf
Fitzgerald c

You'll note that this does not include a first baseman. It doesn't need one. That's why I think the Expos could contend soon. You can always find a first baseman who can bat at least fifth. Consider that, right now, with Andres Galarraga on that horrible season at first, the Expos had more offense than anyone in the division except the Pirates and the Cardinals, and more defense than anyone other than those two, too. That's the #3 club in the division, and they didn't lose Bobby Bonilla. Instead, they gained Barberie. That means

DeShields 2b
Barberie lf
Calderon rf
Walker 1b
Wallach 3b
Owen ss
Fitzgerald c
Grissom cf

is a real possibility. I like it. It has no holes.

So don't lose heart, out there. The sky isn't falling (sorry). Your team may yet win enough games to draw the fans to stay in the frozen north.

Montreal Expos Home Park Performance Factors

	Outs	Runs	Hits	2b	3b	HR	W	K	SH	SF	HBP	IBB	SB	CS	GDP
Home LH Batters	.856	.834	.835	.692	1.085	1.021	.799	.867	.696	.675	.798	.520	.758	.821	.778
Home RH Batters	.846	.963	.849	.944	.814	.914	.815	.833	.933	.799	.969	.993	.770	.789	.713
All Home Batters	.843	.907	.846	.837	.959	.928	.803	.841	.788	.738	.918	.737	.754	.785	.738
Opp LH Batters	.871	1.068	.881	.840	1.225	1.239	.879	.808	.966	.787	1.350	1.428	1.050	.903	.923
Opp RH Batters	.869	1.017	.979	1.148	.594	1.179	.893	.833	.707	.867	.929	.818	.793	.721	.924
All Opp Batters	.859	1.023	.925	.943	.782	1.187	.897	.817	.787	.886	.986	1.020	.848	.822	.913
All LH Batters	.862	.928	.855	.750	1.148	1.113	.833	.844	.787	.713	.910	.785	.837	.854	.829
All RH Batters	.857	.988	.910	1.040	.715	1.039	.852	.834	.786	.833	.932	.923	.791	.769	.811
All Batters	.851	.962	.884	.887	.863	1.050	.848	.831	.787	.797	.951	.848	.794	.805	.817

Conventional Batting Records for Montreal Expos

	G	AB	Run	Hit	2B	3B	HR	TB	RBI	W	K	IW	HB	SB	CS	BRng Eff	GI DP	SH	SF	Avg	Slug	OBP	Runs Ctd
Reyes	83	207	11	45	9	0	0	54	13	19	51	2	1	2	4	.407	3	1	1	.217	.261	.285	16
Galarraga	107	375	34	82	13	2	9	126	33	23	86	5	2	5	6	.478	6	0	0	.219	.336	.268	32
DeShields	151	563	83	134	15	4	10	187	51	95	151	2	2	56	23	.517	6	8	5	.238	.332	.347	74
Wallach	151	577	60	130	22	1	13	193	73	50	100	8	6	2	4	.415	12	0	4	.225	.334	.292	56
Owen S	139	424	39	108	22	8	3	155	26	42	61	11	1	2	6	.354	11	4	4	.255	.366	.321	48
Calderon	134	470	69	141	22	3	19	226	75	53	64	4	3	31	16	.475	7	1	10	.300	.481	.368	85
Grissom	148	558	73	149	23	9	6	208	39	34	89	0	1	76	17	.374	8	4	0	.267	.373	.310	69
Walker L	137	487	59	141	30	2	16	223	64	42	102	2	5	14	9	.385	7	1	4	.290	.458	.349	78
Martinez Da	124	396	47	117	18	5	7	166	42	20	54	3	3	16	7	.422	3	5	3	.295	.419	.332	56
Fitzgerald	71	198	17	40	5	2	4	61	28	22	35	4	0	4	2	.483	5	1	3	.202	.308	.278	17
Foley T	86	168	12	35	11	1	0	48	15	14	30	4	1	2	0	.444	4	1	3	.208	.286	.269	14
Barberie	57	136	16	48	12	2	2	70	18	20	22	2	2	0	0	.267	4	1	3	.353	.515	.435	32
Hassey	52	119	5	27	8	0	1	38	14	13	16	1	0	1	1	.250	5	2	1	.227	.319	.301	11
Santovenia	41	96	7	24	5	0	2	35	14	2	18	2	0	0	0	.364	4	0	4	.250	.365	.255	8
Noboa	67	95	5	23	3	0	1	29	2	1	8	1	0	2	3	.400	1	0	0	.242	.305	.250	6
Martinez De	32	72	8	11	4	0	0	15	2	1	24	0	0	0	0	.083	1	10	0	.153	.208	.164	3
Bullock	73	72	6	16	4	0	1	23	6	9	13	0	0	6	1	.167	3	0	1	.222	.319	.305	7
Williams K	34	70	11	19	5	2	0	28	1	3	22	0	1	2	1	.467	1	0	0	.271	.400	.311	9
Vanderwal	21	61	4	13	4	1	1	22	8	1	18	0	0	0	0	.400	2	0	1	.213	.361	.222	4
Gardner M	27	55	1	5	0	0	0	5	4	1	18	0	0	0	0	.000	0	4	0	.091	.091	.107	1
Nabholz	24	52	5	6	0	0	0	6	1	3	14	0	0	0	0	.125	2	3	0	.115	.115	.164	1
Barnes B	28	49	1	4	0	0	0	4	1	7	19	0	0	0	0	.000	0	3	0	.082	.082	.196	1
Boyd	19	36	1	3	0	0	0	3	2	3	19	0	0	0	0	.000	0	3	0	.083	.083	.154	1
Haney	16	27	1	2	0	0	0	2	1	0	3	0	0	0	0	.000	1	2	0	.074	.074	.074	0
Sampen	43	13	2	3	0	0	0	3	1	0	6	0	0	0	0	.250	0	2	0	.231	.231	.231	1
Mahler R	10	9	0	1	0	0	0	1	0	0	2	0	0	0	0	.000	0	3	0	.111	.111	.111	0
Riesgo	4	7	1	1	0	0	0	1	0	3	1	0	0	0	0	.250	1	0	0	.143	.143	.400	1
Darling	3	6	0	1	1	0	0	2	2	0	2	0	0	0	0	.000	0	1	0	.167	.333	.167	0
Rojas	37	4	0	0	0	0	0	0	0	0	3	0	0	0	0	.000	0	1	0	.000	.000	.000	0
Fassero	51	3	0	0	0	0	0	0	0	1	2	0	0	0	0	.000	0	2	0	.000	.000	.250	0
Ruskin	64	2	1	0	0	0	0	0	0	1	1	0	0	0	0	.000	0	0	0	.000	.000	.333	0
Frey	31	2	0	0	0	0	0	0	0	1	2	0	0	0	0	.000	0	0	0	.000	.000	.333	0
Jones Ba	77	1	0	0	0	0	0	0	0	0	0	0	0	0	0	.000	0	1	0	.000	.000	.000	0
Burke	37	1	0	0	0	0	0	0	0	0	0	0	0	0	0	.000	0	0	0	.000	.000	.000	0
Piatt	21	1	0	0	0	0	0	0	0	0	0	0	0	0	0	.000	0	0	0	.000	.000	.000	0
Long B	3	0	0	0	0	0	0	0	0	0	0	0	0	0	0	.000	0	0	0	.000	.000	.000	0
Schmidt D	4	0	0	0	0	0	0	0	0	0	0	0	0	0	0	.000	0	0	0	.000	.000	.000	0
Wainhouse	2	0	0	0	0	0	0	0	0	0	0	0	0	0	0	.000	0	0	0	.000	.000	.000	0
TOTALS	2209	5412	579	1329	236	42	95	1934	536	484	1056	51	28	221	100	.399	97	64	47	.246	.357	.308	610

Sabermetric Batting Records for Montreal Expos

	Ball Park Adjusted												Runs		Run/					
	AB	Run	Hit	2B	3B	HR	RBI	W	SO	Avg	Slug	OBP	Ctd	Outs	27o	OW%	OG	OWAR	DWAR	TWAR
Barberie	116	15	42	10	1	2	17	16	18	.362	.517	.437	27	79	9.23	.853	3	1.47	0.30	1.77
Bullock	61	5	13	3	0	1	5	7	10	.213	.311	.294	6	50	3.24	.417	2	0.12	0.04	0.17
Calderon	410	68	128	23	2	19	75	45	53	.312	.517	.376	82	307	7.21	.780	11	4.89	0.28	5.17
DeShields	484	78	114	11	4	11	49	79	126	.236	.343	.343	65	403	4.35	.564	15	3.19	-0.04	3.15
Fitzgerald	171	16	36	5	1	4	28	18	29	.211	.322	.283	16	142	3.04	.387	5	0.19	0.00	0.20
Foley T	144	11	30	8	1	0	14	11	25	.208	.278	.266	11	119	2.50	.298	4	-0.23	0.26	0.03
Galarraga	325	33	74	13	1	9	33	19	71	.228	.357	.272	31	259	3.23	.416	10	0.63	0.27	0.89
Grissom	486	72	136	24	6	6	39	29	74	.280	.391	.320	65	371	4.73	.604	14	3.49	1.17	4.66
Hassey	102	4	23	6	0	1	13	10	13	.225	.314	.295	9	84	2.89	.363	3	0.04	0.17	0.21
Martinez Da	340	44	100	13	5	7	40	16	45	.294	.424	.330	48	254	5.10	.639	9	2.72	0.79	3.51
Noboa	82	4	21	3	0	1	2	0	6	.256	.329	.256	6	63	2.57	.310	2	-0.09	0.05	-0.04
Owen S	363	37	95	19	6	3	25	35	50	.262	.372	.324	43	287	4.05	.527	11	1.88	1.92	3.80
Reyes	179	10	41	9	0	0	13	16	42	.229	.279	.292	15	143	2.83	.353	5	0.02	-0.32	-0.30
Riesgo	5	0	0	0	0	0	0	2	0	.000	.000	.286	0	5	0.00	.000	0	-0.06	0.00	-0.06
Santovenia	82	6	21	5	0	2	14	1	14	.256	.390	.256	7	67	2.82	.351	2	0.00	-0.14	-0.13
Vanderwal	52	3	11	3	1	1	7	0	15	.212	.365	.212	4	42	2.57	.310	2	-0.06	0.06	0.00
Walker L	418	56	120	22	2	18	61	35	85	.287	.478	.348	70	312	6.06	.714	12	4.21	1.00	5.20
Wallach	501	59	118	23	0	13	73	42	83	.236	.359	.299	54	398	3.66	.477	15	1.88	1.12	3.00
Williams K	60	10	17	5	1	0	1	2	18	.283	.400	.306	8	43	5.02	.632	2	0.45	0.16	0.61
TOTALS	4650	558	1176	209	36	100	524	411	875	.253	.378	.315	564	3722	4.09	.533	138	25.18	7.11	32.29

Pitching Records for Montreal Expos

	ERA	W	L	Pct	G	GS	CG	ShO	GF	Sv	IP	R	ER	H	2B	3B	HR	BB	IW	SO	HB	WP	BK
Martinez De	2.39	14	11	.560	31	31	9	5	0	0	222.0	70	59	187	32	6	9	62	3	123	4	3	0
Gardner M	3.85	9	11	.450	27	27	0	0	0	0	168.1	78	72	139	21	2	17	75	1	107	4	2	1
Barnes B	4.22	5	8	.385	28	27	1	0	0	0	160.0	82	75	135	24	4	16	84	2	117	6	5	1
Nabholz	3.63	8	7	.533	24	24	1	0	0	0	153.2	66	62	134	35	3	5	57	4	99	2	3	1
Boyd	3.52	6	8	.429	19	19	1	1	0	0	120.1	49	47	115	29	6	9	40	2	82	0	2	3
Haney	4.04	3	7	.300	16	16	0	0	0	0	84.2	49	38	94	20	2	6	43	1	51	1	9	0
Mahler R	3.62	1	3	.250	10	6	0	0	1	0	37.1	17	15	37	6	2	2	15	0	17	0	0	0
Darling	7.41	0	2	.000	3	3	0	0	0	0	17.0	16	14	25	2	2	6	5	0	11	1	4	0
Sampen	4.00	9	5	.643	43	8	0	0	8	0	92.1	49	41	96	22	1	13	46	7	52	3	3	1
Jones Ba	3.35	4	9	.308	77	0	0	0	46	13	88.2	35	33	76	10	2	8	33	8	46	1	1	1
Ruskin	4.24	4	4	.500	64	0	0	0	24	6	63.2	31	30	57	15	2	4	30	2	46	3	5	0
Fassero	2.44	2	5	.286	51	0	0	0	30	8	55.1	17	15	39	7	2	1	17	1	42	1	4	0
Rojas	3.75	3	3	.500	37	0	0	0	13	6	48.0	21	20	42	9	3	4	13	1	37	1	3	0
Burke	4.11	3	4	.429	37	0	0	0	16	5	46.0	24	21	41	7	2	3	14	6	25	4	1	0
Frey	4.99	0	1	.000	31	0	0	0	5	1	39.2	31	22	43	5	0	3	23	4	21	1	3	1
Piatt	2.60	0	0	.000	21	0	0	0	3	0	34.2	11	10	29	7	0	3	17	0	29	0	1	0
Schmidt D	10.38	0	1	.000	4	0	0	0	1	0	4.1	5	5	9	1	0	2	2	0	3	0	0	0
Wainhouse	6.75	0	1	.000	2	0	0	0	1	0	2.2	2	2	2	0	0	0	4	0	1	0	2	0
Long B	10.80	0	0	.000	3	0	0	0	1	0	1.2	2	2	4	2	0	0	4	0	0	0	0	0
TOTALS	3.64	71	90	.441	528	161	12	6	149	39	1440.1	655	583	1304	254	39	111	584	42	909	32	51	9

Sabermetric Pitching Records for Montreal Expos

	Adj	|-Expected-|			|——Opposing Batters——|												Supported				
	ERA	W	L	Pct	BFP	Avg	Slg	OBA	RC/G	GDP	SB	CS	PK	PKE	SH	SF	RSup	RSp/G	W	L	Pct
Barnes B	4.05	6	7	.451	684	.233	.371	.333	4.36	10	20	8	1	6	9	5	66	3.71	6	7	.457
Boyd	3.37	8	6	.544	496	.256	.407	.314	4.24	7	11	9	0	0	2	4	50	3.74	8	6	.552
Burke	3.91	3	4	.468	190	.243	.361	.314	3.65	8	7	1	0	0	2	1	17	3.33	3	4	.419
Darling	6.88	0	2	.222	81	.333	.653	.383	10.43	1	5	0	0	0	0	0	11	5.82	1	1	.417
Fassero	2.28	5	2	.722	223	.196	.266	.263	2.37	4	3	1	0	0	6	0	14	2.28	4	3	.500
Frey	4.76	0	1	.373	182	.281	.373	.374	4.96	6	3	2	0	0	3	2	9	2.04	0	1	.155
Gardner M	3.69	10	10	.498	692	.230	.356	.318	3.68	8	13	17	0	2	7	2	63	3.37	9	11	.455
Haney	3.83	5	5	.479	387	.280	.405	.362	5.42	5	8	6	0	3	6	1	33	3.51	5	5	.457
Jones Ba	3.15	7	6	.577	353	.246	.369	.318	3.54	11	8	6	2	1	7	3	24	2.44	5	8	.375
Long B	5.40	0	0	.316	12	.500	.750	.667	22.28	1	0	0	0	0	0	0	1	5.40	0	0	.500
Mahler R	3.38	2	2	.542	158	.268	.384	.338	4.20	4	3	3	0	0	4	1	11	2.65	2	2	.382
Martinez De	2.27	18	7	.724	905	.226	.311	.282	3.07	14	22	4	3	2	7	3	91	3.69	18	7	.725
Nabholz	3.46	8	7	.530	631	.237	.336	.307	3.47	9	15	11	1	5	2	4	77	4.51	9	6	.630
Piatt	2.34	0	0	.712	145	.230	.357	.322	3.82	4	3	1	0	0	2	0	10	2.60	0	0	.552
Rojas	3.56	3	3	.515	200	.228	.375	.280	3.87	1	5	1	0	0	0	2	21	3.94	3	3	.550
Ruskin	3.96	4	4	.463	275	.241	.371	.333	4.55	1	7	3	0	1	5	0	29	4.10	4	4	.518
Sampen	3.80	7	7	.483	409	.273	.452	.358	5.80	5	16	8	0	0	4	4	51	4.97	9	5	.631
Schmidt D	8.31	0	1	.163	24	.429	.762	.478	16.26	0	0	0	0	0	1	0	0	0.00	0	1	.000
Wainhouse	3.38	1	0	.542	14	.222	.222	.429	5.21	0	0	0	0	0	0	1	1	3.37	1	0	.500
TOTALS	3.51	84	77	.523	6061	.244	.368	.320	4.05	99	149	81	7	20	67	33	579	3.62	83	78	.516

Batting 'Splits' Records for Montreal Expos

	G	AB	Run	Hit	2B	3B	HR	TB	RBI	W	K	IW	HB	SB	CS	GI DP	SH	SF	Avg	Slug	OBP	Runs Ctd
SPLITS for Montreal Expos (all batters except pitchers)																						
vs LHP	1002	1875	207	464	83	10	40	687	193	170	386	20	10	79	29	37	23	10	.247	.366	.312	219
vs RHP	1448	3537	372	865	153	32	55	1247	343	314	670	31	18	142	71	60	41	37	.245	.353	.306	391
Home	941	2217	216	536	95	13	35	762	193	213	436	26	10	106	46	45	30	23	.242	.344	.308	242
Away	1268	3195	363	793	141	29	60	1172	343	271	620	25	18	115	54	52	34	24	.248	.367	.308	368
Grass	638	1611	191	400	56	17	33	589	177	137	329	15	5	61	26	25	18	10	.248	.366	.307	185
Turf	1571	3801	388	929	180	25	62	1345	359	347	727	36	23	160	74	72	46	37	.244	.354	.309	425
April/June	1052	2538	279	622	111	16	44	897	255	259	493	25	12	121	57	39	33	21	.245	.353	.316	295
July/October	1157	2874	300	707	125	26	51	1037	281	225	563	26	16	100	43	58	31	26	.246	.361	.302	315

1991 SPLITS FOR Montreal Expos

BATTING SPLITS

	AVG	AB	R	H	2B	3B	HR	RBI	SB	CS	BB	K	OBA	SPCT
Total	.246	5412	579	1329	236	42	95	536	221	100	484	1056	.308	.357

	#Pit	#P/PA	GB	FB	G/F	G	IBB	HB	SH	SF	GDP
Miscellaneous	22227	3.68	2040	1431	1.43	161	51	28	64	47	97

	AVG	AB	R	H	2B	3B	HR	RBI	SB	CS	BB	K	OBA	SPCT
vs. Left	.247	1875	...	464	83	10	40	193	79	29	170	386	.312	.366
vs. Right	.245	3537	...	865	153	32	55	343	142	71	314	670	.306	.353
Home	.242	2217	216	536	95	13	35	193	106	46	213	436	.308	.344
Away	.248	3195	363	793	141	29	60	343	115	54	271	620	.308	.367
None on	.242	3206	...	775	147	24	59	59	0	0	256	629	.301	.358
Runners on	.251	2206	...	554	89	18	36	477	221	100	228	427	.319	.357
April	.244	652	56	159	24	5	8	52	24	16	48	120	.296	.333
May	.240	934	106	224	35	4	23	99	48	24	107	181	.318	.360
June	.251	952	117	239	52	7	13	104	49	17	104	192	.326	.361
July	.228	806	76	184	27	5	12	69	31	16	69	150	.288	.319
August	.247	943	92	233	50	11	21	89	28	18	79	180	.310	.390
September	.257	958	121	246	44	7	14	113	39	7	69	203	.307	.361
October	.263	167	11	44	4	3	4	10	2	2	8	30	.295	.395
None on/out	.240	1382	...	332	68	13	28	28	0	0	114	258	.300	.369
Scoring Posn	.244	1354	...	330	58	10	19	420	67	24	182	291	.328	.343
Close & Late	.246	1060	...	261	39	7	18	101	49	18	115	212	.322	.347
Bases Loaded	.289	97	...	28	6	0	1	80	0	0	5	13	.287	.381
Batting #1	.232	641	94	149	21	9	10	48	60	24	92	153	.329	.340
Batting #2	.286	667	82	191	32	6	7	56	57	18	45	109	.332	.384
Batting #3	.312	619	92	193	30	8	20	90	36	18	67	91	.378	.483
Batting #4	.229	628	66	144	26	0	17	86	5	4	49	110	.291	.352
Batting #5	.265	618	69	164	39	4	12	74	13	9	42	113	.313	.400
Batting #6	.257	604	55	155	22	6	10	49	30	11	46	102	.310	.363
Batting #7	.215	576	41	124	25	2	11	58	13	9	47	128	.273	.323
Batting #8	.242	537	44	130	32	6	6	47	4	5	61	97	.317	.358
Batting #9	.151	522	36	79	9	1	2	28	3	2	35	153	.206	.184
As p	.108	333	20	36	5	0	0	14	0	0	18	115	.154	.123
As c	.218	555	34	121	26	2	4	55	7	6	47	108	.278	.294
As 1b	.236	607	54	143	22	4	15	64	16	7	43	132	.288	.359
As 2b	.242	624	86	151	20	5	10	55	56	23	98	151	.344	.338
As 3b	.237	620	67	147	26	2	13	80	2	4	56	105	.305	.348
As ss	.260	557	55	145	34	8	5	41	3	6	56	85	.325	.377
As lf	.283	618	86	175	29	6	20	90	35	16	63	99	.349	.447
As cf	.267	664	80	177	25	10	9	52	77	23	40	100	.310	.375
As rf	.295	621	79	183	41	4	14	60	17	13	41	114	.341	.441
Outfield	.281	1903	245	535	95	20	43	202	129	52	144	313	.333	.420
0.0 count	.313	792	...	248	43	7	23	97	...	...	1	0	.319	.472
After (0.1)	.208	2459	...	511	95	17	34	210	...	...	124	704	.249	.302
After (1.0)	.264	2161	...	570	98	18	38	229	...	...	316	352	.355	.379
Two strikes	.174	2494	...	435	72	12	27	165	...	...	215	1056	.242	.245
Grass	.248	1611	191	400	56	17	33	177	61	26	137	329	.307	.366
Turf	.244	3801	388	929	180	25	62	359	160	74	347	727	.309	.354
Day	.233	1502	163	350	55	11	27	150	55	29	150	331	.303	.338
Night	.250	3910	416	979	181	31	68	386	166	71	334	725	.311	.365
Inning 1.6	.248	3585	395	888	159	31	62	370	160	77	310	682	.308	.361
Inning 7+	.241	1827	184	441	77	11	33	166	61	23	174	374	.308	.350
vs.Atl	.303	406	65	123	21	3	10	58	24	7	41	91	.368	.443
vs.ChN	.245	583	63	143	25	6	12	56	25	7	52	123	.306	.370
vs.Cin	.258	392	50	101	21	5	10	48	18	6	41	76	.327	.413
vs.Hou	.242	414	54	100	20	2	5	50	20	8	50	91	.323	.336
vs.LA	.206	369	39	76	9	3	5	34	15	7	41	69	.285	.287
vs.NYN	.237	598	46	142	20	7	4	44	17	13	32	128	.275	.314
vs.Phi	.203	592	49	120	28	3	12	46	27	10	59	113	.278	.321
vs.Pit	.254	606	51	154	31	4	7	48	19	9	38	116	.297	.353
vs.StL	.249	587	54	146	29	4	7	50	15	14	45	95	.310	.348
vs.SD	.266	436	56	116	18	2	9	52	20	9	45	79	.335	.378
vs.SF	.252	429	52	108	14	3	14	50	21	10	40	75	.314	.396

PITCHING SPLITS

	ERA	W	L	SV	SVOP	GS	CG	SHO	IP	H	ER	HR	BB	IBB	K
Total	3.64	71	90	39	67	161	12	10	1440.1	1304	583	111	584	42	909

	#Pit	#P/IP	GB	FB	G/F	BRp9	RA	WP	BK	SH	SF	R	HB	Hld
Miscellaneous	22177	15.40	2011	1542	1.30	12.00	367	51	9	67	33	655	32	44

	ERA	W	L	SV	SVOP	GS	CG	SHO	IP	H	ER	HR	BB	IBB	K
ST	3.56	49	59	0	0	161	12	6	998.2	892	395	76	403	15	622
REL	3.83	22	31	39	67	0	0	0	441.2	412	188	35	181	27	287
Home	2.86	33	35	16	26	68	6	5	639.0	530	203	33	238	15	425
Away	4.27	38	55	23	41	93	6	1	801.1	774	380	78	346	27	484
April	3.75	7	13	4	8	20	1	1	175.0	160	73	13	80	7	82
May	3.76	13	14	5	11	27	2	1	249.0	217	104	23	87	12	164
June	3.70	13	15	8	15	28	1	1	258.0	259	106	20	99	7	172
July	3.08	10	15	6	9	25	3	2	222.1	194	76	16	85	9	142
August	3.77	9	19	6	11	28	2	1	248.1	216	104	15	106	5	151
September	3.61	18	10	9	11	28	3	0	246.2	221	99	22	99	2	170
October	4.61	1	4	1	2	5	0	0	41.0	37	21	2	28	0	28
Grass	4.49	19	27	14	23	46	2	1	401.0	393	200	47	171	12	230
Turf	3.32	52	63	25	44	115	10	5	1039.1	911	383	64	413	30	679
Day	3.95	17	28	12	20	45	2	1	398.2	364	175	38	159	11	262
Night	3.53	54	62	27	47	116	10	5	1041.2	940	408	73	425	31	647
vs.Atl	3.98	7	5	3	4	12	1	1	104.0	107	46	9	41	0	63
vs.ChN	3.71	7	10	6	11	17	0	0	153.0	142	63	15	44	3	98
vs.Cin	4.92	6	6	5	5	12	0	0	106.0	105	58	16	43	2	74
vs.Hou	2.30	10	2	4	7	12	1	0	117.1	89	30	2	40	2	83
vs.LA	3.29	7	5	3	4	12	2	2	104.0	87	38	6	36	3	73
vs.NYN	4.48	4	14	4	6	18	0	0	156.2	151	78	16	93	7	73
vs.Phi	3.69	4	14	1	4	18	3	1	158.2	141	65	10	68	4	99
vs.Pit	3.92	6	12	3	6	18	1	0	156.0	146	68	9	80	8	97
vs.StL	3.30	7	11	3	6	18	2	1	155.1	151	57	9	56	3	95
vs.SD	3.07	7	6	3	8	12	1	0	114.1	91	39	8	40	5	70
vs.SF	3.21	7	5	4	6	12	1	1	115.0	94	41	11	43	5	84

OPPOSING BATTERS VS. PITCHERS.

	AVG	AB	R	H	2B	3B	HR	RBI	SB	CS	BB	K	OBA	SPCT
Total	.244	5345	655	1304	254	39	111	600	149	81	584	909	.320	.368
vs. Left	.249	2269	...	566	114	24	44	259	80	39	286	367	.333	.379
vs. Right	.240	3076	...	738	140	15	67	341	69	42	298	542	.311	.361
ST	.241	3704	442	892	173	27	76	377	105	63	403	622	.317	.364
REL	.251	1641	213	412	81	12	35	223	44	18	181	287	.328	.379
Home	.229	2318	233	530	106	20	33	214	69	36	238	425	.302	.334
Away	.256	3027	422	774	148	19	78	386	80	45	346	484	.334	.394
None on	.239	3057	...	731	141	16	58	58	0	0	311	514	.312	.353
Runners on	.250	2288	...	573	113	23	53	542	149	81	273	395	.331	.389
None on/out	.251	1347	...	338	69	7	25	25	0	0	125	222	.317	.368
Scoring Posn	.248	1377	...	341	63	15	33	474	26	15	198	258	.341	.387
vs 1st Batr	.250	328	...	82	16	2	8	38	6	4	32	65	.318	.384
1st IP	.244	1725	184	421	80	10	40	235	74	24	210	301	.328	.372
Inning 1.6	.243	3583	429	871	163	26	82	397	109	61	391	613	.319	.372
Inning 7+	.246	1762	226	433	91	13	29	203	40	20	193	296	.322	.362
Close & Late	.241	1044	...	252	47	8	12	120	31	13	119	173	.322	.336
0.0 count	.297	768	...	228	48	2	17	99	...	...	35	0	.331	.431
After (0.1)	.221	2316	...	512	97	13	31	201	...	...	107	584	.258	.314
After (1.0)	.249	2261	...	564	109	24	63	300	...	...	442	325	.373	.402
Two strikes	.188	2324	...	438	83	12	26	176	...	...	214	909	.259	.268
Pitch 1.15	.246	1579	...	388	74	6	35	165	60	19	183	253	.326	.367
Pitch 16.30	.225	1000	...	225	50	10	20	129	23	15	110	189	.304	.355
Pitch 31.45	.253	685	...	173	34	9	7	69	12	13	59	136	.315	.359
Pitch 46.60	.250	592	...	148	28	1	11	59	16	14	67	97	.327	.356
Pitch 61.75	.236	581	...	137	24	6	13	65	16	10	53	97	.301	.365
Pitch 76.90	.249	489	...	122	22	3	19	74	9	6	64	67	.339	.423
Pitch 91.105	.279	298	...	83	18	4	6	34	10	4	31	45	.348	.426
Pitch 106.20	.239	92	...	22	4	0	0	1	2	0	14	17	.340	.283
Pitch 121.35	.250	28	...	7	1	0	0	5	1	0	4	8	.344	.286
Pitch 136.50	.167	6	...	1	0	0	0	0	0	0	0	0	.167	.167

III

Player Comments

American League

Starting Pitchers

Brock J. Hanke

		ADJ		ACTUAL			EXPECTED			SUPPORTED		
		ERA	GS	W	L	PCT	W	L	PCT	W	L	PCT
1.	Clemens	2.55	35	18	10	.643	20	8	.719	21	7	.752
2.	Ryan	2.76	27	12	6	.667	12	6	.687	14	4	.763
3.	Wegman	2.83	27	14	7	.667	14	7	.676	16	5	.770
4.	Tapani	2.88	34	16	9	.640	17	8	.669	19	6	.773
5.	Guzman Juan	2.92	25	13	7	.650	13	7	.663	15	5	.760
6.	Key	2.97	33	16	12	.571	18	10	.655	20	8	.706
7.	Abbott	3.00	34	18	11	.621	19	10	.650	21	8	.711
8.	Erickson	3.04	32	20	8	.714	18	10	.643	22	6	.780
9.	Langston	3.11	34	19	8	.704	17	10	.634	18	9	.684
10.	Moore	3.13	33	17	8	.680	16	9	.631	17	8	.661
11.	Bosio	3.21	32	14	10	.583	15	9	.619	16	8	.674
12.	Saberhagen	3.21	28	13	8	.619	13	8	.619	14	7	.643
13.	Morris	3.28	35	18	12	.600	18	12	.608	21	9	.711
14.	McDowell Jk	3.34	35	17	10	.630	16	10	.600	20	7	.734
15.	Krueger	3.55	25	11	8	.579	11	8	.570	11	8	.579
16.	Sanderson	3.55	34	16	10	.615	15	11	.570	17	9	.663
17.	Appier	3.60	31	13	10	.565	13	10	.564	15	8	.633
18.	Wells	3.63	28	15	10	.600	14	11	.559	15	10	.605
19.	Holman	3.64	30	13	14	.481	15	12	.558	14	13	.500
20.	Stottlemyre T	3.70	34	15	8	.652	13	10	.550	14	9	.599
21.	Swindell	3.71	33	9	16	.360	14	11	.549	12	13	.490
22.	Hanson	3.76	27	8	8	.500	9	7	.542	10	6	.652
23.	Tanana	3.81	33	13	12	.520	13	12	.535	16	9	.649
24.	Navarro	3.88	34	15	12	.556	14	13	.526	17	10	.613
25.	Milacki	3.91	26	10	9	.526	10	9	.522	10	9	.524
26.	Hough	3.93	29	9	10	.474	10	9	.520	10	9	.533
27.	Johnson R	3.93	33	13	10	.565	12	11	.519	14	9	.618
28.	Gullickson	3.94	35	20	9	.690	15	14	.519	20	9	.685
29.	Finley C	3.96	34	18	9	.667	14	13	.516	18	9	.649
30.	Hibbard	4.22	29	11	11	.500	11	11	.484	13	9	.571
31.	Brown Kv	4.23	33	9	12	.429	10	11	.483	11	10	.539
32.	Boddicker	4.28	29	12	12	.500	11	13	.477	13	11	.523
33.	Terrell	4.28	33	12	14	.462	12	14	.477	14	12	.528
34.	Nagy	4.39	33	10	15	.400	12	13	.465	9	16	.376
35.	Fernandez Al	4.41	32	9	13	.409	10	12	.462	8	14	.370
36.	McCaskill	4.41	30	10	19	.345	13	16	.463	10	19	.337
37.	Welch	4.87	35	12	13	.480	10	15	.414	11	14	.424
38.	Delucia	5.04	31	12	13	.480	10	15	.396	14	11	.542
39.	Stewart Dv	5.50	35	11	11	.500	8	14	.356	12	10	.555
40.	Gubicza	5.95	26	9	12	.429	7	14	.320	7	14	.339

1. Roger Clemens BOS

If you look at his career, you can see that Roger really doesn't deal well with the giant loads of innings he's been asked to pitch. His real career year, so far, has been the one where he was hurt, and so his arm got a little rest.

Still, it's hard to fault the Red Sox. Their basic battle plan is to mount a .600 offense and fill out the staff with .400 pitchers. That gives them a .500 team, except for Roger. The result is that, however many games over .500 Roger goes, so many will the Bosox. That means that they want to pitch him as much as they can, so as to maximize his value. Year after year, they pitch him right at the limit of his stamina - and then they pay for it in the LCS.

Obviously, the best thing for Roger would be if Frank Viola comes back, so the Sox can lighten up on Roger's load. Also obviously, since Roger keeps ranking #1 even under the strain, he's the very best pitcher in baseball right now.

2. Nolan Ryan TEX

If you read my pitcher article, you now that Nolan is the last of the sixties pitchers. Those are the guys who got light workloads in the Major Leagues when they were young, and who consequently did not tear up their arms. I wonder if they'd change the name to the "Nolan Ryan Award" if he pitched until he was 50?

3. Bill Wegman MIL

FANTASY BEST BUY. Nobody knows who he is. He's 29, and has never been overworked. This year looks just like his 1986 season, except that he gave up far fewer hits and runs. That looks like real improvement, not a fluke. I think he's for real. On the other hand, this is the Brewers....

4. Kevin Tapani MIN

The Mets' career minor leaguer is now 28, and has had two good years in a row. Frank Viola is now on the Red Sox. The only question about whether the Mets or the Twins won the trade is whether Kevin was overworked last year. I think he was; but, if they can keep it under control in 1992, I don't think it was serious.

5. Juan Guzman TEX

I really like him. He doesn't give up homers in the Skydome. If they don't overwork him for just three more years, until his shoulder matures, he could have a spectacular career. Nice strikeout totals, decent control, he's got everything. Another FANTASY BEST BUY until your league discovers him.

6. Jimmy Key TOR

Jimmy doesn't have the strongest arm, and was brutally overworked when he was 27. Still, he's slowly emerging from the shadow of Dave Stieb's reputation, and has a chance at John Tudor's career. When his arm is strong, his hits get down under his innings, and he stops giving up homers. When he's a bit hurt, the hits and homers blow up, as he doesn't have the fine control he needs. Given the arm trouble, I wouldn't pitch him more than 200 innings in a season. I certainly wouldn't do so in 1992, after he had to pitch in a LCS. BAD ROTISSERIE BUY, as the LCS innings put him over the danger line.

7. Jim Abbott CAL

This is not a great one-armed pitcher. This is a great pitcher. If your fantasy league still has the people who think he's a freak, he's a great buy.

8. Scott Erickson MIN

FANTASY LEAGUE WARNING LIGHTS! Scott collapsed in the second half of the season. There could be two reasons for this. First, the hitters could have figured out what he throws. That's very likely; it's just another way of saying Sophomore Slump. He also could have pitched too much. He's over the danger line with the postseason innings as it is, and 204 in the regular campaign is a lot for a rookie anyway. The reason rookies can't handle as much work as veterans is that they tend to press, trying to prove themselves. This wears out their arms faster than veterans do theirs.

9. Mark Langston CAL

Why would you pitch him 246 innings when he couldn't handle 250 two years ago? I don't know that I expect the situation to improve. One of Whitey Herzog's big weaknesses is that he tends to overload his top starters. I'm not saying that Whitey is going to be determining Angel workloads from the front office. I'm just saying that, if you think Whitey's going to change the Rooster's habits; well, not this one.

If he can keep his workload under 225 innings a year, Mark's probably the best lefty pitcher in the league, maybe in the game.

10. Mike Moore OAK

Boy, did I call this one. Mike was murderously overworked by Tony LaRussa in 1989. Predictably, he collapsed in 1990, and his workload went accordingly down. That's the sign of a recovery year, and sure enough. If you look at Mike's career, it's obvious his season's stats will depend on his recent workloads. His limit for not collapsing seems to be something like 210 innings, which is what he got this year. I therefore rate him a decent bet to be OK again in 1992. Not a guarantee, but a good bet.

11. Chris Bosio MIL

Gee, it's beginning to look like Chris has an every-other-year pattern, just like Bret Saberhagen below. That's nonsense, of course. What's going on is that Chris couldn't handle his 234 innings in 1989. This year, he got 204, and should be fine for 1992. GOOD FANTASY BUY, as nobody thinks he's in Mike Moore or Bret Saberhagen's class. He is, though. He's got the arm.

12. Bret Saberhagen KC (NYM)

As mentioned above, and in the pitcher article, Bret Saberhagen does NOT have any mystical every-other-year pattern to his pitching quality. What happened is this: in 1985, the Royals gave him 235 innings in the regular season and then won a 7-game World Series, with Bret pithing three games. That was too much work, and his arm collapsed. In 1986, he got 156 innings, and was fine the next year. Then 257 in '87, and he got worse in 1988. In 1989, he pitched his arm out trying to prove that he could too handle that sort of workload, and trying to keep the Royals in contention. It worked for that year only. The 135 innings in 1990 restored him, but the Royals weren't sure, and so he only pitched 196 last year. That makes him a good bet to perform well for the Mets.

Please note that the only oddity in this whole analysis is the 1989 season, which was Bret's career year. Every other explanation you look at has more holes than that. It's simple. Bret Saberhagen cannot handle 250-inning workloads. He probably can't handle over 230. That still puts him in the top fourth of baseball starters. Now, whether the Mets, who aren't very good about pitching arms, can keep him healthy, I don't know. If they do keep his workload down, he'll move back up to the top five in the rankings. If not, Chris Bosio will be better again.

13. Jack Morris MIN

I think what happened here may be a ballpark adjustment. Jack's 1990 and 1991 seasons are very close, except for a drop of 8 homers and a resultant 37 runs. What that suggests is that one of Jack's pitches can be taken downtown in Tiger Stadium, or one type of hitter can do it. Since he's changing teams, I don't know what to expect of him next year.

I sort of have to admire the man's commercial instincts. The Twins gave him a contract when no one else would, and he showed them no loyalty whatsoever. Of course, they did get a World Championship out of him, so I guess they can't gripe.

14. Jack McDowell CHA

At first glance, it doesn't seem like he picked up much from 1990.. Then you realize that old Comiskey was a pitchers' park and new Comiskey helped hitters. The actuality is that Jack made a significant move, and has placed himself in the class of pitchers who might become true staff aces. Note that I said "might". Jack isn't quite there yet. There are 14 teams in the American League, and Jack ranks 14th among the starters. That's the weakest possible staff ace. Jack still needs to take another step forward. At 26, that's hardly impossible.

15. Bill Krueger SEA

Bill's 34, and this is the first real good year he's ever had. Still, the supporting stats are not at all out of line with his 1989 and 1990 seasons for the Brewers. The Mariners are, at this writing, considering not even offering Bill Krueger a contract. I could not disagree more. For the Mariners to win the division, they have to get lucky. For Bill to have another season like this one would constitute luck, but it's not that much luck. The Mariners have neither a lot of other prospects for getting lucky nor do they have lots of pitching depth. I just don't see that they can afford not to gamble on Bill Krueger. A GOOD ONE YEAR FANTASY BUY.

16. Scott Sanderson NYY

Don Malcolm regarded the Oakland A's discarding of Scott as a real danger signal. He reasoned, and this was before 1991, that losing Scott was a waste of player talent in exchange for money savings. He didn't think the A's had anything like enough pitching depth to just throw away a good journeyman. As it turns out, he was prescient, and he gets some credit for it here.

The Yankees and Scott Sanderson? He's wasting his time there. He's too old to be helping them when and if they get a contender going.

17. Kevin Appier KC

I'm surprised Kevin ranked this low. I thought he was one of the coming staff aces of the American League. I don't think the Royals think he's this weak, either, or they wouldn't have parted with Bret Saberhagen. I do think that Kevin may have a large step forward in store for us. His 1991 supporting stats don't differ very much from his 1990. There's no real obvious reason for the big ERA jump. I suspect a combination of bad luck and Sophomore Slump, and therefore I expect the situation to correct itself. I wouldn't be at all surprised to see Kevin turn in an ERA below 3 or for him to win 17 games next year. One thing the Royals have been doing right: his workloads have been quite reasonable. GOOD FANTASY BUY.

18. David Wells TOR

This, too, may be a case of Sophomore Slump. On the other hand, the drop in strikeouts and the big jump in homers are danger signs of a weak arm. He certainly should be able to handle the workloads he's been getting, so I don't think that's it. Actually, what I want to say is that I want another year or two to get a good read on David. If he can quit throwing that guppy ball, he's going to be as good as the Jays think.

19. Brian Holman SEA

I have a lot more faith in Randy Johnson and Eric Hanson than I have in Brian Holman. Brian gives up more hits than innings, does yield homers, and doesn't strike out that many people. Yes, the ballpark probably does hurt him a little, especially in the homers. Still, the real good pitchers with his strikeout figures throw grounders, not homers. Given that the Seattle infield is very good defensively, that's the best Kingdom strategy. Unless and until Brian starts throwing those ground balls, I think this is the best he's going to get, and he could slide a lot at any time.

20. Todd StottlemyreTOR

There's no real good reason to think he can't duplicate this season for several years. He's 27, he hasn't been really overworked, this year is a natural development from his 1990, and he had this sort of reputation as a kid. He might still move up a step or two, but I imagine this is about it, really. As to whether he's going to go 15-8 again, well, that has a lot to do with the team around him. That team is the Blue Jays, so he may well post that record. GOOD FANTASY BUY, unless you've got some manager who's been following him since he was drafted or something.

21. Greg Swindell CLE (CIN)

I don't know. I wouldn't want to rest my pennant hopes with someone who had had arm trouble after 242 innings in 1988, and who had just gotten 238 again. If Lou can keep the innings down to, say, 210, I think Greg can be the pitcher everyone's been expecting, but I have my doubts for 1992.

22. Eric Hanson SEA

Eric did not respond well to overwork in 1989. I think his lifetime record is probably a reasonable estimate of his true ability. About 3.40 ERA, about 3/2 Won/Lost ratio. That's an awfully good pitcher, you know. Actually, one of the reasons that I expect the Mariners to make some contending noises in 1992 is that I think Eric will stage a comeback to about that. I'd still rather have Randy Johnson, but that's not an insult to Eric. It's faith in Johnson.

23. Frank Tanana DET

Are you kidding? Frank Tanana can still pitch? Well, I guess he can't die until Nolan Ryan does - he's got to bury the old Texan, doesn't he? If you take a look at Frank's supporting statistics, you'll be hard pressed to justify the low ERA. Bit of luck there. Needless to say, BAD FANTASY BUY.

24. Julio Navarro MIL

The Brewers have developed some pitchers, haven't they? Julio's only 25, and there's no reason to expect him to do anything but get better. Well, there's one. The Brewer brain trust gave him rather more innings than a kid should have last year, and they show no signs of not upping the ante. Guys, that's suicide.

25. Bob Milacki BAL

Slowly working his way back from the overwork in 1989. I think he'll get back to that year, but I think the O's ruined his chances to get much better. You really shouldn't be giving young pitchers that kind of load.

26. Charlie Hough CHA

Charlie Hough can still pitch, too? What is this? I thought your legs went first, and I thought you drove off the pitching mound with your legs. I mean, jeez, Charlie Hough is less than two months younger than I am. Still the oddest of the knuckleball pitchers. Gives up homers, but not hits. Doesn't walk very many. Just doesn't pitch like a knuckler man.

27. Randy Johnson SEA

Obviously, the Mariners would really like for Randy to do the things I think he eventually will. His Walks/Innings ratio was the worst of his career; yet, I think he's got his control down at last. Maybe I'm too influenced by the no-hitter. Maybe I make subconscious adjustments for the fact that his style is not well suited to his ballpark (throws hard and up in a homer park). Or maybe it's seeing him occasionally. He just looks like he's ready. Heaven help me, but I rate him a WONDERFUL FANTASY GAMBLE.

28. Bill Gullickson DET

The 20 wins were, of course, a silly joke of Tiger run support. Bill got 5.81 Runs per Game to work with. I'd win 20, too. Bill's Expected Won/Lost - what he'd go with normal support - was 17/12. His Supported Won/Lost was 22/7. Basically, I regard Gullickson as all but through. He can't strike anyone out any more, and he gives up way too many hits. All that's left is that he doesn't walk anyone, either. How he survived 226 innings, I don't know.

29. Chuck Finley CAL

Supposedly on the trading block. I don't think that's the solution. I think the solution is to quit giving him 236-inning workloads. His 1991 stats show little movement except for a 1/3 increase in homers and a 1/4 jump in walks. That looks like tired arm to me. On the other hand, he pitched all year, so his arm got no relief. BAD ROTISSERIE GAMBLE.

30. Greg Hibbard CHA

Sophomore Slump, delayed one year? His homers were way up; his strikeouts way down. It looks like he throws a particular cripple, and the hitters found out what it is. It does not look like a workload problem. The Chisox have gotten less out of more ballyhooed young pitching prospects than anyone, so I can't hold out a lot of hope. They have to pitch him, though, as they don't have anyone else, so he'll get a chance to recover.

31. Kevin Brown TEX

I have no idea what the problem is here. Kevin's hits were way up, with a lesser echo in walks. That's usually the sign of a quality problem, rather than a slump or tired arm. He hasn't been worked enough to get tired, anyhow. I know this: no one can survive in the Major Leagues with a 1/1 strikeout/walk ratio. The guys who strike out this few batters have to have control.

32. Mike Boddicker KC

The Royals signed yet another pitcher who had gotten wildly lucky with his run support. When will they give up? Storm Davis wasn't enough for them? They had to pick up this guy, too? Forget it, Kansas City. Mike Boddicker is bulk, #4 pitching, nothing more.

33. Walt Terrell DET

As far as I can tell, Walt has had one good year (1985) and one lucky one (1987). That's it. He'd probably retire in disgust except that expansion's coming. When his career's done, people are going to think that he pitched in the 30s, against Babe Ruth and Jimmy Foxx.

34. Charles Nagy CLE

Charles really doesn't strike out enough batters for a 25-year-old pitcher. Unless he just stops walking people altogether, you've got to start worrying about whether he's a Major League prospect at all.

35. Alex Fernandez CHA

Alex, on the other hand, strikes out plenty of people for a 22-year-old. His walk totals aren't that awful, either. I like him. A lot. Much more than Jack McDowell. In Randy Johnson's league. A BEST BUY: FANTASY, ROTISSERIE OR REALITY.

36. Kirk McCaskill CAL

Even a quick look at Kirk's 1986 season will tell you all you need to know. He got too much work, and he blew out his arm. Look at the strikeout stats. Cut right in half. He's never gotten the fastball back. Now he's got to learn to pitch like John Tudor or Bruce Hurst, or he's through. He may be able to do that, and expansion is going to give him four or five years to do it, but he's got to change is style completely. Needs a pitching coach.

37. Bob Welch OAK

I predicted this one last year. Every year, the A's have a designated starter. Designated, that is, to try to prove that he can hold up under the workload Dave Stewart can handle. Well, Stewart started out as a catcher, and never strained his arm as a kid.

Yes, Bob can come back. He probably will. If your fantasy league's managers all think he's through, pick him up. But if he gets another 238-inning season, he could really be through, at his age.

And to think. I got started on this whole workload thing by looking at Bob Welch compared to Fernando Valenzuela.

38. Rich Delucia SEA

Has not given a whole lot of evidence that he's a Major League pitcher. He's a 27-year-old sophomore and he doesn't strike too many people out. He does walk too many. Still, the Mariners have no choice but to use him, and he does have an outside chance. I wouldn't gamble a dollar on him, though.

39. Dave Stewart OAK

Finally, at long last, after many years of abuse, Dave Stewart proved to be unable to handle the workload that only Dave Stewart can handle.

40. Mark Gubicza KC

Innings in 1987: 242. Innings in 1988: 270. Innings in 1989: 255. ERAs since then: 4.50 and 5.68. If he sued John Wathan, I'd testify.

National League

Starting Pitchers

Brock J. Hanke

		ADJ		ACTUAL			EXPECTED			SUPPORTED		
		ERA	GS	W	L	PCT	W	L	PCT	W	L	PCT
1.	Glavine	2.26	34	20	11	.645	22	9	.725	25	6	.812
2.	Martinez De	2.27	31	14	11	.560	18	7	.724	18	7	.725
3.	Rijo	2.42	30	15	6	.714	15	6	.697	18	3	.844
4.	Belcher	2.71	33	10	9	.571	12	7	.648	12	7	.617
5.	Morgan M	2.86	33	14	10	.583	15	9	.623	15	9	.621
6.	Harnisch	2.87	33	12	9	.571	13	8	.622	13	8	.597
7.	Benes	2.95	33	15	11	.577	16	10	.605	15	11	.588
8.	Tomlin	2.98	27	8	7	.533	9	6	.603	10	5	.682
9.	DeLeon	2.99	28	5	9	.357	8	6	.602	7	7	.527
10.	Avery	3.00	35	18	8	.692	16	10	.601	20	6	.764
11.	Leibrandt	3.10	36	15	13	.536	16	12	.585	18	10	.630
12.	Smiley	3.12	32	20	8	.714	16	12	.581	20	8	.700
13.	Drabek	3.17	34	15	14	.517	17	12	.572	20	9	.704
14.	Hurst	3.21	31	15	8	.652	13	10	.567	16	7	.683
15.	Maddux G	3.22	37	15	11	.577	15	11	.566	17	9	.657
16.	Smith Z	3.24	35	16	10	.615	15	11	.563	19	7	.715
17.	Ojeda	3.28	31	12	9	.571	12	9	.556	11	10	.521
18.	Martinez R	3.35	33	17	13	.567	16	14	.546	21	9	.685
19.	Smoltz	3.37	36	14	13	.519	15	12	.543	17	10	.637
20.	Greene T	3.38	27	13	7	.650	11	9	.541	13	7	.631
21.	Cone	3.40	34	14	14	.500	15	13	.538	17	11	.601
22.	De Jesus	3.42	29	10	9	.526	10	9	.536	11	8	.579
23.	Tewksbury	3.58	30	11	12	.478	12	11	.513	14	9	.600
24.	Mulholland	3.65	34	16	13	.522	15	14	.504	17	12	.578
25.	Wilson T	3.65	29	13	11	.542	12	12	.503	14	10	.593
26.	Gardner M	3.69	27	9	11	.450	10	10	.498	9	11	.455
27.	Gooden	3.74	27	13	7	.650	10	10	.491	13	7	.651
28.	Hill K	3.97	30	11	10	.524	10	11	.461	9	12	.434
29.	Browning	4.02	36	14	14	.500	13	15	.454	16	12	.584
30.	Barnes B	4.05	27	5	8	.385	6	7	.451	6	7	.457
31.	Black	4.07	34	12	6	.429	13	15	.448	14	14	.495
32.	Viola	4.12	35	13	15	.464	12	16	.442	12	16	.419
33.	Smith B	4.26	31	12	9	.571	9	12	.427	13	8	.624
34.	Burkett J	4.31	34	12	11	.522	10	13	.421	11	12	.490
35.	Bielecki M	4.34	25	13	11	.542	10	14	.417	14	10	.577
36.	Portugal	4.76	27	10	12	.455	8	14	.373	10	12	.477
37.	Deshaies	5.25	28	5	12	.298	6	11	.328	5	12	.289

1. Tom Glavine ATL

Boy did the Braves' pitching staff get straightened out as soon as Bobby Cox got himself down in the manager's office. Starting with this guy. No, I don't think he's a fake or a fluke. But no, I also don't think he'd have done this without Bobby down there. As you will read elsewhere in this book, I think that Bobby Cox has done this sort of thing to three teams now, and that he deserves the lion's share of the credit here.

As for Tom Glavine's future, I'd just as soon have him as anybody. If your league is distracted by the press coverage of Steve Avery, this man could be a GREAT FANTASY BUY.

2. Dennis Martinez MTL

There's not much new to say about Dennis Martinez for old sabermetricians or old readers of these book. It's been clear for some time that this is, and always has been, a top-notch pitcher. He got overworked a couple of years there, notably in 1979 and 1982, and the resultant problems hurt him during what should have been his prime. But at all other times, he's been just great. Now he's 37, and playing out the string with style. His pitching stats haven't varied in shape in years, and there's no reason to expect them to do so for a couple more yet. GOOD FANTASY BUY, if your league, like the sportswriters, haven't caught on.

3. Jose Rijo CIN

Another great pitcher whose reputation follows him at a distance. What happened was New York Hype's dark side. Jose was brought up to the Yankees at age 19, and was awfully good for a 19-year-old. However, he was not Steve Avery or Dwight Gooden, so the New York press panned him. Then he was traded to the other coast, and the press forgot him. by the time he was 24, he'd gotten his game straightened out, but no one paid any attention. He was clearly the ace of the championship Reds team, but he had this injury and.... Right now, Jose Rijo is the best prime pitcher in this league. I'd rather have him than anyone other than Roger Clemens.

4. Tim Belcher LA

Worth Eric Davis. Possibly more. The Dodgers think they can always develop another pitcher. So far, they've been right. Fred Claire also has the sense to hedge his bets with Tom Candiotti.

5. Mike Morgan LA

And Mike Morgan. What happened from 1990 to 1991 is simple enough: Mike stopped giving up home runs and hits. That'll do it. What isn't obvious is that this season is completely compatible with his 1989. The Won/Lost record is much better this year, but that's the luck of the run support. Basically, Mike should be considered to have a few good years left in him. He's too old to be a prime pitcher, and I don't think he's the #5 man in the league over time, but he's good, and he has a 70% chance to be reliable for the next five years.

6. Pete Harnisch HOU

This, too, looks real to me. All the supporting stats are working. Pete's strikeouts are up; and his walks, homers and hits are down. That looks like a jump in class. I don't know that he'll be this good over time, just like I'm not sure about Mike. But Pete is only 25, and it looks like he's got his game under control. He should be close to this good. Again, he has no rep yet, and so is PROBABLY A GOOD FANTASY BUY.

7. Andy Benes SD

Unlike Pete Harnisch, Andy Benes did not perform any across the board miracles. He only did one thing. But that one thing was to get his control down, and nobody was waiting for anything else. With his mere 24 years of age, and his enormous body to put behind the pitches, he should be around for a good long while yet. Of the top pitchers, this is the best bet to actually get better. FANTASY GUARANTEE to be at least good.

8. Randy Tomlin PIT

I've complained more than once about Jim Leyland's shuttling of pitchers between AAA and the big club. He did that to Randy in 1990, but the kid was so good when he was up that even Jim had to give him a try in a rotation spot. His Won/Lost record is a fraud of uncharacteristic bad Pirate run support. After a year and a half of this, I guess I should say I think he's ready. Another GOOD FANTASY BUY, as, again, his reputation is way behind his ability.

After losing Bobby Bonilla, the Pirates have only Bonds, Bell, Van Slyke, the best catching in the league, a good leadoff/first base platoon, Drabek, Smiley, Tomlin here, and a more than acceptable supporting cast. That's why they won by 14 games. And that's why, Bobby Bo or no, the Mets should NOT be your pre-season picks to win the NL East.

9. Jose De Leon STL

This is not a typo. It never is. Jose always pitches completely out of whack with his Won/Lost record. As I get a press pass in St. Louis, and so get to talk to sportswriters, I've tried to figure out why the team can't score for Jose. The best I can do is to get a rumor that the hitters think he's a wimp of some sort. They think he's weak and unreliable, or so it's said. Well, I have this to say. Forget it, guys. He's also your ticket to the division title, if everything else you hope for goes well. If Magrane is back and Olivares is ready, if Lee Smith is not through and the batting order jells, if Jose Oquendo hits .280 again and Felix Jose doesn't slump, then another 16-11 year out of Jose De Leon just might do it. And all you've got to do to get that record is get this man some runs.

10. Steve Avery ATL

Well, he's 22, and Bobby Cox got to manage him, and he sure looks like he's ready. He doubled his innings over 1990, and didn't double his strikeouts, and tripled his homers allowed. But he also stopped walking people and got his hits down below his innings. That will do it every time. And no, he doesn't strike enough people out to justify the reputation his arm has. I rate him a BAR FANTASY BUY, unless your league is full of real tyros. Everyone's heard of him, and no one's heard of Tom Glavine, and Tom's proven more.

11. Charlie Leibrandt ATL

Not to mention - heh, heh - Charlie Leibrandt. If you asked someone to guess who surrounded Steve Avery in the Ballpark Adjusted ERA rankings, how long do you think it would take them to guess Leibrandt and De Leon? This season is compatible with 1990, so it might hold up for a couple of years, even at Charlie's age. I do question, however, if he can handle this many innings per year. He didn't do too well with just ten more five years ago. Still, he strikes out almost as many per inning as Avery does.

12. John Smiley PIT

Has everything back that he had in 1988 and '89, before he was hurt. It's the same shape of supporting stats, too. There's no reason to suspect any permanent damage. The 20 wins, of course, were a fluke of Pirate run support, but he's a legitimate 17-11 man. Still has no rep, so probably still a GOOD FANTASY BUY.

13. Doug Drabek PIT

I put out the overwork warning on Doug. He's had 244, 231 and 235 innings the last three years, and that's not counting the postseason. I don't think anyone can handle that any more, and Doug's is not the strongest arm. Until he demonstrates that he can in fact handle this sort of load, I rate him a BAD FUTURE, FANTASY OR REALITY. The Pirate offense might conceal it for a while, but I think he's headed for trouble.

14. Bruce Hurst SD

Just keeps rolling along. The most consistent pitcher in baseball. Don't you wish that your favorite team had outbid the Padres for him?

15. Greg Maddux CHN

Don Zimmer gave this man 263 innings to pitch. That's "two hundred sixty-three". HORRID FANTASY GAMBLE, and a big worry for the Cubs.

16. Zane Smith PIT

I think this is Zane's true level of ability. Better than your team's #4 starter.

17. Bobby Ojeda LA

Bobby has no consistency at all, and I have no way of making a prediction about him. He's only 34 and he's never been overworked in his life, so he's certainly not through; other than that, I can't say. His ERA should be between 2.50 and 4.50. Basically, what the Dodgers do with him makes sense. They don't count on his, but they keep him around in case he has a hot year. They try him in the rotation as a swing man or #5 starter, until he starts costing them. Then they bench him. When he came over from Boston, everyone compared him to John Tudor, but that's not accurate at all. Bruce Hurst is like Tudor; Ojeda's like no other pitcher I know.

18. Ramon Martinez LA

It is my humble opinion that the Los Angeles dodgers lost the 1991 division title in 1990, when Tummy Lasorda insisted on giving 234 innings to Ramon Martinez. Ramon had never pitched more than 100 innings in the Majors before, and he's physically tiny. If you look at his 1991 stats, what you see is no serious change except that the bottom dropped out of his strikeouts. That, to me, is the sign of a tired arm. Well, Tummy got what he deserved for his folly; but I doubt he's learned.

19. John Smoltz ATL

John seems like he's been around forever, but he's only 25, and has only been in the Majors for four years. Unfortunately, the last two of them have been virtually identical, and they were just this good and no better. He shows every sign of settling into a career as a decent journeyman. The Braves expect more, of course, and he's only 25. Still, if Bobby Cox couldn't get him off the ground....

20. Tommy Greene PHI

At first glance, Greene appears to be another Atlanta pitcher who's come into his own at age 25. However, as the rankings show, he's not really as accomplished as the Braves' lot. I'm not sure I should really attribute this to Bobby Cox, but I'm inclined to. I think that most of the Atlanta kids would have come to about this level of ability with modest management. I think it was Cox who made the difference. It would help if I had some evidence to back this up, other than the rankings; so at this point I'm willing to call it my speculation. I just have a lot of faith in Bobby Cox is all.

Of the group of Atlanta's kids, I think Greene may have the best raw arm. His strikeout totals are very impressive, and without Cox. Therefore, I think he may have more developing yet to do than Avery or Glavine, more refinement. REAL GOOD FANTASY BUY, especially if your league is not full of people who follow deeply enough to get into the Phillies.

21. David Cone NYM

I am not a big David Cone man. He clearly has the best strikeout arm in the National League, but he hasn't done that much with it. His reputation rests on one season, four years ago, when he didn't give up any home runs. He also got a little lucky with run support, and so posted a wonderful Won/Lost record. But the rest of his stats that year look just like the three that followed. The one other oddity in the great year is that it was his worst strikeout year. Rumor has it that he has head problems, and it may be that he has taken to trying to blow everything by the hitters. That could lead to increased strikeouts but also increased homers. At any rate, I rate him a BAD FANTASY BUY, because I think his rep is out of sync with his ability.

22. Jose De Jesus PHI

This is his real level of ability, and he might have another step forward in him. His development has been slow but sure, and there's no reason to doubt this year. At 27, I don't think he's ever going to be a top ten man, but he might be a top 15 someday. Another GOOD FANTASY BUY from the no-media Phillies.

23. Bob Tewksbury STL

A Whitey Herzog mistake. Whitey acquired him from the scrap heap, but didn't think he was a serious Major League prospect as a starter. I can see Whitey's reasoning. Tewks doesn't strike anybody out, and he doesn't control the home rune, either. Most real starters can do at least one of the above. But Bob also doesn't walk anyone, and that can give you this level of quality, if you're reasonably stingy with hits. Bob is. His talents, though, are truly on the borderline, and he's not a kid any more. Any slip in ability, and he'll drop out of the Majors real quick.

24. Terry Mulholland PHI

A good, solid journeyman starter who shows no signs of developing into anything more, or anything less. Your basic, mainline #3 man.

25. Trevor Wilson SF

Young and strong, could move up. However, he already strikes some people out, and his control is decent. He already gives up fewer hits than innings and his homers aren't out of control. For him to improve, he would have to do so across the board. That's not the good developmental sign. The good one is when you've got some guy who's walking five batters a game, and you know what one thing he has to do to start getting everybody out. Trevor might just stall out right here.

26. Mark Gardner MTL

This is a 30-year-old sophomore whose ERA, walks and homers went up, while his strikeouts went down. He was not overworked by any means. He may get something back, as Sophomore Slump is a suspect here, but the indicators are all that he's not going to get too much better. I figure him for just another bulk starter.

27. Dwight Gooden NYM

STILL A HORRIBLE FANTASY BUY, as there are people out there who think he's still a star pitcher just waiting out a string of bad luck. Well, he had the bad luck all right, but it was in the form of brutal overwork when he was very, very young. This is exactly the sort of thing that Craig Wright warns about in THE DIAMOND APPRAISED. However, Craig warns about it happening to college and minor league pitchers. Doc got his in the big time, and will probably never recover. The very mirror image of Nolan Ryan, but the very reflection of Terry Forster.

28. Ken Hill STL

Still has some control trouble, though it's not serious, nor nearly as bad as it was three years ago. Unfortunately, he's started throwing cripples, and his homers are way up. The main problem he has, though, is that he doesn't do well when asked to pitch more than five or six innings. When you get to my suggestion of a modified four-man rotation in the pitcher article, one of the people I'm thinking of is Hill. He could really improve if he got that kind of help.

29. Tom Browning CIN

He's had some luck with run support, and his Won/Lost record overestimates his actual ability. He never was more than a weak #2 starter or strong #3. Also, if you track his career, he doesn't do at all well with workloads of over 230 innings. As he's questionable on that score over the last three years, I rate him a BAD FANTASY GAMBLE, and a good bet to collapse even further in 1992.

30. Brian Barnes MTL

Only 25, could step up. Has to if he wants to stay in the Majors. Unfortunately, he has no one weak spot to work on; he's just not yet quite ready.

31. Bud Black SF

Never more than a journeyman, and he's 35 now; the Giants got just what they should have expected. Why they thought they were close enough to a title to need to fill out their rotation at this cost, I don't know.

32. Frank Viola NYM

Bad year was the result of several seasons of brutal overwork by two braindead organizations. As his arm does not seem to have fallen off, and as he's now moving to a team that plans better, I expect him to make a comeback. GOOD FANTASY BUY, unless the Bosox decide he should work as much as Roger Clemens does.

33. Bryn Smith STL

Won/Lost record was an illusion of run support. Actually, Bryn is on the brynk of being through. He's 36, and hasn't pitched really well in five years. His strikeout figures are reaching the dropout zone.

34. John Burkett SF

Last offseason, ol' Hummm Baby hitched up his jockstrap and told everyone that John here was on the verge of superstardom and was going to lead the Giants back into sweet, sweet contention. I lampooned that in the last book's comment, and see no reason to retract anything. The technical term for what happened to John Burkett is "Sophomore Slump." I expect him to get back most of what he had in 1990, but that's no staff ace. I don't expect him to improve much. He looked like his skills were pretty settled two years ago.

35. Mike Bielecki CHN

A one-year wonder in 1989. The Cubbie lack of depth is all that's kept him in the league. If they score him seven runs a game, he'll win 15; if they score ten, he'll win 20. If not, he's through.

36. Mark Portugal HOU

A half-year wonder, three years ago. Deport him.

37. Jim Deshaies HOU

Supposedly, there are teams who want to trade for him. I can't imagine why. If he were five years younger, he'd look like the Astros blew his arm out with 225 innings of work a couple of seasons past. What kind of pitcher is that? And that's IF he were five years younger.

American League

Relief Closers

Brock J. Hanke

		ADJ		ACTUAL			EXPECTED			SUPPORTED		
		ERA	SV	W	L	PCT	W	L	PCT	W	L	PCT
1.	Henry D	0.75	15	2	1	.667	3	0	.967	3	0	.949
2.	Harvey B	1.60	46	2	4	.333	5	1	.867	4	2	.648
3.	Swift	1.89	17	1	2	.333	2	1	.823	3	0	.869
4.	Farr	1.93	23	5	5	.500	8	2	.818	4	6	.390
5.	Henke	2.15	32	0	2	.000	2	0	.784	1	1	.360
6.	Aguilera	2.22	42	4	5	.444	7	2	.773	6	3	.647
7.	Ward	2.68	23	7	6	.538	9	4	.699	5	8	.416
8.	Henneman	2.88	21	10	2	.833	8	4	.668	8	4	.653
9.	Reardon	2.88	40	1	4	.200	3	2	.668	0	5	.091
10.	Montgomery	3.00	33	4	4	.500	5	3	.650	4	4	.500
11.	Olson G	3.05	31	4	6	.400	6	4	.642	1	9	.054
12.	Russell Jf	3.06	30	6	4	.600	6	4	.640	6	4	.552
13.	Eckersley	3.08	43	5	4	.556	6	3	.638	3	6	.348
14.	Thigpen	3.36	30	7	5	.583	7	5	.597	3	9	.275
15.	Olin	3.51	17	3	6	.333	5	4	.575	3	6	.374

1. Doug Henry MIL

It's only 36 innings, but the Brewers may have something here. Doug's 28, but he's not just a never-was filling in for the disintegration of Dan Plesac. Excepting an apparent injury in 1989, he's been able to master a one-classification jump each season. True, this year he should have been making the transition from AA to AAA ball, but that's OK. There are a lot of pitchers out there who come up for a half year and baffle everyone. What the Brewers need to do to keep him from falling apart is to not worry about next year. He's going to have a Sophomore Slump, as the AL hitters catch up to him. 1992 is, after all, on schedule to be the year he struggles with Major League competition and gets his feet wet. If the Brewers are patient, he might just be the closer they're looking for - in 1993. LOUSY FANTASY BUY for this year.

2. Bryan Harvey CAL

Now the highest paid reliever in history. It is good to be the closer on a Whitey Herzog team. It is not good, however, to get 78 innings of work in a year. BAD FANTASY BUY, but will probably still save his 30. Right now, Bryan is the only young top closer in the game, which does increase his trade value. I think I'd pay him the most of any closer, too.

3. Bill Swift SEA (now SF)

Most people who convert from starter to reliever do so in the minors. Either they're one-pitch wonders who can't get through the lineup twice, or they're guys who throw real hard but lose a couple of mph off the fastball after the first three innings or so. I guess you can figure out that Swift isn't the fastball type, name or no. However, I don't recall his having a one-pitch reputation, either. I know this: his strikeouts were a career high (per inning basis), and they're still not any good. The STATS, Inc. SCOUTING REPORT has him down for a slider and a "sinking fastball", whatever that's supposed to be. If it's a splitter, he might be a one-pitch wonder.

This is the second year he's done well, so it looks like he's for real, whatever it is that he has. He and

Mike Jackson sort of overkill the Giants' reliever problems. I doubt they're worth Kevin Mitchell, though. The principle here is that two players occupy two roster spots, while Mitchell occupies only one. Swift, by the way, is a GOOD FANTASY BUY.

4. Steve Farr NYY

This season resembles his 1988 year in Kansas City, except that this one's under the workload limit. If Steve did in fact give in to overwork in 1989, it might be that he's for real at this level of ability. I have my doubts, based on his age. Very few pitchers suddenly get good at age 31 and then recover from arm trouble at 35. He's a gamble, but then, that's what the Yankees are taking now.

For those of you who remember the "Johnson Principle" from Bill James' old ABSTRACTs, a lot of that principle is expressed there. The principle says that bad teams will drift over time back up towards .500, and good teams will drift back down, too. Bad teams have to take gambles. They lose a lot of them, but they then discard the players who failed. When they win one, they keep him. Meanwhile, the good teams aren't taking any gambles, which means they're not culling any futures. I don't mean to say that Steve Farr is going to take the pinstripes to sweet victory, but he will help them get to respectability.

5. Tom Henke TOR

Tom is one of the few pitchers to have enough arm to survive the effects of overwork. He got 91 innings in 1986, and actually improved. Then 94 in '87 produced a very minor injury and a big strikeout decrease in 1988, but that's about all. Even 89 innings in 1989 didn't tear him apart, though his K's went down again in '90. Last year, though, he finally paid a bit. It wasn't exactly a bad year, but he did need some help from Duane Ward. All in all, he's probably due for a comeback.

As for fantasy, he's NOT THE BEST BUY. He's good enough, but he and Duane are going to split the work, so neither of them should post totals like the guys who close alone will.

6. Rick Aguilera MIN

Rick has been respectable as a closer for three years now. Yes, he was a closer for that half season in New York, before they traded him for Frank Viola. They should have kept him. Platooned with Randy Myers and John Franco, he would have been most effective, and the Mets would have been death in the late innings. Instead, they went for the quick title. They got it, but so did the Twins. The Twins still have Tapani and Aguilera.

7. Duane Ward TOR

Duane is listed here with Tom Henke because both of them posted 20 saves. They're both right handed, so I guess you can't call it a platoon, but that's how it works in Toronto now. I don't know if Duane's arm will hold up in 1992. He got a lot of innings last year, though most of them were not in closer work. In any case, he figures to get a nice light load, splitting time with Tom. Before he's tested that arm, though, I WOULDN'T GET HIM IN A FANTASY LEAGUE. It's not like they have to pitch him or anything.

8. Mike Henneman DET

A decent closer, or maybe better, who is being brutally, brutally overworked by Sparky Anderson, who apparently thinks it's still 1973 and closers can still handle 80 or 90 innings of work. My best bet to collapse in 1992, and therefore a HORRIBLE FANTASY BUY.

9. Jeff Reardon BOS

The opposite story from Henneman. Jeff's ancient, but the Bosox have kept his work way down. His strikeouts haven't collapsed yet, so I think he's still got arm left. GOOD, RELIABLE FANTASY BUY for at least another year now. He should be glad he got away from the Twins; they were overworking him. The Bosox, as I mentioned in their article, are too well organized for that.

10. Jeff Montgomery KC

He has pitched over 90 innings every year since 1989. His ERA has gone up almost a run every year since 1989. His saves have, too, which has occluded the problem. Still, somebody had better have a talk with Hal McRae soon, or Jeff's going to be seeing that nice Doctor Jobe. RANCID FANTASY BUY; but Mark Davis might be a good one. He (Davis, that is) may yet be the KC Closer.

It's worth noting here, where the rankings within the league get really low, that the American League's closer corps is much better then the National's. Jeff here would rate in the top five in the NL. Given that Dennis Eckersley and Bobby Thigpen will probably turn in better years before they're through, this league is loaded with decent relief aces. To finish #10 here is no real slight.

11. Gregg Olson BAL

The same tale as Montgomery, but without the overwork and, consequently, without the obvious excuse. Gregg's strikeouts haven't gone down, nor has he lost control. He just gives up more hits per inning each year than the one before. The only explanation I can think of is that he came up with one real good trick pitch, and the hitters are catching on to it. Still, I'm not comfortable with that. He isn't giving up more homers, which you'd think would be the result of hitters sitting on something. Basically, Gregg is another guy I want to see more seasons of before I offer any conclusions.

12. Jeff Russell TEX

I think this year was just lost to recovering from the 1990 injury. I think he'll return to form by next year. I also agree with the Rangers that his future is as a closer. I rate him a GOOD FANTASY GAMBLE. If you don't get one of the top guys, this is the one I'd pick up. I'm not guaranteeing anything, mind; but I think he's the best bet.

13. Dennis EckersleyOAK

This one is not Tony LaRussa's fault. As distinctly opposed to his handling of starters, which has been homicidal, Tony has always kept Dennis' workload under excellent control. Perhaps that is out of respect for his age. And perhaps the age is all that is wrong with Eck now. He's 37. Most 37 year old players are showing a bit of wear, even the hitters. Perhaps 1990 was one of those "last hurrah" seasons that the truly great hitters often have. I wonder how much his Hall of Fame chances will be hurt by not having his career totals pile up in one specialty?

14. Bobby Thigpen CHA

Predicted. 89 innings in 1990 piling up a record. Under control this year, so might come back. Don't know that I'd bet on it though. Grounds for firing the manager.

15. Steve Olin CLE

Only 26 years old. Might turn into a Major League pitcher someday. On the other hand, he's with Cleveland.

National League

Relief Closers

Brock J. Hanke

	ADJ ERA	SV	ACTUAL W	L	PCT	EXPECTED W	L	PCT	SUPPORTED W	L	PCT
1. Berenguer	1.96	17	0	3	.000	2	1	.779	2	1	.730
2. Williams Mch	2.34	30	12	5	.706	12	5	.711	10	7	.597
3. Smith L	2.59	47	6	3	.667	6	3	.668	2	7	.277
4. Franco	2.93	30	5	9	.357	9	5	.611	4	10	.308
5. Dibble	3.06	31	3	5	.375	5	3	.590	3	5	.315
6. Jones Bar	3.15	13	4	9	.308	7	6	.577	5	8	.375
7. Howell J	3.18	16	6	5	.545	6	5	.572	3	8	.272
8. Landrum	3.23	17	4	4	.500	5	3	.565	3	5	.354
9. Righetti	3.39	24	2	7	.222	5	4	.540	2	7	.188
10. Osuna	3.53	12	7	6	.538	7	6	.520	7	6	.572
11. Lefferts	3.78	23	1	6	.143	3	4	.485	2	5	.256
12. Smith Dv	5.73	17	0	6	.000	2	4	.291	0	6	.075

1. Juan Berenguer ATL

It isn't very often that the league's #1 closer loses his job before the season is through. Yet Alejandro Pena finished the year as the Braves ace. On balance, I agree with that decision. 1991 is completely out of the context of the rest of Juan Berenguer's career, and he's 37 years old. On the other hand, I'd sure keep him around. Odder things have happened to pitchers than finding a few years of third wind in their late 30's. Pena, by the way, is 33.

You might think that, with two journeyman elders as their closer corps, the Braves are in for some trouble. Not necessarily. The closers of the National League are a pretty weak lot right now. Every one of them has a question mark or even more. Many are old, like Juan, Alejandro and Lee Smith. Some are overworked, like Mitch Williams. Some have new managers who haven't been tested, like John Franco. And some are just plain bad.

One feature of the way things get done on this book is that I get the pitcher rankings commingled, rather than separated by league. In the combined closer ranking, Juan Berenguer is only #5. Mitch Williams is #8, Lee Smith #9 and it goes downhill from there. When you consider that the ranking is based on adjusted ERA, and that the American League scored 3/4 of a run more per game than the National, this is pitiful. The AL just plain has all the good closers. And yes, the opposite is true among the starters. Roger Clemens ranks behind three NL men.

When this sort of league disparity happens, the usual suspect is the Designated Hitter. It's plausible. One thing the DH does is let managers keep their middle relievers in longer than in the NL, rather than pinch-hitting for them. That may allow AL managers to get better control of the last-one-inning job that the closer role has evolved into.

Still, the usual suspect is not always the actual culprit, and plausible is not certain. Maybe the AL just went through a spurt of drafting kid closers and it's now paying off. I don't know. I haven't had time to study the issue since I got the rankings. Maybe next year. If you've got some evidence, write me a letter.

2. Mitch Williams PHI

Discarding Mitch was one of the sillier Cub moves. His 1990 collapse had been nothing more than overwork. His comeback this year should have been expected, and I did predict it. On the other hand, the Phillies gave him a ridiculous 88 innings of work, while never contending for the division title, and so I expect him to fall apart again in

1992. HORRID ROTISSERIE BUY., AND A WORSE FANTASY ONE. You might get some saves out of him before the Phillies catch on, whereas in a simulation game, he'll have nothing. What you're looking for, of course, is for Mitch to pitch fewer than 75 innings again. Then he should be on the upswing. No, I have no idea how long he can keep riding the yo-yo.

3. Lee Smith STL

I had "Mr. Lee" down for a disappointment. I figured that, with Todd Worrell gone, Joe Torre would be unable to keep his closer under 80 innings. He'd reason that the big man had always been able to handle big loads before. Well, score one for Torre. He kept the innings down to 73, and got a record performance for it. If the load stays down, Lee Smith should have at least four more years, and Todd Worrell is expected back. GREAT FANTASY BUY. Right now, given a new manager is New York, Lee is the only closer in this league that I would bank on.

4. John Franco NYM

The Mets, of all people, have kept his innings down, and they've reaped the rewards. I don't know if Torborg will continue that. If he does, Franco's going to be good. If John goes over 80 innings, he's going to fall apart. Keep track of the innings at the All-Star break in 1992. You'll know whether to unload him or keep him.

5. Rob Dibble CIN

The following paragraph is worth about $500,000 to Lou Pinella, if he'll only buy the lousy book and read it. Lou, it's like this. You had three reasonable closers, and you chose to give this one more than 80 innings because he got hot early and Randy Myers didn't. You ended up starting Myers and Norm Charlton too, rather than keeping them in the bullpen. Now Myers is gone. You must, absolutely must, return Charlton to the bullpen and share the work. No more than 70 innings per man. With two good men, you have the luxury of being able to do that and not waste opportunities. If you don't, you deserve to have your closer collapse in September, like Dibble just did.

6. Barry Jones MTL

Trading him was a terrible Chisox move. On the other hand, he pitched 88 innings last year. I expect him to fall back some or stay no more than even.

7. Jay Howell LA

Tummy Lasorda, as you know by now if you've been reading this book, has no more idea how to organize a pitching staff than my dear departed grandmother. He's kept Jay's innings down, so he stays healthy. On the other hand, he can't get the work organized, so Jay isn't really a closer, and only gets 16 saves a year. If he were worked correctly, he could pitch 65 innings and save 35.

8. Bill Landrum PIT

Last year, I made a sarcasm about the media perception that you can't win without a top closer. Bill had pitched great, but not really been used as a finishing pitcher. In 1991, Bill didn't pitch nearly as well, but was the sort of regular closer. The media started talking about his great closer ability. All of which just goes to show that you can't win. The media have got it into their heads that you can't win without a top closer, and they're not about to look at such irrelevancies as facts.

9. Dave Righetti SF

Basically, Righetti is through. However, the Giants don't have enough pitching to discard him. Bill Swift probably has the closer job, so I expect Roger Craig to try converting Dave back to a starter. Sorry, Roger, it's too late.

10. Al Osuna HOU

Osuna got 82 innings, which is too many for a closer. On the other hand, he wasn't used to finish games all year. On balance, I think he can do the job, if the Astros give it to him and keep his workload under control. Remember, though, that this is the team that blew up Juan Agosto's arm in two years during which they had Dave Smith to use as well. Al's only one year younger than Mitch Williams, and can't be considered a grade A prospect. But still, he and Mitch are the only two young closers in the league. GOOD ROTISSERIE GAMBLE.

11. Craig Lefferts SD

Couldn't handle 107 innings in 1989 followed by 79 in 1990. Neither can anyone else. He only got 69 this year, so he might come back some. But he's 34, and I wouldn't want to bet on him.

12. Dave Smith CHN

Last year's readers will recall that Dave Smith is one of the linchpins of my innings theories. The Astros kept him under 75 innings for years, and he was the only consistent reliever in the league. Meanwhile, they gave 90 innings to Juan Agosto and he collapsed in just two years. So, does this debacle change my mind? Not really. What I think happened here is that the ballpark adjustment got to Dave. In the Dome, he could pace himself and throw high in the strike zone. No one was going to take him downtown; and, if they did, no one was going to be on base. In Wrigley Field, though, you must pitch down, down, down. You also have to be careful every pitch. What I think happened is that Dave felt the pressure of that, and started pitching some one else's game than his. As to whether he can come back, yes, I think so. If you've got a league full of Cubbie fans who now hate him, he's a REAL GOOD FANTASY GAMBLE.

American League

Catchers

Brock J. Hanke

		OWAR	DWAR	TWAR
1.	Tettleton	4.33	-0.59	3.74
2.	Parrish Ln	1.52	0.91	2.44
3.	Macfarlane	2.23	0.07	2.30
4.	Harper B	2.12	0.12	2.24
5.	Nokes	2.47	-0.55	1.92
6.	Myers G	0.99	0.02	1.01
7.	Hoiles	0.75	0.17	0.92
8.	Fisk	0.57	0.29	0.87
	Karkovice	0.52	0.19	0.71
	Mayne	0.39	0.11	0.50
	Stanley M	0.69	-0.40	0.28
	Orton	-0.04	0.17	0.13
	Borders	-0.46	0.58	0.12
9.	Surhoff BJ	0.08	0.02	0.10
10.	Steinbach	1.18	-1.09	0.09
	Spehr	-0.04	0.03	-0.01
	Dempsey	-0.08	0.02	-0.06
	Merullo	-0.12	0.02	-0.11
	Petralli	0.38	-0.52	-0.14
	Whitt	-0.13	-0.05	-0.19
	Taubensee	0.01	-0.25	-0.24
	Tingley	-0.33	-0.00	-0.33
	Lopez L	-0.34	-0.01	-0.35
	Quirk	-0.20	-0.19	-0.39
11.	Valle	-0.91	0.49	-0.42
	Marzano	-0.45	-0.08	-0.53
	Bradley S	-0.53	-0.01	-0.54
	Ortiz	-0.85	0.25	-0.60
	Melvin	-0.36	-0.26	-0.63
	Geren	-0.72	-0.11	-0.83
	Allanson	-0.61	-0.40	-1.01
12.	Skinner J	-0.84	-0.21	-1.05
	Alomar S	-1.04	-0.01	-1.05
13.	Pena T	-1.37	0.29	-1.08
14.	Rodriguez I	-0.88	-0.34	-1.22

1. Mickey Tettleton DET

Of course he's not this good. What happened here is clear enough. Mickey moved from a hard homer park to Tiger Stadium, which is the best fit in the AL for his talents. Always selective about his pitches, Mickey started sitting on balls in his wheelhouse and made the pitchers pay. The hurlers will adjust this year, and Mickey will come back down to earth. However, earth may not be that far down in this case. Mickey is ideally suited to the ballpark, and he does have that strike zone judgement. Pitcher adjustment, I believe, bothers this sort of player less than others, because they just cannot be made to chase bad pitches. You have to figure out what Mickey can't hit and then throw it for strikes. That's not the same as just being able to throw it. There are always going to be some pitchers that Mickey will be able to punish, as long as he's helped by Tiger.

By the way, if you're wondering what happened to the fifty homer a year men of the 1950s, the ballparks is what happened. Tiger Stadium could not be built now; its dimensions are too small. If all the parks were still like this, the AL would be full of Cecil Fielders and Mickey Tettletons. For Sparky to acquire a team of them is just the man adjusting to his environment. I'm not sure I want to give Sparky credit for that insight, but that's what has happened.

Oh, yeah, Roti ball. Mickey is STILL A GOOD BUY, but he's a better buy in a true simulation league. The walks are worthless to Rotisserie.

Catchers	G	PO	A	Er	TC	DP	PB	SB	CS	CS%	FPct	DI	DG	DW%	DWAR	ERA	ERA Wo/W
Allanson	56	212	22	5	239	1	3	20	16	.444	.979	396.2	2.7	.171	-.48	4.52	1.00
Alomar S	46	280	18	4	302	5	5	21	12	.364	.987	395.1	2.7	.268	-.22	3.92	.90
Borders	101	503	48	4	555	4	13	50	28	.359	.993	699.2	4.7	.425	.35	3.42	.96
Bradley S	65	284	16	2	302	4	3	36	7	.163	.993	404.2	2.7	.281	-.19	4.05	1.10
Dempsey	56	246	23	2	271	5	5	29	12	.293	.993	408.2	2.8	.289	-.17	4.10	.98
Fisk	106	535	53	4	592	5	11	54	37	.407	.993	794.1	5.4	.321	-.15	3.95	1.10
Geren	63	255	18	3	276	2	1	31	14	.311	.989	375.2	2.5	.245	-.27	4.19	.93
Harper B	119	642	31	8	681	7	9	98	28	.222	.988	990.0	6.7	.294	-.37	3.75	1.04
Hoiles	89	433	42	1	476	5	3	49	26	.347	.998	728.2	4.9	.320	-.15	4.19	.84
Karkovice	69	309	28	4	341	6	2	25	19	.432	.988	455.1	3.1	.345	-.02	3.66	.95
Macfarlane	69	389	30	3	422	4	4	21	17	.447	.993	578.2	3.9	.298	-.20	4.06	1.06
Marzano	48	174	20	3	197	0	6	16	13	.448	.985	283.0	1.9	.248	-.19	4.17	1.05
Mayne	80	426	34	6	466	4	2	53	23	.303	.987	607.0	4.1	.304	-.19	3.78	.94
Melvin	71	381	30	1	412	8	3	48	19	.284	.998	571.2	3.9	.261	-.35	4.87	1.11
Merullo	27	79	8	1	88	1	3	15	8	.348	.989	136.2	0.9	.273	-.07	4.02	1.05
Myers G	103	478	37	11	526	7	9	68	25	.269	.979	744.0	5.0	.295	-.28	3.57	1.04
Nokes	129	682	47	6	735	7	11	99	36	.267	.992	992.2	6.7	.233	-.79	4.50	1.06
Ortiz	59	199	18	1	218	2	3	15	13	.464	.995	361.2	2.4	.387	.09	3.64	.98
Orton	28	145	22	1	168	3	1	16	11	.407	.994	205.2	1.4	.407	.08	3.72	1.01
Parrish Ln	111	657	58	2	717	12	19	53	39	.424	.997	912.2	6.2	.440	.56	3.50	.87
Pena T	140	864	58	5	927	14	5	81	40	.331	.995	1156.2	7.8	.310	-.31	3.98	.96
Petralli	66	294	19	9	322	3	3	36	17	.321	.972	403.0	2.7	.124	-.62	4.51	1.01
Quirk	54	294	31	6	331	2	2	38	24	.387	.982	436.2	3.0	.217	-.39	4.27	.91
Rodriguez I	88	517	61	10	588	6	8	36	34	.486	.983	684.0	4.6	.231	-.55	4.39	.97
Skinner J	99	504	37	5	546	4	6	54	28	.341	.991	790.0	5.3	.253	-.52	4.22	.99
Spehr	37	190	17	3	210	2	5	13	14	.519	.986	230.1	1.6	.291	-.09	3.91	1.00
Stanley M	58	240	9	5	254	1	3	34	7	.171	.980	356.0	2.4	.138	-.51	4.65	1.06
Steinbach	116	589	47	13	649	7	6	76	35	.315	.980	941.1	6.4	.155	-1.09	4.69	1.08
Surhoff BJ	127	660	67	4	731	11	11	86	35	.289	.995	1055.0	7.1	.294	-.40	4.21	1.06
Taubensee	25	89	6	2	97	1	4	19	3	.136	.979	181.0	1.2	.130	-.27	4.77	1.15
Tettleton	124	551	56	6	613	2	9	64	40	.385	.990	1004.2	6.8	.231	-.81	4.55	1.04
Tingley	45	222	32	3	257	2	3	20	22	.524	.988	323.1	2.2	.289	-.13	4.20	1.19
Valle	129	670	52	6	728	10	15	46	31	.403	.992	926.1	6.3	.363	.08	3.65	.91
Whitt	20	72	8	0	80	0	1	11	6	.353	1.000	118.0	0.8	.287	-.05	6.41	1.36
TOTALS	***	13491	1144	155	14790	162	214	1469	758	.340	.990	1479.0	10.0	****	****	4.10	

2. Lance Parrish CAL

Still has that good arm, still has good defensive stats overall, too. His With/Without Ratio is excellent, indicating that he's not hurting his pitchers in some subtle way. Given that, I have to wonder why Whitey is shopping him around. Maybe it's the offensive focus, all power and no walks. That may not say "catcher" to Whitey. Still, I think I'd keep him, at least until the dearth at the position corrects itself and there's somebody else to play here.

3. Mike MacFarlane KC

What on earth is Mike MacFarlane doing up here in the rankings? Oh, I see. He got platooned, and turned some doubles into homers. That'll do it, at this position. RANCID FANTASY BUY, unless he keeps this up with his playing time doubled.

4. Brian Harper MIN

Whitey Herzog says that the trade of Harper was his worst mistake with the Cardinals. I disagree. At the time, there were some people who could hit and play good defense as well. Now, the position is going through a recession, just like the economy. Brian Harper is little if any better than he was in 1985, but the position has lost all the people who were superior.

Whitey's worst mistake, by the way, was rushing Luis Alicea up to play second base when Tommy Herr got traded. Not only was Luis not ready; not only did his failure regress his career badly; but Jose Oquendo was in fact ready, and Whitey didn't see it.

5. Matt Nokes NYY

Oh, please. Will somebody develop some catchers in their minor league system?

6. Greg Myers TOR

A rare lefty bat at catcher. Easing him into the lineup by platooning him with Pat Borders didn't hurt for a year, but I would assume the job is now his until he proves he can't hit lefty pitching. Easily the best, possibly the only, young catcher in the game. Figures to come in about #3 at this position in 1992, and as such, is a GOOD FANTASY BUY.

7. Chris Hoiles BAL

He was 27 last year; this should be his peak season. The Orioles are still looking, but who knows? Chris could hold the job for five years before they find anyone.

8. Carlton Fisk CHA

Carlton is exactly 36 days younger than I am. I couldn't post these stats in Little League. On the other hand, if there were any catchers around, the stats plus his age would cost him his job. As it is, he can still play.

9. B. J. Surhoff MIL

Last year, I wrote that Surhoff's problems were the biggest thing keeping the Brewers out of contention. He still isn't exactly helping them, and I think his career is in jeopardy. On the other hand, the Brewers now have more problems than B. J., and have apparently given up on the division chase.

10. Terry Steinbach OAK

There are five part-timers between Fisk and Steinbach. What that says is that Steinbach is inadequate, while Fisk can still play. Or maybe not. Both Terry's and Jamie Quirk's defensive stats are nothing, and both have been decent in the past. There may have been a one-year aberration in the ballpark that foiled the system. Or maybe not; both these guys are old. At any rate, Terry remains the last man in the rankings who can hit at all.

11. Dave Valle SEA

Dave took a brutal press beating in Seattle, as he didn't hit at all early in the year. That was unfair, the position doesn't have any hitters, and the Mariners don't have any options. Still, the M's are close enough to contention to start thinking about addressing problems at the skill positions. If there were any free agent or kid catchers out there, I would suggest they go after them. As it is, they're going to have to work the waiver wire as never before.

12. Joel Skinner CLE

You know, I was never that high on Sandy Alomar Jr. See my comments in the last couple of books. Still, he would probably be dominating this position if he had stayed healthy. All of which goes to show that, when you're snakebit, you're snakebit. The Indians need anti-venin.

13. Tony Pena BOS

This is serious. Tony's 1991 was just horrid, and he's 35. He may have torn his legs up with those oddball catching stances he uses. In short, he may be through, weak position or no. And the Bosox absolutely cannot afford such a hole in their lineup, if they're going to overtake the Blue Jays. They've got to do something, and they've got to do it now, and the only decent gamble out there is Sandy Alomar.

14. Ivan Rodriquez TEX

Ivan Rodriguez is only twenty (20) years old, which is the only excuse for playing him. Neither Mike Stanley nor Gino Petralli can play the position on defense, and the position is weak, and the Texas ballpark inflates offensive stats, so the Rangers could get away with playing Ivan. Still, he is clearly a AA player being murderously rushed.

National League

Catchers

Brock J. Hanke

		OWAR	DWAR	TWAR
1.	Biggio	4.19	-0.52	3.66
2.	Scioscia	2.72	0.42	3.14
3.	LaValliere	1.85	0.45	2.30
	Carter G	1.39	0.45	1.85
	Slaught	1.57	0.24	1.81
	Villanueva	1.71	-0.03	1.68
4.	Santiago	1.64	0.02	1.67
5.	Cerone	1.20	0.14	1.34
6.	Pagnozzi	1.02	-0.03	0.99
	Sasser	0.78	-0.06	0.72
7.	Olson Greg	0.10	0.58	0.69
	Reed Jf	0.44	0.00	0.44
8.	Daulton	0.90	-0.57	0.33
	Hassey	0.04	0.17	0.21
	Fitzgerald	0.19	0.00	0.20
	Santovenia	0.00	-0.14	-0.13
	Nichols C	-0.07	-0.12	-0.19
	Kennedy	0.21	-0.42	-0.21
	Fletcher D	-0.47	0.25	-0.22
9.	Wilkins R	0.09	-0.36	-0.28
	Cabrera	-0.19	-0.10	-0.28
	Girardi	-0.23	-0.06	-0.30
10.	Reyes	0.02	-0.32	-0.30
	Manwaring	-0.19	-0.24	-0.43
	Hundley	-0.66	0.17	-0.49
11.	Decker S	-0.39	-0.16	-0.55
	O'Brien C	-0.94	0.14	-0.80
	Heath	-0.97	0.09	-0.88
	Berryhill	-0.81	-0.22	-1.04
	Gedman	-1.02	-0.06	-1.08
	Lake	-0.97	-0.19	-1.16
12.	Oliver	-0.93	-0.55	-1.49

1. Craig Biggio HOU

The Astros, as I suppose you know, are planning to move Craig out to second base or center field or somewhere, just as soon as they come up with what they think is a real catcher. They could be in for a wait. I'm not completely sure why it is that there are no good young catchers coming up any more, but I do have a couple of guesses as to contributing factors. First, the DH gives American League teams one more place to put a slow hitter than there used to be. Second, catchers don't last as long as other position players, so teams tend to put good bats where they won't wear out. Third, players hit big money only after their sixth seasons, so good young prospects don't want to play the spot where they figure to put in the fewest years. Fourth, catchers pay in offense for the defensive demands of the position, but arbitration and free agency don't pay off for defense behind the plate; so, again, good hitters don't want to catch. Fifth, steroids and bodybuilding have decreased the body fat content of professional athletes so much that there are almost none left of the Ernie Lombardi class of player whose lack of speed had to be hidden behind the plate. And sixth, the few Lombardis that remain just bulk up and play football.

Of these factors all make sense except the second. It is to the player's advantage to play as long as he can, but it is not to the team's, because they stand to lose his services as soon as free agency kicks in. And therefore, if I were running the Astros, I'd keep Biggio behind the plate. Yes, he has a bad throwing arm, but his ERA With/Without Ratio is good. If I had to choose between a catcher who throws base stealers out and one who helps the pitching staff, I'll go with the second guy every time. Besides, the impact of that bat is enormous. Given the current state of NL catchers, Craig figures to win the Astros about three full games over what they're likely

Catchers	G	PO	A	Er	TC	DP	PB	SB	CS	CS%	FPct	DI	DG	DW%	DWAR	ERA	ERA Wo/W
Berryhill	49	214	24	8	246	2	8	33	10	.233	.967	349.2	2.4	.258	-.22	3.58	.87
Biggio	138	889	62	10	961	10	13	126	46	.267	.990	1174.2	8.1	.284	-.54	3.93	.91
Cabrera	17	72	5	1	78	0	3	10	4	.286	.987	111.0	0.8	.226	-.10	4.22	1.23
Carter G	68	355	45	5	405	2	4	59	28	.322	.988	497.1	3.4	.469	.41	2.80	.88
Cerone	80	417	35	6	458	0	6	39	32	.451	.987	564.0	3.9	.385	.14	3.38	.92
Daulton	87	487	30	8	525	5	2	84	18	.176	.985	708.0	4.9	.229	-.59	4.04	1.09
Decker S	77	375	40	7	422	4	7	49	28	.364	.983	569.1	3.9	.298	-.20	3.77	.89
Fitzgerald	53	293	24	2	319	3	2	61	21	.256	.994	409.2	2.8	.331	-.05	3.84	1.08
Fletcher D	45	244	20	2	266	1	1	33	13	.283	.992	334.0	2.3	.462	.26	2.96	.72
Gedman	43	192	13	5	210	3	3	30	10	.250	.976	251.0	1.7	.317	-.06	3.33	.89
Girardi	21	95	11	3	109	1	1	14	6	.300	.972	134.0	0.9	.280	-.06	3.63	.89
Hassey	34	172	12	2	186	1	4	33	9	.214	.989	274.1	1.9	.441	.17	2.69	.70
Heath	45	192	33	2	227	1	6	44	18	.290	.991	324.1	2.2	.391	.09	3.66	1.07
Hundley	20	85	10	0	95	1	1	16	6	.273	1.000	150.0	1.0	.521	.18	3.06	.84
Kennedy	58	237	36	6	279	3	2	44	35	.443	.978	390.1	2.7	.195	-.42	4.50	1.16
Lake	58	277	24	2	303	1	5	34	17	.333	.993	403.0	2.8	.279	-.20	4.22	1.13
LaValliere	104	558	45	1	604	4	5	90	39	.302	.998	844.2	5.9	.425	.44	3.55	1.08
Manwaring	67	315	27	4	346	7	0	35	20	.364	.988	471.1	3.3	.275	-.24	3.99	.98
Nichols C	16	79	13	1	93	2	2	8	9	.529	.989	114.2	0.8	.310	-.03	4.15	1.06
O'Brien C	67	396	37	4	437	7	2	55	26	.321	.991	488.0	3.4	.392	.14	3.54	.99
Oliver	90	497	40	11	548	6	10	70	28	.286	.980	676.1	4.7	.232	-.55	3.94	1.05
Olson Greg	126	712	48	4	764	10	5	95	37	.280	.995	1002.1	7.0	.423	.51	3.35	.88
Pagnozzi	138	668	81	7	756	8	5	86	70	.449	.991	1147.1	8.0	.346	-.03	3.75	1.10
Reed Jf	88	519	29	4	552	7	7	57	28	.329	.993	682.2	4.7	.361	.05	3.60	.89
Reyes	80	375	61	11	447	4	10	38	43	.531	.975	568.1	3.9	.270	-.32	3.86	1.10
Santiago	150	821	98	14	933	14	7	93	57	.380	.985	1296.1	9.0	.351	.01	3.58	1.01
Santovenia	30	109	12	3	124	3	6	17	8	.320	.976	176.0	1.2	.220	-.16	3.94	1.09
Sasser	43	165	13	1	179	0	3	24	10	.294	.994	226.1	1.6	.263	-.14	4.41	1.30
Scioscia	115	677	47	7	731	7	3	82	30	.268	.990	907.1	6.3	.418	.43	3.19	1.12
Slaught	68	338	30	5	373	4	3	42	27	.391	.987	508.0	3.5	.421	.25	3.04	.83
Villanueva	55	259	26	6	291	2	4	42	16	.276	.979	400.0	2.8	.334	-.04	3.44	.81
Wilkins R	82	373	42	3	418	6	6	46	30	.395	.993	539.1	3.7	.251	-.37	4.81	1.34
TOTALS	***	11885	1114	162	13161	131	154	1651	809	.329	.988	1442.0	10.0	****	****	3.69	

to end up with, whereas he's a middle-of-the-pack man at second or center - a man who can easily be replaced.

The same argument applies to Todd Zeile. Todd's right about in the middle of the starters at third base, whereas his value at catcher is about what Craig's is. Todd's replacement behind the plate, Tom Pagnozzi, is another pack man at catcher. All the Cardinals would have to do, to improve their team by about three games, is trade Pagnozzi for a mediocre starting third baseman; a trade they could easily make. Casey Candaele is already a mediocre second baseman.

2. Mike Scioscia LA

One of the things that Fred Claire did right was to acquire Gary Carter and platoon him with Mike here. With the quality of catchers declining every year, the old guys like Carter and Scioscia and Carlton Fisk retain their value relative to the position, even as they age into their 40s. Mike's season is nothing compared to what he could do eight years ago, but no one else can do that now, either.

3. Mike Lavalliere PIT

Another left handed platoon catcher who only needed a replacement rate righty to help his team. And, again like Scioscia, his team went out and got him a good platoon partner. Between them, Lavalliere and Slaught are worth about four games to the Pirates.

4. Benito Santiago SD

Ranking based entirely on playing time; Benito was the only catcher to get into 150 games. Without that, he's just one of the guys, nothing special. One sure sign that his reputation is about two years out of date is that he didn't even throw out that many baserunners last year, and no one noticed.

What follows here is a technical point, so pay attention. There will be quizzes all through the player section. I, personally, downgrade Santiago and all his type of hitter: men in weak-hitting spots who don't get on base. Basically, unless your catcher is Craig Biggio or Mike Sciosia or Mike Lavalliere, you're going to bat the man 7th or 8th. The most important thing for a batter in that spot in the order to do is to AVOID MAKING OUTS. No one expects the #8 guy to drive in runs, and he's sure not going to score many with #9 coming up behind him, especially if he can't run. His job is to just get out of the way of the offensive flow, and pass the inning on to the pitcher so that he can end it and the leadoff man can bat first next time. Santiago, and all the batters like him, don't do that. They end the innings themselves, and they consume a lot of outs for their batting order spot. What you want out of your #8 man is someone like Jose Oquendo or Mike Fitzgerald. That's why I'm always plugging Fitz and

Jose and panning Benito.

5. Rick Cerone NYM

Any time Rick Cerone finishes in the top half of starting catchers, the position is in bad shape. His With/ Without Ratio is wrong, of course; unfairly inflated by contrast to the hopeless Mackey Sasser. Neither Cerone nor Charlie O'Brien is a good defensive catcher any more.

6. Tom Pagnozzi STL

Managed to play 58 more games than Cerone and still finish beneath him. Whitey was right; Pags is not really a starting catcher. The position, though, is just so weak. I mean, look. Pags has the best anti-baserunning arm in the game, and his other indicators are so bad that he still finishes with a DWAR below zero. He's a .260 hitter, and it's an empty .260. The Cards moved him down to 8th every time they gave Jose Oquendo a day off, and Oquendo should be batting ahead of him. Still, Pags finishes in the middle of the pack. Todd Zeile, of course, would be the best catcher in the league. Luis Alicea has hit well over .300 for two years running at Louisville playing third base.

7. Greg Olsen ATL

I was astonished that the whole post-season went by and no one mentioned Greg's catching stances. I mean, the man makes Tony Pena look like a robot. His feature position is a lowered squat where he rests on the sides of his feet and his butt is so low there's no chance of a ball getting under him. Then he improvises. Worst of all, he can actually jump up and move from these positions.

Or maybe this flexibility is just the wave of the future catching athlete. I was in Seattle when the LCS began, and pointed out Olsen's stances to Sue Schumacher, my Spy in the Sound. She said, "So what?" and promptly plopped down into the exact same position that Olsen was in. I asked her if she could get up from it and she popped up like so much blonde toast. Then she admitted to the gymnastics training...

8. Darren Daulton PHI

Why do teams do this sort of thing? I mean, everyone saw Daulton's collapse coming, just like we all saw Storm Davis's. Why do they sign them?

9. Ron Wilkins CHN

Hector Villanueva would have come in 6th, in spite of the low playing time. Hector Villanueva's With/ Without Ratio is good, while Wilkins' is pitiful. Folks, I'm telling you that Hector Villanueva may too be able to catch. Wilkins can't.

10. Gilberto Reyes MTL

This is the only year we'll be rating Gilberto. Mike Fitzgerald is clearly the starter here, but he was hurt all year. Nelson Santovenia is the #3 Expo catcher now, behind Reyes. The reason for preferring Reyes to Santovenia is explained under "Santiago." Reyes has no power, but he gets on base a little and so doesn't hamstring you batting 8th. Every time you start to wonder why they fired Buck Rodgers, just remember, Buck had Fitzgerald sitting on the bench, and thought that Santovenia was a #6 batter.

11. Steve Decker SF

I agree with Roger Craig; I think Decker will be able to play. He doesn't get on base enough to be a real offensive force, but he should develop enough power and batting average to hit 7th and drive in a few runs there. Besides, he's clearly the best defensive catcher the Giants have, and shows signs of becoming one of the best in the league. It's worth noting, though, that Decker would have been a marginal prospect a decade ago. If we get a run of young catchers, he could lose his career before it gets off the ground.

12. Joe Oliver CIN

Job is lost to Jeff Reed, which was obvious to me a year ago. I'm beginning to wonder whether Lou Pinella really understands about the skill positions. He doesn't handle problems at second or center field well, either. I won't rip him for his shortstop handling, though; when it's Barry Larkin who goes down, any replacement is going to look like a horror.

American League

First Basemen

Brock J. Hanke

		OWAR	DWAR	TWAR
1.	Palmeiro	6.01	0.35	6.36
2.	Joyner	5.78	0.52	6.30
3.	Fielder	4.73	0.27	5.00
4.	Hrbek	3.55	0.52	4.06
5.	Olerud	3.68	0.38	4.06
6.	Pasqua	3.59	0.46	4.06
7.	Quintana	3.12	0.47	3.59
8.	Milligan	3.11	0.21	3.32
9.	Mattingly	2.63	0.57	3.20
10.	McGwire	2.09	0.72	2.81
11.	O'Brien P	2.00	0.49	2.49
	Aldrete	1.82	0.17	1.99
12.	Benzinger	1.09	0.24	1.33
	Davis G	1.18	0.06	1.24
	Cromartie	1.00	0.07	1.07
	Bergman	0.65	0.16	0.82
	Martinez Crm	0.45	0.15	0.60
	Brock	0.51	0.09	0.60
	Stevens	0.51	0.05	0.56
	Vaughn M	0.34	0.02	0.36
	Segui	0.10	0.16	0.26
13.	Stubbs	-0.22	0.35	0.13
	Canale	0.01	0.05	0.06
	Martinez Tino	-0.07	0.09	0.01
14.	Jacoby Brook	-0.21	0.19	-0.02
	Jefferson R	-0.53	0.10	-0.43

1. Rafael Palmeiro TEX

BIG age 27 career year. I'd still rather have Mark Grace, but Rafael could convince me if he can keep a respectable amount of this value. There is hope; the power stats weren't just home-park generated, and he did get over the no-walks hump. Still, I don't expect him to remain the best first baseman in the league, or even the second best behind Frank Thomas. I don't really think he can keep up both the power and the batting average.

The two men who are famous for holding age-27 power surges, Stan Musial and Carl Yastrzemski, did not do what Rafael did. Both of them had been league-leading doubles men in their youths, and basically just converted a lot of those doubles to homers, and some singles to doubles. They didn't match their previous doubles highs, though they didn't lose many. What that says is that they developed uppercuts in response to losses of speed (Musial had the early nickname of "The Donora Greyhound"). Palmeiro, though, set career highs in both power categories, which looks much more like a fluke season. As a consequence, I rate Rafael a ROTISSERIE QUESTION MARK. If he holds the homers, he's great; but if he reverts to hitting doubles without the taters, he's going to go for too much money. Yes, I rate him a reality question mark, too, but not as big a one. I expect him to hold the doubles, and therefore some of the value.

2. Wally Joyner CAL (KC)

Apparently a Wally World Class jerk, Joyner can in fact play world class first base. The only question that remains is what chemistry will develop between Joyner and the Royals. There are two basic possibilities. First, Hal McRae and the Royal brain trust might figure out how to deal with the man. That would indicate that the problem wasn't all Wally in the first place, but a bad personality match between Joyner and, according to report, Gene Autry's wife.

The second possibility is that Wally will respond to being discarded by trying to establish his dominance with his new team. That's the Rogers Hornsby syndrome, and it spells trouble. It does help that McRae is no John McGraw, and won't try to overmanage his player. It also helps that Joyner is not coming off a championship year, like Hornsby

First Base	G	PO	A	Er	TC	DP	FPct	DI	DG	DW%	DWAR
Aldrete	46	312	22	2	336	31	.994	310.1	0.6	.493	.09
Benzinger	74	650	38	3	691	57	.996	648.1	1.3	.530	.24
Bergman	49	364	29	1	394	42	.997	379.1	0.8	.552	.16
Brock	25	150	10	0	160	19	1.000	158.0	0.3	.634	.09
Cromartie	29	216	8	1	225	20	.996	222.0	0.5	.463	.05
Davis A	14	116	7	0	123	14	1.000	115.0	0.2	.575	.05
Davis G	36	289	38	8	335	35	.976	299.1	0.6	.450	.06
Eisenreich	15	99	11	1	111	12	.991	105.0	0.2	.569	.05
Fielder	121	1041	82	8	1131	110	.993	1028.0	2.1	.478	.27
Hrbek	129	1140	95	8	1243	110	.994	1082.1	2.2	.580	.51
Jacoby	57	390	33	4	427	29	.991	438.0	0.9	1.262	.81
James C	15	95	8	0	103	7	1.000	110.0	0.2	.613	.06
Jefferson R	26	252	24	2	278	28	.993	227.1	0.5	.562	.10
Joyner	141	1335	96	8	1439	126	.994	1238.0	2.5	.550	.50
Larkin G	39	284	19	1	304	22	.997	241.0	0.5	.611	.13
Maas	37	325	22	6	353	24	.983	323.1	0.7	.414	.04
Martinez Crl	31	229	12	8	249	32	.968	227.2	0.5	.270	-.04
Martinez Crm	43	306	35	3	344	31	.991	317.2	0.6	.586	.15
Martinez Tino	29	248	23	2	273	24	.993	236.1	0.5	.532	.09
Mattingly	125	1097	77	5	1179	132	.996	1073.2	2.2	.605	.56
McGwire	152	1190	99	4	1293	119	.997	1262.2	2.6	.624	.70
Milligan	105	918	81	10	1009	91	.990	893.0	1.8	.461	.20
Molitor	46	389	33	6	428	52	.986	407.2	0.8	.442	.08
O'Brien P	132	1049	84	3	1136	124	.997	1063.0	2.2	.568	.47
Olerud	135	1119	77	5	1201	80	.996	1126.1	2.3	.516	.38
Palmeiro	156	1295	93	12	1400	119	.991	1357.0	2.8	.478	.35
Pasqua	83	510	43	5	558	46	.991	542.0	1.1	.520	.19
Quintana	136	1018	100	8	1126	102	.993	1031.0	2.1	.555	.43
Segui	41	202	22	1	225	22	.996	208.1	0.4	.595	.10
Snyder C	22	133	9	1	143	10	.993	110.1	0.2	1.344	.22
Sprague	22	143	9	0	152	13	1.000	143.0	0.3	.584	.07
Stubbs	92	824	82	8	914	79	.991	789.0	1.6	.577	.36
Tabler	20	182	14	3	199	11	.985	174.0	0.4	.381	.01
Thomas F	56	459	27	2	488	44	.996	476.2	1.0	.551	.19
Vaughn M	48	374	26	6	406	41	.985	352.0	0.7	.377	.02
TOTALS	***	20324	1613	165	22102	1991	.993	1479.0	3.0	2.852	7.51

was. And finally, it helps that Wally can't possibly be as big a jerk as Gregg Jeffries.

3. Cecil Fielder DET

Cecil spent the postseason complaining about not winning the MVP award. His beef was that last year he had been told (by Sparky, no doubt) that the reason he didn't win is that the Tigers didn't win. Along comes 1991, the Orioles are bad, and Cal Ripken wins anyway. Well, Cecil, the problem is this: you have to be better than the other guy, no matter where your team finishes; and you're not, no matter what Sparky says. You get to play in Tiger Stadium, and your stats balloon accordingly, and everyone knows that. You can't play defense, and your game has no breadth, and everyone knows that. Rickey Henderson and Cal Ripken are better players than you are, and everyone knows that, too.

Do I really need to tell you readers that, unless your fantasy game is ballpark-adjusted (fat chance) or includes defense, Cecil is a GREAT FANTASY BUY?

4. Kent Hrbek MIN

You know, there have been a lot of guys like this in sports. Kirby Puckett, Hack Wilson and Oscar Charleston were all pudgy, and they played center field. Charles Barkley plays basketball, for crying out loud. And yet it throws people when Hrbek shows enough agility to field routine ground balls. Why?

5. John Olerud TOR

He's 23, and the men above him are most definitely not, so he's going to catch and pass them all in two or three years. That will leave him second at this spot, behind Big Frank. If you are in a true simulation league, he's a WONDERFUL FANTASY BUY, but only a DECENT ROTISSERIE one, because he takes so many walks. What I want to know is whether he could play third base. He's not fast, but he has a pitcher's arm. I don't suppose we're going to find out with him in Toronto.

6. Dan Pasqua CHA

Everyone above Dan gets to move down one spot. That's because Dan, of course, is not the Chisox first baseman. Frank Thomas is, and he's also the best young player in the league. This is not to say that Dan Pasqua can't play. The new Comiskey proved to be a hitters' park, and Dan picked up six homers at home. More important, he became dangerous enough to be pitched to carefully, and his walk total went way up. I expect both of those to hold, and Dan to move back into the outfield. GOOD FANTASY BUY, as most people don't think much of him.

7. Carlos Quintana BOS

I wrote him off as no prospect a year ago; now, I'm not so sure. He addressed both his most pressing problems, lack of power and mediocre strike zone judgement. He's getting no homers out of Fenway, being right handed; and hasn't yet learned to exploit the Monster for doubles. If he learns to do that, and if the walks aren't a fluke, he could be OK. He's on the wrong team - the Red Sox have to have more than this out of first base and DH - but he could really help a team in a lesser hitters' park. If he goes somewhere, rate him a GOOD FANTASY BUY. If not, I wouldn't gamble on his playing time, what with Plantier and Vaughn.

8. Randy Milligan BAL

This was his third full year in the Majors, and it's a good enough third season to make him a prospect. Unfortunately, he didn't get started until he was 28, and this is not a good season for a 30-year-old. He remains a bad defensive player with too little power for first base. If he could play the outfield, his walks would give him a job at the top of somebody's order, but people put cleanup men at first. On a better team, he's a backup.

Of course, he's a backup on this team too, now that Glenn Davis has signed. Everyone below Wally Joyner and above Milligan here gets to move down another notch.

9. Don Mattingly NYY

I have never liked Mattingly as much as everyone else did, as readers of the SABERMETRIC know well. What I saw was a young hitter with few walks, who was making his living by legging out line drive doubles. I reasoned that the speed that gave him the doubles would leave quickly, and then we'd have on our hands just another power hitter with no strike zone judgement. Pitchers can deal with that, and they have in fact brought Don back to earth. I read him as completely recovered from the injury, because his defensive stats are back to normal. I think this is all there is going to be. HORRID FANTASY BUY, in my opinion, because at least a couple of your fellow managers are going to think he's going to hit 50 doubles again some year.

10. Mark McGwire OAK

Bill James used to warn people against young players with "old player skills." By that he meant young players with 1) a low batting average, 2) lots of power and 3) lots of walks. Bill figured that these players were going to age quickly because they didn't have anything to lose except what age usually gives people. Well, Mark McGwire is sort of the ultimate "old player skills" guy, and he's sure aging in a hurry here. Mark needs to add 50 points to his batting average, and he needs to add them NOW, or he's a backup. And I don't see how he's going to do that unless he gives up a bunch of the power, in which case, he's a backup. BAD FANTASY RISK, and bad risk for the A's.

11. Pete O'Brien SEA

The Mariners had a kid named Tino Martinez, who they expected to take the first base job away from O'Brien. They expected Pete and Alvin Davis to duke it out for DH. Well, Tino was a bust, and so was Alvin, for that matter. Pete's 34, which isn't encouraging. On the other hand, the M's now have Kevin Mitchell, and that frees up their several dozen outfielders and outfield prospects to try out for first base. My money, for what it is worth, is on Alonzo Powell. SPEND A ROTISSERIE DOLLAR ON POWELL, if you hear he got the job. Alvin should come back enough to run Pete off the DH spot. Tino Martinez has acceptable MLEs, but he's done nothing yet on the Mariners.

12. Todd Benzinger KC (LA)

Todd Benzinger absolutely cannot play starting Major League first base. Why do these teams keep trading for him? I just cannot believe that Fred Claire thinks this man can help the Dodgers. The only read I can make on the whole thing is that Fred 1) thinks he can't trade Kal Daniels and will have to play him at first, 2) doesn't think he can get any other help at first, and also 3) doesn't think Eric Karros is any readier than I think he is. Benzinger's a disaster backup in case Kal gets hurt again.

13. Cranklin Stubbs MIL

I do not know what to make of Franklin Stubbs' career, and neither do you, and neither does Don Malcolm.

14. Brook Jacoby CLE

Brook's stats will be found in the third base section, where they belong. He won't get a comment there, though, because he wasn't the most-used third baseman on the A's. What on earth possessed the Tribe to think that this man could play starting first base in the Major Leagues at this age, I do not know. He can still field enough to justify third base on a team with no real options, but that's about it. Right now, his status seems to be sort of itinerant, which is a polite way of saying "finished".

National League

First Basemen

Brock J. Hanke

		OWAR	DWAR	TWAR
1.	Clark W	6.30	0.61	6.90
2.	Kruk	5.78	0.65	6.43
3.	Bagwell	5.83	0.40	6.24
4.	McGriff F	5.93	0.16	6.09
5.	Morris H	4.23	0.39	4.63
6.	Murray E	3.74	0.69	4.43
7.	Grace	2.98	1.03	4.01
8.	Magadan	3.48	0.51	4.00
9.	Merced	3.44	0.12	3.57
	Redus	1.86	0.11	1.97
10.	Guerrero	1.93	0.02	1.95
	Perry G	1.69	0.07	1.75
	McClendon	1.60	0.05	1.66
	Jordan	1.34	-0.04	1.30
11.	Bream	0.96	0.26	1.22
12.	Galarraga	0.63	0.27	0.89
	Hunter B	0.52	0.06	0.58
	Martinez Crm	0.37	0.13	0.50
	Oberkfell	0.28	0.03	0.31
	Donnels	0.15	0.12	0.26
	Litton	-0.48	0.30	-0.18
	Gregg	-0.35	0.10	-0.25
	Benzinger	-0.82	0.09	-0.74

1. Will Clark SF

I'd still rather have Fred McGriff. I'm not completely sure I know what I'm talking about, and yes, I'm trying to do the research to back up my opinion, but I have an argument for McGriff, not just an opinion. My argument is that Fred McGriff, because of his superior on-base skills, consumes far fewer outs than Clark does, batting in the same position. This means that the other San Diego batters get more chances to hit than the Giants do. And thus, while Clark's value per out, as an individual batter, is greater than McGriff's, I think the Padre offense gets more benefit out of the player. Another way of looking at this is that I think Fred McGriff should get some credit for some of the offense that the rest of the lineup generates, because he gave it some of its opportunity. If I ever get this quantified, I may revise the ratings system; for now, though, we stick with TWAR.

2. John Kruk PHI

One of Don Malcolm's favorite players, and I agree. He looks no more like a Major League outfielder than I do, but he can flat hit, and he isn't all that bad on defense. If Ricky Jordan ever does develop (15% chance, outside), John could move back into right field without hurting the Phillies.

And yet, there are several teams, looking at a pennant chase, who could have picked Kruk up for half his value the last three years, and none of them did. Meanwhile, Vince Coleman gets big free agent bucks because he can win superstars competitions.

Oh, yes, GREAT ROTISSERIE BUY, especially if you need batting average.

3. Jeff Bagwell HOU

What happened here is this. The Astros instituted a program of giving their hitting prospects one full month in the Dome to prove themselves; only then were they shipped out. Bagwell, who started the year expecting to play in AAA, regarded this as a godsend opportunity and a show of faith by the organization. His confidence buoyed, he got in a groove and earned himself a job. Eric Anthony, who started the year trying to live up to superstar expectations, regarded the one lousy month as a vote of no confidence, started pressing, and fell apart. It was the same month, but completely different expectations. That's what you get when you impose a system unthinkingly upon human beings.

First Base	G	PO	A	Er	TC	DP	FPct	DI	DG	DW%	DWAR
Bagwell	154	1263	102	12	1377	96	.991	1322.2	2.8	.498	.41
Benzinger	21	124	12	2	138	8	.986	143.0	0.3	.947	.18
Bream	84	656	52	3	711	50	.996	631.2	1.3	.550	.26
Clark W	142	1261	106	4	1371	117	.997	1216.1	2.5	.590	.61
Donnels	13	114	11	0	125	8	1.000	111.0	0.2	.705	.08
Foley T	30	147	9	1	157	8	.994	133.1	0.3	.487	.04
Galarraga	103	875	77	9	961	67	.991	850.2	1.8	.498	.26
Grace	159	1511	164	8	1683	109	.995	1395.1	2.9	.709	1.04
Guerrero	111	947	66	16	1029	72	.984	915.1	1.9	.360	.02
Hunter B	85	621	46	8	675	45	.988	594.0	1.2	.401	.06
Jordan	72	624	37	9	670	38	.987	600.1	1.2	.320	-.04
Kruk	101	719	48	2	769	52	.997	790.2	1.6	.494	.24
Magadan	122	1033	91	5	1129	74	.996	1029.0	2.1	.590	.51
Martinez Crm	32	224	10	6	240	13	.975	222.0	0.5	1.122	.36
McClendon	22	132	10	2	144	12	.986	136.2	0.3	.401	.01
McGriff F	153	1371	84	14	1469	112	.990	1347.0	2.8	.406	.16
Merced	105	911	60	12	983	64	.988	870.1	1.8	.408	.11
Morris H	127	967	101	9	1077	86	.992	1059.1	2.2	.532	.40
Murray E	148	1320	129	7	1456	96	.995	1293.1	2.7	.611	.70
Perry G	60	405	27	5	437	30	.989	424.2	0.9	.381	.03
Redus	45	355	24	4	383	34	.990	346.2	0.7	.437	.06
Templeton	23	147	12	0	159	7	1.000	163.0	0.3	.632	.10
Walker L	39	313	30	4	347	29	.988	337.1	0.7	.461	.08
TOTALS	***	17304	1429	156	18889	1333	.992	1442.0	3.0	2.510	6.48

Not that Bagwell isn't for real, he is. But the system that got the Astros an early year out of him cost them at least one and maybe more of Anthony, who is the sort of player who can carry you to the pennant.

4. Fred McGriff SD

In the long run, Fred McGriff is just going to overwhelm Joe Carter. But, then, Roberto Alomar is going to overwhelm Tony Fernandez. The Jays got a quick division title out of Carter, so they win the trade.

5. Hal Morris CIN

One of the big benefits you sometimes get in hiring another system's ex-manager or ex-GM is that the man may bring a Hal Morris over with him. Morris was messed up in New York, and Lou Pinella knew it. Similarly, Dallas Green knew about Ryne Sandberg and Syd Thrift knew about Bobby Bonilla.

6. Eddie Murray LA (NYM)

I really am beginning to develop some respect for Fred Claire. Murray's finally showing his age, so Fred lets him go. Then he trades pitching for Eric Davis, who solves the right handed bat problem in the Dodger lineup just fine. Then he signs Tom Candiotti as a free agent. Candiotti is better than Belcher, and Davis is better than Murray, and Fred ended up with no more payroll than he would have had he signed Murray.

7. Mark Grace CHN

Not Mark's best offensive year, though it's within the normal range of production. Still, I don't see where he's really any better than this, given a good collection of first sackers in the NL right now. As the only lefty bat in a lineup, he's clearly inadequate. As I said last year, the Cubs would improve if they traded George Bell for Kal Daniels and balanced their order. And I'd still trade Rafael Palmeiro to keep Mark Grace.

8. Dave Magadan NYM

Now, if the front office is to be believed, a third baseman. And yes, he's really about even with Murray at this juncture in their careers. The result of all this movement is that the Mets, having traded Kevin McReynolds and Gregg Jeffries, still don't have anywhere to play Mackey Sasser. I'd have kept Magadan where he was, left Hojo alone and saved Murray's contract. But I suppose the Mets think that moving Dave to third is going to solve their infield defense problems.

9. Orlando Merced PIT

Merced and Redus, like Lavalliere and Slaught, are a big part of the Pirates. And I'll give Jim Leyland credit: first base is not the spot I'd have gone looking for a leadoff platoon. Still, I wish Jim had given John Cangelosi a real shot at the job.

10. Pedro Guerrero STL

To be honest, I didn't expect Pedro to be anywhere near the pack. He's old and his knees are bad. And he has the Cards by the short hairs. They had to offer him arbitration or lose him without the Class A draft choice compensation. And no one will sign him at that price. Now they're talking (I am not making this up) about playing Pedro in left field. Whitey had a bad winter meetings, but he still must be laughing his head off.

11. Sid Bream ATL

Pete DeCoursey loves this guy; thinks he stabilized the Brave infield and has lots of hidden defensive value. But there are a lot of first basemen out there right now who can field grounders. Clark, Kruk (yes he can), Bagwell, Murray (still), Galarraga. They all can play, and Bream just doesn't stick out. No, Brian Hunter can't field with Sid, but Hunter can hit, and is much younger. There's also Francisco Cabrera to develop. I'd let Terry Pendelton worry about captaining the infield defense. And, if you saw the postseason, you saw that Terry does. I question whether Bobby Cox will play Sid next year, so I rate him a BAD ROTISSERIE GAMBLE.

12. Andres Galarraga MTL (STL)

The bad year figures to be an aberration, unless the Expos know something they're not telling. And that may be; Ken Hill wasn't much of a price. Actually, Andres' career makes perfectly good sense up to 1991. He had his peak years right on schedule, and then came down some. There's a big one-year drop there in 1989, but I write that off as a normal fluctuation in the normal progression of the career. In Busch Stadium, new fences or no, Andres figures to pick up some batting points and doubles and lose a lot of homers. I pencil him in for .265 or .270, with maybe 15-18 taters. People will look at that and say it's not a full recovery, but it's just the ballpark. Unless your rules count doubles, though, he's a BAD ROTISSERIE BUY.

American League

Second Basemen

Brock J. Hanke

		OWAR	DWAR	TWAR
1.	Alomar R	5.62	1.02	6.64
2.	Whitaker	4.11	1.41	5.51
3.	Franco Ju	5.16	0.15	5.31
4.	Randolph	3.35	1.43	4.78
5.	Reynolds H	2.62	2.06	4.68
6.	Sax S	3.28	1.39	4.67
7.	Reed Jody	2.62	1.66	4.28
8.	Knoblauch	2.40	1.28	3.68
9.	Gallego	1.94	0.97	2.92
10.	Sojo	0.24	1.60	1.84
	Hill D	0.85	0.76	1.61
	Blankenship L	0.63	0.69	1.32
	Rose	0.26	0.18	0.44
	Brosius	-0.15	0.18	0.03
	Cora	-0.22	0.18	-0.04
11.	Fletcher S	-1.26	1.11	-0.15
	Lewis M	-0.55	0.20	-0.35
12.	Shumpert	-1.25	0.73	-0.52
13.	Ripken B	-1.81	1.25	-0.56
14.	Browne J	-0.67	-0.04	-0.71
	Bell Ju	-1.54	0.31	-1.23

1. Roberto Alomar TOR

I guess we can say he's eclipsed his brother now. If I were to have first pick in a draft where I could keep the player for his career, it would be between Roberto and Frank Thomas. In those one-year leagues, of course, you get someone like Cal Ripken Jr.

I don't know what else to say. He's the best, and he's only 24, so he's going to get better. His career is nothing but the beginnings of a march to the Hall of Fame. He's worth more than Fred McGriff, but Tony Fernandez is worth more than Joe Carter. IF YOU ARE IN ANY SORT OF FANTASY LEAGUE, GET HIM IF YOU CAN.

2. Lou Whitaker DET

Lou and Alan Trammell seem to have set up an oscillating wave in their decline phases. This was Lou's year to be good. If you're trying to figure out which one is the better of the two, here are the parameters: 1) Trammell got hurt and will probably decline faster than Lou, but 2) there is a bit less competition at shortstop, so Alan's relative standing is likely to finish up higher. If I were Sparky, I'd set up two batting order spots, say #2 and #6, that could be platooned between the two of them.

3. Julio Franco TEX

The current holder of the Ernie Banks Award. Plays great on bad teams. If you're wondering why his offense rates below Alomar's and Whitaker's, you need a refresher course in ballpark adjustments. Texas is the best hitters' park, year after year, in the American League. Banks played in a similar park.

There is one danger sign. Julio's defensive stats have been slipping, and he's close to becoming an outfielder, or, like Banks, a first baseman. I don't mean to carry this comparison too far. Banks was a shortstop, not a second baseman. He was also a much better hitter, and especially power hitter, than Julio. But the first three keystone men in the AL here have done nothing but what should have been expected, and I don't really have anything interesting to say about any of them.

As Rotisserie buys, I rate them Franco, Alomar and Whitaker. Lou is too old to bank on, and Alomar is not really the Roti type of player. With what the ballpark gives Julio in batting average and homers, you've got to go with him.

4. Willie Randolph MIL (NYM)

This, of course, is a last hurrah. Combined with Willie's name, though, it got him a wonderful contract out of the Mets, didn't it? As I mentioned in the Bobby Bonilla comment, I'd lead Willie off if I were the Mets. His speed is a question,

Second Base	G	PO	A	Er	TC	DP	FPct	DI	DG	DW%	DWAR
Alomar R	160	334	447	15	796	81	.981	1420.2	7.7	.481	1.01
Baerga	74	161	237	11	409	61	.973	625.2	3.4	.615	.90
Bell Ju	75	103	183	8	294	38	.973	506.1	2.7	.471	.33
Blankenship L	45	70	100	3	173	22	.983	265.0	1.4	.637	.41
Browne J	47	80	109	7	196	17	.964	327.0	1.8	.319	-.06
Cora	80	103	184	9	296	33	.970	565.0	3.1	.392	.13
Fletcher S	85	177	186	3	366	48	.992	636.1	3.4	.666	1.09
Franco Ju	145	294	372	14	680	79	.979	1274.1	6.9	.371	.15
Gallego	134	244	363	7	614	68	.989	1065.1	5.8	.500	.86
Gantner	59	110	190	7	307	31	.977	456.1	2.5	.560	.52
Grebeck	36	62	96	1	159	20	.994	263.2	1.4	.713	.52
Hill D	39	76	89	5	170	23	.971	281.2	1.5	.549	.30
Howard D	25	34	55	1	90	9	.989	156.0	0.8	.469	.10
Hulett	26	29	31	2	62	5	.968	113.1	0.6	.270	-.05
Kelly P	19	34	47	2	83	15	.976	133.2	0.7	.621	.20
Knoblauch	148	246	458	18	722	94	.975	1240.1	6.7	.537	1.26
Lewis M	50	87	140	8	235	29	.966	432.2	2.3	.326	-.06
Newman A	35	52	76	1	129	15	.992	208.0	1.1	.659	.35
Pecota	34	46	34	0	80	8	1.000	143.1	0.8	.503	.12
Phillips	35	106	116	1	223	34	.996	289.0	1.6	.879	.83
Randolph	120	234	375	20	629	96	.968	988.1	5.3	.610	1.39
Reed Jd	150	308	440	14	762	107	.982	1303.0	7.0	.572	1.57
Reynolds H	158	347	458	18	823	132	.978	1391.1	7.5	.619	2.03
Ripken B	101	199	285	7	491	74	.986	819.0	4.4	.625	1.22
Sax S	148	275	439	7	721	107	.990	1297.1	7.0	.546	1.38
Shumpert	144	250	368	16	634	81	.975	1092.2	5.9	.472	.72
Sojo	107	228	326	11	565	78	.981	899.1	4.9	.657	1.49
Whitaker	134	254	361	4	619	90	.994	1062.2	5.7	.588	1.37
TOTALS	***	4772	6915	229	11916	1575	.981	1479.0	8.0	6.806	****

and he doesn't figure to produce anything like this year, but he does get on base, even if his batting average is low. Vince Coleman doesn't. Let Vince hit 7th or so, and use his stolen bases and the numerous outs that Kevin Elster and the pitcher will make to move him along. What's that? You say the Met catcher has to bat behind Vince too? All right, do you really think that Willie Randolph is a better #6 hitter than Vince is?

5. Harold Reynolds SEA

I agree with the Mariners that Harold Reynolds is a most valuable asset. Without him, they'd be weak up the middle, with only Junior holding forth. With Harold, they've got enough there to contend. Nonetheless, I don't agree that they have to stick him up at the top of the batting order. In fact, using Harold there conceals the M's biggest weakness; they have two table setters (Junior and Martinez), and nothing else but power men. The result is that they have to bat Junior third.

If Bill Plummer wants to win, he's either got to come up with a real second hitter, or try this formula:

Junior	cf
Martinez	3b
Buhner, Davis , O'Brien	
or Alonzo Powell	1b, rf or DH
Mitchell	lf
the other one who's hitting	DH, 1b or rf
the best of the rest	rf, DH or 1b
Reynolds	2b
the catcher	c
Vizquel	ss

Bill's reputation is going to rest on making this decision more than on any other factor.

6. Steve Sax NYY (CHA)

Thirty-two is a little old to be setting career highs in home runs and career second-bests in doubles, but Yankee Stadium had a one-year fluke as an extreme hitters' park, so that's what Steve Sax did. Even without that, Steve, like Willie Randolph and Ryne Sandberg, is holding his value very well into his 30s. Actually, Steve reminds me even more of Matty Alou and Manny Mota. He lacks power, and won't take a walk, and is therefore not really what you need at the top of the order. But it looks like he'll hold his batting average until he's 40 and a pinch-hitter. As of now, he's still holding his defense and his base stealing. As a consequence, although he's not what I really look for in a ballplayer, he's an OUTSTANDING ROTISSERIE BUY, particularly if you need average. That will not be hurt one bit by the move to Chicago; new Comiskey was a hitters' park last year.

7. Jody Reed BOS

He's still helping the Bosox, but he's already starting to age. People think of him as a young player, because he's only had four full years, but his first one was at age 26. Men who can't break into the Majors until that age, particularly Red Sox infielders, have some sort of problem. In Jody's case, it's not that he's a weak player, it's that this is a strong position.

8. Chuck Knoblauch MIN

One of the things that the Twins absolutely had to go right in order for them to win, and he did. Long term, I've got my questions about Chuck. He's only 23, but he doesn't do anything real well. Roberto Alomar is only 24, and he's hardly the only real good keystone man out there. For Chuck to rise to the top echelon, he's got to develop some power (unlikely), a real Gold Glove (very unlikely), or learn some strike zone judgement (unlikely again). Basically, he just patched a sucking chest wound in the middle of the Twin defense. As a hitter, well, if Tom Kelly really understood about table setting, he'd get better people to do it that Chuck and Dan Gladden.

9. Mike Gallego OAK (NYY)

Turned in the steadiest year of the guys whose teams need to replace them. Unfortunately for Oakland fans, the team ownership seems to be on an austerity kick, so Mike wouldn't have been replaced, even if he hadn't moved on. The Oakland organization doesn't seem to be too hot at developing infielders. If they were still trying to be a dynasty, they would need to keep Mike. The Yankees don't, but he's not going to start there. He'll be the backup in case Pat Kelly fails. As a consequence, UNLOAD THIS GUY IN A FANTASY LEAGUE NOW.

10. Luis Sojo CAL

Donnie Hill, age 31, finished right behind Luis in the rankings, in only about 3/5 the plate appearances. Luis is not a championship caliber prospect at age 26. Whitey Herzog does not put up with this sort of thing in his infields. Never has.

11. Scott Fletcher CHA

A late-inning defensive replacement; for Steve Sax, it turns out.

12. Terry Shumpert KC

When you're 25 years old, and your team is preparing to hand your job to a trade throw-in, you know you've got problems. Terry's is deciding what career to pursue. Not that Keith Miller is really a throw-in quality player, but Terry Shumpert is.

13. Billy Ripken BAL

I checked. If you subtract this from Cal's TWAR, you still get the MVP. But if you also subtract the TWAR of the #7 man at this position, he doesn't. The question, therefore, is how to get the Cals to let you get rid of Billy.

14. Jerry Browne CLE

Actually, the most-used Indian second baseman was Carlos Baerga, but he's discussed under third basemen, so that Brook Jacoby can be discussed under first basemen. Only on the Indians. Jerry Browne was hurt, of course, but it remains to be seen how much he will ever regain. When the trade was made, I didn't think Franco for Browne was a ripoff at all, but Jerry has proved just too fragile.

National League

Second Basemen

Brock J. Hanke

		OWAR	DWAR	TWAR
1.	Sandberg	5.77	1.09	6.86
2.	Thompson Ro	4.50	1.88	6.38
3.	Samuel	5.12	0.73	5.85
4.	Oquendo	1.87	1.40	3.27
5.	DeShields	3.19	-0.04	3.15
6.	Candaele	2.37	0.72	3.09
7.	Roberts Bip	2.27	0.61	2.88
	Miller K	2.25	0.52	2.78
8.	Lind	0.81	1.86	2.66
9.	Jefferies	2.80	-0.33	2.47
10.	Doran	2.07	0.33	2.40
11.	Treadway	2.13	0.24	2.38
	Teufel	1.60	0.20	1.79
	Ready	1.32	0.32	1.64
	Pena G	1.40	0.23	1.63
	Duncan	1.12	0.41	1.53
12.	Morandini	0.74	0.56	1.30
	Herr	0.56	0.67	1.23
	Backman	0.76	-0.06	0.71
	Lemke	-0.49	0.67	0.18
	Wilkerson	-0.62	0.59	-0.04
	Noboa	-0.09	0.05	-0.04
	Quinones L	-0.22	0.00	-0.22
	Faries	-0.83	0.61	-0.22
	McLemore	-0.60	0.02	-0.58
	Mota A	-0.62	-0.14	-0.76

1. Ryne Sandberg CHN

Right now, my count of Ryne's Bill James Organic Hall of Fame (see in glossary) points is 97.5. Serious contention usually occurs at 100 points, which means that Sandberg is almost there at age 32. He has accumulated exactly zero points for career achievements, although it is certain that he will pile a bunch up, and exactly 2 points for postseason accomplishments. On the other hand, he has made the breakpoint for single season points right on the button five times (200 hits, 100 RBI twice, 30 homers and 40 homers). Given the bias of Wrigley Field, that means that his home park has given him 21 of those points.

No, none of the above is very meaningful. Sandberg is a shoo-in Hall of Famer; counting his points sheds no light upon that. But what else am I supposed to write about? Sandberg is in that grey period, from ages 30 to 35 or so, where his greatness is already established, but his career is not full enough yet to start comparing him to Joe Morgan or Rogers Hornsby or Eddie Collins. If he's still keeping this up at age 36, those comparisons become meaningful, and I start writing about him as a candidate for best second baseman ever. But he could drop right back to where he was in 1986 and 1987. That would leave him well short of the top careers.

After all, Sandberg has exceeded his career totals in batting average, slugging percentage and on-base percentage in every one of the last three years. People don't usually do that at ages 30-32. Right now, we don't know if the power surge that fueled that spurt (Ryno finally learned to exploit Wrigley's home run fences) is real or not. And so, Ryne Sandberg is as bland a player as there is to write about, except to say that for a player of his stats to score 100 runs six times and drive in 100 only twice is a thorough indictment of the Cubbie batting orders of the past decade.

2. Robbie Thompson SF

I read this year as an aberration. Robbie's career peak was probably at age 27, right on schedule. His 1991 looks like 1990 with a hot streak tagged on somewhere. That will happen sometimes, but it usually doesn't hold up. Still, with Roberto Alomar gone, Robbie probably is the second best second baseman in the league, pending the development of Geronimo Pena and maybe Delino DeShields. I give Pena and Delino 60% and 30% chances of overtaking Robbie in the next two years, respectively. I give Jose Oquendo a 98% chance of playing shortstop in two years.

Second Base	G	PO	A	Er	TC	DP	FPct	DI	DG	DW%	DWAR
Backman	36	50	52	2	104	12	.981	222.0	1.2	.332	-.02
Blauser	33	48	66	2	116	15	.983	218.0	1.2	.522	.21
Candaele	109	197	300	9	506	52	.982	868.0	4.8	.461	.53
DeShields	148	285	405	27	717	73	.962	1297.1	7.2	.344	-.04
Doran	87	153	206	7	366	46	.981	695.2	3.9	.426	.29
Duncan	63	118	144	7	269	29	.974	475.0	2.6	.402	.14
Faries	35	66	90	2	158	18	.987	236.0	1.3	.720	.48
Harris L	27	32	49	1	82	12	.988	124.1	0.7	.787	.30
Herr	72	114	148	0	262	33	1.000	476.2	2.6	1.006	1.73
Jefferies	77	144	177	6	327	15	.982	611.2	3.4	.302	-.16
Lemke	109	154	201	8	363	38	.978	596.1	3.3	.551	.67
Lind	147	344	431	9	784	79	.989	1227.1	6.8	.624	1.86
McLemore	19	26	54	2	82	9	.976	150.2	0.8	.377	.02
Miller K	58	120	141	8	269	24	.970	401.1	2.2	.490	.31
Morandini	96	178	247	6	431	45	.986	757.2	4.2	.485	.57
Mota A	26	30	66	3	99	11	.970	219.1	1.2	.231	-.14
Oquendo	118	244	344	7	595	60	.988	904.2	5.0	.650	1.51
Pena G	82	94	141	6	241	27	.975	435.1	2.4	.436	.21
Quinones L	33	45	74	3	122	15	.975	243.1	1.3	.350	0.00
Ramirez R	27	35	52	2	89	9	.978	161.1	0.9	.381	.03
Ready	65	126	143	3	272	22	.989	464.1	2.6	.475	.32
Roberts Bip	68	128	185	7	320	36	.978	563.1	3.1	.488	.43
Samuel	152	298	440	17	755	72	.977	1309.2	7.3	.452	.74
Sandberg	156	267	513	4	784	68	.995	1365.2	7.6	.495	1.10
Teufel	65	100	124	3	227	22	.987	459.2	2.6	1.135	2.00
Thompson Ro	142	316	398	10	724	97	.986	1186.0	6.6	.636	1.88
Treadway	93	156	208	15	379	35	.960	629.1	3.5	.419	.24
Wilkerson	29	51	75	1	127	14	.992	206.0	1.1	.638	.33
TOTALS	***	4109	5731	184	10024	1040	.982	1442.0	8.0	5.683	****

3. Juan Samuel LA

I worte the following before the Dodgers signed Juan Samuel and quit talking about trading him. My faith in Fred Claire is restored.

Juan finally rebuilds his game to where it should be at his current age, and now the Dodgers want to get rid of him. I have a lot of respect for Fred Claire, but this I don't understand. You can start Juan at second and, if he falters, you have the Sharperson/Harris platoon to split between the keystone and third base. And that's assuming that none of the infield prospects works out at third. What's more, Juan represents a legitimate righty power bat to fill in if/when Eric Davis gets hurt again. And he can play center field, too. That's a valuable man to have in an expected pennant race.

By the way, yes, I think the rebuilt game is real. His last four years have constituted a steady improvement from his collapse at age 28 to where he ought to be at age 31. No, he'll never get back to where he was at age 27, but who does? If someone does start him, he's a GOOD ROTISSERIE BUY, as everything he does works for you, but you probably already know that.

4. Jose Oquendo STL

Those of you who don't live in St. Louis may not know it, but Jose is the Cardinal sportswriters' favorite whipping boy. No, I'm not kidding. Why? Well, for the same reasons that he's a LOUSY ROTISSERIE BUY. Jose's game consists of all the things that a casual observer can't see. He takes walks and fields his position dependably. He doesn't run well, which everyone can see. He doesn't have power, and everyone can see that, too. He doesn't make spectacular plays out there, though his pivot is the quickest in the game. But he is always - I mean always - in position, he never gets taken out on the DP, and his hands are unerring. Add that he consumes a minimum of outs, and you've got a valuable, but invisible player. Sure, he had two horrendous 0-for-30+ slumps, but he responded to them by taking walks, and therefore was never a hole in the offense. When he had his one hot streak, the Cardinals made their run at the Pirates.

Unfortunately, though, Jose's very possibly not the best second baseman on his own team. Geronimo Pena is the best prospect the Cardinals have, and the keystone is his spot (yes the Cards tried Pena at third base, and yes his arm isn't up to it). Now, ordinarily, even the worst of managers would see that Jose could play shortstop and move him to make room for the kid. I mean, Geronimo was out of options last year and had to be kept on the Cardinal roster. But Joe Torre has to contend with a Hall of Fame name that is attached to a 36-year-old shortstop. Worse, Ozzie turned in a last hurrah year in 1991, and looks like he can outplay Oquendo until he's 45. Ozzie can't, of course, but the Cards can't very well just cut him loose. And therefore, for all you call-in show fans, let me make you aware that 1) Ozzie

Smith is the very most available of Cardinal trade bait, and 2) if he does move, Geronimo Pena is a ROTISSERIE BEST BUY at second base. In any case, if your league allows holdovers, picking up Pena now is a real good deal.

5. Delino DeShields MTL

Right now, Delino has shown a real hot half season there on the front end of 1990, and a year and a half of this .240-hitting 1991 stuff. It's probably nothing more than sophomore slump, and Delino is only 23, but I do wish the guys who are engraving his Hall of Fame plaque would just hold up a year or two until we get an honest read on the kid. I mean, there's something wrong with a known base stealer who can only hit one double every ten games. If it was just a matter of free swinging in an attempt to bulk up his homer stats, well, fine. He'll get over it. But, right now, we just don't know.

6. Casey Candaele HOU

Candaele may finally have put a respectable talent together at age 31. His 1990 is completely consistent with his 1991. And therefore, referring to the Craig Biggio comment in the catcher section, I have this to say:

Right now, Candaele is about a game and a half worse than Craig Biggio would be at the keystone. But Craig is three or four games better than anything the 'Stros are likely to come up with behind the plate. And therefore, moving Biggio to second base and benching Candaele is going to cost Houston about two games. They should forget it and play Casey.

7. Bip Roberts SD (CIN)

Clearly a leg injury. You've got a man here who loses 23 doubles and half his stolen bases and that's all he loses. It looks like he lost his power, but doubles are Bip's power. The batting average, of course, is just lost leg hits. Basically, stealing the Bipster for Randy Myers puts the Reds right back in contention. Their greatest need in 1991 was a leadoff man so they could get rid of Billy Hatcher. Now they've got one, and he plays the infield on top of it. With Bip at second and Larkin at short, they can afford to get a punchless glove in center field and still have a hot offense. Now if they hadn't traded all their pitching depth for a question mark ace starter....

8. Jose Lind PIT

Last year's book had this typo in it. Yes, in the Pittsburgh team essay. You see, what I was going to do was show how much the acquisition of Jay Bell had helped the Pirates, including what it had done to Jose Lind. What I wrote was, "[besides what the Pirates got out of Bell himself], Jose Lind's offensive stats went up in the #8 slot, because pitchers just don't focus so strongly on the guy who hits before the pitcher as on the table-setter for a team's big three. Altogether, the Pirates gained ** games in shortstop defense, ** games in shortstop offense and another ** games in the form of a better Jose Lind."

The double asterisks should be replaced by "1.35" (DWAR gained at shortstop from 1989 to 1990), "2.6" (OWAR gain at short), and "2.65" (TWAR improvement in Jose Lind from 1989 to 1990). That's a grand total of 6.6 games gained for resisting the temptation to play Felix Fermin. By the way, if you take a look at the DWAR for this position, you'll see that the Gold Glove argument devolves down to Robbie Thompson, Jose Lind, Jose Oquendo and everybody else, including Ryne Sandberg. And if you look at the supporting defensive stats, you'll have to agree with this. Simply put, Lind, Thompson and Oquendo are the shortstops out there at second base. Giving the Glove to Sandberg is a crime against the award. Personally, I'd give it to Lind; I think that, over a period of years, he'll prove out better than the other two, and there's no sorting him and Thompson out this year.

9. Gregg Jeffries NYM (KC)

Keith Miller would have come in 7th, in less playing time. Now both are with KC, where Hal McRae shows every sign of playing Miller at the keystone, where he belongs, and Jeffries somewhere like DH or left field, which is about what he can handle defensively. Hopefully, Gregg isn't so messed up that his bat can't recover.

10. Bill Doran CIN

Now presumably a reserve behind Bip Roberts, Barry Larkin and Chris Sabo, which improves the entire Redleg infield outlook. I guess he's sort of also the outfield reserve, as Roberts will probably move to left if someone gets hurt out there. That makes Doran a supersub, which he is eminently qualified to do. Much, much better than Donuts Duncan. The Reds may parlay Larkin into a dominant team yet.

11. Jeff Treadway ATL

Would you believe that Braves fans, not to mention the sporting press, thought this man had a star season because he hit for a big batting average in Atlanta? Would you believe his manager benched him in the postseason to play someone named Mark Lemke? Would you believe that said Lemke was almost the World Series MVP? Would you believe that your team should do so well as to hire the next Bobby Cox? Would you believe that there's a .320 hitter out there who has lost his job?

12. Mickey Morandini PHI

Randy Ready did better in less playing time, though he would still have come in 12th. I rate Morandini no prospect at all, a ROTISSERIE WORST BUY and a reality worst buy as well. The only thing he has going for him is playing time; the Phillies don't have anyone else. And they won't get into contention until they start addressing this problem, much less the one at shortstop. Pennants are won up the middle.

American League

Third Basemen

Brock J. Hanke

		OWAR	DWAR	TWAR
1.	Martinez E	5.76	0.82	6.59
2.	Ventura	4.66	1.44	6.09
3.	Boggs W	4.82	1.03	5.84
	Phillips	3.96	1.82	5.78
4.	Baerga	4.21	1.16	5.37
5.	Gaetti	2.13	1.65	3.78
6.	Pecota	2.09	0.80	2.89
7.	Gruber	1.83	0.91	2.75
8.	Buechele	1.51	1.21	2.71
9.	Fryman T	2.08	0.60	2.68
	Grebeck	1.97	0.70	2.67
10.	Pagliarulo	1.04	1.09	2.13
11.	Gomez L	1.34	0.43	1.77
	Leius	1.19	0.51	1.69
12.	Gantner	0.42	0.90	1.32
	Barnes	0.89	0.38	1.27
	Seitzer	0.97	0.16	1.13
	Sprague	0.84	-0.00	0.84
	Thome	0.51	-0.04	0.47
	Velarde	-0.02	0.49	0.47
	Livingstone	0.20	0.22	0.42
	Worthington	0.29	0.11	0.40
	Howell Jk	0.19	0.21	0.40
13.	Riles	-0.12	0.40	0.28
14.	Kelly P	0.11	0.15	0.26
	Manto	0.00	0.00	0.01
	Hulett	-0.26	0.17	-0.09
	Law V	-0.34	0.04	-0.30
	Palmer Dn	-0.20	-0.13	-0.34
	Lovullo	-0.43	0.07	-0.36
	Berry	-0.60	0.15	-0.45
	Leyritz	-0.40	-0.15	-0.55
	Jacoby	-1.15	0.45	-0.70
	Sheffield	-0.74	-0.13	-0.87

1. Edgar Martinez SEA

What is it with these on-base types playing third base? Channelling for Eddie Yost? Martinez, Ventura, Boggs and Phillips all take walks and get on base, and none of them can really run. It's a corner on the market of slow leadoff men, retreads from the fifties.

As for Martinez himself, he's the best right now, but Robin Ventura is only 24, while Edgar is, believe it or not, 29. No, you didn't miss about four years of Ed's career there, he has in fact had only two full seasons with the M's. Now, normally, 29-year-old sophomores are a grim lot. But Edgar's years have been good enough to suggest that he was just brought up late, and so there's no reason to figure him to fall back. Yes, at his age, he's probably going to have just a slow decline phase for a career, but it will be a decline phase that looks like he came up at age 24. 1991 was very likely a true measure of his age 29 ability, rather than a fluke. As such, he's a GREAT FANTASY BUY, BUT A WEAK ROTISSERIE ONE, as his walks don't work in the Roti game.

2. Robin Ventura CHA

Now only 24, Robin is about to have the career that his college stats suggested. As you may remember, his slow start in the pros tempted some sportswriters to say that his college career meant nothing. Well, that was not true; he was just being rushed a little. Now he's Roberto Alomar's age, and only about a year behind him. That's legitimate, as Robin is not the player Roberto is, but it still leaves a real good ballplayer here.

The home run surge, by the way, is a ballpark thing. Old Comiskey was one of the all-time pitchers' parks, while New Comiskey turned in a

Third Base	G	PO	A	Er	TC	DP	FPct	DI	DG	DW%	DWAR
Baerga	89	54	181	15	250	14	.940	698.2	2.8	.437	.25
Berry	29	13	48	2	63	3	.968	174.0	0.7	.562	.15
Boggs W	139	88	272	12	372	33	.968	1179.0	4.8	.556	.99
Browne J	14	5	27	6	38	4	.842	105.0	0.4	.430	.03
Buechele	111	87	238	3	328	19	.991	926.0	3.8	.664	1.18
Fryman T	85	45	142	11	198	12	.944	693.0	2.8	.322	-.08
Gaetti	151	111	349	17	477	38	.964	1331.2	5.4	.646	1.60
Gantner	89	50	155	5	210	15	.976	755.0	3.1	.470	.37
Gomez L	104	61	184	7	252	20	.972	909.1	3.7	.463	.42
Gonzales R	26	7	41	4	52	3	.923	110.1	0.4	.686	.15
Grebeck	49	22	49	5	76	6	.934	195.1	0.8	.638	.23
Gruber	111	97	230	13	340	17	.962	977.1	4.0	.578	.90
Hulett	37	18	63	2	83	8	.976	277.0	1.1	.539	.21
Jacoby	67	49	99	3	151	12	.980	535.1	2.2	1.096	1.62
Kelly P	80	43	155	16	214	14	.925	661.1	2.7	.332	-.05
Law V	66	36	60	5	101	7	.950	360.2	1.5	.373	.03
Leius	79	41	100	7	148	8	.953	442.2	1.8	.495	.26
Leyritz	18	10	21	3	34	2	.912	140.1	0.6	.127	-.13
Livingstone	43	31	67	2	100	6	.980	316.0	1.3	.519	.22
Lovullo	21	14	32	2	48	1	.958	126.0	0.5	.481	.07
Manto	32	21	57	6	84	13	.929	260.1	1.1	.377	.03
Martinez E	143	85	293	15	393	26	.962	1228.2	5.0	.512	.81
Pagliarulo	118	56	248	11	315	30	.965	913.1	3.7	.639	1.07
Palmer Dn	50	27	74	6	107	5	.944	400.0	1.6	.278	-.12
Pecota	101	69	157	4	230	15	.983	761.0	3.1	.525	.54
Phillips	46	26	84	5	115	7	.957	331.0	1.3	.501	.20
Riles	69	54	101	10	165	14	.939	485.0	2.0	.494	.28
Schaefer	30	4	20	1	25	3	.960	106.2	0.4	.425	.03
Seitzer	68	45	126	11	182	9	.940	519.0	2.1	.427	.16
Sheffield	43	29	65	8	102	7	.922	369.0	1.5	.262	-.13
Sprague	35	19	61	12	92	2	.870	260.0	1.1	.298	-.06
Sveum	38	26	62	4	92	9	.957	307.2	1.2	.496	.18
Thome	27	12	60	8	80	6	.900	242.1	1.0	.307	-.04
Velarde	50	31	87	8	126	8	.937	321.1	1.3	.522	.22
Ventura	150	134	287	18	439	29	.959	1264.2	5.1	.618	1.38
Worthington	30	26	50	2	78	3	.974	253.1	1.0	.452	.11
TOTALS	***	1649	4618	298	6565	450	.955	1479.0	6.0	5.963	****

first season as a hitters' haven. Robin's home/road homer split was 16/7. That indicates that the power isn't all real, and the pitchers of the AL are going to adjust and take some of it away. I rate Robin as a 15-20 man at his peak in a couple of years, but I wouldn't be surprised to see him fall short of 15 in 1992 and 1993. On the other hand, his nearly equal doubles and homers figures suggest that he was uppercutting; if the pitchers force him to quit that, he could hit some cripples for line drives and convert some of the lost homers to doubles. If he can do that, he will remain a significant power source, and develop into a #3 hitter. I give him a 60% chance of that, and the remaining 40% of becoming the slowest leadoff man in the league.

3. Wade Boggs BOS

The basic difference between Wade and Edgar Martinez is that Wade is 34 years old. They even got started late, both of them. The reason for that, of course, is that Major League development personnel count speed and power highly and plate discipline not at all. The Boggses and Martinezes, in order to get promoted, have to convince their minor league managers that they can hit for average, and that means they have to actually mature their skills.

4. Carlos Baerga CLE

Believe it or not, Carlos Baerga is a real power hitter prospect. As you may know, the Indians moved their fences to another zip code, in an effort to make an entire offense out of Alex Cole. This dumb plan not only backfired (Cole got hurt), it threw all the Tribe's homer stats into a cocked hat. Carlos had a 2/9 home/road split for his 11 homers, which suggests that he's a legitimate 15-20 man at age 23.

He also lacks plate discipline, and so is one of my picks to have sophomore slump. For those of you who haven't followed my reasoning on this, it's as follows: I contend that sophomore slumps are the result of pitchers getting used to having you as a regular batter against them. It takes them a year to get a book on you and find out what you can and can't hit. The second season, they start throwing you the difficult stuff. If you have patience, you can keep your value up by waiting them out; forcing them to throw hard pitches for strikes. If you swing at a lot of pitches, though, they don't have to throw strikes. All they have to do is throw the stuff you don't hit well. Carlos is going to swing at a lot of pitches he can't hit next year, and many of them are not going to be strikes. After a year, of course, he'll have counteradjusted, but it will likely take that long.

I still don't know why the Indians didn't trade Brook Jacoby before the year began, instead of moving him to first base, thereby collapsing his value, and then having to fire sale him.

5. Gary Gaetti CAL

Has not yet recovered all his Minnesota value. If Whitey can get him going full speed again, the Angels may yet win one for the Cowboy. In any case, I agree with the stats that Gary is still the Gold Glove third baseman in the AL.

6. Bill Pecota KC

If you think that Bill Pecota has come into his own as a top third baseman at the age of 32, you should apply to the Met front office for a job. Me? I'll take Keith Miller in trade, thank you, and gamble on Kevin Seitzer getting back on track. Kevin's a mere child of 30, although there's a big question mark regarding 26-year-old rookies of the class of 1987. That's an awfully late arrival, and an awfully big amount of help he got for his rookie bat. Kevin may not have been for real after all.

7. Kelly Gruber TOR

Came on in the second half, and can be presumed ready to resume where he left off. Not that there aren't some warning flags. Kelly's power is really in the 20 homer range, not the 30. His home/road split in 1990, when he hit 31, was 23/8. He still swings at everything, and now that he has a name, the pitchers concentrate more on getting him out. I don't expect him to get back much more than this year; he might move up to #5 or so at the position when he gets back to full-time play. Still, he's a GREAT ROTISSERIE BUY. Everything he does works for you.

8. Steve Buechele TEX (PIT)

Boy did Steve ever cash in a fluke age 30 career year. He's no more than a backup, even for the Pirates. In fact, I'm quite sure he'd never have got the contract he did if the 'Rats weren't so sure Jeff King can't get through a whole year without getting hurt.

9. Travis Fryman DET

What this season indicates is 1) Tony Phillips has fully adjusted to his new ballpark and 2) the As were idiots not to have given him a regular job 8 years ago. Unfortunately, the Tigers haven't given him a regular job either, nor are they likely to. Tony can easily outplay Travis Fryman, but Travis is a hot kid prospect that the Tigers can't just throw away. Normally, they might try Tony at second or even short, but they've got people there, too. That leaves the outfield and DH, where Sparky likes to put the power guys. Well, I guess I don't care where he plays, the Tigers need his leadoff bat to much to bench him. Maybe the silly system of just playing him 30 games at each spot will work.

Yes, that's what this comment is doing here instead of under Phillips. Travis Fryman played a lot more third than Tony, although Tony played more ball overall. Do I have anything to say about Fryman? Well, he's 23, and obviously ready for prime time. He's also another one of those kid power hitters with bad plate discipline. As a consequence, he's going to have a hump to get over somewhere down the line, which suggests a sophomore slump in 1992. His defensive stats suggest he may be an outfielder sooner than the Tigers would like, but his home/road homer splits (8/13) suggest that his power is real, not a Tiger Stadium illusion at all. He's a fantasy league gamble. If he has the slump I predict, he'll be a one-year bust; but if he doesn't, he's going to be worth a lot, particularly in Rotisserie, where his stat profile all works for you.

10. Mike Pagliarulo MIN

Scott Leius, in about half the playing time, ranks only two spots lower. That usually means the job will change hands. Add to that that Leius is younger, and I rate Pagliarulo a very bad bet to get in 200 plate appearances. That also means that I must rate Leius a GOOD CHEAP FANTASY BUY, as his time should increase significantly.

11. Leo Gomez BAL

Takes his walks just fine in AAA ball, but forgets to be patient under the stress of trying to live up to his rep in the big time. I expect him to get over it, and predict that this should be his big breakthrough. IF YOU'RE IN A FANTASY LEAGUE, GET HIM.

12. Jim Gantner MIL

This is not what I mean by a last-hurrah year out of a long-career Hall of Famer. This is a miracle of an injury-free season for Jim. I wouldn't have given a plugged nickel for his chances of getting one in at his age. Still, what his presence in the rankings states, quite forcefully, is that the Indians, A's and Yankees need to get to work on this position.

13. Ernest Riles OAK

Don't be fooled. The position is vacant. Tony Phillips would have rated 4th.

14. Pat Kelly NYY

Either the Columbus stats are a lie, or the Yankee stats are a lie, or there's a weird ballpark adjustment going on here. My vote is for the Columbus stats to be a hot streak. I just don't see how someone with this little plate discipline and this little power can flourish. The only ones who have in my memory are Matty Alou and Manny Mota, and they hit .300 from the day they arrived. The Yankees are trying Pat at second base this year; I would try him at short, given his lack of bat. Even Willie McGee has more power than Pat, and Willie started out able to

National League

Third Basemen

Brock J. Hanke

		OWAR	DWAR	TWAR
1.	Johnson H	6.46	0.03	6.49
2.	Pendleton	5.02	1.44	6.46
3.	Williams MD	4.78	1.09	5.87
4.	Sabo	5.20	0.27	5.47
5.	Zeile	4.24	0.39	4.63
6.	Caminiti	2.43	0.76	3.19
7.	Wallach	1.88	1.12	3.00
8.	Harris L	1.96	0.72	2.68
	Sharperson	1.91	0.20	2.11
	Hollins	1.71	-0.08	1.63
	Wehner	0.96	0.24	1.20
	Walker C	0.66	0.27	0.93
9.	Howell Jk	0.27	0.48	0.75
10.	Buechele	0.53	0.21	0.74
11.	Salazar L	0.60	0.09	0.69
	King J	0.55	0.08	0.63
	Vizcaino	-0.29	0.34	0.05
12.	Hayes C	-0.82	0.74	-0.08
	Hamilton J	-0.14	-0.00	-0.14
	Scott G	-0.35	0.18	-0.17
	Coolbaugh	-0.54	0.23	-0.31
	Wilson C	-0.67	0.05	-0.62
	Presley	-0.66	-0.06	-0.72

1. Howard Johnson NYM (now, apparently, RF)

As long as Hojo's DWAR stay above zero, he's a third baseman. Not the best glove, but certainly an infielder. The idea of signing Eddie Murray to play first, moving Dave Magadan to third and putting Howard out to pasture does absolutely nothing but suppress Mackie Sasser's development. Mackie can't catch. Howard can play third.

But then, this is typical Mets. They finally noticed that their defense was none too good, but they missed that the problems were 1) Kevin Elster's glove can't carry his bat, and 2) they were playing Gregg Jeffries at second base when they had Keith Miller. And therefore they also missed such strategies as 1) trade Kevin McReynolds for Ozzie Smith or some other decent shortstop, 2) install Miller at second, 3) make a reserve out of Elster in case someone gets hurt, 4) trade Jeffries and Vince Coleman for a center fielder, and 5) use the money you just saved on Murray and Coleman to sign Frank Viola. There are no doubt several other plans just as good; this is just the first one I came up with. But to take two of the men who were not the problem and try to solve the problem by moving them is just silly. It also takes the Mets' from having the best regular third baseman around and puts them back in the pack.

2. Terry Pendleton ATL

Sometimes good tactics produce bad results and bad tactics produce good ones. Here's an object lesson. Paying free agent money to a player with Pendleton's credentials as of 1990 was a bad idea. He simply wasn't worth it, unless you believed in miracles. What I figured was that Bobby Cox got hypnotized by the same Pendleton traits that had Whitey Herzog batting him 6th in 1985 and 1986, when he couldn't hit a beach ball. That and maybe Cox thought he'd stabilize the right side of the infield, where the original plan was to play Jeff Blauser at shortstop. I'd have move Blauser to third, as the man can flat hit, and gotten a real shortstop for about $1 million a year less than the Braves pay Pendleton. Still, Pendleton exploded, and the Braves won a pennant that no possible Jeff Blauser bat could have bought them. Bad tactics, good results.

Now for what happened to cause the Pendleton explosion. When Terry came up in 1985, he was a good average, no power, no walks type of hitter, your basic Matty Alou with a hot third base glove. NL pitchers had figures this out by 1986, and

Third Base	G	PO	A	Er	TC	DP	FPct	DI	DG	DW%	DWAR
Backman	20	4	27	2	33	1	.939	120.2	0.5	.281	-.03
Blauser	18	13	28	4	45	1	.911	125.1	0.5	.331	-.01
Bonilla B	67	43	134	13	190	13	.932	520.0	2.2	.513	.35
Buechele	29	22	61	3	86	5	.965	254.0	1.1	1.205	.90
Caminiti	151	128	292	23	443	29	.948	1300.2	5.4	.490	.76
Coolbaugh	54	32	108	7	147	8	.952	457.1	1.9	.470	.23
Hamilton J	33	21	43	5	69	2	.928	203.2	0.8	.351	0.00
Harris L	112	78	153	14	245	16	.943	779.2	3.2	.447	.31
Hayes C	138	85	237	14	336	24	.958	1043.2	4.3	.523	.75
Hollins	34	20	55	7	82	1	.915	254.0	1.1	.277	-.08
Howell Jk	53	33	97	2	132	7	.985	379.0	1.6	1.297	1.49
Jefferies	49	24	93	11	128	7	.914	423.0	1.8	.254	-.17
Johnson H	104	54	172	18	244	11	.926	878.0	3.7	.221	-.47
King J	33	15	62	2	79	0	.975	281.0	1.2	.417	.08
Pendleton	147	108	341	23	472	31	.951	1265.2	5.3	.624	1.44
Presley	16	14	22	3	39	0	.923	139.0	0.6	.239	-.06
Quinones L	19	12	20	3	35	2	.914	136.2	0.6	.184	-.09
Sabo	149	87	244	12	343	22	.965	1286.1	5.4	.400	.27
Salazar L	85	46	149	9	204	6	.956	665.2	2.8	.384	.09
Scott G	31	13	50	2	65	7	.969	235.0	1.0	.531	.18
Sharperson	67	29	68	2	99	5	.980	395.2	1.6	.420	.12
Templeton	17	4	25	1	30	3	.967	104.2	0.4	1.437	.47
Teufel	52	28	78	6	112	4	.946	338.0	1.4	.932	.82
Vizcaino	56	10	26	2	38	1	.947	143.1	0.6	.284	-.04
Walker C	57	22	69	7	98	7	.929	376.2	1.6	.274	-.12
Wallach	148	107	301	14	422	28	.967	1304.1	5.4	.555	1.11
Wehner	36	23	65	6	94	10	.936	231.1	1.0	.598	.24
Williams MD	153	128	292	16	436	29	.963	1307.2	5.4	.549	1.08
Zeile	153	123	290	24	437	18	.945	1316.1	5.5	.421	.39
TOTALS	***	1428	3805	274	5507	316	.950	1442.0	6.0	5.073	****

stopped throwing Pendleton strikes and started making him climb the ladder with outside pitches at his head level. Terry suffered through two truly dreadful years of .230 batting, and an empty .230 it was, too. Whitey Herzog, normally a good filler of lineup cards, kept batting the man 6th, which was just silly. But, Whitey had a plan. He was going to get Terry to hit down on the ball, take pitches, and let some power come from those quick wrists that still make the fielding plays. Well, it worked for a year, 1987, the big age 27 year for Terry. With the high strike taken away from them, pitchers had to come down to Terry's sweet zone. He developed some batting eye, and started hitting, with some walks and some power. It looked like Whitey had finally developed a real #3 hitter.

Unfortunately, the Lords of Baseball restored some of the high strikes in 1988. Terry started watching strikeout pitches go by, and he couldn't stand the frustration. So he started to swing at a few of them, and was soon climbing the ladder again. Still, through all of this, he was trying to develop a real batting eye. It just wasn't working. Then he went to Atlanta, and Bobby cox apparently said, "forget about taking pitches. Swing at what you see." The result was a pitiful 43 walks for a 20-homer man, which is about as few as you can take if you show power. But it was a 20-homer man. And a .319 average man, with almost 40 doubles, batting third on a pennant winner. I still think Whitey was trying the right thing in getting Terry to take pitches, but it didn't work. Letting him swing away finally did. Good tactics, bad results. Bad tactics, good results. Speaking of which, Bobby, has it dawned on you yet that the proper middle of the batting order is Gant third to get on, Justice fourth to hit homers and Terry fifth to drive in runs?

3. Matt Williams SF

Even a worse walks/homers ratio than Terry Pendleton's. You'd think that pitchers could learn to exploit that. They should be able to either destroy his batting average or slash his power by throwing wild pitches at a man who will swing at them. But they haven't for two years now, and I don't know why. Maybe it's because they've already walked Clark or Mitchell and are afraid to throw balls to Matt. In that case, the trade of Kevin is going to hurt Matt badly. Still, until he actually does begin to suffer, you've got to give Matt credit for getting away with it.

4. Chris Sabo CIN

An incurable jerk personally, but he can really and truly play the game. Lenny the Dyke with power but without speed. Rob Dibble with a bat. Scary thought, that.

5. Todd Zeile STL

The best catcher in the National League, bar none. Oh, we're rating him at third base, are we? Well, he's worth about a game and a half over what Mike Sharperson would be in full time play. Sharperson's available, I imagine. At catcher, he'd be worth four or more games over Tom Pagnozzi. Of course, he did steal a hot 17 bases with rested knees. Got thrown out 11 times, but stole 17. The worst managerial move in St. Louis since the days of Solly Hemus.

6. Ken Caminiti HOU

Showed a 9/4 home/road homer split in the Astrodome. If he can keep that up, he'll piece together a career yet. If not, he's a 30-year-old never-was.

7. Tim Wallach MTL

What did you think? He was never going to have an off year? Never going to get old? C'mon, people, he's 34. Give him a break. A fine, fine player, finishing up a career just on the Hall of Fame borderline.

8. Lenny Harris LA

I like Lenny Harris. I'm convinced he can play. I wouldn't platoon him. I'd get rid of either Samuel or Sharperson. Lenny Harris is a year YOUNGER than Jeff Hamilton. A ROTISSERIE BEST BUY.

9. Jack Howell SD

I would assume that this is the last SABERMETRIC that will be discussing Jack Howell as a starter, unless Japan buys the Majors or something. The Padres have made no moves I know of to replace him. I guess they're going to wait for Scott Coolbaugh after all. If they were closer to contention, I might question the wisdom of having nothing behind Scott other than Jack, but this is the Padres, and I guess it won't hurt them to gamble. Now that I think of it, this is one component of the Johnson effect, that teams tend to drift towards .500. Good teams can't afford to gamble, so they can't win one. The Padres can, and eventually will.

10. Steve Buechele PIT

An open sore in Texas, Buechele put in a hot month against a new league's pitchers. No, I don't think he can keep that up. Yes, I know that we're supposed to rate the man who played the most for his team at the position, and the most-used Pirate third baseman was Bobby Bonilla. But Bonilla will get his in the right field section. About Buechele, mark my words: the highest-paid backup infielder in baseball by May. Jeff King can too play.

11. Luis Salazar CHN

The difference between Don Zimmer and, say, Whitey Herzog or Bobby Cox, is this: Both will promote a AA rookie into a Major League starter. Don Zimmer will do so on the basis of a hot spring training. Bobby and Whitey will do so if their analysis of the player's minor league career, WHICH THEY HAVE BOTHERED TO PAY ATTENTION TO ALL ALONG, indicates that the man is ready to start in the bigs. And thus Bobby and Whitey don't end up having to play Luis Salazar because Gary Scott didn't work out.

12. Charlie Hayes PHI

If I were running the Phillies, I'd send Charlie to winter ball to try to learn shortstop, and give Dave Hollins the third base job. Instead, the Phillies sent Charlie to the Yankees, who, according to Peter Gammons, are trying to develop a top defensive infield, so their kid pitchers can win them the title in 1994. Hell, it only took Bobby Cox the same three years, and his third baseman can hit.

American League

Shortstops

Brock J. Hanke

		OWAR	DWAR	TWAR
1.	Ripken C	7.06	3.09	10.14
2.	Vizquel	-0.04	3.00	2.96
3.	Spiers	1.14	1.52	2.66
4.	Schofield	0.60	1.84	2.44
5.	Trammell	1.07	1.33	2.41
6.	Rivera L	0.90	1.50	2.40
7.	Espinoza	-0.34	2.34	2.01
8.	Gagne	-0.03	1.92	1.89
9.	Guillen	-0.69	2.58	1.89
10.	Stillwell	1.05	0.33	1.38
	Sveum	0.19	0.54	0.73
11.	Fermin	-0.80	1.51	0.71
	Diaz Mar	-0.23	0.41	0.18
	Schaefer	-0.30	0.47	0.18
	Weiss	-0.24	0.31	0.08
12.	Huson	-0.58	0.51	-0.07
13.	Bordick	-0.84	0.74	-0.11
	Disarcina	-0.13	-0.00	-0.13
	Gonzales R	-0.66	0.45	-0.22
	Brumley	-0.52	0.26	-0.26
	Howard D	-0.97	0.59	-0.38
14.	Lee M	-1.24	0.77	-0.48
	Hernandez J	-0.90	0.32	-0.58
	Naehring	-0.66	0.04	-0.62
	Newman A	-1.91	1.04	-0.86

1. Cal Ripken BAL

This season poses one of the sabermetric questions that remains as yet unanswered. As you can see, the rest of the AL shortstops were not a winner bunch. Cal's advantage over the second place man, Omar Vizquel, is a ridiculous 7.18. The question is, how much should Ripken be given extra for the advantage, if anything. After all, the people who might compare to him, like Frank Thomas or Ken Griffey Jr. or Roberto Alomar, play positions where there is a lot more competition. Bill James brought up this question when discussing Ernie Banks in the HISTORICAL ABSTRACT, but he didn't attempt to answer it.

I haven't done the work either. Pete Palmer has made a stab at it, with his positional adjustment, but I have a couple of questions with that method as well. My gut feeling is that, in a year like this where one of the top defense positions is undermanned, Ripken should be given the extra credit. The problem occurs when it's not shortstop or catcher or center field that is undermanned. I don't think you can give a left fielder credit for his advantage if the center fielders are strong, because I think it's obvious that the center fielders could all play left if their teams wanted them to. If you have any ideas or methods, please write; this is the question I intend to take up when I've done as much with pitching arms as I can do.

I do know this: CAL RIPKEN SHOULD COMMAND THE ABSOLUTE HIGHEST PRICE IN ANY FANTASY LEAGUE. And also, no other shortstop is worth much more than a dollar.

2. Omar Vizquel SEA

The good news is that the Mariners don't have to shop for a shortstop for the next couple of years, anyway. I mean, they should have to, as Omar's no real prize; but there's just nothing at the position in this league right now. The bad news, of course, is that they have to bat him somewhere. As of now, they not only have to bat Omar, they also have to find a spot for Dave Valle. That's a big fat hole in the Mariner lineup, and they really do need to address it. Odd as it may seem, they might help themselves by trading Omar for a lesser defensive player, but one who can hit a little. There's just nothing out there at catcher to acquire.

Shortstop	G	PO	A	Er	TC	DP	FPct	DI	DG	DW%	DWAR
Bordick	83	137	207	10	354	42	.972	675.2	5.0	.484	.67
Brumley	31	19	76	5	100	9	.950	188.0	1.4	.362	.02
Diaz Mar	65	68	110	7	185	25	.962	359.2	2.7	.445	.26
Espinoza	146	221	434	21	676	112	.969	1189.0	8.8	.607	2.28
Fermin	129	216	374	12	602	73	.980	1092.1	8.1	.531	1.47
Fryman T	71	110	207	12	329	48	.964	604.2	4.5	.497	.66
Gagne	137	182	378	9	569	68	.984	1067.2	7.9	.587	1.88
Gallego	54	42	75	5	122	22	.959	271.0	2.0	.391	.08
Gonzales R	36	46	64	3	113	13	.973	222.1	1.7	.528	.29
Grebeck	25	17	37	4	58	8	.931	135.0	1.0	.305	-.05
Guillen	149	250	439	21	710	89	.970	1286.0	9.6	.619	2.58
Hernandez J	43	48	107	4	159	17	.975	288.0	2.1	.491	.30
Hill D	29	37	82	2	121	12	.983	201.2	1.5	.636	.43
Howard D	63	93	190	11	294	30	.963	515.0	3.8	.478	.49
Huson	116	141	266	15	422	40	.964	765.1	5.7	.438	.50
Lee M	138	194	360	19	573	54	.967	1155.1	8.6	.438	.76
Lewis M	35	41	88	1	130	18	.992	273.0	2.0	.472	.25
Naehring	17	15	50	3	68	7	.956	134.0	1.0	.371	.02
Newman A	55	64	90	2	156	24	.987	300.2	2.2	.643	.65
Riles	20	17	25	1	43	5	.977	101.0	0.8	.320	-.02
Ripken C	160	264	523	11	798	112	.986	1409.2	10.5	.636	3.00
Rivera L	127	179	381	24	584	87	.959	1086.0	8.1	.528	1.44
Schaefer	45	63	83	5	151	23	.967	308.0	2.3	.497	.34
Schofield	132	186	395	15	596	82	.975	1132.0	8.4	.562	1.79
Spiers	127	198	338	17	553	93	.969	1095.0	8.1	.532	1.48
Stillwell	117	162	257	18	437	64	.959	902.0	6.7	.399	.33
Sveum	51	56	125	6	187	24	.968	359.2	2.7	.480	.35
Trammell	91	129	292	9	430	60	.979	762.0	5.7	.579	1.30
Velarde	31	32	64	7	103	16	.932	164.0	1.2	.555	.25
Vizquel	137	223	419	13	655	102	.980	1127.1	8.4	.702	2.95
Weiss	40	64	99	5	168	21	.970	324.2	2.4	.477	.31
TOTALS	***	3637	6885	311	10833	1452	.971	1479.0	11.0	8.437	****

3. Bill Spiers MIL

Another sure sign that the position is all messed up. I doubt that the Brewers think that Spiers is one of their stalwarts. But they're wrong. Bill's not the best defensive shortstop, but he's adequate. And he doesn't sabotage the Brewer batting order. He has some balance to his game. That's important in a DH league, where the batting order is not supposed to collapse at the end with a pitcher. AL managers talk about using the #9 hitter as a sort of secondary leadoff man; Omar Vizquel can't do that, but Bill Spiers can.

4. Dick Schofield Jr. CAL

Before I got these stats, I thought that Schofield might be one of the people Whitey Herzog would let go. But Whitey's ability to see through the muck may be sufficient to see that he can't improve on Dick. Or maybe he can. Ozzie Smith would sure be an improvement, even at his age, as would Jose Oquendo. The Cardinals should have one of them to trade.

If you're thinking that I'm just suggesting this because I'm from St. Louis, and so focus on the Cardinals, think again. Many, many of the management people who change teams bring someone along with them as soon as they can swing the trade. Dallas Green brought Ryne Sandberg from the Phillies to the Cubs, and Syd Thrift brought Bobby Bonilla from the White Sox, along with some others. Joe Torre wanted to bring Devon White over from the Angels, which I thought was a terrible idea. Maybe Joe did know something I didn't there. In any case, I do expect Whitey to bring some Cardinals over, and I don't mean just the bench people like Tim Jones. Hell, maybe Jones could outplay Schofield.

5. Alan Trammell DET

This was an injury season, and we can expect to see Alan return to his normal #2 spot at the position. On the other hand, he is getting to that age where injuries are hard to recover from. I'd want to see another year before I gave a clean bill of health. As such, I have to rate Alan a GAMBLE IN A FANTASY LEAGUE.

6. Luis Rivera BOS

Here's another team that really needs to move up at short, but won't because the player they have is in the top half of the league. Of course, Luis is very, very unlikely to improve, whereas some other teams have kids to gamble on. Also, if Tony Pena doesn't recover, the Bosox are in the Mariners' pickle of having two holes at the end of the batting order. Luis is not Omar Vizquel, but he's no help at the plate.

7. Alvaro Espinoza NYY

Omar Vizquel, only worse and old.

8. Greg Gagne MIN

The Twins have Brian Harper behind the plate, and no offensive holes elsewhere, so they can afford to carry Greg. That has as much to do with their title as anything. Greg is who I think of when I think "typical shortstop." He had a couple of marginal power seasons at his peak, and his glove is steady, so he's going to have a nice career despite not ever rising any significant amount over the replacement rate. The people who can't get over the ten-homer barrier or the .280 batting average are the ones who get cut loose early. Teams keep thinking that Greg might turn in just one more of those good seasons some time when they most need it.

9. Ozzie Guillen CHA

Ozzie has had exactly two seasons in his life that looked like they might promise some offense. Everyone's stats were inflated in 1987, and 1990 was his age 27 peak year. Other than that, he has done nothing to convince anyone he can hit, and in fact he can't. He's got a flashy glove, but all that means is that he's another Omar Vizquel, but older.

10. Kurt Stilwell KC

The Royals finally understand that Kurt's got a shortstop's bat and a second baseman's glove, and they now want to get rid of him. Unfortunately, the available talent at the position is the weakest it's been in a decade.

11. Felix Fermin CLE

An Omar Vizquel wannabe.

12. Jeff Huson TEX

Job now belongs to Dickie Thon. That's an accurate evaluation of Jeff Huson, but the Rangers aren't in contention. Why didn't the Red Sox sign Thon? Because they only sign bats and arms, not gloves, that's why.

13. Mike Bordick OAK

Bordick is 26 and no prospect. He got his one full year in the Majors only because Walt Weiss was unavailable. Weiss has a real chance to come in #3 or even #2 at this position next year.

14. Manny Lee TOR

His 1988 season, at age 24, showed some promise, but he's regressed every year since then. No, I have no idea why. He hasn't been hurt nearly badly enough to do that to him. Right now, he's just marking time until the Jays think Eddie Zosky is ready.

National League

Shortstops

Brock J. Hanke

		OWAR	DWAR	TWAR
1.	Smith O	5.13	2.11	7.24
2.	Larkin B	4.82	1.82	6.65
3.	Bell Jay	3.99	1.90	5.88
4.	Fernandez T	3.08	2.13	5.21
5.	Owen S	1.88	1.92	3.80
6.	Dunston	1.31	1.51	2.83
7.	Blauser	1.92	0.23	2.15
8.	Elster	1.44	0.61	2.05
	Barberie	1.47	0.30	1.77
9.	Thon	0.44	1.07	1.51
10.	Griffin Alf	-0.17	1.18	1.01
11.	Uribe	0.00	0.63	0.63
	Cedeno A	1.01	-0.44	0.57
	Belliard	-0.72	1.18	0.46
	Anderson D	-0.28	0.56	0.27
	Benavides	0.08	0.12	0.20
	Perezchica	-0.01	0.05	0.04
	Foley T	-0.23	0.26	0.03
	Benjamin	-0.86	0.88	0.01
	Shipley	-0.02	-0.02	-0.04
	Offerman	-0.22	0.06	-0.16
	Booker R	-0.27	0.04	-0.23
	Ramirez R	-0.37	-0.04	-0.42
	Templeton	-1.39	0.54	-0.85
12.	Yelding	-0.76	-0.12	-0.88

1. Ozzie Smith STL

Several of the really long-career big-time Hall of Famers, with whom Ozzie would like to be compared, have turned in last hurrah seasons like this. Just a couple of minutes checking produced Joe Morgan, 1982, age 39; Stan Musial, 1957, age 37 and also 1962, age 42; Mike Schmidt, 1986, age 37 (the next year was a big offense year for everyone); and Ted Williams, 1957, age 39. Some of them don't (Frank Robinson, Babe Ruth), but several do. For Ozzie to put on a show entering an option year was no surprize to me. What was a surprize was the vast outpouring of fan sentiment to sign a 36-year-old shortstop to a long-term contract. The Cardinals have Jose Oquendo in place, ready to play short, and the best prospect on the team is second baseman Geronimo Pena, who was out of options last year and had to be wasted on the big league roster. There is also Luis Alicea, who had hit well over .300 the last two years in AAA ball. All these people are at least eight years younger than Ozzie. Needless to say, the new, Whiteyless Cardinal brain trust is not able to sort the situation out.

For those of you who are fantasy league fans, I have the following information: 1) Ozzie is a BAD FANTASY BUY, as he won't come close to last year, and his playing time will go down to give some to Pena. 2) Jose Oquendo is a WEAK FANTASY BUY for simulation games, and a HORRIBLE ROTISSERIE BUY. He won't play full time, making way for Pena, and his offense is non-Rotisserie. 3) Geronimo Pena is a GREAT LONG-TERM BUY, but a lousy short-term one, as he'll be lucky to get in 60 games. 4) If Luis Alicea can get himself traded, he's a GOOD SLEEPER BUY. Whitey had to rush him up when he moved Tommy Herr, and Luis wasn't ready then, but he looks good now if he can only get a regular chance. If your team needs a second or third baseman, get on those call-in phones now.

2. Barry Larkin CIN

The only thing keeping Barry from dominating this position is durability. If he can get back to 140 games a year, he's an 8-WAR man, which means perennial MVP candidacy.

3. Jay Bell PIT

I break down Jay's value to the 'Rats

Shortstop	G	PO	A	Er	TC	DP	FPct	DI	DG	DW%	DWAR
Anderson D	63	68	107	8	183	26	.956	327.2	2.5	.547	.49
Barberie	19	19	48	5	72	7	.931	132.1	1.0	.371	.02
Bell Jay	154	233	480	23	736	77	.969	1327.1	10.1	.538	1.90
Belliard	143	161	355	18	534	50	.966	972.0	7.4	.509	1.18
Benavides	19	26	49	2	77	5	.974	137.2	1.1	.456	.11
Benjamin	51	65	123	3	191	24	.984	308.0	2.3	.725	.88
Blauser	85	75	123	11	209	23	.947	435.0	3.3	.360	.03
Booker R	20	16	29	0	45	2	1.000	115.0	0.9	.372	.02
Cedeno A	64	87	147	15	249	34	.940	561.2	4.3	.248	-.44
Duncan	32	46	68	2	116	12	.983	223.0	1.7	.500	.26
Dunston	142	261	383	21	665	71	.968	1192.0	9.1	.518	1.53
Elster	106	151	298	13	462	39	.972	854.0	6.5	.443	.61
Fernandez T	145	248	437	20	705	79	.972	1262.2	9.6	.573	2.15
Foley T	43	45	71	4	120	12	.967	234.0	1.8	.444	.17
Griffin Alf	109	184	347	22	553	45	.960	933.2	7.1	.517	1.19
Harris L	19	16	46	5	67	7	.925	111.0	0.8	.488	.12
Johnson H	28	45	88	11	144	16	.924	218.0	1.7	.553	.34
Larkin B	118	223	363	15	601	64	.975	1020.2	7.8	.584	1.82
Offerman	49	49	121	10	180	17	.944	349.1	2.7	.373	.06
Oquendo	22	27	22	2	51	5	.961	124.0	0.9	.235	-.11
Owen S	131	184	374	8	566	64	.986	1049.0	8.0	.588	1.90
Ramirez R	44	51	71	6	128	13	.953	267.1	2.0	.312	-.08
Shipley	18	18	30	6	54	5	.889	127.0	1.0	.134	-.21
Smith O	149	244	386	8	638	78	.987	1246.1	9.5	.571	2.10
Templeton	41	54	104	6	164	18	.963	283.0	2.2	.829	1.03
Thon	144	234	409	21	664	65	.968	1258.0	9.6	.463	1.08
Uribe	85	98	216	11	325	37	.966	610.1	4.7	.485	.63
Vizcaino	33	31	74	3	108	14	.972	200.0	1.5	.553	.31
Yelding	72	114	166	18	298	31	.940	587.0	4.5	.325	-.11
TOTALS	***	3199	5745	315	9259	978	.966	1442.0	11.0	7.032	****

in the Jose Lind comment. My estimate there of the net worth of the Fermin for Bell trade is about 6.5 wins a year. Barry Bonds is not 6.5 wins better than what the Pirates would have in left field without him. Therefore, Jay Bell is the Pittsburgh MVP.

He's also one good reason why I don't expect the 'Rats to collapse until/unless they lose Bonds as well as Bobby Bo. As good as Bonilla is, he was only about the #5 cog on the Pittsburgh team, behind Bell, Bonds, Drabek, Van Slyke and Smiley. The Pirates also have the two most potent platoon arrangements in the National League. They are not through yet.

4. Tony Fernandez SD

About even with Jay Bell; the difference in their WAR is a matter of playing time. To convince me that Toronto won the trade in terms of player personnel (they obviously won in the sense that they got a quick division title out of Joe Carter), you have to convince me that Carter is better than Tony. I don't think you can do that, gaudy home run stats or no. Fernandez is also a DECENT ROTISSERIE BUY. The position drops off dramatically after Tony, and most people don't know that.

5. Spike Owen MTL

I thought the acquisition of Owen was a silly move by the Expos, but he's proved me wrong. The change of scenery just plain revived his career. Of course, he's a little old to be helping the team when it finally heaves into contention, so I think they'd be well advised to trade him to a team like, say, the Phillies. They want to move up, and they need a middle infielder, having lost Dickie Thon with only Mickey Morandini to work with. Spike wouldn't hurt the Red Sox, either. If you're wondering who the Expos would play if they did trade Spike, look at Bret Barberie's ratings. Bret Barberie played exactly nineteen (19) games at shortstop.

6. Shawon Dunston

No, he's never going to turn into the All-Star the Cubbies thought he might when they drafted him. He just doesn't have enough discipline, both at the plate and on defense. With his arm and quickness, he should dominate the fielding stats here, but he's regularly out of position and he doesn't anticipate. On offense, of course, he swings at everything. Incompetent Chicago coaching hasn't helped him any.

7. Jeff Blauser ATL

His bat is surely good enough for third base, but the Braves have one of those now. Actually, there are worse defensive shortstops; if

Treadway were a better second sacker, Jeff would be OK in the hole. But it's hard to put both of them out there and then try to convince young pitchers to throw down in the strike zone. Me, I'd put Lemke at second, keep Belliard as a backup and try to trade Treadway. On the other hand, Bobby Cox seems to know what he's doing without my help.

8. Kevin Elster NYM

The problem with Kevin Elster is not his bat. It's not very good, but you could live with it if he played good defense. But he doesn't, and the Mets keep trying to get him to cover for weak infielders elsewhere. This year, the plan is to put him between aged Willie Randolph, who can still hit but whose range is nothing, and a transplanted first baseman. Forget it. He can't do that. Get it through your head, guys, you need another shortstop. The one you've got is a backup.

9. Dickie Thon PHI (TEX)

If you loaded up Dickie's stats through 1983 into Brock2, his age 34 projection probably wouldn't be too far off this year. A couple of books ago, I questioned the Phillies' decision to sign Dickie. I noted that they were not in contention, Dickie was old, and he might not last until they finally got going. Sure enough, the Phils think they're about to make their move, and they let Dickie go. This time they signed Donuts Duncan, who is younger than Dickie was, and better than nothing, but not a whole lot of either. What I would like them to tell me is just what they think they got out of their contract with Thon. How many of those dollars did they get back by finishing two or three games closer to .500 than they would have otherwise?

10. Alfredo Griffin LA

Should be moving down to a non-contender any year now, but Jose Offerman's MLEs are not Major League quality. No, they're not. And they never have been. All that Jose has ever had, and I mean all, is his age. I give him one more year to come up with a decent MLE; if not, I rate him no prospect at all. ANYONE WHO ACQUIRES EITHER ONE OF THESE GUYS IN A FANTASY LEAGUE SHOULD HAVE HIS HEAD EXAMINED.

11. Jose Uribe SF

Still has enough glove that there aren't 12 shortstops ahead of him, so he's a legitimate starter. Does anyone remember that he's all that the Giants have left from the Jack Clark trade? Jose should send Jack part of his salary. If he'd stayed with the Cardinals, he'd be out of baseball by now; he'd never have taken the full time job away from Ozzie Smith, and he'd never have kept starting ability as a backup. He'd be gone and he wouldn't be a millionaire, either.

The willingness of the Giants to keep trying Mike Benjamin demonstrates clearly that they don't read MLEs. Benjamin has never, not for one half of one season, shown anything even remotely resembling a Major League bat. In fact, he's never really shown a AAA bat. As the WAR stats show, his glove makes him exactly a replacement rate player.

12. Eric Yelding HOU

I was surprized quite a bit by Andujar Cedeno's bad defensive stats. I saw him in person and on TV quite a bit, and he sure looks like a Major League shortstop. Nonetheless, the WAR aren't lying; his defensive stats are horrible. He's still young, and the Astros aren't in contention, so he's got a couple of years to learn the position; but he may end up in the outfield. If so, I question his ability to stay in the bigs. He'll have to develop the power to be a middle of the order man, as he doesn't take enough walks to lead off.

Eric Yelding is a player/coach at the Class A level, if anything.

American League

Left Fielders

Brock J. Hanke

		OWAR	DWAR	TWAR
1.	Henderson R	4.61	0.78	5.39
2.	Polonia	4.51	0.26	4.77
3.	Raines	3.18	1.17	4.35
4.	Belle	3.85	0.28	4.13
5.	Gibson K	3.89	0.03	3.92
6.	Vaughn G	2.98	0.76	3.74
7.	Hall	2.98	0.66	3.65
8.	Greenwell	2.90	0.65	3.55
9.	Gonzalez	2.61	0.52	3.13
10.	Orsulak	0.90	1.72	2.62
	Reimer	2.20	-0.01	2.18
	Cotto	1.54	0.27	1.81
	Eisenreich	1.74	0.02	1.76
11.	Maldonado	1.50	0.24	1.74
	Anderson B	1.03	0.24	1.27
12.	Briley	0.62	0.19	0.81
	Griffey Sr.	0.67	0.05	0.71
	Thurman	0.39	0.24	0.63
13.	Moseby	0.58	-0.03	0.55
	Powell A	0.27	-0.00	0.27
	Ducey	0.13	0.02	0.14
14.	Gladden	-0.37	0.45	0.08
	Wilson W	-0.37	0.40	0.03
	Incaviglia	-0.25	0.26	0.01
	Wilson M	-0.16	0.11	-0.05
	Cochrane	0.06	-0.13	-0.07
	Mercedes	-0.31	0.03	-0.28
	Meulens	-0.71	0.24	-0.47
	Daugherty	-0.91	0.07	-0.84
	Shelby	-1.34	0.35	-0.99

1. Rickey Henderson OAK

The sign of the truly killer ballplayer is when he has a bad year, and is over 30 to start with, and still dominates his position. Left field is going through a weak period now - see Barry Bonds - but this is still impressive.

I suppose you can figure out that Rickey, aging, with his team disintegrating about him, and with an offense that relies on taking walks, is NOT THE ROTISSERIE BUY HE USED TO BE. If you've got him, try shopping him around and see if you can fleece someone.

2. Luis Polonia CAL

With Venable and Gallagher gone, and Junior Felix not one ounce better than he appears to be, I would assume that Luis will be moved back to center field, where he probably belongs. I would be a lot more sure of this if Whitey had managed to pick up the big bat he doubtless wants in left. As it is, he's got to fill the outfield, first base and DH with Luis, Hubie Brooks, Von Hayes, Junior Felix and whatever else he can scrabble up. Basically, this means that there are big opportunities for minor leaguers; and in truth, there are a couple who look OK, notably Lee Stevens and Don Barbara. What I don't know is what plans and positions Whitey might have in mind for these guys.

3. Tim "Rock" Raines CHA

A decade ago, Raines and Henderson were mentioned together as the potential "greatest" leadoff men ever, whatever that means. (Is Ted Williams to be considered a "leadoff man?" How about Bobby Bonds? Where do you want to draw the line?) At any rate, Rickey promptly sorted himself out from Tim, and has probably overtaken Billy Hamilton for the best ever complete-career-as-a-leadoff-man type. Both of them as you can see here, sorted themselves out from the other left fielders in baseball. And therefore, although the Chisox lost the one-year one-up trade of Ivan Calderon, I think they have a better chance to win a division with Raines. There are a lot more people who can do what Ivan does than there are who can duplicate Raines at the top of the order.

4. Albert Belle CLE

Every time some damn fool conservative sportswriter wants to talk about some star player as if he were Jack the Ripper, because the player

Left Field	G	PO	A	Er	TC	DP	FPct	DI	DG	DW%	DWAR
Aldrete	16	21	1	0	22	0	1.000	111.0	0.3	.607	.08
Allred	20	42	1	0	43	0	1.000	121.1	0.3	.827	.16
Anderson B	74	82	2	3	87	0	.966	390.1	1.1	.365	.02
Belle	87	166	8	9	183	1	.951	718.2	1.9	.488	.27
Briley	95	122	3	3	128	0	.977	524.0	1.4	.464	.16
Browne J	17	26	0	1	27	0	.963	122.0	0.3	.287	-.02
Carter J	56	94	1	5	100	0	.950	464.1	1.3	.299	-.06
Cochrane	23	28	0	1	29	0	.966	141.0	0.4	.308	-.02
Cotto	38	51	0	1	52	0	.981	184.0	0.5	.507	.08
Daugherty	33	48	1	0	49	0	1.000	227.0	0.6	.414	.04
Ducey	19	26	1	2	29	0	.931	124.0	0.3	.414	.02
Eisenreich	58	74	1	3	78	0	.962	368.1	1.0	.282	-.07
Gibson K	91	157	3	4	164	0	.976	759.1	2.1	.357	.01
Gladden	126	239	4	3	246	1	.988	990.0	2.7	.515	.44
Gonzalez Juan	92	112	1	2	115	0	.983	505.1	1.4	.410	.08
Greenwell	141	262	9	3	274	3	.989	1205.2	3.3	.542	.63
Griffey	26	31	0	0	31	0	1.000	181.0	0.5	.442	.04
Hall M	63	111	4	0	115	1	1.000	484.2	1.3	.676	.43
Hamilton	24	30	1	0	31	0	1.000	134.0	0.4	.659	.11
Henderson R	118	249	10	8	267	1	.970	973.1	2.6	.635	.75
Hill G	21	41	0	0	41	0	1.000	127.2	0.3	1.438	.38
Incaviglia	50	90	4	2	96	1	.979	396.0	1.1	.571	.24
James C	26	48	1	0	49	0	1.000	184.0	0.5	.632	.14
Jones Tr	35	47	0	0	47	0	1.000	191.1	0.5	.613	.14
Kelly	51	100	7	1	108	1	.991	444.0	1.2	.697	.42
Mack	49	103	0	4	107	0	.963	347.0	0.9	.484	.13
Maldonado	66	127	2	2	131	0	.985	553.1	1.5	.951	.90
Meulens	61	115	3	5	123	0	.959	459.1	1.2	.422	.09
Moseby	64	125	1	6	132	0	.955	530.2	1.4	.328	-.03
Newson	16	15	1	1	17	0	.941	100.1	0.3	.341	****
Orsulak	84	158	13	0	171	2	1.000	642.1	1.7	.914	.98
Palmer Dn	29	42	1	3	46	1	.935	182.2	0.5	.315	-.02
Phillips	24	52	0	0	52	0	1.000	175.0	0.5	.674	.15
Plantier	16	29	0	1	30	0	.967	123.0	0.3	.371	.01
Polonia	143	246	8	5	259	0	.981	1249.2	3.4	.422	.24
Powell A	23	31	0	1	32	0	.969	144.0	0.4	.344	****
Raines	132	268	12	3	283	3	.989	1154.2	3.1	.722	1.16
Reimer	61	109	0	5	114	0	.956	452.0	1.2	.348	****
Segui	28	47	1	2	50	0	.960	202.0	0.5	.375	.01
Shelby	26	42	4	1	47	0	.979	170.1	0.5	.755	.19
Thurman	39	68	1	1	70	0	.986	226.2	0.6	.571	.14
Vaughn G	135	315	5	2	322	1	.994	1164.1	3.1	.586	.74
Wilson M	36	60	2	2	64	0	.969	291.0	0.8	.457	.08
Wilson W	41	81	1	2	84	0	.976	258.1	0.7	.562	.15
TOTALS	***	4754	125	107	4986	17	.979	1479.0	4.0	3.132	****

won't talk to the sportswriter with what the writer thinks is proper deference, remember, it could be worse. It could be Albert Belle. And it could be the Cleveland Indians, so the player has no motivation to clean up his act. Speaking of cleaning up, Belle is a cleanup man for a contender waiting for the appropriate trade. I mean it. Belle is exactly the type of player that some team, one bat away from a title, picks up and satisfies for a year or two in order to get over the hump. For precedent, see Jack Clark and Richie Allen. WONDERFUL ROTISSERIE GAMBLE.

5. Kirk Gibson KC

What? Is Kirk Gibson still in baseball? I thought he was DEAD! You say he's rated 5th at a position? Bodybag Gibson? Is the Royals' team doctor named Frankenstein? Next thing, you'll tell me he's learned to catch or something.

6. Greg Vaughn MIL

At age 26, Greg needs to make a big, big step to his peak next year in order to fulfill the superstar tag. Otherwise, he's a journeyman. He needs to make that step in batting average. He already hits homers, though he hits them at home. The big question mark is speed, by the way. No 26-year-old with that much homer power should be hitting that few doubles. If he can't get his swing under control, he can't leg out anything to get the average up. Right now, he's the best bet in the AL to win the Mark McGwire old-man's-skills short career award.

7. Mel Hall NYY

The Cat Man's stats are found under right field. That means that, while Mel played more right field than left, no one played more left for the Yankees than Mel did. That tells you something about the Yankees.

Do any of you remember when Mel was this incredibly hot prospect for the Cubs? Bill James quote was "looks like someone prayed him up." Then Bill went on to say that sometimes even those types don't make it. At the time, there were rumors about Mel's personality. I guess you can figure out that Cleveland is nowhere to send someone with an attitude problem. Neither is New York. I still wonder what might have happened had he ended up with one of the well-organized outfits.

8. Mike Greenwell BOS

The resurgence of the Blue Jays has finally forced the Bosox to take action. Basically, their trouble is that they have this huge hoard of good-hit-no-field people, and they need to convert them into fewer, but better players. What they want to do is keep Plantier and Vaughn, and jettison Brunansky, and trade up the rest of them for a killer player. Unfortunately, all the trade partners want to talk about Plantier and Vaughn. Probably, the Sox will have to package Scott Cooper up with either Greenwell or Ellis Burks to get the man they want.

9. Juan Gonzalez TEX

Juan's stats can be found under center field, which tells you something about the Rangers. I vote for the retirement of Gary Pettis and Juan's move into center. The Rangers tried to sign Danny Tartabull, which suggests that they may agree. If Juan gets a stable spot to play in, I think he'll move up, and so rate him a FIRST RATE FANTASY BUY.

10. Joe Orsulak BAL

Clear proof that the Orioles have too many mediocre center fielders and no left fielders at all. Yes, even after trading Steve Finley. No, I don't think they're well enough organized to do much about it. That is, I think their problems are in the front office, not the manager's chair. They had no business ridding themselves of Frank Robinson.

11. Candy Maldonado TOR

Joe Carter played more at this spot, but he's listed under right field, where he does in fact belong. Moldy did just fine for a fill-in. Now that Mark Whiten and Glenallen Hill are gone, the job devolves onto Rob Ducey or Derek Bell or Turner Ward. Surely one of them is going to move up ahead of Candy. I rate them Bell, Ward and Ducey, because Bell is 23. If you hear that Bell has got the job, he's a GOOD FANTASY BUY. That's Derek Bell, not Candy Maldonado. If they decide Derek needs another year of seasoning, the others, including Candy, are not good buys, as they'll probably share the playing time. Domingo Martinez, by the way, is a first baseman, not an outfielder. He is, however, probably a better DH than Dave Parker.

12. Greg Briley SEA

Had a job handed to him two years ago at age 25, when he showed some signs of deserving it. However, his game has collapsed, particularly his power game, and the M's now have Kevin Mitchell. Greg's failure to develop is one of the two biggest factors (Scott Bankhead is the other) in the slow movement up of the Mariners and, therefore, in the loss of Jim Lefebvre's job.

What the M's did in trading for Kevin Mitchell is what the Bosox are trying unsuccessfully to do. They converted some bulk talent into an All-Star. The reason the M's were able to do that and the Bosox not is that the M's were willing to trade something other than outfielders to get an outfielder. The Sox basically want to make a two-for-one deal within a position. No one wants to be on the back end of that. The M's dealt from their staff and now have outfielders to trade for, say, bulk pitching. That's how you do it, Boston. You just have to have the guts to accept the gamble of a temporary overstock at a spot. The M's have to get something for Briley or Tracy Jones or even Henry Cotto, but they don't have to get an outfielder for them.

13. Lloyd Moseby DET

The job was originally Pete Incaviglia's until he proved to be Pete Incaviglia. T-Bone Shelby and Tony Phillips also played here. Given that the Tigers are not going to play Tony Phillips in the infield, this is probably his spot. I doubt they can win with Moseby.

14. Dan Gladden MIN

That's right, 14th. Dead last. I want to rant a little bit here. For years, absolutely years, the Twins have put up with Dan Gladden in left field and at leadoff. That was absolutely unacceptable behavior. Gladden cannot play well enough to hold down a starting outfield spot in the Major Leagues, much less a hitter's spot. He also absolutely cannot hit well enough to lead off for a championship team. The Twins put up with this because their ballpark encourages them to think about power, not leadoff men, and because they weren't really in contention there.

Then the Twins won the division, and several sportswriters apparently thought it was Dan Gladden's fault, especially after Game 7 of the Series. But the Twins won their division largely because they sat Dan Gladden down some and played people like Shane Mack and Randy Bush. Then they won the LCS and World Series with Kirby Puckett, Chili Davis and a pitching staff. The fact that Dan Gladden scored some critical runs demonstrates nothing except that the rest of the Twin offense was so strong that it was bound to score Dan whenever he did get on base.

The Twins, as you surely know, agree with me and have jettisoned Dan Gladden now that they have become a respectable team. Now the whole world of perfectly respectable Henry Cottos is open to them. Of course, they really should come up with something at least remotely resembling a leadoff man, but one step at a time.

National League

Left Fielders

Brock J. Hanke

		OWAR	DWAR	TWAR
1.	Bonds	6.61	1.14	7.75
2.	Calderon	4.89	0.28	5.17
	Thompson M	3.74	0.82	4.56
3.	McReynolds	3.55	0.75	4.30
4.	Gonzalez L	3.71	0.56	4.27
5.	Mitchell K	3.77	0.32	4.09
6.	Daniels	3.25	0.52	3.76
7.	Bell Geo	3.27	0.02	3.29
	Nixon O	2.12	0.68	2.80
8.	Smith Lo	2.22	0.06	2.28
	Felder	1.62	0.43	2.05
9.	Chamberlain	1.40	0.33	1.73
	Braggs	1.28	0.13	1.41
10.	Clark Je	0.84	0.41	1.25
11.	Hatcher B	0.77	0.36	1.13
	Lindeman	0.90	0.12	1.02
	Ortiz Ja	0.62	0.13	0.75
	Webster M	0.37	0.19	0.56
	Gwynn C	0.35	0.17	0.52
	Mitchell Kth	0.42	0.05	0.47
	Leonard M	0.40	0.06	0.46
12.	Gilkey	-0.33	0.68	0.34
	Jones Chris	0.17	0.10	0.27
	Ward K	0.13	0.07	0.20
	Javier	-0.10	0.24	0.14
	Landrum C	0.10	0.02	0.12
	Sanders	-0.10	0.13	0.03
	Vanderwal	-0.06	0.06	0.00
	Hudler	-0.47	0.33	-0.13
	Davidson M	-0.45	0.26	-0.19
	Carreon	-0.44	0.21	-0.23

1. Barry Bonds PIT

I have a theory as to why this position is so weak. It used to be that left field and first base were manned by a bunch of big ol' dinosaurs who could slug the hell out of the ball, but who were foul poles on defense. Minimum ballpark dimensions and Astroturf changed all that. No more Greg Luzinskis. Nowadays, the guys who can't run don't make it to the Majors at all. They bulk up and play football. And therefore, all the outfielders are potential center fielders. The best ones actually end up there, and the leftovers play left. Barry Bonds, of course, is a center fielder by talent, who just happens to be on the same team as Andy Van Slyke. Milt Thompson and Bernard Gilkey are really center fielders, too; typical Cardinals. Kevin McReynolds played center for a few years. Otis Nixon was a center fielder before he moved to Ron Gant's team. Now, look at the DWAR stats at this position.

2. Ivan Calderon MTL

The best true left fielder in the National League.

3. Kevin McReynolds NYM (KC)

I think he'll improve some in Kansas City. He still has some speed and hits line drives, not fly balls. The only thing that could hurt him would be trying to keep his homer stats up, and he seems too level-headed for that. Since I think Gregg Jeffries will respond well to the move, and since I think Kevin Miller is for real as a second baseman, I think the Royals win the trade real big. It was a typical Mets trade. The Mets get a name to replace a lost free agent name, and get fleeced in the process. Oh, well, it pays the Royals back for David Cone.

4. Luis Gonzalez HOU

Yet another kid outfielder with zero strike zone judgement. And, as a consequence, a prime candidate for sophomore slump. When you'll

Left Field	G	PO	A	Er	TC	DP	FPct	DI	DG	DW%	DWAR
Bass K	22	33	5	1	39	0	.974	159.2	0.4	.708	.16
Bell Geo	146	249	6	10	265	0	.962	1191.1	3.3	.356	.02
Bonds	148	310	12	3	325	1	.991	1279.2	3.5	.665	1.12
Braggs	55	102	1	4	107	1	.963	408.1	1.1	.388	.04
Calderon	122	257	3	7	267	2	.974	1038.0	2.9	.442	.27
Candaele	18	30	0	0	30	0	1.000	112.0	0.3	.642	.09
Carreon	41	65	3	0	68	0	1.000	293.2	0.8	.723	.30
Chamberlain	93	188	4	3	195	0	.985	822.2	2.3	.489	.32
Clark Je	85	139	3	1	143	1	.993	693.0	1.9	.475	.24
Daniels	131	215	9	5	229	0	.978	1033.1	2.9	.532	.52
Davidson M	32	38	0	0	38	0	1.000	143.0	0.4	.638	.11
Felder	42	60	2	1	63	2	.984	238.1	0.7	.600	.16
Gilkey	74	163	6	1	170	1	.994	604.1	1.7	.753	.68
Gonzalez L	131	287	6	5	298	1	.983	1067.2	3.0	.539	.56
Gwynn C	30	28	0	0	28	0	1.000	125.0	0.3	.583	.08
Hatcher B	83	132	4	2	138	0	.986	554.0	1.5	.560	.32
Hayes V	20	55	1	0	56	0	1.000	184.0	0.5	.753	.21
Howard T	34	49	1	1	51	0	.980	188.1	0.5	.525	.09
Hudler	27	43	3	0	46	0	1.000	176.0	0.5	.880	.26
Jackson Dar	21	34	0	1	35	0	.971	141.0	0.4	.423	.03
Javier	52	42	0	0	42	0	1.000	172.2	0.5	.615	.13
Kruk	36	79	4	1	84	1	.988	315.2	0.9	.738	.34
Leonard M	23	24	0	0	24	0	1.000	155.1	0.4	.404	.02
Martinez Crm	16	35	1	0	36	0	1.000	115.2	0.3	.835	.16
Martinez Da	36	30	2	1	33	0	.970	181.2	0.5	.449	.05
McReynolds	123	225	7	2	234	1	.991	949.1	2.6	.580	.61
Mitchell K	99	188	6	6	200	0	.970	820.0	2.3	.492	.32
Nixon O	55	84	3	0	87	1	1.000	348.0	1.0	.758	.39
Roberts Bip	19	39	0	2	41	0	.951	126.2	0.4	.467	.04
Sanders	41	52	3	3	58	0	.948	236.2	0.7	.544	.13
Smith Lo	97	133	5	5	143	2	.965	710.0	2.0	.380	.06
Thompson M	71	159	5	2	166	0	.988	569.2	1.6	.701	.55
Vanderwal	15	24	0	0	24	0	1.000	107.0	0.3	.546	.06
Ward K	30	51	0	1	52	0	.981	202.0	0.6	.476	.07
Webster M	31	26	1	0	27	0	1.000	102.2	0.3	2.217	.53
TOTALS	***	4043	116	73	4232	15	.983	1442.0	4.0	2.794	9.78

swing at anything, it doesn't take pitchers more than a year to figure it out. Then you stop seeing strikes. Obviously, a LOUSY ROTISSERIE BUY.

5. Kevin Mitchell SF (SEA)

The other good real (as opposed to real good) left fielder in the league. Give Woody Woodword some credit. Seattle was chock full of platoon outfielders who could hit, but was having trouble settling on three of them to play regularly. The solution, to get someone better than any of them to solve the problem, is the sort of thing that characterizes winning managements. Now Jay Buhner can be given a lineup spot he can handle, and Mitchell, Junior and Buhner is as good a crew as anybody's.

6. Kal Daniels LA

It's a perfect trade fit. Dodger Stadium is a notorious pitchers' park, so Daniels' walks are undervalued there, while they'd have maximum impact in Wrigley. George Bell has more power than Kal. Because Dodger Stadium is a pitcher's park, home runs are the only way to score there, so Bell's power works better than Kal's on base skills in Dodger. The Bums need a righty bat in the middle of the order, and the Cubs need a lefty. The only question for the Cubs would be whether to lead off Kal or Mark Grace. By the way, if you're wondering what sometimes happens to those guys who seem just headed for the Hall of Fame, take a look at Kal's knees and Eric Davis'.

7. George Bell CHN

I don't think this was what the Cubs had in mind when they signed George, but the Skydome is a hitters' park too. The normal batting stat jump that accompanies a move to Wrigley just didn't occur. As you know if you've read the Cubs essay, I think having Bell and Dawson and Sandberg on the same team constitutes duplication of talent and, therefore, waste of salary money. Since Andre isn't about to agree to a trade, and Ryne plays the infield, the Cubs really do need to trade

George for a lefty power bat like, say, Kal Daniels.

8. Lonnie Smith ATL

Another excellent move by Bobby Cox. If you're going to gamble with cocaine cases, gamble in quantity. That way, you don't have to win all of them. Nixon and Smith are a fine, fine tag team at left field and leadoff, but you wouldn't want to rest your fate with either of them alone.

9. Wes Chamberlain PHI

Needs to step up in class to be what the Phillies are really looking for, and time is running out at age 26. If he has a sophomore slump, he's in trouble, as the Phillies want to contend now. And, as I've said before, these guys who can't take walks are the prime candidates for the second-year woes; Wes isn't going to see too many strikes in 1992. Overall, I rate him a grade B prospect, a #5 hitter at best. The Pirates didn't give away anything they couldn't afford.

10. Jerald Clark SD

Not really a starting quality left fielder, but several teams have piled up more than they need. A couple of quick free agent outfield signings is all the Padres need to vault into contention.

11. Billy Hatcher CIN

The acquisition of Bip Roberts means that the Reds no longer need a desperation leadoff man. I presume that means that Billy Hatcher is through as a Major Leaguer.

12. Bernard Gilkey STL

I cannot for the life of me understand why no one will give Milt Thompson a starting job. Gilkey is no more than a grade B prospect, while Milt has at least five years of championship-quality play left in him. Now the Cardinals have been trapped into signing Pedro Guerrero, and he's the incumbent left fielder. What a joke. If you have any questions as to Whitey Herzog's ability, just look at this pitiful, mismanaged excuse for a team, only two years removed from his touch.

American League

Center Fielders

Brock J. Hanke

		OWAR	DWAR	TWAR
1.	Griffey Jr	6.45	1.34	7.79
2.	White D	5.26	1.87	7.13
3.	Henderson D	4.45	1.58	6.04
4.	Puckett	3.35	1.10	4.46
5.	Devereaux	3.07	1.38	4.45
6.	Cole	3.34	0.30	3.64
	Gonzalez Juan	2.61	0.52	3.13
	Kelly	2.41	0.31	2.72
	Gallagher	1.70	0.98	2.68
7.	Johnson L	0.54	2.04	2.58
	Hamilton	1.84	0.65	2.49
8.	Yount	1.36	0.71	2.07
9.	Cuyler	1.12	0.90	2.02
10.	Burks	1.42	0.33	1.75
11.	McRae B	0.68	0.86	1.54
	Huff	0.93	0.44	1.38
12.	Williams B	1.17	0.18	1.35
	Hill G	1.01	0.13	1.14
13.	Felix	1.16	-0.08	1.08
	Abner	-0.10	0.40	0.30
	Lyons S	-0.24	0.45	0.21
14.	Pettis	-0.21	0.33	0.12

1. Ken Griffey Jr. SEA

Right now, I'd rather have Roberto Alomar, largely because he's kept it up for more years. However, Junior here is two years younger, and his Brock2 projections show him with the potential to be even better than Alomar. In any case, Ken is still PROBABLY A GOOD FANTASY BUY, as the people who don't keep completely up to date still think of him as a kid with potential rather than a proven top All-Star whose only question any more is how high his top end will reach.

The only fly in the fantasy ointment is the possibility that the Mariners could move Junior up in the lineup, to leadoff, to be specific. Given the roster that the M's currently have, laden with slow sluggers, they don't need Ken in the middle of the order. If they do keep him there, their only leadoff prospect is Edgar Martinez. Edgar gets on base, but he's slow. Ken's fast, and he gets on base, too. I don't mean to imply that Ken reminds me of Rickey Henderson or Tim Raines. He's not going to be a career leadoff type with a little excess power. Eventually, as the team around him changes, and as he slows down a bit, he's going to be a #3 man. But right now, on the Mariners as they presently are, he's the best leadoff candidate by far.

2. Devon White TOR

I missed on this one completely. When Joe Torre was hired to manage the Cardinals, he went public with a desire to pick up Devon from the Angels, where he was in trouble. I thought this was silly. I reasoned that Devon's only real good offensive season was 1987, the hitters' year. I saw that Devon is a flashy pure athlete, like Vince Coleman is, and that baseball insiders tend to overrate these guys, confusing ability with skill. Anyway, the Cards made no effort to acquire Devon, as they had rookie Ray Lankford slotted for center field, and the Jays reaped the harvest. Whether Devon will hold up, I still question, as I do with Joe Carter. But the Jays have a division title in hand, and the Cardinals don't.

For those of you who don't read the whole book, I'd like to repeat that this sort of thing is very normal: a management person comes over from one team to another, and has a player in mind to bring with him. Ryne Sandberg came to the Cubs with Dallas Green and Bobby Bonilla came with Syd Thrift. When Joe arrived, I was hoping he had someone in mind; I was so disappointed when it was Devon White. Ah, well, you can't win them all.

3. Dave Henderson OAK

Looks about as much like a center fielder as I do, but his defensive

Center Field	G	PO	A	Er	TC	DP	FPct	DI	DG	DW%	DWAR
Abner	31	71	3	0	74	1	1.000	236.0	1.0	.756	.39
Anderson B	25	52	1	0	53	0	1.000	181.2	0.7	.586	.17
Burks	126	283	2	2	287	1	.993	1074.0	4.4	.424	.32
Cole	100	243	6	7	256	1	.973	792.0	3.2	.443	.30
Cotto	19	41	1	1	43	1	.977	126.2	0.5	.535	.10
Cuyler	150	414	6	6	426	3	.986	1220.1	5.0	.527	.88
Devereaux	147	397	9	3	409	1	.993	1252.0	5.1	.615	1.35
Felix	62	124	1	2	127	0	.984	513.2	2.1	.319	-.06
Gallagher	61	135	6	0	141	1	1.000	468.0	1.9	.739	.74
Gonzalez Juan	92	192	5	3	200	0	.985	647.0	2.6	.523	.45
Griffey Jr	151	359	15	4	378	4	.989	1260.2	5.1	.607	1.31
Hamilton	55	108	0	0	108	0	1.000	383.2	1.6	.536	.29
Henderson D	135	352	10	1	363	2	.997	1170.1	4.7	.669	1.51
Hill G	26	70	0	2	72	0	.972	214.2	0.9	.372	.02
Huff	52	105	3	1	109	1	.991	353.2	1.4	1.290	1.35
Johnson L	157	421	11	2	434	4	.995	1321.1	5.4	.728	2.03
Kelly	73	167	1	3	171	0	.982	641.0	2.6	.307	-.11
Lyons S	34	74	0	0	74	0	1.000	241.0	1.0	.589	.23
Mack	37	58	2	0	60	1	1.000	177.1	0.7	.797	.32
McRae B	149	404	2	3	409	0	.993	1292.1	5.2	.512	.85
Pettis	125	246	4	6	256	2	.977	777.0	3.2	.454	.33
Puckett	144	345	13	5	363	5	.986	1216.2	4.9	.560	1.04
Shelby	26	56	0	1	57	0	.982	138.0	0.6	.566	.12
Venable	27	34	3	0	37	0	1.000	211.0	0.9	.562	.18
White D	156	438	8	1	447	2	.998	1384.0	5.6	.679	1.85
Williams B	84	227	3	5	235	0	.979	746.1	3.0	.407	.17
Wilson W	32	66	0	1	67	0	.985	211.0	0.9	.455	.09
Yount	116	314	1	2	317	1	.994	1012.0	4.1	.519	.69
TOTALS	***	6097	123	69	6289	31	.989	1479.0	6.0	4.662	****

stats are good, and always have been. As he's always been able to hit, which makes him a real good, reliable man to have. He's sort of the mirror image of Vince Coleman. The A's ability to see past what he looked like into what he could do was the last of the brilliant moves that made them a dynasty. They still have the center of that team, but they seem to be on an austerity kick right now. I presume that means that the owner's non-baseball businesses are suffering from the recession, like George Steinbrenner's were when his dynastic ambitions suddenly and inexplicably collapsed. Frequently, a sports team is an overextended mogul's last cash cow.

4. Kirby Puckett MIN

Kirby Puckett and no one else was the World Series MVP. What happened was this: the Twins were facing sudden death with two games to play. The Braves had the wonderful Steve Avery rested and ready to pitch the clinching shutout in Game 6. The Twins did not have any such man on the mound. But Kirby Puckett just decided that he hadn't played enough baseball for the year, and won the game single handedly. Just another exclamation point in a wonderful, Hall of Fame career.

5. Mike Devereaux BAL

This season marks a reasonable advance from Mike's rookie season in 1989, with a sophomore slump in 1990 thrown in between. But these things are supposed to happen from ages 24 to 26 or 25 to 27, not 27 to 29. Needless to say, Mike's growth potential is limited by his age. In fact, I would be very surprized to see him turn in anything like this season ever again. To be specific, I don't think the power will hold. Still, he's shown enough to run Joe Orsulak off the job, and possibly on to the trade block. NOT A REAL GOOD FANTASY BUY, unless no one in your league has ever heard of him or something.

6. Alex Cole CLE

Why a team would decide to play with its ballpark in the hopes of building an entire offense around this man, I will never know. But, then, that's what's made the Cleveland "brain" trust famous, isn't it? I mean, they have no one else on their team who can run like Alex can. No one. It's not just that they aren't the Cardinals, they aren't the Expos. Their team, at its golden best, might turn into a minor league version of the Mariners. They should model their fences on the Kingdome, not the Astrodome.

Alex Cole is an OK player, though his defensive stats suggest he may not be the world's best fundamental outfielder. As long as the Tribe tilts the infield to keep bunts fair, he's going to help with a high batting average and some walks. But it's the infield tilt, not the outfield fences, that help him. He doesn't have the line drive power to hit gappers. All the huge outfield territory does is expose his weaknesses with the glove.

7. Lance Johnson CHA

Good field, no hit. The Pale Hose really can't afford him; not with Ozzie Guillen and Scott Fletcher to put in the batting order too. They've got to get a real bat in at least one of those slots.

8. Robin Yount MIL

That's the second year like this, and he's 36. If you look at the stat lines, you can see what happened. His legs are gone. What's the evidence? Look at the decrease in doubles and the collapse in stolen base percentage.

Nonetheless, I rate Robin Yount a GREAT FANTASY GAMBLE FOR ONE YEAR. What we have here is a top of the line Hall of Famer in his mid-30's, after two bad years. What that says to me is "last hurrah." The last hurrah seasons that people like Stan Musial and Joe Morgan have are a matter of pride and conditioning. What these men do is they go home all winter and work out. When spring training comes, they show up in the best shape of their lives. They blow it out for one last season of remembering, and then the toll of the conditioning workouts is felt, and their bodies do in fact give in. I think Robin feels that threatened right now, and I really expect him to have that last good season in 1992. He's also just one last decent year away from 3000 hits....

9. Milt Cuyler DET

Takes some walks, has some speed, plays on a team that desperately needs a leadoff man. I don't think I'd bench Tony Phillips for him, but he's a good prospect at age 23. He's also one of the people who expose the Rotisserie game for what it is: a completely separate game from baseball. In baseball, this is a hot property. He's young, and he's done something. He has a real offensive focus, so you know where to hit him. He can play some defense. That's a lot of value, but none of it counts in the Roti game. In that game, he's got not that much batting average, some stolen bases and that's it. You also don't get anything for the fact that he's young. You can't keep him long enough. He's not a bad Rotisserie buy, because there are always Roti players out there who don't keep track of kids. But it's a sure tipoff when, the stronger the Roti league, the less of a buy Milt is, because better players will have heard of him.

10. Ellis Burks BOS

Everybody from Bill James to me had Ellis down for a top MVP candidate. Instead, he just collapsed, and at age 27, too. If you want to excuse it as an injury, then you have to face the fact that it's two injuries in five years. The worst part of it, from the Bosox point of view, is that this is the talent that is hardest for them to replace. The Sox farm system specializes in slow sluggers, because the team has to have that power. When they finally get a fast man, and he has the power as well, he's worth his weight in gold. Now, they have to confront the prospect of trading for a center fielder and a catcher at the same time. Their system just isn't going to give them either one.

11. Brian McRae KC

You can write this off as sophomore slump, and that's all it may be, but Brian needs to take a large step forward, or people are going to start thinking he's Billy Ripken, playing only because of his bloodlines. The bad news is his walks, or lack of same. Brian has as bad plate discipline as anyone in the game, and he's supposed to be a leadoff man. The Royals can't win with him batting leadoff. He can't bat anywhere else other than #7 or below. He's young, but he's in trouble.

12. Bernie Williams NYY

Pat Kelly is rated higher, but Bernie played more center field. Of course, Pat's rating is based on more total playing time; it just wasn't all in center. Surprise, surprise; the Yankees did it right. Kelly's no center fielder, and Bernie is. I saw him at Columbus (I highly recommend Columbus for those of you who want to see minor league ball), and he's certainly ready for prime time. He just dominated AAA people.

As a consequence, Bernie's a GREAT FANTASY BUY. He's going to play, and he's going to be at least OK, and he might be better than that.

13. Junior Felix CAL

Dave Gallagher was much better, and he's a real center fielder, but he's 31, and so he's gone for Hubie Brooks. I assume, based on years of watching Whitey, that Junior Felix will be a Herzog special reclamation project. Junior's problem is lack of plate discipline. If he could just take some walks, he'd be fine. Whitey specializes in teaching young hitters to take walks. Sometimes (see Terry Pendelton) it doesn't take, but sometimes it does. Junior's still young enough to give it a try. However, if it doesn't take, he's through. I also expect Junior to be moved to left field, with Luis Polonia moving back to center. Luis is not much of a center fielder on defense, but he's a fully developed player. Junior needs to be freed of fielding distractions.

14. Gary Pettis TEX

No longer a Major League ballplayer. Juan Gonzalez was much, much better, and played decent defense in center. Pettis couldn't even do that.

National League

Center Fielders

Brock J. Hanke

		OWAR	DWAR	TWAR
1.	Butler	5.37	1.31	6.68
2.	Van Slyke	4.75	0.75	5.50
3.	Finley S	4.16	0.90	5.05
4.	Lankford	4.10	0.73	4.82
5.	Grissom	3.49	1.17	4.66
6.	Gant	3.84	0.31	4.15
7.	McGee	3.83	0.20	4.03
8.	Jackson Dar	2.91	0.68	3.59
9.	Dykstra	2.68	0.27	2.96
	Boston	2.16	0.08	2.24
10.	Davis E	1.79	0.39	2.18
	Lewis D	1.09	0.68	1.76
	Howard T	0.82	0.74	1.56
11.	Coleman	1.42	-0.07	1.35
	Hayes V	0.15	0.53	0.68
	Young G	0.05	0.50	0.56
	Espy	0.20	0.08	0.29
	Dascenzo	0.11	0.05	0.16
	Morris Jn	-0.15	0.14	-0.01
	Lofton	-0.24	0.04	-0.20
12.	Walton	-0.49	0.16	-0.33
	Castillo Br	-0.46	0.11	-0.35
	Abner	-0.86	0.36	-0.50
	Winningham	-1.07	0.02	-1.05

1. Brett Butler LA

Don Malcolm doesn't agree with me on this, but I think the acquisition of Butler was the brightest move Fred Claire has made, in a long list of Fred Claire good moves. The Dodgers had big fat holes in center field and leadoff, and Brett Butler was the best available man for both jobs. Actually, Don's problem isn't with Butler per se; he just thinks the Dodgers should have developed Stan Javier and/or Chris Gwynn and saved the money. But the Dodgers were in contention at the time and did not need to gamble at the one batting order spot for which they had no backup.

Don also thought that Brett's age made him a bad gamble against a collapse, but Brett has been the most consistent ballplayer in the bigs for about eight years now. He didn't match his 1990, especially as a base stealer, but he did exactly what should have been expected. I don't know if he'll ever recover as a runner, but he probably has at least three years left at near this level of production. WONDERFUL ROTISSERIE BUY if you need batting average. SPECTACULAR buy in a simulation game of any sort.

2. Andy Van Slyke PIT

I guess we can quit worrying about the effects of that little injury in 1989. As often happens, a chaotic mind belies a reliable ballplayer.

3. Steve Finley HOU

Had his big peak year at age 27, helped by moving to a new league, where the pitchers didn't know him. I doubt he can sustain this level of play, especially with his lack of strike zone judgement. The pitchers will catch on. 1992 should be his National League sophomore slump year. LOUSY FANTASY BUY.

4. Ray Lankford STL

Another kid candidate for a sophomore slump; no strike zone judgement. He is well suited to the ballpark, with line drive power and speed. He does pose the Cardinals a batting order problem. They'd like to bat him leadoff, and probably will, but he doesn't get on base at all. He'd be OK in the #5 slot, but Felix Jose is much, much better. In fact, he is a good #6 man, and nothing more so far.

5. Marquis Grissom MTL

His bat is below average for the position, and he has no business in the top half of the batting order.

Center Field	G	PO	A	Er	TC	DP	FPct	DI	DG	DW%	DWAR
Abner	36	84	1	0	85	0	1.000	258.0	1.1	1.435	1.17
Boston	72	117	1	2	120	0	.983	415.2	1.7	.368	.03
Butler	160	371	8	0	379	3	1.000	1401.0	5.8	.577	1.32
Carreon	22	19	1	3	23	1	.870	126.0	0.5	.165	-.10
Castillo Br	23	37	2	1	40	1	.975	133.0	0.6	.553	.11
Coleman	70	132	5	3	140	1	.979	603.0	2.5	.322	-.07
Dascenzo	58	105	0	2	107	0	.981	392.1	1.6	.341	-.01
Davis E	77	182	5	3	190	4	.984	633.0	2.6	.490	.37
Dykstra	63	167	3	4	174	1	.977	545.2	2.3	.471	.28
Espy	23	41	0	1	42	0	.976	126.1	0.5	.423	.04
Felder	37	67	1	1	69	0	.986	224.1	0.9	.471	.11
Finley S	123	264	11	3	278	2	.989	940.0	3.9	.587	.93
Gant	146	332	7	6	345	1	.983	1275.1	5.3	.408	.31
Grissom	130	344	12	5	361	2	.986	1140.2	4.7	.594	1.16
Hatcher B	51	114	0	3	117	0	.974	377.0	1.6	.373	.04
Hayes V	48	132	2	2	136	2	.985	415.1	1.7	.517	.29
Howard T	41	105	1	0	106	1	1.000	321.1	1.3	.667	.42
Hudler	21	44	0	2	46	0	.957	153.0	0.6	.279	-.05
Jackson Dar	78	205	2	1	208	1	.995	645.2	2.7	.594	.66
Landrum C	18	40	0	1	41	0	.976	129.0	0.5	.403	.03
Lankford	148	365	7	6	378	2	.984	1208.1	5.0	.494	.72
Lewis D	66	156	3	0	159	1	1.000	495.2	2.1	.679	.68
Lofton	19	40	1	1	42	0	.976	145.0	0.6	.424	.04
Martinez Da	30	67	0	2	69	0	.971	258.1	1.1	.286	-.07
McGee	89	189	5	3	197	4	.985	700.1	2.9	.450	.29
McReynolds	31	45	2	0	47	0	1.000	213.0	0.9	.515	.15
Morris Jn	26	44	0	2	46	0	.957	144.2	0.6	.325	-.02
Nixon O	17	45	1	0	46	0	1.000	130.0	0.5	.798	.24
Roberts Bip	29	72	0	1	73	0	.986	218.2	0.9	.505	.14
Van Slyke	133	271	8	1	280	1	.996	1121.1	4.7	.512	.75
Walker C	36	62	4	0	66	1	1.000	265.0	1.1	.660	.34
Walton	100	170	1	3	174	1	.983	577.1	2.4	.416	.16
Winningham	56	90	2	5	97	0	.948	313.0	1.3	.340	-.01
Young G	77	88	4	0	92	1	1.000	312.2	1.3	.721	.48
TOTALS	***	4839	106	74	5019	32	.985	1442.0	6.0	3.795	****

However, he can truly play center field. If the Expos don't get obsessed with making him a leadoff man or something, he'll help them for a decade.

6. Ron Gant ATL

I know there's gas in Atlanta/Fulton County Stadium, but I was sure Ron would rate higher than this. I still think he's the center fielder I'd soonest have in this league. He has the total package: average, power, walks, speed, bat control, the works. His reclamation is the highest tribute to the Atlanta organization.

7. Willie McGee SF

Through as a Gold Glove center fielder, and the Giants are weaning him to left. He hit as empty a .312 as can be done, but it was still .312. Every year, Willie confronts the fact that he absolutely must hit .290 or more to keep a starting job. And every season, despite the fact that every pitcher at the AA level or higher knows he'll swing at wild pitches, he hits that .290. For those of you who don't get to see him too often, what he has that keeps that average up is the ability to swing straight down at pitches at his ankles, and pull them, and pull them hard. That's why he hits into so many double plays: hard ground balls to second base and shortstop.

8. Darrin Jackson SD

What happened to Darrin Jackson here is that he adjusted to his ballpark. Jack Murphy is a mild hitters' park overall, but a wonderful homer park in particular. Jackson developed an uppercut in response and presto. Now, if he can keep it up, he's got himself a starting job. Not an All-Star job or anything, but a starting job.

The reasons it's not an All-Star job, and the reasons why he's rated #8, are: 1) he has no strike zone judgement, and therefore takes no walks; and 2) the 12 doubles indicate that he's undercutting extremely; anything he gets good wood on gets out of the ballpark, nothing bounces off the walls. The combination makes him very fragile. If the pitchers figure out what it is he's hitting for distance, they can stop throwing it, and he's unlikely to respond with enough patience to make them come to him.

Given the above, and that he's already 28, I rate him no more than a 30% chance to keep up a starting ballplayer's level of performance. As I said in the Jerald Clark comment, I think the Padres need to replace both Darrin and Jerald to move up to contender status. I know this: trading Bip Roberts for Randy Myers isn't going to do it. LOUSY FANTASY BUY.

9. Len Dykstra PHI

What I'm tempted to do is just write "Steve Howe" and let the comment go at that.

But that's wrong. What's happened to Steve Howe is that the addiction he's developed happens to be the one that's illegal. Howe is much less danger to himself, and certainly to others, than Dykstra is, but cocaine is a "zero tolerance" infraction, while alcohol is legal. Not to get political here or anything, but that's unjust. Dykstra's the one who should be getting the suspensions, and Howe the wink and nod. But, because alcohol's legal, the price is low, and nobody's living in theft and prostitution to support the habit. Also, it isn't in the control of criminal gangs who will kill rather than be arrested for it, because the punishment for selling it isn't just as bad as that for murder.

10. Eric Davis CIN (LA)

I suppose it's a push as to whether Eddie Murray or Eric Davis is more of an injury gamble as the only righty bat on the Dodgers. What they need, of course, is somebody stable, like George Bell (well, physically stable). They should trade Kal Daniels for George Bell, even if they have to throw someone else in on the deal. As it is, what they need to do with Davis is convince him that defense isn't worth injuries, and keep him away from the outfield walls. That is to say, what they need to do is play him at first base to protect him, and leave Daniels, who they can spare for 50 games, in left.

If Tommy Lasorda is up to that sophisticated an analysis, I'll eat my press pass.

11. Vince Coleman NYM

It's like this: no, there is nothing wrong with Darryl Boston in center field for the Mets. He's not much of a center fielder, but Coleman, despite his speed, is worse. Boston is a better hitter. Coleman claims to be a leadoff man, but he doesn't take his walks, and he's likely to get worse at it without Whitey Herzog to push him, despite his little spurt of patience at the beginning of the year.

But Vince Coleman is a big name, and the Mets paid big money for him, and so they're going to play him, rather than admit they were wrong. And that's why the Mets and the Yankees win so many fewer pennants than they should. They're always trading for some name, and playing it, over someone better.

12. Jerome Walton CHI

I suppose I could be wrong - I wasn't there or anything - but I read this as Don Zimmer's failure. Jerome tried to make a leadoff man of himself in 1990, developing some patience and taking some walks to get on base. But his batting average dropped, and so did his RBI (in the leadoff spot, who cares?) and so Zimmer benched him. Well, what else do you expect Walton to do? He gave up taking pitches and started swinging at everything again. National League pitchers sang a chorus of "Oh, boy, oh boy" and had him chasing ground balls and popups at the plate. That is to say, Jerome Walton's 1991 was the delayed sophomore slump that young outfielders with no strike zone judgement often go through. Whether the new brain trust has enough sense to tell Jerome to go back to what would have worked in 1990, I don't know. I also don't know whether he'll believe them if they do. What I do know is that, if they don't or he doesn't, he's through.

American League

Right Fielders

Brock J. Hanke

		OWAR	DWAR	TWAR
1.	Canseco	5.98	0.16	6.14
2.	Carter J	5.18	0.95	6.13
3.	Sierra	4.76	1.01	5.77
4.	Tartabull	6.07	-0.32	5.75
5.	Winfield	4.73	0.58	5.31
6.	Buhner	3.85	1.11	4.96
7.	Mack	3.79	0.84	4.64
	Hall M	2.98	0.66	3.64
8.	Evans Dw	2.06	0.47	2.53
9.	Whiten	1.03	1.13	2.16
10.	Barfield Je	0.94	1.15	2.09
	Bush	1.68	0.19	1.87
	Plantier	1.70	0.14	1.84
11.	Deer	1.00	0.78	1.78
	Allred	1.57	0.20	1.78
	Martinez C	1.33	0.37	1.70
12.	Brunansky	0.99	0.65	1.64
	Munoz P	0.97	0.40	1.38
	Newson	1.22	0.13	1.35
	Larkin G	0.91	0.07	0.97
13.	Bichette	-0.27	1.12	0.85
	Venable	0.50	0.13	0.64
	Ward T	0.09	0.22	0.31
	Sheridan	-0.31	0.28	-0.03
	Gonzalez Jo	-0.27	0.15	-0.12
	Kirby	-0.39	0.19	-0.20
	Brown J	-0.25	-0.02	-0.26
14.	Sosa	-1.23	0.76	-0.47
	Snyder C	-1.41	0.32	-1.09

1. Jose Canseco OAK

This was supposed to be his peak year. If you run the Brock2 from age 24 on, you get an age 27 season that is truly reminiscent of Mickey Mantle and those guys. But he's not yet fully recovered form his 1989 injury, and he may never be. If he ever does, he's the best hitter in the game, bar none.

This is one situation where sabermetrics and insider opinion agree, but sportswriters often don't see it. The insiders, of course, see his spectacular athletic talents and the formidable distance his home runs travel, and compare that to what other men are capable of. Sabermetricians make ballpark adjustments. And when they make those adjustments, what they see is that his ballpark just robs Jose blind of home runs. In a neutral ballpark, he would threaten fifty; in Texas or Seattle, he'd be well over. As it is, he consistently hits his 16 at home, whether he's in good physical shape or not. When he's healthy, he hits over 25 on the road; when hurt, he doesn't adjust his swing to uppercut that quickly.

As you may have noticed elsewhere in the book, my opinion is that Jose and Eric Davis are injury-prone due to bodybuilding. I think that every person's skeleton has a limit on how much muscle it can support. Eric and Jose have built themselves beyond that limit. And so, every once in a while, they get hurt. Eric exacerbates the problem by playing reckless defense, and he's also thinner in the skeleton than Jose is (just look at them). Consequently, while Eric is a constant gamble, and often a bad one, Jose has a real chance to get his career back and keep it. I'D GAMBLE ON HIM IN A FANTASY LEAGUE, because the payoff is so great, even if you pay top dollar for him.

2. Joe Carter TOR

Every once in a while, the perversities of team managements foil even Dick Cramer's computer programs. If you look at the team boxes, you'll find Joe listed as the Blue Jay left fielder, with Mark Whiten listed in

Right Field	G	PO	A	Er	TC	DP	FPct	DI	DG	DW%	DWAR
Allred	27	63	0	3	66	0	.955	209.0	0.7	.410	.04
Barfield Je	81	178	10	0	188	3	1.000	677.2	2.3	.840	1.12
Bichette	120	248	14	6	268	7	.978	972.0	3.3	.676	1.07
Briley	45	59	1	1	61	1	.984	312.1	1.1	.336	-.01
Brunansky	135	265	6	3	274	2	.989	1096.0	3.7	.521	.63
Buhner	130	240	14	5	259	5	.981	1005.1	3.4	.672	1.10
Bush	33	42	1	0	43	2	1.000	193.0	0.7	.587	.15
Canseco	130	243	5	8	256	0	.969	1078.1	3.6	.393	.16
Carter J	101	190	12	3	205	2	.985	871.0	2.9	.691	1.00
Deer	131	306	8	7	321	4	.978	1137.0	3.8	.549	.76
Eisenreich	42	42	0	1	43	0	.977	223.0	0.8	.292	-.04
Evans Dw	66	113	6	2	121	2	.983	514.1	1.7	.611	.45
Gallagher	23	36	1	0	37	0	1.000	160.0	0.5	.632	.15
Gonzalez Jo	16	30	1	0	31	0	1.000	113.0	0.4	.746	.15
Hall M	63	107	4	3	114	1	.974	479.2	1.6	.485	.22
Hamilton	48	94	2	1	97	0	.990	390.2	1.3	.525	.23
Huff	41	43	1	1	45	0	.978	188.0	0.6	.933	.37
James C	18	30	1	0	31	0	1.000	135.0	0.5	.636	.13
Kirby	16	36	1	0	37	0	1.000	117.0	0.4	.806	.18
Larkin G	48	59	1	2	62	1	.968	312.2	1.1	.293	-.06
Mack	80	132	4	3	139	1	.978	540.2	1.8	.558	.38
Martinez C	52	105	4	2	111	2	.982	424.0	1.4	.591	.35
Meulens	13	29	1	0	30	1	1.000	105.0	0.4	.776	.15
Munoz P	39	72	3	1	76	2	.987	261.1	0.9	.747	.35
Newson	34	33	2	1	36	0	.972	170.1	0.6	.590	.14
Orsulak	67	109	9	1	119	2	.992	397.2	1.3	.870	.70
Pasqua	51	60	3	1	64	2	.984	318.0	1.1	.558	.22
Phillips	23	45	3	1	49	0	.980	135.1	0.5	.861	.23
Plantier	24	44	1	1	46	0	.978	157.0	0.5	.569	.12
Sheridan	26	30	2	0	32	1	1.000	161.2	0.5	.660	.17
Sierra	160	297	14	7	318	3	.978	1401.0	4.7	.556	.97
Snyder C	31	44	2	0	46	0	1.000	192.0	0.6	1.531	.77
Sosa	102	194	5	6	205	0	.971	698.2	2.4	.625	.65
Tartabull	123	189	4	7	200	0	.965	1028.2	3.5	.259	-.32
Thurman	28	37	0	1	38	0	.974	142.1	0.5	.428	.04
Venable	30	34	0	2	36	0	.944	171.2	0.6	.239	-.06
Ward T	41	66	1	0	67	0	1.000	280.0	0.9	1.026	.64
Whiten	105	236	13	7	256	1	.973	881.2	3.0	1.395	3.12
Wilson W	19	29	1	0	30	0	1.000	127.2	0.4	.700	.15
Winfield	114	194	7	2	203	0	.990	976.0	3.3	.521	.57
TOTALS	***	4743	176	102	5021	46	.980	1479.0	5.0	3.142	****

right. But Joe played almost twice as many games here as in left. What happened is this: Joe played more games in left than any other Blue Jay, and he also played more in right. The computer program lists a player at the first position it finds at which this is true. The program finds left field before it finds right field. And so, when it gets to right field, it discards Joe and lists the #2 man, who was Whiten. It's nothing to get excited about, as Joe will move between left and right depending on which Toronto kid wins the remaining job behind him and Devon White.

Actually, two of the kids might be better than Joe next year, though of course Joe will play. There is no chance that Joe will hold this level of value. He thoroughly exploited his new ballpark for home runs, and the AL pitchers will adjust to that. He won't make them pay for the adjustment, because he hasn't the plate discipline to do so. I read him for a big slump in 1992, and warn against him as a BAD FANTASY BUY.

3. Reuben Sierra TEX

Reuben, on the other hand, is almost certain to hold what he has now, and will probably improve. He's going into that notorious age 27 season, and he's in a hitters' ballpark, and he's going to get some help in the offense, if the Ranger management can get a free agent. A GREAT, GREAT FANTASY BUY, and a real MVP candidate if the Rangers should suddenly get respectable.

4. Danny Tartabull KC (NYY)

Danny was hurt during his peak years, and so people overrate the question marks attached to this one good year. In fact, 1991 makes perfect sense in the sequence of healthy years Danny has had. There's no real reason to think Danny's injury-prone, so there is good reason to think he can hold most of this value for a couple of years yet. If he had gotten into Texas or some other good homer ballpark, he could have challenged 40 and become a real offensive monster. As it is, Yankee Stadium willl probably hurt his raw stats. The New York media may then make him press. That's a serious question mark. Having just the one top season really isn't.

5. Dave Winfield CAL

I think Whitey made a mistake in letting him go. The player that Dave most reminds me of is Ty Cobb. Pete Rose, you may not know, was nothing like Cobb, after you adjust for the conditions of the game. Cobb was one of the largest people playing baseball at the time, and a murderous power hitter. Not only are his slugging percentages great, but his isolated power stats are among the very best in his league, year after year. It wasn't just the batting average that made Cobb great. He had size, speed, decent defense and the complete range of hitting skills. He played into his 40s and retired with some value still left. There is no reason to expect anything less of Winfield. He is not through yet. I give him a good chance at 3000 hits and 500 doubles, and a serious, albeit outside, chance at 500 homers.

6. Jay Buhner SEA

Jay won the lottery of Seattle outfielders. It was his development that focused the Mariner situation enough that they could trade for Kevin Mitchell and feel that they had solved their outfield problems. There is some question, though, about where he should bat. If the M's do what I would do, they will start their order with:

Griffey Jr.	cf
Martinez	3b

that leaves Mitchell, Buhner, Henry Cotto, Pete O'Brien and Alonzo Powell to fight over the next three spots. Buhner doesn't hit for enough average to really bat cleanup, much less 5th, but he does take walks, and might bat 3rd. If you don't bat him 3rd, you've got the speed problem that has caused the M's to keep Harold Reynolds at the top of the order and bat Junior in the #3 hole. If you keep Harold at #1 or #2, you end up with power hitters batting way down in the offensive sequence, while Harold Reynolds doesn't get on base that much. It's a problem, and the Mariners should probably try to acquire some speed attached to a real hitter if they really want to win big.

7. Shane Mack MIN

Shane played all over the place, and had real good defensive stats everywhere, including center field. Given Kirby Puckett, right field is probably the best solution, with Randy Bush in left. The real question is whether Shane or Randy will win the competition for leadoff man. Either is better than Gladden was, but neither is exactly the walking machine you really want there. If I were the Twins, I'd try a trade, but I'm not sure with what for bait. Puckett's got too much media value to trade, even though Shane can play center. Kent Hrbek is the only lefty in the lineup. Chili Davis probably wouldn't bring anything like what his value to the Twins is. Like I say, it's a problem.

8. Dwight Evans BAL

Still in the middle of the pack, even at age 40 and with only 270 at-bats. I know the Bosox have got power hitters with no speed coming out of their ears, but I still wouldn't have thrown Evans away. I'd have traded one of the high-profile guys for a big pitching arm, and just let Dewey DH his way into his fifties. He still gets on, and he still hits homers. That's still a hard combination to beat.

9. Mark Whiten CLE

I like Whiten. If he weren't with Cleveland, I'd rate him a ROTISSERIE BEST BUY. As it is, I have to downgrade him to a good buy, just because he's with the Indians. By the way, if you're in a simulation league, rather than in Roti ball, get Dwight Evans instead. The walks count for you in simulation leagues.

10. Jesse Barfield NYY

Now too old to get back what he lost in 1988. That year doesn't look like much was lost to what was thought to be a minor injury, but Jesse never recovered. I'd like Jesse a lot as a reserve and pinch hitter, but the Yankees are still starting him. As it is, in a strong crop of right fielders, he has no real value to a contender.

11. Rob Deer DET

Sparky played him all year, but he wasn't any good. He hit .179 in a hitters' ballpark, and even walks and homers won't overcome that. This is the short career for a player who started with old-man's skills that I mentioned in the Mark McGwire comment. Cut him if you can't trade him; he's through.

12. Tom Brunansky BOS

Rob Deer, only older. Actually, Bruno was better than Rob Deer overall, and actually, they're the same age. But they're still both through.

13. Dante Bichette MIL

If he could only play Gold Glove shortstop, he'd be Omar Vizquel. As it is, he's no prospect. No one should be fooled into playing him over a lousy 15 homers.

14. Sammy Sosa CHA

Not a Major League ballplayer, and his team knows it. But Frank Thomas was hurt, and had to DH, so Dan Pasqua got moved to first base.

National League

Right Fielders

Brock J. Hanke

		OWAR	DWAR	TWAR
1.	Bonilla B	6.25	1.14	7.39
2.	Jose	5.48	1.26	6.74
3.	Strawberry	5.47	0.45	5.92
4.	Walker L	4.21	1.00	5.20
5.	Gwynn T	4.25	0.88	5.14
6.	O'Neill	3.49	1.49	4.98
7.	Justice	3.86	0.62	4.48
	Martinez Da	2.72	0.79	3.51
8.	Dawson	2.90	0.45	3.35
9.	Murphy Dl	2.31	0.58	2.89
10.	Brooks	2.52	0.24	2.76
	Varsho	1.51	0.29	1.80
11.	Bass K	1.26	0.33	1.59
	Williams K	0.45	0.16	0.61
	Sims	0.26	0.03	0.30
12.	Rhodes	-0.22	0.28	0.06
	Smith Dw	-0.26	0.18	-0.08
	Kingery	-0.30	0.13	-0.17
	Anthony	-0.71	0.39	-0.32
	Gonzalez Jo	-0.54	0.15	-0.39

1. Bobby Bonilla PIT (NYM)

Right now, the Mets' player moves stack up like this:

Gregg Jeffries for
Bobby Bonilla
Kevin McReynolds for
Eddie Murray
Keith Miller for
Willie Randolph and
Bill Pecota
Frank Viola for
Bret Saberhagen
Hubie Brooks for
Dave Gallagher

I rate that about even. Bobby Bo is a bit better than Jeffries, but Gregg is younger. The age is gained back in Viola for Bret, but lost again in Miller for Randolph. For 1992 alone, the Mets may have gained a game or even two; but that, added to what the Pirates lost in Bobby, still isn't as many games as the Mets finished behind the Pirates last year. I just don't see that the Mets have become the division front-runner yet.

Let's take a look at the lineup. The latest word is that Bobby is going to play left, with Hojo in right and, of all things, first baseman Dave Magadan at third base. That produces a best-possible batting order of:

Randolph	2b
Magadan	3b
Hojo	rf
Bonilla	lf
Murray	1b
Boston	cf
Elster	ss
someone	c

that's real good 1-4, a gamble 5-6 and real bad 7-8. It's also not what the Mets will do, unless they get lucky with another Vince Coleman injury. What they'll do is:

Coleman	cf
Randolph	2b
Hojo	rf
Bonilla	lf
Murray	1b
Magadan	3b
Elster	ss
someone	c

All that does is to trade quality at leadoff for quality at #6, which is a horrible tradeoff. Well, of course, it also adds another Name to the Met batting order, which is why it will be done.

If you look at that team, it should be obvious that the Mets have done little to address their primary weaknesses, which are offense up the middle and infield defense. Yes, Willie Randolph is a better keystone man, even at age 38, than Gregg Jeffries was; but the Mets should have been playing Keith Miller there anyway. What I don't understand is the desire to move both Bobby Bonilla and Hojo into the outfield, when the resultant third baseman is a converted first sacker. I think they should have just left Dave alone and moved Mackey Sasser into right field. But, then, of course, they wouldn't have Eddie Murray's Name on the team, would they? No, I don't see any reason why Howard John-

Right Field	G	PO	A	Er	TC	DP	FPct	DI	DG	DW%	DWAR
Anthony	37	64	5	1	70	1	.986	280.2	1.0	.759	.40
Bass K	78	123	4	3	130	1	.977	603.0	2.1	.434	.18
Bonilla B	102	172	8	1	181	0	.994	794.2	2.8	.629	.77
Boston	37	20	1	1	22	1	.955	106.1	0.4	.351	0.00
Braggs	26	36	1	1	38	0	.974	141.1	0.5	.529	.09
Brooks	100	166	6	5	177	1	.972	791.1	2.7	.436	.24
Davidson M	32	31	1	0	32	0	1.000	139.0	0.5	.670	.15
Dawson	137	241	7	3	251	3	.988	1183.1	4.1	.461	.46
Felder	44	61	0	1	62	0	.984	220.0	0.8	.519	.13
Finley S	71	57	2	2	61	0	.967	315.2	1.1	.323	-.03
Gwynn T	134	290	7	3	300	3	.990	1175.2	4.1	.568	.89
Howard T	14	27	2	0	29	0	1.000	115.2	0.4	.921	.23
Javier	18	22	1	0	23	0	1.000	126.1	0.4	.587	.10
Johnson H	28	54	3	2	59	0	.966	253.0	0.9	.533	.16
Jose	152	265	14	3	282	2	.989	1301.1	4.5	.628	1.26
Justice	104	204	9	7	220	0	.968	939.1	3.3	.539	.62
Kingery	22	31	0	0	31	0	1.000	115.0	0.4	.651	.12
Martinez Da	58	115	8	1	124	0	.992	437.2	1.5	.881	.81
McClendon	18	19	1	1	21	0	.952	109.2	0.4	.351	0.00
McGee	47	67	0	3	70	0	.957	339.0	1.2	.273	-.09
Murphy Dl	145	285	6	5	296	0	.983	1216.2	4.2	.489	.59
Nixon O	48	88	1	3	92	0	.967	394.1	1.4	.389	.05
O'Neill	148	294	13	2	309	2	.994	1241.2	4.3	.695	1.49
Rhodes	44	87	4	4	95	1	.958	350.1	1.2	.579	.28
Sasser	14	17	3	1	21	1	.952	103.0	0.4	.480	.05
Sims	41	44	4	6	54	0	.889	267.2	0.9	.387	.03
Smith Dw	28	43	3	1	47	1	.979	183.0	0.6	.679	.21
Strawberry	135	208	11	5	224	2	.978	1177.2	4.1	.461	.45
Varsho	43	69	1	0	70	1	1.000	287.0	1.0	.599	.25
Walker L	98	215	6	2	223	2	.991	781.0	2.7	.685	.91
Webster M	27	38	1	2	41	0	.951	165.0	0.6	1.695	.77
TOTALS	***	3777	153	78	4008	28	.981	1442.0	5.0	2.660	****

son should be considered inadequate at third base, except maybe that the Mets now have Bobby Bo.

2. Felix Jose STL

The prototype #5 batter. The job in that slot is to drive in men who are in scoring position with two outs. That's the situation that the top of the batting order is designed to produce. Given that, the attributes of the prototype should be 1) a high batting average, to produce the hits that get the men in from second and third, 2) power, although that is not as important as average in this position, and 3) few walks. What you don't want is for the #5 guy to just pass the opportunity on to the #6 man. Also, for the #5 man to get on first base, when it is assumed that there will be outs already, makes the least use of the walk.

The Cardinal "brain trust", responding to all this, are considering batting Felix in the #3 hole. The "reasoning" is that, if he knows Andres Galarraga is coming up behind him, Felix will develop plate discipline in an effort to get on base. Oh, sure he will. They also intend to bat Todd Zeile #5, in order to "protect" Galarraga, so he can cut down on those strikeouts. This, of course, is if they don't bat Pedro Guerrero #3, in which case they apparently intend to move Felix down to #6.

This is ridiculous, and is puts Joe Torre's technical weaknesses on public display. There is no reason to struggle uphill, when you don't have to. Todd Zeile is exactly the sort of complete hitter that you want to bat #3. Felix Jose doesn't need to take pitches, he needs to bat #5. If Galarraga doesn't recover his bat from 1991, you just bat him #6 and put Pedro at cleanup. It ain't broke, why fix it?

Felix Jose's defensive rating, which labels him a Gold Glove candidate, are not a fluke. Felix, typical Cardinal that he is, is very fast for his position, and does have a true right fielder's arm. I agree with the rankings that Felix, Paul O'Neill and Bobby Bo are heads above the crowd at right field defense.

3. Darryl Strawberry LA

Bizarre as it may seem, there are a LOT of people out there who think that the Dodger one-game second place finish "proves" that signing big free agents doesn't work. I guess they think that what happened to the Braves is an every-year occurrence. Or maybe they think that the Bums would have picked up that crucial extra game if they'd only had Hubie Brooks out there. In fact, the acquisition of the Straw Man is what kept the Dodgers ahead for so long, and Eddie Murray's problems are what kept them from winning, along with Tummy Lasorda's lack of respect for resting Ramon Martinez' pitching arm in 1990. When I noted this for some of the above people, they responded that the Dodgers should have never signed that washed up Murray! When I pointed out that it had been three years since the Dodgers signed Murray, they shut up, but I think it was more from sensing that I was exasperated than from conviction.

4. Larry Walker MTL

Took a nice, convincing step forward in 1991, and established himself as a force for the future. Larry could take more walks and fan fewer times, but I'd still rather have him than Felix Jose, who is two years older, and I like Felix. At 27, Jose probably had his career year in 1991, while Larry was just 25, and should grow for two more seasons. FANTASY LEAGUE BEST BUY, as he's going to be good, and his stats are going to work for you in the Rotisserie game.

5. Tony Gwynn SD

Tony is now 32, and is showing the age in every way other than the triples stat. There is no good reason to expect him to put in another dominant season, though he obviously still has value. What I actually expect is a severe power drop, as he loses the speed that is fueling the triples, and as he retreats to supporting his batting average, which is his central skill, to keep it from sinking below .300. He'll keep the average up, out of pride, and so will RETAIN HIS ROTISSERIE VALUE, but he'll lose ground in any simulation that isn't as artificial as the Roti game.

6. Paul O'Neill CIN

I originally thought that Paul would turn out to be the player that I now think Larry Walker will be. Of course, as he's now 29, there is no chance that will happen any more. He's getting all his homer power out of the ballpark, so I wouldn't trade for him, either. What I do wonder is if he couldn't play center field. His defensive stats are excellent in right, and he has speed. He just doesn't look like he should be able to run. I don't think Lou Pinella is going to take that gamble and find out, and so I think Paul will be sinking down in the pack pretty soon now.

7. Dave Justice ATL

No, this ranking is not wrong. No, he's not a dominant All-Star, though he'd obviously move up in a full season. He's about a 5.5 or 6 game player after the Fulton County gas is taken out of his stats. There is also no reason to expect more than 130 games out of him. Actually, I suspect that he's suffering from bodybuilding his muscles above the strength level that his bones can support, which is what is wrong with Eric Davis and Jose Canseco, too. By the way, you should keep track of these three guys, to see if they have short careers. NOT A GREAT FANTASY BUY, because of the playing time problem. There's always going to be somebody out there who will amortize his stats out to a full year, and expect it to happen, and so overbid for him.

8. Andre Dawson CHI

No, the ranking is not wrong. There is just as much gas in Wrigley as in Fulton County Stadium, and the man is 37. There's a radio sports guy in St. Louis named Mark Eisman, whose name I may have misspelled here. Mark is an Andre Dawson nut, and got me saying that I thought 1990 was a last hurrah year for Andre and that he would come back down a lot in 1991. Then he (Mark, not Andre) gave me a lot of trouble when Andre hit a lot of early homers. Well, Mark, look at the stats. First, Andre did collapse a lot. Second, he kept his homers up only by ruthlessly exploiting his home ballpark. I give him some credit for finally adjusting to the reality of his environment, but the pitchers are going to counteradjust. A VERY BAD FANTASY GAMBLE.

9. Dale Murphy PHI

Held his value by lining some doubles off the wall. If you look at the ballpark adjustment stats for the Phillies, you see that there's an abnormal gap between the homer adjustments for home batters and that for road batters. What that probably means is that there's some idiosyncrasy about Veteran that can be exploited for taters, if you only adjust to it. Murphy is certainly capable of doing that, and thereby having one hell of a last hurrah season. He's also younger than most people think, younger than Andre Dawson, for example. Therefore, he's a GOOD FANTASY GAMBLE, if you have to gamble at the position. Actually, you could allocate some drafting money elsewhere and plan on gambling on Dale, unless you've got a Murphy freak in your league who thinks he's still 30 or something.

10. Hubie Brooks NYM (CAL)

Whitey Herzog thinks that Brooks has something left, which is the most positive thing I can think of to say about Hubie. I'd have kept Dave Winfield, myself.

11. Kevin Bass SF

The idea that Kevin has recovered from his injuries and now makes Kevin Mitchell expendable, is completely without foundation. Roger Craig is flailing, stuck with a team that has a bad development program.

12. Karl Rhodes HOU

Karl is marking Eric Anthony's place until Eric finally develops or the Astros finally give up. He is ranked here only because his 44 games in right were the most on the team. Karl's only 23, and the defensive stats suggest that he might be able to play center. He's going to have to get the average over .250 before anyone will give him a real try, though. What the hell, SPEND A DOLLAR ON HIM IN ROTISSERIE. Anthony might not pan out, after all. Or Steve Finley might get hurt.

American League

Designated Hitters

Brock J. Hanke

		OWAR	DWAR	TWAR
1.	Thomas F	6.86	0.19	7.06
2.	Molitor	6.69	0.08	6.76
3.	Davis C	5.29	0.01	5.30
4.	Baines	4.92	0.01	4.93
5.	Clark Jk	3.98	0.00	3.98
6.	Brett	3.03	0.01	3.04
7.	Downing	2.85	0.00	2.85
8.	Maas	2.64	0.04	2.69
9.	Horn	1.70	0.00	1.70
10.	Parker D	1.61	0.00	1.61
11.	Mulliniks	0.99	0.01	1.00
12.	Davis A	0.93	0.05	0.98
	Jones Tr	0.61	0.14	0.76
	Martinez Crl	0.61	-0.04	0.58
	Tabler	-0.10	0.01	-0.09
13.	Incaviglia	-0.25	0.26	0.01
14.	James C	-0.66	0.34	-0.32
	Romine	-0.49	0.05	-0.44

1. Frank Thomas CHA

Exactly the same age as Roberto Alomar, who didn't go to college. The result of this for the Chisox is that they get Big Crank's peak seasons before he hits arbitration, much less free agency. Just another reason to draft college players.

Frank is clearly the best young hitter in baseball; the only one who reminds me even mildly of Ted Williams. Roberto Alomar is equally clearly the best young overall player. The dropoff after Roberto is steeper than that after Frank, so I'd rather have the middle infielder. Frank should be due for a mild sophomore slump next year, as he got all his homers at home, and the AL pitchers will adjust to whatever he's hitting. But it shouldn't be a severe one, as Frank has the plate discipline to make them throw strikes.

2. Paul Molitor MIL

Mercy, what a hitter. He's 35 years old, and has been injured constantly for a decade, and he can still get 6 3/4 WAR out of his bat alone. If you'd known what was going to happen, wouldn't you have made him a career DH? I ought to be able to use the Brock2 system to get some idea of what his career would have been like without the injuries, but I haven't figured out yet how to mix the actual and theoretical years.

3. Chili Davis MIN

If you'd looked at the Twins at the end of 1990, the last thing you'd have figured they needed was a cleanup man. But it's clear that Chili made a huge difference in their offense, prolonging the offensive sequence so far that it was able to overcome even Dan Gladden at leadoff.

If you look at the Defensive Winning Percentage Top Ten, you'll see Chili listed first, with an absurd figure. Dick Cramer, our master programmer, remembered to put in a minimum playing time requirement, but he forgot to check for defensive innings.

4. Harold Baines OAK

A good pickup that would have helped the A's continue their dynasty if so many other things hadn't fallen apart.

5. Jack Clark BOS

Some people bring up Jack Clark when I talk about short careers of people who started out with old player's skills. But that's not Jack. When he began, Jack was fast. He got hurt early and often, but he piled up some doubles in selected seasons. He was also a real good right fielder for years. In fact, in Fenway, he's probably still a better outfielder than first baseman. He lacks range, but his arm is strong and he has good judgement on fly balls. At first, on the other hand, he's horrible on grounders and inaccurate on the short tosses. The Bosox apparently intend to keep him amidst all the housecleaning, and I agree.

6. George Brett KC

No longer a #3 hitter, and possibly not the DH you'd like to have. It's now, not just "someday soon" that Hal McRae will have to confront the media horror of removing him from the center of the Royal batting order. Another truly great player who had a last hurrah season, in 1990. I predicted that he'd never duplicate it, and I stand by that. I doubt he'll ever really duplicate this one. The 40 doubles he can still hit are the ballpark and nothing else.

7. Brian Downing TEX

Brian's not yet taking advantage of the homers that his new ballpark can give him. As a consequence, he may be able to improve a little. Still, the main difference between Brian and George Brett is that nobody's calling into Texas radio shows demanding that he be batted third out of sentiment.

8. Kevin Maas NYY

At age 27, this should have been his peak season. Instead, this being the Yankees, it was sophomore slump. I figure him to recover some, but not that much. The people who believed all that New York hype, and who expect him to become the next Frank Thomas, are in for a disappointment. Kevin's three years older, and has proven a lot less. What Kevin looks like is yet another young guy with old man's skills. Look at those doubles totals. I figure him for a decade of career or less, and some of that none too good. Somewhere between Tom Tresh and Bobby Murcer.

9. Sam Horn BAL

Don Malcolm's OINKS system shows that Sam has a lot of "bang for the buck" in terms of power and walks versus batting average. The problem, of course, is that he's 28, and he had his peak year in 1990, right on schedule, and he hit .248 that year. Basically, he's a "no prospect."

10. Dave Parker CAL
(now TOR, maybe)

Had his last hurrah in 1990, but may get another year in on the basis of his 13-game hot streak with the Jays. That would be silly. The Cobra finally falls to Ol' Mongoose Time.

11. Rance Mulliniks TOR

The best reason I can think of for keeping Dave Parker.

12. Alvin Davis SEA

I think he'll recover some value, but he's going to be competing with Pete O'Brien for one job on the M's. I give Alvin the 70/30 edge. The Mariners apparently don't. They're talking about letting him go free agent. Unless they know something about injuries I don't, that's silly. They need a lefty bat and a desperation on-base man to bat second if they can't get a real #2 man.

13. Pete Incaviglia DET

His stats are listed in left field, which is accurate. He can still play out there a little, but he has lost all ability he ever had to hit. Young player with old man's skills....

14. Chris James CLE

Glenallen Hill or you or me or somebody has the job.

IV

Everything Else

An MVP Note

Brock J. Hanke

In the advertising, I made the claim that we had predicted the MVPs of both leagues for the last few years. Actually, what I meant was that the MVP of each league has been the person with the highest Total Wins Above Replacement (TWAR) in our lists following. That is true. It has been true ever since I started printing TWARs. However, this year, as it must come to all those who advertise, it didn't happen.

We got Cal Ripken Jr. alright, but who couldn't? Sorry, Cecil. However, our National League TWAR leader was, again, Barry Bonds. The MVP voters, impressed by Atlanta's ballpark stats, gave the award to Terry Pendleton. No, that's not fair. Bonds' team won its division by 14 games. Terry's won by one. I'd have given it to Pendleton too.

I'm not saying the ballpark didn't help Terry's homer stats. What I am saying is that there is indeed a part of the game that goes beyond sabrmetrics. Being in a close race instead of a cakewalk is part of that. However, I do think that Barry Bonds had the best year in the National League from a simple viewpoint of raw production. If the races had been equal, Bonds would have been the MVP.

American League

Total Wins Above Replacement

By WAR

NAME	OWAR	DWAR	TWAR	NAME	OWAR	DWAR	TWAR
Ripken C	7.06	3.09	10.14	Clark Jk	3.98	0.00	3.98
Griffey Jr	6.45	1.34	7.79	Gibson K	3.89	0.03	3.92
White D	5.26	1.87	7.13	Gaetti	2.13	1.65	3.78
Thomas F	6.86	0.19	7.06	Vaughn G	2.98	0.76	3.74
Molitor	6.69	0.08	6.76	Tettleton	4.33	-0.59	3.74
Alomar R	5.62	1.02	6.64	Knoblauch	2.40	1.28	3.68
Martinez E	5.76	0.82	6.59	Hall M	2.98	0.66	3.64
Palmeiro	6.01	0.35	6.36	Cole	3.34	0.30	3.64
Joyner	5.78	0.52	6.30	Quintana	3.12	0.47	3.59
Canseco	5.98	0.16	6.14	Greenwell	2.90	0.65	3.55
Carter J	5.18	0.95	6.13	Milligan	3.11	0.21	3.32
Ventura	4.66	1.44	6.09	Mattingly	2.63	0.57	3.20
Henderson D	4.45	1.58	6.04	Gonzalez Juan	2.61	0.52	3.13
Boggs W	4.82	1.03	5.84	Brett	3.03	0.01	3.04
Phillips	3.96	1.82	5.78	Vizquel	-0.04	3.00	2.96
Sierra	4.76	1.01	5.77	Gallego	1.94	0.97	2.92
Tartabull	6.07	-0.32	5.75	Pecota	2.09	0.80	2.89
Whitaker	4.11	1.41	5.51	Downing	2.85	0.00	2.85
Henderson R	4.61	0.78	5.39	McGwire	2.09	0.72	2.81
Baerga	4.21	1.16	5.37	Gruber	1.83	0.91	2.75
Winfield	4.73	0.58	5.31	Kelly	2.41	0.31	2.72
Franco Ju	5.16	0.15	5.31	Buechele	1.51	1.21	2.71
Davis C	5.29	0.01	5.30	Maas	2.64	0.04	2.69
Fielder	4.73	0.27	5.00	Gallagher	1.70	0.98	2.68
Buhner	3.85	1.11	4.96	Fryman T	2.08	0.60	2.68
Baines	4.92	0.01	4.93	Grebeck	1.97	0.70	2.67
Randolph	3.35	1.43	4.78	Spiers	1.14	1.52	2.66
Polonia	4.51	0.26	4.77	Orsulak	0.90	1.72	2.62
Reynolds H	2.62	2.06	4.68	Johnson L	0.54	2.04	2.58
Sax S	3.28	1.39	4.67	Evans Dw	2.06	0.47	2.53
Mack	3.79	0.84	4.64	Hamilton	1.84	0.65	2.49
Puckett	3.35	1.10	4.46	O'Brien P	2.00	0.49	2.49
Devereaux	3.07	1.38	4.45	Schofield	0.60	1.84	2.44
Raines	3.18	1.17	4.35	Parrish Ln	1.52	0.91	2.44
Reed Jd	2.62	1.66	4.28	Trammell	1.07	1.33	2.41
Belle	3.85	0.28	4.13	Rivera L	0.90	1.50	2.40
Hrbek	3.55	0.52	4.06	Macfarlane	2.23	0.07	2.30
Olerud	3.68	0.38	4.06	Harper B	2.12	0.12	2.24
Pasqua	3.59	0.46	4.06	Reimer	2.20	-0.01	2.18

NAME	OWAR	DWAR	TWAR	NAME	OWAR	DWAR	TWAR
Whiten	1.03	1.13	2.16	Fisk	0.57	0.29	0.87
Pagliarulo	1.04	1.09	2.13	Bichette	-0.27	1.12	0.85
Barfield Je	0.94	1.15	2.09	Sprague	0.84	-0.00	0.84
Yount	1.36	0.71	2.07	Bergman	0.65	0.16	0.82
Cuyler	1.12	0.90	2.02	Briley	0.62	0.19	0.81
Espinoza	-0.34	2.34	2.01	Jones Tr	0.61	0.14	0.76
Aldrete	1.82	0.17	1.99	Sveum	0.19	0.54	0.73
Nokes	2.47	-0.55	1.92	Griffey	0.67	0.05	0.71
Gagne	-0.03	1.92	1.89	Fermin	-0.80	1.51	0.71
Guillen	-0.69	2.58	1.89	Karkovice	0.52	0.19	0.71
Bush	1.68	0.19	1.87	Venable	0.50	0.13	0.64
Sojo	0.24	1.60	1.84	Thurman	0.39	0.24	0.63
Plantier	1.70	0.14	1.84	Martinez Crm	0.45	0.15	0.60
Cotto	1.54	0.27	1.81	Brock	0.51	0.09	0.60
Deer	1.00	0.78	1.78	Martinez Crl	0.61	-0.04	0.58
Allred	1.57	0.20	1.78	Stevens	0.51	0.05	0.56
Gomez L	1.34	0.43	1.77	Moseby	0.58	-0.03	0.55
Eisenreich	1.74	0.02	1.76	Mayne	0.39	0.11	0.50
Burks	1.42	0.33	1.75	Thome	0.51	-0.04	0.47
Maldonado	1.50	0.24	1.74	Velarde	-0.02	0.49	0.47
Horn	1.70	0.00	1.70	Rose	0.26	0.18	0.44
Martinez C	1.33	0.37	1.70	Livingstone	0.20	0.22	0.42
Leius	1.19	0.51	1.69	Worthington	0.29	0.11	0.40
Brunansky	0.99	0.65	1.64	Howell Jk	0.19	0.21	0.40
Hill D	0.85	0.76	1.61	Vaughn M	0.34	0.02	0.36
Parker D	1.61	0.00	1.61	Ward T	0.09	0.22	0.31
McRae B	0.68	0.86	1.54	Abner	-0.10	0.40	0.30
Stillwell	1.05	0.33	1.38	Stanley M	0.69	-0.40	0.28
Munoz P	0.97	0.40	1.38	Riles	-0.12	0.40	0.28
Huff	0.93	0.44	1.38	Powell A	0.27	-0.00	0.27
Newson	1.22	0.13	1.35	Segui	0.10	0.16	0.26
Williams B	1.17	0.18	1.35	Kelly P	0.11	0.15	0.26
Benzinger	1.09	0.24	1.33	Lyons S	-0.24	0.45	0.21
Blankenship L	0.63	0.69	1.32	Diaz Mar	-0.23	0.41	0.18
Gantner	0.42	0.90	1.32	Schaefer	-0.30	0.47	0.18
Anderson B	1.03	0.24	1.27	Ducey	0.13	0.02	0.14
Barnes	0.89	0.38	1.27	Orton	-0.04	0.17	0.13
Davis G	1.18	0.06	1.24	Stubbs	-0.22	0.35	0.13
Hill G	1.01	0.13	1.14	Pettis	-0.21	0.33	0.12
Seitzer	0.97	0.16	1.13	Borders	-0.46	0.58	0.12
Felix	1.16	-0.08	1.08	Surhoff BJ	0.08	0.02	0.10
Cromartie	1.00	0.07	1.07	Steinbach	1.18	-1.09	0.09
Myers G	0.99	0.02	1.01	Gladden	-0.37	0.45	0.08
Mulliniks	0.99	0.01	1.00	Weiss	-0.24	0.31	0.08
Davis A	0.93	0.05	0.98	Canale	0.01	0.05	0.06
Larkin G	0.91	0.07	0.97	Brosius	-0.15	0.18	0.03
Hoiles	0.75	0.17	0.92	Wilson W	-0.37	0.40	0.03

NAME	OWAR	DWAR	TWAR	NAME	OWAR	DWAR	TWAR
Martinez Tino	-0.07	0.09	0.01	Howard D	-0.97	0.59	-0.38
Incaviglia	-0.25	0.26	0.01	Quirk	-0.20	-0.19	-0.39
Manto	0.00	0.00	0.01	Valle	-0.91	0.49	-0.42
Spehr	-0.04	0.03	-0.01	Jefferson R	-0.53	0.10	-0.43
Sheridan	-0.31	0.28	-0.03	Romine	-0.49	0.05	-0.44
Cora	-0.22	0.18	-0.04	Berry	-0.60	0.15	-0.45
Wilson M	-0.16	0.11	-0.05	Meulens	-0.71	0.24	-0.47
Dempsey	-0.08	0.02	-0.06	Sosa	-1.23	0.76	-0.47
Huson	-0.58	0.51	-0.07	Lee M	-1.24	0.77	-0.48
Cochrane	0.06	-0.13	-0.07	Shumpert	-1.25	0.73	-0.52
Tabler	-0.10	0.01	-0.09	Marzano	-0.45	-0.08	-0.53
Hulett	-0.26	0.17	-0.09	Bradley S	-0.53	-0.01	-0.54
Merullo	-0.12	0.02	-0.11	Leyritz	-0.40	-0.15	-0.55
Bordick	-0.84	0.74	-0.11	Ripken B	-1.81	1.25	-0.56
Gonzalez Jo	-0.27	0.15	-0.12	Hernandez J	-0.90	0.32	-0.58
Disarcina	-0.13	-0.00	-0.13	Ortiz	-0.85	0.25	-0.60
Petralli	0.38	-0.52	-0.14	Naehring	-0.66	0.04	-0.62
Fletcher S	-1.26	1.11	-0.15	Melvin	-0.36	-0.26	-0.63
Whitt	-0.13	-0.05	-0.19	Jacoby	-1.15	0.45	-0.70
Kirby	-0.39	0.19	-0.20	Browne J	-0.67	-0.04	-0.71
Gonzales R	-0.66	0.45	-0.22	Geren	-0.72	-0.11	-0.83
Taubensee	0.01	-0.25	-0.24	Daugherty	-0.91	0.07	-0.84
Brumley	-0.52	0.26	-0.26	Newman A	-1.91	1.04	-0.86
Brown J	-0.25	-0.02	-0.26	Sheffield	-0.74	-0.13	-0.87
Mercedes	-0.31	0.03	-0.28	Shelby	-1.34	0.35	-0.99
Law V	-0.34	0.04	-0.30	Allanson	-0.61	-0.40	-1.01
James C	-0.66	0.34	-0.32	Skinner J	-0.84	-0.21	-1.05
Tingley	-0.33	-0.00	-0.33	Alomar S	-1.04	-0.01	-1.05
Palmer Dn	-0.20	-0.13	-0.34	Pena T	-1.37	0.29	-1.08
Lopez L	-0.34	-0.01	-0.35	Snyder C	-1.41	0.32	-1.09
Lewis M	-0.55	0.20	-0.35	Rodriguez I	-0.88	-0.34	-1.22
Lovullo	-0.43	0.07	-0.36	Bell Ju	-1.54	0.31	-1.23

National League

Total Wins Above Replacement

By WAR

NAME	OWAR	DWAR	TWAR	NAME	OWAR	DWAR	TWAR
Bonds	6.61	1.14	7.75	Magadan	3.48	0.51	4.00
Bonilla B	6.25	1.14	7.39	Owen S	1.88	1.92	3.80
Smith O	5.13	2.11	7.24	Daniels	3.25	0.52	3.76
Clark W	6.30	0.61	6.90	Biggio	4.19	-0.52	3.66
Sandberg	5.77	1.09	6.86	Jackson Dar	2.91	0.68	3.59
Jose	5.48	1.26	6.74	Merced	3.44	0.12	3.57
Butler	5.37	1.31	6.68	Martinez Da	2.72	0.79	3.51
Larkin B	4.82	1.82	6.65	Dawson	2.90	0.45	3.35
Johnson H	6.46	0.03	6.49	Bell Geo	3.27	0.02	3.29
Pendleton	5.02	1.44	6.46	Oquendo	1.87	1.40	3.27
Kruk	5.78	0.65	6.43	Caminiti	2.43	0.76	3.19
Thompson Ro	4.50	1.88	6.38	DeShields	3.19	-0.04	3.15
Bagwell	5.83	0.40	6.24	Scioscia	2.72	0.42	3.14
McGriff F	5.93	0.16	6.09	Candaele	2.37	0.72	3.09
Strawberry	5.47	0.45	5.92	Wallach	1.88	1.12	3.00
Bell Jay	3.99	1.90	5.88	Dykstra	2.68	0.27	2.96
Williams MD	4.78	1.09	5.87	Murphy Dl	2.31	0.58	2.89
Samuel	5.12	0.73	5.85	Roberts Bip	2.27	0.61	2.88
Van Slyke	4.75	0.75	5.50	Dunston	1.31	1.51	2.83
Sabo	5.20	0.27	5.47	Nixon O	2.12	0.68	2.80
Fernandez T	3.08	2.13	5.21	Miller K	2.25	0.52	2.78
Walker L	4.21	1.00	5.20	Brooks	2.52	0.24	2.76
Calderon	4.89	0.28	5.17	Harris L	1.96	0.72	2.68
Gwynn T	4.25	0.88	5.14	Lind	0.81	1.86	2.66
Finley S	4.16	0.90	5.05	Jefferies	2.80	-0.33	2.47
O'Neill	3.49	1.49	4.98	Doran	2.07	0.33	2.40
Lankford	4.10	0.73	4.82	Treadway	2.13	0.24	2.38
Grissom	3.49	1.17	4.66	LaValliere	1.85	0.45	2.30
Zeile	4.24	0.39	4.63	Smith Lo	2.22	0.06	2.28
Morris H	4.23	0.39	4.63	Boston	2.16	0.08	2.24
Thompson M	3.74	0.82	4.56	Davis E	1.79	0.39	2.18
Justice	3.86	0.62	4.48	Blauser	1.92	0.23	2.15
Murray E	3.74	0.69	4.43	Sharperson	1.91	0.20	2.11
McReynolds	3.55	0.75	4.30	Elster	1.44	0.61	2.05
Gonzalez L	3.71	0.56	4.27	Felder	1.62	0.43	2.05
Gant	3.84	0.31	4.15	Redus	1.86	0.11	1.97
Mitchell K	3.77	0.32	4.09	Guerrero	1.93	0.02	1.95
McGee	3.83	0.20	4.03	Carter G	1.39	0.45	1.85
Grace	2.98	1.03	4.01	Slaught	1.57	0.24	1.81

NAME	OWAR	DWAR	TWAR	NAME	OWAR	DWAR	TWAR
Varsho	1.51	0.29	1.80	Martinez Crm	0.37	0.13	0.50
Teufel	1.60	0.20	1.79	Mitchell Kth	0.42	0.05	0.47
Barberie	1.47	0.30	1.77	Belliard	-0.72	1.18	0.46
Lewis D	1.09	0.68	1.76	Leonard M	0.40	0.06	0.46
Perry G	1.69	0.07	1.75	Reed Jf	0.44	0.00	0.44
Chamberlain	1.40	0.33	1.73	Gilkey	-0.33	0.68	0.34
Villanueva	1.71	-0.03	1.68	Daulton	0.90	-0.57	0.33
Santiago	1.64	0.02	1.67	Oberkfell	0.28	0.03	0.31
McClendon	1.60	0.05	1.66	Sims	0.26	0.03	0.30
Ready	1.32	0.32	1.64	Espy	0.20	0.08	0.29
Hollins	1.71	-0.08	1.63	Jones Chris	0.17	0.10	0.27
Pena G	1.40	0.23	1.63	Anderson D	-0.28	0.56	0.27
Bass K	1.26	0.33	1.59	Donnels	0.15	0.12	0.26
Howard T	0.82	0.74	1.56	Hassey	0.04	0.17	0.21
Duncan	1.12	0.41	1.53	Ward K	0.13	0.07	0.20
Thon	0.44	1.07	1.51	Benavides	0.08	0.12	0.20
Braggs	1.28	0.13	1.41	Fitzgerald	0.19	0.00	0.20
Coleman	1.42	-0.07	1.35	Lemke	-0.49	0.67	0.18
Cerone	1.20	0.14	1.34	Dascenzo	0.11	0.05	0.16
Jordan	1.34	-0.04	1.30	Javier	-0.10	0.24	0.14
Morandini	0.74	0.56	1.30	Landrum C	0.10	0.02	0.12
Clark Je	0.84	0.41	1.25	Rhodes	-0.22	0.28	0.06
Herr	0.56	0.67	1.23	Vizcaino	-0.29	0.34	0.05
Bream	0.96	0.26	1.22	Perezchica	-0.01	0.05	0.04
Wehner	0.96	0.24	1.20	Foley T	-0.23	0.26	0.03
Hatcher B	0.77	0.36	1.13	Sanders	-0.10	0.13	0.03
Lindeman	0.90	0.12	1.02	Benjamin	-0.86	0.88	0.01
Griffin Alf	-0.17	1.18	1.01	Vanderwal	-0.06	0.06	0.00
Pagnozzi	1.02	-0.03	0.99	Morris Jn	-0.15	0.14	-0.01
Walker C	0.66	0.27	0.93	Wilkerson	-0.62	0.59	-0.04
Galarraga	0.63	0.27	0.89	Shipley	-0.02	-0.02	-0.04
Howell Jk	0.27	0.48	0.75	Noboa	-0.09	0.05	-0.04
Ortiz Ja	0.62	0.13	0.75	Smith Dw	-0.26	0.18	-0.08
Buechele	0.53	0.21	0.74	Hayes C	-0.82	0.74	-0.08
Sasser	0.78	-0.06	0.72	Santovenia	0.00	-0.14	-0.13
Backman	0.76	-0.06	0.71	Hudler	-0.47	0.33	-0.13
Salazar L	0.60	0.09	0.69	Hamilton J	-0.14	-0.00	-0.14
Olson Greg	0.10	0.58	0.69	Offerman	-0.22	0.06	-0.16
Hayes V	0.15	0.53	0.68	Kingery	-0.30	0.13	-0.17
King J	0.55	0.08	0.63	Scott G	-0.35	0.18	-0.17
Uribe	0.00	0.63	0.63	Litton	-0.48	0.30	-0.18
Williams K	0.45	0.16	0.61	Nichols C	-0.07	-0.12	-0.19
Hunter B	0.52	0.06	0.58	Davidson M	-0.45	0.26	-0.19
Cedeno A	1.01	-0.44	0.57	Lofton	-0.24	0.04	-0.20
Webster M	0.37	0.19	0.56	Kennedy	0.21	-0.42	-0.21
Young G	0.05	0.50	0.56	Quinones L	-0.22	0.00	-0.22
Gwynn C	0.35	0.17	0.52	Fletcher D	-0.47	0.25	-0.22

NAME	OWAR	DWAR	TWAR
Faries	-0.83	0.61	-0.22
Carreon	-0.44	0.21	-0.23
Booker R	-0.27	0.04	-0.23
Gregg	-0.35	0.10	-0.25
Wilkins R	0.09	-0.36	-0.28
Cabrera	-0.19	-0.10	-0.28
Girardi	-0.23	-0.06	-0.30
Reyes	0.02	-0.32	-0.30
Coolbaugh	-0.54	0.23	-0.31
Anthony	-0.71	0.39	-0.32
Walton	-0.49	0.16	-0.33
Castillo Br	-0.46	0.11	-0.35
Gonzalez Jo	-0.54	0.15	-0.39
Ramirez R	-0.37	-0.04	-0.42
Manwaring	-0.19	-0.24	-0.43
Hundley	-0.66	0.17	-0.49
Abner	-0.86	0.36	-0.50
Decker S	-0.39	-0.16	-0.55
McLemore	-0.60	0.02	-0.58
Wilson C	-0.67	0.05	-0.62
Presley	-0.66	-0.06	-0.72
Benzinger	-0.82	0.09	-0.74
Mota A	-0.62	-0.14	-0.76
O'Brien C	-0.94	0.14	-0.80
Templeton	-1.39	0.54	-0.85
Yelding	-0.76	-0.12	-0.88
Heath	-0.97	0.09	-0.88
Berryhill	-0.81	-0.22	-1.04
Winningham	-1.07	0.02	-1.05
Gedman	-1.02	-0.06	-1.08
Lake	-0.97	-0.19	-1.16
Oliver	-0.93	-0.55	-1.49

American League

Total Wins Above Replacement

Alphabetical

NAME	OWAR	DWAR	TWAR
Abner	-0.10	0.40	0.30
Aldrete	1.82	0.17	1.99
Allanson	-0.61	-0.40	-1.01
Allred	1.57	0.20	1.78
Alomar R	5.62	1.02	6.64
Alomar S	-1.04	-0.01	-1.05
Anderson B	1.03	0.24	1.27
Baerga	4.21	1.16	5.37
Baines	4.92	0.01	4.93
Barfield Je	0.94	1.15	2.09
Barnes	0.89	0.38	1.27
Bell Ju	-1.54	0.31	-1.23
Belle	3.85	0.28	4.13
Benzinger	1.09	0.24	1.33
Bergman	0.65	0.16	0.82
Berry	-0.60	0.15	-0.45
Bichette	-0.27	1.12	0.85
Blankenship L	0.63	0.69	1.32
Boggs W	4.82	1.03	5.84
Borders	-0.46	0.58	0.12
Bordick	-0.84	0.74	-0.11
Bradley S	-0.53	-0.01	-0.54
Brett	3.03	0.01	3.04
Briley	0.62	0.19	0.81
Brock	0.51	0.09	0.60
Brosius	-0.15	0.18	0.03
Brown J	-0.25	-0.02	-0.26
Browne J	-0.67	-0.04	-0.71
Brumley	-0.52	0.26	-0.26
Brunansky	0.99	0.65	1.64
Buechele	1.51	1.21	2.71
Buhner	3.85	1.11	4.96
Burks	1.42	0.33	1.75
Bush	1.68	0.19	1.87
Canale	0.01	0.05	0.06
Canseco	5.98	0.16	6.14
Carter J	5.18	0.95	6.13
Clark Jk	3.98	0.00	3.98
Cochrane	0.06	-0.13	-0.07
Cole	3.34	0.30	3.64
Cora	-0.22	0.18	-0.04
Cotto	1.54	0.27	1.81
Cromartie	1.00	0.07	1.07
Cuyler	1.12	0.90	2.02
Daugherty	-0.91	0.07	-0.84
Davis A	0.93	0.05	0.98
Davis C	5.29	0.01	5.30
Davis G	1.18	0.06	1.24
Deer	1.00	0.78	1.78
Dempsey	-0.08	0.02	-0.06
Devereaux	3.07	1.38	4.45
Diaz Mar	-0.23	0.41	0.18
Disarcina	-0.13	-0.00	-0.13
Downing	2.85	0.00	2.85
Ducey	0.13	0.02	0.14
Eisenreich	1.74	0.02	1.76
Espinoza	-0.34	2.34	2.01
Evans Dw	2.06	0.47	2.53
Felix	1.16	-0.08	1.08
Fermin	-0.80	1.51	0.71
Fielder	4.73	0.27	5.00
Fisk	0.57	0.29	0.87
Fletcher S	-1.26	1.11	-0.15
Franco Ju	5.16	0.15	5.31
Fryman T	2.08	0.60	2.68
Gaetti	2.13	1.65	3.78
Gagne	-0.03	1.92	1.89
Gallagher	1.70	0.98	2.68
Gallego	1.94	0.97	2.92
Gantner	0.42	0.90	1.32
Geren	-0.72	-0.11	-0.83
Gibson K	3.89	0.03	3.92
Gladden	-0.37	0.45	0.08
Gomez L	1.34	0.43	1.77
Gonzales R	-0.66	0.45	-0.22
Gonzalez Jo	-0.27	0.15	-0.12
Gonzalez Juan	2.61	0.52	3.13
Grebeck	1.97	0.70	2.67
Greenwell	2.90	0.65	3.55

NAME	OWAR	DWAR	TWAR
Griffey Jr	6.45	1.34	7.79
Griffey	0.67	0.05	0.71
Gruber	1.83	0.91	2.75
Guillen	-0.69	2.58	1.89
Hall M	2.98	0.66	3.64
Hamilton	1.84	0.65	2.49
Harper B	2.12	0.12	2.24
Henderson D	4.45	1.58	6.04
Henderson R	4.61	0.78	5.39
Hernandez J	-0.90	0.32	-0.58
Hill D	0.85	0.76	1.61
Hill G	1.01	0.13	1.14
Hoiles	0.75	0.17	0.92
Horn	1.70	0.00	1.70
Howard D	-0.97	0.59	-0.38
Howell Jk	0.19	0.21	0.40
Hrbek	3.55	0.52	4.06
Huff	0.93	0.44	1.38
Hulett	-0.26	0.17	-0.09
Huson	-0.58	0.51	-0.07
Incaviglia	-0.25	0.26	0.01
Jacoby	-1.15	0.45	-0.70
James C	-0.66	0.34	-0.32
Jefferson R	-0.53	0.10	-0.43
Johnson L	0.54	2.04	2.58
Jones Tr	0.61	0.14	0.76
Joyner	5.78	0.52	6.30
Karkovice	0.52	0.19	0.71
Kelly P	0.11	0.15	0.26
Kelly	2.41	0.31	2.72
Kirby	-0.39	0.19	-0.20
Knoblauch	2.40	1.28	3.68
Larkin G	0.91	0.07	0.97
Law V	-0.34	0.04	-0.30
Lee M	-1.24	0.77	-0.48
Leius	1.19	0.51	1.69
Lewis M	-0.55	0.20	-0.35
Leyritz	-0.40	-0.15	-0.55
Livingstone	0.20	0.22	0.42
Lopez L	-0.34	-0.01	-0.35
Lovullo	-0.43	0.07	-0.36
Lyons S	-0.24	0.45	0.21
Maas	2.64	0.04	2.69
Macfarlane	2.23	0.07	2.30
Mack	3.79	0.84	4.64
Maldonado	1.50	0.24	1.74
Manto	0.00	0.00	0.01

NAME	OWAR	DWAR	TWAR
Martinez Crl	0.61	-0.04	0.58
Martinez Crm	0.45	0.15	0.60
Martinez C	1.33	0.37	1.70
Martinez E	5.76	0.82	6.59
Martinez Tino	-0.07	0.09	0.01
Marzano	-0.45	-0.08	-0.53
Mattingly	2.63	0.57	3.20
Mayne	0.39	0.11	0.50
McGwire	2.09	0.72	2.81
McRae B	0.68	0.86	1.54
Melvin	-0.36	-0.26	-0.63
Mercedes	-0.31	0.03	-0.28
Merullo	-0.12	0.02	-0.11
Meulens	-0.71	0.24	-0.47
Milligan	3.11	0.21	3.32
Molitor	6.69	0.08	6.76
Moseby	0.58	-0.03	0.55
Mulliniks	0.99	0.01	1.00
Munoz P	0.97	0.40	1.38
Myers G	0.99	0.02	1.01
Naehring	-0.66	0.04	-0.62
Newman A	-1.91	1.04	-0.86
Newson	1.22	0.13	1.35
Nokes	2.47	-0.55	1.92
O'Brien P	2.00	0.49	2.49
Olerud	3.68	0.38	4.06
Orsulak	0.90	1.72	2.62
Ortiz	-0.85	0.25	-0.60
Orton	-0.04	0.17	0.13
Pagliarulo	1.04	1.09	2.13
Palmeiro	6.01	0.35	6.36
Palmer Dn	-0.20	-0.13	-0.34
Parker D	1.61	0.00	1.61
Parrish Ln	1.52	0.91	2.44
Pasqua	3.59	0.46	4.06
Pecota	2.09	0.80	2.89
Pena T	-1.37	0.29	-1.08
Petralli	0.38	-0.52	-0.14
Pettis	-0.21	0.33	0.12
Phillips	3.96	1.82	5.78
Plantier	1.70	0.14	1.84
Polonia	4.51	0.26	4.77
Powell A	0.27	-0.00	0.27
Puckett	3.35	1.10	4.46
Quintana	3.12	0.47	3.59
Quirk	-0.20	-0.19	-0.39
Raines	3.18	1.17	4.35

NAME	OWAR	DWAR	TWAR	NAME	OWAR	DWAR	TWAR
Randolph	3.35	1.43	4.78	Stubbs	-0.22	0.35	0.13
Reed Jd	2.62	1.66	4.28	Surhoff BJ	0.08	0.02	0.10
Reimer	2.20	-0.01	2.18	Sveum	0.19	0.54	0.73
Reynolds H	2.62	2.06	4.68	Tabler	-0.10	0.01	-0.09
Riles	-0.12	0.40	0.28	Tartabull	6.07	-0.32	5.75
Ripken B	-1.81	1.25	-0.56	Taubensee	0.01	-0.25	-0.24
Ripken C	7.06	3.09	10.14	Tettleton	4.33	-0.59	3.74
Rivera L	0.90	1.50	2.40	Thomas F	6.86	0.19	7.06
Rodriguez I	-0.88	-0.34	-1.22	Thome	0.51	-0.04	0.47
Romine	-0.49	0.05	-0.44	Thurman	0.39	0.24	0.63
Rose	0.26	0.18	0.44	Tingley	-0.33	-0.00	-0.33
Sax S	3.28	1.39	4.67	Trammell	1.07	1.33	2.41
Schaefer	-0.30	0.47	0.18	Valle	-0.91	0.49	-0.42
Schofield	0.60	1.84	2.44	Vaughn G	2.98	0.76	3.74
Segui	0.10	0.16	0.26	Vaughn M	0.34	0.02	0.36
Seitzer	0.97	0.16	1.13	Velarde	-0.02	0.49	0.47
Sheffield	-0.74	-0.13	-0.87	Venable	0.50	0.13	0.64
Shelby	-1.34	0.35	-0.99	Ventura	4.66	1.44	6.09
Sheridan	-0.31	0.28	-0.03	Vizquel	-0.04	3.00	2.96
Shumpert	-1.25	0.73	-0.52	Ward T	0.09	0.22	0.31
Sierra	4.76	1.01	5.77	Weiss	-0.24	0.31	0.08
Skinner J	-0.84	-0.21	-1.05	Whitaker	4.11	1.41	5.51
Snyder C	-1.41	0.32	-1.09	White D	5.26	1.87	7.13
Sojo	0.24	1.60	1.84	Whiten	1.03	1.13	2.16
Sosa	-1.23	0.76	-0.47	Whitt	-0.13	-0.05	-0.19
Spehr	-0.04	0.03	-0.01	Williams B	1.17	0.18	1.35
Spiers	1.14	1.52	2.66	Wilson M	-0.16	0.11	-0.05
Sprague	0.84	-0.00	0.84	Wilson W	-0.37	0.40	0.03
Stanley M	0.69	-0.40	0.28	Winfield	4.73	0.58	5.31
Steinbach	1.18	-1.09	0.09	Worthington	0.29	0.11	0.40
Stevens	0.51	0.05	0.56	Yount	1.36	0.71	2.07
Stillwell	1.05	0.33	1.38				

National League

Total Wins Above Replacement

Alphabetical

NAME	OWAR	DWAR	TWAR	NAME	OWAR	DWAR	TWAR
Abner	-0.86	0.36	-0.50	Daniels	3.25	0.52	3.76
Anderson D	-0.28	0.56	0.27	Dascenzo	0.11	0.05	0.16
Anthony	-0.71	0.39	-0.32	Daulton	0.90	-0.57	0.33
Backman	0.76	-0.06	0.71	Davidson M	-0.45	0.26	-0.19
Bagwell	5.83	0.40	6.24	Davis E	1.79	0.39	2.18
Barberie	1.47	0.30	1.77	Dawson	2.90	0.45	3.35
Bass K	1.26	0.33	1.59	Decker S	-0.39	-0.16	-0.55
Bell Geo	3.27	0.02	3.29	DeShields	3.19	-0.04	3.15
Bell Jay	3.99	1.90	5.88	Donnels	0.15	0.12	0.26
Belliard	-0.72	1.18	0.46	Doran	2.07	0.33	2.40
Benavides	0.08	0.12	0.20	Duncan	1.12	0.41	1.53
Benjamin	-0.86	0.88	0.01	Dunston	1.31	1.51	2.83
Benzinger	-0.82	0.09	-0.74	Dykstra	2.68	0.27	2.96
Berryhill	-0.81	-0.22	-1.04	Elster	1.44	0.61	2.05
Biggio	4.19	-0.52	3.66	Espy	0.20	0.08	0.29
Blauser	1.92	0.23	2.15	Faries	-0.83	0.61	-0.22
Bonds	6.61	1.14	7.75	Felder	1.62	0.43	2.05
Bonilla B	6.25	1.14	7.39	Fernandez T	3.08	2.13	5.21
Booker R	-0.27	0.04	-0.23	Finley S	4.16	0.90	5.05
Boston	2.16	0.08	2.24	Fitzgerald	0.19	0.00	0.20
Braggs	1.28	0.13	1.41	Fletcher D	-0.47	0.25	-0.22
Bream	0.96	0.26	1.22	Foley T	-0.23	0.26	0.03
Brooks	2.52	0.24	2.76	Galarraga	0.63	0.27	0.89
Buechele	0.53	0.21	0.74	Gant	3.84	0.31	4.15
Butler	5.37	1.31	6.68	Gedman	-1.02	-0.06	-1.08
Cabrera	-0.19	-0.10	-0.28	Gilkey	-0.33	0.68	0.34
Calderon	4.89	0.28	5.17	Girardi	-0.23	-0.06	-0.30
Caminiti	2.43	0.76	3.19	Gonzalez Jo	-0.54	0.15	-0.39
Candaele	2.37	0.72	3.09	Gonzalez L	3.71	0.56	4.27
Carreon	-0.44	0.21	-0.23	Grace	2.98	1.03	4.01
Carter G	1.39	0.45	1.85	Gregg	-0.35	0.10	-0.25
Castillo Br	-0.46	0.11	-0.35	Griffin Alf	-0.17	1.18	1.01
Cedeno A	1.01	-0.44	0.57	Grissom	3.49	1.17	4.66
Cerone	1.20	0.14	1.34	Guerrero	1.93	0.02	1.95
Chamberlain	1.40	0.33	1.73	Gwynn C	0.35	0.17	0.52
Clark Je	0.84	0.41	1.25	Gwynn T	4.25	0.88	5.14
Clark W	6.30	0.61	6.90	Hamilton J	-0.14	-0.00	-0.14
Coleman	1.42	-0.07	1.35	Harris L	1.96	0.72	2.68
Coolbaugh	-0.54	0.23	-0.31	Hassey	0.04	0.17	0.21

NAME	OWAR	DWAR	TWAR	NAME	OWAR	DWAR	TWAR
Hatcher B	0.77	0.36	1.13	Mitchell K	3.77	0.32	4.09
Hayes C	-0.82	0.74	-0.08	Morandini	0.74	0.56	1.30
Hayes V	0.15	0.53	0.68	Morris H	4.23	0.39	4.63
Heath	-0.97	0.09	-0.88	Morris Jn	-0.15	0.14	-0.01
Herr	0.56	0.67	1.23	Mota A	-0.62	-0.14	-0.76
Hollins	1.71	-0.08	1.63	Murphy Dl	2.31	0.58	2.89
Howard T	0.82	0.74	1.56	Murray E	3.74	0.69	4.43
Howell Jk	0.27	0.48	0.75	Nichols C	-0.07	-0.12	-0.19
Hudler	-0.47	0.33	-0.13	Nixon O	2.12	0.68	2.80
Hundley	-0.66	0.17	-0.49	Noboa	-0.09	0.05	-0.04
Hunter B	0.52	0.06	0.58	O'Brien C	-0.94	0.14	-0.80
Jackson Dar	2.91	0.68	3.59	O'Neill	3.49	1.49	4.98
Javier	-0.10	0.24	0.14	Oberkfell	0.28	0.03	0.31
Jefferies	2.80	-0.33	2.47	Offerman	-0.22	0.06	-0.16
Johnson H	6.46	0.03	6.49	Oliver	-0.93	-0.55	-1.49
Jones Chris	0.17	0.10	0.27	Olson Greg	0.10	0.58	0.69
Jordan	1.34	-0.04	1.30	Oquendo	1.87	1.40	3.27
Jose	5.48	1.26	6.74	Ortiz Ja	0.62	0.13	0.75
Justice	3.86	0.62	4.48	Owen S	1.88	1.92	3.80
Kennedy	0.21	-0.42	-0.21	Pagnozzi	1.02	-0.03	0.99
King J	0.55	0.08	0.63	Pena G	1.40	0.23	1.63
Kingery	-0.30	0.13	-0.17	Pendleton	5.02	1.44	6.46
Kruk	5.78	0.65	6.43	Perezchica	-0.01	0.05	0.04
Lake	-0.97	-0.19	-1.16	Perry G	1.69	0.07	1.75
Landrum C	0.10	0.02	0.12	Presley	-0.66	-0.06	-0.72
Lankford	4.10	0.73	4.82	Quinones L	-0.22	0.00	-0.22
Larkin B	4.82	1.82	6.65	Ramirez R	-0.37	-0.04	-0.42
LaValliere	1.85	0.45	2.30	Ready	1.32	0.32	1.64
Lemke	-0.49	0.67	0.18	Redus	1.86	0.11	1.97
Leonard M	0.40	0.06	0.46	Reed Jf	0.44	0.00	0.44
Lewis D	1.09	0.68	1.76	Reyes	0.02	-0.32	-0.30
Lind	0.81	1.86	2.66	Rhodes	-0.22	0.28	0.06
Lindeman	0.90	0.12	1.02	Roberts Bip	2.27	0.61	2.88
Litton	-0.48	0.30	-0.18	Sabo	5.20	0.27	5.47
Lofton	-0.24	0.04	-0.20	Salazar L	0.60	0.09	0.69
Magadan	3.48	0.51	4.00	Samuel	5.12	0.73	5.85
Manwaring	-0.19	-0.24	-0.43	Sandberg	5.77	1.09	6.86
Martinez Crm	0.37	0.13	0.50	Sanders	-0.10	0.13	0.03
Martinez Da	2.72	0.79	3.51	Santiago	1.64	0.02	1.67
McClendon	1.60	0.05	1.66	Santovenia	0.00	-0.14	-0.13
McGee	3.83	0.20	4.03	Sasser	0.78	-0.06	0.72
McGriff F	5.93	0.16	6.09	Scioscia	2.72	0.42	3.14
McLemore	-0.60	0.02	-0.58	Scott G	-0.35	0.18	-0.17
McReynolds	3.55	0.75	4.30	Sharperson	1.91	0.20	2.11
Merced	3.44	0.12	3.57	Shipley	-0.02	-0.02	-0.04
Miller K	2.25	0.52	2.78	Sims	0.26	0.03	0.30
Mitchell Kth	0.42	0.05	0.47	Slaught	1.57	0.24	1.81

NAME	OWAR	DWAR	TWAR
Smith Dw	-0.26	0.18	-0.08
Smith Lo	2.22	0.06	2.28
Smith O	5.13	2.11	7.24
Strawberry	5.47	0.45	5.92
Templeton	-1.39	0.54	-0.85
Teufel	1.60	0.20	1.79
Thompson M	3.74	0.82	4.56
Thompson Ro	4.50	1.88	6.38
Thon	0.44	1.07	1.51
Treadway	2.13	0.24	2.38
Uribe	0.00	0.63	0.63
Van Slyke	4.75	0.75	5.50
Vanderwal	-0.06	0.06	0.00
Varsho	1.51	0.29	1.80
Villanueva	1.71	-0.03	1.68
Vizcaino	-0.29	0.34	0.05
Walker C	0.66	0.27	0.93
Walker L	4.21	1.00	5.20
Wallach	1.88	1.12	3.00
Walton	-0.49	0.16	-0.33
Ward K	0.13	0.07	0.20
Webster M	0.37	0.19	0.56
Wehner	0.96	0.24	1.20
Wilkerson	-0.62	0.59	-0.04
Wilkins R	0.09	-0.36	-0.28
Williams K	0.45	0.16	0.61
Williams MD	4.78	1.09	5.87
Wilson C	-0.67	0.05	-0.62
Winningham	-1.07	0.02	-1.05
Yelding	-0.76	-0.12	-0.88
Young G	0.05	0.50	0.56
Zeile	4.24	0.39	4.63

American League

Offensive Wins Above Replacement

All Players

Player	OWAR	Player	OWAR	Player	OWAR
Ripken C	7.06	Sax S	3.28	Allred	1.57
Thomas F	6.86	Raines	3.18	Cotto	1.54
Molitor	6.69	Quintana	3.12	Parrish Ln	1.52
Griffey Jr	6.45	Milligan	3.11	Buechele	1.51
Tartabull	6.07	Devereaux	3.07	Maldonado	1.50
Palmeiro	6.01	Brett	3.03	Burks	1.42
Canseco	5.98	Vaughn G	2.98	Yount	1.36
Joyner	5.78	Hall M	2.98	Gomez L	1.34
Martinez E	5.76	Greenwell	2.90	Martinez C	1.33
Alomar R	5.62	Downing	2.85	Newson	1.22
Davis C	5.29	Maas	2.64	Leius	1.19
White D	5.26	Mattingly	2.63	Steinbach	1.18
Carter J	5.18	Reynolds H	2.62	Davis G	1.18
Franco Ju	5.16	Reed Jd	2.62	Williams B	1.17
Baines	4.92	Gonzalez Juan	2.61	Felix	1.16
Boggs W	4.82	Nokes	2.47	Spiers	1.14
Sierra	4.76	Kelly	2.41	Cuyler	1.12
Winfield	4.73	Knoblauch	2.40	Benzinger	1.09
Fielder	4.73	Macfarlane	2.23	Trammell	1.07
Ventura	4.66	Reimer	2.20	Stillwell	1.05
Henderson R	4.61	Gaetti	2.13	Pagliarulo	1.04
Polonia	4.51	Harper B	2.12	Anderson B	1.03
Henderson D	4.45	Pecota	2.09	Whiten	1.03
Tettleton	4.33	McGwire	2.09	Hill G	1.01
Baerga	4.21	Fryman T	2.08	Cromartie	1.00
Whitaker	4.11	Evans Dw	2.06	Deer	1.00
Clark Jk	3.98	O'Brien P	2.00	Myers G	0.99
Phillips	3.96	Grebeck	1.97	Mulliniks	0.99
Gibson K	3.89	Gallego	1.94	Brunansky	0.99
Belle	3.85	Hamilton	1.84	Munoz P	0.97
Buhner	3.85	Gruber	1.83	Seitzer	0.97
Mack	3.79	Aldrete	1.82	Barfield Je	0.94
Olerud	3.68	Eisenreich	1.74	Huff	0.93
Pasqua	3.59	Horn	1.70	Davis A	0.93
Hrbek	3.55	Plantier	1.70	Larkin G	0.91
Puckett	3.35	Gallagher	1.70	Rivera L	0.90
Randolph	3.35	Bush	1.68	Orsulak	0.90
Cole	3.34	Parker D	1.61	Barnes	0.89

Hill D	0.85	Manto	0.00	Bradley S	-0.53
Sprague	0.84	Velarde	-0.02	Jefferson R	-0.53
Hoiles	0.75	Gagne	-0.03	Lewis M	-0.55
Stanley M	0.69	Vizquel	-0.04	Huson	-0.58
McRae B	0.68	Martinez Tino	-0.07	Allanson	-0.61
Bergman	0.65	Dempsey	-0.08	James C	-0.66
Blankenship L	0.63	Tabler	-0.10	Gonzales R	-0.66
Briley	0.62	Abner	-0.10	Browne J	-0.67
Jones Tr	0.61	Riles	-0.12	Guillen	-0.69
Martinez Crl	0.61	Merullo	-0.12	Meulens	-0.71
Schofield	0.60	Wilson M	-0.16	Geren	-0.72
Moseby	0.58	Quirk	-0.20	Sheffield	-0.74
Fisk	0.57	Palmer Dn	-0.20	Fermin	-0.80
Johnson L	0.54	Pettis	-0.21	Skinner J	-0.84
Karkovice	0.52	Stubbs	-0.22	Bordick	-0.84
Thome	0.51	Cora	-0.22	Ortiz	-0.85
Venable	0.50	Diaz Mar	-0.23	Rodriguez I	-0.88
Martinez Crm	0.45	Weiss	-0.24	Hernandez J	-0.90
Gantner	0.42	Lyons S	-0.24	Daugherty	-0.91
Mayne	0.39	Incaviglia	-0.25	Valle	-0.91
Thurman	0.39	Hulett	-0.26	Howard D	-0.97
Petralli	0.38	Bichette	-0.27	Alomar S	-1.04
Vaughn M	0.34	Schaefer	-0.30	Jacoby	-1.15
Worthington	0.29	Sheridan	-0.31	Sosa	-1.23
Powell A	0.27	Tingley	-0.33	Lee M	-1.24
Sojo	0.24	Espinoza	-0.34	Shumpert	-1.25
Livingstone	0.20	Law V	-0.34	Fletcher S	-1.26
Sveum	0.19	Melvin	-0.36	Shelby	-1.34
Kelly P	0.11	Gladden	-0.37	Pena T	-1.37
Segui	0.10	Wilson W	-0.37	Snyder C	-1.41
Ward T	0.09	Marzano	-0.45	Bell Ju	-1.54
Surhoff BJ	0.08	Borders	-0.46	Ripken B	-1.81
Cochrane	0.06	Brumley	-0.52	Newman A	-1.91

National League

Offensive Wins Above Replacement

All Players

Bonds	6.61
Johnson H	6.46
Clark W	6.30
Bonilla B	6.25
McGriff F	5.93
Bagwell	5.83
Kruk	5.78
Sandberg	5.77
Jose	5.48
Strawberry	5.47
Butler	5.37
Sabo	5.20
Smith O	5.13
Samuel	5.12
Pendleton	5.02
Calderon	4.89
Larkin B	4.82
Williams MD	4.78
Van Slyke	4.75
Thompson Ro	4.50
Gwynn T	4.25
Zeile	4.24
Morris H	4.23
Walker L	4.21
Biggio	4.19
Finley S	4.16
Lankford	4.10
Bell Jay	3.99
Justice	3.86
Gant	3.84
McGee	3.83
Mitchell K	3.77
Thompson M	3.74
Murray E	3.74
Gonzalez L	3.71
McReynolds	3.55
O'Neill	3.49
Grissom	3.49
Magadan	3.48
Merced	3.44
Bell Geo	3.27
Daniels	3.25
DeShields	3.19
Fernandez T	3.08
Grace	2.98
Jackson Dar	2.91
Dawson	2.90
Jefferies	2.80
Martinez Da	2.72
Scioscia	2.72
Dykstra	2.68
Brooks	2.52
Caminiti	2.43
Candaele	2.37
Murphy Dl	2.31
Roberts Bip	2.27
Miller K	2.25
Smith Lo	2.22
Boston	2.16
Treadway	2.13
Nixon O	2.12
Doran	2.07
Harris L	1.96
Guerrero	1.93
Blauser	1.92
Sharperson	1.91
Owen S	1.88
Wallach	1.88
Oquendo	1.87
Redus	1.86
LaValliere	1.85
Davis E	1.79
Villanueva	1.71
Hollins	1.71
Perry G	1.69
Santiago	1.64
Felder	1.62
McClendon	1.60
Teufel	1.60
Slaught	1.57
Varsho	1.51
Barberie	1.47
Elster	1.44
Coleman	1.42
Pena G	1.40
Chamberlain	1.40
Carter G	1.39
Jordan	1.34
Ready	1.32
Dunston	1.31
Braggs	1.28
Bass K	1.26
Cerone	1.20
Duncan	1.12
Lewis D	1.09
Pagnozzi	1.02
Cedeno A	1.01
Wehner	0.96
Bream	0.96
Lindeman	0.90
Daulton	0.90
Clark Je	0.84
Howard T	0.82
Lind	0.81
Sasser	0.78
Hatcher B	0.77
Backman	0.76
Morandini	0.74
Walker C	0.66
Galarraga	0.63
Salazar L	0.60
Herr	0.56
King J	0.55
Buechele	0.53

Hunter B	0.52	Javier	-0.10	Fletcher D	-0.47
Thon	0.44	Sanders	-0.10	Litton	-0.48
Reed Jf	0.44	Hamilton J	-0.14	Lemke	-0.49
Leonard M	0.40	Morris Jn	-0.15	Walton	-0.49
Webster M	0.37	Griffin Alf	-0.17	Coolbaugh	-0.54
Martinez Crm	0.37	Cabrera	-0.19	Wilkerson	-0.62
Gwynn C	0.35	Manwaring	-0.19	Anthony	-0.71
Howell Jk	0.27	Quinones L	-0.22	Belliard	-0.72
Sims	0.26	Offerman	-0.22	Yelding	-0.76
Kennedy	0.21	Rhodes	-0.22	Berryhill	-0.81
Fitzgerald	0.19	Foley T	-0.23	Benzinger	-0.82
Hayes V	0.15	Smith Dw	-0.26	Hayes C	-0.82
Donnels	0.15	Anderson D	-0.28	Faries	-0.83
Ward K	0.13	Vizcaino	-0.29	Abner	-0.86
Dascenzo	0.11	Kingery	-0.30	Benjamin	-0.86
Olson Greg	0.10	Gilkey	-0.33	Oliver	-0.93
Landrum C	0.10	Gregg	-0.35	O'Brien C	-0.94
Wilkins R	0.09	Ramirez R	-0.37	Heath	-0.97
Young G	0.05	Decker S	-0.39	Lake	-0.97
Hassey	0.04	Carreon	-0.44	Gedman	-1.02
Reyes	0.02	Davidson M	-0.45	Winningham	-1.07
Uribe	0.00	Hudler	-0.47	Templeton	-1.39

American League

Defensive Wins Above Replacement

All Players

Player	DWAR	Player	DWAR	Player	DWAR
Ripken C	3.09	Boggs W	1.03	Hrbek	0.52
Vizquel	3.00	Alomar R	1.02	Huson	0.51
Guillen	2.58	Sierra	1.01	Leius	0.51
Espinoza	2.34	Gallagher	0.98	Valle	0.49
Reynolds H	2.06	Gallego	0.97	O'Brien P	0.49
Johnson L	2.04	Carter J	0.95	Velarde	0.49
Gagne	1.92	Parrish Ln	0.91	Schaefer	0.47
White D	1.87	Gruber	0.91	Evans Dw	0.47
Schofield	1.84	Gantner	0.90	Quintana	0.47
Phillips	1.82	Cuyler	0.90	Pasqua	0.46
Orsulak	1.72	McRae B	0.86	Jacoby	0.45
Reed Jd	1.66	Mack	0.84	Gladden	0.45
Gaetti	1.65	Martinez E	0.82	Lyons S	0.45
Sojo	1.60	Pecota	0.80	Gonzales R	0.45
Henderson D	1.58	Deer	0.78	Huff	0.44
Spiers	1.52	Henderson R	0.78	Gomez L	0.43
Fermin	1.51	Lee M	0.77	Diaz Mar	0.41
Rivera L	1.50	Hill D	0.76	Munoz P	0.40
Ventura	1.44	Vaughn G	0.76	Abner	0.40
Randolph	1.43	Sosa	0.76	Wilson W	0.40
Whitaker	1.41	Bordick	0.74	Riles	0.40
Sax S	1.39	Shumpert	0.73	Olerud	0.38
Devereaux	1.38	McGwire	0.72	Barnes	0.38
Griffey Jr	1.34	Yount	0.71	Martinez C	0.37
Trammell	1.33	Grebeck	0.70	Palmeiro	0.35
Knoblauch	1.28	Blankenship L	0.69	Shelby	0.35
Ripken B	1.25	Hall M	0.66	Stubbs	0.35
Buechele	1.21	Brunansky	0.65	James C	0.34
Raines	1.17	Greenwell	0.65	Stillwell	0.33
Baerga	1.16	Hamilton	0.65	Burks	0.33
Barfield Je	1.15	Fryman T	0.60	Pettis	0.33
Whiten	1.13	Howard D	0.59	Hernandez J	0.32
Bichette	1.12	Winfield	0.58	Snyder C	0.32
Buhner	1.11	Borders	0.58	Weiss	0.31
Fletcher S	1.11	Mattingly	0.57	Bell Ju	0.31
Puckett	1.10	Sveum	0.54	Kelly	0.31
Pagliarulo	1.09	Gonzalez Juan	0.52	Cole	0.30
Newman A	1.04	Joyner	0.52	Fisk	0.29

Pena T	0.29	Kelly P	0.15	Merullo	0.02
Belle	0.28	Gonzalez Jo	0.15	Myers G	0.02
Sheridan	0.28	Berry	0.15	Ducey	0.02
Fielder	0.27	Franco Ju	0.15	Tabler	0.01
Cotto	0.27	Jones Tr	0.14	Manto	0.00
Brumley	0.26	Plantier	0.14	Sprague	0.00
Incaviglia	0.26	Newson	0.13	Disarcina	0.00
Polonia	0.26	Venable	0.13	Powell A	-0.00
Ortiz	0.25	Hill G	0.13	Tingley	0.00
Thurman	0.24	Harper B	0.12	Alomar S	-0.01
Anderson B	0.24	Mayne	0.11	Bradley S	0.01
Meulens	0.24	Wilson M	0.11	Reimer	-0.01
Maldonado	0.24	Worthington	0.11	Lopez L	0.01
Benzinger	0.24	Jefferson R	0.10	Brown J	0.02
Livingstone	0.22	Brock	0.09	Moseby	-0.03
Ward T	0.22	Martinez Tino	0.09	Martinez Crl	-0.04
Milligan	0.21	Molitor	0.08	Browne J	-0.04
Howell Jk	0.21	Daugherty	0.07	Thome	-0.04
Allred	0.20	Macfarlane	0.07	Whitt	-0.05
Lewis M	0.20	Lovullo	0.07	Marzano	-0.08
Thomas F	0.19	Cromartie	0.07	Felix	-0.08
Kirby	0.19	Larkin G	0.07	Geren	-0.11
Briley	0.19	Davis G	0.06	Cochrane	-0.13
Bush	0.19	Davis A	0.05	Sheffield	-0.13
Karkovice	0.19	Stevens	0.05	Palmer Dn	-0.13
Rose	0.18	Canale	0.05	Leyritz	-0.15
Cora	0.18	Griffey	0.05	Quirk	-0.19
Williams B	0.18	Romine	0.05	Skinner J	-0.21
Brosius	0.18	Law V	0.04	Taubensee	-0.25
Hulett	0.17	Maas	0.04	Melvin	-0.26
Aldrete	0.17	Naehring	0.04	Tartabull	-0.32
Orton	0.17	Mercedes	0.03	Rodriguez I	-0.34
Hoiles	0.17	Spehr	0.03	Allanson	-0.40
Segui	0.16	Gibson K	0.03	Stanley M	-0.40
Seitzer	0.16	Surhoff BJ	0.02	Petralli	-0.52
Canseco	0.16	Eisenreich	0.02	Nokes	-0.55
Bergman	0.16	Vaughn M	0.02	Tettleton	-0.59
Martinez Crm	0.15	Dempsey	0.02	Steinbach	-1.09

National League

Defensive Wins Above Replacement

All Players

Fernandez T	2.13	Murray E	0.69	Davis E	0.39
Smith O	2.11	Nixon O	0.68	Zeile	0.39
Owen S	1.92	Jackson Dar	0.68	Abner	0.36
Bell Jay	1.90	Gilkey	0.68	Hatcher B	0.36
Thompson Ro	1.88	Lewis D	0.68	Vizcaino	0.34
Lind	1.86	Lemke	0.67	Bass K	0.33
Larkin B	1.82	Herr	0.67	Hudler	0.33
Dunston	1.51	Kruk	0.65	Doran	0.33
O'Neill	1.49	Uribe	0.63	Chamberlain	0.33
Pendleton	1.44	Justice	0.62	Mitchell K	0.32
Oquendo	1.40	Roberts Bip	0.61	Ready	0.32
Butler	1.31	Faries	0.61	Gant	0.31
Jose	1.26	Elster	0.61	Barberie	0.30
Belliard	1.18	Clark W	0.61	Litton	0.30
Griffin Alf	1.18	Wilkerson	0.59	Varsho	0.29
Grissom	1.17	Olson Greg	0.58	Calderon	0.28
Bonds	1.14	Murphy Dl	0.58	Rhodes	0.28
Bonilla B	1.14	Morandini	0.56	Dykstra	0.27
Wallach	1.12	Gonzalez L	0.56	Walker C	0.27
Williams MD	1.09	Anderson D	0.56	Sabo	0.27
Sandberg	1.09	Templeton	0.54	Galarraga	0.27
Thon	1.07	Hayes V	0.53	Foley T	0.26
Grace	1.03	Miller K	0.52	Bream	0.26
Walker L	1.00	Daniels	0.52	Davidson M	0.26
Finley S	0.90	Magadan	0.51	Fletcher D	0.25
Gwynn T	0.88	Young G	0.50	Treadway	0.24
Benjamin	0.88	Howell Jk	0.48	Slaught	0.24
Thompson M	0.82	Carter G	0.45	Brooks	0.24
Martinez Da	0.79	Dawson	0.45	Wehner	0.24
Caminiti	0.76	Strawberry	0.45	Javier	0.24
McReynolds	0.75	LaValliere	0.45	Blauser	0.23
Van Slyke	0.75	Felder	0.43	Pena G	0.23
Hayes C	0.74	Scioscia	0.42	Coolbaugh	0.23
Howard T	0.74	Duncan	0.41	Carreon	0.21
Samuel	0.73	Clark Je	0.41	Buechele	0.21
Lankford	0.73	Bagwell	0.40	Sharperson	0.20
Harris L	0.72	Anthony	0.39	McGee	0.20
Candaele	0.72	Morris H	0.39	Teufel	0.20

Webster M	0.19
Smith Dw	0.18
Scott G	0.18
Hassey	0.17
Gwynn C	0.17
Hundley	0.17
Williams K	0.16
McGriff F	0.16
Walton	0.16
Gonzalez Jo	0.15
Morris Jn	0.14
Cerone	0.14
O'Brien C	0.14
Kingery	0.13
Martinez Crm	0.13
Sanders	0.13
Braggs	0.13
Ortiz Ja	0.13
Merced	0.12
Lindeman	0.12
Benavides	0.12
Donnels	0.12
Castillo Br	0.11
Redus	0.11
Gregg	0.10
Jones Chris	0.10
Heath	0.09
Salazar L	0.09
Benzinger	0.09
Espy	0.08
Boston	0.08
King J	0.08
Ward K	0.07
Perry G	0.07
Hunter B	0.06
Vanderwal	0.06
Leonard M	0.06
Offerman	0.06
Smith Lo	0.06
Noboa	0.05
Dascenzo	0.05
McClendon	0.05
Mitchell Kth	0.05
Wilson C	0.05
Perezchica	0.05
Lofton	0.04
Booker R	0.04
Oberkfell	0.03
Sims	0.03
Johnson H	0.03
Santiago	0.02
Landrum C	0.02
McLemore	0.02
Bell Geo	0.02
Guerrero	0.02
Winningham	0.02
Quinones L	0.00
Fitzgerald	0.00
Reed Jf	0.00
Hamilton J	-0.00
Shipley	-0.02
Pagnozzi	-0.03
Villanueva	-0.03
Jordan	-0.04
DeShields	-0.04
Ramirez R	-0.04
Backman	-0.06
Gedman	-0.06
Sasser	-0.06
Girardi	-0.06
Presley	-0.06
Coleman	-0.07
Hollins	-0.08
Cabrera	-0.10
Yelding	-0.12
Nichols C	-0.12
Santovenia	-0.14
Mota A	-0.14
Decker S	-0.16
Lake	-0.19
Berryhill	-0.22
Manwaring	-0.24
Reyes	-0.32
Jefferies	-0.33
Wilkins R	-0.36
Kennedy	-0.42
Cedeno A	-0.44
Biggio	-0.52
Oliver	-0.55
Daulton	-0.57

National League

Trade Value

All Players

Trade Value is an old Bill James concept that attempts to divine how much value a player has left; that is, how much he should be worth, overall, in a trade. The basic concept involves figuring out how much yearly value the player has established and then figuring out how much playing time he probably has left.

Bill used his Approximate Value as the yearly estimate, but that is one out-of-date method. AV were always hard to compute, and the only reason Bill used them was that he didn't have access to the raw material to do anything more complex. As it turns out, the range of AV values is about twice what the range of TWARs is. Having access to the STATS, Inc. computer makes TWAR easier for me to get hold of than AV would be. Thus, these Trade values are fueled by 2 x TWAR.

Last year, you may recall, these Trade Values were computed using only one year's data. I did get that straightened out with the computer, and these have a full three years to work with. I'm still not sure they're accurate, but I haven't had time to hand check a sample. Next year, I'll know more, and will report to you. Sigh. It's always next year.

Trade Value as of	1/1/92
Bonds	12.562
Bagwell	11.319
Clark W	10.718
Bonilla B	10.660
McGriff F	10.153
Larkin B	8.431
Sandberg	8.421
Johnson H	7.736
Jose	7.719
Strawberry	7.538
Pendleton	7.050
Mitchell K	6.769
Williams MD	6.689
Gant	6.375
Kruk	6.266
Walker L	6.257
Sabo	6.172
Grace	5.884
Gwynn T	5.775
Thompson Ro	5.673
Van Slyke	5.504
Butler	5.473
Bell Jay	5.437
Dykstra	5.284
O'Neill	5.253
Justice	5.205
Morris H	5.185
Magadan	5.034
Calderon	4.960
Fernandez T	4.847
Roberts Bip	4.649
Daniels	4.644
Lankford	4.561
McReynolds	4.546
DeShields	4.467
Zeile	4.367
Merced	4.224
Samuel	4.208
Davis E	4.148
Murray E	4.131
Biggio	4.029
Grissom	3.851
Finley S	3.750
McGee	3.679
Jefferies	3.566
Oquendo	3.516
Gonzalez L	3.475
Wallach	3.430
Martinez Da	3.086
Smith O	3.074
Thompson M	2.990
Owen S	2.941
Bell Geo	2.700
Hayes V	2.552
Coleman	2.516
Smith Lo	2.515
Guerrero	2.483
Doran	2.433
Jackson Dar	2.421
Scioscia	2.414
Candaele	2.386
Hamilton J	2.319
Caminiti	2.308
Harris L	2.307
Galarraga	2.298
Dunston	2.166
Duncan	2.147
Blauser	2.098

Smith Dw 1.923
Walton 1.879
Dawson 1.857
Treadway 1.842
Miller K 1.775
Boston 1.761
Lind 1.721
Daulton 1.666
Sharperson 1.582
Brooks 1.565
Bream 1.469
LaValliere 1.465
Santiago 1.432
Barberie 1.429
Braggs 1.426
Hatcher B 1.382
Wilkins R 1.342
McClendon 1.326
Murphy Dl 1.310
Varsho 1.306
Hollins 1.274
Nixon O 1.271
Howard T 1.195
Redus 1.169
Slaught 1.161
Reyes 1.104
Fitzgerald 1.104
Backman 1.083
Howell Jk 1.072
Carreon 1.057
Felder 1.056
Benzinger 1.032
Elster 1.022
Thon 1.022
Bass K 1.022
Manwaring 0.985
Perry G 0.978
Villanueva 0.971
Ready 0.955
Herr 0.949
Chamberlain 0.905
Lewis D 0.862
Javier 0.851
Teufel 0.848
Hundley 0.847
Jordan 0.835
Sasser 0.820
Wehner 0.819
Pena G 0.786
Hudler 0.770
Pagnozzi 0.768
Oliver 0.754
Gonzalez Jo 0.732
Winningham 0.684
Clark Je 0.679
Morandini 0.577
Kennedy 0.567
Santovenia 0.560
Webster M 0.541
Quinones L 0.526
Presley 0.510
Griffin Alf 0.510
Martinez Crm 0.501
Gregg 0.491
Ramirez R 0.487
Carter G 0.481
Salazar L 0.460
Ortiz Ja 0.448
Walker C 0.434
Lindeman 0.409
Cabrera 0.394
Olson Greg 0.393
Hayes C 0.380
Reed Jf 0.378
Williams K 0.360
King J 0.358
Kingery 0.354
Uribe 0.329
Davidson M 0.329
Foley T 0.325
O'Brien C 0.323
Noboa 0.313
Hunter B 0.307
Anthony 0.307
Templeton 0.299
Buechele 0.295
Gwynn C 0.294
Young G 0.284
Gilkey 0.278
Cedeno A 0.272
Litton 0.267
Yelding 0.266
Espy 0.253
Cerone 0.253
Belliard 0.249
Anderson D 0.246
Heath 0.226
Mitchell Kth 0.215
Decker S 0.192
Leonard M 0.163
Rhodes 0.143
Jones Chris 0.141
Oberkfell 0.140
Donnels 0.134
Dascenzo 0.132
Sims 0.109
Gedman 0.107
Ward K 0.104
Benavides 0.098
Lemke 0.089
McLemore 0.083
Berryhill 0.073
Girardi 0.073
Coolbaugh 0.066
Landrum C 0.061
Lake 0.059
Nichols C 0.045
Fletcher D 0.037
Hassey 0.030
Sanders 0.027
Wilson C 0.025
Booker R 0.024
Vizcaino 0.019
Perezchica 0.017
Benjamin 0.007
Morris Jn 0.001
Vanderwal 0.001

American League

Trade Value

All Players

Trade Value as of	1/1/92
Griffey Jr	12.753
Ripken C	10.923
Thomas F	9.445
Alomar R	8.593
Sierra	8.301
Fielder	8.283
Canseco	8.187
Palmeiro	8.070
Martinez E	7.244
Henderson R	6.822
Ventura	6.820
Franco Ju	6.529
Boggs W	6.200
White D	6.124
Joyner	6.066
Tartabull	5.551
Baerga	5.453
Puckett	5.372
McGwire	5.228
Carter J	5.191
Greenwell	5.000
Mack	4.876
Raines	4.867
Reed Jd	4.701
Henderson D	4.647
Molitor	4.533
Knoblauch	4.529
Davis C	4.477
Polonia	4.461
Hrbek	4.372
Browne J	4.370
Baines	4.307
Reynolds H	4.158
Phillips	4.099
Belle	4.085
Gruber	4.057
Buhner	4.017
Milligan	3.924
Tettleton	3.802
Olerud	3.733
Jacoby	3.723
Quintana	3.680
Whitaker	3.605
Davis A	3.602
Burks	3.525
Kelly	3.519
Pasqua	3.432
Sax S	3.361
Davis G	3.200
Cole	3.117
Clark Jk	3.026
Devereaux	2.981
Barfield Je	2.826
Maas	2.761
Mattingly	2.682
Grebeck	2.597
James C	2.482
Vaughn G	2.392
Vizquel	2.378
Orsulak	2.312
Seitzer	2.286
Trammell	2.216
Sheffield	2.196
Gonzalez Juan	2.195
Ripken B	2.188
Spiers	2.097
Gibson K	2.091
Brunansky	2.087
Fryman T	2.087
Hall M	2.080
Gallego	2.037
Yount	2.036
Stubbs	1.856
Maldonado	1.823
Eisenreich	1.798
Johnson L	1.795
Harper B	1.787
Gallagher	1.718
Cuyler	1.714
Randolph	1.691
Felix	1.682
Rivera L	1.650
Gaetti	1.602
Macfarlane	1.586
Espinoza	1.568
Deer	1.566
Parrish Ln	1.558
O'Brien P	1.549
Brett	1.549
Daugherty	1.544
Hamilton	1.522
Sojo	1.516
Plantier	1.468
Pecota	1.399
Horn	1.399
Schofield	1.391
Martinez C	1.359
Alomar S	1.349
Leius	1.348
Larkin G	1.338
Pagliarulo	1.331
Reimer	1.293
Buechele	1.258
Whiten	1.231
Guillen	1.207
Taubensee	1.151
Stillwell	1.108
Melvin	1.105
Fisk	1.100
Briley	1.084
Merullo	1.067
Aldrete	1.032
Nokes	1.030
Allanson	1.004
Spehr	0.995
Bush	0.992
Skinner J	0.990
Benzinger	0.983
Newson	0.982

Name	Value
Howell Jk	0.958
Cotto	0.941
Williams B	0.937
Gagne	0.901
Gomez L	0.861
Hill D	0.858
Whitt	0.828
McRae B	0.808
Huff	0.761
Allred	0.738
Gonzalez Jo	0.732
Blankenship L	0.728
Incaviglia	0.714
Bichette	0.702
Worthington	0.692
Ortiz	0.691
Bradley S	0.672
Moseby	0.669
Anderson B	0.668
Myers G	0.665
Petralli	0.632
Brock	0.630
Surhoff BJ	0.616
Leyritz	0.607
Gladden	0.605
Sosa	0.602
Weiss	0.595
Hoiles	0.595
Geren	0.586
Munoz P	0.578
Hill G	0.576
Borders	0.576
Barnes	0.576
Newman A	0.574
Martinez Crl	0.546
Martinez Crm	0.532
Pettis	0.522
Karkovice	0.518
Sprague	0.509
Parker D	0.505
Evans Dw	0.453
Sveum	0.448
Law V	0.447
Winfield	0.439
Wilson M	0.430
Fermin	0.429
Tabler	0.427
Riles	0.427
Downing	0.422
Fletcher S	0.412
Steinbach	0.407
Pena T	0.402
Hulett	0.393
Venable	0.391
Wilson W	0.391
Valle	0.388
Velarde	0.338
Thurman	0.333
Mulliniks	0.330
Jones Tr	0.316
Stevens	0.306
Sheridan	0.304
Naehring	0.304
Meulens	0.292
Stanley M	0.261
Mayne	0.257
Bergman	0.256
Gantner	0.236
Cochrane	0.231
Livingstone	0.231
Lyons S	0.229
Romine	0.222
Ward T	0.198
Cromartie	0.197
Thome	0.191
Vaughn M	0.178
Manto	0.166
Abner	0.155
Rose	0.148
Rodriguez I	0.148
Ducey	0.143
Powell A	0.143
Huson	0.138
Griffey	0.135
Segui	0.132
Kelly P	0.121
Marzano	0.121
Lee M	0.108
Diaz Mar	0.092
Cora	0.089
Schaefer	0.084
Orton	0.065
Canale	0.030
Martinez Tino	0.028
Dempsey	0.022
Tingley	0.020
Brosius	0.014

American League

Base Stealing Profit

SB + PkOE - 2(CS + PKO) = Net

	SB	PkOE	CS	PkO	Net
Henderson R	58	10	18	1	32.72
Alomar R	53	4	11	3	31.00
Raines	51	5	15	1	26.29
Cuyler	41	3	10	0	25.43
Franco Ju	36	4	9	3	17.71
Reynolds H	28	4	8	1	15.29
Sax S	31	4	11	0	14.57
Canseco	26	2	6	2	13.14
Knoblauch	25	1	5	2	13.00
Johnson L	26	6	11	0	11.57
White D	33	4	10	4	11.00
Gibson K	18	2	4	1	10.71
Sierra	16	2	4	0	10.57
Trammell	11	0	2	0	7.29
Moseby	8	1	1	0	7.14
Stubbs	13	1	4	0	6.57
Kelly P	12	0	1	2	6.43
Griffey Jr	18	1	6	1	6.00
Molitor	19	1	8	0	5.14
Ripken C	6	1	1	0	5.14
Pettis	29	2	13	1	5.00
Carter J	20	3	9	1	4.43
Winfield	7	1	2	0	4.29
Vizquel	7	1	2	0	4.29
Lee M	7	1	2	0	4.29
Greenwell	15	2	5	2	4.00
Pecota	16	1	7	0	4.00
Maas	5	0	1	0	3.14
Grebeck	0	3	0	0	3.00
Phillips	0	3	0	0	3.00
Kelly	0	3	0	0	3.00
Polonia	48	5	23	4	2.86
McRae B	20	5	11	1	2.71
Huson	8	2	3	1	2.57
Bichette	14	5	8	1	2.29
Orsulak	6	0	2	0	2.29
Espinoza	4	0	1	0	2.14
Anderson B	0	2	0	0	2.00
Quintana	1	1	0	0	2.00

	SB	PkOE	CS	PkO	Net
Joyner	2	0	0	0	2.00
Brett	2	0	0	0	2.00
Mattingly	2	0	0	0	2.00
Cotto	0	2	0	0	2.00
Briley	23	1	11	1	1.71
Puckett	11	0	5	0	1.71
Schofield	8	1	4	0	1.57
Tartabull	6	1	3	0	1.43
Sojo	4	1	2	0	1.29
Gallagher	0	1	0	0	1.00
Lyons S	0	1	0	0	1.00
Martinez Crl	0	1	0	0	1.00
Macfarlane	1	0	0	0	1.00
Brock	0	1	0	0	1.00
Sheffield	0	1	0	0	1.00
Larkin G	0	1	0	0	1.00
Leius	0	1	0	0	1.00
Barfield Je	1	0	0	0	1.00
Hemond	0	1	0	0	1.00
Petralli	0	1	0	0	1.00
Martinez C	0	1	0	0	1.00
Housie	0	1	0	0	1.00
Abner	0	1	0	0	1.00
Cora	0	1	0	0	1.00
Gonzalez Jo	0	1	0	0	1.00
Humphreys	0	1	0	0	1.00
Powell A	0	1	0	0	1.00
Sprague	0	1	0	0	1.00
Fryman T	12	0	5	1	0.86
Devereaux	16	5	9	2	0.57
Pena T	8	0	3	1	0.57
Nokes	3	1	2	0	0.29
Whitaker	4	0	2	0	0.29
Randolph	4	0	2	0	0.29
Sosa	13	2	6	2	0.14
Thurman	0	2	0	1	0.14
McGwire	2	0	1	0	0.14
Thome	1	1	1	0	0.14
Baerga	3	0	2	0	-0.71

	SB	PkOE	CS	PkO	Net
Belle	3	0	1	1	-0.71
Spiers	13	1	8	0	-0.86
Gruber	12	2	7	1	-0.86
Gomez L	1	0	1	0	-0.86
Downing	1	0	1	0	-0.86
Browne J	0	1	0	1	-0.86
Newman A	0	1	0	1	-0.86
Hall M	0	1	1	0	-0.86
Meulens	0	1	0	1	-0.86
Kirby	0	1	0	1	-0.86
Williams B	10	2	5	2	-1.00
Rivera L	4	2	4	0	-1.43
Yount	6	0	4	0	-1.43
Palmeiro	4	0	3	0	-1.57
Mack	13	2	9	0	-1.71
Steinbach	2	0	2	0	-1.71
Ripken B	0	0	1	0	-1.86
Parrish Ln	0	0	1	0	-1.86
Venable	0	0	0	1	-1.86
McCray	0	0	0	1	-1.86
Jacoby	0	0	1	0	-1.86
Webster M	0	0	0	1	-1.86
Maldonado	0	0	0	1	-1.86
Williams K	0	0	0	1	-1.86
Leyritz	0	0	0	1	-1.86
Baines	0	0	1	0	-1.86
O'Brien P	0	0	1	0	-1.86
Buhner	0	0	1	0	-1.86
Borders	0	0	0	1	-1.86
Hill G	0	0	0	1	-1.86
Davis G	0	0	0	1	-1.86
Martinez Crm	0	0	0	1	-1.86
Brown J	0	0	0	1	-1.86
Rodriguez I	0	0	1	0	-1.86
Gaetti	5	2	5	0	-2.29
Tettleton	3	0	3	0	-2.57
Parker D	3	0	2	1	-2.57
Vaughn G	2	1	2	1	-2.57
Riles	3	0	2	1	-2.57
Boggs W	1	0	2	0	-2.71
Brunansky	1	0	2	0	-2.71
Fisk	1	0	2	0	-2.71

	SB	PkOE	CS	PkO	Net
Harper B	1	0	2	0	-2.71
Huff	0	1	0	2	-2.71
Pagliarulo	1	0	2	0	-2.71
Reed Jd	6	0	5	0	-3.29
Stillwell	3	1	4	0	-3.43
Hrbek	4	0	4	0	-3.43
Bordick	3	1	4	0	-3.43
Gonzalez Juan	4	0	4	0	-3.43
Evans Dw	2	0	3	0	-3.57
Incaviglia	1	1	3	0	-3.57
Gagne	11	2	9	0	-3.71
Hoiles	0	0	2	0	-3.71
Fletcher S	0	0	2	0	-3.71
Skinner J	0	0	2	0	-3.71
Valle	0	0	2	0	-3.71
Olerud	0	0	2	0	-3.71
Guillen	21	3	15	0	-3.86
Felix	7	0	5	1	-4.14
Shumpert	17	1	11	1	-4.29
Fermin	5	0	4	1	-4.29
James C	3	0	4	0	-4.43
Thomas F	1	0	2	1	-4.57
Deer	1	0	3	0	-4.57
Hamilton	0	1	0	3	-4.57
Clark Jk	0	1	2	1	-4.57
Ventura	2	0	4	0	-5.43
Pasqua	0	0	2	1	-5.57
Henderson D	6	1	6	1	-6.00
Cole	27	4	17	3	-6.14
Gladden	15	1	9	3	-6.29
Martinez E	0	1	3	1	-6.43
Davis C	5	1	6	1	-7.00
Whiten	4	0	3	3	-7.14
Davis A	0	0	3	1	-7.43
Buechele	0	0	4	0	-7.43
Gantner	4	0	6	1	-9.00
Gallego	6	1	9	0	-9.71
Surhoff BJ	5	0	8	0	-9.86
Benzinger	2	1	6	1	-10.00
Milligan	0	0	5	2	-13.00
Burks	6	1	11	1	-15.29

National League

Base Stealing Profit

SB + PkOE - 2(CS + PKO) = Net

	SB	PkOE	CS	PkO	Net
Grissom	76	3	17	0	47.43
Bonds	42	7	13	0	24.86
Dykstra	24	2	4	0	18.57
Lankford	44	13	20	2	16.14
Jefferies	26	3	5	2	16.00
Smith O	35	5	9	5	14.00
Larkin B	24	0	6	0	12.86
Dunston	21	2	6	0	11.86
DeShields	56	4	23	3	11.72
Davis E	14	1	2	0	11.29
Biggio	19	2	6	0	9.86
Coleman	37	2	14	2	9.29
Roberts Bip	26	3	11	0	8.57
Sandberg	22	5	8	2	8.43
Samuel	23	0	8	0	8.14
Kruk	7	1	0	0	8.00
Harris L	12	1	3	0	7.43
Morandini	13	0	2	1	7.43
Van Slyke	10	1	2	0	7.29
Finley S	34	6	18	0	6.57
Varsho	9	1	2	0	6.29
Pendleton	10	1	2	1	5.43
Murray E	10	1	3	0	5.43
Gant	34	1	15	1	5.29
Daniels	6	1	1	0	5.14
Daulton	5	0	0	0	5.00
Hudler	0	5	0	0	5.00
Fernandez T	23	0	9	1	4.43
Candaele	9	1	3	0	4.43
Calderon	31	4	16	1	3.43
Johnson H	30	5	16	1	3.43
Sabo	19	1	6	3	3.29
Nixon O	0	5	0	1	3.14
Thompson Ro	14	2	7	0	3.00
Mitchell Kth	0	3	0	0	3.00
Perry G	0	3	0	0	3.00
Morris H	10	0	4	0	2.57
Walton	7	1	3	0	2.43
McGriff F	4	0	1	0	2.14
Walker C	0	2	0	0	2.00
Ramirez R	0	2	0	0	2.00
Young G	0	2	0	0	2.00
Sharperson	0	2	0	0	2.00
Miller K	0	2	0	0	2.00
Howard T	0	2	0	0	2.00
Abner	0	2	0	0	2.00
Felder	0	2	0	0	2.00
Thon	11	2	5	1	1.86
Chamberlain	9	0	4	0	1.57
Bass K	7	2	4	0	1.57
Guerrero	4	1	2	0	1.29
Belliard	3	0	1	0	1.14
Dascenzo	0	3	0	1	1.14
Brooks	3	0	1	0	1.14
Redus	0	3	0	1	1.14
Lewis D	0	3	0	1	1.14
Berryhill	0	1	0	0	1.00
Cabrera	0	1	0	0	1.00
Scott G	0	1	0	0	1.00
Duncan	0	1	0	0	1.00
Goodwin	0	1	0	0	1.00
Templeton	0	1	0	0	1.00
Herr	0	1	0	0	1.00
Murphy Dl	1	0	0	0	1.00
Ward K	0	1	0	0	1.00
Litton	0	1	0	0	1.00
Smith Lo	9	1	5	0	0.71
McGee	17	4	9	2	0.57
Clark W	4	0	2	0	0.29
LaValliere	2	0	1	0	0.14
Clark Je	2	0	1	0	0.14
Merced	8	1	4	1	-0.29
Bagwell	7	0	4	0	-0.43
Lind	7	0	4	0	-0.43
Scioscia	4	1	3	0	-0.57
Jackson Dar	5	0	3	0	-0.57

	SB	PkOE	CS	PkO	Net
O'Neill	12	2	7	1	-0.86
Olson Greg	1	0	1	0	-0.86
Landrum C	0	1	0	1	-0.86
Quinones L	0	1	0	1	-0.86
McLemore	0	1	0	1	-0.86
Bullock	0	1	0	1	-0.86
Cerone	1	0	1	0	-0.86
Magadan	1	0	1	0	-0.86
Carreon	0	1	0	1	-0.86
Morris Jn	0	1	0	1	-0.86
Pena G	0	1	0	1	-0.86
Gonzalez L	10	2	7	0	-1.00
Hayes C	3	1	3	0	-1.57
Hatcher B	11	4	9	0	-1.71
Treadway	2	0	2	0	-1.71
Rhodes	2	0	2	0	-1.71
Reed Jf	0	0	1	0	-1.86
Sanders R	0	0	0	1	-1.86
Servais	0	0	0	1	-1.86
Tolentino	0	0	0	1	-1.86
Lofton	0	0	0	1	-1.86
Carter G	0	0	0	1	-1.86
Noboa	0	0	0	1	-1.86
Jordan	0	0	0	1	-1.86
McClendon	0	0	0	1	-1.86
Jones Tim	0	0	0	1	-1.86
Jose	20	4	12	2	-2.00
Zeile	17	3	11	1	-2.29
Doran	5	0	4	0	-2.43
Griffin Alf	5	0	4	0	-2.43
Gilkey	14	2	8	2	-2.57
Wilkins R	3	0	3	0	-2.57
Elster	2	1	3	0	-2.57

	SB	PkOE	CS	PkO	Net
Mitchell K	2	1	3	0	-2.57
Ortiz Ja	0	1	0	2	-2.71
Oquendo	1	0	2	0	-2.71
Thompson M	0	1	0	2	-2.71
Williams MD	5	1	5	0	-3.29
Walker L	14	3	9	2	-3.43
Strawberry	10	3	8	1	-3.71
Blauser	0	0	0	2	-3.71
Backman	0	0	0	2	-3.71
Decker S	0	0	1	1	-3.71
Bell Jay	10	1	6	2	-3.86
McReynolds	6	1	6	0	-4.14
Dawson	4	1	5	0	-4.29
Caminiti	4	1	5	0	-4.29
Grace	3	0	4	0	-4.43
Reyes	2	1	4	0	-4.43
Wallach	2	1	4	0	-4.43
Yelding	11	3	9	1	-4.57
Salazar L	0	1	3	0	-4.57
Justice	8	2	8	0	-4.86
Bonilla B	2	0	4	0	-5.43
Coolbaugh	0	0	3	0	-5.57
Galarraga	5	0	6	0	-6.14
Owen S	2	3	6	0	-6.14
Uribe	3	0	4	1	-6.29
Martinez Da	0	1	0	4	-6.43
Bell Geo	2	2	6	0	-7.14
Bream	0	0	3	1	-7.43
Gwynn T	8	1	8	1	-7.71
Santiago	8	3	10	1	-9.43
Butler	38	6	28	2	-11.71
Pagnozzi	9	1	13	0	-14.14

American League

Top Tens

Ballpark Adjusted

Runs

Player	Runs
Molitor	134
Canseco	117
Palmeiro	111
White D	108
Henderson R	107
Fielder	106
Sierra	105
Franco Ju	103
Thomas F	101
Ripken C	100

Home Runs

Canseco	46
Fielder	40
Belle	39
Ripken C	35
Tartabull	35
Thomas F	30
Tettleton	29
Davis C	29
Gonzalez Juan	28
Buhner	27

Slugging Pct

Tartabull	.604
Ripken C	.590
Canseco	.576
Thomas F	.541
Palmeiro	.537
Griffey Jr	.531
Baines	.507
Joyner	.507
Fielder	.498
Sierra	.498

Strikeouts

Johnson R	228
Clemens	221
McDowell J	181
Appier	166
Candiotti	165
Guzman	160
Langston	159
Abbott	159
Morris Jk	157
Gordon	150

Hits

Player	Hits
Molitor	224
Ripken C	208
Palmeiro	202
Sierra	195
Sax S	193
Franco Ju	191
Puckett	187
Alomar R	187
Polonia	183
White D	180

Runs Batted In

Fielder	132
Canseco	128
Sierra	112
Ripken C	111
Griffey Jr	107
Thomas F	106
Tartabull	105
Joyner	103
Ventura	103
Carter J	101

On-Base Ave

Thomas F	.449
Randolph	.425
Griffey Jr	.412
Martinez E	.412
Boggs W	.405
Franco Ju	.403
Henderson R	.402
Baines	.400
Palmeiro	.399
Tartabull	.396

Walks Allowed

Johnson R	158
Stewart D	117
Guzman	109
Hough	104
Moore M	102
Finley C	101
Langston	101
Fernandez A	101
Morris Jk	98
Welch	95

Doubles

Palmeiro	48
Ripken C	45
Brett	42
Sierra	42
Carter J	42
Fryman T	41
Griffey Jr	41
Reed Jd	40
Alomar R	40
White D	39

Walks

Thomas F	132
Tettleton	100
Davis C	98
Henderson R	97
Clark Jk	93
McGwire	92
Ventura	89
Deer	89
Whitaker	88
Martinez E	83

Offensive WPct

Player	WPct
Thomas F	.818
Tartabull	.804
Griffey Jr	.792
Ripken C	.775
Joyner	.759
Martinez E	.750
Molitor	.725
Baines	.723
Palmeiro	.722
Canseco	.716

Run Support/9 IP

August	6.64
Rogers	6.24
Gardiner	6.23
Stewart D	6.13
Leiter M	6.01
Guzman J	5.97
Gullickson	5.81
Erickson S	5.74
McDowell J	5.53
Delucia	5.49

Triples

Molitor	16
Devereaux	14
Johnson L	13
Anderson B	11
Alomar R	11
White D	10
Greenwell	9
Cuyler	8
Ripken C	7
Polonia	7

Batting Ave

Franco Ju	.339
Palmeiro	.331
Ripken C	.330
Randolph	.329
Griffey Jr	.328
Molitor	.326
Martinez E	.321
Joyner	.317
Tartabull	.316
Thomas F	.316

Defensive WPct

Player	WPct
Davis C	1.001
Phillips	.737
Johnson L	.728
Raines	.721
White D	.679
Henderson D	.667
Gaetti	.646
Ripken C	.636
Henderson R	.635
McGwire	.624

Strikeouts/Walks

Sanderson	5.65
Swindell	5.00
Nichols Rod	4.39
Clemens	3.68
Saberhagen	3.65
Tapani	3.64
Key	3.40
Ward D	3.03
McDowell J	2.59
Appier	2.55

National League

Top Tens

Ballpark Adjusted

Runs

Butler	115
Johnson H	112
Smith O	107
Bonilla B	103
Bonds	101
Sandberg	98
Lankford	97
Bell Jay	95
Van Slyke	94
Finley S	91

Home Runs

Johnson H	41
Williams MD	35
Clark W	29
Mitchell K	28
Strawberry	27
McGriff F	27
Gant	26
Dawson	25
Bonds	25
Sabo	22

Slugging Pct

Clark W	.548
Johnson H	.530
Bonds	.527
Williams MD	.510
Bonilla B	.495
McGriff F	.489
Pendleton	.484
Strawberry	.483
Kruk	.482
Larkin B	.478

Strikeouts

Cone	245
Glavine	222
Maddux G	206
Rijo	192
Benes	149
Harnisch	145
Leibrandt	143
Avery	141
Martinez De	140
Morgan M	138

Hits

Jose	190
Butler	181
Sabo	177
Pendleton	176
Finley S	175
Bonilla B	174
Smith O	172
Zeile	171
Clark W	171
Samuel	170

Runs Batted In

Johnson H	123
Clark W	121
Bonds	115
McGriff F	109
Dawson	102
Williams MD	102
Strawberry	101
Bonilla B	101
Sandberg	98
Murray E	98

On-Base Ave

Bonds	.426
Bonilla B	.402
Butler	.395
McGriff F	.394
Sandberg	.391
Bagwell	.384
Magadan	.383
Smith O	.383
Clark W	.371
Kruk	.368

Walks Allowed

DeJesus J	144
Barnes B	100
Harnisch	95
Smoltz	87
Deshaies	87
Gardner M	87
Belcher	80
Glavine	79
Kile	79
Martinez De	78

Doubles

Bonilla B	44
Jose	42
Johnson H	36
Sandberg	35
Bonds	35
Zeile	35
O'Neill	34
McReynolds	34
Murphy Dl	34
Pendleton	33

Walks

Bonds	115
Butler	107
Sandberg	97
Magadan	92
Bonilla B	92
McGriff F	91
Smith O	86
Johnson H	82
DeShields	79
Bagwell	77

Offensive WPct

Bonds	.801
Clark W	.786
McGriff F	.764
Bonilla B	.750
Kruk	.734
Bagwell	.731
Larkin B	.722
Strawberry	.720
Johnson H	.713
Sandberg	.705

Run Support/9 IP

Hershiser	6.19
Walk	5.71
Rijo	5.64
Smith B	5.48
Whitehurst	5.40
Avery	5.39
Cox	5.28
Downs	5.16
Smith Z	5.13
Gooden	5.12

Triples

Samuel	13
Lankford	12
Gwynn T	12
Kruk	9
Pendleton	8
Clark W	8
Grace	7
Dunston	7
Finley S	7
Dykstra	7

Batting Ave

Gwynn T	.326
McGee	.320
Jose	.313
Clark W	.311
Bonilla B	.305
Pendleton	.305
Morris H	.303
Biggio	.298
Bagwell	.298
Bonds	.297

Defensive WPct

Grace	.709
O'Neill	.695
Bonds	.669
Thompson Ro	.636
Jose	.628
Pendleton	.624
Lind	.624
Murray E	.610
Magadan	.590
Clark W	.590

Strikeouts/Walks

Rijo	4.57
Smith Z	3.62
Whitehurst	3.44
Smiley	3.40
Maddux G	3.38
Cone	3.36
Hershiser	3.27
Benes	3.04
Harris GW	3.03
Mulholland	2.84

Sabermetricians'

Hall of Fame Poll

Brock J. Hanke

I thought we'd get hundreds of responses to the Hall of Fame Poll. I guess I didn't comprehend how much work it is to research all of baseball history. We got ten. However, we got some of them very late, just making it into the book. Also, the ones we have received have been great. One person thought himself obligated to assign at least one point to every player, which is contrry to the instructions, but that did provide a baseline. Anyway, here are the preliminary results, just copied down on a copy of the ballot. The numbers are the average numbers of votes for the players, as if you couldn't guess. It's easy to divide by ten.

Because we've only received ten polls, and because some people sent them in so late, I think there might be more potential voters out there. So I'm giving you another year to vote. There's no copy of the ballot here, so you'll have to find your copy of last year's book, but you can still vote. If you don't have last year's book, and don't want to order it, but do want to vote, send me a letter, and I'll send you a ballot, complete with instructions.

Once again, I'd like to thank Tom Hull for his maniacal work in putting htis thing together. Tom, your dedication is unmatched.

Baseball Sabermetric Hall of Fame Ballot

Rate the following players on a scale from 0 to 10 points.

1871–1879 P	2.2 Jim Devlin	3.8 Tommy Bond	1.6 George Bradley	3.1 Bobby Mathews
6 Al Spalding	3.2 Candy Cummings	2.1 Dick McBride	1.5 George Zettlein	
1871–1879 C	1.9 Pop Snyder	1.8 John Clapp	3.3 Cal McVey	
1871–1879 1B	7.9 Cap Anson	1.6 Tom York	2.4 Joe Start	
1871–1879 2B	2.4 Joe Gerhardt	1.6 Jack Burdock	4.5 Ross Barnes	
1871–1879 SS	4 George Wright	1.8 John Peters	1.9 Davy Force	
1871–1879 3B	3.1 Ezra Sutton	4.6 Deacon White	1.6 Bob Ferguson	3.1 Levi Meyerle
1871–1879 OF	5.3 Charley Jones	5.3 Paul Hines	6.1 Jim O'Rourke	2.5 Orator Shaffer
1.2 George Hall	4.3 Lip Pike	1.3 Dick Higham	.8 Dave Eggler	2 Andy Leonard
1880–1889 P	6.9 John Clarkson	8.3 Tim Keefe	1.5 Tony Mullane	7.1 Charley Radbourn
6.2 Bob Caruthers	4.8 Silver King	4.6 Guy Hecker	6.1 Charlie Buffinton	5.3 Jim Galvin
5 Jim McCormick	2.8 Jim Whitney	5 Mickey Welch	4.4 Dave Foutz	2.2 Charlie Ferguson
2.6 Larry Corcoran	4.2 Will White	1.1 Toad Ramsey	3.4 Matt Kilroy	1.9 Ed Morris
1.6 Adonis Terry	2 Pretzels Getzien			
1880–1889 C	6.8 Buck Ewing	4.8 Charlie Bennett	1.8 Jocko Milligan	2.3 Fred Carroll
1.6 Pop Smith	1.6 Silver Flint			
1880–1889 1B	7.6 Dan Brouthers	7.1 Roger Connor	3.0 Dave Orr	3.3 Henry Larkin
1.7 John Reilly	.7 Charlie Comiskey			
1880–1889 2B	6.8 Bid McPhee	5.1 Fred Dunlap	5.6 Hardy Richardson	3.5 Fred Pfeffer
2.6 Danny Richardson	1.3 Hub Collins	.3 Joe Quinn		
1880–1889 SS	7.2 Jack Glasscock	2.2 Sam Wise	4.5 Germany Smith	.7 Frank Fennelly
5.1 Monte Ward	1.5 Tom Burns			
1880–1889 3B	4.9 Denny Lyons	3.6 Ned Williamson	1.5 Jerry Denny	3 Arlie Latham
1880–1889 OF	6.6 Pete Browning	6 King Kelly	6.5 Harry Stovey	3.6 George Gore
4.1 Tip O'Neill	2.4 George Wood	3.2 Oyster Burns	1.4 Ed Swartwood	2.9 Chicken Wolf
2 Curt Welch	1.2 Abner Dalrymple	1.4 Tommy McCarthy	1.9 Tom Brown	
1890–1899 P	9 Cy Young	9.4 Kid Nichols	8.1 Amos Rusie	4.5 Jack Stivetts
5.1 Clark Griffith	4 Nig Cuppy	3 Frank Dwyer	2.5 Ted Breitenstein	3 Frank Killen
2.7 Sadie McMahon	2.5 Bill Hutchinson	1.8 Pink Hawley	2.1 Icebox Chamberlain	1.3 Mark Baldwin
1.8 Billy Rhines	2 Nixey Callahan	1.2 Brickyard Kennedy	1.4 Jouett Meekin	1.9 Gus Weyhing
1.4 Red Donahue	1.3 Bill Hoffer	1.6 Jim Hughes	.8 George Haddock	
1890–1899 C	4.7 Deacon McGuire	4.1 Duke Farrell	3 Jack Clements	2.3 Chief Zimmer
1.7 Ed McFarland	.8 Heinie Peitz	1.5 Wilbert Robinson		
1890–1899 1B	6 Jake Beckley	1.6 Jack Doyle	1.3 Perry Werden	.9 Tommy Tucker
1890–1899 2B	6.7 Cupid Childs	3.6 Tom Daly	1 Lou Bierbauer	1.4 Gene DeMontreville
1.9 Bobby Lowe	1.6 Kid Gleason			
1890–1899 SS	8.1 George Davis	6.4 Bill Dahlen	6.5 Hughie Jennings	3.3 Herman Long
2.9 Ed McKean	.7 Monte Cross	1.4 Tommy Corcoran		
1890–1899 3B	4.3 Bill Joyce	4.2 Lave Cross	5.7 John McGraw	4.1 Billy Nash
1.3 Billy Shindle				
1890–1899 OF	9.1 Ed Delahanty	7.1 Jesse Burkett	6.9 Sam Thompson	6.6 Billy Hamilton
4.8 Joe Kelley	3.8 Mike Griffin	4.5 Jimmy Ryan	4.4 George Van Haltren	5.6 Willie Keeler
4.1 Mike Tiernan	2.6 Mike Smith	2.4 Kip Selbach	4.1 Hugh Duffy	3.5 Bill Lange
2.3 Dummy Hoy	1.5 Jake Stenzel	.6 Bug Holliday	.5 Patsy Donovan	
1900–1909 P	9.5 Christy Mathewson	7.9 Ed Walsh	8.3 Mordecai Brown	6.3 Rube Waddell
5.6 Addie Joss	7.1 Eddie Plank	4.6 Jesse Tannehill	6.1 Joe McGinnity	5.3 Vic Willis
5 Ed Reulbach	3.6 George Mullin	3.6 Doc White	3.4 Noodles Hahn	4.4 Deacon Phillippe
2.6 Harry Howell	1.8 Al Orth	2.4 Jack Taylor	3.6 Sam Leever	3.5 Chief Bender
3.1 Jack Chesbro	1.8 Bill Dinneen	1.4 Red Ames	.8 Earl Moore	2 Jack Powell
1.6 Orval Overall	1.1 Frank Smith	1.1 Lcfty Leifield	1.4 Jack Pfiester	1.7 Hooks Wiltse
1.6 Ed Killian	1.3 Howie Camnitz	1.1 Bill Donovan		
1900–1909 C	5.5 Roger Bresnahan	3.3 Johnny Kling	2.4 Ossee Schreckengost	1.5 Lou Criger
1900–1909 1B	3.9 Fred Tenney	3.7 Harry Davis	4.9 Frank Chance	1.4 Charlie Hickman
.8 Dan McGann				
1900–1909 2B	9.8 Nap Lajoie	4.6 Johnny Evers	4.2 Miller Huggins	2.3 Jimmy Williams
1.5 Claude Ritchey	1.9 Danny Murphy	2.4 Jim Delahanty		
1900–1909 SS	9.8 Honus Wagner	6.9 Bobby Wallace	4.6 Joe Tinker	2.2 Kid Elberfeld
1.9 George McBride	1.1 Freddy Parent			
1900–1909 3B	6.6 Jimmy Collins	4.1 Tommy Leach	2.9 Bill Bradley	3 Art Devlin
2.1 Harry Steinfeldt	1.1 Sammy Strang	1.4 Wid Conroy	2.6 Hans Lobert	
1900–1909 OF	6.3 Sherry Magee	6.3 Elmer Flick	5.7 Fred Clarke	7.6 Sam Crawford
4.5 Jimmy Sheckard	4.5 Roy Thomas	3.5 Cy Seymour	3.9 Mike Donlin	1.9 George Stone
3 Ginger Beaumont	2.1 Topsy Hartsel	3.2 John Titus	2.8 John Anderson	2.1 Buck Freeman
2.5 Frank Schulte	1.1 Fielder Jones			
1910–1919 P	10 Walter Johnson	9.1 Pete Alexander	5.7 Eppa Rixey	6.8 Stan Coveleski
4.2 Jack Quinn	5.4 Eddie Cicotte	3.8 Babe Adams	3.6 Wilbur Cooper	4.8 Hippo Vaughn
5.1 Joe Wood	2.8 Claude Hendrix	1.8 Joe Bush	1.5 Russ Ford	1.7 Jeff Pfeffer
1.8 Slim Sallee	2.3 Nap Rucker	1.9 Sherry Smith	1.4 Bill Doak	1.9 Hooks Dauss

2.6 Rube Marquard
1.4 Jim Scott
2.2 Jack Coombs
1910–1919 C
2.7 Ray Schalk
1910–1919 1B
1.7 Hal Chase
1910–1919 2B
.6 Bill Wambsganss
1910–1919 SS
2.8 Roger Peckinpaugh
1910–1919 3B
2.7 Larry Gardner
1910–1919 OF
6 Zack Wheat
3.7 George Burns
1 Tilly Walker
1920–1929 P
4.3 Dolf Luque
2.8 George Uhle
1.1 Howard Ehmke
1.3 Red Lucas
1.3 Guy Bush
1920–1929 C
1 Jimmy Wilson
1920–1929 1B
1.7 Joe Judge
1920–1929 2B
1.2 Max Bishop
1920–1929 SS
1920–1929 3B
1.6 Ossie Bluege
1920–1929 OF
5 Kiki Cuyler
3.7 Chick Hafey
.9 Curt Walker
1.4 Bing Miller
1930–1939 P
6.1 Red Ruffing
3 Curt Davis
2.6 Larry French
1.7 Van Mungo
1.6 Monte Pearson
2.2 Johnny Murphy
1930–1939 C
1 Frankie Hayes
1930–1939 1B
2.5 Phil Cavaretta
1930–1939 2B
4.1 Buddy Myer
1930–1939 SS
1.7 Billy Jurges
1930–1939 3B
2.4 Pepper Martin
1930–1939 OF
6.7 Joe Medwick
2.8 Ben Chapman
2 Joe Vosmik
1940–1949 P
4.8 Harry Brecheen
3.1 Eddie Lopat
1.5 Fred Hutchinson
1 Joe Dobson
.9 Rip Sewell
1.1 Hugh Casey
1940–1949 C
1940–1949 1B
1.6 George McQuinn
1940–1949 2B
1.2 Jerry Priddy
1940–1949 SS

1.6 Jim Bagby
1.6 Dutch Leonard
1.1 Rube Benton
4.9 Wally Schang
2 Hank Severeid
4.3 Ed Konetchy
3.2 Stuffy McInnis
9.9 Eddie Collins
.7 George Cutshaw
4.3 Art Fletcher
.8 Everett Scott
7.6 Frank Baker
2.2 Jimmy Austin
9.9 Ty Cobb
5.3 Edd Roush
3.6 Cy Williams
1.5 Dode Paskert
7 Ted Lyons
5.8 Red Faber
4.5 Herb Pennock
1 Lee Meadows
1.7 Ray Kremer
.9 Bill Sherdel
7.3 Gabby Hartnett
2.1 Luke Sewell
9.7 Lou Gehrig
2.3 George Kelly
9.8 Rogers Hornsby
2 George Grantham
6.8 Joe Sewell
6.3 Pie Traynor
10 Babe Ruth
4.8 Ken Williams
3.3 Earle Combs
2.4 Bob Meusel
1.1 Bob Fothergill
9.7 Lefty Grove
5.3 Tommy Bridges
6 Lefty Gomez
.9 Bump Hadley
1.9 Charlie Root
1.4 Pat Malone
2.1 George Earnshaw
7.3 Bill Dickey
2.2 Spud Davis
9.5 Jimmie Foxx
1.5 Ripper Collins
7.3 Billy Herman
1.2 Johnny Hodapp
8.1 Arky Vaughan
1.7 Woody English
5.6 Stan Hack
2.4 Mike Higgins
9 Mel Ott
5.4 Earl Averill
2.9 Cecil Travis
2.7 Lloyd Waner
7 Hal Newhouser
4 Dutch Leonard
2.9 Virgil Trucks
1.6 Al Benton
2 Preacher Roe
.6 Harry Gumbert
2.2 Joe Page
4.9 Walker Cooper
7.5 Johnny Mize
7.6 Bobby Doerr
6.2 Lou Boudreau

2.1 Jeff Tesreau
1.2 Doc Crandall
1.6 Hank Gowdy
2.5 Frank Snyder
3.8 Jack Fournier
3.2 Fred Merkle
4 Del Pratt
4.2 Rabbit Maranville
2.9 Jack Barry
3.8 Heinie Groh
2.8 Milt Stock
7.7 Tris Speaker
4.0 Gavvy Cravath
1.1 Johnny Bates
2.8 Duffy Lewis
5.3 Carl Mays
3.5 Eddie Rommel
2.6 Sam Jones
3.2 Firpo Marberry
1.9 Art Nehf
1 Pete Donohue
2.1 Bob O'Farrell
1 Moe Berg
7.1 George Sisler
2.4 George Burns
7.9 Charlie Gehringer
1.9 Bucky Harris
5.7 Dave Bancroft
2.7 Willie Kamm
7.8 Al Simmons
5 Hack Wilson
2.1 Riggs Stephenson
1.0 Irish Meusel
4.1 Carl Hubbell
4.4 Lon Warneke
6.6 Dizzy Dean
1.5 Bobo Newsom
2.1 Johnny Allen
.8 Clint Brown
1.2 Mace Brown
7.9 Mickey Cochrane
1.2 Babe Phelps
7.7 Hank Greenberg
2.8 Hal Trosky
3.4 Lonny Frey
7 Joe Cronin
1.5 Lyn Lary
5.5 Harlond Clift
2.3 Red Rolfe
7.7 Paul Waner
4.0 Babe Herman
2.6 John Stone
1.7 Gee Walker
4.1 Dizzy Trout
3.9 Spud Chandler
3.5 Howie Pollet
1.9 Johnny Sain
.7 Steve Gromek
1 Tiny Bonham
2.9 Andy Seminick
5.1 Gil Hodges
6.3 Joe Gordon
5.7 Pee Wee Reese

1.6 Larry Cheney
.6 Ray Fisher
.8 Art Wilson
2.1 Steve O'Neill
3 Jake Daubert
1.6 Wally Pipp
3.6 Larry Doyle
3.1 Donie Bush
3.2 Heinie Zimmerman
6.8 Joe Jackson
2.1 Benny Kauff
1.4 Mike Mitchell
1.9 Clyde Milan
6.5 Burleigh Grimes
5.1 Urban Shocker
2.9 Bob Shawkey
2 Jesse Barnes
.7 Rube Walberg
1.3 Earl Whitehill
2.2 Muddy Ruel
7.1 Bill Terry
1.9 Lu Blue
7.9 Frankie Frisch
4.9 Travis Jackson
3.4 Freddy Lindstrom
__ Harry Heilmann
4.6 Heinie Manush
13 Lefty O'Doul
2.9 Charlie Jamieson
2.6 Wes Ferrell
4.3 Fred Fitzsimmons
3 Thornton Lee
3.2 Schoolboy Rowe
1.2 Willis Hudlin
2.4 Joe Heving
5.8 Ernie Lombardi
3.9 Al Lopez
4.8 Dolf Camilli
2 Frank McCormick
5.3 Tony Lazzeri
7 Luke Appling
1.8 Frankie Crosetti
3.1 Billy Werber
7.3 Bob Johnson
5.9 Wally Berger
3.2 George Selkirk
3.2 Doc Cramer
9.1 Bob Feller
4.6 Murry Dickson
1.6 Max Lanier
4.3 Ewell Blackwell
2.4 Johnny Vander Meer
.6 Hank Borowy
2.2 Phil Masi
5.6 Mickey Vernon
3.5 Eddie Stanky
5.9 Phil Rizzuto

2.0 Phil Douglas
2.5 Fred Toney
2.6 Ivey Wingo
2.5 Chief Meyers
3 Fred Luderus
2.5 Buck Herzog
5 Ray Chapman
.9 Red Smith
7.1 Max Carey
2.8 Bobby Veach
7.2 Harry Hooper
.6 Jack Tobin
7.2 Dazzy Vance
4.6 Waite Hoyt
.8 Tom Zachary
2.2 Jesse Haines
.9 Dutch Reuther
1.1 Bubbles Hargrave
4 Jim Bottomley
1.4 Charlie Grimm
2 Marty McManus
2.2 Glenn Wright
3.2 Jimmy Dykes
6.4 Goose Goslin
4 Ross Youngs
3.4 Sam Rice
2.2 Baby Doll Jacobson
5.6 Bucky Walters
4.4 Mel Harder
2.4 Hal Schumacher
1.7 Bill Lee
2.7 Paul Derringer
1.9 General Crowder
3 Rick Ferrell
3.6 Rudy York
1.2 Joe Kuhel
2 Tony Cuccinello
5.7 Dick Bartell
1.7 Pinky Whitney
6.1 Chuck Klein
3 Augie Galan
1.7 Sam West
5.9 Early Wynn
2.7 Claude Passeau
3.1 Mort Cooper
1.6 Tex Hughson
1.1 Al Brazle
2.5 Allie Reynolds
2.4 Jim Hegan
1.2 Elbie Fletcher
1.7 Snuffy Stirnweiss
4.5 Vern Stephens

4.2 Johnny Pesky	2 Eddie Joost	1.9 Eddie Miller	2.5 Marty Marion	
1940–1949 3B	4.5 Bob Elliott	4.6 George Kell	4.1 Ken Keltner	1.7 Whitey Kurowski
3 Eddie Yost	2.3 Buddy Lewis			
1940–1949 OF	10 Ted Williams	9.2 Stan Musial	7.6 Joe DiMaggio	5.5 Charlie Keller
3.2 Roy Cullenbine	5.4 Enos Slaughter	3.2 Bill Nicholson	3.8 Jeff Heath	3.2 Sid Gordon
3.1 Dixie Walker	3.7 Tommy Henrich	2.6 Andy Pafko	1.5 Stan Spence	2.1 Tommy Holmes
2.4 Hank Sauer	1.1 Elmer Valo	3.4 Dom DiMaggio	2.6 Pete Reiser	1.7 Wally Moses
1950–1959 P	9.3 Warren Spahn	7.4 Whitey Ford	6.4 Bob Lemon	7.7 Robin Roberts
7.1 Hoyt Wilhelm	5.3 Billy Pierce	2.9 Curt Simmons	2.8 Bobby Shantz	4.1 Don Newcombe
3.9 Mel Parnell	2.8 Ned Garver	2.6 Johnny Antonelli	2.3 Stu Miller	2.8 Mike Garcia
3.7 Sal Maglie	1.1 Gerry Staley	1.7 Frank Lary	2 Vern Law	1.7 Frank Sullivan
2 Harvey Haddix	1.6 Dick Donovan	1.8 Bob Friend	1.3 Ellis Kinder	1.8 Don Mossi
2.3 Lew Burdette	1.7 Larry Jansen	1.2 Joe Nuxhall	1.9 Johnny Podres	.8 Bill Henry
2.9 Roy Face	1.1 Don Larsen	1.4 Sam Jones	2 Herb Score	1.3 Bob Buhl
2.1 Vic Raschi	2.6 Jim Konstanty	1.5 Carl Erskine		
1950–1959 C	7.9 Yogi Berra	7.4 Roy Campanella	3.3 Smoky Burgess	2.5 Ed Bailey.
2.4 Del Crandall	.9 Stan Lopata	2.9 Sherm Lollar	1.6 Gus Triandos	
1950–1959 1B	3.8 Ferris Fain	3.6 Roy Sievers	1.8 Pete Runnels	2.1 Joe Adcock
1.1 Earl Torgeson	2.7 Bill Skowron	3.5 Ted Kluszewski	1.3 Vic Power	1.3 Whitey Lockman
1950–1959 2B	7.5 Jackie Robinson	5 Red Schoendienst	3.7 Gil McDougald	4.1 Nellie Fox
2 Bobby Avila	3.7 Jim Gilliam	1.4 Billy Goodman	1.5 Frank Bolling	
1950–1959 SS	7.3 Ernie Banks	2.6 Johnny Logan	2.8 Solly Hemus	3.4 Dick Groat
1.1 Woody Held	3.6 Al Dark	2.1 Roy McMillan		
1950–1959 3B	7.4 Eddie Mathews	2.6 Ray Boone	3.8 Al Rosen	1.1 Hank Thompson
1.9 Don Hoak	2.2 Willie Jones			
1950–1959 OF	9.4 Hank Aaron	9.6 Willie Mays	9.8 Mickey Mantle	7.6 Al Kaline
5.6 Richie Ashburn	6.8 Duke Snider	6.1 Ralph Kiner	5.9 Minnie Minoso	5.9 Larry Doby
3 Del Ennis	3.2 Jackie Jensen	2.3 Vic Wertz	2.6 Monte Irvin	2.2 Bobby Thomson
2.7 Harvey Kuenn	3.3 Carl Furillo	1.8 Frank Thomas		
1960–1969 P	8.6 Bob Gibson	7.3 Gaylord Perry	7.1 Don Drysdale	7.5 Juan Marichal
5.2 Jim Kaat	5.3 Jim Bunning	3.2 Larry Jackson	3 Camilo Pascual	7.9 Sandy Koufax
3.5 Mel Stottlemyre	3 Wilbur Wood	2.2 Milt Pappas	2.5 Sam McDowell	3.6 Jim Perry
2 Gary Peters	2.7 Jim Maloney	3.2 Lindy McDaniel	2.1 Claude Osteen	3.8 Mike Cuellar
1.1 Joe Horlen	2.5 Bill Hands	1.7 Sonny Siebert	2.7 Dave McNally	2.5 Dean Chance
1.2 Ted Abernathy	1.2 Don McMahòn	.9 Juan Pizarro	1.1 Bob Veale	3.1 Ron Perranoski
2.1 Denny McLain	1.6 Dick Hall	2.6 Mickey Lolich	1.2 Chris Short	1 Earl Wilson
1.5 Jim Grant	1.8 Al Downing	2.5 Dick Radatz	.9 Ray Sadecki	.9 Jack Sanford
1960–1969 C	5.7 Joe Torre	5 Bill Freehan	4.9 Elston Howard	3.1 Tim McCarver
2 Tom Haller	2.4 Johnny Edwards	2.7 Earl Battey		
1960–1969 1B	7 Willie McCovey	5.9 Dick Allen	8 Harmon Killebrew	6.5 Norm Cash
5 Orlando Cepeda	4.4 Boog Powell	3 Jim Gentile	1.8 Ron Fairly	2.1 Bill White
1960–1969 2B	6.8 Joe Morgan	5.8 Bill Mazeroski	2.4 Ron Hunt	2.4 Dick McAuliffe
1.5 Tony Taylor	2.4 Cookie Rojas	5.7 Bobby Richardson	1.4 Julian Javier	
1960–1969 SS	4.4 Jim Fregosi	2.3 Luis Aparicio	3.7 Maury Wills	2.2 Gene Alley
1.9 Ron Hansen	4.1 Bert Campaneris	4.9 Rico Petrocelli	2.2 Dennis Menke	1.2 Leo Cardenas
1960–1969 3B	7 Ron Santo	3 Brooks Robinson	6.8 Ken Boyer	2.3 Clete Boyer
1 Ken McMullen	1.5 Jim Ray Hart	6.2 Bob Bailey		
1960–1969 OF	9.3 Frank Robinson	2.4 Carl Yastrzemski	8.6 Roberto Clemente	5.4 Jim Wynn
5.5 Rusty Staub	7.6 Willie Stargell	7.5 Pete Rose	6.8 Billy Williams	5.7 Rocky Colavito
6.3 Tony Oliva	5.4 Frank Howard	8.4 Rico Carty	2.7 Johnny Callison	2.3 Don Buford
4.7 Lou Brock	3.3 Vada Pinson	4.3 Bob Allison	2.8 Roger Maris	2.9 Willie Horton
1.6 Felipe Alou	2.3 Willie Davis	2.6 Tony Gonzalez	1.4 Paul Blair	.7 Tommy Harper
1.3 Matty Alou	2.4 Tommy Davis	1.8 Curt Flood		
1970–1979 P	9 Tom Seaver	2.6 Bert Blyleven	8.6 Steve Carlton	7.5 Phil Niekro
8.3 Jim Palmer	7 Ferguson Jenkins	6.4 Tommy John	4.6 Rick Reuschel	3.5 Steve Rogers
6.2 Nolan Ryan	4.3 Luis Tiant	5.8 Don Sutton	3.4 Andy Messersmith	2.6 Jerry Koosman
2.8 Frank Tanana	5 Rich Gossage	1.9 Charlie Hough	4.4 Kent Tekulve	2.8 Vida Blue
1.5 Tom Burgmeier	4.9 Jim Hunter	1.8 Jerry Reuss	2.9 Tug McGraw	1.1 Burt Hooton
2.1 Jon Matlack	2.9 Mike Marshall	2 Clay Carroll	3.3 John Hiller	5.8 Rollie Fingers
4.4 Sparky Lyle	1.2 John Denny	1.6 Gene Garber	1.5 Doyle Alexander	2.1 Ken Holtzman
1.6 Bill Lee	1.5 Rick Wise	1.4 Larry Gura	1.5 Gary Nolan	.9 Terry Forster
1 Rudy May	1.2 Bob Forsch	.7 Randy Jones	.9 Fritz Peterson	1.9 J R Richard
1.3 Dock Ellis	1.5 Dennis Leonard	1.7 Joe Niekro	1.2 Jim Kern	1 Don Gullett
.8 Bill Campbell	5 Paul Splittorff	1.6 Mike Torrez	1.2 Al Hrabosky	1.3 Jim Lonborg
1970–1979 C	7.6 Carlton Fisk	5.7 Ted Simmons	9 Johnny Bench	5.3 Thurman Munson
3.6 Darrell Porter	2.5 Manny Sanguillen	2 Cliff Johnson	2.8 Gene Tenace	1.2 Joe Ferguson
.8 John Stearns	2.8 Bob Boone			
1970–1979 1B	6.1 Keith Hernandez	4.5 Tony Perez	2.5 Andre Thornton	3 Mike Hargrove
2.3 Bob Watson	3.2 Cecil Cooper	2.6 John Mayberry	2.3 Bill Buckner	2.8 Steve Garvey
1.8 Lee May	2 Chris Chambliss			
1970–1979 2B	6.4 Bobby Grich	7.1 Rod Carew	2.6 Davey Lopes	2.2 Dave Cash

2.6 Dave Johnson	1.9 Manny Trillo	2.7 Frank White	1.1 Phil Garner	
1970–1979 SS	4.7 Dave Concepcion	2.6 Freddie Patek	2.2 Mark Belanger	2.9 Rick Burleson
1.5 Chris Speier	3.1 Bill Russell	2.9 Ivan DeJesus	.9 Bud Harrelson	1.4 Larry Bowa
1970–1979 3B	9.9 Mike Schmidt	6.6 George Brett	6.5 Darrell Evans	6.3 Buddy Bell
6 Graig Nettles	4.8 Ron Cey	3.2 Toby Harrah	3 Doug DeCinces	2.7 Bill Madlock
2.4 Sal Bando	1.1 Don Money	2.5 Bill Melton	1.3 Richie Hebner	
1970–1979 OF	8.5 Reggie Jackson	6.2 Dave Winfield	6.5 Reggie Smith	6.2 Bobby Bonds
5.6 Dwight Evans	4.7 Cesar Cedeno	5.4 Jim Rice	5.2 Dave Parker	4.7 George Foster
3.8 Fred Lynn	4 Jose Cruz	4.8 Ken Singleton	3.4 Roy White	3.6 Hal McRae
4.3 Amos Otis	2.7 Brian Downing	2.8 Don Baylor	3.1 Bobby Murcer	2.4 George Hendrick
2.5 Greg Luzinski	1.9 Larry Hisle	2.3 Richie Zisk	1.8 Sixto Lezcano	3.2 Al Oliver
2.1 Oscar Gamble	2 Ken Griffey	2.1 Ben Oglivie	1.6 Jeff Burroughs	1.5 Garry Maddox
1.7 Rick Monday	1.3 Dusty Baker	1.8 Gary Matthews	1.5 Mickey Rivers	1.5 Ron LeFlore
.8 Dave Kingman	1.3 Joe Rudi			
1980–1990 P	5.4 Dave Stieb	6.1 Roger Clemens	4.9 Dennis Eckersley	5.2 Ron Guidry
6 Dan Quisenberry	3.6 Orel Hershiser	3.6 John Tudor	2.6 John Candelaria	2.6 Bob Stanley
3.4 Bret Saberhagen	4.9 Dwight Gooden	3.3 Frank Viola	5.1 Bruce Sutter	4 Fernando Valenzuela
3.2 Jack Morris	2.3 Bob Welch	1 Charlie Leibrandt	1.3 Rick Rhoden	1.1 Mike Boddicker
1.9 Rick Sutcliffe	2.8 Teddy Higuera	1.4 Jimmy Key	1.1 Greg Minton	1.3 Dennis Martinez
1 Mark Gubicza	2.2 Dave Stewart	2.3 Dave Righetti	1.4 Mark Langston	.7 Dan Petry
3.3 Lee Smith	2.7 Willie Hernandez	1.1 Jesse Orosco	1.4 Mike Witt	1.5 Gary Lavelle
.9 Bruce Hurst	2.3 Mike Scott	2 Tom Henke	1.1 Danny Jackson	2.1 Dave Smith
1.3 Mike Flanagan	2.9 Jeff Reardon	.9 Joe Sambito	1.4 Joaquin Andujar	
1980–1990 C	6.7 Gary Carter	4.1 Lance Parrish	3.7 Jim Sundberg	1.4 Tony Pena
1.4 Butch Wynegar	2.7 Mike Scioscia	.6 Terry Kennedy		
1980–1990 1B	6.4 Eddie Murray	4.3 Don Mattingly	4.3 Will Clark	3 Fred McGriff
1.7 Alvin Davis	3.6 Kent Hrbek	1.9 Glenn Davis	2 Mark McGwire	
1980–1990 2B	6 Ryne Sandberg	4.6 Willie Randolph	4.2 Lou Whitaker	2.6 Glenn Hubbard
.7 Tony Bernazard	2.7 Tom Herr			
1980–1990 SS	6.2 Robin Yount	7 Ozzie Smith	6.8 Cal Ripken	5.3 Alan Trammell
3.3 Roy Smalley	3.8 Garry Templeton	2.5 Tony Fernandez	1.6 Dickie Thon	2 Julio Franco
1980–1990 3B	7.8 Wade Boggs	5.4 Paul Molitor	2.4 Tim Wallach	2.6 Howard Johnson
1.5 Bob Horner	3.9 Bobby Bonilla	1.8 Gary Gaetti	1.9 Carney Lansford	
1980–1990 OF	7.4 Rickey Henderson	6.1 Tim Raines	5.5 Jack Clark	5.7 Andre Dawson
4.6 Pedro Guerrero	4.9 Tony Gwynn	4.6 Darryl Strawberry	5.3 Dale Murphy	2.8 Chet Lemon
3 Eric Davis	2.5 Jesse Barfield	3.1 Barry Bonds	2.4 Kirk Gibson	3.6 Kirby Puckett
2.1 Dwayne Murphy	1.8 Lonnie Smith	2 Kevin McReynolds	3.6 Jose Canseco	2.5 Kevin Mitchell
1.1 Kal Daniels	2.1 Brett Butler	2 Andy Van Slyke	1.6 Willie Wilson	2.2 Harold Baines
1.6 Chili Davis	1.1 Lee Mazzilli	.7 Lloyd Moseby	1.4 Phil Bradley	2.1 George Bell
1.5 Willie McGee	2.4 Ruben Sierra			

Write-In Candidates

YOUR NAME:______________________________ AGE:________

STREET ADDRESS:______________________________

____

CITY:____________________ STATE:_____ ZIP:____________

COUNTRY:______________________________

MAIL TO: BBMHOF, 1215 Willow View Drive, Kirkwood, MO 63122

Major League Equivalencies

for
Minor League Players

Brock J. Hanke and Brian Rodewald

What are Major League Equivalencies?

They are basic stat lines which approximate what AAA and AA players would have done had they been brought up by their Major League clubs.

How are they derived?

In the 1985 BILL JAMES BASEBALL ABSTRACT, Bill presented a method for doing MLE's. The method is functionally unchanged from Bill's original. Without going into screaming detail, the method does the following:

1. Adjusts for the minor league ballpark. Bill's original method didn't do this, because Bill had no access to home/road splits for minor league parks, and so could not compute minor league ballpark adjustment factors. Well, I purchased the pertinent data from Howe, who now do all the AAA and AA stats, and got park adjustments made. That Bill doesn't do this, or that his adjustment method is different from mine, would explain why my MLEs are not exactly the same as those found in the STATS Inc. Minor League Handbook.

2. Adjusts for the relative levels of offense in the minor league and the Major League. That is, if the Texas League is scoring 10 runs per game, and the National League is scoring 8, that adjustment is made.

3. Deducts 18% for the difference in quality of play between the Majors and the minors. Oddly enough, this 18% is the same for AAA and AA stats. The varying qualities of the Class-A leagues makes translation from them impossible.

4. Using all the above, computes and uses mysterious "m" and "M" factors. See the Glossary.

Ballpark adjustments are made into the Major League ballpark the player would have moved into. This means that the MLE's are not strictly comparable to each other, any more than any other Major League stats in different ballparks are.

What use are these?

What MLEs do is give you a good handle on how close to ready for the big time a minor league player is. You can quickly see that Eric Karros is not a good reason to let Eddie Murray go, not this year.

For 1992, we've added a new twist. Instead of Slugging Percentage and On-Base Percentage, we have Runs Created and Runs Created per Game. Those of you who are old Bill James readers will realize that these are basic evaluative stats. They give you a good handle on how good a hitter this guy is. A team of him would score about this many runs in a game.

And another new twist. This is the PEAK line. That line is computed by feeding the MLE into Bill's old BROCK2 projection system. Then it's projected out to age 27, which is the strongest year in most careers. If you read a book I did a couple of years ago called THE TOP 150 MINOR LEAGUE PROSPECTS, you'll remember this method. It's experimental, as BROCK2 likes to use rather more than one year as a base, but there it is. It's designed to give you a handle on how good a prospect the man is, by eliminating the age bias. The Peak Line is the best he's ever likely to get. Someday, Eric Karros, someday.

ATLANTA BRAVES

RICHMOND

Name	Age	AB	R	H	D	T	HR	RBI	BB	AVG	RC	RC/G
Bell, Mike	24	331	29	75	10	2	5	23	18	.227	26	2.74
PEAK		513	61	132	18	3	11	56	37	.257	58	4.11
Rodriguez, Boi	26	379	40	97	22	1	8	39	23	.256	41	3.93
PEAK		508	64	138	30	1	13	63	42	.272	68	4.96
Rossy, Rico	28	468	46	110	22	1	2	38	46	.235	40	3.02
PEAK		501	49	118	24	1	2	41	49	.236	46	3.24
Tomberlin, Andy	25	321	38	69	11	2	2	19	28	.215	24	2.57
PEAK		501	76	122	19	3	4	42	49	.244	49	3.49
Willard, Jerry	32	268	34	74	21	0	8	31	30	.276	38	5.29
PEAK		495	63	137	39	0	15	57	55	.277	77	5.81
Woodson, Tracy	29	427	35	108	17	2	7	45	18	.253	40	3.39
PEAK		528	43	133	21	2	9	56	22	.252	52	3.55

GREENVILLE

Name	Age	AB	R	H	D	T	HR	RBI	BB	AVG	RC	RC/G
Alva, John	27	256	27	53	12	1	2	23	14	.207	18	2.39
PEAK		521	55	108	24	2	4	47	29	.207	37	2.42
Casarotti, Rich	25	264	38	68	8	1	0	16	22	.258	24	3.31
PEAK		502	87	142	17	2	0	38	48	.283	56	4.20
Castilla, Vinny	24	259	35	70	17	2	7	44	9	.270	33	4.71
PEAK		522	91	155	36	4	20	81	28	.297	86	6.33
Champion, Brian	24	332	45	75	17	1	7	36	44	.226	36	3.78
PEAK		481	86	124	27	1	15	61	69	.258	69	5.22
Cole, Popeye	26	420	51	102	13	3	2	36	29	.243	37	3.14
PEAK		504	73	131	17	3	3	42	46	.260	52	3.76
Klesko, Ryan	21	419	65	122	22	2	13	68	67	.291	72	6.55
PEAK		463	98	152	27	2	23	82	87	.328	110	9.55
Martin, Al	24	301	38	73	13	2	7	38	29	.243	34	4.03
PEAK		495	82	135	24	3	17	67	55	.273	75	5.62
Morris, Rick	28	338	50	81	16	1	5	42	67	.240	41	4.31
PEAK		459	68	110	22	1	7	57	91	.240	57	4.41
Ross, Sean	24	429	53	121	28	2	8	40	21	.282	55	4.82
PEAK		516	80	159	35	2	13	70	34	.308	83	6.28

BALTIMORE ORIOLES

ROCHESTER

Name	Age	AB	R	H	D	T	HR	RBI	BB	AVG	RC	RC/G
Chance, Tony	27	343	46	77	11	2	10	42	32	.224	34	3.45
PEAK		503	67	113	16	3	15	62	47	.225	52	3.60
Distefano, Benny	30	410	40	97	23	1	13	63	32	.237	44	3.80
PEAK		510	50	121	29	1	16	78	40	.237	59	4.10
Mercedes, Luis	24	356	52	107	11	3	2	27	52	.301	47	5.10
PEAK		476	81	155	17	4	4	48	74	.326	80	6.73
Sheilds, Tommy	27	395	53	102	14	2	5	40	25	.258	39	3.59
PEAK		517	69	134	18	3	7	52	33	.259	54	3.81
Tackett, Jeff	26	419	49	88	14	1	5	39	43	.210	32	2.61
PEAK		492	71	113	18	1	7	44	58	.230	48	3.42
Turner, Shane	29	387	38	97	11	1	1	43	38	.251	34	3.17
PEAK		501	49	126	14	1	1	56	49	.251	46	3.31
Voigt, Jack	26	257	35	62	9	2	5	26	31	.241	27	3.74
PEAK		485	78	126	18	4	12	55	65	.260	65	4.89

HAGERSTOWN

Name	Age	AB	R	H	D	T	HR	RBI	BB	AVG	RC	RC/G
Carey, Paul	24	367	55	88	27	1	13	56	56	.240	51	4.94
PEAK		473	92	128	36	1	24	80	77	.271	89	6.97
Dickerson, Bobby	26	297	29	67	11	2	1	32	8	.226	20	2.35
PEAK		522	64	128	21	3	2	40	28	.245	46	3.15
Gutierrez, Ricky	22	287	41	64	6	2	0	26	48	.223	24	2.91
PEAK		463	90	123	13	3	0	34	87	.266	54	4.29
Hithe, Victor	27	255	40	67	10	3	0	22	32	.263	27	3.88
PEAK		489	77	128	19	6	0	42	61	.262	55	4.11
Holland, Tim	23	492	50	115	19	1	9	63	28	.234	43	3.08
PEAK		511	74	139	23	1	14	63	39	.272	67	4.86
Kingwood, Tyrone	26	313	34	83	14	1	2	32	13	.265	30	3.52
PEAK		516	66	145	24	2	4	47	34	.281	60	4.37
Lehman, Mike	24	325	37	87	22	1	3	40	38	.268	40	4.54
PEAK		487	67	144	34	1	6	53	63	.296	75	5.90
Lofton, Rodney	24	428	67	115	7	2	1	28	40	.269	41	3.54
PEAK		497	95	147	11	2	2	41	53	.296	61	4.71
Robbins, Doug	25	281	39	82	11	1	0	24	59	.292	38	5.16
PEAK		458	70	144	20	1	0	39	92	.314	71	6.11
Shamburg, Ken	25	418	51	109	33	1	10	71	57	.261	58	5.07
PEAK		483	71	138	40	1	16	69	67	.286	85	6.65
Yacopino, Ed	26	262	44	86	15	2	2	41	28	.328	42	6.44
PEAK		490	89	166	29	3	4	55	60	.339	88	7.33

BOSTON RED SOX

PAWTUCKET

Name	Age	AB	R	H	D	T	HR	RBI	BB	AVG	RC	RC/G
Barrett, Tom	32	322	34	80	14	1	0	21	43	.248	31	3.46
PEAK		485	51	121	21	2	0	32	65	.249	49	3.63
Cooper, Scott	24	471	44	122	21	2	9	57	40	.259	53	4.10
PEAK		500	60	144	24	2	14	64	50	.288	75	5.69
Lancelotti, Rick	34	324	35	63	14	1	14	51	36	.194	32	3.31
PEAK		495	53	96	21	2	21	78	55	.194	51	3.45
Pina, Mickey	26	293	32	57	11	1	5	27	23	.195	21	2.40
PEAK		501	70	108	20	2	11	50	49	.216	47	3.23
Plantier, Phil	23	290	55	83	19	3	10	49	53	.286	52	6.78
PEAK		460	110	146	32	4	23	83	90	.317	109	9.37
Stone, Jeff	31	343	50	90	13	8	5	35	24	.262	40	4.27
PEAK		514	75	135	19	12	7	52	36	.263	62	4.42
Twardoski, Mike	27	358	42	84	20	2	2	20	50	.235	36	3.55
PEAK		483	57	113	27	3	3	27	67	.234	51	3.72
Valentin, John	25	320	42	78	21	3	5	39	48	.244	39	4.35
PEAK		478	75	129	33	4	10	58	72	.270	73	5.65
Zupcic, Bob	25	419	56	93	27	1	12	56	44	.222	45	3.73
PEAK		494	86	124	34	1	20	71	56	.251	72	5.25

NEW BRITAIN

Name	Age	AB	R	H	D	T	HR	RBI	BB	AVG	RC	RC/G
Beams, Mike	25	250	20	50	13	1	4	25	27	.200	21	2.83
PEAK		493	52	114	28	2	11	53	57	.231	56	3.99
Blosser, Greg	21	449	48	95	20	3	9	45	61	.212	45	3.43
PEAK		472	79	123	24	3	17	64	78	.261	75	5.80
Byrd, jim	23	290	28	68	8	1	0	14	27	.234	23	2.80
PEAK		495	64	135	17	2	0	36	55	.273	54	4.05
Dixon, Colin	23	272	29	72	16	1	4	20	28	.265	34	4.59
PEAK		491	68	147	31	2	11	61	59	.299	81	6.36
Hendricks, Steve	27	334	20	69	9	1	0	33	32	.207	22	2.24
PEAK		502	30	104	14	2	0	50	48	.207	34	2.31
Housie, Wayne	27	441	57	120	22	1	7	27	51	.272	57	4.79
PEAK		493	64	134	25	1	8	30	57	.272	64	4.81
Milstien, Dave	23	307	36	84	7	1	4	31	44	.274	38	4.60
PEAK		475	71	145	14	1	9	54	75	.305	75	6.14
Paris, Juan	25	416	32	99	17	3	3	41	22	.238	36	3.07
PEAK		514	50	136	23	3	5	48	36	.265	56	4.00
Powers, Scott	25	249	20	51	8	1	0	15	30	.205	18	2.45
PEAK		488	49	115	18	2	0	32	62	.236	44	3.18
Randle, Randy	26	345	33	65	11	1	3	31	27	.188	21	2.02
PEAK		501	62	106	18	1	6	39	49	.212	41	2.80

CALIFORNIA ANGELS

EDMONTON

Name	Age	AB	R	H	D	T	HR	RBI	BB	AVG	RC	RC/G
Amaro, Ruben	27	433	57	115	30	2	1	26	45	.266	45	3.82
PEAK		498	66	132	35	2	1	30	52	.265	58	4.28
Anderson, Kent	28	257	18	43	6	1	1	15	18	.167	11	1.39
PEAK		514	36	86	12	2	2	30	36	.167	24	1.51
Cron, Chris	28	427	45	100	15	1	12	55	33	.234	40	3.30
PEAK		511	54	120	18	1	14	66	39	.235	53	3.66
Curtis, Chad	23	396	50	101	20	2	4	37	36	.255	39	3.57
PEAK		496	82	144	28	2	8	54	54	.290	72	5.52
Davis, Mark	27	392	52	88	14	2	6	33	50	.224	35	3.11
PEAK		488	65	110	17	2	7	41	62	.225	48	3.43
Disarcina, Gary	24	359	37	90	15	2	2	35	20	.251	30	3.01
PEAK		513	67	143	24	3	4	47	37	.279	61	4.45
Grunhard, Dan	28	304	38	65	13	1	4	27	35	.214	25	2.82
PEAK		493	62	105	21	2	6	44	57	.213	44	3.06
Stevens, Lee	24	442	45	112	20	1	10	58	26	.253	44	[illegible]
PEAK		511	69	144	25	1	17	69	39	.282	74	5.44

MIDLAND

Name	Age	AB	R	H	D	T	HR	RBI	BB	AVG	RC	RC/G
Easley, Damion	22	428	46	91	16	2	4	36	41	.213	32	2.56
PEAK		492	78	126	22	2	8	49	58	.256	59	4.35
Flora, Kevin	23	454	60	108	9	7	7	42	27	.238	39	3.04
PEAK		510	94	140	13	8	12	60	40	.275	67	4.89
Howie, Mark	29	476	63	148	20	1	12	76	40	.311	68	5.60
PEAK		507	67	158	21	1	13	81	43	.312	80	6.19
Lawton, Marcus	26	409	48	99	17	4	3	33	20	.242	34	2.96
PEAK		513	72	133	23	5	5	47	37	.259	56	3.98
McConnell, Wall	27	248	25	59	9	1	4	41	34	.238	24	3.43
PEAK		484	49	115	18	2	8	80	66	.238	53	3.88
Salmon, Tim	23	441	62	90	17	2	15	58	63	.204	43	3.31
PEAK		475	100	117	21	2	26	77	75	.246	77	5.81
Williams, Reggie	26	298	48	78	8	2	1	19	44	.262	30	3.68
PEAK		475	86	132	14	3	2	39	75	.278	59	4.64

CHICAGO CUBS

IOWA

Name	Age	AB	R	H	D	T	HR	RBI	BB	AVG	RC	RC/G
Bierly, Brad	29	372	37	77	17	3	10	46	26	.207	32	2.93
PEAK		514	51	106	23	4	14	64	36	.206	46	3.04
Carter, Steve	27	502	62	132	24	7	7	53	25	.263	54	3.94
PEAK		524	65	138	25	7	7	55	26	.263	59	4.13
Guinn, BRian	31	334	36	72	9	1	3	25	33	.216	25	2.58
PEAK		501	54	108	13	1	4	37	49	.216	39	2.68
May, Derrick	23	299	37	81	15	3	2	38	13	.271	31	3.84
PEAK		517	83	157	28	5	5	55	33	.304	73	5.47
McGinnis, Russ	29	361	55	92	15	1	13	55	42	.255	45	4.52
PEAK		493	75	126	20	1	18	75	57	.256	67	4.93
Pappas, Erik	26	275	32	69	16	1	6	37	30	.251	32	4.19
PEAK		489	66	131	29	2	13	61	61	.268	71	5.35
Sanchez, Rey	24	404	46	108	13	4	2	36	25	.267	40	3.65
PEAK		510	72	150	19	5	4	48	40	.294	66	4.95
Smajstria, Craig	30	372	43	94	14	4	2	30	31	.253	35	3.40
PEAK		508	59	128	19	5	3	41	42	.252	51	3.62
Strange, Doug	28	492	60	132	28	4	7	43	33	.268	56	4.20
PEAK		515	63	138	29	4	7	45	35	.268	62	4.44

CHRRLOTTE

Name	Age	AB	R	H	D	T	HR	RBI	BB	AVG	RC	RC/G
Arias, Alex	24	479	66	125	25	0	3	45	40	.261	49	3.74
PEAK		501	86	145	28	0	4	48	49	.289	65	4.93
Crockett, Rusty	25	276	34	55	7	1	1	22	21	.199	17	2.08
PEAK		505	83	116	15	2	3	36	45	.230	42	2.92
Grace, Mike	24	257	21	50	8	0	6	31	14	.195	18	2.35
PEAK		513	62	117	19	0	18	63	37	.228	53	3.61
Knapp, Mike	27	260	19	62	12	0	1	32	16	.238	21	2.86
PEAK		518	38	124	24	0	2	64	32	.239	44	3.02
Paulino, Elvin	25	453	64	111	26	1	22	77	48	.245	63	4.97
PEAK		494	90	134	30	1	33	95	56	.271	92	6.90
Ramsey, Fernando	26	536	75	140	17	5	6	46	31	.261	54	3.68
PEAK		509	84	141	18	4	7	51	41	.277	62	4.55
Roberson, Kevin	24	498	74	121	22	1	17	64	34	.243	56	4.01
PEAK		507	102	138	25	1	25	81	43	.272	79	5.78
Welch, Doug	25	436	43	99	17	0	11	63	22	.227	38	3.04
PEAK		515	69	131	22	0	18	67	35	.254	62	4.36
White, Billy	23	388	50	98	16	3	3	48	57	.253	43	4.00
PEAK		473	78	136	22	4	6	48	77	.288	71	5.69

CHICAGO WHITE SOX

VANCOUVER

Name	Age	AB	R	H	D	T	HR	RBI	BB	AVG	RC	RC/G
Beltre, Esteban	24	338	38	85	10	2	0	24	16	.251	27	2.88
PEAK		516	73	145	18	3	0	40	34	.281	55	4.00
Bernhardt, Cesar	23	267	18	61	11	2	4	21	13	.228	22	2.88
PEAK		515	50	137	24	4	12	60	35	.266	64	4.57
Brown, Curt	25	267	18	61	11	2	4	21	13	.228	22	2.88
PEAK		516	46	132	24	4	11	57	34	.256	59	4.15
Hall, Joe	26	417	32	96	14	1	4	31	16	.230	31	2.61
PEAK		517	49	129	19	1	6	46	33	.250	49	3.41
Hill, Orsino	30	337	31	89	13	1	4	36	29	.264	35	3.81
PEAK		506	47	134	20	2	6	54	44	.265	57	4.14
Lee, Derek	25	310	44	85	25	4	6	35	25	.274	42	5.04
PEAK		503	86	150	42	6	13	70	47	.298	87	6.65
Martin, Norberto	25	329	31	85	8	0	0	16	15	.258	26	2.88
PEAK		517	60	147	15	0	0	38	33	.284	53	3.87
Stark, Matt	27	383	37	101	19	1	11	55	55	.264	51	4.88
PEAK		481	46	127	24	1	14	69	69	.264	69	5.26

BIRMINGHAM

Name	Age	AB	R	H	D	T	HR	RBI	BB	AVG	RC	RC/G
Campbell, Darrin	25	288	36	63	7	2	9	30	25	.219	28	3.36
PEAK		501	84	124	14	3	22	71	49	.248	66	4.73
Chasey, Mark	25	331	39	78	15	2	7	34	67	.236	42	4.48
PEAK		461	66	121	23	3	13	58	89	.262	72	5.72
Coomer, Ron	25	502	77	126	25	4	18	72	55	.251	68	4.88
PEAK		492	95	136	26	4	24	81	58	.276	85	6.45
Foster, Lindsay	25	371	37	78	8	3	1	32	24	.210	24	2.21
PEAK		510	66	122	13	4	2	37	40	.239	44	3.06
Garner, Kevin	26	428	51	105	17	2	20	70	55	.245	61	5.10
PEAK		482	69	127	20	2	28	83	68	.263	83	6.31
Jaster, Scott	26	361	37	95	14	3	9	41	34	.263	46	4.67
PEAK		495	59	138	20	4	15	65	55	.279	74	5.60
Ocasio, Javier	22	397	36	88	7	3	0	28	36	.222	29	2.53
PEAK		494	64	131	12	4	0	35	56	.265	51	3.79
Pledger, Kinnis	23	362	51	78	14	6	13	49	56	.215	45	4.28
PEAK		470	96	120	21	8	27	82	80	.255	87	6.71
Tedder, Scott	26	336	32	98	14	2	0	30	48	.292	44	4.99
PEAK		477	49	145	21	3	0	40	73	.304	68	5.53

CINCINNATI REDS
NASHVILLE

Name	Age	AB	R	H	D	T	HR	RBI	BB	AVG	RC	RC/G
Benavides, Freddie	26	321	21	70	7	0	0	18	13	.218	18	1.94
PEAK		516	42	123	13	0	0	32	34	.238	39	2.68
Casillas, Adam	26	409	37	103	17	3	5	45	40	.252	43	3.79
PEAK		493	52	133	22	3	7	50	57	.270	63	4.72
Garcia, Leo	29	438	42	98	13	4	8	32	28	.224	37	2.94
PEAK		517	50	116	15	5	9	38	33	.224	46	3.10
Gonzalez, Angel	27	300	27	66	9	6	3	36	17	.220	24	2.77
PEAK		521	47	115	16	10	5	62	29	.221	43	2.86
Jones, Chris	28	259	25	57	5	4	8	28	17	.220	24	3.21
PEAK		516	50	114	10	8	16	56	34	.221	51	3.43
Lee, Terry	30	423	60	119	21	4	15	58	53	.281	67	5.95
PEAK		489	69	138	24	5	17	67	61	.282	81	6.23
Lockhart, Keith	27	399	46	95	25	3	8	31	21	.238	40	3.55
PEAK		523	60	124	33	4	10	41	28	.237	54	3.65
Trafton, Todd	28	254	32	66	16	1	8	35	24	.260	33	4.74
PEAK		503	63	131	32	2	16	69	47	.260	70	5.08

CHATTANOOGA

Name	Age	AB	R	H	D	T	HR	RBI	BB	AVG	RC	RC/G
Allen, Rick	24	375	51	89	15	1	5	25	35	.237	36	3.40
PEAK		497	88	133	22	1	10	53	53	.268	63	4.67
Branson, Jeff	25	298	34	74	13	2	2	27	30	.248	30	3.62
PEAK		496	69	136	24	3	5	47	54	.274	63	4.72
Bryant, Scott	24	299	40	86	14	4	9	41	33	.288	47	5.96
PEAK		490	81	153	25	6	21	80	60	.312	98	7.85
Colvard, Benny	25	459	60	122	22	6	21	66	16	.266	62	4.97
PEAK		522	89	152	27	6	32	100	28	.291	94	6.86
Costo, Tim	23	287	30	76	18	2	7	28	20	.265	36	4.61
PEAK		505	71	151	34	3	18	76	45	.299	87	6.64
Lonigro, Greg	26	448	46	111	23	2	7	52	22	.248	44	3.53
PEAK		512	63	136	27	2	10	56	38	.266	62	4.45
Pose, Scott	25	394	59	102	8	3	1	30	67	.259	43	3.98
PEAK		471	82	134	11	3	2	38	79	.285	61	4.89
Sanders, Reggie	24	295	49	88	15	6	9	48	40	.298	53	6.91
PEAK		480	96	155	26	9	20	81	70	.323	106	8.81
Wilson, Dan	23	286	31	69	18	2	2	37	21	.241	28	3.48
PEAK		504	73	140	34	3	5	52	46	.278	66	4.90

CLEVELAND INDIANS
COLORADO SPRINGS

Name	Age	AB	R	H	D	T	HR	RBI	BB	AVG	RC	RC/G
Berroa, Geronimo	27	445	51	121	25	6	8	56	22	.272	51	4.25
PEAK		524	60	143	29	7	9	66	26	.273	65	4.61
Brown, Marty	29	371	40	94	19	1	6	43	31	.253	37	3.61
PEAK		508	55	129	26	1	8	59	42	.254	56	3.99
Kirby, Wayne	28	361	41	89	11	2	1	24	22	.247	28	2.78
PEAK		518	59	128	16	3	1	34	32	.247	45	3.12
Magallanes, Ever	26	286	23	68	10	1	1	21	15	.238	21	2.60
PEAK		511	50	131	19	2	2	40	39	.256	49	3.48
Medina, Luis	29	419	51	115	23	4	11	61	30	.274	52	4.62
PEAK		513	62	141	28	5	13	75	37	.275	71	5.15
Moses, John	34	279	36	69	14	2	1	19	23	.247	25	3.21
PEAK		508	66	126	25	4	2	35	42	.248	50	3.53
Taubensee, Eddie	23	268	33	70	18	2	6	24	19	.261	31	4.23
PEAK		505	83	149	36	4	17	74	45	.295	86	6.52

CANTON-AKRON

Name	Age	AB	R	H	D	T	HR	RBI	BB	AVG	RC	RC/G
Bautista, Ramon	25	274	34	56	8	4	1	24	22	.204	19	2.35
PEAK		503	81	118	17	7	3	39	47	.235	47	3.30
Epley, Darin	25	444	49	107	21	0	6	43	46	.241	44	3.53
PEAK		495	68	132	25	0	9	53	55	.267	63	4.69
Ferretti, Sam	24	295	22	60	10	2	0	19	30	.203	20	2.30
PEAK		493	48	117	19	3	0	33	57	.237	45	3.23
Levis, Jesse	24	376	25	95	15	2	4	38	32	.253	38	3.65
PEAK		500	42	141	22	2	8	52	50	.282	66	4.96
Martinez, Carlos	26	288	40	90	19	1	7	61	18	.313	45	6.14
PEAK		507	79	164	34	2	15	72	43	.323	93	7.32
Ramos, Ken	25	253	35	58	6	2	1	11	23	.229	20	2.77
PEAK		499	86	128	14	4	3	40	51	.257	52	3.78
Sabino, Miguel	24	386	43	80	9	1	4	22	43	.207	28	2.47
PEAK		489	74	118	14	1	8	44	61	.241	51	3.71
Thome, Jim	21	287	39	92	17	1	4	38	35	.321	46	6.37
PEAK		478	82	169	30	2	10	65	72	.354	102	8.91

DETROIT TIGERS

TOLEDO

Name	Age	AB	R	H	D	T	HR	RBI	BB	AVG	RC	RC/G
Allaire, Karl	28	371	45	87	18	3	2	27	50	.235	36	3.42
PEAK		485	59	114	24	4	3	35	65	.235	50	3.64
Clark, Phil	24	349	38	79	11	3	4	37	16	.226	27	2.70
PEAK		517	76	133	19	4	9	52	33	.257	56	3.94
Ford, Curt	31	352	42	84	21	3	2	30	33	.239	34	3.43
PEAK		503	60	120	30	4	3	43	47	.239	51	3.60
Hare, Shawn	25	241	36	67	16	1	8	34	23	.278	35	5.43
PEAK		498	91	150	35	2	22	82	52	.301	94	7.29
Livingstone, Scott	26	317	39	86	11	2	2	49	31	.271	34	3.97
PEAK		493	69	141	18	3	4	45	57	.286	64	4.91
Lyden, Mitch	27	329	27	65	10	1	17	44	12	.198	28	2.86
PEAK		531	44	105	16	2	27	71	19	.198	46	2.92
Mangham, eric	26	365	47	78	11	1	4	28	42	.214	29	2.73
PEAK		487	76	114	16	1	7	43	63	.234	49	3.55
Paredes, Johnny	29	494	65	126	22	3	1	42	37	.255	46	3.38
PEAK		512	67	131	23	3	1	44	38	.256	50	3.54
Rosario, Victor	25	405	47	109	19	8	1	39	16	.269	41	3.74
PEAK		520	73	153	26	9	2	49	30	.294	68	5.00
Rowland, Rich	25	369	44	90	22	0	13	54	47	.244	47	4.55
PEAK		486	73	131	31	0	24	78	64	.270	83	6.31

LONDON

Name	Age	AB	R	H	D	T	HR	RBI	BB	AVG	RC	RC/G
Balthazar, Doyle	24	254	24	58	7	1	1	19	18	.228	19	2.62
PEAK		506	63	131	16	2	3	41	44	.259	51	3.67
Brogna, Rico	22	281	34	68	11	1	10	42	20	.242	31	3.93
PEAK		503	91	142	23	2	29	88	47	.282	88	6.58
Cruz, Ivan	24	426	38	93	19	0	6	40	29	.218	33	2.68
PEAK		507	62	127	25	0	10	54	43	.250	56	3.98
Frazier, Lou	27	423	57	89	8	3	2	34	64	.210	32	2.59
PEAK		478	64	101	9	3	2	38	72	.211	38	2.72
Galindo, Luis	24	259	23	58	5	1	0	17	35	.224	19	2.55
PEAK		480	54	123	12	2	0	32	70	.256	49	3.71
Ingram, Riccardo	25	403	47	96	12	1	14	53	42	.238	45	3.96
PEAK		494	75	131	17	1	24	76	56	.265	75	5.58
Kimberlin, Keith	25	319	23	65	15	3	2	29	20	.204	22	2.34
PEAK		510	49	119	27	5	5	44	40	.233	49	3.38
Reimink, Rob	25	268	32	61	8	1	2	15	43	.228	24	3.13
PEAK		474	69	121	16	2	5	42	76	.255	56	4.28

HOUSTON ASTROS

TUCSON

Name	Age	AB	R	H	D	T	HR	RBI	BB	AVG	RC	RC/G
Anthony, Eric	24	293	36	82	17	1	6	39	17	.280	34	4.35
PEAK		512	79	157	31	2	15	70	38	.307	84	6.39
Cedeno, Andujar	22	323	31	81	15	4	4	35	13	.251	30	3.35
PEAK		518	70	150	27	6	10	62	32	.290	72	5.28
Cooper, Gary	27	378	54	96	19	4	10	47	43	.254	45	4.31
PEAK		494	71	125	25	5	13	61	56	.253	65	4.76
Lofton, Kenny	25	507	59	130	15	11	1	32	34	.256	47	3.37
PEAK		509	71	143	17	10	1	45	41	.281	61	4.50
Mota, Andy	26	430	41	106	15	2	1	29	15	.247	32	2.67
PEAK		518	60	137	19	2	1	40	32	.264	50	3.54
Nelson, Rob	28	340	25	69	14	1	11	39	32	.203	29	2.89
PEAK		503	37	102	21	1	16	58	47	.203	47	3.16
Rhodes, Karl	23	289	28	61	14	1	1	29	24	.211	20	2.37
PEAK		499	68	126	27	2	3	41	51	.253	53	3.84
Rhode, Dave	24	231	23	72	7	2	1	25	34	.312	30	5.09
PEAK		475	55	159	17	4	3	48	75	.335	82	7.01
Simms, Mike	25	280	34	56	15	1	10	37	23	.200	24	2.89
PEAK		503	85	116	30	2	26	79	47	.231	68	4.74
Tolentino, Jose	31	282	28	67	19	4	4	32	28	.238	29	3.64
PEAK		500	50	119	34	7	7	57	50	.238	58	4.11

JACKSON

Name	Age	AB	R	H	D	T	HR	RBI	BB	AVG	RC	RC/G
Dean, Kevin	24	267	23	55	10	4	1	23	35	.206	21	2.67
PEAK		482	54	115	20	7	3	40	68	.239	53	3.90
Hubbarb, Trent	28	432	54	112	20	2	1	28	43	.259	41	3.46
PEAK		500	63	130	23	2	1	32	50	.260	52	3.79
Hunter, Bert	24	363	39	81	17	6	1	30	37	.223	31	2.97
PEAK		493	67	126	25	8	2	43	57	.256	58	4.27
Kellner, Frank	25	296	32	69	7	4	1	17	18	.233	22	2.62
PEAK		511	70	133	14	6	2	42	39	.260	52	3.71
Madsen, Lance	23	392	38	75	19	4	4	35	27	.191	26	2.21
PEAK		506	74	118	28	5	8	51	44	.233	53	3.69
Mikulik, Joe	28	468	53	120	17	4	8	65	27	.256	47	3.65
PEAK		520	59	133	19	4	9	72	30	.256	55	3.84
Prager, Howard	25	339	39	91	24	1	6	45	34	.268	41	4.46
PEAK		496	69	145	37	1	12	64	54	.292	80	6.15

KANSAS CITY ROYALS

OMAHA

Name	Age	AB	R	H	D	T	HR	RBI	BB	AVG	RC	RC/G
Berry, Sean	26	354	49	83	21	8	8	43	39	.234	42	4.18
PEAK		489	80	124	30	11	14	64	61	.254	73	5.40
Brunfield, Jacob	27	382	49	91	15	5	2	34	28	.238	34	3.15
PEAK		512	66	122	20	7	3	46	38	.238	48	3.32
Clark, Dave	29	343	35	92	24	3	9	51	25	.268	45	4.84
PEAK		513	52	138	36	4	13	76	37	.269	70	5.04
Cole, Stu	26	425	51	99	14	5	2	30	34	.233	36	2.98
PEAK		500	71	126	18	6	3	41	50	.252	53	3.83
Leonard, Jeffrey	36	249	22	54	9	1	7	39	11	.217	21	2.91
PEAK		527	47	114	19	2	15	83	23	.216	45	2.94
Liriano, Nelson	28	280	39	68	16	8	2	28	26	.243	31	3.95
PEAK		503	70	122	29	14	4	50	47	.243	59	4.18
Moore, Bobby	26	476	52	102	14	3	0	27	31	.214	31	2.24
PEAK		506	68	119	16	3	0	33	44	.235	42	2.93
Morman, Russ	30	304	36	71	15	3	5	39	35	.234	32	3.71
PEAK		493	58	115	24	5	8	63	57	.233	54	3.86
Pulliam, Harvey	24	333	27	76	19	1	4	29	26	.228	29	3.05
PEAK		503	54	130	31	1	9	54	47	.258	61	4.42

MEMPHIS

Name	Age	AB	R	H	D	T	HR	RBI	BB	AVG	RC	RC/G
Bridges, Tony	23	361	29	73	10	0	2	26	28	.202	22	2.06
PEAK		502	59	122	17	0	4	40	48	.243	47	3.34
Koslofski, Kevin	25	282	35	34	14	3	5	34	27	.121	13	1.42
PEAK		498	100	79	29	6	14	53	52	.159	39	2.51
Laureano, Frank	24	347	49	95	15	3	2	29	50	.274	42	4.50
PEAK		477	80	143	23	4	4	47	73	.300	73	5.90
Long, Kevin	25	393	51	98	16	3	2	30	36	.249	37	3.39
PEAK		499	79	137	22	4	3	45	51	.275	60	4.48
Pedre, Jorge	25	351	36	80	24	1	5	50	20	.228	31	3.09
PEAK		513	68	131	37	1	10	58	37	.255	61	4.31
Robinson, Darryl	24	339	36	88	14	3	2	30	14	.260	32	3.44
PEAK		519	70	149	24	4	4	50	31	.287	63	4.60
Toale, John	27	244	35	62	13	0	5	36	24	.254	27	4.01
PEAK		501	72	127	27	0	10	74	49	.253	59	4.26
Walker, Hugh	22	395	34	82	14	5	2	36	24	.208	27	2.33
PEAK		508	65	128	21	7	4	46	42	.252	54	3.84

LOS ANGELES DODGERS

ALBUQUERQUE

Name	Age	AB	R	H	D	T	HR	RBI	BB	AVG	RC	RC/G
Bean, Billy	28	240	21	58	16	2	1	21	15	.242	21	3.12
PEAK		518	45	125	35	4	2	45	32	.241	50	3.44
Brooks, Jerry	25	398	39	95	14	2	9	49	18	.239	35	3.12
PEAK		518	67	137	20	2	16	66	32	.264	64	4.54
Davis, Butch	34	261	33	66	13	3	5	26	12	.253	26	3.60
PEAK		526	66	133	26	6	10	52	24	.253	57	3.92
Goodwin, Tom	23	474	50	104	13	1	1	27	37	.219	30	2.19
PEAK		502	74	130	17	1	2	38	48	.259	50	3.63
Hansen, Dave	23	235	25	58	8	1	3	24	31	.247	23	3.51
PEAK		479	68	136	19	2	9	53	71	.284	70	5.51
Hernandez, Carlos	25	315	36	89	17	1	6	26	15	.283	36	4.30
PEAK		517	73	158	30	1	13	67	33	.306	80	6.02
Karros, Eric	24	450	53	116	24	3	15	61	37	.258	54	4.37
PEAK		501	77	143	29	3	24	82	49	.285	87	6.56
Munoz, Jose	24	357	29	95	12	1	0	40	13	.266	29	2.99
PEAK		521	53	153	20	1	0	41	29	.294	58	4.26
Offerman, Jose	23	267	35	64	5	1	0	17	30	.240	20	2.66
PEAK		487	84	135	12	2	0	35	63	.277	54	4.14
Rodriguez, Henry	24	416	37	91	16	1	7	41	16	.219	30	2.49
PEAK		521	65	130	23	1	13	58	29	.250	56	3.87

SAN ANTONIO

Name	Age	AB	R	H	D	T	HR	RBI	BB	AVG	RC	RC/G
Baar, Bryan	24	332	23	62	15	0	7	35	14	.187	20	2.00
PEAK		519	54	115	26	0	17	61	31	.222	51	3.41
Barker, Tim	24	377	48	93	16	1	1	32	54	.247	35	3.33
PEAK		477	74	132	22	1	2	40	73	.277	60	4.70
Castillo, Braulio	24	279	34	71	15	1	5	33	21	.254	29	3.76
PEAK		504	79	143	29	2	13	63	46	.284	74	5.53
Finken, Steve	26	364	37	89	15	1	3	33	37	.245	33	3.24
PEAK		492	58	129	22	1	5	44	58	.262	57	4.24
Magnusson, Brett	24	339	47	76	17	1	7	45	46	.224	33	3.39
PEAK		480	87	123	26	1	14	60	70	.256	68	5.14
Traxler, Brian	24	360	35	78	19	0	5	42	36	.217	30	2.87
PEAK		494	64	123	28	0	10	53	56	.249	59	4.29
White, Mike	24	239	16	58	10	1	1	25	7	.243	18	2.69
PEAK		525	46	143	24	2	3	46	25	.272	55	3.89
Young, Eric	25	435	56	103	14	1	2	24	46	.237	35	2.85
PEAK		494	78	130	18	1	3	41	56	.263	54	4.01

MILWAUKEE BREWERS

DENVER

Name	Age	AB	R	H	D	T	HR	RBI	BB	AVG	RC	RC/G
Brantley, Mickey	31	451	61	117	16	3	11	61	33	.259	50	4.04
PEAK		513	69	133	18	3	13	69	38	.259	61	4.33
Canale, George	26	262	28	52	9	1	7	37	44	.198	25	3.21
PEAK		469	61	103	18	2	16	57	81	.220	58	4.28
Cangelosi, John	29	287	55	73	7	1	2	20	51	.254	30	3.79
PEAK		467	89	119	11	2	3	33	83	.255	53	4.11
Carillo, Matias	29	399	44	94	16	3	6	44	28	.236	36	3.19
PEAK		514	57	121	21	4	8	57	36	.235	50	3.44
Kmak, Joe	29	281	27	57	15	1	1	26	24	.203	19	2.29
PEAK		507	49	103	27	2	2	47	43	.203	37	2.47
Listach, Pat	24	273	41	59	9	2	1	25	39	.216	22	2.78
PEAK		477	92	119	18	3	3	38	73	.249	53	4.00
McIntosh, Tim	27	437	55	110	17	5	12	73	32	.252	49	4.05
PEAK		512	64	129	20	6	14	86	38	.252	62	4.37
Montoyo, Charlie	26	377	54	77	12	1	8	36	60	.204	34	3.06
PEAK		472	82	106	17	1	13	51	78	.225	55	4.06
Olander, Jim	29	469	70	133	30	5	7	61	55	.284	65	5.22
PEAK		492	73	140	31	5	7	64	58	.285	73	5.60
Smith, D.L.	29	279	27	50	6	1	1	17	24	.179	14	1.65
PEAK		506	49	91	11	2	2	31	44	.180	27	1.76

EL PASO

Name	Age	AB	R	H	D	T	HR	RBI	BB	AVG	RC	RC/G
Ashley, Shon	25	455	58	114	22	3	22	67	52	.251	61	4.83
PEAK		491	80	136	26	3	32	95	59	.277	94	7.15
Byington, John	24	468	40	104	21	1	8	60	18	.222	35	2.60
PEAK		521	62	132	26	1	13	60	29	.253	58	4.03
Escatera, Rubin	27	409	68	106	21	3	5	45	45	.259	44	3.92
PEAK		495	82	128	25	4	6	55	55	.259	60	4.41
Faulkner, Craig	26	247	26	62	15	0	9	31	14	.251	28	4.09
PEAK		509	65	136	32	0	23	78	41	.267	76	5.50
Jacas, Dave	27	478	69	102	21	4	5	35	43	.213	37	2.66
PEAK		505	73	108	22	4	5	37	45	.214	43	2.92
Jackson, Kenny	27	396	51	98	20	4	15	44	24	.247	46	4.17
PEAK		519	67	128	26	5	20	58	31	.247	65	4.49
Jaha, John	26	445	83	126	31	1	27	91	59	.283	79	6.69
PEAK		481	103	143	34	1	35	102	69	.297	109	8.71
Tatum, Jim	24	455	67	120	21	4	16	87	47	.264	59	4.76
PEAK		492	93	144	25	4	25	83	58	.293	93	7.22

MINNESOTA TWINS

PORTLAND

Name	Age	AB	R	H	D	T	HR	RBI	BB	AVG	RC	RC/G
Brito, Bernando	28	421	53	104	16	1	19	66	20	.247	49	4.17
PEAK		525	66	130	20	1	24	82	25	.248	63	4.31
Brown, Jarvis	25	427	50	117	4	5	2	30	26	.274	42	3.66
PEAK		511	72	152	7	5	3	45	39	.297	62	4.66
Bruett, J.T.	24	338	41	91	5	3	0	29	29	.269	32	3.50
PEAK		500	74	148	10	4	0	39	50	.296	60	4.60
Hale, Chip	27	346	36	79	15	3	1	30	34	.228	29	2.93
PEAK		501	52	114	22	4	1	43	49	.228	44	3.07
Jorgensen, Terry	25	447	59	127	26	0	8	48	39	.284	58	4.89
PEAK		501	79	154	31	0	12	64	49	.307	82	6.38
Reboulet, Jeff	28	384	40	90	25	3	2	37	41	.234	37	3.40
PEAK		497	52	116	32	4	3	48	53	.233	51	3.61
Rodriguez, Victor	30	264	29	76	16	0	4	26	15	.288	33	4.74
PEAK		520	57	150	32	0	8	51	30	.288	67	4.89
Sheaffer, Danny	30	323	37	93	14	1	1	34	18	.288	35	4.11
PEAK		521	60	150	23	2	2	55	29	.288	60	4.37
Sorrento, Paul	26	400	48	117	28	1	9	63	45	.293	60	5.72
PEAK		488	66	149	35	1	13	66	62	.305	86	6.85
Webster, Lenny	27	319	34	76	17	0	5	27	17	.238	29	3.22
PEAK		522	56	124	28	0	8	44	28	.238	49	3.32

ORLANDO

Name	Age	AB	R	H	D	T	HR	RBI	BB	AVG	RC	RC/G
Capellan, Carlos	24	360	36	83	10	1	0	26	20	.231	25	2.44
PEAK		513	67	134	17	1	0	36	37	.261	48	3.42
Delima, Rafael	24	387	39	91	15	4	4	40	40	.235	37	3.38
PEAK		492	64	131	21	5	7	51	58	.266	63	4.71
Garcia, Cheo	24	487	51	131	24	4	8	66	38	.269	58	4.40
PEAK		503	66	149	27	4	12	63	47	.296	78	5.95
Gilbert, Shawn	27	520	61	126	13	4	3	34	45	.242	46	3.15
PEAK		506	59	123	13	4	3	33	44	.243	46	3.24
Kvasnicka, Jay	24	287	42	74	11	3	4	24	46	.258	36	4.56
PEAK		471	85	135	20	5	9	54	79	.287	75	6.03
Masteller, Dan	24	363	38	84	15	4	5	31	36	.231	35	3.39
PEAK		494	67	130	23	5	10	55	56	.263	65	4.82
McCreary, Bob	24	339	22	66	9	1	2	20	21	.195	19	1.88
PEAK		510	47	117	16	1	5	40	40	.229	43	2.95
Ortiz, Ray	24	462	52	108	19	3	8	63	41	.234	45	3.43
PEAK		498	74	132	23	3	13	59	52	.265	67	4.94
Parks, Derek	23	252	27	51	15	0	6	27	26	.202	23	3.09
PEAK		491	78	120	32	0	19	67	59	.244	68	4.95

MONTREAL EXPOS

INDIANAPOLIS

Name	Age	AB	R	H	D	T	HR	RBI	BB	AVG	RC	RC/G
Cordero, Will	20	361	41	95	16	3	9	44	24	.263	44	4.47
PEAK		504	83	154	25	4	21	79	46	.306	91	7.02
Diaz, Alex	23	370	41	90	14	3	1	18	24	.243	32	3.09
PEAK		507	75	142	22	4	2	44	43	.280	60	4.44
Haney, Todd	26	512	57	161	32	2	2	32	41	.314	74	5.69
PEAK		500	61	163	32	2	2	51	50	.326	79	6.33
Kremers, Jimmy	26	290	28	70	14	0	9	35	35	.241	35	4.30
PEAK		485	56	126	25	0	19	67	65	.260	72	5.42
Mack, Quinn	26	417	29	114	19	7	5	41	11	.273	47	4.19
PEAK		522	43	150	25	8	8	58	28	.287	70	5.08
McPhail, Marlin	31	320	34	88	23	1	6	31	26	.275	43	5.00
PEAK		509	54	140	37	2	10	49	41	.275	69	5.05
Shines, Razor	35	472	51	119	27	0	6	50	57	.252	54	4.13
PEAK		491	53	124	28	0	6	52	59	.253	57	4.19
Vanderwal, John	26	479	70	141	35	7	12	60	70	.294	86	6.87
PEAK		476	77	146	35	6	14	70	74	.307	94	7.69

HARRISBURG

Name	Age	AB	R	H	D	T	HR	RBI	BB	AVG	RC	RC/G
Cassels, Chris	23	297	28	66	15	0	9	40	19	.222	29	3.39
PEAK		508	71	133	29	0	24	79	42	.262	74	5.33
Cianfrocco, Archi	25	453	58	141	21	8	6	63	37	.311	71	6.14
PEAK		503	74	167	25	8	9	64	47	.332	91	7.31
Faulk, Jim	24	267	26	67	10	2	3	38	35	.251	30	4.05
PEAK		482	59	135	20	3	8	51	68	.280	68	5.29
Hernandez, Cesar	25	417	48	105	16	1	9	43	24	.252	44	3.81
PEAK		512	76	142	22	1	15	65	38	.277	69	5.04
Katzaroff, Rob	23	556	77	160	21	1	2	42	52	.288	65	4.43
PEAK		495	85	158	21	1	3	47	55	.319	74	5.93
Kosco, Bryn	25	379	42	90	24	3	7	48	46	.237	45	4.20
PEAK		488	67	129	33	4	12	61	62	.264	72	5.42
Martin, Chris	24	294	24	66	10	0	4	29	21	.224	24	2.84
PEAK		506	56	129	20	0	10	52	44	.255	56	4.01
Natal, Bob	26	335	38	85	16	2	9	44	47	.254	45	4.86
PEAK		478	63	129	24	3	16	64	72	.270	76	5.88
Santangelo, F.P.	24	461	63	112	12	6	3	34	72	.243	50	3.87
PEAK		472	80	129	15	6	4	44	78	.273	63	4.96
Stairs, Matt	23	502	71	165	30	8	9	63	64	.329	95	7.61
PEAK		481	81	170	30	7	12	71	69	.353	109	9.46

NEW YORK METS

TIDEWATER

Name	Age	AB	R	H	D	T	HR	RBI	BB	AVG	RC	RC/G
Donnels, Chris	26	271	33	71	16	1	6	41	42	.262	35	4.72
PEAK		473	65	131	29	2	13	60	77	.277	77	6.08
Gardner, Jeff	28	476	54	119	19	3	1	41	57	.250	44	3.33
PEAK		491	56	123	20	3	1	42	59	.251	50	3.67
Hansen, Terrel	25	349	39	81	17	1	10	46	27	.232	34	3.43
PEAK		505	74	131	27	1	20	72	45	.259	70	5.05
Hundley, Todd	23	431	46	101	20	3	11	49	34	.234	43	3.52
PEAK		501	76	136	26	3	20	73	49	.271	77	5.70
Jimenez, Al	25	319	27	51	7	1	4	23	27	.160	15	1.51
PEAK		502	63	97	14	2	9	43	48	.193	37	2.47
Leiper, Tim	25	268	25	57	9	1	1	22	24	.213	18	2.30
PEAK		500	60	121	19	2	3	38	50	.242	48	3.42
NcDaniel, Terry	25	380	47	80	19	4	7	31	34	.211	32	2.88
PEAK		500	81	120	27	5	13	59	50	.240	61	4.33
Roseboro, Jaime	26	264	25	67	10	0	1	21	19	.254	22	3.02
PEAK		503	56	136	20	0	2	41	47	.270	54	3.97
Torve, Kelvin	32	319	42	75	17	1	7	36	42	.235	34	3.76
PEAK		486	64	114	26	2	11	55	64	.235	57	4.14

WILLIAMSPORT

Name	Age	AB	R	H	D	T	HR	RBI	BB	AVG	RC	RC/G
Burnitz, Jeremy	23	432	52	78	11	5	21	56	74	.181	44	3.36
PEAK		464	90	105	15	6	37	94	86	.226	84	6.32
Dozier, D.J.	26	241	32	54	8	3	5	19	27	.224	23	3.32
PEAK		488	78	119	18	6	13	56	62	.244	62	4.54
Hernandez, Rudy	24	328	25	57	6	0	0	14	47	.174	16	1.59
PEAK		477	50	100	11	0	0	26	73	.210	35	2.51
Howell, Pat	23	255	28	58	4	1	1	17	15	.227	17	2.33
PEAK		510	79	136	11	2	3	41	40	.267	51	3.68
May, Lee	24	282	18	46	6	2	1	12	19	.163	12	1.37
PEAK		508	48	101	14	4	3	34	42	.199	34	2.26
McBride, Loy	25	268	15	46	10	0	3	19	23	.172	14	1.70
PEAK		501	40	103	21	0	8	43	49	.206	41	2.78
Navarro, Tito	21	449	45	106	6	2	2	28	51	.236	35	2.76
PEAK		482	70	136	11	2	4	42	68	.282	60	4.68
Williams, Paul	23	435	40	92	21	1	5	47	48	.211	34	2.68
PEAK		488	64	123	26	1	9	51	62	.252	60	4.44
Zinter, Alan	24	400	29	71	10	3	6	37	42	.178	25	2.05
PEAK		492	52	105	15	4	11	49	58	.213	48	3.35

NEW YORK YANKEES

COLUMBUS

Name	Age	AB	R	H	D	T	HR	RBI	BB	AVG	RC	RC/G
Hughes, Keith	28	414	57	105	18	3	7	60	48	.254	47	4.11
PEAK		493	68	125	21	4	8	71	57	.254	59	4.33
Humphreys, Mike	25	403	63	107	22	2	8	48	50	.266	52	4.74
PEAK		487	92	141	28	2	13	63	63	.290	79	6.16
Leyntz, Jim	28	263	44	65	23	1	10	43	31	.247	37	5.05
PEAK		492	82	122	43	2	19	80	58	.248	74	5.40
Lovullo, Torrey	26	386	66	98	23	2	9	67	47	.254	49	4.59
PEAK		485	96	131	30	2	14	63	65	.270	74	5.64
Lusader, Scott	27	278	43	74	12	3	6	29	22	.266	34	4.50
PEAK		510	79	136	22	6	11	53	40	.267	65	4.69
Ramos, John	26	367	47	106	18	1	9	55	45	.289	53	5.48
PEAK		484	70	146	25	1	14	65	66	.302	83	6.63
Sax, Dave	33	264	41	71	19	1	7	48	41	.269	39	5.46
PEAK		476	74	128	34	2	13	87	74	.269	75	5.82
Stankiewicz, Andy	27	363	42	92	11	2	1	36	24	.253	32	3.19
PEAK		516	60	131	16	3	1	51	34	.254	47	3.30
Walewander, Jim	31	400	73	84	11	1	2	34	56	.210	30	2.56
PEAK		482	88	101	13	1	2	41	68	.210	37	2.62
Williams, Bernie	23	299	47	83	13	3	7	33	31	.278	41	5.12
PEAK		491	100	152	24	5	17	72	59	.310	91	7.25

ALBANY

Name	Age	AB	R	H	D	T	HR	RBI	BB	AVG	RC	RC/G
Davis, Russ	22	469	52	99	23	1	8	53	45	.211	41	2.99
PEAK		492	82	126	27	1	14	60	58	.256	66	4.87
DeJardin, Bobby	25	476	68	136	20	0	2	49	57	.286	57	4.53
PEAK		489	81	151	22	0	3	45	61	.309	70	5.59
Knoblaugh, Jay	26	331	48	91	15	1	10	46	39	.275	48	5.40
PEAK		486	81	141	23	1	18	69	64	.290	82	6.42
Masse, Billy	25	352	62	101	16	1	10	57	43	.287	53	5.70
PEAK		488	103	151	24	1	19	73	62	.309	91	7.29
Phillips, Vince	23	477	65	127	26	1	8	78	52	.266	59	4.55
PEAK		488	87	146	29	1	12	62	62	.299	81	6.39
Silvestri, Dave	24	507	89	129	31	4	20	77	76	.254	79	5.64
PEAK		474	107	134	31	4	27	86	76	.283	97	7.70
Snow, J.T.	24	472	72	128	32	1	13	70	61	.271	70	5.49
PEAK		482	92	144	34	1	19	74	68	.299	91	7.27
Vargas, Hector	26	341	46	92	19	1	1	36	41	.270	40	4.34
PEAK		485	73	138	28	1	2	43	65	.285	64	4.98
Viera, John	24	305	48	79	10	2	5	37	37	.259	36	4.30
PEAK		485	96	139	18	3	11	58	65	.287	73	5.70

OAKLAND A'S

TACOMA

Name	Age	AB	R	H	D	T	HR	RBI	BB	AVG	RC	RC/G
Afenir, Troy	28	252	26	54	11	2	7	29	16	.214	22	3.00
PEAK		517	53	111	23	4	14	60	33	.215	48	3.19
Coachman, Pete	30	293	49	70	14	1	1	28	36	.239	27	3.27
PEAK		490	82	117	23	2	2	47	60	.239	48	3.47
Fox, Eric	24	500	65	119	21	5	4	39	42	.238	45	3.19
PEAK		500	83	134	23	5	6	49	50	.268	62	4.57
Hemond, Scott	26	313	38	75	17	4	2	23	29	.240	30	3.40
PEAK		495	70	128	28	6	4	46	55	.259	60	4.41
Howitt, Dann	28	430	44	101	24	4	10	55	36	.235	45	3.69
PEAK		508	52	119	28	5	12	65	42	.234	56	3.89
Jennings, Doug	27	318	33	75	15	1	2	34	35	.236	28	3.11
PEAK		495	51	117	23	2	3	53	55	.236	48	3.43
Komminsk, Brad	31	258	29	67	13	3	4	33	21	.260	29	4.10
PEAK		509	57	132	26	6	8	65	41	.259	61	4.37
Simmons, Nelson	29	409	36	98	17	1	5	51	35	.240	37	3.21
PEAK		507	45	121	21	1	6	63	43	.239	48	3.36
Witmeyer, Ron	25	414	49	96	17	3	11	61	42	.232	43	3.65
PEAK		495	75	129	22	3	18	68	55	.261	71	5.24

HUNTSVILLE

Name	Age	AB	R	H	D	T	HR	RBI	BB	AVG	RC	RC/G
Armas, Marcos	22	300	35	64	17	1	7	47	16	.213	26	2.97
PEAK		512	93	132	32	2	20	73	38	.258	70	4.97
Buccheri, James	23	335	42	67	16	0	0	20	63	.200	26	2.62
PEAK		458	78	111	25	0	0	32	92	.242	50	3.89
Conte, Mike	24	353	32	76	11	0	5	26	22	.215	26	2.53
PEAK		510	64	126	18	0	11	52	40	.247	53	3.73
Correia, Rod	24	286	22	60	11	1	1	20	28	.210	21	2.51
PEAK		495	50	120	21	2	3	38	55	.242	49	3.53
Dattola, Kevin	24	280	34	62	14	2	0	16	32	.221	24	2.97
PEAK		488	75	124	27	3	0	37	62	.254	53	3.93
Neel, Troy	26	358	56	95	22	0	21	60	73	.265	68	6.98
PEAK		457	82	128	29	0	33	93	93	.280	103	8.45
Paquette, Craig	23	371	44	92	18	1	7	52	25	.248	38	3.68
PEAK		506	83	144	27	1	14	65	44	.285	73	5.44
Tinsley, Lee	23	298	41	63	8	4	2	21	47	.211	26	2.99
PEAK		469	88	118	16	6	5	43	81	.252	58	4.46
Vice, Darryl	25	282	40	65	12	1	0	24	56	.230	27	3.36
PEAK		462	77	119	22	2	0	34	88	.258	55	4.33

PHILADELPHIA PHILLIES

SCRANTON WILKES-BARRE

Name	Age	AB	R	H	D	T	HR	RBI	BB	AVG	RC	RC/G
Batiste, Kim	24	437	38	110	20	2	1	29	8	.252	34	2.81
PEAK		530	59	149	27	2	2	45	20	.281	57	4.04
Campusano, Sil	25	291	31	66	10	1	5	33	17	.227	24	2.88
PEAK		512	72	130	20	2	12	57	38	.254	58	4.10
Fletcher, Darrin	25	291	27	72	11	1	5	35	17	.247	27	3.33
PEAK		512	61	140	21	2	12	59	38	.273	65	4.72
Grotewold, Jeff	26	264	23	59	11	2	3	26	19	.223	22	2.90
PEAK		503	54	122	22	4	7	48	47	.243	53	3.76
Legg, Greg	32	333	41	83	12	2	2	29	32	.249	30	3.24
PEAK		502	62	125	18	3	3	44	48	.249	50	3.58
Peguero, Julio	23	480	49	112	16	3	1	27	29	.233	35	2.57
PEAK		509	71	138	20	3	2	41	41	.271	55	4.00
Scarsone, Steve	26	384	36	90	16	2	4	26	14	.234	30	2.76
PEAK		518	60	131	23	3	7	49	32	.253	54	3.77
Schu, Rick	30	334	48	93	25	2	9	40	37	.278	48	5.38
PEAK		495	71	138	37	3	13	59	55	.279	77	5.82
Wade, Scott	29	295	34	67	11	2	6	30	24	.227	27	3.20
PEAK		509	59	116	19	3	10	52	41	.228	49	3.37

READING

Name	Age	AB	R	H	D	T	HR	RBI	BB	AVG	RC	RC/G
Austin, Pat	26	314	42	80	19	1	2	29	33	.255	33	3.81
PEAK		491	75	133	31	1	4	46	59	.271	62	4.68
Brown, Dana	25	260	29	55	4	1	2	19	22	.212	17	2.24
PEAK		502	73	121	10	2	5	41	48	.241	46	3.26
Dostal, Bruce	27	344	50	94	10	2	3	25	46	.273	39	4.21
PEAK		485	71	133	14	3	4	35	65	.274	59	4.53
Lindsey, Doug	24	299	19	67	11	0	1	25	16	.224	20	2.33
PEAK		514	43	131	21	0	3	40	36	.255	49	3.45
Longmire, Tony	23	308	32	78	20	1	6	41	26	.253	35	4.11
PEAK		499	70	144	35	2	15	68	51	.289	81	6.16
Milette, Joe	25	339	38	73	8	2	2	21	29	.215	24	2.44
PEAK		501	72	123	14	3	4	41	49	.246	48	3.43
Riesgo, Nikco	25	341	44	77	16	1	9	48	38	.226	35	3.58
PEAK		492	82	125	25	1	18	67	58	.254	69	5.08
Robertson, Rod	24	399	38	85	17	0	6	37	26	.213	30	2.58
PEAK		509	67	125	24	0	11	54	41	.246	55	3.87
Ryan, Sean	23	421	40	88	19	0	5	50	41	.209	32	2.59
PEAK		493	68	123	25	0	9	51	57	.249	57	4.16
Waller, Casey	24	384	46	87	22	1	8	38	42	.227	38	3.45
PEAK		490	78	126	30	1	15	63	60	.257	69	5.12
Williams, Carey	25	401	40	97	19	2	4	45	21	.242	35	3.11
PEAK		515	65	138	27	2	7	52	35	.268	60	4.30

PITTSBURGH PIRATES

BUFFALO

Name	Age	AB	R	H	D	T	HR	RBI	BB	AVG	RC	RC/G
Espy, Cecil	29	380	54	106	23	7	2	33	27	.279	46	4.53
PEAK		514	73	143	31	9	3	45	36	.278	65	4.73
Garcia, Carlos	22	445	47	105	17	5	6	46	25	.236	39	3.10
PEAK		510	78	141	23	6	11	60	40	.276	69	5.05
Meyer, Joey	30	280	21	67	11	1	5	27	12	.239	24	3.04
PEAK		527	40	126	21	2	9	51	23	.239	48	3.23
Miller, Keith	29	424	49	98	23	6	8	53	53	.231	46	3.81
PEAK		489	56	113	27	7	9	61	61	.231	57	4.09
Redfield, Joe	31	341	46	83	17	5	6	38	41	.243	39	4.08
PEAK		491	66	120	24	7	9	55	59	.244	60	4.37
Schulz, Jeff	31	417	42	111	17	3	2	41	32	.266	42	3.71
PEAK		511	51	136	21	4	2	50	39	.266	54	3.89
Tubbs, Greg	29	358	55	87	15	7	3	27	37	.243	37	3.69
PEAK		498	77	121	21	10	4	38	52	.243	55	3.94

CAROLINA

Name	Age	AB	R	H	D	T	HR	RBI	BB	AVG	RC	RC/G
Crowley, Terry	24	459	49	113	14	5	7	37	36	.246	46	3.59
PEAK		503	69	139	18	5	11	58	47	.276	68	5.04
Edge, Greg	27	344	36	71	9	1	1	19	30	.206	22	2.18
PEAK		506	53	104	13	1	1	28	44	.206	33	2.22
Estep, Chris	25	296	29	39	16	1	4	29	27	.132	14	1.47
PEAK		499	76	84	31	2	11	46	51	.168	37	2.41
Pennye, Darwin	25	445	43	107	18	6	5	35	19	.240	40	3.20
PEAK		519	64	139	23	7	8	55	31	.268	62	4.41
Romero, Mandy	24	317	24	64	11	0	3	26	37	.202	23	2.45
PEAK		487	50	115	19	0	7	43	63	.236	50	3.63
Schreiber, Bruce	25	318	21	72	10	1	1	19	17	.226	22	2.41
PEAK		514	44	131	18	2	2	40	36	.255	48	3.38
Young, Kevin	23	255	31	82	18	5	3	28	13	.322	41	6.40
PEAK		514	75	179	38	9	9	70	36	.348	102	8.22
Zambrano, Eddie	25	262	24	61	16	2	3	25	18	.233	24	3.22
PEAK		508	59	132	33	4	8	54	42	.260	62	4.45

ST. LOUIS CARDINALS

LOUISVILLE

Name	Age	AB	R	H	D	T	HR	RBI	BB	AVG	RC	RC/G
Brewer, Rod	26	362	26	66	16	1	4	34	25	.182	21	1.92
PEAK		504	47	104	24	1	7	43	46	.206	41	2.77
Fernandez, Joey	26	299	26	58	11	1	6	21	40	.194	23	2.58
PEAK		480	52	104	19	2	12	51	70	.217	52	3.73
Figueroa, Bien	28	257	12	43	7	1	0	9	14	.167	10	1.26
PEAK		522	24	87	14	2	0	18	28	.167	22	1.37
Jones, Tim	29	288	22	61	8	1	3	19	26	.212	20	2.38
PEAK		504	39	107	14	2	5	33	46	.212	39	2.65
Maclin, Lonnie	25	306	23	73	9	1	2	24	11	.239	22	2.55
PEAK		521	51	138	17	2	5	45	29	.265	53	3.74
Martinez, Julian	25	382	34	71	16	1	6	26	45	.186	27	2.34
PEAK		489	59	107	23	1	11	50	61	.219	50	3.53
Ross, Mike	26	239	13	41	7	1	2	13	10	.172	11	1.50
PEAK		515	39	101	17	2	6	38	35	.196	35	2.28
Royer, Stan	24	493	31	103	23	4	8	48	31	.209	37	2.56
PEAK		510	44	123	26	4	12	58	40	.241	57	3.98

ARKANSAS

Name	Age	AB	R	H	D	T	HR	RBI	BB	AVG	RC	RC/G
Abreu, Frank	24	239	14	44	8	1	1	12	33	.184	14	1.94
PEAK		479	38	105	19	2	3	35	71	.219	44	3.18
Brannon, Cliff	24	367	27	80	19	1	2	26	20	.218	25	2.35
PEAK		513	50	128	29	1	4	45	37	.250	51	3.58
Christian, Ric	25	263	17	48	8	2	0	13	20	.183	13	1.63
PEAK		505	44	108	18	4	0	31	45	.214	37	2.52
Fernandez, Jose	24	263	27	46	10	1	7	15	43	.175	20	2.49
PEAK		469	70	99	20	2	19	62	81	.211	59	4.31
Fiore, Mike	26	419	36	85	24	2	5	30	31	.203	30	2.43
PEAK		502	54	113	30	2	8	48	48	.225	50	3.47
Martinez, Luis	26	259	16	55	12	1	1	19	23	.212	18	2.38
PEAK		497	37	116	24	2	2	38	53	.233	46	3.26
Ross, Mike	26	237	18	45	13	0	4	16	10	.190	14	1.97
PEAK		515	52	109	30	0	11	52	35	.212	45	2.99
Sellick, John	26	361	34	69	13	1	10	38	30	.191	26	2.40
PEAK		499	61	106	20	1	18	61	51	.212	52	3.57
Shireman, Jeff	26	344	29	65	8	1	1	16	32	.189	18	1.74
PEAK		495	53	105	13	1	2	32	55	.212	37	2.56
White, Charlie	25	307	19	56	10	2	1	17	23	.182	16	1.72
PEAK		506	43	108	19	3	2	36	44	.213	38	2.58

SAN DIEGO PADRES

LAS VEGAS

Name	Age	AB	R	H	D	T	HR	RBI	BB	AVG	RC	RC/G
Azocar, Oscar	27	336	32	82	18	2	4	31	15	.244	29	3.08
PEAK		526	50	128	28	3	6	49	24	.243	50	3.39
Higgins, Kevin	25	376	33	89	10	2	2	27	31	.237	29	2.73
PEAK		503	55	133	15	3	4	42	47	.264	54	3.94
Mota, Jose	27	352	35	84	8	1	1	23	37	.239	27	2.72
PEAK		498	49	119	11	1	1	33	52	.239	42	2.99
Staton, Dave	24	351	38	76	15	1	14	52	29	.217	34	3.34
PEAK		501	77	125	24	1	29	86	49	.250	75	5.39
Taylor, Will	23	440	51	93	9	2	3	20	38	.211	29	2.26
PEAK		498	83	125	13	2	5	43	52	.251	51	3.69
Vatcher, Jim	26	370	42	80	22	3	11	42	36	.216	37	3.44
PEAK		494	69	117	31	4	18	68	56	.237	66	4.73
Walters, Dan	25	271	24	71	18	0	3	26	15	.262	27	3.65
PEAK		513	56	147	36	0	8	56	37	.287	69	5.09
Ward, Kevin	30	255	32	68	14	3	3	26	39	.267	31	4.48
PEAK		477	60	127	26	6	6	49	73	.266	67	5.17

WICHITA

Name	Age	AB	R	H	D	T	HR	RBI	BB	AVG	RC	RC/G
Cisarik, Brian	27	367	49	92	21	2	3	37	46	.251	39	3.83
PEAK		489	65	123	28	3	4	49	61	.252	57	4.20
David, Greg	25	293	31	65	10	0	3	33	29	.222	23	2.72
PEAK		496	67	124	19	0	7	46	54	.250	53	3.85
Harris, Vince	24	364	55	92	11	1	0	28	44	.253	32	3.18
PEAK		485	90	137	17	1	0	37	65	.282	57	4.42
Hilleman, Charles	26	278	33	65	16	1	4	32	20	.234	25	3.17
PEAK		503	72	127	30	2	9	53	47	.252	59	4.24
Lopez, Luis	21	433	31	101	15	1	1	30	13	.233	29	2.36
PEAK		522	56	146	22	1	2	43	28	.280	56	4.02
McWilliam, Tim	25	292	28	76	17	1	4	40	24	.260	31	3.88
PEAK		503	59	143	31	2	9	58	47	.284	71	5.32
Redington, Tom	23	376	39	94	20	0	3	41	47	.250	38	3.64
PEAK		482	65	138	28	0	6	49	68	.286	69	5.42
Sherman, Darrell	24	478	66	124	15	2	2	35	52	.259	46	3.51
PEAK		490	83	141	18	2	3	43	60	.288	63	4.87
Valentin, Jose	22	429	52	94	19	3	10	49	39	.219	39	3.14
PEAK		494	90	130	25	3	19	70	56	.263	74	5.49
Velasquez, Guillermo	24	477	51	124	23	2	13	71	33	.260	54	4.13
PEAK		507	71	146	26	2	20	75	43	.288	81	6.06

SAN FRANCISCO GIANTS
PHOENIX

Name	Age	AB	R	H	D	T	HR	RBI	BB	AVG	RC	RC/G
Coles, Darnell	30	308	26	75	18	1	3	40	17	.244	27	3.13
PEAK		521	44	127	30	2	5	68	29	.244	50	3.43
Lewis, Darren	24	292	38	84	10	6	1	32	26	.288	34	4.41
PEAK		498	77	156	19	9	2	50	52	.313	75	5.92
Parker, Rick	29	278	25	70	8	5	3	25	17	.252	26	3.38
PEAK		518	47	131	15	9	6	47	32	.253	54	3.77
Santana, Andres	24	425	51	113	6	3	1	21	23	.266	35	3.03
PEAK		513	77	151	10	3	2	42	37	.294	59	4.40
Wilson, Jim	31	405	379	102	24	0	11	47	30	.252	44	3.92
PEAK		512	479	129	30	0	14	59	38	.252	61	4.30
Wood, Ted	25	477	55	124	31	4	6	66	56	.260	54	4.13
PEAK		489	67	139	34	4	8	57	61	.284	75	5.79

SHREVEPORT

Name	Age	AB	R	H	D	T	HR	RBI	BB	AVG	RC	RC/G
Clayton, Royce	22	466	60	116	20	5	3	48	43	.249	45	3.47
PEAK		493	86	142	24	5	5	50	57	.288	69	5.31
Cooper, Jaime	26	362	41	74	8	1	1	17	24	.204	21	1.97
PEAK		506	72	114	13	1	2	33	44	.225	39	2.69
Guerrero, Juan	25	457	56	138	39	1	13	67	32	.302	71	6.01
PEAK		507	74	146	45	1	19	82	43	.323	101	7.95
Hosey, Steve	23	393	56	104	20	3	9	52	39	.265	48	4.48
PEAK		492	93	147	27	4	17	71	58	.299	87	6.81
Lewis, Dan	24	405	47	106	29	1	9	65	35	.282	49	4.42
PEAK		499	74	145	37	1	16	70	51	.291	83	6.33
Patterson, John	25	445	58	118	30	9	3	41	21	.265	49	4.05
PEAK		517	81	150	37	10	5	56	33	.290	74	5.44
Smiley, Reuben	23	308	41	63	7	2	3	22	38	.205	22	2.42
PEAK		482	93	119	14	3	7	45	68	.247	54	4.02
Tucker, Scooter	25	339	35	87	27	1	3	20	19	.257	35	3.75
PEAK		513	65	145	43	1	6	55	37	.283	69	5.06

SEATTLE MARINERS
CALGARY

Name	Age	AB	R	H	D	T	HR	RBI	BB	AVG	RC	RC/G
Amaral, Rich	30	319	51	92	21	1	2	23	35	.288	38	4.52
PEAK		496	79	143	33	2	3	36	54	.288	68	5.20
Blowers, Mike	27	307	36	73	16	1	6	38	26	.238	29	3.35
PEAK		507	59	121	26	2	10	63	43	.239	54	3.78
Brundage, Dave	27	339	48	87	18	2	2	20	46	.257	35	3.75
PEAK		484	69	124	26	3	3	29	66	.256	57	4.28
Cockrell, Alan	29	406	49	97	22	1	7	52	29	.239	37	3.23
PEAK		513	62	123	28	1	9	66	37	.240	52	3.60
Hood, Dennis	25	301	33	43	8	1	7	27	22	.143	14	1.47
PEAK		506	89	90	16	2	18	57	44	.178	40	2.60
Howard, Chris	26	276	20	55	10	1	6	23	11	.199	18	2.20
PEAK		516	50	114	20	2	14	57	34	.221	48	3.22
Jackson, Chuck	29	457	52	108	23	4	10	55	24	.236	42	3.25
PEAK		523	59	123	26	5	11	63	27	.235	52	3.51
Lennon, Pat	24	385	48	106	24	4	10	47	30	.275	49	4.74
PEAK		503	79	152	33	5	18	77	47	.302	90	6.92
Martinez, Tino	24	410	62	112	29	4	13	55	53	.273	59	5.35
PEAK		482	91	145	36	4	22	81	68	.301	99	7.93
Springer, Steve	31	388	40	82	20	1	11	45	18	.211	31	2.74
PEAK		526	54	111	27	1	15	61	24	.211	45	2.93

JACKSONVILLE

Name	Age	AB	R	H	D	T	HR	RBI	BB	AVG	RC	RC/G
Bolick, Frank	26	464	68	115	16	0	14	72	75	.248	60	4.64
PEAK		471	81	125	18	0	17	63	79	.265	72	5.62
Boone, Bret	23	471	64	117	15	2	16	74	63	.248	61	4.65
PEAK		478	90	136	18	2	25	79	72	.285	88	6.95
Bowie, Jim	27	443	50	134	22	0	8	66	32	.302	62	5.42
PEAK		513	58	155	25	0	9	76	37	.302	72	5.43
Campanis, Jim	24	383	36	92	9	0	13	48	33	.240	41	3.80
PEAK		500	64	135	14	0	24	77	50	.270	74	5.47
Gonzalez, Ruben	25	305	26	70	12	0	3	39	33	.230	27	3.10
PEAK		493	53	127	22	0	7	46	57	.258	57	4.20
Manahan, Anthony	23	405	66	99	20	2	6	44	49	.244	45	3.97
PEAK		483	105	136	26	2	11	58	67	.282	73	5.68
Pennington, Ken	26	317	31	75	13	2	5	28	23	.237	30	3.35
PEAK		503	59	128	22	3	10	53	47	.254	59	4.25
Wetherby, Jeff	28	261	38	73	14	2	6	36	31	.280	38	5.46
PEAK		492	72	138	26	4	11	68	58	.280	73	5.57
Williams, Ted	27	266	46	56	9	4	3	16	19	.211	21	2.70
PEAK		513	89	108	17	8	6	31	37	.211	42	2.80

TEXAS RANGERS

OKLAHOMA CITY

Name	Age	AB	R	H	D	T	HR	RBI	BB	AVG	RC	RC/G
Capra, Nick	34	470	60	117	28	3	4	31	75	.249	55	4.21
PEAK		474	61	118	28	3	4	31	76	.249	58	4.40
Fariss, Monty	24	479	68	119	26	8	11	59	78	.248	65	4.88
PEAK		470	83	130	27	7	15	67	80	.277	82	6.51
Green, Gary	30	300	29	59	4	1	2	24	30	.197	18	2.02
PEAK		500	48	98	7	2	3	40	50	.196	32	2.15
Hasselman, Bill	26	430	47	101	19	1	7	48	52	.235	43	3.53
PEAK		485	63	123	23	1	10	51	65	.254	61	4.55
Mauer, Rob	25	445	62	124	35	3	17	63	82	.279	80	6.73
PEAK		466	77	141	38	3	24	84	84	.303	105	8.72
Millay, Gar	27	251	31	54	10	1	5	23	50	.215	27	3.70
PEAK		459	57	99	18	2	9	42	91	.216	51	3.83
Peltier, Dan	24	337	31	71	14	3	2	25	37	.211	27	2.74
PEAK		490	59	119	23	4	4	43	60	.243	53	3.86

TULSA

Name	Age	AB	R	H	D	T	HR	RBI	BB	AVG	RC	RC/G
Burton, Mike	25	348	32	74	15	1	5	36	41	.213	29	2.86
PEAK		489	58	118	23	1	10	51	61	.241	56	4.08
Frye, Jeff	25	480	69	129	27	8	3	30	51	.269	57	4.38
PEAK		494	83	145	30	8	4	52	56	.294	74	5.72
Harris, Donald	24	434	35	86	14	5	7	40	18	.198	29	2.25
PEAK		519	60	120	19	6	13	57	31	.231	52	3.52
Hernandez, Jose	22	290	27	61	14	4	1	15	18	.210	21	2.48
PEAK		507	69	129	28	7	3	45	43	.254	56	4.00
Morris, Rod	26	367	33	87	14	5	0	26	21	.237	29	2.80
PEAK		509	54	130	21	7	0	39	41	.255	51	3.63
Rohrmeier, Dan	26	399	50	103	17	1	4	46	44	.258	41	3.74
PEAK		489	70	134	22	1	6	47	61	.274	62	4.72
Sable, Luke	26	324	24	83	9	5	0	25	18	.256	28	3.14
PEAK		510	44	139	16	7	0	40	40	.273	55	4.00

TORONTO BLUE JAYS

SYRACUSE

Name	Age	AB	R	H	D	T	HR	RBI	BB	AVG	RC	RC/G
Bell, Derek	23	430	64	131	19	6	10	66	40	.305	64	5.78
PEAK		495	92	165	24	6	17	76	55	.333	101	8.26
Ducey, Rob	27	252	39	64	8	1	7	28	36	.254	30	4.31
PEAK		481	74	122	15	2	13	53	69	.254	63	4.74
Fields, Bruce	31	248	20	54	8	0	2	15	19	.218	17	2.37
PEAK		511	41	111	16	0	4	31	39	.217	38	2.57
Knorr, Randy	23	327	20	74	17	0	4	30	16	.226	25	2.67
PEAK		515	45	136	30	0	10	56	35	.264	61	4.35
Martinez, Domingo	24	441	44	120	13	1	14	59	28	.272	52	4.37
PEAK		509	66	152	17	1	23	79	41	.299	84	6.35
Pederson, Stu	32	356	35	81	17	1	7	39	46	.228	35	3.44
PEAK		487	48	111	23	1	10	53	63	.228	53	3.81
Quinlan, Tom	24	447	40	93	20	3	8	35	51	.208	38	2.90
PEAK		488	59	118	24	3	13	57	62	.242	61	4.45
Schunk, Jerry	26	313	23	67	7	0	4	20	6	.214	19	2.09
PEAK		525	51	123	13	0	8	46	25	.234	43	2.89
Suero, William	25	379	35	64	15	1	1	20	27	.169	18	1.54
PEAK		507	66	102	23	1	2	33	43	.201	35	2.33
Zosky, Eddie	24	488	49	112	15	2	5	27	25	.230	37	2.66
PEAK		515	69	134	18	2	8	50	35	.260	55	3.90

KNOXVILLE

Name	Age	AB	R	H	D	T	HR	RBI	BB	AVG	RC	RC/G
Cedeno, Domingo	23	329	36	68	7	4	1	22	25	.207	22	2.28
PEAK		502	79	124	14	6	2	40	48	.247	49	3.50
Delarosa, Juan	23	375	34	75	11	1	4	29	14	.200	22	1.98
PEAK		520	73	126	19	1	9	50	30	.242	49	3.36
Deloach, Bobby	25	355	37	88	15	2	5	34	21	.248	34	3.44
PEAK		512	67	140	24	3	10	57	38	.273	65	4.72
Gianelli, Ray	26	353	48	91	14	2	8	34	55	.258	46	4.74
PEAK		473	73	130	20	3	13	59	77	.275	73	5.75
Kent, Jeff	24	435	61	104	32	1	12	54	68	.239	57	4.65
PEAK		472	85	127	36	1	19	71	78	.269	83	6.50
O'Halloran, Greg	24	342	34	81	13	2	8	48	23	.237	34	3.52
PEAK		508	68	136	22	3	17	68	42	.268	70	5.08
Thompson, Ryan	24	394	43	88	14	2	8	37	22	.223	33	2.91
PEAK		513	77	131	21	2	15	63	37	.255	61	4.31
Yan, Julian	26	342	40	89	15	2	16	54	19	.260	45	4.80
PEAK		510	73	141	24	3	29	90	40	.276	85	6.22
Young, Mark	26	310	38	67	10	2	1	19	45	.216	25	2.78
PEAK		476	69	113	17	3	2	35	74	.237	48	3.57

Glossary

APPROXIMATE VALUE

This Bill James method computes the worth of a single player's single season. It relies on the rawest of stats, without ballpark adjustments. It also does not interpolate between its basic breakpoints. As a consequence, Approximate Values are, in fact, very approximate. They are only used for quick evaluations or when you have just the rawest of stats to work from. Bill used AV to get a quick handle on a player season for which he didn't or couldn't compute something more comprehensive.

New BASEBALL SABERMETRIC APPLICATION

As it turns out, the range of Approximate Value figures is about the same as twice the range of Total Wins Above Replacement. Since TWAR is a much more reliable stat, and since a computer can calculate TWAR even faster than AV, BASEBALL SABERMETRIC uses 2xTWAR instead of Bill's AV. Actually, you won't see any AVs in the book; the only use we've made of AV was as a feeder stat for Trade Value (qv.).

The breakpoints and point values for Bill's AV are:

FOR PITCHERS

1. Games Pitched

   30-54 games = 1
   55-79 games = 2
   80+ games = 3

2. Innings Pitched

   40-89 = 1
   90-139 = 2
   140-189 = 3
   190-239 = 4
   240-289 = 5
   290-339 = 6
   340+ = 7

3. 2*(Wins+Saves)-Losses

   6-13 = 1
   14-23 = 2
   24-35 = 3
   36-49 = 4
   50-65 = 5
   66-83 = 6
   84+= 7

4. Wins

   18+= 1

5. League ERA leader= 1

6. League Save leader = 1

7. Compute:
   Pitcher's Decisions*
   (League ERA + 1 - Pitcher's ERA)
   /13

   Round statistically, and add to the above.

   NOTE: Item #7 will be a negative number if the Pitcher's ERA is more than 1.00 above the league ERA. That will reduce the total AV, rather than increasing it. If the AV should fall below zero, then it is equal to zero.

NON-PITCHERS

1. Games Played

   10-49 = 1
   50-99 = 2
   100-129 = 3
   130+ = 4

2. Batting Average

   .250-.274 = 1
   .275-.299 = 2
   .300-.324 = 3
   .325-349 = 4
   .350-374 = 5
   .375-.399 = 6
   .400+ = 7

3. Slugging Average

   .300-.399 - 1
   .400-.499 = 2
   .500-.599 = 3
   .600-.699 = 4
   .700-.799 = 5
   .800+ = 6

4. Home Runs*100/At-Bats

   2.5-4.9 = 1
   5.0-7.4 = 2
   7.5-9.9 = 3
   10.0+ = 4

5. Walks*100/At-Bats

   1.0-1.9 = 1
   2.0-2.9 = 2
   3.0+ = 3

6. Stolen Bases

   20-49 = 1
   50-79 = 2
   80+= 3

7. High RBI and Low Slugging Percentage

   70+ / .400- = 1
   100+ / .500-= 2
   130+ / .600-= 3

8. Primary Defensive Position

   Second, Third or Center = 1
   Shortstop = 2

   Catcher (10-79 games) = 1
   (80-149 games) = 2
   (150+ games) = 3

9. Range Factor (qv.)

   Above League Average for all but Catchers and First Base = 1

10. Assists

    100+ first base only = 1

11. Fielding Average

    Above League Average at Position = 1

12. Double Plays

    Shortstop or Second Base

    90-119 = 1
    120-149 = 2
    150+ = 3

13. Assists Plus Double Plays Outfielders Only

    12+= 1

14. Opposition Stolen Bases Catchers Only

    Below League Average = 1

15. 200+ Hits = 1

16. League RBI leader = 1

17. Take total to this point and multiply by the Largest of:

    Player's At-Bats/500 or
    Player's Plate *Appearances/550

    Round statistically.

BALLPARK ADJUSTMENT

This is the concept of adjusting a players' stats to reflect the biases of the home ballpark in which he plays half his games. The objective is to come up with a stat line that is "what the player would have done if he played the same number of games in each ballpark," or "what the player would have done in a neutral ballpark."

There are various methods of doing this, but the basic approach is always to compare the player's stats at home with his stats on the road. The ELIAS BASEBALL ANALYST does the silliest thing possible with this information, which is to compute the ratio of the two splits. This results in an adjustment not to a neutral ballpark, but to all parks EXCEPT the home park. I'm not sure what method PETE PALMER uses for his Linear Weights, but, knowing Pete, I'm sure they're much more reasonable than the ELIAS. For the last two years, what we have done is to compute the following formulas for both the batting and pitching stats for a team, for the National and American Leagues:

NL: (11R + H) / (6R + 6H)
AL: (13R + H) / (7R + 7H)

where R and H are the road and home stats. Then we multiplied the results by each player's stats, to get a ballpark adjusted figure. This year, we did something a little more complicated with the formula. We made three sets of adjustment figures: one for lefty batters, one for righty batters, and one for the whole. The component stats were both the team's batters of the appropriate hand and also the team's pitchers' opposing batter lines for opposing batters of the appropriate hand. The only reason for generating the total figures was to work with switch hitters.

BILL JAMES HALL OF FAME METHOD
(ORGANIC HALL OF FAME SYSTEM)

This method is used to evaluate a player's chance of making the Hall of Fame. it is NOT designed to determine whether the player "should" make the Hall; just whether he is likely to do so. That is, this is an evaluation of the apparent statistical criteria which the Hall of Fame voters do in fact use in determining who should be voted into the Hall.

PITCHERS

1. Wins

   15-17 = 2
   18-19 = 4
   20-22 = 6
   23-24 = 8
   25-29 = 10
   30+= 15

2. Strikeouts

   200-249 = 2
   250-299 = 3
   300+ = 6

3. Winning Percentage of .700+ and 14+ Wins

   = 2

4. ERA (50+ games or 150+ innings)

   2.00-2.99 = 1
   1.00-1.99 = 4

5. Saves

   20-29 = 2
   30+= 5

6. No-Hitter = 1

7. League Leader

   ERA = 2
   Games = 1
   Wins = 1
   Innings= 1
   Winning Percentage = 1
   Strikeouts = 1
   Shutouts = 1
   Saves = 1
   Complete Games = 0.5

8. Career Wins

150-174 = 5
175-199 = 8
200-224 = 10
225-249 = 15
250-274 = 20
275-299 = 25
300+ = 35

9. Career Winning Percentage (200+ decisions)

.550-.574 = 1
.575-.599 = 3
.600-.624 = 5
.625+ = 10

10. Career ERA Below 3.00 = 10

11. Career Saves

200-299 = 10
300+ = 20

12. Games Pitched

700-849 = 10
850-999 = 20
1000+ = 30

13. Career Strikeouts

3000-3999 = 10
4000+ = 20

14. World Series

Game Started = 2
Game Won = 2
Relief Appearance = 1

15. LCS Win = 1

NOTE: Total Points for Post-Season play are limited to 20.

16. MVP = 8

17. Cy Young Award = 5

18. All-Star Game Pitched In = 3

19. Gold Glove = 1

20. Rookie of the Year = 1

NON-PITCHERS

1. Batting Average (only for seasons of 100+ games)

.300-.349 = 2.5
.350-.399 = 5.0
.400+ = 15.0

2. 200+ Hits = 5

3. 100+ RBI = 3

4. 100+ Runs Scored = 3

5. Home Runs

30-39 = 2
40-49 = 4
50+= 10

6. Doubles

35-44 = 1
45+= 2

7. 100+ Walks = 0.5

8. League Leader

Batting Average = 6
Home Runs = 4
RBI = 4
Runs Scored = 3
Hits = 2
Stolen Bases = 2
Doubles = 1
Triples = 1

9. Career Hits

2000-2499 = 4
2500-2999 = 15
3000-3499 = 40
3500+ = 50

10. Career Home Runs

300-399 = 3
400-499 = 10
500-599 = 20
600+ = 30

11. Career Batting Average (1500+ games)

.300-.314 = 8
.315-.329 = 16
.330+ = 24

12. Games Played at Catcher Only

1200-1399=15
1400-1599 = 30
1600-1799 = 45
1800+ = 60

13. Games Played at Shortstop

1900-2199 = 15
2200+ = 30

14. Games Played at Second Base

same as #13

15. Games Played at Third Base

2000+ = 15

16. Games Played at Second, Short or Third Combined (in ADDITION to above)

2500+ = 15

17. If the player has a career batting average of .275+ and has played 1500 games at either Second Base, Shortstop or Catcher (do NOT combine)

= 15

18. MVP Award = 8

19. All-Star Game Played = 3

20. Gold Glove = 1

21. Rookie of the Year = 1

22. Regular Player on a World Champion

Shortstop = 6
Catcher = 6
Second Base = 5
Center Field = 5
Third Base = 3
Left Field = 2
Right Field = 2
First Base = 1
DH = 1

23. Regular Player on World Series Loser

Shortstop = 5
Catcher = 5
Second Base = 3
Center Field = 3
Third Base = 1

24. Regular Player on LCS Loser

Shortstop = 2
Catcher = 2
Second Base = 1
Center Field = 1
Third Base = 1

MANAGERS

1. Managed 100+ Games = 2

2. World Champion = 8

3. World Series Loser = 5

4. LCS Loser = 3

5. EACH 200 Career Wins = 1

6. Team Won 100+ Games = 1

DEFENSIVE AVERAGE

This is a method of evaluating defense in very high detail, devised by Pete DeCoursey.

DEFENSIVE EFFICIENCY RECORD (DER)

This is the percentage of all balls in play that a team has turned into outs. Double Plays do NOT count twice. For seasons in which Play-by-Play data is available, this is a direct counting stat. For earlier seasons, the following computation is used to estimate the DER:

1. Compute:

Putouts-Strikeouts-Double Plays
-2*Triple Plays
-Opposition Caught Stealing
-Outfield Assists

2. Compute:

Total Batters Faced-Strikeouts
-Hits-Walks-Hit by Pitch
-.71*Errors

3. Average Computations 1 and 2 above. This is called Plays Made.

4. Compute DER=

Plays Made (#3 above) divided by
(Plays Made + Hits - Home Runs + .71*Errors)

DEFENSIVE WINNING PERCENTAGE

This is an estimate made by Bill James on the basis of long analysis and observation. The chart is a little old and, therefore, out of date, but it is still the best estimate of defensive contribution available.

The Chart below is used to give the defensive player a number of Points, each of which converts into a hundredth (.01) in the winning percentage. The Chart contains, for each defensive position, four separate criteria, each with its own number of possible points. It is arranged so that each position has a "40-point" criteria, a 30-point, a 20-point and a 10-point. This gives a total possible of 100 points, each of which is worth .01. Therefore, a perfect score would be worth a Defensive Winning Percentage of 1.000. Naturally, the standards for this sort of achievement are, essentially, impossible. The Criteria at the various positions are:

CATCHERS

40-point Opposition Stolen Bases per Game divided by the League Average.
30-point ERA when he is in the game minus League ERA.
20-point Fielding Average.
10-point Assists per Game.

FIRST BASE

40-point Fielding Average.
30-point Assists per Game.
20-point Number of 363 Double Plays involving the player.
10-point Errors made at Third Base and Shortstop.

SECOND BASE

40-point Compute:
Player's Double Plays / Games Played /
(Team (Hits + Walks) / Game).
30-point Range Factor (qv.) - Double Plays per Game.
20-point Fielding Percentage.
10-point Team Defensive Efficiency Record

THIRD BASE

40-point Range Factor (qv.)
30-point Fielding Percentage.
20-point Compute:
Player's Double Plays / Games Played /
(Team (Hits + Walks) / Game).

10-point Team Defensive Efficiency Record.

SHORTSTOP

40-point Range Factor (qv.) - Double Plays / Game
30-point Compute:
Player's Double Plays / Games Played /
(Team (Hits + Walks) / Game).
20-point Fielding Percentage.
10-point Team Defensive Efficiency Record.

ALL OUTFIELDERS

40-point Range Factor (qv.)
30-point Fielding Percentage.
20-point Career Assists * 162 / Games Played.
10-point Team Defensive Efficiency Record.

DEFENSIVE WINS ABOVE REPLACEMENT (DWAR)

This process needs to be followed for EACH defensive position the player has played. Then, the various DWARs are added together to get the player's total DWAR.

1. Compute the Player's Defensive Winning Percentage (qv.) at the position.

2. Select the appropriate Game Assignment from the following chart:

   Shortstop = 11
   Catcher = 10
   Second Base = 8
   Center field = 6
   Third Base = 6
   Right Field = 5
   Left Field = 4
   First Base = 3

   NOTE: DH has no defensive value at all, and so will provide no DWAR component.

3. Compute the player's Defensive Games at the position =

   Defensive Innings at the position / 9

3. Compute DWAR =

   Defensive Winning Percentage at the position *
   Game Assignment for the position *
   Defensive Games at the position

EXPECTED WINNING PERCENTAGE

This is the winning percentage that a pitcher "should" have had in a perfect and completely just world. It is computed by applying the Pythagorean Method (qv.) to the Pitcher's Ballpark Adjusted ERA and the League's Average Runs Per Game. That is, it strips away the illusions of the pitcher's ballpark and his team's offensive contribution.

EXPECTED WINS / EXPECTED LOSSES

EWins are computed by multiplying the pitcher's Expected ERA (qv.) by his actual number of decisions, statistically rounding the result to an integer. ELosses are the actual decisions minus the EWins. Surely that is what you expected.

the FAR RIGHT END OF THE NORMAL CURVE

As you may know, there is a statistics distribution called "normal"; you may have heard of it under the name "bell curve" or "normal curve". The normal curve represents the distribution of almost everything, provided that you are examining the whole possible population. Thus, the distribution of baseball talent among the whole of the human race is the normal curve.

However, professional baseball players are not chosen randomly from the whole human race; they are chosen precisely for their ability to play baseball. They are the very best small part of the curve, the part that is on the "right end" of the "normal curve". The importance of this distinction is this: the whole normal curve has most of its people in the middle, with a small number of really great or really bad performers. The right end, on the other hand, has most of its people at the bottom (the left side of the right end, if you're following me), and can be turned on its side and treated as a talent pyramid.

There are a lot of consequences of the difference between a normal distribution and a pyramid distribution; you'll note several in this book. To keep things straight, remember that a talent will be normally distributed if the population you're talking about was selected by some method that is unrelated to the talent at hand. For example, the baseball talent of concert pianists is distributed normally. However, if your population is chosen by some method related to the talent to be examined, you will get the pyramid talent distribution, so the distribution of baseball talent among Major League baseball players is the pyramid. The distribution of talent in a minor league is the funny-looking trapezoid you get if you take a pyramid and lop (truncate) the top off.

FAVORITE TOY

This is a method for estimating the player's chance of attaining a goal, given whatever head start he already has. For example, Don Malcolm of the San Antonio Trotters wants to finish his career with 3000 walks (that hog - but that PATIENT hog). He is now 27 years old and has already accumulated 1492 walks (thereby officially discovering first base). He computes as follows:

1. Compute the number of the given event that has to happen before the goal is attained. For example, Malcolm needs 3000-1492=1508 walks.

2. Estimate the number of years remaining in the player's career as

   24 - .6*current age.

   For example, Malcolm, at age 27, has 24 - .6*27 = 24-16.2 = 7.8 years remaining in his nefarious career.

   NOTE: Any player over 37 years old is automatically assumed to have 1.5 years left; that is, if he is still playing.

3. Compute the following:

   3 * this year's events +
   2 * last year's events +
   1 * two years ago's events / 6.

Then compare that to 3/4 of this year's events. If the 3/4 figure is greater, use it instead. This gives you an estimate of how fast the player is proceeding towards his goal.

For example, Malcolm took 133 walks this year, 153! last year and only 98 the year before. The computation gives 3*133 + 2*153 + 98 = 803, which, divided by 6, yields 133.8. Checking, 3/4 of this year's 133 is 99.75. That is less that 133.8, so 133.8 it is. Malcolm is taking, on the average, 133.8 walks per year, which means that he is roughly as lazy as Jack Clark.

4. Multiply #3 by #2. This gives you the estimated number of the event that will be attained before the career ends.

For example, Malcolm's #3 is 133.8 walks per year, while his #2 is 7.8 years left. Multiplying, we get an estimate of 133.8 * 7.8 = 1043.6 before Malcolm drops dead 3/5 of the way to first (no doubt from being beaned by an irate catcher). Doesn't look like Malcolm's going to make it. BUT,

5. Compute:

(#4 / #1) -.5. This gives you the estimated chance that the goal will, in fact, be reached.

For example, Malcolm computes (1043.6 / 1508) - 0.5 = .6921 - 0.5 = .1921. That is, there's almost a 20% chance that Malcolm will turn in a long, injury-free career, and get those 3000 free passes (not usable for special engagements).

MAJOR LEAGUE EQUIVALENCIES

A method devised by Bill James for deciphering what a minor league player's basic stats might be if he were to play in the majors. You start by adjusting Runs, Hits, Doubles, Triples, Homers, Walks and Strikeouts; from those you can compute the other basic stats. The method gets long and involved and works like this:

1. Adjust the minor league stats (R, H, D, T, HR, BB, SO) for the minor league ballpark.

2. Compute, but do not use yet, the minor league's Runs Per Game and divide by the Major League's R/G, to get the league context out of the way. In Bill's original presentation of this, in the 1985 ABSTRACT, he did not do this, because he didn't have minor league ballpark adjustments to work with. We got ours from Howe Sportsdata, which is now the official statisticians for all AAA and AA teams.

3. Multiply #2 above by .82 to adjust for the level of competition. Oddly enough, it's the same .82 for AAA ball as for AA ball. This gives you a factor called "m," which you'll use in the next step. You also need the square root of "m," which is called "M"."

4. Multiply each individual stat by a factor Bill determined, making use of "m" and "M" above. The factors are:

Runs = "m"
Hits = .98 x "M"
Doubles = "M"
Triples = .85 x "m"
Homers = "m"
Walks = "m"
Strikeouts = 1.05

5. Adjust for the Major League ballpark.

6. Now, you can also compute At-Bats. This is done by taking the minor league At-Bats and subtracting the minor league Hits to get minor league Outs. Then you add those Outs back to the final, adjusted Major League Hits to get Major League At-Bats. That allows you to compute Batting Average, Slugging Percentage and On-Base Percentage.

OFFENSIVE GAMES (OG)

A player's offensive games are established by computing the portion of his team's games that he, personally, consumed. Now, while it is generally assumed that offensive opportunity is presented to players in the form of Plate Appearances, that is not true for the team as a whole. The team gets 27 outs in which to do its damage, not some set number of trips to the plate. Therefore, a player's Offensive Games are computed by looking at the number of OUTS that the player consumed and dividing by 27, which is the number of outs to a game. ("As it turns out," the extra-inning games just about exactly balance the rain-shortened games and the lost ninth innings of home teams that are already ahead.) The computation is:

Player's Outs Created / 27.

OFFENSIVE WINNING PERCENTAGE (OW%)

A Bill James method designed to answer the question, "If a team had all it's players just as good as this one is, what would that team's winning percentage be?" This is computed, as you might guess, by applying the Runs Created method to the Pythagorean method after ballpark adjusting the whole. It is done as follows:

1. Compute the player's Runs Created (qv.), and divide it by the player's Outs Made (including such things as sacrifice flies and caught stealings). Then multiply by 27 to get the players "Runs Created Per 27 Outs" or "Runs Created Per Game."

2. Compute the team's Runs Per Game as follows:

Team Runs Scored + Team Runs Allowed
divided by
Twice the Team's Games Played (usually 162*2=324, but not always)

3. Divide #1 by #2 to get the ratio of what the player did to what the League's teams did in the player's ballpark.

4. Square #3 to start the Pythagorean ball rolling.

5. Compute:

#4 / (1 + #4)

to complete the Pythagorean process. This will give you the player's OW%.

OFFENSIVE WINS ABOVE REPLACEMENT (OWAR)

Compute:

(Player's Offensive Winning Percentage (qv.) - .350 (the Replacement Rate)) *
Player's Offensive Games (qv.)

This gives you the amount by which the player is better than the hypothetical Replacement Player and multiplies that by the player's playing time in games. That gives you the number of games the player won for his team in his personal offensive window of opportunity.

PETE PALMER'S LINEAR WEIGHTS

Pete is the only old-line sabermetrician still in the business of producing sabermetric analysis. His basic approach is called "linear weights." LW is not a baseball concept, but a normal method of mainline statistics. In statistics, linear weights means assigning a value to each part of a whole and evaluating the whole by summing up the parts. So, to evaluate the runs contributed by a hitter, Pete assigns a value (called a "weight") to a home run, another to a triple, a double, a single and so on. Some values, like that for a strikeout, are negative. Then Pete sums all the values up and gets his answer.

Pete gets the weights he gives each event by correlating the sums for teams to the actual number of runs the team scores. That is, he applies the same standard that Bill James does, standard deviation of formula runs against actual team runs. Even using the same standard, Bill and Pete disagree on which of their methods works best. The issue of argument is an addition to linear weighting called "curve fitting"; Pete's methods meet the standard better than Bill's if he uses curve fitting, but Bill's methods work best if curve fitting is not allowed."

Pete's curve fitting method involves applying a multiplier to his original linear weights such that the final formula generates the very best correlation to actual team runs for an individual year. Bill thinks that this is a bad method because it doesn't generate one formula that you can apply year after year; Pete likes his additional accuracy. In any case, the differences are quite small, and Bill and Pete agree on such things as rankings in almost every case.

You can find a much fuller explanation of Pete's methods in the book he produced with John Thorn, TOTAL BASEBALL. TB is an expensive book, but is essential for sabermetricians. Pete and John also produce an annual update to TOTAL BASEBALL, but it is very expensive indeed. You can find early Thorn and Palmer in their two books THE HIDDEN GAME OF BASEBALL and THE PITCHER. Also, Eliott Cohen edits an annual called the BASEBALL ANNUAL in conjunction with Thorn and Palmer. Of the three, Palmer is the sabermetrician. John Thorn is a book packager and Cohen is a magazine editor.

POSITIONAL ADJUSTMENT

A portion of Pete Palmer's Linear Weights method for evaluating the overall contribution of players. Pete evaluates their offensive contribution, and then their defense, and then adds in this factor, based on the individual player's defensive position. The adjustment involves finding out what the average player at the position hits and comparing it to what the average player overall hits. Pete figures that a shortstop who hits well is worth more than a first baseman who hits the same.

While no one argues with Pete's premise here, there are arguments against this method. The one I tend to bring up is that, during certain periods in baseball history, the very best superstars - the great hitters who could play anywhere on the diamond - were loaded up at one key position, and therefore had to "compete" with each other for positional adjustment. For example, in the dead ball era, superstars were loaded into the shortstop slot, with the result that Honus Wagner and his crowd get very small positional adjustments for playing this very valuable position. The same thing happens to the Willie Mays / Mickey Mantle / Duke Snider / Richie Ashburn / Larry Doby crowd in center field in the fifties, an era in which shortstops didn't hit much. Frankly, I wish Pete would base his adjustments on something more global than individual years; but, then, that's the argument against curve fitting, too.

PYTHAGOREAN METHOD

A method for finding out what the winning percentage of Team A against Team B should be, given the number of runs per game that Team A scores against Team B pitching is and what the number of runs per game that Team B scores against Team A pitching is.

This concept is often applied with "the league as a whole" in the place of Team B, and a player's record instead of Team A. Thus, this method gives us such useful results as batters' Offensive Winning Percentages and Pitchers' Expected Won/Lost Records.

The method is:

1. Divide Team A's Runs/Game (against Team B) by Team B's R/G against Team A.

2. Square #1 to start the "Pythagorean" concept.

3. Compute:

#2 / (1 + #2)

to complete the Pythagorean process. This will give you Team A's winning percentage against Team B.

For example, let's say that the Cardinals score 5 runs per game against the Mets, and that the Mets score only 4 per game against the Cards (yeah, right, Hanke):

1. 5/4 = 1.2

2. 1.2 squared = 1.44

3. 1.44/(1+1.44) = 1.44/2.44 = .590

Thus, if these Cardinals got to play those Mets for 162 games, the Cardinal wins should total .590 x 162 = 95.58, for a probable record of 96 and 66. This should give you an idea of what sort of advantage it takes to win 100 games.

PYRAMID DISTRIBUTION OF TALENT

See "Far Right End of the Normal Curve".

RUNS OF SUPPORT PER GAME

The number of runs that a pitcher's team scored for him, per game.

STOLEN BASES PROFIT METHOD

A method devised by Brock J. Hanke for evaluating the actual contribution of base stealers. It relies on the fact that the positive value of a stolen base is almost exactly half the negative value of a caught stealing. In the method, stolen bases and bases gained on errors made while trying to steal bases are summed and caught stealings and pickoffs are subtracted at double value. The result is the "profit" the base stealer made for his team, expressed in bases. Please not that bases are not of that much value themselves; it takes about 4 1/2 of them to make a run.

SUPPORTED WINNING PERCENTAGE

Computed by applying the Pythagorean Method (qv.) to the pitcher's ERA (NOT ballpark adjusted) and his Runs of Support Per Game (qv.). This gives you the winning percentage the pitcher "should" have had, given the support his team's batters gave him. It is NOT as good a measure of pitching quality as Expected Winning Percentage (qv.), but it does give you a good handle on what the pitcher's actual pitching luck (or clutch ability, if you must) was like, as opposed to his luck in getting runs scored for him.

For example, Jose de Leon had the worst Runs of Support figure in the National League. His actual record was 7-19, no surprise. His expected Won/Lost record of 11-15 indicates that he was actually a much better pitcher than 7-19, but his Supported Won/Lost of 8-18 shows that luck wasn't a factor in his pitching, just in the support he got.

SUPPORTED WINS/SUPPORTED LOSSES

SWins are computed by multiplying the Supported ERA (qv.) by the pitcher's actual number of decisions, and statistically rounding to an integer. SLosses are the actual decisions minus the SWins.

TRADE VALUE

This is computed by combining the concepts of Approximate Value (qv.) and the Favorite Toy (also qv.). The idea is to estimate how much value the player would have left to give his new team if he were traded. The computations are:

1. Estimate the number of years left in the player's career by the method used in the Favorite Toy, which is

24 - .6*Player's Age.

Remember that, if the player is over 37 years old, he still gets 1.5 years minimum.

2. Estimate the player's established Approximate Value Per Year. You can do this by the following computation:

3*this year's AV +
2* last year's AV +
1*two years ago's AV
all divided by 6.

If the player you're dealing with doesn't have 3 years in yet, just use this year's AV. The whole process yields an estimate, after all.

3. Compute Trade Value as:

a. (#2 - #1) squared
b. #a * (#1 + 1) * #2 / 190
c. #b + (#2 * #1 * #1 / 13)

NOTE: This year, due to programming constraints, our Trade Values only use the AV for 1990, which means that they are a bit off, quite a bit in some cases (Bip Roberts, Jose Oquendo). We will get this fixed next year. Also NOTE that we use 2xTWAR for AV (see Approximate Value in this Glossary).

TRUNCATED PYRAMID DISTRIBUTION OF TALENT

See "Far Right End of the Normal Curve". This is the distribution of talent in the minor leagues.

Mad Aztec Press
Order and Response Sheet

On the last page is our 1992 Order and Reader Response Sheet. You can include this in with your Hall of Fame Ballot, or send it in separately. There are spaces for backordering all four years' worth of this book. There are boxes to check if you think you'd buy a different format of book from us. So fill 'er out and send 'er in.

Please don't get confused if you want to order from STATS, Inc. Their order sheet is on the reverse leaf of ours. Both are on the "last page." You can photocopy both sides, of course.

The other projects mentioned on our sheet are very much alive. I'm trying to sell them to larger publishers, or in a distribution deal. This year's success with Elysian Fields Press gives me good hope. As you can see by the titles, the other projects are designed to have a wider appeal than just to sabermetricians. So, if you check one of these off, there is a real chance you'll actually get to own one.

Of those books, the BALLPARK BOOK is designed to combine the general fan's interest in pictures and stories about old ballparks with the sabermetrician's desire for information. The idea is to give each ballpark a picture or two and a general essay, and then discuss the effects it has had on the players who played there.

The other one is just what it's title says, a handbook for people who want to know what baseball statistics amount to, both the traditional ones and the sabermetric. In addition, I'll write real honest journalism essays on the important developers in the field, from Bill James, Pete Palmer and Dick Cramer right back into the 19th century.

Well, enough of the hard sell. thanks for joining us this year, and welcome back in advance for 1993.

Yours for a nice normal year where the favorites finish first,

Brock J. Hanke

Bill James FANTASY BASEBALL

If You Like Fantasy Baseball, You'll Love Bill James Fantasy Baseball...

"Hi. This is Bill James. A few years ago I designed a set of rules for a new fantasy baseball league, which has been updated with the benefit of experience and the input of a few thousand owners.

The idea of a fantasy league, of course, is that it forges a link between you and your ballplayers; YOU win or lose based on how the players that you picked have performed. My goal was to develop a fantasy league based on the simplest and yet most realistic principles possible — a league in which the values are as nearly as possible what they ought to be, without being distorted by artificial category values or rankings, but which at the same time are so simple that you can keep track of how you've done just by checking box scores. There are a lot of different rules around for fantasy leagues, but none of them before this provided exactly what I was looking for. Here's what we want:

1) ***We want it to be realistic.*** We don't want the rules to make David Cone the MVP because of his strikeouts. We don't want Vince Coleman to be worth more than Bobby Bonilla because he steals lots of bases. We want good ballplayers to be good ballplayers.

2) ***We prefer it simple.*** We want you to be able to look up your players in the morning paper, and know how you've done.

3) ***We want you to have to develop a real team.*** We don't want somebody to win by stacking up starting pitchers and leadoff men. We don't want somebody to corner the market on home run hitters.

I made up the rules and I'll be playing the game with you. STATS, Inc. is running the leagues. They'll run the draft, man the computers, keep the rosters straight and provide you with weekly updates. Of course you can make trades, pick up free agents and move players on and off the inactive list; that's not my department, but there are rules for that, too. It all starts with a draft..."

- Draft Your Own Team and Play vs. Other Owners! Play by Mail or With a Computer On-Line!
- Manage Your Roster All Season With Daily Transactions! Live Fantasy Phone Lines Every Day of the Baseball Season!
- Realistic Team and Individual Player Totals That Even Take Fielding Into Account!
- The Best Weekly Reports in the Business!
- Play Against Bill James' Own Drafted Teams!
- Get Discounted Prices by Forming Your Own Private League of 11 or 12 Owners! (Call or write for more information)
- Money-Back Guarantee! Play one month, and if not satisfied, we'll return your franchise fee!

All This, All Summer Long — For Less Than An Average of $5 per week.

Reserve your BJFB team now! Sign up with the STATS Order Form on the next page, or send for additional Free Information.

Two Big Hits from
Bill James and STATS, Inc.

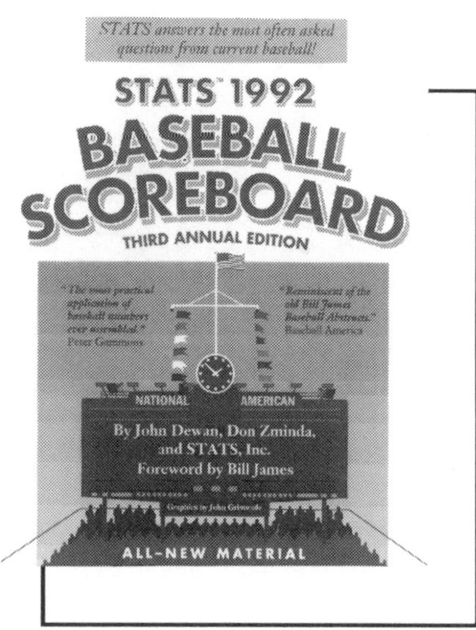

STATS 1992 Baseball Scoreboard

All New for 1992!

- The Unique STATS Analysis Used by the Teams, Networks, and NOW YOU!
- Find Out the Answers to Questions Like:

  "Who Has the Best Zone Ratings?"
  "Does AstroTurf Really Affect Hitting?"
  "Which Pitchers Eat Lefties?"
- Over 100 Questions Answered Using Baseball's Most In-Depth Database
- Available February, 1992

"Brilliant . . . reminiscent of the old Bill James Abstracts!" — ***Baseball America***

Bill James/STATS 1992
Minor League Handbook

New in 1992! **Available November 15, 1991!**

- Exclusive Bill James' Major League Equivalencies
- Official Minor League Stats from Howe Sportsdata International
- Minor League Career Records
- Minor League Leader Boards

"The Next Step for the Serious Baseball Fan!"

Order Now! Use the STATS Order Form on the last page of this book.

STATS Order Form

Product	Quantity	Your price	Total
Bill James Fantasy Baseball Franchise		$25 deposit	
STATS 1992 Baseball Scoreboard		$12.95	
Bill James/STATS 1992 Minor League Handbook		17.95	
The Scouting Report: 1992		15.95	
Bill James/STATS 1992 Major League Handbook		17.95	
Discounts on previous editions while supplies last:			
Bill James/STATS 1991 Major League Handbook		9.95	
Bill James/STATS 1990 Major League Handbook		9.95	
STATS 1991 Baseball Scoreboard		9.95	
The STATS Baseball Scoreboard (1990)		7.95	
U.S. – For First Class Mailing – add $2.50 per book		2.50	
Canada – all orders – add $3.50 per book		3.50	
Subtotal			
Subtract $1.00 per book if you order 2 or more		– $1.00	–
Total			

☐ Yes, I can't wait! Sign me up to play Bill James Fantasy Baseball in 1992. Enclosed is my deposit of $25.00 on the franchise fee of $89.00. A processing fee of $1.00 per player is charged during the season for roster moves.

Team Nickname: ____________________ ____________________ (example: Dayton Mutants)

Would you like to play in a league with a team drafted by Bill James? Yes No (circle one)

Would you like to receive information on playing BJFB on-line by computer? Yes No (circle one)

Please Rush Me These Free Informational Brochures:

☐ **Bill James Fantasy Baseball Info Kit**

☐ **STATS Fantasy Football Info Kit**

☐ **STATS On-Line Brochure**

☐ **STATS Year-End Reports Brochure**

☐ **STATS Reporter Brochure**

Please Print:

Name____________________________________Phone__________________

Address____

City____________________________State__________Zip_______________

Return this form (don't tear your book; copy this page) to:

STATS, Inc.
7366 N. Lincoln Ave
Lincolnwood, IL
60646-1708

Method of Payment (U.S. Funds only):

☐ Check (no Candian checks) ☐ Money Order ☐ Visa ☐ MasterCard

Credit Card Information:

Cardholder Name____

Visa/MC #_______________________________________Exp. Date__________

Signature____

For faster credit card service: call 1-800-63-STATS to place your order, or fax this page to 1-708-676-0821.

mad

Mad Aztec Press
1215 Willow View Drive
Kirkwood, MO 63122

ORDERS

________ copies of Baseball Sabermetric 1992 @ $15.95 per copy = ________

________ copies of Baseball Sabermetric 1991 @ $15.95 per copy = ________

________ copies of Baseball Sabermetric 1990 @ $15.95 per copy = ________

________ copies of The 1989 Baseball Abstract @ $13.95 per copy = ________

+ $2.00 postage if Canada
or $5.00 if foreign (not Canada) = ________

NOTE: All monies in U. S. funds ONLY

TOTAL = ________

I WOULD AT LEAST CONSIDER ORDERING:

Conditions of the Game ☐
(the sabermetric Ballpark Book)

The Encyclopedia of Baseball Statistics ☐

My Name and Address (send ordered books to):

Name: ________________

Address: ________________

____

City: ________________

State: ______ **Zip:** ________ **Country:** ________

Don't cut this sheet out! XEROX it! Keep your book in good condition!